THE
BLACK
POWER
IMPERATIVE

Also by Theodore Cross

Black Capitalism (1969)

Behind the Great Wall (with Mary Cross, 1979)

THE
BLACK
POWER
IMPERATIVE

Racial Inequality
and the
Politics of Nonviolence

Theodore Cross

New York
FAULKNER
1984

Library of Congress Cataloging in Publication Data
Theodore Cross, 1924-
  Ethnic America.

  Includes bibliographical references and index.
  1. Minorities—United States—History.
  2. United States—Ethnic relations.

                                        84-80109
ISBN 0-916631-00-1

First Printing: September 1984
Second Printing: July 1985
Copyright © 1984 by Faulkner Books
870 Seventh Ave.
New York, N.Y. 10019
Printed in the United States of America

Acknowledgments

I BEGAN WORK on this book more than twelve years ago. Over such a long period it is difficult to recall all of those whose writing and ideas have shaped one's thinking.

To anyone who has read even casually on the subject of power, it will be evident that my indebtedness is very great to a number of people. First, there are the works of the celebrated philosophers of power: Tolstoy, Hume, Hobbes, Dostoevsky, Locke, Machiavelli, Bentham, Rousseau, Gandhi, Gibbon, and John Stuart Mill. I am indebted to them.

Among more recent scholars and writers, I am indebted to J. Kenneth Galbraith, who, more effectively than any person, has exposed coercive power as a driving force of contemporary capitalism. Here, I mention also the important writings of Lasswell, Mosca, Commons, Weber, Pareto, and C. Wright Mills.

Either in or out of the context of power, no serious consideration of the subject of race discrimination is possible without benefit of the works of Gordon Allport, Lester Thurow, and Gary Becker. I am indebted to them.

Many distinguished philosophers and commentators have written on the subject of redress as it affects considerations of justice and fairness. Four particularly influenced my views. They are John Rawls, Boris Bittker, Thomas Nagel, and Hannah Arendt.

Over the years, the writings of Robert Heilbroner, Robert Browne, William Chafe, Martin Delany, W. E. B. DuBois, Franz Fanon, George Frederickson, Charles Hampden-Turner, T. George Harris, Julian Jaynes, Christopher Jencks, Winthrop Jordan, Robert Lekachman, Arnold Schuchter, and Richard Sennett have pushed my thinking in new directions.

I am grateful also to the commentators who have forcefully argued the case for restraint in the use of public and private power to deal with issues of racial inequality. These include Milton Friedman, Alexander Bickel, Edward Banfield, Owen Fiss, Alan Dershowitz, George Gilder, Nathan Glazer, Robert Novak, Daniel Moynihan, Irving Kristol, George Will, Robert Nozick, and, particularly, Thomas Sowell.

My work on this book had its origins in reflections and ideas I developed during the years I worked as a consultant at the former federal Office of Economic Opportunity during the Johnson and Nixon administrations. I am indebted to Sargent Shriver, the first director of the Office of Economic Opportunity. More years ago than I care to remember, he provided me with the chance to test my ideas against a number of self-help efforts funded by the federal government. I am grateful also to Donald Rumsfeld, former counselor to President Nixon and director of the Office of Economic Opportunity. In the spring of 1970, Rumsfeld arranged for me to express my

v

ideas on black economic development to President Nixon at a Cabinet meeting. This opportunity gave legitimacy to my views on the importance of proprietary power to the progress of black people and advanced efforts I had under way to test this thesis. I am also grateful to a number of OEO and White House aides who served in the late 1960s—particularly Donald Lowitz, Richard Cheney, Robert Finch, Carol Khosrovi Marshall, Marvin Feldman, Bill Walker, Dick Ramsden, Len Garment, Rocco Siciliano, Maurice Stans, Gary Baden, Arthur Fletcher, Abe Venable, the late Bob Kunzig, Paul London, Vic Sparrow, Milton Moskowitz, Sam Doctors, Sue Davis, Eric Stevenson, and Connie Good. Despite considerable political opposition, a number of these officials and consultants helped advance the funding of my plan for the creation of the Opportunity Funding Corporation, a national experiment using various financial devices for augmenting the economic power of blacks and other racial minorities.

I acknowledge my obligation, also, to staff and friends of the Office of Economic Opportunity who opposed the Opportunity Funding Corporation initiative. They did so on a principled basis and in some cases for reasons I later came to support. These include Jeff Faux, Senator Jake Javits, Gar Alperovitz, Roy Innis, John McClaughry, Leon Sullivan, Carl Perkins, Alex Mercure, Sar Levitan, Darwin Bolden, and Bill Spring.

For research, editorial aid, and discussion on particular points I am greatly indebted to Peter Slavin, Linda Epstein, Barry Schwartz, Robert Schaevitz, Justin Clifford, Robyn Bantel, Isaac Schkop, Llewellyn Gerson, Michael Shulan, Richard Pious, and Ruth Darmstadter. For editing and tightening arguments I express thanks to Ellen Ryan, Victoria Mathews, and Helen Kelly. I express particular thanks to Philip Rosenberg for his close and exacting critique and suggestions as to some early drafts.

I am indebted to Lori Jacobs for her extraordinary skill and patience in editing the final manuscript and proofs. For infinite patience and assistance in the preparation of charts and exhibits I express my thanks to Tony Gigante, and to George Curtin and the staff at The Nimrod Press.

My profound thanks to Elaine Kursch and Joann Scanlon who have worked over manuscript pages with infinite skill and care.

I am grateful beyond words to Bruce Slater who, in many respects, was my partner in this enterprise. His research, rich insights, critiques, and exhaustive editing were of inestimable value.

My thanks to Rochelle Lewis, my dear friend and colleague who for thirty years has been a constant source of encouragement and support.

Needless to say, responsibility for views expressed are mine alone. I accept responsibility for any errors in fact or judgment.

THEODORE CROSS

For Mary

Preface

IN 1619, TWENTY AFRICAN NEGROES arrived in the American colony of Virginia. In time, this small group of black slaves would be followed by tens of thousands more. At the start of the American Revolution, no census had been taken, but it is known that the black population then numbered at least half a million people. Interrupted only by a slave embargo established by Congress in 1807, the steady stream of African immigrants continued, ceasing largely a century ago. Today, 28 million Negro citizens, mainly direct descendants of these former slaves, claim an American heritage that substantially predates that of very large numbers of, if not most, American whites.

As we enter these last decades of the twentieth century—360 years after the arrival of the first black people, and more than a century after the liberation of all Negroes from slavery—one would expect that sufficient time had passed for them to have attained a proportionate share of the nation's income, wealth, and positions of power and esteem. But this is not so. After all these centuries, black citizens, in economic and political terms, remain a deeply inferior—if not, in many respects, an outcast—minority.

Hundreds of studies have been published on race discrimination and inequality. But prior to this time, no comprehensive effort has been made to explain the subordinate position of blacks in the United States in terms of unequal holdings of power. This is the first part of my undertaking. I will show why the collective mode of judging the qualifications of people, which we call race discrimination, must be viewed as an intensely coercive form of private and public power. I will then explain how this power has arrested the economic development of black people in the United States and suppressed their capacity to attain those powers and liberties necessary for success in a competitive economy. I will describe the economic measures and political benchmarks by which unequal power positions of the races should be defined and measured. I will identify the forces of prior advantage and incumbency which keep the black condition from changing for the better even when power in the form of race discrimination is no longer present. I will show why, by all accepted standards of fairness, our society will remain unjust, and probably dangerously so, unless, within established constitutional processes, the state uses its power to take certain overriding corrective measures which, under ordinary circumstances, would be viewed as profoundly unfair and which, in the most odious way, involve loss of freedom for the majority.

Toward the end of this book, I work out specific alternatives to the forms of public aid and assistance that have sapped the strength of blacks and held them back. Here, I hasten to promise that I will not burden the reader with exhortations for greater corporate responsibility, special race commissions, blue-ribbon task forces, or banal pleas for Marshall Plans in the inner city.

My thesis here is that for blacks, the distribution of power in American society is the single issue of overriding importance. The unequal position of Negroes may be understood only in terms of unequal holdings of power. The merit of each and every item on the black agenda must be judged by the single criterion of whether it detracts from or enhances the economic and political strength of black people. For these reasons, the policies I urge require the systematic cultivation of black power in all the legitimate forms that a constitutional democracy protects.

Clearly, many of the suggestions I propose are foreign to liberal orthodoxy. Furthermore, I do not expect their immediate adoption as goals of the Congressional Black Caucus. My ambition is the more modest one of praising black power, of working toward rehabilitating it from the opprobrium that it now carries, and legitimizing it as a liberal and progressive strategy. Attending this is my hope that some of these proposals may receive places high on the black citizen's agenda for the 1980s.

THEODORE CROSS

Princeton, New Jersey
June 1, 1984

CONTENTS

CONTENTS

PART THREE

Banquets and Breadlines: The Racial Distribution of American Wealth

PART FOUR

The Ethical Premise of Countervailing Power

CONTENTS

PART FIVE

The Gathering of Power:
The Shape of a Black Agenda

"*Every body continues in its state of rest, or of uniform motion in a right line, unless it is compelled to exchange that state by forces impressed upon it.*"

—*Sir Isaac Newton*
Principia Mathematica *(1687)*

Part One

The Origins
of
Unequal Positions

"At nature's great table, there are no plates for some."
—*T.R. Malthus (1798)*

Power in the Beginning:
The Original Bias
Toward an Equal Start

"Liberty, or Freedom, signifieth the absence of opposition; by opposition, I mean external impediments of motion."

—*Thomas Hobbes,* Leviathan *(1651)*

IN THE BEGINNING, the world was ruled by power. Nature's power, presented as life-threatening violence, was the essential condition that confronted man when he first reared up on his hind legs a million or more years ago. As one of nature's frailest creatures, vulnerability was man's natural state. And powerlessness was his original position.

Despite her savage and remorseless ways, nature's power on earth functioned in remarkably random and unpremeditated ways. The killer instinct of the poisonous snake played no favorites. Power in the form of landslides, floods, and blizzards operated with no pattern or predictability. Hungry packs of wolves did not search out specific victims. Driven apparently by the laws of chance, smallpox epidemics were not seen to target preselected individuals. Thus, natural power showed certain traits that we now identify with the concept of justice. There was, in fact, an elegant evenhandedness in the petrifying process by which the power of the rampaging tiger destroyed human or animal life.

Natural power acted not only upon individuals, but also upon *groups* of people. For various reasons, people survived or failed not only as individuals, but also as tribes or societies. Throughout the many centuries of mankind's struggle to maintain life, nature's power also applied its evenhanded ways to the life prospects of groups on earth. Plagues and tidal waves evidenced no natural group or tribal discrimination. The accidents and imponderables of droughts and famines showed no meanness of narrow pur-

3

pose, no systematic plan to single out any tribe for favorable or unfavorable treatment. Everyone was exposed, but no kinship or racial groups were unequally exposed because of some environmental, biological, or divine curse.

Human Power: The Assault on Open Access

From the earliest times, economic scarcity was one of nature's most terrifying forms of power or constraint. Neolithic farmers were bowed down and broken by their skimpy harvests. Before that, small ape-like men fought it out with animals or other men over a minor discovery of grubs. Everywhere, human life and behavior were controlled by nature's power reflected in her unrelenting denial of abundance.

But once more, a natural law of equal opportunity governed the limited distribution of goods. Individual people were indeed unequal in strength, cunning, or intelligence; thus, survival success would necessarily be unequal among individuals. Yet, access to scarce resources was general and open to all. The sterile sand continents of the Middle East did not favor any one of its nomadic tribes over any other; the blessings of the lush meadows of central Europe were not set aside for any particular agricultural society. In no part of the world was stoop labor or degrading work assigned by nature or fate to untouchable or subordinate castes. Under the original rule of open access, the best places for hunting and fishing were never restricted or allocated by a decree of nature. Within any given ecological habitat or niche each person and each group had "an equal go."

With the passage of time, however, the original pattern of equal access was to change. A new form of power entered the world. This was human power. Adopting the brute forces of violent power discovered in nature, tribes of men warred with each other to win superior hunting grounds or private water rights. To win economic advantage, prisoners of war were captured, indentured for work, and put on allocated rations. Instead of competing head to head for the scarce resources that were open to all, nature's rule of open opportunity was subverted. People in most societies joined forces with others to protect themselves against competition from strangers or rivals. Special user and kinship rights to natural resources were established through the force of weapons or of tribal decrees. Racial conventions and skin-color privileges emerged whose purpose was to keep specific groups in or out of coveted places. Everywhere it turned out that areas of restricted entry for privileged or protected groups were substituted for creation's original rule of open access to all.

4

Possibly the quest for power served merely to satisfy imperfectly understood human needs or yearnings; but its use was also mankind's pragmatic strategy for moderating the constraints of natural scarcity. Through various instruments of human power and contrived advantage, the greater burden of natural scarcity could be shifted to weaker groups; an unequal share of the world's abundance could, in turn, become the protected claim of more powerful groups. In the process, human power made wide-ranging modifications in nature's free-flowing and evenhanded scheme of random constraint, open competition, and equal opportunity.

Fences, Taboos, and Restricted Entry

In a world ruled by power, nature arranged, nonetheless, certain benevolent provisions of freedom. By freedom I mean quite literally the capacity to escape or defeat the power of others. Under the original grant of freedom, some animals managed to outrun their natural predators; as often as not, ground rodents dodged the talons of the hawk; in a truly remarkable display of liberty, a flip of feathers sent a bird into a flight that confounded the ground predator, not to mention the otherwise invincible power of gravity.

It happened then that mobility as a form of freedom or escape from power was a superb strategy for improving life prospects. Conversely, it followed that any curtailment of a creature's natural grant of liberty or mobility increased the risks of bodily harm as well as the chances of a short life. To this end, the life expectancy of a bird with a broken wing was as short as that of a toothless tiger.

Freedom in the form of physical mobility was also central to the capacity for *human* survival and well-being. Throughout recorded history, people have escaped hunger and poverty by the simple tactic of moving to another place. They have removed themselves from servitude or oppression by fleeing to a land of freedom and open opportunity. Bowed down by a hostile climate or oppressive neighbors, they have made their way to a more benign or more open society. And barring some physical handicap or accident, each person was endowed with the same liberty to get up on his two legs and walk or run to some other place.

But once more human power altered the natural access to liberty. From the earliest times, some people curbed the mobility of other people by constructing walls, fences, and defended boundaries. Invisible barriers and codes of allowed behavior were erected by law, custom, or taboo. Restricted areas of permitted human movement were prescribed by force, custom, or state-ordered apartheid. Agreed-on place assignments—often

5

connected with defined human or racial characteristics—frequently limited human motion in space or time. These fences, seen and unseen, defined opportunities, altered the distribution of luck, and, in the process, imposed unequal life risks.

Power Surrendered for Protection

Freedom was also shaped by the capacity for diversity, or the ability to find multiple solutions to the constraints of shortages. Creatures of different species could often coexist successfully in the same habitat simply because they used different resources. Cattle, unlike humans, could live on grass. Giraffes fed on acacia leaves at the tops of trees, free of competition except from other giraffes. Pigs could eat almost anything. Mankind, in turn, was endowed with a generous share of natural talent for pursuing diverse strategies. True, man could not breathe under water. Nor could he fly like a bird c eat only once a month in the style of a boa constrictor. But man did have two hands and an opposable thumb. He had the ability to thrive on practically any diet and an even more remarkable ability to live and propagate in the tropics, the desert, or the arctic.

This adaptive trait of having or being able to work out alternative solutions to human demands was an indispensable requirement for success and well-being. The rule applied not only to all species, but also to all individuals, classes, and tribes within the human family. It usually followed then that the groups and institutions that became dependent on a single source of goods or sustenance would, in time, come to harm. Where the ability to find alternative sources of supply, or to provide for oneself, was abandoned, left to lie fallow—or possibly even purposefully subverted by some other group—an almost certain consequence was the emergence of inequality in life prospects.

No groups of humans appeared to have a predetermined aptitude either for avoiding dependency or for discovering multiple solutions to the problems of survival and success. But in many societies, nature's scheme was overturned. A powerless state of human dependency was imposed on certain groups by law, patrimony, or custom. Security or protection was conferred on designated tribes in exchange for the surrender of their abilities to pursue freedom or diversity. Under community rules or treaties, the capacity to fend for oneself, or to pursue diverse approaches to the travails of life, was blocked, sabotaged, or utterly bargained away. Dependency's frail lifeline was a foolish and risky departure from nature's plan which always had conditioned survival and success on the retention of a proper store of freedom of choice.

Power and Freedom as the Guardians of Well-Being

The ideal of freedom, then, was profoundly rooted in the exigencies of human survival. The pursuit of life has always been less precarious for those who had alternatives. But the blessings of freedom have never offered much of value without the power necessary to exploit and protect these freedoms. For example, a person may not rationally consider himself "free" to eat meat if it turns out that he lacks the power to capture or purchase it. Similarly, an individual is not in fact free to compete with another person to win control over a scarce resource if either of them lacks the price of admission, or the power to insist on access, to the place where the competition is to be staged. The freedom to study, learn, and improve one's skills counts for little if one lacks the power to insist on permission to enter the established places where instruction takes place. Self-evidently, my freedom to pursue my life unmolested is of no benefit to me without the power to prevent you from picking up a club and ending my life. In simple terms, *freedom is always incomplete without power*. Paradoxically, this conclusion also implies that one way freedom is created and maintained is through coercion— at least enough coercion to compel others not to interfere with one's liberty to explore a wide variety of means of human fulfillment and survival.

In endowing living creatures with the capacity to survive, nature obligingly supplied some natural means of coercion. The cobra, for example, has a lethal fang. The kangaroo can flatten a man and kick his heavy nylon net to shreds in a matter of seconds. Even the humble skunk's ability to be left alone is universally respected. In nature's scheme, these powers were nicely balanced, thus providing a sort of spontaneous environmental regulator. Every day for tens of thousands of years, a certain number of tigers were powerful enough to capture and consume a certain number of gazelles. And, on the same days, a certain number of gazelles were free to escape the tiger and live another day. It appears that this interplay between power and freedom guarded the delicate balance of life on earth. And in life's competition it was the capacity for human power, in conjunction with the possession of liberty, that was the infallible determinant of which groups and individuals would survive, fail, or prosper.

Human Intelligence: Power Discovered in Technology

In a world where life prospects were largely regulated by one's relationship to power and liberty, mankind managed to create a uniquely superior position for itself. Despite all the environmental pressures that beat upon him, man not only has improved his liberties but has also become the most powerful of all creatures.

What human trait made this possible? Surely not physical power, for man's endowment in natural weapons was puny indeed. He not only ranked low in strength and agility, but, compared with many predators, his senses of vision, hearing, and smell were dull. He did, however, have one distinctly superior trait which separated him from all other forms of animal life. This was the special quality of his brain. Man had the superb advantage of being self-aware, innovative, and capable of calculation, foresight, and planning. Most important, man could imagine himself in new or hypothetical situations and, in the process, create power in the form of weapons and defenses that would protect him when the events he anticipated actually happened. Man did not delude himself when he designated his species *Homo sapiens,* for this unique human intelligence enabled him to countermand many of nature's most powerful orders.

The spear and the club were perhaps the first clues that only man could create power in the form of extensions of himself. Cro-Magnon man perfected the animal hunt. Some aboriginal man conceived the salmon spear and the rabbit snare. Nets, nooses, fences, weirs, and ambushes were the early technology of constraint. A bow and arrow, and finally a rifle, could quickly extinguish the life of an otherwise superior adversary. Man caged the tiger instead of being caged by it. He rode on the back of the wild stallion, harnessed the ox, and even forced the powerful elephant to work. As a superb learning, report-receiving, and data-storing creature, man embarked on millions of searches for information that would enhance his powers and liberties and so extend his tenure on earth. His fine mind examined every aspect of what he saw; his remarkable brain lingered over every complexity and nuance. Decisively, then, man used his brain to free himself from of nature's constraints. He discovered escape routes from the natural forces of floods and famines. He decoded the habits of the predator, and, as a result, he could plan to be in another place when the predator struck. Very early in his history, man invented agriculture; in so doing he overturned nature's original order that he was to forage for food. In time, man learned to flood deserts, drain swamps, and clear jungles. One by one, nature's potentially conquering forces were conquered by man, and at each step, human liberty was expanded by the sheer force of human intelligence. In time he mapped and controlled the world.

As a result of the evolution of human innovation, nature's original scheme of equal access gave way to new forms of protected advantage. At any particular place or time in history a tribe that was terracing hillsides and converting swamps into rice fields was likely to be living better and enjoying more freedom and leisure than another tribe that had not happened on the idea or learned it from others. Those tribes that had discovered the pointed spear, the net for trapping animals, and, regrettably, the automatic rifle were also likely to enjoy a superior standard of living. Once more, the general access to innovation, learning, and technology was frequently blocked or rationed by edicts or taboos usually promulgated by groups holding superior weaponry or political power. Again, these were contrived inequalities which ran counter to nature's even hand. There appeared to be no decree from on high that endowed any one ethnic or tribal group with special access to, or talent for creating, the technology that contributed so greatly—and unequally—to human power and freedom.

Power as Competence

Massive differences in the ability to use power were derived from the possession of tools, weapons, and technology. But for the vast majority of humans, the capacity for power was best measured by the human trait we know as competence. The traits of competence are the same as those of power generally. Competent people are proficient at blunting nature's harms. The competent control outside events and adapt to pressures and changes that threaten their well-being. Competent people possess qualities of independence and self-sufficiency. They find means of penetrating natural barriers and man-made rules. The competent persuade others to do their bidding. They fend off predators; they dam rivers; they bring the wild animal to heel; the competent are, and have been, successful in growing corn, finding a cave, or fashioning a lean-to. The competent look into the future, calculate risk, and choose the superior escape route or the preferred path to attack a stronghold. Always the competent are alert, decisive, forceful, and get things done. Human power belongs to them uniquely.

In particular, competence power is discovered in the form of human energy, known as work or labor. From the earliest times, good, hard work, skillfully performed, has always provided a superior escape route from the constraints of economic scarcity and need. Human energy, in the form of purposeful and useful work, has provided mankind with forts, moats, and other defenses against the depredations of others. Most important, individual competence—usually in the form of skill and the capacity to deliver labor—provided the essential reward power that came to drive the competitive markets of Western societies. Hence, it was the competent who were in a tactical position to confer favors on others and thereby influence behavior in the marketplace by winning transfers of desired goods, labor, and credit. The incompetent, on the other hand, could offer few, if any, rewards. Accordingly, under competitive markets as originally conceived, they had little power in the sense of the ability to influence the economic or political behavior of other people.

Just as some people were physically strong and others weak, nature parceled out individual competence unequally. Some people were superior warriors, skilled huntsmen, master craftsmen, or adept at finding cover. Other individuals were skilled at developing or using tools, or were proficient in herding cattle or growing crops. While individual competence was apportioned unequally, the inherent capacity for competence and intelligent action appeared to be randomly distributed among kinship or racial groups. Anthropologists measured different-sized brains, skulls, and rib cages. Yet no genetic characteristics declared that certain groups would be suited for plantation agriculture and domestic service or that other groups would be particularly adept at manning assembly lines and building financial institutions. Nor were there predetermined or biological characteristics among tribes that made some of them inherently more skillful than others in developing the many tools, weapons, and other man-made extensions of human power and freedoms. No ethnic group had a special capacity for breeding high or low achievers. No tribe or race stood accused from birth of incompetence, stupidity, or sloth.

Yet, once more, human power produced an unequal development of competence. Inadequate nutrition dulled human wit; isolation from education or mental stimulation blunted perceptions and intelligence. Shortages of goods and shelter turned human desires away from study or intellectual pursuits. The desire to acquire the skills necessary to build upon one's natural endowment of competence was frequently curtailed by outside human power manifested in the form of caste, servitude, or limited group expectation. Property qualifications, as well as class or racial restrictions, were frequently imposed by law or custom as conditions to the right to enter institutions controlling education, training, and apprenticeship. Despite the presence of these forces—whose effects were often mistaken for natural inequalities—it appeared that a detached and orderly universe stubbornly provided the blessings of an evenhanded law of equal opportunity. Every time that a gifted child was born of an outcast or a lower-class family, nature emphatically refuted man's power embodied in his concept of caste, class, or racial superiority.

Language as Power

Man's capacity for language has always been a decisive element of human power, often ranking in coercive impact with the use of outright force. Power emanating from the human voice box charms and seduces. It manipulates, mesmerizes, and makes others behave according to the power holder's will. Over the centuries, speech uttered and understood has persuaded people to hate, to shun, to kill, or to wage war. Rulers and philosophers have used language to cause people to surrender valuable rights, to reject freedom or self-reliance, to assume with good grace a position of dependency and vulnerability. Birthrights sold, unfulfilled lives, unfocused aspirations, and acceptance of assigned stations in life have been the sure product of the skillful use of controlling words or propaganda.

The ability to be silent, or to silence others, may control the behavior of others with the same force as speech or writing. Distracting and diverting others from what the deceiver wants most for himself have been achieved by transmitting or withholding information, by educating people or not educating them, by palming off falsehood as truth. Language has always been particularly forceful when it sends up smokescreens, jams transmissions, and releases decoys and Trojan horses. Half-truths, deceptive rhetoric, and confusing innuendo may render a rival group confused, misdirected, and unable to assert power, to keep its head down, or otherwise protect its interests. In particular the power of language "co-opts" and controls when it disingenuously says that it endorses the goals of those it seeks to manipulate. Masters of language—particularly those who believed that their bodies housed a superior form of life—could, and did, cause the uneducated or uninformed to spend their lifetimes calling wrong numbers, sorting out double-talk, checking false leads, attending the wrong press conferences, and applying at the wrong offices.

In the book of nature, no population group had superior access to the power of speech. Armed only with human voice boxes, the individual amplifiers all had equal wattage. Each and every tribe or ethnic group had equal access to the powers of language. In time, however, human technology radically altered the potential for using the power of language. The printing press allowed certain groups to make their voices heard above all others. Electronic transmission made it possible for language to be communicated to millions instead of mere thousands. Those groups controlling newspapers, textbooks, and radio and television stations came to hold a greatly disproportionate share of the power and influence of speech. The people who owned or presided over mass media were virtually guaranteed an audience for their broadcasts. But lesser voices, together with curbstone speakers and the underground press, were rarely successful in winning more than a handful of listeners or readers.

Magnified millions of times over the original power of the human voice, mass media was frequently used to control human potential, predetermine attitudes, and assign people to certain reservations or positions of restricted privilege. On a mass basis, group reputations could be destroyed, prejudices confirmed, character and competence attacked, and superior or subordinate positions ratified. Captive populations could literally be created and fenced in simply as a result of the fact that all of the audible messages in a particular society declared that this or that economic or political position or obligation was inevitable, necessary, or just. For these events to occur, all that was required was that, by accident or plan, mass communications come into the hands of people who shared a common opinion that certain other people were predestined or obligated to hold inferior, outcast, or second-class status.

The use of loudspeakers as power to advance one's position and to hold other people in place was not necessarily a consciously selfish or self-seeking act. Widely broadcast consensus opinion constrained others with equal force even when it was driven by generous or altruistic intentions. Hence, the uncontradicted consensus opinion of media loudspeakers could successfully instruct people that they were "helpless victims of a cycle of poverty," that they were "incurably hard core," or that "they should send their children to schools attended by other children of their race or class." By this process, the natural liberties and powers of groups of people could be blunted and repressed. In many places in the world, people walked the plank to the tune of music composed by loving, caring, and compassionate protectors.

Throughout the centuries, control over the written word, or the word most often heard, has been vested in various groups. Media power was sometimes held by the church, by press barons, by newspaper conglomerates, or by network television empires. With careless accusations of conspiratorial power, we sometimes refer to these groups as press or media overlords. There is rarely any evidence of the presence of a conspiracy. We have identified nevertheless the locus of great power. The institutions and classes of citizens that own or have control over movable type, printing presses, and telecommunications have always been located very close to the fuse boxes of society's power. Other citizens of lower rank who perhaps were not considered eligible to receive broadcasting licenses or to obtain credit and capital necessary to engage in important communications enterprises were, for these reasons, almost wholly removed from the centers of a nation's power system.

Power as Tools and Machinery

From the earliest times, tools have been used to extend the bounds of human freedom as well as to curtail human liberty. Anthropologists believe that the first rudimentary tools appeared in Kenya some 2.5 millions years ago. Apparently, the first tool was the digging stick. Later, some remarkably innovative minds conceived the mechanical power of the lever, the wheel, the cart, and the wheelbarrow. By these technological devices, man magnified the force of his work. Step by step, he developed a marvelous collection of ways in which to get more work done without working as hard himself. Some brilliant innovator harnessed the energy of oxen, another developed the rake, and yet another conceived the potter's wheel and the buffalo-drawn plow. All of these devices were magnificent additions to man's capacity to free himself from nature's constraint of enforced labor and foraging for food.

Inch by inch, mile by mile, mankind expanded the frontiers of liberty through the capital of new technology. Then, in the nineteenth century, the steam engine revolutionized commerce, industry, and the human prospect. No longer did it require a company of men and a dozen horses to haul a few tons of goods from London to Liverpool; nor did it take a man or child half a day at a hand loom to make a few yards of cloth. The industrial age had arrived. Economic success, it was now discovered, came about not only through the power of labor but also through the ability to avoid or leapfrog the constraint of labor by replacing it with machines that did the work.

As in the case of other acquired powers, this newfound freedom from human toil was unequally distributed. Those who owned or controlled the capital goods that reduced or eliminated work often won great riches and advantages. Groups that as a result of custom, rule, ethnic expectation, or prior circumstance relied on the work of their hands and backs were almost always economically backward and powerless. In many societies, labor-saving agricultural machines drove landless workers onto welfare rolls or forced them to seek industrial employment, for which they were usually unprepared. Unquestionably, the sum total of all human economic freedom was greatly enlarged by the appearance of capital goods, but the impact of technological capital on human liberty and opportunity was unequal as long as those whose work was displaced by a new machine did not have a prior claim on the new work or rents that the machine created.

An important result of the process of advanced toolmaking and technology was the creation of surplus value. Industrial technology allowed people, virtually for the first time, to produce goods of significantly more value than the cost of producing them. This newly created value could then be invested as capital to create new technology, machinery, and automated labor substitutes. The shrinking importance of labor and the increasing powers of rents and dividends from machinery resulted in profound redistributions of economic power. Groups having little or no control over capital and machinery tended to toil at the bottom of the economy whether it was wealthy or poverty-ridden. Other groups that possessed or owned capital occupied the positions at the top. As a result, labor power today—unless organized in the form of a successful cartel—is frequently a measure of economic impotence, just as control of capital and technology is an excellent means of determining who has society's power and the right to use it.

From time to time, various social philosophers of the romantic stripe have glorified the ideal of a primitive society, free from the burdens of machines, property, and surplus value. Ironically, it has often been those who enjoyed the superior powers and liberties inherent in their command over machinery and access to property rents who have urged propertyless groups to stick to their work and to avoid the painful burdens of owning capital. Those who have heeded this advice have usually accepted employee status as the end point of their economic aspirations. We shall presently see how this cast of mind—the desire to be always the employee, never the employer—has acquired a peculiar tribal bias which, in an economy driven by various forms of capital and technology, has virtually precluded certain ethnic groups from obtaining any significant share of the current store of economic and political power.

The Power Principle and Group Well-Being

The forces governing human wealth and well-being have not changed greatly since the dawn of history. For all groups in a given society, the prospect for improved incomes, greater holdings of property, and more favorable life chances generally is profoundly influenced by the group's relationship to the instruments of power. Acquiring and holding power have indeed become strategic principles well adapted to preserving life and protecting people from its perils. As a group, blacks, for example, have done poorly when much stronger people, often acting in league, have used power against them. In instances where minority and outcast people have done well—owning their own homes, being able to afford good college educations, holding secure and prestigious positions—they have done so in large part because they, or others acting on their behalf, have acted powerfully. It is indeed true that successful groups compete effectively by using powers to reward others as well as to coerce them. Often they compete successfully on equal terms and on level playing fields; but just as often, successful individuals and groups advance their economic status by joining special-interest groups, acquiring favored positions, erecting barriers against others, establishing exclusive turfs, and blocking competition from possible rivals. This has always been true, it remains true today, and there is no reason to suppose that it will not be true tomorrow.

Hereafter, I shall use the word "power" to mean access to, or the ability to use, all those sanctions, rewards, inducements, and reins that people in an advanced society use to control their environment and influence the behavior of others. I will sometimes use the word somewhat loosely, to mean those liberties that flow from standing erect and being proud and self-sufficient. In this sense, the well-being of blacks and other minority groups may be viewed as a function of independence and a capacity for self-nourishment. This conclusion is consistent with the history of the progress of other minority and lower-ranking groups. Establishing a strong and well-defended position of group self-sufficiency has invariably provided a plate of armor behind which oppressed groups have protected themselves and nurtured their kin in the face of animosity, neglect, and indifference on the part of the majority.

Clearly, power and freedom from coercion do not assure well-being. Command over power and liberty does not guarantee circumstances that lead to a full and happy life. Yet, when any group is denied some fair share of the ability to coerce, as well as some freedom from the coercive powers of others, the probabilities are overwhelming that most members of that group will have a less than equal share of the material goods any rational person would want. It turns out, then, that a firm grip on some of society's power becomes a necessary, although not a sufficient, condition for economic, social, and political well-being.

Indisputably, the issue of who holds power is not an exclusive concern of blacks and of others at the bottom of the pecking order. The compelling need to pay close attention to one's place in the hierarchy of power has become a general imperative. In a modern industrial society, the traditional virtues of self-sufficiency and of going it alone on the frontier are less useful than in the past. In a nation where pioneers have long since been replaced by wage earners and professionals, the well-being of most citizens depends largely on whether others are persuaded to engage them in trade, commerce, or employment. Increasingly, too, success in our society has been regulated by adversary proceedings in which goods are won, goods are claimed, and disputes resolved through courts, administrative hearings, strikes, and group demands. In America today, these are the forces that explain wealth, advantage, and success just as surely as do daring, diligence, and attention to work.

Edmund Burke once wrote, "I know of nothing sublime that is not some modification of power." Despite this blessing by the great philosopher, the explicit act of seeking power has always been judged as vulgar and offensive. It sometimes follows then that a group that is running far behind others will choose to look in another direction, perhaps to a society that outlaws competition, rewards unequal competence equally, or promises that everyone will have an equal share of the society's jobs, food, and produce. But experience in other nations and societies reveals that no matter what the intended arrangement, it is always the powerful who do well. The emperors, overlords, and tribal chiefs of the past lived well because they were powerful. The privileged elite and party bureaucrats in Marxist societies enjoy advantages because they, too, are powerful. And heaven help people—or races of people—in America today who fail to become well-trained soldiers.

CHAPTER TWO

The Dynamics of Contemporary Power

"I do not say it is good, I do not say it is bad. I say it is the way it is."

—Charles Maurice de Talleyrand (c. 1800)

BY ALL NORMAL PROCESSES of observation one concludes that power creates for itself superior station and material well-being. A state of powerlessness, in turn, produces subordinate positions and marginal economic status. These are stubborn and unalterable facts. This being so, we profit from inquiring further into some of the important traits and uses of contemporary power. We shall then be in a position to understand the connection between majority power and the unequal position of black people in the United States today.

In simplest terms, we know that power is the ability to cause others to do something they would otherwise not do, or to refrain from doing something they are planning to do. In everyday life, we see power in the American household. In a mundane example of human power, a mother says to her child, "Turn off the TV; do your homework; hold your head up; clean your room." If the child does what he or she is told, successful power is at work. And the mother has it!

But we are interested here in much more complex power arrangements. We are concerned particularly with *group* power. What standard levers of power do groups use to influence other groups? How are superior group positions and advantages won and maintained? What are the instruments of coercion that groups use to spoil the chances of their opponents, while improving their own prospects and those of their clients? How do groups use power to prop up losers and rob potential winners of the fruits of their labor and ambitions? How, particularly, does the intellectual process of assigning a person to a class or group translate into a telling form of constraining power or oppression?

The mechanics of power present unfamiliar terrain. Let us pick our way through it and note what is relevant or useful. I will mention here only what I believe is necessary background for the more important explanation ahead of how power connects with the idea of race or skin color.

The Power of Information

We have already seen why human intelligence is an indispensable prior condition to the use of those powers that are distinctly human. To persuade, or indeed force, another person to do one's bidding requires the presence of a human brain capable of receiving information, observing events, pondering situations, perceiving a target, tracing potential scenarios, and forecasting behavior. In order to influence the behavior of others, human intelligence must continuously grasp, store, and decode countless varieties of information. Because information is such an important element of the power process, people with command over superior information tend to be, on that account, powerful. People with little information, or with access only to the information doled out by the powerful, tend to be on that account powerless. Thus, we now have a major precondition for the presence of human power: human intelligence, but human intelligence insofar as it is combined with access to the *signals of information* that intelligence can recognize and convert into the ability either to constrain people or to cause them to change opinion or direction.

The modern democratic state illustrates this principle. In a nation where people govern themselves, the voter may influence the policies of a political candidate by either granting or denying him his ballot. But without information about the candidate's record or attitudes, the citizen in a voting booth has no more political power than a chimpanzee randomly pulling the levers of a feeding machine in a psychology laboratory. In the marketplace, too, the consumer, like the voter, has the theoretical power to put the uncaring or dishonest manufacturer or merchant out of business by withholding money or trade. But no such power exists unless the buyer has the appropriate information as to what and from whom he is buying—that is unless he is, as we usually say, an "informed" consumer.

Similarly, courts of law may be mighty instruments of state power. But without necessary information to make judgments and issue decrees, even a court will be altogether helpless. In 1973, for example, a team of skilled investigators armed with the power to subpoena witnesses had to search for months before it could detect and then prove that the Detroit Edison Company was using a "black dot" racial coding system to channel promotions of black employees into lower-paying job categories. In another Detroit case, dozens of lawyers spent thousands of hours locating, sorting, collating, and comparing 40,000 pupil transfer slips in order to provide the courts with information that would prove that the Board of Education was using its official powers to racially segregate the city's schools. Thus, without access to information even the state itself, the repository of sovereign power, may become altogether weak and helpless.[1]

In general, the principle can be stated as follows: No person or institution may employ power without the appropriate information required for rational thought, judgment, and planning. In turn, this means that the degree of power one possesses will depend largely upon one's position with regard to *access* to information. Power is necessarily unequal when one party to any competitive transaction knows what's going on and the other party doesn't. So, too, adversary political and economic positions are always unequal when one group is largely unaware of its strategic and tactical position and another group possesses all the information it needs to rationally choose the most advantageous course to advance its policies and goals. To a surprising extent, the principle of information inequality alone accounts for the fact that many of the civil rights organizations designed to advance the status of blacks in the United States tend to be relatively powerless. These organizations often possess many of the trappings of power—troops willing to rally to a cause, a collective will to produce change, and the ability to sound the call to arms—but the organizations remain impotent because of a woeful inability to secure strategic information from others.

The rule that power derives from access to information applies to the protection of our most important and cherished liberties. In a very real sense, the freedoms intended to be derived from the Bill of Rights, as well as from civil rights legislation, will not be realized in practice unless one has access to certain necessary information. Each of us theoretically enjoys the fundamental liberties of freedom from certain illegitimate exercises of power such as rigged juries, "redlined" lending districts, racially gerrymandered voting districts, and racially motivated decisions in employment. But, in fact, these promised liberties are merely abstract and fuzzy assurances unless the people affected have access to, or command over, *information* as to whether, by what processes, and by whom these liberties are being denied. Without this information, minorities may not even know that race discrimination is being used as a weapon against them, much less be in a position to do anything about this unlawful restriction of their protected liberties.

Because power always depends on information, intelligence-gathering activities must be understood as an integral part of the acquisition and maintenance of power. This explains why governments and other powerful institutions frequently tap telephones, send up spy satellites, and dispatch agents into the innermost citadels of rival governments or large corporations. The various domestic and foreign intelligence agencies of the United States Government spend upward of $3 billion a year and employ over 51,000 people in the gathering of information. Formal intelligence operations are always missions of power.

How Secrecy Disarms Power

Since control and possession of information are indispensable to the exercise of power, it stands to reason that those who hold power will often try to block access to information as a means of maintaining the power balance in their own favor. The practice of secrecy thus becomes a fundamental trait of the power user. It is easy to understand why, for example, the Federal Bureau of Investigation does not publish lists of those under surveillance. Such secrecy obviously serves a legitimate investigative purpose. But it is not so readily apparent why the U.S. Government does not widely publish lists of the subsidies it regularly pays to racially segregated institutions. And what purpose is served by the Department of the Treasury's policy of maintaining lists of hundreds of financial institutions which are not in compliance with federal affirmative-action employment regulations, yet giving these lists no publicity whatever. Similarly, school boards throughout the country do not disclose their policies in siting newly constructed schools in cities with large black populations; neither do they publish the ratio of black teachers to white teachers, or the expenditures per pupil allocated according to racial groups. These facts have to be pried out of most public institutions, and this can be done only by those already in possession of enough information to know what to ask, whom to ask it of, and where to look for the desired facts. In cases where information is denied, the process of secrecy is an integral part of the power strategy by which an institution husbands its own power and, in so doing, denies power to others.

The habit of secrecy and the tendency to cover up facts and processes are also natural traits of powerful organizations in our society other than the government. Labor and business organizations guard their powers as well as their freedoms by controlling information. Plumbers' unions, for example, have fought determined and costly court battles to keep secret the fact that only a small fraction of their membership is recruited from the ranks of racial minorities. Insurance companies and credit institutions spend huge amounts in legal fees before agreeing to surrender information about the percentage of loans or investments they have in minority communities. Ask a major corporation about its voluntary community outreach programs and a full and only moderately embellished answer will be received. Ask the same corporation about its minority recruiting policies, about the ways it sets opportunities for the advancement of blacks, or about the institutional process by which it determines the effect on minority employees of the location of a new plant. The answers will, at best, be evasive. The reason for silence or evasion is not necessarily one of bureaucratic ignorance or of corporate rigidity. Nor can one necessarily conclude by the presence of evasive tactics that institutional opposition to the advancement of black people is at work. But one can be quite sure that institutional freedom and power are being protected.

It can be concluded, then, that many powerful business and governmental organizations mislead others simply because this mode of communication is inherent in the very nature of organizational power. The possession of great power virtually commands equivocation or the withholding of information; and in many cases, organizations are powerful precisely because they do this. Powerful organizations survive best in dim light; they thrive in total darkness.

Empowerment is therefore a process not only of securing and processing available information, but also of legitimately obtaining at least partial command over society's established instruments for *requiring* the production of information. No group that has been removed or isolated from power, either in its private or public form, may come to power until it understands its needs to win access to information, until it wins the power to command intelligence and, finally, until it secures in hand the information necessary for the display or use of power. Unquestionably the most important of all these instruments for forcing disclosure of information is the government subpoena. Any person or group armed with subpoena powers is strong indeed. Reciprocally, one can count on the fact that people or groups whose members rarely hold or control the subpoena power will also tend to be the same people who in any particular society also occupy subordinate economic and political positions.

Some groups that aspire to power confidently believe that powerful institutions will voluntarily turn over information needed by the weak. But this is living in a fool's paradise. The magician never reveals his tricks. And the powerful almost never make other people powerful.

Hiding Who Has Power

Concealing information from the powerless not only serves to enhance power, but also benefits the powerful by camouflaging the locus of power itself. Thus, powerful people usually deny that they have power and almost always deny that they want or seek it. The powerful sometimes hide their power by falsely claiming that power is in the hands of others, such as puppet heads or token personnel. Members of the federal government have been particularly adept at the deceptive siting of power. During the early 1970s, for example, when the nation was seriously considering welfare reform, the White House made all decisions while falsely informing the public that the Department of Health, Education, and Welfare was calling the shots. Similarly, the Federal Reserve Board has consistently responded to protests over bank credit discrimination by falsely declaring that Congress, not the Board, had the power to direct the flow of credit into minority communities. In 1972, President Nixon declared that he had no power to enforce the law requiring certain local school districts to achieve racial balance by busing children. This was, in fact, a traditional act of power exercised through simple disclaimer of the possession of power.

The plain conclusion is that those who want power must first find out who has it. In order to stop air pollution, to block the sale of dangerous food, or to curb racial discrimination, one must discover who controls these activities, who, if anyone, profits from them, and who has the power to stop them. One must work skillfully through the labyrinths of concealment that lead ultimately to the commander-in-chief. He is often located not in the White House or its corporate equivalent, but in a dingy brownstone building many blocks across town.

Power in Flock Effect:
Imposing One's Will Through Group Action

People who are bereft of most of the familiar instruments of power— money, the ability to be skillful at a task, access to political spoils, and connections with the mighty—tend to seek power, if they seek it at all, by means of concerted or unanimous action. This seemingly innocent term conceals one of the most effective forms of human power. A familiar law of physics is that force is greatly multiplied when individual units of power are combined in place and time. Examples of concerted action or consensus effect are familiar. Raindrops falling randomly on a roof will present no threat to the structure, but the roof will cave in if all the water is deposited on one part of it at a single point in time. Many animals use flock effect to achieve power. Hawks sometimes hunt in pairs to catch squirrels which could elude a single predator by hiding around tree trunks. A wolf pack has a cooperative strategy for killing a moose, one wolf going for the vulnerable nose while another attacks the hindquarters.

Humans, too, are much more powerful when they act in groups. Voting coalitions, protest marches, group sit-ins, hunger strikes, and product boycotts are familiar examples of the power of gathering in crowds. So too are vigilante posses, economic blacklists, all-white primaries, and whites-only codes in labor unions. A rebellious form of consensus power appears in the ancient practice known as the "collective mutiny." For blacks, the collective acts of feigning ignorance and breaking tools were the first uses of consensus power employed during the slave period. Today, as always, group energy effect always adds up to much more force than the sum total of the units of energy involved. For outcast groups of people who have little or no access to any of a society's positions of power—state office, legislative positions, high offices in major corporations—the power of consensus or concerted action is usually the only means of asserting greater influence and winning the attention of people who are otherwise unconcerned.

Although power through concerted action may take such highly visible forms as a work stoppage or a protest march on the nation's capital, the force of group effect will just as often operate in a silent and altogether invisible manner. People who are the targets of group prejudgments or prejudice are familiar with this force. In economic terms, for example, the restriction on black opportunities is about the same whether people openly display their prejudice or covertly decide not to hire black clerks, artisans or business managers. Thus, if members of a majority group, acting without plan or premeditation, happen upon a collective decision to exclude blacks from certain public schools, the constraint is just as great as it would be if open, violent, and virulent race prejudice were at work. When, as used to be the case, the majority of people quietly acts in concert to reject or boycott Negro labor, a severe economic force is brought to bear on blacks, even though none of what we think of as the traditional instruments of force, terror, or violence has been employed.

If, as already noted, access to information is the first principle of power, the second principle is collective action. In accordance with the first requirement which insists on controlling who gets information, the first step toward successful revolutionary change in government power has always been the seizing of all radio stations and newspapers. In accordance with the principle of collective action, the second task of almost any revolutionary government is the banning of private collective action —usually by outlawing the assembly of more than five people unless they have first obtained a police permit. Thus, the powers that a totalitarian state represses provide sure clues to the mechanics of power assured in a free society.

If power is found in consensus, and if power-building is consensus-building, it follows that power disappears whenever consensus dissipates. Everyday examples of this phenomenon are familiar. A strike threat buckles and loses its force if a significant number of strikers withdraw from the common mutiny and decide to go back to work. The will of a great nation to fight a war becomes paralyzed when it is beset by internal dissensions over its moral right to conduct that war. The power of a great political party ebbs and disappears when its ranks split. An economic cartel loses its force if one or more members withdraw, cut prices, or decide to trade with or employ those who were previously boycotted.

Notice in this connection that the sudden fragmentation of an earlier consensus lies at the very root of the powerlessness of blacks today. Over a period of only a few years, the force of the black movement achieved under the great unifying influence of Dr. Martin Luther King, Jr. declined and dissolved. For a number of years black organizations have been feuding with one another over goals, tactics, and government funding. Running counter to the political objectives of large numbers of poor blacks, a new breed of middle-class Negroes has strong economic disincentives which prevent them from vehemently pressing for tighter antidiscrimination laws and stricter affirmative-action rules. Because of these divisions and disputes, blacks in the United States still count for little as a political force; nobody worries very much about their pain or plans, and they no longer exert much political or economic pressure on the American majority. Black people rarely succeed in enlisting government power to act on their behalf. And the more they proclaim that they are "Republicans who happen to be black" or "Democrats who happen to be Negro," the more clearly they announce, too, both their group virtue as well as their political impotence.

In a world terrorized by nuclear weapons and lone snipers one sometimes forgets that collective action is still the driving force behind most forms of usable worldly power. The Revolutionary War rallying cry, "United we stand, divided we fall," was not just a slogan to boost morale. It was then and is today a concise and accurate statement of the power process.

The Power-Deficient Environment

Another word for consensus is "organization," in the sense that consensus requires the presence of people who are willing to think and act alike for a common purpose. The absence of consensus, then, amounts to disorder, disorganization, and sometimes even chaos. In this impotent condition, people act randomly, often competitively, never in concert or collusively, and obviously not as a unified body. Such disorganized, random, and nonpurposeful behavior constitutes a vacuum state which I shall call a "power-deficient environment."

Without making any judgment for the moment about how such a situation might have evolved, it seems clear that the so-called urban ghetto is a prime example of a power-deficient environment. Events there occur more often by accident than as a result of plan or design. Work patterns tend to be part-time, irregular, and uncoordinated. Commercial transactions are often completed as the result of an accidental meeting; just as often, they fail to happen because of a lack of common planning or purpose. People tend to allow themselves to drift into even the most important life decisions, such as marriage, childbirth, and jobs. In the inner city, there is often neither formal nor informal political action, just as there is often no concerted effort by any group to protect itself against crime, drug abuse, or commercial exploitation. As members of a power-deficient environment, the urban poor do not command income, retain money, accumulate reserves, or create a hedge against catastrophic or unexpected events. In many cities, low-income minorities have no local zoning boards, no school districts, no banking institutions, no ward organizations, and no other institutions through which they can act collectively for a common purpose.

In sharp contrast is the power-intensive environment. A traditional suburb of a major city, for example, acts collectively for its citizens' protection. Through mutually agreed upon zoning restrictions, it protects itself against the influx of the poor and blacks. It sends large delegations to the state capital when a new road threatens to divide it. Every election day, it dispatches ten times more voters per capita to the polls than does the urban ghetto. The middle-class American suburban community acts cooperatively through a variety of collective institutions to protect its children, its safety, its health, its housing, its recreational facilities, and its employment. It represses competitive and divisive tendencies in favor of common leadership and a plan. More because of its abiding community consensus than because of its money, it virtually bristles with all the signals of power.

It is important, then, that we understand that power may have a *territorial status*. There are power-intensive places or communities just as there are power-deficient ones. And in many cases, the determining factor is the presence or absence of organization or consensus.

Power on the Cheap:
Threats and Coercive Bluffing

In life's competition, tribal groups, as well as individuals, discovered in the manner of the orangutan how to win superior positions not only by force but by a *show of force*. The reasons were pragmatic. Like energy, power is subject to the rules of conservation. No matter how great one's power, limitations on resources, energy, and influence always exist. To overcome these limitations, man has developed two basic ploys for signaling power without using it: the bluff and the threat. Essentially, any indication of a willingness to use power constitutes a threat. The threat becomes a bluff when the threatening party knows—but the threatened party does not—that the threat either cannot or will be carried out. In either case, both the threat and the bluff permit one to magnify one's power by gaining the effects of power without expending any resources or energy. For example, a labor union may not have the strength to strike both General Motors and Ford, but both companies can often be brought to terms if the union does not disclose which company it intends to strike. In war, multiple enemies may sometimes be kept at bay if one makes power displays on two fronts, without committing to either. Throughout history, some of the most important successes in the use of diplomatic power have occurred not as a result of explicit military power displays, such as troop movements, but rather as a result of hints or bluffs.

In the modern world, threat power has become a common manipulator of human behavior. Governments use threat power in international affairs;

welfare officials use the subsistence check as threat power. The grading system in schools and, for teenagers, the keys to the family car are also forms of threat power. In all cases the power principle is the same: obtaining control or obedience by threatening painful adverse consequences.

In political and economic practice, the threat and the bluff have been greatly disparaged. However, the threat as well as the bluff may be invaluable and acceptable for human protection and advancement. In fact, the traditional democracy both confers and protects nonviolent threat power in the hands of the people. This includes the right to threaten to organize for collective bargaining, the right to threaten to strike, the right to threaten to run for public office, the right to threaten to vote as a bloc, or the right to threaten to boycott a presidential nominating convention. In these examples, the government overtly and constitutionally protects not only a collusive act, but also the threat to use the coercive power of collusion or unanimous action.

Power on Deposit: The Institutionalization of Threats

The principle of power conservation not only gives rise to threat strategy but also supports the idea of institutionalized power. Institutionalized power is power in storage: threats saved up, constraint operating in permanent form. Like a charged battery, institutionalized power emits signals of force and constraint even when no one is turning the crank of the power generator. The development of institutionalized power has been a major evolutionary strategy that people have developed over the centuries to establish superior positions for themselves and to deal with the threats and depredations of others.

Let us look at a simple example of the institutionalization of power. If I have to chase you off my front field every time you steal my vegetables, my power is not institutionalized. This is so because no permanent constraint is in place. On the other hand, if I build an electric fence around my front field, then my power has been converted into permanent form. Now I can sit on the porch and drink mint juleps knowing that I am more or less secure. The fence represents power institutionalized; it provides constraint both day and night. Having created a store of constraining power by building the fence to keep strangers away from my front field, I am now free, if I wish, to use my energy to chase trespassers off my back field.

In this example, threat power takes the form of a tangible constraining barrier. Another way to institutionalize power is to establish a reputation for tracking down and punishing those who persist in stealing vegetables. Better yet, one might arrange for the passage of the public law forbidding and punishing theft, in which case public law enforcers would do the actual work of providing an effective barrier to theft. Threat power, moreover, sometimes takes the form of social custom, etiquette, or taboo. Codes of expected behavior, backed by only an occasional sanction, such as an act of ostracism or public criticism, apply the same threat power as the presence of an electric fence. In the same manner, traditional taboos against mixing the races in schools or employment enforce themselves without dealing out punishments or sanctions in individual cases. When the sabre has been rattled once or twice, the code of behavior is publicly understood. It is not necessary to expend energy power to chase each and every violator off prohibited turf.

From the earliest times, the foundations of public law have rested on the power of the institutionalized threat. Hammurabi's price control laws were obeyed not because Babylonian merchants were actually drowned daily, but because of the king's stated intention, and apparent ability, to have these price gougers drowned. From time to time, the handgun lobby in the United States demonstrates its ability to remove from office a congressman who has the temerity to introduce a gun-control bill. This occasional act of political terror has been sufficient to keep much of the rest of Congress in line. Highly visible and believable institutionalized power acts as a kind of watchdog agency. Once an institution has established credible evidence of its ability to bring others into compliance with its will, the club, the boycott, the strike, or the protest march may become unnecessary. For many years, Reverend Jesse Jackson successfully policed "fair" employment practices in Chicago by exploiting the leverage he gained with a few demonstrations of boycott power. Jackson was fond of saying, "It only takes one phone call from Breadbasket to send them scurrying. They move as soon as they hear your footsteps coming." For good or for bad, Jackson used institutionalized threat power to enact his own set of affirmative-action laws.

In southern communities a generation earlier, institutionalized threat power was on the other foot. Armed police officers or squads of vigilantes simply took an occasional stroll through the black districts of southern cities and towns. Without the need to show violence, a highly effective form of threat power was at work: keeping black people off the streets after 9 P.M., requiring deferential behavior, making it clear that black voter registration —or perhaps even interracial dating—would not be tolerated.

In recent history, minority groups have experimented only tentatively with consensus power in its stored or institutionalized forms. Blacks have tended to rely instead on less sophisticated and impermanent manifestations of sporadic consensus power, usually in the form of an ephemeral act of group revolt or a demonstration of temporary outrage. From time to time the moral force of charismatic leaders has produced marches on state capitals as well as other forms of collective action and pressure. But an isolated instance of, say, 10,000 blacks marching on Washington or on Selma, Alabama is a far cry from a massive reservoir of institutionalized power that is capable, *on demand,* of organizing 10,000 blacks to march on Washington or Selma—or of even credibly threatening to organize such a march. Among black organizations, only the trade union of sleeping car porters and the Southern Christian Leadership Conference have approached this degree of organized and institutionalized power. And today, with the catalytic force of Martin Luther King, Jr. and A. Philip Randolph no longer on the scene, there is no viable body of institutionalized black power in this country capable of putting significant nonviolent black consensus pressure into action. Indeed, throughout the country there are many organizations of "black educators," "black engineers," "black lawyers," and so forth. These are loose affiliations of black people that display no power traits whatsoever.

Only a few years ago, many black groups were actively calling for institution building, thus directly addressing the issue of their need for group empowerment. They urged the creation of civil rights organizations, legislative caucuses, lobbying bodies, centers for teaching economic and political power, rural agricultural collectives, and urban community development corporations. These are precisely the kinds of bodies that, independent of individual leadership, tend to gather a stored-up capacity for pressure and persuasion. People who scoff at such proposals and who put them down as mere posturing or rhetoric will do well to restudy the mechanics of collective power. Using the threat force of collective action *without actually fighting* or taking overt action has always been a potent weapon of those who are otherwise powerless.

When Power Provides Loopholes

In crudest terms, the intensity of power is measured in inverse ratio to the number of choices left to the object of constraint. A gun pointed at a person's head is an example of almost total constraint, for, in this case, the options narrow virtually to one. The same could be true of, say, a truly punitive tax imposed on racially segregated institutions. In these situations, there are no "loopholes," "moral obligations," "guidelines," "hiring objectives," or "ambiguities of language." There are no sanctuaries in which the target of raw power may take refuge.

A court order, on the other hand, may or may not have the same power intensity as a mugging or a holdup, depending on the circumstances of those at whom the order is directed. For example, a judge's order requiring citizens of a community to register their children in racially balanced public schools may appear to leave those subject to the order with no options. But this is so only until loopholes are discovered. One family may move its residence to an all-white suburb; another may organize an all-white private school. When these escape hatches are discovered by the people intended to be constrained, a force that at first appears to be an irresistible exercise of government power largely dissolves. For good or bad, government power has been foiled. For others, however, the constraint is total—particularly for those who have neither the choice of changing their addresses nor the money to organize racially segregated academies.

Many "orders" issued by the state amount to little more than advice or entreaties. For example, suppose that a state-supported university has a long record of racial discrimination in the employment of teachers. A court order may be issued requiring that within five years the faculty of the university must achieve a minority membership roughly proportional to the population mix of the surrounding community. If such an order were a true command, the university would be almost totally constrained. On the other hand, the court may issue an "order" simply calling upon the institution's faculty recruiters to search the country for black teachers, but may permit them to hire purely on such a basis as they see fit. In this case, only a modicum of constraint is placed upon the university, leaving it free to do as it wishes as long as it puts on a suitable show of attempted compliance to satisfy the court that it is acting in good faith.

In identifying the presence of power or constraint, therefore, one must not confuse entreaties with commands, or expectations with orders. The implications of the difference are crucial for public policy. Interest groups working for the advancement of minority groups have often been bought off by orders that seemingly grant their wishes, only to discover later that these so-called orders were, in fact, not binding on anyone. A well-known declaration of good intentions masquerading as constraint is contained in the 1977 Statement of the Declared Racial Policies of United States Firms With Affiliates in South Africa, the so-called Sullivan Principles. In the late 1970s, at least 100 major U.S. corporations doing business in South Africa subscribed in writing to the Sullivan Principles without limiting, in any way, their freedom to employ anyone they chose. The Sullivan Principles provided:

"[We] support the following operating principles:

1. Non-segregation of the races in all eating, comfort and work facilities.
2. Equal and fair employment practices for all employees.
3. Equal pay for all employees doing equal or comparable work for the same period of time.
4. Initiation of and development of training programs that will prepare in substantial numbers, Blacks and other non-whites for supervisory, administrative, clerical and technical jobs.
5. Increasing the number of Blacks and other non-whites in management and supervisory positions.
6. Improving the quality of employees' lives outside the work environment in such areas as housing, transportation, schooling, recreation and health facilities.

We agree to further implement these principles. Where implementation requires a modification of existing South African working conditions, we will seek such modification through appropriate channels.

We believe that the implementation of the foregoing principles is consistent with respect for human dignity and will contribute greatly to the general economic welfare of all the people of the Republic of South Africa."

The rhetoric of this declaration rings with conviction. Many university student activists of the 1970s, who sounded the alarms of protest, accepted the Sullivan statement as a landmark of racial progress. But one looks in vain for something in the words that obliges anyone to do anything. This example serves as a warning. Whenever powerful organizations all too readily submit to apparent constraint, it is useful to look for the loopholes that convert an order into a mere entreaty. For a command to function as such, it must contain a clear delineation of duties and sharply defined rules of behavior. The order must set forth a date and a specific place, must precisely describe a quantifiable commodity that must be appropriated or an action that is obligatory. There can be no loopholes, no advisory commissions to recommend change, no slippery avenues of escape.

No Power Without Sanctions

The exercise of coercive power requires the real, or apparent, ability and willingness to deliver or suspend pain or penalties. Over many years, for example, public schools in the South were free to disobey the Supreme Court school integration decision in *Brown v. Board of Education* because no police officials, state governors, or states' attorneys were disposed either to enforce the law or to impose fines or penalties for even the most flagrant violations of law. Also, for many years, Congress was noticeably opposed to the Court's school integration orders and took no steps to enforce them. Similarly, construction unions working on government jobs openly ignored government-ordered racial employment requirements and felt no pressure to do otherwise because the Office of Federal Contract Compliance Programs had sent clear signals that its rules were not to be taken seriously.[2] Many large financial institutions holding government deposits have consistently disobeyed federal rules prohibiting employment and credit discrimination, knowing full well that the United States Treasury does not withdraw its deposits for infractions of its equal opportunity rules. Thus, the presence of a watchdog person or agency that is willing and able to impose sanctions is indispensable to creating even the most rudimentary form of constraint. Organizations that lobby for so-called voluntary regulation do not subject themselves to even the slightest degree of constraint. They are merely asserting normal human aspirations for institutional autonomy. Similarly, other organizations that campaign "for flexible goals for minority employment" should not be viewed as submitting to a rule against job bias: they, too, in many cases are simply asserting their desires to employ white people in preference to black people.

Notice, however, that the powerful will often conciliate or blunt assertions of the will of others by creating government watchdog agencies having only theatrical or mock power. Consider, for example, the U.S. Civil Rights Commission. The word "Rights" in the name of the Commission conveys the idea of constraint or obligation, but the Commission is, in fact, merely an advisory body. Similar elements of mock power may be discovered also in the charter of the Equal Employment Opportunity Commission. The EEOC appears to bristle with power; it issues great sheaves of regulations. Business corporations rail against its "oppressive" rules and red tape. The powers of the EEOC are said to be intolerably arrogant and oppressive. But this agency, like other citizen bodies, is in many respects an ornamental agency of exhortation. Its powers are essentially conciliatory. It may advise and entreat, but like any ordinary citizen it is obliged to go to court in order to win the right to command adherence to its mandates. One should never confuse its powers with those of agencies having the power to compel. The Federal Communications Commission, for example, has the power to revoke broadcast licenses. For many years, the Federal Trade

Commission made binding laws of commerce. When the Securities and Exchange Commission tells a corporation to jump, the usual reply is, "Where, when, and how high?" The hortatory orders of scores of mock administrative bodies—organizations that abound in the field of minority rights—must be distinguished from those that truly have the powers to adjudicate or command.

The ability to levy fines or even to impose jail sentences—the normal forms of government sanctions—is not necessarily sufficient for the effective exercise of power. Indeed, major corporations often treat even large government fines as mere slaps on the wrist, writing off the loss as just another, and usually tax-deductible, cost of doing business. But public or peer humiliation is another matter. When, for example, pressure groups succeed in publicly humiliating corporate executives who break laws, or in morally isolating a corporation as an "outlaw" from the mainstream of respectable behavior, the pressure groups may, in effect, be issuing public commands. Their de facto regulatory powers are considerable even though they have no formal right to make laws or to activate established processes of legislative or executive action.

Violence as Power

Despite all we have said about the subtle and hidden processes of power, the fact remains that much of the power in the world, whether in private or state hands, emerges from the capacity to commit acts of violence. Plainly and simply, man has borrowed and adapted nature's original terrors. Very early in history, humans became the planet's most effective and notorious users of raw power in the form of brute force. In an effort to diminish the potential for chaos and self-destruction implicit in this fact, most societies have limited the right to use violence and terror by reserving this power for use only by the state. Indeed, the great German sociologist Max Weber has defined the state as neither more nor less than an institution possessing a monopoly on the legitimate use of force within a given territory.

This state monopoly over the use of violence implicitly requires that the state use its powers to suppress the private use of violence by individuals or bands of individuals. Nevertheless, private violence, usually in covert form, has been tolerated by the state to a surprising degree. The state is especially likely to avert its eyes and allow the use of private terror when the political objectives of the terrorists are in harmony with the state's own aims or even in line with the personal beliefs of law enforcement officials. In American history, the most notorious examples of this phenomenon were the lynchings of black people, midnight raids on Negro neighborhoods, and other acts of terrorism conducted by white citizens' councils and members of the Ku Klux Klan. That whites were rarely, if ever, punished for such acts reflected not only the private sympathies of southern sheriffs, but also the official policies of state and federal governments which, through most of the history of the nation, approved and nurtured a public apparatus of racial caste and subordination.

Despite such glaring exceptions, it generally remains true that the right to use violence is reserved to the state. As a result, it often follows that those groups in a society that control the instruments of violence are the real, although often secret, powers behind a government. Identifying the locus of power in this way is always valid in a totalitarian state. If, in a particular society, one discovers that considerable power is held by an industrial clique, by a merchant class, or by an aristocracy of peers of the realm, one will usually find that these groups also have a rather firm influence over the military and the central police. In contrast, the minor staff officers and the foot soldiers in the military will tend to be drawn from the same groups that work as clerks and functionaries in banks and industrial organizations. Even in a constitutional republic such as the United States, we learn a great deal about who holds economic and political power by identifying the civilian groups that head and oversee the activities of the military. In this respect, the process of identifying the locus of power in a particular nation or society has not changed since Edward Gibbon first analyzed the nature of the power of Rome.

Power in a Candy Box

The use of force or deprivation is only one side of the mechanics of human power. Obviously, people may be influenced or held in place by offering them pleasure as well as by threatening them with pain. The ability to convey rewards is no less real as a form of power than the ability to inflict punishment, although reward power is not nearly so absolute and automatic in its operations. Thus, where brute force leaves the object of power little choice but obedience, the offer of rewards permits a certain latitude in response. Those who are being subjected to influence or temptation are, after all, technically free to repudiate favors that tend to curb their auton-omy. On the whole, however, if the treasure offered is sufficient, resistance requires an unusual degree of fortitude. In actual practice, few instruments of power have been as efficient as taking a person to the top of a mountain and showing him a kingdom below, presenting him with a vicuna coat, or demonstrating the capacity to deliver money to a Swiss bank. Since the earliest history of mankind, power has consistently disarmed other power by corrupting it, by paying it to not do its duty or to desert its individual or group purposes.

This cynical but indisputably valid view of much of human motivation means that no successful analysis of power relationships is possible without determining who controls, or has the means to buy, the loyalty or sympathetic attention of others. To a large extent, many of the power relationships that we consider legitimate and proper turn on who owns wealth, who controls large pools of money, who fills job openings, and who controls the award of prizes and prestigious positions. Especially in a democratic state, the process of barter has become the motor force of government. A despotic emperor has very little need for negotiation and exchange because he is able to control the behavior of his subjects by simple unilateral commands. But an official of a constitutionally governed republic rarely possesses such absolute authority; the coercive power of the state is usually dispersed among countless government branches and agencies. To move the state into action, it is necessary to assemble a coalition or consensus of agencies and constituencies. This is where reward power comes into play, for it is often the most effective instrument either for forming or for breaking the alliances that ultimately produce legislative or executive commands.

In the workings of America's two-party democracy, for example, Republicans always find themselves having to take steps to make peace with labor unions, just as Democrats, who can generally count on union support, have to come to terms with industrial leaders. A congressman from the Second District frequently strikes a bargain with a congressman from the Ninth, ensuring support for appropriations that benefit the other. A representative from Harlem who may be a member of the House Defense Appropriations Committee may trade his vote to save aircraft manufacturing jobs in California for a California congressman's reciprocal support of a federal job development program in Harlem. One hand, as they say, washes the other. These practices are lawful, legitimate, and are, in fact, encouraged under democratic forms of government.

In an exchange system where people advance their political and economic goals by making connections and building alliances, power begets power and wealth creates additional wealth. Those who already have the economic or political strength to influence the outcome of the government's decision-making process are usually able to secure government decisions that will in turn assure them of a greater share of society's goods and wealth. Groups with superior political bargaining power are in a position to claim a larger share of public franchises, deposits, contracts, and subsidies. The powerful who win access to the spoils of political victory may use these resources to purchase further economic or political advantages. Weaker groups with no delegates in the centers of power, or with delegates who have little of the wherewithal to barter for the favor of the legislative and executive branches of government, are thus likely to receive a smaller share of society's goods.

Foreswearing the Power of the Purse

While the nation's governance has always swung on the hinge of political barter, political theorists express a sturdy faith that a sort of ad hoc equilibrium will prevail: big business's generosity to the Republicans will be matched by the intensive voter-registration drives of the AFL-CIO's Committee on Political Education on behalf of the Democrats. In theory, and often in practice, the danger of monopoly control over the force of government has been mitigated by the presence of strong countervailing forces. Yet, for various reasons certain classes of citizens—particularly the black minority in the United States—have come up short in terms of bargaining chips. These groups never sat as chairmen of the great committees of Congress; they seldom occupied posts in government where they could disburse public funds; they had no access to the war chests of large corporations or of labor unions. Members of these groups almost never sat on licensing boards where they could grant permits and thereby enhance the economic as well as the political positions of their constituencies. Blacks and other low-status groups almost never held posts on city education or health boards where they could barter favors in exchange for new schools, streetlights, hospitals, and other benefits for their communities or their friends. In the eyes of the United States Constitution, these low-ranking groups had an equal voice and vote; yet, possessing none of society's standard means of rewarding others, they became almost wholly subject to governance by a more powerful majority. Those who lived outside the centers of power were generally obliged to entrust their hopes for group progress, a better life, and equality of opportunity to the goodwill—or guilt feelings—of dominant groups that had established access to all of the bargaining chips and favors that drive the forces of the political and economic marketplace.

Exclusions from power—be they separations either from trafficking in favors or from the coercive process—tend to be advertised as self-chosen. For this and other reasons, outcast groups have often disdained the role of political barter in allocating positions in a democratic state. Many minority spokesmen, particularly, have taken a high ethical line. Admirably straight-laced, they have steadfastly insisted that it was not right or proper to employ the machinery of politics to buy rights, liberties, or equal opportunity. They repudiated the degraded politics of cloakroom conciliation. They stood morally superior to the grubby legislators who horse-traded votes, jockeyed for favorable assessments, voted their prejudices, and thereby made the laws of the nation. Often, the less powerful sought instead to perfect their civil rights and to improve their economic positions by appealing to the generous spirit of the mighty. Many Negro leaders, in particular, beseeched powerful segregationists in Congress to abandon their political attacks against the proponents of racial integration. In the name of justice and fairness, black civil rights groups made nationwide pleas for equal treatment of the races and for the appointment of blacks to policymaking positions. Allied with the League of Women Voters and other groups of compassionate and often idealistic whites, they urged reluctant Presidents to adopt statesmanlike declarations in favor of the protection of voting rights. They agitated furiously for racial justice with every weapon available other than the standard articles of the powerful.

In foreswearing use of the standard horse-trading techniques of elected assemblies, blacks and other low-ranking groups were denying themselves access to established institutions of human power. They were rejecting the means of protection and advantage which, since the dawn of civilization, have controlled people's chances for surviving, for living in decent circumstances, and for otherwise realizing the fulfillment of their human potential. In a utopian society, we are told, weaker groups will be well protected and nourished by the strong. But in a world regulated by power, those at the bottom who repudiate the classic techniques of political barter tend to assure themselves a permanent position as well-pacified clients of the more skillful operators of the machinery of state.

Power as Proprietary Positions

In the first chapter, we showed how coercive power developed in the form of a number of rudimentary proprietary arrangements. A defined hunting or fishing territory was necessarily an instrument of power since it excluded entry by others whose freedoms were, to that extent, restricted. One person's possession of a digging stick and a cave necessarily meant that another person could not use them. The sum total of one particular tribe's proprietary holdings—its tools, its spears, its undisclosed or protected fishing holes, its stores of surplus food or water, its fenced-off agricultural plots—was an excellent measure of the tribe's power and well-being.

As mankind developed the idea of proprietary power, the simple concept of tribal real estate or tools was left in the dust. A dazzling array of property entitlements emerged, each of which protected the advantage of some as it denied advantage to others. The industrial revolution produced factories and machinery whose owners or managers necessarily decided who would or would not be allowed to take employment. The proprietors of large financial institutions determined who, or which groups, would be granted or denied credit. The heads of large insurance companies necessarily decided whose commercial undertakings were bondable and, therefore, who was qualified to bid on private or government contracts. In modern times, those who had, or controlled access to, certain computers had an exclusive franchise to grant or deny the power of information. Institutions possessing special sources of information, or having technical equipment that could process information faster than others, could literally force third parties to pay huge economic rents for the superior information the owners or makers of the computers possessed.

In modern society, the power holder's most valuable property rights took the form of intangible property. These were enforceable promises, or freedom limitations, undertaken by others. These proprietary intangibles included promissory notes, bonds, and other indentures. Add to that patents, government contracts, and franchises. These intangibles, defended by the power of the state against use or appropriation by others, included such further proprietary rights as price supports, tax subsidies, cost-of-living allowances, and labor contracts. Even diplomas, test scores, racial expectations, seniority arrangements, a favored chance of admission to an educational institution, and tenured employment became articles of proprietary power or advantage. In all of these examples of contemporary property power, there was the presence of a protected advantage that always included the right or ability to defend a position and exclude others from it.

The distribution of these proprietary intangibles often became the most reliable indicator of modern economic power. Invariably, the powerful owned or controlled these proprietary intangibles, and the powerful were known because they had them. Possibly the single most important badge of the powerlessness of blacks in America has been their total separation from either ownership or influence over the standard instruments of capital and proprietary power. Until very recently, black people rarely controlled or owned any part of capitalism's standard supply of intangibles. Nor did they participate in the contractual economy under which labor, capital, and goods were allocated according to the standard promissory arrangements and property entitlements of the modern industrial state. In this sense, the economic position of blacks was structurally backward. In fact, throughout the first half of the twentieth century, the status of the American Negro was still determined in the feudal tradition of class which prescribed menial forms of obligatory employment and virtually proscribed ownership of the instruments of capital. And even in the contemporary contest for economic success and advantage, black people continued to be armed as poor men with spears and rifles while the white majority had exclusive control over all the heavy artillery of the capitalist state.

On Self-Funded Positions

In the mistaken belief that World War II had not ended, Private Teruo Nakamura of the Japanese Imperial Army spent thirty years in hiding on the Indonesian island of Morotai. In excellent physical condition, he was lured back to civilization by the playing of the Japanese national anthem. For three decades, he had survived on a diet of wild bananas and potatoes.

This humble little tale reminds us of how much can be accomplished on the basis of a simple ability to take care of one's self. The reason is obvious. A self-sufficient individual is less vulnerable to the threats of the powerful and therefore less subject to their power. The Japanese islands depended on imported raw materials to make everything from battleships and airplanes to gunpowder and bullets. When their sea lanes were cut off, surrender was inevitable. But Private Nakamura depended on nothing but his own survival skills. As long as the bananas and potatoes held out, he could wage war indefinitely.

Examples of the principle are legion. The employee who reports a pollution violation in his employer's factories is well advised first to make sure that his retirement benefits are vested and protected. A charitable foundation supporting a voter-registration drive among uninfluential groups would do well to assure itself that its tax-exempt status will stand up under the challenge of those who prefer to keep political power to themselves. The professor who is still working toward a tenured university appointment is probably less likely than his tenured colleague to distribute controversial pamphlets on campus.

For the same reason, blacks who have successfully challenged power, or reached for power in their own right, have tended to be those with well-guarded economic flanks. Self-employed blacks operating agricultural cooperatives in the South have always been more effective in civil rights drives than their counterparts who held domestic employment. Teachers and civil servants with legally protected jobs were stronger than fellow blacks with equally remunerative but less secure jobs. The blacks who launched the successful lunch-counter sit-ins and voter-registration marches of the 1960s were often unemployed students protected by prior arrangements for bail, babysitters, grocery money, and legal fees. The great master of nonviolent black power, A. Philip Randolph, organized the black pullman porters while remaining relatively immune from retaliation by the railroads because he was never in their employ. To further enhance his independence, Randolph got his money from clambakes in Harlem and never accepted funding from white foundations.

Following the general rule, the weakest of black organizations have been those most dependent on the benevolence of others. When the black Mortgage Bankers Association decided in the late 1960s to challenge the credit discrimination policies of large financial institutions, it found itself powerless to do so because its funding support was drawn largely from the very organizations it intended to challenge. Associations of black building contractors have traditionally been handcuffed by the fact that their income consists chiefly of optional charitable gifts from large construction companies. As a result, most black organizations have been obliged to be content with such palliatives as training grants and token entrepreneurship assistance. Almost without exception, these Negro organizations have been unwilling and unable to mount major challenges to race discrimination in jobs or performance bonding in the construction trades. Facing a similar dilemma, the hundred-odd National Urban League affiliates have no capacity to challenge corporations that abandon efforts to monitor their equal opportunity practices, since almost all the League's funding is provided by business interests. Indeed, in past years, many of the League's staunchest corporate contributors have been simultaneously spending much larger sums lobbying to defeat equal opportunity proposals that the League was fighting to enact. The conclusion is clear: The ready ability of black organizations to secure funding from white business interests is less often a useful measure of organizational success in attaining political or economic objectives than it is a reliable symptom of the timidity of their programs. In the kingdom of the powerful, it is almost axiomatic that the tame and the meek can get money whenever they want it. Cute little pussycats get their catfood set out for them in pretty little bowls, but lions and tigers have to make do for themselves.

Recognizing this law of worldly power, organizations that seek to command rather than entreat always insist on remaining self-funded. To be effectively self-funded, an organization must avoid acquiring money by appealing to guilt, kindness, compassion, or a sense of noblesse oblige; a willingness to act on such motives is always optional on the part of the donor. A self-funded organization, on the other hand, tends to acquire money under obligatory arrangements. Regrettably, it turns out that this can most effectively be done by appealing to such motives as self-interest, fear, and political or commercial advantage. Unfortunately, this elementary truth brings us right back inside the vicious circle whose perimeter we have been exploring. Significant power is hard to achieve without obligatory funding; obligatory funding is hard to achieve without the power to satisfy needs, inspire fear, bestow advantages, or inflict punishment. Later, we will explore ways to break out of this vicious circle. Here we will be content to warn of its existence.

The Outcomes of Unequal Power

Certain elementary rules concerning the effects of power may be stated with some confidence. For example, we know that when people are confronted by power held by others they tend to stop what they are doing and pay attention. We know, too, that stronger power wins over weaker power. In contests between unequal powers, the stronger person will usually prevail. To be sure, it may happen in a particular contest that luck or accident will reverse the expected outcome; but we may wager with confidence that after a sufficient number of contests of strength have taken place, the victor's prize, as well as the superior position, will be awarded to the stronger person. In our society, this person will be the individual who possesses the traditional power traits of human intelligence, competence, daring, and the capacity for hard work. Yet, power's rewards of success will also tend to move toward those who have access to connections and influence; gains will be made as well by those with the ability to deploy society's political and other coercive forces. The conclusion that superior power prevails is not merely an expression of the cynic's rule. It is a simple statement of how the world works. The rule applies in physics, politics, war, economic exchanges, and sporting events. The power advantage is a truism every child either knows intuitively or learns very early in life. Anyone who believes otherwise must be treated as something of a romantic contemplating outcomes in some world other than our own.

I have just stated the singular rule about power which applies to contests among individuals. But there is also a *collective rule* of power: When two groups are dissimilarly situated with respect to holdings of power, the members of the weaker group will also tend to lose in contests against members of the stronger group. Again, this does not mean that in any particular contest each member of the weaker group will lose when pitted against a member of the stronger group. The collective rule is simply that over a period of time, competitive outcomes will favor members of the stronger group. A corollary of this rule of group power is that when two groups are dissimilarly placed with respect to holdings of power, they will not be made or become equal by receiving the *same treatment* from whoever supervises or sets the rules of the contest. Thus, if for some reason, wise or foolish, it is decided that, because of historical circumstances or otherwise, it is unfair for one group to win most of the contests and that, instead, inequalities in outcomes should be more evenly distributed between the two groups, the intended results will not occur if the rules of the contest are evenhanded and apply across the board to both groups. The apparent reason for this is that superior power is not only superior but also tends to reproduce itself because it wins so much more often and builds new power based on previously won advantage.

Positions of unequal power will also control outcomes in any competitive *economic* contest. In the scheme of American capitalism, the winners tend to be those with economic power in the sense of superior skills and productivity. But the winners will also tend to be the powerful in the sense of those who skillfully use coercive force to create demand for their own work or goods, to organize collective bargaining units, or to use politics for economic advantage. Winning positions in life will also be awarded to those who inherit proprietary positions or who, for reasons of caste, class, or inheritance, sit behind barricades that defend educational, economic, and political entry or advantage. Thus, a capitalist system is not only an economy, but a *political* economy. It will choose as winners the smartest and the most talented, but it will also award its prizes to the most powerful, even if these are not necessarily the smartest, most talented, or most meritorious.

The collective rule which confers the most desirable prizes and positions on the powerful does not depend much on the state of the economy. In declining economies or revitalized economies, under supply-side economics or demand-regulated economics, under bloated governments or lean ones, the rules are the same. The stronger parties will hold or improve their positions. In many instances, they will, in fact, improve their positions at the direct and observable expense of the weaker parties. The history of most ethnic groups in the United States confirms this rule of group power. Those groups that arrived here with inferior power holdings did not raise themselves to equal positions simply by sitting back and waiting for help from the benign forces of competitive markets. They attained positions equal to the majority by actively seeking power and by reaching out for and assuming a wide range of positions of power and advantage in the political and economic system.

There is a considerable tendency among the powerful to deny in the strongest possible terms the existence of the rule that distributes goods according to the sum totality of the power operating in a particular transaction. Moreover, in recent years, particularly, much of the public has been persuaded that the driving force of capitalism springs from a basic altruistic instinct of the capitalists. Players in the contest—especially newcomers to the game—are counseled to rely on faith that others will treat them fairly, if not generously. Capitalists of the evangelistic stripe have widely distributed reports and studies concluding that earnest corporate responsibility movements and private acts of voluntary charity are capable of rescuing those who are oppressed or do badly. But these conclusions are fanciful ones that serve principally the interests of well-defended people. Capitalism is indisputably a self-seeking system. Each person in a capitalist society necessarily tries to improve his own economic position using every coercive or noncoercive advantage permitted by law. Operating according to its ethic of rational pursuit of self-interest, capitalism grants no quarter to the weak. And for rich and poor alike, the principal lever used to improve each person's lot is human power in all the many forms we have described.

This brings us to a third rule about power which has been noted many times: Superior positions are almost never surrendered except to superior power. This rule is no less true of the behavior of progressives than of conservatives. Most liberals, for example, will happily spend billions of dollars of government money authorizing CETA grants, "innovative" housing programs, food stamp programs, and other efforts that protect the weakness of the poor. Antipoverty warriors, whose politics may be described as progressive, may be counted upon to work endless hours in shaping social experiments to improve the lives of the less fortunate and, in the process, smother them with the kindness of a close and sincere embrace. But one may rest assured that traditional liberals and other "concerned" groups have very little interest in empowering blacks or other powerless groups. In fact, the most dedicated progressive voters will conscientiously instruct blacks to abjure power and seek aid. With a few notable exceptions—voting rights for blacks and a brief experiment with poverty law services and community self-determination initiatives—virtually every social program ever devised in this country to alleviate the condition of blacks or of the poor confirms the proposition I have stated.

Power as Risk Reduction

Despite the commanding importance of power in human affairs, human intelligence has never developed a satisfactory definition of this elusive concept. But perhaps we are now much closer to an understanding of power's function and purpose. Power depends upon, derives from, and, in fact, may be defined as the *ability to control risk*. The person who successfully seeks power invariably studies his situation with reference to risk or advantage. If, for example, the person is a jobless black man, he begins to move out of a powerless position as soon as he asks what he can do to reduce the risk that his unemployment will continue. This may lead him to the idea of acquiring training and skills that would reduce the economic risk of continuing joblessness. He may inquire about other measures he can take to *improve the odds* that others will seek his trade, extend credit to him, or invest in his entrepreneurial endeavors. He investigates structural changes that can be made in society's selection processes, hoping to *reduce the risk* that he and other members of his group will be denied admission to desirable positions in the academic, political, business, or professional worlds. He begins to think about how power held by others, or by the state, may be turned to his advantage by causing this power to be used to open new doors, to confound the strategy of opponents, and to neutralize the superior strength of competitors.

As we strive to understand power and how it operates, we may speak of constraint, of consensus, of organization, and of unity; we may analyze power's need for information and self-sufficiency, its tendency to command rather than entreat, its close identification with the control of capital and property; we may examine the many ways in which power hides itself and uses the standard tools of threats, bluffs, and rewards. We may go further and show how power equates with skill and competence, particularly with the ability to motivate others to enter into new trading, credit, or employment relationships. But in the end, our inquiry comes down to the fact that *power is always an attack on risk probabilities*. Power describes essentially the ability to minimize the risk of losing what one has while maximizing the likelihood of winning more. Power has always been the means by which humans deal with unseen and unknowable perils. Power is the best way yet devised to get through life's bold gamble. Powerlessness, in turn, simply means life lived at long odds. It is no accident that people without power play the numbers, while people with power leave nothing to chance.

The Legitimacy of Power:
The Commanding Force of Nonviolence

"The strongest is never strong enough to be always the master, unless he transforms strength into right, and obedience into duty."

—*Jean Jacques Rousseau (1762)*

THE POWERS OF NATURE have no moral dimension. When the lion strikes down the gazelle, it is impossible to pass judgment on the morality or the ethics of the attack. We may feel pity or sorrow for the rabbit carried off by the hawk but find it irrelevant to criticize the raptor for taking unfair advantage of a weaker creature. One weeps for the victims of the power of natural disasters such as floods or hurricanes, but these, too, are acts of natural power having no moral content whatever.

Human power, in contrast, has always carried a moral or ethical quality. Once a man, or a human institution, decides to use coercive weapons or pressures, a moral judgment will be made about the act of power. An important consequence of this is that one's success in using pressure or coercion of any kind will depend, to a considerable extent, on whether or not the people affected by the action, as well as society as a whole, judge the use of power to be fair, moral, or just.

Particularly, society tends to approve of those exercises of human power that it regards, for one reason or another, as "legitimate." This means that the efficiency and force of any exercise of power is automatically enhanced if its use is seen as proper or legitimate, whereas even the most forceful and commanding measures lose their strength if they are perceived as illegitimate or improper uses of power. In most societies governed by a combination of public laws and group codes of behavior, coercive power classified as legitimate and allowable gains an added measure of strength simply by being so classified. Conversely, exercises of power perceived as illegitimate and therefore forbidden have their effectiveness blunted by this pejorative label.

The practical effect of moral judgments in undercutting or enhancing power is immediately understood when one considers the civil rights struggles in the southern states during the 1960s. Two power users—black demonstrators and white police officers—stood in opposition to each other. The public responded immediately by judging the morality of each group's behavior, and the outcome of the struggle depended largely on whose behavior was felt to have the greater claim to legitimacy.

Thus, success in acting powerfully and in winning public support for one's power requires some educated guesses about prevailing public sentiments. Those who seek power must be prescient, intuitive, and watchful enough to know when their own actions, or the actions of an adversary, will be viewed as legitimate. The effective user of power needs to know when a particular course of action will be viewed as "violent," "arbitrary," or "subversive" or when, instead, it will be seen as "nonviolent," "justifiable," or even "heroic."

In the preceding chapter, we examined the mechanics of power and the various motivations that induce people to defer to those who are powerful. We were concerned largely with the naked power of coercion, whether in the blunt form of sheer physical force or in subtler forms, such as the threat, the bluff, temptation, or intimidation. But the fact is that commands are often obeyed simply because they are made by individuals or institutions perceived as having the legitimate right to make them. Thus it is important to ask the following questions: Why do people obey established power? What are the differences in form between power that is or is not perceived as illegitimate? What are the standard trappings of legitimacy that tend to persuade the public to support or permit the pressures of special-interest groups? What specific forms of power are perceived as rebellious, harmful, or not in the public interest? Under what circumstances will the use of such extreme pressure as mass marches, mutiny, boycott, and similar measures be seen as legitimate?

These issues are important to judgments that we will make later about right and might of certain forms of power that whites have traditionally used against blacks. Equally, these characterizations about the legitimacy of power are binding on blacks and other groups that wish to influence, and press their way into, economic, political, and educational institutions in the United States.

Legitimacy, Consent, and the Duty to Obey Power

Ever since the French philosopher Jean Jacques Rousseau popularized the idea of a social contract over 200 years ago, one of the fundamental principles of our political theory has been the notion that the legitimacy of power derives from the consent of those over whom power is exercised. Even a forceful or violent act tends to have legitimacy if the person against whom it is directed consents to it. To take the simplest example, football players, prizefighters, and hockey players all practice various forms of violence in their professions, yet they are not condemned for it. This is so simply because those whom they attack consented in advance to those limited forms of violence permitted under the rules of the game.

The consent that gives rise to a sense of duty to obey the power, and to acquiesce in the outcomes it produces, need not be drawn up in writing or published as a *magna carta*. The permission that confers legitimacy on power may take the form of a formal vote, a constitutional convention, an exchange of glances, a silent nod, or even the tacit endorsement of a political process. This means that even when an outcast or subordinated group accepts rules of economic or racial etiquette made by others and consistently behaves according to the latter's demands or expectations, the power of the rulemaker tends to acquire legitimacy.

Consent may lend legitimacy to a wide variety of power arrangements used for the distribution of material goods and advantages. By agreement, for example, money and goods could be allocated according to chance, according to merit, according to the principle of absolute equality, or even according to some quite arbitrary system wherein those who are physically strong, weak, blue-eyed, or black-faced get extra daily rations. If it were agreed in a constitutional convention that the blue-eyed people would run the banks and lunch at expensive restaurants, these arrangements would enjoy a certain inherent legitimacy even though it were perfectly apparent that the allocations were both foolish and harmful to society as a whole. As long as the parties to the contract consent to its provisions, they are all morally obliged to accept the outcomes of the competition conducted within the rules set forth in the contract. And power that enforces those outcomes always has the strongest claim to legitimacy.

Once we understand the significance of consent in power relationships, we are ready to draw a very important distinction between legitimate and illegitimate power. Raw force is obeyed when there is no other choice, but legitimate power is obeyed, for the most part, because people *feel an inner obligation* to do so. This feeling of *wanting* to obey power transcends and reinforces the fear that is the traditional motor force lying behind an act of obedience to coercive force. The very highest stage of success in the use of power is attained when one succeeds in creating circumstances where people who obey power do so not because they *have to* but because they *want to*. On this question, the great philosophers of power—Machiavelli, Hume, Tolstoy and Clausewitz—agree. They find the locus of power in the will of the person being commanded, not in the person issuing the commands.

Besides the element of mutual consent, there is a wide range of circumstances that confer the feeling of wanting to obey or to protect power. People typically feel a duty to obey power when it has the authoritative cloak of formal law. In this case, even highly objectionable orders elicit a sense of obligation. For example, court decrees ordering the racial integration of a public school often provoke strong disagreement on the part of parents and school officials, who often feel the orders are profoundly unjust. Nevertheless, most people feel obligated to obey them. This explains why, given a choice, the successful power user is always well advised to try to enlist state power as an ally, for state power is almost always dressed in the cloak of legitimacy. In general, a person, group, or movement seeking to gain and exercise power will do much better, all other things being equal, by working within and through "the system" than by a rebellious effort to "fight city hall." For this reason, successful power always strives to get itself registered or validated by formal processes—preferably by the state or other body to whom people feel a duty of obedience.

Of course, the government is not the only institution capable of inspiring the feelings of a duty to obey. Members of private groups often feel a similar duty to obey group commands. This sense of obligation may arise because members have agreed to be bound by the will of the majority of the group; it may be attributable to the charismatic qualities of a group leader perceived as a person who should be obeyed; or it may derive from a sense of loyalty to a common group purpose. The failure of movements without powerful leaders is often due not only to dissension and disagreements—conditions which always subvert power—but more especially to the lack of both the sense of obligation and the sense of group loyalty that a leader often inspires. Conversely, a unified and cohesive organization may fall apart if events somehow undo the perceived legitimacy of the leader. The deposed monarch, the impeached president, and the community leader caught in a corrupt act usually discover that their moral force—the desire of people to obey them—evaporates long before their titular powers are taken away.

Power's Paradox: Strength in Vulnerability; Weakness in Impregnability

Absolute power compels obedience, but the despotic character of absolute power—not the least important feature of which is its perfect insulation from retaliation by others—tends to destroy the claim of legitimacy. One of the many seemingly paradoxical yet nonetheless valid rules of power is that power tends to acquire legitimacy if the person or institution using it can be hurt while using power. The other side of this proposition holds that uncontrolled power—power without attendant vulnerability—tends to be seen as illegitimate.

This is true of government power as well as of private coercion. Nothing is so flawed in the public mind as a power that cannot be questioned or punished by others. Military power represented by the Dresden fire bombings in World War II produced far greater human slaughter than Hiroshima, yet the Dresden raids are seen as far more legitimate. In part, this was because Dresden was a defended city and, indeed, hundreds of American and British pilots lost their lives flying bombing missions over Germany. Japan, on the other hand, was virtually unprotected from atomic weapons. So we see that a sort of "bully rule" governs the collective conscience, giving legitimacy to the gunfighter in the open street at high noon—a state of grace that it absolutely withholds from the mugger in a dark hallway at night.

The requirement that the power user accept the risk of self-harm underlies almost all theories of successful power in the form of civil disobedience. In Birmingham, Alabama, in the early 1960s, a black person found it a risky business to sit in the front of a bus, march his child into a segregated school, or sit at a lunch counter reserved for whites. But part of the reason why these acts of protest were seen as legitimate was not simply because their political aims were considered just, but also because the acts of rebellion and law-breaking carried a considerable risk of personal danger.

Once a nonviolent group demonstrates that its members are prepared to accept hurt—to pay the penalty that legitimacy insists upon—many forms of otherwise impermissible protest will acquire legitimacy and strength. Of course, there is an obvious catch here for anyone planning a winning strategy. For if it is true that a movement wins public admiration and support by running the risk of self-harm, it is no less true that the movement advocating such a strategy severely diminishes the number of people willing to join it. People naturally tend to admire and honor a martyr, but they tend just as naturally to try to avoid becoming one.

The requirement that a person or group holding or using power assume some risk of harm applies to economic power as well as to physical and political power. In fact, the prospect of self-harm has long been the fundamental price regulator of the powers governing in our economic system. For example, the possibility of being hurt by a competitor—or by a customer free to withhold his trade—is theoretically our most important power mechanism of control over farm, manufacturing, and retail prices. On the other hand, invulnerable market power—that is, monopoly power—is seen as illegitimate precisely because the monopolist is unaccountable, unrestrained, and immune to the competitive harms inherent in a marketplace full of rivals.

Race discrimination in employment, credit, and other forms of commerce—the collective act of ganging up on members of a stigmatized group and refusing to trade with them—is an example of an illegitimate form of power. This is so in large part because the actors who use the coercive power of a racial boycott—and thereby often establish a closed shop for their enterprises—are wholly insulated from the penalties of competitive forces which, under normal circumstances, would punish unfair or inefficient economic decisions.

The American tendency to look with suspicion at invulnerable power is, of course, at the roots of our theory of constitutional government. The concept of tripartite government is based on the idea that permissible power is vulnerable power. Each branch of government is seen as legitimate, in large part because each branch is susceptible to punishment and correction by other powers. Presidents can thus veto the decisions of legislatures, and legislatures can overrule those vetoes. The courts can declare the acts of either the President or Congress unconstitutional, and the courts may in turn be "overruled" by the admittedly drastic remedy of amending the Constitution. Add the fact that all elected officials are subject to being voted out of office and we see that the constant exposure to risk of harm is one of the main factors legitimizing the official power of almost every officeholder in our system. Only officials who are exposed to these potential risks command a stable and legitimate government—one that the public feels a duty to obey.

The fact that the United States Government has not, in any important sense, been politically accountable to its black citizens may explain to some extent the low opinion of the legitimacy of government held by a good many blacks, as well as the erosion of their sense of duty to obey public power.

The entirely predictable decline in perceptions of government legitimacy resulting from this state of affairs became especially evident during the late 1960s and early 1970s, when many black power movements openly acknowledged in words and acts that they felt little loyalty to city, state, and federal governments. Thus, not only do legislative measures that enhance black political power, such as voting rights legislation and remedial redistricting of election districts, have the benign effect of drawing blacks into democratic processes, but these redistributions of power also confer much greater legitimacy on government itself. So we see that stability and legitimacy of government are enhanced rather than undermined by the presence of a great many active and unfettered pressure groups.

It is important to notice that the events creating black people's perceptions of government illegitimacy happened by no means exclusively in the distant past. In very recent years, police officials, public prosecutors, and judges in southern states have been insulated from accountability to unlawfully disenfranchised black voters. These officials could come to no political or administrative harm by refusing to indict or convict whites for crimes against blacks. Over a long span of history, tens of thousands of local governing bodies in the United States have been wholly protected from political accountability to Negro citizens. Public health care organizations, local zoning boards, farm loan agencies, public welfare agencies, state-administered employment agencies, and school boards have been free to establish administrative rules and procedures serving only the needs and wishes of the white population. Even today, few, if any, of the thousands of all-white suburban zoning boards in the United States incur any risk of not being returned to office as a consequence of adopting rules that effectively keep blacks from living in white communities. In the United States, the power to educate—and to deny education—has been largely in the hands of administrative officials who never lost a post—or even heard of anyone losing one—as a consequence of allocating better or greater public educational resources to whites. In view of these circumstances, profound questions may be raised about the legitimacy of the political power holdings of a considerable number of white officeholders in American society. The reason for this is not simply that black people failed to use political processes to punish malfeasance in office but that through various unconstitutionally improper and coercive devices blacks were systematically denied admission to the political parties and access to the voting booths where punitive or countervailing political power could be brought to bear.

Legitimate Power's Iron Link With Nonviolence

In prehistoric times, force and violence may have been the ultimate sources of power, but in most Western societies nothing robs power of its legitimacy as effectively as excessive reliance on these primitive weapons. As America learned in Vietnam, power often diminishes as the level of violence and inflicted pain escalates. The reason is clear. Excessive force provokes public revulsion and backfires on the power user. Instead of feeling a duty to obey power, national and world opinion condemn and rebel against it. Ordinarily, then, a group embarking on violence as an empowerment tactic embarks, too, on the path to self-destruction. A clear example is provided by some of the more militant factions within the "black power" movement of the 1960s and 1970s. Whatever claim to legitimacy the Black Panther party might ever have possessed disappeared completely when it adopted and endorsed the strategy of "offing the pigs." Savage and violent strikes at another person or institution may produce temporary advantage, but in the end the politics of terror must come to naught. Late in his career Napoleon wrote, "What astounds me most about the world is the impotence of force to establish anything." In modern times Gandhi established the principle that the successful power user not only strives to undermine the moral authority of his oppressor but also avoids any use of violence, thereby protecting the authority—and hence the power—of his own movement. One of the great masters of power in our time, Dr. Martin Luther King, Jr., confirmed Gandhi's rule which now and forever more he would have black people obey: "In our protest, there will be no cross burnings. No white person will be taken from his home by a hooded Negro mob and brutally murdered. There will be no threats or intimidation."

Power, Virtue, and the Public Interest

The public perception of the ideological goals of an organization, a pressure group, or a movement greatly affects its claims to legitimacy. Power becomes much more acceptable when it is perceived as necessary to "save democracy," to "preserve law and order," to protect society against "subversive elements," or to "right a wrong." Public sentiment will often confer legitimacy on forceful measures taken by individuals whom the public judges to be aggrieved. Compelling moral force of this sort can even confer legitimacy on acts of civil disobedience. In this case, the concept of legitimacy may be turned upside down with state power becoming illegitimate as private power becomes legitimate. Dr. Martin Luther King was thus able to commit nonviolent but illegal trespass and unlawfully resist arrest without having his acts of defiance condemned as illegitimate acts of power. The inherent injustice in the racial laws of the South was viewed by the national conscience as sufficient reason for not complying with the laws of the South.

Some years earlier, the governors of Alabama and Mississippi had tried essentially the same tactic. They, too, turned to civil disobedience, defying federal law in an effort to preserve racially segregated schools. The governors asserted that their actions were highly principled; they pictured themselves as defending the liberty of Americans to associate with "their own kind." Americans as a whole, however, dismissed the position of the southern governors as unjust, self-serving, and distinctly contrary to the national interest.

The fact that the public ethic is generally reluctant to confer legitimacy on power and pressure unless they appear to be altruistic in motivation presents a profound dilemma for the self-help efforts of special-interest groups. In the case of blacks, for example, it is frequently difficult to show why bloc voting on their part is not only in their interest but also in the *public* interest. Similarly, those who defend affirmative-action programs are under great pressure to show not only why such an unusual process is just, but also how the country as a whole will benefit. Public school busing pressures fail, in large part, because the public at large does not perceive a benefit to the public as a whole. If the time comes again when blacks and other minority groups believe it necessary to resort to the pressure strategies of nonviolent civil disobedience, they will be able to win general support for their actions only if they succeed in convincing the majority that these unusual pressures are in the interest of the entire society.

The Illegitimacy of Power Used to Eliminate Inequalities

We showed earlier that a condition of vulnerability, in the sense of being open to the risk of competitive harm, is an indispensable element in any power user's claim to legitimacy. It follows, then, that the weak frequently acquire power and strength simply by appearing weak. One of the most notable traits of the American psyche is that public sympathy tends to run in favor of the underdog. This does not mean, however, that the actions of those operating out of an unequal or disadvantaged position automatically enjoy the benefit of legitimacy. On the contrary, the American system of competition is, in fact, built on presumed economic and social *inequality*. The drive to be one step ahead of the next fellow is an integral part of the American ethic and is a principal ingredient in the education of the young. Only somewhat less enthusiastically, general approval attends the corollary that the less competent and less industrious should drop to the bottom. It follows that inequalities and disadvantages are seen as acceptable and that the use of power to eliminate them has little claim to legitimacy. This is true of both state and private power. State action veers decidedly toward illegitimacy whenever it forces one individual to transfer money, goods, or an economic benefit to another solely for the purpose of creating equality. In a like manner, private power tends to be seen as illegitimate if its explicit purpose is to divert money from a public or private purse to help the weak catch up to the strong.

This persistent opposition to using public or private power to rearrange inequalities explains, in part, why extreme economic differences continue to be accepted and approved by the vast majority of the American people. It appears that 5 percent or less of the American population owns perhaps half of all the private wealth of this country. This great inequality provides a remarkable departure from the natural sense of fairness that, say, children would have in dividing a cake. Yet the vast majority of Americans would view any effort to use government taxing power for the express purpose of equalizing such immense differences as decidedly un-American, if not seditious and collectivist. To a surprising extent, these opinions are shared by rich and poor alike.

To be sure, government powers may legitimately be used to mitigate the effects of extreme inequalities, as long as these powers serve such laudable purposes as preventing starvation and preserving public order. Thus, public power may tax the affluent in order to provide welfare assistance, food stamps, and other forms of public aid for those in need. But in America, no political group has ever succeeded in winning legitimacy for coercive measures designed to promote economic equality.

Legitimacy Conferred on the Power to Redress Undeserved Inequalities

There is one overriding exception to the general rule that denies legitimacy to the use of power for the purpose of rearranging unequal positions.

This occurs under the principle of redress. We noted earlier that countervailing power acquires legitimacy when it is brought to bear to curb or neutralize power that has acquired a monopoly or invulnerable position. But in the case of redress, the sweep of permissible power is much broader. Legitimacy tends to attach to countervailing power where the power user has been harmed or has been put at a disadvantage by uses of power that society considers unfair or improper. In evaluating the moral position of those attempting to use power to even up advantages, Americans tend to ask the following questions: Is the party using pressure to bring about change responsible for his own position? Are those who hold dominant power responsible for creating or maintaining the unequal situations? Does a group enjoying a superior advantage owe its position to acts that forcefully blocked or unfairly impeded the progress of a disadvantaged group?

In other words, before the collective conscience passes judgment on the legitimacy of any effort to use power to rearrange unequal positions, it wants to know if anyone is *culpably* responsible for creating the subordinate conditions or inequalities. If the public considers certain holdings to be illegitimately won, public power will probably refrain from protecting those holdings from being challenged by other power. Moreover, despite the strong public commitment to protect the private ownership of property, the state will, in many cases, order redistributions of property or competitive advantage. Whenever a winning or superior position is judged by the public to be undeserved or improperly won, the advantage gained becomes highly vulnerable to pressure for redistribution.

If a powerful group—racial or otherwise—within a society has become economically or politically superior to another group, and if the difference has been achieved in whole or in part by blocking off the risk of competitive harm or loss from competitive efforts on the part of members of the less powerful group, serious questions then arise as to the legitimacy of the power and positions held by the first group. It is quite difficult to get people in our society to subscribe to the general proposition that unequal economic positions should be equalized, but it is not so difficult to convince them that positions should be readjusted when one party has improperly insulated himself from competitive failure by entering the game with a stacked deck. Coercive power will rarely be seen as legitimate if it is used simply to give the underdog what the upper dog has, but it can win widespread support if it is aimed at restoring or recreating the balance of competitive risk.

The downtrodden thus have no right, according to the American ethic, to trade places with the powerful. But the American sense of the legitimacy of power requires that members of the superior group must always remain subject to the competitive risk of losing their places to the underdogs. To the extent that whites in America have arranged economic and political contests with blacks in a manner that assured places to whites and freed them from competition with blacks, a strong case can be made that the superior power holdings of whites have weak moral footings and are significantly lacking in legitimacy. This, in turn, introduces the possibility that the use of countervailing power by blacks and others to reorder these positions may claim for itself a considerable degree of legitimacy.

The legitimacy that is accorded to countervailing or corrective power is self-limiting. As soon as countervailing or corrective power has restored the risk of losing a competitive contest, any further use of redistributive power will probably be seen as illegitimate. Said another way, once the absolute power of the dominant group is subjected to the sting of correction and accountability, the legitimacy of its position is restored; those who would further cut back the superior positions of others no longer have legitimate grounds for doing so. We commonly see this phenomenon in antitrust settlements where economic power that has been adjudicated illegal or illegitimate is restrained by court order, but only for a specified period of time during which injured parties are granted a temporary umbrella of protection in order to recover competitive strength. Justice does not insist on equality or equal positions; its ends are served once vulnerability to the power of others has been reestablished.

Halo Effect:
Power Augmented by Association

Whenever a person or group honored and admired by the general public supports a cause, the perceived legitimacy of the cause is almost automatically enhanced. This is as true for freedom marchers as for white citizens' councils wishing to maintain the color line. In this regard, political movements are no different from razor blade companies and breweries; they all seek "authority figures" such as war veterans, clergymen, football heroes, and entertainment stars to endorse their product. A salient example of this phenomenon is provided by the black movement in South Africa, which has persistently weakened its own cause by its failure to win allies in the small but prestigious black middle class, which for generations has been in awe of whites. South African whites, in turn, have skillfully denied black groups the advantage of associating their movement with prestigious people by funding and rewarding a solid front of "system blacks" who administer state-ordered apartheid in the black townships and homelands.

Of course, the converse of this "halo principle" is also true. Nothing erodes the legitimacy of a movement as quickly as its association in the public mind with despised or disreputable persons. In past years, southern congressmen effectively delayed serious federal civil rights legislation by invoking the names of Thomas Jefferson and the Founding Fathers. But their cause quickly lost legitimacy when it became linked in the public mind with the actions of those who defended the "American way" by bombing black churches and orphanages. Suddenly, the power of these legislators evaporated, and the civil rights bills passed.

An organization's association with reputable or disreputable ideas affects perceived legitimacy as drastically as its association with revered or despised persons. When the Communist party was the most visible and vocal champion of black rights in the 1930s, the legitimacy of the black movement was greatly damaged. In the early 1960s, the black power movement gained a bad name—from which it has yet to recover—from its association in the public mind with a handful of radical militants who did their crusading with machine guns and Molotov cocktails. In recent years a number of black politicians have undermined a wholly admirable black political agenda by hinting that "there will be race riots and blood on the streets if you don't pass my bill." In the same manner, the perceived legitimacy of the women's movement has been greatly impeded because the general public has too often associated equal rights with lesbianism and hostility to traditional concepts of the family. In defending the legitimacy of its power, a successful protest movement is always very careful about whom it allows in its tent.

Vested political and economic positions are often effectively defended by associating the power of one's opposition with immoral, improper, or unpatriotic values. Thus, equal opportunity pressures may be successfully disparaged as illegitimate on the premise that they are stimulated by "outside agitators" or that they "seriously undermine economic liberty." And lawful agitation by loyal citizens for certain government welfare programs may be perceived as illegitimate if the objectives of these citizens are publicly identified with socialism, the decline of free enterprise, or "the overly protective welfare state." Hence, to a great extent, the outcome of a struggle for power may be controlled not by the inherent force of the constraint employed, or by the force of reasoned argument, but rather by whoever is most successful in identifying his cause with certain symbols that the public loves and respects.

Moral Authority as Power's Safe-Conduct Pass

An important feature of the concept of legitimacy—one that is of particular concern to minority and other pressure groups—is that people will generally guard and support the right to use power that they consider legitimate even if they disagree with the objectives of this power and feel no obligation to obey it themselves. For example, many people who dislike and distrust the power of trade unions will nevertheless defend the union's right to act powerfully on behalf of its members.

The legitimacy of the power of trade unions is conferred to some extent by the fact that collective bargaining organizations are officially recognized by public law in the Wagner Act. However, there are many special-interest organizations that possess considerable legitimacy not formally conferred by the state. In most cases, this legitimacy derives from the manner in which the organizations do business. For example, the Legal Defense Fund, formerly associated with the National Association for the Advancement of Colored People, limits its pressures for institutional change to the accepted and honored processes of the courts. The highly acceptable way in which the Legal Defense Fund pursues its goals adds immeasurably to the organization's perceived respectability and, in turn, to its power. In abjuring public demonstrations, civil rights marches, and organized boycotts, it surrenders useful instruments of collective power but gains in exchange a degree of legitimacy it would lose if it adopted the more militant coercive techniques of confrontation and direct action.

In addition to winning support from more or less neutral observers, legitimacy benefits a movement or organization by giving it added strength and stability. Consider, for example, the power embodied in such collective action as a group boycott. Most people view such negative pressures as somewhat subversive, making it difficult for boycotts to acquire stability and momentum and to achieve permanent economic or political changes. Occasionally, however, the public may confer strong feelings of legitimacy on such a movement. This happened during the Montgomery, Alabama public transport boycotts of the early 1960s, when the public sense of injustice was stirred by the unfairness of racial segregation. At the beginning of the struggle, the police forces of Birmingham possessed all the legitimacy of state authority. Because of this, they appeared amply capable of defending white supremacy against all comers. But once the fire hoses and police dogs were turned on nuns and children, the perceived legitimacy of the police as an institution declined rapidly, as did their power. Here was the very rare event of the official power of the state becoming wholly illegitimate and, on that account, impotent. And by acting unjustly and ruthlessly, the city of Birmingham succeeded in transforming the fragile protest efforts of the transportation boycotts into a durable and powerful civil rights movement.

The overall conclusion may be stated simply. Winning a public judgment of legitimacy is the first precondition for the effective use of power. One cannot hope to develop a successful political strategy for winning and using power without first understanding how power is controlled by public notions of fairness and culpability, by public perception of power's vulnerability, and by whether or not the pressure being used conforms to the established processes to which all have consented. Those who understand the importance of legitimacy and win it for themselves and for their cause receive a ticket to act forcefully without a need to engage tanks or armies. Where there is opposition to one's goals, there is no better way to cripple the will to resist than by devising a means to capture the collective conscience of the public. The most successful pressure groups invariably bind themselves to this requirement of legitimacy. They struggle mightily to achieve intellectual and moral respectability for their power. Once this coveted status is attained, they strive not to impose their will on others but to appeal so strongly to the demands of legitimacy and justice as to conquer the mind and make others want to obey the will of the conqueror.

If black people in the United States succeed in pressing their demands on whites, it will not be simply because they have finally learned the secret of how to make others behave according to their will. Nor will they come to power simply because they have used newly discovered political muscle to set up a system of public sanctions with well-publicized conditions for their removal. Power's state of grace will descend on blacks when they have mounted a stark and morally compelling display of economic injustice. Their drive for affirmative action and other corrective rights and compensatory positions will prevail, if ever, when whites choose to accept the black agenda simply for the reason that they have no answer to its overwhelming moral authority.

CHAPTER FOUR

Power in Free Markets:
To Each According to His Merit

"In spite of their natural selfishness and rapacity, though they mean only their own conveniency, though the sole end which they propose from the labors of all the thousands they employ be the gratification of their own vain and insatiable desires . . . they are led by an invisible hand . . . without intending it, without knowing it, to advance the interest of society."

—*Adam Smith,*
The Wealth of Nations *(1776)*

IN CHAPTER ONE, we made two fundamental points. The first was that in most political and economic settings the material well-being of individuals and groups, as well as their protection from the various perils of life, has depended on their relationships to power. Those who were in a position to influence, persuade, or conquer the will of others were better off; those, in turn, who had little autonomy or self-sufficient means, or were otherwise unsuccessful in freeing themselves from coercion by others, were badly off. Possibly, this is not the way things might or should have been; but this, to quote Walter Cronkite's felicitous phrase, is "the way they were."

The second point was that under nature's original scheme natural power provided for a general rule of open access or opportunity. No master plan stated that the road from rags to riches was to be traveled more often by certain tribal or ethnic groups. Nor were life's scarcities or menial positions more often assigned to any particular clans or castes. But mankind made drastic revisions in the original scheme. Throughout history, and in virtually all societies, the rule of open access was overturned. No matter what the professed ideology of a particular society might be, positions of privilege or disadvantage were reserved for certain groups, and whenever this happened, human power was almost invariably an active agent as well as the responsible force.

Prior to the emergence of free-market systems in the tradition of Adam Smith, the economic status of people, and the allocations of goods and positions among them, was determined by coercive power. This power took the form of feudal place or fixed life assignments. Under the feudal tradition, nature's provision of open access and equal opportunity was ignored. The power of the sword, the warrior, and the obligation of feudal duty established holdings of wealth and set the pattern for economic exchanges between people. But the eighteenth-century philosophers who articulated the theory of the democratic state—and its handmaiden, free-market capitalism—repudiated many of the coercive rules of the feudal state which for centuries had assured certain groups a good place for themselves, while ascribing a subordinate position to others. In place of the established power arrangements of predetermined or caste position, a new ideology of free markets chose as its centerpiece the concepts of open access and individual liberty. Thus, in 1776, the year in which Thomas Jefferson proclaimed the free spirit of a new republic in his Declaration of Independence, Adam Smith, an expatriate Scotsman in London, issued his treatise, *The Wealth of Nations,* one of the great philosophical works of all time. It proved to be the new economic charter for modern nations, just as Jefferson's document became the model for most political constitutions in the free world today.

In economic terms, these great documents of government repudiated coercive power as a legitimate means of distributing goods and resources. Instead they insisted on establishing a wide range of freedoms: freedom of commercial association, freedom to choose one's trading partners, freedom to deny or to grant credit, freedom to select one's employees without interference from others, and the freedom to deny or permit entry into private places where commercial or employment activity was taking place. The single most important blessing that the philosophers wished to protect was the liberty of each individual to choose—particularly in commercial transactions—what was good for himself or herself. Indeed, one of the most important individual freedoms that the state was supposed to protect was the liberty to do business with people—or refuse to have commerce with them—based on considerations of race, class, or any other indicia of rejection that the person in commerce chose to use. And one of the most important rules of government was that while these freedoms to choose trading partners were being exercised, the head of state, as well as the state itself, was to stand by as a benign observer, committed in a fundamental way to a policy of nonintervention or nonuse of state power.

The Unadvertised Role of Power
in the Free-Enterprise System

The idea of individual liberty, in fact, substituted a new form of power as the driving force of the economic system. This was the power to activate others by rewarding them. Thus, the power of brawn, force of arms, and feudal obligation gave way to a different set of human powers in the form of individual skills, diligence, and the ability to produce and sell goods that other people wanted. Under these new power arrangements, there was to be no coercion. People parted with their goods or money because someone else had revealed his power to persuade them and others that his goods, his labor, or his capital was better or more reliable than that offered by competitors.

On the surface it appeared there was little room for traditional coercive power to operate in the libertarian scheme. Presented to the citizen instead was a cornucopia of choices. According to the free-market theory, workers would be free to select from a rich assortment of enticing jobs and opportunities, while employers enjoyed the privilege of choosing among the thousands of employees who made themselves available for work. Merchants, bankers, and investors could shop comparatively and could select from the wide offerings of management services and entrepreneurial skills available to them. At the same time, managers and entrepreneurs were free to choose those offerings of capital and credit that pleased them most.

But there was a catch in Adam Smith's vision of economic freedom. Beneath all of the formal freedoms lay the hidden presence of powerful constraint. The economists of liberty insisted that all participants in the economic system—like political candidates in a democracy—should submit themselves as competitors in a contest for popular choice. As the philosophers saw it, only if each "free" person faced the constraint of having to deal with the presence of rivals or competitors would the system of economic liberty provide for public well-being. Examples of competition acting as a constraint upon individual economic liberty are familiar. In a marketplace regulated by competing rivals, the grain merchant who persistently overcharges his customers lays the groundwork for his own economic failure since his competitors will undersell him and lure away his customers. Similarly, the liberty of the usurer to charge an excessive rate of interest will be punished not by the power of the cop on the beat enforcing the antiusury laws, but by the neighborhood banker whose perception of his own advantage tells him it makes competitive sense to offer a lower interest rate.

Standard libertarian theory held that workers would be protected against exploitation and the unnecessary risk of physical harm simply by the unbridled self-interest of competing employers. The coal mine operator would not, in truth, be free to pay workers an exploitative wage because a competing mine operator could outbid him for the workers' services. Similarly, unsafe mines went bankrupt as dangerous conditions sent miners to work in safer shafts. Because of the constraints of competition, there was no need for government watchdogs to provide protection against various forms of physical or economic harm. The libertarians held that precisely because individuals are self-seeking, society as a whole would be well served. In a free market, the public interest would be unintentionally advanced by the pursuit of private gain. This was the explicit theme of Adam Smith's *The Wealth of Nations*.

The philosophers of economic freedom set one precondition that must prevail before the free market would be permitted to use its competitive powers to work out its solutions to problems of allocating economic goods. Obviously, this condition was the presence of competition. The workings of a free market were acceptable only as long as strong rivals were competing for individual economic advantage. Moreover, the rivals must not be permitted to act collusively to set prices, to divide the available work, or to collectively boycott or refuse to compete for the goods or labor of a person or a particular group of people. Therefore, if in a particular situation, people joined forces against certain players and refused to compete for their labor or goods, the central government as the natural policeman of the free market would be obliged to come to the rescue of competition. Except in these limited instances, however, the libertarian scheme, with its implicit assumption that the sum total of all individual freely expressed desires will add up to social good, has generally prevailed.

Hustling marketplace competitors thus became the economic statesmen who shaped our laws of commerce, credit, and employment. For two centuries, the notion that regulatory power is automatically generated by competition, first promulgated by Adam Smith and later refined by David Ricardo, T.R. Malthus, and John Stuart Mill, has been the bedrock of American economic thought. Even today, the laborer, the industrialist, and the banker are constrained far more by the forces of competition than by the abominated rules of the central government in Washington.

We see then that, contrary to popular belief, coercive power was never rejected in the free-market plan. Adam Smith's markets were always regulated by the power of the mighty club of competition. The participants in these markets were never free to do exactly what they wanted. Coercive power in the form of the pain and punishment of competition was, in fact, viewed as a necessary protector of liberty, for it guaranteed that people would not—or at least would not for long—use their liberties in such a way as to do mischief to others, curtail the liberties of other citizens, or harm the public interest.

Competition's Provision for Individual Justice

Power in the form of competition played a second role in regulating economic liberty, and it is this function particularly that concerns us here. According to libertarian theory, competition among rivals was expected not only to police the public interest, but also to safeguard individual interests. Under the market system, anyone treating another person in an undeserved or unfair manner was automatically "punished" by rivals who would step in and set the balance right. If, for example, a company refused to hire the best person for a job because of racial considerations, some rival would be sure to hire the person and gain the benefit of his or her talents. The necessary consequence of having a rival looking over every competitor's shoulder was fair and evenhanded treatment for all. In the marketplace constructed by Western man, the pain and penalties of competition acted as kind of a surrogate for the evenhanded forces and laws of the natural world.

What a remarkable system was this grant of individual opportunity and freedom regulated only by competition! Not only did people competing with one another act as an economic parliament, but, without establishing any formal economic courts, the people as a whole also sat in judgment on each other by serving as de facto judges and juries in disposing of individual grievances.

The determination of individual merit, protected by a rule of equal access or opportunity in the competition to display merit, was left to the automatic processes of the marketplace. Each person was to hire or work for whomever he pleased. Goods, credit, and capital were to be allocated according to the individual judgments of people who were free to act on their own perceptions of their self-interest. Each person voting with his money would ensure that others would get exactly what they deserved. The principles of voting democracy were thus applied to the governance of the economic treatment of each citizen.

Particularly in modern times, certain defects have shown up in the thesis that free markets necessarily serve the public interest. Competition has never displayed sufficient regulating force to provide for the safety of drugs, toys, clothing, or automobiles. Industry has never provided forces of competitive oversight sufficient to keep streams free of toxic wastes or to protect the health and safety of its workers. A serious defect in the stern self-regulating market economy has been revealed, too, in its frequent inability to provide enough work. Nevertheless, the libertarian economic tradition has been durable. The remarkably successful economic history of the United States continues to be taken as evidence that the forces of unfettered competition are sufficient to weaken class barriers and are capable of producing, in the long run, a rough and ready approximation of social justice. "Up by the bootstraps" has been the credo of countless American millionaires whose childhoods were bleak and deprived. The children of first-generation peasant immigrants have risen to become great surgeons, historians, and lawyers. And the rags-to-riches miracles continue to confirm beliefs that the free-market system, if left to its own devices, can work for all.

Competition's Protection for the Outcast

It is self-evident that, in most nations and societies, there have always been social outcasts or pariahs. Traditionally, these groups have been denied the benefits of open competition; they have been assigned, instead, a fixed place or station in the economic life of most nations. People who would otherwise compete for their economic offerings have, instead, shunned them, ganged up against them, and boycotted their labor and produce. Of course, traditional libertarian dogma proclaimed that punitive powers of competitive markets would open doors and crush barriers that stood in the way of the progress of these groups. Depending on individual ability and diligence, it was said that outcast groups would also tend to rise to the top as competitors actively sought to win out over their rivals by bidding for the services of the most qualified persons, even when they belonged to a stigmatized class or race. Thus, 100 years ago, as today, the positive powers of competition were always seen as ideal protectors of social, racial, or religious outcasts.

Looking back to 1776 and earlier, we now see how Americans have been extraordinarily unfaithful to the ideal of free and open markets. For several centuries, black people in the United States received no protection what-soever from the iron fist of competition. Without benefit of competition or evaluation of individual ability, their assigned economic place was that of serfs, sharecroppers, and later domestic and agricultural menials. Curi-

RACIAL JUSTICE DISPENSED BY THE COERCIVE POWER OF FREE MARKETS

Racial bigots beware: How the self-seeking goals of large numbers of competitors operating in markets open to all are expected to provide the necessary sanctions to punish race discrimination, weed out prejudiced people, and provide sup-port to the efforts of qualified blacks to rise to the top.

- No matter how economically or educationally handicapped any racial group may be, the group will nevertheless contain a signif-icant core of highly talented and ambitious people, some of whom will in fact rank higher in qualifications and abilities than the aver-age level of qualifications and abilities of members of the most privileged groups.

- The normal human instinct to advance one's individual or institu-tional interests will cause people to seek out these highly qualified members of disadvantaged groups and award them educational and economic places in firms and institutions in preference to less qualified people who happen to come from privileged groups.

- As long as no outside pressure, particularly the government, is allowed to interfere with the competitive market forces that auto-matically punish bigots and confer advantages on those who act without racial bias, members of minority groups will sense better opportunities, seek improved educational skills, and increasingly equip themselves to compete more effectively with members of more advantaged groups.

- As a result of the push and pull of these competitive processes, increasing numbers of formerly outcast racial groups will grad-ually rise to the top of the economic, educational, or professional ladder and, in time, will reach economic, educational, and profes-sional parity with the majority of the population.

ously, most whites have never recognized the startling inconsistency of this arrangement. Because black people were believed to belong to a biologi-cally inferior race, genetically distinct from the rest of American society, their exclusion from the safeguards of the marketplace was never viewed as a violation of the integrity of the merit system. Accordingly, Adam Smith's grand design, which created open markets and allowed each person to rise or fall according to competitive judgments of his or her merits, never applied to or protected black people in the United States. Shunned, rejected, and often loathed, the feudal concept of "place" was, and in many cases still is, reserved for the American Negro.

Nevertheless, the force of competition stands as an impressive protector of the opportunities of racial minorities. Today, the ambitious white entrepreneur is likely to be competitively well advised to employ a competent member of an outcast race. To the shrewd buyer, industrialist, or housewife, powerful competitive forces tend to enforce a rule of racial neutrality under which the skin color of an artisan, merchant, or plumber is irrelevant to the job to be done. Entirely aside from the presence of race relations commissions and litigious civil rights advocates, the sheer competitive pressure to get the best person for the post is a potent guardian of the opportunities of blacks. In fact, there is good reason to believe that today there is less profit in the practice of racial bigotry than at any other time in the economic history of the nation. But competition's provision of economic justice for the American Negro is a very recent phenomenon.

Two important conclusions emerge. The first of these is that, contrary to standard opinion, capitalism places just as much emphasis on coercive power as it does on liberty. Strong supporters of the view that free markets always work for the best completely ignore the fact that when this happens it is because *punitive market power,* inherent in the contest among competing rivals, has commanded this happy result. The second point is that capitalism, in its classic and theoretical form, was never an inherently racist economic power system. It did not by its nature depend on the subjugation of blacks or of other outcast groups. In its classic form, not only did capitalism refuse to reserve places or privileges for any particular ethnic group, but its competitive powers systematically punished those who did. In this sense, the forces of capitalism had many of the dispassionate and evenhanded qualities of nature's power, after which, in many respects, it appears to have been modeled.

CHAPTER FIVE

Power in Strong-Arm Economics: To Each According to His Brawn

"The Lion, the Ass, and the Fox went hunting together. Their luck was good, and at the end of the day the Lion asked the Ass to divide the spoils. The Ass divided everything into three equal portions and invited the Lion to take his pick, whereupon the indignant Lion leaped upon the Ass and devoured him on the spot. He then turned to the Fox and invited him to make a new division. The Fox hastily piled everything into one great heap, save for a few odd scraps, and asked the Lion to choose. The Lion asked the Fox who had taught him to divide so well.
"'The Ass,' replied the Fox."

—Aesop's Fables *(550 B.C.)*

ACCORDING TO FREE-MARKET THEORY, the only permissible form of coercive economic power resided in the natural sanctions and controls of the competitive process. Thus, under the open-market arrangement, the forces of the marketplace automatically endorsed skill and hard work by rewarding them with success and money, and in an equally self-regulating way, punished ineptitude and laziness by meting out the pain of economic failure. No other coercion or intervention was allowed. Government power stood by and watched as private contestants, acting presumably in a rational and self-seeking way, chose the best qualified person for the job. For several centuries in the United States, these were the principal rewards and punishments that the American economy knew. It is true that large numbers of competitors, who invariably professed dedication to free-market solutions to economic problems, sometimes used political power to make occasional raids on the public treasury. But, on the whole, coercive power was held at bay. In the formative years of the American economy, there were no subsidies for the people who drilled for oil, no tax deductions to advance the interests of real estate developers. Indeed, the economic system knew no government power in the form of equal opportunity laws, minimum wage rules, affirmative-action guidelines, set-asides for minority contractors, or job preferences for returning war veterans.

From the beginning, it was predictable that most contestants would not rest easily under an economic system that permitted them no way to get ahead other than by submitting their competence, the quality of their produce, or the reliability of their capital to open bidding. Understandably, then, the more aggressive participants in the economic contest took steps to assure themselves success and to mitigate the rigors of economic failure. They learned to protect themselves and their friends from the uncertain outcomes of open competition; they developed a host of schemes to stack the economic deck in their own favor and against their competitors; they blocked potential rivals from entering the playing fields of competition; they closed doors to competitors who wished to sit at the bargaining tables where goods and labor were traded; they lobbied for and obtained public laws protecting themselves against the perils of competitors entering their trades or turfs; in the name of economic justice they sponsored ostensible social reforms, which, in fact, did little more than feather nests and protect jobs. "Reward the workers, not the shirkers," was the official doctrine of the ardent advocates of free enterprise and open competition. But, in fact, these fierce defenders of free markets were quick to claim their share of coerced benefits in the form of government handouts, trade assocation protection against "unfair" competition, and guaranteed prices for certain politically favored enterprises.

Gradually, then, coercive power was introduced into the marketplace. It grew in strength each year. Foremen, nurses, school teachers, blue-collar workers, and large manufacturers all learned to manipulate the techniques of pressure and power. Home builders, commodity brokers, and dairy farmers helped themselves and hobbled the competition by picking up the election tabs of congressmen and state legislators. Throughout the nation, economic outcomes were increasingly determined by the heft of the club and the depth of the purse of political action committees and special-interest lobbies. And whenever a brand-new form of coercive force or pressure was brought to bear, the established masters of economic coercion always discovered and proclaimed good moral reasons why the competitive process should be overruled and why they, and not others, should go to the head of the line.

When Power Restricts Employment and Levies Tribute

Of all the economic schemes devised by man for making gains through the use of coercive power, few have so effectively served their users as human consensus power expressed in the noncompetition pact. Without any overt display of force or violence, people developed collective economic advantage simply by banding together and agreeing not to compete with one another for the labor, trade, or goods of third persons. Thus, if all employers in a particular area decided that they would accept workers only at certain wages and on certain terms, the available workers had no choice but to accept those terms. Or if employers decided, in common with other employers, that only certain types or classes of people would be acceptable as employees, borrowers, or tenants, those who did not fit into the accepted class were effectively removed from the competitive protection of the marketplace. Often operating in the disguised form of a trading group, a professional association, or a benevolent protection league, the collective agreement to exclude or limit marketplace participation by others became a potent weapon of economic force. Over the years, realtors, lawyers, druggists, farmers, securities dealers—not to mention believers in the inherent superiority of white people—have been signally successful in relieving themselves of the distasteful pressures of competition from certain categories of people.

The labor union represents the most important example of coercive economic power embodied in the standard noncompetition pact. Despite some recent setbacks, the labor union has, in fact, become the most significant manifestation of coercive economic power in the Western world. The most important economic gains in capitalistic economies have been won not by large corporations acting in league with one another, but rather by trade unions operating on standard cartel principles. Winning has been achieved by limiting the right to bargain individually, restricting the numbers of those eligible to work, erecting barriers to keep out qualified but unwanted workers, and denying employers any labor whatsoever unless all members of the designated pool of labor are hired on collectively satisfactory terms.

True to established economic principles that contrived shortages of goods or labor will raise the price of the commodity, those who have worked in unionized industries have invariably done better. No economist has successfully measured precisely which portion of labor income is due to the coercive muscle of collective bargaining, but the fact that extra income is created is undeniable. While most people on fixed incomes and in nonunionized occupations have suffered considerably as a result of the high inflation rates of the late 1970s, the major trade unions have almost always succeeded in keeping their members' wages protected against a deteriorating dollar. From 1967 to 1979, real earnings in highly organized industries such as steel, aluminum, transportation, utilities, trucking, railroads, automobile manufacturing, and mining rose much faster than in trades that were not organized.

A special feature of labor union power concerns us here. This was the almost universal practice of generating greater bargaining power by limiting membership in the group permitted to apply for work. Recognizing the outstanding advantages of contrived labor scarcity, members of trade unions have almost invariably had an economic interest in keeping out newcomers to the union—especially those who were strangers, social outcasts, or otherwise considered as undesirable associates in the marketplace. It followed that those groups that, by historical accident or through unequal social or political power, did not have a proportionate share of members of labor unions tended on the whole to earn less than groups with fuller union membership. And groups with disproportionately small membership in trade unions were obliged, in disproportionately large numbers, to enter the nonunionized labor market, where employer bargaining power was usually superior. The combination of two forces—collective bargaining and membership restrictions in the bargaining unit—almost invariably restricted the economic progress of racial minorities and other groups that were at the bottom of the pecking order.

In some cases, the coercive power of labor turned to the use of outright force. Fuller participation in the age of affluence has sometimes been attained through urban riots, bridge closings, industrial sabotage, threatened blackouts, and other marginally criminal acts. The objective was to disrupt, to threaten, and to inflict unbearable cost. Unlike several other countries in the Western world, the use of violence to make economic gains has not been the American economic norm; yet, in many industries the threat of force lurks in the background as a hidden club. As in a game of Russian poker, the big stick tends to be brought out from under the card table when the competitive bargaining process works against an aggrieved group.

Those who have delivered the most impressive economic force have been groups large enough, or so essential to economic activity, that no matter how illegitimate their weapons, they could, in fact, defy the power of the state. Thus, the most financially profitable work stoppages often occurred in firehouses, police stations, and nursing homes. There were strikes in schoolrooms, post offices, and sewage treatment facilities. Sanitation workers kept even with, or moved ahead of, rising currency inflation by leaving mountains of refuse on city streets. Few instruments of economic power were as potent as a threatened strike by hospital workers. Policemen sitting at home discovered that they could be an even greater public menace than the looters and rioters from whom they were supposed to guard the public. In many cases, the open competition in which rivals submitted their industry and talent for selection in the marketplace was altogether suspended. Large numbers of power groups in American society were able to levy tribute on society as a whole and, with the exception of the airport controllers strike action in 1981, most of them were only faintly amused by public pleas that they should abandon the use of force and resubmit themselves to the competitive rigors of the marketplace.

Power in the Executive Suite: Disparities Between Pay and Performance

The use of coercive power to win a premium in excess of one's economic worth or productivity has been a standard strategy of those at the top as well as at the bottom. With the aid of friendly directors, cooperative lawyers, and obedient consultants, business executives in the upper reaches of corporate America devised a wide variety of employment contracts, golden parachute agreements, "shark repellent" bylaw restrictions, and other protective devices that paid them handsomely for bad as well as good performance. In common with academic professionals and blue-collar workers, the most fervent executive advocates of free enterprise consistently fought to remove themselves from the competency tests of the free market.

Many of the economists of freedom were skeptical about the long-term benefits to society of so-called free collective bargaining. They longed to reinstate the old-fashioned sanctions of the traditional free market; they yearned for the old days of the weekly economic report card, which adjudicated the quality of a person's industry and productivity by whether or not Friday's paycheck was waiting in the office. But coercive power has now taken firm control of the nation's marketplace. Tens of millions of unionized electrical workers, printers, plumbers, construction workers, railroad workers, street sweepers, and executive bureaucrats are bargaining from positions where they frequently extract compensation far greater than the intrinsic value of their work.

In such an economy, it was a serious disadvantage not to have one's own cartel. Formidable handicaps, particularly, faced outcasts and other low-status groups that had no access to powerful organizations such as labor unions, governing boards of large corporations, bodies determining qualifications, and other certifying units that came to be so important in adjudicating success and failure in the American economy.

Raiding the Treasury: When Political Muscle Is the Arbiter of Economic Success

The deployment of coercive power to temper and control the harsh penalties of the market economy was not an innovation of the labor movement. Long before workers had learned to use organized pressure and consensus power to alter the outcome of the competitive process, other influential persons had been enlisting government power to help them get ahead. Tapping the public treasury in favor of preferred groups has, in fact, been one of the oldest and most venerable of American traditions. The second item of legislation passed by the First Congress in 1789 was a shipping preference similar to modern maritime subsidies. Later, in 1841, the Land Redemption Act provided certain settlers with up to 160 acres of farmland at $1.25 an acre. Before the emancipation of the slaves, the Homestead Act of 1862 gave 162 acres, without charge, to 1.6 million white families who agreed to settle and farm what had formerly been public lands. Particularly in the post-World War II years, the list of favored or subsidized groups rapidly expanded to include, among many others, tobacco farmers, bankers, real estate owners, dairy operators, small businessmen, war veterans, and automobile manufacturers. Over the years, those groups that have been most successful in improving their fortunes by establishing direct claims against the public treasury have tended to be the politically powerful. Other groups with no political power have, in large measure, been left to the tender mercies of free markets and, in some cases, of markets rigged against them.

The economic history of the United States essentially confirms the power principle. The drive for access to the places of competition became a drive for preferred or protected places on the playing fields. The competition among groups to win as many places in institutions as the merit of individual members would warrant became, instead, a struggle to achieve fixed quotas or entitlements. Even the most dedicated champions of limited government responded to pressure rather than merit or need. Under the conservative Administration of Ronald Reagan the U.S. farm subsidy program grew to $20 billion—nearly seven times the average yearly cost during the 1970s. The civil rights movement, too, became a contest between opposing interest groups for special allotments and preferences. In order to explain who gets ahead in the United States it has now become relevant, though not determinative, to ask who holds coercive power and who doesn't, who are the rulers and who are the subjects—rather than simply who are bright and ambitious and who are lazy or dull of mind. Two full centuries after the founding of a republic dedicated to open competition in private markets, it appeared that the politically powerful in American business, labor, and professions working with clubhouse cronies and cooperative congressmen were collecting upwards of $50 billion a year in government preferments and subsidies, a sum which in 1980 was about twice what the government was spending on its programs for the poor.

The Tendency of the Powerful to Save Free Markets for the Weak

Despite some recent moves to evict the forces of coercion from the marketplace and to restore greater weight to competition in the economy, we have come to live in a nation where coercive power, either in government or private form, is deeply involved in controlling our economic fortunes. Hard work, open competition, and long hours on the job are often prescriptions for the good society rather than for what society has become. The fact remains that effort and ambition contribute a great deal more to income when one has the credentials and certificates our society often requires before it will hear of, or recognize, effort and ambition. In the United States, one is indeed likely to win a job by learning skills and then applying for work; but one also gets ahead in life by first winning an apprenticeship post and then learning the necessary skills once one has secured a position. Wealth and success are not only a product of diligence and ambition to get ahead, they are the result, too, of seniority agreements, government franchises, mineral grants, work permission cards, farm allotments, interest-free loans, and protected employment. Political power, regrettably, is one of the major driving forces of the American economy.

In recent years, a number of groups, whose members have not heretofore been full participants in the benefits of the American affluence, have acquired a clearer sense of the dynamics of the creation of wealth and poverty in this country. Despite exaggerated and cherished claims to the contrary, they have come to see that American economics and money acquisition are intimately connected to politics, connections, and influence. Often viewing the economy from a distant servant's wing, they have, nevertheless, carefully noted how the acquisition of desirable goods and services often is determined by coercive market power and the relative strength of pressure groups. In common with others who now hold higher rank, the outcast groups have learned to improve their fortunes through the commands of quotas and credentialization, as well as through the market forces of skill, diligence, and training. They have become adroit at seeking out government protection and subsidies. They have lined up special tickets of admission for their friends and relatives by learning to write the rules and regulations. Like many other Americans, they have begun to improve their living standards by reaching for a risk-free economic life of protected position which determinedly defends itself against the penalties of failure under the sanctions of the established market system. This may be perverse of them, but particularly where prior position and categorical rules have kept them out, many of them have sensibly decided that they will make little progress in the competition for power unless they too seek out preassigned positions and categorical rules to get themselves in. This economic strategy perforce takes the world of American capitalism as it is rather than as it was conceived by the Founding Fathers, or as it is nostalgically and simplistically viewed by many political conservatives and other advocates of free-market principles.

It seems then that, over a span of 100 years, a remarkable economic change has occurred. Instead of submitting themselves to the judgments of free markets, the powerful in America have become in all respects economic protectionists benefiting greatly from the many coercive arrangements that guard position and advantage. Ironically, now that blacks and other formerly outcast groups are permitted to openly compete for advancement whites consistently instruct them in the virtues of *not* being protectionists. Blacks, particularly, are constantly reminded of the old bromide that the only way to get ahead is to borrow a dollar and build a better mousetrap. Successful white businessmen, who back their skills and diligence with the full armory of coercive political and economic weapons available to them today, nevertheless preach to struggling minorities the rags-to-riches pieties of Horatio Alger. While those at the top of the economic pyramid salute politics, property, and other forms of coercive power, minority groups are constantly admonished that they should pledge sole allegiance to the now often unheeded verities of Adam Smith.

There is a special bite to the irony of this story. As we shall see in later chapters, the majority of whites—those legendary followers of Adam Smith—have not only become confirmed economic protectionists, but they have done so, to a considerable extent, at the direct expense of the black people who, for so many years, they faithfully protected from the blessings of either competition or power.

Part Two

The Race-Trait
Belief System
as
Power

"... When you control a man's thinking you do not have to worry about his actions. You do not have to tell him to stand here or go yonder. He will find his 'proper place' and will stay in it. You do not need to send him to the back door. He will go without being told. In fact, if there is no back door, he will cut one for his special benefit. His education makes it necessary."

—Carter G. Woodson
The Miseducation of the Negro *(1933)*

CHAPTER SIX

Power in Classifying People:
To Each According to His Group

"The human mind must think with the aid of categories. . . . Once formed, categories are the basis for normal prejudgment. We cannot possibly avoid this process."

—Gordon W. Allport,
The Nature of Prejudice *(1954)*

SOLEMNLY AND FROM ON HIGH, individuals in much of the Western world were instructed to compete. In fact, in a free society, one of the most praiseworthy acts of citizenship was to submit one's competence to the competitive judgments of the marketplace. Nevertheless, we have seen that most employers, workers, traders, and capitalists abhorred competition. As a result, the protectionists took charge of a large part of the economy. They set up barriers that blocked entry to the market by others; they established private economic preserves where competitors couldn't reach them; they denied work licenses to potential rivals; they used political power to win public subsidies, grants, and contracts. These were only a few of the wide-ranging coercive measures employed by the powerful as well as the competent to ensure favorable economic decisions for themselves.

Less apparent to the untrained eye was a related form of consensus power. This took the form of the collective mode of observation, thinking, and reaching conclusions about the qualifications or traits of people. Through a process of classifying people—and acting in a predetermined way dictated by the class mode of judgment—certain groups were held in fixed and subordinate positions. Those, in turn, who made and enforced decisions in accordance with the established classifications were assured a dominant and advantageous position for themselves without submitting their worth and abilities to the pain and penalties of open competition. This was an important form of coercion that operated in the economic system. Let us examine how this power worked.

On Classification and Constraint

In Chapter One, we saw how human intelligence enabled people to become powerful by learning, remembering, and applying information about the observable traits and habits of other creatures. Man was thus able to stalk, ambush, and ensnare. But the human brain could do much more than observe, memorize, and recall. Among other things, it could compare, differentiate, and, above all, classify and generalize. In particular, the capacity to generalize and classify generated human power: It enabled people to make class distinctions and thereby contain and limit the freedoms of others.

How do classifications and generalizations enable one set of people to constrain another? Think back tens of thousands of years. Imagine a meadow full of edible beetles. Thousands of them are busy in their own ecological niche, unobtrusive and almost undetectable because nature has provided them with good cover. But man's intelligence was on the case. He remembered that on more than one occasion he had found these beetles hiding under a hard, gray object he called a rock. From this he concluded that other beetles would be found under other rocks. Note that this generalization—"beetles tend to hide under rocks"—is also a prediction both about what beetles will do and about what man should do to find them. These predictions told primitive man how to conduct a sensible search for beetles. He was no longer limited to relying on memory and thus limited to returning again and again to the same rock. In this way, beetles were brought under man's control because man knew exactly what they were going to do.

"Living under rocks" was a trait man had correctly associated with the behavior of beetles as a class of insects. As man mentally classified other creatures and observed habits associated with these classes, he developed a long and accurate list of predictable creature behaviors. By classifying animals and making generalizations about the traits associated with each class, man was able to predict behind what rocks and in what caves, bushes, and fields different species would feed, nest, forage, or hide.

Until man made the beetle/rock connection, beetles enjoyed relative freedom. But once man constructed his mental dossier on beetle-class behavior, the jig was up. The poor beetles, coded alike in appearance and the victims of built-in biological rules of behavior, were finished once man had deciphered their biological code. Man scooped them up as he pleased. To be sure, the ability to develop species-trait classifications is not unique among humans, but, as far as we know, no other species learned to classify so efficiently or to use the class-behavior prediction as an extension of its will.

If a human being could classify objects and animals, it is not surprising that by the same mental process he also came to classify groups among his own species. Human subgroups—with attendant behavior expectations— were created according to height, weight, sex, race, nationality, hair color, skin color, religion, personality, and habits. In each case, traits were linked —sometimes accurately, but perhaps more often inaccurately—to membership in the class. Thus, people not only classified one another as French, Italian, or Jewish, but also stereotypically as French and therefore amorous, Italian and therefore hot-tempered, Jewish and therefore avaricious. Such stereotyped generalizations occasionally described positive traits, but more often than not had pejorative implications and served as cautionary reminders about undesirable types of behavior believed likely to be encountered in any dealings with the groups about whom these generalizations had been made.

In this way, class membership came to control not only the ways in which people thought about each other, but also the ways in which they treated each other. Economic selections, voting decisions, friendship choices, the selection of neighbors, schools, teachers, and business associates came under the control of the class-trait expectation. Once the class had been identified and fixed traits correctly or incorrectly assigned to members of the class, individuals in the class were seen as having these class traits and usually as not possessing other traits or capabilities that didn't belong to the class. In this human tendency to judge one another according to class membership or rank rather than individual ability, we now begin to perceive the potential of a serious threat to individual liberty. If people judged each other according to class-trait expectations, what was to become of the philosophers' rule that markets were to be open, free, and driven only by considerations of *individual* competence and productivity?

Group Imperatives as Judgments of Qualifications

Trait classifications produced not only behavioral assumptions but also collective value judgments. Some trait classifications denigrated and stigmatized entire groups, while others conferred respect. A few classifications were value-free. In the United States, for example, an essentially neutral judgment attaches to people with white complexions and blue or brown eyes. A person of Scandinavian or English ancestry living in the United States expects neither an inferior nor a privileged position. These groups do not have to bear the burden of any major constraining stereotypes.

Class-trait expectations relating to various ethnic groups are far from consistent throughout the world, indicating that stereotypes are often neither accurate nor objective pictures of human traits or behavior. The Englishman's stereotyped image of the German is quite different from the "typical" German who inhabits the Italian imagination. The American image of the "average" Japanese is totally unlike the Chinese image of the same individual. What is more, stereotypes also vary in a specificity that depends on many factors, the most important of which is undoubtedly the extent of contact between the peoples involved. Koreans, for example, tend to have one stereotyped image of the Japanese and a completely different image of the Chinese, whereas Americans tend to lump Chinese, Japanese, and Koreans together as "Orientals," all of whom are imagined to share common traits. It is true, then, that these class-behavior generalizations tell us less about the people they describe than about the people making the generalizations. It is thus not surprising that once a class-trait generalization has been formed, it tends to be rigid, ritualistically followed, and well defended against reexamination or revision. These trait associations have often survived for remarkably long periods of time with little or no objective validation. In many cases, there appear to have been powerful human needs to hold on to these trait prejudgments and protect them from countervailing forces of corrective education and contradictory information.

Not all class-trait generalizations are pejorative. Those describing characteristics of elite classes tend to be laudatory, entitling supposed possessors of these traits to favorable treatment. In the United States, these benefits, and the sense of superiority that goes with them, accrue to people who are classified as Protestant, graduates of Harvard College, members of certain clubs, or, until recently, those whose names were listed in *The Social Register*. The public respect and attention one derives from being included within elite classes invariably confer power. People listen to, and are often swayed by, those they assume to belong to honored groups. Power accrues, therefore, to all those included within the select circle sometimes called "the establishment." Few dare offer these individuals an undesirable table at a restaurant, complain if their dogs destroy shrubs, or refuse their children admission to selective institutions. In fact, as a general rule of economics, those who enjoy establishment status are likely to be in great demand. One aspect of this enviable status is almost assured employment, invitations to join the boards of corporations, and opportunities to participate in "sure-thing" investment opportunities. This is power indeed!

Once class-trait value judgments come to exist, they tend to evolve into imperatives or taboos that shape the conduct of all concerned in an almost obligatory fashion. Groups seen as dependable, upstanding, and business-like tend to have their members selected for responsible positions through which they can demonstrate these ascribed talents. Conversely, members of groups regarded as shiftless and undependable tend to be excluded from positions through which they could prove the falsity of these charges. This form of selective competition, in which outcomes depend on class membership, often produces long-standing and seemingly indelible negative judgments that act as self-fulfilling prophecies. Alexis de Tocqueville stated that God, being all-knowing, "had no need to make generalizations." Man—a good deal less than perfectly rational and omniscient—created generalizations and then used them both to honor himself and to denigrate and sometimes even to enslave others.

Power in the Derogatory Class Prejudgment

Predictable behavior is more characteristic of some classes than of others. Certain classifications—most notably those connected with the laws of physics—are associated with a very high order of predictability. For example, the statistical probability approaches absolute zero that the random moving molecules of a volume of liquid will suddenly align themselves in the shape of a Michelangelo sculpture. Similarly, the chemical properties or traits of classified substances such as mercury or potassium can be identified with considerable precision: The behavior of these elements can be predicted with great certainty. In contrast, medical science produces a level of predictive accuracy somewhat below that of physics. For example, a person diagnosed as a diabetic is likely to develop a specific set of signs and symptoms, but may not necessarily do so.

Class-trait associations within the more subjective behavioral sciences are even more difficult to establish and are even less reliable. Observations about human behavior are notoriously unreliable because there is a natural tendency to see what one expects to see. What is more, even when the trait descriptions are accurate and unbiased, there is absolutely no way of knowing whether the traits in question are inherent characteristics of the population or whether they have evolved in response to specific circumstances and would disappear under other circumstances. For example, in our society, certain racial groups are often stigmatized as lazy. Even if there were any truth to this accusation—which is extremely doubtful—this "socialized" laziness might well be nothing more than a resigned response to restricted competitive opportunities which the race-trait expectation demands. In this sense, many of the supposed traits of various groups are undoubtedly artificial creations.

Some class imperatives reliably predict behavior while others either force or prevent that behavior. And the degree of constraint will vary with time and place. For example, in sixteenth-century England, an individual could reliably be assumed to follow the same profession or trade as his father. In mid-twentieth-century America, one could predict—with only a slight risk of being wrong—that a brain surgeon or a tenured professor at a major university would be male. If, today, one were to choose at random the name of a chief executive of one of the 2,000 largest corporations in America, one could be almost certain that that person would be neither black nor female. We can make these predictions because class-trait expectations operate so pervasively in shaping reality. This is a form of coercive power that uses no visible force or violence. The noose is tightly drawn by class-trait expectations that become fixed and controlling in society's behavioral and value systems.

The coercive powers of class judgments profoundly control the lives of those to whom they are applied, but very few people stop to ask whether their class-trait forecasts are true. Nor do they ask themselves whether the class forecasts are true only because people generally thought they were true and because individuals within the class had no choice but to obey the class expectation and thus *make* it true. In fact, many class imperatives are not true at all, but are mere superstition, wishful thinking, or taboo. On a regular basis the most respected scientists and investigators proclaim many of our racial codes to be false. Meticulous laboratory studies demonstrate to the general public that many common assumptions about classes of people are not true at all. Yet many people still cling dogmatically to the humbug of class or race mythology.

False class-trait judgment unfortunately constitutes the basis for many important decisions in our society. Although we like to think of ourselves as truth seekers fervently guarding our open minds and our free press, in fact, we often prefer certainty to truth. We tend to be intellectually lazy and find that accepting trait classifications is an easy way to make life's decisions, especially when everyone else seems to be acting on the same pre-judgments. By nature, we try to avoid the anxieties generated by challenges to our settled knowledge, especially when these challenges threaten the grand or minor status we have either achieved or acquired by birth. Those who live under the protective wing of a favorable class-trait imperative are understandably reluctant to give up their beliefs, while those who have fallen victim to the curse of a collective slander are unlikely to win reinstatement. They face a long and often futile uphill fight before society will even pretend to judge them on their individual merits.

Defending Power Through Selective Observation

Class-trait expectations—and the power they generate—are protected by the selective nature of human memory. People tend to read and listen to information that confirms their beliefs and to ignore information that challenges these beliefs. For example, several years ago, many people in New York City found support for racial bias when the press reported widely that the first two political appointments made by a New York City mayor were blacks who had had prior difficulties with the Internal Revenue Service. The black borrower who defaults on a loan is remembered long after thousands of whites have defaulted. If an academic institution employs a black person in a high post and she or he fails to do a satisfactory job, people are likely to find in that single failure a confirmation of their racial-trait expectations, while hundreds of whites who were fired from similar posts are taken as exceptions to the general rule of white competence. Every time people read of a particularly heinous crime committed by a black youth, a record of the event is securely locked in the human memory bank.

There are other ways in which the human mind defends against relinquishing class-trait expectations. People tend to attribute typical behavior of members of a class of people to all individuals within the class. For instance, if a group of 100 people averages 5' 8" in height, we have no precise information about the actual height of any one of the individuals in the group. Yet we don't always remember to think logically. For example, it is known that minority individuals score *on the average* between 100 and 200 points below the national median on established tests for college admission. But this particular statistical fact offers no evidence whatsoever of the actual score of any individual black person applying for admission to a college. Educators will nevertheless often declare that so-and-so had a very high score "for a black person," as if surprised that the usual poor performance of blacks generally didn't rub off on the particular applicant.

This tendency to transfer notions about typical behavior to individual behavior operates broadly when economic selections are made. Consider decisions to grant credit. The lender supposedly determines the credit-worthiness of individuals; the average performance of the class into which the person fits should thus be largely irrelevant. Yet class-trait expectancies are so deeply embedded that many, if not most, lenders regularly use typical behavior to form invalid assumptions about individual behavior, refusing credit to teenagers or the elderly because, on the average, members of these groups have poorer credit ratings than those of the whole population. Or lenders may refuse credit to individual blacks because, on the average, blacks earn less than whites and have less stable job histories. Under present conditions, a credit rule that rejects all black applicants may indeed be a rational and efficient way to conduct the affairs of a banking institution. But this manner of judgment does not make any sort of valid statement about the creditworthiness of any particular black person applying for a loan.

Tightening the Drawstring: The Widely Shared Class-Trait Expectation

Power, I have proposed, is a function of human consensus. To the extent that the consensus is widely held or tightly organized, those who join in it can exercise very great power. For example, if only a small minority of the population believes that young men with long hair have a weak work ethic, the economic freedoms of people in this class are not rigidly constrained because a sufficient number of competitive employers not bound by the consensus will override the adverse minority opinion. But if, instead, an overwhelming majority accepts the proposition that, say, women as a class are passive individuals who will tend to shy away from competition in business transactions, this expectation will greatly reduce the career oppor-tunities of women as a class. This in turn would mean that women would have few chances to disprove the generalization and set the record straight.

Of course, in time, most class-trait imperatives are questioned. Very powerful forces are at work that tend to *correct* faulty class-trait ex-pectations. If, for example, many people confuse the species traits of a cobra with those of a garter snake, the class-behavior expectation will probably be cleared up very rapidly. The same is true in all cases where those who subscribe to the belief system will become seriously harmed or put at a disadvantage by clinging to this erroneous belief system. Unfortunately, the belief system about blacks has never been effectively challenged in American society because blacks are so universally believed to be less diligent and less competent than whites. Because America enjoys an overstocked labor pool with a plentiful supply of skilled workers, those who decline to hire talented blacks suffer virtually no competitive disadvantage in acting out their racial biases, while those who are both principled and courageous enough to ignore racial taboos gain little or no competitive edge by doing so. One of the few notable exceptions occurs in the field of organized sports, where skilled performers have always been in short supply. In 1947, when the Brooklyn Dodgers broke baseball's color line, they virtually forced other teams in their league to follow suit or to fall by the wayside as the more open-minded teams gained a tremendous competitive advantage by signing black athletes. Indeed, in eight of the next ten years the National League championship was won by teams dominated by black superstars. Nothing so stirring illustrates the dramatic impact of black athletes as the fact that after the integration of baseball, black players won the National League Rookie of the Year Award six out of the next seven years and the National League Most Valuable Player Award ten out of the next fifteen. Obviously, any team willing to ignore this trend and cling to its old prejudices paid heavily for the privilege.

Unfortunately, the lesson taught by baseball and other team sports has not been readily transferred to other areas of the economy. Instead of drawing the conclusion that blacks can compete with whites on equal terms if given a fair chance, white America has, on the whole, solaced itself with the generalization that what is true of athletes is due to a genetic or cultural advantage and may not be true in other areas of human endeavor. Yet, outstanding success at team sports is surely only partly a matter of legs and wrists and brawn, but partly also a matter of leadership, daring, perseverance, and other such intangibles that would be of considerable value in any sort of economic activity. Trait expectations, however, do not easily give way to considered judgment. Unless those who are unfairly stereotyped hold power in the form of private or public means to punish those who promote and act on inaccurate and self-serving classifications—in something like the direct and unanswerable way that Jackie Robinson, Ernie Banks, Willie Mays, and Henry Aaron "punished" baseball's white supremacists—the objective fact of individual competence will almost never rescue an individual from the strong arm of an entrenched racial stereotype.

Stereotypes Etched in Stone: When the State Adopts a Class-Trait Prejudgment

Class stereotyping has many potent ways of ratifying itself. When the state adopts and proclaims class-trait expectancies, the belief system is virtually guaranteed acceptance and continuity. Over a century ago, the Supreme Court declared in the *Dred Scott* decision that Negroes were "beings of an inferior order, and altogether unfit to associate with the white race."[1] The force of this opinion unquestionably served to legitimize the coercive force of class-trait expectations. If the state adopts an opinion, it is generally assumed to be valid and reliable. In addition, the state has the power to act on its announced beliefs. A state-adopted class-trait imperative may thus become the rationale for unchallenged restrictions on careers, licenses for political activities, access to public institutions, or choices in housing. Traditional Jim Crow laws and federal restrictions on government-financed home mortgages in ethnically integrated areas are examples of state power used to reinforce class- or race-trait expectations.

With similar force, an agency of the state may adopt a class-trait expectation. A public school may classify a child as retarded, autistic, or brain damaged. Such determinations are often established by subjective or unscientific means. The class designation may have been influenced by where the child lives, his skin color, or his parents' behavior. As an instrument of state control, these judgments may have crippling effects. Children who are marked early are very likely to be judged, graded, and treated by peers in accordance with the trait classifications. And the child's career expectations may be severely limited by received opinion.

An even more powerful reinforcement of class-trait belief systems arises when the subjects themselves of unfavorable stereotypes come to believe the derogatory things said of them. Just as any child if told often enough that he is a bad boy may despair of convincing anyone to the contrary and may choose instead to act out the identity assigned to him, so a whole people may be infected by the negative assessment of themselves. In their capacity for doing psychological damage and limiting freedom, these self-imposed class expectations can program behavior so that a subjugated class becomes an unwitting accomplice of its oppressors. Over the course of many generations, a great many blacks have indeed come to believe that as a class they were suited to carry luggage, to sweep, and to clean latrines. It even became a point of pride that they, above all others, had the physical endurance to do heavy labor or to work in front of hot steel furnaces, where they had been assigned as a class. Very large numbers of them came to accept the class judgment that they were not suited for entrepreneurial activity, that they had no right or competence to organize themselves for political activity, that they had no business challenging the views of whites. They came to believe that as members of a special racial group they would benefit by avoiding the humiliations of attending integrated schools or entering other places where they were clearly not wanted. Not many decades ago many black people in the South were known to blacklist or ostracize other blacks who opened professional offices or retail stores in violation of society's racial taboos. Thus, in a very real sense a self-adopted class-trait expectation caused very many Negroes to join in the majority plan that assigned inferior status to them. It has been observed before that no form of power is less costly and more efficient for a dominant class than to have an underclass put on the chains of its own enslavement.

The Class-Trait Judgments in the Marketplace

We noted earlier that competitive markets were intended to liberate society from the class expectations of the feudal period. Under the libertarian plan, economic and professional positions conferred by birth or class membership were erased and supplanted by judgment based on individual merit. Early in the history of the free-market economy, the practice of making rational economic judgments of individual competitors did indeed play an important part in economic decisionmaking. During the long period of village capitalism in England, the intelligent employer, trader, and investor could base his judgments on simple and direct observations of the individual skills, character, and prior accomplishments of those with whom he did business. From personal observation, the wool trader in a small community in England knew which workers were competent and industrious and which were dull or lazy. He had direct and often firsthand knowledge about which firms had refused deliveries of wool or had defaulted on contracts. Even in the early stages of industrialization, the small manufacturer was likely to have intimate knowledge about the personal characteristics of his potential suppliers and customers.

In this sense, competitive capitalism was off to a proper start, as required and approved by the philosophers of liberty. But as the marketplace grew, the factory system proliferated and specialization increased; no person or firm could possibly know or even come to know the qualifications of the people whose services or participation were required. General Motors counted its employees in the hundreds of thousands. At any one time, the Chase Manhattan Bank had hundreds of thousands of borrowers, most of them personally unknown to management. As the economy became larger and more complex, the case-by-case method of laboriously scanning the entire marketplace for craftsmen, vendors, or borrowers—each individually evaluated by current and past performance—became a painfully protracted, if not impossible, way to run one's economic life.

The solution to the dilemma was found in a return to selection according to class-trait associations. Economic man now began to manage business by looking for positive class traits and by rejecting applicants presumed to be a liability because of negative class traits. Each applicant was no longer considered individually. Instead, people were selected or rejected principally because they were presumed to have or not have commercially useful traits on the basis of their membership in certain classes, whether these classes were defined in terms of race, family connections, education, place of origin, or any other criteria assumed to be relevant for the purpose at hand. Inevitably, some of these class-trait predictions did have a certain validity for forecasting talent and industriousness. It stands to reason, for example, that lawyers from the top law schools will tend, on the whole, to have more on the ball than graduates of a backwater diploma mill. But for every valid class-trait generalization in widespread use, scores of other class prejudgments have amounted to little more than easy, but wholly arbitrary, means of ducking one's economic homework. Choosing employees from among the graduates of a particular high school and excluding those from other schools may have been a convenient way to screen or limit the potential applicant pool, but did little to assure a work force consisting of the best available talent. Recruiting trainees only from among the sons of current employees, members of the local Rotary Club, or people of one's own skin pigmentation satisfied a natural tendency to build and maintain networks of camaraderie, but at the cost of economic rationality. Thus, we have turned full circle as economic freedom has evolved into its own form of neo-feudalism, which requires that people be sorted and evaluated according to classifications often as irrelevant as the medieval system that assigned each citizen his "place" and expected him or her to know it.

Nowhere is the intense force of the collective mode of judgment more ritualized than in the credit industry, an industry that exerts an incalculable impact on the economic well-being of all those who come into contact with it. Over the course of time, collective thinking has produced a very broad catalogue of credit exclusions. These categories are familiar: "school dropouts," "women," "teenage drivers," and, in recent years, residents of certain postal zones. Those charged with the responsibility for allocating credit have generally acted on the principle that the appearance of prudence, rather than prudence itself, is the highest virtue. Instead of dispensing credit only after a careful evaluation of individual risks and rewards, they have tended to limit funds to those certified in advance as safe or proper.

The class-trait imperative clearly denied huge segments of the population the benefits of market competition. The collective "rubber stamp" severely restricted or regulated access to employment, credit, neighborhoods, businesses, clubs, trade associations, government contracts, and accrediting and educational institutions. Fortunately, many class members did not have the mark of inferiority and outcast status physically branded on their foreheads. As a result, they could shake the class-trait stigma and claim superior rank by the simple strategy of taking up membership in a new class. But that privilege was not available to everyone. When the brand of class membership was physically indelible, coercive power often became oppressive power, and, even in the United States, class became caste. In one of the great tragedies of American history, one group of people, in particular, stood accused from birth. Contrary to the most fundamental tenets of the Republic, they were determined by the color of their skin to carry the traits of Sambo as well as the mark of Cain.

CHAPTER SEVEN

The Ethnic Prejudgment as Power: To Each According to His Race

"When they were burning John Huss, a gentle little old lady came carrying her faggot to add it to the pile."

—*Albert Camus*
Carnets *(1942-1951)*

AS TO THE NATURAL INCLINATION of man to take care of his neighbor, the economists of freedom were cynics. Accordingly, they framed their economic selection system around a premise of individual self-interest. Forget vague and unenforceable concepts of economic justice, they said. Let the self-seeking desires of individual competitors settle all those futile debates over commercial ethics, business morality, and who was or was not getting his fair share of the economic pie. Engaged in business near my home in Princeton, New Jersey is "Warmhearted Bill's TV Repair." The day may come when Bill will decide to take the unusual step of hiring a female repairperson. But when that happens, most economists at Princeton University would declare that it should be not because Bill is warmhearted—or because he has been ordered to do so by the state—but because, in employing the particular woman he chooses to hire, his customers, and, so, his profits, will be better served.

But the classical theory of human profit motivation has proven to be only partially true. Man is a creature of complex motivations, not merely a one-track seeker of money. He is not unfailingly aggressive, ambitious, and competitive. Instead of pursuing the icy logic of financial self-interest, our theoretically rational and self-seeking economic man often defied Adam Smith's cardinal rule of economics: He sometimes, in fact, maximized risks and minimized rewards.

The Preference for Status Over Profit

In postulating financial self-interest as the prime motive of human beings, standard economic theory never made adequate allowance for one enduring quality in most people that seriously contradicted and consistently prevailed over the motive for economic gain. This quality was man's obsessive quest for prestige, position, and status. Ralph Waldo Emerson observed that the solar system had "no anxiety about its reputation"; but Samuel Johnson identified the major flaw in free-market economic theory: "Every man has a lurking wish to appear considerable in his native land."

It followed that economic man almost without exception deeply yearned for the respect of his superiors, the celebration of his virtues by his peers, and the faithful deference of his subordinates. He discovered self-esteem in hobnobbing with prestigious and preferred people. For people in commerce and trade, as in other endeavors, the prospect of not only associating with "one's own kind," but also mixing with people of a "better" kind has always been one of life's most prized objectives.

The quest for esteem and self-esteem was necessarily accompanied by a corresponding fear of loss of face. Associating with certain individuals of low repute was one of the surest ways to diminish one's esteem in the eyes of others. Accordingly, economic man might have had a considerable interest in money gain, but, at the same time, his interest in avoiding the "wrong" neighborhood, the "wrong" associations, the "wrong" schools, and the "wrong" seats at sports events was equally as great. This desire to maximize status often overrode the drive for profit which had been counted on by free-market theorists as the police force that would assure a meritocratic society that the most qualified people would rise to the top.

Over the centuries, the preference for status over profit introduced an important element of coercive power into the marketplace with profound economic consequences. Once economic man ceased to be a food-gatherer, self-employed sheepherder or private tiller in the fields, his work required close association with large numbers of other people. Selling services, hiring labor, or working in a shop or factory required physical and social contact with others. As the industrial revolution proceeded, people increasingly stood next to each other on assembly lines or in locker rooms; they shared company restrooms and cafeterias. Under twentieth-century capitalism, lending or borrowing money and using other people's capital, machines, or land could not be arranged without the intimate contact of a conference, possibly a shared meal, or the bodily contact of a handshake. Thus, everyday commerce, particularly when it took the form of divisions of labor, presented large numbers of economic exchanges in which the quest for status caused people to choose contact and association with highly regarded groups and to take active steps to avoid stigmatizing contacts and transactions with outcast groups.

As American capitalism matured in the twentieth century, the search for status over profit accelerated as large bureaucracies replaced small firms. As organizations grew in size, profit typically belonged to institutional owners who were not actively engaged in the management of the firm. As a consequence, the financial success of the firm became increasingly less important to the people who worked for it, and social or ethnic contacts on the job frequently became correspondingly more important than hiring the most talented or diligent worker. The money incentive to employ the most qualified person diminished as the person doing the hiring became increasingly removed from direct participation in the profits of the business organization. In large financial institutions, the desire to lend money to a person highly motivated to repay a loan often become a less urgent consideration than the prestige and connections of the prospective borrower. Particularly when the founding entrepreneur was no longer on the scene, the quest for status and comfort frequently overturned the meritocratic ethic of the capitalist that one should seek out and do business only with the best-qualified person. In time, the substitution of the comfort motive for the profit motive became a controlling force in the selection of employees, managers, contractors, borrowers, and other players in capitalism's daily competition.

In recent times, the fierce determination of most humans to avoid associations with disesteemed people has shown signs of abating. Yet, there is a persistent human need to avoid contact with outcast groups. Only a few years ago civil service workers at City Hall in New York City felt intolerably contaminated when welfare mothers were put to work beside them. Recently, the British press quoted a lowly Cockney boy who "expressed distress about eating an orange that had been picked by a nigger." Even the man sentenced to be hanged was sufficiently concerned with his self-esteem so as not to want to share his gallows with a polecat. If one lost one's job, so be it. But disaster became catastrophe if one lost it to a person who was held in very low regard by society. In the late twentieth century, many white people in the United States were prepared to recognize a profound ethical claim underlying black pressures for affirmative action, yet one had to admit that the loss of one's job to an outcast person was an intolerable assault on the human ego, as well as on the pocketbook.

Position Advantage Won Through the Collective Degradation of Others

Status typically flows from one's admission into a charmed inner circle. And the essential pleasure of preferred status lies in its scarcity, for tickets of admission into the "best" places are always in short supply. Under conditions of natural shortages, man had always competed for the scarce resources necessary for survival. In the modern world—especially the parts of it with relatively abundant material goods—the scarce commodity known as status also became the object of extremely fierce competition.

The competition for status has always marched hand in hand with trends in other forms of rivalry in the marketplace. Just as economic man found ways to circumvent the rule that his economic competence must be submitted to evaluation by the market, so, too, he devised schemes for avoiding one-to-one competition for status. The chief of these techniques involved setting up ascriptive arrangements for controlling and rationing the main ingredients of status. Although it was possible to win status through skill, diligence, and hard work, it was also possible to accomplish precisely the same end by gathering the respect society automatically assigned to people who were members of an esteemed class. By winning admission to the "right" class, one could short-cut the competitive process and acquire automatic entitlement to superior status without necessarily proving oneself.

The presence of esteemed classes necessarily required the existence of disesteemed or stigmatized classes. In most multiracial societies, those selected for degraded status were members of racial minorities. Race provided a convenient criterion for assigned inferiority and it has proven, over the course of history, to be more suitable for this purpose than such old standbys of discrimination as creed, political persuasion, speech patterns, or religion. In a racial system of classification, where physical characteristics provided the clues to the agreed-upon code of inclusion or exclusion, relatively unintelligent people could enjoy the power of awarding and denying status. In deciding who was "in" and who was "out," even children and dull-witted adults could immediately tell the players apart. In addition, racial classifications were largely immutable from birth. Members of religious sects could change or abandon their religions, philistines could acquire an education, and hippies could cut their hair. But the distinguishable physical characteristics of many races were largely unalterable. The process of granting or denying status as a consequence of membership in a racial class tended to be especially attractive to the lowliest members of the racial majority. In the 1970s, a poor white in the South who had murdered a black man explained to the press: "If I ain't better'n a f . . . n' nigger, then what the hell am I better'n of?" Back in 1858, Senator Trumbull of Illinois stated the same point more elegantly. "White labor," he declared, "cannot be respectable and honorable when it is brought into competition with black labor."

The goal of advancing one's status through the collective degradation of others is more easily accomplished when the negative stereotype tends to reflect, or coincide with, a society's distribution of economic and political power. Because of the normal tendency of people to fight back, a successful class stereotype usually stacks the deck against a weaker party. Moreover, when a less economically advanced group is chosen for collective disrepute, the superior group is able to shun the outcasts without losing the economic profits that might have come from successful commercial transactions with their designated inferiors. For these and other reasons, the majority usually singled out for degraded status such economically weaker groups as Chinese "coolies," Mexican "wetbacks," Filipino "boys," white "hillbillies," and others who, because of a condition of prior peasantry, servitude, or immigrant status, had not achieved normal levels of participation in economic and political power.

Little is known about the psychological forces that cement the social consensus assigning opprobrium and degradation to certain races. For reasons few understand, certain ethnic groups seem to react to certain other groups with inexplicable feelings of loathing, repugnance, and dread of contagion. Caucasians have long harbored these primitive taboo-like fears with regard to blacks, fears that apparently go far back in history and have prevailed in a wide variety of settings. In nineteenth-century Wolverhampton, England, as well as in twentieth-century South Boston, Massachusetts, the white population's aversion for dark-skinned people was virulent and nearly universal. Almost anywhere in the United States, one could find many whites who said either openly or behind cupped hands: "Blacks smell, they are violent, they breed like rabbits." More recently in the United States, one tends to hear self-contradictory complaints: "They don't want to work," "They are welfare cheats," and "They steal our jobs." In both cases the class proscription is dedicated to the degradation and subordination of the black race.

Americans spend a good deal of time telling both themselves and the world that these intense feelings of racial loathing are largely a matter of the past. Yet the fact remains that feelings of revulsion and the fear of contamination still reach paranoid and panic proportions. In the 1960s, a Mississippi highway patrolman found to be otherwise sane, fired a gun loaded with buckshot through a college dormitory window at a group of black coeds. In court, the patrolman could not "for the life of him" explain why he had done it. In the 1970s, plans for introducing gradually integrated housing into such communities as Forest Hills, New York, and Cicero, Illinois, produced riots. In the early 1980s, the Ku Klux Klan was again on the march in the South and Midwest, and outbreaks of Klan activities were reported in northern areas such as surburban New York and New Jersey. In some parts of the country, black children were still spat upon when they entered previously all-white schools.

It would be erroneous to conclude, however, that the United States suffers from some special curse. Degradation according to racial caste is a worldwide phenomenon. The Chinese are persecuted in Indonesia; gypsies are reviled outcasts in Hungary and Rumania; Indians were despised and expelled from Kenya. Crimean Tartars and Volga Germans are oppressed in the Soviet Union, while the Burakumin barely survive in the ghettos of Osaka, Japan. The pariah Bihari minority has been forcibly driven out of Bangladesh. It seems that everywhere the privilege of giving an underdog a daily kick in the hindquarters provides comfort to people who claim, or aspire to, membership in a superior caste.

The Racial Prejudgment as Coercive Power

Let us now see how the racial mode of making decisions operated as a form of coercive power working in the marketplace for labor, goods, and capital. As we shall see, its effect was to completely erase both natural and benign powers built into free markets, powers intended to bring economic harm to people who made selections according to race or class rather than according to individual qualifications and merit.

It is self-evident that people operate as either buyers or sellers in the market. Racial prejudgment occurs on the buying side of the market whenever the user of labor, capital, goods, or services rules out, or refuses to use, the work, money, goods, or services offered by members of a specific racial group. On the selling side, the racial mode of decisionmaking operates whenever someone who offers work, capital, goods, or services on the market declines to consider offers from buyers, borrowers, or even employers who come from a particular racial group. Both of these processes of making economic judgments may be called *primary* forms of race discrimination. The important point to notice is that whenever the racial prejudgment occurs, coercive power is at work because the judgment tends to limit or block the freedom of the outcast person to enter certain jobs or places where economic benefits may be obtained.

A secondary form of racial prejudgment occurs whenever members of a racial majority reject or ostracize members of *their own group* who agree to trade with a castigated racial group. This *secondary* form of racial prejudgment is a particularly potent form of economic power because it reinforces and makes certain that no one will depart from the original racially biased economic decision. This may be illustrated by a specific example. Consider the owner of a diner who has to choose between hiring a white short-order cook of average talents or a much more competent black cook. In a racially harmonious world, the rational choice would obviously be to hire the black person, who would thus increase the owner's profits by attracting more customers because of faster service and tastier meals. The effect of primary discrimination is to make the owner willing to forego the economic advantage of having a better cook in order to avoid contact with a black employee. Yet forces of economic rationality still remain in effect and may cause the black person to be hired for the job, since the employer who is willing to disregard his personal prejudices may still reap the economic benefits of employing the highly skilled black cook. But this is no longer the case once secondary discrimination comes into play. Thus, if the diner's patrons decide that they would rather eat somewhere else than dine on food that they see is being prepared by a black cook, the traditional sanctions of competitive markets are suspended. And the rewards for ignoring race in order to encourage the hiring of the best qualified person are wholly removed from the economic transaction. Here, employing the most efficient cook will unqualifiedly cost the owner money. Normal competitive incentives are turned upside down, since hiring the less competent white cook will actually *increase* the owner's profits. So we see that secondary racial boycotts have the power to transform racial prejudice from a possibly costly and inefficient luxury into a sound and rational business practice. Secondary racial decisions furnish the added benefit of allowing employers to practice racism with a good conscience. The employer may now look the disappointed job applicant in the eye and say, "Believe me, I've got nothing against Negroes. If I had my way, I'd hire you in a minute. But my customers would put me out of business in a month, and that wouldn't do either of us any good."

The dimensions of racial prejudgments as a form of economic power thus begin to emerge. In its several forms, race discrimination takes on the characteristics of an economic boycott or blacklist. To be sure, the trade and employment embargo erected against outcast groups has never been total.

In a market economy, where getting the wherewithal to eat and survive depended entirely on being chosen by someone, a total boycott of racial minorities from all employment would have been equivalent to a policy of racial genocide. To avoid this unacceptable consequence, the rules against freely choosing from the offering of goods, labor, or even the management or entrepreneurial competence of outcast groups have never been absolute or inviolable. In the main, people who belonged to stigmatized groups competed among themselves for special, and often segregated, work. They plied their trade in the ghettos or darky towns of urban or rural America. These economic arrangements were always acceptable to whites as long as Negro people obeyed the racial taboos and did not seek out contacts with the majority in ways that made the latter uncomfortable.

The racial division of labor served a number of functions. First, it isolated the minority in physical space and so protected whites from fears of contamination and loss of status. At the same time, the daily sight of racial divisions of tasks was a constant and valued reminder to whites of their superior rank. Another function of task reservation by race was to fortify the ideology of group degradation while still permitting members of the majority to give lip service to the ideal of free and open competition: "Who says blacks are not allowed to compete? We see them competing every day for jobs as janitors, laundresses, stoop laborers, and equal opportunity counselors." And, according to the race-trait expectation, blacks were seen as uniquely qualified for competition in these particular jobs.

While Marxist rhetoric rarely speaks the truth about American institutions, it has accurately identified possibly the most important function of the racial selection system. The etiquette of race guaranteed white families and employers a source of labor needed for the disagreeable tasks that whites did not wish to perform. Black slavery and economic Jim Crow— backed by wretched and segregated public education for Negro children —did, moreover, provide the white majority with a low-cost supply of menial workers. In this manner, power embodied in the race prejudgment served economic needs as well as the demands of feelings of racial contamination.

Power Defended: Using Ideology to Validate the Racial Prejudgment

In embracing the racial mode of selection, the robust, hard-boiled, and free-swinging profit maximizer of American capitalism had clearly gotten himself bound up in a bundle of contradictory racial conventions and taboos. These rules ran contrary to the capitalist manifesto that merit, and merit alone, should govern decisions in the marketplace. For even if blacks as a group had lower job skills and educational attainments, there were necessarily many blacks who were better qualified than many whites who were in fact chosen for particular positions or awards. Further, the racial prejudgment created a fundamental conflict with society's values since Americans as a rule, and especially those Americans who came from puritan stock, always had a passion for fairness.

In order to stay on the right side of the angels and at the same time maintain the apparent legitimacy of a racially biased economic order, it was necessary for the majority to construct an ideology to justify their racial prejudgments. The majority had to discover and circulate reasons of principle for adopting the racial codes that ranked whites higher in the hierarchy of esteem. This was no easy matter in a nation that took pride in declaring itself a democratic melting pot.

The answer lay in equating the racial prejudgment with established concepts of "just deserts." Inequalities had always existed as a necessary and proper result of a free-market economy. No one had ever objected to inequalities as long as they were in some sense deserved. All that was needed to legitimize racial codes, therefore, was an explanation of them as a rational outgrowth of the collective inferiority of the outcast group. If this inferiority could be established, the system was just and there would be no occasion for the white majority to feel guilty or ashamed. As a result, the simple and unexplained racial prejudgment became converted into the racial-*trait* prejudgment.

The racial-trait prejudgment was codified in the drearily familiar profile of blacks as carefree, happy-go-lucky people who were less competent than whites and had a marked tendency to be dull-witted, amiable, childlike, and shiftless. This theory of collective racial inferiority was then applied in almost all major areas of commercial and professional life. The competence of blacks in such minor and disreputable arts as gambling and pimping was conceded, as were their talents for athletic and theatrical performance and their talents as pentecostal ministers, faith healers, and operators of minstrel shows. But as to their competence for more serious endeavors, the slanders were sharp and explicit. In every executive suite, the same self-serving theme prevailed: "Blacks are extravagant and lazy. How can they be entrusted to own a factory, run a mill, or manage a bank?" In this manner, the collective decision to exclude all blacks, without regard to individual talent or diligence, from participation in the economic and political affairs of the nation was justified as fair, rational, and deserved.

It has always been true in the United States that a great many blacks—until recent years perhaps the majority—were uneducated and unskilled. But the theory that fundamental social and environmental social handicaps necessarily prevented any members of the group from being educated or well-trained was clearly unsound. The distinguished accomplishments of many blacks were so evident that even the most determined bigot often found it difficult to maintain the racial prejudgment. To deal with this inconsistency, a secondary doctrine of racial disrepute was devel-

THE CIRCULAR DEFENSE OF THE RACE-TRAIT PREJUDGMENT

Person 1: The trouble with blacks is that they are lazy.

Person 2: But government figures show blacks get just about as much of their income from work as whites, and much more often than whites have both husbands and wives working.

Person 1: Yes, they are working, because the government forces me to hire unqualified blacks in preference to qualified whites.

Person 2: But government statistics show that businessmen often ignore government antidiscrimination laws and affirmative-action program requirements.

Person 1: You are right. That's because blacks are shiftless and lazy and white people won't obey a law that isn't fair.

Person 2: But blacks were making gains and winning better jobs and incomes before 1969 when affirmative action really began.

Person 1: Yes, that's because before 1969 all those eggheads and do-gooders in the big corporations insisted on hiring all those unqualified Negroes.

oped. Thus, many whites came to believe that whenever a black person was successful the achievement was due to error or dishonesty.

In New York City not too long ago, disappointed white job seekers openly argued that black apprentices who scored high on an aptitude test should nevertheless be denied membership in the union local because they had probably cheated on the test or had received help from white friends. In other instances, other arguments were trotted out to explain away the accomplishments of blacks. Highly successful black businessmen were rudely assumed to be either half-breeds, fronts for a white man, the undeserving beneficiaries of white patronage, or simply not as successful as they appeared to be. The mental gymnastics required to deny the undeniable were often ludicrously reminiscent of Adolf Hitler's efforts to deal with a similar dilemma when he had to confront Einstein's achievements as a scientist. Hitler first argued that the theory of relativity was a hoax, then that it was not Einstein who had conceived it, and finally, that Einstein was not a Jew at all.[1]

As an ideology that whites could unconditionally embrace, the charge that blacks, as a group, were flawed still presented logical threats to the position of whites. If blacks were, in fact, less competent, less assertive, and less hard-working than whites, there had to be some reason. Was it possible that these defects had something to do with the way blacks had been treated by whites? If so, then the traditional thesis that blacks in some sense "deserved" their inferior station was out the window, for in that case whites would be held responsible for the supposed handicaps of blacks. But if one could show—preferably in a testing laboratory, in a high court of law, or perhaps, by resort to biblical authority—that black people had unequal native endowments, then one could continue treating them as unequal with a clear conscience. The result was "scientific" racism—the theory of the innate biological inferiority of blacks. The point was simple: Blacks were a subspecies of *Homo sapiens* and, as such, lacked a full complement of the normal human traits of intelligence, sensitivity, and competence. If whites could establish this thesis, all the ducks would fall into place. The racial atrocities of the past would seem less than outrageous. If natural superiority was a fact of life, affirmative action would be considered as merely a generous gift to black people, with no moral or legal base whatsoever. Laws prohibiting race discrimination were seen not as a means of protecting the merit system, but rather as a sop to an unfortunate group that lacked the stuff to compete.

The early promoters of "scientific" racism offered a wide repertoire of unproven assertions. In all events, it was concluded that blacks were congenitally uneducable in either the ordinary or the more sophisticated activities of commerce. Negroes, it was asserted, had an inborn inferior work ethic. People of African descent had a biologically inbred incapacity for managing capital and a genetically transmitted tendency toward poverty and unemployment. They also suffered from an inherited proclivity for prodigality. In the rush to maintain the ideology of race, it was widely published that the black minority was further burdened by an inborn and pathological tendency to lie, steal, loaf, gamble, and drink on the job. Thus, a racially stratified economic system which might seem unjust to a sentimentalist or a liberal turned out not to be unfair at all, for one could hardly expect the employer, the voter, the banker, or the college admissions officer to argue with Mother Nature.

In summary, we see that the mode of judging people which we call "race discrimination" is simply one of many of the important forms of coercive economic power that block or erase the ability of the normal competitive forces of free-market capitalism to provide for open access and equal opportunity. Even generous and compassionate people in the highest ranks of society, particularly those who work tirelessly "for the uplift of blacks," have observed the standard racial prejudgments and in so doing have removed any possibility of restoring capitalism's vaunted system of built-in penalties for those who valued the accident of race over the bargaining force of individual competence. Moreover, even though some participants in the market contest were prepared to adopt a racially neutral mode of selection, their benign presence in the market could not restore the competitive equilibrium as long as they were socially or economically bound over to third parties who were economically powerful and clung determinedly to powerfully held racial feelings. All of these racial sentiments and taboos which controlled virtually every economic selection process were then fortified by strict dogma that universally proclaimed the natural superiority of white people.

Thus it came about that capitalism's natural drift toward recognizing and rewarding economic competence and diligence was, in one more instance, converted into a system of partially closed or coercive markets. Capitalism's fierce ethic which insisted on its players seeking out and paying well for the services of the most qualified persons yielded to rigid tribal traditions of predetermined place and controlled opportunity. Here, in the fixed conventions of race, feudalism found its successor in racism. And in the process, many of the justly revered principles of Adam Smith were sabotaged and finally smashed.

Mob Justice: Majority Power Codifies the Race-Trait Belief System

"The property which every man has in his own labor, as it is the original foundation of all other property, so it is the most sacred and inviolable . . . to hinder him from employing this strength and dexterity in what manner he thinks proper without injury to his neighbour is a plain violation of this most sacred property."

—Adam Smith
The Wealth of Nations *(1776)*

THE IMPLACABLE DRIVES of the race-trait prejudgment demanded of its believers that they do certain things: shun Negroes; segregate them in order to avoid contact and contamination; scapegoat them as clowns and losers; hold them in servile and menial status. These were the universal imperatives of both the northern and southern traditions of black subordination.

Power was generated in the first place through simple and universally obeyed rules of private etiquette or custom. These codes of behavior control required that all Negroes obey—and act out their plans and movements in life in accordance with—a class prejudgment of inferior competence and prescribed subordination. We have seen that these fiats of racial inferiority essentially took the form of quarantine and boycotts directed with varying degrees of intensity against all Negro people. But much greater forces were also brought to bear. First, there was a consistent use of the power of terrorism and intimidation to strictly regiment the activities of Negroes and to define the acceptable limits of their economic, social, and political behavior. Second, there was a long history of enactments of formal laws by which the sovereign powers of federal, state, and local governments were employed to physically segregate Negro people and to enforce the limited zones of activity and entry that whites had assigned to them.

Using these powers, whites, acting as a unified political body, legislated *inferior* opportunities and status for blacks as surely as today the government sometimes legislates *superior* opportunities and status for them. In recent years there have been widespread efforts to deny that whites have used public or private power to control Negroes or to hold them in place. Let us now review, in very precise terms, how the demands of the race imperative were incorporated into the public as well as the private laws of American society.

The Official Laws of Race

Racial codes have long been part of the official laws of many states. Commonly, these laws punished the simple condition of membership in the black race. In 1807, for example, Ohio passed its first black code restricting the right of black citizens to move about freely. In 1808, after a race war in Cincinnati, an ordinance was enacted requiring any black who moved to the city to post a bond of $500 within thirty days. In 1859, Arkansas passed a statute requiring blacks to choose between enslavement and exile. Contrary to general beliefs, the codes that regulated the mobility or economic position of blacks were never restricted to southern states. In 1660, the Boston Town Meeting passed a law forbidding the employment of free black artisans. In 1712 the Connecticut Assembly provided that no free black could buy land.

Neither the Civil War nor the enactment of the Thirteenth Amendment to the Constitution put an end to the official racial codes. The infamous Jim Crow laws of the South, enacted during the Reconstruction period, banned interracial marriages and multiracial religious worship, as well as the mixed seating of blacks and whites in street cars, saloons, buses, theaters, and hotels. The force of the state was employed also to separate the races in restaurants, waiting rooms, baseball parks, taxicabs, and places of employment. Under a carefully crafted system of state control, public laws were issued that decided how, when, and where the vast majority of black people would live, work, worship, eat, and raise their children. The total powers of the state were used to humiliate and subjugate the Negro person.

In due course, many of the official racial laws came under constitutional attack. In 1821, a black man successfully challenged the ordinance of the District of Columbia and other cities requiring free Negroes to appear before the mayor with their freedom papers and to post a "peace bond" of $20 signed by a respected white man who guaranteed their good behavior. In time, the Supreme Court overturned state laws prohibiting interracial marriage and local laws segregating public parks, buildings, and schools. The Court ordered the U.S. Department of Housing and Urban Development to rescind its regulations granting federal mortgage insurance only in racially segregated communities. Little by little, with stubborn resistance all along the way, the official codes of race were repealed, the final step, perhaps, being taken on June 7, 1972, when the state of Louisiana expunged its laws prohibiting mixed dancing, marrying, and other forms of intimate association between blacks and whites.

But great powers usually find ways to rule small powers, and the potent demands of the race-trait imperative would not be denied by the simple refusal or inability of the government to enforce the ideology of race. The majority simply turned to an underground system of *private law* to enforce the same racial codes that formerly had been enforced by the official laws of the state. By private means, the codes of race were remodeled but not dismantled.

People Acting Like Governments: The Advent of Private Citizens' Laws

People commonly operate under the incorrect assumption that a coercive act that controls or regulates human liberty does not qualify as a law unless it is issued under the auspices of the established political machinery of the state. For example, in a republic governed by a constitution one would normally expect that the way to guard the safety of one's child would be to invoke parliamentary laws that keep child molesters in jail. One might expect, too, that the way to protect one's property would involve calling the police or going to court and invoking a formal legal writ of trespass. Yet it is perfectly possible, instead, to protect people from harming others by private agreements backed in turn by privately agreed-upon sanctions. For example, people in a given community may come to a private understanding that certain potentially dangerous groups or threatening classes of people will not be allowed to enter certain parks, schools, and playgrounds. In an entirely unofficial but still effective and forceful way, people who are in control of theaters, restaurants, hospitals, and hotels may effectively "protect" their clientele by coming to a written or unwritten understanding that certain disreputable groups of people will not be permitted to enter these premises. By collective agreement, enforced by social ostracism and occasionally by unofficial threats of violence, an entirely private set of rules of etiquette may be enacted which provide that specified schools, professions, and careers will be reserved for certain classes or categories of citizens. As long as the private agreement exists and applies across the board, and as long as people obey the agreement and punish or shame those who disobey it, most of the requirements for a law exist. We may call these unofficial agreements "private citizens' laws." Indeed, before the coming of official law formally enacted by the state, it is probable that society was largely governed by these sorts of cooperative exchanges of private promises and conventions made for mutual protection, advancement, or advantage.

There is almost no public awareness of the extent to which the power of the official lawmaking process has been displaced or supplemented by citizens' laws. For example, from time to time, state governments have decided to "protect" American Indians from their presumed tendency to profligacy by enacting official laws that stipulate that no bank may lend money to this particular class of citizens. But, on even more occasions, private banks in the United States have accomplished precisely the same result, in a wholly extraparliamentary way, by using consensus power mentioned earlier—in this case by coming to a mutual understanding with other banks that all American Indians were not appropriate credit risks. The traditional credit practice of "redlining" Negro neighborhoods may be viewed in the same way. Without resorting to the official sanctions of legislatures, financial institutions in effect outlawed mortgage credit in black communities. Private banking institutions have been able to legislate this result by the simple process of acting in a common manner and for a common purpose. In this regard, public laws abolishing redlining practices should be viewed simply as the process of a public law overriding a prior private citizens' law.

To draw up and promulgate private laws it is not necessary to hold a formal convention and to write a formal contract or charter. Every society contains a body of customs, conventions, and taboos which people obey as if it were a system of law. Thus, it was a custom, not a law, that commanded the Spartans to throw retarded children over the side of a cliff. It was by custom that the American Indian amputated the nose of an unfaithful wife. In some cultures, unwritten edicts rather than published laws required that female babies be drowned. Hindus in India observed an entirely unwritten law that made one out of seven people untouchable and employable only in such lowly occupations as tanning hides and handling human and animal wastes. Whites in the United States had a similar, but less harsh, set of customs and taboos governing the behavior and opportunities of Negroes.

These private laws, made outside officially constituted legislatures, have always regulated a large part of our nation's social and economic life. The private labor union, particularly, has been a potent instrument of unofficial legislation. In many communities, trade unions have issued and enforced rules providing that union members only are permitted to run subways, deliver mail, wire buildings, or build automobiles. Nationwide labor agreements in many industries override local ordinances as to working hours and health and safety conditions affecting millions of families. Under collective bargaining agreements, teachers' unions in major cities, rather than officially elected bodies, make the laws that set school hours and determine the number of children permitted in a classroom. Uniformed fire officers' associations, rather than elected officials, in effect pass local laws requiring that three pumpers and two ladder trucks will respond to every box alarm. In some cities police "benevolent" associations lay down the law as to the work shifts that govern the hours when it is safe for members of the public to go out in the streets. Associations of landlords have agreed on standardized lease regulations which effectively enact parietal rules about television sets, pets, and—for much of American history—the race of the tenants in apartment buildings.

The private codes of commerce blend imperceptibly into the private codes of race. Without exchanging word or gesture, real estate agents, usually with the full concurrence of homeowners, have passed a host of private laws stipulating that Jews cannot live in communities such as Bronxville, New York, or Lake Forest, Illinois. Entirely outside of legislatures, private laws have been enacted by which insurance companies write fire insurance policies only on properties having specified and approved ZIP codes. The lenders who collectively deny credit, the real estate agents who refuse to show property, and the local homeowners who do not wish to be shunned at church suppers are the originators of many of our land use laws. No need for old-fashioned Jim Crow. It is private citizens, and not official town meetings, who pass the most effective laws prohibiting the introduction of racially integrated low-income housing into the so-called stable white neighborhoods.

Contrary to popular myth, the great private lawgivers in our society were not necessarily the large corporations or financial institutions. The powerful lawmakers were not even the Presidents, county sheriffs, assemblymen elected by people, and other "legal seated" folks. The statute writers of whom I speak did not work out of the White House, Congress or the courts. Sometimes, indeed, they were people of exalted station or members of ruling classes. But most often they were ordinary citizens, usually non-elected and nonappointed, who nevertheless legislated in an almost sovereign manner through the simple process of collectively acting out their common desires, fears, and racial expectations. In the mid-1960s, Birmingham's notorious Public Safety Commissioner Bull Connor was not referring simply to the police or the state legislatures when he declared, "Down here, we make our own law."

The important feature of a citizen's law is that, unlike official enactments by the state, it is never subjected to constitutional review. Citizens' laws may indeed be reversed by a countervailing legislative enactment, but there is no right of constitutional redress in the courts. The reason for this is that private citizens' laws are by definition made by the people rather than by an official governmental body whose formal enactments are considered "state action" and therefore limited by the Constitution. If, for example, virtually all citizens were to act upon a fixed custom or rule of etiquette to the effect that blue-eyed people only were to hold certain scheduled jobs, live in certain neighborhoods, or go to certain schools, these codes of behavior would not be treated as official enactments of law. Accordingly, the state could not be successfully charged with lawbreaking if it simply permitted its citizens to use their private powers to make and obey such a rule of social etiquette. On the other hand, if the state acting through executive order or through a parliamentary body were to officially enact the same set of rules, the state would be guilty of constitutional lawbreaking. Beyond any doubt, the government would then be violating established constitutional rules that guarantee citizens equal protection of the law. In the United States, this insulation of citizens' laws from constitutional oversight and protection has provided the white majority with very broad and unrestricted powers to make private laws limiting the abilities of racial minorities to enter a wide range of places, institutions, and positions. Thus, unless the legislatures choose to forbid private lawmaking, the Constitution shelters from judicial oversight not only individual bigotry but a wide range of private legislation that converts private bigotry into obligatory behavior.

Vigilante Power: When Punishment Becomes the Business of Bullies and the State Does Nothing

Private citizens' laws did not simply regulate behavior where no prior formal law existed. A prime function of the private codes of race was to reverse or repeal official parliamentary laws. And this was often true of formal and official laws which demanded that the state use its powers and confer its benefits without racial distinction. The use of private terror and the threats of violence—together with collective agreements not to enforce public laws—were the standard instruments for maintaining a constitutional subterfuge by which equal treatment was publicly proclaimed while unequal treatment was privately legislated. In this connection, the most barbarous of all uses of citizens' laws was the effective repeal as to Negroes of the common law prohibiting the murder of another person. On countless occasions in the twentieth century, "protective associations" of lynching parties privately executed black men for "boastful remarks," "insulting a white man," or for seducing, or merely approaching, a white woman. In the summer of 1955, the battered corpse of 14-year-old Emmett Till, a black youth from Chicago, was pulled out of the Tallahatchie River in Sumner, Mississippi. His crime—violating the private code of the South by whistling at a white woman. At about the same time, government-appointed civil rights commissioners heard testimony that by common consent coroners in Lowndes County, Alabama, ruled as "suicide" the death of a number of blacks who had been tied in chains and found in a branch of the river. These unpunished private acts of collective violence not only cemented the codes of racial segregation and control but, in effect, repealed the public law guaranteeing the right of impartial trial to those accused of a crime.

The use of the threat of violence as a means of private governance and regulation of the black race continued to be an effective weapon of racial control well into the second half of the twentieth century. Fair-minded citizens are usually so incensed at private acts of violence against blacks that they fail to observe the overriding lawgiving process by which terrorism and intimidation tolerated by the state still cut wide swaths through the law and act as repealers of our most sacred constitutional rights.

The private organizations and institutions that reversed state laws requiring equal treatment of the races are well known. Standing as ultimate enforcers of the private racial codes that repealed the official laws of crime were the Ku Klux Klan, the so-called white citizens' councils, and other ad hoc vigilante terrorists. At the peak of its power in 1925, the Klan had 3 to 6 million members, a quarter of the national male Protestant population. In the 1920s, the head of the Klan claimed without excessive exaggeration, "I am the law in Indiana." Many years later the powers of the Klan had declined, yet, in some communities, it continued to influence the enforcement of public laws. During the early 1970s, a white spy for the National Association for the Advancement of Colored People who had infiltrated the

Ku Klux Klan testified that a deputy sheriff in Oklahoma informed him that he as a Klan member could go out and kill "any nigger you see, and the law'll be behind you." It is not known on how many occasions the state stood by as an observer but failed to prevent or punish the murder of Negroes. Ironically, the United States Government officially counts water fowl migrating from Canada into the United States but has never undertaken an official census of the lynchings of Negroes. The NAACP has estimated that between the Emancipation Proclamation and World War II, 2,771 black men were executed by public lynching.

The official laws of the state prohibited the use of force to restrict economic opportunities, yet private lynchings and other forms of violence against blacks provided otherwise. For many generations, private vigilante groups in the South burned down black business establishments that trespassed over the line of permissible economic activity. Black farmers who offered their produce for direct retail sale instead of through established white intermediaries were the victims of attacks by arsonists. The most famous incident of public lynching to protect white economic positions occurred in East St. Louis in 1917.[1] Thirty or more blacks were clubbed and stabbed in a dispute over the hiring of Negroes in plants holding war contracts. In the southern states the essential conditions of labor peonage were reestablished. Terror and violence, backed by economic sanctions and threats often condoned by the state, assigned the black man to a fixed employer, a fixed place of labor, a fixed wage, and usually denied him the ability to withhold his work. Violence or threat of violence was a standard measure to deal with Negroes seeking any employment, capital, or entrepreneurship that was deemed "out of place."

The citizens' laws of Jim Crow, which assigned fixed places to members of the black race, were not limited to the southern states. Whites in the North established a comprehensive set of racial codes and place assignments. Boasting an open society, free of loathesome southern racial prejudices, northerners condescendingly regarded southern whites as bigots because formal laws of race were enacted and Jim Crow signs were publicly displayed. Yet, in many of the northern states, racial terrorism was an integral part of the apparatus for controlling Negroes without resorting either to formal public law or to visible signs of boycott or exclusion. Hastily organized neighborhood vigilante groups were commonly employed as the guardians of racial place assignments. In 1973 a black family did not remain long in a white neighborhood in Detroit after rocks were thrown through its windows, its German Shepherd puppy was stabbed to death, and garbage was dumped in the family kitchen. For centuries most of

Staten Island, a borough of New York City, had been entirely, but unofficially, off-bounds for blacks. Then, in 1972, a white family rented a house in Staten Island to a Negro family. The neighbors responded by shooting bullets through the windows. When the Negro family insisted on moving in, the building was burned to the ground. Clearly visible to any black family that might consider violating the northern etiquette of racial place were posters which screamed: "No niggers," "Nigger be warned," "Return our American rights."[2] Unlike most radical political terrorists who seek to advance an alien ideology, the northern terrorists who enforced the ordinary codes of race never stood far from the political mainstream. They spoke for the racial objectives, if not the political methods, of the majority. Capitalists, labor unions, educational institutions, churches, and politicians of all parties sincerely believed in and published the ideology of an inferior black race. But their manifestos were frequently carried out by thugs and bullies who were never curbed by the state.

Today, an opinion very much in vogue among whites and some blacks is that the behavior codes currently imposed on blacks in the United States are ones of class and not of race. To hold this view requires one to ignore the fact that poor whites have always systematically attacked poor blacks while middle-class whites continue to threaten, and feel threatened by, middle- and upper-class blacks. The violence that is frequently directed at middle-class blacks is illustrated by the following 1979 news item:

> "Four hours after the members of a black I.B.M. executive's family moved into their split-level house in a predominantly white community here, an explosion and fire drove them screaming into the streets...."[3]

In general, the underlying purpose of such attacks has been to enforce a private code of race relations—to keep blacks, regardless of their economic level or class, out of white neighborhoods, schools, and, frequently, jobs. There are indeed class codes just as there are racial codes. To admit the existence of one is not to deny the existence of the other. The racial codes, however, were the ones that society often enforced (or permitted to be enforced) through acts of terror, intimidation and violence.

North Follows South: The Private Racial Codes of Education and Neighborhood Protection

The scene of some of the most intense and significant private legislation in American history has been the emotionally charged area of public education of young people. In most southern states, official race segregation in public education prevailed. White parents' fears of racial contamination produced state-designated "separate but equal" school systems in which children continued to be segregated by race long after the Supreme Court found public school segregation unconstitutional. In northern states, white people congratulated themselves on the fact that segregated education had never been the official law of the land. Segregation was nevertheless the operating principle of a majority of public school systems. Commonly observed principles of racial etiquette required that blacks and whites live in separate neighborhoods. As a result of this living arrangement, it necessarily followed that children who went to neighborhood schools would go to school only with children of their own race. The racial segregation of public education was buttressed further by a common understanding among school officials that new school buildings would be constructed in black *or* white areas but not in the border areas where the races might be drawn together from across both sides of the racial dividing lines. Society's unofficial prohibition against building new boundary schools accounts for the fact that a number of almost exclusively white public schools still could be found in Detroit in 1970, even though school enrollment in the city as a whole was 64 percent black.[4]

In passing constitutional judgments as to whether the pupil imbalances created by race codes in education should be reversed by cross-district busing of pupils, the United States Supreme Court has consistently insisted on attaching different culpabilities and consequences to "official" compared with "unofficial" racial segregation. But an intelligent person had to struggle mightily to find any pragmatic differences between the two arrangements. Measured either in statistical terms of racial outcomes or by the degree of restriction on educational choice, there was little distinction to be made. Private agreements or understandings as to educational place assignments, as long as they were universally observed and respected, produced precisely the same results as official segregation explicitly enunciated in state law or by official policies.

The common etiquette of racial selection that separated the races, and at the same time segregated education, was buttressed once more by a host of private lawgivers operating outside elected legislatures. Acting under so-called codes of ethics, landlords, mortgage bankers, and real estate agents made industry agreements that prevented racial mixing of neighborhoods, apartment houses, and mobile home parks. The code of ethics of the National Association of Real Estate Boards, which was binding on all members, stated that it was unethical for realtors to show or sell property in a white neighborhood to a black person since doing so might change the racial composition of the neighborhood. For many generations in the North, until the Supreme Court outlawed the practice, racial segregation became contract law in many communities by virtue of restrictive convenants in deeds. In the post-World War II period, hundreds of thousands of newly constructed homes, such as those in Levittown, Pennsylvania, were restricted by contract to Caucasian use. Although the original builder of these homes later denounced racial discrimination in housing, the original sales agreement for his houses contained a clause stating, "No dwelling shall be used or occupied by members of other than the Caucasian race, but the employment and maintenance of other than Caucasian domestic servants shall be permitted." This provision was standard if not obligatory in the real estate industry at the time.[5] The collective powers of private members of the real estate industry, acting in unison and for a common racial purpose, created rules having all the force of public law.

Even within nominally integrated schools, private codes of racial segregation found ample scope to pursue their agenda. Here the private law-making force was the built-in racial beliefs of teachers, many of whom expected black children to demonstrate inferior academic abilities. This led to a tracking system that was little more than a faintly camouflaged brand of racial segregation. In California in the early 1970s, for example, 27 percent of the children classified as "educable mentally retarded" were black even though blacks constituted only 9 percent of the student population. When a judge ordered retesting of some of the children, each of the minority children whose parents had claimed racial discrimination scored well above the 75 IQ cutoff point.[6] There was little question that the original scores had been influenced by the racial expectations of the teachers administering the tests. Segregation, in short, takes many subtle forms and, like a stubborn weed, reasserts its presence despite all efforts to eradicate it. Ethnically segregated tracking within individual schools is merely a smaller-scale version of a larger system of racially gerrymandered school districts, which are in turn merely a single facet of a larger racial selection process that insists upon racially restricted residential options, allocated job opportunities, and controlled entrepreneurial endeavors.

"Eat My Bread; Sing My Song":
The Purchase of Compliance With the Codes of Race

We have seen that the demands of the racial selection system caused whites to forego potential economic gains by shunning employment and commerce with qualified blacks even when Negroes offered talents superior to those of competing whites. Whites also made affirmative payments for the luxuries of racial segregation. Without particular regard for either merit or need, jobs were provided, credit granted, welfare allotments okayed, and housing set aside for Negroes who knew and kept their economic place. The result was the erection of an elaborate system of public grants and private stipends used to purchase compliance with the codes of racial etiquette. Here, too, the private power of the purse was sometimes employed in cases where the coercive powers of the state were not constitutionally permitted to be used to enforce Negro behavior. The use of money power to control blacks was sometimes a telling statement of public beliefs in the superior value of the lives of white people. In an infamous chapter of American history, the U.S. Public Health Service, in the 1930s, conducted a syphilis experiment at Tuskegee, Alabama. Under this project, 399 black men "voluntarily" participating in the experiment on the continuing effects of syphilis were provided with free medical care—except that their cases of syphilis went untreated—free rides in limousines with government decals on the doors, free hot meals on examination day, modest cash payments of $35, and the promise of inexpensive burials at government expense. No whites were recruited for—or paid to take part in—the important medical experiment.

The fact is that today, as in the past, the power of the purse may be used wholly to reverse great constitutional guarantees when a recipient of monies is in sufficient need or in a state of ignorance. It was widely reported in the 1960s, for example, that petty bureaucrats in Lowndes County, Alabama, delayed the enforcement of the Supreme Court's antisegregation decision in public education by providing free food, medical care, and shoes for poor black children, as long as they attended racially segregated schools. Similarly, on many occasions, southern employers have let black workers know that continuation of their employment, or the chances of promotion to better jobs, depended on their not exercising the right to vote. Blacks who joined public protest movements could frequently count on having their farm loans called in at the bank. Negroes who agitated for integrated schools were not likely to find a ready market among whites for their farm produce. Under such circumstances, constitutional guarantees of the right to equal education, the right to vote, and the right of peaceable assembly had little, if any, value. The potential for major infringements of civil rights was considerable whenever a target group had to work for, borrow money from, sell agricultural products to, or rent houses from another clan that preferred to be bound by restrictive racial codes rather than by a principle of equal opportunity.

Public payments continue to be used to control blacks, although rarely to purchase acquiescence in the repeal of their constitutional rights. In recent years, antipoverty allotments, "black capitalism" grants, revenue-sharing funds, and government contract awards have been employed to purchase the political allegiance of black leaders. Reverend Judge Stringer, mayor of Hobson City, Alabama, expressed no surprise that in 1974 former Governor George C. Wallace, America's most outspoken segregationist, received 20 to 25 percent of the black vote in Alabama. "Not long before the election, George saw to it that we got $153,000 in road funds," Stringer explained. In Chicago in the 1950s, black Congressman Ralph H. Metcalfe spent many years comfortably ensconced in Mayor Richard Daley's patronage system. One can only speculate whether it was a genuine regard for Daley's politics or simply a realistic respect for the mayor's control over public-service jobs that persuaded Metcalfe at the 1968 Democratic National Convention to argue from the podium against seating a Georgia delegation led by the black legislator Julian Bond. In very recent years, considerable economic and political rewards, including invitations to the White House, have been bestowed on "qualified" blacks who have been willing to speak out against busing, affirmative action, food stamps, and the denial of tax subsidies to segregated schools.

Money talks and large aggregations of money have the power to command. Acting in harmony with the collective racial views of the individuals who controlled them, large financial institutions have been a vital cog in enforcing the etiquette of racial behavior. In 1971, the U.S. Senate Judiciary Committee determined that a group of Boston savings banks (the so-called Boston Banks Urban Renewal Group) had appointed itself guardian of racially homogeneous neighborhoods. By denying federally insured mortgages to blacks wishing to purchase homes in white neighborhoods while letting mortgage money flow freely to blacks buying homes in all-black Roxbury and certain areas of nearby Dorchester, the banks were able to legislate and enforce racial zoning policy more effectively than the state could have done had it been so minded. A similar consortium of New York City banks and insurance companies used their mortgage powers to enforce society's rule that specified districts in Queens to be reserved either for blacks or for whites.[7]

If institutional money became such a potent enforcer of the racial codes, what, we ask, has become of the Negro financial institutions. Why didn't they tend to moderate or reverse the racial codes? The answer is that through all of our nation's history, black-owned financial institutions have controlled only a minuscule portion of the nation's credit. Increasingly dependent on the charitable inclinations of whites, black-controlled banks have never been disposed to challenge the racial codes desired by their benefactors. Even if they possessed the will to skirt the codes of race, the black-owned banks lacked the economic strength to make any important exceptions to established private injunctions against the financing of blacks moving into white communities or extending credit to white firms that might employ blacks in positions outside the purview of the etiquette of race. Black banks were regulated by state and federal officials who were white; black banks depended on white banks for loan participation and emergency credit needs. On the whole, the Negro banker survived at the sufferance of whites and thus was unable and unwilling to buck the private laws of race.

To be sure, the force of money has always been influential in American society. We all know how it nominates political candidates, elects lawmakers, and enacts many, though by no means all, of our most familiar public laws. But money had a special potency in enforcing racial etiquette. A reason was that almost everybody who had wealth, property, or substantial disposable income not only shared the standard racial fears and expectations but also benefited from enforcing the rules which assigned Negroes to a rigid though unpublished schedule of permissible positions.

When Racial Etiquette Is Tantamount to Economic Licensing

Public concern with the injustice of physical segregation of the races often obscures the economic side of virtually every code of racial behavior. Thus, a private code preventing blacks from residing in the best neighborhoods is tantamount to an economic code restricting them from access to the people who have information and contacts leading to the most desirable jobs. Racial segregation in public schools or universities is equivalent to economic legislation to the effect that young blacks are not entitled to all the wide-ranging opportunities for contacts and good luck which are part of the great blessings afforded by capitalism's insistence on free and open markets. Equally, a private code excluding blacks from business clubs and social gatherings is tantamount to private legislation denying blacks access to business credit, valuable contracts, and entrepreneurial ideas and opportunities. The political practice of both major political parties of retaining blacks in government as spokesmen for racial progress or as petty bureaucrats, rather than in positions of government power, also legislates unequal economic opportunities for blacks in that, unlike whites, it leaves them virtually bereft of any power to use public position to win economic advantages for themselves and their friends. Thus, many of the racial taboos that controlled personal mobility and social behavior must be considered equivalent to restrictive economic opportunity legislation. The economic chains would have been no more binding had whites used the explicit criterion of race as a condition for official licensing of jobs, credit, public contracts, and other economic awards.

How Jim Crow Reserved Jobs in the North

It is still commonly believed that in the North, the economic codes of Jim Crow applied only to professional baseball and to obtaining room assignments at the best hotels. The fact is that through the potent forces of private Jim Crow, it was publicly decided throughout the United States that blue- and white-collar jobs, business credit, government contracts, and opportunities for entrepreneurship were reserved to whites. Of all the private racial codes operating in the United States, the racial codes of job reservation were perhaps the most rigid and enduring. In virtually every area of economic endeavor there were cohesive and universal understandings, both written and unwritten, as to the proper and acceptable careers for a black person. Deeply etched in the brains of all who controlled capital, jobs, and credit were the rules of a nationwide blacklist and a companion "white list." Under these codes of private Jim Crow, blacks could be dining car waiters, housemaids, yard workers, low-level civil service workers, postal clerks, and slaughterhouse employees. By force of the same codes, blacks could not be plumbers, welders, railroad trainmen, sheetmetal workers, carpenters, elevator installers, or electricians. The prohibition against black electricians, in fact, is one that has endured for an extraordinarily long period of time. The 1960 U.S. Census reported only seventy-nine Negro electrical apprentices in the entire nation. In the early 1970s blacks were not even a measurable percentage of railway workers. Construction unions nationwide were 1.7 percent of iron workers, 0.2 percent of the plumbers and sheetmetal workers, and 0.4 percent of the elevator constructors.[8]

Even when the job reservation codes within particular trades broke down, the better jobs were still held for whites. Blacks, for example, were permitted to work as short-haul or city truck drivers while positions as long-haul drivers were reserved for whites. In many cities black workers were qualified to ride on the back of garbage trucks, but only white workers sat up in the cab. In steel factories the "hot jobs" in front of the blast furnaces were usually reserved for blacks. The system of racial etiquette in employment was so firmly in place in the U.S. economy that, in fact, no conscious

Before antidiscrimination laws forced bigotry to go underground, the racial codes were put in writing

The Racial Prerequisite for Membership in Trade Unions

Early Twentieth Century

BROTHERHOOD OF LOCOMOTIVE FIREMEN	"He shall be white born, of good moral character, sober and industrious, sound in body and limb, his eyesight shall be normal, not less than eighteen years of age and able to read and write the English language."
BROTHERHOOD OF RAILWAY CARMEN	"Any white person between the age of 16 and 65 years, who believes in the existence of a Supreme Being, who is free from hereditary or contracted diseases, of good moral character and habits. . . ."
CLERKS AND FREIGHT HANDLERS UNION	"All white persons, male or female, of good moral character."
MASTERS, MATES AND PILOTS UNION	"White person of good moral character, in sound health, and a firm believer in God, the Creator of the Universe."
WIRE WEAVERS UNION	"Christian, white, male of the full age of 21. . . . Foreigners applying for admission must declare citizenship intentions and pay an initiation fee of $1,000."

Source: Herbert Hill, Black Labor and the American Legal System: I. Race, Work, and the Law, Washington, D.C.: The Bureau of National Affairs Inc., 1977, pp.19-20.

act of racial prejudgment was necessary to make it work. There was virtually no bank, insurance company, factory, school, college, employment office, coal mine, or oil rig where white skin color was not an implicit requirement for admission, employment, or advancement.

Most of the racial codes that regulated the economy were enforced by unwritten custom and unpublished etiquette, but before public opprobrium attached to racial bigotry the codes were reduced to writing. Labor unions were particularly explicit, their bylaws often specifying membership in the white race as a prerequisite for admission to the union. Corporations, too, sometimes took the trouble to spell out their racial rules of employment entitlement. At the beginning of World War II, the president of North American Aviation stated company policy:

"While we are in complete sympathy with the Negro, it is against company policy to employ them as aircraft workers or mechanics . . . regardless of their training. . . . There will be some jobs as janitors for Negroes." [9]

Government power mirrored the private forces of job regulation. Until well after World War II, the Army and Navy were essentially segregated institutions, with the Army putting blacks in all-black companies and regiments, the Navy assigning them as messmen or to other menial duties. At the same time it was generally understood that the federal government at large would employ blacks only as janitors, elevator operators, and messengers. As late as 1960 there were almost no Negroes holding positions in even the middle ranks of the federal civil service. For nearly 200 years the White House staff and other executive branches were manned entirely by whites. The high-sounding posts which a few blacks now hold in the ghetto way stations at the White House and in the government bureaucracy did not exist.

In one of the remarkable ironies of the racial history of the United States, the Supreme Court was one of the most faithful observers of the racial codes of employment. Twenty-one years after the Court's decision to desegregate public schools, the twenty-one laborers employed at the Court—primarily maintenance and heavy cleaning men—were all black, while the nineteen skilled craftsmen—carpenters, painters, electricians, plumbers, and stonemasons—were all white. Without exception, the twenty-two charwomen were black, yet all but one of the secretaries to the Justices were white. All of the Justices' messengers were black. [10]

Congress, the mightiest of official lawgivers, was also a potent enforcer of the racial codes of job reservation. When Congress ultimately decided, in the Civil Rights Act of 1964, to bar race discrimination in the hiring practices of private businesses, professions, and educational institutions, it chose to exempt itself from the provisions of the Act. Ten years later, documents were produced showing that the offices of nineteen congressmen and one United States senator routinely discriminated against blacks. Typical job order requests to the Congressional Placement Office read: "White . . . no pants suit" (from the office of Rep. James J. Delaney, a New York Democrat), "prefer no minorities" (Rep. Tennyson Guyer, an Ohio Republican), "no southern accents . . . white only" (Rep. Edward Boland, a Massachusetts Democrat), "prefer VA resident . . . white only" (Republican Senator William Scott of Virginia). Republican Representative Albert Johnson of Pennsylvania demanded, "Republican only . . . no minorities . . . no Demos," but Congressman Johnson's biases weren't exclusively racial. He also specified, "no water signs (Scorpio, Pisces and Cancer)." A 1974 survey by the Congressional Placement Office showed that 80 percent of 150 job requisitions made by members of Congress stipulated racial requirements.[11]

The Racial Codes for Allocation of Capital and Credit

We have already shown how the power of money—granted or withheld —was employed by the state to reinforce private rules governing black employment, housing, and education. Add to this a comprehensive set of credit and investment codes which American business used to circumscribe or repress the process of black capital formation. Long-standing traditions of commercial banking, moreover, laid down a strict convention providing that black people, even when endowed with unusual entrepreneurial talent and drive, might borrow money to buy a Cadillac car or a television set but almost never to start up a new business enterprise. All of the fast-moving games of the capitalist—acted out through letters of credit, bond indentures, and broker loans—took place on fields of combat totally closed to admission by black people. The Horatio Alger bootstrap borrowing opportunity, by which class barriers were traditionally shattered, was definitively reserved for whites.

The standard exceptions to the ethnic codes of commerce fine tuned to rules of race. Credit and capital were made available to black entrepreneurs for intragroup endeavors whose tendencies were to maintain segregation and distance between the races. Thus, at a very early date, whites began to grant credit to segregated funeral homes, hotels for blacks only, life insurance enterprises catering to blacks, and banks doing business exclusively in black communities. Even in the most difficult economic times, credit continued to flow to blacks for purposes that served the ends of the race-trait expectation.

During the Nixon administration it became fashionable in government and in banking circles to fight race discrimination by trying to create a new class of black capitalists. This seemingly enlightened movement had two basic though unspoken thrusts. It was assumed first that blacks would be racially segregated capitalists, and second that they should function in activities most informed business people would generally consider marginal. Frequently, then, it was the castoff or racially segregated project that caught the fancy of white bankers who were bent on doing favors for black entrepreneurs. In Pittsburgh in the late 1960s, black groups, aided by a government-assisted credit, purchased a nail factory which had become obsolete because the seller of the factory had begun to manufacture prefabricated homes. In several cities, large metropolitan banks financed the purchase by blacks of nearly bankrupt inner-city hotels which had lost their trade to suburban motels. Traditionally, inner-city rib shops and fast-food operations were common vehicles of "black capitalism" stipends. Black-oriented publications and black advertising agencies promoting products to be sold to blacks were also favored objects of credit issued to black entrepreneurs. Only in extremely rare cases was credit offered to enable blacks to buy into enterprises in the mainstream of the American economy or to start up a new enterprise whose product, service or place of business was not oriented toward minority affairs. On the whole, much of the minority capitalism effort was directed toward financing enterprises that had most of the earmarks of something the cat had dragged home. The financial risk in bankrolling these enterprises mattered little to the credit institutions involved since, in most cases, the loans were guaranteed by the federal government. As in other instances, private power in the form of money used to regulate and limit black opportunities was subsidized by public funds.

Commercial control through the credit codes of race which allocated funds to segregated or racially stereotyped business activities were usually justified by the thesis that blacks do not have the stuff and starch to compete with whites in the mainstream economy. Often, too, credit was restricted to limited ghetto-based activities on the premise that a black-owned enterprise could not be successful if it tried to overcome the prejudices of white customers. In this manner, the economic handicaps arising from prior discrimination justified present discrimination, and secondary discrimination ascribed to unnamed third parties enforced a racial code for which the credit grantor could disclaim any responsibility.

The Racial Boycott:
Adam Smith's Clawback Disarmed

We recall from our earlier discussions in Chapter Four that the major force in the free market which was counted on to protect fair economic treatment of blacks and other minorities was the power of the market to punish. This power took the form of sanctions or harms that would presumably befall any competitor who made commercial selections according to race rather than individual qualifications. To this end, it was postulated that the racial bigot who rejected talented or qualified black employees or borrowers would see his own commercial enterprise lose out to a competitor who was more interested in employing talented people than in selecting ones who were members of a favored race. The personnel or subcontracting officer who recruited or purchased under a "whites only" policy would stand in jeopardy of losing his job since his firm would be placed at a competitive disadvantage by another firm that was less interested in irrelevant racial qualifications. A fundamental thesis of market capitalism was that there would always be a greedy competitor, relentlessly seeking to make a buck, who would choose the best qualified person for the job, for the loan or for the contract, and, in the process, inexorably drive the bigot out of business. This jeopardy of risk of economic harm facing the racial bigot was the famous "clawback" of competition which made the marketplace—rather than the courts or the legislators—the arbitrator of fair and racially neutral economic selections.

But the theory of market punishment held up only as long as there were, in fact, competitors who were disposed to attach greater commercial importance to abilities such as competence, ambition, and willingness to engage in hard work over racial considerations. The potential for clawback in the marketplace ceased once racial choices or individual prejudices became racial codes of behavior. Since race discrimination was a nearly universal practice, there never were any competitors—be they employers, lenders, or traders—who were willing to seek out economic advantage from a competitor's bigotry or lapse of judgment. In reality, then, the risk of clawback effect became totally inoperative the moment whites—through implicit understanding with other whites—could and did assure themselves that they would come to no competitive harm by treating blacks as a class of undifferentiated inferiors and incompetents.

In practice, then, the corrective power of the marketplace was suspended. The merchant who refused to hire a well-qualified black clerk was never punished by the marketplace since all competing merchants, bound as they were by the mercantile codes of race, were never inclined to take competitive advantage of the merchant's error. The banker who refused credit to the well-qualified black entrepreneur never lost a good loan to another banker since the latter also observed the same racial codes. The white investor, contractor, and manufacturer could always safely indulge a "whites only" trading preference since they, too, could safely count on no competitor taking advantage of their racial prejudice. Racial bigotry was in the saddle and prejudgment never became misjudgment because everybody was loyal to the same racial codes of commercial behavior. Of course, free-market theory insists otherwise, but there is no record, to my knowledge, of anybody in the United States ever going broke by observing the codes of race discrimination.

In these ways, the benign sword of competition was supplanted by the bludgeon of the racial cartel. Large corporations, labor unions, and the OPEC oil ministers have a reputation as the most effective fixers and riggers of economic markets. But, in fact, the united economic front presented by whites against the commercial offerings of blacks in the United States made a number of the world economy's most powerful cartels look like ineffectual trade associations or economic discussion groups. Here in the universal boycott of the black race was great power—invisible yet obsessive and ubiquitous—insisting on menial employment, mandating total obedience, and always drawing tight nooses around the freedoms and aspirations of tens of millions of Negro people.

Why Private Race Discrimination Is Tantamount to Race Legislation

The proposition that universally obeyed race discrimination is tantamount to race legislation may be illustrated by a fictional parable, which, nevertheless, accurately reflects the process of private lawgiving in the United States.

Let us suppose that as a result of a worldwide catastrophe there were only 100 human survivors on earth, all living on one island. Following the theory of the social contract, this group of 100 people decides to write a constitution establishing a tripartite system of government similar to that now prevailing in the United States. The government consists of a chief executive, a high court of law, and a parliament of ten elected people. In the tradition of liberal democracy, these three bodies are charged with making, interpreting, and administering the laws while the rest of the population goes about the business of building a civilization on the island. The constitution provides for a traditional bill of rights which guarantees equal treatment under the law.

Now suppose that the parliament decrees in its wisdom that it would be most efficient and in the best interests of the majority if all necessary tasks on the island were allocated by a *majority* vote. The parliament then votes that nobody will be obliged to cook meals, tend to garbage, and carry firewood except A, B, and C, who will do these menial chores according to a schedule and for a wage decided upon by the parliament. A, B, and C will not be *forced* to do these jobs; nor will they be arrested and thrown in jail if they choose instead to sit on the beach and stare into space. They are perfectly free to run away to another part of the island and live on berries and roots. But if A, B, and C don't care for berries and roots, and if they want to earn wages to buy food and shelter, no options will be open to them other than to do the appointed jobs at the wages designated by majority vote of the parliament. In the meantime, everybody else is allowed and encouraged to do whatever his or her abilities permit.

Clearly, if the new constitution of this island reads the same as the one in the United States, A, B, and C could go to court and the judges would have to declare that the act of the parliament was unconstitutional in that it violated the guarantee of equal protection of the law and was otherwise in conflict with the bill of rights.

But what if the people as a whole hadn't turned the system of job allocation over to their parliament? What if they had decided there was another way to skin a cat? It might have come about that a similar understanding about job reservation had evolved by common consent and custom agreed on at cocktail parties, wedding celebrations, and business get-togethers. A, B, and C would still be the ones to cook the meals, carry the wood, and take out the garbage. There would still be no law preventing A, B, and C from running off and living in the wilds; nor would there be any law preventing D and E, or anyone else, from violating the custom and doing the menial chores themselves. It was universally expected, however, that anyone who broke with the custom would lose a lot of friends, find it difficult to get into country clubs, have his children ridiculed in school, and perhaps on occasion have a "censure" rock thrown through his picture windows. Ultimately, then, everybody fell in line with the custom except for a handful of people generally regarded as misfits and troublemakers.

Confronted with this situation, A, B, and C would have been totally correct to have concluded that the new society had effectively enacted precisely the same law as in our parliamentary version of the tale. It wouldn't have mattered to *A, B,* or *C* that there was no law on the books prohibiting him from working at other than his assigned tasks. There was no law prohibiting him from flapping his arms and flying either—simply because he could not do it. The social system acting on its own enforced the "law" of job selection as effectively as nature acting on her own enforces the "law" of gravity.

If, as is clearly the case, the United States Constitution forbids the people acting through its legislatures to enact Jim Crow laws reserving certain jobs for members of the white races, why, we may ask, under the same Constitution, may the majority of the people, acting in concert and frequently in conspiracy, draw up, obey, and privately enforce the very same set of Jim Crow rules they are forbidden to adopt and enforce publicly? If the majority of citizens acting through established legislative assemblies have no constitutional authority whatsoever to require that certain classes of people shall live in one neighborhood while other groups shall live in other neighborhoods, why may the same majority of citizens adopt and enforce informal racial codes to the same end? If, as the Supreme Court has declared, the people acting through the powers of the state may not "confer benefits or impose disabilities" on certain racial groups, why may the same people, acting as a collective force and using all the powerful and respected institutions of society, impose and enforce exactly the same disabilities and benefits on a racial group?

As the Constitution has been interpreted by the courts, these are idle and impractical speculations. No matter how tightly drawn or observed, the private economic codes and conventions of race are considered to be a constitutionally permissible form of private lawgiving. Private laws are not subject to judicial review. Hence, these racial codes of etiquette may be overridden only at the discretion of legislatures which, by definition, are controlled by the same groups that imposed the private racial codes in the first place. Under these circumstances, there is some risk that the Constitution, which has so often come to the rescue of blacks in the past, may have some of the characteristics of a claim check on the back of which is written, "Not Responsible for Damage or Loss."

Illegitimate Power and the Codes of Race

Before leaving the subject of race and cartel force, we must note that the economic codes of race employed elements of power that had all the characteristics of illegitimacy that we described in Chapter Three. The racial codes were imposed outside formal legislative processes, and so were not subject to the constitutional review in courts which surely would have struck them down if they had been acted on by a formal assembly of the people. The codes established a "heads I win, tails you lose" rule of economics in which a white man was rarely placed in a position where he took any competitive risk of losing his job or position to a black person, or of being discharged for lapse of duty if he employed an incompetent white person rather than a skilled and diligent Negro. Inherent in the codes of race was a massive violation of Western ideals of fairness in that whites announced in advance a set of rules that called for an open contest for jobs, money, and positions and then proceeded to play the game according to a different set of rules under which blacks were free to enter the contest only if a majority of whites agreed to open the contest to them. And finally the economic codes were enforced—and to this day in some cases are still buttressed—by terrorism. Thus, the power inherent in the racial codes must be deemed profoundly illegitimate, not because it represented superior power, but rather because the power operated from an *invulnerable* position which, for all the reasons stated, had been neither fairly won nor subject to being dislodged in competitions open to all contestants or voters.

We may now begin to gauge the terrible mischief produced by the power embodied in the rules of race. The codes of racial subordination nullified the value of black education. The rules of race removed all career advantages in acquiring skill and training. They undermined self-confidence, chilled human ambitions and kept people unfulfilled. They defamed black labor and disparaged its produce and entrepreneurship. They made a virtue of human apathy while punishing or ignoring qualities of daring, imagination and willingness to take risks. They defended privilege and improved the fortunes of undeserving people. By closing down the routes to conventional economic gain, the codes of race often turned people toward underground or criminal economic activity rather than in the direction of productive work. Without question the rules of race created an environment of unequal competitive powers under which the economic lifeline of black people was threatened unless they asked for favors, demanded tribute, or accepted gratuities from the powerful.

The State as an Outlaw: The Eviction of Blacks From Political Power

"You know and I know what's the best way to keep the nigger from voting. You do it the night before the election. I don't have to tell you any more than that. Redblooded men know what I mean."

—*Senator Theodore G. Bilbo (1946)*

IN THE UNITED STATES, the race-trait prejudgment was a universal mode of economic, political, and social selection. It was, moreover, the intellectual and emotional force that established the social and economic codes of race. But the contradictory requirements of voter democracy and of popular sovereignty presented whites with a persistent dilemma. Since elected legislative bodies and officials had the constitutional power to abolish the codes of race, or punish people who obeyed these conventions, the imperatives of black subordination could be safeguarded only as long as Negroes were not permitted to influence the public power that controlled the political and lawmaking processes. In short, the nation would be safe for racial segregation and enforced inferiority only as long as political democracy was not extended to Negro people.

Particularly in the South, where the concern with race was a public obsession, and where vigilante terrorism was an established means of carrying out the conventions of Negro inferiority, it was essential that whites retain the power to suspend the enforcement of public laws requiring evenhanded punishment of whites for acts of violence against blacks. Thus, if the private codes of racial subjugation were to remain in force, it was necessary that whites, and not blacks, hold firm control over all of the political processes that selected judges, jurors, police chiefs, sheriffs, public prosecutors, and other law enforcement officers. For these and other reasons, American politics became racist politics, with membership in the white race serving as an express and necessary condition for holding the powers of public office.

We shall now see that Negro history was not simply a story of how black people were placed beyond the protection of the law; the underlying constitutional structure of the nation totally excluded them from the making of laws or from sharing in the laws' wide-ranging benefits and powers. Until very recently, the racial stipulation in political selections has been an integral feature of American democracy.

The Original Exclusion

The question of race and politics entered the early deliberations of the Founding Fathers. In the course of drafting the Constitution, a major disagreement arose between the northern and southern states as to whether slaves should be counted in apportioning congressional representation among the states. In order to swell its ranks in Congress, the South, with its large slave population, argued for inclusion of blacks in the head count—although for all other purposes, blacks were to be classified as "nonsentient beings." The northern states contended, with impeccable logic, that if slaves were to be considered chattels in the eyes of the law, they could neither be citizens nor voters. Therefore it was clear that they ought not to be counted in determining congressional representation. The debate was long and acrimonious, and the question was resolved only when the Founding Fathers settled upon the notorious Three-Fifths Compromise. Each slave would be counted as three-fifths of a person for the purpose of determining the southern Census count. But slaves would not be allowed to vote, or even to cast three-fifths of a vote. Owning a slave made a man count as a man and three-fifths, at least insofar as his congressional representation was concerned, but being a slave still made a man count as no man at all.

Throughout much of the South, however, it was the condition of race itself, rather than slave status, that determined a man's eligiblity for full citizenship. In the original constitutions of the southern states only Tennessee, Kentucky, and North Carolina permitted free Negroes to vote. Even in the North, free blacks were often explicitly denied the vote. Although New Jersey's first constitution extended the franchise to all residents "of full age who were worth fifty pounds of proclamation money," this requirement was amended in 1807 by an explicitly racist "qualifying act" specifying that only white males could vote. Over the next half century, state after state followed New Jersey's lead, with New York placing extremely severe restrictions on black voters in 1811, Pennsylvania totally denying them the vote in 1838, and Ohio taking the same step in 1850. Prior to 1865, only Maine, Massachusetts, New Hampshire, Rhode Island, and Vermont allowed blacks to vote without qualification, and less than 6 percent of all blacks in the North lived in these states. Even northern abolitionists, in their campaign against slavery, did not suggest that blacks should be given full political rights.[1]

Thus, the Union's victory in the Civil War may have freed the slaves, but it did not win them the political powers free men need to protect their individual liberties. On the contrary, in the years immediately following the war several northern states, including New York, Ohio, Wisconsin, Michigan, and Kansas, voted down referendums calling for Negro suffrage. What is more, the federal government took no steps to force the defeated South to guarantee Negro suffrage. As a result, southern whites, many of them former Confederate leaders, were able to maintain control over the state governments they had led in insurrection. In 1865 and 1866, white political hegemony produced the infamous "black codes," which, in effect, reimposed servitude on the emancipated slaves. Many states adopted vagrancy laws that specifically permitted the arrest of Negroes who showed no visible means of support. Laws prohibiting blacks from possessing liquor or from buying farmland were enacted in many states. In South Carolina, blacks were required by law to go to bed early, rise at dawn, and speak respectfully to their employers.[2]

When Negroes Held Political Power

Following the Civil War, Congress was controlled by northern Republicans who had every reason to hope that the huge potential southern black vote would remain loyal to the party of its emancipator. Congress responded to the black codes with the Reconstruction Act of 1867. This legislation placed most of the former Confederate states under military rule and required them to draft new constitutions barring state discrimination against black voters. Union soldiers were placed in charge of registering black voters. As was to happen 100 years later, after the enactment of the federal Voting Rights Act of 1965, many whites were surprised at the black voter turnout. In the 1860s, as in the 1960s, black people whom whites assumed both needed and wanted to have their "betters" make their laws and run their lives suddenly became intensely political. By the end of 1867, federal voting rolls in the South showed 703,000 registered blacks and only 627,000 registered whites. Here, in the sudden politicization of blacks, was an early appearance of the "dangerous and alien" political influence that southern journalist Henry Grady was to warn about twenty years later.[3]

Historians differ about the importance of black political power during the Reconstruction period. One student of Reconstruction politics maintained that "only five years after Lincoln's proclamation, the 4 million ex-slaves were politically dominant in the South and held the balance of power in the nation." Another authority contended that "Negroes were not in control of the state governments at any time anywhere in the South." Indisputably, however, American blacks held greater political power in the United States during the immediate post-Reconstruction period than at any other time, including the present.[4]

During the Reconstruction years, black political strength was most impressive at the state level. In the 1870s, blacks in Mississippi held 42 percent of the seats in the state legislature and also served as secretary of state, state superintendent of education, and lieutenant governor. In 1870, blacks were elected speakers of the house in Alabama and in Mississippi. A Negro was chosen president of the senate in Louisiana. In South Carolina's first Reconstruction legislature of 1868, black delegates outnumbered whites by more than two to one. Twenty-eight percent of Mississippi's 1870 legislature was black, and the percentage in Alabama was nearly the same. During the 1868-1890 period, 670 blacks in the South served in state assemblies and another 124 in state senates.[5]

Negroes, however, were not permitted for long to maintain their political strength in the southern states. With the fading of the northern Republican dream of riding to national power with the backing of southern black voters, the Union Army grew increasingly weary of protecting blacks from the violence of whites. At the same time, the determination of southern whites to disenfranchise blacks intensified. As a result, after 1876 the black presence in Congress declined rapidly. Only nine of the twenty-two blacks elected to Congress during this period served beyond 1880, and only five survived past 1890. When North Carolina's George H. White surrendered his seat in the United States House of Representatives in 1901, Congress again became a white enclave and remained so for the next twenty-eight years. And blacks disappeared from the state legislatures even more rapidly. Seventy-three Negroes served in the Alabama legislature during Reconstruction. All were gone by 1876.

Any lingering hope of reestablishing black political influence in the South was dashed by the Hayes-Tilden Compromise of 1877. In this compact between North and South, southern Democrats agreed to award nineteen disputed electoral votes to Rutherford B. Hayes, the Republican presidential candidate, thereby enabling him to defeat his Democratic opponent,

Samuel J. Tilden, by a single vote, 185 to 184. In return for southern votes, the newly elected President withdrew the remaining Union troops from the South. The racial politics of the South were thereafter restrained by nothing but the consciences of southern whites. Although northern liberals professed the deepest commitment to protecting the civil rights of blacks, they

PRIOR TO EVICTION: THE CONSIDERABLE POWER OF THE BLACK ELECTORATE

Blacks in Congress in the Post-Civil War Period

NAME	STATE	LEVEL OF OFFICE	TERM(s) OF OFFICE
Hiram R. Revels	Miss.	U.S. Senate	1870-1871
Blanche K. Bruce	Miss.	U.S. Senate	1875-1881
Joseph H. Rainey	S.C.	U.S. House	1869-1879
Robert C. DeLarge	S.C.	U.S. House	1871-1873
Robert B. Elliot	S.C.	U.S. House	1871-1875
Alonzo J. Ransier	S.C.	U.S. House	1873-1875
Richard H. Cain	S.C.	U.S. House	1873-1875 1877-1879
Robert Smalls	S.C.	U.S. House	1875-1879 1881-1887
Thomas E. Miller	S.C.	U.S. House	1889-1891
George Washington Murray	S.C.	U.S. House	1893-1897
John A. Hyman	N.C.	U.S. House	1875-1877
James E. O'Hara	N.C.	U.S. House	1883-1887
Henry P. Cheatham	N.C.	U.S. House	1889-1893
George H. White	N.C.	U.S. House	1897-1901
Benjamin S. Turner	Ala.	U.S. House	1871-1873
James T. Rapier	Ala.	U.S. House	1873-1875
Jeremiah Haralson	Ala.	U.S. House	1875-1877
Josiah T. Walls	Fla.	U.S. House	1871-1877
Jefferson F. Lone	Ga.	U.S. House	1869-1871
Charles E. Nash	La.	U.S. House	1875-1877
John R. Lynch	Miss.	U.S. House	1873-1877 1881-1883
John Mercer Langston	Va.	U.S. House	1889-1891

Source: Joint Center for Political Studies, National Roster of Black Elected Officials, Vol. 6, August, 1976, Washington, D.C., p. lvi.

readily abandoned their commitment to the black cause in exchange for victory in a presidential election. At the cost of only a single presidential election, the white South thus secured the first leg of a long-term contract that reestablished white political supremacy in the South for almost a century.

Deprived of protection from both Congress and the executive branch in Washington, blacks were once more exposed. Superficially, it might have appeared that as long as the Fourteenth and Fifteenth Amendments, particularly—guaranteeing blacks the rights to vote as well as the right to "equal protection of the laws"—remained on the books, blacks had at least theoretical political strength for protecting full citizenship rights. Unfortunately, the United States Supreme Court had already put an end to this romantic notion with a series of rulings that, in effect, put the foxes in charge of the henhouse. In *The Slaughterhouse Cases* of 1873 and the *Reese* and *Cruikshank* decisions of 1876, the Supreme Court ruled that the responsibility for preserving black voting rights fell to the states, which were free to do as they wished as long as they did not commit the technical error of making race an explicit criterion for disenfranchising the black voter.[6]

The Supreme Court had pointed out the road to total disenfranchisement of the Negro voter. Over the next twenty-five years, southern whites amassed a byzantine array of legal and extralegal techniques for keeping the franchise for themselves. The instruments of disenfranchisement included poll taxes, property and residency qualifications, literacy tests applied in a racially discriminatory way, gerrymandered political districts, inaccessible polling places, concealed ballot boxes, complicated voting rules, hostile registrars, racist sheriffs, economic sanctions against blacks who went to the polls, and, if all else failed, direct and unambiguous shotgun intimidation. The success of these stratagems may be gauged by the results of the 1888 and 1892 Florida gubernatorial elections. In the 1888 contest, the defeated Republican ticket gathered 26,845 votes, most of them black. In 1890, Florida changed to the multiple-box system in which ballots for each contested office had to be placed in separately labeled boxes—one for congressmen, one for governor, a third for sheriff, and so on. Designed to confuse illiterate blacks into casting invalid votes, the system worked so well that in 1892 the Republican ticket pulled only 8,681 votes, barely a third of its total four years earlier.[7] Southern whites had made a good start toward creating a protected political environment where they could enjoy the political freedoms of internal differences and debates without running political risk that blacks might gain power by throwing their weight behind one of the competing white candidates.

Whites Briefly Divided

By the mid-1880s, white Democrats in the South were easily winning their campaign to control all courthouses, state assemblies, county commissions, and sheriffs' offices. At that point, a temporary division in the ranks of the white electorate snagged otherwise smooth progress, suddenly bringing to the fore white fears that blacks might seize the balance of electoral power created by divided factions of white voters. This split occurred when poor southern whites, seeking a more equitable distribution of land and wealth, launched a full-scale political war against the conservative landed class. Splitting off from the Democratic party of the South, Populist leaders openly courted black voters. Like the Republicans before them, the Populists had little interest in working toward equal rights or political power for Negroes. Rather, their strategy was based on the hope of using blacks as one element of a coalition that would produce a political majority. Nevertheless, their need for black votes obviously carried with it the need to resurrect the black voter and to protect black suffrage.

The Populist alliance of whites with blacks presented an intolerable threat to the traditional forces of white supremacy in the South. In the end, the fear of mounting black political power prevailed over the desire for economic reform, and Populist leaders were finally persuaded to abandon their always shaky defense of black suffrage. In one of the sorriest spectacles of American political history, the poor whites of the South in effect decided that it was more important to keep blacks down than to improve their own lot if improvement meant sharing power with the black minority. Rallying around the flag of white supremacy, the white South closed ranks to end the danger of black power. Here was an issue that transcended economic differences and plunged the South into a new era of race-baiting "nigger politics." In the half century to follow, tens of thousands of southern politicians were to win office on the single-issue ticket of racial supremacy.

The aborted Populist revolt of the late nineteenth century failed to achieve its purposes, but it at least illustrates the potential strength of blacks in southern electoral politics today. Now that the fight to keep racial segregation has been lost, the Democratic party in the South no longer has a single overriding issue capable of uniting whites and giving the party monopoly power over southern politics. In fact, in 1984, the Republican party claimed eleven of the twenty-two United States senators in southern states. In Mississippi, a black independent candidate for the Senate ruptured Democratic solidarity so severely that in 1978 the state's first publicly chosen Republican senator was elected. As the Republican party continues to gain strength in the once "solid South," blacks may once again endeavor to exploit their potential power as swing voters either by seating their own candidates or by negotiating alliances with either of the major parties.

The Magnolia Strategy

Capitalizing on the defeat of the Populist revolt, the southern states rewrote their constitutions so as once more to disenfranchise blacks. Mississippi took the lead in 1891 with the establishment of onerous voting requirements that effectively blocked all but a very few black votes. Known collectively as the "Magnolia strategy," the Mississippi voting codes were widely emulated throughout the South.

The keystone of this program of systematic disenfranchisement was a $2 poll tax, by no means a small levy in a day when poor blacks often worked for well under a dollar a day. To make matters worse, the fine print of the law required that the tax be paid no later than the first day of February, nine months before the election. Needless to say, no one bothered to explain this technicality to blacks, who all too often showed up at town courthouses with their voting money only to be told they were too late. As a further impediment, the poll tax had to be paid cumulatively; if the voter failed to register in 1890 and 1892, the entry fee jumped to $6 in 1894. Poor whites also tended to be excluded from voting, but this did not threaten racial control. The effect of the poll tax was to leave the more affluent whites of the South in charge of government, and these governing whites could usually be counted on to protect their less affluent brethren from the economic encroachment of blacks.

The one drawback of the poll tax system—the fact that some blacks could afford to pay—could be remedied. Thus was born the second mainstay of the Magnolia strategy, the so-called literacy test required of all voter registrants. According to Mississippi law, a prospective voter had to be able either to read and understand the United States Constitution or to offer a reasonable interpretation of it. The criteria for determining what constituted a "reasonable" interpretation of a document that Mississippi Senator Theodore Bilbo once claimed, "damn few white men and no niggers at all can explain," were left entirely to the discretion of white voting registrars. If any doubt existed as to the purpose of this legislation, Senator Bilbo clarified the matter once and for all in a letter of instruction to election officials:

> "If there is a single man or woman serving [on a registration board] . . . who cannot think up questions enough to disqualify undesirables then write Senator Bilbo or any other good lawyer, and there are a hundred good questions which can be furnished."[8]

The point certainly wasn't lost on the perhaps mythical black man who showed up to register at a Mississippi county courthouse, only to be confronted by a registrar asking him what "habeas corpus" meant. After a moment's reflection, the prospective voter replied, "Habeas corpus—that means this nigger ain't gonna register today." Nor was the purpose of the law lost on Atlanta mayor Andrew Young, who vividly recalled the day in 1955 when his brother tried to register to vote in New Orleans. Young's brother, a former U.S. Navy lieutenant and a graduate of the Harvard School of Dental Medicine, was informed by the registrar that he had failed the literacy test.[9]

Following Mississippi's lead, North Carolina, Alabama, Louisiana, Virginia, and Oklahoma adopted their own versions of the Magnolia strategy. Southern political leaders made no secret of the real purpose of these diabolical requirements. According to Carter Glass, a delegate to the Virginia constitutional convention and later a U.S. senator, the laws were designed purely and simply "to discriminate to the very extremity of permissible action under the Federal Constitution with a view to the elimination of every Negro voter who can be gotten rid of legally, without materially impairing the numerical strength of the white electorate."[10] Most whites were not as frank about their objectives as was Senator Carter Glass. Supremacists always insisted that literacy tests were designed to exclude the ignorant vote rather than the Negro vote.

Beyond any question, the Magnolia strategy was a resounding success. In 1896, Louisiana had 130,000 eligible black voters; in 1900, after amending its constitution, only 5,000 remained on the rolls. And when Virginia remodeled its constitution, it reduced 147,000 black voters to a mere 21,000.[11] These results, whites were to contend, proved conclusively the apathy of colored voters and their indifference to who holds political office.

Disenfranchisement Through Reprisals

In addition to openly discriminatory voting requirements and a dazzling maze of bureaucratic machinations designed to bamboozle those few blacks lucky enough to find loopholes in the system, southern whites also had at their disposal a considerable arsenal of extralegal and quasi-legal techniques for keeping blacks out of politics. Disproportionately poor even by southern standards, blacks were especially vulnerable to economic retaliation. Generally dependent upon whites for employment, blacks in many parts of the South were made aware that they could lose their jobs if they registered to vote. School boards often threatened to dismiss black teachers who attempted to vote. The use of the economic club to enforce political disenfranchisement persisted into the middle of the twentieth century. In 1957, a Mississippi registration official provided the House Judiciary Committee of the Congress with a precis of the system in operation:

> "The [White Citizens] Council obtains the names of Negroes registered from the circuit court clerks. If those who are working for someone sympathetic to the Council's views are found objectionable, their employer tells them to take a vacation. Then if the names are purged from the registration books they are told that the vacation is over and they can return to work." [12]

The carrot as well as the stick played a role in keeping southern blacks out of federal, state, and local politics. Imposing economic sanctions on politically "uppity" blacks was tempered to some extent by an awareness that, in common with their white brethren, black voters and influential members of the black community could be manipulated and bought by favors. Black schools received charitable grants on the condition that they taught the virtues of racial accommodation; black leaders who discouraged protest and happily rode on Jim Crow buses received public grants; blacks who spoke up for the superiority of white political judgment were awarded bank credit, good jobs, and steady promotions in the jobs they already held. Even in recent years, the rule of purchased accommodation has prevailed in some of the most progressive cities in the South. [13]

Curiously, in their almost paranoid sensitivity to the supposed dangers of black voting, white southerners have been far more alarmist than the situation objectively warranted. After Reconstruction and the death of the Populist movement, the South was for generations so solidly Democratic that the party's nominees usually rode into office in uncontested elections. In effect, the official November contests were mere formalities; Democratic primaries actually determined who would hold office. In practical terms, this meant that even if blacks were permitted to vote in fairly substantial numbers, their votes would be utterly meaningless as long as they were denied access to primary elections. If blacks could be excluded from the primary but allowed to vote in the final (token) interparty election, Negroes would, for all practical purposes, be casting their ballots after the election had been held. Thus, although the Fourteenth and Fifteenth Amendments prohibited explicitly discriminatory election laws, and although the Supreme Court might at any moment overturn the implicitly discriminatory voting codes white southerners cherished so dearly, the all-white primary seemed secure simply on the grounds that the Democratic party was not an official government agency and that its rules were thus not subject to the prohibitions of the Constitution. Indeed, in 1935 the Supreme Court en-

DIVIDE AND CONQUER

As recently as 1980, racially gerrymandered voting districts in Mississippi effectively disenfranchised black voters by distributing them in four congressional districts.

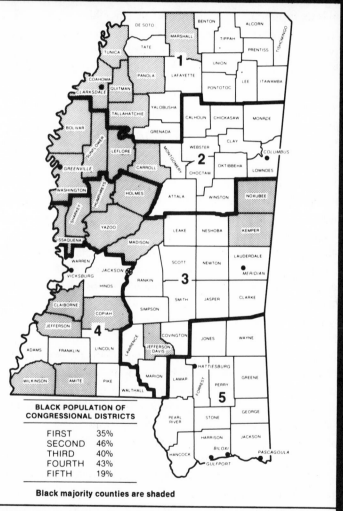

**BLACK POPULATION OF
CONGRESSIONAL DISTRICTS**

FIRST	35%
SECOND	46%
THIRD	40%
FOURTH	43%
FIFTH	19%

Black majority counties are shaded

Source: U.S. Bureau of the Census, General Population Characteristics, Vol.1, Part 26, Series PC(1)-B, "Census of Population: 1970", Table 35, pp.87-109 ; and U.S. Department of Commerce, Bureau of the Census, Congressional District Atlas, "Districts of the 95th Congress".

dorsed this logic when it ruled that the congressional power to regulate elections did not extend to party primaries, which it described as "private" contests not involving state action.[14]

The Supreme Court's decision protecting the all-white primary was finally reversed nine years later when the Court belatedly acknowledged that the white primary was, after all, an unconstitutional device. Gradually, southern states began to abandon their cherished white primary laws. But a few white supremacists still fought on. In 1948, Herman Talmadge, the winner of that year's gubernatorial election and later a United States senator, promised to fight for a white primary. "I don't know whether I can get it 100 percent white," he conceded, "but I'm going to get it as white as I can."[15]

The Racial Gerrymander and the Art of Down-Home Politics

Although the explicitly racist political laws of the past no longer remain on the books, racial conservatives in the North and the South still retain formidable official means for neutralizing the political power of blacks. An important instrument for suppressing black voter influence lies in the ability of whites—through their control of southern legislatures—to draw and redraw voting districts. In both the North and the South, blacks have tended to dwell in geographically concentrated groups. Although whites almost everywhere have insisted on the ghettoization of blacks, whites have had to deal with the necessary consequence that racial segregation enhances potential black political force. For example, in a number of counties in west Mississippi and in the black belt running northeast from Alabama through Georgia and South Carolina, the black population may exceed 80 percent of the total population. Such heavy concentrations of black voters theoretically allow a group that is merely an ethnic minority in statewide terms to put its own slate of officials in office in local elections.

The white response to this threat has been the political gerrymander. Whites always controlled the state legislature which, in turn, determined voting districts. Thus, it was a relatively simple matter to draw voting districts so that concentrations of black voters were dispersed among many districts, all of which still had safe white majorities. In this manner, the black vote was diluted and became politically ineffectual. Southern political leaders have been far more adept at this art than their counterparts who cloned and installed similar political arrangements in the North.

The success of the gerrymander strategy is shown by the fact that although the sixteen states classified by the Census Bureau as southern contain 53 percent of the nation's black population, only three congressional

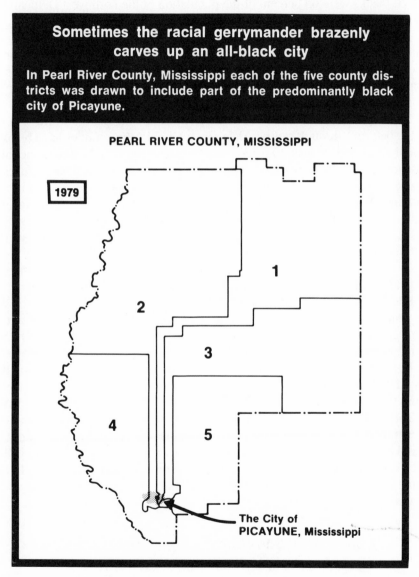

Sometimes the racial gerrymander brazenly carves up an all-black city

In Pearl River County, Mississippi each of the five county districts was drawn to include part of the predominantly black city of Picayune.

PEARL RIVER COUNTY, MISSISSIPPI

1979

1

2

3

4

5

The City of
PICAYUNE, Mississippi

districts in the South have a black voting majority. In contrast, the other thirty-four states, containing only 47 percent of the black population, have eleven predominantly black congressional districts.[16]

Prior to the redistricting process conducted after the 1980 Census, a classic example of the racially gerrymandered congressional districts appeared in Mississippi.[17] When the federal Voting Rights Act was enacted in 1965, blacks were 65 percent of the population of the northwest Delta area along the Mississippi River, from the Tennessee border south to Vicksburg. As blacks began to register to vote in the late 1960s the Delta was carved up into horizontal east-west slices, providing whites with secure voting majorities in all five of Mississippi's congressional districts. State legislators conceded that the purpose of east-west carve-ups of a north-south concentration of blacks was to "maintain our southern way of life."

Much the same story may be told of Alabama and Georgia. A distinct black belt runs through central Alabama, where sixteen counties have black populations greater than 40 percent but not one of the state's congressional districts is more than 40 percent black. The Alabama legislature has diffused black voting power by drawing the district lines so that these black counties fall into five of the state's seven congressional districts. In Georgia, a distinct black belt runs throughout the central part of the state. These largely black counties, however, have been apportioned among six of the state's ten districts.

It would be pointless to go into further detail, showing how, on a state-by-state basis, the South has effectively shut out black citizens from its political life. The brilliantly successful strategy of southern politicians may be summed up by the fact that the five states of the Deep South—Alabama, Georgia, Louisiana, Mississippi, and South Carolina—are each at least 25 percent black, yet they did not send a single black man to the U.S. House of Representatives from 1900 to 1972, when Georgia's Fifth Congressional District elected Andrew Young. In 1984, all thirty-six of the congressmen from these five Deep South states are once again white.

The carving up of black voter concentrations is even more blatant at the local level. To cite only one egregious example, when Pearl River County, Mississippi, was divided into five districts, the predominantly black city of Picayune was carved up so that one segment of it belonged to each of five county districts; this enabled Pearl River County to elect five white supervisors in 1979.

Diluting Black Voting Strength: Annexations, At-Large Elections, and Other Ruses

Reveling in their inspired ploys, the legislatures of southern states seemed to delight in conferring the vote on blacks, on the one hand, while simultaneously nullifying its force on the other. Blacks often discovered that the moment they become numerous enough to elect a local judge, justice of the peace, police chief, or school board, these positions suddenly become appointive rather than elective offices. And when a growing concentration of black voters in any city threatened to give blacks a powerful voice in a city government, the annexation of overwhelmingly white surrounding suburbs was sufficient to reestablish white political power. In 1968, Jacksonville, Florida, probably set a record in this regard when it annexed all 827 square miles of surrounding Duval County, thus suddenly transforming itself into the largest city (in land area) in the United States. Other cities that have annexed surrounding suburban areas and thus diluted the voting strength of inner-city blacks include Charlotte, Memphis, Houston, Indianapolis, Jackson, Shreveport, Baton Rouge, and Savannah. In many southern cities the power-diluting effects of political annexations were reinforced by federally subsidized black housing developments constructed just outside city election district limits.

Conversion to an "at large" election system is a common ploy for taking the vote away from blacks once they think they have gotten it. This measure provides that members of a city or county governing body are to be elected from a political area as a whole (where blacks are outnumbered by whites) rather than from individual wards or districts (where blacks frequently outnumber whites). As a result, minority neighborhoods obtain no representation on school boards, city councils, or county governing boards whose decisions are vital to black interests. Mobile, Alabama is a classic example. In 1980, Mobile was 36 percent black, but the city had never had an elected black city official. In 1980, the Supreme Court upheld the Mobile at-large election system on the grounds that it did not explicitly discriminate against blacks and that blacks had not proved that the system was specifically designed to exclude them.[18] The political injury to blacks is palpable, but proof of discriminatory intent is hard to come by.

Finally, briefly note two other electoral devices currently popular in the South, the so-called runoff and the "open" primary. Under the runoff primary system, if no candidate wins a majority of the total vote in the original primary election, the top two finishers then square off in a second primary to determine the winner of the nomination. This makes it extremely difficult for black candidates to be nominated unless blacks constitute a majority of the entire electorate—a condition that exists in virtually no southern electoral district. Thus, in congressional and other statewide election contests in the South, even if a black candidate is able to "lead the pack" in the first contest when several whites are competing, in almost all cases he will lose the runoff primary in a one-on-one, black-on-white contest. This was the case in the 1984 Democratic primary in Mississippi's Fourth Congressional District, a district that was 43 percent black. Henry Kirksey, a black state senator, led a four-candidate field in the original primary but failed to obtain a majority of the total vote. In the runoff three weeks later, Kirksey was defeated in a direct black-white contest by Britt Singletary, a 29-year-old white lawyer. In 1984, runoff primary laws were in effect in nine states. It was no coincidence that all of them were in the South: Alabama, Arkansas, Florida, Georgia, Mississippi, North Carolina, Oklahoma, South Carolina, and Texas.

Black representation in state legislatures has been disproportionately low in the states where "voting-at-large" rules leave large concentrations of blacks without an effective political voice.

1979			
Legislative Body	Number of Black Members in Legislative Body	Percent Black	Percent Black Population of State
Arkansas-House	3	3.0%	18%
Florida-Senate	0	0.0%	15%
Florida-House	4	3.3%	15%
North Carolina-Senate	1	2.0%	22%
North Carolina-House	3	2.5%	22%
South Carolina-Senate	0	0.0%	30%
Virginia-House	4	4.0%	19%

Source: Joint Center for Political Studies, National Roster of Black Elected Officials, Washington, D.C., Vol.9, 1979, pp. x-xi, 14, 52, 169, 201, & 226.

Louisiana employs a variant known as the open primary system, in which all candidates from every party are lumped together in a single primary election. If one candidate receives a majority of the total vote, he is elected, not simply nominated, to office. If no candidate receives a majority in the open primary, the top two finishers meet in the general election even though they may well be from the same party. This system is even more prejudicial to blacks than the runoff primary because it precludes the running of independent candidates in the general election, inasmuch as one must finish either first or second in the open primary in order to win a place on the general election ballot.

In sum, whites have used their control of state assemblies in the South to craft a maze of election laws designed to keep political power away from blacks and to preserve white control over government power. A number of federal judges in the South have invalidated some of the most flagrant devices used to disenfranchise blacks. But court challenges are laborious and uncertain and, in the end, appeals must face a Supreme Court which now tends to strike down only the most explicitly discriminatory voting rules and practices.

The Politics of Terror

The removal of blacks from positions of power has always been accomplished by multifaceted strategies. In circumstances where the labyrinth of statutes and administrative rules failed to keep politics in the hands of whites, the forces of terrorism stood prepared to plug up the breach. During the Reconstruction years, when the black electorate expanded as radical Republicans in the North pressed their campaign to enfranchise blacks in the defeated South, white violence escalated proportionately. In 1870, President Grant warned Congress that "the free exercise of franchise has by violence and intimidation been denied to citizens in several of the states in rebellion." During the Populist rebellion of the late 1880s, several blacks held local elective offices in Crittenden County, Arkansas. In a single day, all of these blacks disappeared, corralled by white vigilantes and forced at gunpoint to flee across the river to Tennessee.[19]

The strategic use of terror to keep blacks away from the polls never required daily or even monthly doses of violence. Those in charge signaled their power in much the same manner as the bandit in old western movies who took control of a saloon by the simple act of placing his gun on the bar for everyone to see. In much the same spirit, Ku Klux Klan cadres burned crosses on street corners and hung effigies of blacks with the warning sign: "This nigger voted."[20] During a 1948 march through Wrightsville, Georgia, the Klan's Grand Dragon warned that "blood will flow" if blacks tried to vote in the upcoming primary. With little reason to doubt that the Klan meant business, most blacks stayed home. One Negro who did not, a World War II veteran named Isaac Nixon, paid the price. In 1948, he was shot after voting, but Nixon lived long enough to name his killers. A few months later, the two men that the dying man named as his attackers were acquitted by an all-white jury.[21] In Liberty County, Florida, twelve blacks managed to register to vote in 1956. After the Klan had left burning crosses in front of their homes, eleven of the twelve went back to the voting registrar and asked that their names be removed from the rolls. In 1964, blacks who were publicly demonstrating for the right to vote in Alabama were clubbed by state troopers; a Unitarian minister was murdered; and a white woman sympathizer was shot and killed by the Ku Klux Klan.[22]

Ultimately, the federal Voting Rights Act of 1965 cut down most of the quasi-governmental machinery that kept blacks out of voting booths and party conventions. Yet terrorism still persists, albeit marginally, as an extralegal method of achieving what the public law may no longer do. The firebombings of homes and dynamiting of cars no longer play the roles they once exercised in southern politics, but intimidation and violence have not disappeared from the political scene. Older blacks, particularly, know their political place. Past terrorism has left a legacy of fear. It would be too much to expect that in less than a generation, memories of the harsh punitive measures taken by whites would fade away from the consciousness of blacks who might contemplate political activity.

Controlling the Black Vote in the North

Northerners congratulate themselves, as well as their ancestors, for never having employed the explicitly racist tactics of the literacy test, the all-white primary, and the poll tax. The record suggests, however, that northern tolerance for black political activity had little to do with concerns for safeguarding Negro civil rights or access to political power. Until 1940, only 22 percent of all blacks in the nation lived in the North, where they were usually outnumbered by whites ten to one. Even as late as 1980, there was no northern state with a black population exceeding 15 percent. Having in mind the forces that northern whites consistently mounted to protect themselves from the competition, or presence, of blacks in schools, neighborhoods, and jobs, the generosity of white northerners in conferring the vote on blacks reminds one of Adam Smith's comment on emancipation generally: "The late resolution of the Quakers in Pennsylvania to set at liberty all their Negroes may satisfy us that their number is not very great."

Like their brethren in the South, northerners had a determined, though in their case unadvertised, commitment to white political control. Prior to the Civil War, blacks were permitted by law to vote in only five New England

KEEPING POLITICAL POWER
AWAY FROM BLACKS

Both the poll tax and the literacy test have been abolished, but southern whites have developed a versatile collection of ruses which they still use to preserve and consolidate their political control over blacks.

State legislatures, local election officials, and influential political figures maintain white political supremacy by:

- racially gerrymandering election districts by carving up concentrations of black voters and distributing them within a number of predominantly white districts.

- annexing all-white suburban areas to a municipality in order to prevent urban blacks from becoming a citywide majority.

- changing elective offices to appointive positions when white candidates or incumbents are threatened by black majorities or pluralities.

- establishing at-large election systems where black candidates must compete in a large, predominantly white, voting district instead of having the opportunity to run in a single-member district where blacks are a voting majority.

- instituting runoff primaries to ensure that a successful black candidate winning a plurality of votes cannot win a party's nomination when white voters have split their votes among several white candidates.

- switching polling places in black precincts on the eve of an election.

- effectively disenfranchising rural blacks by requiring voter registration only during regular work hours and only at a county courthouse that may be fifty miles or more away from areas where large numbers of blacks live and work.

- intimidating black voters by placing voting booths in all-white clubs, schools, or churches.

- holding periodic purges of the voting rolls forcing blacks to constantly resubmit themselves to psychologically threatening and complicated reregistration procedures.

- using economic reprisals, such as denying credit or threatening employment of blacks who make a move toward running for political office.

- handing out special work details on election day in order to prevent blacks from getting to the polls.

- using economic pressures to persuade blacks to sign absentee ballots that are already made out with the names of white candidates.

Sources: Examples are based on author's interviews with black political leaders in the South. For detailed analysis of election ruses employed to keep blacks under white political domination see: Voting in Mississippi: A Right Still Denied, Lawyers' Committee for Civil Rights Under Law, Washington, D.C., 1981; Chester Goolrick, Paul Lieberman and Ken Willis, "In Southern Voting, It's Still White Only," The Atlanta Constitution, December 7-10, 1980; and U.S. Civil Rights Commission, Political Partcipation, Washington, D.C., 1968.

states: Maine, New Hampshire, Massachusetts, Vermont, and Rhode Island. Immediately after the Civil War, northern legislators promptly rejected black suffrage rights in Wisconsin, Connecticut, Kansas, Ohio, Michigan, and New York. Elsewhere in the North, blacks were either prohibited by law from voting or had to meet a property requirement that, in effect, disenfranchised most of them. When eligible blacks did vote in the southern states, they were subject to considerable harassment and abuse. In 1831, Alexis de Tocqueville noted that blacks in Philadelphia could not appear at the polls without being mistreated. The extreme antiblack sentiment evident in Boston in recent years was rampant in that city as early as the mid-nineteenth century. In 1850, a southern senator noted that in Massachusetts "the voters absolutely drove them [Negroes] from the polls at an election, and scorned and spit upon them." [23]

Terrorism as a means of keeping political power from Negroes was not a common practice in the northern states. Instead of disenfranchising blacks, both political parties in the North tended to control Negro votes by purchasing their ballots and politicians. Around the turn of the century, to cite one of the more garish examples, Springfield, Ohio's white voters were divided almost fifty-fifty in party affiliations, leaving the city's 1,500 black voters with a potentially decisive role in determining election outcomes. But the black population of Springfield was poor and politically unsophisticated; it was not likely to organize collectively to exploit its potentially powerful swing position. It appears that on each election day Springfield's black votes were tracked down and bought. In Philadelphia, too, it was common practice to purchase black votes. In 1899, W.E.B. DuBois reported that the black vote was controlled at the white political clubs, where bosses doled out money in return for the precinct's black vote. DuBois stated that "the business of the club is to see that its precinct is carried for the proper candidate, to get jobs for some of its boys, to keep others from arrest and to secure bail and discharge for those arrested." The going price for a vote in those days, DuBois noted, was "fifty cents and a drink of whiskey." Forty years later, in 1940, the Republican machine still controlled black as well as white politics in Philadelphia, the only change from DuBois' day being that the price for each vote had risen to $2. [24]

Bargaining for Negro votes reached its apogee in Chicago, the terminus of the black railroad migration route from Louisiana, Alabama, Arkansas, and Mississippi. Since 1876, blacks have been regularly elected to the Illinois state legislature from the South Side of Chicago. All of the first three northern blacks elected to Congress were from Chicago. None of them were crusading champions for black rights; virtually all owed their political success to qualities of unstinting loyalty to their white bosses. One black man, William Dawson, who served in Congress from 1942 until 1970, was consistently effective in securing the black vote for Chicago Democrats. He particularly distinguished himself in his efforts on behalf of John Kennedy in the 1960 presidential election. In fact, Kennedy's margin of victory in Dawson's congressional district was more than three times his victory margin in the entire state of Illinois, an important state in Kennedy's narrow victory in the Electoral College. It has been reported that Kennedy offered Dawson the Cabinet position of Postmaster General, a post usually offered to loyal party hacks. According to historian Arthur Schlesinger, Jr., however, Dawson was offered the post with the prearranged understanding that he would turn it down. If this is so, the Dawson manipulation foreshadowed what was to become a common political practice during the Nixon, Ford, Carter and Reagan administrations. Public honors and harmless posts were bestowed on blacks, while government power was reserved for the important clients of white America.[25]

The political gerrymander, so effective in the South in defusing bloc voting by blacks, was never consistently exploited in the North. In fact, in some instances, northern and midwestern politicians took measures that facilitated political participation by blacks. An example was St. Louis, Missouri, where in 1968 the black population was about 47 percent of the total. In this case, the Missouri state legislature constructed a black majority congressional district when it could easily have split the black vote between two white majority districts. The motive for this benevolent districting decision is unclear. It may have been either to ensure a Democratic (albeit black) seat in Congress or to limit black voter influence to only one district. In any event, the consequence in 1968 was that William Clay, a black man, was elected to Congress from the First District. What is more, in many other large northern cities, district lines have been drawn so that blacks can more readily be elected to Congress. In New York, Chicago, Philadelphia, Cleveland, Baltimore, St. Louis, Detroit, and Los Angeles, whites have faced up to—and politically recognized in the redistricting process—the realities of very large black minorities, in some cases constituting 30 percent or more of the total vote.

But, until recent years, there was more racial gerrymandering against than in favor of blacks. In 1966, for example, the Ohio state legislature drew a district line right through the middle of the black community of Columbus, thus effectively dividing the black population. As a result, Columbus' Negroes—making up 20 percent of the city population—were represented in Congress by two conservative Republicans. Much the same thing happened in Cincinnati, where concentrations of black voters were allotted to two congressional districts. In each of these districts, the potential strength of the black vote has been diluted by the inclusion of a sizable portion of suburban Hamilton County, which has historically voted overwhelmingly Republican.

One of the most flagrant examples of racial gerrymandering in the North occurred in the city of Indianapolis. Prior to 1970, most of the approximately 100,000 black residents of the city were bunched in the Eleventh Congressional District, where black voters played a key role in congressional elections, providing just enough votes to allow a liberal white Democrat, Andrew Jacobs, Jr., to win reelection repeatedly. In 1972, the Republican-controlled state legislature split the black sections of Indianapolis into three congressional districts and thus added over 50,000 conservative white suburbanites to the Eleventh District. As a result, Jacobs was defeated by a slim margin in the 1972 election. Although he was able to regain the seat later, blacks in Indianapolis are still divided into three congressional districts, where they hold only a fraction of the electoral power they once held.

Blacks Pledged to Whites at Nominating Conventions

The delegate selection process at political nominating conventions has been a prime means of keeping political power away from blacks. In the post-Civil War years, the Republican party flirted briefly with issuing delegate invitations to Negroes. In fact, immediately following the ratification of the Fifteenth Amendment in 1870, blacks were integrated into the proceedings of the Republican national conventions. But the number of participating black delegates dwindled after 1892, once again removing blacks from any influence within the party. In 1968, only twenty-six black delegates were present at the convention that nominated Richard Nixon. At the 1972 convention, this figure had risen to fifty-six delegates—4 percent of the total. In 1980, Ronald Reagan was nominated by a GOP convention whose delegates were less than 3 percent black.[26]

Until recently, blacks have not been better represented at Democratic conventions. No black person attended a Democratic presidential nominating convention until 1924. In 1936, the first year the majority of black voters favored the Democratic party in a presidential election, twelve blacks (1 percent of the total) were convention delegates, and one of them was actually selected to second Roosevelt's nomination. In 1972, when 26 percent of all the votes cast for George McGovern were those of Negroes, the delegate total at the convention that nominated him was 15 percent black. This figure represents the high-water mark for black participation at Democratic national conventions. In 1976, 90 percent of all black voters supported Carter, providing him, many people believe, with the critical margin necessary for election. Black representation at the 1976 convention, however, had fallen to 10.8 percent. In 1980, the black delegate total was 14.4 percent.[27]

The body count of black delegates at nominating conventions is not an adequate measure of black political power. Because of the way in which convention delegates are selected, black delegate selections are more likely to represent white interests than any identifiable black constituency. Although party leaders always choose a certain number of black faces, the selections tend to give the nod to safe blacks with demonstrated loyalty to a lily-white party hierarchy. In some instances, presidential aspirants screen black delegates who run pledged to their candidacies. A record for raising racial issues is grounds for being denied a delegate invitation. Thus, when blacks do win a place in a state delegation to a national nominating convention, they are often loyal supporters of either a white presidential candidate or the white-controlled party apparatus. Of course, white delegates are also manipulated by the party apparatus, but when this happens they represent whites. The important point is that because of the way political power is organized in the party hierarchy, the people who pull black delegate strings tend to be white.

Prior to Jesse Jackson's 1984 presidential bid, blacks had mounted a serious attempt to influence the nominating process at a national convention only once. At the 1972 Democratic convention, Shirley Chisholm, then a congresswoman from New York, controlled a handful of delegates and attempted to use them to influence the party platform. But the McGovern forces were firmly in control of the convention and her effort failed. In 1984, presidential nominee Walter Mondale had a firm hold on at least 200 black delegates, frustrating Jackson's efforts to use his 300 black delegates as a bargaining force. At no time in history have blacks entered a convention with control over their delegate power.

State Power Provides Safe Conduct for Racial Caste

In a succinct statement of the ideal of popular sovereignty, President Lincoln once said that no man was good enough to govern another man without the latter's consent. Yet for 100 years or more following the emancipation of the Negro, whites consistently blocked Negro people from either consenting or denying their consent to the policies and actions of the officials who governed them. To this end, white people did not simply employ ethnic bloc voting (a strategy they currently deplore when it is used by blacks) as a means of excluding blacks from achieving a parity of political status. They used the sledge hammer powers of violence as well as the nonviolent—but altogether sovereign—forces of state legislation and party rules. Backed by these sanctions, the racial political strategy was implemented through all-white primaries, poll taxes, literacy tests, and collusive voter-registration tactics. The imperative that reserved all political power to whites was reinforced through voter-district gerrymandering, election-at-large rules, and discriminatory redistricting. The strategy was made permanent in the minds of millions of black people through widely publicized visions of lynching parties and nightriders in white robes and hooded masks. Thus did the ancient voices of racial subordination become embodied in a carefully engineered apparatus of state control of the American Negro.

We are now in a position to see the connection between the economics of exclusion and the politics of exclusion. Through the skillful use of racial etiquette, backed when necessary by the force of the state, blacks were held in a separate labor market, evicted from craft and industrial employment, and removed from access to the normal flow of capital, credit, and investment. A system of fixed racial sector incomes, and attendant economic and social degradation of the Negro, was enforced through private and public codes mandating the physical segregation of Negroes in neighborhoods, schools, churches, parks, factories, and transportation. The racially stratified economic scheme was then doubly safeguarded by a host of political stratagems which took extreme measures to prevent blacks from using political power to break or erode the economic boycott that had been mounted against them. In so doing, white people provided constitutional safe conduct for an enduring system of racial caste.

CHAPTER TEN

Control Through Racial Defamation, Tokenism, and Discrediting Black Power

"Tyranny over the mind is the most complete and most brutal type of tyranny; every other tyranny begins and ends with it."

—Milovan Djilas,
The New Class *(1957)*

POWER EMBODIED IN RACIAL LEGISLATION, economic boycott, and the codes of Negro etiquette provided the major building blocks of racial control and subordination. But these forces were nurtured and fed by a further apparatus of power that established the right of whites to govern and the duty of blacks to obey. The Negro's low opinion of himself—as well as his sense of his lowly economic, political, and educational position in a society controlled by whites—was secured through the massive human powers of propaganda and persuasion. For two centuries or more, the use of power manifested in language and symbols of racial inferiority was, in fact, a central feature of the political governance and economic regulation of the American Negro. Although recently moderated and in some cases dismantled, the published ideology of black inferiority continues to be recruited in the cause of producing inferior status and diminished self-respect.

Throughout the history of the nation, the character of black Americans has been systematically attacked, ridiculed, and defamed. At one time or another, nearly every legislature, court of law, school, social club, business organization, and church has openly taught the codes of black contamination and disrepute. Toys, games, postcards, movie posters, and cookie jars have depicted blacks as lazy, ignorant, comical, stupid, amoral, unclean, and—in recent years—as a class of persons requiring special nurturing, protection, and support. Year after year, generation after generation, the defamation of black people—a message universally believed, shared, and communicated—has viciously undermined the expectations of black children and cut down the repute and standing of all members of the Negro race. The savage power of human language has rarely been used in a more devastating and injurious way.

Racial Defamation Proclaimed by National Heroes

The original slander of the character of black people in America probably began no later than that day in 1619 when the first twenty African Negroes arrived in Virginia as indentured servants. During the colonial period, the daily speech of millions of ordinary white folks on the subject of the qualities of people of the black race is neither reliably nor generally recorded, but the words of great national heroes and other influential people have been set down for all to read. In fact, the assault against the Negro character was led at the very highest level of our society. Thomas Jefferson expressed his low opinion of the Negro race, declaring that blacks are equal to whites "in memory" but "in reason much inferior . . . and in imagination dull, tasteless and anomalous." When the intellectual achievements of black men such as Benjamin Banneker, the self-taught black mathematician and astronomer, were offered to refute Jefferson's thesis, the author of the Declaration of Independence announced his suspicion that Banneker had assistance from whites and supported his claim by noting, "I have a long letter from Banneker, which shows him to have a mind of very common stature indeed." [1]

Even Abraham Lincoln, the Great Emancipator, was a declared white supremacist. His views on race were expressed in his 1858 debates with Stephen A. Douglas: "I, as much as any other man, am in favor of having the superior position assigned to the white race . . . ," he said, adding that there is a "physical difference" between blacks and whites "which will ever forbid the two races living together on terms of social and political equality."

Later, in 1862, President Lincoln called Negro leaders to the White House and addressed them as follows:

> "There is an unwillingness on the part of our people, harsh as it may be, for you free colored people to remain with us. . . . Your race suffers very greatly, many of them by living among us, while ours suffer from your presence. . . . If this be admitted, it affords

a reason at least why we should be separated. . . . You and we are different races. We have between us a broader difference than exists between almost any other two races. Even when you cease to be slaves, you are yet far removed from being placed on an equality with the white race. You are cut off from many of the advantages which the other race enjoys. It is better for us both to be separated." [2]

The human desire to rescue the life of a less fortunate person produces, it seems, a parallel need to defame the character of the victim who is often said to be unable to save himself. Cassius Clay, America's leading white abolitionist, was determined to rescue the Negro from slavery, but at the same time he was bent on giving the colored man a bad name. "I have studied the Negro character . . . ," Clay said. "They lack self-reliance. We can make nothing of them. God has made them for the sun and the banana."

Until World War II, all American Presidents expressed themselves as overt racists. Theodore Roosevelt demanded that "race purity must be maintained." In a letter to a friend he wrote, "Now as to Negroes, I entirely agree with you that as a race and in the mass, they are altogether inferior to whites." Speaking to a group of black students at a North Carolina college, President William Howard Taft stated: "Your race is adapted to be a race of farmers, first, last, and for all time." [3] Woodrow Wilson, who enjoyed the largest percentage of the black vote received by any Democrat up to the time of his presidency, broke campaign promises he had made to blacks by segregating the city of Washington as well as the civil service. In the liberal as well as conservative tradition of race relations, Wilson explained that segregation was "in the best interests of the colored people." [4]

Presidents Warren G. Harding and Calvin Coolidge spoke as self-appointed experts on genetics and race. Harding declared in favor of immigration quotas on the basis of inherent "racial differences" and the difficulty of assimilating anyone but northern Protestants. On the subject of Negroes, President Coolidge broke his customary silence: "Biological laws show us that Nordics deteriorate when mixed with other races." On signing the U.S. Immigration Act of 1924, Coolidge said: "America must be kept American." Herbert Hoover asserted: "Immigrants now live in the United States on sufferance . . . and would be tolerated only if they behaved." President Dwight Eisenhower never publicly declared the Negro race to be inferior, but his private view of the Supreme Court's school desegregation decision is well known. Chief Justice Earl Warren reported that the President took him aside at a White House dinner in 1954, while the Supreme Court was deliberating its decision in *Brown v. Board of Education,* and lobbied for his southern friends, saying: "These are not bad people. All they are concerned about is to see that their sweet little girls are not required to sit in school alongside some big overgrown Negroes." For most of our history, the White House has stood on the side of the common bigot. The official opinion of American heads of state has ranged from ridicule and innuendo to outright racial slurs.[5]

By the last quarter of the twentieth century, overt racial insults had become bad manners, if not bad politics. To be sure, the halls of government still harbored a handful of unreconstructed segregationists who continued to play the "nigger politics" of the Old South. On the whole, however, successful politicians in both the North and South no longer could afford to echo Virginia's United States Senator William Scott's 1973 declaration that "the only reason we need ZIP codes is because niggers can't read."[6] This is not to say that considerable political mileage cannot be made from racial slurs and innuendo, provided they are subtle enough not to offend the "liberal" sentiments to which all but the most intransigent reactionaries have learned to pay lip service.

The most potent and respected force in government spearheaded the defamation of Negro people. The Justices of the Supreme Court officially declared and maintained the dogma of the subhuman character of the Negro. Possibly the most revered of all American jurists, Chief Justice Roger Taney, had announced in the *Dred Scott* decision of 1857 that Negroes are "beings on an inferior order, and altogether unfit to associate with the white race, either in social or political relations; and so far inferior that they had no rights which the white man was bound to respect."[7] An official and almost unanimously proclaimed dogma of Negro inferiority prevailed in the teachings of the Supreme Court until the turn of the century.

By the middle of the twentieth century, defamation by judicial decree, like the racial slur in politics, had largely disappeared from official court opinions. An exception was President John Kennedy's first appointee to the federal bench, William Harold Cox of Mississippi. Still serving in the early 1980s, Judge Cox was known to be a bigot as well as an uneducated man. In a 1962 decision he wrote:

> "I think the court could take judicial note of the illiteracy that is prevalent among colored people; and I do know that of my own knowledge. And the intelligence of colored people don't compare ratio-wise to white people. I mean, that is just a matter of common knowledge."[8]

The racial fulminations of Judge Cox are unique, distinctly uncharacteristic of the judicial behavior of most federal judges in either the South or the North. Cox is important, however, because his archaic opinions from the bench were an unqualified restatement of the national judicial consensus that had prevailed for two centuries.

The consensus view of the bad character of Negro people has always been marked by minor differences in opinion as to the nature of the ethnic defect. Some whites insisted and declared that blacks were cheerful, well-adjusted, and happy-go-lucky; others saw them as sluggish, moody, and hostile. Polling the nation, one invariably got conflicting opinions. Was the black man really stupid but warmhearted? Was he generous but unrealistic? Or was he crafty, cool, and larcenous? Were black people generally devious and irresponsible, or were they, on the contrary, obedient and loyal to a fault? Gone today is the image of a grinning black sambo or of a childlike ninny. Not many people refer any more to blacks as "niggers" or "coons." And if they do, society's punishment may no longer be a gentle reprimand. But the process of subtle racial defamation grinds on. In fact, people who pride themselves on their freedom from racial prejudice consistently publish their backhanded insults: "He shows great promise for a black man," "For a black applicant his scores are very high," or "This is the most intelligent, honorable, and dedicated Negro you could ever hope to meet." Patronizing statements of this order were often agents of racial control; they frequently paved the way, and provided a screen, for the admission of carefully selected, and frequently bland or deferential Negroes into the middle ranks of the establishment.

The Literature of Racial Slander

The collective opinion that pinned inferior qualities and qualifications on people of the black race has been shaped not only by the degrading words of America's Presidents, heroes, and lawmakers, but also by the ostensibly authoritative declarations of the country's standard encyclopedias. Lodged in millions of homes, schools, and public libraries, these works have assiduously taught that black people were retarded, slothful, and otherwise inferior to whites. In all of the standard texts published during the half century following emancipation, a universal theme of racial disrepute was introduced into the minds of hundreds of millions of white and black children. These standard works did not speak in whispers as some people do today; they virtually shouted their white supremacist opinions so that even the most backward intellect would grasp the idea of the natural inferiority and contamination of Negro people. The following passage is from the eleventh edition of the *Encyclopedia Britannica,* which I read as a child:

> "Mentally, the Negro is inferior to the white. . . . The Negro children were sharp, intelligent, and full of vivacity, but on approaching the adult period a gradual change set

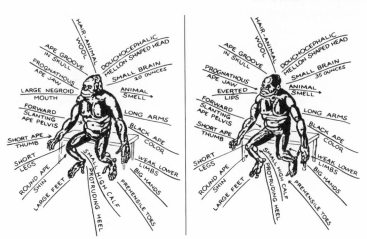

SCIENTISTS SAY NEGRO STILL IN APE STAGE

Races Positively Not Equal

(1)   The Negro's head shows the archaic form. The front of the Negro's skull is much smaller than the white man's, thus giving the Negro less room for the higher faculties, such as affection, self control, will power, reason, judgment, apperception, orientation and a feeling for the relationship of personality to environment.

(2)   Formation determines the amount of intelligence that will be reflected just as the size and shape of a glass pitcher determines the size and shape of the water in it. If this were not so there would be no law governing intelligence and one organism would reflect as much mind as another regardless of its construction.

(3)   The Negro's whole skull capacity is much undersize so that the black brain weighs 35 ounces as against 45 ounces for the Caucasian brain.

(4)   In the Negro the cranial bones are very thick and the cranial sutures unite early in life. This checks the development of the brain and explains the sudden stunting of the Negro intellect shortly before puberty.

(5)   The Negro's hair is flat and without a center core or duct. It is not a true human hair but resembles the wool of the lower animals and it can be felted.

(6)   The Negro's eyeball is tinged with yellow as is the ape's. The jaws protrude so that the facial angle of the Negro is 70 degrees as in the ape. The white man's facial angle is 82.

(7)   The Negro's nose is concave at the bridge as is the ape's. The nostrils turn up and show the red inner lining. The lips are everted and show the red mucous membrane.

(8)   In the white man the alveolar arch and palatine area of the mouth became shortened and widened and the tongue became shortened and more horizontally flattened which allows for greater refinement in pronunciation while the Negro palate and tongue remained apelike (macro-

dont) and he is unable to pronounce sibilant sounds. Sibilant sounds are unknown in Negro dialect.

(9)   The Negro carries stench glands as does the dog and in his natural state these may serve as a means of identification in place of a name. This stench (from extra sweat glands) is partly under control and is put out when the Negro is excited.

(10)   The black skin of the Negro has nothing to do with climate. It is caused by animal coloring matter between the true and the scarf skins. It is proven the world over that black and yellow skins are signs of mental and spiritual inferiority and that no tinged race can create a civilization.

(11)   A few mulattoes may appear to be brilliant but this brilliance never allows them to invent or create which shows they have not bridged the gap between the black and white, for no archaic form can become modern.

(12)   The Negro is much closer to the ape than any other race physically, and consequently mentally, for form must determine mental and moral qualities and like must produce like. Every race is different physically and thereby mentally. With the Negro, the body—hence mind—is the lowest of all.

(13)   No amount of imitation and apeing will instill a creative or inventive instinct into the Negro nor will education or sympathetic aid.

(14)   The Negro has had just as long as the white man to develop. Tens of thousands of years have passed by and the Negro has not produced a civilization. Where is his art, his science, his religion? What single aspect of civilization has he contributed to present-day culture?

(15)   The Negro has no morals. He is not immoral but non-moral. Without the white man to control him the Negro reverts to savagery and practices torture, cruelty and witchcraft. The Negro is a natural cannibal and on his native doorpost may be found choice cuts of human flesh. In Africa the Negro even sells his dead relatives and will eat human flesh after it has become decomposed.

(16)   As the black genes of the Negro are more powerful than white genes—the Negro has thereby destroyed every white civilization that he has come in contact with or has left that civilization stagnant and rotting and dependent upon the last drop of white blood from outside to keep it going.

(17)   Negro blood which differs from all other human blood and has a sickle shaped cell has destroyed Egypt, India, Carthage, Greece, Rome, and caused the deep animal sleep to fall upon China, Portugal, Spain, and Turkey.

Unless the Negro race with its deadly sickle celled blood is separated from the white race it will completely destroy America.

Mongrelization of the Races
Would Destroy White Christian Civilization

*—Source: from a handbill distributed
in the South in the early 1970s.*

in. The intellect seemed to become clouded, animation giving place to a sort of lethargy, briskness yielding to indolence. We must necessarily suppose that the development of the Negro and white proceeds on different lines." [9]

For centuries, the entire weight of Anglo-Saxon intellectual tradition subscribed to the doctrine of Negro incompetence. In the Western world, there were no Darwins, Mendels, or Freuds disposed to insist that there was no rational or scientific basis for the dogma of Negro inferiority. Even blacks themselves were powerless to contradict effectively the deeply ingrained opinion of racial inferiority. Negroes were caught in a classic double bind; if, as virtually all whites believed, blacks were inherently of subhuman intelligence, how could one reliably accept the opinion of any black person to the contrary?

Political and academic power arrangements further guarded the doctrine of black inferiority. As a race Negroes were barred from all posts of political, educational, and commercial position or prestige, where their visible presence, or performance, might serve to contradict the prevailing stereotype. Also, under society's racial codes as to who was entitled to hold power, Negroes had no access whatsoever to important communications media and, therefore, lacked the power to make their voices heard. All schoolbooks were published and written by whites. All magazines, journals, and news media were controlled by whites and, accordingly, reflected the conventional racial dogma. Even today, few of the standard school primers or textbooks proclaim the attainments of black people such as Dr. Charles Richard Drew, a pioneer in the preservation of blood plasma; Dr. Daniel Hale Willams, who performed the first successful open-heart surgery; or Dr. Percy L. Julian, who discovered cortisone. Until recently the accomplishments of black leaders and heroes such as Dr. W.E.B. DuBois, Harriet Tubman, Crispus Attucks, and Richard Allen were essentially unknown since they have never been taught in America's schools. Nor were American school children, black or white, ever informed that astronomy was taught in African schools at a time in history when white people in England were still living in mud huts and dressing themselves in the skins of wild beasts. The rich heritage of black pioneers, lawmen, stagecoach drivers, cowboys, and miners in the West never surfaced in textbooks or juvenile fiction. Young people were instructed instead in the proper place of Negroes from books such as *The Bobbsey Twins,* which told the story of Jujube, a colored boy doll, and Flossie, the little white girl who owned him. Flossie "always took pains to separate Jujube from the rest by placing the cover from the pasteboard box between them." [10]

162

Clowns and Braggarts: The Tyranny of Mass Media

The power of print media no longer leads the hound pack in the field of racial disparagement. Regrettably, that honor now goes to television. The single most influential communications force in the history of mankind continues to degrade blacks, assign unflattering traits to them, and reaffirm traditional prejudices and role assignments. The average American family watches television four hours a day, a fair portion of which consists of shows that present blacks in silly or servile roles. One of television's most influential statements about black people was the highly successful situation comedy *Beulah,* an early 1950s show about a black woman who became America's favorite maid. Nearly thirty years later, the television message about the qualities of blacks has not changed significantly. In the mid-1970s, the incompetent buffoonery of Stepin Fetchit was recreated in the inanely grinning J.J. on *Good Times.* Redd Foxx in *Sanford and Son* portrayed a poor, lazy, superstitious junk dealer surrounded by a host of other comic black characters. *What's Happening* featured an overweight, unintelligent teenaged clown who was always getting into trouble. When TV detective *Baretta* needed inside information, he inevitably turned to his informer, a streetwise black pimp created to add comic relief to what was considered one of the most violent shows on television. In 1980, *The Jeffersons,* a long-running hit which at times ranked as the nation's most popular show, was watched regularly by over 40 million viewers. The main character, a black man named George Jefferson, was a loud-mouthed, arrogant fool. If white children failed to learn from their parents that black people were shiftless and irresponsible fakes, television situation comedies more than adequately filled the gap in their instruction.

A 1979 study by the United States Commission on Civil Rights reported that blacks and other minorities continue to be presented on television as blatantly negative racial stereotypes. The study reported that blacks are portrayed disproportionately more often than whites as comic figures, and black teenagers more often have no identifiable occupation. In contrast, white males are much more often portrayed as mature, successful, glamorous, and prestigious characters. The survey found that blacks and other minority males are used in comedy roles nearly three times as often as whites.[11]

Roots, one of the most successful dramas in television history, is frequently cited as a persuasive example that television, although controlled wholly by whites, nevertheless presents diverse points of view and on occasion is willing to criticize majority viewpoints. For eight nights in 1977, 130 million Americans watched scores of cruel and sadistic whites maim and rape innocent and "sensitive" blacks. Later, in *Roots II,* 130 million people in the United States watched the vicious terrorism of the Ku Klux Klan, the race riots of the Woodrow Wilson era, and a slew of military officers who brutalized blacks. In the orgy of public guilt that followed the airing of this series, it might have been expected that whites would suddenly become more attentive to the current grievances of blacks. In truth, however, the message of *Roots* was self-congratulatory, not self-critical. Blacks were delivered from bondage because good whites finally prevailed over bad whites. Blacks won civil rights not because they were able to mobilize their forces to liberate themselves, but because charitable and caring whites saved them from the lynchers and tormentors. In the tradition of benign colonialism, helpless and childlike Negroes were portrayed as eternally grateful to their white saviors.[12] *Roots* told one-half of the story of black progress down the road to freedom—the part that was most soothing to the consciences of whites. But what of black courage, independence, and self-help? One looks now for *prime time* television which tells the story of the protest marches at Selma, of the North Carolina lunch-counter sit-ins, or of A. Philip Randolph's successful march for jobs in 1941.

Roots, of course, was entertainment, not a lesson in affirmative action. But entertainment for the masses also shapes public opinion. For the foreseeable future, American children will be nursed on television. For most people, television will shape attitudes and opinions and will create or smash desires for new knowledge. In a society that has renewed its flagging interest in protecting segregated schools and neighborhoods, hundreds of millions of whites will continue to learn to think about blacks not from meeting or reading about black doctors, lawyers, and businessmen, but from watching large numbers of blacks parading on television as comics and as incompetent braggarts. It appears that in the absence of black influence over television programming, station ownership, or commercial sponsorship, Negroes will, as they have in the past, submit their reputations to whatever jokes and slurs whites continue to find engaging or profitable.

Control *Through Tokenism: Limited Access Sustained*

The rising influence of the civil rights movement in the 1960s, coupled with the emergence of a new national awareness that the racial codes could no longer be defended, brought an end to much of the published dogma of racial inferiority. Textbook racial stereotypes were censored. Cream of

Wheat boxes depicting the smiling and servile Rastus were taken off the shelves. Nigger Head Stove Polish was marketed under a different brand name. The time had arrived in American history when a careless indulgence in a racial slur could drive a high official from office. Racial defamation in the form of speech was still protected, but throughout the nation, an overt act of race discrimination in employment, credit, or housing became a punishable offense. There was now reason to assume that the greater society would no longer use the massive power of the media to publish the traditional agenda of black contamination, incompetence, and laziness.

While overt attacks on the character of Negroes went underground, defamation of Negro qualifications continued in a more subtle form. Instead of directly disparaging black people, the culture of black inferiority continued to be spread by a milder form of racial derogation which we have come to know as the institutional or corporate responsibility movement. This movement—which almost without exception declares the incompetence and inadequacy of black people whenever it sets about to do good works—began in earnest after urban riots in the Watts section of Los Angeles in 1965.

During this period, American industry was profitable, but under intense public attack by civil rights groups because large corporations had no place for black people except as chauffeurs, messengers, and sweepers. In consequence, corporate public relations personnel were engaged to deflect charges of race discrimination. Company press agents, supported by newly appointed vice-presidents of urban and community affairs, publicized the thesis that if Negroes were more often indigent, unemployed, and working in lowly jobs, the reason had little to do with racially discriminatory business practices of the past or present. The explanation, instead, was that blacks as a group were undermotivated, unwilling to accept education, and culturally unqualified for employment. What is more, widely publicized corporate outreach programs to hire the so-called hard-core unemployables sent an unmistakable message to Negroes and whites: One should not blame the business community if segregated black schools were not properly educating black children or uncovering their hidden academic talents. Nor were the racial codes of American employers to be blamed if black parents failed to discipline their children, neglected their educations, and failed to see that they remained in school. Thus the token job, the token loan, as well as the token admission of a black person into a white university became both a slightly open door as well as a reaffirmation of Negro inadequacy. Publicized admissions of select individuals directed a spotlight on black failings and sent an unmistakable message that Negroes as a group were lacking in the normal qualifications and abilities that would cause them to participate in the life of American institutions in the same proportion as whites. No public attention whatsoever was directed to the many hundreds of thousands of Negro American adults who, over many decades, had completed college educations but throughout their entire adult lives were unable to secure industrial or professional employment that was even remotely appropriate to their skills and attainments.

Trust Us! The Disarming Shibboleths of Good Works

After the publication of the Kerner Commission Report of 1968, the business community began to take positive steps to demonstrate high-minded intentions to repair the Negro problem. If schools had failed blacks, American business would itself now take on the responsibility of providing better education for them. Bankers, industrialists, and insurance executives would embark on a campaign to teach the black poor to read. There is no evidence that the highly publicized corporate educational grants and programs, which peaked in the early 1970s, made any measurable contribution to the reading skills of young blacks. But these programs did succeed in deflecting the attention of blacks and liberal whites from the workings of an economic system that for several centuries had been closed to blacks, whether educated or not. The truth was that the reasons for the very low rate of participation by blacks in the economic system were mixed and complex. Race discrimination did exist, and blacks in large numbers were unprepared. But for much of the business world, a simpler view prevailed; the fault was laid almost exclusively at the doorstep of uneducated, unmotivated, and footloose young blacks who were addicted to the dole and preferred handouts to honest work. Neither race discrimination practices that then existed nor the chilling effects of past occupational restrictions were seen as the cause of black inequality or as a serious barrier to the upward progress of blacks. Thus, under the umbrella of corporate benevolence, the defamation of the black character continued unabated. In clear and simple terms, blame for racial inequality was put squarely on the shoulders of blacks, their families, their deplorable educational values, and their irresponsible social habits.

As the corporate responsibility movement proceeded in the early 1970s, it soon became clear to the public relations industry that private sponsorship of the improved education of the black man greatly enhanced the public image of a number of major corporations. The herd instinct took charge and hundreds of large companies hopped on the bandwagon of corporate care and concern for the disadvantaged. Dozens of corporate street schools were established for black high school dropouts. In all major cities, tingles went down the spines of the confirmed believers in corporate benevolence as newspapers and television stations proclaimed the fact that corporate charity for inner-city schools had increased "tenfold." With great ceremony, Michigan Bell Telephone Company in Detroit trumpeted the stirring news that it had "adopted" Northern High School, 98 percent black at the time. The Chrysler Corporation followed suit with a grand public ceremony at which it, too, "adopted" the predominantly black Northwestern High School. High-minded executives at the Chase Manhattan Bank summoned the nation's media to announce that Chase Manhattan had conceived of a unique and "innovative" Harlem street academy for delinquent ghetto youths and unwed black mothers. Major corporations selected their most dispensable executives and sent them off to ghettos to teach math, reading, and prudent bookkeeping. The Greyhound Corporation, which, since its founding, had hired only white bus drivers, sponsored a number of urban conferences at which hundreds of dedicated liberals from business, government, and academia were told about Greyhound's new scholarship programs for minorities. During this period, the radical chic—young white lawyers, bankers, and foundation executives—were the establishment trendsetters. And deprived young blacks were the necessary stage props whose presence, either singing at charity balls or attending street academies funded by corporate good works, testified to the continuing handicaps and inadequacies of black people. Sharing the same paternalistic attitudes as the Abolitionists a century before, corporate America in the 1960s assumed protective trusteeship over the education and guidance of young blacks as well as responsibility to repair the many other social and emotional failings that they attributed to Negro families.

The corporate responsibility movement gave significant attention to the spiritual uplift of blacks. It was everywhere agreed that black youngsters, in particular, deserved a break. In the summer of 1969, under the sponsorship of the New York Coalition of Businessmen, a group of hand-picked black youths from Harlem was shipped off with considerable press fanfare to spend a few days in the exclusive all-white suburb of Darien, Connecticut, where the youngsters would learn the "ecology of the seashore." Later that summer, the Coalition announced that these youths were to be permitted to camp for a weekend in the private hunting preserves of Gardiners Island, Long Island.[13] Of course, most whites aspired to bring strength, independence, and competence into the lives of their own children. But for black children the spiritual objective shifted. "Bring sunshine into the lives of a ghetto kid" was the 1983 slogan of one of New York City's most prestigious charitable organizations.

During the urban riots of the 1960s, virtually no Wall Street or State Street law firms employed blacks, and no downtown businessman's club was open to them in any major city. In common with other cities with large black populations, the Atlanta Chamber of Commerce was closed to membership of blacks. The Harvard Business School and its peer institutions did not admit black students except under rarest circumstances. None of the "Big 8" firms, which controlled most of the accounting profession, would risk offending a client by sending a black associate to work on the annual audit. But the competition among these business and professional groups to help disadvantaged blacks was dedicated and profound. And in the pursuit of corporate good works they competed as determinedly as they were determined not to compete for the employment or recruiting of those they had decided to support or succor.

Once more press offices of large institutions were engaged in promoting the missionary efforts. Once or twice a year in New York City it was announced that leading personages in law, industry, and banking had agreed to inconvenience themselves for one Saturday a year. At 9:00 A.M. sharp, like an old-fashioned board of working overseers, these worthies and their teenaged children departed from the East Side of Manhattan, each to spend a day in Harlem engaged in what they called "painting bees" and "garbage cleanups." If the public at large had not already absorbed the message about the deep-seated handicaps of blacks, publicized gestures such as these made them abundantly clear. Influential whites were sending powerful racial statements: Black people were congenitally sloppy and neglectful of their neighborhoods, which would stand no chance at all of being cleansed if it weren't for the benevolent intervention of their congenitally tidy white brethren. In this way, great powers made superficial but satisfying amends for past injuries and at the same time securely propped up the ideology of Negro inferiority.

Sloganeering Oils the Chains

During the decade 1965-1975, the full extent of the black handicap could be viewed in the hotel ballrooms of dozens of cities, where white businessmen gathered to congratulate each other on how they were combatting black poverty by granting soft loans and technical assistance to black-operated "mom and pop" stores in East Harlem and other ghettos. Metropolitan Life agreed to grant mortgages in the Bedford-Stuyvesant and Roxbury ghettos; Safeway announced that it would "consult" with and "give" advice and encouragement to aspiring black supermarket operators; Swift, the meatpacking firm, "helped" six Negroes establish ice cream parlors; John Hancock "pledged" to buy stock in a new black-managed bank to be opened in Roxbury. At one gathering of businessmen, the chairman of a large metropolitan bank solemnly intoned: "Isn't it time somebody stood up and said business should participate because it's the right thing to do—the humanitarian, the moral, the Christian-like thing to do?" Insofar as commercial exchanges with the Negro were concerned, most large corporations still tended to the view that American capitalism was a charitable activity.

Indeed, some corporations were engaged in serious minority employment efforts and commercial exchanges that went considerably beyond the stage of slogans and charades. But in the late 1960s and the early 1970s, serious commitment to establishing regular commerce with Negroes was limited to a few companies, and even then transactions were invariably couched in charitable terms. Every loan, every investment or act of employment was described as "give," "grant," "pledge," "adopt," or "encourage." Condescension and a profound sense of noblesse oblige, rather than a desire to make way for integration, opportunity, and enlarged black bargaining power, marked the executive's view of his disadvantaged neighbor.

Possibly the climax of the great corporate responsibility movement occurred in the early 1970s at a government-sponsored conference on black problems held in the White House's Indian Treaty Room. The meeting was attended by the President, a number of carefully screened blacks, and scores of business leaders. Minority groups have since discovered that invitations to attend meetings at the Indian Treaty Room should be declined. Whether the agenda is minority capitalism, the grievances of migrant workers, or Indian fishing rights, the Indian Treaty Room has become known as a place where the people invited leave with less than they had before they entered. This conference was no exception. For a number of hours, the blacks in attendance remained calm and respectful while white businessmen wrung their hands over what to do about the recent riots in ghetto neighborhoods. Finally, one of the President's leading campaign contributors stated: "I submit, Mr. President, that the problem of these [black] people is motivation." At this point, a large number of blacks spontaneously left the room, to the bewilderment of the speaker and a great many prominent business executives. Thus, under the guise of good works, racial disparagement continued to be the underlying theme of the virtuous.

As the 1960s came to an end, ecology replaced the plight of blacks as the focus of corporate social responsibility. Major companies now stumbled over one another in a new contest to be the first to give dollars for clean water. Corporate executives turned to backpacking for a cleaner environment; they neglected, or altogether forgot, their erstwhile duties as antipoverty warriors in the inner cities. Forgotten, too, were the seminars in which whites agonized about their need to make a "meaningful contribution" to the welfare of the disadvantaged Negro. The large life insurance companies had quietly withdrawn their mortgage lending programs earmarked for inner-city blacks and replaced these efforts with newsletters on the duties of corporate responsibility. Chase Manhattan Bank had abandoned its street academies for the rehabilitation of black illiterates and drug users. The corporate-sponsored Hank Aaron scholarship funds fell into disuse. The decline of the corporate responsibility movement appeared to be closely connected with the decline in Negro agitation. With the exception of serious race riots in Miami for a few days in the spring of 1980, the ghettos were quiet.[14]

In some cases, the roadshow movement survived. As late as 1983, a few large insurance companies were still dispatching retired executives to the ghettos to act as literacy volunteers. In this difficult economic period, 50 percent or more of black teenagers in the United States who wanted work could not find it, yet the Youth Motivation Task Force of the National Alliance of Businessmen continued to instruct black youths that problems in finding employment were due to their casual habits of wearing Nike running shoes to job interviews rather than to shortages of jobs or persisting institutional preferences to employ whites.

Peddling a Mythology of Black Capitalism

The federal government also employed symbols to influence crowds. Washington agencies such as the former Office of Economic Opportunity, the Small Business Administration, and the Office of Minority Business Enterprise set up public relations shops with funding from Congress. These agencies had no power to make economic rules regarding commerce between blacks and whites. They had no authority to order affirmative action or to bar the use of racial criteria in making economic selections. But the government agencies assiduously worked to keep themselves in business by staging token, although highly visible, black-assistance activities.

It was under the aegis of the government's minority capitalism programs that tokenism as a form of propaganda reached its highest state of elaboration. In the 1960s, the Republican party had not yet conceded the black vote to the Democratic party. During this period, President Nixon made skillful use of publicized government efforts to assist black entrepreneurs as a lever to win some black support for the Republican party without incurring the detriment of fundamental, costly, and politically unpopular economic reforms. In a skillfully mounted effort to stroke dissident blacks and appease liberal whites, the Nixon administration's public relations troops launched a campaign to catapult a handful of well-known black athletes into entrepreneurial status. By presidential order, established bank-chartering safeguards were waived as black-owned banks with aggregate deposits no greater than the petty cash account at a minor branch of New York's Citibank were organized and widely heralded as "potent new instruments of black economic power." The heads of the nation's largest corporations appeared before press photographers as they made token deposits in the new black banks. Ten years later, no inroad whatsoever had been made in the huge capital ownership gap between blacks and whites. Indeed, black financial institutions were struggling for mere survival rather than for economic influence. But the original ballyhoo of government-sponsored minority capitalism had been so effective that very large numbers of blacks and whites remained persuaded that Negro people had, at last, become true partners with whites in the ownership and control of American capital.

The truth was that the black capitalism programs implemented by the government from 1969 to 1977 were almost a total failure from the point of view of drawing a significant number of black people into positions of capital control and ownership. From the viewpoint of whites who orchestrated the black enterprise programs, the outreach efforts were perhaps a success, at least insofar as they accomplished the purpose of persuading members of the black community, as well as liberally minded whites, that something of importance was being done about the economic plight of racial minorities. Remarkably, too, most of the strident black community groups which, for a brief time, had been the scourge of corporate America were successfully pacified. The bottom line of the effort was that under white protection, black enterprise continued on a trivial scale and, in virtually all cases, was pursued as before on the ghetto reservation.

Suicide by Siding With Superiors

Throughout the nation's history, blacks have never been free of complicity in limiting the opportunities and expectations of members of their race. For many years after the abolition of slavery, Negroes who worked to establish educational institutions for their people commonly supported the prevailing belief of whites that the outside limit of Negro educational aspirations should be instruction in industrial and normal schools. Black politicians often ingratiated themselves with the white-controlled patronage system by publicly declaring the desirability of separate schools, playgrounds, and neighborhoods. Every act of unequal racial treatment— whether voting disenfranchisement, job segregation, or laws against interracial marriage—found a large number of black apologists and collaborationists. Their opinions of the limited place of the Negro in American society were, perhaps, as effective in holding the racial line as were the Jim Crow proclamations of even the most highly esteemed whites.

The debilitating effects of the racial slander were most pernicious when broadcast from the pulpits of black heroes. For many generations, the limits of black economic and professional ambitions were set by Booker T. Washington, whose sense of racial etiquette was predicated on a firm belief in the patient, faithful, and accommodating character of the American Negro. Read his words! Would any black child who heard—and whose family taught—the message of Washington's famous Atlanta Compromise speech be likely to aspire to become a congressman, an industrialist, or a poet?

"No race can prosper til it learns that there is as much dignity in tilling a field as in writing a poem. It is at the bottom of life we must begin, and not at the top. Nor should we permit our grievances to overshadow our opportunities.

"To those of the white race . . . were I permitted I would repeat what I say to my own race: 'Cast down your bucket where you are.' Cast it down among the eight millions of Negroes whose habits you know, whose fidelity and love you have tested in days when to have proved treacherous meant the ruin of your firesides. Cast down your bucket among these people who have, without strikes and labour wars, tilled your fields, cleared your forests, builded your railroads and cities, and brought forth treasures from the bowels of the earth. . . . Casting down your bucket among my people, helping and encouraging them as you are doing on these grounds, and to education of head, hand and heart, you will find that they will buy your surplus land, make blossom the waste places in your fields, and run your factories. While doing this, you can be sure in the future, as in the past, that you and your families will be surrounded by the most patient, faithful, law-abiding, and unresentful people that the world has seen. As we have proved our loyalty to you in the past, in nursing your children, watching by the sick-bed of your mothers and fathers, and often following them with tear-dimmed eyes to their graves, so in the future, in our humble way, we shall stand by you with a devotion that no foreigner can approach, ready to lay down our lives, if need be, in defence of yours, interlacing our industrial, commercial, civil, and religious life with yours in a way that shall make the interests of both races one. In all things that are purely social we can be as separate as the fingers, yet one as the hand in all things essential to mutual progress." [15]

As history's most influential black supporter of white racial stereotypes, Booker T. Washington was greatly esteemed and honored by white opinion makers. His views were widely published by the white press. Wealthy whites lined up to make generous donations for the erection of monuments in memory of the words and achievements of a leader whose thesis of accommodation nevertheless drew tight circles around the ambitions of black people. In contrast, the vigorous teachings of other black spokesmen such as Dr. W.E.B. DuBois, who called on members of his race to aspire to equal standing with whites, were buried, suppressed, or lost.

The teachings of Booker T. Washington illustrated the common tendency of little powers to identify with, and support the objectives of, great powers. In Booker T. Washington's name, Negroes frequently taught their children that accommodation to racial segregation was right and virtuous. Loyal to his instructions, black people often turned their backs on young blacks who had career plans that didn't fit in with the protocols of race. Delegations of prominent local Negroes led by local ministers were known to pay calls on politically active blacks and persuade them to compromise their hopes and principles in the name of avoiding trouble. The limited "teach or preach" option available to highly educated blacks was published wisdom in black schools and households. Thus, blacks were held in place not only because no one with power in the white community took them seriously, but also because other blacks often taught each other that no one—black or white—should take them seriously.

The Voices of Vulnerability: Purchasing the Rhetoric of Black Spellbinders

Booker T. Washington may have been the white man's favorite Negro, but no responsible person ever accused this great man of being on the white man's payroll. Yet large sums of money and grants were, in fact, available to other Negroes who agreed to teach the virtues of racial subordination and accommodation. After World War I, the major political parties in the United States hit upon the strategy of hiring black spokesmen. To this end, a nationwide network of black speakers' bureaus was established and financed by whites. Black "spellbinders" were sent out to address Negro

SHOOTING ONE'S OWN TROOPS:

Today, as well as a century ago, large numbers of influential blacks have scuttled the efforts of other blacks to press for equal rights and for broader economic and political participation.

- "We colored men should not get involved in American politics because that would distract us from our efforts to build a strong economic base and a sound moral character." (circa 1870)

- "As a Negro, I am strongly in favor of literacy tests as a prerequisite for voting as these requirements will encourage members of our race to seek a good education." (circa 1880)

- "The colored man should be in favor of a poll tax and property ownership as preconditions to voting as these requirements will encourage Negroes to work hard and to be thrifty." (circa 1885)

- "Negroes should encourage the use of the multiple-ballot box system as this ensures that only intelligent people will be able to vote and this will result in the election of responsible officials who will look after the interests of the black man." (circa 1890)

- "I am opposed to enacting a federal antilynching law as that would intrude on states' rights and only encourage whites to take further reprisals against blacks." (circa 1920)

- "I am opposed to agitation for the rights of citizenship as the only answer for the colored man is to be patient, make himself competent, and give no occasion for anyone to find fault with him." (circa 1925)

- "As a Negro, I am opposed to pressing white employers to hire Negroes since whites will most certainly employ members of our group as soon as we have been through an apprenticeship period and have shown ourselves worthy and qualified." (circa 1930)

- "I am against affirmative-action pressures for admission of blacks to elite educational institutions since most blacks will be better off in settings where academic pressures are not so great." (circa 1980)

- "I am against political activism to advance the economic position of ghetto blacks because I doubt the ability of our people to rise in one great leap from our agricultural backgrounds into a jet and computer society." (circa 1981)

- "I am against government tampering in the marketplace for black labor because unregulated markets serve black interests and because political reforms do not generate individual ambition, investment, and hard work." (circa 1980)

- "We blacks should be opposed to legislation forcing racial integration in schools and neighborhoods because history has repeatedly shown the folly and futility of government tampering with local folkways and habits." (circa 1980)

Note: Some late nineteenth and early twentieth century materials bearing on how blacks have supported the restrictive racial policies and attitudes of whites may be found in August Meier, Negro Thought in America 1880-1915 (Ann Arbor: University of Michigan Press, 1963); also see C. Vann Woodward, Origins of the New South 1877-1913 (Baton Rouge: Louisiana State University Press, 1951); and Louis R. Harlen, ed., The Booker T. Washington Papers (Urbana: University of Illinois Press, 1972).

religious, fraternal, and political organizations. The speaker's function was to mollify black leaders, keep black voters in line, and promise blacks "a piece of the action." The speakers' bureau movement saw a significant revival in the late 1960s. In the main, this movement took the form of appointing black people to highly visible but wholly uninfluential government posts. During this period, black spokesmen were often named to government positions with all the pomp and fanfare usually reserved for presidential appointments. Job titles were impressive and the pay was excellent. The job of most appointees was to appease other blacks, to negotiate with Negroes on behalf of whites, and to stand as visible symbols of newly won black influence. Others were employed merely to carry good news to the ghettos that better hospitals, schools, jobs, and rat exterminators were on the way. From the beginning, some black officials detected a degree of hypocrisy in the race relations industry of the federal government. Black officials who found it unacceptable to act as spellbinders and pacifiers of other blacks left government service, yet, if they wished to match in industry the substantial salaries that they had been receiving in public office, they left office quietly, and without calling press conferences to explain why they were departing.

The ready ability of a sitting government to win the services of black pacifiers was particularly apparent during the 1972 presidential election campaign, when a number of black community and political leaders in the South mounted major campaigns to reelect President Nixon. This effort seemed odd to many political observers since, among other offenses to black people, President Nixon had sought to appoint at least one good friend of Jim Crow as a Justice to the Supreme Court. While couching his policies with sugar-coated pieties about the evils of racial discrimination, the President had nevertheless offended most of the nation's blacks by explicitly instructing members of his cabinet to "go slow" in enforcing laws requiring public school integration in the South. Throughout his presidency, President Nixon steadfastly refused to meet with or consider the grievances of black leaders. With such a record, how could the President hope to win the votes of rank-and-file southern blacks? Regrettably, the cynic's answer is correct. Using the traditional coin of American politics, the President simply directed political support and community grants to the campaigns and constituencies of a few key black politicians in the South. In consequence, a number of black politicians had the President to thank for helping them remain in office. They would obligingly repay the political debt by urging Negro voters to support the President.

To be sure, there is nothing particularly unusual or venal in speaking kind words about one's patron. Many black politicians, like whites before them, invariably speak favorably about the person who controls political patronage. Yet, during this crucial period when black political power was germinating, Negro political support in the South for President Nixon undercut much of the black political agenda and stranded the activists who were pressing for tighter antidiscrimination laws in employment and stricter federal enforcement of court orders requiring the integration of public schools. Then, as today, the ability to mount black political power to integrate industry, to advance affirmative action, to win wider minority economic opportunities through legislation, and to make officials who were friends of Jim Crow politically accountable to black voters was frequently surrendered in common barter: generous pork barrel for the collaborating black politician and for his clients and constituents.

Blacks Orchestrate the Redemption of George Wallace

White politicians in the South—particularly Alabama's Governor George Wallace—were masters of the political strategy of using blacks to ensnare other blacks. For many years Wallace's name was virtually synonymous with southern white supremacist opinion, yet he was frequently successful in winning the political support of black mayors in a number of predominantly black Alabama cities. Instead of adopting the bolder strategy of organizing collectively to defeat Wallace and possibly elect a racial moderate, a number of black mayors competed for the favors of the Alabama governor who controlled the public purse strings of federal revenue-sharing as well as other grants for poor communities. This tactic served Wallace well in 1982 when, as possibly the South's most infamous racial bigot, he was overwhelmingly elected governor of Alabama with the support of 79 percent of the state's black voters. The spectacular irony of the event was that black voters used their newly won political power to return to office the very man who had fought so determinedly to prevent them from winning that power in the first place. The political events in Alabama were not unusual. In many of the poorest counties in the South, blacks were in the majority, yet, in the early 1980s, whites held every political job that mattered. White sheriffs, district attorneys, and circuit court clerks were consistently returned to office by black voters who commonly deplored the militants who "stirred people up" and cursed the "out-of-state agitators" who told people that black politicians could make their lives better. In these ways did former shoeshine boys and field hands, with the potential power to elect and control governments, line up once more for their allotments of brushes, polish, and rakes.

George Wallace was merely one of many southern politicians adept in the strategy of purchasing black political allegiance. White supremacists—such as Strom Thurmond of South Carolina, Herman Talmadge of Georgia, and Jamie Whitten of Mississippi—long ago discovered that if they rescued an individual black constituent from a pressing personal or family problem and publicized their good works, they could win black voter support while steadfastly voting against black interests in Congress. In a similar manner, the power to appoint Negroes to government jobs has been consistently used by southern segregationists to pacify blacks, capture their political support, and manipulate their votes. While there has never been much political mileage to be won by a U.S. senator in appointing a white constituent to a minor government post, the naming of a black person to the same position has become a powerful political statement. Just as an attack on a single black person has often been viewed as an attack on the black race, so, too, a favor granted to one black individual tends to be looked upon as a blessing bestowed on the entire race. Through the processes of racial favors, economic and political advantage have been defended by whites and power has often been safely kept out of the hands of blacks.

To be sure, there have been important exceptions to the practice of disarming blacks by conferring on a few of them the appearance rather than the reality of participation in government power. The designation of Andrew F. Brimmer as a member of the Federal Reserve Board in 1966, the appointment of Thurgood Marshall to the Supreme Court in 1967, and the naming of William T. Coleman as Secretary of Transportation in 1975 are examples of blacks who were awarded positions of considerable power and influence. But these were rare exceptions. Since the days of Reconstruction, most blacks in the executive branch, as in the theater, have played the roles of briefcase carriers and coat holders for the powerful. In recent years, the rules of race are unchanged. Whites in the inner circle of the executive branch make the decisions; blacks who sit in the outer circle are frequently paid and garlanded, provided that they ratify the decisions made by their superiors who sit inside.

Marketing the Illusion of Equal Power

In allocating power according to race, the corporate world has traditionally moved in tandem with politicians. Until recent years, blacks never held corporate posts above the rank of orderly or messenger. The talents and skills of black people had not changed overnight, yet suddenly, in the late 1960s, Negroes began appearing by the scores as elected company officers. In most corporations, the customary title was assistant vice-president in charge of urban affairs. Blacks were employed in large numbers to be the minority affairs spokesmen in the corporate world. In major companies a Negro community affairs officer was usually designated to announce, in a particular city, that a consortium of white banks was about to "grant unprecedented" business loans to black businessmen. During periods when the codes of race discrimination in employment were an integral part of the process of corporate personnel selection, black men were paid generous salaries to speak out about the "splendid community outreach efforts" of their employers. Black bankers, whose financial institutions were either created or propped up by minor credits hastily gathered by passing the hat among white institutions, were chosen as spokesmen to publicly disclose that the greater business community "had mounted a new grass-roots commitment to solving social ills." In most cases, the charter of assistance was devised by whites, but black executives were drafted to mouth the shopworn business jargon about the "newly emerging business interface with changing urban conditions" and the "small beginnings of a giant new business initiative" in favor of minority communities. Invariably, Negroes were recruited to announce—but never to commit or authorize—new business contracts with black contractors. White executives decided when a black bank was safe enough to act as a depository of corporate payroll accounts. However, when the minority bank had proved its qualifications, black people on both sides handled the ribbon-cutting ceremony and announced the making of the initial $10,000 deposit.

In large corporations and other organizations, blacks were also paid and celebrated for being experts on race relations and as reliable guides to the proper solutions to the problems of Negro status. When black grievances presented the prospect of serious racial strife, Negroes everywhere were hired to lecture other blacks on why laws against race discrimination, government minimum wage requirements, and affirmative-action rules were the true culprits in causing racial inequality. Before the rotary clubs and sewing circles of America, blacks in corporations were employed to downplay the importance of race discrimination and to congratulate their employers on helping inner-city blacks deal with their problems of low motivation, broken families, and a near-incorrigible preference for life on the streets. Eager cadres of corporate blacks in significant numbers became evangelical ministers who, in the face of unemployment rates among college-educated blacks that were twice or more the rate of peer whites, preached a simple gospel of family, morality, and hard work. As sometime experts on the probable effects of their own manipulation, blacks employed in industry were often asked the somewhat insulting question, "How will such and such a course of corporate public relations play in the black community?" Thus, in the corporate as in the political world, there remains even today a lingering element of truth in Frederick Douglass's statement: "Slaves were expected to sing as well as to work."

Keeping Power by Discrediting Black Power: Soft-Soap From the Supply Side

We have seen that the forces of the race-trait belief system manufactured the familiar political instruments of power that limited Negro freedoms: strict codes of racial etiquette, restrictive racial legislation, barriers against entry into places where commerce and education were taking place, and threats against blacks who crossed over the established circles of racial segregation. We have seen also that the race-trait expectation generated power in the form of the standard literature of racial defamation. Thus, for several centuries, the spoken and written word consistently impugned and disparaged the powers of the colored man to think for himself, to perform a task, to govern his life, or to work diligently for a self-selected goal.

Beginning in the latter half of the twentieth century, whites in very large numbers began to moderate the dogma of racial superiority. They loosened, and in many cases abandoned, the codes stipulating that membership in the white race was a necessary qualification for entry into certain jobs and other desirable places. Many of the traditional barriers and taboos that kept blacks laboring in segregated work forces and studying in segregated schools were removed. At the same time, the racial party line, by which the power of human language had been employed to discredit or slander the competence of black people, was greatly moderated or went underground.

But a new attack on the competence of black people took shape. Instead of validating their superior positions by asserting that they were superior people, whites now began to certify the superior positions they held by disparaging the use by black people of power to improve their own positions. Insistence on equal opportunity was, indeed, the legal right of the black man, but assertions by him of such political or economic power as was necessary to reach a position to compete on an equal footing were considered inappropriate and unwarranted, if not subversive to the economic and political system.

As a result, the use by blacks of pressures in the form of strict enforcement of antidiscrimination laws, pressure for withdrawal of government support for institutions that recreated racial segregation, the development of black political organizations in order to influence government, and other similar strategies came under intense verbal assault by whites. In public and private institutions, there was widespread dramatization of the injustices and harms inherent in virtually every strong measure advocated by black political and economic strategists. The use of various forms of nonviolent black power—the single most effective strategy in the history of the economic and political progress of the Negro race—was systematically maligned.

In the early 1980s, the disparagement of black power and self-help initiatives, as well as the deprecation of any use of government power to expand the choices and opportunities of blacks, took many forms. Once more, bogus rhetoric, sloganeering, and unsubstantiated accusations were the essential weapons of black pacification. When blacks proposed the use of nonviolent protest measures to press large corporations to hire or upgrade more blacks, the latter were charged with seeking a free ride and rejecting the American ethic of hard work and self-reliance. When blacks called for legislation that would open new economic doors and greater opportunities for racial integration, the proposal was disparaged by identifying it with the sins of a bloated government bureaucracy. Whenever blacks sought to use the leverage of government power to expand their educational choices, they usually received a stern lecture to the effect that by seeking special preferences they would only harm their self-image as well as their group reputation among whites. Advocates of black political organization and pressure were patronized as dupes of socialism and international racism. Lily-white political arrangements, well-defended against black influence, were held up as synonymous with such virtues as patriotism, loyalty, freedom, public safety, and traditional family values. Conversely, even the most traditional and legitimate forms of nonviolent black pressure were linked with publicly recognized evils such as disloyalty to the flag, economic decline, stirring up racial tensions, and crime in the streets. Campaign slogans used when blacks ran for public office published the contamination and decay that black mayors would bring to the cities: "If you love Philadelphia"; "Atlanta is too young to die"; "Don't let Birmingham become another Atlanta"; and, in Chicago, "Before it's too late."

The overleaf provides a historical sampling of some of the standard admonitions that have been used to persuade blacks to refrain from bringing political power to bear on their own behalf. Many of these slogans are so shallow, false, and patently manipulative as to insult the intelligence of black people. With few exceptions, they tend to be delivered in tones that are patronizing or contemptuous. Nevertheless, these slogans and warnings appear to have achieved considerable success in appeasing traditional black activists and undercutting the will of other blacks to adopt more vigorous strategies in dealing with the essential predicament of black powerlessness.

Black Power and Self-Inflicted Wounds

As was the case in the original defamation of black competence, the disparagement of black power was most disarming when the attack was spearheaded, or appeared to be spearheaded, by blacks. Prior to the civil rights movement of the late 1950s, too, a strong body of black opinion gave its stamp of approval to racial segregation and roundly criticized the use of black agitation and protest to remove it. As was true of the black speakers' bureaus of two generations ago, there is, today, no current shortage of gifted black intellectuals to lead the ideological attack on black political action. In recent years, particularly, a number of black economists and politicians have joined the assault on the use of pressures, protest, and legislation to draw more blacks into the economic and educational mainstream. Dire admonitions were posted for black people to see and obey: "Don't endanger the efforts of whites to provide voluntary integration of public schools." "Don't pursue racist policies of organizing black voters to elect blacks to political office." "Don't press business organizations to use race as a positive factor in assigning blacks to desirable jobs." "Don't band together to pressure the government to award franchises and government contracts to blacks." "Draw near to us in the workplace and in educational institutions, but not in relationships predicated on confrontation or power." Blacks, in large numbers, dismissed black pressure groups as extremists. Black mayors in small towns in the South scoffed at black political activists as a fringe on the left. Black businessmen assured other blacks that black political candidates do more harm than good. Just as influential blacks a century ago were often parties to the defamation of the character of black people, today there are similar groups of blacks who, today, are active agents in the disparagement of greater black influence. It is difficult to overestimate the debilitating effect of these groups on the validity of black grievances and, hence, on the legitimacy of corrective power.

RECIPE FOR INEQUALITY: A CENTURY OF PIOUS
POWER AND PARTICIPATION ARE AGAINST

Racial segregation is in your interests and you only harm yourself by agitating for mixing with whites. (1850-1964)

- "I am opposed to agitation to eliminate slavery because plantation life offers Negroes food, shelter, and the opportunity to become civilized." (circa 1850)

- "I am opposed to pressuring government officials to allow Negroes to leave agricultural work and become factory workers because it has been established that the noise of the factory tends to cause Negroes to doze off, daydream, and hurt themselves." (circa 1900)

- "I am opposed to your trying to pass laws eliminating voting restrictions because I believe Negroes need a period of apprenticeship before they can take full advantage of the rights of citizenship." (circa 1910)

- "I am opposed to opening up white colleges and universities to admission by Negroes because special industrial schools for training Negroes will protect their sense of self-esteem and prevent their being harmed by climbing the evolutionary ladder of progress too rapidly." (circa 1925)

- "I am against your running black candidates for political office because, if elected, they will be unable to deal with the white establishment on your behalf." (circa 1935)

- "I am against removing Jim Crow restrictions that prevent blacks from doing business in white neighborhoods because black communities afford black businessmen a place to flourish with little, if any, competition from whites." (circa 1935)

- "I am opposed to changing government mortgage insurance rules to permit Negroes to buy houses in white neighborhoods because that would cause a drastic drop in property values, which would cause Negroes to lose their entire investments." (circa 1946)

- "I am opposed to using court pressures to mix the races in schools and playgrounds because that would provoke whites, increase the ranks of the Ku Klux Klan, and harm the psyches of black children as a result of self-comparison with the white children with whom they will be associating." (circa 1950)

- "I am opposed to your pressing the government for careers as policemen, firemen, and government workers because this would cause Negroes to withdraw in large numbers from the most promising opportunities they have in nursing, domestic service, teaching, and in the ministry." (circa 1950)

Affirmative integration is against your interests and you hurt your people by seeking government policies that force it on whites. (1965-1980)

- "I am opposed to all forms of affirmative action because it is already proven that these pressures have halted the ongoing improvement in the lives of black people."

- "I am opposed to all federal programs and government meddling that cheapen dollars, making it impossible for minorities to pay their bills."

- "I am opposed to strong affirmative-action pressures to advance blacks into high teaching posts in major universities as that would create the impression among students and others that blacks don't have what it takes to compete in the intellectual world of whites."

- "I am opposed to blacks in large cities using political power to win government contracts for themselves and their friends because it teaches them that wealth can be produced without toil and hard work and propagates fantasy visions of free goods."

- "I am opposed to using the government fiscal powers to help blacks acquire ownership of capital because the economic future of blacks will be much more secure if they seek qualifications that will permit them to hold a steady job in large and reliable corporations."

- "I am opposed to all the civil rights activities of a strong federal government and instead I would restore states' rights so minorities will have more say and so their families and neighborhoods can flourish."

- "I am opposed to your organizing voter coalitions and playing power politics because that will only backfire against Negro candidates by causing white voter backlash, which will serve to elect conservatives opposed to your interests."

- "I am against Congressional Black Caucus pressures for stronger enforcement of EEOC rules because that would encourage the belief among Negroes that jobs are a gift from heaven rather than won through hard work and qualifications."

- "I am opposed to all liberal reforms favoring blacks because these rules hamper my ability to get rid of the bureaucratic red tape that has made wreckage of the lives of Negroes."

- "I am opposed to blacks running black candidates for mayor or the city council because their election could cause white businessmen to leave the center city and thus cause blacks to lose their jobs."

In the politics of race relations today, as well as 100 years ago, we may discern a standard rule of power. Powerful people invariably defend their own interests in the name of the interests of the people they seek to control. Those who wish to command obedience often do so most successfully by convincing the persons whose freedoms they wish to circumscribe that the orders they are asked to obey are intended to serve the best interests of those who are to be subject to them. Slavery in the United States was ideologically founded on this principle of benevolent authority. In the American South, Jim Crow, also, found its legitimacy in the notion that the white man knew what was best for the black man and that grateful black people should be content with, and even prefer, restrictions on their freedom. The modern corporate responsibility movement, too, is predicated on the well-publicized idea that blacks should be grateful that successful white businessmen are willing to stand guard over black progress, protect black people from economic failure, and, particularly, decide whether affirmative action, racial quotas, and similar pressures are or are not in the best interests of Negroes. Indeed, the so-called supply-side economic thesis has been made to order for blacks and whites who wish to preserve existing power relationships. Blacks, in many cases, urge other blacks to rally behind tax cuts for the wealthy. They rail against the welfare chiselers and loafers. They broadcast the virtues of markets unguarded against race discrimination. They praise the pretentious mythology of government grants to black entrepreneurial training. They rush to support evangelical commentators who characterize capitalism as an altruistic or charitable enterprise. They support the supposedly unique blessings that will flow toward blacks if Negro people will simply accept the wise policies of those with the economic and political power to set those policies.

Implicit in every public justification of unequal power holdings is the proposition—always supported by large numbers of blacks—that it is wrong, futile, and unpatriotic to use any form of power or pressure to overcome the handicaps of prior oppression. Here, one is reminded of the post-Civil War assurances of the great abolitionist William Lloyd Garrison, who, observing the end of slavery and the enactment of the Thirteenth Amendment, expressed his certainty that "without special help—black men and women would win their way to wealth, distinction, eminence, and official station." [16]

In the 1930s, redcaps in railway terminals worked for tips. No one offered them salaries until they were organized by a Negro man, Willard

WELL-PUBLICIZED BROMIDES THAT SELL FALSE OR INSINCERE REASONS WHY BLACKS SHOULD NOT PRESS WHITES FOR FURTHER GAINS

A political democracy protects protest but often undermines the desire to use it by calling it undemocratic or unpatriotic.

- "I am against pressures to integrate the armed forces because integration would lower morale among the troops and hinder the war effort."

- "I am against federal laws opening up public facilities to Negroes because I believe local governments should decide whether blacks and whites should eat together in public places."

- "I am opposed to lunch-counter sit-ins because they hurt the tourist trade and the city's bond rating."

- "I am opposed to lobbying to establish a holiday to honor Martin Luther King, Jr., because another day off from work would severely diminish American productivity."

- "I propose to eliminate poverty by cutting regulatory red tape so we will have a stronger economy that can afford to hire our less fortunate citizens."

- "I am opposed to blacks using political power to win government contracts and to press for more important positions in large corporations because these pressures hurt the productivity of the nation and its ability to compete with foreign interests."

- "I am opposed to blacks pressuring us to enact the Humphrey-Hawkins full employment bill because this fosters the impression abroad that Americans want to be cared for."

- "I am against overly strict enforcement of antidiscrimination laws because the problem is not too much race discrimination but too much government interference with free competition."

- "I am against government efforts to aid minority entrepreneurs because these efforts use valuable federal resources without doing anything to help those who are too poor, too weak, or too afraid to compete."

- "I am opposed to black civil rights groups trying to get court fines against whites who discriminate because that would be vindictive and we Americans believe that bygones should be bygones."

- "I am against the publication of instances of racial discrimination and injustice because that only interferes with our ongoing efforts to find better jobs for blacks and to improve race relations."

- "I am opposed to affirmative action and stronger enforcement of equal opportunity laws because that would slow our ability to build a revitalized system of free enterprise disciplined by the competitive forces of the marketplace."

- "I am opposed to protest and agitation by blacks because these activities afford the Soviet Union an opportunity to spread propaganda that our system does not work and is inferior to theirs."

- "I am opposed to Negro agitation and protest because black power is as wrong as white power and two wrongs don't make a right."

Townsend of the Transport Workers Union. No one offered the black housemaids of New York or Chicago a minimum wage until government commanded it. The end of racially segregated schools, all-white primaries, and race discrimination in credit and employment was never the natural outcome of an easy and automatic evolutionary process. In each case, these gains were the result of intense political pressures. In every instance, things got better because people—particularly black people—struggled to make them better. Yet, in the 1980s, large numbers of blacks continued to be among the strongest advocates of the proposition—refuted, it would seem, by 350 years of history—that if the economic and political marketplaces were only left to their own devices, conditions for blacks would get better by themselves.

Today, many blacks who view themselves as powerless to affect American economic or political policies praise the therapeutic marvels of the unchecked marketplace that denied them admittance for 300 years. Publicizing the altruistic plans of whites to use the proceeds of wealth, profits, and tax cuts to voluntarily invest in the economic endeavors of the Negro— a group demonstrably lacking in access to the powers necessary to compete on equal terms with whites—many blacks, it would seem, are once more leading other blacks down the path of continued powerlessness and persisting subordination to the will of others. Under such circumstances, it is regrettable that now, as frequently in the past, the badge of a black skin has sometimes become the mark of the pigeon. In the face of the near-terminal economic decline that beset many millions of Negroes in the late 1970s and early1980s, large numbers of black people have showed unusual determination to persuade their brothers to keep their noses in the trap.

Part Three

Banquets and Breadlines: The Racial Distribution of American Wealth

"If someone takes away your bread, he suppresses your freedom at the same time. But if someone seizes your freedom, rest assured, your bread is threatened."

—*Albert Camus*
Bread and Liberty

CHAPTER ELEVEN

Black and White Incomes: 350 Years to Equality

"You can't get away from arithmetic."

—The Great McGinty
Paramount Pictures
(1940)

UNDER THE TUTELAGE OF MILITANTS on the left, many black people in the United States have come to blame the free-enterprise system for racial inequality. In fact, the problem for blacks has not been free enterprise but closed enterprise. The marketplace that was to be free and open to all was, in fact, almost completely restricted in favor of entry by whites. Backed by strong racial traditions, skin-color taboos, and the peer pressures of established racial etiquette, a powerful economic and political consensus mounted by the white majority decided in advance when, where, and under what circumstances blacks would work, what kinds of jobs they would hold, and what wages they could receive. In the United States, there has never been an open competition for black labor, capital, entrepreneurship or executive talent. At no time in history, including the current period, have blacks received adequate protection from the vaunted "invisible hand" of free and open competition. We see then that blacks have never been hurt by free enterprise. They have, instead, been waiting for it.

The necessary effect of an economic cartel that displaces free competition and substitutes controlled markets is to shift income and wealth from one group to another. This has been true of almost every effort to close entry to markets dating from the early price fixers of Babylonia down to the labor union movement of modern times. The restrictive boycott mounted against blacks in the United States appeared to be no exception. Because of the long-standing restrictions on black participation and advancement in the economic affairs of the country, it is probable that whites were able to carry off somewhat more than their earned share of the national income and wealth. Later on, I shall offer proof of a direct causal connection between the income inequalities of blacks and the coercive forces of the codes of race discrimination. In the meantime, let us measure the extent of the income differences between races. How great is the income gap between blacks and whites? Relative to whites, are the incomes of blacks improving or declining? Are the normal competitive forces that tend to produce greater income for people who are improving their skills and education now working in favor of blacks? These are some of the questions we must answer if we are to reach a realistic assessment of the economic position and prospect of blacks in America today.

Income differences are by far the most effective means of assessing relative economic power of individuals or groups. For whenever income is transferred to another person, some form of economic power is working— either in the form of skills, hard work, ingenuity, persuasion, coercion, or proprietary advantage. Moreover, income is easily quantifiable, requiring no value judgments or subjective interpretations. Unlike other gauges of well-being, such as the place where one lives, the value of one's car, or size of one's home, income as a barometer of economic health is free from biases of folkways, group habits, and tastes. What is more, in this country, income has long been a traditional yardstick for success and achievement. For these reasons, I have adopted annual income figures as the most objective way to compare black and white economic power and well-being.

Before we proceed to make comparisons, an explanatory note is in order. Hereafter in the text, unless otherwise stated, all income figures for various types of families and individuals will be *median* figures, as opposed to average or *mean* figures. The median figure is derived by ranking all incomes from highest to lowest and then selecting the one that falls exactly halfway down the list. In other words, half the families in the country will have incomes higher than the median family income, and the other half will be lower. The average or mean, in contrast, is derived by adding all income and dividing this total by the number of families in the population one is trying to measure.

Economists generally have found median figures preferable to mean for most analytical purposes because they are less likely to be distorted by atypical instances within the population. For example, if one family among ten in a community had an annual income of $1 million and the other nine had incomes of $5,000 each, the mean or average income for the group would be $104,500 ($1,045,000 ÷ 10). However, the figure of $104,500 would not accurately reflect the well-being of the group as a whole. The median income, on the other hand, would divide these ten families into groups: one with five families, each earning $5,000, and the other with four families, each earning $5,000 and with one family earning $1 million. The median, then, would be exactly $5,000, a much more representative and accurate, although less-than-perfect, picture of the group's economic profile. The median figure best shows how the "middle man" or typical fellow is doing.[1]

We will compare black and white incomes generally, as well as certain categories of income and types of income receivers. By "income" I am referring to money or cash income, including wages, salaries, income from rental property, interest, dividends, unemployment compensation, and welfare payments, but excluding in-kind transfers such as food stamps, housing subsidies, and health benefits, as well as government expenditures in such broad areas as special education and manpower programs.[2]

The figures I use are drawn from the U.S. Bureau of the Census, which employs standardized statistical sampling techniques and reports the annual incomes of families and individuals, cross-tabulated by such factors as race, sex, age, region, education, occupation, and marital status. For Census purposes, a family is "a group of two of more persons related by blood, marriage, or adoption, residing in the same household." Individuals living alone—a growing segment of the population—as well as the increasing numbers of unmarried couples living together, are not classified as families.

Black Family Incomes Less Than Three-Fifths of Whites'

In 1981, the median annual income for white families was $23,517. The comparable figure for blacks was $13,267. In other words, the black median income was only 56 percent of the white median income. Stated another way, in 1981 the average black family was living, or trying to live, on an income of $56 for every $100 available to the average white family.[3]

Most other ethnic groups, excluding newly arrived Hispanics and Chicanos, have equaled or bettered the national median for whites. Specifically, families of Russian, Polish, Italian, and Irish descent have had median incomes greater than those of white families. Yet the income of blacks, most of whose ancestors have been in this country well over 100 years longer than all of these ethnic groups, has been consistently lower.

Family incomes in the United States were first measured in the 1940 Census, an inexact and tentative effort. The 1940 Census considered only

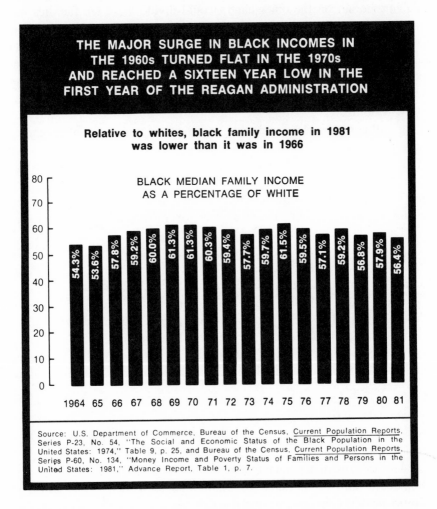

THE MAJOR SURGE IN BLACK INCOMES IN THE 1960s TURNED FLAT IN THE 1970s AND REACHED A SIXTEEN YEAR LOW IN THE FIRST YEAR OF THE REAGAN ADMINISTRATION

Relative to whites, black family income in 1981 was lower than it was in 1966

BLACK MEDIAN FAMILY INCOME AS A PERCENTAGE OF WHITE

Year	%
1964	54.3%
65	53.6%
66	57.8%
67	59.2%
68	60.0%
69	61.3%
70	61.3%
71	60.3%
72	59.4%
73	57.7%
74	59.7%
75	61.5%
76	59.5%
77	57.1%
78	59.2%
79	56.8%
80	57.9%
81	56.4%

Source: U.S. Department of Commerce, Bureau of the Census, Current Population Reports, Series P-23, No. 54, "The Social and Economic Status of the Black Population in the United States: 1974," Table 9, p. 25, and Bureau of the Census, Current Population Reports, Series P-60, No. 134, "Money Income and Poverty Status of Families and Persons in the United States: 1981," Advance Report, Table 1, p. 7.

wage and salary income, which allows us to make only general comparisons with later income data. This qualification aside, the differences between the races were staggering. According to the 1940 Census, white families had a median income of about $1,325; the nonwhite median, composed primarily of blacks, was about $490, or only 37 percent of the average white family's income.[4] In stark terms these figures reveal the degraded status of Negroes in America prior to 1940.

After World War II, the first official estimate of national median income by race took into account a broader range of income sources. In 1947, the national median income of white families was about $3,200. Although the quality of jobs held by blacks was higher than usual as a result of wartime labor shortages, the 1947 median for nonwhites, still mostly blacks, was only $1,600, or 50 percent of the white figure. By 1950, the postwar recession had abated and blacks had made some gains; median earnings of nonwhites grew to 54 percent of the white median. Throughout the 1950s, black family incomes fluctuated in the general vicinity of half that of whites. In 1958, a minor recession, which characteristically hurts blacks more than whites, dropped nonwhite income within a single year from 54 percent to 51 percent of white income.

When President Eisenhower left office in January 1961, nonwhite median incomes stood at 53 percent of the white figure. During the three years of the Kennedy administration, blacks made no significant gains on whites. Although national awareness of the problem of poverty was on the increase, Congress enacted no important social legislation until the 1960s. In short, nonwhite incomes relative to white incomes remained unchanged during the Truman, Eisenhower, and Kennedy administrations: 53 percent in 1951, 53 percent in 1963.[5]

In 1964, the U.S. Bureau of the Census began annual publication of income figures for blacks as distinct from nonwhites in general. In that first year of Lyndon Johnson's presidency, black incomes were still running only 54 percent of white incomes, but blacks began to advance immediately thereafter. They not only improved their absolute economic position, for the first time since World War II, but also began to narrow the income gap. Over the next five years—1964 to 1969—the median black family income moved 7 percentage points closer to the median for whites, reaching 61 percent in 1969, the narrowest the gap has been to date.[6]

No one knows exactly why black incomes surged during this five-year period. Possible factors were the generally favorable labor market, the fact that fewer young blacks were leaving school, increasing union membership among blacks, and a lessening of racial prejudice. Black income gains were also undoubtedly affected by certain programs designed to strengthen the bargaining power of blacks generally. These included federal support of minority economic self-help programs, voter-protection legislation, and intensive federal support of rural and inner-city community-action activities.

This period also brought comprehensive fair employment legislation and the beginning of a whole set of executive orders imposing federal affirmative-action employment requirements on major employers. It is probable, too, that civil disturbances contributed to black economic progress during these years, as freedom marches, lunch-counter sit-ins, and burnings and

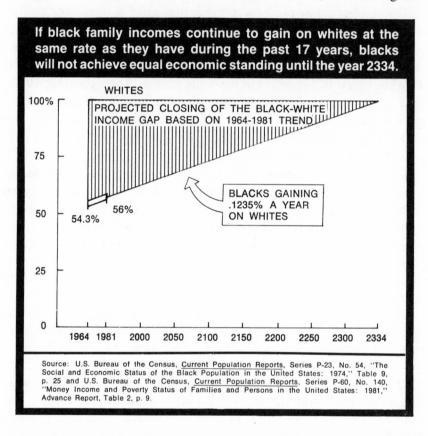

If black family incomes continue to gain on whites at the same rate as they have during the past 17 years, blacks will not achieve equal economic standing until the year 2334.

WHITES

PROJECTED CLOSING OF THE BLACK-WHITE INCOME GAP BASED ON 1964-1981 TREND

BLACKS GAINING .1235% A YEAR ON WHITES

54.3%   56%

1964 1981   2000   2050   2100   2150   2200   2250   2300   2334

Source: U.S. Bureau of the Census, Current Population Reports, Series P-23, No. 54, "The Social and Economic Status of the Black Population in the United States: 1974," Table 9, p. 25 and U.S. Bureau of the Census, Current Population Reports, Series P-60, No. 140, "Money Income and Poverty Status of Families and Persons in the United States: 1981," Advance Report, Table 2, p. 9.

lootings in thirty or more urban ghettos during the late 1960s undoubtedly put pressure on major institutions to open job markets that had formerly been closed to blacks.

Whatever the cause of this increase in relative black incomes, the trend peaked in 1969 and then turned downward. Commentators who supported the noninterventionist racial policies of the Nixon administration—perhaps somewhat embarrassed that blacks should start to lose ground right after President Nixon's election—suggested that this decline was due to a faltering economy. This, however, does not appear to have been the case. From

1970 through 1973, the gross national product rose 33 percent, from $982 billion to $1,306 billion, yet each year during the period black family income relative to white declined.

The erosion of the relative black position continues to the present time. Census figures show that the black median income in 1981 was 56 percent of the white median, or approximately where it stood fifteen years earlier in 1966. Thus, *in terms of relative family income, blacks have made no progress since 1966.*

Long-term projections give no grounds for optimism. Even under the assumption most favorable to blacks, a progressive straight-line continuation of the minuscule gains made between 1964 and 1981 would show black family incomes not catching up with those of whites until the year 2334. In more realistic terms, the negligible increases in black family income over the past seventeen years, largely offset by the net loss over the past ten years, strongly suggest that blacks will not catch up with whites, or even markedly improve their position relative to whites, without the intercession of some radical new force to alter economic power in favor of black people.[7]

The Black-White Dollar Gap

Percentages tell only part of the story. People pay for groceries and medicine with dollars, not percentages. Let us focus therefore on a comparison of black and white *actual* dollar income.

One way to assess this difference is to compare the *aggregate national income* of blacks and whites, adjusting for the relative size of the populations. In 1979, the black population in the United States received a dollar income of $114 billion, or 7.2 percent of the total national dollar income of about $1.6 trillion. In that year, blacks constituted approximately 11.5 percent of the population. Had blacks received their proportionate share of the total, their aggregate income would have been 11.5 percent of the total, or $181 billion instead of the $114 billion they actually received. Hence, for 1979, the aggregate black-white income gap or shortfall may be calculated at about $67 billion. In absolute dollar terms, blacks have been losing ground steadily. Inflation exaggerates the loss, yet nineteen years earlier, in 1960, the total dollar gap was only about $17 billion.[8]

In 1964, black family median income was a meager $3,700. By 1979, this sum had increased by 213 percent to $11,600. During the same period, white family income increased from $6,800 to $20,500, a slightly smaller improvement of 199 percent. If the influence of inflation is subtracted, these gains shrink to 34 percent for blacks and 28 percent for whites. In either case, on the basis of *percentage* increase, blacks showed more progress than whites over this fifteen-year period.[9]

To understand the significance of the figures, these gains must be assessed against their relative starting points. Consider an analogy. Assume

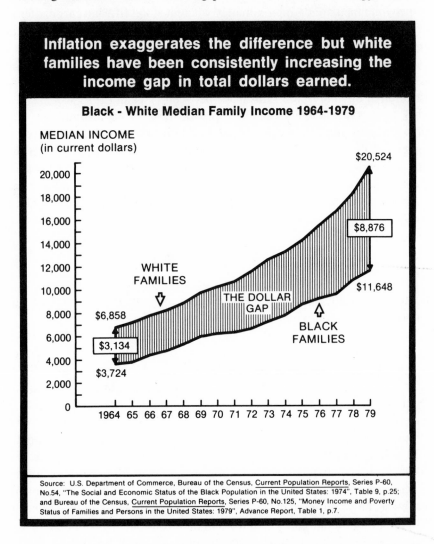

Inflation exaggerates the difference but white families have been consistently increasing the income gap in total dollars earned.

Black - White Median Family Income 1964-1979

MEDIAN INCOME
(in current dollars)

Source: U.S. Department of Commerce, Bureau of the Census, Current Population Reports, Series P-60, No.54, "The Social and Economic Status of the Black Population in the United States: 1974", Table 9, p.25; and Bureau of the Census, Current Population Reports, Series P-60, No.125, "Money Income and Poverty Status of Families and Persons in the United States: 1979", Advance Report, Table 1, p.7.

that one year ago I received an allowance of one-half pound of meat per week. Recently, my allowance was doubled, or increased by 100 percent. This means that I am presently receiving one pound of meat per week, a huge percentage improvement. But suppose someone else received two pounds of meat per week last year and his ration was also increased by 100 percent. This means that today he is receiving four pounds a week compared with my one pound. My ration increased by one-half pound while his increased by two pounds, placing him even further ahead of me than before— *yet the percentage increase was the same* for both of us.[10]

This hypothetical situation fairly represents the relative progress of black and white incomes. Since blacks started with a very low median dollar income, their large percentage increases do not constitute evidence of emerging equality, especially since whites made much greater dollar gains during the same period. Over these fifteen years, the median black income gain was $7,924 while the median white income gain was $13,666. Based on the 1964 to 1979 experience, this means that *the family income gap between blacks and whites is actually increasing at the rate of about $380 per year.*[11]

If blacks are to close the income gap, their incomes must increase in real dollar amounts at least as fast as those of whites. In that event, black income as a percentage of white income would necessarily increase, even though the absolute dollar gap would remain the same. In time, near parity would be achieved as the constant dollar gap became an even smaller percentage of a much larger dollar figure. But this has not occurred. In the fifteen years between 1964 and 1979, the dollar gap, unadjusted for inflation, has grown from $3,000 to $8,875. Adjusting for inflation to show the actual buying power of those dollars reveals that the gap has grown only slightly, from $7,730 to $8,875. Whites, in short, have shown no signs of relinquishing their commanding lead. In a decade and a half of economic depression and expansion, civil unrest and civil peace, high inflation, and civil rights legislation, the dollar income gap between blacks and whites has expanded, not narrowed.

The Exaggerated Effect of Female-Headed Families

The overall black-white family income gap may be fully understood only in connection with the influence of female-headed families. In 1970, 31 percent of black families had a female head of household, compared with only 9 percent of white families. By 1979, the figure for blacks had increased to slightly over 40 percent, while for whites there was only a small increase, to 11.5 percent. Thus, in 1979, black families were about three and one-half times more likely to be headed by a woman than white families. This female-head-of-household statistic may be the single most important indicator of the serious state of the black economic condition. Since the median income for women in the United States is only 60 percent of that for men among full-time workers, the median income figure for all black families as a whole is drastically lowered by the number of black female-headed families. Specifically, while the median income for a family headed by a white female was $11,464 in 1979, the black female head of household had a median income of only $6,907. Families headed by black women had incomes only 60.2 percent of those of white female-headed families and only 33.7 percent of the incomes of all white families.[12]

But the fact that black female single-adult families are a much larger share of all black families than their white counterparts can account for less than half of the black median family income gap. In other words, if all female-headed families, black and white, were left out of the calculations, and if it were assumed that income figures for each type of family remained the same, black median family income would become at most 77 percent of the white figure. Although this difference in family composition explains a considerable portion of the difference in income, a significant 53 percent of the income gap still remains unexplained.[13]

The performance of black families headed by a male, with incomes close to 80 percent of whites in 1979, is often cited to show how much the female-headed black family acts as a drag on black income generally. The great importance of this factor should not be underestimated. But much of the strong performance of black male-headed families is due to the fact that there are more black married-couple families with both spouses working and producing income, 59 percent of blacks versus 48 percent of whites. When we consider black husband-wife families where the husband is the sole provider, their comparative family income plummets to only 64 percent of the income of their white counterparts.[14]

Black and White Age Differences

Two other considerations—age and regional differences—have often been cited to explain the black-white income gap. While these factors have some effect on comparative income differences, the effects are not significant.

The matter of age is first. In any population age bracket, the median age for blacks is lower than that for whites. Not surprisingly, then, in 1978 just over 9 percent of black heads of households were under 25 years of age, as compared with only 6.4 percent of white family heads. Since, as a rule, at all age brackets through middle age, younger people earn less than older people, it is reasonable to expect black heads of households to earn lower median incomes simply because, on average, they are younger. On closer examination, however, this explanation, however simple and appealing, proves to be false. Let us see if black incomes would rise significantly if, as a group, they were not younger than whites, and moreover, if in all age categories within the population the percentage of blacks equaled the percentage of whites. If we recompute median black family income accordingly (i.e., on the assumption that black family heads have an age distribution identical to that of whites), based on 1978 figures, we find that black median family income figures would increase by only $610 a year. Adjusting the age distribution of the black population to equal that of the white population only improves the gap by 3.3 percentage points. One reason for the fact that age differences do not explain much of the black-white family income gap is that a larger percentage of black families than of white families are headed by persons in the prime earning years, 25 to 54. This would tend to offset the effect of younger black heads of household. The critical point to observe is that at all age brackets, blacks earn much less than whites. Depending on the age group, black incomes range from 44 percent to 66 percent of the earnings of whites. Thus, even for the age group where blacks make the best showing, those 65 years and over, black incomes are still 35 percent lower than comparable white incomes. This refutes the common misconception that lower black earnings are due to the lower average age of blacks.[15]

The argument that blacks earn less because as a group they are younger than whites, and young people earn less than older people, ignores the fact that what makes the black population as a whole younger than whites is not just the large number of young black adults but the very large group of black children and teenagers. On the whole, these groups are too young to be wage earners. The median age of blacks and whites in the wage-earning years is thus much closer than for the black and white populations as a whole.

Distortions Caused by Where Blacks Live

It is commonly said that the black-white income gap has been overstated because the figures fail to take geographical differentials into account. Families in the South are generally about 15 percent more likely to be poor than families in the North and West. Blacks still live in the South in disproportionately large numbers; about 51 percent of all black families are southern, as compared with 31 percent of all white families. Because of regional differences alone, blacks ought to be significantly poorer than whites. The problem with this argument lies in the fact that the geographical factor alone only accounts for a small portion of the racial income gap. Even if the figures are adjusted to eliminate the influence of geographical differences, black median income would improve by only $521 a year, raising the 1979 black-white income share from 56.8 to 59.3 percent. Obviously, then, geographical distribution is not a great factor in the overall black-white income gap.[16]

Another way to explore the question is to greatly exaggerate actual regional distribution by race and observe what happens to income. Assume that 100 percent of all blacks live in the South, the area where earnings are lower, and earn what southern blacks actually earned in 1979. On those assumptions, black median income in 1979 as a percentage of white would fall from about 57 percent to only 52.6 percent. This shows that the regional concentration of blacks in the South is not a significant factor in explaining the overall black-white income gap. Similarly, if 100 percent of blacks lived in the region where black incomes were the highest, the North Central where their median income was $13,128, the figure would improve from 57 percent to only 64 percent. Again, this shows that even when we select the most favorable regional distribution, the income shortfall would still be 36 percent. The conclusion to be reached is that although geography contributes to income inequality, it does not do so in a decisive way. Even if all southern blacks moved to the North and earned what northern blacks earned, a 36 percent differential would still exist.[17]

In-Kind Payments and Off-the-Books Income

Other key factors influencing the black-white family income gap relate to the way in which the Census Bureau defines and measures income. Unfortunately, it is very difficult to assess certain of these factors quantitatively. First, as mentioned earlier, the Census Bureau records only *cash income*. While this may have been a reasonable procedure a generation ago, over the past two decades government assistance to the poor in the form of noncash benefits or *in-kind* transfers—such as food stamps, housing subsidies, health care aid, job training assistance, and the like—has increased tremendously. These noncash transfers often produce many of the benefits of cash, namely, a better standard of living. Therefore, it is properly argued that excluding these in-kind benefits from tabulations of family and personal income artificially overstates the black-white income gap, inasmuch as they accrue more often to the poor and hence to blacks. The question, of course, is whether or not the black-white income gap would be significantly narrower if these noncash benefits were included in family and personal income calculations.

Unfortunately, it is not possible to calculate the extra value accruing to blacks because of these government in-kind benefits. Even if the estimated annual gross value of such benefits were $15 billion, and if blacks, who comprise 30 percent of the total poor in the nation, claimed 30 percent, or $4.5 billion, the black-white median income gap would not be narrowed substantially. This sum of $4.5 billion is only 4 percent of all black income received in 1979. Moreover, those who receive nonmoney income are blacks and whites whose incomes are well below the national median; raising their income by inclusion of in-kind benefits does not affect the median of either group.[18]

A further question is what the effect is on the income gap of unreported or "off-the-books" income. To avoid income tax, Social Security tax, and loss of welfare benefits, many families seriously underreport some types of income and fail to report others. In many businesses, such as restaurants, shops, casinos, and other individually owned enterprises where receipts tend to be in cash, an estimated $250 billion a year is off the books. In 1978, the Census Bureau compiled independent income estimates made by various government agencies including the Bureau of Economic Analysis, the Social Security Administration, and the Veteran's Administration. These estimates concluded that half the underreported income in this country was earned through interest and dividends, while public-assistance income was shown to comprise only 2.3 percent of all unreported income. As we will show in Chapter Fourteen, interest and dividend income flows almost exclusively to whites. The massive tax evasion in off-the-books income is thus likely to involve whites predominantly since whites receive all but a small part of the types of income that are traditionally hidden from the government.

Indeed, there is every reason to believe that if all income in this country were reported to the Census, the black-white income gap would, in fact, expand.[19]

Let us now briefly review the effects of the various statistical factors described above. When the major distorting factors are taken into account, the family income gap may be subject to qualifying adjustments upward or downward, but never adjusted more than 10 percent. No calculable adjustments, however, contradict the basic conclusion that massive and persisting family income differences do exist. Despite whatever computational biases there may be, one may assume that differentials have been fairly consistent over the past ten years (1969 to 1979), and that during this period there was a distinct downward trend of black incomes as a percentage of white.

Income Earned Through Work: Who and How Much

The black-white family income gap must be viewed in terms of how well blacks are doing in the "nonassisted" or "market" economy. In a market economy, income from salary, wages, interest, and dividends is the norm, whereas income from public assistance is a measure of the extent to which the free marketplace is failing to provide for a part of the population. For this reason, it is important to examine the income relationship between black and white families, without taking into account what the government provides to "take up the slack." The objective is to obtain a picture of the income gap that measures the abilities of families to get along in the economic system, to earn money, and even to earn excess income to be saved and invested for further earnings. The moment we do this, we find that, in fact, the gap between blacks and whites in the nonassisted or market economy is much wider than the traditionally published 40 percent shortfall in black family income.

To begin to understand how the free market has operated to exclude or ignore blacks, we must first obliterate the myth that blacks subsist principally on government assistance. In 1979, slightly over 81 percent of black families had incomes from wages and salaries, a figure very close to the 83.8 percent for whites. True, blacks earn less than whites for the work they do, but in any given year the percentage of earned black income is just about the same as for whites. In fact, while whites derived 75 percent of their total income from wages and salaries, blacks derived *more*—80 percent—from this source.

The standard stereotype is therefore directly the opposite of the truth. *Black earnings from wages and salaries are a higher percentage of their total income than white earnings from wages and salaries.*[20] Yet, the majority of whites persist in their beliefs that black people are the drones in American society.

Now let us consider how blacks and whites compare in terms of *unearned* income, particularly in the area of public assistance. Blacks receive proportionately much more of their income from public assistance than do whites. In 1979, 4.1 percent of all black family income came from public welfare sources, as compared with only 0.4 percent of all white family income. On the other hand, the point must be made that virtually none of the other traditional sources of unearned income commonly available to whites as full participants in the American economic system is available to blacks.

The significant fact is that whites derive about *five times* as much of their income from private property income (dividends, interest, rentals, etc.) as do blacks. In 1979, blacks received about $1.2 billion from private property

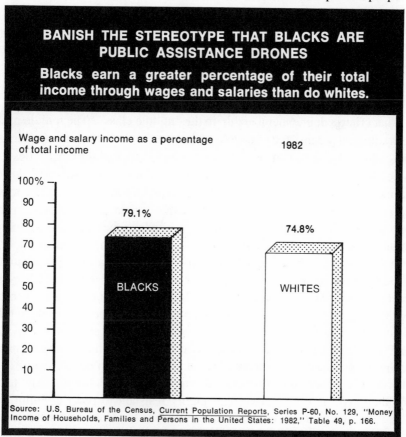

BANISH THE STEREOTYPE THAT BLACKS ARE PUBLIC ASSISTANCE DRONES

Blacks earn a greater percentage of their total income through wages and salaries than do whites.

Wage and salary income as a percentage of total income

1982

79.1%

74.8%

BLACKS

WHITES

Source: U.S. Bureau of the Census, Current Population Reports, Series P-60, No. 129, "Money Income of Households, Families and Persons in the United States: 1982," Table 49, p. 166.

or investment income. Whites, however, received a little over $87 billion —over 6 percent of their total income.[21]

The Growth of the Black Middle Class

Up to this point, we have regarded income differences from the standpoint of the *entire* population. Let us now examine various specific income groups. Are some groups of blacks doing better or holding their own better than blacks as a whole? What percentage of blacks earn at subpoverty levels between $2,000 and $4,000 a year? What percentage earn $25,000 or more? Are these groups growing or shrinking? Within the entire black population, do we find evidence of intragroup mobility? In terms of dollar earnings, are black people moving more in one direction than another? The group trends help us to understand the overall national trend and, in some cases, may point to what lies ahead.

First, let us examine the comparative percentages of whites and blacks who hold middle-class status. To know what is happening to blacks as measured by middle-class yardsticks is very important. If blacks were to reach the point where they held middle-class status in the same percentages as whites, a great leap toward racial equality would be achieved.

What criteria define membership in the "middle class"? The middle class has traditionally consisted of people with strong family attachments, people who value education and participate actively in community activities. Is home ownership, a savings account, a white-collar job, or a particular dollar income the determining factor, or is it a combination of all these factors? We certainly can't determine who is in the middle class and who isn't simply by polling people for their opinions of where they stand in the status hierarchy, for Americans are somewhat notorious for their often comically distorted class perceptions. The black pullman porter earning $72 a month in 1925 used to think of himself as part of the American upper middle class because he owned one share of General Motors and was making an income near the top of the black pay scale pyramid. Nelson Rockefeller once told an audience that the tax burden falls "on the average person like you and me." A decidedly upper-class wag once commented that a middle-class person is someone who still eats his salad off his main dinner plate. It is difficult to see how economists could improve on this definition. The term "middle class" is a subjective one, highly resistant to precise definition.

In 1979, the median income for all families in the United States, regardless of race, was $19,684. Rounding this, we can take the figure of $20,000 as a reasonably accurate signpost of middle-class status at the beginning of the current decade.

In 1979, the Census Bureau reported that about 27 percent of black families have incomes of $20,000 or better. This is clearly the brightest news so far reported in this chapter, for it seems that a full quarter of all black families have made it to the middle class. On the other hand, in the same year, 52 percent of white families had incomes of $20,000 or better.

By this measure, whites were twice as likely to be in the middle class as blacks. Clearly, the black-white inequality in holdings of middle-class status is very great.[22]

But, the reader might ask, "Why ignore the 'lower middle class' by using the median figure as the lower limit of middle-class status?" Does the pic-

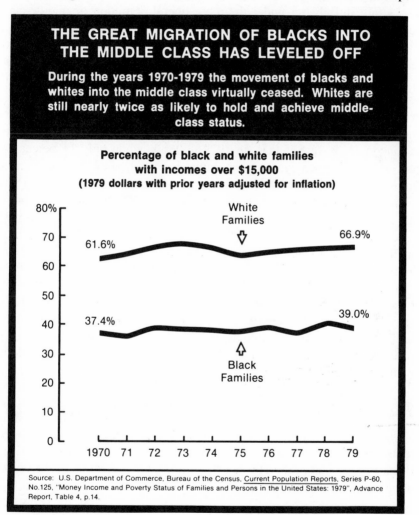

THE GREAT MIGRATION OF BLACKS INTO THE MIDDLE CLASS HAS LEVELED OFF

During the years 1970-1979 the movement of blacks and whites into the middle class virtually ceased. Whites are still nearly twice as likely to hold and achieve middle-class status.

Percentage of black and white families with incomes over $15,000
(1979 dollars with prior years adjusted for inflation)

White Families

61.6% → 66.9%

37.4% → 39.0%

Black Families

1970 71 72 73 74 75 76 77 78 79

Source: U.S. Department of Commerce, Bureau of the Census, Current Population Reports, Series P-60, No.125, "Money Income and Poverty Status of Families and Persons in the United States: 1979", Advance Report, Table 4, p.14.

ture change drastically if we include the "marginally middle class" or those who have almost "made it"? Even if we lower the dividing line, we find that the black-white middle-class disparity remains virtually unchanged. If we drop the figure to $15,000 and look at the comparative percentages of families with incomes greater than $15,000, we find that 12 percent of black families had incomes between $15,000 and $19,999. This means that 39 percent of black families had incomes of $15,000 or better. But 15 percent of white families had incomes of $15,000 to $19,999, putting 67 percent of white families above the $15,000 line. In other words, relative to whites, blacks fare little better under the more liberal definition of middle-class status. Whites are still almost twice as often "middle class or better."

As great as this gap is, the important point is, of course, that blacks have been moving rapidly into the middle-class range. The trends suggest, however, that even over the long term it is unlikely that they will catch up with whites. Using the lower definition of middle class (which is most favorable to advocates of the thesis that blacks are making very rapid progress), we find that in 1955, more than two decades ago, 36 percent of white families had incomes above $15,000 (in 1979 dollars), while only 11 percent of nonwhite families enjoyed similar status. By 1960, nonwhites were up to almost 20 percent, but whites were outpacing them at 46 percent. This trend continued through the 1960s and the first half of the 1970s. All in all, in the past twenty-four years an additional 31 percent of white families (from 36 percent in 1955 to 67 percent in 1979) have moved into the lower middle, middle, and upper classes, as compared with only 28 percent of nonwhites (from 11 percent in 1955 to 39 percent in 1979).[23]

During the middle and late 1960s, black progress into the middle class (those with incomes $15,000 and above) was so rapid that it appeared that parity might be achieved by the end of the century. But since 1970, black families have been moving into the middle class more slowly (37.4 percent in 1970 versus 39 percent in 1979). The prospects for reaching middle-income equality with whites now appear to be quite dim.

The Myth That the Majority of Blacks Are Middle Class

Writing in 1973, Ben Wattenberg and Richard Scammon celebrated the "robust and growing black middle class." Their widely discussed article, "Black Progress and Liberal Rhetoric," arrested the attention of the reader with a powerful and widely quoted opening paragraph:

"A remarkable development has taken place in America over the last dozen years: For the first time in the history of the republic, truly large and growing numbers of American blacks have been moving into the middle class, so that by now these numbers can reasonably be said to add up to a majority of black Americans."[24]

This study has profoundly influenced government policy and public attitudes toward the economic progress of blacks. The study provided scholarly confirmation of the thesis that further government intervention in the economy on behalf of blacks was no longer required. In light of what is known today, the Scammon-Wattenberg conclusions must be considered inaccurate. But very important, too, is the fact that at the time they were written, they were not correct.

The basic flaw in the reasoning of this study lies in the definition of middle class. Wattenberg and Scammon defined "middle class" as annual family income, outside the South, to be in excess of $8,000. Even in 1971, this was much too low. In fact, at that time, the Bureau of Labor Statistics defined $7,200 as the *lower* standard budget for a family of four. The Bureau wrote that $7,200 represents a "minimum of adequacy" and does "not conform in certain respects to prevailing customs and buying practices"—that is, to the collective judgments of these families concerning what is necessary for a satisfactory standard of living.[25]

Viewing the incomes of "working class" families from that historical perspective, the incongruence of the Scammon-Wattenberg definition becomes clear. In 1971, auto workers nationwide were averaging from $16,000 to $20,000, and steelworkers were making over $16,000. It was indeed correct that half the black population outside the South was earning $8,000 a year in 1971, but this in no way justified the conclusion that half of the black population was, at the time, middle class. In fact, in 1971, 72 percent of all black families in the United States earned below the national median income. Yet, the totally false idea that a majority of blacks have made it into the middle class is deeply rooted in the minds of tens of thousands of politicians and others who make public policy and shape public opinion. Possibly more than any other factor, the Scammon-Wattenberg thesis has undermined the legitimacy of affirmative measures to deal with black inequality.

Statistical Legerdemain: Equality Among Young Married Blacks in the North

The progress of certain successful black groups has been cited as a statistically significant harbinger of general black progress. Back in 1970, Daniel P. Moynihan, then counselor to President Nixon, studied the economic performance of young black married families living outside the South. His contention was that the best indicator of black progress would be this group, young and relatively free from the effects of past discrimination. In that same year, the Census Bureau reported that among families outside the

South in which both husband and wife were present and in which the head of household was *under 35 years of age,* incomes of blacks and whites were "more or less equal." [26]

This dramatic statement left the civil rights groups gasping for breath. Commenting on this finding a year later, Senator Moynihan wrote:

> "Now this surely is an event: young couples from an oppressed minority starting their lives as full equals, in income terms at least, of their contemporaries in the majority group. . . .

> "This is not the end of it. In young families outside the South, where both husband and wife worked, black incomes were higher than white." [27]

Given the indisputable government figures I have presented so far, showing black incomes running almost without exception 40 percent behind whites, even the most naive observer would immediately be suspicious of the meaning and implications of the claim that young black couples were starting off life as the equals of whites.

The basic fallacy in the young-black-and-white-couples-starting-off-equal thesis lies in a fundamental misuse of statistical method. The figures cited purport to support a conclusion about a large population group when, in fact, they relate to a very small part of this population group. The black group in question—young married-couple families living outside the South—is so small in relationship to the total black population that it cannot cogently speak to the greater question of overall progress of blacks. In 1970, the group of husband-and-wife families outside the South in which the head of household was under 35 years of age comprised only *10 percent* of all black families and only 17 percent of all white families in the United States. [28]

We must be wary of the significance to the overall black population of an event embracing only 10 percent or less of the black population. In addition, the exclusion of blacks in the South—where, in 1970, 52 percent of all black families resided and earned only 57 percent of what whites earned—seriously compromises the meaningfulness of the statistics. The comparison also screens out the intractable problem of families with a female head of household—36 percent of all black families in 1970, 40 percent in 1979. Missing, too, are data about young black males in the North who either are not married or have broken marriages. The comparative black-white income gap is not known, but the huge dimensions of the gap are generally suggested by the very high unemployment rate—upwards to 50 percent—prevailing for young, single black males.

BLACK AND WHITE INCOMES

In short, by careful gerrymandering of statistical categories, one may discover 10 percent good news. The news has been broadcast widely and has now been accepted by many as strong evidence of an overall trend toward equality. The remaining 90 percent of blacks who are doing badly are either dismissed as insignificant or are ignored. This thesis of black-white equality somewhat resembles the effort of the statistician who goes to Wall Street and finds 100 business school-trained blacks earning the "national white mean" and on that basis proclaims that the nation is on the threshold of achieving racial equality.

There is another serious fallacy inherent in the thesis that young black and white couples are starting off equal. Not only are the family comparisons based on very small samples, but the samples are not matched; that is, the *composition* of the black and white groups compared is different enough to make comparisons invalid. It is a basic rule of statistical comparison that no valid generalizations can be derived from a comparison of two groups unless the groups are reasonably comparable internally. For example, suppose I were to announce that black families in the relatively affluent New York City suburb of New Rochelle earned 30 percent above the national white median or, say, 40 percent above the white median in the poor rural state of West Virginia. What does such a claim mean about the relative positions of blacks and whites in America? Virtually nothing, for the social and economic compositions of the groups being compared are so different that they render absolutely meaningless any generalizations from this information.

How does this conclusion apply to the young-black-couples thesis? The important question is not whether the two groups—black and white husband-wife families living in the North with the head of household under 35—have equal incomes, but whether they are similar enough in terms of intellectual, social, and economic variables to be considered statistically comparable. It is certainly obvious that these two groups have important characteristics in common and appear superficially to be "peer groups": Both are married, both are young, and both live outside the South. Less clear, but equally true, is the fact that they vary greatly in other important characteristics.

Chief among these differences are the characteristics of the average female in each group. The mean earnings of married black women in the Moynihan group were, in 1970, actually 130 percent of the corresponding figure for white wives. A number of factors help to explain this rather surprising statistic. When they do work, married white women work less intensively than married black women—that is, they have more part-time employment. As a result, the total income of the group is lower. White women, especially those who are highly educated, tend more often to be casual or part-time workers, whereas married black women at all family income levels tend more often to be intensive workers. Thus, 52 percent of the black wives who worked in Moynihan's group were year-round workers, compared with only 36 percent of the white wives. How comparable, then, are these two groups in terms of economic well-being when black wives must do significantly more work to achieve this parity.[29]

There is also very strong evidence that the incomes of the white group are reduced significantly because white husbands with working wives tend to be relatively low earners: The earnings difference between black men with working wives and those with nonworking wives tends to be slight. It appears, then, that the young white male whose wife works is likely to be a "poorer provider" than his white peers whose wives do not work. It is therefore quite probable that in the white community a "working wife" is more often a signal of the husband's weakness as a provider than in a black community, where working wives traditionally have been, and still are, a neutral statement about the economic strength of the husband. To test this hypothesis, let us look at the relative performance of husband-wife families with and without working wives and also at the performance of the husbands themselves when their wives are working and when they are not.

In husband-and-wife families living in the North and West, and with the household head under 35, we find that the median income of black families with two spouses working was 55 percent higher than in black families with only the husband working. In contrast, working wives increased the median income of white families by only 13 percent.[30]

What do these figures tell us? Let us recall that in 1970 the median income for black husbands whose wives did *not* work was 76 percent of that of white husbands. But in families where the wives worked, the mean income of the black husbands leapt to 90 percent of the mean income for white husbands—a dramatic difference. In addition, this difference almost entirely results from different levels of performance on the part of white husbands, depending on whether or not their wives work. In 1970, the mean income of black men outside the South and under 35 years of age with working wives was only $126 lower than the median income of black men with nonworking wives, or $6,978 versus $7,104. For whites, however, the mean income of white men with working wives was substantially below the median income of white men with nonworking wives, or $7,777 versus $9,373—a difference of $1,596. *In other words, as a breadwinner, the married black male in the North and West performed equally as well whether his wife worked or not.* The same emphatically cannot be said of the young white husband.[31]

These figures substantiate the conclusion that the white man with a working wife tends to be a relatively poorer provider than other white husbands.

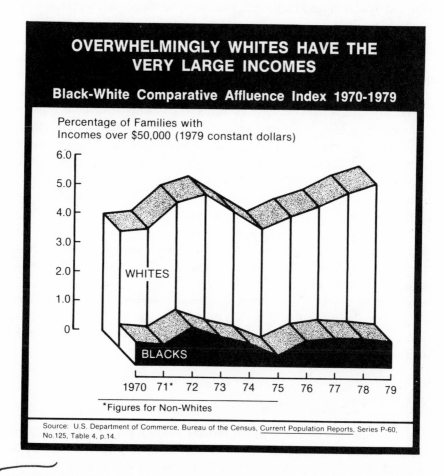

OVERWHELMINGLY WHITES HAVE THE VERY LARGE INCOMES

Black-White Comparative Affluence Index 1970-1979

Percentage of Families with
Incomes over $50,000 (1979 constant dollars)

WHITES

BLACKS

1970 71* 72 73 74 75 76 77 78 79

*Figures for Non-Whites

Source: U.S. Department of Commerce, Bureau of the Census, Current Population Reports, Series P-60, No.125, Table 4, p.14.

If a white husband is successful, there is no reason for his wife to work, and she probably will not. Indeed, successful white males have traditionally discouraged their wives from working except as part-time volunteers or in other capacities that similarly signal the fact that the wife's employment is a matter of preference rather than a reflection on the husband's earning power. But among black people, a working wife is an event that often signals family economic strength; it is not an intimation of economic failure.

These considerations all lead to the conclusion that claims about the income parity of young black and white couples do not refer to comparable families. Select groups of economically strong blacks are being compared with groups of economically weaker whites. The family comparisons thus essentially boil down to a declaration that black women, by working more often and by earning at a higher rate than white women, add more than white women to family earnings, and that white men whose wives work tend to be relatively poor earners.

There is one other significant factor in the demographics of young whites and blacks in the North that tends to make the two groups appear more equal than they actually are. We are all aware that place of residence is a factor that greatly affects income, for it is well known that urban incomes are, as a whole, far in excess of rural incomes. The black population outside the South is almost entirely urban (95 percent), whereas the white population in the North and West is only 71 percent urban. The comparative performance of young whites in the North is therefore greatly reduced, simply because the population sample contains more than six times as many rural families as the black population sample to which it is benignly compared. To the extent that this factor skews the overall figures, claims about income parity can be reduced to the vague and meaningless statement that urban blacks in the relevant age category earn more than rural whites in the same age group, but less than urban whites.[32]

In sum, under analysis all the hoopla about equality among young black and white married families in the North does not hold up. It appears to have been something of a rhetorical flourish that does, however, well serve the noninterventionist politics of our time.

The Black-White Income Gap at the Top

A thorough view of how well any group is doing must show the comparative performance of those at the top of the economic pyramid. As may be expected, the comparative economic inequality of the races in the high-income groups far exceeds the overall disparities in the middle or, as we shall see later, at the bottom.

In 1959, when the national median family income for all races was about $5,400, Census policymakers did not consider it useful to categorize family incomes above $25,000 a year. The highest bracket reported was "$25,000 and up." In that year, only 0.1 percent of nonwhite families had incomes exceeding $25,000, compared with 0.8 percent of white families. By 1969, when the median family income had climbed 74 percent, or 38 percent after adjusting for inflation, only 0.6 percent of black families had incomes over $25,000 in 1969 dollars, while 4 percent of all white families had incomes at or above this figure. By 1969, the Census questionnaire was revised to include a bracket of $50,000 and up. About 4,300 black families fell in this new category, but they represented only 0.1 percent of all black families;

IN CORPORATE AMERICA WHITES ONLY ARE THE WINNERS AT THE TOP

- The 802 highest paid chief executives earned a total of $245.1 million in 1978.
- The group had compensation averaging $306,000.
- The lowest paid member of the group earned $81,000.
- The highest paid executive in the group earned $3,423,220.
- Not one of these highest paid executives was a black person.

Source of reported salaries: Forbes, June 11, 1979, p. 117.

---

white families were about eight times more likely to be in this top bracket. By 1979, the figure for black families had risen to 0.9 percent, but whites continue to move into affluent circumstances far more rapidly than do blacks.[33]

In 1979, the Census Bureau created a new upper bracket to show families with incomes of $75,000 or above. While only 0.2 percent of black families had incomes over $75,000, 1.5 percent, or nearly eight times as many white families, had incomes in the highest bracket.[34]

The fact that the big winners in American society are almost exclusively white is confirmed by the results of several studies of executive compensation. Not one of the 800 most highly compensated chief executives in 1978—with annual remuneration ranging from a high of $3,423,220 to a low of $81,000—was a black person. The total compensation received by this very small and elite group was $245 million, *not one dollar of which found its way to a person in the black community*. Among blacks, the truly big winners tend to be a few score of highly compensated athletes and entertainers. That there should not be a single black person in the top executive group is extraordinary when one considers that in 1979 there were 25 million blacks in the United States and they made up 11.6 percent of the American population.[35]

Summing Up

In the first part of this chapter, I showed that all economic indices disclose a very large income gap between blacks and whites. Despite claims to the

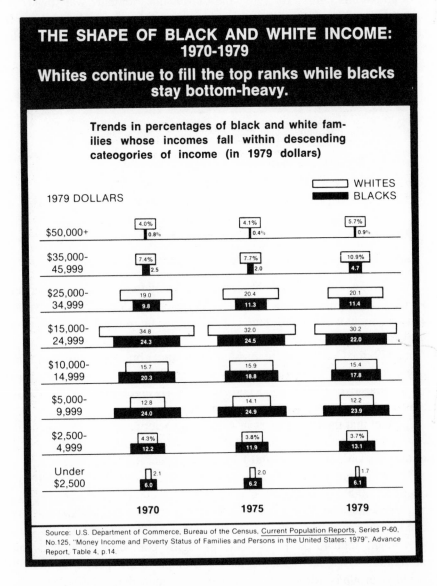

THE SHAPE OF BLACK AND WHITE INCOME: 1970-1979

Whites continue to fill the top ranks while blacks stay bottom-heavy.

Trends in percentages of black and white families whose incomes fall within descending cateogories of income (in 1979 dollars)

1979 DOLLARS

☐ WHITES
■ BLACKS

1979 DOLLARS	1970 White	1970 Black	1975 White	1975 Black	1979 White	1979 Black
$50,000+	4.0%	0.8%	4.1%	0.4%	5.7%	0.9%
$35,000-45,999	7.4%	2.5	7.7%	2.0	10.9%	4.7
$25,000-34,999	19.0	9.8	20.4	11.3	20.1	11.4
$15,000-24,999	34.8	24.3	32.0	24.5	30.2	22.0
$10,000-14,999	15.7	20.3	15.9	18.8	15.4	17.8
$5,000-9,999	12.8	24.0	14.1	24.9	12.2	23.9
$2,500-4,999	4.3%	12.2	3.8%	11.9	3.7%	13.1
Under $2,500	2.1	6.0	2.0	6.2	1.7	6.1

1970   **1975**   **1979**

Source: U.S. Department of Commerce, Bureau of the Census, Current Population Reports, Series P-60, No.125, "Money Income and Poverty Status of Families and Persons in the United States: 1979", Advance Report, Table 4, p.14.

contrary, there appears to be no valid basis for assuming that blacks as a group are making, or will make, important gains. Although the income gap narrowed impressively in the 1960s, the 1970s brought no additional gains. In fact, black family incomes in 1981 were less than three-fifths of whites', a bit lower than where they stood in 1966. Projecting the trend of the past seventeen years (1964 to 1981) forward on a straight-line basis, black incomes will not catch up with white incomes until the year 2334. If the negative 1969 to 1981 trend continues. the income gap will widen, bringing black family income relative to white back to the 1950 line by the end of this century. Even if this latest trend reverses, it is probable that for the foreseeable future, whites will continue to open the aggregate dollar gap between the incomes of the two races, just as they have been doing for the past thirty-five years.

The principal claim to emerging black equality has rested on the progress of the black middle class. Yet there is no basis for the commonly held impression that the black middle class now includes 50 percent of the overall black population. Blacks at or above the national median income (in 1979 approximately $20,000) constitute only 26.7 percent of the total black family population. The number of middle-income blacks increased rapidly during the 1960s, but during the 1970s, blacks, like whites in the lower-income brackets, moved much more slowly toward middle-class status.

In the upper-income brackets, the gap is much greater. Compared with blacks, white families are six times as likely to have incomes of over $50,000 a year. At the very top of the income scale, black faces are almost never seen. The tunnel vision of liberal America invariably concentrates its attention on the huge number of blacks at the bottom of the economic ladder. It almost always neglects the far greater disparity in black representation at the top.

CHAPTER TWELVE

People in Poverty:
The Expanding Black Underclass

"There had lived a simple agrarian folk who had not changed with industry, who had not farmed with machines or known the power and danger of machines in private hands. They had not grown up on the paradoxes of industry. And then suddenly the machines pushed them out and they swarmed on the highways."

—*John Steinbeck,*
The Grapes of Wrath *(1939)*

VIEWING THE ECONOMIC POSITION of blacks primarily in terms of average family income is, in a sense, misleading. The comparison of the incomes of the average black family and the average white family does indeed give us a fairly clear picture of how often blacks come up short in our racially skewed economic system; yet the comparison does not fully tell us how far short they fall. It is, one might say, like comparing the health records of two groups wholly in terms of days missed from work due to illness, but ignoring dramatic differences in mortality rates. The economic position of blacks in America cannot be comprehended unless one not only understands how the "average" black family is doing, but further observes the numbers and the trends affecting blacks at the bottom of the economic ladder. Moreover, the relative economic powers of the groups do not come into view unless one understands the extent to which blacks, in very large numbers, lack sufficient economic strength to compete with enough vigor to win even the material necessities of life. For these reasons, let us now turn to the complex issue of black poverty in America.

Blacks in Poverty Four Times as Often as Whites

Since the mid-1960s, poverty in this country has been defined by the Bureau of the Census solely on the basis of income. For purposes of measuring poverty, both earned and unearned income are taken into account, including federal, state, and local public assistance in cash, but excluding

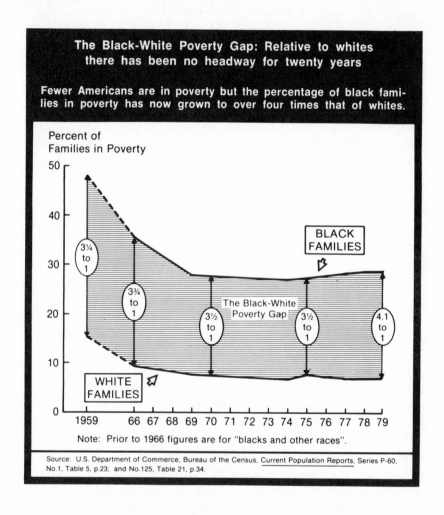

The Black-White Poverty Gap: Relative to whites there has been no headway for twenty years

Fewer Americans are in poverty but the percentage of black families in poverty has now grown to over four times that of whites.

Percent of
Families in Poverty

BLACK FAMILIES

The Black-White Poverty Gap

WHITE FAMILIES

3¼ to 1   3¾ to 1   3½ to 1   3½ to 1   4.1 to 1

1959 66 67 68 69 70 71 72 73 74 75 76 77 78 79

Note: Prior to 1966 figures are for "blacks and other races".

Source: U.S. Department of Commerce, Bureau of the Census, Current Population Reports, Series P-60, No.1, Table 5, p.23; and No.125, Table 21, p.34.

such noncash support items as subsidized housing, food stamps, Medicare, and Medicaid. Poverty "thresholds" have been established for individuals and families, based on the number of people present in the family, the number of children present, the sex of the family head, and the place of residence (whether farm or nonfarm). All families are then classified according to these four characteristics, and those with incomes below the "threshold" income assigned for the particular category are included in what government statisticians euphemistically term the "low-income" population. In 1979, for example, the poverty threshold for a nonfarm family of four was $7,412. All nonfarm families with four members living together and having incomes of less than $7,412 were officially classified as poor.[1]

In 1979, the poverty gap between black and white families was much wider than the income gap and even wider than the unemployment gap. While less than 7 percent of all white families were classified as poor, 28 percent of black families fell below the poverty line. In other words, more than one out of every four black families lived on an income less than the income standard set by the U.S. Government as minimally necessary to subsist. In contrast, only one out of every fifteen white families lived on an income below this standard.

Blacks, therefore, were four times as likely as whites to be living in poverty. To look at this inequality another way, black families accounted for about 10 percent of all families in the nation, but over 31 percent of all families classified as living in poverty.[2]

Intact Black Families Twice as Often Poor

Presented with these huge differences between the races, social commentators have attempted to explain, in various ways, the statistical factors responsible. As one might expect, statistics are colored by ideology; many of the factors that are cited to explain away lower black median incomes have been trotted out again to account for the very high rates of poverty among blacks.

For example, the disproportionate poverty of blacks is often blamed on the fact that a very large number of black families are female-headed. In 1979, more than 40 percent of all black families were headed by females, as compared with 11.6 percent of white families. The poverty rate for black families headed by a woman was 49 percent, compared with only 22 percent for white, female, single-parent families. Black, female, single-adult families in poverty accounted for 72 percent of all black families in poverty, about 46 percent of all female-headed families in poverty, and over 22 percent of all families in poverty—white and black, male and female. Unquestionably, particularly in the black community, there is a very high correlation between the absence of a male and poverty in the family.[3]

This does not mean that if blacks and whites had the same percentages of female-headed families, the black-white poverty gap would disappear. Thus, if black families were headed by females only as often as white families (11.6 percent) and if black poverty rates remained unchanged, the ratio of black to white families in poverty would drop but only to a ratio of

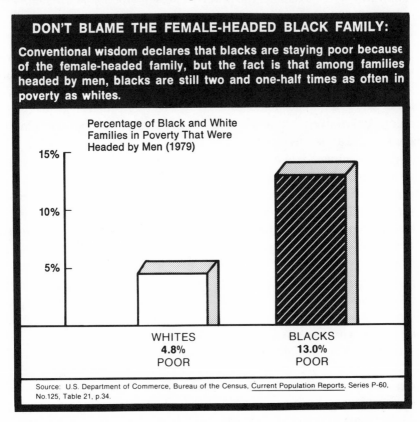

DON'T BLAME THE FEMALE-HEADED BLACK FAMILY:

Conventional wisdom declares that blacks are staying poor because of .the female-headed family, but the fact is that among families headed by men, blacks are still two and one-half times as often in poverty as whites.

Percentage of Black and White Families in Poverty That Were Headed by Men (1979)

WHITES
4.8%
POOR

BLACKS
13.0%
POOR

Source: U.S. Department of Commerce, Bureau of the Census, Current Population Reports, Series P-60, No.125, Table 21, p.34.

2.5 to 1. Thus a significant gap still remains. The presence of a very large black-white poverty gap among groups other than the female-headed family confirms that having black skin is the major problem. In 1979, 4.8 percent of all white families with a male parent present were classified as poor, while 13 percent—2.7 times as many—of similar black families fell into this category. For husband-wife families with heads between 25 and 44 years of age, the white poverty rate was 4.2 percent in 1978. The comparable black rate was 7.6 percent.

This means that intact black families *whose head is in his or her prime earning years* are nearly two times as likely to be living in poverty as are similar white families.[4] The black female-headed family is a handy scape-goat for racial conservatives. But it accounts for only part of the huge poverty gap that exists between blacks and whites.

Age, Education, and Poverty Rates

The position is also taken that blacks are more often poorer than whites simply because they are, on the whole, younger. The median age of the black population is indeed some seven years younger than the white median age, largely because black families have more children than white families (1.54 per black family; 1.01 per white family). These factors, it is argued, lead to a higher incidence of poverty among blacks because young people earn less than older people.[5]

This position collapses when we examine the poverty rate between blacks and whites of *equal* age. If the poverty rates are compared for black and white families with heads of similar ages, we find that the gap is always at least 3.5 to 1 and reaches a high of 5 to 1 for the 60-to-64 age group. Black families with heads under age 25 were 3.8 times as often in poverty in 1979 as white families with heads in the same age group. For black families with heads in their prime earning years—25 to 44—the poverty rate was 27.6 percent, compared with only 7.3 percent for whites in the same age bracket. The same disparities prevail when individuals instead of families are com-pared. Poverty rates for every age group of blacks run from 2.7 to 3.8 times higher than for white individuals of the same age.[6]

Age is thus no more a significant factor in accounting for unequal poverty than in accounting for the lower median income of blacks. Even if there were no age disparity between the black and white populations, the overall black poverty rate for families would decrease by only 1 percentage point, to 26.7 percent, changing the poverty gap from 4.1 to 1 to 3.9 to 1. For individuals, as distinct from families, the gap, currently 3.5 to 1, would narrow to only 3.3 to 1. While age does affect one's chances of being poor, age in and of itself is not a significant determinant of the poverty gap.[7]

The fact that black families tend to be larger than white families—3.66 and 3.22 members, respectively—is often assumed to account for the higher incidence of poverty among blacks. Under analysis, however, this hypoth-esis does not stand up. The fact is that the black poverty rate for each family size runs from 2.5 to 4.2 times higher than the white poverty rate. No matter how small or large the size of a black family, it is far more likely to live in poverty than a similar white family.[8]

Probably, the most commonly cited explanation of the high black poverty rate is the lower educational attainments of blacks. The exaggeration of this factor becomes clear when we compare the poverty rates of blacks and whites with equal years of schooling. Here, we find that in 1979 white families headed by a person with four years of high school had a poverty rate of only 5.1 percent. By contrast, 19.9 percent—or almost four times as many—of similarly educated black families were poor. One might expect to

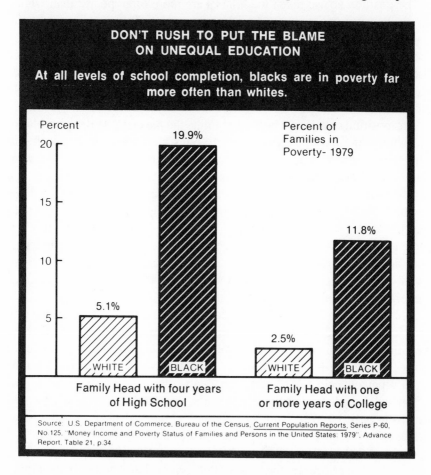

DON'T RUSH TO PUT THE BLAME ON UNEQUAL EDUCATION

At all levels of school completion, blacks are in poverty far more often than whites.

Percent

Percent of Families in Poverty- 1979

19.9%

11.8%

5.1%

2.5%

WHITE   BLACK   WHITE   BLACK

Family Head with four years of High School

Family Head with one or more years of College

Source: U.S. Department of Commerce, Bureau of the Census, Current Population Reports, Series P-60, No 125, "Money Income and Poverty Status of Families and Persons in the United States: 1979", Advance Report. Table 21, p.34

find greater racial equality among families headed by a person with one or more years of college. However, Census figures for 1979 show that black families headed by a person having some college experience were more than five times as often in poverty as similar white families (2.5 percent for whites; 11.8 percent for blacks).[9]

The admittedly great differences in the quality of education available to blacks as opposed to that available to whites do not account for the huge differences in poverty rates. *Blacks with some college experience show family poverty rates more than twice as great as whites with high school educations only.* Even young blacks (ages 22 to 34) with some college experience show poverty rates twice as high as whites with only high school diplomas.[10] It is difficult to imagine more lugubrious statistics than these. The black-white income deficit that prevails when blacks have equal or better education is powerful evidence that low educational attainments of blacks do not explain the poverty gap.

Another factor affecting the calculation is the fact that the black poverty population, like the black population as a whole, is largely concentrated in urbanized metropolitan areas. More than 78 percent of all black families live in metropolitan areas, nearly three-quarters of these in inner cities. Nearly 60 percent of all *poor* black families were living in central cities in 1979—up from 46 percent in 1969 and 39 percent in 1959. By comparison, only 55 percent of the white families in poverty lived in metropolitan areas in 1979, and less than half of those were in the areas designated by the Census as central cities.[11]

The important point here is that the Census Bureau's definition of poverty considers only those characteristics mentioned earlier—family size, number of children, sex of head of household, and farm or nonfarm residence. It does *not* distinguish between families living in higher-cost urban areas and those living in lower-cost urban or rural areas. Particularly, the national poverty index does not account for the relatively low purchasing power in urban ghetto areas. Abundant evidence shows that goods and services are considerably more expensive in black inner-city areas such as New York City, where there are approximately 114,000 poor black families or about 7 percent of all poor black families in the United States. The cost of living in New York tends to be about 16 percent higher than the national cost-of-living figure, and a similar situation exists in most of the other large metropolitan areas where most poor blacks live. In effect, then, the poverty figures actually understate the real gap because the limited money available to poor blacks buys less than the same amount of money in the hands of poor whites living in less expensive locales. For this reason alone, the official poverty gap, showing nearly *four times* as many black families in poverty as white, should be regarded as an extremely conservative figure.[12]

No Poverty at All?

In recent years, the Bureau of the Census has been criticized for greatly overstating the extent of poverty in the United States. The thrust of the criticism derives from the fact that the Census Bureau omits from its calculations of income many noncash benefits received by the poor. As Herbert Stein, former Chairman of the President's Council of Economic Advisors, wrote:

"There is very little poverty in the United States despite recent Census Bureau estimates that there were almost 26 million people in poverty in 1975. These estimates exclude the effect of food stamps, Medicaid and subsidized housing, which are so great as to remove from the 'poverty' category most of the people who seem to be in that category when account is taken only of money income."[13]

Some economists have estimated that these in-kind transfers for the benefit of the poor may total as much as $20 billion a year. Clearly, if the poor were actively *receiving in cash* these sums, which would average out to approximately $3,720 per poor family in 1979, very few poor families in the United States would not rise above the poverty threshold inasmuch as the mean income deficit for poor families in 1979 was only $2,697 per family.[14]

In fact, though, the assumption that values of this magnitude find their way to the hands of the poor is absurd. A large portion of the money spent by the government for the benefit of the poor accrues to the nonpoor members of the bureaucracy who administer these programs, particularly those who administer manpower training programs, education, and health services. Goods and services of considerable value do of course reach the poor and, to some extent, alleviate the exigencies of poverty. But the question that concerns us here is whether these in-kind government subsidies, not counted in official income calculations, are being disproportionately claimed by blacks, thereby lessening the reported racial poverty gap. It does seem probable that blacks, concentrated in urban areas where particularly heavy government in-kind expenditures are made, are claiming a disproportionate share of the total in-kind benefits. But the distortion cannot be great. If we assume that the actual value to the entire low-income population of total in-kind benefits is $10 billion a year, and if we assume that blacks receive a hugely disproportionate share of these benefits, say 50 percent, then the black poverty rate would still be more than double that of whites.[15]

The assertion that no poverty exists in the United States appears to be inspired more by political opposition to government support programs than by careful examination of the facts. Any person who believes that there is little poverty in this country or who doubts that America's poor are disproportionately black would benefit from visiting any one of the dozens of backward counties of the rural South. Bolivar County, Mississippi or the Third World slums of the South Bronx would be a good place to start.

Government assistance may distort the poverty picture, but the distortion results from understating the problem, not exaggerating it. This occurs because, as stated earlier, the official poverty computation includes cash benefits received from the government. Inasmuch as one of the purposes of

MOST BLACKS ARE NOT ON WELFARE AND MOST WELFARE BENEFICIARIES ARE NOT BLACK

But Very Large Percentages of Blacks Are Dependent on Government Support Outside the Free-Market System

FEDERAL GOVERNMENT PROGRAM	1981	PERCENT OF BENEFICIARIES WHO ARE BLACK
Aid to Families With Dependent Children		44.4%
Food Stamps		34.2%
CETA Public Service Jobs		33.0%
Medicaid		34.9%
Public Housing		36.0%
Education for the Disadvantaged (1976)		34.5%
Supplemental Security Income		27.4%

Data obtained from the Department of Labor and other government sources as reported in The New York Times, June 2, 1981, p. B11.

poverty statistics is to measure who is and who is not "getting by" in the American market economy, the inclusion of government benefits obscures the full extent to which particular racial groups are not "getting by" on their own in the unassisted marketplace.

In 1975, the Bureau of the Census calculated, but did not publish, figures that excluded from income statistics various types of public assistance and government transfer payments. These figures show that for white families comprised of two or more persons the poverty rate would rise from 7.7 percent to 8.2 percent if public-assistance payments were excluded. If, in addition, those families receiving public assistance lost their Social Security benefits, the white poverty rate would further rise to 8.8 percent. This is a

14.3 percent increase over the actual poverty rate. For blacks, the change is similar but slightly larger—from 27.1 percent to 29.5 percent if public assistance is excluded, to 31.2 percent if Social Security payments are also excluded from the calculations. In all, this adds up to a 15 percent increase—an overall increase about the same as that for whites.[16] Thus, we see that the black-white poverty ratio remains about the same even when welfare and other government payments are eliminated.

The Black Freeloader Myth

Of course, the percentage of poor black families actually receiving public assistance is much larger than the relative number of poor white families receiving aid. In 1978, slightly over 58 percent of black families below the poverty line were receiving money assistance from the government, while only 30.5 percent of poor white families were claiming it. Racial conservatives have often pointed to this statistic as corroboration for their beliefs that blacks are generally lazy and temperamentally inclined to sponge off the welfare system rather than work to raise their standard of living.[17] But once again, the derogatory racial stereotype does not square with the facts. First, it should be noted that one reason whites claim a lesser percentage of public-assistance income is that the poor among them more often have other sources of support to fall back on. Whites, having a longer history of employment, are more often in a position to claim unemployment insurance and Social Security benefits, both of which are tied in amount and eligibility to prior employment. In 1978, the percentage of whites below the poverty level receiving private and public pensions and similar benefits was higher than the rate of poor blacks, or 12.4 percent versus 10 percent. More important, perhaps, poor whites tend to have stronger work records on which the payments are based and therefore receive larger dollar sums by way of government transfer payments. Finally, poor whites have traditionally received dividend and interest income over five times as often as poor blacks, or 22.7 percent versus 4.4 percent.[18]

Those who believe America's favorite myth, that blacks could pull themselves out of poverty if they would only go to work, close their eyes to the very large numbers of blacks who are in poverty despite the fact that they are employed. We showed in the last chapter that blacks, in fact, earn a much greater percentage of their income through wages and salaries than do whites. The companion statistic is *that blacks not only comprise a dis-*

proportionately large section of the poor, but they also make up a dis-proportionately large number of the working poor. Of all white families that have at least some income from work, 4.8 percent are poor. Over 18 percent of black families with earnings income fall below the poverty threshold, nearly four times the rate prevailing for whites. Also, of families dependent solely on earnings for their incomes, a greater percentage of blacks fall in the poverty class than do whites—over two times as many. In 1978, 19 percent of all white families received all their income from earnings as compared with 29 percent of all black families. Yet 85 percent of these black families earned enough to pull themselves above the poverty line. For whites, the comparable figure was 93 percent. Thus, depending on earnings to get out of poverty is a more effective strategy for whites than for blacks. Or, to put it another way, blacks are less likely than whites to be able to pull themselves out of poverty on the strength of their earning power. Roughly 7 percent of white families depending entirely on earnings fail to make it above the poverty line. For black families, the failure rate is 15 percent.[19]

Despite the huge disparities in poverty rates between working blacks and working whites, many white Americans—and, recently, many blacks, too—cling tenaciously to ancient race-trait stereotypes that explain black poverty as the result of an inadequately developed work ethic.

Trends Affecting the Black Poor

It is instructive to observe what happens when one raises the floor definition of poverty. Many people feel that everyone in the United States should be assured a standard of living significantly higher than the Census Bureau's official "subsistence" level. To accommodate this more liberal view as to what constitutes poverty, the Census Bureau publishes data on those people living on incomes less than 125 percent of the official poverty level. Under this new definition, in 1979, $9,265 became the threshold for a nonfarm family of four. Even at this new threshold, the black-white poverty ratio is still 3.6 to 1.[20]

A strong case may be made, however, for the fact that even the benchmark of 125 percent of the official poverty threshold is insufficient. A better view, perhaps, of the extent of poverty in the United States is obtained if we make the altogether reasonable assumption that any family living on less than half the national income norm should be regarded as poor. Since the national *median* income for 1979 was slightly under $20,000 let us take $10,000 as our new family poverty threshold for a family of four. When this adjustment is made, it turns out that *more than two out of every five black families* (43.1 percent) were poor in 1979, compared with 17.6 percent of white families.[21]

These figures dramatically emphasize the extent of poverty—especially black poverty—in contemporary America. Are there any indications that this picture is changing? Are blacks emerging from poverty? Is the poverty gap between blacks and whites increasing or diminishing?

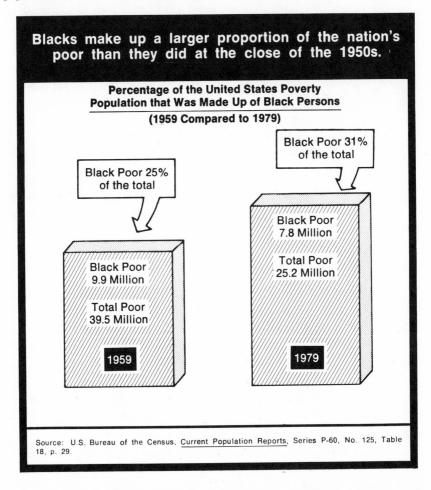

Blacks make up a larger proportion of the nation's poor than they did at the close of the 1950s.

Percentage of the United States Poverty Population that Was Made Up of Black Persons

(1959 Compared to 1979)

Black Poor 25% of the total

Black Poor 31% of the total

Black Poor 9.9 Million

Total Poor 39.5 Million

1959

Black Poor 7.8 Million

Total Poor 25.2 Million

1979

Source: U.S. Bureau of the Census, Current Population Reports, Series P-60, No. 125, Table 18, p. 29.

In 1959, by the official government subsistence level measure, the black poverty population numbered about 1,860,000 families, or about 45 percent of the black population. The official white poverty population included 6,027,000 families, or roughly 15 percent of all white families. In the ten years from 1959 to 1969, as the official poverty cutoff line was raised from about $3,000 to $3,800 for a nonfarm family of four, the official black family poverty rate declined sharply, from 48 percent to 28 percent. The net reduction in the number of poor black families between 1959 and 1969 was 494,000. At the same time, the official white poverty rate dropped a greater amount—by more than one-half, from 14.8 percent to 7.7 percent. Thus, in the decade of the 1960s, there was decided economic progress for both races. But the relative status of poor whites improved somewhat more than that of poor blacks.[22]

In the next ten-year period, from 1969 to 1979, blacks did not fare as well. Since 1969, the black poverty rate for families has dropped less than one-half of one percent, from 28 percent to 27.6 percent. The actual number of black families in poverty has increased, since during this period the total black population increased by approximately 3 million persons. Over 300,000 more black families were poor in 1979 than in 1969. This slippage nullified most of the gains of the 1959-to-1969 decade. The 300,000 additional black families who slipped into poverty from 1969 to 1979 canceled out over 60 percent of the gains achieved in the previous decade. In contrast, the white family poverty rate declined slightly between 1969 and 1979, dropping from 7.7 percent to 6.8 percent. This means that in 1979, 88,000 fewer white families were poor than in 1969. In sum, the figures of the last twenty years show that while blacks have made gains, they have been, and continue to be, disproportionately poor—almost four times as often as whites. Over any period five years or longer from 1959 to the present, whites have emerged from poverty at a greater rate, and, of course, in far greater numbers than blacks.[23]

It is, of course, impossible to predict what will happen to black poverty percentages over the next decade or generation. If traditional liberal values were to be reasserted in America, many legislative initiatives would be possible—broad-scale public-service employment legislation and expanded funding of community development employment programs to name two. Such acts could directly attack and reduce the black-white poverty gap. Moreover, if a national minimum family income plan were enacted, the poverty gap between the races would be statistically dissolved, although the lingering social problems associated with disproportionate black poverty might well persist for a considerable time.

It is possible, too, that the supply-side economic thesis that would encourage business development and growth could cause more money to trickle down to the poor, thereby reducing poverty among both blacks and whites. But as we shall show later, it is very unlikely that less government regulation, greater investment in automation and technology, and more labor competition are going to cause blacks to *close* the poverty gap. The opposite result is more likely to be the case.

Barring any major liberal political initiatives—which seems highly unlikely in today's political climate—the picture to emerge is bleak. During the 1970s, blacks lost rather than gained ground in both an absolute and a

THE CRITICAL STATE OF BLACK AMERICA AS IT ENTERED THE 1980s

	Black	White
Children in Poverty	41.2%	11.0%
Teenage Unemployment	36.5%	13.9%
Illegitimate Births	48.8%	7.3%
Female-Headed Families	40.5%	11.6%
High School Heroin Users	8.0%	0.7%
Vitamin C Deficiencies	4.7%	2.2%
Covered by Health Insurance.	57.7%	80.9%
Life Expectancy at Birth (Years)	68.3	73.5
Infant Mortality (per 1,000 births)	23.5	13.3
Maternal Mortality (per 100,000 births)	26.5	9.0
Homicides (per 100,000 population)	39.7	5.8

Note: Except where indicated, figures are percentages and are for the latest year available. When available, "black only" data are used; otherwise figures are for non-whites.

Sources: U.S. Bureau of the Census, Current Population Reports, Series P-23, No. 80; Series P-60, No. 120; U.S. Bureau of Labor Statistics, Employment and Earnings, January 1980; and Dr. William A. Darity and Edward W. Pitt, "Health Status of Black Americans, The State of Black America—1979," The National Urban League, New York, 1979.

relative sense. Even if one considers the black progress made during the 1960s, the total picture derived from the last two decades gives us no basis for predicting that the poverty gap is tending to close. Projecting recent trends into the future, it is impossible to see any point in time when black poverty will be no higher than that of whites generally, or for that matter, of other formerly disadvantaged white ethnic groups in the United States.

Black Children in Poverty

Of all the poverty statistics, the ones that describe the prospects of black children present the most serious threat to the stability of our society. The economic and social conditions that increase the risk of racial unrest and civil disturbances are not simply present inequalities, but rather the way that these inequalities are perceived to have the power to unfairly control the destiny of children. Politically, people seem to be infinitely patient when, for various reasons, their own lives and aspirations are limited or blocked. But these same people will not tolerate indefinitely economic or social arrangements that crush, or restrict, the opportunities of their children.

Since 1960, many millions of black children have been raised in poverty conditions. Many of that generation are now adults. In most cases, their skills, aspirations, and habits are now permanently formed. To the extent that very large numbers of this group are now poor, they are likely to remain so. In 1979, almost a generation later, about two-fifths of black children under the age of 18 were still being reared under circumstances the government regarded as deprived.[24] Two out of every five American black children brought into the world today will grow up under seriously handicapped economic conditions. This is a very large group, and it will bear a commensurate risk of chronic disease, mental retardation, inferior education, drug addiction, and the sense of personal frustration that so often leads to criminal behavior. The unequal life chances faced by over 40 percent of black children make a mockery of the disposition of most politicians today to look the other way and applaud the black middle class which emerged in the 1960s and maintains only a fingertip grip on an economic status precariously close to the fringes of poverty.

CHAPTER THIRTEEN

Black Unemployment: More Than Twice as Often and Still Losing Ground

"Throughout history the powers of single black men flash like falling stars, and die sometimes before the world has rightly gauged their brightness."

—W.E.B. DuBois (1868-1963)

WE HAVE MEASURED the economic powerlessness of black people in the United States by comparing how they rank with whites in various categories of income. The black family poverty rate, presently about four times as great as the rate for whites, highlights huge differences in relative command over income. Even this meager ability to attract resources appears to be in further decline. For more than a decade blacks have become an increasingly larger percentage of the nation's poor. Considering income as a whole, the average black family has been earning about 40 percent less than the average white family. While the ratio of black to white family income improved dramatically for blacks during the 1960s, no overall improvement has been recorded thereafter. After a decade of public preoccupation with social programs designed to make life easier for black people, we find that in 1981, the ratio of black to white median family income stood at the same level as it did fifteen years earlier in 1966.

Of course, factors other than annual income reveal a person's economic status or power to attract income. Some relevant questions are: Am I working? If so, how steady is my job? How great is my risk of losing it? If I do lose it, how good are my chances of getting another? What legal or economic arrangements, if any, are in place that improve my chances of holding my job or finding a new one?

When we measure the economic differences of race we must take into account such factors as involuntary unemployment, underemployment, and quality of employment. These qualitative features of a wage earner's work life may be more important than the statistician's measures of comparative income because they help explain the reasons that incomes of particular groups are higher or lower. So we turn now to the question of how blacks compare with whites in regard to group positions of employment and unemployment. As we might expect, we will discover that the most important feature of black economic powerlessness is a much weaker capacity to sell labor in the middle and upper reaches of the economy.

Good Times or Bad: Twice as Often Unemployed

The single most critical observation we can make about the relationship of black unemployment to white unemployment is that over the last twenty-five years, through both good and bad economic times, black unemployment has remained at a level very close to twice that of whites.[1]

From 1954 to 1979, the white unemployment rate fluctuated greatly, moving from a low of 3.1 percent to a high of 7.8 percent. These two extremes occurred only six years apart. In 1969, when the white rate was 3.1 percent, nonwhites were unemployed at the rate of 6.4 percent. In 1975, one of the years of greatest hardship since the Depression of the 1930s, the unemployment rate for whites soared to 7.8 percent. Following the 2-to-1 pattern, unemployment skyrocketed to 13.9 percent for nonwhites in general and to 14.7 percent for blacks. The 1979 figures show a white unemployment rate of 5.1 percent, as compared with a nonwhite rate of 11.3 percent, or a ratio of 2.2 to 1.

The most recent recession confirms the past. In the summer of 1982, a year of very serious economic problems, the black unemployment rate was 18.9 percent—slightly more than twice the white rate of 8.4 percent.[2]

Paradoxically, the 2-to-1 ratio of black to white unemployment is a phenomenon of the mid-twentieth century, the period of greatest black progress. Despite the degraded status of blacks prior to World War II, the ratio of black to white unemployment was low. Indeed, in 1930, the first year during which the Census measured unemployment by race, white male unemployment actually exceeded unemployment for black men—5.4 percent for white males and 5.1 percent for black males. This equal unemployment rate, so very different from the situation prevailing in recent years, was largely the result of the geographic distribution of the races during the 1930s as well as the nature of the work available at that time to blacks. Somewhat sheltered from unemployment by their low economic status, blacks in the agrarian South could still find cotton and vegetables to pick at a time when whites in the industrial North had difficulty getting jobs as factory workers and managers. The mass layoffs of the Great Depression years had little effect on blacks; they had almost no manufacturing positions

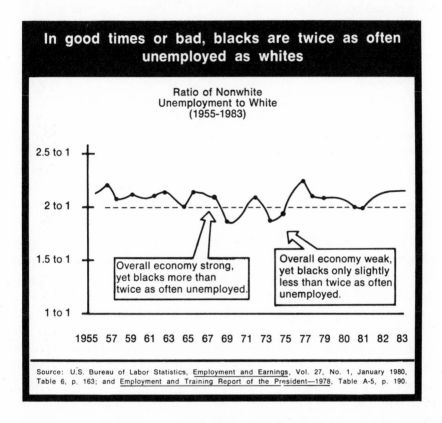

In good times or bad, blacks are twice as often unemployed as whites

Ratio of Nonwhite
Unemployment to White
(1955-1983)

2.5 to 1

2 to 1

Overall economy strong, yet blacks more than twice as often unemployed.

Overall economy weak, yet blacks only slightly less than twice as often unemployed.

1.5 to 1

1 to 1

1955 57 59 61 63 65 67 69 71 73 75 77 79 80 81 82 83

Source: U.S. Bureau of Labor Statistics, Employment and Earnings, Vol. 27, No. 1, January 1980, Table 6, p. 163; and Employment and Training Report of the President—1978, Table A-5, p. 190.

to lose. Even in the depths of the Depression, blacks in the North escaped the brunt of the blow simply because there were still shoes to be shined, messages to be delivered, and household work to be done. Racial stereotyping in employment, like the slavery system preceding it, provided blacks with a certain amount of job security. As late as 1940, before the coming of war brought an end to the Depression, the nonwhite unemployment rate was only 25 percent higher than the rate for whites.[3]

The high demand for labor during World War II helped blacks break through many traditional barriers, and by 1945 many were gainfully employed at wartime jobs. But with the end of the war, blacks became vulnerable to the forces of conventional industrial unemployment. When 16 million men, mostly white, returned home from war and began to look for work, the urgent need for black manpower totally evaporated, and blacks lost some of their wartime gains. From that point on, the percentage of unemployed blacks began to climb. By 1948, the first year for which the Labor Department provided annual unemployment data, nonwhite males posted an unemployment rate 1.7 times that of white males. Two years later, the ratio reached the 2-to-1 level, the level that has now prevailed for three decades.[4]

In spite of more than thirty-five years of relative postwar prosperity, a sustained effort by the federal government to reduce job discrimination, the imposition in some industries of quota hiring of blacks, some voluntary efforts to find jobs for inner-city blacks, and the expenditure of tens of billions of dollars in federal manpower and training programs for minorities, relative unemployment rates remain unchanged. *The comparative rate of unemployment for blacks as against whites has not improved for over a third of a century.*

The 2-to-1 unemployment ratio—the essential and apparently intransigent underpinning of black inequality—may be better understood by noting how various subgroups influence the total. These class breakdowns tend to throw some light on the reasons for the persistent racial differences.

A reasonable first step would be to separate men from women. While women in general experience higher unemployment rates than men, black women fare relatively better than black men. In 1950, for instance, while the unemployment rate for nonwhite men was 2 times that of white men, the rate for nonwhite women was only 1.6 times that for white women. Black men have closed the gap but black women continue to have a lower unemployment ratio in relation to whites. By 1979, nonwhite men were 2.3 times as often unemployed as white men, while nonwhite women were 2.1 times as often unemployed as white women.[5]

The Special Predicament of Black Teenagers

The hardest hit victim by far is the black teenager. Although the rate of unemployment among black teenagers has climbed steadily throughout a quarter of a century, the reasons for this are mixed and complex. Black teenagers have fewer skills and less education to offer employers. Minimum wage laws, insofar as they discourage the hiring of unskilled laborers, probably work particularly against young blacks. If employers must pay a fixed minimum wage to young people, they are likely to soak up the entire labor pool of young whites before they turn to young blacks. Black teenagers are located predominantly in cities, and jobs tend increasingly to be found in the suburbs. No doubt, too, the limited job opportunities traditionally offered blacks continue to dampen the motivation of black teenagers to press for conventional employment. Whatever the reasons—and all of these factors undoubtedly play some role—the predicament of the black teenager is the single most serious aspect of the economic problem of the black race in the United States.

The statistical trends are devastating. In 1954, the nonwhite teenage unemployment rate was about 1.4 times the white rate. By the 1970s, black teenagers were, on the average, 2.3 times as often unemployed as white teenagers. By the end of the decade, in 1979, 36.5 percent of black teenagers were unemployed, or 2.6 times the rate for white teenagers. In the summer of 1981, the ratio had climbed further to 3 to 1. For the first time in history over 50 percent of young blacks were unemployed.[6]

Many people have the impression that black teenage unemployment has been grossly overstated by the Census Bureau. The stereotypical view of black teenagers standing on a street corner or in a barroom shooting pool and hustling drugs leads to the sweeping conclusion that the hundreds of thousands of black teenagers the government says are seeking work really are not. But this conclusion flies in the face of the government count. Until it is shown that the Census Bureau is actually counting teenagers who are really not seeking work, the statistics remain unrefuted. Four to five out of every ten black teenagers who want to work are unable to find employment.

Recent critics of the teenage unemployment statistics take the position that the published unemployment ratio overstates the labor market problem of black youths because many of those classified as unemployed are teenagers who are in school and who are not, in fact, looking for full-time work. Also, it is said that many of those who are in school do not suffer serious economic hardship since they are merely unable to secure part-time jobs. It serves little purpose to dispute whether the calculations of the Labor Department are correct because the gravity of the black teenage labor problem becomes very clear when we consider the indisputably ominous trends in the percentage of teenagers actually employed. In 1954, nonwhite male teenagers were slightly *more* likely to have either a full- or part-time job than white male teenagers, about 52 percent to 50 percent, respectively. Since that time, the percentage of nonwhite male teenagers holding jobs has steadily declined, while the rate for similar whites has remained relatively constant over the past twenty-five years. In 1980, only about 26.5 percent of all nonwhite male teenagers held either a full- or part-time job compared with 52 percent of similar whites.[7]

The steadily widening gap between the percentage of black and white teenagers who are actually working shows the magnitude of the economic problem of black youths; more important, it shows how an ever-increasing black underclass is being produced in the United States.

The "Solid Black Family Man":
Still Twice as Often Without Work

Critics of Census calculations suggest that the very high black un-employment rate gives an inaccurate portrait of black opportunities in our society. The hardnosed "we-made-it-and-so-can-they" position assumes

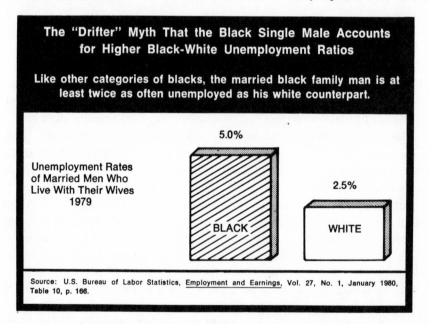

The "Drifter" Myth That the Black Single Male Accounts for Higher Black-White Unemployment Ratios

Like other categories of blacks, the married black family man is at least twice as often unemployed as his white counterpart.

Unemployment Rates of Married Men Who Live With Their Wives 1979

5.0% BLACK

2.5% WHITE

Source: U.S. Bureau of Labor Statistics, Employment and Earnings, Vol. 27, No. 1, January 1980, Table 10, p. 166.

that the very high overall black unemployment rate is really the result of a substantial core of drifters and very weak earners who are surrounded by an otherwise healthy economic group. According to this view, what is needed is a new calculation of the black-white unemployment ratio that leaves out the "poor performers": teenagers, older people, men without families, married men living alone, and abandoned wives. It is said that meaningful black-white unemployment comparisons should consider only the employment records of "solid family men." [8]

This line of reasoning sounds appealing in the abstract, but it does not produce much in the way of favorable results. In 1979, nonwhite married men ages 20 to 64, with spouses present, were unemployed at the rate of 5 percent; white married men who lived with their wives had a rate of 2.5 percent. This is exactly the 2-to-1 unemployment ratio found in the population as a whole.

Not long ago, things were looking up for the black family man. In the decade between 1962 and 1972 the black-white unemployment ratio for married men living with their spouses dropped from 2.5 to 1 to 1.7 to 1, so that in the early 1970s it may well have been true that "solid black family men" were showing a more favorable performance compared with their white peer group. But since 1972, the ratio has steadily deteriorated. By the end of the decade, nonwhite family men were twice as often unemployed as similar whites. [9]

Unemployment and the Lower Average Age of Blacks

The disproportionately higher black unemployment rate is often explained in terms of the lower average age of the black population. This point was first and most effectively made by black economist Thomas Sowell in his book, *Race and Economics*. Profesor Sowell's logic is straightforward. Younger adults are more likely to be unemployed than older adults. Since the black population contains a higher proportion of younger workers—the median age of blacks in America is 23.5 years, compared with 29.6 for whites—Professor Sowell concluded that this age difference accounts for much of the higher unemployment rate. [10]

As mentioned earlier in connection with black-white income differences, a serious problem with this argument lies in the fact that the largest factor contributing to the lower average age of the black population is the much greater percentage of black children. For blacks, the percentage of the population below the age of 16 is huge—32.4 percent, compared with 24 percent for whites. But these black children, not expected to be employed or employable, are not and should not be counted as part of the unemployment statistics. The question is not whether blacks *as a whole* are

younger, but whether black workers, or potential workers, are younger.
The average age difference between the black and white civilian work force is not great. If one interpolates within age brackets for the working force of both races, the gap in the age differential between blacks and whites is an insignificant 0.9 years.

Differences in the average ages of blacks and whites are a specious explanation for the higher unemployment rates of blacks

In all age groups, black males are at least twice as often unemployed as white males.

	1979		
AGE GROUP	BLACK UNEMPLOYMENT RATE	WHITE UNEMPLOYMENT RATE	RATIO OF BLACK TO WHITE UNEMPLOYMENT
16-19	34.1%	13.9%	2.5-to-1
20-24	18.4%	7.4%	2.5-to-1
25-34	9.4%	3.6%	2.6-to-1
35-44	6.3%	2.5%	2.5-to-1
45-54	5.4%	2.5%	2.2-to-1
55-64	5.1%	2.5%	2.0-to-1
65+	6.3%	3.1%	2.0-to-1

Source: U.S. Bureau of Labor Statistics, Employment and Earnings, Vol. 27, No. 1, January 1980, Tables 3 & 5, pp. 158 & 162.

The fact is, black men at every age level are at least twice as often unemployed as white men of the same age. In 1979, black men in their prime earning years, 25 to 54, were 2.5 times as often unemployed. Black men over 55 did comparatively better, but their unemployment rate was still more than double that of their white counterparts.[11]

Black Education and Unemployment

If the average citizen is asked to explain why blacks are twice as often unemployed as whites, he would probably answer that they don't meet the educational requirements for a great many of the jobs in today's labor market. Let us examine this commonly held belief.

Blacks have made extraordinary gains in education in recent years. Since 1940, the median number of school years completed by young blacks has increased by almost 50 percent; in terms of average years of school completed, young blacks between the ages of 20 and 29 are now practically equal to their white peers. Yet there have been no corresponding gains in employment rates. During this period of major educational gains by blacks, the unemployment ratio among young blacks compared with whites of the same age has remained virtually constant.[12]

Government statistics show that high school completion does not alter the established 2-to-1 black-white unemployment ratio. Since 1967, the ratio of nonwhite to white unemployment for those who have completed high school has remained close to the unemployment relationship between blacks and whites as a whole. What is more, blacks who in 1978 had college experience of one to three years were still unemployed two and half times as often as their white peers. Even black college graduates are twice as likely to be unemployed as white college graduates.[13]

It is certainly true that the education received by black children is of a much lower quality than the training whites are likely to acquire with equal years of schooling. Yet even with this taken into account, one would still expect to find a significantly smaller unemployment differential between blacks and whites with the same years of school completed than that between blacks and whites in the entire population. One finds no such thing. Blacks do improve their chances of avoiding unemployment by staying in school. But education is very disappointing as a force helping blacks to *close* the unemployment gap. At various levels of educational attainment, a black person is twice as likely as a white to find himself without a job. The young black male who completes high school is still twice as likely as the white youth with a high school degree to find himself unemployed after graduation. And if the black student goes on to a college degree, he or she will still run double the unemployment risk faced by white fellow graduates. In other words, no matter how much education they have, blacks do not win employment security on an equal footing with whites. Except for those holding professional or postgraduate degrees, the impact of a racially skewed job market remains constant at every educational level.

Other Minorities Doing Better

The experience of other minority groups in America provides a sharp contrast to the persistent unemployment gap between blacks and whites. Italian, Irish, and Russian immigrants arrived in this country in great numbers between 1850 and 1930, well after the emancipation of blacks. Most of these immigrants had been peasants in their native countries, yet these groups are now unemployed significantly less often than blacks. Indeed, the

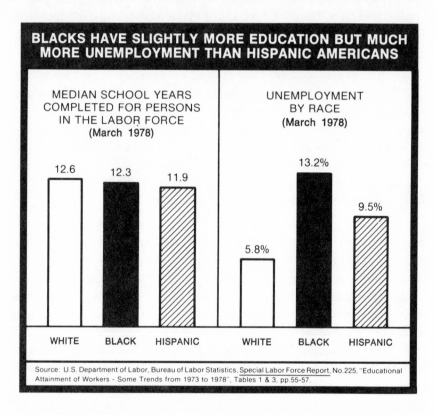

BLACKS HAVE SLIGHTLY MORE EDUCATION BUT MUCH MORE UNEMPLOYMENT THAN HISPANIC AMERICANS

MEDIAN SCHOOL YEARS COMPLETED FOR PERSONS IN THE LABOR FORCE (March 1978)

WHITE	BLACK	HISPANIC
12.6	12.3	11.9

UNEMPLOYMENT BY RACE (March 1978)

WHITE	BLACK	HISPANIC
5.8%	13.2%	9.5%

Source: U.S. Department of Labor, Bureau of Labor Statistics, Special Labor Force Report, No.225, "Educational Attainment of Workers - Some Trends from 1973 to 1978", Tables 1 & 3, pp.55-57.

unemployment rates for Italian-, Irish-, and Russian-Americans are equal or very nearly equal to the overall rate for all American whites. Oriental-Americans have done particularly well with a lower unemployment rate than the population as a whole. In 1970, for example, the unemployment rate for whites was 4.5 percent; for blacks, 8.2 percent; for Chinese-Americans, 3.35 percent; for Japanese-Americans, 2.5 percent. Even the Spanish-speaking Americans, principally from Mexico, have surpassed blacks in employment despite lower educational levels and the ostensible handicap of a language barrier. In 1978, blacks were unemployed at a rate of over 13 percent, but the rate for Spanish-speaking Americans was only 9.5 percent.[14]

The Decline in Black Labor Force Participation

Another way to look at the success of a group in getting and holding employment is to consider the percentages of work participation or of people working rather than the unemployment rates. The labor force participation figure is a good indicator of the economic well-being of various groups because it takes into account a larger population than the unemployment figure. It includes those who are "sitting on the sidelines," such as welfare recipients, the discouraged, the elderly, the physically disabled, and those who for some reason do not wish to work. It is a particularly useful indicator because of the fact that it counts discouraged workers. The unemployment rate, however, excludes discouraged workers. It tells us what percentage of the population is looking for a job but can't find one. In contrast, the labor participation rate is arrived at by dividing the number either employed or seeking work by the total noninstitutionalized population, ages 16 to 65 and including those not seeking work.

In 1948, the percentage of nonwhite men in the civilian labor force was in fact slightly higher than the percentage of white men, 87.3 versus 86.5 percent. Throughout the early and mid-1950s, labor force participation by both nonwhite and white men was about the same, although both slowly declined. This is consistent with our earlier observation that the unfavorable unemployment gap between blacks and whites did not begin to develop until after World War II. The early 1960s saw the beginnings of a significant trend. While white male labor force participation continued to decline at the steady rate of about one-half of a percentage point per year, with the decline slowing as 1970 approached, nonwhite participation began to slip at an increasingly faster rate until 1977, when it reached 71 percent. This compared with a white male participation rate of 78.6 percent, a difference of over 6.5 percentage points.[15]

The general decline in the overall civilian labor participation rate may be traced in part to removal of people from the work force by the liberalization of retirement policies and disability benefits. Probably, the displacement of workers by the increasing automation of manufacturing is an important factor. The decline also may be related to demographic trends such as the fact that teenagers, who look for work less frequently than adults, have become a relatively larger proportion of the population. However, taken individually or collectively, these factors do not explain why the black male labor participation rate has been dropping so much faster than the white rate. Indeed, because whites are more likely than blacks to hold those unionized jobs offering the most attractive retirement benefits, it would seem likely that they would retire from the labor force at an earlier age,

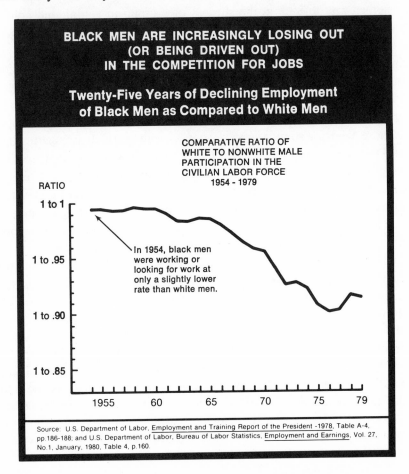

BLACK MEN ARE INCREASINGLY LOSING OUT (OR BEING DRIVEN OUT) IN THE COMPETITION FOR JOBS

Twenty-Five Years of Declining Employment of Black Men as Compared to White Men

COMPARATIVE RATIO OF WHITE TO NONWHITE MALE PARTICIPATION IN THE CIVILIAN LABOR FORCE 1954 - 1979

RATIO

In 1954, black men were working or looking for work at only a slightly lower rate than white men.

Source: U.S. Department of Labor, Employment and Training Report of the President -1978, Table A-4, pp.186-188; and U.S. Department of Labor, Bureau of Labor Statistics, Employment and Earnings, Vol. 27, No.1, January, 1980, Table 4, p.160.

thereby making the white rate lower than the black. Yet, exactly the opposite has occurred, and no satisfactory reason has as yet been suggested to explain the much steeper decline in the black labor force rate. The problem is especially vexing when we examine the participation rates of men in their prime earning years, 35 to 44. There we find that the white labor force participation rate has dropped from 98 percent in 1948 to 96.4 percent in 1979, while for nonwhites the decline has been from 97.2 percent to 90.9 percent—a drop nearly four times as great.[16]

If the 1960 to 1979 decline in the nonwhite labor force participation rate were to continue, only about 68.5 percent of working-age nonwhite males would be in the labor force by 1985. The figure would further drop to 63 percent by 1995. Thus, one of the most ominous problems facing blacks is that in periods of recession or prosperity black men are consistently becoming a smaller percentage of the national labor force.

These facts raise many thought-provoking questions. Do current welfare laws persuade more blacks than whites to stop working? Is a factor of continuing race discrimination discouraging increasing numbers of blacks from entering the labor market? Are blacks, blocked from labor, entrepreneurial, or capital markets for reasons of past or present discrimination, transmitting to their children and peers an ethic of low-employment expectations or disenchantment with the kinds of jobs generally available to them? Is an increasingly automated society where robots replace unskilled labor driving unskilled blacks out of the job race more rapidly than whites? There does not appear to be any convincing proof to strongly support or refute any one hypothesis. Yet, of all observed statistical trends affecting the black race—other than the sharp increase in black women receiving public relief—none is more alarming than the steep decline in the labor force participation of black men.

One may expect these trends affecting black men generally to grow worse as the years go by. This is because the trends in work participation affecting young black men are even more unfavorable. In 1954, young white and nonwhite males, 16 to 17 years of age, participated in the work force at approximately the same rate. By 1979, however, white males in this age bracket had increased their participation by 17 percent while nonwhite males of the same age had a 32 percent decrease in participation. Several decades ago in 1954, nonwhite males 18 to 19 years of age actually showed stronger labor force participation than whites of the same age, about 78.5 percent compared with 70.5. But this edge rapidly dissipated over the next twelve years. In the years since 1965, the white participation rate in this age bracket has increased to almost 75 percent, but the black participation rate has dropped 13 percent to less than 58 percent.[17]

The poor performance of young blacks in the job market is frequently blamed on minimum wage laws. It is said that since unskilled and undereducated blacks are more often "not worth" the minimum wage, the labor market turns instead to young whites whose education and skills tend to be superior. But this explanation does not square with the facts. For the fourteen years during which young black labor participation steadily declined, young blacks had so dramatically improved their educational attainments

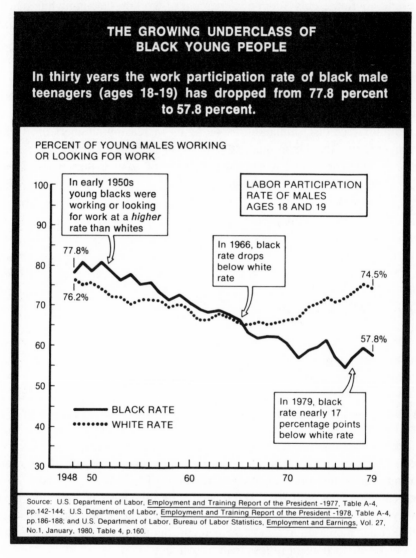

**THE GROWING UNDERCLASS OF
BLACK YOUNG PEOPLE**

In thirty years the work participation rate of black male teenagers (ages 18-19) has dropped from 77.8 percent to 57.8 percent.

PERCENT OF YOUNG MALES WORKING
OR LOOKING FOR WORK

In early 1950s young blacks were working or looking for work at a *higher* rate than whites

LABOR PARTICIPATION RATE OF MALES AGES 18 AND 19

77.8%

In 1966, black rate drops below white rate

74.5%

76.2%

57.8%

━━━━ BLACK RATE
••••••• WHITE RATE

In 1979, black rate nearly 17 percentage points below white rate

1948 50   60   70   79

Source: U.S. Department of Labor, Employment and Training Report of the President -1977, Table A-4, pp.142-144; U.S. Department of Labor, Employment and Training Report of the President -1978, Table A-4, pp.186-188; and U.S. Department of Labor, Bureau of Labor Statistics, Employment and Earnings, Vol. 27, No.1, January, 1980, Table 4, p.160.

that they graduated from high school at about the same rate as their white peers. In view of this improving level of education, one might expect that increasing numbers of blacks would be performing well enough to justify receiving the minimum wage. Yet this has not happened. The labor force participation of black youths has dropped catastrophically during the very period when their gains in numbers of years in school have been greatest.

Even when one considers the fact that many schools push young blacks through to graduation with inadequate attention to academic achievement, one still must face the fact that striking improvements in numbers of school years completed by blacks have had a disappointingly negligible effect on their comparative labor participation rate.

Black Unemployment During Economic Recession

Whenever the nation enters a recession, there is virtually no time lag between the national increase in unemployment and the concomitant doubling of this increase among nonwhites. For example, when white unemployment jumps from 3 to 6 percent, the rate for blacks quickly doubles, from 6 to 12 percent. Assuming a black labor force of 10.4 million, more than 624,000 additional blacks are almost immediately out of work. This correlation between black unemployment and changes in the national economy has been evident throughout all recessions since World War II.[18]

The effects of a recession are particularly harsh in the inner cities. In 1979, for example, the general unemployment rate for nonwhites was 11.3 percent, but the rate for nonwhites in poverty areas was 13.8 percent, and for nonwhites in metropolitan poverty areas 15 percent. Impoverished communities act like powerful amplifiers, multiplying the effects of unfavorable changes in the economy.[19]

These multiplied effects of recession are somewhat mitigated in the long run by the fact that when the economic cycle reverses, blacks eventually regain their losses. Yet even here, the negative side outweighs the positive, for blacks regain their prerecession economic position much more slowly than do whites. This lag in the ability of blacks to recapture their significantly lesser share of the job market was demonstrated as the nation moved out of the severe 1974 to 1975 recession. In the first two years of recovery, 1975 to 1977, the white unemployment rate declined slightly more than 20 percent, but nonwhite unemployment went down by only 6 percent. Andrew F. Brimmer, a leading black economist and former Governor of the Federal Reserve System, noted: "In fact, after two and one-half years of substantial economic expansion, blacks as a group ended up with a relatively smaller proportion of the nation's jobs." Blacks not only lose proportionately twice as many jobs as whites during an economic recession, but are also subject to the additional problem of a lengthy job recovery period.[20]

A number of conclusions may be drawn from the comparative un-employment statistics and trends over the last thirty years. In general, job shortages will probably become more severe as more teenagers and women, particularly white women, enter the labor force. Accordingly, most fore-casts suggest that unemployment will increase in the years ahead, while overall participation in the labor force will decrease. As technology dis-places low or semiskilled work and more highly educated people and partic-ularly hitherto inactive white women enter the job market, it seems that very large numbers of black men may expect to have a very difficult time.

When these elements are combined with the fact that over 40 percent of all black children are presently being reared in conditions of poverty, we see that the future offers little basis for optimism. A heavy tide is running against these black children. Hundreds of thousands of them are being reared in public housing, places not conducive to expectations that reach far above the underground economy. Out of school and out of work at age 18, most of them are poor now, and there is a depressing abundance of reasons for concluding that most of them will remain poor in the years ahead.[21]

The Quality of Black Employment

The relative economic power of blacks to effectively exchange work for money may not be gauged adequately by the percentages of those holding or not holding jobs. Of equal importance is the relative *quality* of the jobs held. To what extent have blacks ceased to be the porters, maids, and bootblacks in our economy? Compared with whites, how often are they now represented in such higher-paying occupations as over-the-road truck drivers, factory workers, skilled craftsmen, engineers, lawyers, foremen, and firemen? To what extent have they moved into positions as craftsmen, professional people, and managers? What is the racial distribution and what are the trends in the distribution of upper-echelon positions such as cor-porate vice-president, practicing architect, and partner in a law firm?

The distribution of jobs by race is clearly important for a number of reasons relating to the psychological, political, and social context of black life. In economic terms, people in higher-paying jobs are less vulnerable to the risk of unemployment; their aggregate earnings, including benefits, are greater; they are generally better equipped to wield political influence and to exploit friendships and job connections to their advantage and to the advantage of their children. The quality of one's job greatly affects one's sense of self-esteem, economic security, and accomplishment. This may explain why success in marriage, in friendships, and in intellectual and cultural pursuits is closely tied to success in work. What is more, the high self-regard that goes along with economic or professional success is frequently transmitted to children, just as the failures and frustrations of unsuccessful parents may undermine the ambitions of their offspring. Finally, in our society, the quality of the job one holds greatly determines the respect one receives from family, peers, and society generally. For a shunned and outcast group such as blacks, nothing contributes so much to a higher repute for the group as the appearance of large numbers of them not simply employed, but performing successfully in respectable and challenging work.[22]

With this as background, a brief historical note on the quality of black employment is useful. At the turn of the century, the black population consisted of about 10 million people. Over half of all black men and women were—to use the Census Bureau term in those days—"gainfully employed" as agricultural workers, either working for wages or working as sharecroppers. Blacks typically spent twelve to fourteen hours a day in fields earning about $1 a day. In 1910, about 42 percent of all black women were employed as household domestics. Blacks had virtually no representation as craftsmen, professionals, or managers. There were, of course, exceptions. There were black religious leaders, human rights advocates, and politicians; there were, of necessity, black nurses, midwives, teachers, lawyers, and ministers needed to operate the segregated institutions of the South.[23] A handful of blacks managed to achieve considerable affluence in commercial activities protected in many cases against competition from whites by policies of racial segregation.

Sure signs of progress first appeared with the publication of the 1960 Census data. The economic pressures from the production demands of World War II had lowered racial barriers. Blacks had begun to advance into craft and white-collar jobs, notably in clerical positions, and to a lesser extent into professional and technical positions. Over 3 percent of black men and 7 percent of black women were classified as either professionals or technicians. With increasing agricultural mechanization and lower farm employment in the South, the number of black farm laborers plunged to about only 7 percent of all black workers. However, less than 2 percent of black men held managerial positions, and only 10 percent of black men were employed as craftsmen. About 14 percent of black men were classified as nonfarm laborers and 16 percent as service workers. Nearly one-quarter of the black male laborers were classified as factory operatives. The greatest improvement in the quality of jobs held by blacks—mirroring the impressive growth in black incomes—occurred during the 1960s when black males, the group traditionally bearing most of the brunt of racial discrimination, made solid gains. From 1960 to 1979, the percentage of black males in professional and technical jobs rose 262 percent. And blacks have increased their presence in managerial positions by a striking 331 percent.[24] Professor Richard B. Freeman has summarized the great occupational progress of blacks after World War II in the following terms:

> "There was a dramatic collapse in traditional discriminatory patterns in the market for highly qualified black Americans. . . . Black and white occupational distributions have tended to converge, as black women moved from domestic service to factory and clerical jobs, and as black men increased their representation in craft, professional and managerial jobs."[25]

Curiously, these important improvements in the occupational status of blacks have not been reflected in comparative overall income statistics. As we have seen, the median black-white family income figure has remained relatively unchanged since 1967, in a period when, as Professor Freeman states, "black and white occupational status is tending to converge." Yet if black occupational gains were so impressive, why did black family income as a percentage of white actually decline during the same period? Why did the great surge in the number of blacks earning middle-class incomes apparently come to an abrupt halt in 1970? Why were there virtually no income gains among blacks in the higher-income brackets?

The answers are not clear. Certain countervailing forces are well known, the most important factor being the fact that the occupational gains by blacks necessarily include only *employed* blacks. Millions of unemployed and unemployable black males reap no benefit from this progress. Occupational gains also tend to make one forget the large and increasing numbers of unemployed black mothers whose only income, in many cases, is public assistance. Furthermore, much of the progress of the 1960s was the work of the group Professor Freeman calls the "black elite." Yet this group, consisting of college graduates under 35 years of age, is negligible in size, only 3 percent of the black population ages 14 and over. The gains of these few superior performers have had little effect on the economic well-being of the black population as a whole, which since World II has consistently experienced an unemployment rate double that of whites and a poverty rate triple the white rate. These huge negative forces combine to retard overall black progress. We receive a false impression to the contrary because of the high visibility of still very modest numbers of blacks recently occupying managerial and other positions of responsibility or power.[26]

The visible phenomenon of blacks doing better is to some extent a classic illustration of media controlling the content of a message. Successful blacks are everywhere in view. We see them at elite college commencements, as television newscasters, in highly visible government posts. At the same time, the black pullman porter and the black yardman are gone. On television, George Jefferson, the black entrepreneur-hustler, has replaced Beulah, the black maid. All of this imposes a kind of tunnel vision that shuts out the complete view of the large majority of blacks whose incomes,

BLACKS STILL HOLD LARGE (AND SOMETIMES INCREASING) PERCENTAGES OF THE LOW-PAYING AND MENIAL JOBS

	BLACK EMPLOYMENT AS A PERCENT OF THE TOTAL WITHIN EACH OCCUPATION		
	1960	1970	1979*
Private Household Workers	49.6	52.7	33.1
Laundry and Dry Cleaning Operatives	33.2	26.4	24.9
Taxicab Drivers and Chauffeurs	17.8	22.8	28.0
Nonfarm Laborers	23.3	20.1	17.4
Janitors	26.2	22.7	24.6
Cooks	20.8	19.5	19.3
Farm Wage Workers	23.3	20.4	20.9
Lodging Cleaners	55.8	38.9	40.4
Practical Nurses	15.1	21.8	18.6
Gardeners	18.1	17.2	16.1

* 1979 figures for non-whites, 90 percent of whom were black.

Source: U.S. Bureau of the Census, 1960 Census of the Population, Subject Reports, Series PC(2)-7A, "Occupational Characteristics", Table 3, pp.21-30; U.S. Bureau of the Census, 1970 Census of the Population, Subject Reports, Series PC(2)-7A, "Occupational Characteristics", Table 2, pp.12-27; and U.S. Department of Labor, Bureau of Labor Statistics, Employment and Earnings, Vol. 27, No.1, January, 1980, Table 23, pp.174-175.

opportunities, and achievements are far behind those of whites. This distorted view of black progress tends to be further corroborated by the policies of large corporations that hard-sell to the public the still relatively token presence of black managers and middle-management executives.

Contrary to public beliefs, the percentage of black workers in low-paying jobs has not decreased in recent years. In 1979, 33 percent of all household workers in the nation were black. Over 40 percent of all lodgings cleaners were black. Blacks are still heavily concentrated in the menial occupations of gardener, laundry worker, janitor, and cook.[27]

While still a tiny percentage of the black population, the increasing number of black middle-management personnel, combined with a continuing stagnation of very large numbers of blacks in menial positions, illustrates the trend toward stratification of the black population. This schism tends to undermine the ability of the black minority to pull itself up as a political group. The economic differences that divide the black population often translate into opinion differences that polarize blacks and thwart their potential for unified political action. Certainly, no race is homogeneous in political and economic attitudes, but with blacks in the United States, the natural cementing force of race and past oppression, around which a strong political consensus could be organized, is being held at bay by extreme intragroup class differences.

Obviously, the occupational gains made by blacks in recent decades are important. But additional factors must be noted to put this progress in a realistic perspective. First of all, whites are pushing ahead into higher positions as fast as blacks are replacing them in the lower positions. When the figures show greater percentages of blacks moving into clerical positions (4.9 percent in 1960, 7.6 percent in 1979), it must thus be remembered that in these posts the white percentage is decreasing because whites are moving even higher into professional and managerial jobs, not because they are dropping on the economic ladder. As in the past, whites continue to occupy posts as file clerks, bank tellers, key punch operators, postal clerks, and typists, but their children are more often than in the past likely to become accountants, engineers, lawyers, and other professionals. Some blacks are taking up the slack as typists, clerks and tellers. They are earning more than in the past, but in the context of the entire occupational range they are not catching up with whites. Whites are still at least twice as likely to be professionals and managers. Blacks, on the other hand, are still twice as likely to be service workers, laborers, and farm laborers.[28]

The "Doublespeak" of Census Classifications

The scope of recent black employment progress tends to be distorted by the Census Bureau's broad and ambiguous job classifications. When the Census classifies a black person as a "manager," one does not know whether he or she is the assistant manager at a laundry and is grossing $200 a week or the manager of a branch bank that loans $200 every ten minutes. "Craft positions" include relatively low-paid construction sweepers as well as highly paid pipe fitters. The Census term "female technician" does not indicate whether the worker carries specimens from lab to lab or analyzes the specimens' contents. Nor does the Census provide information about the distribution of jobs within these broad classifications. In many cases, great economic differences exist between the top of the class and the bottom of the class; the claim that blacks now constitute such and such a percentage of a particular job class is not particularly meaningful until we realize that blacks are much more often at the bottom of the class in question, while most of the top jobs are held by whites.

Here is a concrete example of the distortion. The Census classification of "professional and technical workers" embraces electronics engineers, professors of physics, social workers, and elementary school teachers. From 1960 to 1970, the percentage of black professional and technical workers reportedly increased by 120 percent. But 10 percent of that increase was accounted for by a tripling of the number of black social workers.[29]

The percentage of nonwhites employed as "professionals and technicians" more than doubled during the period 1960 to 1979, and in the case of men more than tripled. But a closer look at this category designation, which includes diverse skills and talents, shows that within this broad classification nonwhites were much more likely to be found among the technicians than among the professionals. In 1970, a year in which figures for "blacks only" are available, blacks are reported to occupy a favorable 5.4 percent of all professional and technical positions. But blacks comprised only 2.3 percent of the accountants, 1.6 percent of the authors, 1.8 percent of the designers, 1.2 percent of the engineers, 1.3 percent of the lawyers and judges, and 2.2 percent of the doctors. Conversely, they were 6.5 percent of the librarians, 7.8 percent of the registered nurses, 9 percent of the medical and dental technicians, and 15.3 percent of the social and recreational workers. Stated differently, blacks were 9 percent of all medical and dental technicians, but only 2.2 percent of the doctors; 9.4 percent of the elementary school teachers, but only 3.3 percent of the university faculty; 15.3 percent of the social workers, but only 3.1 percent of the social scientists.[30] The percentage of blacks working in the physical sciences as physicists, chemists, biologists, and so forth is not even included in the Census table because practically no blacks hold these positions. Thus, we see that the term "professional and technical" gathers in and upgrades a large number of black technicians and lumps them together and makes them appear to be statistically equal to large numbers of high-ranking white professionals.

Perhaps the Census Bureau's most ambiguous category is "white-collar worker." We know that in 1960 only about 14 percent of nonwhite men and less than 19 percent of nonwhite women were in white-collar jobs. By 1979, the figures had increased to about 27 percent and 50 percent, respectively. But the most remarkable growth for blacks holding white-collar jobs has been in the clerical category. Between 1960 and 1979, the percentage of nonwhite male clerical workers rose from 5.2 percent to 7.6 percent. The change for nonwhite women was much greater—from 8.7 percent in 1960, to 29 percent in 1979.[31]

Finally, government pressure on industry to upgrade employment conditions for racial minorities has led to a tendency to overstate black occupational progress. Industry has less to fear from government equal opportunity compliance officials when black salespeople are classified as managers and when black technical assistants are called technicians. The 1970 Census sample showed 632,000 black professional and technical workers. How often, one must ask, is a black clerical assistant classified as a technical worker? In how many cases were the 32,000 blacks classified as "engineers" really working as laboratory aides?

The loose job classifications adopted by the Census Bureau not only make it difficult to obtain an accurate picture of the economic status of blacks but actually serve as one of the most important obstacles to black economic progress generally. As open invitations to statistical deception, the Census Bureau's broad classifications stand in the way of efforts to expose the myth that black people as a whole are gaining on whites.

No Blacks at the Top

The fact that blacks account for one-half of all private house cleaners and a third of all garbage collectors would be more acceptable if *some* blacks were found at the top of the economic pyramid. But this is not the case. A 1976 survey of the 1,000 largest corporations, banks, utilities, insurance companies, and investment and pension funds did not find a single black person among the several thousand high executives holding the titles of president, chairman of the board, vice-chairman of the board, chairman of the executive committee, or chairman of the finance committee. In 1978, *Ebony* magazine's annual survey of the "100 Most Influential Black Americans" did not mention even one black serving as an official in a major American corporation. The only black businessmen in the survey were officials of black-owned corporations, banks, and life insurance companies.[32]

In the late 1970s, it appeared that the black person supervising the greatest number of employees in the United States was Louis M. Callaway, Jr., manager of the Ford Motor Company's 3,800-worker assembly plant in Chicago. This is an important post. Yet, if this plant were counted as an independent company, it would rank three hundred forty-seventh among *Fortune*'s 500 largest industrial corporations.

Similar patterns appear in the professions. A 1979 survey reported in *The National Law Journal* showed that among the 3,700 partners in the nation's fifty largest law firms, only twelve were black.[33] As late as 1984, it was difficult to identify any black person at or near the top of any major corporation or professional firm.

The Cost of Being Unequal

What is the dollar cost of unequal employment participation by blacks in the economy? Using data from the Census Bureau and the Bureau of Labor Statistics, we can make a rough estimate of what unequal rates of unemployment and unequal salary and wage scales are costing blacks in terms of earnings they would otherwise realize. The calculation is done in two steps. First, we determine the amount of earnings lost to blacks because they find themselves in lower-scale jobs with consequently lower wage rates. This is done by multiplying the average level of black employment during 1978 (8,925,000 workers) by $2,897, the difference in mean earnings between blacks and whites ($10,541 white mean earnings versus $7,644 black mean earnings). When we do this, we find that blacks who worked in 1978 would have had about $25.9 billion in additional earnings had they been remunerated at the mean rate for whites.

Second, 12.6 percent of blacks were unemployed in 1978 compared with 5.2 percent of whites. If blacks had had the same rate of unemployment as whites during that year, an average of 755,000 additional blacks would have held jobs and gained income from earnings. If we assume that these blacks were hired without bias and were paid at the white mean, we find that an additional $8 billion in earnings were lost to blacks because of higher unemployment rates. This makes an estimated total of about $34 billion lost due to lower wage rates and higher unemployment.[34]

This huge figure summarizes the earnings lost to blacks because of their unequal access to the job market. As staggering as it is, the real total is probably much higher, for my estimate does not include the large numbers of black people who are missed in the Census survey. Of greater importance, the estimate does not include the loss of potential contributions by black people to the gross national product, contributions that would have been made had blacks been generating incomes equal to the national mean. Also the estimate does not include other dollar costs, such as welfare payments, housing subsidies, manpower programs, extra police protection, and drug programs, expenses directly or indirectly attributable to racial in-

ESTIMATED BLACK EARNINGS DEFICIT DUE TO LOWER WAGES AND HIGHER UNEMPLOYMENT RATES

1978 (Billions of Dollars)

SOURCE	AMOUNT
Unequal wages and salaries	$ 25.9
Unequal unemployment rates	$ 8.0
Total	$ 33.9
Total Black earnings—1978	$ 82.7
Amount Blacks would have earned had they been earning equally with Whites	$116.6

Source of the statistics used for calculations: U.S. Department of Labor, Bureau of Labor Statistics, Employment and Earnings, Vol. 26, No. 1, January 1979; and U.S. Bureau of the Census, Current Population Reports, Series P-60, No. 123, "Money Income in 1978 of Families and Persons in the United States," Table 58, p. 237.

equality. The dollar calculation does not, of course, begin to touch the toll in human terms: greater rates of family discord and family breakup, higher rates of alcoholism and drug addiction, malnutrition, substandard housing, disease, loss of self-respect, and high infant and adult mortality rates.

These costs have no balance sheet because no accountant can measure them.

CHAPTER FOURTEEN

Latecomers to the Feast:
The Black-White Wealth Gap

"He is defiled and must live outside the camp."

—Leviticus *13:46*

FEW OF US NEED to be convinced that holdings of property and wealth are closely related to the possession of power. Indeed, the ownership, or even simply the control, of property and capital touches at the very heart of social, economic, and political influence. It is useful to consider some of the reasons that this is so. Once the link between propertied status and power has been established, the critical political importance of wealth to blacks in the United States will become clear. Holdings of capital and wealth by black people will be seen not simply as one of the many economic measures that we use to determine whether or not equality, or progress toward equality, has occurred. An established black wealth base will be understood, also, as a necessary political condition that must prevail in order that black people possess the overall power they need to bargain their way toward equal economic status with whites.

In making the connection between wealth and power, the first point is that in a free society, ownership of property or economic surplus confers an exemption from the constraints of economic struggle. The person of means, like the provident squirrel with a goodly store of acorns, is relieved of the need to toil. If unemployment occurs, a modest store of property in the form of a savings account, a family allowance, a pension right, or a dividend income expectation gives an individual the freedom of not being obliged to accept the first job to be offered. Even when unemployment is not threatening, having property, money in the bank, or some other form of stored-up resource ensures the freedom to refrain from work or to leave an unwanted job and seek another position without undue apprehension about making ends meet during the jobless period. Under the most ideal conditions, the control of wealth, in self-owned or even in borrowed form, affords the delights of independent entrepreneurship and the chance ultimately to accumulate a larger store of property.

It has become fashionable in some circles for people of means to denounce their wealth as producing burdens rather than freedoms. Yet with few exceptions, the rich persist in enduring the bondage of property ownership with its attendant evils, such as the worries about maintaining a summer place in the Hamptons, the necessity of making difficult decisions about which preparatory school their children should attend, and the obligation to pay exorbitant sums for gasoline to keep both their cars and their boats running. Oddly enough, despite lamentations about the intolerable burdens of wealth, the rich get little sympathy on this score other than from each other.

Perhaps this is because only those who must make do without a plentiful bankroll fully appreciate the extent to which affluence in our society is a prerequisite for the full realization of certain civil and political liberties and rights—rights meant to be free for all citizens but which, in fact, have to be paid for. Equal justice, for example, is fundamental to our scheme of human rights, yet the fact is that justice tends to be unequally apportioned according to one's ability to pay for it. Regrettably, in both civil and criminal judicial contests, justice is, to some extent, purchased. Whether as a defendant in a criminal action or as a participant on either side of a civil suit, litigation is an expensive activity which, like yacht racing, is not likely to reward the person who attempts it with insufficient funds. Without property—and the economic power that property confers—the state's promise of equal justice is paper-thin.

Ownership of property also greatly affects one's access to political power, which, as we have seen, often becomes converted into economic power and well-being. Although the Constitution gives each individual an equal right to aspire to political office, as a pragmatic matter, access to the political power derived from holding elected office is demonstrably unequal. The law usually permits an individual to spend an unlimited amount of personal funds in seeking public office. Possibly as a result, at least 25 percent of the members of the U.S. Senate are millionaires. Moreover, money always speaks loudly and clearly to elected legislators. In the frequent and intense struggles for legislative votes, the most effective barrage of pressure comes from a senator's or congressman's contributors back home. The poor may cajole and plead with legislators to do what is "right," but the political heat that effectively persuades invariably comes from the propertied groups which have the capacity to provide financial support in the next political campaign.

Except in the rarest cases, having great wealth contributes far more to political success than having been born in a log cabin or in a black ghetto. When Thomas Jefferson was at work drafting the Constitution, he contemplated that only property owners would be enfranchised. In many respects, this is precisely what happened.

Ownership of even modest amounts of wealth or business capital has particular importance for minority groups that face opposing power in the form of negative prejudgments of race discrimination. A private business, for example, acts as a bulwark against employment discrimination. The white-owned bank, life insurance company, or retail establishment may decline to hire black executives, but the barriers of race discrimination do not so seriously impede the black person capable of finding economic independence, say, as a self-employed banker, life insurance executive, or retailer serving his own race. True, a black person who owns his own catering house, tailor's shop, or construction firm may find that his clientele is severely limited in its purchasing power, but his most valued freedom is that he does not have to go on his hands and knees to others to ask for the job, contract, or production order for which he has been prejudged as unqualified. Also, the black barber operating his own shop, the black funeral director with his own establishment, or the black storekeeper cannot be fired because of his political views. For these individuals, economic livelihood does not depend on refraining from voting, keeping quiet about school segregation, or declining to challenge unequal expenditures of public money. It appears that this is why self-employed black farmers in the South, even though poor, were always more effective marchers for civil rights than those who were employed by whites.

Finally, the attainment of propertied status by Negroes presents a powerful and direct attack on the fundamental psychology of racial stereotypes. It almost goes without saying that in our society the ownership of property is intimately related to the distribution of status and respect. In a society that values material things, property introduces one to the envied propertied class. As James Madison observed, "The most common and durable division is between those who hold and those who are without property." Dr.

James Freeman Clarke, a black Unitarian minister in New England, tellingly commented over a century ago on the social importance of making money, especially as it applied to black people:

"No race in this country will be despised which makes money. If we had in Boston or New York ten ourang-outangs worth a million dollars each, they would visit in the best society, we should leave our cards at their doors, and give them snug little dinner parties. We long for the time when there shall be colored people as rich as Croesus in every part of this dear New England." [1]

In recent decades, many traditional social values have tumbled, but the bourgeois sense of the respectability that inheres in property ownership has survived H. Rap Brown, the marches on the White House, and the student revolts of the 1960s. Therefore, a wealthy black person is not only an economic bastion protected from the racial hostility of others, but he or she stands also as a living refutation of the repressive black race-trait stereotype that, when confronted with a sufficient number of disarming examples of success, must, in time, abandon the group expectation of economic failure. Entrepreneurially won wealth in the hands of blacks, particularly, tends to subvert the common belief that blacks are born to labor while whites are born to employ blacks.

In measuring the capacity to use property to influence the behavior of others, the actual ownership of the property is frequently a mere technicality. For example, it is not the owners and stockholders, but the managers and controllers of the nation's corporate wealth, who decide whether serious efforts will be made to break down discriminatory practices within the nation's corporations. The executive managers of wealth and of corporate capital decide whether or not places of employment near black communities will be relocated to all-white suburban areas. The controllers and managers, rather than the owners of corporate wealth, negotiate the labor contracts that provide or omit the seniority clauses assuring whites, who are beneficiaries of racially discriminatory labor practices in the past, that they will retain their positions in the future. It is the managements, and not the actual owners, of the great aggregations of banking wealth in the United States who decide whether mortgage and commercial loan disinvestment will or will not occur in black communities. And finally, it is the chief executives, and not the owners, of corporate capital who decide whether or not middle managers will be chastened or dismissed for failing to meet affirmative-action goals. For these reasons, it is just as important for blacks to concern themselves with who *controls* wealth as with who *owns* it.

In the United States, the concentration of economic power at the top is great. In 1983, the managers of pension funds controlled one trillion dollars, a third to a half of the equity investment capital of the nation. In the same year, the senior management of 300 of the largest banks in the United States controlled an even greater sum of private lendable funds. Only a score of all white executives at the top of the largest life insurance companies controlled the investment of $600 billion of stocks, bonds, and mortgages. Here were important concentrations of power where the attitudes and decisions of those in charge profoundly affected the economic and political fortunes of citizens generally, and of racial groups in particular. To the extent that black economic power and well-being depend on the distribution of corporate wealth, the assessment will, in large measure, turn on the question of whether blacks hold executive positions where the levers of investment and credit are manipulated.

To what degree have blacks participated in this important process of wealth and capital formation, ownership, and control? To what extent are black people making greater claims on wealth than in the past? Compared with whites, are they losing or gaining in the competition for the control and ownership of property, capital, and wealth?

In this inquiry, we receive very little assistance from the U.S. Census Bureau. The government has found the subject of wealth differences among groups of citizens to be a somewhat embarrassing topic for official inquiry. Particularly, the measure of wealth inequalities of blacks has been a matter on which the Census counters of the federal government have been habitually mute. Since our government does very little official research on holdings of wealth, we must rely mainly on private and unofficial sources.

Black and White Wealth: Trends Over the Last Century

During the early days of black slavery, the question of black ownership of property was, of course, moot. The black slave usually owned nothing. As a person, he was a lawful form of property. However, among free blacks, there were entrepreneurs of daring, energy, and ingenuity. Antony Johnson, a black man, arrived here in 1621 and soon accumulated enough wealth to buy his freedom and purchase five indentured slaves and 250 acres of property in Northampton, Virginia. In 1762, a young black businessman, Samuel Fraunces, paid $2,000 for a mansion in what is now downtown Manhattan. He opened Fraunces Tavern, still one of the most famous restaurants in New York City. By 1830, there were 3,777 black slave owners.

In the 1850s, a black plantation aristocracy prospered in Louisiana. In New Orleans, Thomy Lafon, a black merchant, financier, and money lender, did well enough to leave an estate valued at half a million dollars, a vast sum in those days. In 1856, the real estate holdings of black Philadelphians had reached $800,000. The land holdings of blacks in New York were worth over $1 million. Free blacks owning stocks, bonds, and annuities prospered in Cincinnati, Washington, and Boston. At the outbreak of the Civil War, thousands of freedmen had achieved considerable economic success as entrepreneurs in catering, life insurance, tailoring, and sail-making, and as provisions merchants.

In the 1860s, the total real and personal wealth of free black persons was conservatively placed at $50 million. Professor Lee Soltow's authoritative analysis of the 1870 Census estimates that "a rather surprising 19 percent of nonwhites held wealth." [2]

The fact that free blacks were making good progress in commerce prior to the Civil War must be put in perspective. If wealth in the free black community totaled approximately $50 million, it then follows that black wealth per capita, assuming a free black population of 488,000, was about $102 a head. Professor Soltow's analysis of the 1870 Census essentially confirms the accuracy of these figures. It shows the average wealth of black adult males to be $74 per person, based on a total aggregate wealth of the $80 million held by black males in 1870.

Now compare this figure with average white holdings. Professor Soltow has found that white males in 1870 had about thirty-six times the wealth of black males. The per capita figure for white males was about $2,700 based on an aggregate white personal wealth of about $23 billion. [3]

Now let us see what clues there are as to what happened to black-white wealth ratios in the century following the Civil War. In 1967, the U.S. Office of Economic Opportunity surveyed American households and found that the net wealth accumulation of whites, including equity in homes and businesses, cars, stocks, savings, government bonds, etc., was then about $1.1 trillion. The aggregate holdings of these resources by blacks were reported to be about $22.7 billion. This meant that blacks, who constituted about 11 percent of the population, owned roughly 2 percent of all assets. In other words, the ratio between black and white holdings of wealth was in the magnitude of 5 to 1. [4]

This government survey showing a massive gap between the average wealth of whites and blacks has been the most powerful single statement of the extent to which blacks are almost totally absent from the propertied and entrepreneurial classes of the nation. Yet, there is a far more serious gap in the composition of resources held by black and white families. In 1967, blacks—then about 11 percent of the overall population—had only 1.1

percent of all money in banks and government bonds. Black families, on the average, had just under $300 per family in banks and other financial institutions, compared with about $2,950 for white families. Black ownership of stocks was estimated at a minuscule 0.13 percent of the total.

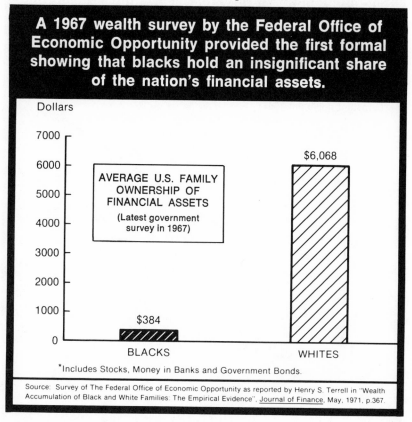

A 1967 wealth survey by the Federal Office of Economic Opportunity provided the first formal showing that blacks hold an insignificant share of the nation's financial assets.

AVERAGE U.S. FAMILY OWNERSHIP OF FINANCIAL ASSETS
(Latest government survey in 1967)

$6,068

$384

BLACKS   WHITES

*Includes Stocks, Money in Banks and Government Bonds.

Source: Survey of The Federal Office of Economic Opportunity as reported by Henry S. Terrell in "Wealth Accumulation of Black and White Families: The Empirical Evidence", Journal of Finance, May, 1971, p.367.

Finally, when all financial assets are included, black families in 1967 had average holdings of only $384, compared with $6,068 for the average white family.

It is impossible to make any precise comparisons between the apparent black-white wealth gap prevailing in 1870 and the situation determined by government estimate in 1967. In the first place, in 1870 the Census was counting black males whereas the Office of Economic Opportunity was counting families in 1967. Second, there is no way to determine whether the government was counting the same items as wealth in 1870 as it was in 1967. Nevertheless, as long as we confine our comparison to *wealth ratios,* the variations should not greatly affect any comparisons we choose to draw.

A superficial glance at the statistics tells us that the racial gap in personal wealth has narrowed from the 36-to-1 ratio between the mean wealth of

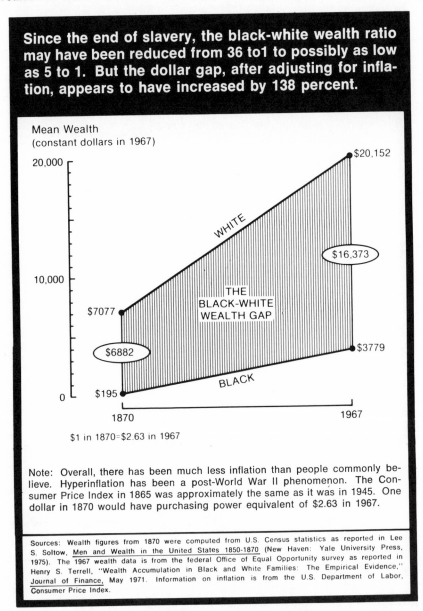

Since the end of slavery, the black-white wealth ratio may have been reduced from 36 to1 to possibly as low as 5 to 1. But the dollar gap, after adjusting for inflation, appears to have increased by 138 percent.

Mean Wealth
(constant dollars in 1967)

20,000

$20,152

WHITE

$16,373

10,000

THE
BLACK-WHITE
WEALTH GAP

$7077

$6882

$3779

0    $195

BLACK

1870   1967

$1 in 1870=$2.63 in 1967

Note: Overall, there has been much less inflation than people commonly believe. Hyperinflation has been a post-World War II phenomenon. The Consumer Price Index in 1865 was approximately the same as it was in 1945. One dollar in 1870 would have purchasing power equivalent of $2.63 in 1967.

Sources: Wealth figures from 1870 were computed from U.S. Census statistics as reported in Lee S. Soltow, Men and Wealth in the United States 1850-1870 (New Haven: Yale University Press, 1975). The 1967 wealth data is from the federal Office of Equal Opportunity survey as reported in Henry S. Terrell, "Wealth Accumulation in Black and White Families: The Empirical Evidence," Journal of Finance, May 1971. Information on inflation is from the U.S. Department of Labor, Consumer Price Index.

white and black males in 1870 to a much more modest 5-to-1 ratio between the assets of white and black families 100 years later. Yet, it must be borne in mind that this closing of the percentage gap has much less significance than would have been the case if the two races had started off with a much smaller difference between them. Since blacks after emancipation held near zero wealth, even very slight increases appear as very great reductions in the percentage gap between blacks and whites.

It would be comforting to conclude that if blacks have managed to cut the gap by something like a factor of seven in a little under 100 years, then they must be fast approaching parity with whites. In fact, however, it appears that the gap has been narrowing so slowly that if we project forward on a straight-line basis the same percentage gains that occurred in the 1870 to 1967 period, we find that blacks would not catch up with whites for nearly five centuries. It appears that in 1870, the black-white wealth ratio stood at 2 percent. Approximately 100 years later, in 1967, the ratio had risen slowly to 18 percent. Thus, the per capita ratio of black wealth to white wealth over the century appears to be closing only at the rate of 0.16 percentage points a year. Moreover, as we show later, the wealth gains one would have expected to have occurred as a result of the greater opportunities generally available to blacks in recent years have not produced significant improvement in the black-white wealth ratio.

Indeed, if we look at actual dollar amounts rather than ratios, we see that whites are not only far ahead of blacks in terms of total wealth but are actually increasing the dollar gap. After adjusting for inflation during this period of approximately 100 years, we find that in 1870 the average white held assets valued at about $6,900 more than the assets of the average black. In 1967, the dollar gap had grown by 138 percent to $16,400. Writing in 1975, Professor Soltow puts all these figures in stark perspective when he points out the following:

> "[A]verage wealth for nonwhites today is less than that of whites in 1870. Nonwhite wealth in 1962, corrected for changes in prices and changes in age composition, was only 40 percent of white wealth in 1870." [5]

Black Wealth Today

If in 1967 blacks had held financial resources on a parity basis with whites, they would have had aggregate assets of about $37 billion. Their actual holdings were valued at only $2.3 billion. In these terms, in 1967, the financial asset gap between blacks and whites amounted to $35 billion or $5,600 per family. This figure, computed from an Office of Economic Opportunity study done in the late 1960s, tends to be confirmed by Census

Bureau tabulations of dividend and interest income. In 1978, black families and unrelated individuals had slightly over $1 billion in income from dividends, interest, and rent. Whites, on the other hand, enjoyed about $67 billion from these sources. On a per capita basis, this translates to about $41.50 of dividend, interest, and rent income for every black, compared with about $360 for every white.[6]

If both blacks and whites earned the same rate of return on these financial assets, the relative per capita dividend and interest income would reflect the relative holdings of invested wealth. On this basis, black per capita wealth in 1978 would be about 11.6 percent that of whites. If, in fact, blacks had a greater cash yield on such assets—a very likely event since blacks have much more invested in savings accounts than whites, who have a much greater percentage invested in low-yielding equity securities—the real wealth gap would increase beyond the 9-to-1 ratio.

A 1982 study by Andrew Brimmer, former Governor of the Federal Reserve Board, estimated black wealth in 1982 at $144.6 billion. The corresponding figure for the country at large was $6,189.7 billion. On this basis, blacks held 2.34 percent of the nation's total wealth.

A recent paper released by the Joint Center of Political Studies in Washington, D.C., has estimated current black holdings of wealth based on probability samplings made in 1979. The study concluded that the black-white family wealth ratio is considerably more favorable to blacks than either the Office of Economic Opportunity or the Brimmer study would have suggested. The Joint Center conclusion was that the overall average personal wealth of the black family stands at about 36 percent of the white family. But the key measure of economic status and power—holdings of stocks, mutual funds, certificates of deposit and other liquid assets—continues to show almost insignificant participation by blacks in the fruits of American capitalism. The Joint Center study concluded that black households in 1979 had average financial assets of only $2,200 per family compared with over $20,000 for white families.[7]

Black Savers: A Stereotype Turned Upside Down

Although blacks, on the average, own far less property and surplus value than do whites, they have a greater proportion of liquid assets in savings accounts. They also have a much greater percentage than whites of non-income-producing assets such as real estate, motor vehicles, and consumer durables. Consequently, a smaller percentage of their assets take the form of business equity, stocks, bonds, and other securities.

Curiously, life insurance is one form of asset accumulation in which a surprising reversal of expectable disparities exists. A 1966 University of Michigan survey of consumer finances shows that at every income level a greater percentage of black families than white families owned life insurance. In periods of inflation, this works to further diminish black financial strength because the face amount of life insurance policies is payable in fixed dollars that rapidly diminish in real purchasing power.[8]

One of the most persistent articles in the canons of American racial stereotypes is that blacks are less financially responsible and more improvident than whites. This idea, however, like many other widely accepted racial stereotypes, is refuted by the facts. Studies have shown that at any given income level, blacks are not less financially responsible and more improvident than whites. A study prepared for the University of Michigan by three outside economists shows that blacks spend less on consumer goods and save more than whites with comparable incomes.[9]

Professor Milton Friedman has explained this phenomenon in terms of the different lifetime income expectations of the two racial groups. Because blacks have less job security than whites, and because blacks are able to increase their incomes at a much slower rate, they tend to place relatively heavier emphasis on savings as a nest egg or cash reserve to hedge against possible financial hard times. Whites, in contrast, working on a more secure financial base with greater prospects of job security and income advances, tend to think of savings less as protection against a "rainy day" than as an investment strategy for wealth accumulation.[10]

As with life insurance, the greater tendency of blacks to keep dollars in savings accounts has not served them well in recent years, when ownership in real estate and select groups of securities has provided greater protection against inflation. But the significant point here is that the relatively greater rate of purchase of life insurance by blacks, as well as their relatively greater tendency at all income levels to save money—even in the face of inflationary pressures—testifies to the fact that black families are strongly committed to providing for the future. As is the case with whites, there are very large percentages of improvident blacks; but the common notion that blacks as a group are not future-oriented and are less capable of adopting middle-class economic values is pure mythology.

The Triviality of Black Capitalism

In recent years, the government has generated considerable publicity for various federal programs designed to foster so-called minority capitalism.

In the eyes of many of its advocates, government support of minority entrepreneurship was meant as a means of building black economic and political clout and, to some extent, of protecting participating blacks from racial discrimination.

Instead of supporting black economic power aspirations, however, minority capitalism became the Nixon administration's means of addressing black economic problems "on the cheap." At a cost to the government of only a few hundred million dollars a year, new black entrepreneurs, who were often black athletes, could be displayed at political fund-raising dinners where they were expected to provide testimonial evidence of the disappearance of racial inequalities. The cynical government effort to manipulate black voters, as well as to throw dust in the eyes of white liberals who supported pressures for wider black participation in the economy, has not received much attention in studies of the Nixon presidency.

How important is black capitalism in the United States today? In 1977, the Census Bureau counted about 230,000 black-owned businesses, comprising approximately 1.6 percent of all firms in the nation. In the total American economy, these black businesses occupy a minuscule position. The gross receipts of black business endeavors were $8.6 billion, accounting for about two-tenths of one percent of the national total of about $4.4 trillion.

To place black business in a readily understandable perspective, the combined gross receipts of all the 230,000 black business efforts in 1977 were about the same as the sales volume of Western Electric, at that time the eighteenth largest industrial corporation in the United States.[11]

Most black businesses are very small operations of the mom-and-pop variety and therefore do not represent transferable or inheritable value. According to the 1977 Census Bureau survey of minority-owned businesses, about 83 percent of all black firms reported no paid employees and average gross receipts of a mere $11,800 per firm. Of the 17 percent of black-owned firms with paid employees, the average number of employees per firm was only four. According to *Black Enterprise,* in 1982, the combined annual sales of the twenty-five largest black businesses were about $1.2 billion. This combined sum was just about equal to the sales of only one relatively unknown corporation, Pacific Resources of Honolulu, which ranked two hundred fifty-eighth in the United States in terms of annual sales.

The combined annual sales of all of the twenty-five largest black enterprises in 1982 were equivalent to about five days of sales of Exxon.[12]

The mini-boom which appeared to be developing in black enterprise beginning in the late 1960s has been cooled by unfavorable economic con-

STILL WAITING FOR CAPITALISM: THE TWENTY-FIVE LARGEST BLACK BUSINESSES

In 1982 there were 258 industrial corporations in the United States each having annual sales greater than the combined total of the 25 largest black-owned businesses.

RANK	COMPANY & LOCATION	EMPLOYEES	TYPE OF BUSINESS	1982 SALES*
1	Motown Industries Los Angeles, California	231	Entertainment	104.300
2	H.J. Russell Construction, Inc. Atlanta, Georgia	500	Construction/development/ communications	103.850
3	Johnson Publishing Company, Inc. Chicago, Illinois	1,586	Publishing, cosmetics & broadcasting	102.650
4	Fedco Foods Corporation Bronx, New York	725	Supermarkets	85.000
5	Wardoco Incorporated New Haven, Connecticut	17	Commercial fuel oils	84.393
6	Thacker Construction Company Decatur, Georgia	475	Construction/engineering	77.300
7	G & M Oil Company, Inc. Baltimore, Maryland	57	Petroleum sales	62.096
8	Soft Sheen Products, Inc. Chicago, Illinois	570	Manufacturer & distributor of hair care products	55.000
9	Vanguard Oil and Service Company Brooklyn, New York	51	Petroleum sales	53.000
10	The Jackson Oil Company Baltimore, Maryland	53	Petroleum sales	50.801
11	M & M Products Company, Inc. Atlanta, Georgia	380	Manufacturer & distributor of hair care products	43.000
12	Johnson Products Company, Inc. Chicago, Illinois	541	Manufacturer of hair care products & cosmetics	42.400
13	Dick Griffey Productions Los Angeles, California	95	Entertainment	41.200
14	The Smith Pipe Companies, Inc. Houston, Texas	85	Oilfield pipe & supply sales	35.000
15	Systems and Applied Sciences Corp. Riverdale, Maryland	800	Computer and electronic data systems	34.000
16	Wallace & Wallace Enterprises, Inc. St. Albans, New York	10	Petroleum sales	32.000
17	Grimes Oil Company, Inc. Boston, Massachusetts	35	Petroleum sales	31.906
18	Housing Innovations, Inc. Boston, Massachusetts	125	Real estate development/ construction	29.230
19	Teleport Oil Company San Francisco, California	30	Petroleum sales	28.000
20	L.H. Smith Oil Corporation Indianapolis, Indiana	39	Petroleum sales	27.000
21	Inner City Broadcasting Corporation New York, New York	250	Radio & TV communications	24.500
22	Community Foods, Inc. Baltimore, Maryland	275	Retail foods	23.000
23	Robinson Cadillac-Pontiac, Inc. Atlanta, Georgia	58	Auto sales & service	22.379
24	American Development Corporation North Charleston, South Carolina	300	Manufacturing	21.000
25	Restoration Supermarket Corporation Brooklyn, New York	150	Retail grocery	21.000

* Millions of Dollars

Source: Black Enterprise, June 1983, p. 68; and Fortune, May 2, 1983, p. 226.

ditions and persistent racial stereotyping. Particularly, the politicization of the government's black capitalism effort has led to a persistent ghettoization of black entrepreneurship. In most cases, bank credit and government loan guarantees have been offered black entrepreneurs only when their plans contemplated segregated business activities. White institutions are frequently enthusiastic about sending money and credit backing to blacks, but less generous when the black entrepreneur proposes to integrate white neighborhoods or to enter the mainstream of American capitalism.

The low expectations attached to black entrepreneurship have changed of late, but they prevailed through the mid-1970s and seriously retarded the efforts of blacks to win capital bases in the heartland of the American economy.

Examining the current list of the largest black enterprises, one is struck by the fact that virtually all of them are service-oriented. Most notably, in 1982, twenty-six out of the top 100 black businesses were automobile dealerships. Perhaps even more startling is the fact that in 1977 nearly one out of every eleven black businesses was either a barber or beauty shop. Not one of the leading black businesses is truly capital-intensive. Among them, there are no blacks controlling production of electronics, electricity, chemicals, or heavy machinery; the list shows no black-owned oil production, coal mines, cattle ranches, or land holdings of any importance. Black business operates on the fringes of American capitalism, where competition is most intense and where there is little opportunity to create and transmit significant durable wealth by gift, sale, or inheritance. Andrew Brimmer has noted that the heavy concentrations of black businesses in low-growth industries render their prospects for the future particularly bleak.[13]

At first glance, it might seem that there is an advantage to the black community as a whole in the fact that black business, being service-oriented and therefore labor-intensive, should be able to provide jobs for black workers. But the weight of black business as a force for wider employment opportunities for black people is negligible. The 100 largest black businesses in 1982 had a total of only about 22,500 employees. On the reasonable assumption that most employees of black businesses are black, the 100 largest black enterprises account for about one-quarter of one percent of the total of 9 million black jobs in the United States. According to the 1977 Census Bureau survey, about 165,000 blacks were employed by all black-owned business enterprises, a figure that represents less than 2 percent of all black jobs that year. American Telephone and Telegraph alone employed more than 100,000 blacks in 1977, approximately five times as many as the 100 largest black businesses combined and almost two-thirds as many as all black businesses in the nation.[14]

Banks and life insurance companies have long been considered to be the traditional bastions of black economic enterprise. In 1982, there were thirty-eight black-owned life insurance companies, many of which could trace their antecedents back to the chartered black mutual aid and beneficial societies of the 1880s. Representing the combined historical product of black initiative and the long-standing refusal of white-controlled companies to insure blacks, these thirty-eight black life insurance companies had combined assets of $740 million in 1982.

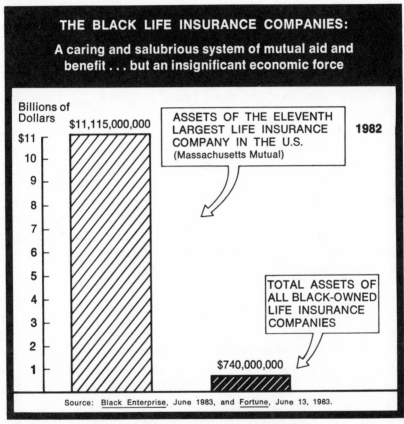

THE BLACK LIFE INSURANCE COMPANIES:

A caring and salubrious system of mutual aid and benefit . . . but an insignificant economic force

Billions of Dollars

$11,115,000,000

ASSETS OF THE ELEVENTH LARGEST LIFE INSURANCE COMPANY IN THE U.S. (Massachusetts Mutual)

1982

TOTAL ASSETS OF ALL BLACK-OWNED LIFE INSURANCE COMPANIES

$740,000,000

Source: Black Enterprise, June 1983, and Fortune, June 13, 1983.

This figure must be put in perspective. The combined resources of all the black-owned life insurance companies were about 1.2 percent of the assets of the Prudential Life Insurance Company alone. North Carolina Mutual Life Insurance Company, the largest of the black companies, had assets of $200 million, roughly equal to 1.8 percent of the resources of Massachusetts Mutual Life Insurance Company, the eleventh largest life insurance company in the United States. Even the relatively small white-controlled Mutual of Omaha, which ranked sixtieth in 1981, had more than twice the assets of all black life insurance companies combined.

The black life insurance industry may be a good morale booster for blacks, but as an economic force both within the insurance industry and within the American economy as a whole, it is simply too small to matter.

What about the widely publicized black banks? Like the black life insurance companies, black-owned and -operated banks are a product of black zeal and determination, as well as of credit discrimination by white banks that have traditionally been reluctant to extend credit to black farmers and businessmen. Again, the arithmetic of black banking is dismal. In 1982, there were forty-four black-owned and -operated banks in the United States with aggregate assets of about $1.3 billion. This represents less than one-tenth of one percent of the nation's total banking resources and in the aggregate less than the assets of any one of the 168 largest banks in the country.[15]

Clearly, an overall black banking force of $1.3 billion in assets—averaging out to approximately $57 per head for the black population—is of little economic consequence other than as a stimulus to black esprit. Black banks have been burdened by heavy losses associated with the generally low incomes and weak economic positions of their customers. This, in turn, means that the black banks have been handicapped in the competition for banking capital and deposits. Consequently, black banks have been capable of furnishing capital sufficient to support only the most tentative steps toward economic development in the black community.[16]

Who Controls Black Wealth?

To understand an army, one must know not only who owns it, but also who commands it. In order to understand ecclesiastical power, one does not ask who owns a church, but rather who are its cardinals and bishops. So, too, in a highly developed economy where the separation of capital ownership from its management is the rule, one must ask who are the chiefs who control the huge economic and political power represented by the great national store of plants, machinery, and investment capital. The question of the control of wealth may be divided into two parts. To what extent do blacks control their own wealth? And to what extent do they share control over corporate wealth in general? We will deal with the second question first.

The total value of corporate wealth in America may be estimated to be between $7 trillion and $8 trillion. The executives who control the deployment of this gigantic store of value also control the vast economic and political power at its disposal. For example, the senior management of

Citicorp, a very large bank, owns an infinitesimal percentage of the shares that control the $130 billion of the bank's resources. Yet the senior management of the bank, governed only by regulatory forces, competition, and the rather soft hand of oversight by a board of directors, possesses the power to decide to what extent, if any, portions of the huge resources will be invested in mortgages in Harlem, in business credits to minority entrepreneurs in the South Bronx, or in nursing homes in the black Bedford-Stuyvesant area of Brooklyn. With Citicorp as with other large banks, billions of dollars are loaned to nations such as Poland or Argentina—nations neither particularly stable nor particularly friendly to the United States—while insignificant sums are committed to underdeveloped black communities in the United States. This allocation of credit is not simply the inevitable outcome of the bankers' imperative to commit very large sums of money to supposedly secure borrowers. These investments of funds are the product, too, of the collective goals, prejudices, and stereotypes as well as the rational views of the people holding posts at the top of the banking institutions.

Very great concentrations of economic power are vested, too, in the heads of America's great industrial corporations. They choose whether to locate plants, machinery, and jobs where blacks live, where whites live, or in areas accessible to both. They decide whether candidates for employment should be drawn largely from the local and often all-white high schools or from a larger cross-section of the community. These and countless other decisions mentioned earlier have a profound effect on the employment prospects of the black population. To what extent do blacks share in exercising the corporate power that makes decisions that are so critical to their life chances?

As we have already noted, even after the progress made in recent years, blacks have become pegged as a class of lower and middle managers of American business. They almost never appear in line positions of power in any large banks or industrial corporations. Of course, many corporations, responding to the vogue that developed during the late 1960s, have invited blacks to serve as corporate directors, but the power of an individual director is negligible. In nine out of ten large corporations, the board of corporate directors merely rubber-stamps management decisions. A person must be naive indeed to believe that black corporate directors in this country hold anything more than token power.

A number of large corporations currently employ blacks in management positions as vice-presidents exercising various responsibilities. But black executives are usually concentrated away from centers of power—often in areas of community relations, urban affairs, and minority recruiting. The fact that not one of the top 500 corporations in America employs a black person in its high posts as either president, chairman of the executive committee, or chairman of the finance committee—or for that matter as a senior line executive—adequately sums up the near total separation of blacks from the corporate powers that affect their opportunities and careers.

This conclusion was confirmed in a 1970 study conducted by the Race Relations Information Center of Nashville, Tennessee. After surveying "the 3,182 senior officers and directors in the executive suites and boardrooms of the nation's top fifty corporations," the study reported that the only three blacks to be found were serving as company directors. Not one was a senior executive.[17] A cursory examination of the top ranks of the Fortune 500 corporations confirms that the very high-ranking executives in corporate America continue to be exclusively white.

If blacks have no influence over the deployment of the general wealth of corporate America, do they at least control the uses and allocations of whatever modest wealth "belongs" to them? Since the total wealth represented by pension funds, bank resources, savings and loan assets, and the assets of life insurance companies is approximately $4 trillion, and since black incomes run about 60 percent of white incomes, we may assume blacks have a valid claim of upwards to 60 percent of their population share of these resources. On this assumption, about 7 percent of life insurance resources, pension funds, savings and loan, and banking assets may be considered, in an equitable sense, as "belonging" to, or set aside for, blacks. In dollar terms, this works out to approximately $280 billion. Since blacks occupy almost none of the very senior policymaking positions in banking, life insurance, or pension fund investment management, it becomes clear that blacks exercise no participating control whatsoever over the investment allocation of their own money.[18]

Given the present precarious state of the black economy, most blacks might very well decide that "their money" would be more safely invested in white enterprises. Alternatively, large numbers of blacks might also want to stipulate that their assets be invested in the shares of large, sound, and profitable mainstream corporations with strong minority employment records. Voting collectively, blacks might also prefer not to have their funds invested in shares of corporations that have lagged badly in minority employment or in those that bankroll the political opponents of affirmative action. Or, contrary to the established policies of the majority of whites who control pension funds, many blacks might want to cast a ballot that their funds be withheld from the shares of banks lending funds to support South African apartheid. But participatory democracy is only a partial likeness of American capitalism. Blacks have no choice in these matters. In no sense do blacks in America participate in decisions that control the investment of any part of large institutional funds.

There is, indeed, a very low level of awareness among blacks of how their share of institutional capital is invested. For example, blacks who deposit their money in local savings institutions may be forgiven for assuming that this money is plowed back into the black community in the form of investments and loans. For many years, savings and loan companies mounted a national advertising campaign keyed to the slogan, "Invest in Your Community." In May 1975, however, representatives from twenty cities described to the Senate Banking Committee where the deposits made by black people were going. Not far from the typical case was that of the Interstate Building Association with twelve offices in the District of Columbia. The population of the District of Columbia was then about 71 percent black. In 1973, the Interstate Building Association had $55 million loaned to suburban residents, almost all of whom were white, and only $185,000 loaned to District of Columbia residents.[19]

Before leaving the topic of control of wealth, we should consider one industry of overwhelming importance to the issue. This is investment banking. Investment banking firms as such neither own nor control large sums of private capital, yet, they exercise important influence over who does and does not have access to credit, capital, and other means of wealth formation.

The investment banking industry is notable in having almost no blacks in management positions. In fact, the industry has been cited repeatedly as a persistent laggard in the employment of racial minorities. In 1973, less than one percent of all securities salespersons were black. There were no black partners or senior officers in any of the fifty largest firms dominating the investment banking or brokerage industry. In the early 1980s, no black person held a post near the top of any large investment banking firm. At that time, no black person had ever been publicly identified as holding a position in the high executive ranks of the large institutional money managers who invested and reinvested hundreds of billions of dollars of public and private pension funds. Blacks who have entered the investment banking industry are heavily concentrated in municipal finance transactions, where, for political reasons, the employment of a manager with black skin is often an economic and political advantage to the investment firm. The nearly total separation of blacks from capital allocation decisions is one of the most formidable barriers that isolate blacks from the mainstream of American capitalism.[20]

White America's Disproportionate Claim to Government-Sponsored Wealth

In the United States, government power is an important source of private wealth formation. The legendary private fortunes created by government sponsorship were amassed many decades ago, when blacks were not considered eligible to ride the gravy train of government largesse. Blacks were almost exclusively employed as agricultural and domestic laborers when the government made its grants—exclusively to whites—of real estate, utility and railroad franchises, mineral rights, and broadcast licenses. The value of these various grants, licenses, and franchises may today be counted in the hundreds of billions of dollars.

The contemporary equivalent of these awards is the government contract. In 1980, U.S. government contracts to the private sector totaled about $100 billion. Of this vast sum, $3.4 billion, excluding loan packaging, went to minority enterprise. This averages out to $134 per minority person, contrasting sharply with a government expenditure of $459 a year per person for the population as a whole.[21]

Most government contract money is awarded to large defense contractors and corporations whose managements or stockholders, as we have already noted, are predominantly white. No racial prejudice here, but obviously the government awards advance the economic position of those groups— almost entirely white—that have holdings of the shares of these companies. But there is frequently a more direct racial impact resulting from the business-as-usual allocation of federal contracts. Consider, for example, contract awards in the predominantly black District of Columbia. In 1974, *The Washington Post* reported that only 1.9 percent of the dollar value of the District's construction money went to minority firms (a circumstance recently changed by the coming to political power of black people in the District). These skimpy awards made to blacks sketch out the closed economic circle in which blacks are confined in most cities. In part, because of past discrimination, very few black firms have the financial strength to undertake and fulfill large government contracts. In this sense, the award of major contracts to white firms seems inevitable. And, as a result, black firms are unlikely to gain the competence and financial strength needed to turn things around.

Blacks are thus in the *Catch-22* position of the man whom no one will hire because he doesn't have experience and who can't get experience because no one will hire him. Indeed, the figures regularly published by the Department of Defense and other agencies confirm that the federal government's efforts to help blacks break out of this self-perpetuating mold are negligible. Most whites, forgetting perhaps that their ancestors received huge government grants and privileges allocated under strict "whites only" policies, are distressed that the government should now make even limited contract set-asides for minority bidders.

Whatever one's view of the advisability of favored treatment of minority contractors, the current token level of awards accomplishes little except to dupe inexperienced liberals into believing that black capitalism is on the march, while in fact, affirmative-action policies in their present form shape small expectations only and contribute little or nothing toward the building of an important and necessary black economic base.[22]

Wealth in the Ground: Whites Riding a Runaway Freight Train; Blacks Running Alongside

There are few societies—the United States included—where economic and political power are not closely connected with the control and ownership of land. The landless status of the black population is a critical feature of their almost complete isolation from the instruments of capital. Just as blacks essentially work for capital owned by whites and operate machines owned by whites, so, too, they have traditionally worked land owned by whites.

W.E.B. DuBois estimated that in 1875 blacks in the United States owned about 3 million acres of land. Over the next forty years black landholdings actually grew—to 8 million acres in 1890, 12 million in 1900, and 15 million in 1915. Since that time, however, there has been a steady decline in black land ownership. Today, there are less than 5 million acres of black-owned farmland, and black land ownership is being reduced at the rate of about 300,000 acres per year.[23]

The loss of land by blacks reflects, in part, migration patterns. Blacks began to leave the rural South in the early years of this century. During World War I, many blacks abandoned their farms to work in war industries in the North. During World War II, thousands more left to join the armed forces or to try their luck in northern urban centers where they hoped to escape poverty by finding better employment opportunities. Black ownership of land had reached its peak before these great northward migrations. Although most of the acreage held by blacks in the early part of the century was farmland, the holdings also included what is now the hugely valuable Sea Islands of South Carolina and the Citronelle Oil Field in Alabama.[24]

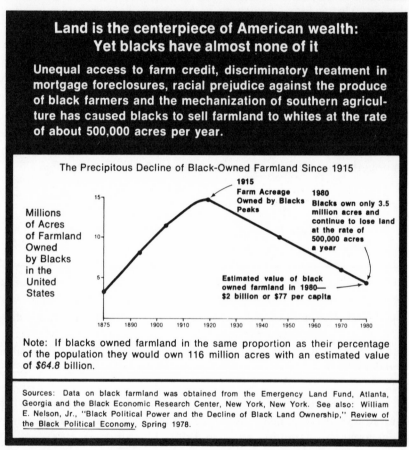

**Land is the centerpiece of American wealth:
Yet blacks have almost none of it**

Unequal access to farm credit, discriminatory treatment in mortgage foreclosures, racial prejudice against the produce of black farmers and the mechanization of southern agriculture has caused blacks to sell farmland to whites at the rate of about 500,000 acres per year.

The Precipitous Decline of Black-Owned Farmland Since 1915

Millions of Acres of Farmland Owned by Blacks in the United States

1915 Farm Acreage Owned by Blacks Peaks

1980 Blacks own only 3.5 million acres and continue to lose land at the rate of 500,000 acres a year

Estimated value of black owned farmland in 1980— $2 billion or $77 per capita

Note: If blacks owned farmland in the same proportion as their percentage of the population they would own 116 million acres with an estimated value of $64.8 billion.

Sources: Data on black farmland was obtained from the Emergency Land Fund, Atlanta, Georgia and the Black Economic Research Center, New York, New York. See also: William E. Nelson, Jr., "Black Political Power and the Decline of Black Land Ownership," Review of the Black Political Economy, Spring 1978.

Over the years, other forces, too, have contributed to the decline in black land ownership. Whites controlled the legal system of the South and were able to manipulate it to acquire large amounts of black-owned land. The legal technique for the eviction of blacks was the so-called partition sale, which took place when blacks died without making wills. By buying up a single share from an uneducated black heir, whites could force an auction sale of the balance. Land foreclosure sales occurred in every recession, and those standing by to make bargain purchases were invariably white. The disposition of southern banks to permit payment moratoria on farm mort-gages during difficult times was a banking judgment not made on a racially neutral basis. Thus, land in the South was transferred from blacks to whites by the banking practice of denying blacks relief on mortgage payments while granting breathing space to whites. The mechanization of southern agriculture also drove blacks to sell agricultural land that they could not farm efficiently without the machinery they could neither afford nor finance through white-owned banks. Even when government-assisted farm credit became available during the 1930s, it was administered locally by white officials who exclusively preferred white applicants to blacks.

Blacks and the Real Estate Boom of the 1970s

Compounding the outright loss of land, blacks have also failed to claim a significant share of the wealth benefit from the huge appreciation in real estate values that has taken place in recent years. Since 1970, the value of homes and farmland has risen dramatically. The increase in values during the decade appears to have been sixfold or more. According to the National Association of Realtors:

"Single-family homes constitute the single largest category of assets in this country. . . . Taken together, single-family structures have an aggregate value in the neighborhood of $2.3 *trillion*. A number of this magnitude must be put into perspective. The $2.3 trillion represents one-fourth of the entire wealth of this nation. If divided evenly among every man, woman, and child it would amount to a bit over $10,000 per person." [25]

Being poor in land and in home ownership, blacks have not benefited from this vast source of wealth appreciation. To measure the extent of the inequality in real estate wealth gains, let us work on the assumption that wealth derived from land and home ownership follows the established racial pattern of wealth ownership in general. If this is so, then upwards to 98 percent of the sixfold appreciation of home and land values accrued to whites; only 2 to 3 percent went to blacks. During the 1970s, therefore, whites probably added about $9,000 per capita to their wealth holdings; blacks probably added only $1,300 on a per capita basis.

It is likely, however, that these figures greatly overestimated the black wealth gain, since whites generally own real estate in suburban, farm, and other areas where the most dramatic value increases have occurred; blacks, however, tend to own real property in remote rural communities and in marginal and less desirable urban areas. [26] Thus, we see that for reasons having very little to do with current race discrimination, but strongly connected with race discrimination of the past, it is likely that the truly colossal gains in the value of U.S. real estate that have occurred in recent years have redounded almost entirely to the benefit of whites.

It is probable, too, that any forces tending to close the black-white wealth gap have been blunted due to surges in recent years in the value of *commer-*

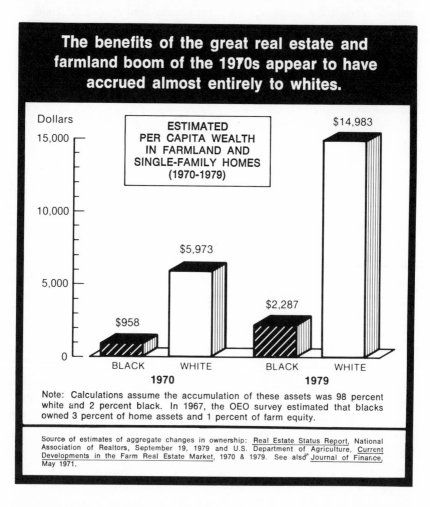

The benefits of the great real estate and farmland boom of the 1970s appear to have accrued almost entirely to whites.

ESTIMATED PER CAPITA WEALTH IN FARMLAND AND SINGLE-FAMILY HOMES (1970-1979)

Dollars

15,000 —

$14,983

10,000 —

$5,973

5,000 —

$2,287

$958

0

BLACK WHITE BLACK WHITE
1970 **1979**

Note: Calculations assume the accumulation of these assets was 98 percent white and 2 percent black. In 1967, the OEO survey estimated that blacks owned 3 percent of home assets and 1 percent of farm equity.

Source of estimates of aggregate changes in ownership: Real Estate Status Report, National Association of Realtors, September 19, 1979 and U.S. Department of Agriculture, Current Developments in the Farm Real Estate Market, 1970 & 1979. See also Journal of Finance, May 1971.

cial real estate. Here is a huge ocean of value where black participation in ownership is very slight indeed. Virtually, all the urban office building properties—where values have increased by hundreds of billions of dollars in recent years—are owned by whites. Also, the spectacular farmland boom of the 1970s (only partially moderated in the mid-1980s) has been enjoyed almost entirely by white people since black holdings of farmland have now been reduced to an insignificant figure.

OPEC's Gift to White America

Unquestionably, the spectacular increase in the dollar value of petroleum wealth during the 1970s has had a significant effect on blunting the progress toward the closing of the wealth gap between blacks and whites. It appears that during the decade of the 1970s, the market value of petroleum and natural gas reserves in the United States alone increased from about $100 billion to about $700 billion. The astronomical increase in the dollar value of U.S. oil and gas reserves during this period was more than twenty times the aggregate estimated U.S. black-owned wealth in 1967. Perhaps half of this added value, or about $300 billion, accrued to the benefit of private individual investors and to the essentially U.S.-owned producers other than the international oil giants. Many thousands of petroleum multimillionaires have been created during the past ten years, but there are no indications that blacks as investors in shares or as mineral rights owners shared to any important extent in this huge increase in the value of national wealth.[27]

In recent years, a handful of blacks, owning small farms in the so-called Tuscaloosa Trend in southern Louisiana, are reported to have had oil or gas finds on their properties.[28] But virtually all the major new oil discoveries have benefited groups other than blacks. Spectacular new oil and gas producing areas such as the western Overthrust Belt, the Anadarko Basin of Oklahoma, and the Williston Basin of western North Dakota are not black man's territory. Black oil wildcatters are virtually unknown and there are almost no blacks living in any of the areas of the country where the hundreds of billions of dollars of new oil and gas discoveries have been established in recent years. Oil and real estate predominate in the very large Forbes 400 American family fortunes. Their combined wealth in 1982 was about $92 billion.[29] John Johnson, owner of *Ebony* magazine, is the only black person mentioned in this roster of the wealthiest Americans.

In one of the remarkable ironies of history, the 50 million barren acres of land the white man didn't want and reserved for the American Indians now appear to contain nearly 5 percent of the nation's oil and natural gas reserves, one-third of its strippable low-sulfur coal, and one-half of its privately owned uranium. Taking into account underdeveloped properties, upwards to 25 percent of all U.S. mineral wealth may be located on Indian lands. The undeveloped value of potential coal reserves on Indian land alone may approach $1.5 trillion, a sum sixty-five times the estimate of *all* black-owned wealth in 1967.[30]

Black people, on the other hand, have virtually nothing in the ground. Faithfully responding to two decades of government promises that entrepreneurial wealth grows on trees in the ghettos, blacks in very large

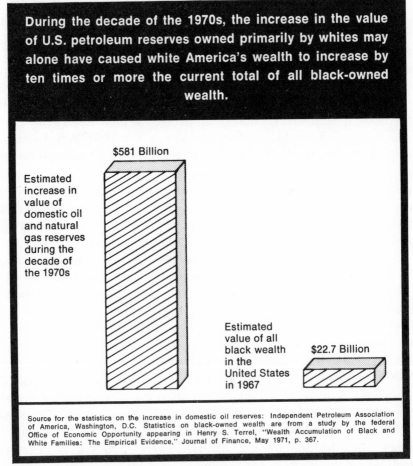

During the decade of the 1970s, the increase in the value of U.S. petroleum reserves owned primarily by whites may alone have caused white America's wealth to increase by ten times or more the current total of all black-owned wealth.

$581 Billion

Estimated increase in value of domestic oil and natural gas reserves during the decade of the 1970s

Estimated value of all black wealth in the United States in 1967

$22.7 Billion

Source for the statistics on the increase in domestic oil reserves: Independent Petroleum Association of America, Washington, D.C. Statistics on black-owned wealth are from a study by the federal Office of Economic Opportunity appearing in Henry S. Terrel, "Wealth Accumulation of Black and White Families: The Empirical Evidence," Journal of Finance, May 1971, p. 367.

numbers still plug away toward financial independence as proprietors of rib shops and filling stations in the inner cities.

The Trend in the Black-White Wealth Gap

Several centuries of government indifference to measurement of the black-white wealth gap means that any effort to plot the curve of the relative progress of black people is highly speculative. The black wealth figure may be $145 billion (or 2.34 percent of the national total) as estimated by Andrew Brimmer, or $211 billion (or 3.4 percent of the national total) as estimated by the Joint Center for Political Studies.[31] Or the figure may be significantly different from either computation. Whatever the ratio, conventional wisdom usually states that black wealth will now rapidly catch up with that of whites. Following this reasoning, it may be shown that in the decade 1964-1973, minority bank assets grew by 1,300 percent to over $1 billion. In just one year, 1973, sales of the top 100 black businesses were up 25 percent, reaching $70 million. From 1969 to 1972, black manufacturing firms increased in number by 38 percent, from 2,981 to 4,116. Black transportation and public utilities firms increased by 30 percent, from 16,733 to 21,738.[32] Viewing the black entrepreneurial landscape, one can identify scores of instances where entrepreneurial activity is up 1,000 percent or more, simply because there was no such activity at all a mere decade ago.

In the overall scheme, however, these gains are trivial. Even if black property and business ownership were to make spectacular gains in the near future, this would still be only a drop in the great ocean of white America's wealth, which must now be counted in the trillions of dollars. This conclusion may be considered against the background of the great 1982-1983 surge in U.S. stock market values, which had at one point added (not counting pension funds) about $400 billion to the personal wealth of Americans. These gigantic sums—added suddenly after a decade of stock market stagnation—appear to have accrued almost entirely to whites since blacks have and always had insignificant holdings in securities.

Even if specifically intended to favor blacks, targeted intervention by the government in *income* policies is not likely to affect the black-white wealth gap, which is both huge, intractable, and apparently growing in dollar amount. If the government sincerely wished to confer significant propertied status on black people, it would be obliged to take drastic steps to use its huge federal purchasing and fiscal powers to stimulate large-scale wealth formation among blacks. It would be necessary, too, for the federal government to establish major economic homesteading rights for blacks in areas of government-awarded franchises, just as was done for whites over the past century. It would be necessary also to finance the purchase by blacks of *major* segments of the nation's capital instruments. Federal black capitalism programs—focusing as they do on blacks becoming small-scale operators rather than serious proprietors of important mainstream enterprises—have had spiritual or psychological value only. Aside from turning blacks away from the important centers of economic action and power, their impact has been trivial. They have had negligible effect in reducing the huge wealth differences between the races.

The Appendage to American Capitalism

Whatever one's view of the wealth statistics, a single conclusion is inescapable. Black people in the United States function essentially as appendages to the body of American capitalism; they are not connected in any significant way with capitalism's most important objective, the creation of surplus value or wealth. The machines, the plants, the oil wells, and the stock certificates, which represent capital value and play such an important part in contributing to individual and institutional economic freedom and power, are owned and controlled entirely by whites. The economy of whites has a *capital base*. It alone owns the means of production and engages in production of goods. Blacks, on the other hand, have a labor-based economy. They have no capital; blacks own almost no machinery, and they do not control any noticeable part of the means of production.

As an economically isolated and subordinate group, blacks import and buy the goods they need from the economic mainstream where virtually all resources are owned and controlled by whites. There is no reliable evidence, in either short-term or long-term trends, that the huge racial gap in relative wealth positions will change or be rearranged in favor of blacks. The control of capital, particularly in corporate hands, plays such an important role in the allocation of employment and other valued positions that there is little likelihood that economic power at the top will be used to break down or greatly moderate the very large inequality between the races in employment and other economic opportunities.

Blacks, finally, are totally bereft of the economic clout that they need to be politically influential. Liberals focus all their attention on racial inequalities in income and poverty rates, yet the massive capital and wealth deficit faced by blacks is, and always has been, one of their most formidable and enduring handicaps. The separation of blacks from the means of production in the United States—their position as laborers for machinery owned by others and as users of goods made by others—continues to present a pitiful condition reminiscent of southern journalist Henry Grady's recollection of a Georgia funeral, of which he said that Georgia had provided only the corpse and the hole in the ground—all else being imported.

CHAPTER FIFTEEN

The United States Congress:
The Backwaters of Black Politics

"We have always been directed by others in all the affairs of life. . . .
The Anti-slavery Societies, the Abolition Societies, whose ostensible
work has been to do battle for the Negro's elevation, have never . . .
thought it safe for them to advance colored men to places of trust."

—Rev. Richard H. Cain,
    a black minister in the South (1865)

THE THEORY OF FREE-MARKET CAPITALISM was that people would achieve economic gains and well-being through the application of the human powers of competence, skill, and hard work to purely economic tasks. The fact was, however, that the American economy became profoundly politicized. Not only did people do well because they possessed powers inherent in having superior economic skills; they made economic gains, too, because of their ability to influence the powers of the state. Thus power, in a political sense, became an important determinant of individual wealth and prosperity. Public benefits, such as superior public education, better health care, and neighborhood amenities, were invariably claimed by those groups that had political influence. Additionally, politically well-entrenched groups customarily used the machinery of government to enact laws and to secure public rulings that directly protected or advanced their economic interests. Put bluntly, the politically powerful are able to—and do—vote themselves government jobs, subsidies, franchises, protective contracts, and at times, wonderful Christmas trees of economic benefits.

To what extent do blacks influence important decisions in government? As a group, are black people able to shape the political decisions that affect their own affairs? Are blacks instrumental in selecting those who are chosen to exercise the formidable powers of public office? Are they in a political position to remove from office those officials who inhibit the progress of Negroes or treat them, either on the streets or in the law courts, as unequals under the laws of the country? To what extent do they share in the political spoils and pork-barrel benefits that other American minority groups have so diligently employed to improve their economic and social status? To what extent are blacks in a political position to be instrumental in passing fair employment ordinances and similar economic rules that are likely to improve their employment and other opportunities? Do blacks have any "say" on such standard domestic issues as food stamps, school lunches, Medicaid, subsidized housing, job training, aid to education, or welfare reform? In a broad sense, our answers to these questions will help us discover whether or not the changes wrought by the civil rights movement of the 1960s have altered traditional black-white political power arrangements.

A few cautionary words. To avoid being misled as to where political power actually resides, one must be very careful not to confuse real power with the trappings of power. At times, the President of the United States, a man of almost unrivaled power in the world, has been known to carry his own luggage and to spurn the use of government limousines. On the other hand, there are a number of wholly uninfluential presidential appointees who appear on television and expatiate on high government policy yet in real life do little but carry the briefcases of others. The most minor ministers in government—both black and white—often travel in limousines guarded by the Secret Service. The important point to remember is that power always throws dust in the eyes of those whom it wishes to influence or manipulate. Theatrical manifestations of power are never dispositive on the issue of who actually has power. Power, we must remember, is always a matter of the ability to command or influence others. For this reason, we must disregard titles and trappings and ask instead: Who stands at the gates of admission? Who authorizes the issuance of the checks? Who approves budgets? Who pulls the strings attached to the tens of thousands of government marionettes who often strut and posture while remaining totally subject to the will of others?

Just as power must not be confused with glory, petty power should not be mistaken for grand power. This distinction may depend on time and place. In Oklahoma, for example, the governor of the state is considered to be a very powerful man. But when he comes to Washington his power shrinks. He is merely one of fifty governors who happens, at that moment, to be in a city populated by hundreds of very powerful senators, Supreme Court Justices, and chairmen of congressional committees. Measured by his capacity to make and implement major policy decisions, the power of the governor of Oklahoma—compared with that of the director of the federal Office of Management and Budget, the chairman of the Federal Reserve Board, or even the chief staff assistant to the chairman of the Senate Judiciary Committee—is minimal.

The distinctions between power and glory, and between grand power and petty power, are central to an assessment of black political influence in the United States. For many centuries, whites have facilitated their continuing rule over Negroes by the simple device of persistently blurring these power distinctions. Those who hold powerful posts and command esteem have frequently misdirected blacks to search for glory instead of influence. People who walk the corridors of great power have succeeded in convincing blacks that their interests would be best served if they settled for superficial tokens of political influence. By accepting prizes and honors, blacks have tended to perpetuate the continuation of their inferior, if not outcast, political status. Successful management of the theater of power has always been an important feature of the racial script that calls for the separation of Negroes from the seats of power.

Loyal Lieutenants: Black Congressmen in the Post-Depression Years

If a visitor from another world were to arrive in the United States, he would, in time, notice that one out of every eight faces in the general population is black. If he paid a visit to our Congress and prior to his arrival had no knowledge of the history of race relations in this country, he would expect to find a more or less random distribution of congressional seats among racial groups. The visitor would then calculate that about fifty-three black people should sit in the House of Representatives and another twelve in the Senate, for a total of sixty-five black members of Congress. But when he actually counts blacks on Capitol Hill, he reaches twenty and stops. He thus discovers that blacks have only 30 percent of the congressional representation they would have if racial parity existed. Since he has learned that Congress is the chief lawmaking body in the United States, he correctly concludes that the extreme shortage of black faces in Congress is important evidence that Negroes, as a group, are much weaker politically than are whites.

If, in seeking further knowledge, our visitor called for some American history books, he would discover that the disproportionately small number of blacks in Congress today is, in fact, a relatively large representation compared with the way things used to be. Until 1869, eighty years after the ratification of the Constitution, Congress was an entirely white enclave. Following the emancipation of the slaves and the end of the Civil War, the first black legislators, Joseph H. Rainey of South Carolina and Jefferson F. Lone of Georgia, were seated, in 1869. During Reconstruction, twenty more black congressmen followed them to Washington. But in the last two decades of the nineteenth century, the white South gradually reestablished its former exclusive hold on congressional seats. By 1901, all blacks had been purged from Capitol Hill. For the next twenty-eight years, from 1901 to 1929, not a single black person served in Congress. But in April 1929, a startling event occurred. Oscar De Priest, a Negro Republican from Chicago, entered the House of Representatives. Some of his colleagues might have mistaken him for a messenger boy; many most certainly wished he had been. Once De Priest had broken the modern color barrier, thirty-five other blacks followed him into the House and one black man, Edward W. Brooke of Massachusetts, was elected to the Senate.

Until recently, black members of Congress have usually owed their elections to urban white political machines that used black elected officials as a means of controlling the black vote. In sharp contrast to most black congressmen today, earlier black legislators were a timid and deferential group. De Priest, for example, was elected with the backing of Republican party leaders in Chicago and apparently never aspired to much influence in Congress. On a few occasions, De Priest chided his House colleagues on race discrimination in government employment. Generally, however, he sat quietly in the House throughout his three terms. During the period in which he sat in Congress, he did not introduce a single piece of legislation. A rock-ribbed Republican fiercely loyal to the party of President Lincoln, De Priest strongly opposed large increases in federal aid to the unemployed during the first years of the Depression, explaining that he did not want America to go to the "dole system." At one point in his career, he generated minor headlines by crusading against communism.

De Priest was defeated in 1934 by Arthur Mitchell, a black Democrat who was even more deferential to whites. On occasion, Mitchell criticized De Priest for his "bombast, ballyhoo and noise" about race. Mitchell, once a protégé and disciple of Booker T. Washington, and clearly sharing his patron's accommodationist views of the proper means of black advancement, refused to sign an NAACP-sponsored petition calling on Democratic leaders to pass an antilynching bill.

BLACKS ELECTED TO CONGRESS SINCE THE TURN OF THE CENTURY
No Appearances at All Until 1929

Name	State/City Represented	Tenure
Senate		
Edward W. Brooke	Massachusetts	1967-79
House		
Oscar De Priest	Chicago	1929-35
Arthur W. Mitchell	Chicago	1935-43
William Dawson	Chicago	1943-70
Adam Clayton Powell, Jr.	New York	1945-67; 1969-71
Charles C. Diggs, Jr.	Detroit	1955-80
Robert N. C. Nix	Philadelphia	1958-79
Augustus F. Hawkins	Los Angeles	1963-
John Conyers, Jr.	Detroit	1965-
Louis Stokes	Cleveland	1969-
William L. Clay	St. Louis	1969-
Shirley Chisholm	New York	1969-83
George W. Collins	Chicago	1970-72
Ralph H. Metcalfe	Chicago	1971-78
Ronald H. Dellums	Berkeley	1971-
Parren J. Mitchell	Baltimore	1971-
Charles B. Rangel	New York	1971-
Walter E. Fauntroy	Washington, D.C.	1971-
Andrew Young	Atlanta	1973-77
Yvonne B. Burke	Los Angeles	1973-79
Barbara C. Jordan	Houston	1973-79
Cardiss Collins	Chicago	1973-
Harold E. Ford	Memphis	1975-
Julian Dixon	Los Angeles	1979-
Mickey Leland	Houston	1979-
Bennett Stewart	Chicago	1979-81
William H. Gray, III	Philadelphia	1979-
Melvin Evans	Virgin Islands	1979-81
George Crockett	Detroit	1980-
Harold Washington	Chicago	1981-83
Augustus Savage	Chicago	1981-
Mervyn Dymally	Los Angeles	1981-
Katie Hall	Gary	1983-85
Alan Wheat	Kansas City	1983-
Major Owens	New York	1983-
Edolphus Towns	New York	1983-
Charles Hayes	Chicago	1983-

When Mitchell retired in 1943, Democrat William Dawson, another black man, won Mitchell's congressional seat. Dawson remained on Capitol Hill for twenty-six years, retiring in midterm in 1970. Some of his constituents on Chicago's South Side considered him an Uncle Tom. In the view of the Democratic party machine in Chicago, however, Dawson's primary job was to deliver Chicago's black vote, a task he managed effectively. Dawson was instrumental in the election of Richard Daley as mayor of Chicago and faithfully delivered the black vote in Daley's later campaigns for reelection. In the 1960 presidential election, John Kennedy carried Illinois by only 9,000 votes, yet Dawson's First Congressional District gave him a 30,000-vote margin. On Capitol Hill, Dawson didn't rock the boat and concentrated on uncontroversial matters in the Government Operations Committee. Dawson's relaxed attitude toward civil rights issues was comforting to old-guard Democrats in Congress, as was his solid support for the Vietnam War, during which a disproportionate number of blacks served in combat. In 1966, Dawson was rewarded for loyal service to the party with an appointment to the honorary post of vice-chairman of the Democratic National Committee.

The first assault on the traditional view of the black congressman as a species of plantation overseer occurred with the election to Congress in 1945 of Harlem's controversial Adam Clayton Powell. Powell was the first black congressman who owed his election to blacks rather than to a white-controlled political machine. Powell's ability to deliver black votes was considerable, but, unlike Dawson, he did not do so without something in return—often for himself, often for his constituents. It is generally recognized that in 1956 Powell made a deal with the Eisenhower administration to abstain from supporting Adlai Stevenson in the latter's second bid for the presidency if the Justice Department would suspend its investigations of Powell's income tax returns. Venality aside, here for the first time was an example of a black political figure bargaining from a position of strength.

During the 1960s, Powell made the powerful House Education and Labor Committee his private fiefdom. When bills he did not like were referred to the committee, he simply sat on them, while bills he approved were pushed through the committee immediately. In this regard, Powell was no maverick; he behaved precisely as did other influential committee chairmen in the House and Senate.

But members of the House were not accustomed to such independent and arbitrary behavior on the part of a black colleague. Powell, too, was adept at making enemies among members of Congress. He had, indeed, violated Booker T. Washington's twin injuctions that blacks should stay out of politics and avoid threatening the white man's self-esteem. Accordingly, when the political fortunes of the flamboyant representative from Harlem began to flag, there was no shortage of congressmen ready to move in for the kill.

Powell's political decline began when a Harlem widow sued him for slander and won a large judgment. Powell refused to pay, and in 1966 was found guilty of criminal contempt for ignoring subpoenas issued in efforts to enforce the judgment. To avoid arrest, Powell moved to Bimini, where he took up residence with a 26-year-old white receptionist from his Washington office. The following year, the full House, exceeding the recommendations of the select committee that had been investigating Powell's affairs, voted to remove him from the Ninetieth Congress. The charges were contempt and misuse of public funds—the latter stemming from a six-week European junket he had taken with the receptionist and another woman employed on Capitol Hill. In the special election held to fill his then vacant seat, Powell won overwhelmingly. Reluctantly, the House agreed to seat him in the new Congress, but fined him $20,000 for alleged misuse of payroll and travel funds and stripped him of his seniority. Powell also forfeited his committee chairmanship along with his elegant office and staff perquisites.

In 1969, the Supreme Court ruled that the responsibility for punishing a sinning member of the House rested with the voters, not with Congress. The Court decided that the House had acted unconstitutionally in excluding Powell in 1967. By then, however, Powell's political popularity had dramatically declined. In 1970, he lost the Democratic primary by 1,950 votes to Charles Rangel. Adam Clayton Powell, the cocky and self-confident nemesis of bigots and liberals alike, died of cancer in 1972.[1]

The charges lodged against Powell of nepotism, manipulation of travel funds, payroll abuse, and other acts of personal corruption were essentially true. Still, the House's refusal in 1967 to seat him was a transparently racist act on the part of his congressional colleagues. If exclusion from the House were a suitable punishment for corrupt behavior, evenhanded treatment would have called for the exclusion of large numbers of congressmen, a group once defined by the celebrated wit Ambrose Bierce as "the only uniquely American criminal class."

In spite of his early promise as an independently powerful black political figure, Powell did little to advance the black cause. On too many occasions, his philandering in Bimini was of greater importance to him than attendance at debates on civil rights measures before the House of Representatives.

Nevertheless, as head of the Education and Labor Committee, Powell provided important support for President Johnson's "Great Society" programs, particularly antipoverty, voting rights, and job discrimination initiatives. On more mundane issues, Powell was also a courageous pioneer. He was the first black to swim in the congressional swimming pool, and his staff integrated the House restaurant, which as late as 1946 did not seat blacks. In contrast, the other black member of the House at the time, Congressman Dawson of Chicago, never publicly questioned this particularly offensive example of congressional Jim Crow.[2]

Blacks in Congress in the 1980s: Potential Vote Brokers at Last

Today, black members of Congress are a brand-new breed. As a whole, they tend to be strong, self-assured, and, when necessary, prepared to incur the enmity of whites. In terms of talent, intelligence, and political savvy, they stand considerably higher than the congressional average. In terms of the verbal finesse and sleight-of-hand techniques that characterize many successful congressmen, the blacks in Congress rank with the best.

Parren Mitchell, a Democratic congressman from Baltimore, is a good example of this new style of forceful black leadership. Mitchell is one of the most influential congressmen in the House, and recent years have seen him emerge as a prominent spokesman for both black and white liberals. Chairman of the Black Caucus from 1977 to 1978, Mitchell has been a principal counselor on black economic objectives and strategies. A former sociology professor at predominantly black Morgan State College, Mitchell is a powerful orator who has been described as "one of God's angry men." To some extent, Mitchell's ability to remain independent of the major forces in the Democratic party is due to the circumstance that he needs little or no electoral support from whites to remain in office. His district—Maryland's Seventh Congressional District—is almost three-quarters black.

Black Congressman John Conyers, Jr., from Detroit, also holds a black political base. Conyers is well known for having introduced in 1972 an impeachment resolution that charged President Nixon with usurping the war-making powers of Congress. Twice, in 1971 and again in 1973, Conyers ran against Carl Albert for House Speaker, an act of defiance he undertook primarily to protest the stodginess of Democratic leadership. He is generally credited with "keeping the fires burning" on the Humphrey-Hawkins full employment bill. He once stalked out of a Black Caucus meeting with President Carter over this issue, which he and many others considered critical to black progress. As chairman of the Judiciary Subcommittee on Crime, Conyers was also instrumental in the passage of the Speedy Trial Act of 1973.

Ronald Dellums of California is unquestionably one of the most effective black representatives on the Hill. A charismatic figure, Dellums is heir to Adam Clayton Powell in his skill at deflating the bogus rhetoric of many congressmen who profess to be undying friends of black Americans. In a body of moderates, he has chosen a radical course to jar his colleagues and the public into awareness of humane alternatives to present economic and political arrangements. Unlike Mitchell and Conyers, his constituency is not predominantly black. Yet, he has been outspoken on racial and defense issues without suffering for it at the polls. California's Eighth Congressional District, covering Berkeley and parts of neighboring Oakland, is politically the most radical district in the country. Both the militant student movement of the 1960s and the Black Panther Party were born within the borders of Dellums' district, which he has represented since 1971. This constituency has given Dellums a power base that has enabled him to become a national spokesman against some of the least engaging features of American capitalism. In addition to chairing the House District of Columbia Committee, Dellums sits on the Armed Services Committee, where he is a leading foe of defense spending. He has used this forum to conduct extra-official hearings on racism in the military and U.S. war crimes in Vietnam. Son of a longshoreman, Dellums is a former Marine, social worker, and university lecturer.

Until her retirement in 1983, Congresswoman Shirley Chisholm of Brooklyn was another forceful presence in the House. A star at the 1972 Democratic National Convention, the self-proclaimed "unbought and unbossed" Chisholm won the votes of 152 delegates for the presidential nomination. Among liberal blacks and whites, however, she had severe critics; they argued that she sacrificed the interests of the poor to those of established powers in Brooklyn politics. She was Secretary of the Democratic Caucus and a favorite of House Speaker Thomas P. ("Tip") O'Neill, who made a place for her as the first woman on the House Rules Committee. Disillusioned with the retreat from the programs of the "Great Society," Chisholm, who had represented the Bedford-Stuyvesant and Bushwick sections of Brooklyn since 1968, announced that she would not seek reelection in 1982. On the subject of right-wing evangelical groups, she declared, as she hung up her political hat: "They've paralyzed the people with three words: family, morality, and flag."

Other influential black congressmen include Charles Rangel of Harlem, a high school dropout and veteran of the Korean War who ousted Adam Clayton Powell in 1970. He has become an important member of the powerful House Ways and Means Committee as well as the leading congressional expert on narcotics problems. Congressman Rangel has also been an articulate critic of Reagan tax policies in terms of their negative impact on the poor and racial minorities. Louis Stokes of Cleveland, chairman of the House Ethics Committee and the brother of former Cleveland Mayor Carl Stokes, was one of the moving forces behind the Black Caucus's boycott of Nixon's 1971 State of the Union address. William Clay of St. Louis is a former union business agent who has specialized in union legislation. He authored the labor management section of the Civil Service Reform Bill and was instrumental in securing House approval for liberalization of the Hatch Act, which prohibited federal employees from engaging in political activity. Walter Fauntroy, elected in 1970 as the nonvoting delegate from the District of Columbia, has played an important role in organizing the Black Caucus. Fauntroy chairs the important Domestic Monetary Policy Subcommittee of the House Banking, Finance and Urban Affairs Committee. Cardiss Collins of Chicago first went to Congress by winning the special election held to fill the seat left vacant when her husband, George W. Collins, died in office in 1972. She has since emerged as a significant political figure in her own right, chairing the Black Caucus during the Ninety-sixth Congress. Harold Ford, a surprise winner of a House seat from Memphis in 1974, won a key seat on the powerful Ways and Means Committee.

The senior black congressman is 78-year-old Augustus Hawkins of California's Twenty-ninth Congressional District, which includes Watts in Los Angeles. Although Hawkins authored most of the original Humphrey-Hawkins full employment bill, he never assumed leadership on the full employment issue. In 1985, Hawkins became chairman of the Education and Labor Committee. Previously, he had served as head of the House Administration Committee. Some blacks feel that Hawkins could have been more aggressive in using his seniority to advance the black agenda in Congress.

Three black congressmen elected in 1978, Julian Dixon of Los Angeles, Mickey Leland of Houston, and William Gray of Philadelphia, are likely to become vigorous spokesmen on black issues. Shortly after his arrival on Capitol Hill, Dixon became the first freshman congressman to chair the District of Columbia Subcommittee of the House Appropriations Committee. Controlling the pursestrings of the city's budget. Dixon's power in Washington rivals that of Mayor Marion Barry. From 1983 to 1985, Dixon chaired the House Ethics Committee. William Gray, a third-generation baptist minister, proved to be a deft broker between the Black Caucus and the House leadership in the 1983 contest over budget restoration of social and jobs programs. In 1985, Gray assumed the chairmanship of the House Budget Committee, probably the most important position ever held by a black politician in the United States. Mickey Leland is a highly charismatic speaker and the darling of Texas's Eighteenth District (41 percent black and 31 percent Mexican-American). In 1985, Leland became chairman of the Black Caucus and headed the House Select Committee on Hunger.

In 1980, four additional blacks were elected to Congress. Two were from Chicago: Gus Savage, a fiery orator and publisher of a weekly newspaper on Chicago's South Side, and Harold Washington, who has since left the House to become mayor of the city but was replaced in 1983 by yet another new black representative, Charles Hayes. Also elected in 1980, Merv Dymally, a native of Trinidad and former Lt. Governor of California, upset nine-term veteran of the House Charles Wilson in the Democratic primary. In Detroit, George W. Crockett, the elder statesman of the city's black community, was elected to fill the vacancy created when Charles Diggs was forced to leave Congress on payroll-padding charges. Crockett, a former judge, serves on the House Judiciary and Foreign Affairs Committees.

Four new black members were elected to the House in 1982. Edolphus Towns, a black social worker, was elected to the Brooklyn seat vacated by scandal-ridden Frederick Richmond. Major Owens, also of Brooklyn, assumed Shirley Chisholm's seat. Two more blacks were elected in significant victories because they were chosen despite, rather than because of, their color. Alan Wheat, in Kansas City, was elected in a district that was only one-fifth black. Katie Hall won in an Indiana district that is only one-quarter black. However, she lost her seat in 1984 when a disappointing number of white voters failed to support her reelection bid.

The black delegation in the House has a good complement of educators and statesmen. It has acquired a deserved reputation for strong, purposeful, and energetic leadership. But the high visibility and personal qualities of many blacks serving in Congress appear to have misled the press into exaggerating the powers and prowess of black legislators. By any realistic measure, the black population, despite its political cohesion, does not have a position of legislative strength on Capitol Hill. The black congressional delegation has not succeeded in becoming a moving force in influencing the behavior of the President, other members of Congress, or the business establishment. Most recent Presidents have either ignored black legislators or have paid mere lip service to their pleas to move ahead with the black agenda. Department of Justice officials routinely table complaints of black congressmen over the failure of federal agencies to withdraw funding from organizations discriminating against blacks. Third-tier officials at the Defense Department merely listen politely to the complaints of black members of Congress about the still meager allocation of military contracts to black businessmen.

Moreover, black legislators today are essentially powerless to affect legislative agendas; they do not play an important part in legislative strategy, timing, or bargaining. Despite the impressive political solidarity prevailing within the Black Caucus, the number of blacks in Congress is too small for them to become an effective voice. In most matters of special concern to black voters, black representatives in Congress are in a position to do little more than run through the legislative motions. The mentality that used to look to the NAACP for recourse or redress is gone, yet black legislative power is not yet in place. Black congressmen still stand by as observers of a lawmaking process in which the nation's legislative programs are first moved, shaped, and then either enacted or defeated by whites.

One might expect that voting rights legislation combined with some favorable congressional district reapportionment would have increased the influence of southern blacks in Congress. But this is not so. Very few blacks have been elected to Congress from the Deep South. Ever since Andrew Young left the House in 1977 to become Ambassador to the United Nations, 9 million black people—more than a third of the entire black population of the United States—have been represented in Congress entirely by whites. As we shall see, a very large number of these southern white congressmen not only ignore the black political agenda but still vote a strong white supremacist ticket.

Congressional Committee Chiefs: Blacks on the Slow Track

Numbers alone do not reveal the full extent of black legislative impotence. Because of the importance of seniority and committee membership in the congressional decision-making process, members of Congress are decidely not equal. Legislation is made and killed by committees and by congressional leadership, and in these leadership posts, black influence counts for even less than one might imagine on the basis of a straight black-white head count.

Like almost any large organization, Congress is hierarchical. The official leadership of each party in the House and Senate is composed of the majority and minority leaders and whips, the chairmen of certain key committees and subcommittees, and the ranking members of the minority party on these same committees and subcommittees. People who hold these posts are the great powers in Congress. In the past generation, these powers in Congress have included such men as Rayburn, Martin, McCormack, Boggs, Hays, Mills, Ford, Dirksen, Wright, Rhodes, Fulbright, Johnson, Eastland, Long, McClellan, Mansfield, Baker, O'Neill, and Byrd. There are and have been no comparable black figures.

An assessment of black legislative power requires a close look at the congressional committees; most legislation is enacted or defeated in these committees. The committee chairman plays a key role in this process. He is uniquely able to influence the voting behavior of committee members through his control of their advancement within the committee system and because of his special powers over bills important to them. For years, committee chairmen were unrivaled autocrats. Rank-and-file committee members—and, indeed, Congress as a whole and occasionally even Presidents—danced to the legislative tunes they called. A chairman could singlehandedly kill a bill he opposed by declining to hold hearings on it or by refusing to call the committee into session to vote on it. Committee members were loath to cross a chairman for fear of retaliation through any of the various forms of punishment at the chairman's disposal.

Despite a series of reforms that have stripped the House committee chairmen of their powers to act capriciously, the chair retains formidable powers and prerogatives. A chairman acts as a floor leader when a committee bill reaches the full House. He selects committee members for the all-important House-Senate conference committees that negotiate compromises between competing House and Senate bills. Moreover, a chairman must "sign off" before a subcommittee can hold a hearing on a bill. The chairman retains the power to choose the staff of the full committee and to approve the selection of subcommittee staff members. Although he no longer chooses his committee members, his preferences are frequently honored. While a chairman may no longer block bills by arbitrary fiat, he is in a position to delay them by stalling subcommittee hearings and by delaying calling the full committee into session. Under the right circumstances—for example, in the closing weeks of a session—his ability to delay a measure may be equivalent to defeating it.

Committee chairmanships have been almost exclusively reserved for whites. Until recently—with the exception of Adam Clayton Powell's chairmanship of the important House Education and Labor Committee—no black has ever headed a committee with important jurisdiction and influence within the House. In recent years, the situation has drastically changed. In 1985, Congressman William Gray assumed the chairmanship of the House Budget Committee. Here at last, a black was in a position to play a commanding part in the annual haggling over the nation's resources. In 1985, blacks also chaired several other House committees. Congressman Parren Mitchell chaired the Small Business Committee; Augustus Hawkins assumed control over Adam Clayton Powell's former forum, the House Education and Labor Committee. Congressman Ronald Dellums chaired the District of Columbia Committee and Representative Dixon chaired the House Standards of Official Conduct Committee. Three blacks also served as Chairman on special House Select Committees: Charles Rangel (Narcotics), Mickey Leland (Hunger) and Louis Stokes (Intelligence). The lineup in the House of chairmanship power suggests that blacks are not likely candidates for election to the powerful chairs that control taxation, military policy, foreign affairs, law enforcement, banking, and appropriations. In assigning high posts in the councils of legislative bodies, white legislators (both Democrats and Republicans) tend to be racial conservatives.

It is often suggested that the political power of blacks in Congress should be measured by their ability to influence legislation of particular concern to blacks. If one accepts this racial but pragmatic standard for measuring power, black political weakness is still very great. With the exception of William Gray's chairmanship of the House Budget Committee, no black congressman has ever been in a position—by virtue of holding a committee chairmanship or other high post in the Congress—to influence, say, such critical matters as the impact of monetary controls on black unemployment, the effect of energy policy on the poor or the enforcement of affirmative-action employment rules in the over $300 billion defense industry.

Because of established seniority rules, the prospects are not bright for black congressmen to assume other key committee chairmanships. The only blacks within striking distance of an important committee chairmanship are Judiciary Committee member John Conyers and Charles Rangel of the Ways and Means Committee. Yet, in each case, two or three other members of the House hold greater seniority. For the foreseeable future, it remains likely that vacancies in the chairmanships of key House committees will be filled by whites. If control of the House were to shift to the Republican party, blacks would be removed from eligibility for drawing any top congressional posts. Conservative blacks have achieved federal office through presidential appointment, but in 1985 there were no black Republicans in the House of Representatives.

It is useful to consider how different the political situation of blacks might be today if, over the past twenty years, one or two of the most powerful

THE BEST SHOWING SO FAR:

Black Subcommittee Chairmen in the United States House of Representatives 98th Congress—1984

Subcommittee	Committee	Subcommittee Chairman
Oversight	Ways and Means	Charles Rangel
Criminal Justice	Judiciary	John Conyers
Employment Opportunity	Education and Labor	Augustus Hawkins
Postal Personnel and Modernization	Post Office and Civil Service	Mickey Leland
Domestic Monetary Policy	Banking, Finance and Urban Affairs	Walter Fauntroy
Government Activities and Transportation	Government Operations	Cardiss Collins
Fiscal Affairs and Health	District of Columbia	Walter Fauntroy
Judiciary and Education	District of Columbia	Mervyn Dymally
Government Operations & Metropolitan Affairs	District of Columbia	William Gray
District of Columbia	Appropriations	Julian Dixon
Postal Operations and Services	Post Office and Civil Service	William Clay
Small Business Administration Authority	Small Business	Parren Mitchell
Military Installations and Facilities	Armed Services	Ronald Dellums
Public Assistance and Unemployment Compensation	Ways and Means	Harold Ford

committee chairmanships in Congress had been held by blacks. A hypothetical example of traditional political vote brokering comes to mind. According to historical experience, an estimated thirty senators and seventy-five congressmen, most of them from southern states, may generally be counted on to vote in favor of almost any bill for which the quid pro quo is another bill that will raise import duties on foreign textiles. Such a textile duty bill would be of paramount importance to all congressmen from the textile manufacturing states of Mississippi, Arkansas, South Carolina, North Carolina, Virginia, Georgia, Alabama, Tennessee, New York, Pennsylvania, Massachusetts, and California. In some of these states, textile labor accounts for as much as 40 percent of the total labor force.

Now suppose that a black person of considerable seniority chaired the House Ways and Means Committee or the Senate Finance Committee. A black chairman of either of these committees would have the power to advance, or to seriously delay, textile import duty legislation on the committee agendas. He or she could also greatly influence the voting of a substantial number of other committee members. In the American tradition of pressure groups, the committee chairman would then be able to use this power over the destiny of a textile duty bill to advance such initiatives as full employment legislation, government contracting in favor of minorities, welfare reform, and other measures of great importance to blacks. Lacking this ability to bargain from the heights of committee legislative strength, black lawmakers have been powerless to advance legislation that has always ranked high on the black agenda. A powerful case may be made for the proposition that the presence of a black person chairing the House Ways and Means Committee would increase black political influence and stature in the United States considerably more than the election of two or three more blacks to the Congress.

Blacks have done slightly better in the chairmanships of subcommittees in the House of Representatives. But even here, their assignments have been stereotyped according to race and job function. In a few cases, however, blacks have held subcommittee chairmanships that confer some potential leverage in negotiations with other members of the House.

By far the most important of the subcommittee posts held by blacks in recent years have been the Education and Labor Committee's Employment Opportunities Subcommittee chaired by Augustus Hawkins, the Banking, Finance, and Urban Affairs Committee's Domestic Monetary Policy Subcommittee chaired by Walter Fauntroy, and the Oversight Committee of Appropriations chaired by Charles Rangel. As we shall see in Chapter Twenty-two, these posts carry certain powers that could be used to great advantage in expanding the economic opportunities of blacks.

What of the black presence as rank-and-file members of House committees? Blacks sit on all three of the most powerful committees in the House—

Appropriations, Rules, and Ways and Means—and on several other major committees. Blacks also sit on many of the more important subcommittees of the House. But in no instance is the black presence on any of the major committees more than a token representation. For example, blacks have three seats on the fifty-five-member Appropriations Committee and two seats on the thirty-five-member Ways and Means Committee.

The legislative power of blacks in Congress may be summed up in two figures: twenty and ten. There are only twenty blacks in the House, and half of them—ten members only—have over ten years of seniority. Because blacks are not present in the House in significant numbers, they are necessarily spread thin on committees; because they were previously present in even lower numbers, few of them have sufficient seniority to command the chairmanship of choice committees or subcommittees. Until black representation and seniority increase, it is unrealistic to expect black legislators to make further gains through the committee system. Even an intense and successful effort to elect more black representatives would not bear fruit for many years.

The Congressional Black Caucus: A Bid for Solidarity

Beginning in the mid-1970s, the Congressional Black Caucus has become the focal point of black efforts to increase black strength within the legislative branch. Founded in 1969 as an outgrowth of the so-called Democratic Select Committee, the Caucus has become a generally cohesive group that presses for legislation and government measures it sees as helpful to black political and economic interests. Assessments of the political effectiveness of the Black Caucus vary, with some observers concluding that the Caucus constitutes a formidable political force that white politicians, including the President, must fear and respect, while others dismiss it as a largely ineffective school for inexperienced and uninfluential legislators. The truth lies somewhere between these two extremes.

The Caucus first commanded a national audience during the Nixon administration. In order to focus national attention on President Nixon's insensitivity to black problems, the Caucus boycotted Nixon's 1971 State of the Union address. After repeatedly refusing to discuss black problems with members of the Caucus, Nixon finally agreed to a meeting at which the Caucus presented him with sixty-one recommendations for government action. The White House was then pursuing what it called its "southern strategy," that of courting white southern votes, playing down the black social agenda, and virtually writing off the black vote. Accordingly, Nixon either rejected or ignored the Caucus's recommendations. In turning his back on Caucus recommendations, the President was clearly pursuing a pragmatic—and, as it turned out, politically shrewd—course of action. At that time, backlash against militancy in general—and radical activists in particular, such as Eldridge Cleaver, Bobby Seale, and Huey Newton—was turning the nation to the right on racial and other issues. As a result, the majority of voters, northern and southern, Democratic and Republican, were not enthusiastic about fifteen black legislators calling a meeting with the President and making political demands on him. Tradition, dating back to the early days of the NAACP, allowed blacks to be admitted only one by one into the Oval Office. Hence, the very element that gave the Caucus strength—the fact that it set itself up to negotiate as a single unit and sought to meet as a body with the President—was seen as the most disturbing feature of this new phenomenon of black politics.

Despite a number of early setbacks, the Caucus became increasingly skilled at winning a bigger say in the House of Representatives. An important element of its early strategy was to gain seats on important House committees. The Caucus won its first major success in 1971. In the face of resistance from both Speaker Carl Albert and Committee Chairman F. Edward Hebert, the Caucus insisted on a seat for Ronald Dellums on the Armed Services Committee. The Caucus refused to back down, and Dellums, a vocal critic of the Vietnam War and of Pentagon spending, was appointed.

Throughout the early 1970s, the Caucus continued to concentrate on winning seats on choice committees. The Caucus was successful when its strategy was carefully plotted and when Caucus members were adroit in taking advantage of political breaks. First, the early retirement in the early 1970s of an unusually large number of senior House members opened committee seats. Second, the House leadership during that period was extremely vulnerable to internal political pressure. The years 1972 to 1976 saw previously unassailable House leaders fighting to retain their positions and acquire allies. When black members offered themselves as willing supporters of the threatened leadership in return for appointment to certain committee seats, deals could usually be made. The Caucus was frequently able to persuade House leaders pressing for reform in the House's time-encrusted procedural rules to support Caucus bids for committee seats in exchange for Caucus votes in support of reform. By exploiting these circumstances, the Caucus managed to win for its members a record level of influence and power. In fact, by the end of the 1970s, congressional leadership was far more responsive to black political influence than was President Carter, despite the fact that his election was, in large measure, due to black support.

Another sign of growing Caucus strength was the fact that members of Congress began "lobbying" the Caucus just as the Caucus had earlier lobbied other congressional groups. The results of this strategy included several enactments of varying significance to the black population, including an extension of voting rights legislation, the strengthening of civil rights protection in law enforcement, enactment of the Humphrey-Hawkins full employment resolution, expanded youth employment programs, and prohibitions on the import of Rhodesian chrome. During the 1970s, the Caucus was also influential in establishing the House Assassinations Committee, in passing home rule legislation for the District of Columbia, in persuading the Carter administration to alter its originally unfavorable *amicus curiae* brief in the *Bakke* case, and in creating public works legislation that reserved $400 million in government contracts for minority firms.

It must be remembered that a prime purpose of the Caucus was to create a black political force whose solidarity would produce influence greater than the sum total of the votes of individual Caucus members. Thus, an accurate assessment of the congressional strength of the Caucus must consider not only the results achieved, but also the means used by the Caucus to bring about change. A certain pragmatism characterized Caucus dealings in the late 1970s. On occasion, the Caucus used bloc-vote trading—in effect, offering a number of black votes as a negotiable commodity to be bartered for votes in favor of legislation important to the Caucus. In 1973, for example, the Caucus struck a bargain with southern congressmen. Black support for renewed farm subsidies was exchanged for southern support of a minimum wage bill. The important point to remember here is not that minimum wages were necessarily good for blacks, but that blacks *wanted* minimum wages, bargained hard for them, and won. In the process, old political enemies became political allies, and both groups gained from the alliance.

As long as political power in the House is divided among two parties and many special-interest groups, bloc-vote trading will probably continue to be an effective negotiating tool for the Caucus. But the importance of this tactic should not be exaggerated. According to one black congressman, the bloc of votes available for trade by the Caucus has often included less than half the Caucus's votes. These defections occur simply because sometimes it proves politically infeasible for individual Caucus members to vote for or against certain measures. Caucus strength naturally diminishes to the extent that it is unable to bind its members to a unanimous Caucus position. A group such as the Caucus projects political power not only on those occasions when it votes as a bloc, but whenever it demonstrates to other congressmen its almost certain *disposition* to vote as a bloc. To the extent that solidarity is undermined by defections from the group position, the power of the Caucus is profoundly diminished.

The Caucus has been criticized from time to time for insufficient unity. Often, this criticism results from the somewhat naive assumption that black politicians are so bound by racial identity that they can readily put aside their political and ideological differences. But this is almost never the case. The truth is that much divides, as well as unites, the members of the Black Caucus. There are major differences in individual backgrounds, political views, and constituencies. Some Black Caucus members represent predominantly poor blacks in depressed areas while others serve middle-class black constituencies in rather affluent communities. Some members have strong special-interest groups to contend with and placate. For example, Mickey Leland's Houston district is oil company territory, while Berkeley student activists are a powerful force in Congressman Ron Dellums' California district. The members also operate under different political philosophies. Some, like Charles Rangel, represent the respected and pragmatic "to get along, go along" school of congressional politics; others, like Dellums, have brought black militancy into the House and have no intention of turning down the heat on whites. Some Caucus members believe that representing the public interest as a whole is their primary job; others put black objectives first and foremost, contending that the ethnic approach to political change best serves the public interest. The activities of some members of the Caucus are heavily weighted toward the protection and furtherance of individual career objectives—a goal that in itself serves the cause of greater black influence and prestige. These expected sources of diversity within the Caucus necessarily undermine solidarity and significantly weaken the consensus power and influence of the body. While diversity is a highly desirable condition in most free institutions, its presence is absolutely lethal in an organization that is in the early stages of power building.

A mark against the Caucus has been its unwillingness to develop its potential for the successful lobbying of congressmen elected from districts with large numbers of black voters. While the Caucus has effectively employed this tactic on several occasions, notably in the vote on home rule for the District of Columbia, it has never incorporated this pressure device as an integral part of its political strategy. This reluctance to build fires in legislators' home districts may be partially the result of the fears of some members of the Caucus of offending big-league liberals. In some cases, the still-powerful teachings of Booker T. Washington rule the roost. When this happens, black accommodation to the nation's rearguard fight against racial integration is often justified on the ground that black pressure strategies are counterproductive because thay produce a backlash harmful to blacks. However, this conclusion is shortsighted. Backlash effect, as we shall later show, is invariably exaggerated and is often a red herring employed to check the desires of blacks to assert greater political strength.

The fact remains that there are sixty-five congressional districts in the country with white incumbents and black populations exceeding 20 percent; twenty-one white incumbents represent districts where the electorate is over 30 percent black. The potential is considerable for using political pressure on white congressmen from these districts to advance black political objectives.

White Congressmen With Black Constituents

Of course, the race-trait mode of making up one's mind is not a failing peculiar to whites. Many blacks believe that blacks have a uniquely superior perspective on black problems which no white person can have. This naturally leads to the conclusion that black legislators are best equipped to effectively represent black interests. Up to this point, our black legislative head-count measure of black political influence has assumed the truth of this thesis. But the American political process is more complex. White congressmen are, to a considerable extent, accountable to black voters. Accordingly, the earlier statement that only 5 percent of the House of Representatives is black does not necessarily provide an adequate measure of the accountability of elected representatives to the wishes—or potential pressures—of black voters.

There are at least sixteen congressional districts with a white representative in Congress where black voting strength exceeds 30 percent. There are at least fifty additional districts with white incumbents where black voting strength exceeds 15 percent. In many cases—particularly in the North— congressmen in these districts count on the black voter as an integral part of the Democratic coalition and would have difficulty remaining in office if the black voters in their district were seriously alienated.

Black influence over white members of Congress has been diminished in the North by several factors, including gerrymandering of voting districts along racial lines, the decline in liberal concerns about racial inequality, low voter turnout among blacks, and the presence in many urban districts of highly vocal white ethnics—particularly Polish-, Italian-, and Jewish-Americans—who are often hostile to blacks and black political objectives. But the great majority of the white congressmen elected from northern

BASES OF POLITICAL POWER BUT STILL SHORT OF A BLACK MAJORITY:
Congressional Districts Where Black Voting Strength Is Greater Than 30 Percent

1985

Congressman and Party	State and Congressional District	Percent Eligible Black Voters Within District
Ben Edreich (D)	Alabama—Sixth District	31%
Lindsay Thomas (D)	Georgia—First District	30%
Charles Hatcher (D)	Georgia—Second District	32%
Wyche Fowler (D)	Georgia—Fifth District	60%
J. Roy Roland (D)	Georgia—Eighth District	32%
Corrine Boggs (D)	Louisiana—Second District	41%
Cathy Long (D)	Louisiana—Eighth District	36%
Steny Hoyer (D)	Maryland—Fifth District	31%
Webb Franklin (R)	Mississippi—Second District	48%
Wayne Dowdy (D)	Mississippi—Fourth District	41%
Peter Rodino (D)	New Jersey—Tenth District	51%
Walter Jones (D)	North Carolina—First District	32%
Tim Valentine (D)	North Carolina—Second District	36%
Floyd Spence (R)	South Carolina—Second District	32%
Robert Tallon (D)	South Carolina—Sixth District	37%
Norman Sisisky (D)	Virginia—Fourth District	37%

congressional districts where there are a large number of black voters have voting records in Congress that most black interest groups would applaud. And to a certain extent, these congressmen may be viewed as part of a black influence bloc within Congress. However, the collective political power that accrues to blacks because of this congressional representation is not nearly as important as the black legislative influence that would develop if a number of these congressmen were participating fully as

Black Caucus members dedicated to vote on bills under a tightly organized bloc-voting agreement.

In the South, too, numerous white congressmen with large black constituencies have responded positively to the political aspirations of their black constituents. These include Wyche Fowler of Georgia, Charles Rose of North Carolina, Corrine Boggs of Louisiana, and Beryl Anthony of Arkansas. On the other hand, there are far more old-school racial conservatives— at least twenty in 1985—who still covertly, and sometimes overtly, play the racial politics of the Old South. In an almost knee-jerk fashion, they vote against positions favored by the Black Caucus.

Among southern congressmen representing districts at least 25 percent black, some of the close friends of Jim Crow include William Dickinson of Alabama, Robert Livingston and Henson Moore of Louisiana, and Floyd Spence of South Carolina. There are many other congressmen from the South with smaller, but still significant, black constituencies who seldom, if ever, support Black Caucus initiatives. In fact, as surely as they attend black funerals and honor black heroes, they vote almost to a man against measures such as voting rights legislation, the withdrawal of federal funds from racially segregated institutions, and anti-redlining credit measures. Jamie Whitten of Mississippi is one congressman with a particularly offensive record on racial issues. Because of the immense power he wields in the House as chairman of the House Appropriations Committee, Whitten has been a persistent thorn in the side of black politicians. Despite the fact that blacks comprise 22 percent of the eligible voters in his congressional district in northern Mississippi, Whitten is consistently returned to Congress. His career stands as eloquent testimony to the failure of southern blacks to take measures to punish their tormentor at the polls.

In sum, the political weakness of southern blacks in Congress has two important features. The first is numerical. In 1985, there were only two black members of Congress from the entire South—Harold Ford of Tennessee and Mickey Leland of Texas—and throughout the twentieth century to date, no blacks have been elected to Congress from eight other southern states. The second feature is that the blacks in the South tolerate, and leave in office, at least twenty white congressmen who are not merely deaf to cries for compassion but whose voting records display extreme hostility to black efforts to integrate and progress. And these congressmen continue to be reelected without serious opposition from districts with very large black populations.

True, the gerrymandered congressional district, the runoff primary system, and white economic manipulation of black voters have conspired to reduce black political influence in these districts. In the main, however, these congressmen do not represent black political interests *because blacks neither organize politically nor vote in sufficient numbers to make their congressmen take black concerns into account.* Possibly, black voters may never be politically strong enough to banish the congressional cloakroom jokes about darkies and loose shoes, but voting blacks in the South clearly already have sufficient strength to purge much of the voting behavior in Congress that is harmful to them. On the issue of racial injustice, blacks consistently lecture whites in stern and unforgiving moral tones, but thus far, they have failed to make any of their political opponents tremble.

The Legislative Superpower: No Blacks at All

Largely by accident, the constitutional design of the selection process for election to the U.S. Senate almost guarantees that the Senate will be an all-white legislative body. To the continuing disadvantage of the black voter, United States senators are elected on a statewide basis instead of one from each of two districts within the state. Since no state has a black population of more than 35 percent—and even the heavily black-populated states tend to have only 20 to 30 percent blacks—there are no opportunities in Senate contests for blacks to take advantage of large or near-majority black voter concentrations. In recent years, many Senate incumbents have been in trouble with voters generally, but the black vote has not been one of their serious problems. The difficulty blacks have experienced in mounting successful election campaigns for statewide offices was highlighted in the 1978 Senate contest in Virginia. During his term as Secretary of the Navy, Republican Senate candidate John Warner had opposed the efforts of Chief of Naval Operations Elmo Zumwalt to integrate the Navy. Warner also went on record as an early opponent of the extension of the Voting Rights Act. Blacks were organized and prepared to block Warner in his Senate bid; yet Warner squeaked into office despite a heavy black vote against him. Had Warner been required to run for the Senate from the eastern half of the state, which included heavily black Richmond, rather than in the state at large, he could easily have been defeated.

In modern times, the only black person to be elected to the Senate has been Republican Edward W. Brooke of Massachusetts, whose election in 1966 was largely the product of his liberal white electorate rather than an organized campaign of black voters. In fact, only 4 percent of the Massachusetts voting-age population is black. Senator Brooke served only two terms and was defeated for reelection in 1978. Nevertheless, Brooke's twelve years in the Senate are worth examining because they show what a single black senator can and cannot accomplish.

Never a man of strong personal magnetism, Edward Brooke was nonetheless a senator of considerable influence. Almost without exception, whites in all walks of life tend to look upon blacks as experts on racial issues; Brooke accordingly stood out in the Senate as *the* expert on black issues, much as the token black on the board of a large corporation or university tends automatically to be typecast as an expert on minority affairs. The stereotype of wisdom acquired by racial attribute gave Brooke considerable authority in the Senate. Furthermore, as a member of the relatively small Republican Senate minority, Brooke was able to cull influence from the prominent committee positions that twelve years in office had earned him. He was the ranking Republican on the Banking, Housing, and Urban Affairs Committee, the ranking Republican on its Urban Affairs Subcommittee, and the third-ranking Republican on its Labor-HEW Subcommittee.

In the 1970s, Brooke campaigned in the Senate on behalf of busing to achieve school desegregation, government-funded abortions for poor women, housing for the poor, and other minority-backed efforts. Toward the end of his Senate career, he became known as an effective leader on civil rights and social welfare legislation. It was often a lonely fight. Writing about the struggle over busing in 1975, one publication noted that Brooke "led the opposition to the anti-busing amendments almost singlehandedly, staying on the Senate floor for long hours every day of the eight-day debate." Few other liberals took the floor to speak against the amendments.

Opinions have varied as to Brooke's role in the 1969 Senate defeat of President Nixon's nomination of Clement F. Haynsworth to the Supreme Court. Unquestionably, Senator Robert Griffin of Michigan played a major role in the Republican opposition to Haynsworth, but Brooke was the first to publicly express distaste for the nomination and wrote a letter to the President urging him to withdraw Haynsworth's name. This was an act of considerable courage; it had long been regarded as heretical for a senator to oppose a Supreme Court nomination by a president from his own party. For this reason, and also because of Brooke's status as a black and a Republican, his opposition to Haynsworth conferred legitimacy on the Democratic resistance to the nomination. Brooke must also be credited with gathering many of the seventeen Republican votes that were ultimately cast against Haynsworth. Brooke's success in the Haynsworth affair, as well as in the later rejection of G. Harrold Carswell for the Court, shows the crucial roles blacks can play as elected officials within the Republican party. Even in periods of nationwide conservatism, when the problem of racial disadvantage is not high on the agenda of the party in power, the party nonetheless

---

As long as a substantial minority of whites won't vote for a black person, blacks are unlikely to be elected to offices where candidates are chosen on a statewide basis

In the 1982 Elections:

- Sixty-six major party candidates ran for the United States Senate. None were black.

- Seventy-two major party candidates ran for Governor of their states. Only one, Thomas Bradley of California, was black. He lost.

- Of the three hundred or more major party candidates seeking statewide office below the level of Governor, fourteen were black. Five of them won.

---

derives legitimacy when racial minorities are included among its members and particularly when one or more hold high elective office.

After swamping his Democratic opponents in the 1966 and 1972 Senate races, Brooke lost his seat in the 1978 election to two-term Congressman Paul Tsongas, who captured 55 percent of the Massachusetts vote. Brooke's defeat came as no surprise; he had been hounded for months by bad publicity that grew out of his headline-making divorce and its subsequent investigations. The divorce trial brought to light the fact that Brooke had lied to the state about his personal finances. Although no charges were brought against him, damage had been done. Opinion polls showed that his credibility with voters had plummeted. As a result, the usual sources of campaign funds were no longer available. But there was certainly more to Brooke's defeat than financial accusations and divorce in a heavily Catholic state. In Tsongas, Brooke faced an able, attractive candidate with considerable voter appeal. The fatal blow, however, may have come from Senator Edward Kennedy, who had given Brooke's Democratic opponents only token support in 1966 and 1972 but threw himself into Tsongas' campaign, even going on the stump with him for a few days.

Brooke's career is an important case study of black political power in several ways. His presence illustrated the potential that even one black senator can have in shaping legislative forces. Even more important is the fact that Brooke was essentially elected to the Senate by whites. His career thus stands as an important refutation of the charge often made by blacks that a Negro cannot be elected to office in any state or district with a large white majority.

While the influence of one person may be great, black political power is always controlled by the cold reality of arithmetic. The fact is that the United States Senate, with its huge lawmaking, treaty-ratifying, and judicial confirmation powers, now has no black members. This circumstance stands by itself as a compelling statement of the triviality of black political influence in the United States. In the minds of many blacks moreover— including the nonaligned black nations of Africa—the fact that not one of the 100 Senate seats is held by a black person raises some serious questions about the political legitimacy of both major political parties in the United States.

As with the House of Representatives, the absence of blacks from the Senate is not dispositive of the issue of black influence in that body. We must still ask about the influence of black voters on other members of the Senate. In states with a large and strong black electorate, most senators recognize that they owe some measure of accountability to their black constituents. For example, even Senator Strom Thurmond, that wily old expert at playing the racial politics of the Old Confederacy, has found it profitable to court the black voters in South Carolina. His tactics have included gestures such as securing government favors for black colleges and enrolling his daughter in an integrated school. These measures have permitted the senator to otherwise pursue one of the most determinedly antiblack voting records in the Senate. Although his attempts to woo black voters were relatively unsuccessful in his 1978 reelection campaign, when he received only 3 percent of all black votes, it appears that his assurances of personal friendship for blacks, combined with his highly skillful showcasing of black underlings, have succeeded in preventing a large anti-Thurmond turnout by blacks, who constitute 30 percent of the state's population, but a far smaller proportion of the state's active voters.[3]

In general, the influence of black voters on the politics of southern senators has not been great. Because of the statewide election system and the lack of sophistication among black voters, few of the racial hardliners in the Senate from southern states have much to fear from black political action.

Senators who have consistently voted against Black Caucus-supported initiatives include Jesse Helms and John East of North Carolina, John Stennis and Thad Cochran of Mississippi, Jeremiah Denton of Alabama, John Warner of Virginia, and Russell Long of Louisiana. In general, they have successfully played Thurmond's theme of voting no on civil rights and affirmative integration while holding themselves out as fast friends of the black voter.

A number of the Senate traditionalists from the South have scrupulously put blacks on their staffs, publicized gestures of fiscal generosity toward black institutions, and prior to each election have made a considerable effort to "chat up the black vote." Defenders of the color line understand that now that blacks have the vote, this is merely a charade necessary for holding office. Yet, in many cases, successful manipulation of the still inexperienced black voter keeps power in the hands of racial traditionalists as effectively as did the literacy tests of a generation ago. Additionally, the political tenure in the Senate of the old guard is well protected by the favors it sends back home as a result of its firm hold on senior committee posts. And, in many places in the South, the racial conservatives are abetted too, most particularly in Texas, by a black electorate that still squabbles and stumbles over itself.

During the 1970s, many of the old-school southern segregationists such as Eastland of Mississippi, Talmadge of Georgia, McClellan of Arkansas, and Allen and Sparkman of Alabama left the Senate. The senators who have replaced them comprise a mixed group. The emergence of the GOP in the South has produced a number of arch-conservative Republicans, including Warner of Virginia, Helms and East of North Carolina, Mattingly of Georgia, Hawkins of Florida, Denton of Alabama, and Cochran of Mississippi. This group has continued to play the game of undying friendship for Negroes and dedicated support for toothless and unmonitored declarations of equal opportunity. The very large numbers of eligible black voters in these states have been too passive and disorganized to close ranks against them. However, several southern senators, including Dale Bumpers and David Pryor of Arkansas, Ernest Hollings of South Carolina, Lawton Chiles of Florida, Howard Heflin of Alabama, and James Sasser of Tennessee, have progressive voting records. By nature or by virtue of the nature of their constituencies, they have been sensitive to the political wishes of minority voters in their states. But for these senators racial politics puts the shoe on the other foot. The threat of racial voting backlash from whites often prompts the prudent southern liberal to project racial conservatism while quietly voting a more liberal racial agenda.

What about senators from states in the North? To what extent are they held politically accountable to the large black populations, particularly in the heavily industrialized Northeast? There are at least a dozen senators who represent the six northern states where blacks comprise at least 10 percent

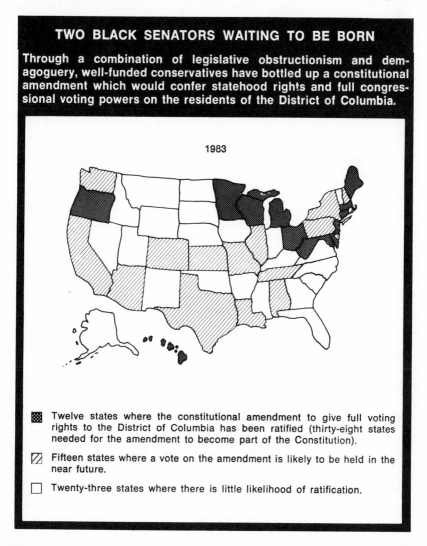

TWO BLACK SENATORS WAITING TO BE BORN

Through a combination of legislative obstructionism and demagoguery, well-funded conservatives have bottled up a constitutional amendment which would confer statehood rights and full congressional voting powers on the residents of the District of Columbia.

1983

Twelve states where the constitutional amendment to give full voting rights to the District of Columbia has been ratified (thirty-eight states needed for the amendment to become part of the Constitution).

Fifteen states where a vote on the amendment is likely to be held in the near future.

Twenty-three states where there is little likelihood of ratification.

of the voting-age population. Of course, not all northern senators with large black constituencies worry much about the black vote. For example, there are very large numbers of blacks living and voting in Wilmington, Delaware, but since the Wilmington half of the state doesn't elect a U.S. senator, black voting strength in Delaware—about 14 percent of the total—is no threat to Delaware Senator William Roth, Jr., whose voting record on black issues ranks with those of conservative diehards from the South. Most other senators from heavily black northern states have relatively progressive records on race-related issues. Liberal Democrats from states with large numbers of minority voters can count on strong support from blacks on election day, as can Republican Charles Mathias of Maryland, who regularly receives much larger shares of the black vote than most other Republicans. Democrat Carl Levin of Michigan, a strong supporter of legislative initiatives to increase black opportunities, owed his election victory in 1978 over incumbent Robert Griffin to black voters. Levin received 91 percent of the black vote and needed every bit of it to eke out a close victory.[4]

No clear reading can be had on the extent to which the voting behavior of senators from the northern states with large numbers of black constituents is, in fact, influenced by their black constituents. It is probable that most Senate liberals vote favorably on black-related bills simply because they are liberals. Black voter influence is a factor, but is probably not the major influence it would be if, for example, there were, as in the case of the House, two dozen seats where white incumbents had to deal with black voter percentages running over 30 percent or more.

Without question, the black political organizer's fondest dream would be the election of a sufficient number of black senators needed to achieve proportionate racial representation. If blacks were sitting in the Senate in proportion to their population percentage, there would be a total of about twelve black United States senators. Tightly organized in a caucus similar to that in the House, twelve black senators would be an awesome legislative force. The Senate leadership would face a brand-new power center with which it would have to deal and come to terms on routine as well as important legislative business. The opportunities for legislative horse-trading of votes in favor of initiatives favored by racial minorities would be limitless. Confirmation of presidential appointments and the passage or defeat of many important legislative packages often ride on considerably less than twelve votes. A tightly knit black caucus of twelve United States senators would often hold the balance of voting power in the legislative branch. The now slowly dawning awareness of black political power in the country would mature overnight.

Despite the recent successes of blacks in elective politics—between 1971 and 1976 the number of black elected officials doubled in all offices nationwide—there is little chance that a black person will be elected to the

Senate in the foreseeable future. The Edward Brooke phenomenon of 1966 to 1978 is not likely to be replicated soon in a nation increasingly coming to the view that too much has already been done for Negroes. Only in Mississippi does the black electorate reach 30 percent of the total electorate. In no state does it appear that whites in sufficient numbers are prepared to vote a black into office as a United States senator. While there are signs of change in white voter attitudes in a few states, particularly among liberals in some urban areas, many black elected officials express the opinion that lieutenant governorships are the highest posts that black politicians can realistically hope to claim in any contest where voting is on a statewide electoral basis.

White on White: Deputized Congressional Power

Legislative power, like other forms of power, is rarely retained exclusively in the hands of the person to whom it has been formally entrusted. In Congress, too, the proverbial "man to see" is frequently not the "boss." As in any organization, power in Congress tends to shift whenever the boss is away, overworked, skillful in the art of delegating authority, or lazy. Almost every member of Congress today has at least a dozen aides at his disposal, a good share of whom hold law, masters, or doctoral degrees. A few high-ranking members of Congress have as many as seventy assistants.

The huge power of the congressional staff is evident in the role staffers play in the lawmaking process. Staff members draft most of the 20,000 bills introduced into Congress each year. When the meaning or intent of a piece of legislation is in doubt, the staffers are called upon to interpret what they have written, not only during debate but even after the bills have been passed. Staff members actively lobby staffers in the employ of other congressmen for the passage or defeat of particular bills. The staff role in the committee process is an especially important feature of staff power because staff members organize and schedule committee hearings, set the agenda, select witnesses, and prepare questions for their bosses to ask. Staff members, rather than legislators, usually deal with lobbyists and government agency functionaries. Not only do staff members take an active part in the critical sessions during which bills are "marked up," but staffers also advise members on how to vote and sometimes even control their votes.

Ten thousand strong on Capitol Hill, staff members attract little attention from the press, yet their quasi-legislative functions warrant the conclusion that they constitute an invisible government within Congress.[5]

The most influential aide on a committee or subcommittee is normally either the staff director or the general counsel. The most important staff presence in a member's office is usually the administrative assistant and one or more of the legislative assistants. Most congressmen have one legislative assistant; most senators have several. Some of these staff aides are delegated so much authority that it would be correct to regard them as surrogate members of Congress.

High in the constellation of aides in both parties are the assistants to the House and Senate leadership. They exercise influence in various ways. They screen information before it reaches the leaders for whom they work and are thus able to choose which bills move into the legislative hopper and which are discarded. Leadership staff members act as troubleshooters, advisers, and decisionmakers. Conferring with them is for all practical purposes the functional equivalent of dealing with a member of the leadership.

Categorically, there are no public institutions exercising federal government power, today, where black people have been so completely removed from power as in the staffs of the United States Congress. These delegated powers are, and always have been, reserved almost exclusively for whites. Of the roughly 5,000 professionals employed on Capitol Hill, perhaps 100 could accurately be termed "staff superpowers." A survey of these highly influential staff persons in the Ninety-sixth Congress showed that all of them were white. None of the professional aides serving either the House or Senate leadership were black. Of the eighteen standing committees in the Senate, not one had a black staff director and only one had a black general counsel—the Budget Committee, which does not write legislation. And none of the subcommittees had a black staff director or general counsel.

The most striking fact is that in 1978 no senator, including those with outstanding reputations for liberalism on racial matters, had hired a black person to fill any position as legislative or administrative assistant. The count showed that seventy-five of the nation's 100 senators—three out of four—employed no blacks in professional positions on either their personal or their committee staffs.[6] The senators who are most eloquent in proclaiming the equal dignity of black people appear to have virtually no interest in conferring equal power.

The complete separation of blacks from staff power in Congress is well illustrated by the House delegation from Ohio. In 1977, the staff of Representative Louis Stokes, a black man, was all black. Otherwise, the approximately 280 full-time employees serving Ohio's twenty-two white congressmen included a total of twenty blacks, none of whom held a professional position.[7] With staff positions in Congress, the statistical disparity between black and white employees is so great that if Congress were a large corporation, the Equal Employment Opportunity Commission would have an airtight case of racial discrimination. But, of course, no such case can be brought because Congress has exempted itself from every equal opportunity law it has passed.[8]

The mechanism that maintains all staff power in white hands is simple, efficient, and, remarkably, often colorblind. The selection process largely replicates the manner in which incumbency perpetuates itself in other institutions. Recruitment for congressional staff posts is generally by word of mouth, with most professional openings filled on the basis of recommendations and referrals by insiders who already work on the Hill or did so in the past. The insider's network includes lobbyists, consultants to committee staffs, and members of the executive branch who deal with Congress. Because this network is white, it almost necessarily works to recruit whites, thus producing a self-perpetuating group of almost all-white congressional staffs. In many cases, a member of Congress who might be receptive to hiring a black aide is deterred either by the racial feelings of constituents back home or by what he imagines their sentiments to be. In any case, members of Congress are under little or no pressure to find black aides, and whites in Congress rarely profit politically from hiring them other than at the token level. Thus, the lily-white quality of congressional staffs appears to be less the product of deliberately race-conscious employment decisions and more the natural result of a white-controlled hiring system that perpetuates itself through the employment of friends, classmates, and peers.

Insignificant as they were to start with, there was a further decrease in both the number and influence of black staffers in the Ninety-seventh Congress, which convened in January 1981. For the first time in nearly three decades, the Republicans took control of the United States Senate. As a result, hundreds of positions on the staffs of Senate committees were filled by Republican chairmen. The new GOP committee heads assigned these staff positions to their political operatives and cronies, just as the Democrats did when they controlled the Senate. Few Republican senators owe any political debt to blacks. Few GOP senators have any political need to court the goodwill of black voters by naming blacks to staff posts. Arch-conservative GOP committee chairmen such as Senators Jesse Helms of Agriculture or Strom Thurmond of Judiciary—all of whom have consistently opposed efforts to bring blacks into the political and economic mainstream—cannot be expected to name any blacks to fill staff positions other than at the assistant deputy level. Without a doubt, Republican control over the selection of committee staffs further reduced the already minuscule black input into the deliberations of the United States Senate.

Black Holdings of State Political Office

The media coverage that occurs whenever blacks move into posts in Washington is so extensive that the importance of black activities in state and local politics is often overlooked. In some ways, however, a group's political power at the state and local levels is a superior measure of its influence. Elected state officials control state budgets that exceed $25 billion. It is at the state and local levels that decisions are made about the funding of public services in predominantly black neighborhoods, school districts, public hospitals, libraries, and recreation facilities. Policies in effect at the state capital and in city hall are often of greater significance to black citizens than the activities of the federal government in Washington. A black alderman may have more impact on the lives of his constituents than he would if he were a member of Congress. Major black-controlled cities haven't even begun to test their authority to legislate equal opportunity and affirmative-action measures affecting resident corporations.

Initiatives with profound racial consequences such as the redrawing of congressional district lines, the annexation of suburbs by large cities, the establishment and implementation of voter-registration procedures, and the determination of qualifications for getting on the ballot are among the important political decisions left to the discretion of state legislatures. State and local legislative bodies also decide whether or not to make the sort of political arrangements that effectively disenfranchise blacks—"runoff" primaries for state and federal offices and elections "at large" in cities with heavy concentrations of black voters. State legislatures also check or release the political power of blacks through their authority to ratify or reject proposed amendments to the U.S. Constitution. A major example of the potential impact of local power on black political power nationally is the proposed amendment that would grant voting representation in Congress to the District of Columbia. Adoption of this measure by three-fourths of the state legislatures would undoubtedly increase the number of blacks in the United States Senate from zero to two.

Measured in terms of total numbers elected to office in the past decade, blacks have made substantial gains at the state and local levels. In 1969, there were 1,185 black elected officials in the United States. A decade later, 4,607 blacks held elective office—a 288 percent increase. But the political power attached to the office counts for the most. Measured in these terms, blacks at the state level still wield virtually no political influence.

In the early 1980s, the so-called New Federalism of the Reagan Administration was rapidly shifting power to the states. If anything, these policies

BLACKS ARE AN EMERGING FORCE IN STATE POLITICS BUT WHITES ARE STILL IN CHARGE

1982	Black	White	Percent Black
State Governors	0	50	0.0%
State Lt. Governors *	0	43	0.0%
Secretaries of State **	2	46	4.2%
State Attorney Generals	0	50	0.0%
State Senators	73	1,908	3.7%
State Representatives	257	5,244	4.7%
County Board Members	392	18,665	2.1%
Mayors- Cities with Pop. Greater than 200,000	9	63	12.5%
Mayors- Cities with Pop. 75,000-200,000	14	176	7.4%
Total	747	26,268	2.8%

*Seven States do not have an office of Lt. Governor.
**Alaska and Hawaii do not have a Secretary of State.

Source: National Roster of Black Elected Officials, Vol. 12, Joint Center for Political Studies, Washington, D.C., 1982, and Washington Information Directory 1983-84, Congressional Quarterly Inc., Washington, D.C., 1983, pp. 811-828.

were shifting power away from blacks. States'-rights initiatives confer increased power on state governors. In 1984, there were no black governors or lieutenant governors. The only black state governor in American history, P.B.S. Pinchback, served as governor of Louisiana for forty-eight days in 1871, after the incumbent governor was impeached and convicted. In 1978, more than a century after Governor Pinchback's brief moment of glory, two blacks served as lieutenant governors in Colorado and California. Neither is still in office.

The absence of black state governors, like the void of black United States senators, reflects the inability of black candidates to succeed in statewide elections. Where voting districts are small and the concentration of black voters high, black candidates can, and often do, win office, as the careers of many black congressmen illustrate. But since blacks are in a minority in every state, the racial tag in contests for state office becomes a handicap instead of an advantage, with the result that election to statewide office is an almost insurmountable task. A multiple-party system, whose effect would be to split the white vote among numerous candidates, might permit the election of a black to an important statewide office. But the two-party system is solidly entrenched in the United States and, in most cases, neither of the major parties is disposed to nominate a black person, except, possibly, as a junior running mate to attract black voters to the ticket.

Blacks have served in statewide office as secretaries of state in Michigan and Wisconsin, as superintendent of public instruction in California, as state treasurer in Connecticut, and as state comptroller in Illinois. Blacks have also been elected on a statewide basis as state supreme court justices— one each in Alabama, California, Florida, and Pennsylvania, and one justice elected to the state court of appeals in North Carolina. In the 1982 elections, fifteen blacks ran for statewide office but only five of them won—Oscar Adams, Justice of the Alabama Supreme Court, Allen Broussard of the California Supreme Court, Henry Parker, Treasurer of Connecticut, Richard Burris, Comptroller of Illinois, and Richard Austin, Secretary of State in Michigan.[9]

As would be expected, blacks have had far more success in electing blacks as members of state legislative assemblies than in electing them to offices chosen from a statewide ballot. As late as 1950, not a single black served as a state legislator in the South; only a handful held office in the North. By 1979, blacks held 307 of the 7,482 seats in all of the state legislatures. This was remarkable progress, attributable in large measure to the enactment of the federal Voting Rights Act of 1965. Yet racial parity in representation remains far in the future. In 1979, the 307 black state legislators held only 4 percent of the seats in all state legislatures, only one-third of the seats blacks would have held if there had been equal racial representation.[10] No matter what is done to correct inequities in election procedures, a heavy tide will continue to run against blacks, particularly those seeking statewide office, as long as there is a significant minority of whites who won't vote for a black person for any public office.

The black political success rate varies greatly in the states. In 1979, Tennessee, a state with a black population of approximately 15 percent, had a legislature that was 9 percent black. In contrast, both Alabama and Georgia had black populations greater than 25 percent, yet in 1979 the

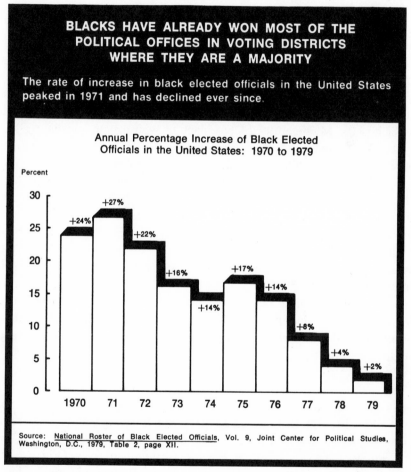

BLACKS HAVE ALREADY WON MOST OF THE POLITICAL OFFICES IN VOTING DISTRICTS WHERE THEY ARE A MAJORITY

The rate of increase in black elected officials in the United States peaked in 1971 and has declined ever since.

Annual Percentage Increase of Black Elected Officials in the United States: 1970 to 1979

Source: National Roster of Black Elected Officials, Vol. 9, Joint Center for Political Studies, Washington, D.C., 1979, Table 2, page XII.

Alabama legislature was only 11 percent black, and in Georgia, blacks held no more than 10 percent of the legislative seats. In other southern states, blacks were underrepresented to an even greater degree. In Arkansas, for example, 3 percent of the legislature was black, although the state had a black population of 17 percent. In Mississippi, a state where over 37 percent of the population was black, only seventeen of 174 legislators were black in

1979. A black delegation of 4 percent of the total sat in the 160-member Florida state legislature; the same percentage prevailed in the 170-seat North Carolina General Assembly. In 1979, there were no blacks whatsoever in the state senates of Florida, South Carolina, and Texas.

These extreme fluctuations are the result of many factors: differences in the degree of black voter activity, differences in the intensity of the determination of whites to keep political power away from blacks, variations in the relative skills of local political parties in defusing black issues, differences in the racial attitudes of judges sitting on voting rights cases, as well as a multitude of other factors.

As one might expect, blacks have been far more successful in securing legislative positions in the North and in the West. Black holdings of legislative positions were particularly strong in California, Illinois, Maryland, Massachusetts, Michigan, and Ohio, each of whose state legislatures had racial makeups that mirrored the black percentage of the state's population. For reasons not altogether clear, among northern states, Delaware and New Jersey had very low black representation in their state legislatures.

In local offices, as distinguished from the state office level, blacks have made little more than token progress. Although blacks hold roughly 4 percent of all state assembly seats, they have been only about half as successful in winning elective office at the county level. Of approximately 18,400 positions on county governing bodies in the nation in 1979, only 351, or slightly under 2 percent, were held by blacks.[11] Despite the presence of large numbers of eligible black voters, whites in the South continue to be adept at retaining white political power at the county level. A 1975 study revealed that blacks made up a majority of the population in 101 southern counties; yet in almost two-thirds of these counties, blacks held no seats on the county governing body.[12]

Of course, the most notable and publicized gains by blacks have occurred in the cities. In 1984, there were 225 black mayors in the United States, and blacks held the mayor's office in eleven of the nation's largest cities: Chicago, Philadelphia, Los Angeles, Detroit, Birmingham, New Orleans, Atlanta, Washington, Newark, Oakland, and even Richmond, cradle of the Confederacy. Other cities that had black mayors and populations over 100,000 were Berkeley, California; Hartford, Connecticut; Dayton, Ohio; Charlotte, North Carolina; Gary, Indiana; Spokane, Washington; and Roanoke, Virginia.

Certainly, a few of these political victories gave blacks the dubious privilege of presiding over urban insolvency, poverty, and decay. Crime, dilapidated housing, lengthening welfare rolls, and murderously high unemployment rates marked life in cities such as Newark, Detroit, and Gary. But Chicago, Richmond, New Orleans, and Oakland could be counted as cities in moderately good economic health. The victories of black mayoral candidates in Los Angeles and Atlanta were major political triumphs. And the election of Mayor Harold Washington in Chicago and Wilson Goode in Philadelphia in 1983 must be counted as the most important events in the recent political history of black America.

In most cases, black mayors have proven to the white business establishment that in heavily black-populated cities black mayors are more effective peacekeepers than are white mayors. This explains, in part, the white voter support and financial backing that black mayoralty candidates have received. Campaign experience also shows that black mayors do not succeed in winning elections on a civil rights ticket; nor are they likely to be reelected when their campaigns are marked by racial militance. In fact, the record of black mayors so far wholly refutes the stereotype that black politicians are likely to turn city governments over to radicals, hate mongers, and a racial spoils system. The black mayors—traditionally an anathema of machine Democrats, conservatives, and opponents of ethnic politics—represent a major step in the fuller integration of blacks into the American political mainstream.

In medium-sized and small cities and towns, election results show a very strong correlation to race. Black mayors were found in such predominantly black communities as Compton, California; East St. Louis, Illinois; East Orange, New Jersey; Pritchard, Alabama; and Highland Park and Pontiac, Michigan. To be sure, most of the 225 black mayors in the United States governed small rural southern cities. In 1979, 66 percent of all black mayors were from the South, and 68 percent were elected in towns with populations of less than 5,000. In economic terms these mayors carried little influence. Most of them governed tiny black-belt rural communities having very high levels of illiteracy, unemployment, and poverty.[13]

Blacks as School Board Officials

There are few activities in our society where the connection between political power and economic prospects for those who have it has been more evident than in public education. School board officials influence individual school budgets, teacher qualifications, curriculum quality, academic standards, allocations of computer training resources and classroom size and discipline. For these reasons, a critical measure of the ability of blacks to compete for educational resources is the extent of black representation on the approximately 17,000 local school boards in the country. The good news to report is that more blacks are to be found on school boards than in any other public office. Of the 4,607 blacks holding elective positions in the nation, nearly one-quarter sit on local school boards. The bad news is that *blacks hold only one percent of all school board seats.* This tiny percentage ultimately works to deprive blacks of control over the forces affecting the education of their children, especially in large cities and in communities with a large black school population. A notorious example of the patrimonial relationship that tends to prevail in many public school systems is the school board of Boston, Massachusetts, where no black person held a seat on the Boston School Committee until 1978, even though black students outnumbered white students.[14] Black parents, in very large numbers, may be faulted for not lighting the fires of learning in the minds of their children at home, but they may not be blamed when majority power has systematically prevented them from controlling what happens at school.

There is no satisfactory way to grasp the magnitude of shortfall in black political influence in the United States. One must inevitably rely on statistical measures, despite an acute awareness that numbers alone cannot tell the story. This is particularly so when, as is the case in the United States, all the imperial powers in government are held by whites. In a color-blind society, one would expect that blacks, who make up almost 12 percent of the population, would claim roughly the same percentage of elected officials. In 1984, however, blacks held *approximately one percent* of all federal, state, and local elected government posts. The numerical disparity is so huge that one may confidently state that in the United States there is very little political power-sharing between blacks and whites. Indeed, a trend toward greater black political influence has developed since the enactment of voting rights legislation. Yet, despite upbeat news stories and soothing rhetoric from the centers of power, there can be little doubt that black people in the United States have been and, for the immediate future, will be essentially governed by whites.

CHAPTER SIXTEEN

Blacks in the Executive Branch:
Walter Mittys and Lord High Nobodies

"The eagle suffers little birds to sing."

—*William Shakespeare*
Titus Andronicus *(1593)*

THE FOUNDING FATHERS feared an imperial presidency and, in many respects, this is precisely what they got. Pause for a moment to consider the
extraordinary powers of the American chief of state. The President controls
an annual federal budget approaching a trillion dollars; he has stewardship
over a federal work force of 2 million workers; he commands possibly the
strongest military in the world. Add to these powers the President's authority over law enforcement, over the central police, and over the intelligence
forces. Then consider his power to name federal judges and heads of the
central bank—officials whose lawgiving and regulatory edicts often survive
for generations after the President has left office. Next, look to the President's appointive powers. With the authority to name or dismiss thousands
of highly placed officials, he effectively controls most of the policies and
efforts of a hundred or more government departments and agencies that
regulate commerce, employment, credit, and investment in a nation that
still possesses the largest and most important economy in the world. These
indications of the broad sweep of the presidential authority show the huge
importance of the executive power to the lives of citizens and groups of
citizens that are competing for position and advantage in the United States.

In addition to his formal constitutional powers, the President has command over a wide range of informal but traditional instruments of political

control: patronage granted or withheld; government grants made or denied; appointments made or refused, to ambassadorships, presidential commissions, and other coveted posts. So pervasive is the presidential power in the United States that the voting attitudes and policies of every congressman, senator, mayor, local alderman, and corporate chief are, to a major extent, influenced by the presidential carrot and the stick. We see, then, that the standard civic text's portrayal of the office of the President as the branch of government that administers and enforces the law is a grossly inadequate and seriously misleading statement about the true nature and scope of the presidential authority.

In an economy where the distribution of goods and money among many different claimants is controlled in large part by political power, the ways in which the presidential power is exercised is of utmost importance to black people, as it is to other groups that fall far short of average levels of income and wealth. For blacks particularly, the power of the President to translate his individual views or prejudices into government policy is uniquely important. This is so because of the American tradition of governance by presidential executive order. In many instances, through the process of executive decree, the President's wishes may be freely converted into the law of the land without the approval of other branches of government that might otherwise oppose his wishes. The unilateral presidential power to make law is sometimes used in startling and unprecedented ways. In 1941, when America faced the necessity of tooling up for an impending war, President Roosevelt summarily imposed affirmative racial integration on much of the nation's private industry. Twenty years later, again without the prior approval of Congress, President Kennedy issued a series of executive orders requiring tens of thousands of corporations to actively recruit and employ blacks and other racial minorities. Acting on federal constitutional interpretations prohibiting state-supported racial segregation, we now see that either President Eisenhower or any of the other Presidents who preceded him might have used the presidential powers to enforce the mandates of the Constitution to peremptorily abolish dual public school systems maintained by the states. In fact, by virtue of instructions to the Department of Justice, a President so minded might have invoked constitutional authority under the broad protections of the federal Bill of Rights to impose antilynching protection within the states, a guarantee which for so many years Congress and state legislatures stubbornly refused to enact. The presidential executive power to deal with broad issues affecting race relations is truly dazzling in its scope.

In considering the relationship between blacks and presidential power, the questions we ask are: Who controls the great powers of the executive branch? Who has controlled them in the past? Who, in the nature of things, is likely to control them in the future? Since the executive power, like other power in a democracy, is, in theory, shared, who are the people invited to enter the inner circle where one influences the executive authority? Who are the people and special-interest groups that are in a position to win presidential favors and successfully block, before they happen, the handicaps and penalties that the White House has the power to impose? Do blacks ever have inside access to this great power of the presidency? Do they influence it from the outside? What are the pressures operating in American politics that tend to persuade a President to accommodate, or to oppose, the political goals of most blacks?

No modern democracy with a white majority—the United States, of course, included—has ever elected a black person to head its government. In fact, with the exception of John F. Kennedy, a Roman Catholic, and Herbert Hoover's Vice-President, Charles Curtis, who was part American Indian, all American Presidents and Vice-Presidents have been white Protestants. Although the nation was never constitutionally established as a white Christian state, for much of its history it has essentially acted as if it were.

Recent years have witnessed a revolutionary change in the racial attitudes of American citizens. There would be no problem today in nominating and electing a second-generation Italian, Greek, Pole, or Irishman to the White House. Even the naming of a presidential candidate with a Hispanic background is not beyond the realm of possibility. But in terms of the racial politics that pragmatically govern eligibility for the very highest office, it appears that two groups, Jews and blacks, still remain beyond the pale. This does not mean, of course, that the political circumstances of these two races are comparable. Residual anti-Semitism today would almost surely defeat a Jewish candidate nominated for the presidency by either major party—if indeed, such a candidate could be nominated, an unlikely event given the near certainty of his defeat. Yet, despite this racial disability, American Jews hold considerable power, as evidenced by a substantial number of seats in the United States House and Senate, a fair share of state governorships, an impressive presence on federal and state judicial benches, and the possession of key leadership positions in banking, industry, journalism, and communications.

In contrast, for blacks there are no alternative sources of power to compensate for the unofficial rules that de facto exclude them from eligibility for the top executive post. The fact that in the collective view of the national electorate a black person is effectively disqualified by race from holding the nation's highest office can hardly be seen as a vestigial remnant of a once powerful discriminatory force. The situation is, rather, business as usual, the culminating exclusion in a political system that methodically denies blacks access to power all the way up and down the line. From time to time, an apparent exception may appear to the rigid tradition that denies power to blacks, but as we shall see, these exceptions almost invariably turn out to be afterthoughts or token blacks permitted to enjoy the celebrity that comes from proximity to power. Almost never do these highly visible and celebrated blacks influence government power or hold it in their own right.

Eisenhower to Johnson: Blacks as Ambassadors to Other Blacks

Since the early days of the American republic, and especially in the twentieth century, every President has had an inner circle of influential aides and assistants. Their duties are wide ranging; their power considerable. They write the memoranda that shape presidential policy and often decide what the President shall read and whom he shall see. They dispense presidential favors to members of Congress just as they chide or punish Cabinet members who fail to remain in line. Those close to the President are often more important than the President in determining the administration's posture on issues such as affirmative action, welfare reform, full employment, minority contracting, open housing, school desegregation, and criminal justice. When a President must fill a vacancy for a high agency position or for a Supreme Court seat, a presidential aide is frequently responsible for recruiting candidates and recommending nominees. Above all, it is the staff that seizes on an otherwise dormant issue, brings it to the surface, and elevates it to presidential caliber.

In modern times, the presidential stand-ins have become increasingly influential in running the nation's affairs. Unelected and never mentioned in the Constitution, many of these aides have, in effect, become "assistant presidents." The major presidential policymakers of the past include names such as Harry Hopkins under Roosevelt, McGeorge Bundy under Kennedy, Bill Moyers under Johnson, H.R. Haldeman and John Ehrlichman under Nixon, Donald Rumsfeld under Ford, Hamilton Jordan in the Carter administration, and Edwin Meese and James Baker in the Reagan Administration. The men who make up the inner circle of the President's staff have always been exclusively white. The White House proudly proclaims itself to be an equal opportunity employer, and, in a sense, this is true if one counts the blacks who invariably serve the coffee and guard the doors and the aides who sit in the Executive Office Building next to the White House. But the President's lieutenants who drink the coffee at the famous breakfast meetings where national policy is settled are invariably white men. The important "Saturday night" dinners where great issues are decided are attended by White House officials of the highest rank, who almost without exception are white. Blacks in government, however, are frequently invited to make appearances at the plenary and ceremonial meetings where the great decisions made earlier are announced to the public.

The all-white composition of White House power which has prevailed for centuries has no connection whatsoever with the intense racial sentiments that could motivate, say, a conservative racial extremist in the House or the Senate. Governance by whites is virtually an inbred rule of behavior which people unconsciously perform just as they would tie a necktie or climb stairs without cognitive awareness of what they are doing. In recent years, the reservation of White House staff power to whites might have served a secondary function. On a great many issues, opposition to presidential policies can be beaten by deciding the issues in the inner circles of government. In this manner, the uncomfortable forces of democracy may be blunted. In this way, too, the nagging pressures of the black agenda can often be contained by dealing with them *in camera*.

The first break in the whites-only tradition of White House executive staff occurred in the Eisenhower presidency. After the 1954 Supreme Court school desegregation ruling, Eisenhower appointed a black man, E. Frederick Morrow, a highly regarded attorney and former Commerce Department official, to the post of White House Counselor for Special Projects. Morrow's appointment marked the beginning of a long period during which there was one, and usually only one, place in the White House reserved for a black special assistant, just as there later came to be a customary "black seat" on the Supreme Court and on the boards of many public institutions. According to the custom that developed, the black person in the White House post was almost invariably designated as an assistant for minority affairs. His job was to act as the President's established "bridgehead" to the black community. He was to serve as an advance man and spokesman for the decisions the government reached in discharging its traditional responsibility for protecting and helping Negroes. Morrow was the first of a long line of black appointed officials who served, in effect, as ambassadors to domestic blacks.

Morrow's duties in the Eisenhower administration, by his own account, were trivial, if not menial. He was in charge of security for the Executive Office Building; he coordinated the welcome-home ceremonies when Eisenhower returned to the White House after recuperating from his heart attack. Removed from any active role in domestic policymaking, Morrow's most significant responsibility was analyzing Negro voting patterns for the administration. Morrow's own words best describe his place:

> "No matter how vigorously I may disagree in my own mind about certain top-level advice that has been given, it is not wise for me to interject my own ideas. I have to sit back and watch developments and deplore the fact that in my estimation a lot of these actions will lead to real difficulty." [1]

President Kennedy's well-known friendship and concern for blacks won him great popularity with black voters. Only two blacks, Andrew Hatcher and Frank Reeves, served on the White House professional staff during the Kennedy administration. Democratic National Committeeman Reeves never intended to stay long at the White House. To this end, he was pencilled in to fill the first vacancy on the District of Columbia Governing Commission. While awaiting an opening, Reeves served as a special assistant to Kennedy, functioning as the President's liaison to the black community. Soon after his appointment to the Commission, personal income tax problems led Reeves to resign from both the Commission and the White House staff.

Andrew Hatcher was by far the more visible black member of the Kennedy team. A newspaperman who had worked on the Kennedy campaign staff, Hatcher served as Deputy to Press Secretary Pierre Salinger, a major figure in the Kennedy White House. Filling in for Salinger, Hatcher occasionally ran press conferences. He also played a public relations role for the Kennedy administration internationally, serving as a general ambassador of goodwill to black African nations.

For the first time in recent history, the Kennedy years saw the executive branch move to the forefront of the struggle for civil rights. It was during the Kennedy administration that issue was joined with Governors Ross Barnett of Mississippi and George Wallace of Alabama over the racial integration of state universities. The executive branch assumed an active role both in plotting strategy and in developing the tactics by which the federal power could be used to ensure racial integration of public institutions in the South. In these struggles to break white supremacy, the economic and political future of black America was at stake, yet there is no suggestion that any blacks in the White House were either influencing the strategy or calling any of the shots. The great civil rights confrontations of 1961 and 1963 saw blacks outside the White House join forces with white Kennedy lieutenants to win the major civil rights victories of that time. The stars of the White House team—Burke Marshall, Harris Wofford, Lewis Oberdorfer, Ramsey Clark, and Nicholas Katzenbach—were all white men. As with the original emancipation in the last century, it is clear from press accounts in the early 1960s that blacks were not necessary parties in planning or carrying out their second liberation.

The White House staff under Lyndon Johnson again included only two blacks, Hobart Taylor, Jr., and Clifford Alexander, Jr. Here, for the first time, blacks were issued a modicum of power. Taylor, an attorney, had backed LBJ's bid for the vice-presidential nomination in 1960 and was the son of a wealthy Texas oilman who was a longtime friend and political supporter of the veteran Texas senator. When the Kennedy-Johnson ticket was elected, the younger Taylor became one of the Vice-President's special assistants. He was appointed director of the Committee on Equal Employment Opportunity under Kennedy, but did not join the White House staff until Johnson succeeded to the presidency. His title was Associate Counsel to the President, and throughout his tenure at the White House he headed the White House Equal Employment Opportunity Committee.

There are sharp differences of opinion about Taylor's influence in the White House. Some blacks viewed him as a traditional "corporate Negro," faithfully serving the interests of whites. Historian Arthur Schlesinger, Jr., quotes Robert F. Kennedy as feeling "contempt for Taylor" because "I thought he was so ineffective." [2] Taylor, however, apparently played some role in the formulation of Kennedy's executive order that established the President's Committee on Equal Employment Opportunity. Taylor also influenced the design of the Federal Contract Compliance Program, which attacked discriminatory hiring practices in firms holding government contracts. Although Taylor's responsibilities under Johnson suggest some black influence on affairs of state, this influence was confined to the standard black domestic issues. After a year in the Johnson White House, Taylor left to become director of the Export-Import Bank. Like many others favored by presidential appointment, Taylor was in great demand as a director of large corporations. He served on the boards of A&P, Aetna Life, Sohio, and Westinghouse Electric.

Clifford Alexander, a black man of considerable personal force and ability, joined the White House staff in 1964. Alexander was a National Security Council analyst when he was chosen by President Johnson to become the President's Deputy Special Assistant. Increasingly, Alexander won

Johnson's admiration. In 1965, the White House staged a highly successful conference on civil rights, while at the same time adroitly avoiding a side-show of demonstrations and political embarrassments. It appears that Alexander worked chiefly on legislation and speeches on issues such as civil rights and narcotics. After two years in the White House, Alexander was appointed chairman of the Equal Opportunity Commission—successor to the original President's Committee on Equal Opportunity—while continuing to serve as an active member of the White House staff. By all accounts, Alexander's influence in the Johnson administration was unprecedented for a black White House staffer, but his troubleshooting missions were usually limited to the special concerns of members of his own race. Alexander was to later serve in a much more visible role in the Carter administration.

There was one forceful black presence in both the Kennedy and Johnson administrations who was not officially employed in the government. Louis Martin was editor of the *Michigan Chronicle,* a black newspaper, as well as a veteran of Democratic politics. A friend of Kennedy's brother-in-law Sargent Shriver, Martin joined the Kennedy organization during the 1960 campaign. His wisdom, political contacts, and close relationship with Shriver won Kennedy's trust. After the election, Martin became the Democratic National Committee's Deputy Chairman for Minorities, a position he held throughout both the Kennedy and Johnson administrations. He not only succeeded in turning the office into an effective base from which to influence domestic policy but managed to spend so much time at the White House that many observers believed he was on the staff. One of his first assignments for Kennedy was on a six-man committee headed by Shriver, which recruited and screened candidates for the several hundred highest political appointments. Martin did not neglect the opportunity to actively integrate the federal government. Under President Johnson, Martin continued as a major outside recruiter, working with John Macy, then chairman of the Civil Service Commission, to fill staff vacancies in the upper ranks of the federal bureaucracy. Nicknamed the godfather of black politics, Martin was partly responsible for bringing influential blacks such as Robert Weaver, Thurgood Marshall, and Andrew Brimmer into the government, thus playing a critical role in the eventual integration of the Cabinet, the Supreme Court, and the Federal Reserve Board. Once in office, these appointees—with Martin's encouragement—in turn often named other blacks as their subordinates.

In 1963, Bayard Rustin proposed a massive march on Washington to protest the Jim Crow voting laws of the South. At this time, Martin advised

President Kennedy on how to deal with the potentially explosive confrontation. But Martin's role was not restricted to putting out "brush fires" in the black community. Throughout the Johnson presidency, Martin was an influential figure in many broad civil rights issues. He helped draft the Voting Rights Act of 1965 and actively lobbied Congress in support of its passage. The importance of his contribution to integrating the United States Government is illustrated by President Johnson's refusal to inform senators of the appointment of Thurgood Marshall to the Supreme Court until Martin could be present for the historic formalities. Martin is unquestionably one of the great unsung black figures in American political history. Although widely acknowledged to have had more influence on Presidents Kennedy and Johnson than any black staff member before him, history books barely mention him. Few Americans have even heard his name.

Blacks in the Nixon-Ford White House: More Ceremony but Less Influence

The Nixon presidency saw no black figure inside the White House even approach the level of Louis Martin's influence under both Kennedy and Johnson. On the whole, President Nixon's use of blacks in the White House was traditional: superintending political patronage in black districts, mounting black capitalism roadshows to win black voters, and working up self-congratulatory publicity to hail minority programs. The virtues of paternalism were so securely held in the Nixon White House that the staff often neglected even to invite black officials to hear about aid and rescue missions that were being planned for their constituents. In 1969 and 1970, I attended more than half a dozen White House staff planning sessions on major minority-enterprise programs. Not a single black person was present at any of those meetings.

Initially, the leading black person on the Nixon White House staff was Robert J. Brown, a public relations man from North Carolina. His influence in the Nixon administration was marginal, as symbolized by the fact that his office was not in the White House but in the adjoining Executive Office Building. Harry S. Dent, a presidential assistant and at one time a close friend of Brown, wrote that during Nixon's first term Brown worked on black voter efforts, organized a White House staff prayer breakfast group, and went South "to tell blacks and the public all the good things Nixon had been doing to improve the lot of blacks."[3] Brown attended Cabinet meetings, regularly consulted with the Secretary of Commerce on the black capitalism program, and chaired an interagency task force designed to direct government aid to minority communities. These responsibilities reflected more show than substance. During the late 1960s, funds for minority-enterprise programs were lodged not in the Secretary of Commerce's office but in the Office of Economic Opportunity, then headed by an important and capable Nixon confidante, Donald Rumsfeld.

Nixon reshuffled all his black presidential aides after his reelection in 1972. Brown returned to his public relations firm and was succeeded as Special Assistant to the President by Stanley S. Scott, a journalist on the White House communications staff who had previously been assigned to black media. Like Brown before him, Scott had little influence in the White House. With his usual political acuity, Nixon had sensed the growing strength of the "silent majority"—the large blue-collar and white-collar classes opposed to liberal programs for helping minorities—and was already committed to the so-called southern strategy, which was aimed at augmenting and then capturing the white backlash vote. The Republican party had ceded black votes to the Democrats and had set its sights instead on the southern white majority which made up the backbone of Democratic voting strength in the South. Between the southern strategy and the White House's later preoccupation with the Watergate scandal, the few black programs already implemented quickly faded away. Signs of their demise were visible: Scott was no longer invited to Cabinet meetings, and his staff, which under Brown had included more than a half dozen aides, was whittled down to a secretary and one assistant.

In the Nixon White House, three other black aides worked on the Domestic Council headed by John Ehrlichman. Norman Ross dealt with natural resources policy, Sally Anne Payton handled District of Columbia affairs, and Norris Sydnor was on the minority programs desk while doubling as White House troubleshooter on such minority matters as discontent among black servicemen stationed in Europe. The presence of four blacks in White House staff positions was a numerical increase over the Kennedy and Johnson years, but Negro influence on domestic policymaking, even within the narrower sphere of black issues, decreased during Nixon's presidency. The singular unimportance of blacks in the Nixon administration is illustrated by the fact that none of the so-called high-level black White House staff members is even mentioned in Nixon's memoirs or in any of the major narrative accounts of the Nixon administration.

In racial matters as in so much else, the Ford White House continued the patterns established by its predecessor. The highest-ranking black in the Ford administration was John Calhoun, a former White House public relations specialist who was appointed as the President's Special Assistant for

Minority Affairs shortly after Ford took office. Calhoun was working with several strikes against him in his effort to function as an effective black voice in the White House. In the first place, the Ford administration had little commitment to minorities, including almost no interest in courting them for either vote gathering or political manipulation. In the second place, there was no coherent minority program for Calhoun to administer and no inclination within the administration to fund any program he might back. Calhoun's authority within the White House is illustrated by the fact that he reported to the White House Public Liaison Director rather than directly to the President. His "staff" consisted of a single secretary. Despite these impediments, Calhoun managed some impressive accomplishments. He improved the level of government funding of minority colleges and hospitals and is credited with fending off cuts in funds for minority business enterprise.

Under President Ford, three blacks enjoyed places on the Domestic Council. Richard Parsons worked on civil rights, law enforcement, and drug abuse; Norman Ross continued to deal with natural resources policy; and Arthur Fletcher, a man of unusual stature and ability, helped formulate urban policy. Another black in the Ford White House, Aaron Spaulding, was one of four or five staff members who counseled on personnel appointments within the administration.

In sum, neither the Nixon nor the Ford White House evinced any inclination toward delegating power or even listening seriously to blacks. Usually isolated in the Executive Office Building and mainly invited to the ceremonies at which decisions that had already been made were rubber-stamped, blacks on the executive staff had almost no contact, influence, or leverage with the President.

Blacks in the Carter White House: Democracy's Tokens With One Exception

President Carter's contribution to the racial integration of American government was chiefly his appointment of large numbers of blacks to the federal bench. Despite its proclaimed interest in blacks and their concerns, the Carter White House had no commitment whatsoever to bringing blacks into serious White House posts.

At the epicenter of power in the Carter White House were seven high-level staffers—Hamilton Jordan, who functioned from the start as Chief of Staff and was ultimately given that title, Press Secretary Jody Powell, Assistant for Intergovernmental Affairs Jack Watson, Jr., Counsel to the President Robert Lipshutz, Staff Director Alonzo C. McDonald, Domestic Policy Assistant Stuart Eizenstat, and Congressional Liaison Officer Frank Moore. In accordance with tradition, this inner circle was all white. Although the Carter administration claimed to have some black "brain trusters" on the payroll, there is no evidence that their brains were used by the all-white palace guard.

The White House staff that Carter had promised in his election campaign to slash by 30 percent grew by nearly 30 percent to 655 names.[4] Among these were a record number of black faces. In 1979, the Executive Office of the President employed twenty-three blacks—far more than could be found in any prior administration. At the onset, the senior member of this group was Martha E. (Bunny) Mitchell. As the top-ranking black at the White House, Mitchell enjoyed a modified version of the traditional title. Her title was Special Assistant to the President for Special Projects. Perhaps the two "specials" in her title were the tipoff to the importance of her job, for in the Orwellian world of Washington politics nothing is less special than a special assistant or a special project. In any case, Ms. Mitchell was never qualified by experience, influence in the black community, or closeness to the President to have any impact whatsoever on the policies of the Chief.

Blacks who had actively supported the Carter election campaign were disappointed, and in many cases angered, by the Mitchell appointment. Many blacks had hoped that an important White House post would go to a black person with proven political skills and influence. Mitchell brought to the White House only what little political experience she had gleaned in her former position as chairwoman of the D.C. Women's Political Caucus and as a part-time consultant to various government agencies. At the time, one could have made a list of scores of blacks with higher standing and experience in government.

Criticism of Mitchell began to build from the moment her appointment was announced. It was charged that inexperience prevented her from being an effective voice for blacks inside the White House. While her most important responsibility was black affairs, she complained of the "animosity and unwillingness of some blacks both inside and outside the administration to work with [her] on specific problems." By October 1978, it was apparent that she could not function as an effective liaison to black groups; she resigned to become the Executive Assistant to the Deputy Administrator of the Small Business Administration. Thus was the highest-ranking black person in the White House relegated to a secondary position in the federal bureaucracy.[5] And in accordance with the standard racial script, she was dispatched to an agency primarily concerned at that time with minority affairs.

Inspired by the Carter campaign promises to post minorities in the highest places, black voters expected to achieve unprecedented levels of influence in the government. In fact, the talented groups of blacks appointed to the White House staff at the beginning of the Carter presidency often possessed intellectual credentials superior—in some cases far superior—to those of the white staffers working with them in the White House. Nevertheless, Negroes on the Carter staff never held posts or responsibilities of sufficient importance to make their names generally recognizable either on Capitol Hill or to moderately well-informed students of American politics. In May 1978, after less than eighteen months of the Carter administration, more than a third of the blacks holding White House staff positions departed. Some of those leaving were among the highest-placed blacks in the executive branch—men such as Lawrence A. Bailey, Deputy Assistant for Intragovernment Affairs, Kurt Schmoke, Assistant Director of the Domestic Council, and Dennis O. Green, Associate Director in the Office of Management and Budget.

These mass resignations might have been expected to place political pressure on the President. They didn't. The resignations were completely ignored by the press, civil rights groups, and others in government—an unmistakable indication of how low Carter's black staffers ranked in the White House pecking order. The reasons for the departures are not altogether clear. It is clear that Hamilton Jordan was considerably less interested in black problems in 1978 than John Ehrlichman had been in 1970. Carter had used blacks to get elected, but it became increasingly clear that the White House was not the place where he would pay them back.

Shortly before the mass resignations, Carter had offered Mayor Richard Hatcher of Gary, Indiana, the position of Presidential Liaison to the Black Community. Hatcher refused, citing problems in Gary which demanded his attention. It is probable that Hatcher saw that his function, like that of many dozens of blacks before him, would be to pacify the black community without any concurrent grant of power to influence the President on its behalf. The proposal that Hatcher would report to Hamilton Jordan rather than directly to the President sent signals to the black community that the steadily worsening economic condition of blacks in the late 1970s was not an urgent White House concern.

As Kennedy and Johnson had done before him, Carter turned to Louis Martin, the tried-and-true black counselor to Presidents. In October 1978, Martin took over as the White House Special Assistant for Minority Affairs.

He readily acknowledged his status as a "pinch hitter" for Carter in the President's efforts to overcome the disenchantment of black Americans with his administration. Carter assured Martin that he would enjoy the same type of personal relationship with the President in this administration as he had with Presidents Kennedy and Johnson. Martin was, indeed, given an office in the East Wing of the White House instead of in the usual Executive

RACIAL STEREOTYPING IN THE UNITED STATES GOVERNMENT

How the Executive Branch Continues to Choose Its Members According to a Racially Restrictive Selection System

- In cabinet and other appointments it generally selects blacks for equal opportunity, housing, or community affairs posts where a major part of the job is to communicate or negotiate with other blacks.

- It almost never selects blacks for posts where the incumbent has broad access to secret, military, or diplomatic information.

- It prefers blacks in staff posts and in the custodial agencies and it rarely places blacks in positions of line government authority.

- It designates black officials to announce new social programs or to announce the curtailment of programs but it almost never empowers them to plan or to construct new social initiatives or to determine which ones will face budget cuts.

- The highest-ranking black in the White House is usually designated Special Assistant to the President for Minority Affairs.

- It systematically invests blacks with the trappings of power when in fact their positions are largely showcase and decorative.

- It often selects blacks for ambassadorships to African nations while the top embassy posts in the capital cities of our strategic allies and of our foremost adversaries always go to white diplomats.

- It never names blacks to the inner circle of presidential advisers who have daily access to the Chief Executive.

- It consistently denies that it stereotypes blacks in making government appointments but in practice invariably does precisely that which it denies.

Office Building annex; yet, he appears to have had very limited personal contact with the President. A careful search of newspapers and black publications has failed to produce any material that might suggest Martin had political muscle within the Carter administration even remotely resembling what he had enjoyed many years earlier under Kennedy and Johnson.[6]

In addition to Louis Martin, several other blacks, many of them talented professionals, joined the Carter staff in midterm. With the exception of

Martin, however, the names of these individuals remain unknown even to the most avid readers of political journals. No black person in the Carter White House was ever linked by the media to any major happenings in government. The memorable events of the Carter presidency—rapprochement with China, the Mideast peace negotiations, the Iranian crisis, the battle against inflation, and the SALT II negotiations—all occurred without the visible assistance or participation of any black person. Camp David, one can be sure, was not formally closed to blacks. Yet then, as in the early 1980s, there was no political need for the White House to invite black government officials and—just as serious a matter—no need even to have them *appear* to be receiving invitations.

There is a well-known rule in the economics of race relations to the effect that the higher a black person has moved in terms of personal education and qualifications, the greater the gap between his income and the income of his white peer group. In other words, race discrimination bites hardest at the top. Only recently have there been exceptions to this rule. Yet, the traditional rule applies with particular force in political life. In the Carter administration, as in all previous presidencies, black officials who enjoyed nominally high ranks were likely to be concerned exclusively with black affairs, while low-ranking black bureaucrats were more likely to be assigned duties regarding general matters of state. In other words, the higher a black official rises, the more the race-trait expectation takes hold and regulates his duties. And the higher the black person rises on the federal bureaucratic ladder, the greater is his supposed "expertise," not only in matters of race relations but also in all of the economic and social pathologies that are presumed to afflict members of the black race.

Blacks and Other Presidential Powers: Money, Budgets, and National Security

To fully appreciate the decidedly outcast and often bizarre role of blacks in the executive branch, we turn to a cluster of powerful organizations that serve the White House. The most important are the Council of Economic Advisors, the Office of Management and Budget, and the National Security Council. The very names of these institutions suggest great power because they preside respectively over nothing less than the state of the economy, the government's money, and the security of the United States.

The Council of Economic Advisors, known as the CEA, was created in 1946 to study the economy, to watch the apparent impact of the government's economic policies, and to guide the President in setting new policies. Possibly, the course of the business cycle may be beyond governmental control, but to the extent that anyone in the executive branch bears any responsibility for shaping the economic fortunes of the nation, that responsibility rests with the Council of Economic Advisors.

As we have seen repeatedly, economic policies are rarely racially neutral. To cite examples, the decision to cool off inflation at the expense of greater unemployment is likely to put blacks out of work two times or more as often as whites. A government decision to encourage massive investment in labor-saving manufacture of robots will have a much more severe impact on lower-skilled black labor than on white workers. These and many other similar factors explain why the racial composition of the Council on Economic Advisors, as well as its institutional attitude toward the concerns of blacks, is a matter of great importance to black Americans. There are, in fact, scores of highly placed black economists in the United States. Like their white peers, they come in all the colors of the political spectrum: middle-of-the-roaders, pragmatists, Keynesians, Marxists, and Friedmanites. In 1979, the Council of Economic Advisors had thirty-two full-time employees, only one of whom was black—and he was a junior staff economist, the lowest professional level.

Perhaps the most influential of all the presidential councils is the Office of Management and Budget (OMB). Like the Council of Economic Advisors, OMB deals with money matters. The difference lies in the fact that OMB has line authority over government spending. OMB is the agency chiefly responsible for the preparation of the President's budget. OMB, uniquely, has the manpower to examine and evaluate the unending range of government programs. All agency heads must submit their annual appropriation requests to OMB, which ultimately proposes an agency-by-agency budget to the White House. After comment by the Domestic Council, National Security Council, and the Council of Economic Advisors, OMB's proposals go to the President for final action before submission to Congress. Congress may, of course, tinker with the budget here and there, adding funds for its pet projects and cutting appropriations for programs it deems unnecessary. On the whole, however, little is altered at the congressional review stage. In other words, the budgetary power—and the critical ability to use the budget to whip the federal bureaucracy into line—essentially rests with OMB. And the budget is the key to what the government does or does not do, which programs are put into operation and which are ignored, which prosper and which starve.

If one were to select a single place in government other than the Oval Office where the claims and aspirations of minority groups could best be protected, the choice appears to narrow down to either the Justice Department or the OMB. It is at OMB, for example, that funds are allocated or denied to inner-city housing, education, and health care programs, or to minority business enterprise. Appropriations for voting rights law enforcement, for administration and oversight of the criminal justice system, and for aid to public schools are essentially controlled at OMB. Control over the funding of hundreds of government agencies gives OMB the power to shape the policies of those agencies, including the enforcement of federal laws controlling employment and credit discrimination in thousands of large corporations and labor unions. If, by directive, the head of OMB were to require a civil rights compliance review of all private programs receiving federal grants or assistance before authorizing the disbursement of government funds, the pressures for compliance would be compelling. In fact, it is probable that such an initiative would be far more effective than a doubling of the law enforcement capabilities of the civil rights division of the Justice Department.

As of the beginning of the Reagan Administration in 1981, only four blacks had held middle-to-upper-echelon posts at OMB. Two of them—an Assistant General Counsel and a Deputy Associate Director for Program Evaluation and Implementation—were appointed during the Nixon-Ford years. After the 1976 presidential election, many blacks shared the unrealistic view that a black person would be named to head OMB. Instead, down-home politics prevailed, and the job went to President Carter's crony Bert Lance. Carter did, however, appoint a black man, Dennis Green, as one of OMB's six associate directors. Only two steps removed from the top of the agency, Green was apparently the first black person ever to participate substantively in drawing up the federal budget. It is in some ways fortunate for the general advancement of blacks that once a government post has been occupied by a black person, the human tendency to stereotype endows the seat with the incumbency of race. When Green resigned after sixteen months to return to an executive position at Ford Motor Company, Carter appointed Frank Raines, a black who was then a member of the White House Domestic Council.

Unlike most of the larger but less important federal bureaucracies, such as HHS and HUD, OMB has always been entirely dominated by whites. In 1977, blacks comprised 22 percent of OMB's white-collar employees at the staff level, but they held only three of the sixty-one jobs at the three highest

GS levels and not one of the twenty-six jobs at the top two levels.[7] Control over any government's budget is nearly tantamount to the overall power to govern. For this reason, OMB is one of the first places to look in order to determine if blacks are moving up or down in the world.

The National Security Council is the third member of the important Councils in the executive branch. By the terms of the Constitution, the President is the Commander-in-Chief of the nation's military forces, but the National Security Council sits at the center of the entire American military intelligence network. In times of national emergency, such as the Cuban Missile Crisis of 1962, the National Security Council usually shapes the choices the President will consider. It falls to the NSC more than to any other organization to classify an enemy weapon as "offensive," to choose whether to make only a minor flapdoodle over the presence of MIGs in Cuba or to designate them as "unacceptable." The strategic judgments upon which the President's most critical command decisions are based are more likely to come from the National Security Council than from any other source within the defense establishment. Here again, we find that the level of trust and respect is very low for black opinions and authority in matters of great national urgency.

The National Security Council has eight permanent members: the President, the Vice-President, the Secretary of State, the Secretary of Defense, the Director of the Central Intelligence Agency, the Chairman of the Joint Chiefs of Staff, the Assistant-to-the-President for National Security Affairs, and his deputy. In 1977, the National Security Council's staff consisted of fifty-six people. Although eight of them were black, the nine highest-ranking staff members were white. Indeed, the blacks on the staff were so junior in grade that only two of them earned more than $20,000 a year.[8] Since the National Security Council was created in 1947, no black person has ever held any important staff post on the Council.

The absence of black faces in any important position at the National Security Council is a serious affront to blacks and somewhat reminiscent of the more blatant racism that once prevailed at the Federal Bureau of Investigation, the CIA, and the officer corps of the military services. Many blacks read the racial composition of federal security and intelligence agencies as a public statement that top government officials are unwilling to entrust blacks with military secrets or information critical to national security.[9] These views are strongly reinforced by the very heavy representation on the part of blacks in many top posts of domestic agencies whose activities are far removed from national security.

The Cabinet: Special Seats for Blacks

For nearly 200 years, the Cabinet Room in the White House was as segregated as the theaters of Memphis or the transit system of Birmingham. Not until 1957 did a black person—J. Ernest Wilkins, an Assistant Secretary of Labor under Eisenhower—ever attend a Cabinet meeting. However, neither Eisenhower nor his successor John F. Kennedy ventured to break the

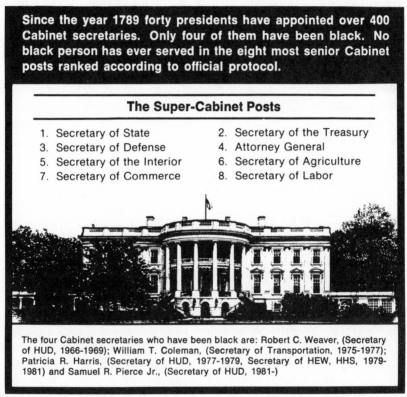

Since the year 1789 forty presidents have appointed over 400 Cabinet secretaries. Only four of them have been black. No black person has ever served in the eight most senior Cabinet posts ranked according to official protocol.

The Super-Cabinet Posts

1. Secretary of State
2. Secretary of the Treasury
3. Secretary of Defense
4. Attorney General
5. Secretary of the Interior
6. Secretary of Agriculture
7. Secretary of Commerce
8. Secretary of Labor

The four Cabinet secretaries who have been black are: Robert C. Weaver, (Secretary of HUD, 1966-1969); William T. Coleman, (Secretary of Transportation, 1975-1977); Patricia R. Harris, (Secretary of HUD, 1977-1979, Secretary of HEW, HHS, 1979-1981) and Samuel R. Pierce Jr., (Secretary of HUD, 1981-)

color barrier by appointing a black to a Cabinet position. Finally, in 1966, a century after the Civil War, President Johnson broke with tradition and appointed Robert C. Weaver as Secretary of the new Department of Housing and Urban Development. In recent years, Cabinet posts have often been awarded on a ceremonial basis to honor women and blacks. At the same time, government power has moved away from most Cabinet posts. To some people it may appear almost as though a sort of governmental block-busting operation were in effect here, with the President's Cabinet playing the role of a once ritzy neighborhood now in the process of being down-graded as minority tenants move in.

Obviously, some Cabinet posts are far more formidable than others. The Departments of Justice, Defense, and State have jurisdiction over great issues, but other departments are concerned with much narrower issues and constituencies. Among the least important of these are the Departments of Housing and Urban Development and Health and Human Services. Both departments are charged with administering programs designed primarily to help the poor, blacks, and other groups on the margins of society. Neither secretary has much regulatory authority. Although the overall budgets of these departments are large, only a relatively small portion of their funds may be used for discretionary programs from which a power base can be built.

The most influential Cabinet posts almost inevitably go to persons who are trusted friends of the President or, for some other reason, enjoy his personal confidence. Presidents who grew up living next door to whites, went to school with whites, were trained to trust the competence of whites, and entered into businesses or professions controlled entirely by whites will naturally name whites to their Cabinet. The occasional Cabinet appointment that does not favor someone personally close to the President usually goes to a well-tested member of the establishment. As a result, names like Mc-Cloy, Schlesinger, Richardson, Weinberger, and Harriman move in and out of many administrations, always at the highest levels. With the selective process so heavily slanted toward establishment figures or intimate associates of the President, blacks claim no important posts even when racially neutral selections are made.

In the entire history of the United States, none of the highest Cabinet posts—Secretary of Defense, Secretary of State, and Attorney General—have ever gone to a black person. In fact, there has never been a black Secretary of the Treasury, Commerce, Agriculture, Labor, Energy, Education, or Interior. All the black Cabinet members in American history can be counted on the fingers of one hand: Robert Weaver, Secretary of HUD under Johnson; William Coleman, Secretary of Transportation under Ford; Patricia Harris, Secretary of HUD, then Health, Education and Welfare renamed Health and Human Services in 1980 during the Carter administration; and Samuel R. Pierce, Secretary of HUD under Reagan.

Sub-Cabinet Posts: Deputies for the Colored

In addition to naming the members of his Cabinet, the President also appoints approximately 1,500 sub-Cabinet officials and other high-ranking members of the executive branch. These officials serve at the discretion of either the President himself, a Cabinet secretary, or an agency head. Some are placed in GS categories, while others are given positions outside the regular bureaucracy. Excluding U.S. attorneys and other law enforcement officials, these 1,500 appointees fall into three categories: (1) executive schedule personnel, such as Cabinet secretaries, undersecretaries, assistant secretaries, directors of bureaus, services, or administrations, heads of independent agencies, members of commissions, and so forth; (2) holders of GS-16, -17, and -18 positions, whose duties are political in nature—helping to make policy, directing administration programs, or serving as aides to key political appointees; and (3) ambassadors. The record of presidential appointments of blacks to influential positions in these three categories has indeed been dismal.

The Nixon Administration. Richard Nixon campaigned in 1968 on a pledge to give black Americans "a piece of the action." Although no black person was ever appointed to serve in the Nixon Cabinet, Nixon did compile a better record than most Presidents in appointing blacks to higher-level government jobs. Certainly Nixon's record surpassed the performance of either John Kennedy or Lyndon Johnson, whose main initiative had been the appointment of Robert Weaver as Secretary of HUD. During its five-and-one-half-year life span, the Nixon administration named blacks to approximately seventy-seven noncareer jobs in the executive branch.

Few Presidents have drawn greater enmity from blacks than President Nixon. His record for minority appointments is, thus, all the more impressive, especially when one considers that blacks, of whom most are Democrats to begin with, did not readily accept service in the Nixon administration. During Nixon's first eighteen months in office, Negroes were offered eighty-three high-level posts in the government. Only twenty-one accepted. Arthur A. Fletcher, for example, calculates that he was the seventh black to be offered the post of Assistant Secretary of Labor for Employment Standards by the Nixon administration.[10]

In accordance with tradition, the highest posts went to blacks in departments primarily interested in black economic, social, and housing matters. Thus, three blacks served as full assistant secretaries in HUD. Even within other departments, high-ranking blacks usually functioned in areas of particular concern to blacks. In addition, the Department of State boasted the predictable roster of blacks—at least a dozen—with ambassadorial or similar positions related to African nations. The job titles held by blacks during the Nixon administration reveal the way people at the top almost always match race and job function: Director of Equal Opportunity; Director and Deputy Director of Minority Business Enterprise; Assistant Secretary for Fair Housing and Equal Opportunity; Director and Assistant Director of the Community Relations Service; Director of the Federal Contracts Compliance Program; Director of the Job Corps; Director of Civil Rights; and so forth. In the main, the jobs held by blacks during these years, as in later administrations, tended to be "support" positions rather than "line" posts where command could be exercised.

The major exception to the practice of appointing blacks to limited responsibilities in race-related areas was undoubtedly Nixon's selection of Benjamin Hooks as a Commissioner of the Federal Communications Commission. This was probably the most important black appointment since Andrew Brimmer had been appointed to the Federal Reserve Board in 1966 and Thurgood Marshall to the Supreme Court in 1967. Hooks, a vigorous and able public servant, later became Executive Director of the NAACP.

The willingness of an increasing number of blacks to accept presidential appointments during the latter part of the Nixon administration was probably due in part to a decrease in the frequency with which other blacks charged that those who went to work for Nixon were sellouts and Uncle Toms. At the same time, the early 1970s evidenced a growing feeling among many minority spokesmen that conservatism was on the march and that Nixon would be reelected. It was also time for blacks to make room for themselves on the bandwagon. Many a community organizer of the Great Society years now heard himself saying, "I can get more money for my people working from the inside than from the outside."

The Ford Administration. The only nonelected president in American history is Gerald Ford, whose major effort, on succeeding to the White House, was to stabilize the executive branch in the wake of Watergate. Ford left most Nixon appointees in office, for the most part making appointments only when a resignation, retirement, or death produced a vacancy.

Ford did, however, make one Cabinet appointment that was, in the eyes of many, a breathtaking break with traditional job stereotyping. He selected William T. Coleman, Jr., a distinguished Philadelphia lawyer, chairman of the NAACP Legal Defense and Educational Fund, and former law clerk to Supreme Court Justice Felix Frankfurter, as Secretary of Transportation. For two years, Coleman presided over the department's 73,000 employees, exercising jurisdiction over three huge sectors of the economy: airlines; railroads; and automobile transport. Riding herd on these three major energy consumers gave the Transportation Department unprecedented influence over the government's energy and environmental policy. To Coleman fell the responsibility for deciding in 1976 whether the Franco-British Concorde SST would be permitted to land at U.S. airports, a decision with profound implications for America's diplomatic relations with France and England. In the end, the actual decision was much less important than the fact that a black person made it. The Coleman appointment, particularly in relation to the Concorde issue, was a milestone event in American Negro history. Few people have considered its importance in eroding the unwritten code that provides that black people are not yet ready to hold major power.

The Carter Administration. During the 1976 presidential campaign, Jimmy Carter proclaimed an unprecedented commitment to black aspirations for social and economic justice. Despite his near-fatal "ethnic purity" gaffe—compounded by remarks about "black intrusion into white neighborhoods"—the nation's black leadership rallied behind him. The black vote proved crucial to Carter's narrow victory over Ford.

After the election, black leaders came to Washington to claim their winnings. Andrew Young assured them that Carter was aware of his debt to black Americans and would pay it in full. "We're going to get at least two Cabinet posts," Young said. "Two *full* Cabinet posts." When the UN ambassadorship was mentioned as a possible post, Young dismissed it as a token that blacks need not settle for. Few black leaders expected a minority person to be named to any of the super-Cabinet positions, but there was some reason to hope that the attorney generalship might go to a black person, possibly Congresswoman Barbara Jordan of Texas. Instead, Carter stuck by racial tradition and offered Jordan the top spot at HEW, a safe and relatively noncontroversial slot. Jordan rejected HEW.[11]

Blacks had been led to believe that if a Negro was not named Attorney General, the appointment would then go to a white person with a strong civil rights record, possibly John Doar, a Justice Department lieutenant under Robert Kennedy and counsel to the House Judiciary Committee during the Nixon impeachment hearings. The announcement of Carter's nominee came as a shock to blacks. Carter chose as his Attorney General former U.S. Appellate Court Judge Griffin Bell, never a friend, and sometimes a foe, of civil rights. Much of the difficulty in sustaining the appointment arose from the fact that Bell had once written a letter strongly supporting President Nixon's nomination to the Supreme Court of G. Harrold Carswell, Bell's colleague on the Fifth Circuit bench. Although Bell turned out to be a superior Attorney General and an evenhanded administrator of justice, his nomination dramatized the inability of blacks to curb or influence either the

President or the Senate on a matter of great concern to minority citizens. Carter may have owed his election to blacks more than to any other group, yet this did not prevent him from somewhat cavalierly ignoring their wishes and winning Senate confirmation of Bell by a 72-21 margin. To many people, the Griffin Bell appointment was viewed as an egregious double-cross of black voters and, more than any other recent political event, should have persuaded blacks that their destiny was not always secure in the hands of the Democratic party.

Elsewhere in the Carter Cabinet blacks held their traditional assignments, winning sixty-seven sub-Cabinet posts which ranged in importance from a secretaryship at HUD to an "executive assistant to the assistant secretary for community planning and development." Patricia Harris, a woman of unusual strength and talent, was assigned to head HUD, an agency with virtually no influence on the affairs of state. She was later upgraded to head HEW-HHS, where the regulatory power is somewhat greater but where budgets are still almost entirely mandated by law. Another Carter appointee, Eleanor Holmes Norton, did a remarkable job in straightening out the affairs of the Equal Employment Opportunity Commission. But in terms of racial stereotyping, this appointment broke no new ground. As a result of a political compromise, the Commission lacked the usual rulemaking powers of most government agencies and did not have the authority to hold hearings or issue orders. Carter's appointment of Clifford Alexander as Secretary of the Army was an innovative step because it put a black man in a position of considerable influence in the military. But cynics noted that this appointment was a further instance of blacks being assigned to be the boss of other blacks. At the time of the Alexander appointment, 30 percent or more of all Army recruits were black.

Unquestionably, the most important advances made by blacks during the Carter administration were in the federal judiciary and in federal law enforcement generally. As we shall see in the next chapter, some of these changes were truly revolutionary. Wade H. McCree, a black, was named Solicitor General and was thus entrusted with arguing the majority of the federal government's cases before the Supreme Court. Drew Days III, a black man, was appointed Assistant Attorney General in the Civil Rights Division of the Department of Justice. Other notable exceptions to political stereotyping were the appointments of James Joseph as Undersecretary of the Interior and Quentin Taylor as Deputy Administrator of the Federal Aviation Administration in the Department of Transportation. In most respects, however, Carter danced to the same racial melodies as other presidents before him. Blacks continued to show up in very large numbers as ambassadors to black nations and in agencies handling equal employment, open housing, and community-service activities.

Andrew Young: Power Aborted

Carter's appointment of Andrew Young as Ambassador to the United Nations presents a complicated study in black political influence. Until his forced resignation in 1979 over a charge that he had held an unauthorized meeting with a representative of the Palestine Liberation Organization, Young was the best known and perhaps the most effective of all Carter's black appointees. While Carter insisted that Young's appointment was the keystone of his campaign to place more blacks in high government posts, Young himself, as noted earlier, did not have an especially high regard for the position. His opinion was sound. The United Nations ambassadorship has often served as a place to park troublemakers where they could do little harm. It has also served as a political dumping ground both for great men who have passed their prime and for men who stood in the President's way. Any aspirant to a high government post would certainly rank the UN ambassadorship below at least a dozen jobs in the Cabinet or White House.[12]

Early in Young's career as UN ambassador, the White House announced that as one of his vice-presidential tasks Walter Mondale would have responsibility for American policy on Africa. The London *Economist* observed, "While not admitted to as such, this step was plainly a sign to Mr. Young and to those his words have angered that he is not a spokesman on Africa, official or unofficial."[13] Nevertheless, in his two and a half years at the UN, Young often emerged as a leading spokesman for administration foreign policy. In African affairs, he played an important diplomatic role which greatly transcended the traditional activities of a UN ambassador. Where diplomats before him had failed, Young greatly improved America's relations with African and other Third World nations. He skillfully conducted negotiations in support of Western plans for a peaceful transition to majority rule in Zimbabwe-Rhodesia. He was also the first black person in American history to be given a standing invitation to attend meetings of the National Security Council. Through his persistent independence and integrity, Young made a unique contribution to respect for and self-respect among blacks. Young's extravagant charges of racism in government nevertheless demonstrated to blacks and whites that it was possible to be a part of a white-controlled government and yet retain enough independence to be openly critical of that government. Never a faceless assistant for minority affairs in the White House, Andrew Young was the black community's most visible link to American government. Yet most whites in the United States agreed with the negative assessment of Henry Kissinger: "Ambassador Young should learn discipline or not continue his post." [14] Important testimony to the potential of an emergent political force in the black community is the fact that despite his controversial and uncompromising approach to his job, Young survived as long in office as he did.

Blacks in the Independent Agencies

Roughly speaking, independent bodies in the federal government may be divided into two groups: those that can and do issue commands and those that simply do research, manage programs, and automatically disburse money largely in accordance with the dictates of others. The former can be called "command agencies," the latter, "custodial/disbursing agencies." In many ways, the power distinction is the same as that between staff and line authority in either the military or a large business corporation. The distinction may be blurred on occasion, but it is nevertheless valid.

The command groups include such agencies as the Federal Reserve Board, the National Labor Relations Board, the Federal Trade Commission, and the Securities and Exchange Commission. These bodies enjoy some or all of the governmental powers to subpoena witnesses, make administrative law, issue rulings, hold hearings, and impose sanctions. The functions of many custodial and disbursing organizations are broad, but their legal authority is limited. Included in this group are the U.S. Commission on Civil Rights, the Equal Employment Opportunity Commission, the General Services Administration, and the Small Business Administration.

The thirteen major command or regulatory agencies in the American government have fifty-eight top positions. Due to fixed terms of appointment and turnover during the decade 1969 to 1979, an estimated 125 to 150 people held jobs as board members, commissioners, or chairmen. Only five were black: Harold Jenkins at the National Labor Relations Board (1963-present); Andrew F. Brimmer (1966-1974) and Emmett J. Rice (1979-present) at the Federal Reserve Board; and Benjamin Hooks (1972-1979) and Tyrone Brown (1977-1981) at the Federal Communications Commission. [15]

Of all the command agencies in the federal government, the Federal Reserve Board is the most influential. Here, poised to challenge the President and Congress, is an economic adversary possessed of power second only to the President. In the history of the Board, two black men—Brimmer

SKIN COLOR IS NO LONGER A CONDITION TO ENTRY INTO GOVERNMENT SERVICE BUT IT CONTINUES TO BE AN IMPORTANT FACTOR IN DECIDING WHO WILL HOLD GOVERNMENT POWER

The largest number of black presidential appointees have always been posted at or near the top of custodial departments and other agencies that worry about blacks, the poor, and Third World nations.

Nixon Administration

James Farmer	Assistant Secretary of HEW for Administration
Samuel J. Simmons	Assistant Secretary of HUD for Equal Opportunity
Stanley B. Thomas	Assistant Secretary of HEW for Human Development
John L. Jenkins	Director, Office of Minority Business Enterprise
H.R. Crawford	Assistant Secretary of HUD for Housing Management
John H. Powell	Chairman, Equal Employment Opportunity Commission
Arthur Fletcher	Assistant Secretary of Labor for Wage and Labor Standards

Carter Administration

Patricia R. Harris	Secretary of HUD, Secretary of HEW, HHS
Eleanor H. Norton	Chairwoman, Equal Employment Opportunity Commission
Randolph Blackwell	Director, Office of Minority Business Enterprise
Drew Days III	Assistant Attorney General, Civil Rights Division
Goler Butcher	Administrator for Africa, Agency for International Development
Chester McGuire	Assistant Secretary of HUD for Fair Housing and Equal Opportunity
Ernie Green	Assistant Secretary of Labor for Employment and Training

Reagan Administration

Samuel R. Pierce	Secretary of HUD
Robert Wright	Associate Administrator, Minority Business, Small Business Administration
Clarence Thomas	Assistant Secretary of Education for Civil Rights
Rosslee Douglas	Director, Office of Minority Economic Impact, Energy Department
Melvin Humphrey	Director, Office of Small and Disadvantaged Business Utilization, Transportation Department

Other blacks have been appointed to high government posts in this period where race was not relevant to the job function. Some of these appointments include: Nixon Administration: James Cowan-Assistant Secretary of Defense, John Reinhardt-Assistant Secretary of State, Benjamin O. Davis-Assistant Secretary of Transportation and Benjamin Hooks-Commissioner, Federal Communications Commission. In the Carter Administration: Wade H. McGree-Solicitor General, Chester Davenport, Assistant Secretary of Transportation, Quentin Taylor-Deputy Administrator, Federal Aviation Administration, James A. Joseph, Under Secretary of the Interior, Azie T. Morton, Treasurer of the United States, and Emmett J. Rice-Governor of the Federal Reserve Board.

and Rice—have served as one of its governors. A House of Representatives study in 1976 noted that in over sixty-three years the "Fed" has had no women and only four black men among the 1,000 directors of its twelve regional banks.[16]

Blacks did much better in the custodial, disbursing, and advisory bodies. Between 1969 and 1979, seven blacks were members of the Equal Employment Opportunity Commission alone, more than the total number of blacks who served on the thirteen regulatory commissions mentioned earlier. Blacks have also been appointed in very large numbers to posts in such black-oriented and relatively powerless agencies as the Civil Rights Commission, the Community Services Administration, and the Office of Personnel Management. The heaviest assignment of high black officials has always been made at the two giant custodial departments of the federal government. From the beginning of the Nixon administration through the end of the Carter administration, at least seven blacks served as Cabinet officer heads or as undersecretaries or assistant secretaries of HUD and HEW/HHS.

Blacks in the General Bureaucracy: Still at the Bottom but Doing Much Better

In racial composition, the federal bureaucracy bears many similarities to the National Football League. A very large number of the players are black, as are the assistant coaches. But the head coaches are all whites. Ironically, the concentration of blacks on the lower rungs has worked to give blacks a certain degree of influence over government actions. Black bureaucrats are fully as capable of dampening government initiatives as are their white counterparts. The legions of black civil servants, with jobs protected by law, have at times blocked programs they opposed and advanced initiatives they favored. Even in conservative times, momentum in the federal bureaucracy has sometimes permitted blacks to move forward with programs that superiors in government preferred to curtail.

Numerically speaking, the federal government has been, and is, the nation's most influential discriminator *in favor of* blacks. The very high rate of employment of blacks in government is the natural outcome of the sixty years of their steady migration into the nation's capital, as well as of recent governmental affirmative-action employment policies. In 1977, 387,000 blacks held jobs in the federal government—16 percent of the total federal work force. If only the Washington, D.C. federal work force is counted, the figure rises as high as 35 percent. Another 330,000 blacks served in the nation's armed forces, 16 percent of the country's fighting forces. Clearly, then, blacks held a far greater percentage of positions in government than their proportion of the total population.[17]

The progress of blacks into the white-collar ranks of the civil service has been rapid. In 1912, there were 23,000 blacks working for the federal government, but only a few more than 1,000 blacks held positions in what was then known as the "federal service." From the Civil War through the 1940s, almost all black government employees were handling mops, running errands, and working in the mailrooms. In fact, separate washrooms and lunchrooms for blacks were the rule in federal government buildings until Eisenhower's first term as President in the early 1950s. By 1977, in contrast, more than 8,000 blacks earned salaries of more than $25,000 in government jobs in Washington.[18]

Despite the progress in recent years, blacks are still heavily concentrated at the bottom of the federal government bureaucracy. In the Army, nearly one out of three soldiers is black, but blacks comprise only one out of sixteen officers. While blacks held about 16 percent of all civilian full-time federal jobs as of late 1977, about half were in positions such as elevator operator, mail carrier, security guard, maintenance worker, and so forth. Blacks are highly concentrated at the lower end of the GS pay scale. At the GS-1 through GS-4 levels, over 21 percent of the groups consisting of trainees, clerical helpers, and technical aides in 1977 were black. By contrast, only about 3.5 percent of the employees at the three highest grades GS-16, -17, and -18 were black. At any GS level with a starting salary of more than $20,000, blacks made up no more than 5.5 percent of the total work force. The most major void in blacks at the top was probably in the postal service. Although 21 percent of all postal service employees were black, blacks held none of the thirty-one highest-paying positions at headquarters in Washington.[19]

Blacks and the Reagan Administration

Six weeks after Ronald Reagan's landslide victory in 1980, the director of his transition team, Edwin Meese, announced that more than one black person would be appointed to posts in the new Cabinet. Meese declared further that the President was "committed to putting blacks in nontraditional roles." "Reagan's staff," he said, "would have no ambassadors to black people."[20] Several blacks of national repute, including Thomas Sowell, Gloria Toote, Jewel Lafontant, Edward Brooke, Arthur Fletcher, and Marva Collins were mentioned as possible Cabinet secretaries by various members of Reagan's transition team. Yet when all the posts were filled, the only black Cabinet member was Samuel R. Pierce, Jr., a New York lawyer. Once more, racial etiquette prevailed and, contrary to Meese's promise, Pierce was appointed to the traditional black post, Secretary of the Department of Housing and Urban Development. It soon became clear that Pierce would not carry much influence in the Reagan team. In the summer of 1981 it was widely reported in the national press that at a White House conference of city officials, President Reagan mistook Pierce for a black mayor. The incident suggested that the President had not met with, or consulted, his HUD Secretary on many occasions. The event confirmed also—as the Reagan Administration openly conceded—that black concerns ranked near the bottom of the presidential agenda.

The Reagan White House named a traditional top-ranking black staffer, Melvin Bradley. His original title was Senior Advisor of Policy Development, later upgraded to Special Assistant to the President. For the first few months of the Reagan Administration, Bradley's main duty was to recruit other blacks to serve in government posts.

After the 1982 fiasco in which President Reagan advocated tax exemptions for private schools that discriminated on the basis of race, Melvin Bradley was assigned the task of alerting the President to policy decisions that would offend Negroes. It was widely reported in 1983, however, that Bradley was not consulted when the Administration came out against racial promotion quotas in the New Orleans Police Department.

In 1981, considerable publicity attended the appointment of Thaddeus Garrett, a black man and an ordained minister, as an aide and consultant on domestic affairs to Vice-President Bush. Garrett's assignments included White House coordination of the Atlanta child murder investigation as well as the problem of the increasing influx of minority workers into the United States. In many respects, Mr. Garrett's job was that of apologist to blacks for the Reagan Administration. He said in mid-1983, "It's a fireman-type job being a minority in any administration." [21]

After the first five months of the Reagan presidency, no black had been appointed to any of the approximately 100 positions as undersecretary, assistant secretary, or deputy secretary of any of the thirteen Cabinet departments. [22] Later in 1981, several blacks were appointed to second-level sub-Cabinet posts, but, again, almost exclusively to black-oriented assignments. Reagan's black appointees held the standard titles of their race: Deputy Assistant Secretary for Fair Housing at HUD; Assistant Secretary for Civil Rights at the Education Department; and Director of Civil Rights at the Department of Transportation.

As expected, a black man, William Bell, was appointed chairman of the Equal Employment Opportunity Commission, a position that had previously been held by five other blacks. The appointment was strongly opposed by civil rights groups on the ground of inadequate qualifications. Bell had never supervised more than four employees and the post would require him to administer an agency with over 3,300 workers. Under pressure from civil rights groups, the Bell appointment was finally withdrawn by the White House. The Bell nomination was important for two reasons. It marked the first time in the memory of most people that blacks had ever opposed the appointment of another black person to any government post. This opposition in turn signaled increasing political sophistication among black politicians and spokesmen who were now sensing how ruling powers sometimes use black appointments to manipulate or demean.

While the yeast was still rising in the Bell affair, President Reagan once more used his appointive powers to offend blacks. In February 1982, he nominated a black man, the Rev. B. Sam Hart, a right-wing evangelical minister, to serve on the U.S. Commission on Civil Rights. This time, blacks everywhere noted that the White House computer screens had performed the unusual feat of finding a black person who was politically opposed to each and every item on the civil rights agenda. Reagan was also forced to withdraw this appointment when a number of conservatives in the Senate strongly opposed the selection. The manifest inadequacy of the qualifications of Bell and Hart revealed no particular racial animosity in the Reagan Administration, but rather a kind of throwaway neglect of black appointments and concerns.

Looking back over the five prior presidencies, the Reagan Administration stood out as uniquely insensitive, unaware, and unaccountable to the aspirations of black people. This was politically understandable. The Administration had been elected by white voters over the opposition of black voters; its sources of financial support were not only whites, but in a great many cases whites who thought blacks had been brought along too fast. Officials in the Administration neither had nor cared about having access to blacks. Yet, in the Reagan Administration the traditional theater of pacification was in place. In early 1982, the President proposed to permit federal tax exemption for racially segregated educational institutions but, as he did so, he publicly proclaimed that he was opposed to racial discrimination in "every fiber of my being." As in other matters, the President was persuasive. His praise was effusive for the television film *Blacks in the Military*, which ended with Marian Anderson singing the "Star Spangled Banner" at the launching of *S.S. Booker T. Washington*, a merchant ship under the command of Captain Huge Mulzac, the country's first black skipper. In 1984, a presidential election year, hardly a month went by in which a black entertainer was not celebrated in the Rose Garden of the White House.

In the tradition of Presidents before him, President Reagan publicly stated on many occasions that he was "always on the lookout for qualified blacks," a statement that not only tended to demean the qualifications of blacks generally, but also served to excuse him later on when almost no additional blacks were appointed to his Administration. One should not regard this as a break with the past. The Reagan Administration was simply a florid example of deep-seated institutional resistance to sharing power with Negroes. Since the Eisenhower years, farce or fantasy has attended virtually all claims that blacks in the executive branch were participating team members or influential in shaping the policies of government.

Paternalism and Caste: *"Not Yet Ready to Hold Power"*

In Europe during the Middle Ages, a natural order of class prevailed. People of different classes often worked together and lived near each other, but each individual retained rights and duties attached to the class to which he or she belonged by birth. According to the strict class designations of the time, kings commanded, nobles protected, and peasants obeyed. Authority was a prerogative of birth. In the United States, the idea of fixed prerogatives of birth ran counter to the principles of individual freedom, open opportunity, and upward mobility. In practice, too, birthright in the United States conferred only modest political advantages. There were, however, fundamental duties that attached to being black. In all governing bodies, councils, and caucuses a racially determined etiquette of either exclusion or subordination prevailed over the liberal values of open access and equal opportunity. For several hundred years in the United States, the rules of caste provided that it was the sole prerogative of whites to govern blacks.

Gone now from the federal government are the rigid exclusions of our racist past. In the executive departments and agencies of the federal government, blacks work in very large numbers. In most cases, the jobs they hold carry generous pensions, and the work is protected by law. Gone from government are the repressive racial conventions—prevailing less than a generation ago—which required even highly educated blacks either to work at menial posts in the federal bureaucracy or to seek work elsewhere. Beginning in the late 1960s, black people moved rapidly into the higher civil service grades as well as into a number of sub-Cabinet and higher-level agency posts. Although blacks were undeniably present in considerable numbers in the executive branch of government in the early 1980s, by no means could they be said to constitute an influential political presence. With few exceptions, almost all highly placed blacks were lodged in custodial agencies and departments far removed from levers of the executive authority. Over the years, a number of whites holding high posts in government have publicly challenged presidential policy, often with historically significant results. But only a handful of blacks have ever been in a position in the executive branch either to make policy or to influence it by publicly or privately expressing dissent.

Hence, we see that the ugliest features of white supremacist beliefs are dead or dying, but the white sense of responsibility for the lives of blacks remains very much alive. Liberal whites, in particular, continue to have a solicitous and somewhat condescending sense of duty to help and govern the black minority. Although many whites have agitated for more black faces in higher government posts, the vast majority of whites—both progressives and conservatives—still cling to beliefs that in the important nerve centers of government, black officials simply don't have the stuff "to get things right." Thus, instead of sharing the general responsibility of government with blacks, contemporary political custom now delegates to blacks responsibility for the affairs and concerns of other blacks. In consequence, a kind of political ghetto has been established in Washington, a politically zoned area in which blacks are assigned the task of managing the social and economic problems viewed as endemic to the black race.

An incident from my personal experience illustrates the persistent view of most whites that equal opportunity rules stop at the gates to power. On March 24, 1970, thirty-one congressional and executive branch leaders had breakfast with President Nixon. The purpose of the meeting was to discuss the President's plans for implementing Supreme Court decisions outlawing public school segregation. This was not a routine government conference on food stamp safety nets, welfare rules, minority enterprise, or other social programs at which black officials are invariably in attendance and sometimes even in charge. The issue of enforcement of school desegregation rules was, instead, a great structural issue affecting the lives of almost everyone in the United States. The issue was so important, in fact, that no black person in government was invited to the breakfast. If, indeed, a black official had stumbled into the meeting, his or her presence would have been a matter of general embarrassment.[23]

The racial composition of the officials attending this meeting on public school desegregation makes an important point about government process as well as power. Many black people did then, and still do, oppose the busing of school children to achieve racial integration. A significant number of blacks, indeed, have registered strong opposition to many other standard initiatives of the liberal agenda. Yet, their opinions on the issue of school desegregation were neither heard nor invited except when they were known in advance to endorse a decision already made by whites. Once advised of the decision—on which they had voted neither yea nor nay—black people would be asked once more to rededicate themselves to the policies and programs of wiser and more experienced elders. Despite glowing manifestos to the contrary, blacks were not part of the discussion. They were never where the action was. The navigation of the ship of state was firmly in the hands of whites.

CHAPTER SEVENTEEN

The Power to Decide:
Black Robes and White Judges

"We need to join together and move on to the courthouse."

—*Martin Luther King (1965)*

MORE THAN 200 YEARS AGO, in 1772, Lord Chief Justice Mansfield outlawed slavery in England. The great jurist legislated emancipation by judicial fiat. In the landmark case of *Somerset v. Steward* he wrote: "The state of slavery is so odious that nothing can be suffered to support it." Finding no natural or positive law that justified human servitude, he ruled that a black man, James Somerset, must go free and might not be removed by force from England and returned to enslavement in the West Indies.

Nearly a century later, also reaching its decision without benefit of any written law on human slavery, the Supreme Court of the United States came to the contrary conclusion. In a famous decision taught to every school child, Dred Scott was remitted to his master in the slave state of Missouri. Writing the Supreme Court's majority opinion, Chief Justice Taney declared that chattel servitude was the natural state of Negro people:

"They are beings of an inferior order, and altogether unfit to associate with the white race either in social or political relations; and so far inferior that they had no rights which the white man was bound to respect."[1]

The particular outcomes of these two court proceedings are much less important to us here than how they display the awesome powers of the judiciary in most Western societies. In interpreting constitutions and so-called natural laws, courts of law have truly staggering powers to control the lives of people and to shape the destinies of nations, groups, and individuals.

Particularly, the judicial powers of the state weigh heavily in determining the economic and political claims and prospects of racial groups. In any given year, the success of blacks and other minorities in winning hundreds of thousands of jobs in the United States depends on whether judges decide that certain corporate hiring practices, plant relocation decisions, and employment or job-testing procedures are legally acceptable. It is courts, rather than legislatures, that decide whether white people have a right to send their children to all-white—and often fiscally privileged—public schools. Law courts, today, are the centers of government power where it is ultimately decided whether and when affirmative-action policies in employment, housing, credit, and contracting are a proper or unacceptable means of integrating society or of redressing prior injustices. For blacks and whites, for rich and poor, the epoch-making decisions of the American judiciary consistently confirm the pragmatist's view that the power of the sovereign is often in the hands of whoever has the authority to interpret the laws of the state.

Two circumstances working in combination—the majestic force of the courts in the American scheme of government and the past history of the American judiciary—have produced deep-seated concerns among black people as to the instincts and intentions of people chosen to hold the judicial power. If, to most whites, these fears often appear to border on paranoia, consider briefly the role of the American judiciary in providing safe conduct for the rules and etiquette of race. For many generations, judges in the United States consistently denied equal protection of the law to Negroes in all parts of the country. Federal and state criminal justice systems, alike, steadfastly refused to punish law enforcement officers who collaborated in the public lynchings of black people in the southern and border states. Law courts acted as the backbone of southern white supremacy and to this end upheld the rules requiring all-white juries, police forces, prosecuting officers, and political primaries. For a century or more, the judiciary consistently gave its stamp of approval to officially segregated schools, buses, libraries, washrooms and public parks—arrangements it piously declared to be in the best interests of Negroes. In the name of states' rights—or a declared absence of jurisdiction—federal and state courts charged with safeguarding the Bill of Rights determinedly looked the other way when southern sheriffs and state attorneys refused to prosecute whites who committed violent crimes against Negroes.

In the northern states, too, de facto segregation or discrimination in public education, health care, and employment was protected by federal and state judges who shared the same distaste and contempt for the Negro as did their brothers who sat on the benches in the South. All of the tricks and subterfuges used to politically gerrymander, disenfranchise, and otherwise contain the political rights of blacks in northern states and cities were successful in large measure because they always had the full cooperation of state and federal courts.

Particularly, it was the *federal* judiciary in the South that blacks had the greatest reason to fear. Historian Donald Strong sums up the reasons:

> "A federal judge in the South was a white southern politician before he became a judge. He had grown up with a set of values and loyalties before becoming a jurist called upon to enforce federal laws that often clashed with these values. . . . His personality was formed in a society that segregated everything from maternity wards to cemeteries." [2]

Aside from the explicitly racist opinions of judges in the past, and the recurrence of those attitudes from time to time in recent years, Negro people, at this stage in the history of their race, have a uniquely political and economic stake in the decisions as to who holds the power to prosecute, to try facts, to determine the law, and to judge guilt or innocence. In recent years, the judiciary has become a major, if not the single most important, force for *expanding* the opportunities, powers, and liberties of blacks. Even the conservative Supreme Court of Warren Burger has often supported black economic and political objectives on issues such as affirmative action, voting rights protection, and school desegregation. For several generations, blacks and other civil rights groups have consistently brought their most troublesome social, economic, and political problems to the courts for arbitration and in a very large number of cases have received favorable answers.

For all of these reasons, most blacks have singled out the judiciary as a great power in their lives. And those who have studied the effects and distribution of power in American society may well conclude that the ability to affect judicial outcomes, by becoming judges or influencing those who appoint judges, is indispensable to the overall effort of black people to move up toward social, political, and economic equality with whites.

Blacks and the Judicial Head Count

To what degree do blacks actually influence the great powers inherent in the judicial process? To answer this question, we must know to what extent the elected officials who actually appoint judges are accountable to black voters. We must find out to what extent the committees of the various bar associations and the attorneys general who recommend the appointment of

Gains Through Years of Judicial Conserva

- For the first time, the Supreme Court strikes down a Jim Crow law. Oklahoma's "grandfather clause," limiting voting to prior voters ruled unconstitutional. *Guinn v. United States*, 238 U.S. 347 (1915).

- A city may not set aside certain city districts or blocks for occupancy by blacks. *Buchanan v. Warley*, 245 U.S. 60 (1917).

- Negroes may not be prohibited from serving on juries. *Norris v. Alabama*, 294 U.S. 587 (1935).

- Picketing against racial discrimination in employment not barred by the Norris-LaGuardia Act. *New Negro Alliance v. Sanitary Grocery Co.*, 303 U.S. 552 (1938).

- All-white primaries ruled unconstitutional. *Smith v. Allwright*, 321 U.S. 629 (1944).

- Craft unions must represent black and white workers on equal terms. *Steele v. Louisville and Nashville Railroad Co.*, 323 U.S. 192 (1944).

- State courts may not enforce deed covenants restricting occupancy of real estate to whites. *Shelley v. Kraemer*, 334 U.S. 1 (1948).

- Where educational resources are unequal in a state university system, blacks must be admitted to the white school in that system. *Sweatt v. Painter*, 339 U.S. 629 (1950).

- Blacks may not be required to sit apart in state university classrooms. *McLaurin v. Oklahoma State Regents*, 339 U.S. 637 (1950).

- Interstate railroads may not set aside special tables for Negroes in dining cars. *Henderson v. United States*, 339 U.S. 816 (1950).

- Public school systems may not segregate black and white students. *Brown v. Board of Education of Topeka*, 347 U.S. 483 (1954).

- For the first time, the Supreme Court invalidates a racially gerrymandered voting district. Tuskegee, Alabama redistricting plan that changed voting district from a square to an "uncouth twenty-eight-sided figure" in order to remove almost all blacks from the city limits ruled unconstitutional. *Gomillion v. Lightfoot*, 364 U.S. 339 (1960).

:tivism, and Strict Constructionism (1915-1980)

- A black woman may not be held in contempt of court for refusing to reply to questions from a judge who refused to address her except by her first name. *Hamilton v. Alabama,* 376 U.S. 650 (1964).

- The Constitution does not prevent Congress from outlawing private race discrimination in a private business which caters to the public. *Heart of Atlanta Motel v. United States,* 379 U.S. 241 (1964).

- Poll tax ruled unconstitutional in all elections. *Harper v. Virginia Board of Elections,* 383 U.S. 666 (1966).

- Laws prohibiting interracial marriage ruled unconstitutional. *Loving v. Virginia,* 388 U.S. 1 (1967).

- Attorneys fees must be awarded to successful plaintiffs in civil rights suits. *Newman v. Piggie Park Enterprises,* 390 U.S. 400 (1968).

- Civil Rights Act of 1866 interpreted to outlaw racial discrimination in the sale or lease of real estate. *Jones v. Mayer,* 392 U.S. 409 (1968).

- Tests that screen out a disproportionate percentage of minority candidates are unlawful unless the test is shown to be a valid indicator of job performance. *Griggs v. Duke Power Co.,* 401 U.S. 424 (1971).

- Busing of school children may be ordered to achieve racial integration of public schools previously segregated by public law or official practice. *North Carolina v. Swann,* 402 U.S. 43 (1971).

- The President may order industry to set minority hiring standards as a condition of awarding federal contracts. *Contract Association of Eastern Pennsylvania v. Schultz,* 442 F.2d 159 (3d Cir. 1971), *certiorari denied* 404 U.S. 854 (1971).

- Back pay for workers may be ordered in employment discrimination cases even when the employer acted in good faith and did not intentionally exclude minorities. *Albermarle Paper Co. v. Moody,* 422 U.S. 405 (1975).

- Corporations may provide special training programs for blacks to redress specific acts of prior discrimination. *U.S. Steelworkers v. Weber,* 443 U.S. 193 (1979).

- Congress may set aside portions of federal works contracts exclusively for minorities. *Fullilove v. Klutznick,* 448 U.S. 448 (1980).

363

judges are representative of blacks. Do blacks exercise any political influence over the United States senators who, in practice, appoint federal district court judges in the United States? Do black people share control of the traditional avenues of patronage that lead to judgeships? To what extent do blacks influence the powerful judiciary committees in the legislative branch, which are constitutionally charged with approving the appointments of judges? And finally, there are the most critical questions of all: What is the racial composition of the courts? How often do blacks sit as judges? How well are black people represented on the highest tribunals, where final constitutional decisions are made, many of which have a profound bearing on whether or not government power will be used to advance or retard the economic or political position of blacks?

To answer these questions, the first place we look to is the pinnacle of American judicial power, the nine-member United States Supreme Court. One Justice—Thurgood Marshall, appointed by President Johnson in 1967—is black. For most of our nation's history, however, the vast majority of citizens—both black and white—believed that black people were too ignorant and too untrained to exercise the judicial power. Those beliefs are duly reflected in the history of appointments to the Court. Since the founding of the nation, over 100 justices have sat on the Supreme Court. With the exception of Thurgood Marshall, they have all been white. But the racial belief system that separated blacks from judicial power has been definitively penetrated. In fact, most observers agree that, in common with a number of other important institutions in our society, the Court has now, in effect, been racially politicized. For the foreseeable future there will probably be a permanent black seat on the Court. Since blacks make up about 12 percent, or one-eighth, of the U.S. population, it cannot be said that they are numerically underrepresented on the Court.

It is important to note, however, that voting power in a court consisting of only a few members is not analogous to a large legislative assembly where small voting blocs form alliances, bargain with coalition builders, delay votes, and maneuver to exercise political power from an essentially minority position. In a judicial body made up of less than a dozen members, the question of whether the proportion of black members closely mirrors the composition of society as a whole is not really important in terms of technical voting power. The presence or absence of a single black judge, say, on the Supreme Court will have only marginal impact on the decisions of the Court. It is true that a so-called black voice may bring a new perspective to the Court's deliberations, but the single vote counts for little except when the other Justices are divided. Of far greater significance to America's black population is the general attitude of other members of the Court toward racial issues and, particularly, their view of the constitutional responsibilities of the judiciary in dealing with racial problems.

Blacks Sitting in the Federal Courts

The question of the accountability of the judicial power to blacks should never be equated with the single issue of how the Supreme Court happens to stand on racial issues. This is the case in large part because only a small fraction of all federal court controversies ever reach the Supreme Court. Issues tend to be settled in the federal judicial system's twelve courts of appeals which act as the courts of last resort for the vast majority of federal litigants. These federal courts of appellate jurisdiction are extremely powerful lawmaking bodies.

Until 1949, when President Truman appointed William H. Hastie to the Court of Appeals for the Third Circuit in Philadelphia, no black had ever served on any federal appellate court in the system's 160-year history. In 1961, President Kennedy appointed Thurgood Marshall to the Court of Appeals for the Second Circuit. In 1966, President Johnson appointed two blacks to the federal appeals bench, Spottswood Robinson, III, to the District of Columbia Circuit and Wade H. McCree to the Sixth Circuit. Neither President Nixon nor President Ford named any blacks to any of the federal appeals courts. At the end of the 1979-1980 federal judicial term, there was a total of nine black federal appellate judges, all but one Carter appointees. By naming eight blacks to serve with the 123 white appellate judges, President Carter lowered the ratio of whites to blacks on U.S. courts of appeals from 62 to 1 to 14 to 1, giving blacks an unprecedentedly high 7 percent presence on the federal appeals bench.

Since lower-court federal judges issue orders and decide cases as individual judges, the federal district courts provide the only federal forums where a black person sitting as a judge holds the unilateral power to control the day-to-day judicial business of the nation. This is, in fact, one of those rare circumstances in our society where a black person may determine the rights and liberties of whites. In 1980, there were fifty-four black federal judges— about 11 percent of the total. Thus, racial parity has been reached in the judicial head count at the federal district court level.

In terms of black participation in the exercise of high government powers, the court appointments of President Carter placed the federal judiciary at the top. He named thirty blacks to the federal district courts and eight more to the courts of appeals. The total of thirty-eight black judges appointed by him was more than twice the number of blacks sitting on the federal bench when he entered office. Indeed, over a third of the 298 judges named by Carter were blacks, women, or Hispanics. President Carter literally changed the face of the federal judiciary. In contrast, as of April 1983, only three of the 121 federal judges appointed by President Reagan were black.[3]

Blacks and the Judicial Power in the South

One of the most striking accomplishments of President Carter's single term of office was the integration of the federal judiciary in the southern states, a remarkable feat for which he has never received proper credit. After the South lost a series of public school racial integration decisions beginning in 1954, southern politicians quickly perceived that as long as the federal judiciary in the South was sympathetic to Jim Crow traditions, laws mandating school integration, voting rights, and open housing could be nullified or skirted in the courts. From the viewpoint of those fighting the rearguard action against racial integration, it was a matter of great urgency to keep blacks off the federal bench in the South, particularly the federal district courts where individual judges retained direct supervision over school desegregation and voting practices. As late as 1978, no black sat as a federal judge in Alabama, Arkansas, Florida, Georgia, Kentucky, Louisiana, Mississippi, North Carolina, South Carolina, Tennessee, Texas, or Virginia.

Two factors were largely responsible for the preservation of almost total white control of the southern federal judiciary. The first was the highly conservative makeup of the Senate Judiciary Committee. The second was the time-honored tradition known as "senatorial courtesy," a rule of legislative etiquette by which federal judicial appointments do not clear the Senate unless the appointments are supported by senators from the states where the judges would have jurisdiction.

For many years, Senator James Eastland of Mississippi, who retired from the Senate in 1978, supported by a number of like-minded southern senators, was able to use the veto powers of the Senate Judiciary Committee to block or discourage the appointment of black federal district court judges. According to creditable accounts, when President Kennedy appointed Thurgood Marshall to the Second Circuit in 1961, Eastland refused to vote the nomination out of the Senate Judiciary Committee. He finally demanded the appointment of his law school roommate, Harold Cox, to the federal district court in Mississippi, in return for committee approval of Marshall's appointment. Eastland reportedly met Attorney General Robert Kennedy in a Senate hallway and said, "Tell your brother when I get Cox, he gets the nigger."[4] Cox was appointed and to this day sits on the federal bench in Mississippi, where—in a manner at odds with the vast majority of his judicial peers—he has repeatedly insulted blacks from the bench and, ignoring clear law or precedent, ruled against them in civil rights cases.

In 1978, President Carter made the first significant dent in this nearly impregnable bastion of white supremacy when he pressed the Senate to approve the nomination of Robert F. Collins, who became the first black judge to take a seat on the federal bench in the South. With the support of Senator Edward Kennedy, who briefly succeeded Eastland as chairman of the Senate Judiciary Committee in late 1978, Carter later added eight more blacks to the federal bench in the South. These appointments, which received little publicity at the time they were made, were to significantly change perceptions of millions of southern whites and blacks as to who is entitled to hold great power in American society.

What about judicial power at the state level? State courts have always been, and still remain, predominantly white. In 1979, there were approximately 21,000 state and local judges in the United States. About 550, or 2.6 percent of the total, were black, most of them concentrated in the northern states. Approximately 70 percent of all the elected black judges were from only six states: California, New York, Michigan, Illinois, Pennsylvania, and Ohio. In contrast, only two of Mississippi's 237 judgeships were held by blacks and only five of Alabama's nearly 400. There were no black judges in Virginia and only one in South Carolina. In 1979, in all the southern states combined, there were only forty elected black judges at the state level. In addition, one invariably found a lower percentage of blacks the higher one went in the state court system. In 1982, in the entire country, only five black judges served on the state courts of last resort—one each in California, Florida, North Carolina, Pennsylvania, and Alabama.[5]

It is important to notice the close link between political power and the judicial power held by black people. Usually, blacks have been successful in winning significant representation in the judiciary in those states where they have developed political strength. In states where Negroes are politically inactive or, for some reason, blocked from making their voices heard, appointments of blacks to the bench are uncommon.

Blacks and the Police Power

For the ordinary citizen, the judicial power of the state is far more often represented by a police officer than by a judge sitting on the bench. In a very real sense, the law is what the policeman on the street tells the citizen rather than what a judge rules or a personal attorney advises. The police officer decides when to stop and frisk a suspect. It is the police officer, and not the courts, who decides whether to make most arrests. Obviously, a police officer doesn't ask the permission of a court to shoot at a fleeing suspect. Although the courts have handed down numerous decisions curbing the police power, the fact remains that police discretion is still very broad. Most police matters, after all, are settled on the scene by a cop deciding who should return what to whom, who owes whom an apology, who should be asked to leave the premises. These are not, to be sure, the sort of monumental decisions that are written up in law reviews and weekly news magazines, but they nevertheless have a great deal to do with the question of the power, status, and self-respect of black people and, most particularly, where they can and do go in life.

It goes without saying that policemen are not necessarily evenhanded administrators of their discretionary powers. In particular, a white officer who was raised in a segregated community, attended segregated schools, learned black inferiority at his mother's knee, and who associated predominantly with fellow officers of his own race will often be influenced in exercising police power discretion by the race of the person with whom he is dealing. As a result, it is well-known that blacks are disproportionately harassed, searched, insulted, and arrested. From arrest to imprisonment, there have always been differences in the treatment of the races. Blacks have a higher arrest rate than whites, when arrested they are more likely to be prosecuted, they have more limited opportunities to post bail and plea bargain, and they are subjected to more rigorous standards of parole than whites. To a certain limited extent, these differences may be attributable to the higher crime rate among blacks, but far more important is the fact that a great deal of racial bias exists in the exercise of the power of police discretion. In its 1980 annual report, Amnesty International, the London-based Nobel Peace Prize recipient, singled out police officials in the United States as offenders against international standards of fair treatment of accused people:

> "Police brutality, especially toward members of ethnic minorities, is widespread and severe, resulting in death in many cases. Although it is probably not due to official policy, it is undoubtedly able to occur so frequently because it is officially tolerated." [6]

Police discretion is subject to a certain amount of oversight and control by senior police officials, and, to a greater extent in recent years, by the courts. Yet the racial composition of the police force still remains the single most important factor in determining whether police-administered justice will be reasonably color-blind, This means, in turn, that the racial makeup of the police force at all levels must be recognized as a vital index of any minority group's participation in the administration of justice. In terms of the impact of the state on their daily lives, the racial composition of the police may indeed be more important to blacks than the racial makeup of the law courts.

In 1974, the International Association of Chiefs of Police and the Police Foundation published the results of a survey that covered 493 state, county, and municipal forces in the nation. It found that approximately 4 percent of state police were minority-group males. In California, the state with the largest number of black state police, blacks comprised only 107 of 5,592 officers. Despite these very low percentages, the figures actually testify to huge progress. Only a decade ago, no motorist or car thief ever encountered a black state trooper.

The major cities with large black populations still lag significantly in the numbers of minority police officers. In New York City, for example, a city 25 percent black and with the largest black population in the nation, only 7.7 percent or 2,419 out of 31,232 police officers were black in 1974. By 1977, the percentage had not changed significantly, with about 1,800 black officers out of a smaller police force of about 25,000. There were seventy-six black sergeants, eighteen black lieutenants, and eight black police officers with the rank of captain or above, most of whom had completed twenty years of service and were eligible for retirement.[7]

Information on the number of black police chiefs in the United States is difficult to obtain. The Joint Center for Political Studies publishes annually a *National Roster of Black Elected Officials,* but most police chiefs are appointed and are therefore not included. According to the 1979 *Roster,* blacks were the *elected* chiefs in nine very small towns, eight in Louisiana and one in Missouri. Blacks have also held office as police chiefs in Atlanta, Detroit, Newark, Gary, and Washington, D.C. In 1984, the top black lawmen in the country were Houston Police Chief Lee P. Brown and Benjamin Ward, Commissioner of the New York Police Department.

The law enforcement official who has always loomed large in the lives of blacks—especially in the southern states—is the county sheriff. In many rural southern counties, the "law" is what the sheriff says it is. For millions of black people, the unchecked power of the southern sheriff continues to be symbolized by the cattle prods, police dogs, and fire hoses used on black demonstrators under the orders of Sheriff Jim Clark in Selma, Alabama. Of approximately 3,000 sheriffs in the United States holding office in 1979, only fifteen were black. There were no black sheriffs in heavily black-populated states such as Arkansas, Florida, Georgia, Illinois, Louisiana, Mississippi, New York, North Carolina, Ohio, Pennsylvania, and Tennessee.[8] Mounting black political power in the southern states has yet to flow down into equivalent holdings of day-to-day police power.

Blacks as Prosecuting Officials

Once an arrest has been made, the power to prosecute leaves the hands of the police officer and becomes a matter of prosecutory discretion. Settling all criminal cases by actual trial would impose an impossible burden on judges and prosecuting officers. Hence, the vast majority of cases are disposed of by the prosecuting officers. Under this plea-bargaining system, the accused trades the presumption of innocence and the right to trial by jury for the best deal that can be worked out between his lawyer and the prosecuting attorney. While the practice of settling criminal cases in this manner has been severely criticized, it is now a firmly entrenched part of the American criminal justice system.

The plea-bargaining system transforms the local or state prosecuting officer into one of the single most important power holders in the criminal judicial system. For this reason, the number of blacks in state and federal prosecuting attorney's offices is another critical index of the judicial system's accountability to the black population. Over the past century, the authority of blacks in the federal or state law enforcement process has ranged from nonexistent to minuscule. The U.S. Attorney General, the chief law enforcement officer of the United States, has always been a white man. Although recent years have seen the appointment of a few blacks among the numerous deputy attorneys general, the senior deputies responsible for the core activities of the Office of the Attorney General have always been white. Similarly, all fifty state attorneys general are white and have always been white—with the single exception of Edward Brooke of Massachusetts, who thus enjoys the distinction of being the only black state attorney general as well as the only black United States senator in the past 100 years.

The federal prosecuting authority is considerably decentralized, with the bulk of the work falling to the approximately ninety-four U.S. attorneys scattered throughout the country. The U.S. attorneys enjoy considerable prosecuting discretion on a large number of matters that range from civil rights violations to political corruption. Officially, U.S. attorney appointments are made by the President, but as in the case of federal judges, these selections tend to be made by the senators from each state in a process similar to that used to select federal judges. This practice of senatorial courtesy may explain in part why no black person served in any U.S. attorney posts until the Kennedy administration. Again, blacks made major inroads during the Carter administration when President Carter appointed six black lawyers as U.S. attorneys. As of April 1983, the Reagan Administration had appointed ninety-three U.S. attorneys. Only one was black.[9]

Blacks and the Central Police

Until recent years, the Federal Bureau of Investigation, America's national police force, has maintained an open friendship with Jim Crow. J. Edgar Hoover, who ran the FBI with an iron fist for the half century until his death in 1972, rarely bothered to conceal the virulence of his racial prejudices. "As long as I am director, there will never be a Negro special agent of the FBI," he often said. For more than forty years, the only blacks in the Bureau were dubbed "honorary agents." In reality, they acted as little more than personal servants, retainers, chauffeurs, or office boys to Hoover. In 1961, Attorney General Robert Kennedy insisted that every branch of the Justice Department increase its hiring of minorities. But Hoover stood firm, stating that he "was not going to lower standards just to integrate the Bureau." Ultimately forced to yield to Kennedy's pressure, Hoover responded with token hirings. By the end of 1967, only ten blacks had been sworn in as FBI special agents.[10]

The effect of Hoover's prejudice was not restricted to the maintaining of a lily-white staff at the FBI. His notorious racial attitudes also played a large role in determining the investigatory agenda of the FBI. Aside from his persistent and well-known efforts to discredit Dr. Martin Luther King as a sexual libertine and agent of world communism, Hoover insisted that the Bureau practice selective enforcement of the nation's civil rights laws. He was a staunch protector of massive disobedience in the South, and his usual obsession with law and order disappeared whenever the Bureau was called upon to enforce voting rights legislation in southern states.

While overt policies of assigning blacks to custodial roles no longer prevail at the Bureau, hiring practices in the FBI still bear the imprint of Hoover's preference for whites. Until 1979, no black held a senior position in the Bureau; until 1978, no black was ever placed in charge of any one of the Bureau's then fifty-nine field divisions. In 1980, there were only two black agents-in-charge of field divisions, one in Indianapolis, the other in Atlanta. Of the 7,882 special agents in the Bureau in 1980, only 226 were black—less than 3 percent.[11]

Blacks and the Legal Profession

Not only do lawyers provide this country with 2 percent of its gross national product, but they also constitute the nation's single most powerful professional class. The vast majority of our legislators are, and always have been, lawyers. Once laws are passed, lawyers as defense counsel, lawyers as prosecutors, lawyers as litigating attorneys, lawyers as trial judges, and lawyers as appellate judges oversee how, when, and whether the laws will be enforced. In our increasingly complex and regulated economy, lawyers play ever more central roles in major business, industrial, and financial decisions. Only after the issues have passed through the hands of countless attorneys does one get answers to questions as diverse as where a Boston child will go to school and where the National Football League's Raiders will play football. It seems that virtually no aspect of American life is unaffected by the powerful hand of the legal fraternity. Chief Justice Charles Evans Hughes once called the United States the greatest law factory the world has ever known. Since Hughes' death over thirty years ago, this "factory" has grown enormously, to the point where it now produces 40,000 new lawyers annually.

To what extent do blacks share in the powers and benefits that flow from membership in this important, quasi ruling class? How readily do blacks gain access to the profession? Do they hold their share—or any share—of high positions in it? If not, are they at least making progress toward full participation?

It is generally believed that the first black lawyer in the United States was Malcolm B. Allen, admitted to the Maine Bar in 1844. He was indeed a rarity. Some prestigious law schools in the North admitted a very small number of Negroes during the latter part of the nineteenth century, while in the South, several all-black law schools emerged during the Reconstruction period. However, by 1930, there was no law school in the South that was open to the admission of black students. The first break in this solid wall of the white legal establishment occurred in 1935, when the University of Maryland Law School was ordered to admit a black man. Four years later, the University of Missouri Law School was racially integrated. Still, two of the nation's most prestigious law schools, the Universities of Texas and Virginia, did not admit any black students until 1950. Even in the post-

World War II era, most of the selective law schools of the Northeast operated under strict limiting admissions quotas for blacks. The screening net was so inflexible that for years the vast majority of black lawyers in the United States were educated at the all-black Howard University Law School in Washington, D.C. Whether gifted or incompetent, lazy or ambitious, Howard graduates were trained almost exclusively to serve the limited commercial and personal needs of other Negroes.

During the 1960s, blacks began to move more rapidly into the legal profession. Nationwide, there were 2,100 black law students by 1970, 4,800 by 1974, and 5,300 by 1978, when the total national law student enrollment had reached 121,600. In 1970, there were approximately 275,000 lawyers in the United States, but only 4,200—about 1.5 percent— were black. By 1979, the percentage of black attorneys had risen to about 2.5 percent of the total.[12]

In 1980, blacks made up between 0.5 and 1.5 percent of overall bar association memberships. Until the late 1950s, the American Bar Association categorically refused to admit black members. As a result of the exclusion of blacks from the ABA, Negro lawyers founded the National Bar Association in 1925, and the organization still has 8,500 members today. The exclusion of blacks from many state and local bar associations does not have merely the simple consequence of depriving Negroes of the social and professional advantages of rubbing shoulders with white members of the bar. One of the important consequences of the racial segregation of bar associations is that black lawyers, who are not participating members of mainstream bar associations, are never entered on the selection track leading to judicial appointments. Nor do they participate in the deliberations that precede bar association recommendations and endorsements with regard to candidates for the bench.

The marginal position of blacks in the power centers of the legal profession is revealed particularly in statistics of black membership in elite law firms in major cities. In 1979, a survey conducted by *The National Law Journal* showed only twelve black lawyers among the more than 3,700 partners in the nation's fifty largest law firms.[13] The sixty-eight leading law firms in New York City, Los Angeles, and Washington, D.C. had a total of 3,443 partners in 1983. Only twenty of them were blacks.[14] Suits against law firms charging racial bias have been common. One of the most prestigious New York City law firms, Cravath, Swaine, and Moore took the legal position in 1975 that the process of choosing law firm partners is altogether exempt from federal laws against employment discrimination. One could hardly ask for a clearer example of the tendency of some of the most distinguished members of the bar not only to view their firms as white men's clubs, but also to view the principle of equal justice or opportunity as

THE CORRIDORS OF LEGAL POWER ARE ALMOST LILY-WHITE

Some of the largest and most prestigious law firms in New York City had no black partners and fewer than one percent black associates in 1983.

LAW FIRM	PARTNERS		ASSOCIATES		Percent Black Lawyers in Law Firm
	Total	Black	Total	Black	
Cahill Gordon & Reindel	56	0	150	1	0.48
Cravath, Swaine & Moore	51	0	147	0	0.00
Curtis, Mallet-Prevost, Colt & Mosle	36	0	74	1	0.91
Hughes Hubbard & Reed	53	0	115	1	0.60
Kaye, Scholer, Fierman, Hays & Handler	74	0	135	2	0.95
Milbank, Tweed, Hadley & McCloy	72	0	144	0	0.00
Phillips, Nizer, Benjamin, Krim & Ballon	41	0	51	0	0.00
Proskauer Rose Goetz & Mendelsohn	71	0	123	0	0.00
Rosenman Colin Freund Lewis & Cohen	68	0	125	1	0.52
Stroock & Stroock & Lavan	52	0	105	1	0.64
Sullivan & Cromwell	73	0	158	1	0.43

Source: Legal Times, August 8, 1983, p. 38.

applying to everyone but themselves.[15] As any layman could have predicted, however, the courts did not permit the legal profession—an American enterprise with annual volume approaching that of the steel industry in the United States—to continue the practice of admitting whites only into partnership status.

Conclusion

Although most whites believe that blacks are overreacting when they accuse the American legal system of oppressive racism, the suspicious view that many blacks take of the criminal justice system may, in fact, be readily corroborated by a simple reading of a few indisputable facts drawn from the legal history of the United States. In 1870, 33 percent of all prisoners in the United States were black; in 1890, 40 percent of all prisoners in the South were black. In 1939, 44 percent of the U.S. prison population was black. In 1978, blacks made up roughly 11.5 percent of the population, but they were over 40 percent of the federal prison population and 48 percent of the state prison population. In 1974, 65 percent of black prisoners had not completed high school and 46 percent had incomes of less than $2,000 a year when arrested.[16]

Disproportionate rates of poverty and illiteracy do not explain the skewed statistics. Numerous and uncontradicted studies have shown that blacks, on the average, receive longer sentences than whites for comparable crimes and are executed more often for serious crime. Although many more whites than blacks have been convicted of murder over the last fifty years, over 53 percent of those executed have been black. The Law Enforcement Assistance Administration reports that between 1930 and 1979 a total of 1,754 whites and 2,066 blacks across the nation were executed, with 1,659 executions of blacks occurring in the South. In southern states, blacks were executed for murder more than twice as often as whites and an astounding nine times as often for rape.

In the late 1970s, the largest death-row populations in the country were in the states of Florida, Georgia, and North Carolina. In Florida, the death penalty is authorized for first-degree murder, distribution of heroin, and rape of a child under 11. The jury is allowed discretion in recommending mercy based on the circumstances of the crime, but the recommendation is not binding on the court. In the year and a quarter after the statute went into effect, nine of the seventeen men awarded the death penalty were black, and 78 percent of the death sentences imposed on blacks were imposed even though the juries had recommended mercy. In Georgia, the death penalty is authorized for first-degree murder, rape, armed robbery, and kidnapping. In the first year after this statute went into effect, five of the ten men on death row were black and three of them had been sentenced to die for crimes other than murder. In the year and a quarter after North Carolina decreed the death penalty for first-degree murder, arson, rape, and burglary, thirty-two people were given death sentences—twenty-one were black and one was an

American Indian. Again, over half of the blacks were sentenced to die for crimes other than murder.[17]

The conclusion that pronouncements of death sentences have more to do with the race of the accused than with the severity of crimes committed is consistently verified by correlations between the race of the victim and the sentence handed down by judge or jury. In many parts of the country, courts continue to protect the right of whites to use violence against blacks without fear of retribution. In many cases, even the murder of a black man does not appear to be a crime severe enough to warrant the death penalty. A study of death-row inmates in Texas, Florida, and Georgia, conducted by the Southern Poverty Law Center, found that while 54 percent of all murder arrests resulted from the killing of a black, only 5 percent of all death-row inmates had murdered blacks. Conversely, 45 percent of all death-row inmates were blacks who had killed whites. In sharp contrast, no white person had been sentenced to death for killing a black person despite the fact that the percentages of arrests for these crimes were similar.[18]

At the nonviolent end of the list of criminal offenses, the race of a convicted person is also an important factor in sentencing decisions for white-collar offenses. In 1970, for example, whites convicted of income tax evasion received an average sentence of nearly thirteen months in jail, while blacks convicted of the same crime received about twenty-eight and a half months.[19]

Of all the political and social burdens that weigh heavily on the black race, few have been so onerous as its separation from the judicial power of the state. This distance from power is not deplored simply by bleeding hearts and zealots on the left. Large numbers of conservative blacks— including those pursuing traditional careers in law, finance, or business —assign the highest importance to bringing an immediate end to the established system of nearly all-white control over the judicial and the police authority. However uncomfortably the idea of judicial power-sharing may rest on the shoulders of many whites, black people have in this respect incisively cut through to the heartland of power: Their rights and opportunities as citizens, as well as their opportunities to reach equal status with whites, will be best protected by a firm hold on the levers of judicial power, complemented by a strong political position which will give them a major voice in the process by which judges and prosecuting officials are appointed or elected.

Part Four

The Ethical Premise
of
Countervailing Power

"Freedom is not enough. You do not wipe away the scars of centuries by saying: Now you are free to go where you want, do as you desire."

—*Lyndon Johnson (1965)*

CHAPTER EIGHTEEN

Majority Power as the Cause of Black Inequality

"I constructed four miniature houses of worship—a Mohammedan mosque, a Hindu temple, a Jewish synagogue, a Christian cathedral—and placed them in a row. I then marked 15 ants with red paint and turned them loose. They made several trips to and fro, glancing in at the places of worship, but not entering.

"I then turned loose 15 more painted blue; they acted just as the red ones had done. I now gilded 15 and turned them loose. No change in the result; the 45 traveled back and forth in a hurry persistently and continuously visiting each four, but never entering. This satisfied me that these ants were without religious prejudice."

—*Mark Twain*
On Experimental Design *(1896)*

WHENEVER IT IS ASKED why blacks in the United States have a lower social and economic status than whites, the answers often serve the interests of the speaker rather than the truth. Robert Shelton, the Imperial Wizard of the Ku Klux Klan, would say that the black race was unequal because God had made it so. In an unguarded moment, the late George Meany once explained, "It's because they don't like to work." Arthur R. Jensen, the psychologist and behavioral geneticist, might say that blacks are unequal because the genes controlling native intelligence are different in blacks than in whites. Daniel Moynihan, formerly a sociologist and now a United States Senator from New York, might point to the decay in the fabric and integrity of the black family. Many economists today, particularly of the neo-conservative school, explain that blacks are unequal because they have become victims of the liberal social policies of an overprotective government that has robbed black people of their incentives to work. Another group of contemporary sociologists would undoubtedly say that blacks are unequal for the simple reason that they are the most recent group of poor immigrants to arrive in our cities.

All of these explanations are flawed. *Blacks are unequal because whites have made them so.* While other forces have contributed to the unequal status of the black race, black inequality is essentially the natural, logical, and *provable* result of the commanding forces of economic and political power embodied in the social and economic practice that we call "racial caste" or "subordination." In earlier chapters, I have shown the nature and range of this immense coercive power; in this chapter, I will demonstrate its causal effects. I will show not only that sovereign power was brought to bear against blacks in the form of the rules of racial subordination, but also that the codes of race were *effective* in the sense that they essentially account for and explain the extreme economic differences that presently exist between blacks and whites.

The question of causality is not simply an interesting academic or metaphysical riddle. Establishing the genesis of racial inequality and identifying the parties responsible is vital to the task of convincing members of both races of the legitimacy of using power in the form of political demands by or on behalf of blacks. It is not enough, therefore, that blacks and their allies simply organize a power consensus of sufficient strength to bring about economic or political gains; they must first ensure that the vast majority of citizens are sympathetic to their grievances and perceive the changes they seek as both just and deserved. Deeply embedded in the American ethic of fairness is the belief that it is not inequality per se, but only *undeserved* inequality that provides the ethical basis for the right of either public or private power to call for redress.

Before proceeding to show, in a positive sense, that black inequality in the United States is essentially the result of the codes of race and pressures of the etiquette of race subordination, we may first satisfy ourselves that it is not essentially the result of anything else. To this end, let us examine some of the most common hypotheses that are currently advanced to explain the political and economic inequality of blacks.

Fated to Fail: The Thesis of Natural Inferiority

In the United States, as well as in much of the Western world, there has always been a school of racial theory known as "scientific racism." According to this view, blacks as a group labor under a natural handicap of lower intelligence as well as an inborn deficiency in other mental attributes and motivational drives. It is then argued that these deficiencies not only explain why whites naturally achieve a superior economic and political position but also justify the continuation of a hierarchical system in which whites rule over and consistently do better than blacks. Historically, it was this theory of the genetic inferiority of the black race that provided the ideological underpinnings for American slavery, southern Jim Crow, South African apartheid, African colonialism, and the denial of self-rule to many nations of blacks.

It is not often recognized that the theory of genetic inferiority consists of two distinct propositions. The first is the simple claim that a genetic disadvantage actually exists. The second claim is that the defect produces the unequal performance that is observed. On the face of it, the first claim seems to be an uncomplicated issue of plain biological fact: Either there is or there is not a difference in the genetic makeup of the two races that affects various types of mental functions and motivational drives. Unfortunately, genetic science has not yet progressed to the point where it has become possible to "read" chromosomes clearly enough to produce a simple yes or no answer. At present, therefore, so-called scientific racism is faced with the hard and inescapable fact that there is absolutely no scientific evidence to support its theory of the inferior genetic endowment of blacks.

So far, however, scientific racists have argued their case by other means. If genetic inferiority cannot be demonstrated in a laboratory, they say, it can at least be inferred from evidence of a different sort. Let us test intelligence, they propose, and see whether blacks are as intelligent as whites. But notice that such a test could not possibly *prove* the genetic or inherent inferiority of one group or another. At most, it could prove one group to be *measurably* less intelligent—but whether or not this difference had a genetic origin or resulted from some other factors—differences in infant nutrition, diet, education, or social background, for example—would be merely a matter of conjecture. In addition, reliance on measures of intelligence determined by intelligence tests brings us into the middle of one of the hottest controversies in the contemporary behavioral sciences. These tests clearly measure something, but grave doubts have been expressed as to whether they measure anything that can validly be equated with the vague and rather grand-sounding attribute we call intelligence. It may well be that these tests measure nothing more than the ability to feel comfortable in a certain type of testing situation and to function well under the limited conditions of such a test. It may be that the tests are so culturally biased that they automatically penalize anyone not at home in the cultural setting of the test makers. Indeed, it has been argued with some cogency that the tests have unwittingly been designed to reflect middle-class values. As a result, children of rural families, of the poor, and of large numbers of blacks who take these tests do so with a built-in disadvantage.

These considerations leave scientific racism with nothing to back it up but a completely circular logical process that starts with the conceded fact of black economic inequality and then attempts to explain this inequality by positing a genetic deficiency in intelligence. Unable to find genetic evidence to support its theory, scientific racism leaps to the conclusion that genetic inferiority can be inferred from scores on so-called intelligence tests, which may well be the result of many economic, cultural, and environmental factors which have nothing to do with native intelligence. How such a theory lays claim to the name "scientific" is a mystery. It makes as much sense as claiming that the United States produces fewer chess champions than Russia because Americans are less intelligent than Russians and then proving this theory by using the ability to play championship chess as the measure of intelligence.

Yet even if the reasoning of scientific racists were not circular, they would still be a long way from proving their point. So far, we have examined only the chain of faulty logic by which they attempt to establish the genetic inferiority of blacks. Most scientific racists assume that once they have proven—usually through below-average results on standardized tests—that blacks labor under a handicap of inferior intellectual equipment, they have answered the original question about the causes of economic inequality. In fact, they have not, because once again they are making an inference about a causal relationship and are assuming that this inference constitutes proof of the very question at issue.

For the moment, let us make the assumption—which very few students of human intelligence or genetics would accept—that blacks, as a group, are inherently lagging in certain mental traits that contribute to success in contemporary Western societies. These deficiencies might involve racial differences in the capacity for ambition, desire for money, fondness for work, and need for achievement or recognition by others. In fact, let us assume the greatest degree of inequality in intelligence that any advocates of scientific racism have yet postulated—that the mean black intelligence as measured by IQ tests is, on a scale of 100, 15 percentage points below that of whites. Let us also assume—again an assumption for which there is absolutely no evidence—that blacks lag behind whites in other behavior traits relevant to economic success at exactly the same 15 percent rate. Can we then say we have found the root of black economic inequality?

Not in the least. The simple fact remains that even if all the unsubstantiated claims of the scientific racists were true, and even if their circular logic were completely valid, blacks should still have been far more successful in our society than has been the case. For example, even if the mean intelligence of blacks were, in fact, 15 percent lower than the white mean, there would still necessarily have to be a very large number of blacks with IQs far higher than the white mean. The fact that on the average Americans are taller than Europeans does not mean that any American is taller than any European; nor does it mean that no European is taller than the average American. Similarly, the fact—if it were a fact—that blacks are less intelligent than whites would not mean that any white is smarter than any black; nor would it mean that no blacks are smarter than the average white. All theories of scientific racism concede this. Scientific racism argues for a lower *mean* intelligence, but invariably concedes the statistical inevitability of the presence of a very large number of blacks who, according to standardized tests, are far more intelligent than a very significant number of intelligent whites.

What, we then ask, happened to this group of highly intelligent blacks? If, in fact, intelligence and related genetic endowments were equally apportioned among the races, blacks, constituting roughly 12 percent of the population, would be found in approximately 600 offices occupied by the most senior 5,000 business executives in the nation. But if we instead accept scientific racism's notion of a 15 percent black intelligence shortfall, a few hundred of these top executives would still be black. But there are no blacks in such positions. Obviously, then, some force other than unequal native intelligence must be at work to explain the total absence of blacks from the highest management posts of large corporations.[1]

Scientific racists might, of course, respond with the rather silly and cynical explanation that intelligence scores do not correlate with success in business or commerce. But if this is so, then the proposition that blacks don't do as well because they are less intelligent falls apart completely.

The inability of scientific racism to explain other shortfalls in the performance of blacks applies to a whole range of activities where it is assumed that intelligence contributes to economic or professional success. Even granting the most extreme deficiencies in human abilities ever postulated by racist theory, we would expect to find a significant number of blacks in all kinds of human endeavors. But this is not the case. Instead, we find, for example, that for many generations there were no black partners in any major accounting firms in the United States; we find that there were no black detectives on any police force in cities such as New York or Chicago; we find that until very recently there have been no black professors at any of the major universities in the country. Until recent years, almost no blacks in the country held positions as engineers, bankers, industrialists, insurance officials, stockbrokers, or retail merchants. Literally scores of other professional and business activities had no blacks in them whatsoever. No extant theory of scientific racism or unequal black intelligence can explain these circumstances. Even assuming the 15 percent group intelligence and motivational shortfall, there would still have been millions of individual blacks not only qualified for these positions, but more qualified than many of the whites who attained the posts.

Clearly, then, even if it were true, as the scientific racists argue, that the mean level of black intelligence falls 15 points below the white mean, some other forces must be precluding black success. All current theories of genetic inferiority force us to this conclusion.

Let us now consider some tasks generally assumed to require a lesser degree of intelligence but a higher disposition for hard manual labor. If we adopt the racist thesis and assume that the capacity of desire for hard work is not randomly distributed among the population, and that blacks, once again, rank 15 percent lower than whites on some hypothetical scale that measures the disposition to work hard, we would still expect the percentage of, say, black construction workers to reflect these measured shortcomings. In fact, until very recently, the percentage of blacks in some construction trades did not even reach one-half of one percent. We would also expect to see some blacks as railroad firemen, ironworkers, plumbers, machinists, and state policemen. But we know that until recently virtually no blacks were in these fields.[2] Interstate truck driving is not a job requiring unusual intelligence or capacity to reason, yet until recent years this was a lily-white occupation.

Finally, history itself refutes the genetic theory of racial economic inequality in an even more positive way. In the pre-Civil War period, blacks attained a very firm economic footing as artisans, in the skilled trades, and in the transportation industry, positions that they lost only after a long period during which white labor used violent tactics to drive blacks out of the market. The admirable success record of black entrepreneurs prior to the Civil War completely refutes the notion that blacks suffer from some congenital defect that represses entrepreneurial skills or drives. Much the same sort of unanswerable evidence comes to us from the history of the performance of blacks from other parts of the world.

If blacks were by nature less intelligent or otherwise less well-equipped for material success, how is it that blacks in Latin American countries have so often achieved important posts and distinctions that far exceed the relative performance of blacks in the United States? As Professor Thomas Sowell has pointed out, blacks who have come to this country from the West Indies are consistently more successful than blacks born and raised here.[3] As early as 1901, blacks in New York City from the West Indies were known as the "black Jews"; they showed entrepreneurial traits equal to or exceeding whites'. This finding is altogether inconsistent with the theory of genetic inferiority and suggests instead the existence of some force operating on blacks who were raised in the United States. The success of West Indian blacks in the United States strongly suggests that it is not race, as such, that produces unequal incomes and attainments, but the particular cultural expectations and experience that people of the black race either bring to the United States from elsewhere or grow up with in the United States.

Manifest Destiny: Putting the Blame on Cultural Differences

The second theory commonly advanced to explain unequal black incomes and professional attainments places the blame on the cultural burdens of the African heritage, which supposedly retard the ambitions and abilities of many blacks. Historical forces such as climate, tribal traditions, and communal work patterns are said to continue to handicap blacks in competing successfully in a sophisticated modern system of competitive and industrial capitalism. In its most extreme form, this theory holds that by Western standards blacks suffer from a kind of cultural lag or pathology that causes them to be relatively unambitious, uneducable, and dependent. Like its handmaiden, scientific racism, the theory of cultural inferiority is an ugly slur on the traditions of an ancient and distinguished people.

In cataloging the accomplishments of black people in early African history, historian John Henrik Clarke points out that at the time Aristotle was laying the foundations of Western thought, the great culture of Ethiopia had been flourishing for 450 years.

In the Middle Ages, students from all over the world came to Timbuktu in the area of northwest Africa which is now Mali to study law and surgery at the University of Sankore. As W.E.B. DuBois writes:

"Always Africa is giving us something new. . . . On its Black bosom arose one of the earliest, if not the earliest, of self-protecting civilizations, and grew so mighty that it still furnishes superlatives to thinking and speaking men. Out of its darker and more remote forest vastnesses came, if we may credit many recent scientists, the first welding of iron, and we know that agriculture and trade flourished there when Europe was a wilderness." [4]

It is frequently said that the most disabling handicap that brought blacks to their present state of economic inequality is the lack of a commercial tradition that would enable them to adapt easily to contemporary economic conditions. This, too, is pure fiction. Ghana, Dahomey, and several of the Ivory Coast nations had early and rich mercantile traditions. Historian John Hope Franklin has commented on the commercial achievements of early Africans:

"The interest of early Africa in the outside world can best be seen in the great attention that was given to commerce. The tendency of tribes to specialize in some phase of economic activity made it necessary that they maintain commercial intercourse with other tribes and with other countries in order to secure the things that they did not produce. Some villages, for example, specialized in fishing; others concentrated their talents on metallurgy; while others made weapons, utensils, and so on. In tribes where such specialization was practiced, tradesmen traveled from place to place to barter and to purchase. Upon returning they were laden with goods which they sold to their fellows. Some tradesmen from the West Coast went as far north as the Mediterranean and as far east as Egypt, where they exchanged their goods for the wares of tradesmen from other parts of the world. It is to be recalled that the travels of the kings and emperors did much to stimulate this international traffic. Africa was, therefore, never a series of isolated self-sufficient communities, but an area that had far-flung interests based on agriculture, industry, and commerce. The effect of such contacts on the culture was immeasurable. It can only be said here that these routes of commerce were the highways over which civilization as well as goods traveled and that Africa gave much of her own civilization to others and received a good deal in return." [5]

Professor Eugene Genovese brings this historical record up to date in his discussion of the skills West African peoples brought to America in the slave ships:

"Peoples who filled the slave ships brought magnificent skills with them. . . . Throughout the Americas the Africans displayed a high level of mechanical skill, and where they had the chance, as in Cuba, they often came to dominate particular trades. . . . In Virginia, while the majority of free Negroes were farmhands and unskilled labor mechanics, artisans were found everywhere and in significant numbers. . . . The notion that Negroes were incapable as craftsmen grew up during the late antebellum period—in the face of overwhelming evidence to the contrary." [6]

Once again, the mercantile achievements of free blacks in the United States in the last century completely refute the notion that blacks are somehow not culturally suited for successful commercial endeavors. Prior to the intensely repressive post-Reconstruction and Jim Crow periods when blacks were forcibly evicted from every trade in sight, blacks participated widely in the American economy. The pre-Civil War achievements of blacks as professionals, landowners, and entrepreneurs are well documented. Before Reconstruction, the great majority of the skilled workers in the South were black. Fair numbers of skilled black tradesmen and craftsmen could be found working as railroad brakemen, ironworkers, cabinetmakers, plumbers, sailmakers, carpenters, stonecutters, wharf builders, coopers, millwrights, confectioners, druggists, engravers, typesetters, and photographers.

Widespread repressive measures were, indeed, imposed on blacks during the Reconstruction period when whites set about to undermine the black economic base and quickly to reestablish white economic and political control. But nothing in the history of black labor suggests any Negro cultural barriers different from, or more formidable than, those that handicapped the impoverished peasant immigrants who came to this country from Ireland and Italy and whose descendants now respectively earn incomes at 7.5 and 13 percent *above* the national norm.[7]

Powerful evidence, too, that there is no inherent cultural barrier—or for that matter, genetic handicap—is the proven success of blacks in those fields or circumstances where it is known that whites *chose not to discriminate* against them. At the same time, of course, the success of blacks in these special occupations and in economic sectors where discrimination did not prevail points the finger of responsibility directly at race discrimination as a cause of black inequality. The relative success of blacks as teachers and physicians serving their own people is a useful example. In a number of areas where, for some reason, race discrimination could not block achievement, blacks were, in fact, successful. Thus, black attainments were significant in the fields of scientific research and discovery, literature, and historical and educational inquiry. As long as segregation etiquette was observed, blacks also did relatively well in banking, restaurant operation, life insurance, and funeral direction. In these situations, Negroes were either catering to the special needs of the black community or were pursuing racially segregated activities, which whites did not find threatening or contaminating and therefore did not try to curtail. Whites did not write insurance on black lives, so blacks succeeded in that field. Black banks never sought a white clientele, so blacks did relatively well in banking. Because blacks were not competing or mixing with whites in these activities, they were allowed to, and did, succeed. Conversely, in trades where discrimination was written into trade union charters or was known to be particularly intense, the black success rate fell far below the black norm in other fields of endeavor. As mentioned earlier, the construction trades—possibly the most virulently racist trade unions in the country—are preeminent examples. There has always been a disproportionately low number of black workers here—for example, in 1971, electricians, 1.8 percent; plumbers, 1.2 percent; and sheetmetal workers, 1 percent.[8]

The consistent tendency of black success or failure rates to fluctuate directly with the presence or absence of known race discrimination largely removes both the genetic and the cultural explanations for black inequality. The high performance rates of blacks in activities where they were accepted or tolerated and their low penetration of activities and trades where they were not wanted tend rather to suggest that the codes of race are fundamentally responsible for what occurred.

Everybody's Scapegoat: The Black Family

Few serious scholars today would defend the thesis that indigenous tribal traditions are the black man's principal burdens. But a variant of the thesis of cultural handicap contends that the "root cause" of black economic inequality is the black family as it has evolved in the American setting. The position is that the black family, characterized by matriarchal households, absent fathers, high illegitimacy rates, and low levels of family ambition transmitted from generation to generation, is the single greatest inhibiting factor blocking the economic progress of the black race. In recent years, this thesis has focused principally on the black male who, according to popular stereotype, tends to be footloose and largely absent from the home. He is pictured as invariably sitting on the stoop instead of grabbing his lunch pail and providing for his wife and offspring.

Among blacks and whites the so-called pathology of the black family is everybody's favorite culprit. Dr. Martin Luther King, Jr. stated the consensus view: "The shattering blows in the Negro family made it fragile, deprived, and often psychopathic." In 1965, the famous Moynihan report on the Negro family put the case more bluntly:

> "[A]t the center of the tangle of pathology is the weakness of the family structure. Once or twice removed, it will be found to be the principal source of most of the aberrant, inadequate, or antisocial behavior that did not establish but now serves to perpetuate the cycle of poverty and discrimination. . . ."[9]

It must be conceded that the black family has become weakened and has not coped well with the vicissitudes of American capitalism. But there is no single explanation for this. The most careful historical research available today shows that the black family, despite preconceptions to the contrary, was a stable institution under slavery and remained so for at least the next three generations after emancipation, or through the first quarter of the twentieth century. After undertaking a detailed analysis of marriage

---

WE ALL KNOW THE BLACK FAMILY, DON'T WE?

It's a slow moving dependent outfit that:

- has a *smaller* percentage of its income from nonwork sources than white families.

- is *just as likely* as a white family to have income from wages or salaries.

- when the family is intact is 22 percent *more likely* to have both spouses working.

- has children who are currently completing school *at the same rate* as whites.

Source: U.S. Bureau of the Census, Current Population Reports, Series P-60, No. 120, Table 1, p. 7; No. 118, Table 30, p. 117; No. 119, Table 38, p. 150, Table 26, p. 105, and Series P-20, No. 314, Table 1, p. 7.

---

records, slave registers, and Census data, Professor Herbert G. Gutman's well-known study concluded that nuclear families and stable marriages typified black families:

> "Most slaves married, raised families, and, unless sale occurred, lived together until death. Most mothers had all their children by the same father. Most children grew up in two-parent families . . . What they [blacks before and after Emancipation] showed demonstrates that the origins of late twentieth-century urban black poverty and the suffering associated with it are not found in the inability of slave field hands and common laborers to maintain durable families. That is the message from these thousands of ex-slaves." [10]

If, as Professor Gutman's research shows, the black family structure remained intact into the 1920s, it follows that the forces operating on black families to bring about the high instability rates of recent years are to be found in recent history. One then looks to such social and economic forces as economic discrimination against the black male as a breadwinner, racial restrictions on admission of blacks to institutions that prepare people for a competitive economy, and, in recent years perhaps, a welfare system that rewards broken families.

Whatever the reason for the breakdown of the black family, the empirical evidence is strong that the nature of the black family unit is not the major cause of black inequality. Census statistics, particularly, refute the hypothesis that defects in the black family are the prime cause of the economic differences between blacks and whites. If the root of the problem lay in the black family, one would expect, for example, the incomes of intact black families to come closer to white family norms. But they do not. In 1979, poverty among black families with husband and wife living together was

---

If the instability of the black family is the principal economic problem, why do blacks still do much worse than whites when their families are intact?

1979

- Poverty among intact black families is almost three times that of white families.

- Unemployment in black husband-wife families living together is nearly twice the rate of comparable white families.

- Intact black families earn only 77 percent of white husband-wife families despite the fact that they have both spouses working 14 percent more often than whites.

Source: U.S. Department of Commerce. Bureau of the Census, Current Population Reports, Series P-60, No. 129, Table 25, p. 104; Series P-60, No. 130, Table 21, p. 95; and U.S. Department of Labor, Bureau of Labor Statistics, Special Labor Force Report, No. 237, Table A, p. A-8.

---

almost three times as prevalent as poverty among similar white families. Unemployment of the husband in husband-wife black families was two times more frequent than in white husband-wife families. In the South, where the family trauma supposedly attending migration to the urban North was not present, black families were broken only 6 percentage points less often than black families in the North and West. Yet these southern black husband-wife families earned only 74 percent of the income of white husband-wife families in the South.[11]

The positive gains made in recent years by intact black husband-wife families are often cited to prove that the sociological failings in the black family (the "footloose" black male and his stereotyped unwed or deserted female counterpart) are the major causes of racial inequality. But America's favorite myth holds very little truth. The strong performance of black married couples is due primarily to the fact that so many black families have two earners contributing to family income; in 1979, black intact families had two breadwinners 22 percent more often than comparable white families. Moreover, the very poor relative economic performance of black husband-wife families where the male is the sole breadwinner entirely refutes the position that everything works well for blacks who stay married. In families where the male is the only earner, black family incomes in 1979 were only 64 percent of white families where the male is the only breadwinner. And since 1972, this group of intact black families with the male as the single breadwinner has made no gains on similar white families.

It is rather clear then that the laudable tendency of black couples to have two people on payrolls is the main reason for the stronger performance of black married couples. For black married couples, having two jobs in the family is a far more successful strategy for staying even than is setting up business with the male at the head and as the sole earner. Under such circumstances, not much can be said for the opinion that for blacks, the surest way out of poverty is to arrange for black families to be headed by men. Clearly, other very powerful outside forces have been working to hold blacks back.[12]

The Fiction of Blacks as Peasant Newcomers to the Cities

The recent repudiation of traditional liberal views on racial issues has spawned a host of new theories to explain black inequality. Currently, one of the most common of these is the "recent immigrant" theory of the cause of black economic differences. This thesis is identified particularly with Professor Edward C. Banfield. Writing in 1974, he said, "Today, the Negro's main disadvantage is the same as the Puerto Rican's and Mexican's, namely that he is the most recent unskilled, and hence relatively low-income, migrant to reach the city from a backward rural area."[13]

Professor Thomas Sowell, the black economist, has refined this argument and stated it more precisely. He suggests that black Americans have undergone what amounts to three immigrations: the first in 1619 as slaves, the second in 1863 as freed men, and the third in the 1920s with the mass movement from the rural South to the urban North. Sowell contends that this last immigration is the true equivalent of the experience of peasants who came from Ireland, Italy, and Western Europe. Professor Sowell, who was 50 years old in 1980, then said of himself:

"I'm the equivalent of a second generation American . . . a native of Gastonia, North Carolina, whose parents moved to New York when [I] was a child. . . . After all, the first Kennedy lived and died a laborer. It was the third generation before they came into the money."

Viewed in this perspective, blacks, as very recent immigrants to the cities, are making progress that is considerably ahead of the accomplishments of comparable European immigrants who required several generations to reach economic parity with the nonimmigrant white population. Professor Sowell's argument appears formidable when one considers that in 1960, 65 percent of all blacks living in metropolitan areas outside the South were born in the South, and predominantly in the rural South.[14]

The logical structure of this position may be restated as follows: In general, agrarian or peasant people earn less than professionals and urban dwellers. Peasant immigrants to the United States may therefore be expected to earn less than established urban families. Black immigrants from the American South to northern cities should really be viewed as recent immigrant peasants. From this it follows that because of their recent peasant status blacks can and should be expected to have much lower incomes than whites. Accordingly, one should not be unduly alarmed by present black inequalities. Like all immigrant groups before them, blacks simply need time to adapt to an industrial society, educate their children, build institutions, and engage in party politics. Then, like other ethnic groups before them, they will finally make their way to equality with other Americans.

The recent immigrant theory of the origins of black inequality is simple and seductive. But despite its superficial appeal, the logic of the recent immigrant thesis is at total variance with historical facts. First, the thesis fails to account for what has happened to over one-half of the black population in the United States. About 51 percent of all blacks—more than 13 million people—still live in the South. Their ancestors first arrived in the seventeenth century, and they have lived in the South for 300 years. But blacks in the South, whether one regards them as peasants or not, have always earned a small fraction of what whites earn. In no sense can these southern blacks be regarded as recent immigrants. Thus, the recent urban migration theory totally fails to explain the gross poverty and income differences affecting over one-half of the black population.[15]

But let us for the moment ignore the southern blacks whose inequality cannot in any way be attributed to their status as recent immigrants. Let us assume, instead, that the "peasant newcomer" thesis is intended only to explain disproportionate black poverty affecting the other half of the black population which lives in the North. If this theory has any validity, we would then expect to find that black immigrants to northern cities would take about as long to equal national mean incomes as it took other peasant immigrant groups. If blacks are held back by nothing more than their unfamiliarity with the urban setting, the effects of this unfamiliarity should subside for them much as they have for other peasant immigrants. Is this in fact happening?

Black migration to northern cities is by no means a recent event. By 1930, the black migration to the North was well under way. New York City then had a black population of 328,000; Chicago, 234,000; Philadelphia, 220,000; Detroit, 120,000; Washington, D.C., 132,000; and Cleveland, 72,000. Thus, millions of blacks today who are or should be entering their prime years of earning and achievement are, in fact, the *grandchildren* of these early "immigrants" who came to the large cities prior to 1930. Like the Kennedys today, they are two generations away from "urban pioneer" status. But where, we ask, is the black A.P. Giannini, Spyros Skouras, or Andrew Carnegie? After all this time, the descendants of these urban pioneers should surely have provided us with a few success stories. Considering the huge number of third-generation northern blacks living in the large cities in 1950, why were blacks at that time predominantly sweepers rather than assistant sales managers, mailroom clerks rather than accountants' helpers, maids and chauffeurs rather than apartment house managers? In 1950—a time in our history when millions of blacks were in a position to claim a *three-generation* heritage in a northern setting—there was only a tiny black middle class; in 1950 the vast majority of urban blacks were still domestic or industrial menials.[16]

The experience of other ethnic newcomers to the United States also refutes the recent immigrant theory of black inequality. Compare, for example, Americans of Spanish origin, chiefly Puerto Rican and Chicano, who have arrived in the urban North much more recently than most blacks and who, like blacks, live principally in the cities. Despite language barriers and a recent peasant background, their economic performance has already significantly surpassed that of blacks. Compared with blacks, Americans of Spanish descent have a smaller percentage of families living in poverty, a lower unemployment rate, a higher median family income, and a higher rate of participation in the labor force. It does not make sense to say that blacks today are simply experiencing the deprivations and disadvantages of urban newcomers when Spanish-speaking peasant newcomers who came to urban settings in the United States more recently are doing much better than blacks.

The history of European immigrant groups also refutes the "peasant newcomer" theory of black inequality. Italian-Americans, for example, arrived in our cities as poor, uprooted peasants. The vast majority left the most depressed areas of southern Italy. Like Irish immigrants before them, they brought neither capital nor skills and were thus forced to work at the menial low-paying jobs avoided by native-born whites. Beginning in the late nineteenth century, Italian immigration peaked in 1914 at more than 280,000 per year. Yet, only a little more than two generations later, as a group, Italian-Americans had incomes equal to white median levels. In 1971, the median family income of Italian-Americans was $11,600, exceeding the overall United States family median by over 13 percent.[17] At that time, many Americans of Italian background had risen to the top of industry and the professions. Considering the blacks who began to migrate to northern cities in the 1920s, can it be said that they are making economic progress even remotely comparable to Italian-Americans? Hardly.

Moreover, there are few signs that for blacks the normal improvement in the economic position of "recent immigrant groups" is actually occurring. During the years from 1970 to 1979, black incomes increased much more slowly than did white incomes. During the 1970s, there was little evidence that the "migrants" to the North were making a significant move toward economic parity. Indeed, in 1970, black median family income in the Northeast was about $7,800—71 percent of the white figure of about $11,000. In 1979, the figures were $12,000 for blacks and about $21,400 for whites. During this ten-year period, then, black family income as a percentage of white actually dropped from a little over 71 percent to 56.5 percent. In the North Central region, where this acculturization of the "black peasant newcomer" was presumably occurring, the percentage of black to white family income dropped from well over 73 percent to a little over 62 percent. The relative decline in black incomes has been most dramatic in the West, with median black family income falling from 77 percent of white income in 1970 to 62 percent in 1979. On a comparative basis, blacks in the North and West are doing much worse than they were in 1970. Only in the South—where blacks have been "newcomers" for over 300 years—has the percentage improved slightly from about 56.5 percent to 58 percent.[18]

Looking at the matter from the vantage point of the early 1980s, the black-white unemployment gap has been constant for an entire generation, and there are no statistical indications that it will ever close. Poverty rates for blacks compared with whites have shown no progress. The wealth gap is vast—probably 10 to 1—and apparently almost totally resistant to change. In sum, the notion that the major problem of blacks is that they are relatively recent agrarian peasants arriving in the cities and, like other groups, they will catch up economically is totally inconsistent with the economic history of the past twenty years. In fact, there is no convincing evidence to show that blacks as a group are catching up at all.

An important study directly refutes the recent immigrant theory of black inequality. Professor Stanley M. Masters, analyzing data from the 1960 Census, has shown that for black families in the North, there is no significant income difference between families headed by blacks born in the South and families headed by northern-born blacks. The annual earnings of southern-born black males are actually higher than those of black males born in the North. First-generation male immigrants from the South are more likely to be employed and less likely to be poor than males from families with one or more generations of experience in the urban North. Southern-born black men with at least five years in the North have higher median incomes and are less likely to be at the bottom of the income ladder than northern-born blacks of the same age.[19]

The recent immigrant analogy is a fiction. From the standpoint of historical fact and logical argument, it is pure fable. Accepting this fiction lulls many blacks into the probably unwarranted belief that their situation will improve if the free-market economy is allowed to function without interference. Moreover, the myth undermines certain important interventionist strategies that have served blacks well while it supports as well laissez-faire domestic policies that, for a century or more, have completely failed to help blacks catch up to whites. The sooner blacks eliminate the recent immigrant fiction from their thinking, the sooner they will stand a chance of sorting out their case and moving on to what they can, and probably must, do to improve their fortunes.

America's Favorite Myth: Racial Inequality and Unequal Education

Unequal education is the factor most commonly cited to explain black inequality. In most national polls, Americans consistently turn to inferior schooling as the principal handicap to black progress. Is this opinion founded on fact?

There is no question that both blacks and whites improve their economic chances through education. But, in the past, blacks have derived much less gain from education than whites. For example, in 1978, the black male who had graduated from high school compared with the black male who had completed only elementary school improved his income by 36 percent; the white male high school graduate earned 66 percent more than his counterpart who did not go to high school. This means, in effect, that in past years, whites were offered a significantly greater economic inducement for staying in school than were blacks. The most striking evidence that unequal education has not been the driving force behind racial inequality lies in the extreme patterns of inequality that have existed independent of levels of education. In this connection, the most significant statistic is that as late as 1977, black male college graduates (of all age groups) were still earning less than whites who had only completed high school: $11,522 for blacks compared with $11,879 for whites.[20]

Although young blacks who have stayed in school have made important gains in recent years, the fact that in past years black incomes have failed to outperform those of whites with much lower educational attainments is powerful evidence that we must look beyond educational differences to find the reasons to explain the massive black-white income gap.

Other Census figures discredit the theory that unequal education is the major contributor to income inequality. For example, at all levels of educational attainment, up to college, blacks are up to 2.5 times as often unemployed as whites with the same years of school completed. In 1978, black families headed by a person with one year or more of college experience had a poverty rate of about 4.5 times greater than the rate for whites with the same college experience.[21] The huge disparity in the poverty levels of educated blacks and their comparable whites cannot be explained by differences in the quality of education received by blacks and whites. A small difference in poverty levels could be so explained, but not a rate of 4.5 to 1.

Blacks consistently receive sermons from whites and other blacks promising that they can close the income gap by staying in school and getting "a good education." The fact of the matter is that blacks have been staying in school in increasing numbers—and, as we have shown, have gained little by it in their efforts to close the income gap. Between 1970 and 1977, the median number of years of schooling completed rose 3.3 percent for young blacks between 25 and 29 years of age and 2.5 percent for blacks between the ages of 30 and 34; whites in the same age brackets showed increases of only 1.6 and 2.4 percent, respectively. Yet, during these years, blacks in these age groups made no gains.[22]

By 1977, the education gap had closed to the point where young blacks and young whites had nearly identical median years of completed education. (In the 25-to-29 age group, the median number of years completed was 12.6 for blacks, 12.8 for whites; in the 30-to-34 age group, the median number of years completed was 12.4 for blacks and 12.8 for whites.) But, although the education gap had largely closed, the comparative unemployment rates (2 to 1) were unchanged, the poverty rate (3 to 1) was

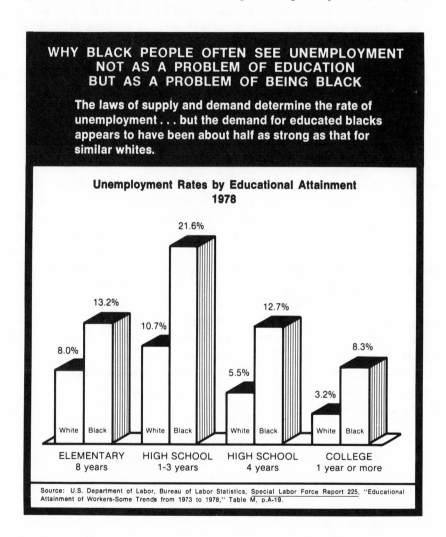

WHY BLACK PEOPLE OFTEN SEE UNEMPLOYMENT NOT AS A PROBLEM OF EDUCATION BUT AS A PROBLEM OF BEING BLACK

The laws of supply and demand determine the rate of unemployment . . . but the demand for educated blacks appears to have been about half as strong as that for similar whites.

Unemployment Rates by Educational Attainment 1978

Source: U.S. Department of Labor, Bureau of Labor Statistics, Special Labor Force Report 225, "Educational Attainment of Workers-Some Trends from 1973 to 1978," Table M, p.A-19.

unchanged, and the black-white family income ratio (60 percent of whites) remained constant.[23]

The lower quality of education available to blacks is certainly an important factor and would explain, to a great extent, why blacks with the same years of schooling as whites would earn much less. Still, the quality of schooling cannot account for the huge and persistent differences in economic performances among blacks and whites.

As already mentioned, until recently, black college graduates have always earned about the same as white high school graduates. To be sure, the quality of black education is a key factor here, and it is theoretically possible that given the schooling generally available to blacks, a black college graduate is no better educated than a white high school graduate. But even if this argument could be sustained, it would effectively clinch the point that it is not inferior education per se that explains the economic inequality of blacks. For the poorer quality of black education—according to which unequal black incomes are explained—has its roots in public and private race discrimination. Until the 1960s, almost all elite educational institutions either excluded or severely curtailed the enrollment of blacks. In the states where most blacks lived, they were almost never permitted to enter state university systems except for those that were racially segregated, fiscally starved, and educationally inferior. Until recent years, expenditures for public education have always been grossly unequal for blacks. Hence, the immense differences in the quality of education open to blacks are directly related to the intense race discrimination that has always governed the appropriations of public funds in virtually every city, town, state, and local school district. Thus, insofar as responsibility for black economic inequality can be placed on unequal education, it must be remembered that, in most cases, unequal education has been the direct result of strict racial barriers prevailing in both private institutions and in public school systems.

Going down the path of unequal education in search of the responsible cause of black economic inequality simply leads us once more to the codes of black inferiority.

Racial Burdens Mistaken for Class Burdens

The position is frequently taken that blacks suffer more from class prejudice than from racial prejudice and that class differences essentially explain persistent economic differences between blacks and whites. Advocates of this thesis often point to the fact that while racial prejudice has clearly diminished over the past few decades, black unemployment has risen sharply.[24] If the black economic condition has thus deteriorated in the face of diminishing discrimination, doesn't this prove that race discrimination is not as important as we think in its effect on black inequality? The position may then be taken that if things worsen as racial discrimination abates, economic differences may be due to persistent class differences or to other forces distinct from race prejudice.

This conclusion completely mistakes the nature of black employment in 1948 as compared with 1978. No one would seriously argue that because blacks had virtually no unemployment in 1860, race discrimination was not holding them back. The fact is that there was no black unemployment because blacks were fully employed as noncompensated agrarian slaves. In other words, unemployment figures by themselves may not tell us very much unless we know something about the quality of the employment available to the portion of the population listed as unemployed. Television executives, because they move from job to job, may well have a higher unemployment rate than sharecroppers. Still, all things considered, it is probably better to be a television executive than a sharecropper. Exactly the same point can be made about the unemployment situation of blacks three decades or so ago. Blacks then had much lower unemployment rates be-cause they did not work in occupations where they would be subject to traditional risks of industrial unemployment. They worked as bootblacks, field hands, domestics, and porters; they earned little, but the work was steady. In the past thirty years, however, blacks have begun to move into an industrial society and are now subject to the rigors of industrial un-employment. A comparison of black unemployment figures in the present with those of the past thus tells us very little about the reasons for the changes in the economic condition of blacks over the past twenty or thirty years. The deterioration of black unemployment rates over the long term certainly does not permit us to assign "class differences," rather than "race differences," as the responsible cause for persisting black inequality.

The thesis that class differences explain the subordinate status of blacks has been most effectively articulated in the work of Professor Edward Ban-field. In the first edition of his book, *The Unheavenly City,* he writes:

> "If, overnight, Negroes turned white, most of them would go on living under much the same handicaps for a long time to come. The great majority of New Whites would continue working at the same jobs, living in the same neighborhoods, and sending their children to the same schools."

In a later revision, published in 1974, the Banfield statement was modified to read, "The situation of most Negroes would be far from satisfactory if there were no prejudice at all." [25]

Professor Banfield's position has been important in shaping government policy. His position deserves careful examination. Professor Banfield is saying that, to a considerable extent, blacks will continue to remain poor because they are already poor. This certainly makes sense. In a capitalistic society such as ours, where having a grubstake is a huge economic advantage, it is unquestionably much easier to make money if one has money. "To him that hath shall be given, and from him that hath not shall be taken away" is a biblical aphorism that continues to control all but a few of the economic transactions in this world. Thus, if I were provided with a sample of 100 5-year-old children and were asked to predict which of them would wind up with incomes that would place them in the top economic bracket by the time they were 40, which would have middle-class incomes, and which would be poor, it wouldn't be necessary for me to administer intelligence tests and sketch psychological profiles of the children. I could probably achieve a fairly high degree of accuracy of prediction simply by asking how much each of their fathers was making right now. To the extent that Professor Banfield is merely saying the same thing in a different way, it is difficult to quarrel with him. Poor blacks would tend, on the whole, to remain poor even if they became white "overnight," simply because poor people, on the whole, tend to remain poor.

But it appears that Professor Banfield is saying more. He is suggesting that because a certain tendency of economic class tends to perpetuate itself, racial discrimination plays an insignificant role in the plight of blacks. The real question is not whether blacks are suffering from class disadvantage *or* from racial prejudice. It is a question of whether they are laboring under a dual handicap of class disadvantage *and* racial prejudice. There is no reason to assume that the two are mutually exclusive. Consider, again, my sample of 5 year olds. Anyone who has observed American society in action would undoubtedly feel confident that class is an excellent predictor of economic success. The children of upper-class parents will indeed tend to remain in the upper class when they reach maturity, although a certain small percentage will undoubtedly fail and slip back into the middle and lower classes. And the children from lower-class backgrounds will, on the whole, remain so, despite a small number who manage to make their way up into the middle class and an even smaller number who make it all the way to the top. But the question here is whether the force of race prejudice enters into the picture too. It appears quite clear that we have every reason to believe it does. If our hypothetical sample contained twenty lower-class blacks and twenty lower-class whites, it might well be that we would be right in thirty of these forty cases if we predicted that the poor children would remain poor in adult life. This gives us a measure of the extent to which class determines economic well-being. But it might also well be that eight of the ten lower-class children who grew up to better their economic position were white, while only two black children succeeded in climbing out of the lower class. This difference—eight out of twenty white children as compared with only two out of twenty black children—would give us a measure of the extent to which racial prejudice and discrimination affect and control economic well-being.

In other words, Professor Banfield is undoubtedly right in declaring that if a community of poor blacks suddenly turned white overnight, most of them would remain poor. He might just as well have said that in any given community of poor whites, most will remain poor. However, the question that must be asked is whether poor or lower-class whites manage to climb out of poverty at a greater rate than blacks. It is all well and good to say as Professor Banfield does that "the situation of most Negroes would be far from satisfactory if there were no prejudice at all." This may be true. But the fact remains that ample evidence suggests that even though the situation of most blacks might be far from satisfactory if there were no race prejudice at all, blacks would nevertheless be far better off than they are today.

In particular examples, the positive evidence is overwhelming that race and not class is the critical and dominant factor. If lower-class status and not race is the essential problem, why have college-educated blacks—people obviously showing middle-to-upper-class traits—traditionally earned about the same as white high school graduates who are usually from the middle or lower class? If being from the "lower classes" rather than belonging to the wrong race is the critical problem of most blacks, why have blacks never penetrated industries such as the construction trades, which have always filled the majority of their jobs from middle-to-lower-class families? If the essential problem is one of class behavior rather than racial status, why is it that even today blacks have found it almost impossible to secure positions as firemen and policemen, positions traditionally filled by members of low-income-to-lower-middle-income families. If class rather than race is the problem, why is it that, in 1983, when the Democratic nomination for Chicago's mayor went to a black person, the traditional Democratic support in the city's white ethnic neighborhoods disappeared so fast that even the Republican party was astonished? If class and not race is the basic handicap, how is the conclusion to be reconciled with all the situations we have demonstrated in which blacks have done so much better when race discrimination rather than class discrimination has been removed? These circumstances point clearly to the factor of race rather than class as the essential culprit in producing the differences we observe.

The opinion, so widespread today, that lower-class status rather than racial status is the essential problem facing blacks contradicts many other patterns of social behavior that we may observe around us. For example, is it class hostility or racial animosity that has caused whites in the South and in many parts of the Middle West to organize segregated academies that exclude black school children without regard to class background? Is class or racial discrimination the motive behind the widespread practice of gerrymandering of voting districts so as to split up heavy concentrations of black voters in order to create "safe" districts for whites? Is it class discrimination or race discrimination that is operating in the tens of thousands of American business, luncheon, and country clubs that exclude blacks from membership without regard to their business or professional background? Can it be that the many trade unions, in all parts of the country, that still exclude blacks from their memberships are doing so because the particular blacks who would like to drive trucks or pour concrete are of a lower class than that of the whites who are now members of those unions?

When, as NAACP legal complaints have proven many times, real estate agents steer prosperous black families into black neighborhoods and apartment developments rather than into white suburban communities, is that because whites don't want to associate with poor and disadvantaged families or because they wish to avoid living next door to blacks? Is it because of race or class prejudice that poor and mostly lower-class whites in many areas of Boston, Louisville, and other cities use violence to resist court-ordered busing of black children to their white neighborhood schools? Do many of the state university systems of the South still maintain racially segregated campuses because whites don't want their children socializing with blacks or because they don't want them mingling with students from lower-class families? In recent years, school boards across the country have been obliged to close large numbers of public schools because of shrinking student populations. If, as many people contend, these school authorities are not motivated by racial considerations, why is it that the racially segregated schools—either predominantly black or predominantly white—are invariably the ones that are kept open, while the racially integrated schools are the ones selected for closure.[26] Similar examples of unmistakable racial prejudice as opposed to class bias may be found in virtually every daily newspaper.

This does not deny that class attitudes are an impediment to upward progress of blacks just as they are for whites. But the evidence is overwhelming that for blacks there has been the massive additional burden of intense race dicrimination. Race discrimination is a fact of life; it is a powerful economic and social force which has dominated the life of virtually every black person reared in the United States. The presence of continuing codes of race must be acknowledged and publicized even if the publicity has the effect of causing many blacks to oversimplify the reasons for inequality and to blame *all* their problems on a "racist" white society.

The Positive Proof That the Rules of Race Caused Black Inequality

We have produced strong evidence that factors such as educational differences, differences in family stability, and class and cultural differences are not the prime causes of black inequality. Since in each case these forces do not satisfactorily explain what has occurred, we are repeatedly thrown back to the explanation of race discrimination. What affirmative proof is there that the extreme racial inequalities, whose presence everybody must acknowledge, are traceable to the codes of race?

We know definitely that universal racial codes of occupational exclusion could have stunted black ambitions and diminished desires among blacks to acquire training for jobs society would not award. Practical experience tells us, too, that the racial codes that insisted on allocating menial jobs to blacks while placing blue-collar or white-collar posts off limits could logically have had the effect of holding blacks in lowly positions where incomes were low. We know, too, that universally observed codes of employment under which employers hired all available white labor before they turned to black job applicants could and should have produced higher rates of unemployment among blacks. We know, too, that if major business schools limit their credentials to whites, a likely outcome of the admissions codes is the production of very few blacks with technical training and skills to hold business posts of the upper rank. If, by reasons of race, certain people are ineligible for certain rewards, one may infer that ineligibility is a cause of those people not winning any of the rewards. Common sense tells us that all of this *could* have happened and was *likely* to happen. But is this, in fact, what did occur? Can the causal connection between the known racial codes of exclusion and unequal racial results be proven in some affirmative sense?

Only a generation ago, the evidence of a causal link between racial discrimination and unequal black positions was inescapable. In fact, it was often possible to collect the "smoking revolver" type of direct proof that put the issue beyond doubt. These exhibits usually took the form of spoken or written messages. For example, when I was a child, signs hanging in shop-windows as well as classified advertisements commonly declared "only whites need apply." There were *never* any black clerks inside these shops; the inference of a causal connection was impressive, though not conclusive. In the past, the charters of many labor organizations had a "Caucasian-only" clause; until 1959, the Brotherhood of Railway Trainmen had such a written provision. And there were no blacks working as trainmen, although they had been railroad workers before the adoption of the Caucasian-only clause.

As a young lawyer, I saw hundreds of Caucasian-only covenants in deeds. There were no blacks in the neighborhoods for which the deeds were filed. When I was in the U.S. Navy in 1942, the rules required two lines for blood donors—one for blacks, one for whites. And, in fact, blacks were in the black line and whites in the white line. When I was married in Louisville, Kentucky, there were two marriage logbooks in the city hall—one for whites, the other for nonwhites. And so it goes. It would require only a few days' research for any college student to produce from public records hundreds of documents containing Caucasian-only clauses in charters of clubs, religious organizations, fraternal societies, labor unions, and universities. The wills of hundreds of thousands of people who died in the last 100 years restricted charitable gifts to members of the Caucasian race. Millions of blacks living today recall being explicitly told that they were rejected for employment, credit, or admission to an educational institution *because* they were black. Many light-skinned blacks recall and have testified to having been discharged from employment *because* their employers later discovered they were Negroes.

In addition, there are reams of anecdotal evidence that is highly persuasive on the question of whether the codes of race produced and maintained black inequality. American blacks of great distinction—whose careers ultimately overcame the rules of race—would be able to provide direct connections between race discrimination and unequal positions. Mrs. Rosa Parks, for example, was a college graduate. However, on December 1, 1955 when she refused to yield her seat on a Montgomery, Alabama bus to a white man, she was employed as a seamstress. Roy Wilkins, a man of unusual gifts, used to tell how he worked successively as a redcap, a dishwasher, a pullman-car waiter, and a cleanup man in a St. Paul slaughterhouse. Any research institution with the determination and resources to do an oral history of race relations in the United States could produce mountains of direct evidence of race discrimination. It could also produce huge amounts of evidence that, in particular cases, race discrimination was the driving force in producing unequal economic positions.

In today's society, however, one rarely encounters "smoking revolver"-type evidence of racial discrimination, except perhaps at cocktail parties and in tasteless jokes told to confidants. The overt expression of racial bias is strongly frowned upon even among people who regularly use racial criteria in making their economic and professional decisions. Far fewer whites today than ten years ago will give racially biased answers to such questions as "Should blacks be allowed to live wherever they can afford to live?" Nevertheless, the race-trait prejudgment that used to proclaim itself so loudly in written language still controls human behavior. It is deeply embedded in our value system and conventions. In the minds of most white people, the sight of an individual black person still triggers judgments of inferior competence, lower educational attainments, and lesser knowledge of the ways of the world.

Indeed, the fact that this racial belief system has, as it were, gone underground makes it all the more difficult to deal with because it is almost impossible to convince a person that his beliefs are not valid when he himself may be unaware that he holds such beliefs. An employer who has never hired a black to fill a responsible position or a married couple that has never had a black in their home except as a domestic servant may all profess themselves willing to employ and socialize with blacks and may openly deplore the absence of qualified black workers or the shortage of blacks in their social sets. How is it possible to determine whether these professions are sincere or whether they conceal racial sentiments which continue to control who gets what? In a large number of cases, blacks are denied consideration for positions not because the people making the selections harbor strong animosities toward blacks or because these people believe Negroes are congenitally incompetent, but rather because the managers of the institutions, associations, or businesses in question do not notice black people, or simply don't think of them as being potential candidates for the positions in question. How do you prove that a person who, in effect, looks through you just as if you were transparent is making unfair judgment calls against you? In individual cases, it is not possible to tell.

When Improbable Outcomes Identify a Culprit

But it is possible, by means of statistical analysis, to determine whether an institution or an economic system is operating on racial principles. At first glance, this may seem like a contradiction, for if we can't be certain that any particular individual is acting in a racially biased way, how can all these uncertainties add up to a certainty about the overall system? In fact, however, there is nothing at all contradictory here; we make such calculations all the time. For example, if the winner of the state lottery is the lottery commissioner's first cousin, our suspicions may be aroused, but we don't know definitely that any hanky-panky was involved. In an honest lottery, the commissioner's cousin's chances to win are rather slim—but then again, the chances of any particular individual to win are slim. The outcome seems unlikely, but that's about all we can say. If, however, relatives of the commissioner win the next three lotteries in a row, the odds against this happening by chance become so astronomically high that we would have to be very naive to avoid drawing the inference that the lottery was fixed. Or consider a more mundane example—and one closer to the experience of blacks in our society: Imagine that you invite a man you work with to bring his wife to your house for dinner. He explains that he has theater tickets for the night in question. Even if your next invitation is rebuffed you would probably not be justified in concluding that he has some reason for not wanting to be in your company. But if the rejections go on long enough, there will be a point at which this conclusion is justified, and, in fact, inescapable. The odds are so heavily stacked against your friend's having bona fide social commitments on so many randomly chosen nights that it is quite reasonable to draw an inference of bad faith.

Exactly the same reasoning can be applied to a proof of racial prejudice with exactly the same commonsense results. When a black person is rejected for a job for which he or she is superlatively qualified, it may be that an even more outstandingly qualified white happened to have preceded him or her into the employment office. It may even be that the black person just happened to have rubbed the personnel manager the wrong way. These things can happen and don't necessarily indicate racial bias. But when they happen thousands upon thousands of times, when we find *white high school* graduates sitting at the desks *black college* graduates were not considered qualified to occupy, when blacks with secure and well-paying jobs are turned down for mortgages that go to whites with shakier credit ratings, we can be reasonably certain that all the excuses and justifications offered on a case-by-case basis simply do not account for the extraordinary and improbable results we see.

Today, too, a broad range of circumstances with highly unusual statistical outcomes are, by themselves, acceptable proof of racial discrimination, as well as of unequal positions resulting from that discrimination. For example, Detroit, Michigan had a black population of 44 percent in 1969 compared with 21 percent in New York City. Yet only 1.3 percent of New York City teachers were black compared with almost 17 percent in Detroit. Making adjustments for possible lower professional attainments of black teachers, what factor other than racial discrimination could account for these disproportionate percentages? There are almost limitless examples of similar circumstances with improbable statistical outcomes that can only be explained by the presence of race discrimination. For example, can anything other than discrimination explain why no black law school graduates were admitted to the Pennsylvania Bar during the ten-year period 1933 to

There is no reason why blacks and other minorities should be proportionately distributed in all walks of life, yet only a significant factor of occupational restrictions tied to skin color adequately explains the extremely low representation of blacks in jobs requiring only minimal levels of schooling.

Occupation	Percent of Jobs Held by Blacks 1960
Locomotive Engineers	0.2%
Bank Tellers	0.5%
Textile Weavers	0.6%
Telegraph Operators	0.6%
Ticket Agents	0.8%
Tool and Die Makers	0.9%
Office Machine Repairmen	1.3%
Electricians	1.4%
Carpenter Apprentices	1.8%
Firemen	1.9%
Telephone Operators	2.5%
Cabinetmakers	2.7%
Railroad Switchmen	2.7%
Dispatchers	3.2%
Policemen	3.7%

Source: U.S. Bureau of the Census, 1960 Census of the Population, Special Studies, "Occupational Characteristics," Series PC(2)-7A, Table 3, page 21.

1943? Or why the state of Mississippi had only two or three practicing black lawyers until the early 1950s? According to a government study, black credit applicants with assets in excess of $20,000 were rejected at the rate of 22 percent; white applicants with the same resources were turned down at the rate of only 14 percent. In California in the early 1970s, 27 percent of the students classified as "educable mentally retarded" were black, even though blacks made up only 9 percent of the student population of California.[27] Clearly, race discrimination played a large part in the hundreds of thousands of decisions that produced these extremely unequal results.

Statistics delineating very unusual patterns of employment have always provided the most potent evidence of a system of job allocations by race in the United States. Differences in the distribution of jobs have been such that they cannot possibly be explained by factors other than race. As late as 1970, blacks comprised only about 11 percent of the population, yet they held an extraordinary 53 percent of positions as private household workers, almost 39 percent of the jobs as lodgings cleaners, 26 percent of the laundry and dry cleaning work force, and 23 percent of the janitorial work force.[28] Many economic and educational factors contributed to this extraordinary skewing in the distribution of menial work, but even when the probable effects of the other factors are subtracted, one is left with a statistical anomaly that virtually forces the conclusion that either official or unofficial protocol of job reservation according to race had been in effect for a long time.

We see then that there is a great range of economic circumstances where improbable economic outcomes can be explained only in terms of policies of racial discrimination and subordination. This conclusion is particularly strong where virtually no blacks have been represented in particular trades requiring little or no education.

But the next question is, can we also show a direct causal connection between racial discrimination on the one hand and lower black incomes and unequal positions and performance on the other? Once again, we return to the statistical disparities mentioned earlier. While never incontrovertibly proving the point, these statistics send strong signals that majority power in the form of race discrimination has been the single most critical factor in lower black incomes. In fact, there is a wide variety of circumstances where patterns of racial inequality are so striking that we are left with no conclusion but that race discrimination has been the essential culprit.

Race Discrimination Outlawed: Blacks Forge Ahead

Probably the most convincing proof that race discrimination is directly responsible for black inequality is of the empirical kind, familiar to the laboratory scientist. The standard principle of scientific observation, as well as of laboratory experimentation, is that when an existing phenomenon or pattern of behavior persists for a long period of time and then suddenly

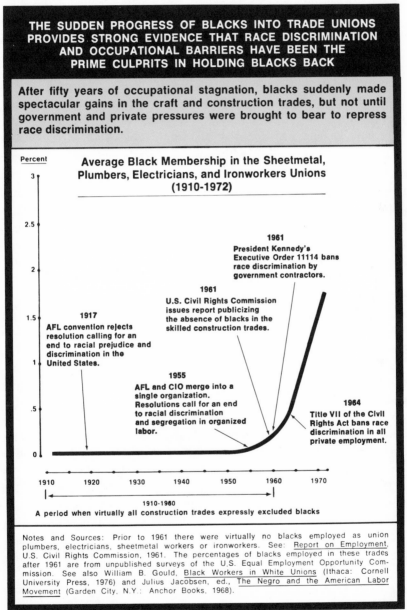

THE SUDDEN PROGRESS OF BLACKS INTO TRADE UNIONS PROVIDES STRONG EVIDENCE THAT RACE DISCRIMINATION AND OCCUPATIONAL BARRIERS HAVE BEEN THE PRIME CULPRITS IN HOLDING BLACKS BACK

After fifty years of occupational stagnation, blacks suddenly made spectacular gains in the craft and construction trades, but not until government and private pressures were brought to bear to repress race discrimination.

Percent

Average Black Membership in the Sheetmetal, Plumbers, Electricians, and Ironworkers Unions (1910-1972)

1961
President Kennedy's Executive Order 11114 bans race discrimination by government contractors.

1961
U.S. Civil Rights Commission issues report publicizing the absence of blacks in the skilled construction trades.

1917
AFL convention rejects resolution calling for an end to racial prejudice and discrimination in the United States.

1955
AFL and CIO merge into a single organization. Resolutions call for an end to racial discrimination and segregation in organized labor.

1964
Title VII of the Civil Rights Act bans race discrimination in all private employment.

1910   1920   1930   1940   1950   1960   1970

1910-1960
A period when virtually all construction trades expressly excluded blacks

Notes and Sources: Prior to 1961 there were virtually no blacks employed as union plumbers, electricians, sheetmetal workers or ironworkers. See: <u>Report on Employment</u>, U.S. Civil Rights Commission, 1961. The percentages of blacks employed in these trades after 1961 are from unpublished surveys of the U.S. Equal Employment Opportunity Commission. See also William B. Gould, <u>Black Workers in White Unions</u> (Ithaca: Cornell University Press, 1976) and Julius Jacobsen, ed., <u>The Negro and the American Labor Movement</u> (Garden City, N.Y.: Anchor Books, 1968).

disappears, one looks to see if some new force or element has been introduced into the chain of events. This kind of inquiry often leads to the discovery of the factor that was causing the phenomenon in the first place. The causes of many physical diseases have in fact been discovered by systematically introducing or removing various suspected chemical agents and seeing whether or not a physical problem goes away or the patient gets better. In this manner, events that happen together in time and space are in fact often identified as reliable causal agents. The conclusion that a cause has been reliably detected is particularly convincing when, in a series of experiments, the observed phenomenon consistently, or quite suddenly, goes away when the suspected "culprit" is removed or withdrawn.

Now note what has happened to black people in cases where race discrimination has been removed or withdrawn. I showed earlier in this chapter how blacks have fared much better in economic and professional settings and fields where, for one reason or another, whites *chose* not to discriminate against them. But blacks have also done much better in settings where race discrimination was less intense or where whites were forced to be objective in making competitive judgments (e.g., choosing winners in sports events). Also, we noted that blacks have done comparatively better in regions of the country where race discrimination was less intense. For example, the economic gap between blacks and whites in the South has always been much greater than that between blacks and whites in the North. These circumstances suggest that race discrimination has been strongly implicated in producing unequal economic results.

But the most telling proof at hand of the culpability of racial prejudice is the fact that blacks have almost consistently performed much better immediately following efforts on their part, or on the part of the government, to remove discriminatory practices of whites. The construction trades—traditionally all-white preserves—once more furnish us with excellent examples of proof. For several generations (roughly 1900-1960), blacks had almost no participation in the construction trades, areas of labor activity where very little general school learning is required. We also know that during this long period of time many, if not most, specialty unions excluded blacks, often by written provisions in union charters. Yet, black participation in these trades suddenly leaped manyfold during the decade of the 1960s, when intense federal legislative and executive pressures were being exerted to reduce race discrimination on the part of construction employers and labor unions.

We know that during this short span of years, blacks as a group didn't suddenly raise their qualifications to perform in these trades. We know, too, that after fifty years of economic stagnation, blacks didn't suddenly acquire ambition, new work motivations, or self-discipline, the lack of which current economic conservatives assert as the cause of black inequality. But the fact that stands out most vividly is that during this short period of time there was in fact a massive and sudden abatement in race discrimination practices

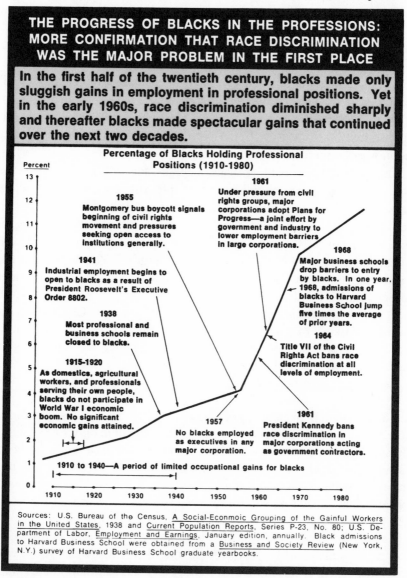

THE PROGRESS OF BLACKS IN THE PROFESSIONS: MORE CONFIRMATION THAT RACE DISCRIMINATION WAS THE MAJOR PROBLEM IN THE FIRST PLACE

In the first half of the twentieth century, blacks made only sluggish gains in employment in professional positions. Yet in the early 1960s, race discrimination diminished sharply and thereafter blacks made spectacular gains that continued over the next two decades.

Percentage of Blacks Holding Professional Positions (1910-1980)

1955 Montgomery bus boycott signals beginning of civil rights movement and pressures seeking open access to institutions generally.

1961 Under pressure from civil rights groups, major corporations adopt Plans for Progress—a joint effort by government and industry to lower employment barriers in large corporations.

1941 Industrial employment begins to open to blacks as a result of President Roosevelt's Executive Order 8802.

1968 Major business schools drop barriers to entry by blacks. In one year, 1968, admissions of blacks to Harvard Business School jump five times the average of prior years.

1938 Most professional and business schools remain closed to blacks.

1964 Title VII of the Civil Rights Act bans race discrimination at all levels of employment.

1915–1920 As domestics, agricultural workers, and professionals serving their own people, blacks do not participate in World War I economic boom. No significant economic gains attained.

1957 No blacks employed as executives in any major corporation.

1961 President Kennedy bans race discrimination in major corporations acting as government contractors.

1910 to 1940—A period of limited occupational gains for blacks

Sources: U.S. Bureau of the Census, A Social-Economic Grouping of the Gainful Workers in the United States, 1938 and Current Population Reports, Series P-23, No. 80; U.S. Department of Labor, Employment and Earnings, January edition, annually. Black admissions to Harvard Business School were obtained from a Business and Society Review (New York, N.Y.) survey of Harvard Business School graduate yearbooks.

in the United States which coincided with a sudden and very sharp increase in the representation of blacks in construction trades. Here, in the sudden positive change in black fortunes, was convincing evidence that race discrimination had been a major force holding blacks back in the first place. Other examples of sudden progress of blacks confirm the same conclusion. For half a century prior to 1960, there was almost no progress whatsoever of blacks winning professional and managerial positions. Yet with the advent, in 1964, of civil rights laws outlawing race discrimination, blacks made spectacular moves into these professions. The gains were, in fact, explosive after 1968 when major business colleges dropped the barriers against the admission of blacks. In many occupations, the gains were 500 percent or more in just a few years. Surely blacks did not suddenly become qualified to enter executive and business positions. Instead, the fences were dropped and blacks marched in. Here is potent proof that race discrimination was the problem in the first place!

The sharp improvement of black incomes generally, which coincided with various government initiatives to prevent discrimination against blacks, further confirms the conclusion that race discrimination was the major historical force holding blacks back in the first place. Census figures show that from 1910 to 1940 there was virtually no improvement in the occupational status of blacks in the United States.[29] Yet, look what happened when the nation began to attack race discrimination. After President Roosevelt's 1941 order banning race discrimination in defense industries, black incomes not only surged but, in fact, only six years later in 1947 had gained a massive 14 percentage points on whites. True, this was a prosperous period when almost everybody was doing better. But the huge gains that blacks made on whites—coinciding with a period when race discrimination in employment was neutralized—were absolutely unprecedented.

Then again, after the enactment of the Civil Rights Act of 1964 banning race discrimination in all forms of employment, black incomes surged once more, rising from 54 percent of whites' to 61 percent in only five years. Of course, during this period as well as in the earlier World War II years, blacks were benefiting also from strong economies. But there had been strong economies before, the World War I years, for example. Yet, blacks appear to have made no significant occupational gains during the World War I period. It seems clear that the reason for this is that racial caste was very much a fact of American life during World War I and its aftermath. Only a combination of economic boom and the breakdown of racial caste was sufficient to break the back of Jim Crow in the South and of racial occupational restrictions in the North.

Other evidence that race discrimination has been the important factor in holding blacks back appears when we compare the historical pattern of the

THE TIMING OF KNOWN HISTORICAL TRENDS IN IMPROVEMENT OF BLACK INCOMES PROVIDES CONVINCING EVIDENCE THAT RACIAL DISCRIMINATION IS AN UNDERLYING CAUSE OF BLACK INEQUALITY

Significant black income gains did not occur until employer discrimination was suppressed by increasing public pressures and by government intervention.

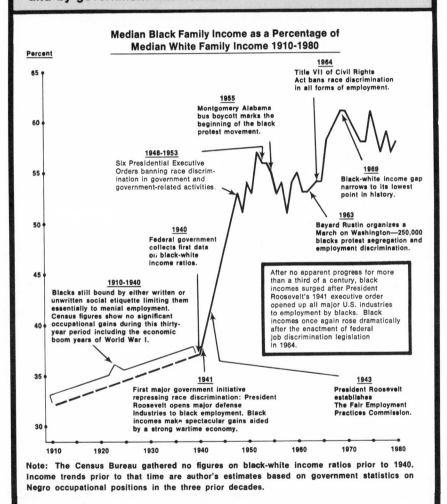

Median Black Family Income as a Percentage of Median White Family Income 1910-1980

Percent

1964
Title VII of Civil Rights Act bans race discrimination in all forms of employment.

1955
Montgomery Alabama bus boycott marks the beginning of the black protest movement.

1948-1953
Six Presidential Executive Orders banning race discrimination in government and government-related activities.

1969
Black-white income gap narrows to its lowest point in history.

1940
Federal government collects first data on black-white income ratios.

1963
Bayard Rustin organizes a March on Washington—250,000 blacks protest segregation and employment discrimination.

1910-1940
Blacks still bound by either written or unwritten social etiquette limiting them essentially to menial employment. Census figures show no significant occupational gains during this thirty-year period including the economic boom years of World War I.

After no apparent progress for more than a third of a century, black incomes surged after President Roosevelt's 1941 executive order opened up all major U.S. industries to employment by blacks. Black incomes once again rose dramatically after the enactment of federal job discrimination legislation in 1964.

1941
First major government initiative repressing race discrimination: President Roosevelt opens major defense industries to black employment. Black incomes make spectacular gains aided by a strong wartime economy.

1943
President Roosevelt establishes The Fair Employment Practices Commission.

Note: The Census Bureau gathered no figures on black-white income ratios prior to 1940. Income trends prior to that time are author's estimates based on government statistics on Negro occupational positions in the three prior decades.

Source: U.S. Bureau of the Census, <u>1940 Census of the Population</u> and <u>Current Population Reports</u>, Series P-60, Nos. 123 & 127. The data on the lack of occupational gains by blacks prior to 1940 are from the Census Bureau's <u>A Social-Economic Grouping of the Gainful Workers of the United States</u>, 1938.

413

incomes of comparable blacks and whites—particularly blacks and whites who show similar attitudes toward education and the need to get ahead. Again, look at the government statistics we cited earlier. Discounting and rediscounting all the probable effects of the fact that the quality of education available to blacks has been lower than that available to whites, can one think of a reason other than race discrimination to explain why young blacks with college experience are 2.3 times as often unemployed as whites? Can there be any reason other than race discrimination to explain why as late as 1978 young blacks with some college education fell into poverty 2.3 times more often than their white peer group? Or why, until 1978, black male college graduates had median incomes less than white high school graduates?[30] In the latter cases, particularly, blacks who were necessarily showing considerable academic ability and drive for self-improvement were doing less well than whites who clearly had significantly lower abilities, ambitions, and drive. It is true that highly educated young blacks ages 18 to 34—only about 1.5 percent of all black wage earners—now show earnings equal to or sometimes higher than their white peers, but this happily shows a *current* reduction in discrimination against highly educated blacks. It does not diminish the force of the position that race discrimination has been the prime force in producing unequal economic positions.

In assessing the probable causes of black inequality, we repeat once more one of the most important statistics: Until 1978, black college graduates always earned less than white high school graduates. No qualitative differences in black education can explain away this extraordinary difference in results. This is, and will remain, powerful if not clinching proof that puts the lie to the revival of the thesis that race discrimination has not been an important force in causing the lower incomes and unequal poverty rates of blacks.

Discrimination's Power Frustrated: The Success of Other Ethnic Minorities

A convincing explanation of why certain events have happened still falls short of satisfactory proof unless the explanation also accounts for other circumstances that appear to be inconsistent with it. An important fact that we must now consider is that a number of other ethnic groups have suffered intense racial and religious discrimination; yet, in many cases, they have made very significant, if not superior, economic progress.

Let us stop again here to recall an important rule of causation. A force such as racial discrimination may cause an event or effect, but this does not mean that it will do so in every case or even in most cases. Smoking, for instance, is certainly a cause of lung cancer, but only a very small percentage of people who smoke actually contract lung cancer.

How does this consideration apply to the question of racial discrimination? The fact is that forces of race discrimination may produce serious and permanent harm in some settings and not in others. And the fact that race discrimination does not produce inequality in some situations does not in any way eliminate it as the responsible cause in other situations. It is well known, for example, that Japanese-Americans have been the victims of intense discrimination in the United States, yet earn considerably above the national norm—specifically, 33 percent above the national median in 1969. Jewish-Americans, who have experienced even greater race prejudice, earn about 34 percent above the national mean. Before we can determine what these statistics tell us about the effects of race discrimination on economic performance, we must ask whether in certain crucial ways, the experience of the ethnic groups in question is comparable with the black experience. In order to pin down the forces responsible for black inequality, we must show that the experience of other groups subject to racial discrimination but nevertheless doing well is or is not comparable with the black experience. The comparability of the settings in which race discrimination occurred must be confronted before we can deal with the rhetorical query that is so often posed to blacks: "We were able to make it—why not you?" or "Jews made it without affirmative action, why not you?" [31]

Jews in America and in Europe have experienced intense and cruel oppression, yet their economic and professional achievements have been great. Once or twice every century, a significant percentage of the European Jewish community has been annihilated. At many points in history, the structure of Jewish family life in the eastern areas of Europe, which was the ancestral home of so many American Jews, has been utterly shattered. At many times and in many places, there have been systematic and state-sponsored efforts to defile or obliterate Jewish language and culture. In the United States, Jews were despised, reviled, and segregated.

Despite similarities in the treatment of Jews and blacks, the circumstances of Jews and blacks have not been comparable. Jews in the United States were never sold into slavery; they were never declared by the highest court in the land to be of "an inferior order and altogether unfit to associate with the white race, either in social or political relations." Jews in this country were not officially stigmatized by the state; they were never wholly removed from the protection of the law. Unlike blacks, there was never a period when American Jews were ever denied legal control over the rearing and instruction of their children. Jews were never treated as articles of property who could not own capital, sell labor for wages, or make a commercial promise. Jews in America were never prevented, either by official law or by private terrorism, from learning to read or write. Their freedom to vote was never curtailed. Only the most naive person would conclude that the Jewish and black experiences in the United States were even remotely comparable.

Throughout American history, two entirely different forces of racial prejudice have been at work. Negroes were black; Jews were white. The barriers of prejudice were high for Jews, but the barriers were penetrable. Louis Brandeis and Benjamin Cardozo, both Jews, became Justices of the Supreme Court. If Frederick Douglass, a black man of remarkable talents, had chosen a legal career, he could not under any circumstances have won an appointment even to a lower federal judgeship. The great black intellectual W.E.B. DuBois could not have taught at Harvard University under any circumstances, yet a small quota of Jews were eligible for appointments to high academic posts in the most elite universities in the country. Hence, the main difference between the ethnic barriers blocking Jewish progress and those in the path of blacks was the degree of flexibility or penetrability. American society was willing to allow a Jew to be an exception to the general rule of exclusion. No exceptional status was ever granted the black man.

The field of politics further illustrates the profound difference between the racial barrier opposing blacks and Jews. Presidents Theodore and Franklin Roosevelt each appointed one Jewish member to his Cabinet; neither appointed a black. Nor, for most of our history, could any of the nation's politicians or its most liberal-minded citizens have conceived of a black person in the President's Cabinet. Consider, for example, a black man possessing remarkable qualities of intellect, wisdom, and leadership, who in 1937 ultimately became the nation's first black federal judge. Unlike Henry Morgenthau, a Jewish man of modest talents, this man, Judge William Hastie, and other Negroes with comparable qualifications, could never have served in the Cabinet of the President. Numerous Jews have served in the United States Senate, but from the end of Reconstruction to the present there has been only one black senator—Edward Brooke of Massachusetts, first elected in 1966. Until very recently, there had been no black mayors of major cities and no black had ever been elected governor of a state. Jews have been granted considerable acceptance for high political posts, whereas, until recently, blacks had not been accepted at all. Stated another way, the doors to public and private power have been open to Jews. For blacks, they were invariably closed.

Of course, there have been strict barriers to the admission of Jews into the top ranks of the professions and commerce. But there has also been a long tradition of exceptions, quotas, and loopholes. Despite powerful feelings of anti-Semitism prevailing in the major law firms of New York and other large cities, it has been commercially expedient for many generations to have a certain number of Jewish partners, yet until the early 1970s, none had any black partners. The large national accounting firms had a tradition of admitting a Jewish partner or two—but *never* a black partner. To this day, large numbers of engineering, architecture, commercial banking, investment banking, and utilities firms have only partially resisted accepting Jews in management or professional posts. But until very recently, these institutions, without exception, were closed to blacks. In fact, the largest securities auction market in the world, the New York Stock Exchange, had no black member until 1971 when public pressures and publicity forced the transfer of a seat to a black person. The pain from liberty denied is always relative. For blacks the pain was unacceptably intense for anyone seriously seeking a career in business, the professions, and elsewhere in the workplace above the rank of menial. For Jews, on the other hand, the punishments were variable, capable of being endured, and frequently overcome.

There were also profound differences in the content of the race-trait attribution that controlled the processes of decision and admission. Blacks were universally believed to be shiftless, lazy, and incapable of professional achievement. The racial defamations leveled against Jews were equally odious, but often took the form of attributing to the Jewish people an almost supernatural talent for successful commercial activity. Jews were despised for traits held in esteem by our economic system and looked down upon for the very characteristics that presupposed success. Jews were held to be clever and devious, and were therefore expected and allowed to function in roles where such traits were considered appropriate. Blacks, on the other hand, were paralyzed and frozen in place by a set of attributed traits that rigidly classified them as incompetent misfits in America's commercial and industrial society.

The author Susan Jacoby recalls an event that vividly illustrates the essential difference between the black and the Jewish experience:

> "I remember an edgy conversation fifteen years ago between a black girl from Howard University and a Jewish girl from Radcliffe. The Jewish girl was describing the quota system her father overcame to gain admission to law school in 1937: My Dad told me, 'Even though they rigged the game, we just made up our minds to be ten times as good as they were and beat them by their own lousy rules.' The black girl said, 'But what if they don't even let you into the rigged game?' " [32]

Not only was the intensity of racial discrimination of a different order, but the targets of the attack were differently fortified to withstand it. Jews faced ethnic prejudice with the advantage of centuries-old traditions and skills in the learned professions. Transmitted by scholars from generation to generation, Jewish learning was well protected against all efforts to destroy it. Jews, like Asians and many white European ethnic groups, brought with them to the United States a unique armory of collective practices and support institutions. Indigenous to Jewish culture and traditions was a wide assortment of schools, synagogues, hospitals, old-age homes, societies for aiding, feeding, and caring for people of Jewish background. Unlike many black organizations—often created and financed by whites on behalf of blacks—B'nai B'rith, an international organization created to protect Jews from defamation and other harms, was organized, controlled, and financed by Jews.

In commerce, too, there has been a long history of exceptional Jewish strength. Although many Jews, particularly those from Eastern Europe, came to America as impoverished peasants, a great many others came from European families that had successfully practiced competitive capitalism for many centuries. Because of restrictions in religious law, Jewish communities were obliged to produce their own food and clothing to ensure that these items met religious standards. Thus, the Jewish ghetto in Europe had an independent and balanced economy. It was an importer of raw materials and an exporter of manufactured or processed goods. Conversely, prior to the Protestant Reformation, religious strictures prohibiting Christians from lending money at interest virtually awarded Jews an unchallenged monopoly by default; this was to become the banking industry of Europe. The economic power of Jews in finance and banking was considerable. It was no accident that Queen Isabella of Spain turned to Jews to finance the voyage of Columbus, one of the great capitalistic ventures of the fifteenth century.

The renowned Jewish reverence for education afforded the Jewish people the greatest possible protection against the downward mobility that intense racism might otherwise produce. Jews fiercely resisted any attempt to destroy their culture or the transmission of knowledge. Within the Jewish family and community, the standards of education for the male were uniformly rigorous. Jewish groups have long traditions of financing the studies of promising young men. Although the principal purpose of instruction was the preservation of Jewish tradition and religion, education and training produced knowledge and competence in commercial and professional activities. Traditions of excellence in professions and trade provided Jews in

Europe and in the United States with the independence and freedom required to compete successfully for power in discriminatory societies.

In total contrast, blacks in America have always been extremely vulnerable to the intense prejudice they faced. Blacks did not come to America voluntarily but were abducted from their homelands. Instead of bringing traditions and institutions with them, they were brought here by slave traders who made a concerted, and in most cases successful, effort to obliterate the supportive culture of the people they sold into slavery. By law, blacks were not even permitted to investigate their heritage. The languages of Africa were purposefully erased from the black culture in America, and for 200 years, blacks were forbidden to learn to read. In time, inferior and racially segregated schools were meagerly financed by whites who then decided what would be taught to Negroes. As wards of whites, blacks were uniformly instructed in the white vision of natural white supremacy and in the innate and unfortunate inferiority of blacks. All instruction, controlled as it was by whites, taught that whites had superior intelligence, creativity, productivity, and leadership qualities. Black parents, having no control or authority over the academic instruction of their children, watched them grow to venerate white heroes and benefactors, while the accomplishments of Negroes during the Civil and Revolutionary Wars were ignored. A fiercely racist society, which marked all black men as failures, permitted no black role models to light the fires of ambition or learning in the minds of Negroes. Black colleges and trade schools were established, financed, and controlled by whites to channel blacks toward petty economic endeavors and to teach them to set low aspirations for themselves and for their children.

Self-help institutions comparable with those that Jews established or brought with them to this country were never available to Negroes. For most of the history of Negroes in this country, black organizations were discouraged or banned as subversive. Virtually all organizations designed to advance the economic and social status of blacks—including the National Urban League and the National Association for the Advancement of Colored People—were dependent on funding by whites, and for the most part became handmaidens of white economic and political interests. Organizations billed by liberal whites as seedlings of black economic power were no such thing. In the years following the black urban riots of the late 1960s, insignificant tokens of minority capitalism were fostered by the federal government with a white-controlled agenda dedicated to serving and maintaining rather than empowering Negro people. By the late 1970s, a small group of tiny and undercapitalized black banks had emerged, backed usually by large metropolitan banks that wanted to get the monkey of racism off their backs. Yet, by no stretch of the imagination have black people ever owned or controlled any influential instruments of American capitalism. Indeed, to this day, black communities are almost entirely untutored in commerce, finance, accounting, law, and credit. Black neighborhoods in the United States are importers of goods and services; they control no capital or manufacturing activity. They have no jurisdiction over employment except through agencies and development corporations erected and funded by whites. Except through the courts, black communities have no political or economic means of significantly influencing the employment decisions in any major corporation.

The overall conclusion then must be that black people were subjected to far more rigid controls over their persons and aspirations than were American Jews. Only in the case of Negroes was the weight of government power brought to bear in the cause of racial segregation and humiliation. Because of the unique stranglehold of slavery and the only slightly less repressive post-slavery experience of Jim Crow, Negroes, unlike Jews, wholly lacked, and were not permitted to develop, the collective strength and the institutional self-support system necessary to repel the blows that were delivered against them. Nothing in the black experience suggests that blacks should have made their way to equal standing with the Anglo-Saxon majority simply because Jews were successful in doing so.

To be sure, there are other nonwhite minorities who have withstood the repressive force of race prejudice far more successfully than blacks. As early as 1969, Chinese-Americans had attained a median family income of over $10,500, 77 percent higher than that of black families and 8 percent higher than the median family income of whites. Many Chinese, like blacks, were brought to America as railroad workers and coolies where they labored and lived in near-slave status. Japanese-Americans, too, had a superb economic performance. Locked in detention centers during World War II, they now have family earnings in the United States that are about 30 percent above the national white median.[33]

Once more, there were important differences between the Asian-American experience and the black experience. Americans of Asian descent were never bred as chattel for slavery. Asian-Americans were always allowed the right to control their children's development; on rare occasions only were they denied the right to own property or to participate in commerce and elections. Because of major language differences, whites never controlled the schools, minds, spirits, and sense of identity of Asian-American children. Unlike blacks, Asian-Americans were never taught in public schools the essential backwardness and savagery of their race. Asian-Americans were not politically active, but they were never denied access to economic power in the form of running business institutions and other money-oriented endeavors. The racial subordination of Asian-Americans was never an official ideology incorporated in the laws of the state.

Other now successful ethnic groups—for example, Irish-Americans and Italian-Americans—were also objects of the most intense hatred and discrimination in this country. But they, too, were never an uprooted or abducted people; they were never officially removed from the protection of the law; they were never traded as chattel or prevented by law from learning to read or write. They brought their language, institutions, religion, and traditions to America. For the simple reason that their skins were white, white ethnics were able to slip unobtrusively into the mainstream of American society. To compare the experience of these groups with that of blacks shows a complete insensitivity to the unique tragedy of the black experience in the United States.

Small Expectations: How Blacks Obeyed the Orders of a Controlled Marketplace

The inescapable connection between race discrimination and the unequal economic position of blacks leads us now to state the relationship between the codes of race and conventional economic doctrine. Call to mind, first, a fundamental proposition of free-market economics—one often cited by the great contemporary economist Dr. Milton Friedman: "The market tells people what to produce and what not to produce." [34]

This simple axiom of economic behavior has never been seriously challenged or refuted. True, supply creates its own demand, but reciprocally, too, demand creates supply. Certainly, no economist would seriously disagree with Dr. Friedman's proposition. How does this statement apply to the economic control of Negroes in the United States?

In a few simple examples, we may remind the reader how the sanctions of coercive power, as well as the incentives of reward power, dictate behavior in a market economy. The examples are familiar to any student of high school economics. Low prices for beef, for instance, cause people to stop producing beef. If demand dries up for popcorn or horse-drawn carriages, rational people will stop manufacturing them. Prizes and negative sanctions in the market also control career decisions. Thus, the payment of high salaries for the skills and services of graduate masters of business administration will, in time, produce an ample supply of graduate MBAs; low salaries, or no bids at all in the marketplace for MBAs, will, in time, cause people to stop seeking and attaining the degree of MBA.

In precisely the same manner, rewards and penalties of the market may operate selectively in favor of or against the economic development of certain groups. Thus, in a fanciful example, a national boycott—no economic demand at all—against Eskimo refrigerator salespeople will, in time, eliminate any supply there may be of Eskimo refrigerator salespeople. On the other hand—again in a fictitious and exaggerated sense—strong selective demand for Eskimo refrigerator salespeople is likely to produce a large supply of these particular persons. These examples lead to the general statement of economic behavior that over the long term, aggregate demand forces at work in the market determine who, when, and whether people will aspire to, prepare themselves for, and enter specific careers.

In 1973, Senator John C. Stennis of Mississippi declared that if federal employees were to be appointed solely because they were members of the Negro race, it would discourage and prevent qualified white people from bothering to apply. Senator Stennis' logic was impeccable. He was also faithfully stating the laws of economic supply and demand.

True, some people wholly ignore traditional economic incentives. Some people seek training for careers where there are no visible job openings. Others will apply themselves diligently to their school books and deliberately pursue employment where opportunities are limited and the pay is low; still others will work and study for the sheer pleasure of study and work. Since human motivation is complex, the effect of the demand curve on human behavior cannot be mathematically modeled or reliably plotted. But, on the whole, we may say with some confidence that people respond to the rewards and sanctions in the market. They do pretty much what the market tells them will bring financial rewards; above all, they will avoid those activities that they expect will bring them losses or pain.

It is true, too, that people are remarkably adept at shifting behavior in response to changing sources of demand power in the marketplace. At this moment, for example, the demand is very slight for militant blacks skillful at scolding white people who are attending seminars for businessmen on urban problems. Ten years ago, however, there was a great demand for blacks gifted at lambasting the system. On the other hand, the demand today is very strong for black urban affairs officers, particularly those who can convincingly reassure other blacks that Negro people are making good economic progress. In United States politics, the demand is high for blacks who wish to be ambassadors to African nations; the demand is much lower for talented blacks who aspire to influential posts in the State Department or in the White House. Currently, the demand at elite universities for gifted and well-prepared black students is insatiable; a generation ago, there was no demand at all. Happily, a strong demand exists today for well-trained black professionals; and, in accordance with normal expectations, the number of black professionals is rapidly expanding. Happily or unhappily— depending on one's political view—the demand is currently very high for articulate blacks who are willing to travel the country and tell other blacks how liberal policies of the Great Society have "eroded their incentives and made a tragic wreckage of lives." Possibly, the demand is ever higher for black people who, in the name of equal opportunity, convincingly praise the existing power arrangements that put whites on the fast track while reserving the back seat for black people in all affairs of state. In each case, demand finds its supply.

We know, then, with some precision how the powers of penalties and payments operate in the marketplace; we know with fair certainty, too, the ways people respond to these forces. What then has been the probable effect, over the years, of market power on blacks?

Let us now state a number of conclusions as to the effects of a racially biased market demand system, each the predictable effect of the incentives and sanctions of market power as embodied in the laws of supply and demand.

For many generations, the market for labor unmistakably rewarded blacks for being domestic servants, shoeshine boys, and agricultural workers. Reading the market correctly, blacks did precisely what the market told them to do. They did indeed become servants, shoeshine boys, and agricultural workers. In fact, they acquired a virtual monopoly on these jobs.

For a century or more the production orders of the market sent unmistakable wage and price signals to blacks telling them not to bother to produce young people with college diplomas, since the economic opportunities were only marginally worse for black college dropouts. Blacks had no trouble figuring out what the market wanted, and huge numbers of young blacks obeyed the production orders of the market. They did not produce many college-educated people or young people with aspirations to win college diplomas.[35]

For as far back as any living person can remember, blacks by the tens of millions were informed and indoctrinated by standard signals of the marketplace that they could not excel in academic, business, and professional endeavors. Responding once more to the demand levels of the market, black people rarely undertook the efforts to educate or otherwise prepare themselves so as to excel—or perform even moderately well—in these endeavors.

Since the founding of this country, young blacks have been earnestly instructed—by both blacks and whites—that their economic options were limited because Negro people possessed inferior capacities to acquire skills and to develop motivation for achievement. Confirming these signals, the market told blacks that it did not want black investment officers, entrepreneurs, stockbrokers, or security analysts. Once more, blacks figured out what the market wanted and they did precisely what the market told them to do. They produced no people qualified to perform these activities.

The market, which about a century ago erected a universal economic boycott against blacks in most of the skilled blue-collar trades, told blacks in no uncertain terms not to produce or train plumbers, electricians, or construction workers. As expected, blacks once more obeyed the market. None prepared themselves to be plumbers, electricians, or construction workers.

In recent years, particularly, the market has frequently sent price messages posting greater economic rewards for urban blacks pushing drugs, pimping, and snatching purses than for blacks working toward entry and advancement in the lawful trades where whites were preferred. Again, unfortunately, many blacks obeyed the production orders of the market. Of course, these blacks were always at liberty to do otherwise. No one tortured them until they obeyed these messages. But the market forces were powerful and persuasive. When asked what he would do if he awoke one morning to find that there was no show business, the black singer Sammy Davis, Jr. replied, "I'd probably run numbers."

The etiquette of the political marketplace closely followed the rules of the market economy. It sent clear signals to blacks stating that they should not bother to produce politicians, legislators, and judges. The messages were equally clear that blacks need not bother to vote for black politicians, legislators, and judges since their votes would always be nullified by gerrymander or overridden by whites. Once again, most blacks obeyed these production orders of the political marketplace. In very large numbers, they failed to vote. And almost never did they put up black candidates for political office.

The market sent unmistakable signals to blacks that they would be more likely to prosper and make their way if they flattered whites and acted in an obsequious manner toward them. Perceiving what the market wanted, blacks in the past produced a disproportionately large supply of deferential, self-effacing, and uncomplaining people.

The model of supply and demand applied to public and private education. The market posted unambiguous messages to blacks that their children would not be well served by the diligent pursuit of education, nor would they profit from reaching out for careers in which whites would shun and avoid them. Here, too, the market's production orders were followed. Black adults often discouraged their children from seeking advanced education, and as a result black people in the United States produced a very large supply of uneducated, nonprofessional, and poorly motivated people.

Once more in recent years, the market posted special pricing messages for black males. Among these were strong market signals—embodied particularly in the public-assistance system—that they and their families would economically gain if they deserted their families and refrained from taking work. Hearing the market's signals, large numbers of black men— particularly those with little education and limited skills—faithfully obeyed the production orders of the marketplace. In all too many cases, there was far greater profit for blacks in acquiring an addiction to foster care and economic protection than in seeking one's fortune in a closed economy.

Here, then, in the racial orders of the marketplace was market power brought to bear against total market weakness. Here, along the well-marked trails of acceptable career choices, were subordinate and menial positions assumed as an almost reflexive response to the communicated signals of anticipated pain or absence of rewards. Here, in the ubiquitous guideposts of marketplace racial etiquette, were black people softly manipulated by the rewards and tokens promised for compliant behavior. Here, for a whole race of people, economic freedom was surrendered and human confidence collectively shattered by communicated and well-proven assurances of certain failure. It is often said that every American success story starts with a kid who hated to lose. It may be said with equal truth that just as many stories of failure start with the kid who is not permitted to win.

Not only were the economic fortunes of black people controlled by the standard racially coded signals of the private marketplace, but those signals were repeated, nurtured, and amplified by the power of the state. In fact, until very recently, the state never challenged the racial orders of the marketplace or withdrew its own support for the orders.

It is possible, of course, that blacks could have ignored the orders of the marketplace. They could have shrugged off the collective charge of incompetence in employment, trade, and management as simply an unwarranted and unfair defamation. They could have totally disregarded the market signals that said that a well-developed work ethic and a desire for achievement were not desirable traits in black people. They could have refused to buy the charade of black capitalism that channeled them into the bush leagues of American capitalism. If, from the beginning, there had been a base of black economic self-sufficiency and strength, it is conceivable, too, that successive generations of American blacks could have stubbornly ignored all the social insults and sanctions that whites used to enforce the production orders embodied in racial economic codes. Indeed, one can imagine that significant numbers of blacks with tenacious determination might have unceasingly prepared themselves, in the same proportions as whites, for the highest and most prestigious positions. Pressing hard for careers at the top, thousands of other blacks might have trained to become lawyers, physicists, architects, or other professionals despite the fact that such positions, as well as the educational opportunities needed to obtain them, were absolutely closed to the members of their race. Yet, to pursue such a course would have been foolish and irrational behavior. Long before the advent of the behavioral sciences, people had well learned that human beings act sensibly and adopt for themselves, repeat, and transmit to their children the games and strategies that have permitted them to survive. They tend to shy away from activities that cause undue anguish and frustration, or that do not nurture happiness and success.

Racially prejudiced people, strong opponents of black progress, as well as those who take an idealistic view of functioning of free markets cling to the recurrent theme that the economic backwardness of blacks in the United States is due to forces other than the orders of the marketplace. Increasingly, those who express this opinion rest their case on assertions that racial inequality is simply society's retribution for loose living, unwanted offspring, and the failure of blacks to hold their families together. Indeed, there is an expanding body of opinion today that the race prejudgment of inferiority universally applied to a group of people in the United States for over three centuries should not be regarded as a major force that has sapped the ambitions of black people, repressed their desires for education, and left millions of them vocationally disabled. But logic, common sense, empirical evidence, and our knowledge of the actual workings of the marketplace require a different conclusion. As responsive people governed in large part by economic forces, blacks in the United States are today largely a product of market commands issued by whites. Their obedience to the rigid racial orders of the market, as well as the social, educational, and economic effects of obedience in the past, is today their greatest misfortune.

If our conclusion is correct that the lower levels of skills, aspirations, and educational achievement among blacks are, in fact, the direct result of the coercive power of a 200-year market boycott which suspended economic demand for them in the general marketplace for labor and capital, the important question we now ask is what will happen if the tides of economic power are reversed? What will happen to the motivations, skills, and educational achievements of future generations of young blacks if countervailing power is brought to bear to reverse the boycott and create a high and concentrated level of market demand—expressly targeted toward black people—for those skills, motivations, and educational allotments? If, indeed, racially restrictive regulations and discriminatory rules in the marketplace have chilled the desires of large numbers of blacks to become entrepreneurs, capitalists, and holders of institutional power, will a new set of rules generating a special demand for black people in these positions create a new supply of Negro bankers, professionals, industrialists, and venture capitalists?

These questions bring us to the consideration of the important, complex, and highly controversial issue of public policy that is generally known as "reverse discrimination." They lead us also to consideration of certain other countervailing power strategies whose purposes are to lift the selective racial embargoes that whites have imposed on the marketplace as well as to motivate whites to accept, finance, and employ blacks in a much wider range of economic, academic, and professional endeavors.

The Scars of Memory:
Racial Inequality in a
Discrimination-Free Society

"Whether the stone hits the pitcher or the pitcher hits the stone, it's going to be bad for the pitcher."

—*Miguel de Cervantes (1605)*

A RULE OF ORGANIC BEHAVIOR well-known to physicians is that most things get better by themselves. This, too, is an article of faith with traditional economists. If a troubled economic body, like an ailing human body, has the capacity within itself to correct whatever is wrong with it, there is little reason for prescription or intervention from without which might actually delay recovery or cause further complications.

In a society that prizes individual liberty above most other values there is a special reason for insisting that the economic body be allowed to cure itself. Prescriptions for outside intervention in economic affairs always take the form of governmental or private coercion of one sort or another. These commitments of power inevitably restrict someone's liberties. In these circumstances, some outcomes that are achieved may be worth such a price, but if the results we want will happen anyway, by an automatic or evolutionary process, then these coercive measures mean that we are sacrificing our liberties for little or no gain. So, too, in the case of possible cures for racial inequality, our freedoms are hanging in the balance; the use of state power on behalf of blacks—or the employment of collective protest and pressures on their part—is justified only if the body economic does not appear to contain within itself forces sufficient to repair positions that are viewed as unacceptable or unjust.

We have already seen that the principal, although not the sole, cause of black inequality in America has been the force of the collective race-trait prejudgment which, for several centuries, imposed a general quarantine on the economic activities of Negro people. Insofar as this is the case, it is possible that the simple act of removing this force will permit blacks to win economic equality with whites. Indeed, there is abundant precedent among certain other minority groups where equality has been achieved without resorting to collective pressures or outside intervention. Let us make some estimates as to whether this is likely to be the case for blacks in the United States.

Let us suppose that racial discrimination in the United States, like yesterday's toothache, simply goes away. We can then imagine a brand-new state of national consciousness in which people make up their minds about each other's traits and qualifications without regard to skin color. Whites will no longer view the circumstance of having a black face as standing for inferior competence, intelligence, reliability, or diligence. Gone, too, will be the remaining hard core of Americans who still believe that they are somewhat superior beings who, simply because they are white, are entitled to a greater share of wealth, status, privilege, and deference. Nowhere in the United States will people call the police if they see a colored person walking along the street without a delivery uniform. Almost never again will glaring white parents confront and intimidate black school children as they enter a formerly all-white public institution. In no community will public officials prevent blacks from moving into town or keep them off municipal payrolls.

These changes in the way people think would present a truly revolutionary change in the American way of life. But let us assume, nevertheless, that all of this comes about. What are the likely consequences of the suspension of racial prejudgments? Would the astronomically high unemployment rate that plagues black youths eventually drop to a level no higher than the level that prevails for whites? Would the most vigorous and best-qualified black people readily rise to the top in professional and educational attainment? Would the black middle class catch up with the white middle class and swell, as in the case of whites, to become 60 percent or more of the black population? Would new generations of blacks be able to overcome the sense of futility, reduced ambition, low self-image, and other effects that years of race discrimination have established and reinforced? Would blacks, for the first time in our history, begin to form and control capital in their own right? Would a significant portion of the American people's store of personal wealth eventually be acquired by blacks? Would the names of blacks begin to appear at the very top executive ranks of major banking and commercial institutions? If, in this new discrimination-free society, one randomly selected a name from the registry of a state police force, the roster of congressmen, the membership of a plumbers' union, or a list of those holding professorial chairs at a great university, would the chances be about one in nine that the name of the person chosen would be that of a black person?

Since we are assuming a condition of racially neutral public policies and private judgments, we must, for the moment, also assume that our hypothetical post-racist society will not engage in policies of so-called reverse discrimination or race-conscious affirmative action. Government policies requiring the affirmative admission of blacks into white-controlled neighborhoods, schools, business organizations, government institutions, and other centers of power will not be permitted. Statutes, rules, and corporate practices that affirmatively allocate employment, contracts, bidding rights, credit, and business franchises to black people will either be exorcised or permitted to lapse. In a racially neutral society, skin color cannot count either way. However, I shall assume the continued existence of public laws that prohibit people from considering race as such when making economic, professional, and educational selections. In all of these areas, a racially neutral selection system would be enforced by the state.

As we consider what is likely to occur in a post-racist society, we must take into account both the natural forces of open competition, which would tend to produce economic and political parity between blacks and whites, and the inertial forces, which tend to perpetuate present racial inequalities. Let us deal with the latter first.

The Power of Information:
The Strategic Superiority of the White Position

All other things being equal, two individuals of equal ability and competence possess equal degrees of negotiable currency in the form of economic bargaining power. By this I mean that their abilities to influence the selections of others through the standard tokens of work, goods, or innovation should be about the same. But this does not mean that equal success or advancement will necessarily attend equal talent or merit. The results of ability or qualifications will be greatly affected by power conferred by outside circumstances or advantages.

One of the most important of these forces—one which perhaps overwhelms all other variables in its impact on life chances—is relative access to the power of information. In both political and economic competitions, the moderately intelligent person will be able to fare well and make sound decisions if he or she has access to a generous flow of fresh and accurate information. On the other hand, a highly intelligent and gifted person receiving only a narrow flow of dated or limited information will make incorrect or shortsighted decisions and be much more subject to manipulation by others. This, in turn, will produce a much greater likelihood of economic or political failure.

Information, and the accompanying power it confers, is often simply a function of the proximity of people in time or space. A young man growing up in a sturdy working-class setting is likely to know or be known by someone who also knows the person in charge of employing union apprentices. A businessman and his children will, in all likelihood, have social contacts with bankers and other economically influential people and will thus have special access to the valuable economic information that results from this relationship. When the owner of a local hardware store needs temporary summer help in his lawn care department, the children of his friends and neighbors will have this information before any ads are placed in the help-wanted section of the newspaper. The conclusion must be that, wholly apart from any considerations of favoritism or nepotism in the making of economic selections, people who are in close contact with people who have the power to confer economic benefits will have an economic advantage deriving from access to and possession of superior information about those benefits. So we see that the information advantage is a critically important element in the economic power which supplements, and frequently subverts, the traditional personal powers of talent and qualifications.

In the United States, racially segregated living, education, and work patterns have denied blacks access to this sort of free-flowing economic information, except insofar as it applies to the limited economic activities carried on within the black community. Even in a discrimination-free society, history will have left its mark. The isolating effects of segregated neighborhoods, education, and jobs will persist long into the future. Because black teenagers currently have less than their share of parents with valuable contacts in the business community, they will claim less than their share of information about summer jobs offering good prospects for later success. Because young black high school graduates have little or no access (as neighbors or through parental friendships) to shop stewards and to other officials in the strongest unions, these young people will continue to hear about and win less than their proportionate share of apprenticeship and training positions. Because aspiring young black businessmen mature in a society where they are physically isolated from the mainstream of white commerce and business connections, they, too, will have less than their proportionate share of information about marketing and credit opportunities and they, for this reason alone, will continue to be less successful in competition for opportunities and positions where the possession of information is an important economic factor. In other words, even if young blacks were to become as equally qualified as young whites and even if they were treated by society as a whole in a racially neutral fashion in terms of judgments made about their qualifications, they would still start off their careers and operate from an economically handicapped position because of the fact that prior segregation will almost uniformly deny them equal access to the hugely important form of power created by information advantage.

Undoubtedly, much of the white information advantage for young people develops in the nation's tens of thousands of predominantly white public schools. This competitive edge accrues particularly to young people who attend the privileged all-white suburban public schools. Many observers have noted that in the United States today, the most exclusive schools are not private institutions but rather the elite public schools located in affluent and virtually all-white suburbs. It is here that the information advantage of whites is overwhelming. The advantage lies not simply in the high quality of academic instruction, but also in the quality of economic information that flows into these essentially segregated schools which educate the children of whites. Once more, information on employment opportunities tends to be transmitted into those predominantly segregated schools where economically successful white parents send their children. Conversely, information about these students and their abilities tends, in turn, to flow outward into industry and other places of economic opportunity. In this manner, the distribution of economic information is channeled in a racially biased manner even among people who meticulously make their economic selections in a manner that is wholly free of racial bias.

Without affirmatively ordered cross-district school busing—not permitted in a discrimination-free society—these predominantly white schools would maintain their present racial makeup because of the racial composition of the communities they serve. The immense differences in income and wealth among blacks and whites—previously established largely as a result of policies of racial subordination and discrimination—will tend to prevent blacks from "buying their way into" the more enriched neighborhoods and sending their children to the better schools where so much valuable economic information is found and exchanged. Even employers with genuinely racially neutral hiring policies would perpetuate the formerly discriminatory system if, as is likely to be the case, they maintain current policies of recruiting from predominantly white schools where their children, and the children of their friends and current employees, go to school. Once more, then, racially neutral hiring practices superimposed on unequal information handicaps created by past race discrimination are certain to reproduce and ratify existing racial inequalities. Unequal information power forces that result.

Past discrimination will continue to produce many other forms of information advantage for whites in a society that no longer engages in racial discrimination. The fact that the barriers of race are dropped does almost nothing to redistribute or equalize the information inequities produced by prior segregation. For example, a student in a black college—or on any one of the all-black campuses of many of the state universities in the South—will not have white roommates and friends to provide information about job opportunities obtained through parents who influence the employment decisions of large manufacturing companies and of other employers. As long as racially neutral admissions policies are pursued in predominantly white educational institutions, blacks, whose average educational achievement levels and tuition-paying capacities fall far short of whites, will less likely be admitted, and therefore will be less likely to win access to the information network that is an invaluable adjunct to a college education. Because of present segregated patterns of employment, teenage offspring of black parents who belong to traditional black fraternal societies and clubs are not likely to have access through their parents or relatives to valuable employment and entrepreneurial information. Instead, the most current and coveted economic information is much more likely to be claimed by the offspring of whites who belong to white men's clubs, business leagues, and associations whose members are an integral part of the economic mainstream.

Unless public policies are adopted that break up the superior ability of whites to claim economic and professional information, whites and blacks will always be working with different currency and resources no matter how faithful society may be in its pursuit of equal opportunity. Thus, persisting conditions of racial segregation in places that, on the surface, appear to have nothing to do with economic success will continue to handicap blacks. As long as racially segregated living patterns remain unmolested, each generation of blacks will be starting off at a disadvantage, as will the next and the next.

It is true that the economic information power of blacks would increase somewhat if all employment openings and other entrepreneurial and marketing opportunities had to be widely advertised. But even when efforts are made to equalize information power through advertising, the communication process invariably tends to be pro forma. Help-wanted advertisements are placed, but insiders and their friends have the first crack at claiming openings. In fact, in most cases, the best jobs are often filled prior to posting; those who don't know of an opening from some inside source usually stand little chance of competing. Naturally, then, the inside information network belongs to whites because whites hold almost all the inside posts. Even if race discrimination in employment disappears, the white proprietary hold on information power will persist: Whites will feed information to other whites because with very few exceptions they live with other whites and because whites and blacks have very little of the informal leisure-time contacts that are often the basis of preferential recommendations for choice jobs. There are very few opportunities for valuable economic information to reach blacks until that information has been thoroughly combed through and digested by whites.

The information disadvantage that handicaps otherwise well-qualified blacks is simply one aspect of the dual economic system I have referred to earlier. Just as ghetto blacks, particularly, import goods and services from a still-distant mainstream economy controlled by whites, so, too, do blacks import economic information. And by the time they finally get it, the information is picked over, stale, and of relatively little value. No known quantitative techniques measure the continuing disadvantage to blacks that results from their isolation from valuable information. The conclusion that the disadvantage must be very great is simply one that a thoughtful person readily deduces from observation and common sense.

One way to gauge the extent of segregation disadvantage is to look at the racial composition of America's urban public schools. In 1957, 68 percent of New York City's public school population was white. The percentage steadily decreased to 29 percent in 1977. If current trends continue, the percentage of whites will drop to 15 percent by 1987. From 1968 to 1976, Los Angeles lost 37 percent of its white pupils and was only 37 percent white in 1977. During the same period, Chicago lost 40 percent of its whites and was only 25 percent white in 1977; Houston lost 45 percent to become 34 percent white; Detroit lost 61 percent and became 19 percent white; Philadelphia lost 25 percent to become 32 percent white; Miami lost 27 percent and became 41 percent white; Dallas lost 45 percent and became 38 percent white; Cleveland lost 30 percent to become 38 percent white; and Washington, D.C. lost 45 percent of its few white pupils and was left with a minuscule 4 percent white student population in 1977.[1]

The increasing concentration of blacks in large cities may give them some political power, but this advantage comes at the cost of denying them access to the information network of the economic and educational mainstream. In our hypothetical post-racist society, where race-conscious policies to force integration of schools and neighborhoods will not be permitted, blacks will be blocked from access to the most current and profitable information as long as present patterns of segregation persist. And this situation will continue to be exacerbated as long as whites flee from cities and urban plant shutdowns and relocations continue.

It must be recognized that the upward mobility of low-income *whites* is also severely limited by information disadvantage, since whites, in common with blacks, practice "class segregation" in schools, clubs, and choice of friends and neighbors. Indeed, the economic information disadvantage of lower-class whites may, in some respects, be as great as that faced by the great mass of poor blacks. But the question that concerns us here is not whether lower-class whites are handicapped in their efforts to improve their lot, but whether, in a discrimination-free society, blacks as a group have a reasonable chance of overcoming the racial handicaps that enforced separation from society's power has imposed upon them in the past. As long as whites practice class segregation in schools, neighborhoods, clubs, and recreational associations, blacks will be disproportionately burdened by the information disadvantage for the simple reason that, compared with whites, blacks are four times or more likely to be members of lower economic classes. Class discrimination and segregation are said to be a handicap about which blacks can have no legitimate complaint. But this position is indefensible when lower-class status is in large part the result of inferiority imposed by a prior system of racial quarantine or caste.

So concerned have liberals been about the distressing economic and living conditions in many of the nation's black communities that they have almost totally failed to see this fundamental economic handicap which affects almost all blacks, one that has nothing to do with unequal education, motivation, upbringing or job skills. From the standpoint of access to economic information, blacks are simply located in the *wrong* neighborhoods and places. They face the massive additional power disadvantage of attending schools and social gatherings where no important economic or job information penetrates. The churches and fraternal lodges that usefully serve their social needs serve them poorly in economic terms since they provide blacks with none of the information they need to compete on an equal footing in the mainstream economy. The high wall that must be penetrated by blacks is not only the well-known barrier of the race-trait prejudgment, but the well-defended information advantages of whites which the racial proscriptions of our past have firmly set in place.

Born With a Superior Resumé: The White Ladder of Connections

Since the beginning of time, people have quite naturally tended to look after those closest to them. In a very large majority of cases, employers will sooner hire a friend, relative, or neighbor rather than search out a better-qualified stranger. Nepotistic decisions will be made as long as the difference in competence is not dramatically great or critical to the success or failure of the employer's enterprise. A very strong case can be made for the proposition that nepotism is a healthy practice and a necessary element in our economic freedoms. It must be recognized, however, that nepotism is an important and ubiquitous means of gaining and protecting wealth and income advantage in a capitalist society.

Even if race discrimination were suddenly to disappear, there would be nothing to stop people from continuing to make their economic selections on the basis of nepotism or some other form of favoritism. The successful whites who dominate the rosters of bank officials, contracting officers, union officials, and plant foremen will obviously continue to have children, nephews, nieces, brothers, and brothers-in-law who are also white. Trace out the chain of friends, friends of friends, and acquaintances of friends of almost any person holding economic position or power and one will find another white person. As nepotistic favors flow outward and then return home, a closed and all-white system is created. Through this network, the unique position whites have achieved relative to blacks (at least in part because of prior discrimination) will perpetuate itself even if racial discrimination were suddenly eliminated from the social map.

In a racially neutral society, nepotism may be expected to operate at the political end of the economy as well as on the market side. Here, once more, whites who refrain from race discrimination will still fortify their advantages. To the extent that valuable public contracts, zoning variances, public deposits, and franchises are awarded to friends, associates, and members of the party in power, they will be awarded to whites. Holders of high political office will appoint colleagues who will be white, as will be their successors. The political patronage system that rewards friends and supporters will inevitably confer judgeships on whites. For generations to come, the momentum of political incumbency will overwhelmingly favor whites, who in all likelihood will continue to use cronyism to the advantage of other whites. Blacks will claim little of the economic advantage that accrues to the friends and relatives of those holding political power. Although the media have directed a great deal of attention to the black politician, he or she is, in fact, a rare creature. In 1983, whites had a virtual monopoly on political power: They held 99 percent of all elected offices.[2]

Blacks, too, have their families, friends, and fraternal organizations where favoritism and nepotism are practiced. But the potential for black gains from these practices and connections is not significant simply because blacks have so few desirable positions to pass around among themselves. Consider for a moment specific examples of the immense differences in relative power of the two races to favor friends and relatives in economic transactions. The millions of white members of the Knights of Columbus, the Benevolent and Protective Order of Elks, and the Lion's Club are the plant foremen, the shop stewards, and the important hiring officers of our society. In contrast, the black Elks, the black Knights of Pythias, and the black Shriners tend to be the assistant managers, the urban affairs officials, and the deputies in our economic system. Blacks have few fraternal or blood brothers who are heads of unions or who are the personnel officers in corporations or the admissions officers at selective colleges. They almost never have brothers or uncles who own or control a bank or have line authority to lend money within financial institutions. Much more often, the beneficiary of black nepotism will find a marginal job in an inner-city bank or a post office, a minor post in a corporation, or perhaps a government-guaranteed loan to start a fast-food franchise awarded by another black who has recently succeeded to procurement authority in the federal government. Black nepotism is and will be petty nepotism; grand nepotism—often in the form of very large public works contracts, franchises, and natural resource grants—is and will be reserved for whites. And garden-variety nepotism which carries no racial purpose or intent whatsoever will stack the deck in favor of whites.

Seniority: Substituting Incumbency for the Racial Prejudgment

Economic success depends on a lot of things: enterprise, self-discipline, intelligence, political skills, a knack for taking tests, not to mention capacity for hard work. But one of the most important factors in the achievement of economic success is simply that of having held a job for a long period of time. Through contract, custom, or law, the merit principle is often overturned in favor of a single criterion—the length of time a person has held a job. Seniority arrangements are a distinct form of market power which confers job tenure and promotion advantages on people who hold positions and, in turn, restricts the ability of others to compete for those positions and to enter, and move freely within, the economic system. The seniority system is also a key element in the protection of white economic power and advantage. The firefighters' department of the District of Columbia provides a good example. In 1982, the department was 70 percent white in a city that was 70 percent black. Without the intervention of affirmative action, it is certain that, for many years to come, the large majority of promotions in the department will go to whites.

If American society had observed racially neutral selection processes from its beginning, the coercive power of the seniority system would clear people for promotions, or mark them for layoffs, in a racially neutral manner. But seniority rules imposed on the results of centuries of race discrimination simply reinforce black subordination and white economic dominance. If racial discrimination were to disappear overnight, those who have seniority would still enjoy superior incomes, superior chances of promotion, and superior job security in the case of manpower cutbacks.

Consider some examples of how seniority rules successfully defend the positions of whites. The 1975 budget crisis in New York City required layoffs that cost certain departments of the city government as much as 40 percent of their entire black male work force. Prior to 1967, Trans World Airlines had no black pilots, co-pilots, or flight engineers. By 1975, this company had twelve blacks employed in these positions, but this gain was placed in jeopardy by a proposed manpower cutback made strictly according to seniority rules and with no apparent regard to race. Had this cutback gone into effect—fortunately, it did not—it would have eliminated the entire black TWA professional airborne work force. In the course of state budget cutbacks in the fall of 1981, four out of five Maryland state employees receiving layoff notices were women or minorities. In Detroit, where three of every five members of the work force were black, four of every five of the nearly 3,000 city employees laid off in 1980 and 1981 were black people.[3]

The racial impact of seniority rules occurs most visibly in trade unions. Organized labor still controls 25 percent or more of all blue-collar jobs in the United States. These unionized posts are of prime importance to blacks; it is here that many blacks hope to make their first entry into skilled employment. The provisions of the seniority clauses in collective bargaining agreements are not necessarily racially motivated, but they strongly favor whites while blocking the advancement of blacks who, as newcomers to the labor unions, invariably lose out under the "last-hired, first-fired" rule. As a sacrosanct employment right defended by organized labor both in the courts and by threat of strike, seniority rights alone will cause black workers to bear more than their share of reduced workweeks, shift changes, uncom-

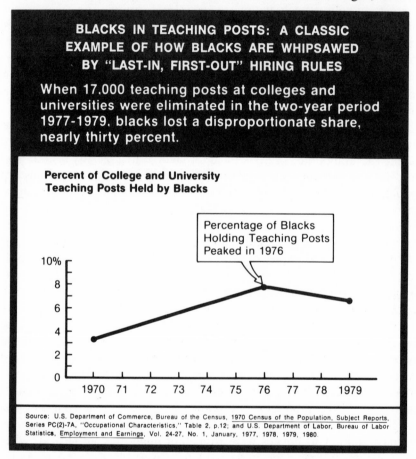

BLACKS IN TEACHING POSTS: A CLASSIC EXAMPLE OF HOW BLACKS ARE WHIPSAWED BY "LAST-IN, FIRST-OUT" HIRING RULES

When 17,000 teaching posts at colleges and universities were eliminated in the two-year period 1977-1979, blacks lost a disproportionate share, nearly thirty percent.

Percent of College and University Teaching Posts Held by Blacks

Percentage of Blacks Holding Teaching Posts Peaked in 1976

Source: U.S. Department of Commerce, Bureau of the Census, 1970 Census of the Population, Subject Reports, Series PC(2)-7A, "Occupational Characteristics," Table 2, p.12; and U.S. Department of Labor, Bureau of Labor Statistics, Employment and Earnings, Vol. 24-27, No. 1, January, 1977, 1978, 1979, 1980.

pensated workdays, and holidays without pay. The familiar assurances published by labor leaders to the effect that seniority rules are necessary to protect black jobs are blatantly hypocritical and are insulting to the intelligence of black people.

Another important way in which seniority and its handmaiden, job tenure, confer most of their benefits on whites is illustrated by selections for positions in the academic world. For a multitude of reasons, blacks urgently need to progress into many more prestigious positions in the academic community. Yet, seniority arrangements in academia impose almost insurmountable obstacles to qualified blacks. In the early 1980s, probably 3 percent or less of the tenured posts at the college and university level were held by blacks. The percentage was much smaller in the smaller elite private institutions. Although blacks may now compete for entry-level appointments as instructors or other nontenured positions, most universities and colleges are currently seriously overtenured. As a result, few new tenured posts will open up for many years and those positions that become available will be claimed mainly by whites who are already on the tenure track. Despite affirmative-action requirements in academic appointments, blacks are, in fact, currently losing ground in their efforts to win significant representation in the teaching profession. The barriers of tenure and job seniority rules are major culprits. Once again, it is sheer nonsense to defend a tenure appointment system as fair and free from racial bias when all the candidates eligible to be chosen for promotions are inside the eligible pool as a result of an educational system that, for two centuries, systematically excluded Negroes from the pool of eligibles without regard to their talents, diligence, or academic promise.

Crony Capitalism: The Racial Effects of Pressure, Pull, and Friends in Court

Superior access to the economic advantages of information, nepotism, and seniority privileges tells only part of the story of why whites hold superior powers to perpetuate their advantage in the competition for wealth, education, and status. A very important feature of the white power advantage lies in the disproportionate ability of whites to make gains and protect wealth through coercive pressures. These pressures which, in theory, are frowned upon in a merit selection system count for a great deal in almost any economic scheme. Coercive power is frequently employed, for example, in "asking for" or, in effect, insisting upon an economic favor. There is power in the form of the disposition of a patron or an influential friend to "go to bat" for another person whose abilities have been overlooked or unfairly— or for that matter, fairly—appraised. There is the huge range of situations where access to jobs, credit, or education is facilitated because of the economic power process that we normally call "pull." In a highly politicized system of admissions such as that which exists in the United States, the process of "pull" or "influence" strongly reinforces the habits of the system to choose whites in preference to equally qualified blacks.

There is no way of measuring or proving the extent to which coercive power enters into or controls the millions of employment and other economic decisions that are made every day. We may best approach the question simply by imagining what is likely to happen in a number of situations. Consider, for example, the tens of thousands of times every day an employer somewhere exerts some coercive pressure on an employee or supplier to do him or a friend an economic favor. The distribution of coercive power is so arranged in our society that the beneficiary of pressure or "pull" will, with overwhelming frequency, be white. If the banker or lender uses his position to induce a homeowner to employ the banker's son, friend, or relative, then the beneficiary of that "pull" will in all likelihood be white. Economic relationships such as landlord-tenant, customer-supplier, banker-borrower, and salesman-purchasing agent are invariably fraught with opportunities to use coercive pressure to win economic advantage for oneself or one's friends. With few exceptions, whites are the current players in these power arrangements. In manipulating them the participants will almost necessarily help other whites, even if there is no racial intent to do so.

In many other transactions that determine economic well-being, the use of political power to create economic advantage will invariably favor whites. Whenever, for example, political pressure is brought to bear on real estate developers or on other commercial people to employ the services of firms owned by town selectmen or their friends, the beneficiaries of this sort of political coercion are bound to be white, because 99 percent of the real estate developers, commercial people, and selectmen in America are white. Whenever a United States senator or state legislator is invited to become a "no investment required" partner in a real estate development project whose success depends on government permission, it is again 99 percent certain that all those who profit from the political relationship will be white. Indeed, one of the most characteristic features of the American economy is the huge network of daily economic transactions that take place between the public and private sectors. Even excluding indictable acts of political corruption, these transactions produce gains counted in billions of dollars each year. Because of the extreme racial disparity in political power allocations, these winnings will almost never go to blacks. As far as one can see into the future the pork-barrel, log-rolling, and other vote-buying appropriations—which even the least cynical among us notices nearly every day in the newspaper—will almost always improve the incomes of whites. It is true that every few years the Senate makes a pass at breaking up the cozy ties between government officials and private contractors, but the old-boy network is durable. It survives even the most dedicated efforts at reform.

It must be recognized, too, that economic favors and political pressures are sometimes effective in winning the admission of students to academic institutions. As long as this is the case, whites, once more, will be the winners, since blacks are almost never counted among the important and well-heeled alumni who have either influence or friends with influence in colleges and graduate schools. In student admissions, most educators turn their backs on these important lapses in the merit system; yet, as long as these procedures exist—under circumstances where there is no countervailing reverse discrimination in admissions that favor blacks—the sub rosa pressures on the educational admissions system will cause blacks to be admitted in lower percentages than whites.

Labor unions are another important instrument of coercive power in the American economy where whites will reinforce their economic position vis-à-vis blacks. Despite some membership losses in recent years, most large unions continue to win income gains significantly exceeding the gains of nonunion labor as well as the general rate of inflation. Because the strongest unions which control the highest-paying jobs are disproportionately white, collective bargaining gains accrue largely to white workers. In fully integrated unions such as the United Automobile Workers, the economic forces of collective bargaining probably benefit the races equally. Also, blacks are the chief beneficiaries of labor power gains made by certain predominantly black municipal and hospital unions. Here, blacks are uniquely powerful. But the fact remains that in the strongest unions, blacks are a far smaller portion of the membership than their percentage of the population would suggest, and many of the unionized jobs they do hold are at the lower end of the skill and wage scales. On the whole, then, in a discrimination-free society, trade union power would contribute importantly to the perpetuation of white economic dominance.

Of course, blacks, to a limited extent, have demonstrated a modest ability to use direct action, protest, and boycotts to win fuller participation in the American economy. But once again, we must remember that these are race-conscious acts of coercion that will not be permitted by the rules we have established for our hypothetical post-racist or discrimination-free society. A white-dominated economy, which permits and protects traditional coercive pressures other than race-conscious pressures, will necessarily fortify the superior white position.

White Is Lucky: On the Racial Distribution of Chance

The Irish have a proverb: "Good luck beats rising early." No matter how determinedly a society keeps opportunities open to all, economic well-being is often determined by incidents that can be attributed to nothing but plain and simple good or bad luck. It follows that any current or historical circumstance that alters the lottery of individual or group chances will greatly change economic outcomes. Almost all views of the prospects for achieving racial equality in the United States overlook the important influence of luck.

We noted earlier how nature's original scheme distributed various forms of power in a remarkably random fashion. Environmental power or risk treated individuals, as well as groups of people, without apparent discrimination. Rain fell on everyone in a democratic fashion. Poisonous snakes and man-eating tigers struck out at people randomly. No particular tribe had a special inborn capacity to find favorable hunting grounds or to survive a drought or a famine. The fortunes and accidents of life were not biased in favor of, or against, any single group.

Today, there are many circumstances in which the ordinary laws of chance still prevail. For example, black and white people have equal chances to win a state lottery or at a Las Vegas roulette table. The poor black dirt farmer in the South faces the same risk as the poor white farmer of having his crop ruined in a hailstorm.

In most cases, however, "luck" is not randomly distributed across the population. Some groups are better fortified against bad luck and better situated to come upon good luck. The same is true of individuals within groups. Consider, for example, a white man and a black man each having a revolutionary idea for a new way to sew buttonholes. The white man is much more likely to be a member of a club, a fraternity, a prestigious social group, and so forth. In the course of making his daily rounds, he happens to run into a wealthy investor who decides to set him up in business. This chance encounter may be regarded as mere "luck," and in a sense, it is. But the entrepreneur was lucky because he was in a position to be lucky. The overwhelming odds are that the black man with the same new product idea will have no such ability to move about in ways that can improve his luck. He may tell his idea to associates every bit as often; he may broadcast his vision to all within earshot, but he is far less likely to have the good luck of his words falling on the ears of anyone in a position to finance or advance the project.

Even if race discrimination disappears, whites will continue to be in a position to claim the luck advantage. Whites are already present in neighborhoods, schools, clubs, and social gatherings where superior luck will make an important contribution to economic and professional success. The pure chance of being offered a good job, an investment opportunity, or an important contact that will open an exciting new career is, and will be, far superior for whites. Unless society is forced to racially integrate across the board through coercive processes, the pure laws of probability will help whites because most economic good luck happens in places, neighborhoods, institutions, and gatherings attended by whites. Whites, too, have the full social mobility needed to improve their luck. They can make random appearances, seize on propitious circumstances, and, in fact, make a career of going to only those clubs, parties, and institutions where one will, in time, encounter successful people, new opportunities, or a friend in court. Because whites have greater mobility in the mainstream society, they are able, so to speak, to put on a suit and go anywhere to improve their luck. And blacks will possess this mobility not as a result of the simple removal of racial bias, but only when the luck disadvantages of prior segregation are removed by opening up every institution not only to access but to actual participation and presence. Social policies, it is said, should not attempt to alter the distribution of economic luck. But restraint in this regard has little to commend it when the luck of the deal has been radically altered in favor of the group that controlled both the deal and the shuffle.

Blacks frequently rail against the so-called five-o'clock shadow, a convenient shorthand term describing the present circumstances in which whites work on a daily basis with blacks but then return in the evening to their all-white neighborhoods and their segregated country clubs, sports events, and dinner engagements. Most blacks consider this sort of social segregation as only a minor irritant, but it is, in fact, a major source of the perpetuation of economic inequality. Even when job and credit opportunities are held open on an equal basis for all, social isolation forecloses to blacks their fair share of the random social encounters that so often can be the "lucky break" that makes the difference between a lackluster career and meteoric success.

For the foreseeable future, too, the incidence of bad luck will work against the life prospects of blacks as long as the vast majority continue to live in neighborhoods where violent crime rates are high, drug addiction rates are ten or more times the national norm, and police protection is substandard. Blacks in the rural South and in northern cities alike face far greater prospects of disease, infant mortality, and lower life expectancies because of poor public sanitation and health care. This increased exposure to environmental bad luck will affect the life chances even of middle-class blacks as long as they live in higher-risk inner-city communities. Indeed, if all blacks turned white tomorrow, they and their children would still face a far greater risk of accident in the workplace and death at an early age simply because of where they live, work, and go to school. The black bad luck disadvantage would be neutralized only by an unacceptably coercive national plan that would enforce racial integration of all facets of social life.

Automation and Robots: Blacks Hold the Vulnerable Jobs

Labor-saving machines—not being human—know nothing about race or creed. Nevertheless, the impact of the computer and robot is as racially biased as if the machine were a blatantly unreconstructed racist. The reason for this is that an economy that increasingly replaces labor with machines will necessarily first displace the repetitive human tasks which are most often performed by people with lower skills. Since blacks make up a disproportionately large part of the unskilled work force, they are necessarily the first to be displaced by automation.

The full effects of automation on employment generally are not known. Wassily Leontief, the Nobel laureate economist, sees the tide of technology moving onward leaving in its wake a vast army of unemployed. Others take the more sanguine view of the great economist Adam Smith that work-saving devices create as many, if not more, jobs as they eliminate. Regardless of which view is correct, there can be little doubt that while machines create jobs for some, they also eliminate the jobs of the unskilled, primarily black work force. For example, the introduction of complex computer-controlled, work-saving servomechanisms usually takes work away from unskilled people—more often blacks—who would otherwise perform the routine and repetitive tasks of which the machine is capable. At the same time, the new technology provides jobs for highly trained individuals—more often whites—who are equipped by education and training to design, repair, program, finance, and operate this equipment.

Agricultural labor, in particular, has a long history of technological unemployment. In the South, particularly, harvesting machines—invariably owned by whites—have made millions of black field workers obsolete. Cotton-dusting airplanes and mechanical crop pickers have replaced hundreds of thousands of black cotton choppers and sharecroppers. Many of these people migrated north, and their children now make up much of the army of the urban poor. The introduction of earth- and material-moving equipment has eliminated the jobs of low-skilled black diggers and porters. For centuries, the tobacco-picking industry resisted the machine. The leaves on a single tobacco plant ripen at different times and require picking by deft hands. In the South, picking tobacco has always been a black man's job. But in 1971, an industrial breakthrough occurred. A four-legged, four-wheeled mechanical defoliator—whose labor-saving economies could pay for it in two years—began moving down the rows of tobacco plants in eastern North Carolina. The machine could strip leaves from the stalk as gently as human hands. In the 1970s, the tobacco harvester was expected to precipitate a farm-to-city migration of 50,000 black field workers and farmers from North Carolina alone. In 1978, California farmers introduced mechanical harvesters for fresh-market tomatoes. The research office of the California legislature estimated that by 1982 nearly 20 percent of the harvest jobs associated with ten major crops would disappear.[4]

On construction sites, steam shovel equipment replaced black ditch-diggers but rarely threatened the jobs of masons, plumbers, and steel erectors, most of whom were unionized and white. Inevitably, direct-reading check-scanners will replace tens of thousands of key punch operators, the vast majority of whom are semiskilled black women working in the major metropolitan banks of New York City, Philadelphia, and Chicago. In short order, fully automated bank tellers will eliminate the need for large numbers of black bank tellers who have only in recent years been entrusted with the handling of currency. In years to come, the introduction of mail-sorting machines will almost certainly eliminate the jobs of tens of thousands of black postal workers. Mechanized robots of all kinds will cut deeply into the very heavy employment of blacks as assembly-line workers and urban transit operators. The introduction of advanced communications techniques and electronic mail will displace a huge number of blacks as messengers and letter carriers. Wherever the robot rears its head, black jobs are directly in the line of fire.

No intelligent person—black or white—would question the need to restore enterprise, growth, and productivity to a flagging American economy. But there is a serious and unequal racial impact in government efforts to stimulate growth through subsidizing the introduction of new technology. For many years, Congress has encouraged the development of mechanization through tax credits and accelerated depreciation allowances. Government grants to universities have been earmarked for agricultural research aimed at the technological replacement of farm labor. In the 1980s, the state

Occupation	Number of Black Workers 1980	Percentage of Total Jobs Held by Blacks—1980	Reason for Projected Decline in Employment
Cleaners and Servants	262,194	53.4%	Mechanized Commercial Cleaning Services
Clothing Ironers	46,056	40.4%	Synthetic Fibers and Automatic Pressers
Farm Laborers	151,255	16.9%	Robot Planters, Sorters, and Harvesters
Packers and Wrappers	115,200	19.2%	Mechanical Sorting and Packaging
Sewers and Stitchers	156,812	19.9%	Automatic Fusing Machines
Postal Service Workers	68,970	24.2%	Electronic Mail and Optical Mail Scanners
Transit Workers	114,920	22.1%	Automatic Transportation Systems
Textile Workers	72,998	22.6%	Computer-Controlled Looms and Knitters
Typists	158,565	15.5%	Electronic Voice Transcribers
Steel Workers	63,802	14.6%	Computerized Production
Automobile Washers	33,970	21.5%	Self-Service Car Washes
Loggers	19,008	19.9%	Automatic Tree Harvesters
Bakers	13,965	10.5%	Continuous Mix Systems
Metal Molders	14,025	25.5%	Automatic Sand Slingers
Assembly-Line Workers	175,864	15.2%	Industrial Robots

Prepared by author from statistics appearing in: U.S. Bureau of Labor Statistics, Employment and Earnings, Vol. 28, No. 1 (January 1981), Tables 23 and 30, pp. 180, 187.

NTO BLACK-HELD JOBS
n the Readily Mechanized Employment
Massive Declines in the Next Decade

Occupation	Number of Black Workers 1980	Percentage of Total Jobs Held by Blacks—1980	Reason for Projected Decline in Employment
Paper Mill Workers	59,860	16.4%	Automatic Continuous Pulp Digestors
Boiler Tenders	9,996	14.7%	Thermostat Control Systems
Library Attendants	20,064	13.2%	Home Computer Access to Library Files
Telephone Operators	49,928	15.8%	Automatic Switching Devices
Stock Clerks	66,092	12.4%	Computerized Storage and Retrieval Systems
Welders	78,888	11.4%	Robotic Arc Welding
Cashiers	167,832	10.8%	Universal Product Code Scanners
File Clerks	69,984	21.6%	Electronic File Retrieval
Tailors and Dressmakers	21,017	15.8%	Computer-Controlled Stitching
Messengers	15,974	16.3%	Telecommunications and Electronic Mail
Fabric Cutters	42,987	16.1%	Computer-Guided Laser Scissors
Gardeners	97,963	16.3%	Robot Lawn Mowers and Sprinklers
Key Punch Operators	57,988	21.8%	Optical Scanners and Readers
Stenographers	9,984	15.6%	Automatic Dictation Machines
Private Mail Carriers	37,950	23.0%	Electronic Mail

of California, with an annual budget allowance in excess of $72 million, developed, through its state university system, an array of labor-saving harvesting machines that require only a small fraction of the manpower previously used to harvest by hand.[5] As the nation moved into the 1980s, supply-side efforts in the form of tax credits and special depreciation allowances were granted by the federal government to industry to stimulate the modernization of factories and to "reindustrialize" a capital-deficient American economy. Once more, blacks, as the weakest economic group, will be most profoundly affected by the elimination of the jobs that robots and other work-saving machines can readily perform.

It has often been observed that automation provides benefits as well as disadvantages for blacks. This thesis, particularly, has been the focal point of the exhortations of conservative economists to persuade blacks to give unqualified support to reindustrialization efforts. Insofar as technology, in the words of Edward C. Banfield, "enables unskilled workers to do things formerly done by more skilled workers," it may actually help blacks. But whether or not blacks actually gain this benefit is, to say the least, open to question. It appears more likely that new jobs created by automation will be first claimed by whites with greater skill, work experience, and connections. To the extent that blacks move up and claim the jobs formerly held by whites, automation may indeed contribute to a higher black standard of living. Technology may indeed raise living standards across the board and thus moderate black poverty and improve black incomes. But whites will collect disproportionate advantages since they are best fortified against job displacement. It is market power that counts and whites have it! Thus, the anticipated effect of increased automation should be to leave the black-white income gap intact, or even increase it.[6]

There is no proof whatsoever of the Marxian thesis that blacks in America are capitalism's essential exploited surplus labor pool, which, under the tycoon's ruthless mandate, must shift blacks and other caste menials from one low-paying sector of the economy to another. In fact, both chattel slavery and the later abuses of southern agricultural sharecropping were totally at odds with every respectable form of free-market ideology. But it is unquestionably true that because of their lower skills, blacks as a group are more often displaced not only by seniority's "last-hired, first-fired" rule, but also by the fact that robots and other technological methods can and will be used to perform low-skilled jobs. In any evenhanded competition, blacks lose more jobs to machines and will have to run harder to catch up. The decline of smokestack industries and their replacement by the new form of economic power represented by the miracles of robotics, fiber optics, tele-communications, silicon chips, and computer-aided design and manu-facture are, in fact, the most formidable current threats to the catch-up efforts of black people in the United States.

The severe threat of the microelectronic revolution to black employment does not mean that black people, in the manner of the early nineteenth-century Luddites, should go about the country smashing machinery or otherwise forestalling technological innovations in the hope of saving black jobs. But the special economic vulnerability of black America must be confronted and publicized. Government assurances that free markets driven by robots and computers are the salvation of millions of untrained blacks must be refuted as pure sloganeering, lacking any foundation in logic or fact. Blacks must deal with the threat of automation by promoting aware-ness among blacks generally of precisely how the larger good to society of technological change disproportionately benefits whites. This, in turn, will focus attention on the need for disproportionate efforts on the part of blacks to develop personal skills as well as the economic and political powers necessary to claim a much greater share of the rents—and specialized white-collar employment—that the computers and robots will produce.

The Steamroller of White Property Power

The tides of technology, which swamp some while propelling others forward, have a uniquely harmful impact on the ability of black people to make gains through the strategy of hard work in conventional blue-collar employment. But the forces of automation are only one facet of much broader coercive effects resulting from distribution of holdings of property, wealth, and proprietary positions. Because of the respect accorded property owners in the American scale of values, blacks may not be regarded as the social or economic equals of whites until a significant number of blacks become and are perceived as solid property owners and capitalists. Even if racially discriminatory attitudes were suddenly to cease, Negroes would continue to be regarded as an inferior social class because they are not a propertied class. Of even greater importance is the fact, as noted earlier, that property itself is a major element of economic power. Those who control wealth and capital tend to control allocations of employment, credit, contract awards, investment, and admissions to institutions that are stepping-stones to economic, political, and social gains.

In this regard, across-the-board racial equality cannot come about in America until a significant number of black families establish themselves as formidable property owners with all the collateral powers and prerequisites that wealth confers. Even though some blacks have become wealthy as sports and entertainment superstars, the fact that Negro wealth is largely

---

HUGE WEALTH DIFFERENCES BETWEEN BLACKS AND WHITES POSE AN OVERWHELMING BARRIER THAT IS LIKELY TO KEEP BLACKS AT THE BOTTOM AND ALL BUT ENSURES THEIR REMAINING THERE

In a society where the control of wealth and capital stands for economic and political power, blacks own or control none of the essential ingredients.

- Stocks, bonds and bank accounts held by blacks are less than 0.7 percent of the national total.

- Black-owned or -operated firms account for only two-tenths of one percent of the gross receipts of the nation's businesses.

- Black-owned or -controlled banking resources are only seven-hundredths of one percent of the national total.

- Farmland is one of America's great appreciating assets with a current value in excess of $600 billion. Blacks hold only one-tenth of one percent of the total acreage.

- Blacks own virtually none of the nation's in-ground petroleum and natural gas reserves now estimated to be worth nearly $700 billion.

- Black ownership of single-family homes is valued at only 3.4 percent of the national total of $2.3 trillion.

- Blacks own no significant portion of the nation's office buildings, industrial parks, shopping centers, or other commercial real estate now estimated to have a value over $800 billion.

- Blacks have almost no stake whatsoever in the major communication resources including newspapers, television and radio stations, book publishers and cable television networks.

The source of the data on black ownership of financial assets is the federal Office of Economic Opportunity study as reported by Henry S. Terrell, Journal of Finance, May 1971. Information on black-owned firms is from the U.S. Bureau of the Census, 1977 Survey of Minority Owned Businesses. Black banking assets are documented in the June 1980 issue of Black Enterprise. Data on the value of the nation's farmland are from Current Developments in the Farm Real Estate Market, U.S. Department of Agriculture, 1979. The source for the value of domestic petroleum reserves was the Independent Petroleum Association of America, Washington, D.C. Ownership and values of single-family homes are discussed in Real Estate Status Report, National Association of Realtors, September 19, 1979. The value of commercial real estate is calculated from data in The Statistical Abstract of the United States—1978. The token presence of blacks in the communications industry is discussed in Black Enterprise, July 1980. For a detailed analysis of the wealth holdings of blacks and whites see Chapter Fourteen.

---

traced to such sources and has little or no base in the economic mainstream diminishes, rather than improves, the traditional reputation of the black race as a group of financially insubstantial people.

We have seen that the wealth gap between whites and blacks is truly astronomical in proportion. Yet, we must ask, what are the chances of blacks closing the wealth gap in a discrimination-free society? What are the chances, too, of blacks taking control of a significant element of corporate capital and using this position to bootstrap further economic gains?

We like to think of the United States as a pure meritocracy in which people with starch and drive rise to the top, largely unaided or unhandicapped by family or class background. Unfortunately, this image of American society is only partially true. Although a considerable amount of interclass mobility is possible, family wealth has a powerful influence on the economic well-being of the next generation. The offspring of affluent and upper-middle-class parents have an easier time getting jobs, an easier time passing standardized admissions tests, an easier time acquiring skills and training, an easier time starting up new businesses, and an easier time securing venture capital and borrowing money. Millions of relatively affluent whites run family-owned businesses handed down from one generation to the next. Some of these families are very wealthy; others have less impressive wealth. But the important point is that most of them have been very successful in keeping important company jobs—as well as wealth—in the family. Many large companies come to mind where the job opportunities of the founders' grandchildren have been assured: Ford Motor Company, McGraw-Hill, Anheuser-Busch, and the Hearst Corporation, to name only a few out of many thousands. In 1981, the chairman of the giant E.I. du Pont de Nemours Company was a great-great-great-grandson of the founder of the du Pont Company. Literally, millions of smaller family-controlled white enterprises are run on the principle of keeping key positions in the family. For the foreseeable future, young blacks will have little chance to move into a successful family business for the simple reason that there are and will be very few of them to move into. Even if race discrimination were to vanish from the face of the earth, black families—unlike millions of whites—will not be in a position to use family business advantages to fortify themselves against economic adversity or as a base to build further wealth and power.

This is not to call into question the practice of taking care of one's own by handing down to them the fruits of one's own labor. Being able to do so is, after all, one of the primary motivating ingredients in a great many successful careers. The point, though, is to take measure of the tremendous headwinds blacks face because of this freedom that we properly protect. Whites hold almost all wealth in America and have thereby provided their heirs, counted in the many millions of people, with spendable wealth as well as job security derived directly from the ownership of capital by their parents. Blacks have almost no wealth and, as a result, have almost no ability to pass on this form of job security and economic self-sufficiency or advantage to future generations.

As the barriers of race discrimination disappear, what are the chances that blacks will ultimately achieve a propertied status comparable to that of whites? With race prejudgment gone, one might expect normal competitive forces eventually to shatter white monopoly control over the means of production and to redistribute these instruments of economic power along nonracial lines. We might expect, too, that as schools of business continue to be open to blacks, black graduates will, in time, find their way into the high corporate posts that control industrial wealth. Freed from the chains of racism and fired with the ambition for material success, blacks could be expected to organize new banks, insurance companies, and high-technology enterprises. In time, too, the great and unequal fortunes held almost exclusively by whites would be reduced by estate tax levies as well as by the inevitable tendency of some sons and grandsons to dissipate their inherited fortunes. This is at least the outcome posited by the thesis of pure competition.

What makes such a scenario unrealistic, however, is the fact that the American economy is not nearly as open and fluid as it was in the past. In the nineteenth century, a poor immigrant boy from Scotland, Andrew Carnegie, assembled the largest steel manufacturing enterprise in the world. He was able to do so because he lived in a frontier society where no steel industry existed. In California in 1928, an Italian immigrant, A.P. Giannini, founded the Bank of America, which was to become the largest and most influential financial institution in the free world. The American banking industry was in its infancy at the time, and California was a frontier state. Irish immigrants such as the Bradys and the Kennedys built great fortunes in copper mining and real estate when much of the West was relatively undeveloped. All of America was wide open to frontier opportunity when the young immigrant Thomas Mellon was brought by his father from northern Ireland to Pittsburgh, where he prospered as a banker during the spectacular period of economic growth that followed the Civil War. When the United States was a frontier society, there was no shortage of immigrants to exploit and lay claim to the resources of an empty continent. But during these years, blacks were either legal chattels or labored under the rules of Jim Crow. The only immigrants who were permitted to stake out these claims were white.

Today, the open opportunities of a frontier society no longer exist, except in a few relatively specialized new fields such as computer technology. Most of the natural wealth of the United States has already been claimed. Major oil fields, for example, are either already in the hands of whites or will be discovered in the next decade by large oil companies or by well-financed individuals who, in almost all instances, will be white. Even if race discrimination were to wholly disappear from the United States, black people have no prospect of organizing an oil exploration or production company with even one-ten thousandth the resources of any of the major petroleum companies or of the great individual wildcatters of our time. Unless the government were preferentially to set aside public lands for the development of mineral interests by minorities—a policy not permitted in a color-blind society—it is inconceivable that, in terms of ownership of mineral resources, blacks could catch up, given the profoundly inferior position of their present holdings. It is too late in the economic history of the United States to conceive of significant amounts of increasingly scarce natural resources being discovered or developed by black capital or black entrepreneurs.

Gone, too, are most of the prospects for creation of private wealth through the award of government-issued or -created monopolies. Thousands of television and radio broadcasting franchises—in the twenty largest cities alone, worth many billions of dollars—have been issued exclusively to whites over the past fifty years. These valuable grants were issued without charge at a time when discriminatory government policies systematically excluded blacks from competing for these awards. Generations ago, when blacks were still agrarian peasants in the South and were separated by law or custom from equal access to education, employment, and capital, whites staked out the huge railroad land grants, electric and gas utility monopolies, and licenses to operate domestic airline routes and interstate trucking franchises. Whites now hold hundreds of billions of dollars of wealth accumulated from these public sources. Blacks hold no market share whatsoever.

Insofar as a nondiscriminatory society would open the market to black entrepreneurial talent, the racially motivated economic awards of the past would seem to be correctable. But, in fact, the claims have already been made, banked, and distributed. The seeds of racial discrimination have by now become full-grown trees. In the field of government-created wealth, the ordinary forces of competition offer little prospect of blacks ever catching up unless state power is employed to make explicitly race-conscious advantages or property awards to them.

Real Estate Wealth: Blacks Hopelessly Behind

Ownership of real estate has always been a vital index of holdings of both economic and political power. Over 200 years ago, John Adams insightfully made the point: "[T]he balance of power in a society accompanies the balance of property in land." One of the great impediments to the ability of blacks to equalize economic power and position is the huge gap between blacks and whites in the ownership of real estate. In the United States, once abundant and undeveloped land was originally granted almost exclusively to whites, beginning when aboriginal title to thousands of square miles was issued by the English Crown. The Land Preemption Act of 1830 provided farmland, at a cost of $1.25 an acre, almost exclusively to white settlers. The United States Homestead Act of 1862 transferred 160 acres, without any charge whatsoever, to each of 1.6 million families, apparently nearly all of them white. During the last century, the great railroad barons extracted from the government title to vast amounts of western land acreage at a time in our history when all of the people who made the awards could not conceive of a black person working even as a pullman porter much less as a railroad entrepreneur.[7]

Most of the small real estate holdings in black hands during the nineteenth century steadily slipped away as a result of partition sales, delinquent tax sales, and various legal maneuvers. It appears that at the turn of the century blacks owned as much as 12 million acres of land, primarily farm property in the South. Yet, the Emergency Land Fund, a nonprofit group seeking to reverse the decline in black-owned farmland, has estimated that in 1978 less than 5 million acres of farmland in the United States remained in black hands. The Land Fund calculated that property was being lost by blacks to whites at the rate of 300,000 acres per year. Even if this downward trend in black land ownership were halted, it is difficult to imagine any competitive force capable of reversing the process and establishing parity between blacks and whites in land ownership. To gauge the magnitude of the gap in the ownership of real estate, consider simply the fact that there are approximately one billion acres of prime farmland in the United States, having a value in 1980 of perhaps $600 billion. In order for blacks to reach parity in the ownership of farmland they would have to raise one-eighth of this sum, or approximately $75 billion. And these figures do not take into account commercial property—probably valued in the trillions—virtually all of which is held by whites; nor do the figures include quality residential real estate, which again is almost exclusively owned by whites. All in all, the massive disparity in real estate holdings—the great fortress of economic power in America—may be the most serious impediment to the ability of blacks in a society without racial discrimination to make their way to wealth equality with whites.

In recent years, the outlook for closing the real estate wealth gap between blacks and whites has become bleak indeed. The forecast is particularly grim when we view current trends in home ownership. Economic forces at work in recent years—skyrocketing land values, steadily rising construction and mortgage interest costs—have greatly slowed the overall growth in home ownerhsip of Americans generally. But these conditions have dealt a particular blow to the small but emerging class of middle-income blacks. In past years, whites have had an almost exclusive hold on propertied class status, not only because of real estate mortgage credit discrimination but more particularly because very few blacks could earn or raise the sums necessary for down payments on homes. Also, home ownership for whites received an additional boost since whites predominantly earned sufficient incomes to take advantage of federal tax policies that give homeowners unlimited tax deductions for mortgage interest and real estate taxes. But blacks, as the quintessential renters in our society, were not receiving any part of the federal tax favors since, in far more cases than whites, their rents were being used to carry landlord mortgages on real estate owned by whites.

As a result of rapidly escalating prices of houses and unacceptably high mortgage interest rates prevailing in recent years, both young whites and young black families have been essentially frozen out of the home ownership market. But 50 million or more whites already own their homes, often financed by long-standing mortgages written on very favorable terms. Blessed with established equity in homes that in most cases have risen manyfold in value, whites, in very large numbers, are still able to trade up to the ownership of bigger and more expensive homes. Moreover, young whites are often in a position to receive help from parents who stake them to a down payment on a house. Few blacks have the same opportunity. And very few blacks have the basic trading currency in the form of ownership in a home equity. Under economic conditions prevailing in the early 1980s, it appeared that blacks would continue to be the property users and tenants in our society. Higher incomes for some blacks, and the prospective end to race discrimination in mortgage credit, offered little comfort to most blacks since oppressive conditions in housing and mortgage markets, in effect, declared a general moratorium on staking out further claims except for those who had already established their holdings.

Black Entrepreneurship: When the Elephants Compete With Chickens

If blacks, unlike whites before them, have little chance of establishing wealth positions as a result of federal grants, subsidies, tax policies, and real estate ownership participation, what then are the prospects for blacks overcoming the wealth disadvantage by establishing new business enterprises? Despite some recent setbacks in world technological leadership, it continues to be almost impossible to overrate American ingenuity, especially as evidenced by the remarkable ability to produce new wealth. Many of today's largest fortunes are of relatively recent vintage. Since World War II, newcomers such as the Ludwigs, Fribourgs, Lands, Pritzkers, Bechtels, Hewletts, and Newhouses have become stupendously wealthy. Their fabulous success—as well as that of tens of thousands of others building wealth on a somewhat more modest scale—is often held up as an entrepreneurial model for blacks. In a discrimination-free society, why couldn't blacks match these outstanding accomplishments? In theory, they probably could. But in gauging the likelihood of this happening, let us not forget our earlier calculations showing the absolute triviality of black capitalism and how far behind blacks are in the competition for wealth. In 1982, the *combined* sales of the twenty-five largest black businesses were less than the sales of the two hundred fifty-eighth largest industrial corporation in the United States. This suggests that even if blacks established a dozen or more new multi-billion-dollar enterprises every year—a rate much higher than that of whites—in the foreseeable future, a successful minority capitalism strategy could not make even a minor dent in the wealth gap between blacks and whites.

What about the prospect of blacks developing new wealth by exploiting technological advances? In an open society where second-class business status attached to race was removed, blacks could certainly make gains, gains at least relative to where they now stand. But the continuing headwinds are fierce. In a discrimination-free society, the elimination of affirmative action would cut a huge swath in black admissions to superior business schools. And, today, the fact is that most new firms that are developing entrepreneurial wealth by exploiting high technology are headed by young people with superb graduate business training. Without affirmative action and special preferences, few blacks will have the educational credentials to make their competitive way into the large corporations where job positions can be used as springboards to start up new firms.

The venture capital advantage will continue to accrue almost exclusively to whites simply because whites possess virtually all such high-risk capital. Thus, even if blacks stood shoulder to shoulder with whites in technological developments and entrepreneurship, the economic gains resulting from black innovations would accrue disproportionately to whites. One needs hundreds of millions of dollars to exploit a Polaroid or Xerox patent, for example, and today only whites possess the resources necessary to develop such innovations. For example, Dr. Edwin Land, the inventor of the Polaroid camera, today owns only 15 percent of the shares of the company he founded. Land has indeed fared well, but so have other investors, venture capitalists, and bankers, almost invariably white, who have made a greater total profit from his ideas. The black inventor of the 1990 equivalent of instant photography is likely to lay claim to a huge fortune, but his or her wealth is likely to be only a small percentage of the total value of the enterprise; in any capital-intensive effort the bulk of the ownership will go to backers who for the foreseeable future will almost certainly be white. In the early 1980s, large numbers of venture capital funds were doubling their wealth every few years. Under the rule that "them that has gets," the startling increases of wealth taking place in these firms almost always enrich white capital. For obvious economic reasons, the firms that solicit venture investors do a heady business among wealthy whites and don't even bother to call on blacks.

The persistence of inherent racial handicaps in capital formation is confirmed by recent experience. For the past ten years, the world of entrepreneurship has been relatively open to blacks. Young blacks have graduated in large numbers from prestigious business schools. Business credit once closed to them is now available. But there are almost no signs of successful start-ups of potentially important new business enterprises in which blacks play a significant part. In recent years, thousands of new firms have raised huge sums of capital—literally billions of dollars—by selling shares publicly. Yet a careful search fails to disclose any publicly funded new business start-up of any consequence, outside sports and entertainment, in which a black person is the principal entrepreneur.

A strong case can be made, then, that economic power is so aligned in our society that neither the forces of entrepreneurial innovation nor obsolescence—both of which normally take wealth from some and confer it on others—currently works in favor of equalizing the economic status of black people in the United States.

Given the huge wealth shortfall, combined with the formidable obstacles that block new black capital formation and entrepreneurship, the prospects are slight that blacks, emulating immigrant whites before them, will be able to catch up. The libertarian promise that blacks can now bootstrap wealth in the Horatio Alger tradition is completely visionary. And the disadvantage of being admitted at the end of the banquet is even greater if, as may very well be the case in the United States today, the ability of the party as a whole to produce is in decline.

The Unequal Ability to Bankroll Political Power

In the United States today, just as a century ago, political power tends to follow wealth, the ownership of property, and the control of corporate assets. But the relationship is also reciprocal. Political power, once won and held, is readily used to increase economic advantage. The nearly exclusive hold whites enjoy over national, state, and local politics permits them to use noneconomic means to open the economic gap between the races even wider. As noted earlier, as large as the economic gap between the races may be, the black shortfall in political power is even larger. In Congress, blacks have a small fraction of the representation that parity would call for. In the executive branch they have only ceremonial representatives; despite recent black appointments to the bench, judicial power in the hands of Negroes is trivial. On a national basis, only one percent of all elected officials are black. Hence, there is no political base in the United States from which blacks are likely to derive much economic gain.

What of the future? If current trends continue, blacks will not make more than modest political inroads from which concurrent economic gains can be leveraged. There is no black wealth in the country sufficient to finance major election campaigns, and there is no prospect in the foreseeable future for such wealth to develop. Even in a society void of racial prejudice, black politicians—except at the urban level where whites have conceded the inevitability of black political control—are not likely to gain access to the sort of institutional wealth that would be required to make them competitive with serious white major-party candidates. Fourteen loans from two friendly Atlanta banks, totaling $1.5 million, kept Jimmy Carter's campaign alive during the critical spring of 1976. No such "old-boy network" banking credit is, or ever has been, available to blacks. The classic technique of funding campaigns through deficit financing may be a common procedure among whites; it is not a resource black candidates can count on. For the foreseeable future, the financial network of bankers, doctors, lawyers, and corporate executives who support candidates will support white candidates because the network itself is white. And the white old-boy network will continue to collect economic dividends owed by the politicians whom it has sponsored, financed, and, in some cases, put in office.

The skyrocketing costs of elections, which in recent years have spawned a host of political fund-raising techniques, are almost certain to lead to the election of few blacks to political office. The overwhelming majority of institutions that fill the lobbyists' suitcases with cash are, and will remain, white. And the candidates that receive the cash will almost certainly be white. The political stripe or persuasion of the vaunted corporate political action committees that handle hundreds of millions in political contributions may be middle-of-the-road or conservative. But, as long as the roots of American capitalism that feed the PACs are all white, the politicians on the auction block will also be white. This result is not dictated by current racial discrimination or favoritism. It is simply the natural outcome of two centuries of American history during which all holdings of individual and corporate wealth and other power holdings have been concentrated in the hands of white people.

It is comforting to imagine that as America evolves toward a more open society with lowered or no barriers of race discrimination, a condition of economic parity between blacks and whites will ultimately prevail. This, after all, is the result demanded by the theories of freedom and open selection prevailing in the United States. But the outlook in the real world leaves little room for such optimism. The workings of an economy never match pure economic and political theory. The fact is that the forces of economic history have produced certain structural biases in our economic sytem. For example, a long series of events in the United States—particularly the unwillingness of the American people to tolerate balanced budgets—has produced a bias toward inflation. A different set of events—including the unwillingness of the American people to tolerate or accept the commercial offerings of black people—has produced a deep-seated bias against accepting the tender of Negro citizens. Just as the bias toward inflation restricts the development of credit and investment generally, the bias against black people determinedly allocates resources to white people and at the same time restricts the aspirations, growth, and progress of the Negro sector of the economy. Momentum effect mandates inequality even when responsible people act without racial consciousness or bias. It is true that a discrimination-free society will blunt the effects of bias and will confer greatly improved economic opportunities for blacks; but without the backing of reverse discrimination, it is difficult to see where blacks will find sufficient economic or political power to successfully assault—from the profoundly inferior position they now occupy—these stoutly held positions in white territory. Economic and political power recognize the consequences of history and, while proclaiming equal dignity and opportunity for all, will nevertheless favor those who hold the upper hand.

Racial Equality and Interracial Marriage

In many societies that tend to assign inferior economic status to particular ethnic groups, interracial marriage has been a traditional and important means open to immigrant groups to improve their economic circumstances. Daughters of first-generation Irish, German, Polish, and Italian immigrants have frequently married into more affluent families who have been in this country longer. Sons of uneducated peasant migrants to America from Italy or Ireland have made their way into company employment and perhaps married a vice-president's daughter. Cultural and religious traditions as well as class barriers often discourage these marriages, but they have nevertheless occurred in very large numbers. The opportunity of white ethnics to overcome class barriers and to become part of the national melting pot has been a major factor in assisting all European immigrant groups to achieve incomes now equal to or above the national mean. Hispanics in America, too, are being assimilated very fast with resulting reductions in their economic deficit.

The opportunity to moderate economic differences through interracial marriage is rarely open to blacks. At one time or another at least forty states had laws forbidding marriage between blacks and whites. Today, the obstacles to interracial marriage still remain great, mostly in the form of intense social taboos. Unlike Hispanics, blacks are not gaining by melting.

If Americans were ever able to overcome the superstitions of race, widespread intermarriage between the races would undoubtedly produce the final and complete economic solution to black-white economic differences. But even among people who make racially neutral decisions in employment, housing, and admission to educational institutions, interracial marriage is unlikely to occur. Presumably, the disappearance of all vestiges of racial discrimination would produce many more marriages between blacks and whites. But to the extent that class barriers prevent this—and the present class differences between blacks and whites are very great—intermarriage is not likely to act as a significant force in closing the economic gap between blacks and whites.

Education as a Force for Racial Equality

Up to this point, we have identified a number of incumbency advantages that, independent of race discrimination, tend to maintain the superior position of whites and enable them to transmit advantages to their children, their friends and, particularly, to other whites. Let us now consider some of the countervailing forces that may help to narrow the gap between the races. The equalizing force cited most often in discussions of racial inequality is education. What is the likelihood that over a period of time improved educational opportunities for blacks—better schools, more years spent in school, and better training for jobs—will greatly equalize opportunities for acquiring income, wealth, and economic status generally?

Confidence in the magical power of education to level class differences is deeply embedded in the American national ethic. This belief accords with traditional economic theory. One who takes advantage of education tends to improve his or her competence. Competence, economists tell us, improves the marginal productivity of labor and hence increases the statistical probability that it will be employed. Thus, education and training are key elements of economic power. Under this theory, it follows that if the quality of education offered blacks is improved, and blacks steadfastly pursue the instruction offered, they should gradually move up the economic scale toward parity with whites.

But do the facts bear out this theoretically appealing proposition? As we showed in Chapter Eighteen, government statistics show that, while blacks gain from increased education, the marginal dollar value of increased education has not necessarily risen as educational attainments rose. One of the most important empirical and theoretical studies of black economics of our time shows that discrimination against blacks tends in fact to be *greater* if blacks are better educated than they are now.[8]

The fact is that over the past decade the black-white income gap has not narrowed, even though race discrimination has diminished and black educational gains have been significant. During the period 1970 to 1977, young blacks improved their median years of education from 12.2 to 12.6, nearly equaling the white median of 12.8 years. In fact, by 1977 young blacks were completing high school in almost the same percentages as young whites. In addition, the number of blacks who had completed one or more years of college increased 150 percent during the years 1970 to 1977. But black income gains during these same years were disappointing. The incomes of families headed by young blacks ages 25 to 34 in 1969 were only 66 percent of the incomes of comparable white families. By 1978, this same group of black families had incomes only 59 percent of what similarly placed whites earned. Even discounting the inferior quality of education available to most blacks, the educational gains of young Negroes were not producing much in the way of monetary rewards for young blacks generally.[9]

HOW EDUCATION HAS FAILED TO DELIVER EXPECTED ECONOMIC GAINS TO BLACKS

IN 1979:

- Black high school graduates ages 18-24 earned about the same as white youths who attended elementary school only.

- Young blacks ages 22-34 with a high school diploma were 3.5 times as likely to be poor than similar whites.

- Blacks, ages 25-34, with one to three years of college earned about the same as whites of the same age who had graduated from high school but had not gone on to college.

- Blacks between the ages of 25-34 with some college experience were 2.5 times as likely to be unemployed as whites of the same age and educational experience.

- Young blacks from 22 to 34 years of age with some college experience were in poverty 2.8 times as often as their white counterparts.

- Young black high school graduates ages 25-34 were 2.3 times as likely to be unemployed as similar whites.

- Blacks, ages 25-29, with a high school diploma earned less than whites of that age who dropped out of high school.

Source: U.S. Bureau of the Census, Current Population Reports, Series P-60, No. 129, Table 53, p. 220; No. 130, Table 13, p. 52; and the U.S. Bureau of Labor Statistics, Special Labor Force Report, No. 240, Table M, p. A-23.

A persuasive part of the case against education as a reliable force for modifying the disadvantage of race is the fact that greatly improved educational attainments among young blacks are not mitigating their unemployment rates. Since 1950, the percentage of young blacks 25 to 34 completing high school has more than *tripled*. This is a spectacular achievement that has been accomplished in only one generation. Yet the unemployment rate among young blacks is still at least twice the rate among young whites, and the gap has been constant for nearly thirty years. There is no discernible evidence here that more years in school have had a salutary effect on the black-white poverty gap. In 1979, 5.1 percent of white families headed by a person with a high school diploma were living at the poverty level. In contrast, 19.9 percent of similar black families were poor, almost four times as many. For families whose head had one or more years of college in 1979, the black povery rate of 11.8 percent was more than four times the white rate, 2.5 percent. Even at the highest levels of educational attainment, the black poverty rate is four times the white rate—the same ratio that applies to black and white families generally. [10]

Of course, years of school are not as important as the quality of education received. Nevertheless, the huge inroads blacks have made in high school completions and in college attendance should have produced much greater gains in employment rates and other economic measures. The fact that relative to comparable whites, blacks who remain in school have received a smaller economic payoff clearly indicates that schooling is not the panacea it is thought to be. And under no circumstances do the Census statistics support the frequently made statement that blacks with similar schooling do as well as whites.

There is, however, one group for whom education has delivered many of the promised rewards. In 1978, young black male college graduates 25 through 34 attained earnings 93 percent of the earnings of their white peers. This is very strong evidence that a college education now pays off handsomely for young blacks. But other factors have been at work too. Very strong affirmative-action policies, especially on the corporate level, have brought highly educated blacks into good jobs they would not otherwise have held. In fact, large firms have stumbled over one another to place educated young blacks in visible and well-paying entry positions. So much is this the case that it may well be affirmative action rather than improved education that accounts for much of the recent gain. This suspicion is confirmed by the fact that in the past a college education has been a highly disappointing economic resource for black people. Traditionally, in fact, the gap between black and white incomes *widened* the further one went up the scale of educational attainment. Note in this connection, too, that black high school graduates, a group much less frequently the beneficiaries of affirmative-action programs, have lagged badly despite educational gains. The young black male high school graduate still has an unemployment rate three times that of his white counterpart. [11]

To gain some perspective on the widely touted performance of this group of young educated blacks, a few other factors should be noted. The encouraging statistics showing superior earning performance by young college-educated black men refer only to those who are, in fact, employed. For the group as a whole, however, high educational achievement does not seem to have any appreciable effect on relative unemployment rates. For young blacks ages 25 to 34 with some college experience, the unemployment rate in 1978 was 6.8 percent, 2.3 times the rate for whites. This suggests that education may help blacks earn more when they do find jobs but does little to actually help them find jobs or improve their employment security. Only time will tell whether highly educated young blacks are being showcased by corporations at high entry salaries for political, legal, and public relations reasons, or whether they are moving up into stable positions where five to ten years from now they will be earning at, or close to, parity with their white counterparts.[12]

When Education Is a Purchasable Commodity: Blacks Irreducibly Vulnerable

At many points in this book, we have shown how, in economic and political terms, whites enjoy the advantage of incumbency. Whenever blacks take a step forward, whites take two. Whites hold the citadels and passes and are not likely to surrender many of them to blacks. In our society, education must also be viewed in terms of a defended advantage. To the extent education contributes to higher incomes and career attainments, the advantage of education in a post-racist society will be nearly all white.

At the lower levels of schooling, through high school, whites will continue to claim superior public education. Funding of public education on a local rather than a statewide or federal basis means that the more affluent white communities will have much more money for public education than will black communities. Even if race discrimination disappears from every economic and educational activity, white children will be far better prepared for the foreseeable future to claim the jobs with high knowledge requirements which the microcomputer and robot revolution is bound to produce. In the all-black inner-city schools which at least 56 percent of black school children attend, illiteracy is often the norm, and most children read and compute well below grade level. Even in a society free of race discrimination, these conditions are not likely to change for the better because poverty alone, even excluding racial prejudice, will perpetuate this educational disadvantage. True, there are isolated instances where dedicated and innovative teachers and administrators have converted the educational deserts of the inner cities into places where black students get excited about learning and compete successfully with suburban white children for admission to quality colleges. But these are rare events that never occur on a citywide basis. Affluent and middle-class whites will continue to go to advantaged neighborhood schools while the huge mass of poor blacks will continue to go to inferior neighborhood schools. To the extent that education is important in controlling life chances, an educational policy based on the neighborhood school concept is virtually certain to reproduce racial inequality.[13]

If the incumbency advantage favors whites in public education, it becomes truly overwhelming in private education. In the early 1980s, the comprehensive annual fees at the most selective private universities were as high as $13,000, putting the total four-year cost of one person's education at a private institution of the highest quality somewhere in the neighborhood of $52,000. At high-quality state universities, the fees ranged from $3,000 to $5,000 per year. Considering the fact that in 1979 whites in the $50,000-a-year-and-over income bracket outnumbered blacks 84 to 1, it is certain that whites are overwhelmingly better equipped to pay for the costly educational advantages offered by the highest-quality universities.

Scholarship aid programs available at most colleges are not likely to moderate the white advantage. The cost of tuition is only part of the unusually heavy financial burden that low-income students face in going to college. Particularly, the student who plans on a post-secondary education must be able to afford to remain out of the work force for four years, at least as far as full-time work is concerned, and also must support himself or herself, or have access—usually from family sources—to some alternative means of support. White parents are obviously much more likely than black parents to be financially capable of supporting the higher educational pursuits of their children. Thus, to the extent that economic considerations control the ability to pursue higher education, blacks will be significantly underrepresented in the pool of applicants to college and graduate school. Even massive new appropriations for scholarship assistance—a prospect not currently considered by the most affluent private institutions which, in fact, are cutting back on aid and grants—would alter the underlying economic handicaps of low- and middle-income blacks contemplating higher education.

The importance for blacks of winning admission to, and being able to carry the financial load at, the nation's selective institutions cannot be overemphasized. The elite colleges and universities have played an almost mandarin role in our society. They send their graduates on to the best law firms, the best jobs in banking, the most successful medical practices, and the highest levels of the corporate boardroom. If, for example, the post of Justice of the Supreme Court were selected as a premier post of power and prestige in the United States, we find that of the 102 people who have served as Justices, nine attended Princeton and at least twenty-nine—including five of the nine members of the Court in early 1984—at one time went to either Yale or Harvard. The selective colleges and universities are in the most literal sense the preparatory schools for the highest posts in the governmental, corporate, financial, and academic power structures. The prospect of blacks catching up with whites in terms of the ability to find their share of places at the top of the American political and economic system depends to a surprisingly large extent on their ability to meet the demands, financial and otherwise, of these highly ranked educational institutions.[14] Anyone scanning the graduating rosters of some of these colleges and universities in the early 1980s would conclude that these institutions were becoming increasingly populated by white students from affluent suburban communities such as Scarsdale, Greenwich, and Grosse Pointe. Soaring college tuitions alone seem to have dictated this result.

Unequal Incomes and Success on Standardized Tests

Black civil rights groups have correctly identified the standardized admissions test as one of the most formidable barriers preventing blacks from moving up into positions where credentials count. One need not go into either the question of race and intelligence or the question of testing bias to conclude that current testing arrangements greatly favor whites.

The Educational Testing Service in Princeton, New Jersey, has published statistical information showing that, racial considerations aside, family income is the most important determinant of success on standardized tests. Poor people of *all* races score much lower on standardized tests than do students from middle-class or upper-income families. This means that for *economic reasons alone,* blacks as a group will score much lower on standardized tests and will tend to be disproportionately screened out even under admissions and testing processes wholly free of racial bias.[15]

The crushing effect of tests on blacks seeking jobs subject to even low-level competency requirements is revealed in the math and verbal tests recently given by the Pentagon. Black men and women scored an average of 24 percent on tests of developed ability in math and reading compared with an average score of 56 percent for whites. For college-bound students, the disparity in test achievement may be even greater. Of the 9,128 students nationwide whose verbal Scholastic Aptitude Test scores in 1983 were 700 or higher—the highest score being 800—*only sixty-six were black.* [16] Without the benefit of affirmative action or quota allocations of positions to blacks, it is *almost certain* that as long as competency tests are

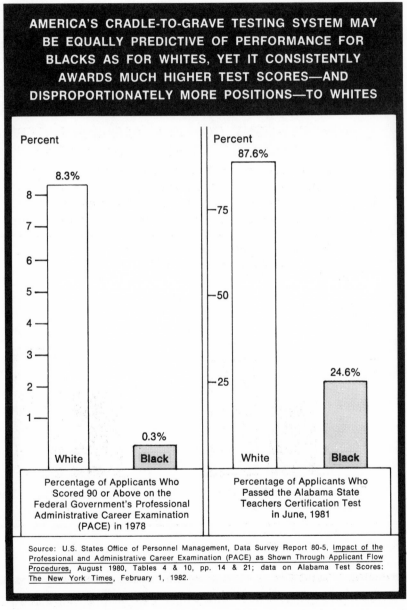

AMERICA'S CRADLE-TO-GRAVE TESTING SYSTEM MAY BE EQUALLY PREDICTIVE OF PERFORMANCE FOR BLACKS AS FOR WHITES, YET IT CONSISTENTLY AWARDS MUCH HIGHER TEST SCORES—AND DISPROPORTIONATELY MORE POSITIONS—TO WHITES

Percent

8.3%

0.3%

White   Black

Percentage of Applicants Who
Scored 90 or Above on the
Federal Government's Professional
Administrative Career Examination
(PACE) in 1978

Percent

87.6%

24.6%

White   Black

Percentage of Applicants Who
Passed the Alabama State
Teachers Certification Test
in June, 1981

Source: U.S. States Office of Personnel Management, Data Survey Report 80-5, Impact of the Professional and Administrative Career Examination (PACE) as Shown Through Applicant Flow Procedures, August 1980, Tables 4 & 10, pp. 14 & 21; data on Alabama Test Scores: The New York Times, February 1, 1982.

used to control admissions to training and jobs, there is little prospect that young blacks will take places pari passu alongside of whites. Under established testing procedures, the *measured* gap between blacks and whites in demonstrating ability in mathematical reasoning, clerical skills, reading comprehension, and vocabulary is profound. There is no racially neutral strategy in sight that is likely to reverse this.

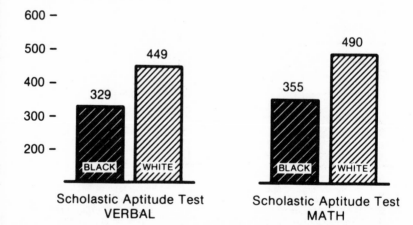

WHEN A SOCIETY RECENTLY EMERGING FROM A SYSTE **HIGHER EDUCATION TO DEPEND ON PERSON/** **EQUALLY MAKING THE OPPORTUNITY FOR HIGHE**

HOW CURRENT COLLEGE ADMISSION TESTING TENDS TO SCREEN OUT BLACKS

On the average, blacks score more than 120 points below whites on standardized tests for college admissions. In fact, in any given year only 10 to 20 percent of blacks will score at or above the white mean.

Mean Scholastic Aptitude Test Scores for College-Bound Students (1976-1977) Grade Scale-200-800

Scholastic Aptitude Test VERBAL — BLACK 329, WHITE 449

Scholastic Aptitude Test MATH — BLACK 355, WHITE 490

Source: Educational Testing Service, Princeton, New Jersey, Statement submitted to U.S. House of Representatives, Subcommittee on Civil Service, May 15, 1979, p.6 and Appendix M.

There is no evidence whatever of a plot on the part of whites to use test scores to screen out black people. But, the undeniable fact is that the racial difference in test scores has the effect of screening out blacks from virtually any activity where competency tests are used. In the past five years, more than thirty states have adopted some sort of minimum competency test (MCT) for public school systems. In 1979, nineteen states required the examinations for high school graduation. Many states use the test for pro-

F RACIAL CASTE PERMITS THE OPPORTUNITY FOR ONOMIC CIRCUMSTANCES, THE SOCIETY IS UCATION DEPENDENT ON RACIAL STATUS

POVERTY STATUS ALONE DENIES EQUAL EDUCATIONAL OPPORTUNITIES TO BLACKS

The poor score lower than the rich and blacks are four times as likely to be poor than are whites.

1973 - 1974

College Board Scores of Students	Mean Family Income of Students in Each Range
750-800	$24,124
700-749	$21,980
650-699	$21,292
600-649	$20,330
550-599	$19,481
500-549	$18,824
450-499	$18,122
400-499	$17,387
350-399	$16,182
300-349	$14,355
250-299	$11,428
200-249	$ 8,639

Source: College Bound Census, 1973-1974, College Entrance Examination Board, Princeton, New Jersey, 1974; U.S. Bureau of the Census, Current Population Reports, Series P-60, No. 120, "Money Income and Poverty Status of Families and Persons in the United States: 1978" (Advance Report), Table 21, p. 33.

motion from junior to senior high school. In Tampa, Florida, where the tests have been under legal challenge by racial minorities, blacks comprised only about 19 percent of the 1979 senior high school class. But 64 percent of the

4,200 students who failed the Tampa examination three times were black. Clearly, if similar results prevail in other testing situations, blacks will be disproportionately barred from graduation and will therefore be less often able to find employment or go on to higher education. In the absence of special education or preparation advantages, the effect of current testing practices would be to cause blacks to fall even further behind. Regardless of whether one approves or disapproves of standardized tests, and without regard to whether or not the tests are fair or unfair, culturally biased or balanced, racially biased or racially neutral, blacks will consistently fall behind in admissions to employment career training and to higher education if the tests continue to be used in their present form.[17]

The testing barrier in a discrimination-free society is almost insurmountable in terms of opening up teaching opportunities for blacks. With considerable truth, licensing examinations for the teaching profession have been characterized as an "academic electric chair" for prospective black teachers. In Florida, only 37 percent of students from the predominantly black Florida A&M University are passing the state's competency test, a passing rate similar to many other black colleges across the South. In California, seven out of ten minority teachers flunked the state's first licensing examination given in 1982. In Arizona, three out of four blacks failed.[18] Even the most ardent supporter of affirmative action in education would not accredit incompetent teachers. So be it! But the notion that noninterventionist government policies will somehow overcome testing barriers and produce blacks in the teaching professions at the same rate as whites is pure nonsense.

Standardized tests for college admissions probably present the most serious testing barrier. An American College Testing Program study reported the following norms for entering freshmen in the fall of 1975:

"Blacks had the lowest average scores of any group with a composite of 12.2 on a scale of 1 to 36. The overall national average was 18.7 for the program's four tests of academic ability—English, mathematics, social studies, and natural sciences. For whites alone, the average was 20.0."[19]

A College Entrance Examination Board study completed in 1977 shows blacks averaging approximately 100 points below the overall average on the verbal part of the Scholastic Aptitude Test and about 115 points lower on the mathematical part. This means that about 85 percent of the black scores were below the average white scores. In 1977, the president of the University of North Carolina publicly stated that "at the Chapel Hill flagship school the average test score for entering blacks was about 250 points below the average white score." Similar racial differences in test scores prevail in major graduate programs. Devastating statistics such as these portend a gloomy future for blacks who lose the advantage of affirmative action and are obliged to compete on an equal footing for admissions to various educational institutions.[20]

IQ tests, which purport to test native intelligence and are widely used to classify children, confirm the huge testing barrier for blacks. A test of 1,800 black children in five southeastern states (where scores generally are about 5 points below the national norm) shows only about one-tenth of the black students scoring at the white mean or better, and approximately 18 percent of all black students scoring in the retarded category with an IQ of 70 or lower. Once again benefits and burdens associated with a class reinforce the positions of those who disproportionately fall into membership in the class. And standardized tests, which sort people by class, defend the white economic advantage without reference to the separate issue of test fairness.[21]

One must not think of standardized tests merely as an occasional hurdle for admission to only some of the coveted places in our society. The fact is that the United States operates a cradle-to-grave testing program starting in kindergarten and going up to the bar examination or graduate school. As *The Economist* of London has put it: "Illinois real estate salesmen, Philadelphia firemen, and Liberian seamen" all fall under the jurisdiction of standardized tests. Testing controls entry to a huge proportion of the American employment market. As long as blacks have significantly lower scores on these tests, the white class advantage will necessarily be fortified.

An additional test barrier is now in place. The widespread practice of taking "cram" courses in order to improve scores on standardized tests delivers a major blow to the potential for greater black admissions to academic institutions. Taking cram courses is a rational practice for test takers. Government studies show that coaching or practice courses for scholastic aptitude tests do in fact improve test results, even though, according to official College Entrance Examination Board doctrine, these tests supposedly measure only natural aptitude rather than learned skills. If the practice of test coaching continues, whites will continue to be in a position to confer additional advantages on themselves because they are in a far superior position to pay tuition at the coaching or preparatory schools. Neither poor blacks nor poor whites have the $400 tuition usually required for enrolling in test coaching courses. Because of disparate poverty rates, blacks lack the financial means to purchase coaching assistance four times or more often than do whites.

America's Latest Discrimination:
The Computer's Children Are White

Possibly the most serious aspect of the educational advantage lies in the privileged access by whites to the powerful economic force represented by the microcomputer. Microcomputers are firmly entrenched in white schools and high-quality computer education, today, is going almost exclusively to young whites. This is a matter of great importance because of the changing nature of job markets. Government statistics show how the U.S. employment economy is rapidly dividing into two tiers. On the top we have the high-skill and highly paid positions mainly connected with computers, robots, telecommunications, and other forms of high technology. On the bottom is the lower tier of mostly dead-end occupations such as janitors, clerk-secretaries, food workers, and other service positions held in very large numbers by blacks. Those young people who are computer literate will have a fair chance of winning employment in the first tier. Youths who for any reason have little understanding of, or proficiency with, computers are likely to be preparing themselves for second-tier positions, including many of the current blue-collar positions which are rapidly disappearing in the United States.

There are many reasons why computer advantage lines up on the side of young whites. Whites predominantly go to the well-funded schools that can afford computers. Blacks in massive numbers go to inner-city and rural schools that can barely afford to purchase textbooks. Even if a particular school can afford computer facilities, there will be far more students competing for computer time in overcrowded and underfunded inner-city schools than will be the case in suburban institutions. In an age where public funds for education are being sharply reduced, public schools are increasingly relying on parental gifts for computer instruction. This necessarily means that black students in the ghetto schools will fall behind.

A 1983 National Science Foundation study showed that youngsters in the 12,000 most affluent public school districts are four times more likely to have access to a computer than students in the 12,000 poorest districts.[22] Moreover, for personal economic reasons alone whites stand a far better chance—two to one or better—of growing up in a family that has sufficient income to buy a microcomputer and the necessary software for use at home.

When we look to find other factors that advance or discourage computer literacy the advantages are almost entirely white. How many black families, for example, are financially able to send their children to the burgeoning computer camps where affluent white youngsters by the thousands gain an important leg up in the competition for jobs in the emerging high-technology economy that is rapidly replacing smokestack America? How do blacks overcome the handicap of the circumstances that not only do affluent school districts have richer budgets for buying computers, but, further, computer company equipment donations are less likely to go to poor schools because they do not represent a rich potential market for subsequent purchases? Proportionately blacks are far more often attending

EVEN IN A SOCIETY THAT NO LONGER PRACTICES RACE DISCRIMINATION, THERE IS A HIGH LIKELIHOOD OF THE EMERGENCE OF A BLACK TECHNOLOGICAL UNDERCLASS

- The wealthy and mostly white public school districts are able to pour money into the purchase of computers while poorer and blacker districts remain without them.

- White families are three to four times as likely to be financially capable of purchasing personal computers and software for instruction in the home.

- White parents by reason of background, education, and employment are far better equipped to help their children obtain access to computer terminals and to prepare and encourage them to learn computer skills.

- White parents are in a much stronger economic position to send their children to computer camps and to pay tuitions for special coaching in computer training and technology.

- In times when limited public funds are available for education, the ghetto and poverty area schools disproportionately attended by blacks go without computers while parents in affluent public school districts are able to take up the slack through private gifts of computer equipment.

- Computer equipment and software publishers commonly make equipment gifts to the affluent and usually white school districts whose students are expected to be the computer users of the next decade.

- Academic admission standards at quality institutions educating students in computer science and technology tend to disproportionately screen out black applicants who because of prior education and background tend to achieve significantly lower test scores.

underfunded public schools. How do they cope with the fact that these schools much more often lack the funds to employ expensive computer teachers who can easily find high-paying computer-related jobs in industry?

In the United States today, parents and offspring alike are terrified at the prospect of confronting the use of a personal computer. But even more terrifying is the prospect of not having the money to buy a personal computer or being reared in a school district that can't afford them. Educationally speaking, whites are poised to take advantage of, or ride out, the computer revolution. Blacks must view it as an oncoming, and terrifying, steamroller.

The suggestion that America is building a technological black underclass is likely to be refuted by illustrations of young blacks who have made their way, and in a few cases are leading the microcomputer revolution. These gains must be put in perspective. Groups are equal only if comparable percentages within the groups are also equal. Thus, if, hypothetically, a few hundred black graduate engineers who design computers are earning the same amount as, or more than, tens of thousands of whites doing the same work, this is no evidence of equality or of the impending equality of the races generally.

This caveat must also be made about the superior economic performance of many young black college graduates. The young group of college-educated blacks in question is very small, consisting of about 200,000 people. Black male college graduates who were under 35 in 1978 made up less than one percent of the total black population; the over 4 million whites in this category are roughly 2.5 percent of the general white population. The success of such a small group of blacks points more to the increasing inequality *within the black community* than to a higher success rate for blacks generally. And the overriding and inescapable fact remains that the vast majority of young blacks simply are not gaining on their white peers as a result of improved educational attainment.[23]

Waiting for the Tooth Fairy: Economic Growth and Racial Equality

If the educational opportunities offered in a society free of race discrimination appear insufficient to help blacks close the gap, let us examine other possible forces within the economy that might help them to catch up. Many blacks rely on the benefits of general economic development and growth, counting on across-the-board improvements in the national standard of living to better their lot. But this expectation is unwarranted. In the past ten years, in fact, the United States economy has not expanded rapidly. After adjustments for inflation are made, it is questionable whether the nation's largest corporations—particularly the large ones disposed to employ blacks—have made any gains in profits at all in recent years.

Looking back over the past decade, government policy has only sporadically pursued the objective of economic expansion. The Federal Reserve

Board has consistently resisted inflationary pressures by holding back on employment growth. The emasculation of the Humphrey-Hawkins full em-

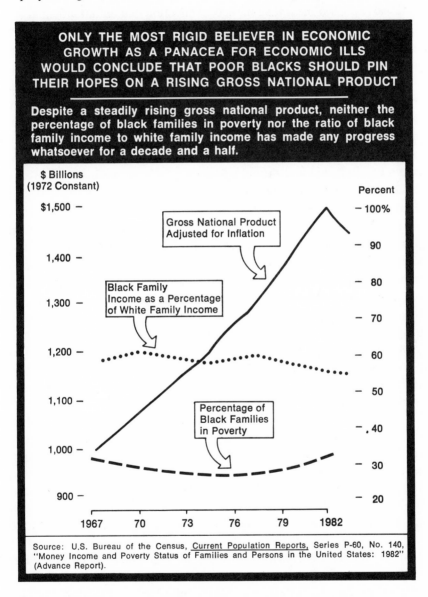

ONLY THE MOST RIGID BELIEVER IN ECONOMIC GROWTH AS A PANACEA FOR ECONOMIC ILLS WOULD CONCLUDE THAT POOR BLACKS SHOULD PIN THEIR HOPES ON A RISING GROSS NATIONAL PRODUCT

Despite a steadily rising gross national product, neither the percentage of black families in poverty nor the ratio of black family income to white family income has made any progress whatsoever for a decade and a half.

$ Billions (1972 Constant)

Percent

Gross National Product Adjusted for Inflation

Black Family Income as a Percentage of White Family Income

Percentage of Black Families in Poverty

Source: U.S. Bureau of the Census, Current Population Reports, Series P-60, No. 140, "Money Income and Poverty Status of Families and Persons in the United States: 1982" (Advance Report).

ployment measure in Congress in 1978 is a fairer statement of the greater national concern about inflation than about full employment. But even if expansionary policies were pursued, there is no indication that they would disproportionately help blacks and thereby reduce the economic gap. The effort to reindustrialize America is not likely to produce new jobs in the traditional industrial heartland of steel production and automobile and tire manufacturing where black employment is highly concentrated.

Does history provide us with any insight as to what economic growth generally is likely to do for blacks? The feelings of suspicion many blacks share about the promised benefits of a strong economy go back prior to the Civil War, when, for many generations, the cotton economy of the South was booming without conferring any economic benefits whatsoever on indentured slaves or emancipated workers. While the history of slavery and of economic Jim Crow tends to produce negative expectations about the chances of blacks to close the economic gap, more recent history does not provide us with much useful evidence.

Between 1960 and 1969, a period of rapidly expanding economic growth and employment, blacks did make very important gains at all levels of the income ladder. During this period, also, black incomes made some gains on white incomes. But the causal connection between these events is blurred because this period in history was also marked by the enactment of anti-discrimination laws and the presence of other intensive race-conscious forces working in favor of blacks. These were years of fair employment legislation, intense civil rights pressures on employers, and affirmative-action initiatives. No doubt, a rapidly growing economy greatly improved the black economic condition generally, but by no means can it be certified with any certainty that the strong demand thrust of the economy in this period was the major force accounting for black gains.

In the earlier World War II period, during the boom years of 1941 to 1946, blacks also made significant economic progress. In fact, during this period, blacks also made some catch-up gains on whites. But, once more, the evidence is confused by the civil rights pressures of the early 1940s, which forced defense plants to open to black employment and produced President Roosevelt's fair employment order No. 8802 of 1941. The black gains during the World War II years appeared to be a combination of intense government pressures *plus* a booming economy.

If we examine the period 1969 to 1975, the results are not encouraging. All economic factors were positive during this six-year period. The official gross national product of the United States, adjusted for inflation, increased from $1.36 trillion to $1.53 trillion. The total number of persons employed in the nation increased from 78 million to 85 million. Corporate profits were, in real terms, up 21 percent. Aggregate overall national wealth, adjusted for inflation, rose from $4.8 trillion to $5.6 trillion. Yet, through-out this period, black unemployment remained constant at twice the white rate. Incomes of black families as a percentage of white family income remained essentially unchanged. The ratio of the black poverty rate to the white poverty rate held about constant or increased slightly above the his-toric 3-to-1 ratio. In other words, general economic growth appeared to have little or no ameliorating effect on the racial economic gap.

THE LONG-TERM ECONOMIC HISTORY OF THE UNITED STATES REFUTES THE PROPOSITION THAT BLACKS GAIN MUCH ON WHITES BY SIMPLY EXPANDING THE ECONOMIC PIE
No Material Occupational Gains by Blacks During a Fifty-Year Period of Great Economic Expansion

Changes in Relative Occupation Status of Black and White Males - 1910-1960

Year	Occupational position of black males relative to white males
1910	.780
1920	.781
1930	.782
1940	.775
1950	.814
1960	.821

Source: Occupational position ratios taken from Stanley H. Masters, Black-White Income Differentials (Academic Press, 1975) p.46, and Dale L. Hiestand, Economic Growth and Employment Opportunities for Minorities (Columbia University Press, New York, 1964) Table XII, p.53.

Some conservative economists favoring market-oriented solutions to black economic problems would contend that affirmative action was hold-ing blacks back and probably nullified the catch-up gains they would have derived from a growing economy. But there is no evidence whatsoever that this is true. In fact, as we show later on in this chapter, the economic settings where affirmative-action policies have prevailed are consistently ones where black economic and professional progress have been most dramatic.

The long-term view suggests that economic growth as such is not suf-ficient to cause blacks to catch up to whites. Professor Gary S. Becker, who some years ago completed pioneering studies in the economics of racial discrimination, charted the occupational progress of blacks relative to whites over a long period of history, from 1910 to 1950. He concluded that the relative occupational position of blacks did not change significantly during these forty years. Using Becker's research as a framework, Professor Dale Heistand studied black progress in seven occupations. He found that black males gained during the high labor demand war years of the 1940s,

THE DUBIOUS SLOGAN THAT A RISING ECONOMIC TIDE LIFTS ALL BOATS

In the United States from 1970 to 1978:
- **Median family income in real terms grew 6.5 percent.**
- **In constant dollars the gross national product grew 34 percent.**
- **Nearly 16 million new jobs were created.**
- **One million people moved out of poverty.**
- **Personal wealth multiplied dramatically.**

Yet during the same period:
- **Black family income as a percentage of whites declined slightly.**
- **The unemployment rate differential between blacks and whites worsened by 28 percent.**
- **141,000 additional black families moved into poverty while a net number of 185,000 white families ceased to be poor.**
- **The labor force participation rate of black males dropped three times as much as the decline for white males.**
- **Joblessness among black teenagers increased from 2.2 times to 2.6 times the rate for white teenagers.**
- **Black wealth already a minuscule percentage of white wealth declined further in relationship to whites.**

Source: U.S. Department of Commerce, Bureau of the Census, Current Population Reports, Series P-60, Nos. 118, 119 and 120, Series P-23, Nos. 38 and 80; and U.S. Department of Labor, Bureau of Labor Statistics, Employment and Earnings, Vol.27, No.1, January, 1980.

but made no material improvement in any other decade from 1910 through 1960. On a scale of 100, the job positions of black males moved only from 78 to 82 during this fifty-year span of time. Yet, during this same fifty-year period, national wealth increased tenfold, the gross national product increased almost fifteenfold from $35 billion to $500 billion, and family income, adjusted for inflation, doubled. One would expect the general economic growth of the country to have had the effect of closing the economic gap between the races. But it didn't.[24] Here is the strongest evidence that blacks who count on economic growth to rescue them are leaning on a weak reed. While it is almost certain that economic growth should improve black incomes in an absolute sense, there is no particular reason why it should be expected to cause the black-white economic gap to close. As long as whites hold all economic and political power—along with a near monopoly position in educational advantages—why should growth in the future do what growth in the past has failed to do?

In recent years, a number of blacks have put their faith in the economic development strategy known as "supply-side economics." Under this strategy, the view is expressed by government economists that economic stimulants such as income tax cuts, reductions in federal spending, reduced government regulation of business, and accelerated depreciation write-offs will draw the rich out of their unproductive tax shelters, encourage business activity, and put people—particularly black people—back to work. If supply-side strategies do revitalize the economy, the policies will undoubtedly help some blacks. But, once more, there is no reason to expect that the policies will help blacks to catch up with whites. The superior economic and political power of whites—not to mention their superior educational prowess and skills—has always placed them in a superior position to claim advantages in a growing economy and to defend these advantages in a sinking one. Economic growth achieved through the "trickle down" techniques of supply-side theorists may well address the issue of helping the overall economic lot of blacks, but it does not address the issue of racial inequality. In past periods of economic growth, blacks have often made significant gains on whites. This occurred during World War II and, once more, during the decade of the 1960s. But each of these periods was also marked by very strong presidential executive orders and congressional legislation blocking race discrimination in industrial employment and, in many cases, mandating the employment of blacks.

It appears, then, that when black leaders look wistfully to economic development and industrial reinvestment as forces for racial progress, they are really counting on two social goods. First, they expect that, in absolute terms, black incomes will rise. This is a reasonable expectation. Second, they assume that general economic growth creates a national milieu within which whites will somehow share prosperity with blacks. This second assumption is questionable. It is certainly true that in times of adversity whites look with a particularly suspicious eye at affirmative action and other initiatives directly aimed at helping blacks often at the expense of whites. But the corollary—that economic growth provides a reliable environment capable of *causing* blacks to catch up with whites—does not appear to be valid. The simple historical fact is that prosperity and economic growth, as such, have not closed the gap. Whenever the catch-up did occur, something else—usually government coercion, race-conscious preferences, or an express redistribution of privileges and power—was added to the recipe.

Evenhanded Tax Policies Favor Whites

It is almost certain, too, that the tax policies used in recent years to energize a supply-side economic growth strategy raise further barriers to efforts of blacks to catch up with whites. The reason for this is that the standard set of tax reforms usually called for by supply-side economists strongly favors the wealthy and other high-income groups which are composed almost exclusively of whites. For example, in 1981, the federal death tax in the United States on wealth transfers was virtually abandoned as to any wealthy taxpayer in the hands of a competent tax lawyer. Capital gains taxes were reduced and if skillful tax advice was available, huge percentages of family and corporate income could be sheltered from taxation. Generous new tax shelters were created by Congress through liberalized investment tax credits and accelerated depreciation deductions. In the early 1980s a huge tax shelter industry had developed in the United States whose business was to help millions of wealthy people—doctors, dentists, corporate executives, and successful small businessmen—avoid taxes.

Whatever the outcome of these tax policies in terms of curbing inflation and stimulating employment and economic growth, several results seemed almost certain. The wealthy, who were almost exclusively white, would keep much more of their wealth and incomes. Since, on a relative basis, blacks had almost no wealth and were only a tiny percentage of the high-income families that benefited from the tax relief skewed toward the wealthy. The logical effect of the tax cuts was to enlarge the after-tax income of whites, thus tending to increase the black-white income gap.

Under the supply-side agenda, important tax relief was established, too, for people with middle-income economic status, where whites outnumbered blacks at least two to one. Tax breaks for the poor, who were disproportionately black in very large percentages, were no relief at all since their tax bill was slight to zero. While some "help-the-rich-first" tax policies may benefit the economy as a whole and while some of these benefits may leak through to those below, it is preposterous to declare that aid to the prosperous will do anything to cause the lowly toilers in our society to *catch up* with the affluent.

In no sense is it accurate to state, as many pejorative editorials contend, that the tax policies of the early 1980s took money from blacks and gave it to whites. But at the same time, it is clear that these policies fortified the

FEDERAL TAX SUBSIDIES OF UPWARDS TO $50 BILLION A YEAR REDOUND PRIMARILY TO THE BENEFIT OF WHITES

Since blacks as a group hold very little individual or corporate wealth, and count very few people with very high incomes or major property holdings, long-standing federal tax subsidies in the form of deductions from taxable income and tax subsidies for capital formation or investment almost exclusively benefit whites and are, therefore, likely to further open up the wealth gap between blacks and whites.

Federal Income Tax Break	1981 Revenue Loss to the U.S. Treasury	Percentage Accruing to Those Earning $30,000 or More
Mortgage interest deductions	$19,602,000,000	74%
State and local tax deductions	17,844,000,000	82
Capital gains deductions	13,231,000,000	82
Charitable deductions	8,836,000,000	84
Property tax deduction	8,679,000,000	75
Consumer credit interest deduction	8,246,000,000	76
Interest on state and local bonds	4,599,000,000	100
Capital gains deferral on home sales	967,000,000	78
Politician contributions deductions	80,000,000	66

Note: In 1981, only 15 percent of all black families had incomes over $30,000 compared with 35 percent of all white families. In 1981 only 0.1 percent of all black families had incomes over $75,000 compared with 2.3 percent of all white families.

Source of figures on tax subsidies and benefit percentages: Congressional Budget Office (1983).

economic position of affluent and predominantly white families. Economists, on the supply side, promised a wonderful unleashing of black enterprise and wealth formation as a result of tax relief for wealthy whites and for successful corporations. But there was no reason given why funds generated from tax savings would be invested in black businesses or, for that matter, in other enterprises that would provide jobs for blacks at a greater rate than they provided jobs for whites. On the contrary, the funds generated by tax savings would more likely be invested in work-saving machinery and other technology where the investment and employment benefits would be disproportionately claimed by whites because of their much stronger foothold in finance as well as professional, technical, and other positions requiring skills and education.

During the period of transition to supply-side economics in the early part of the 1980s, it was to be expected that the government's bread and circus formula would be working overtime. But the supply-side theater in Washington, which portrayed blacks bootstrapping their way to affluence, appeared to be designed more to keep black people from making waves than to float new black entrepreneurs. In 1980, for the first time in many decades, wealthy people in the United States—among whom blacks were very rarely counted—were very close to political power. This was a golden political opportunity for the affluent, and they wasted no time in loading more cargo on their boats under the new banner of tax reform and business deregulation. Even when skin color was not a qualification, very few black people were eligible for invitation to the party.

When Inequality Is in the Pipeline, Competition Is Not Enough

Entering the 1980s, the philosophy of public affairs commonly termed "libertarian" or "neoconservative" dominated the economic affairs of the nation. According to this theory of government, the special, and perhaps only, economic duty of the state was to protect its citizens from any breakdown in competitive markets. The libertarian view insists that if competitors in the marketplace were free from government controls and were permitted to make decisions on the basis of financial self-interest, they would choose the most qualified people, regardless of race. Competitors would not practice racial discrimination because they would be harming themselves both economically and professionally if they allowed racial attitudes to prevent them from choosing the most qualified people to perform economic, professional, and educational tasks. Left alone, it was argued, the marketplace would be self-correcting, self-regulating, and—for disadvantaged groups—self-improving. In a truly open and competitive environment, racial minorities would eventually find their way to parity with the majority. Professor Walter Williams, a black man and an authority on black labor, stated the case succinctly: "Black people do not need any special programs. All they need is for government to get off their backs." [25] How valid is this view? The likely effects of racially neutral and fully competitive labor markets cannot be predicted with any certainty, but history does provide us with some clues.

EQUAL TREATMENT CEASES TO BE EQUAL WHEN UNEQUAL POSITIONS HAVE BEEN CREATED BY DISCRIMINATORY TREATMENT IN THE PAST

The self-righteous and sometimes simple-minded distinctions that freeze racial inequality while society congratulates itself for no longer being racist

- "We protect you against racial bias in admission to institutions of higher learning, but we can't protect you from the fact that the long history of discrimination against your race in public education will almost certainly cause your children to lose out in the competition for admission to places in higher education."

- "We protect you against race discrimination in employment, but we do not protect you if you lose your job as a result of your employer moving to a racially segregated white community, where your position must necessarily be claimed by a white person."

- "We protect you against racial discrimination in suburban housing, but don't ask us to protect you against zoning and density restrictions which, as a result of previous economic discrimination against you, will almost always price members of your race out of these neighborhoods."

- "We protect you against race discrimination in job promotions, but our laws are unable to protect you against seniority rules which, as a result of prior race discrimination, cause almost all promotions to go to whites."

- "We protect your right to take part equally in voting, but we do not protect you against the restrictive effects of voting at-large election systems, which our parents created to ensure that black candidates could not be elected."

- "We protect you against discrimination in the granting of mortgage credit, but we cannot protect you against credit redlining by postal ZIP code, which accomplishes precisely the same result."

- "We protect you against racial segregation in public schools, but we do not protect you against prior decisions to racially segregate neighborhoods where the schools are located, even if, as a result, your children will necessarily go to all black schools."

The barely perceptible gains by blacks during the century following the end of the Civil War are of little value to this inquiry. This was a period marked by closed markets and intense racial discrimination which, as I have shown earlier, appears to explain much of the racial inequality that persists today. The very poor performance of blacks relative to whites during this period proves nothing in terms of the likely effect of the substitution of free markets for racially biased markets.

The tendency of more openly competitive markets to help blacks did show up during the World War II period and again in the late 1950s and early 1960s when pressures were increasing for fairer employment practices. While the positive effects of much less race discrimination in our markets seem to have been spent, there is evidence here that reduction in race discrimination contributes significantly to black progress.

Of particular interest to us is the most recent fourteen-year span during which race discrimination was on the wane and legislation against ethnic bias imposed a considerable degree of racial neutrality on economic selections. As noted earlier, blacks made economic gains during the period 1965 to 1979, but they made no overall progress toward parity with whites. At best the evidence shows intolerably slow progress, and at worst a steady deterioration in comparative economic positions. The poverty gap between the races worsened from a ratio of about 3.5 to 1 in 1965 to over 4 to 1 fourteen years later in 1979. Black family income as a percentage of white family income rose only slightly, from 53.6 percent in 1965 to 56.8 percent in 1979. Particularly discouraging was the steady drop in black-white family income percentage, from a high in 1969 of 61 percent to under 57 percent in 1979. During this same period, racial prejudice in the United States seemed to be dissipating. Yet, despite the new openness, whites were adding dollars of income much faster than were blacks. In 1965, the dollar gap between black and white families was $3,365. By 1979, the dollar gap had increased to $8,876, a sum much greater than the rate of inflation.

Of very great importance is the fact that racially neutral selection choices imposed as a result of job discrimination laws have done nothing to alleviate the critical plight of the black teenager. In fact, the comparative economic situation between young blacks and whites has steadily worsened for many years. In 1954, the nonwhite teenage unemployment rate was 16.5 percent, slightly higher than the 12 percent rate prevailing for white teenagers. By 1980, over 38 percent of black teenagers were looking for work and unable to find it, compared with the white teenage unemployment rate of 15.5 percent. Repealing minimum wage laws would possibly enable unskilled black youths to find employment at low wages. This strategy would no doubt bring some young blacks into low-level employment, but the unemployment differential between black and white teenagers is massive. It is unlikely that a gentle force such as the removal of minimum wages will significantly close the overall gap. Common sense tells us that young blacks

ADVOCATES OF UNREGULATED MARKETS AS A SOLUTION TO THE PROBLEMS OF BLACK INEQUALITY HAVE SHORT MEMORIES OF THE ECONOMIC HISTORY OF THE UNITED STATES

Over the first half of this century, an unregulated market system:

- established skin color as an unwritten but necessary qualification for admission to industrial, white-collar, and executive employment.

- used strikes, violence, and terrorism to evict blacks from positions they previously held in skilled and craft jobs.

- set in place a semifeudal sharecropping system that virtually reinstated the prior system of chattel servitude for the southern Negro.

- organized all-white craft and trade unions with charters, bylaws, or unwritten rules which explicitly denied membership to Negroes.

- established a nationwide banking and credit system that limited investment and business credit to members of the white race, and thereby maintained Negroes as a nonpropertied and nonentrepreneurial class.

- established skin color as an express requirement to participate in competition for government franchises, contract allocations, land grants, and mineral development privileges.

- set up a bonding and insurance system that explicitly denied life insurance, fire insurance, and contract performance bonds to members of the black race.

- established a "whites first" order for hiring under which public utilities, financial corporations, and insurance companies exhausted all available white labor before it employed any members of the black labor force.

- created a nationwide trade association of real estate brokers that adopted a universally observed code of ethics forbidding its members from offering Negroes land, homes, apartments, or commercial property in white neighborhoods.

- barred all Negro businessmen and professionals from the economic and professional benefits of memberships in trade associations, chamber of commerce organizations, rotary clubs, and other gatherings attended by whites.

- provided generous private funding to a racially segregated network of agricultural and trade schools that channelled Negroes onto the lowest rungs of the economic ladder and taught them little except that they were a race of low performers.

are not going to find much comfort in perfectly competitive markets. Unemployed young whites are likely to have better skills than jobless young blacks. As a distinctly economically weaker group, unemployed black youths are not going to claim the disproportionately greater share of jobs that they need in order to begin to catch up with young whites.[26]

While it is clear that blacks need open and racially neutral markets to hold their present position and, perhaps, to make some incremental gains on whites, it appears on the whole that, without the aid of special pressures or intervention, open competition is not likely to carry sufficient force to bridge the gulf. It seems that whatever the state of the economy in future years, whites will continue to move ahead of blacks for the simple reason that they hold far superior positions of economic power and protection. In the vast majority of economic contests, the two racial groups will be bargaining from unequal positions and with different currencies. Such historical data as we have confirm this conclusion.

The Myth That Affirmative Action Hurts Blacks

Many proponents of free markets as the ideal solution to the problem of black economic inequality contend that the main reason blacks have not made economic gains on whites is that the government has not, in fact, adopted racially neutral policies. The position is that open markets have not been allowed to work their benign effects because government power has been used to force affirmative action and racial quotas on employers and other institutions. It is strongly contended that blacks have actually suffered as a result of these affirmative-action policies. This thesis goes against all the evidence. Wherever we do find gains by blacks, there is a close connection between these gains and the presence of strong affirmative action. For example, during the 1970s, Census figures show that black men in managerial positions dramatically increased from 2.8 to 6.9 percent of the total, a 146 percent increase. Clearly, this is due in large part to the fact that affirmative action had been particularly strong in business school admissions and in admissions to management posts in large corporations.[27] Gains in these fields were much less dramatic during the 1960s (1.6 percent to 2.8 percent), a period usually characterized as the "pre-affirmative action era." Additionally, the huge increase during the 1970s of blacks in government posts, in higher education, and in state and local police forces is unmistakably attributable to especially strong affirmative-action policies prevailing in these fields—policies that, in many cases, involved strict ethnic employment quotas ordered by the courts. Further, the great progress that

In no period in history has there been a more profound and sustained fall-off in patterns of economic, social and educational discrimination against blacks than that which has occurred during the past fifteen years (1964-1979); yet if, in the future, black incomes continue to gain on white incomes at the same rate as they did during this fifteen-year period, blacks would not catch up to whites until the year 2244.

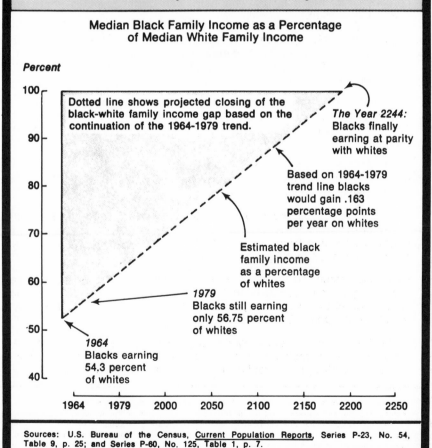

Median Black Family Income as a Percentage
of Median White Family Income

Percent

Dotted line shows projected closing of the black-white family income gap based on the continuation of the 1964-1979 trend.

The Year 2244: Blacks finally earning at parity with whites

Based on 1964-1979 trend line blacks would gain .163 percentage points per year on whites

Estimated black family income as a percentage of whites

1979 Blacks still earning only 56.75 percent of whites

1964 Blacks earning 54.3 percent of whites

Sources: U.S. Bureau of the Census, Current Population Reports, Series P-23, No. 54, Table 9, p. 25; and Series P-60, No. 125, Table 1, p. 7.

How Important Gains by Blacks Are Linked With

- In 1969, President Nixon imposed affirmative-action employment requirements on most building and construction trades. During the 1970s, the percentage of black plumbers and electricians in the construction trades increased 59 and 46 percent, respectively.

- In many U.S. corporations, affirmative-action policies in the recruitment of young black executives began in the early 1970s. During the 1970s, the percentage of black males who held managerial positions increased by nearly 150 percent.

- In the mid 1960s, business and professional organizations implemented affirmative-action programs in various professional occupations. From 1968 to 1980, the percentage of blacks holding professional or technical jobs increased by 63 percent.

- Under court or administrative orders, many city fire departments instituted affirmative-action employment plans during the 1970s. From 1970 to 1980 the percentage of black firemen increased 132 percent from 3.4 to 7.9 percent.

- Beginning in the late 1960s, affirmative-action admission plans were initiated by most of the nation's law schools. From 1970 to 1974, the number of blacks attending law school more than doubled.

- During the 1970s, many law firms established affirmative-action plans in the employment of associates. In that decade the number of black attorneys nearly tripled, and from 1970 to 1979 the percentage of black members of the bar increased by 67 percent.

- A government-mandated affirmative-action program was introduced at Digital Equipment Company in the early 1970s. Thereafter, the minority work force at this company grew from 2.2 percent of the total employment in 1970 to 8.5 percent in 1975.

- In the four years following the enactment of the Voting Rights Act of 1965, black voter registration in the southern states increased by nearly 50 percent. By 1976, the potential black vote had doubled.

Sources: Information on the numbers of black managers, professionals, lawyers, plumbers, electricians, firemen and university faculty is from the U.S. Bureau of the Census, 1970 Census of the Population, "Occupational Characteristics," and the U.S. Bureau of Labor Statistics, Employment and Earnings, January 1977-81. Law school attendance by race was reported in Walter J. Leonard, Black Lawyers (Senna & Shih, 1977). A report on the affirmative action plan at Digital Equipment Company appeared in Newsweek, September 26, 1977. Voter-registration statistics are from the Voter

Strong Role Played by the Federal Government

• Beginning in the late 1960s, Harvard University introduced affirmative-action policies in the admission of black students. During the years 1968 to 1970, the percentage of blacks in the freshman class increased almost three-fold from 3 percent to 8 percent.

• Beginning in 1977, President Carter committed his presidency to strong affirmative-action policies in the appointment of blacks to the federal bench. His appointment of thirty-eight black judges (more than all other Presidents before him combined) tripled the number of blacks serving as federal judges within a period of only four years.

• Prior to 1970, black-owned firms received negligible government contract awards. Preferential contract award policies were instituted by the federal government beginning in the early 1970s. Thereafter, the level of contract awards to black firms rose more than tenfold, from $344 million in 1972 to nearly $4 billion in 1980.

• In the early 1970s, colleges and universities, some threatened by a cut-off of federal funds, adopted affirmative-action plans in faculty hiring. In just six years from 1970 to 1976, the percentage of nonwhite faculty members increased 42 percent.

• In 1961, registered minority apprentices in the skilled craft trades were only 2 percent of the total. After government affirmative-action plans were imposed in the late 1960s, the percentage of black apprentices employed in these trades increased ninefold from 1961 to 1971.

• Only ten blacks served as special agents in the FBI in 1967. After the death of J. Edgar Hoover in 1972, strong affirmative-action measures were instituted to recruit minorities. By 1980, there were 226 black special agents at the FBI, an increase of 2,160 percent.

• At the 1964 Democratic National Convention, only 2.8 percent of the delegates were black. In 1968, the Party made special efforts to recruit black delegates. That year, 6.7 percent of all delegates at the national convention were black. Four years later in 1972, the 452 black delegates comprised close to 15 percent of the entire convention.

Education Project in Atlanta, Georgia. Harvard College's minority enrollment figures were obtained through its Office of Admissions. Data on Carter's black appointments were from the White House Personnel Office. The Office of Management and Budget supplied the information on government contract awards. The FBI personnel information is from Bureau's Office of Public Affairs. The Joint Center for Political Studies in Washington, D.C. compiles the data on black delegate totals.

blacks made in the blue-collar trades—positions largely closed to them in the past—is inconceivable without the presence of intense affirmative-action pressure on recalcitrant labor unions and employers. The number of black federal judges in the country tripled during the years 1977 through 1980. This clearly occurred not as the result of an open and racially neutral selection process, but as a direct consequence of expressly race-conscious judicial appointments made by President Carter.

A compelling case for the effectiveness of affirmative action is made in a study prepared by the Labor Department during the Reagan Administration. The study, which examined hiring practices at 77,098 businesses between 1974 and 1980, found that minority employment grew 20.1 percent at companies covered by affirmative-action requirements, but only 12.3 percent at companies with no government contracts or other special hiring obligations.[28]

There is no evidence whatsoever that affirmative action has hindered rather than helped blacks. On the contrary, the visible gains blacks can point to during the 1970 to 1979 period—when black families' incomes were, on the whole, losing ground compared with whites'—are specifically associated with areas of employment and opportunity where intense affirmative-action policies prevailed. Almost always the big guns of racial quotas have been in place in those situations where major gains have occurred.

In the most fundamental sense, the gloomy prospect that presently exists for achieving racial parity is explainable in terms of unequal power. In the United States, whites fill almost all the upper rungs of the ladders of wealth, power, education, and prestige. Whites control almost all of the franchises, patents, licenses, and monopoly positions that resist normal competitive forces. Whites are invariably the landowners, the high budgetary officials, and the all-powerful lawgivers who allocate wealth, income, advantage, and opportunity. Whites control almost all of the existing institutional sources of public and private power and influence. Whites hold literally 99 percent of the economic and political tickets of admission to positions of status, prestige, and comfort. In almost every grab or competition for power in this country white people win. All of the circumstances of our economic history have combined to produce a social, economic, and political system in which whites are uniquely positioned to make the advantageous decision at the right time. Whites, and essentially only whites, have the financial independence to withstand the harms of making the wrong decision at the wrong time. Under these circumstances, blacks are still likely to make progress with the aid of better education, openly competitive markets, and an expanding economy. But the chances American blacks have of crossing the great economic and political gulf that separates the races are about as good as those that nineteenth-century Zulu warriors armed with assegai spears had of successfully attacking a fortress defended by one of the machine gun regiments of Cecil Rhodes.

Underlying our view of what will happen in a post-racist society is the assumption of the death of racial traditions and taboos by which hundreds of millions of whites in this country have lived for 300 years. But can we really be expected to purge ourselves of the personal and collective racial biases that have persisted for so long? Obedient for centuries to the taboos of race, can we now be counted on to rid ourselves of the subconscious mental orders that are triggered by seeing a black face? Can we banish the instructions that are so deeply ingrained in our psyches that often we are not aware of the extent to which our decisions are based on the racial-trait prejudgment? Is it realistically possible or probable that any legal or ethical injunction calling for evenhanded treatment of blacks is capable of obliterating the ways in which we have made up our minds and conducted our economic affairs through our entire national history? We purport to be a raceless state, but can we truly be or become one when the objective of banishing racial prejudice has been achieved nowhere in the world? Even if one could give positive answers to all of these questions, we must still face the deeper meaning of the conclusions we have drawn about the fate of blacks in a discrimination-free or a post-racist society. The tragic paradox of our time is that a society that tries to become, and may eventually succeed in becoming, open may in fact remain closed because it simply cannot escape its past.

CHAPTER TWENTY

Reverse Discrimination:
The Case for Countervailing Power

> *"[T]o criticize inequality and to desire equality is not, as is sometimes suggested, to cherish the romantic illusion that men are equal in character and intelligence. It is to hold that, while their natural endowments differ profoundly, it is the mark of a civilized society to aim at eliminating such inequalities . . . as have their source, not in individual differences, but in its own organization. . . ."*
>
> —*Richard Henry Tawney*
> Equality *(1931)*

WE HAVE SHOWN THAT a major tenet of liberal wisdom is indeed correct. Blacks in the United States hold their places at the bottom of the economic ladder because whites put them there. In recent years, particularly, the blame for Negro inequality is often placed elsewhere—on defects in the black family; on flaws in the work ethic of the black male; on protective policies of governments. We have examined these and other explanations. But in each case we find an anterior cause. In each instance the trail leads to a central culprit, which is the repressive force of race discrimination or caste.

Under these circumstances, the human mind often turns to thoughts about winning back what was improperly denied, about restoring blacks to positions they might have occupied had the collective power of the white majority not been employed to keep them as social and economic outcasts. But primitive instincts for getting even have been superseded by man's laws of justice. Bringing countervailing power to bear to redress the damage caused by the prior constraints of caste is an appropriate way to address black grievances only if the use of that power may be shown to be both legitimate and just. Within the framework of Western law, redress is feasible but revenge is not; the reordering of positions unfairly won is thinkable but retaliation is not. What, then, is the moral base that blacks must establish if they are to justify the use of private pressure groups, as well as the power of the state, to redress their positions?

In recent years, the question of the enforced preferential treatment of blacks in our society—and the use by them and by others of private pressures as well as state power to achieve that end—has created a tempest of philosophical and legal controversy. In dealing with this issue, it is clear that two great American values are at stake and are in necessary conflict. On the one hand, the principle of equity seems to call for some policies that involve the use of countervailing power: usually enforced affirmative action or reverse discrimination. On the other hand, the principle of individual liberty—together with certain additional considerations of equity—seems to require that such policies be renounced. How can these conflicting values be reconciled?

Champions of the primacy of individual choice often assert uncritically that we make a bad trade whenever we sacrifice liberty for equity. Yet society can hardly function without such trade-offs. Far from being inimical to the American ideology, these compromises are woven into the fabric of our society and are so commonplace that they often go unnoticed or are taken for granted. Would any libertarian object to the standard rule that prohibits the playing of loud music at unreasonable hours? Would any libertarian criticize the action of the mother who takes a cookie from her son and gives it to the younger sister from whom he took it? Yet in both cases, liberty—the freedom to listen to the music or to eat the cookie of one's choice—is restricted in order to do right by others—the neighbors who are entitled to a night's sleep or the sister who deserves a cookie of her own. Unless liberty is tempered by equity, society will quickly degenerate into a jungle, with the only law being the right of the strongest to exercise their liberties as they see fit.

The point about balancing equity and liberty is simply a restatement of our original self-limiting rule about power. Power—the ability to curtail the freedoms of others—tends to lose its strength unless it is perceived as representing or achieving equity. Power that is not backed by a public sense of legitimacy is mere force, a form of strength that people will neither encourage, protect, nor feel a duty to obey. Reverse discrimination as a form of power that restricts liberty of choice is subject to the same rule. No person will for long obey its commands unless its purposes and processes are perceived as legitimate.

State Power Used to Override the Private Codes of Race Subordination

We will first take up the question of why and when principles of equity justify the use of state power to block the liberty of an individual or a group to practice the custom of racial discrimination. We will then move on to the much more difficult question of why private and sometimes state power may be used affirmatively to force people to have transactions with others—to do business with outcast groups, to employ them, or to admit them to certain institutions.

Clearly, one of our most cherished national liberties is the freedom to associate with whomever we please. This freedom of association includes the liberty to choose our friends, neighbors, and associates—as well as the freedom to do business with people of our own choice. In fact, for several centuries in the United States, it was considered a violation of a person's most important freedoms for the state to deny him the liberty to choose his associates in employment, commerce, or trade. What is more, it was also considered an intolerable interference with individual freedom for the state to restrict the individual's right to set the terms of that association or to curb the privilege of withdrawing from the relationship. So sacrosanct in the American tradition was the liberty of contract that for many generations the United States Supreme Court tolerated almost no state or congressional restrictions upon it.

A consequence of the unconditional protection of the liberty of association and contract was, of course, the protection of the *liberty to be racially prejudiced* in one's associations and commercial selections. The general guarantee of freedom to associate with whomever one pleased placed one under no obligation to have fair or rational reasons for these choices. It was simply one's inalienable right to refuse to deal with another because of his black skin or blue eyes or red hair. Traditionally, this freedom to make, and act upon, categorical prejudgments about people was tolerated under the widest range of commercial, professional, and personal circumstances. Whether one was running a personal household, a factory, a union hall, a bowling alley, a barbershop, or a social club, the freedom to be a racial bigot was protected by the state. Expressing this traditional ideal of liberty, the distinguished American economist Milton Friedman has written:

> "I believe strongly that the color of a man's skin or the religion of his parents is, by itself, no reason to treat him differently, that a man should be judged by what he is and what he does and not by these external characteristics. I deplore what seems to me prejudice and narrowness of outlook of those whose tastes differ from mine in this respect and I think

the less of them for it. But in a society based on free discussion, the appropriate recourse is for me to seek to persuade them that their tastes are bad and that they should change their views and their behavior, *not to use coercive power to enforce my tastes and my attitudes on others.*" [Emphasis added.] [1]

But, racial discrimination is not simply a matter of "attitudes," "tastes," and "views" to be dealt with only by speech that "convinces" people to change their views. Race discrimination—as a mode of making up one's mind about the qualities or qualifications of others—is a matter of human behavior toward others. And when racial prejudgment is joined in by others, it is a form of intensely coercive behavior that, like other socially harmful uses of human power, must invariably be dealt with by much stronger measures than mere persuasion. The process by which race discrimination as a form of behavior converts itself from a benign form of *liberty* into a destructive form of coercive *power* is a vital matter. Let us develop it further to show the point at which race discrimination, as a form of behavior, becomes an intolerably coercive act that a free society must prevent. Examples of various forms of race discrimination will clarify the issue.

Suppose I spend much of my time thinking highly derogatory and hostile thoughts about black people and making defamatory and insulting statements about the black race. The nation will probably tolerate my prejudices, however deplorable they may be. To almost any extent, in fact, American society will protect my freedom of speech. In fact, all of us should be grateful every time a judge rules in favor of allowing the most repugnant private statements of racism. Of course, many people feel that the majority should step in and make a law that prevents racial defamation. Some attitudes toward neo-Nazi demonstrations in the Jewish community of Skokie, Illinois, illustrate this position. But the strongest case can be made for the proposition that in the matter of free speech, no power on the part of the state should be invoked to prevent racial slurs. I would suggest, too, that the result would be the same even if it were proven that white and black children had come to believe in and act on the truth of the racial insults they heard from their parents and others.

Now suppose that instead of just thinking or speaking the racial prejudgment, I carry my thoughts into action. Assume, for example, that I make a personal rule that no black person will be allowed to enter my house. Assume, furthermore, that I establish a strict family code that my child may not go to any birthday party given for a black child. I next remove my child from a private school that has decided to admit black children. In fact, I instruct my child to cross the street whenever he or she encounters a black person.

In all of these cases, without enlisting the support of the state or others, I have enacted a personal "Jim Crow" code of behavior governing myself and my family. Most people today would no doubt despise me for my bigotry. And if I instruct my child to turn her head and pass the other way if she encounters a black child who, say, is a helpless victim of a hit-and-run accident, there would probably be no end to the public opprobrium visited upon me. But certainly, in these cases, there is no reason to enact civil rights legislation or to call out a U.S. marshal in order to force me to change my ways. The point is that we are free to conduct our personal and family lives in this way. And, if we wish, we may determine that the decision about whom we will choose to help, or not help, will, in fact, depend on the race of the person calling for help. For the state to protect this kind of individual freedom to be a bigot is very difficult medicine for many liberals to accept. But, in this particular case, the liberty of the bigot is still protected and should be guarded by the state.

Now, let us advance the reasoning further to an example where racial bigotry takes the form of group action. This is where the real trouble begins in terms of one person's liberty abridging the freedoms of another person. This occurs because collective action, as we saw earlier, always introduces a high degree of coercion or force. Suppose I belong to a birdwatching, bowling, or drinking club. The club brazenly posts a sign, "No black people allowed." This is a gross racial insult. Good and responsible citizens of any color will not go near the place. Here, for the first time, race discrimination takes the form of group behavior. There will be differences of opinion, but a strong case can still be made for the fact that the state may not force the members of the club to take down the sign. Thousands of private clubs have this rule today. The only difference is that they do not hang a sign announcing the conditions of admission. Indeed, the racial codes of the association restrict the liberties of blacks, but blacks can watch birds, bowl, or drink in clubs of their own. Thus, the damage done by the racial prejudgment is essentially that of an offensive racial insult rather than a serious restriction on important liberties of those against whom the insult is directed.

But let us suppose the racial insult takes the form of a kind of behavior that blocks people from pursuing employment or trade in a supposedly open and competitive society. Let us assume, then, that the sign "No blacks allowed" hangs outside the only businessmen's eating club in town or outside the offices of a plumbers' or carpenters' union hall. Or, suppose the sign is posted at the headquarters of a private association that fixes the professional qualifications of dentists, lawyers, or engineers. The group defamation is no more offensive than before; yet, almost intuitively, we sense a greater need for society to curtail the individual freedom of association expressed in the racial prejudice. The reason for this is that these collective rules of the bigot—unlike exclusion from a birdwatching club—now threaten more than the inner feelings and freedoms of blacks in seeking recreation. The rules now seriously curtail the commercial or professional opportunities of blacks. The discriminatory code directly impinges on the ability of one group in our society to earn money, to eat, and to pay rent and medical bills. We have now reached the point where the liberties of blacks are intolerably restricted by the bigots' pursuit of their liberties.

Clearly, the state has, or ought to have, the right to take measures over and beyond persuading people, in Professor Friedman's words, "that their tastes are bad and that they should change their views and their behavior." When liberty has been used to curtail or deny altogether an *important* liberty of others, the majority may call upon the state to prevent such abuses. The liberty of group association does not give anyone the right to abridge the liberty of blacks to enter professions and trades or to pursue their economic livelihoods.

Let us look more closely at examples of the restriction of the liberty of others to make free choices in employment or occupation. We shall see that something quite unexpected happens when people, acting in common with other people, decide to pursue *identical* acts of freedom. Suppose that I am a master electrician and I decide that I will not hire an extremely well-qualified black person as my apprentice. Indeed, I set down a personal Jim Crow code governing myself alone. I am willing to accept the consequence that my racial bias may cost me money. Do I have the right to make such bigoted and possibly economically foolish decisions?

If we assume that my prejudice is not shared by the rest of the electricians in the nation—that is to say, they have different racial tastes from my own or, in any case, have a sufficient profit incentive to hire the well-qualified black person—then a case can be made for my right to be as bigoted as I choose. But if it turns out that the great majority, if not all electricians, will not employ black apprentice electricians, the electricians have, in effect, through their private and parallel behavior, made a public economic law prohibiting blacks from becoming electricians. The electricians have effectively established skin color as a requirement for holding an electrician's license. Of course, this particular licensing statute is not found in the records of the legislature, but, as we have shown earlier, it nonetheless has most of the characteristics of statute law.

This example is not hypothetical. In the United States, a private consensus among whites has "legislated" numerous racial codes that have prevailed over many generations. Blacks could be pullman porters, but they could not be firemen on trains; blacks could be schoolteachers, provided

---

UNIVERSALLY PRACTICED RACE DISCRIMINATION IS A STANDARD FORM OF CARTEL POWER

In allocating places and opportunities according to race rather than merit, whites in the United States have used the full armory of coercive weapons commonly employed by the traditional combination in restraint of trade.

In common with a classic cartel, the collective racial prejudgment mounted against black people:

- used collusion and gentlemen's agreements to keep targeted groups out of jobs and markets.

- allocated employment, credit, and capital through the commands of law and private agreement among cartel members, rather than through free-market forces of open competition.

- employed public resources and subsidies to enrich cartel members and to aid—or prop up—favored groups or classes of citizens.

- ostracized defectors and deputized vigilantes to punish those who broke the exclusionary rules of the cartel.

- resorted to the use of terrorism and violence whenever it could not accomplish its goals by nonviolent means.

- provided special franchises, loans, job privileges, government contracts, and exclusive bidding rights for cartel members.

- used legislatures and government agencies to enact licensing laws and administrative rules that safeguarded the favored position of members of the cartel.

- established customs, rules of etiquette, and gentlemen's agreements to prevent potential competitors from acquiring the training and skills necessary to equip them to perform the tasks or to take advantage of the opportunities that the cartel wished to reserve for its own members.

- proclaimed its fervent and undying devotion to unrestricted employment and free trade while steadily pursuing the closed membership objectives of the cartel.

- called for open competition and a fair fight, but not until it had succeeded in becoming the biggest kid on the block.

---

they did not teach white children; blacks might join the construction trades as sweepers, but not as plumbers. Everywhere the racial stipulation had the effective requirements of a law. It was obligatory, imposed by coercion, and backed by sanctions. To a large extent, the economic, political, professional, and academic activities of the nation were controlled by these largely private racial codes established by the white majority simply exercising its collective liberty to discriminate against blacks.

The conclusion is inescapable. One might possibly allow me, as a master electrician, the liberty to be a bigot. But this is tolerable only as long as I am part of a minority or eccentric group. If my prejudice is shared by the majority, the state must step in to prevent me from converting my racial prejudgment into a form of public power that is the equivalent of legislative action. It is precisely *because* everyone else is behaving in the same manner as I am that I cannot be allowed the freedom to pursue my individual bigotry. This may seem at first glance to be a philosophically inconsistent argument: How can I lose my right to act in a certain way simply because the majority is in agreement with me? In fact, however, political theory is not a matter of cold, abstract logic. It must constantly be tempered by common sense. For example, if I burn leaves in my backyard in the fall, I am probably doing no harm. And since I am doing no harm, the state has no right to interfere with my right to dispose of my rakings as I see fit. But if everyone starts burning leaves, the air may become intolerably polluted. The state may now prohibit the burning of leaves. My bonfire in and of itself contributes no more pollution to the atmosphere than it did when I was the only one setting fire to leaves. But it has now become part of a general practice that produces a serious health hazard.

Exactly the same point is to be made about racial prejudice. And for this reason the difference between majority prejudice and minority prejudice is very great. When the minority engages in private racial discrimination, the majority does not feel it as more than a minor irritant. But when the majority embarks on private racial discrimination, it exercises virtually sovereign power in its control over the economic opportunities and life chances of the minority. This explains why collective behavior—whether arrived at by explicit or tacit agreement—that excludes certain groups from access to such necessities as employment, trade, or education may, and must, be prevented by the state. The sanctions employed by the state for this purpose may be far more severe than simple exposure of the offending parties to the influence of speech, which may or may not persuade them to curtail their harmful activities.

So we see that there is, indeed, a fundamental freedom to contract, trade, and employ as we please. And part of this freedom includes the liberty to entertain sentiments of racial prejudice. But the freedom to make racially bigoted choices, like the freedom to make unsafe products or to blow smoke in an elevator, has to be curtailed by the state when it has become a universal form of public behavior that seriously curtails, in the manner of a public law, those freedoms, needs, and opportunities of others that society views as important to human life.

Reverse Discrimination: When Public Power Requires Affirmative Integration

Most people will concede that the state has the right to command its citizens *not* to consider race when making certain economic and educational decisions. Does it follow from this that the state may sometimes have the right to affirmatively command a person to accept, admit, or deal with members of a certain race in an economic, professional, or educational relationship? Laws against racial discrimination and laws ordering affirmative action are both significant restrictions on liberty. Yet they clearly differ in the degree of constraint. In policies of enforced reverse discrimination, the abridgement of liberty is extreme; it affirmatively forces people to employ, admit, trade, and go to school with certain groups.

When the state protects the original liberty to choose whom one will employ or with whom one will do business, it is protecting two values. First, it is protecting liberty as an end in itself. Second, to some extent, it is protecting the principle of merit, the principle upon which our economic system is based. Whenever free people make their economic choices in a rational manner, the expected result is that in most cases the qualified or meritorious person will be chosen. The important point to notice is that when the state blocks the liberty to discriminate, it is, indeed, curtailing individual freedom, but it is not undermining the merit principle. On the contrary, one of the important missions of laws prohibiting race discrimination is, in fact, the enforcement of the merit system.

But reverse discrimination totally confounds the merit system. The moment any authoritative agency, be it the state, an individual, or an institution, orders affirmative outcomes based on race, it is not only restricting individual liberty, it is also attacking the merit principle that antidiscrimination laws seek to defend. Whenever a university, corporation, or labor union is ordered to admit a certain number of blacks or other racial minorities, implicitly it is also being ordered to deny whites their expected right to be judged on the basis of their individual worth or competence. Insofar as the merit principle is regarded as a universal standard of equity, the state may thus not order affirmative racial discrimination or racial quotas without undermining the principle it is seeking to uphold.

Under these circumstances, is it legitimate for the state to require people to employ those against whom they may not discriminate? May banking institutions be ordered to extend credit to particular racial groups against whom they once discriminated? May institutions of education be ordered to admit people, or classes of people, whom they or others have excluded in the past? May the state proceed further and instruct people that under certain circumstances they *must* trade, or refrain from trading, with certain racial groups in order to neutralize the harmful effects of past discrimination? If so, in specific instances, on what moral and ethical basis can we legitimize such extraordinary abridgements of personal liberties?

To answer these questions requires us to examine the merit principle much more closely. The fact is that the merit or competence principle does not have an exclusive claim on our sense of justice; no single standard can be used to determine what constitutes equity in all cases. An important element of equity is the principle of restitution, of making people whole when they have been wronged. This principle of *redress* often overrides simple considerations of merit in determining the just outcome of any competitive process. To each according to his contribution is the principle of distribution prevailing in the United States. But in our society this principle has always been qualified by an overriding principle of justice or redress.

Competition From Blacks Subverted: When the Merit Principle Yields to the Principle of Redress

Let us see how the principle of redress applies to the situation of blacks in America. Let us begin with some general examples of how and when the idea of redress overturns the normal rule that calls for selections according to merit or individual competence. Although the examples that follow may be fanciful at times, they illustrate how the strict application of the merit principle is inconsistent with almost everyone's sense of equity.

Suppose I offer, in accordance with established specifications, to plow your field for $50 while my competitor offers to plow it for $100. Assume that it appears we will both do equally competent jobs. Clearly, at this point, under the usual principles of merit, I am definitely entitled to get the work. Let us suppose further that I am able to do the job for the lower price of $50 because I worked hard, saved my money, and bought a tractor which makes my work more efficient. In the competition for the contract to plow the field, I have a distinct advantage, but it is not an undeserved or unfair advantage. Indeed, even if I had been lucky and had won the tractor in a lottery, nevertheless, under the merit principle, I would still be entitled to the job of plowing the field because luck is usually regarded as deserved. I am entitled to the fruits of my good luck just as you would have been entitled to the fruits of yours had you been lucky enough to win the lottery.

Notice, too, that even if my advantage is very great and my present wealth is already huge, most people would acknowledge that I deserve to be awarded the contract on the basis of my lower bid. This would be so even if my competitor recently broke his leg, has an incurably ill child in need of expensive medication, and desperately needs the income to feed his family. Feelings of sympathy may, in fact, persuade our hypothetical farmer to award the contract on the basis of need, but he is under no obligation to do so. The extra $50 the farmer would have to pay to have his plowing done by the needier but more expensive bidder would, in essence, be a charitable donation and is for this reason a purely discretionary matter. As the person with the superior competence, I am entitled to the contract. I would, in fact, have ground for complaint if the farmer chose to be charitable at my expense by denying me the job I deserved. "If you want to give my competitor money he hasn't earned, that's your business," I might tell the farmer. "But don't take it out on me by denying me the right to the job I won fairly." The point is simply this: Hardship in itself is not generally regarded as a suitable basis for upsetting the usual application of the merit principle, even though we can all imagine instances in which the concerned parties might agree to waive the merit principle in favor of various humanitarian considerations.

Now let us consider a somewhat more difficult case. Suppose it turns out that my competitive advantage was unfairly won in that I stole the tractor from my competitor. Or suppose my competitor has no tractor because I set his on fire. Or suppose the reason my competitor was unable to finance the purchase of a tractor was that I, his competitor, had spread maliciously false rumors to the effect that his credit or workmanship was bad. Or suppose my competitor had no tractor because I was an active party to an unlawful conspiracy in which it was agreed that all banking and commercial people in our particular county would boycott my competitor, both as an equipment borrower and as a contractor to plow fields. Under these circumstances the merit or competence principle is in trouble as a rule for deciding who should be awarded the contract. The question of restitution or redress now enters the situation. This happens because my superior competence to plow the field is directly traceable to my having improperly acquired the advantage I enjoy. Yet, despite the wrongs I have perpetrated, I am still the low bidder and, in this sense, demonstrably better qualified to plow the field. Should I be allowed to enjoy the benefits of my immoral and illegal act?

We now see that we have reached an example that begins to parallel the situation of blacks in the United States today. As the victims of past discrimination, their position is similar to the worker whose tractor was maliciously burned. For hundreds of years they have suffered the disadvantages resulting from unfair—and often state-supported—boycotts which excluded them from the competitive markets. Conversely, whites have enjoyed the fruits of this unfair competition and now find themselves in possession, as it were, of almost all the tractors. For whites simply to agree, under these circumstances, to stop discriminating hardly sets the balance right. Some sort of redress or restitution seems to be required.

But what sort? As our tractor fable shows, it must be a restitution that permits the unfairly disadvantaged competitor to realize the value of the contracts he would have filled if he had not been unfairly deprived of his chance to compete. This, in essence, is what the principle of affirmative action is designed to accomplish. It maintains that whites cannot simply agree to stop burning black people's tractors and consent to open competition because open competition—when one side has all the tractors—is not fair competition if the tractors were unfairly acquired in the first place.

The principle of affirmative action is often incorrectly described as merely searching harder for qualified blacks and other minorities. But, in fact, the principle calls for far more. It often makes awards to lesser qualified people and thus, in the interests of greater equity, wholly rejects the principle of merit. The principle of affirmative action, when viewed in its most extreme form, in effect calls for awards of contracts to blacks in similar proportions to those that would have prevailed had they possessed the tractors they would have won had they not been the victims of hundreds of years of unfair competition in the form of economic racial boycotts.

Indeed, opponents of affirmative action should note that far from being an extreme remedy, the procedure often does not go as far as the principle of equity would seem to require. For example, an affirmative-action college admissions policy will admit many blacks into colleges to which they would not have been admitted on the basis of their scores on standardized admissions tests or their high school records. But once they are in college the advantage ends. Favoritism in admissions is a one-shot advantage; it does not give minority students a fair share of the various competitive advantages their white middle-class classmates will always enjoy—relative economic security, a tradition of higher education, and a familiarity with the worlds of white-collar and professional work. It does not give minorities the network of white middle-class contacts that will help them get good jobs after college. The application of racial quotas in the hiring or promotion of a black person does indeed neutralize a competitive disadvantage on a single occasion, but this single act of favoritism in no way compensates its beneficiary for a lifetime of enforced exclusion from the economic advantages of integrated public education, of the social mobility routinely accorded whites, and of access to political power and control of capital. In terms of our tractor fable, an affirmative-action program gives the victims of prior boycotts the single contract they would have had had they not been unfairly excluded from the competition, but it does not provide them with the central instrument of power advantage—the tractor that makes it so much easier for their competitors to do the same work.

This is not to say that affirmative-action programs in their present form are not beneficial to blacks, or to propose that a rigid program be established to raise the black population automatically and instantaneously to the average white standard of living. Such a program would be economically impossible, politically unacceptable, and undesirable in many ways. The harms from America's caste system cannot be obliterated; justice simply requires efforts to moderate those harms. Affirmative action is a small, tentative attempt toward a modicum of redress. Far from giving blacks an unwarranted advantage, affirmative action goes only a small way toward equalizing the unfair advantage whites enjoy. In a sense, the situation of American blacks may be compared with a man unfairly sentenced to a long prison term for a crime he did not commit. Affirmative action is a program for giving him a job when he is finally released. But this doesn't restore the income he lost while he was in prison. Nor does the grant of a job reverse, or compensate for, the damages resulting from years of prison isolation.

When Renewed Competition Carries Insufficient Force to Redress Positions Unfairly Won

One more example will help explain why a boycott or other suspension of the competitive process that is sustained over a long period of time may not be adequately repaired by simply breaking the boycott and restoring competition. Assume that for five generations a labor union has practiced nepotism in that it has admitted to apprenticeship and membership only lineal male descendants of other members. Assume, too, that it is the practice of all the men in the union to adopt the name "Plumber." Therefore, after a century or more, it turns out finally that all the plumbers in the country have the surname "Plumber." Clearly the family of Plumbers (today's members of the union) are the best-qualified plumbers. Probably, too, their sons (also named Plumber) have the proper exposure to tradition, skills, and learning models to make them better-qualified apprentices than a random selection from the public as a whole (which had long ago lost interest in going into plumbing). Over many generations a great many people with the potential skills to plumb buildings have been prevented from entering the profession, including many who would have risen to the very top. We have here a classic restraint-of-trade situation in which the present competence and motivation to go into plumbing of people who are not named Plumber have been improperly impaired by the ancestors of current Plumbers. Even more important is the fact that the current Plumbers, even if they stop discriminating against people who are not named Plumber, are still current beneficiaries of a skill and training advantage unfairly acquired as a result of the prior boycott. These advantages have been transmitted, generation by generation, down the line.

Clearly the family of Plumbers has an entitlement to their position based on the very highest qualifications. But under principles of equity or redress, they have a very weak claim to their group position of advantage. If adjustments seem to be in order, once again there will be differences of opinion as to how the unfair entitlement should be corrected. Certainly nobody wants his house plumbed by an incompetent person whose skills or aptitude is inferior for any reason. Yet, unless the principle of redress as a standard element of distributive justice is to be abandoned, the merit principle may have to yield somewhat to some government intervention or "affirmative action." In the interest of correcting an undeserved advantage, various coercive processes may have to be brought to bear to set aside "non-Plumber" families for favored treatment. The Plumbers as a family may argue, "Let's now pass antidiscrimination laws and let bygones be bygones. Let the objectively most qualified person for the job prevail." But given their present superior competitive position, the Plumbers may accept such legislation *without losing a single plumbing job*. In this situation, justice is incomplete without some affirmative redress.

Countervailing Power Not Justified in Seeking Equal Results

Opponents of the use of policies of reverse discrimination and other forms of countervailing power to redress the competitive position of black people commonly take the position that these remedies seek to make people equal and, therefore, should be rejected out of hand as forms of socialism.

But this is a totally incorrect view of the objectives of reverse discrimination. Socialism as a doctrine takes the position that the state has the inherent right to use its power to equalize holdings of personal wealth by taking money from those who have and giving it to others who haven't. Socialism, therefore, looks upon *equality* as possibly the highest economic and social good. Affirmative action, however, isn't interested in equality. It honors and protects present inequalities. It enthusiastically supports the doctrine of Adam Smith that society is best served in an economic and political sense when gifted and hard-working people are disproportionately compensated. But affirmative action protects present inequalities only as long as they are *fairly* won and emerge from positions fairly won. Once it appears that groups have used collusive power to subvert the competitive processes that award places according to ability and hard work, affirmative action steps in and redresses unequal competitive positions that have been won through monopoly or collusive power. Affirmative action therefore abhors any form of allocation that insists on equal results. Countervailing race discrimination, instead, sets *equity* or economic fairness as its highest good.

The remedy of affirmative action, which offends so many whites when applied to racial matters, is in fact quite commonplace in our legal system. For example, when undeserved positions, advantages, or holdings are the result of commercial falsehood, cartel behavior, fraud, or some other behavior that society condemns or outlaws, the courts usually require more than the mere cancellation of the unfair advantage. When for years a patent medicine company successfully markets a product on the basis of untrue advertising, the courts will often go beyond ordering the company to stop telling untruths. They will usually make the company spend money telling the public the truth about the limited therapeutic value of the product. If a manufacturing or mining company has been polluting the air and streams of a particular town for fifty years, a judge, having decided that the pollution is now wrong even though it was once legally permitted, not only may require the company to stop polluting but also may order it to take "affirmative action" to clean up the air and water. If several corporations establish dominant positions in certain markets by illegal activities in restraint of trade, the corporations are required not only to suspend their improper activities, but also to affirmatively take steps to yield or share the market advantage that was improperly won. In fact, in order to carry out the principle of affirmative action, judges often provide the victims with a temporarily protected economic position of advantage.

In other words, there are many areas of commercial and competitive life where we find nothing offensive to our sense of justice in requiring favored economic treatment for certain classes of people, as long as their condition of diminished competitive power has been the result of wrongs, trespasses, or unfair dealings committed by a stronger group. In such cases, the claim of fairness or "just deserts" is an overriding one and displaces the usual standard of competence or merit in making selections. The principle of redress does not necessarily require the payment of money damages, but instead reorders competitive positions so as to create, as best as can be done by fallible human beings, a situation in which the competition can proceed as if the acts of misappropriation had never occurred.

Requiring the Innocent to Give Up Places of Advantage

The principle of redress requires that the burden of repairing harm should be borne by those responsible for creating the harm. But what about possible claims against the innocent beneficiaries of an unjust act of another person? If innocent people happen to gain from an unfair competitive practice, do they have an unquestioned right to keep their gains simply because the unfair practice was not of their making? This is the fundamental issue that is presented when whites, today, oppose affirmative action on the ground that they should not be held responsible for the racially repressive actions of their parents or ancestors.

This situation is often covered by the principle of equity known as "the rule of unjust enrichment." According to this rule, a *wholly innocent party* may be required to surrender a superior position or advantage if that position or advantage was acquired through the fraud, misappropriation, or unjust act of another person. A familiar example involves the individual who innocently purchases a bargain item, only to learn later that he bought it so cheaply because it was misappropriated property. Despite the fact that he bought it in good faith, he is not allowed to keep it. The wrongfully taken property must be returned to its rightful owner. If a life insurance policy is obtained by the insured in a wrongful manner, the innocent beneficiary is frequently not permitted to keep the money even if wholly innocent of wrongdoing.

The claim today of blacks in the United States for redress in the form of adjustments in competitive positions between the races does not necessarily rest on an assertion of wrongdoing by the particular people who will lose out as a result of policies of reverse discrimination. The claim rests, to a considerable extent, on the proposition that whites as a group are beneficiaries, at least in part, of holdings and positions unfairly acquired in the past. With considerable moral force, blacks may take the position that since whites retain at least partially undeserved holdings—the unearned privilege of going through life with the political and economic advantages of having a white skin—whites may be required, for the moment, to submit their competitive positions to readjustment claims. This claim to redress is not only consistent with standard principles of economic justice, but may, in fact, be *required* by those principles.

Whites in the Professions: Spoils of a Protected Marketplace

Let us consider a number of aspects of the current white economic advantage and trace out how positions of dominance by whites have been won through noncompetitive processes where ordinary principles of equity would call for readjustments of the competitive position of the black population. Consider, first, the holdings or advantages of whites in the learned professions. In the United States today, there are approximately 13 million lawyers, doctors, dentists, accountants, engineers, and other professionals. These professionals are predominantly white. Only a few years ago, they were virtually all white. In most cases, the people who hold these positions are well qualified and, in this sense, deserve the advantageous positions they hold. But in practically every case, these professionals hold partially undeserved positions. And these positions are, in part, a result of unfairness—and often constitutional illegality—in the process by which they were chosen. For example, in most cases, these white professionals, whether in the North or the South, moved through a public educational process where, contrary to constitutional principles of equal treatment, they received the benefit of public educational resources that were, in many cases, over twice or more as great as those that the state afforded to blacks. In a great many cases, these professionals had the advantage of secondary and advanced *private* school education. Almost without exception, these private schools were assisted by the state because they enjoyed tax exemption and other public benefits. Again, with few exceptions, these private schools and colleges were entirely closed to the competitive admission of blacks. Except for the very young professionals practicing today, medical and law schools were either closed to blacks or limited by highly restrictive racial quotas. Admission to the professional societies that issued licenses to practice was in almost all cases closed to blacks. The public or private bodies that certified professionals to practice regularly used racially discriminatory criteria for qualification. The selective hospitals where internships and residency requirements had to be met were closed to blacks either by custom or by law. In many parts of the country, state and federally operated law libraries and other professional libraries were closed to non-whites. Until recently, law firms, accounting partnerships, and engineering firms observed a fixed racial code of employment that excluded blacks as apprentices, associates, or partners.

We may confidently state that in no sense did the millions of white professionals enjoying the advantages of their positions *today* enslave, defraud, or oppress blacks. But they are, nonetheless, beneficiaries of a fundamentally unjust selection system that produced unfairly acquired advantages which blacks may now call into question. By custom or law, all professional posts and advantages were allocated to whites who on that account were, and are now, somewhat better off.

Blacks Evicted From Blue-Collar Trades: Back-Door Income Transfers to Whites

The professions hold only a small, although disproportionately influential, number of the positions of superior advantage in American society. Let us look at other positions that involve far greater numbers of people, namely, the skilled and semiskilled labor force. At the turn of the century, a million or more blacks worked in the mining, manufacturing, and transportation industries. Blacks, moreover, worked in great numbers as plumbers, mechanics, printers, carpenters, and other craftsmen. In the middle of the last century, blacks probably outnumbered whites as bricklayers, painters, and textile workers.[2] There then followed a half century of occupational eviction as blacks in very great numbers were forced out of skilled trades. The instrument of job eviction was often violence. More often, forced removal was accomplished by covenants restricting work to whites. Scores of unions, including the American Federation of Labor, amended union constitutions so as to limit membership to "white males." It was the consistent practice of public licensing boards to refuse professional permits to black plumbers and electricians, thereby protecting whites from competition by blacks. Almost universally, white firms refused to employ blacks in the blue-collar trades. In industrial plants, whites uniformly refused to work with blacks. Where blacks were present, whites went on strike to force blacks out of jobs. In the North as well as the South, acts of terrorism enforced the occupational evictions. Either by universal agreement or vigilante force, black jobs became white jobs. In some cases, blacks were forcefully eliminated from entire industries. In the depths of the

Great Depression, the American labor movement lived by a rule, "No jobs for Negroes until every white man has a job." The white population banded together and, in effect, denied work permits to blacks unless they were willing to labor as maids, bootblacks, and postal clerks. And all along the line, whites benefited by eliminating blacks as competitors; in the process, they won some economic and educational advantages for themselves and their offspring. Few people working in blue-collar trades—or whose parents worked in blue-collar trades—hold positions or advantages derived from selection processes that were open to competition from blacks. Even the rugged "up by the bootstraps" corporate executive who takes great pride in the fact that he started off in his company many years ago as a lineman's apprentice or as an assembly-line helper is necessarily a product of a pervasive and long-standing racial cartel or combination that without exception denied apprenticeships and other entry positions to black people no matter how well qualified they were.

In questioning the application of the principle of redress to black Americans one might ask, "What would have occurred if these forceful misappropriations of blue-collar positions had not taken place?" One can only guess. We do know that until recently blacks were rarely to be found in the trades in which they had freely participated prior to and after the Civil War. Clearly, over the years, many millions of whites, through coercive and noncompetitive means, have improperly improved their opportunities and transmitted some unearned advantages to their friends and children. These children and grandchildren now comprise the group asked to submit to affirmative action.

To put this abstract black claim for redress in perspective, let us try to quantify, in the most general way, a dollar measure of the advantage won by whites through the long traditions of improper boycotts against blacks. In 1979, the aggregate dollar income gap between blacks and whites stood at about $67 billion. If only one-half of this difference were attributable to the combined effects of racial job codes, unequal public expenditures for public education, and other acts of force or control in employment, then blacks would have been improperly impeded to the extent of about $33.5 billion a year. Or, to put it the other way around, whites, as a class, by subverting the rules of open competition, have misappropriated from blacks and have improperly transferred about $33.5 billion annually to themselves. If one sets a customary capitalization rate of 10 percent to this unfairly won annual income advantage of $33.5 billion, the aggregate value of the *undeserved income holdings* of white labor becomes a current capitalized sum of about *$335 billion*. It is in terms of a figure of this magnitude that the redress claim of the black population may be measured.[3]

When Capitalism Won't Let You Play: Wealth Gathered in Competitions Closed to Blacks

The economic advantages that American society has historically attached to skin color appear most dramatically in regard to holdings of property, capital, and wealth. We recall that whites, who comprise about 88.5 percent of the population, own about 98 percent of all financial assets. Conversely, blacks, with 11.5 percent of the population, hold not much more than one percent of these resources.

Of course, one cannot possibly determine how much white wealth—which appeared to top $6 *trillion* in 1983—was acquired in or derived from transactions where the competitive rights of blacks—or their property rights in their labor—were violated. But even the most cursory reading of U.S. history makes it clear that the legitimacy of a great deal of the wealth of whites is subject to considerable question. Untold billions of dollars were acquired by whites over the course of almost two and a half centuries through the misappropriation of the products of slave labor. Hundreds of millions of dollars more were derived from the sale of slaves, their wives, and their offspring. The agricultural, manufacturing, and real estate wealth of the South was founded, in large measure, on the profit from forced and unpaid black labor. Misappropriations in the form of sharecropping and other sequestrations of Negro labor and property continued after the Civil War and persisted well into the first half of the twentieth century.

Of even greater importance is the fact that the established policy of state and federal governments has been to create wealth in the hands of whites while holding back its grants and benefits from blacks. In past generations, literally trillions of dollars of private wealth in the form of government land grants, petroleum and other mineral rights, and radio and television franchises were issued without charge to whites under blatantly unconstitutional administrative rules and procedures allowing whites and whites only to stake out claims or applications. Direct government awards of wealth to private citizens under whites-only government policies account, today, for holdings of land, franchises, and broadcasting rights with current values in the hundreds of billions of dollars.

What is more, the great body of private and corporate wealth in this country arises out of the private entrepreneurial racial codes, which for a century or more were permitted and often encouraged by the state. As shown earlier, free blacks in the last century were well established as merchants, commercial property owners, and sometimes as manufacturers. Here again, occupational eviction often took place. By common consent, schools of business would not educate black businessmen, banks would not finance them, and potential white customers would not trade with them. The administration of licensing laws, building permissions, and public franchises—in combination with the racial codes of contracting and trade— assured that virtually *all new capital formation for a century or more would take place only in the hands of whites.* The state, always controlled by whites, stood by, protected, and often subsidized these exclusions of blacks from the competition. Since these actions by the state overtly favoring the white race were unconstitutional lawbreaking on its part, one can hardly conceive of a stronger claim for redress than the deep-seated racial disadvantages directly attributable to that lawbreaking.

The extraordinary success of the white population generally in the United States in accumulating the many trillions of dollars of personal wealth that they hold today was, in very great measure, due to certain personal qualities and achievements that were theirs. As a group, they were shrewd, inventive, and hard-charging. The processes of wealth formation by whites in the United States are not even remotely comparable to those of South Africa, where an entire economy was built on the backs of slave labor. But in the United States, a certain unmeasurable, but undeniably very large, amount of the holdings of whites was acquired by cheating blacks out of the protection of open competition. A great nation that purported to have no racial policies except neutrality had, in fact, a back-door policy under which the state favored whites and subsidized them for two centuries or more.

It is not sufficient to argue that because of other disadvantages blacks would have lost out in the competition for wealth. First, we do not know that to be the case; second, if this had been the case, prior racial discrimination and oppression would have been largely responsible for their losing; and finally, outcomes from rigged competitions, even when combined possibly with other economic forces, may not be permitted to stand without some recompense. Much time, indeed, has expired since literally billions of dollars of federally owned petroleum and other public rights were issued to whites in lotteries or grants in which blacks were not permitted to stake their claims. Other forces, too, have intervened to augment or rearrange white holdings of mineral resources. But, nevertheless, the claim of blacks remains strong. They may not ask for the petroleum, or for the minerals in the ground, or for the airwave franchises that have already been granted to

AMERICA'S LONG HISTORY OF 100 PERCENT

For 300 Years the American Colonies, the
Untold Billions of Dollars of Public Wealth

1675—Massachusetts Bay Colony cedes plantation rights in six-square-mile tracts to "worthy" individuals. The population of the Colony included black slaves as well as free blacks. Neither were treated as "worthy" individuals eligible for land grants.

1683—Maryland and Virginia establish fifty-acre land grants to settlers who pay their own way across the Atlantic. Blacks were given a free ride in slave ships and thus were not eligible for grants.

1785—The federal Ordinance of 1785 authorizes the sale of 640-acre tracts to settlers for $1 per acre. As slaves, blacks were legally prohibited from owning property.

1800—The federal government establishes liberal credit privileges in the western territories for buyers of public land at a price of $1 an acre. Slaves not eligible and free blacks generally considered uncreditworthy.

1830—The federal Preemption Act grants land settlers rights to purchase up to 160 acres each at $1.25 per acre. The vast majority of blacks are still slaves and ineligible to own property. No evidence of significant participation by free blacks.

1850—The beginning of the massive federal land grant program for private railroad companies. Outright awards of 130 million acres frequently include property for twenty miles on either side of roadbeds. These lands later found to contain billions of dollars of petroleum and mineral reserves. Black businessmen never considered qualified to acquire, finance, or operate railroad franchises.

1862—The Homestead Act grants settlers 160-acre tracts of federal land without charge. Over 250 acres of public lands transferred almost exclusively to whites in the most important land grant program in American history. Negro claimants blocked by lynch mobs, intimidation and refusals of local authorities to protect their claims.

Sources: A thorough historical summary of American public land grants may be found from Stephen L. McDonald, The Leasing of Federal Land for Fossil Fuel Production (Baltimo Conquest of the Skies (Boston: Little Brown & Co., 1979). Information on the history of rac Broadcast Regulation (New York: St. Martins Press, 1973). Government procurement data a

RACIAL QUOTAS IN FAVOR OF WHITES

States and the Federal Government Allotted Exclusively to Members of the White Race.

1889—In the celebrated Oklahoma Land Rush, 150,000 white settlers scramble to claim the choicest land. Savage lynchings, Ku Klux Klan terrorism and Jim Crow legislation kept Negroes out. Later the heirs and successors of white settlers were to discover billions of dollars of petroleum resources on these lands.

1920—The Mineral Leasing Act authorizes the federal government to lease public land for the exploration of oil, gas, and other minerals. Affluent Negroes need not apply. Race discrimination in public awards was the established policy of the federal government in the 1920s.

1926—The federal Air Commerce Act authorizes the granting of monopoly air routes to qualified aviators. The nation's airlines are born. Twenty thousand white pilots learned their trade in the rigidly segregated World War I Army Air Corps ensuring that the ownership of commercial aviation would be lily white.

1927—The federal Radio Act authorizes the award of radio station broadcast franchises to private citizens. Under settled policy of the federal government, no grants were made to Negroes. Radio broadcast licenses currently valued in the billions of dollars are now held almost exclusively by whites.

1939—The Federal Communication Commission issues the first licenses for television broadcast stations. No grants made to Negroes until token awards of the late 1970s. In 1980, all major television franchises, valued at $5 billion to $10 billion, held exclusively by whites.

1941—Government contracting becomes a major factor in the sales, revenues, and profits of private enterprises. Race discrimination in government contract awards becomes the official policy of the United States government. During the years 1941 to 1980, approximately $3 trillion in contract awards were made almost exclusively to white-owned firms.

er Wolf, Land in America (New York: Pantheon Books, 1981). Mineral rights information is
n Hopkins University Press, 1979). The history of aviation is detailed in Carl Soberg,
television franchising appears in Erwin G. Krasnow and L.B. Longley, The Politics of
the federal Office of Management and Budget.

whites. But some readjustments are called for when the government parcels out future property and wealth.

Education and Politics: Special Subsidies and Set-Asides for Whites

So far, we have shown how for a period spanning several centuries markets for labor, capital, entrepreneurship, and the professions set aside all their benefits for whites and in the process created unfairly won wealth holdings whose legitimacy may now be drawn into question by blacks. But whites also set aside exclusively for themselves other public resources which have contributed in large part to the huge income and wealth advantage that they currently enjoy in the competition with blacks. Of greatest importance, here, are the competitive advantages held by whites, today, which flow from centuries of public education in which learning resources were set apart for exclusive enjoyment by white people.

It may not be disputed that whites, as a class, have an overwhelming advantage over blacks in terms of meeting the requirements for admission to educational institutions today. But are those advantages deserved in the sense of having been won fairly? We know that the future success of, say, 5 million young adults in management professions and in entrepreneurial endeavors will be greatly influenced by their success in competition for admission to colleges, universities, and graduate schools. Over the next ten years, the future success of 35 to 40 million others will be determined in the same way. But to what extent are whites justly entitled to this competitive advantage? The social and economic head start in life created by the white economic advantage, the greater ability of higher-income whites to perform better on standardized admissions tests, and the advantage of safe and segregated suburban schools are all partially the products of a long-term process in which open competitive access was denied to blacks and in which whites and only whites qualified for employment and other benefits. The superior personal connections and credentials of whites, and their superior ability to provide for their children and to pay for higher education, are derived at least in part from long-standing economic arrangements in which the life chances of blacks were systematically blocked and violated, while those of whites were protected and subsidized. On top of this is the long history of public schooling in the United States, schooling in which blacks not only were unconstitutionally segregated, and thereby removed from all important educational competition, but were also denied equal expenditures of public educational funds. For this and other reasons, the unequal educational prospects that whites enjoy today have deep roots in unlawful actions committed in the past. Most whites in the United States today who have positions of economic or professional advantage must necessarily accept the fact that they were won under a long-standing system of repression in which the state was an unconstitutionally active participant.

In addition, we must consider the degree to which whites have unconstitutionally used political power for the explicit purpose of creating and protecting white economic advantages. While it is true that economic gains won through the garden-variety pulls and pressures of American political bargaining should not be disturbed, economic advantages gained by whites through any *unconstitutional* use of state power must be considered vulnerable to claims for reordering or redress of competitive positions. And when the state breaks its own laws in order to subsidize, enrich, or protect the economic position of whites only, the claim of blacks tends to be a strong one indeed.

The nearly exclusive hold that whites presently have over important positions of political power may be traced, in a large number of cases, to elections held under unlawful or unconstitutional procedures. We saw earlier that in the post-Civil War period, blacks in the South secured positions of political power in both the United States Congress and in southern legislatures. Starting, however, in the 1870s, blacks in the South were evicted from Congress and the state legislatures by force, intimidation, and statute. Thereafter, until the 1960s, every trick that whites could devise was used to disenfranchise blacks and keep all political power to themselves. To this day, scores of congressmen from the southern states derive the advantage of elective incumbency from unconstitutional rules where, by one illicit means or another, voting was closed to blacks. A dozen or more United States senators from the southern states hold positions acquired at a time when blacks were officially disenfranchised or were harassed, terrorized, or dismissed from jobs for trying to vote. The United States Congress, particularly, is an institution where it is clear that a great many blacks would have been elected to public office—and would still hold office—if constitutional voting procedures had been in effect since the turn of the century. Blacks were in Congress in good numbers after the Civil War. The likelihood is very strong that they would be there today had they not been unconstitutionally barred from voting and putting up candidates for election to public office. Since blacks constitute approximately 24 percent of the population of the eleven southern states that made up the Old Confederacy, an equitable redistribution of political power might assign to blacks as many as twenty-six congressmen and five United States senators. During the Reconstruction period, southern blacks were, in fact, well on their way to representational parity.

The fact that all Senate and House seats from the deep southern states are still held by whites is powerful evidence of the fact that the unconstitutional voting system of the past is still paying political dividends to whites today. Affirmative action as a form of redress is not constitutionally permissible to adjust unfairly acquired political positions. The unfairly won advantage of these incumbencies may not be disturbed. For many years to come, whites in the South will undoubtedly continue to reap the economic as well as political benefits of elective posts gained at least in part by unconstitutional processes.

As we saw earlier in Chapter Nine, the northern states, too, employed unconstitutional means to keep all political power in the hands of whites. Segregated housing, gerrymandered voting districts, all-white political caucuses, and, in some cases, terrorism were used to discourage black political activity and, in the process, to allocate almost all political power to whites. With this force in hand, whites almost everywhere may, today, take fullest advantage of their prior misappropriation of political power as well as of the lawbreaking activities of their ancestors. In the process, they retain the superior and necessarily partially undeserved power to use the apparatus of the state to channel wealth and economic opportunities into bank accounts, industries, and other endeavors owned by whites.

When Reverse Discrimination Sheds Innocent Blood

The position that standard rules for dealing with unjust enrichment require a reordering of competitive positions between blacks and whites is by no means free from practical and theoretical difficulties. There are two particularly serious problems. First, the claim of any wrongfully disadvantaged group to an adjustment of competitive positions must be made against those whose superior position can be shown to have been unjustly won. A claim loses its moral force whenever enforcement of the claim on behalf of a disadvantaged group has the effect of taking positions or advantages away from people who, indeed, are members of a dominant group, but who are for some reason not beneficiaries of improper processes of the past. Second, the demands of justice require that any adjustment of the competitive positions in favor of the disadvantaged group should not benefit members of the group who have not suffered any injury. The problem, in short, is this: Most will concede that blacks as a whole have suffered at the hands of whites, and that whites as a whole have often enriched and empowered themselves at the expense of blacks. Adjustments, therefore, seem to be required. But how can such adjustments be made without benefiting individual blacks who have not been harmed and without penalizing individual whites who have in no way profited from the wrong?

Who are the members of the white majority community who may not in any way be said to have increased their welfare and competitive position at the expense of blacks? The fact is that there are almost none. Whites whose ancestors in the United States go back many generations may indeed be morally innocent today but, nevertheless, occupy economic positions at least partially traceable to unconstitutional educational advantages and to several centuries of impermissible and often unconstitutional protection from black competition. All whites whose families have been in the United States for a number of generations are necessarily products of segregated or dually funded school and university systems; they are beneficiaries of a long history of economic opportunities protected against competition from blacks and the unconstitutional denial to blacks of their democratic right to use political power to hold the system open to equal access by the races. In particular cases, many of this group of whites may indeed count themselves, today, as poor or disadvantaged. But, whatever their position, their ancestors claimed or should have claimed the advantages accruing from an unqualifiedly racist economic and educational selection process that granted and set aside economic, political, and educational advantages for whites as surely as it denied or took them away from blacks.

But what of the millions of whites in the United States whose ancestors came to this country as nineteenth-century, often peasant immigrants from countries such as Italy, Poland, and Ireland? These immigrants—often greatly discriminated against after their arrival—have no reason to accept the claim that their economic position today is due in any measure to the exploitation of blacks. In fact, they will declare with great force that the advantages they have today were earned only after overcoming great obstacles, often comparable to those faced by blacks. Yet, on closer examination we can see that even the so-called white ethnic population has considerably benefited from racial codes mounted against blacks. The immigrant whites were, as often as other whites, the beneficiaries of the violence and terror that were used to accomplish the occupational eviction of blacks from trades such as plumbing, printing, and carpentry. Indeed, in many cases, white ethnics, organized into trade unions, have been the driving force behind employment codes excluding blacks from apprenticeship training programs; in untold cases, white ethnics have been the explicit beneficiaries of racial occupational restrictions and other economic codes of limited entry that protected whites from competition from blacks. In industries such as construction, shipping, mining, rubber, textiles, trucking, heavy manufacturing, and utilities, white ethnics consistently benefited from job protection arrangements and overtly menacing tactics that excluded blacks. In Buffalo, Cleveland, Detroit, Pittsburgh, Boston, Baltimore, New York, and other large cities, Polish-, Irish-, Italian-, German-, and Scandinavian-Americans were deeply involved in, and benefited from, the process of forcible removal of blacks from trades and industry.

Immigrant American groups were major participants in erecting the racial codes that excluded qualified blacks from jobs as policemen, firemen, and schoolteachers. White immigrant groups, like other white groups that arrived in the United States earlier, benefited from the most harmful of all forms of publicly approved discrimination—a racially segregated public school system designed to give blacks an inferior education and to provide superior educational benefits to whites. White ethnics in large numbers not only used the political system to economic advantage, but also were prime actors in politically disenfranchising blacks and in unconstitutionally manipulating state power to prevent blacks from voting and influencing the political process. Although white ethnics have had a difficult time and have reached economic parity with others only by overcoming huge obstacles, they, too, in common with the majority of the white population, enjoyed a considerable measure of educational, political, and economic advantage derived from a racial selection system that, with the concurrence and support of the state, expressly and consistently established skin color as a condition for admission or participation.

The main groups that have not benefited from race discrimination in employment, education, health care, contracting, credit, and investment appear to be immigrants to the United States who have arrived only in the past decade. Their numbers are certainly not great enough to warrant rejecting the black claim for redress. Clearly, millions of whites in the United States may in all truth claim that they have never participated in the long process of savage racial attacks directed against blacks. But it is a rare white person who can state with confidence that he has gained no economic, political, educational, or other advantage because of the competitive restrictions and other racial codes of exclusion set up by his ancestors or by others who went before him. To this extent, all whites in the United States are children of an apparatus of economic and political protection that conferred advantages on whites as surely as it imposed disabilities on blacks.

Unjust Enrichment: When Reverse Discrimination Rewards the Unharmed

The second major problem arises when state or private power reorders economic or other positions in favor of blacks who, in fact, have sustained no injury. We know that the black population as a whole has a mean family income 40 percent short of that of whites. We know, too, that black wealth holdings and other positions of advantage make up a small fraction of the white mean. But our system of justice is generally interested in redressing the position of individuals, not in correcting the mean or median positions of groups. Nevertheless, under standard principles of class restitution, groups may pursue redress if they can show that *most, if not all* those within the group, have suffered improperly or unconstitutionally imposed harm. We then must ask: Are there large numbers of blacks in the United States who hold what we may call "uninjured status"?

It is safe to say that almost all blacks in America today have been handicapped to some degree by the collective racial codes of enforced inferiority of the past and, to a lesser degree, by the racial prejudgments of the present. The number of blacks alive in the United States today who have not, to some extent, been held back as a result of their parents and grandparents having suffered the burden of enforced illiteracy, segregated education, and unequally funded public schools must indeed be minuscule. The descendants living today of highly educated and gifted blacks who were obliged to work as postal workers and office clerks when they were well qualified to be college professors, lawyers, and bankers have inherited an undeserved legacy of cultural and economic disadvantage. Even bright and well-prepared young black law and business students in school today carry the burden of an ancestral tradition where nonpropertied status, as well as total isolation from the entrepreneurial and professional machinery of American capitalism, was imposed on their parents and their parents' parents. Given the extent to which parental economic advantage is a major factor in determining the life prospects of offspring, most young blacks who are alive today address life with opportunities stunted by low incomes and high poverty rates directly traceable to the oppressive racial economic rules of the past.

Almost all blacks in the United States today are politically weaker because their ancestors were unconstitutionally denied the self-protection that democracy grants its citizens in the form of voting rights and the right to run candidates for public office. Because of past discrimination, blacks will generally have few, if any, friends and relatives in high places who can help them in the same way that highly placed whites help other whites. For all blacks the curtain of segregation isolates them from the central network of economic information, connections, and opportunity discovery. To be sure, individual blacks often overcome these and countless other handicaps. And increasing numbers of them attain achievements comparable to many of their white peers'. But in all cases, they do so against greater odds than whites must overcome to reach the same destination. Thus, all blacks, without regard to their individual skills, ambitions, and dexterity, carry extra baggage. For the tough-minded and the tenderhearted alike, a great and undeserved disaster has struck them all.

Birthrights Denied: The Life Chances of Black Children

We have seen that whites by the hundreds of millions made some significant gains—and transmitted these gains to their children—as a result of the public and private racial codes that told black people which trade schools they could go to, which jobs they might hold, what tests for admission they might take, for what commercial purposes they might borrow money, and for what kinds of public awards or contracts they might apply. Under circumstances such as these where the power of the state was so profoundly implicated in the economic subordination of the black race, the claim for redress or restitution is powerful indeed. But the force of the position is best gauged when we measure the detrimental effects of past racial discrimination on black children. If one chooses at random 100 black and 100 white infants born today, one may predict with statistical certainty that four or more times as many of the black children will be born into poverty. A black child will be born to illiterate parents three times or more as often as a white child. The mean income of the black child's parents will be less than three-fifths that of the white child's parents. The life expectancy of the black child will be over six and a half years less than the white child's.

We do not know for certain how to gauge the extent to which these massively unequal life chances are the result of a long chain of repressive acts perpetrated by whites. But we do know that to a very great extent every black child born today will enter life with the neutrality of luck and the arbitrariness of natural talent profoundly altered by past and present acts of race discrimination.

Herein lies the ultimate justification for a policy of restitution or reverse discrimination. It is based on each black child's claim today to a repair of his or her life's chances. About forty years ago, the great French writer Antoine de Saint-Exupery concluded his book *Wind, Sand and Stars* with an account of a trip he took in the third-class compartment of a train crammed with immigrant workers being shunted out of France during the early days of World War II.

"I made my way along those passages, stepping over sprawling bodies and peering into the carriages (he wrote). In the dim glow cast by the nightlamps into these barren and comfortless compartments I saw a confused mass of people churned about by the swaying of the train. . . .

"I sat down face to face with one couple. Between the man and the woman a child had hollowed himself out a place and fallen asleep. He turned in his slumber, and in the dim lamplight I saw his face. What an adorable face! A golden fruit had been born of these two peasants. . . .

"I bent over the smooth brow, over those mildly pouting lips, and I said to myself: This is a musician's face. This is the child Mozart. This is a life full of beautiful promise. Little princes in legends are not different from this. Protected, sheltered, cultivated, what could not this child become?

"When by mutation a new rose is born in the garden, all the gardeners rejoice. They isolate the rose, tend it, foster it. But there is no gardener for men. This little Mozart will be shaped like the rest by the common stamping machine. This little Mozart will love shoddy music in the stench of night dives. This little Mozart is condemned.

"I went back to my sleeping car. I said to myself: It is the human race and not the individual that is wounded here, is outraged here. I do not believe in pity. What torments me is not this poverty . . . : what torments me is not the humps nor the hollows nor the ugliness. It is the sight, a little bit in all these men, of Mozart murdered." [4]

Let us now restate the black claim for redress in terms of obligations that we usually consider to be basic human rights. Under traditional principles of equity—often important enough to be protected in the national charters governing civilized peoples—black people, in common with all humans, had and still have certain rights. These are minority rights which, under the Constitution of the United States, the majority may not take away. Blacks, for example, had the right to absolute protection from being held in slavery by the majority. They had the right to the protection of their homes, their cattle, and their crops from midnight raids by vigilante terrorists. They and their wives had the right to be protected by the state from acts of rape and abuse. They had the right to protection from public lynchings for crimes, whether those crimes were committed or not. They had a right that neither the state—nor the people acting with the same force as the state—might set them aside as an outcast class of menials. They had the right that the majority not segregate them, or enforce through the courts racial covenants that would herd them into special enclaves. They had the right that their children not be subject to the massive economic and social disadvantages that this enforced isolation necessarily brought about.

Black people in the United States had the right that the state might not officially slander them in the presence of their children. According to accepted principles of justice, they had the right that the highest judicial body in the land not declare their race to be "excluded from civilized governments and the family of nations."[5] In circumstances where the state provided medical care, blacks had the right to the same kind of care as whites. When charged with wrongdoing, blacks had the right to trial by their peers without hindrance on the part of state officials. Blacks had the right to whatever friendships, connections, and advantages might come their way from intermarriage or from associations with members of any race. Blacks had the right to equal advantages of public education, and to freely purchase private education whenever it was subsidized by the state. They had an absolute right that the force of the state not be employed to prevent them from voting or holding public office. They had the right to live under the rule of law in which any right granted to whites had to be unequivocally granted to blacks. They had a right that the state do nothing to block any of these rights.

In all these ways whites violated the most fundamental economic and human rights of blacks. Under standard principles of redress, observed in most parts of the Western world, blacks now have the right to use non-violent collective pressure, as well as to enlist the power of the state, in an effort to restore themselves to positions they would have held if their rights had not been violated in these many ways.

Part Five

The Gathering of Power:
The Shape of a Black Agenda

"Every great movement must experience three stages: ridicule, discussion, adoption."

—*John Stuart Mill (1859)*

The Politics of Empowerment and the Bases of Black Strength

*"We cannot avoid
Using power.
Cannot escape the compulsion
To afflict the world,
So let us, cautious in diction
And mighty in contradiction,
Love powerfully."*

—*Martin Buber*
(1878-1965)

ALMOST WITHOUT EXCEPTION, black people in the United States are born into a state of powerlessness; they are reared in a condition of powerlessness; as adults they live in communities of powerlessness. Even when their professional, management, or business attainments are very great, individual blacks in the United States are seldom in a position where they are feared, obeyed, or greatly respected by whites. Powerlessness—with its handmaiden qualities of obedience, deference, and withdrawal—is still the norm of black life in America.

What is the nature of this impotence? What are the forces and benefits that continue to hold blacks in check? Why is it that other groups in the nation—war veterans, teachers, farmers, senior citizens, and certain ethnic minorities—exercise great influence in the country, while blacks as a group or as individuals are mere bystanders whose interests and aspirations are largely ignored? Must black people simply resign themselves to being controlled, manipulated, and buffeted about? Or if they would end this state of affairs, where do they look to expand their circumscribed say in the economic life of the nation? What measures do they take to rid themselves of the keepers and protectors who hold them back? How do black people take leave of their junior partner status in running the ship of state? Where do blacks look to acquire the strength to negotiate with and take positions alongside the mighty?

The Minority Position: The Culture of Disunity

Standing guard over all other factors that prevent blacks from coming to power is the essential limiting force of the minority position. In certain African nations, the sheer overwhelming numbers of blacks ultimately compel ruling whites to yield power to them. The pattern of change in these countries is familiar: first, a colonial state of total black disenfranchisement, followed by a period of mock parliaments and token black officials, followed, then, by the sharing of government power, and ending with the ultimate transfer of the power of the state to blacks. In the United States, however, blacks are a small minority: They may occasionally plan public demonstrations and protests; as a special-interest group they may lobby for the political or economic policies that they believe will help members of their race. But in the last analysis, blacks in the United States simply do not have the legions of people necessary to enforce their demands either by direct agitation or through formal political action. Blacks make up only 11.5 percent of the population of the nation; although this small number is by no means fatal to power acquisition, the numerical minority position is a supremely difficult hurdle to overcome.

The powerlessness of blacks is also closely connected to group attitudes and habits that have emerged as rational adaptations to historical forces applied against them. Many blacks still bear the imprint of their traditional schooling in subservience and deference to others. It appears that, to a great extent, the racial mythology of inferiority and group character disparagements of the past still produce, today, a shared sense of inadequacy, resignation, and depression. The sense of powerlessness that prevails among so many blacks today is in large part the result of the self-doubt of adults and the lowered expectations of children produced by long-standing occupational racial codes and government insults that have placed low ceilings on Negro aspirations as well as opportunities. Moreover, in the case of large numbers of poor blacks, national welfare and assistance programs, often designed with blacks in mind, have acted as a potent constraining force that has unquestionably discouraged assertions of political strength and economic independence.

The collective powerlessness of blacks in America may be traced further to deep-seated divisions among them as to what kinds of strategies will best secure their common interests in achieving equality. Economic and class differences among blacks—far exceeding those prevailing in society generally—discourage the emergence of the group consensus or unity that is always a prerequisite for the acquisition of power. As a result of these divisions and other forces, blacks have lacked effective leadership. Except for a brief period during which Dr. Martin Luther King, Jr. seemed on the verge of emerging as the national spokesman for a unified black consensus, no black person—except possibly the Baptist preacher Reverend Jesse Jackson in recent years—has attained sufficient inspirational influence to stimulate a national black awakening and to impose a common program on the group. The problem of leadership has been magnified, too, by the refusal, for a century or more, of the professions, and the foreign service, and the great institutions of learning in America to open their doors to gifted black people and so enable them to produce political statesmen and leaders.

In great measure, the collective impotence of the black minority is tied to the inability of black spokesmen to find a towering and clearly defined symbol of racial injustice. To the great credit of a nation that genuinely aspires to become a raceless state, there is no equivalent of South Africa's Robbens Island in the United States; only occasionally are blacks provided with the moral advantage that occurs when a diabolical figure such as Sheriff Jim Clark or Governor George Wallace appears on national television. Great injustices continue to persist, but unlike the highly visible segregated lunch counters and closed voting registrars' offices of the 1950s, black grievances now lie obscured in the bewildering economic statistics of the Census Bureau. Gross inequalities persist, but without some highly visible symbol of injustice, blacks cannot organize around their grievances.

The state of black powerlessness and dependency is particularly exacerbated by the refusal of most black people to perceive the problem of Negro inequality as one of unequal power. Almost all black organizations still insist on pursuing a standard liberal agenda in which charity, fiscal aid, and service to the poor are preferred to strategies of economic and political empowerment. Blacks in alliance with liberal whites have enacted a comprehensive but enervating program of rescue missions: public housing, aid to the cities, job enrichment programs, and corporate volunteerism ("give a black kid a job"). This network of aid and relief programs, in the absence of any significant power transfers, has reinforced long-standing habits of black dependency and has worked at cross-purposes with the drive for political and economic influence.

Another factor contributing to black weakness is the often expressed fear that collective gains achieved by assertions of black power will be nullified by the presumed "white backlash" that is expected to follow from any significant move toward black empowerment. Nurtured by whites and blacks, these fears tend to make blacks as leery of achieving power as they are weary of lacking it. Nothing is more inimical to the growth of black strength and influence than the ready acceptance by blacks of the received wisdom of whites—and indeed of most blacks—who, in complete defiance of proven concepts of power, denigrate the influence of protest, ridicule the idea of bloc voting, and hoot at the pursuit by blacks of the politics of group consensus. ("You can't eat ballots and demonstrations, old man.")

The continuing enfeeblement of blacks also owes a great deal to a long tradition in the black community of preferring policies of patience, trust, and economic "uplift" programs over a strategy based on political action, nonviolent demonstrations, labor stoppages, and consumer boycotts. The strong religious tradition of blacks was, indeed, the tower of strength that sustained the successful marches and protests of the 1960s, but the spiritual blessings now appear to be mixed. It seems likely that blacks would have more power in this world if it weren't for a strongly held conviction on their part that Providence will take care of them in the next. The notion that the meek will inherit the earth may provide reassuring comfort to poor blacks, but it is hardly an inducement to stop being meek.

Plain, old-fashioned deception and self-deception are key ingredients in black weakness. Thus, political power is transferred from blacks to whites every time black voters support rearguard segregationists who cynically and corruptly send government helicopters and ambulances to the assistance of black children while consistently voting against the interests of their parents. The black political voice is diminished every time a southern black mayor campaigns for the election of a racial conservative who pays off his political debts to blacks with morsels of federal revenue-sharing funds while steadfastly opposing empowering initiatives such as affirmative action and the appointment of black judges to the federal bench. Loss of the will to use political power to protect vital black interests invariably develops when blacks, in common with other powerless groups, deceive themselves in beliefs that they have reliable friends in court and that they don't need power in their own right because these friends will unselfishly let them in on the action. Since the beginning of time, powerless people have persisted in tying themselves down by rationalizing the continuation of the impotent positions that they despise but fear to try to change.

The weakness of blacks today is due in considerable part to the tendency of many blacks to confuse power with glory, whether in the field of government, business, or education. For example, the limited power that blacks do have tends to ebb whenever an influential black spokesman accepts an unimportant post as presidential adviser on minority or African affairs; in the eyes of whites and blacks, black power dissipates whenever a black politician seizes an opportunity to take a display ride around the world in Air Force One, while never being offered a place of attendance in matters of great national significance, such as arms reduction, Middle East treaty negotiations, or national fiscal policy. Black political influence is demeaned when black civil rights leaders are seen publicly vying with one another to appear on a podium with white political candidates whose programs on behalf of blacks are largely confined to occasionally praying with them in a church associated with Frederick Douglass or delivering the black power salute at meetings of the Congressional Black Caucus. Efforts on the part of blacks to protect and advance their interests are undermined whenever black spokespeople praise and publish the rhetoric of powerful officials in government who sidestep or evade the enforcement of laws encouraging racial integration while consistently proclaiming their friendship for the black race. Power must necessarily be weakened by its continuing courtship of the oppressor, by its cuddling up to the restrictive views of the racist, and its fawning over those in power who would use public funds to subsidize the means of keeping blacks out of important institutions.

At the core of the impotence of members of the black minority is the fact that they possess no *formal* power. After a decade and a half of institutional huffing and puffing about getting blacks into important government posts, no black person in the United States—with a handful of exceptions—holds any of the established seats of political or economic power. Almost no blacks in government, industry, banking, or education have positions that are even close to the power centers where orders are issued, budgets are cut, and important policy decisions are made. The derivative power that comes from holding office belongs entirely to whites.

Finally, and overwhelming in importance, black people are powerless because of the power ineligibility status that, in the United States, goes with having black skin. White people by the scores of millions have black people pegged as unqualified to hold power because they are incompetent, untrustworthy, or lazy. And the possible escape hatch for blacks in the minds of the nonracist sector of society is nevertheless plugged up by the balance of the white population who although unprejudiced are nonetheless beholden to the image that prejudiced whites have of blacks as losers and incompetents. Thus, even in the minds of people who hold no racial prejudice, blacks are not credible as political candidates—nor does anybody want them on their ticket—since a very large percentage of the population will not vote for them because of their race. Whites and blacks know with considerable certitude that except in special circumstances, blacks will not be nominated as serious contenders for public office, and this prevents others from working for their nomination. Nonprejudiced and prejudiced

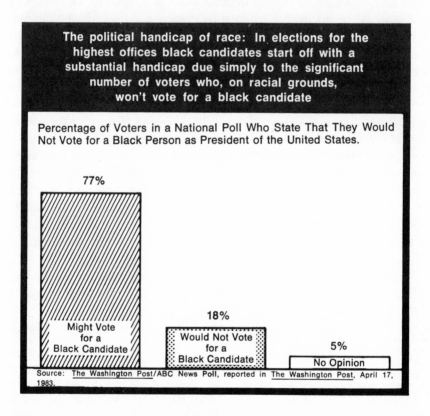

The political handicap of race: In elections for the highest offices black candidates start off with a substantial handicap due simply to the significant number of voters who, on racial grounds, won't vote for a black candidate

Percentage of Voters in a National Poll Who State That They Would Not Vote for a Black Person as President of the United States.

77%
Might Vote for a Black Candidate

18%
Would Not Vote for a Black Candidate

5%
No Opinion

Source: The Washington Post/ABC News Poll, reported in The Washington Post, April 17, 1983.

people alike view blacks as incapable of mounting, organizing, and funding a political candidacy, with the result that very few blacks or whites will take the risk of working toward that end. Just as an officeholder who is not eligible for reelection loses most of his influence once his lame-duck status becomes known, blacks have little influence to start with simply because congenital lame-duck status conferred by racial attitudes makes them essentially ineligible to hold the powers of public office.

For blacks, the same power ineligibility status tends to prevail in education, commerce, and employment. Hence, to put up the name of a black person for nomination as president of a college, a bank, or a large corporation is usually a futile act. Among racists and nonracists, alike, the memory imprint that still produces the rigid taboos of race denies black people power's passport of having a white skin. Impotence—and ineligibility to hold power—in fact precedes them, even before they enter a room.

Blacks are powerless, finally, because of the opprobrium that society assigns to any overt strategy of embracing power as a political strategy. Power in itself is a taboo in Western society. In the United States, for example, it is possible to be pro-rich, pro-poor, pro-military, or pro-big business. It is possible to be pro-environment, pro-civil rights, pro-farmer, pro-Hispanic, and, indeed, *pro-black*. But it is virtually impossible to be pro-power. Black empowerment must be cautiously pursued because the overt espousal of power as a platform or an objective is intolerably subversive in the eyes of most Americans—black or white.

Given the massive disparity in power holdings in this country, where can blacks turn for relief? Where can they find the tools needed to dispel the various social, economic, and political forces that continue to render them powerless? How can they successfully resist having whites tell them where to go and where to sit? How can Negroes turn in their often empty rhetoric of militance for a share of the sure but quiet ability to tell others what to do?

Consensus as a Condition for Black Empowerment

From time to time, black utopians have advocated total withdrawal from the American mainstream and the establishment of a black homeland in Africa, Alaska, or the Deep South. With good cause, these separatist movements have always petered out. Aside from the insuperable logistical problems in relocating 27 million black people, separatist theories suffer from the inherent weakness of their assumption that blacks would greatly benefit by taking economic and political control over the rural and underdeveloped areas where inevitably they would be concentrated. Even if black sovereignty in these communities could be achieved, the separatist idea would be an altogether unsatisfactory strategy. In a sense, after all, blacks already have their poverty-stricken "homelands" in the United States in such places as Gary, Indiana, the Bedford-Stuyvesant section of Brooklyn, and Lowndes County, Alabama. Blacks already dominate the poorest, the most unproductive, and many of the declining industrialized regions in the country. Indeed, the pursuit of group self-sufficiency must be a central part of the strategy of black advancement, but self-sufficiency cannot be found in the social and economic backwaters of our society. Driving whites out in order to take economic and political control of a ghetto may eliminate some flagrant exploitation and profiteering; it may provide blacks with a political base for winning greater influence in state and national politics; but, as a long-range strategy for establishing blacks as a prosperous and influential people, it makes about as much sense as organizing a mutiny to take over the helm of the *Titanic*.

Power is to be discovered, then, only in the American economic and political mainstream. Only here do blacks connect with vast pools of American capital, win accreditation from elite educational institutions, gain the benefits of secure high-level jobs, acquire the political skills that have been the birthright of the white majority, and take possession of their fair share of seats in important legislative and judicial bodies. To seek a power base in the black ghetto of the United States is, fundamentally, a contradiction in terms. The ghetto is, by definition, a disorganized and power-deficient place where powerless people are housed or, in many cases, simply warehoused. To win power, blacks must go where power is.

Thus, the road to empowerment is reasonably clear. Blacks must shed their habits of dependency, cease to toady to the powerful, discover collective power on their own, and cultivate and assert it with all the intensity that characterizes other powerful special-interest groups. United action is not only the fundamental characteristic of human power which blacks must exhibit; it is also the necessary first stage leading to more sophisticated levels of empowerment. In later stages of power development, strength is found in legislative bodies, executive positions, and control of large institutions. Other ethnic groups have used formal institutional bases to defend and augment their power—Italians in sanitation, Irish in police, and Jews in public education—and, in each case, ethnic unity provided the initial point of entry.

Since the eclipse of black militancy in the mid-1970s, it has become fashionable to ridicule the idea of united action by blacks and other minority groups. The scoffing comes mainly from established liberals whom power has served well and who, in fact, flirted briefly with black radicalism in the days when Huey Newton and Stokely Carmichael were media events. Concerted action, they now declare, with all the cynical wisdom of those who have learned from experience, has been given its chance and has failed. On this score, they are about as right as those who said on the eve of Valley Forge that the American independence movement was dead. The inescapable fact is that the principles of power, true since the origins of early man, do not change. Powerless people aggregate power through concerted action. Such action may take the form of a protest march or of a boycott. It may present itself as positive collective action in support of a particular political candidate or punitive group action to remove a candidate from political office. The important point is that power insists that the human action be purposeful, acted out in concert, capable of being controlled, and credibly advertised and proclaimed as such.

The collective power that blacks must achieve should not be confused with the simple happening of mass action. There is no power at work, for example, if great numbers of blacks randomly appear in the course of a week in front of the Lincoln Memorial. Similarly, no power whatsoever is functioning if in every election 90 percent or more of all black voters faithfully and predictably give their vote to candidates of the Democratic party. Thus, when in 1982 blacks provided victory margins for Governors Mario Cuomo in New York and Mark White in Texas, or when their heavy but predictable turnout helped defeat incumbent congressmen in Alabama, North Carolina, South Carolina, and Virginia, very little black political power was at work. There is political significance in mass action only if the collective act appears to be purposeful and capable of being reversed or scrubbed once certain objectives are either won or determined to be un-winnable.

We see, then, that the most difficult aspects of group empowerment are achieving, maintaining, and controlling consensus. There must be a central command, an agreed-upon objective, and the ability to move as a group toward or away from the chosen target. All collective action, be it political or economic, succeeds or founders depending on whether or not it success-fully maintains a quasi-military—but always nonviolent—discipline and spirit that unify the group and cause it to press forward toward its selected goals.

Marches, Vigils, and Protest: Power's Debut for the Disenfranchised

As in the case of other groups separated from society's standard instru-ments of coercion, group agitation and collective protest have been the traditional form of consensus power used by blacks in the United States. Black protest first began hundreds of years ago when slaves surreptitiously broke tools on southern plantations. The record of successful black protest over the past fifty years is impressive. Only when threatened by a Negro march on Washington, in 1941, did President Roosevelt sign the historic presidential order that opened up the defense industry to black workers. As a result, black incomes and employment status in the United States showed greater gains during the World War II years than at any other time in

American history. A. Philip Randolph's second threatened march on Washington in 1948 produced President Truman's Executive Order 9981 ending segregation in the armed forces. The Montgomery, Alabama, bus boycotts and the later Freedom Rides of the 1960s were undeniably the catalysts that persuaded the Interstate Commerce Commission to ban racial segregation on interstate carriers. The opening of public facilities to blacks was never volunteered; it was the direct result of the lunch-counter sit-ins which began in Greensboro, North Carolina in the early 1960s. Two black protest marches at Selma, Alabama in the early 1960s touched the conscience of the nation. In rapid succession there followed the Voting Rights Act of 1965, federal funding of grassroots organizations in nonwhite communities, legal services for the poor, and legislation prohibiting discrimination in employment and housing. Blacks made huge income gains in the 1960s, traceable in large part to expanded economic opportunities created as a result of the decision of large numbers of blacks, in alliance with sympathetic whites, to converge in mass protest at particular places and times.

Always there are strong public forces working against black empowerment through protest and agitation. In recent years, a number of new pressures have emerged that reinforce society's general opposition to direct action. For example, the determination of racial conservatives—as well as most liberal politicians—to persuade blacks to look to corporate voluntarism, economic growth through laissez-faire economic policies, and even private charity, in lieu of agitation and self-help, co-opts even the most dedicated efforts to mount political action. Nevertheless, the potential of mass protest remains great. Where grievances carry compelling moral force and lie within the corrective power of presidential executive order, the credible threat of mass protest will be a potent and efficient agent of change. If black incomes continue to lose ground relative to whites', if black unemployment and the percentage of black children being reared in poverty continue to remain at unacceptably high levels, or if government continues to temporize with the enforcement of civil rights laws, blacks must and will march again.

Routine boycotts and collective economic action—now enjoying comprehensive protection from the Supreme Court—are also capable of producing consistent gains for blacks. Product boycotts may be successfully mounted against corporations that still refuse to hire blacks or ignore laws prohibiting racial discrimination. Picketing and mass deposit-withdrawal strategies used against financial institutions practicing mortgage redlining of black communities are effective methods for changing institutional credit practices. The refusal of large corporations to license black distributors, to deal with black wholesalers, and to advertise in black-owned media may be successfully reversed by selective patronage boycotts. Demonstrations and sit-ins at construction sites where blacks have been excluded from work forces consistently produce more gains for blacks than the so-called hometown or voluntary solutions encouraged by the federal government. These forms of collective action are the contemporary counterparts of "The League for Fair Play" and the "Don't Buy Where You Can't Work" movements of the 1920s and 1930s. As a combined form of political and economic power, these measures are legitimate, almost always protected by law, and highly effective in expanding the opportunities of blacks and easing their way into places that have been heretofore closed.

Potentially the strongest—but commensurately most risky and in some cases illegitimate—weapon of protest is the declaration of a general strike. The general strike has been employed as a political and economic weapon in other countries but not in the United States. The probable effect of a general strike by black workers on black political and economic objectives is uncertain. Clearly, under present patterns of employment, large segments of the private sector could not be manned solely by whites and thus could not function without black workers. As long as black workers did not assert a right to strike the government as an employer, a general work stoppage of black workers could generate massive and entirely lawful pressure on economic and political institutions. Unquestionably, the general strike is a potential instrument of black protest that cannot be ignored. Decades ago, work stoppages and strikes by black workers would have only slightly inconvenienced the general society. The nation would not have suffered greatly without the services of its black maids and bootblacks. Moreover, in the segregated society of the past, strikes by black teachers, nurses, and welfare workers would have produced greater distress to blacks than to whites. Today, the much wider—though still inadequate—black participation in the economy greatly alters the balance of economic power. An essential feature of black power today, unlike a generation ago, is that black workers are indispensable to the wheels of industry, banking, and government.

The strategy of direct action always includes the possibility of blacks bringing pressure on institutions by embarking on a systematic course of urban demonstrations. In theory, the power of civil disturbances appears to be very great. But this response, leaning as it does toward violence, tends to undermine the legitimacy of black power. The consequences of widespread urban disturbances are imponderable. Who, we must ask, is to gain when all the redlined tenements are reduced to rubble or ashes? Up to what point will white Americans tolerate revolt? The closer blacks push the issue toward revolt or insurrection, the greater becomes the likelihood of crushing reprisals. In many respects, the urban revolt—like a nuclear warhead—is not a weapon at all, for the simple reason that it cannot be used to achieve a political objective. Besides, blacks now have, in fact, a far superior resource that they can deploy. They have the mighty weapon of the vote.

A decade or two ago, blacks had no political voice. Their only source of power was agitation and mass action. Today, however, the most potent ingredients of black strength are found in conventional politics. Properly conceived and carried out, black politics has, in fact, all the potential for becoming a strong, legitimate, and constitutionally protected national striking force. How is this great force to be developed and brought to bear?

The Sleeping Giant: Black Voting Strength in the South

The fountainhead of formal black political power reposes in the voting potential of blacks in the southern states. Despite past migrations of blacks into northern cities, one-half of the total black population still lives in the South. In the southern states, this confers on blacks a disproportionate voting strength that has yet to be exploited. In Mississippi and South Carolina, for example, blacks make up more than 30 percent of the population, as they do in twenty-seven congressional districts scattered throughout the South. In Georgia, Alabama, and Louisiana, as well as in forty-eight congressional districts in various southern states, blacks constitute well over 20 percent of the population. Blacks are 35 percent or more of the eligible voters in major southern cities such as Atlanta, New Orleans, Birmingham, Savannah, Charleston, Durham, Richmond, and Baltimore. In scores of black-belt counties, precincts, and state assembly districts throughout the South, black voters actually outnumber whites.

Without even considering how black power in the South can make itself felt on the national, economic, and political scene, we notice immediately its potential impact on the economy of the South. Forty-eight percent of the entire United States black labor force is in the South. New laws encouraging the unionization of southern workers would produce significant economic gains for working blacks. Electing more black state legislators and organizing campaigns to remove from office the traditional lawmakers who guard the South's traditional "right-to-work" laws would be highly advantageous to black labor in the South. By installing some black representatives in key legislative posts at the state level where voting districts are gerrymandered against the election of Negroes, blacks would be able to reform district lines without having to rely on the creaky and often unfriendly machinery of southern courts of law. Because a wide range of economic

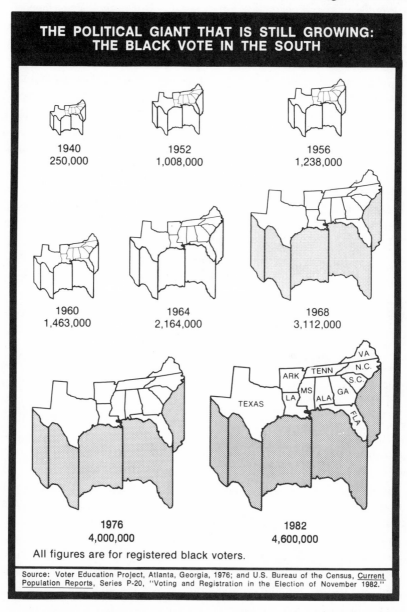

THE POLITICAL GIANT THAT IS STILL GROWING: THE BLACK VOTE IN THE SOUTH

1940
250,000

1952
1,008,000

1956
1,238,000

1960
1,463,000

1964
2,164,000

1968
3,112,000

1976
4,000,000

1982
4,600,000

All figures are for registered black voters.

Source: Voter Education Project, Atlanta, Georgia, 1976; and U.S. Bureau of the Census, Current Population Reports, Series P-20, "Voting and Registration in the Election of November 1982."

benefits generally flow from political victories, it is certain that government contracts, state and local patronage, favorable licensing decisions, and public franchises and grants in favor of blacks would ride piggyback on black political winnings. Clearly, the South offers a most fertile territory to mine black power.

Looking at the concentrations of black voting strength in the South, we see at least forty-eight congressional districts where blacks are at least 20 percent of the population. These are the bases where ballot politics can be used to elect congressmen who are friendly to black political and economic objectives.[1] The 1984 Democratic primary balloting provides a suggestion of what may lie ahead. In seven congressional districts in Georgia, Alabama, Arkansas, and Mississippi, Jesse Jackson won pluralities. In seven other southern districts, he was outpolled only by voters who favored sending uncommitted delegates to the nominating convention.

The immense potential influence of an organized southern black voting bloc comes into view against a backdrop of presidential elections. In 1976, the black vote for Carter in Mississippi was about ten times the President's overall margin of victory in that state. In Louisiana, the figure was about three times; in Texas and South Carolina, 1.6 times; in Florida, 1.4 times. Obviously, massive black abstentions or vote shifts would have thrown a number of southern states—and therefore the outcome of the election, which was very close—to President Ford. If 30 percent of the black vote in Texas and only 4 percent of the black vote in Mississippi had shifted from Carter to Ford, Ford would have won the presidency by 274 electoral votes to 264. A shift to Ford of 34 percent of the black vote for Carter in Texas, Louisiana, Mississippi, Florida, South Carolina, and Maryland would have given Ford a significant victory of 319 to 219 electoral votes. It is clear then that, as long as the pollsters' computers were accurately briefing the opposition, any black leader capable of delivering 10 to 15 percent of the black vote in the South would have had significant bargaining power in negotiations with both presidential contenders.[2]

Except in districts where blacks are a majority, two conditions are required for black voting power to achieve national impact. First, the general election must be close enough for black swing votes to play a decisive role. Second, southern whites must be of divided opinion on the candidates. A large predicted white voter turnout in the South for one candidate or the other will swamp the black vote and obliterate its potential value either as a decisive factor in the election outcome or as a bargaining chip for negotiation with established candidates.

The force of the black vote in the South can be displayed to best advantage in presidential primaries. In a post-primary national election such as the

Carter-Ford contest, black leaders, even if organized, could have done little more than bluff; the shift of black votes away from Carter would have resulted in the election of President Ford, a then unacceptable alternative to most blacks. The situation is quite different, however, in state Democratic presidential primaries where blacks can pick and choose among a number of reasonably acceptable candidates. In this case, the black vote, if properly controlled and manipulated, can be awarded to whichever candidate makes the most satisfactory political deal with the black electorate. As we shall show later on, presidential primaries are also occasions for running black favorite sons who carry delegate votes and bargaining strength with them to the national nominating conventions.

Political power invariably requires the actual or apparent ability to *concentrate* voting or other political activity in time and place. It is not sufficient to show simply that in theory one might have committed a politically powerful act; one must demonstrate the apparent ability to comit it. In one respect, blacks in the South have met this test of political power. They have repeatedly shown their ability to concentrate votes for candidates they favor. For example, in a dramatic display of voter sophistication, blacks in 1966 awarded 89 percent of their votes to a Democrat in one of two off-year United States Senate contests in Virginia, while giving 91 percent of their support to the Republican in the other. In the same year, Ernest Hollings, a white protégé of Robert F. Kennedy, running for the United States Senate from South Carolina, received over 97 percent of the black vote. He won by a margin of only 12,000 votes over conservative Republican Congressman Marshall Parker, a protégé of Senator Strom Thurmond, then one of the nation's leading opponents of racial equality. Blacks gave Hollings 65,000 votes and were clearly responsible for his victory.

In 1968, blacks again demonstrated their ability to concentrate votes for favored candidates. Liberal Democrat Robert W. Scott won 99 percent of the black vote and defeated James Gardner, a Ku Klux Klan apologist, for the governorship of North Carolina. The margin of victory was only 70,000 votes in an election in which blacks apparently gave Scott 200,000 votes— three times his margin of victory. The black vote was again highly influential in the 1976 congressional elections. Supported by 93 percent of the black vote, Tennessee Democrat James Sasser defeated the Republican incumbent, Senator William Brock. Since, overall, Sasser won only 53 percent of the Tennessee vote, the concentration of black votes was obviously crucial to his success. At least six southern members of the House of Representatives owed their election in 1976 in large part to the black vote.[3]

In one major respect, however, blacks have failed to demonstrate the credibility of their political power. They have never shown an ability to *swing* their vote from one candidate to another. Without the demonstrated capacity to deliver a centrally controlled black vote, they will not be seen as a force that can either save a candidate from defeat or, at the last moment, snatch a victory away from him by switching their allegiance to another candidate. Until they develop this ability, they will not have the power to make candidates come to them.

In the South, the increase in the sheer number of black voters has been a great boon to the potential for black political empowerment. The federal government's voter-registration drive, the abolition of poll taxes and literacy tests, the reduction in harassment of black voters, the emergence of black candidates, and rising black political awareness have combined to nearly triple the southern black voter registrations during the period 1960-1982. This dramatic increase in the size of the black electorate could easily be augmented by concerted voter-registration campaigns and by getting out the vote of registered nonvoters. In national election years, according to Census figures, southern whites have voted at a rate nearly 25 percent higher than southern blacks. This means that there are still large, untapped reservoirs of unemployed black strength. The black vote in Mississippi and South Carolina could well be raised to 30 percent of all voters in the state; in Georgia, Alabama, and Lousiana, blacks could easily become 25 percent of the electorate. This would give blacks a commanding influence in gubernatorial, mayoralty, state assembly, and presidential elections where whites are running against other whites. And in voting districts where blacks are a majority or a near majority, black candidates by the scores could be elected to office.

The Electoral College in the North: Where the Sum of Black Power Is Greater Than Its Parts

A peculiar irony of the black political condition is the fact that black voters owe much of their potential strength to race discrimination and segregation. Just as concentrated black voting power in the South is an end product of agrarian slavery, so black voting power in the cities of both the North and the South is a result, in great part, of northern policies of residential segregation. All of the largest cities in the United States have significant black minorities. In New York City, blacks make up approximately 25 percent of the population; in Chicago, 40 percent; and in Philadelphia, approximately 38 percent. Approximately 45 percent of the populations of Memphis, St. Louis, Charleston, and Cleveland are black, while in Atlanta, Newark, Detroit, Baltimore, New Orleans, and Gary the figure exceeds 50 percent. Over 70 percent of the population of Washington, D.C. is black.

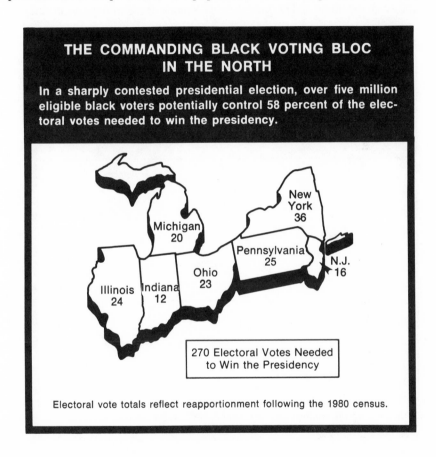

THE COMMANDING BLACK VOTING BLOC IN THE NORTH

In a sharply contested presidential election, over five million eligible black voters potentially control 58 percent of the electoral votes needed to win the presidency.

New York 36

Michigan 20

Pennsylvania 25

Ohio 23

N.J. 16

Illinois 24

Indiana 12

270 Electoral Votes Needed to Win the Presidency

Electoral vote totals reflect reapportionment following the 1980 census.

In the country's ten largest cities, the eligible black vote could produce almost 4 million ballots.

Although black migration into the large cities has slowed in recent years, the black birth rate remains high, and the flight of whites from the cities appears to be continuing. If present trends hold, Cleveland, Memphis, Philadelphia, Chicago, and St. Louis may all have black majorities by 1990. An important bellwether of the probability of ultimate black urban political control is the fact that at least fifteen of our twenty largest cities have increasingly smaller minorities of whites in their public schools. Since young people inevitably grow up to voting age, demographics alone point to the possibility of black urban political control within a generation. After the Democratic National Convention of 1980, Mayor Edward Koch of New York warned President Carter: "If you don't carry the cities, you ain't gonna be the next President." The landslide of Ronald Reagan's election did not

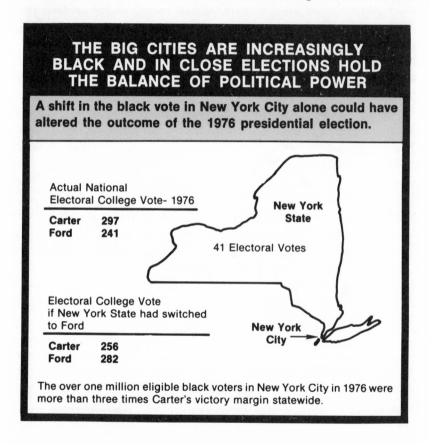

THE BIG CITIES ARE INCREASINGLY BLACK AND IN CLOSE ELECTIONS HOLD THE BALANCE OF POLITICAL POWER

A shift in the black vote in New York City alone could have altered the outcome of the 1976 presidential election.

Actual National
Electoral College Vote- 1976

Carter   297
Ford   241

New York State

41 Electoral Votes

Electoral College Vote
if New York State had switched
to Ford

Carter   256
Ford   282

New York City

The over one million eligible black voters in New York City in 1976 were more than three times Carter's victory margin statewide.

bear out Koch's prediction. But in a closer contest, the urban vote—and particularly an increase in the black urban vote—would have tipped the scales in Carter's favor.

The concentration of blacks in the cities will clearly produce many more urban elected officials responsive to the local needs of blacks. Urban political power is also likely to confer some economic gains on urban blacks. But how do these large urban voting blocs produce black strength in national elections? To answer this question one must look to the large northern industrialized states whose electoral votes are very important to any successful presidential bid. The potential here is impressive. In a tightly contested race, the half million expected black votes in Philadelphia and Pittsburgh alone could hold the balance of power controlling Pennsylvania's twenty-five electoral votes. In a close presidential election, blacks could hold the balance of political power in Ohio, with the 300,000 eligible black voters in the six cities of Columbus, Akron, Dayton, Cleveland, Youngstown, and Cincinnati representing a margin of control over Ohio's twenty-three electoral votes.

Four other northern states offer even more important opportunities for blacks to control the outcomes of presidential elections. The Electoral College delegations of Michigan, Illinois, New Jersey, and New York make up over 35 percent of the votes necessary to win the presidency. In a close election, this huge bloc of electors could be controlled by more than 2 million eligible black voters in New York City, Detroit, Chicago, Newark, Buffalo, Jersey City, and East St. Louis. If white voters in these four states were divided, blacks as swing voters would have nearly preemptive powers in national elections. Black voters in these states might also achieve a commanding position in senatorial and gubernatorial elections if, once more, whites were closely divided. Here, in merely four of the most populous states capable of swinging ninety-six electoral votes in a presidential election, is the black political homeland.

The formidable political power of blacks was revealed in the 1976 presidential election. In many northern states, whites were almost equally divided between Carter and Ford, but the heavy black vote for Carter provided the necessary margin for a Democratic victory. In New York, Pennsylvania, Ohio, Wisconsin, and Missouri, Ford would have been the winner if white voters only were counted. But heavy black turnouts for Carter actually reversed the decision of the white voters and gave the 116 electoral votes of the five states—truly a commanding bloc—to Carter.

For any group aspiring to swing-vote status, the ability to tip an election is much more likely to be present in gubernatorial and senatorial campaigns. Indeed, it is safe to say that today few candidates for governor or senator in New York, Illinois, Pennsylvania, Michigan, or New Jersey could be elected if their politics were unacceptable to blacks in New York City, Chicago, Philadelphia, Detroit, or Newark. A candidate for the governorship of Ohio must make peace with the quarter of a million black voters in Cleveland, Columbus, and Cincinnati. At the same time, whites in great numbers are not yet prepared to vote for blacks for these offices—with the result that recent gains in black voting power have still left blacks far short of any realistic prospect of electing a black U.S. senator or governor in any state. At this stage, black influence in the statewide contests rests primarily in the potential to deny or grant these high public offices to the various white politicians contending for them.

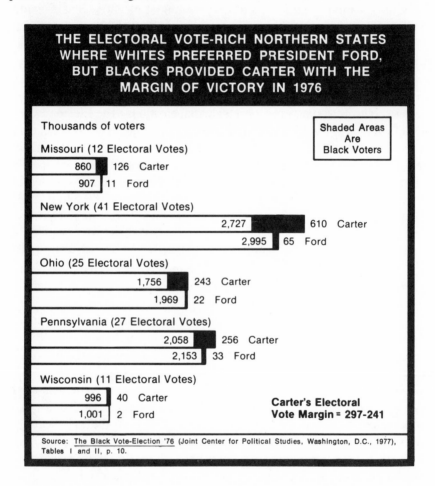

THE ELECTORAL VOTE-RICH NORTHERN STATES WHERE WHITES PREFERRED PRESIDENT FORD, BUT BLACKS PROVIDED CARTER WITH THE MARGIN OF VICTORY IN 1976

Thousands of voters

Shaded Areas Are Black Voters

Missouri (12 Electoral Votes)
860 | 126 Carter
907 | 11 Ford

New York (41 Electoral Votes)
2,727 | 610 Carter
2,995 | 65 Ford

Ohio (25 Electoral Votes)
1,756 | 243 Carter
1,969 | 22 Ford

Pennsylvania (27 Electoral Votes)
2,058 | 256 Carter
2,153 | 33 Ford

Wisconsin (11 Electoral Votes)
996 | 40 Carter
1,001 | 2 Ford

Carter's Electoral Vote Margin = 297-241

Source: The Black Vote-Election '76 (Joint Center for Political Studies, Washington, D.C., 1977), Tables I and II, p. 10.

Mayoral elections are another matter. Black mayors have appeared on the political map of the United States with ever-increasing frequency. It goes without saying that these victories provide an important underpinning for the black urban elective power base. These mayors not only hold city hall, but also often head and control their party's delegations to state and national conventions. Mayors generally control patronage, government contracts, city deposit accounts, and other public perquisites that confer political influence. Eleven large cities had black mayors in 1984: Chicago, Los Angeles, Philadelphia, Detroit, Atlanta, Newark, New Orleans, Richmond, Birmingham, Oakland, and Washington, D.C. In years to come, the prospects are good for the election of additional black mayors in Cleveland, Memphis, St. Louis, and Baltimore. As natural spokesmen for urban constituencies whose support will be needed by statewide and national candidates, the black mayors will have an increasingly greater impact on national political decisions, nominations, and appointments.

Black Influence in Presidential Primaries: The Favorite Son Bargaining Card

We have already noted how primary elections offer a striking opportunity for the development of political influence. For blacks, primaries are truly beautiful because, unlike general elections, nominating contests are often marked by intense competition among many candidates representing a considerable range of political opinion. This means that candidates in primaries are obliged to court various constituencies, including minority votes and special-interest groups, in order to assemble a winning plurality or majority. But in a general election, the choice is much more restricted. As the candidate choices narrow, usually to two, minority influence drains away; in most cases, the black voter's options dwindle to a choice between staying at home on election day or voting for the candidate who, for many blacks, is seen as the lesser of two evils.

This point was illustrated in 1974 when George Wallace faced four challengers in the Democratic race for governor of Alabama. Early in the campaign Wallace needed to woo the black vote in order to win a primary plurality. At this point, blacks had some power to negotiate the terms under which their greatly needed support would be delivered. But once the primary was over, their power wilted because Wallace no longer needed their votes. The white Democratic vote, divided in the primary, was now united behind him, assuring him a victory over his Republican opponent.

By skillfully working the primaries, black voters could have influenced the politics of candidate Jimmy Carter in the 1976 presidential election. But blacks made the same crucial error that has plagued them for most of their political history. Instead of securing concrete assurances of executive support for legislative policies as well as a specific commitment to appoint blacks to high-level government posts, blacks fell victim to a well-conceived public relations campaign aimed at winning their support at the lowest possible price, while the Democratic party paid much greater attention to the demands of other constituencies within the party.

Liberal opposition to Carter (alienated by his infamous gaffe about the value of "ethnically pure neighborhoods") did not sustain its momentum during the primary months. Blacks and civil rights sympathizers succumbed to the loudspeakers on Carter's bandwagon, which endlessly reminisced about how little Jimmy Carter had played with black children as a boy. Endlessly the nation heard the story of Carter's courageous act in hanging a portrait of Martin Luther King, Jr. in the halls of the Georgia State Capitol. No mention was made, however, of Carter's praise for George Wallace and Lester Maddox during his 1970 gubernatorial campaign. Southern Democrats later delivered the South solidly to Carter in the general election. Racial conservatives understood Carter's need to hang a certain amount of black political window dressing.

Without making any concrete promises to black people, Carter's press efforts paid off handsomely in millions of black votes. In the early Florida primary, black ballots enabled Carter to deal a smashing blow to the presidential aspirations of George Wallace. By May 1976, the campaign was gathering momentum. In the Michigan and Wisconsin primaries, black voters once again put Carter over the top. Suddenly, with the Carter bandwagon rolling, it was too late for blacks to exact any commitments. Their options were gone, and they had no choice but to support Carter in the general election. The only alternatives at that time were Ford and Reagan, both of whom held views highly unsatisfactory to the majority of black voters. In the national election, Carter won the black vote overwhelmingly, without having made a single political commitment to black people. Yet, without the heavy black vote for Carter, President Ford would have been elected to a full term. This gift to Carter, it is pleasant to think, should have counted for something. It didn't. The moment the black vote was assured and victory won in the general election, Carter's interests, like those of dozens of Presidents before him, turned to the pressures and needs of other constituencies.

Betrayed in 1976, blacks should have avoided the primary mousetrap in the next national election. But once again, in the 1980 primary season, blacks sat like dignitaries on the reviewing stand and let the parade pass them by. Again, no effort was made to coordinate strategies prior to the onset of the primary season. Blacks never even tried to achieve a consensus on what course to follow or, for that matter, on which candidate to support. A majority of the Congressional Black Caucus supported Senator Ted Kennedy while most black mayors, fearful of losing important federal subsidies for their cities, lined up behind President Carter. Some influential black spokesmen even flirted with the idea of going Republican. The result was that on primary day the rank-and-file black voters, having received no clear signal from their leaders, disastrously split their votes between the two front-running Democratic candidates. As a consequence, black political power counted for naught.

The moment the primary results were in, blacks found, not surprisingly, that there was little they could do to influence the balance of the contest. The 484 black delegates at the 1980 Democratic National Convention in New York City made up 29 percent of the total required to nominate a presidential candidate, yet they were unable to play a significant role. They owed their allegiance not to any black candidate or cause, but to one or the other of the white presidential aspirants. Yet, if they had been unified, they could have been influential players in the fight over convention rules. A united black front threatening to bolt the Carter fold on the vote over the "open convention" rule could have forced the President to make some concessions to the black delegates on platform policy issues or appointments in his second administration. No such threat ever materialized, and Carter campaign strategists were able to keep their black delegates in line without having to make any concrete assurances of support for black legislative or political goals. When the rules fight was won and Carter's renomination assured, the President turned to appeasing Senator Kennedy, organized labor, and white liberals, all of whose votes he would need if he was to have a chance to win in November. As ever, the black vote was safely in the bag.

The lessons of the past are clear. If blacks are to acquire a significant political voice, they may not allow their political moves to await the outcome of presidential nominating conventions. Their best opportunity for shaping presidential policy is during the primary season, when Democrats can be forced to compete for the black vote. Black politicians must take steps early in the campaign to arrive at the convention with a solid bloc of delegates. Once the primary process narrows the field to one, it is very likely that all the Democratic presidential candidates will have escaped the clutches of black political power without having made definitive commitments to policies favored by the large majority of Negro people.

Blacks Must Control Their Delegates

The key to convention power is, of course, "control." Power asks not only how many delegates you have on your side, but also who controls them. Traditionally, most black delegates have been handpicked by whites and pledged to support white candidates. As such, blacks have been unable to use delegate influence to advance the interests of black America. Black political power will not be firmly in place until black candidates not only control a large bloc of black delegates but also hold the allegiance of the vast majority of black delegates at the convention. Majority candidates would then no longer be able to nullify black strength by dividing it.

How can such control be achieved? Again, the key to the puzzle lies in the geographic concentration of black voters. To see how this works, it is necessary to understand the delegate selection process. Although delegate selection rules change somewhat every four years, delegates to the national convention are chosen for the most part on the basis of the primary or caucus vote received in areas that usually correspond to congressional districts. A bird's-eye view of the potential for developing black balloting power within these districts is provided by looking at the racial count. There are forty-nine congressional districts in the nation where black population concentrations are greater than 30 percent, sixty congressional districts where blacks make up more than 25 percent of the total, and eighty congressional districts where the black population exceeds 20 percent of the total. A well-organized campaign aimed at maximizing the black potential in these districts could conceivably send as many as 200 black delegates to the nominating conventions. Since there are many additional districts with black population concentrations between 10 and 20 percent of the total, the final black delegate total could become even larger.

Black political bargaining power will persist only as long as in the early stages of a campaign the black delegates maintain distance from major candidates. To ensure that these delegates remain independent for as long as possible, they must go to conventions pledged, until released, to various black favorite son candidates. In this manner, the force of an undivided bloc is maintained and maximum black voting strength is delivered in exchange for maximum political advantage.

There is a long list of primary states where black favorite sons could win a sizable number of convention delegates. Looking over the field for future elections, blacks could run Congressman William Gray in Pennsylvania, Mayor Thomas Bradley of Los Angeles, or Congressmen Ronald Dellums, Merv Dymally, Augustus Hawkins, or Julian Dixon in California and Congressman Parren Mitchell in Maryland. State Senator Henry Kirksey could be the favorite son in Mississippi; Congressmen John Conyers or George Crockett or Coleman Young, mayor of Detroit, in Michigan; and possibly Congresswoman Cardiss Collins or Representatives Gus Savage or

Charles Hayes in Illinois. In Georgia, Mayor Andrew Young of Atlanta would be the ideal candidate; in Ohio, Congressman Louis Stokes. In New Jersey, the presumable favorite son would be Mayor Kenneth Gibson of Newark; in Tennessee, Congressman Harold Ford; in New York, possibly Congressmen Charles Rangel, Edolphus Towns, Major Owens, or Franklin Thomas, head of the Ford Foundation. Other black favorite sons could include Mayor Ernest Morial of New Orleans, Congressmen William Clay or Alan Wheat of Missouri, former Mayor Henry Marsh of Richmond, Virginia, Congressman Mickey Leland in Texas, Walter Fauntroy in the District of Columbia, and Mayor Richard Hatcher of Gary, Indiana, or Willie Lewis Brown, Jr., Speaker of the California Assembly.

A variation on the strategy of running a host of local black favorite son candidates would be to field a slate of regional black favorite son candidates. The regional favorite son strategy has advantages when fear of retaliation from party regulars and reluctance to break off traditional party loyalties make it difficult to find a favorite son to run in the major states where there is important black political strength.

A third variation on the favorite son strategy would be one of running the same candidate in every state primary. Naturally, this candidate would need to have sufficient national appeal to win a large number of delegates in every region across the country. A national black candidate greatly admired by a significant percentage of Americans would undoubtedly attract more voter attention than would a selection of favorite sons. As seen in the 1984 presidential primaries, the remarkable spectacle of a black person running for the nation's highest office changes whites' views of who is entitled to seek power, derails the standard litany of American media politics, and presents a striking event of great national interest and appeal.

An important advantage in running a national black candidate would be the possibility of the candidate's qualifying for matching federal campaign funds. A candidate seeking federal money must receive private contributions of $5,000 or more—in individual donations of $250 or less—in at least twenty different states. If these qualifications are met, the candidate is then eligible to receive funds on a dollar-for-dollar basis up to a certain limited amount dictated by federal law. The ceiling was initially set in 1976 at $5 million, but the total dollar amount available to each candidate has been raised every election year to coincide with the rate of inflation. Black favorite sons seeking delegates in only one state would not meet these qualifications and thus would be limited to private donations. But a well-known national black candidate would have little trouble meeting federal funds qualifications in twenty states.

Whether the black strategy is national, regional, or local favorite son candidacies, the goal is the same: to capture and acquire control of a sizable number of delegate votes and to use them as bargaining chips at the nominating convention. If black voters were excited enough at this prospect to turn out at primary elections and party caucuses at about the same rate as white voters do, it is not inconceivable that blacks could arrive at the national convention armed with 500 or more controlled delegates.

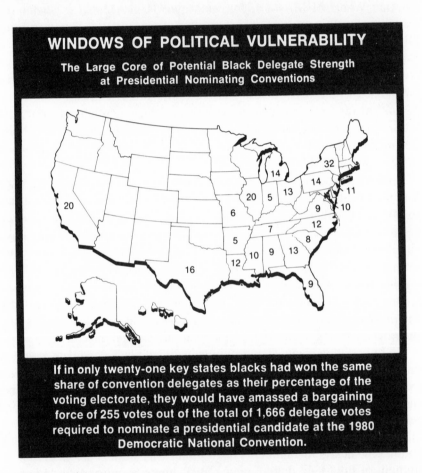

WINDOWS OF POLITICAL VULNERABILITY

The Large Core of Potential Black Delegate Strength at Presidential Nominating Conventions

If in only twenty-one key states blacks had won the same share of convention delegates as their percentage of the voting electorate, they would have amassed a bargaining force of 255 votes out of the total of 1,666 delegate votes required to nominate a presidential candidate at the 1980 Democratic National Convention.

The prospect of success at a national nominating convention increases greatly if blacks are able to make successful alliances with Hispanics and other minority voters with policy objectives very similar to their own. By 1985, it is expected that Hispanic voters will outnumber blacks. Even today, very large Spanish-speaking U.S. populations have huge political influence in states such as Arizona, California, Colorado, Florida, New Mexico, and New York. A successful alliance with Hispanic voters could easily add another hundred delegates to the minority presence at every Democratic convention.

Obviously, the more delegates controlled by blacks, the greater their chance of swinging the convention to the white candidate of their choice. But even a few score of delegates can be a significant force. For years, Chicago's Mayor Richard Daley was a powerful national politician and sometimes even a presidential kingmaker; yet he controlled no more than 100 delegates to the Democratic National Convention. Potentially, blacks can be three times as strong. This is not pie-in-the-sky politics; it is a reasonably predictable conclusion about the leverage effects of well-known principles of minority politics.

"Let's Make a Deal":
Black Strength in General Elections

Under the present two-party system where the major parties do not compete for the black vote, the superior route for black entry into the political system lies through the Democratic state nominating primaries. Encouraging multiple candidates, exploiting divisions within the Democratic party, nurturing divisive tendencies in the Republican party, and nominating black favorite sons are the most effective strategies for blacks seeking to influence the direction of future presidential initiatives, executive orders, and appointments. There are, however, a few exceptional cases where blacks may wield considerable power in the general presidential election.

Let us examine some election results to see how minority power sometimes prevails over majority power. In the 1976 Carter-Ford contest, Ford received only 8 percent of the black vote, with 90 percent going to Carter and 2 percent to third-party candidates. Among white voters, however, 51 percent of the ballots favored Ford while 47 percent named Carter, with third-party candidates again drawing 2 percent. Had the black vote in 1976 not been so nearly unanimous, Ford would easily have been elected on the strength of his 51-47 margin over Carter among white voters. Indeed, if Ford could have pulled as little as 23 percent of the black vote, he would have had a popular majority.

In any apparently close election such as this one, a black leader with sufficient influence to persuade any significant portion of the black vote to stay home on election day, or even to vote Republican, could bargain from a position of significant political strength. In fact, in the Carter-Ford contest, the person who could influence large numbers of black voters might have exacted substantial platform and black appointment commitments from either candidate—from Carter for delivering the votes that would save him from defeat, from Ford for minimizing the black vote in the Carter column.

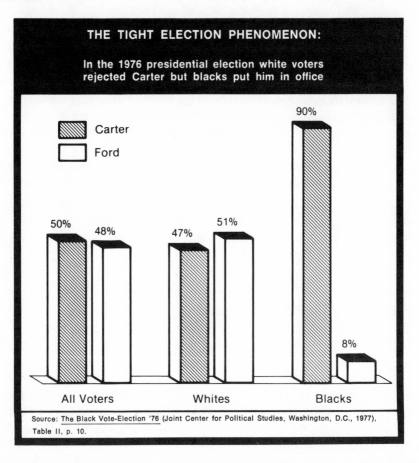

THE TIGHT ELECTION PHENOMENON:

In the 1976 presidential election white voters rejected Carter but blacks put him in office

Carter

Ford

90%

50% 48%

47% 51%

8%

All Voters   Whites   Blacks

Source: The Black Vote-Election '76 (Joint Center for Political Studies, Washington, D.C., 1977), Table II, p. 10.

The Electoral College results in 1976 highlight even further the huge political power that blacks possessed but failed to use. First, let us consider what would have happened if black voters en masse had been dissatisfied with, say, Carter's preelection promises to use executive power to advance the economic development of blacks and had simply stayed at home on election day. With the black vote, Carter won 297 electoral votes, only twenty-seven more than he needed to win the presidency. Without these votes, he would have captured only eighty-one electoral votes, and Gerald Ford would have amassed 457. This is due to the fact that in thirteen states—Alabama, Florida, Louisiana, Maryland, Mississippi, Missouri, New York, North Carolina, Ohio, Pennsylvania, South Carolina, Texas, and Wisconsin, accounting for 216 electoral votes—*Carter lost the white vote but still carried the state*. Thus, if blacks hadn't turned out for Carter, there would have been a landslide victory for Ford.[4]

Now let us consider a much more realistic hypothesis. If only one-tenth of the black voters who voted for Carter had instead boycotted the election, the states of Mississippi and Ohio would have shifted to Ford, giving him a 273-265 electoral vote victory. Again, assuming that all parties perceived that the election would be close, any black leader with control over even a small percentage of the black vote in these two states would have had considerable bargaining leverage with either Ford or Carter. Having computers and access to accurate polling of voter preferences is generally believed to be a vested advantage of the white politician. But in this instance the special knowledge that computers and polling provide apprises mainstream candidates of the closeness of impending votes in particular states' voting districts and forces them to come to terms with black voters in situations where, without the information, the latent power of the black voter would have been ignored.

Other very minor shifts in black voting patterns in the 1976 presidential election could have assured a Republican victory. If only one in every five blacks in New York State had switched his or her vote in 1976, Ford would have been returned to the White House. If in Texas Carter had polled only 68 percent of the black vote instead of the 96.8 percent he actually received, he would have lost the state to Ford. Most dramatically, if a mere 6,000 blacks who voted for Carter in Mississippi had switched to Ford, and only 4,000 black voters in Ohio had switched their votes, Ford would have won the election with 273 to Carter's 265 electoral votes.

The Carter-Ford election of 1976 was not the first time the black vote provided a critical margin of victory in a presidential election. Although the event passed largely unnoticed, blacks played a crucial role in the 1948 election. President Truman's directive that the armed forces be desegregated and his support for a Presidential Fair Employment Practices Commission won him significant black support. Overall, President Truman carried 303 electoral votes to Thomas E. Dewey's 189, a seemingly safe margin. Yet Truman lost the white vote in California, Illinois, and Ohio. Without the black support he received in those three states, seventy-eight electoral votes, and thus the presidency, would have gone to Dewey.[5]

Again, twelve years later, President Kennedy's razor-thin victory over Richard Nixon would not have occurred save for the black vote. Kennedy carried the popular vote by only 118,000 ballots—less than one-tenth of one percent of the overall vote. But nationwide, he polled about 75 percent of the black vote. In Illinois, Kennedy defeated Nixon by only 9,000 votes

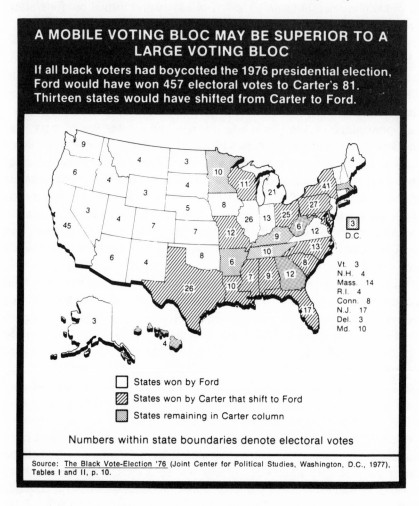

A MOBILE VOTING BLOC MAY BE SUPERIOR TO A LARGE VOTING BLOC

If all black voters had boycotted the 1976 presidential election, Ford would have won 457 electoral votes to Carter's 81. Thirteen states would have shifted from Carter to Ford.

Vt. 3
N.H. 4
Mass. 14
R.I. 4
Conn. 8
N.J. 17
Del. 3
Md. 10

☐ States won by Ford

▨ States won by Carter that shift to Ford

▩ States remaining in Carter column

Numbers within state boundaries denote electoral votes

Source: The Black Vote-Election '76 (Joint Center for Political Studies, Washington, D.C., 1977), Tables I and II, p. 10.

after piling up a 250,000-vote margin in black precincts. The black vote also rescued Kennedy in Texas, where his 46,000-vote plurality would have vanished had it not been for the 150,000-vote lead he gathered in the black precincts of the state. Kennedy lost the white vote in Michigan, New Jersey, Missouri, and North Carolina, yet carried all four states because of his heavy support from black voters. If a mere 9,000 blacks in Illinois and 10,000 blacks in Missouri had stayed home that day, the election would have been thrown into the House of Representatives.[6]

In retrospect, one now sees that because of the Reagan landslide, the black vote as such was helpless to affect the outcome of the 1980 presidential election. The voting power of blacks always depends on rather close elections where their ballots can tip the scales to one candidate or another. But political power depends not on hindsight but on what the major parties and candidates *knew* prior to the election. Polls conducted in the late stages of the election campaign showed Ronald Reagan with only a slim lead. At this point, the black vote, organized as a swing voting bloc, could have maneuvered with considerable force.

Possible scenarios may be sketched out. In the atmosphere of uncertainty that prevailed as election day approached, a politically cohesive black voting bloc, capable of swinging as a unit from one candidate to another, could have won major concessions from candidate Carter and perhaps from candidate Reagan. By threatening to support the Republican nominee or the third-party candidate, John Anderson, blacks could have exacted firm policy commitments from Carter, who knew he would need a large black vote in order to hope to win reelection. It is even conceivable that had blacks been in a position to present candidate Reagan—politically hard-pressed in October 1980—with the opportunity of claiming the black swing vote, a political deal might have been cut in which there would have been no presidential backtracking on civil rights enforcement, no presidential assaults on busing for racial desegregation, and some moderation of the economic policies that appeared to stifle black progress during the early years of the Reagan Administration. Later in his Administration issues arose— the Martin Luther King holiday bill, tax subsidies for schools that exclude blacks, and voting rights legislation—where Reagan, the racial conservative, in fact demonstrated his capacity to back down on "matters of principle" in the interests of saving Republican candidates from major black-voter backlash. Despite the landslide defeat of incumbent President Carter in 1980, even aborted negotiations between black leaders and presidential candidates would have been a dramatic display of black political might.

Of course, the potential negotiating influence of the black vote evaporates almost entirely when an enormously popular President is already in the White House, and when his nomination and reelection are assured without regard to how skillfully blacks concentrate and manipulate their votes. Also, even when a close national election is predicted, the black vote loses much of its influence with the Democratic candidate if the Republican alternative is an arch conservative unacceptable to the large majority of blacks. In normal circumstances, where an election is seen as close and the contenders are a moderate Republican and a liberal or somewhat conservative Democrat, blacks can increase their influence by endeavoring to strike a bargain with either candidate. But, as suggested earlier, as long as

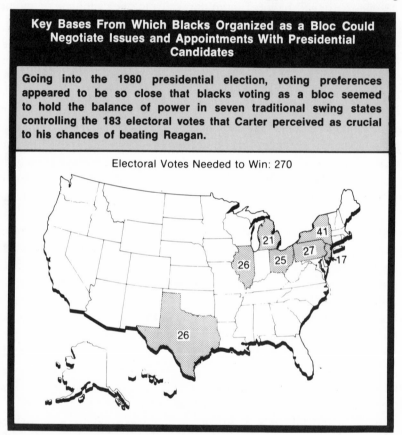

Key Bases From Which Blacks Organized as a Bloc Could Negotiate Issues and Appointments With Presidential Candidates

Going into the 1980 presidential election, voting preferences appeared to be so close that blacks voting as a bloc seemed to hold the balance of power in seven traditional swing states controlling the 183 electoral votes that Carter perceived as crucial to his chances of beating Reagan.

Electoral Votes Needed to Win: 270

the two-party system prevails and by its very nature greatly limits the political choices of blacks, the far superior strategy lies in exerting political influence by manipulating the presidential primaries.

Blacks as Nonvoters: The Silent Minority

So far, we have considered the great potential for developing a formidable political sword if the black vote, or any significant part of it, could be delivered or withheld as a controllable quid pro quo. But black political power does not entirely depend on finding means to manipulate a voting bloc. Important black political force is latent, too, in the sheer numbers of black voters. In the 1976 national election, only 49 percent of the eligible black voters actually went to the polls, compared with about 61 percent of the eligible whites. In primaries, when black voting strength usually has its highest potential influence, the black voter participation rate customarily drops to 20 percent or in some instances to a catastrophic 10 percent.[7]

The borough of Brooklyn in New York City is typical of the highly disorganized and apathetic quality of the black vote. In Brooklyn's Twelfth Congressional District in 1978, 54 percent of the population was black, and 20 percent was Hispanic. In the neighboring Thirteenth District, Jews were a voting majority. That year, the Twelfth District had a black congresswoman, Representative Shirley Chisholm, and the Thirteenth a Jew, Representative Stephen Solarz. Each was easily reelected in 1978, with 88 and 81 percent of the vote respectively. But 85,000 votes were counted in the heavily Jewish district while only 29,000—approximately one-third as many—were tabulated in the majority black district.

Now consider the powerful influence that black voters would have if they went to the polls as often as Jews, a much smaller numerical minority. As an example of the comparative politicization of the two groups, consider the turnouts of Jews and blacks in the 1976 senatorial primary in New York State. Jewish-Americans cast 33 percent of the total vote in this election, although they comprised only 14 percent of the population. On the other hand, blacks, who also comprised about 14 percent of the population, cast only 11 percent of the total vote. Politicians believe—and it is their *beliefs* that make them accountable to minorities and other interest groups—that the vote among the Brooklyn-based and often lower-income Hassidic Jews approaches 100 percent. This perception confers huge political power on a very small minority.[8]

Jews comprise only 3 percent of the national population yet their political influence even on a nationwide basis is striking. A 1976 campaign memorandum warned presidential candidate Morris Udall that "three-quarters of a million Jewish votes are certainly enough to be decisive in a close election, and even more influential considering that these votes tend to be cast as a bloc and clustered in big electoral vote states."[9] Each element of this statement should, in theory, apply also to the black vote, for the potential strength of the black vote is four times as great as that of the Jewish vote. But the unused voting potential of very large numbers of blacks does not pose a comparable threat. In Congress, for instance, the political influence of Jews is so great that an issue such as the Israeli occupation of the West Bank of the Jordan has been virtually taboo as a debatable issue. On the other hand, issues that most blacks regard as nondebatable, such as federal day-care assistance or federal income support, are either ignored or casually debated and tabled in Congress.

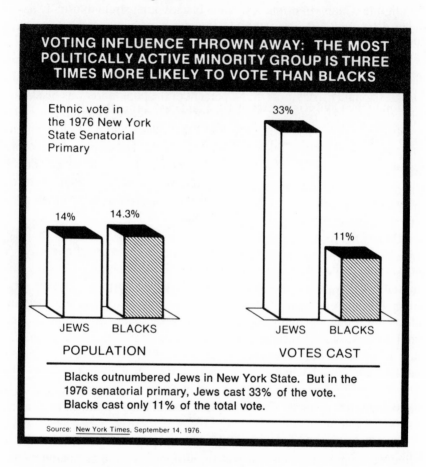

VOTING INFLUENCE THROWN AWAY: THE MOST POLITICALLY ACTIVE MINORITY GROUP IS THREE TIMES MORE LIKELY TO VOTE THAN BLACKS

Ethnic vote in the 1976 New York State Senatorial Primary

14% 14.3%

JEWS   BLACKS

POPULATION

33%

11%

JEWS   BLACKS

VOTES CAST

Blacks outnumbered Jews in New York State. But in the 1976 senatorial primary, Jews cast 33% of the vote. Blacks cast only 11% of the total vote.

Source: New York Times, September 14, 1976.

If the voting rate of America as a whole—59.2 percent in the presidential year 1980, 46 percent in the 1978 off-year elections—is generally termed a national disgrace, the black rate of participation can be more properly described as catastrophic. In 1978, only 37 percent of all blacks went to the polls, but for blacks ages 18 to 20, the voting participation rate was only 15 percent; for blacks ages 21 to 24, 25 percent. If these low turnout rates continue, especially among young blacks, the prospects are very poor for the next generation of blacks to acquire political power in the United States. In some states, the congressional districts have been redrawn by court order expressly to assure black voting success. Here is truly a remarkable event: an invitation by the powerful to share power! Yet blacks—and especially young blacks—still fail to turn out to elect their candidates or to defeat those who oppose black interests.[10]

The 1978 midterm elections show how black influence, even in an election important to black interests, evaporates because of low voter turnout. In Texas, black voters, who together with Hispanic-Americans make up close to one-third of the state's electorate, had good reason to defeat the reelection bid of Senator John Tower, whose voting record included opposition to the Civil Rights Act of 1964 and the Voting Rights Act of 1965. The vote in black precincts went overwhelmingly against him, but the turnout was so low, averaging about 25 percent, that Tower squeaked into office. An increase of only 2 percent in the black vote would have defeated him. In removing him from office, blacks might have permanently eliminated from the Senate a politician who has proved to be one of the most formidable opponents of black economic and political progress.

In the same year, the same 2 percent increase in the black vote in Texas would in all likelihood have elected Democrat John Hill to the governorship instead of Republican William Clement. In Virginia, an increase of less than one percent of the black vote would have defeated freshman Republican Senator John Warner. Indeed, modest increases in black voter turnouts at congressional elections in 1978 would probably have resulted in the defeat of Republicans Floyd Spence of South Carolina, Samuel Devine of Ohio, and William Dickinson of Alabama, all of whom were arch conservatives, if not racial segregationists.

If the black sleeping giant is willing to wake up and stir his stumps, he can virtually write his own ticket. We noted earlier that if all black voters had stayed home on election day of 1976, Gerald Ford would have been a landslide winner, with 457 electoral votes to Jimmy Carter's eighty-one. But, as we know, the black vote gave Carter a narrow victory. What if the black voter turnout had equaled that of other dedicated voting groups? If, matching the turnout of Jewish voters, 75 percent of the eligible blacks had voted following the pattern set by blacks who did vote—90 percent for Carter and 8 percent for Ford—they would have shifted the electoral votes of California, Illinois, Michigan, New Jersey, Oklahoma, Oregon, and Virginia to Carter. The result would have been 432 electoral votes for Carter against 106 for Ford. In other words, *black voters in the 1976 presidential election had the potential to create an Electoral College landslide either way.*[11]

Many political observers feel that the potential for enhanced black political power derived from either increased voter participation or aggressive bloc voting is exaggerated. They warn that as soon as whites become aware of mounting black voter activity, a backlash will cause the white vote to increase and thereby swamp any black gains. This possibility certainly cannot be rejected out of hand, but it cannot be accepted uncritically, espe-

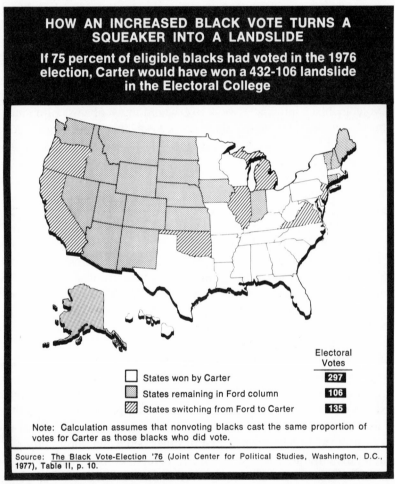

HOW AN INCREASED BLACK VOTE TURNS A SQUEAKER INTO A LANDSLIDE

If 75 percent of eligible blacks had voted in the 1976 election, Carter would have won a 432-106 landslide in the Electoral College

Electoral Votes

☐	States won by Carter	297
▓	States remaining in Ford column	106
▨	States switching from Ford to Carter	135

Note: Calculation assumes that nonvoting blacks cast the same proportion of votes for Carter as those blacks who did vote.

Source: The Black Vote-Election '76 (Joint Center for Political Studies, Washington, D.C., 1977), Table II, p. 10.

cially since the backlash argument—that blacks are better off voting *issues* rather than *race*—is a key element in the theology behind the nation's fifty-year history of keeping political power in white hands. Is the backlash argument relevant to the question of blacks increasing their voting strength, or is it merely another instance of defeatist propaganda put forward to discourage black political action?

To some extent, the question can be answered by looking at the Jewish experience. Anti-Jewish prejudice still runs high in America, yet Jews have been relatively successful in playing the politics of race. Blacks are 11.5 percent of the population; Jews are only 3 percent. Yet in the Ninety-sixth Congress elected in November 1978, there were twenty-three Jews in the House of Representatives and seven in the Senate.[12] A black person has never been elected governor of any of the fifty states. Jews have served as governors of New York, Pennsylvania, Maryland, and Rhode Island. Jews have served in the President's Cabinet as Secretaries of State and Treasury, as Attorney General, and as Director of the National Security Council, but the nation has never witnessed a black person in these powerful and sensitive posts. Four Jews have been appointed to the Supreme Court, but only one black has made it to the Court. America's Middle East foreign policy, shaped in great measure to accommodate Jewish political power in the United States, has consistently supported the autonomy of Israel despite the tremendous economic pressures from the oil-producing Arab states and many large U.S. oil companies. Jewish candidates have never found backlash to be a serious problem; why should blacks be unduly concerned by the thrust of it? The demonstrated strength of the Jewish vote shows that if the power of the minority is sufficient, determined, and functioning within traditional boundaries of legitimacy, racial backlash is not an insuperable obstacle.

Blacks who continue to look upon the exhortation to get out the vote as an overdone and meaningless piece of Fourth of July rhetoric should note one compelling item of election statistics: *The number of eligible blacks who did not vote in the 1976 presidential election was greater than the winning margin achieved by either candidate in twenty-five states accounting for 384 electoral votes.*[13]

Despite admonishments from friends of Jim Crow and nervous doubts expressed by cap-in-hand liberals about the wisdom of blacks pursuing ethnic political power, the evidence is strong that a greatly expanded black voter participation rate represents the best hope for the attainment of a commanding black political force.

Blacks as a Third Political Force: No More Free Lunches for Democrats

Power is found in consensus. But consensus confers only the potential for power. This potential cannot be realized and converted into force without an instrument—an organized pressure group, a protest march, a boycott, a strike—by which consensus makes power itself felt. In politics, this instrument is the *political party*. Since the acquisition of political power is the end objective, we must then ask whether black political interests might not be better served by organizing a black political party. Would blacks, as a group that already votes with up to 90 percent uniformity, be more or less powerful if they had their own political place wholly independent of the two major parties? This is not a hypothetical question. In Chicago's Cook County there are in fact two Democratic parties—one white, one black.

The present American political system in which two parties take turns governing the country is customarily perceived as amply serving the needs of blacks; but the two-party system is, in fact, a major impediment to the goal of black power and to the overall political strategies that greater power in black hands could set in place. Indeed, the political weakness of blacks is, in a sense, structurally built into the limited options provided by our two-party system. For sixty years following emancipation, the black vote was the Republican party's greatest asset. No matter what positions the party of Abraham Lincoln took, blacks continued to vote Republican. For generations, when both political parties were fighting antilynching bills, blacks still kept "Abe Lincoln's picture on the wall." Even as late as 1932, most blacks remained loyal to Republican Herbert Hoover. Franklin D. Roosevelt was largely responsible for shifting the loyalty of blacks to the Democratic party, and this shift was soon converted to unflagging devotion. Next to the political action committee of the AFL-CIO, the automatic black vote has been the single greatest resource of the Democratic party for the past five decades. The virtually all-white Democratic party leadership expects and succeeds in getting blacks to rubber-stamp the candidate it nominates. In return, blacks are granted almost no bargaining power within the party. Their votes, taken almost as a birthright by Democratic politicians, are essentially powerless to shape platform issues. This is especially true when the interests of blacks run counter to the interests of organized labor and other party constituencies whose loyalty the Democrats must be careful to maintain. In every election, one sees a Democratic party whose candidates pay public tribute to the emerging political power of blacks and accord black leaders all the honors to which the latest debutante is entitled. But these ceremonies rarely distract the party from propitiating racial conservatives and ignoring equal opportunity manifestos when necessary to meet the demands of important constituencies.

Locked into a political marriage that serves them badly when it serves them at all, black leaders have been surprisingly slow to give serious consideration to the organization of a black political party which might well hold the balance of power in close elections and keep the leaders of both parties from wandering away from them after elections.

For a great many reasons, the case for a black political party is strong. A black party would tend to reinforce the political solidarity that already exists among black voters. This is especially important at a time when there are increasing ideological differences within the black community—differences produced in part by the growing economic schism between poor blacks and the new corporate and professional black elite. A black political party would tend to neutralize these class differences and focus attention on the vital economic and political interests of the group as a whole. Of greater importance, a black political party would give blacks a mobile political striking force. Precisely because the essential impotence of the black vote derives from the fact that it is a faithful vote that always supports the Democratic ticket, a black party, created and perceived as an independent political base, would make the black vote negotiable and therefore strong. A black political party would help blacks swing their vote from one candidate to another, thus enabling them to win far greater influence over the policies of all candidates, including political independents.

A black political party would also be able to organize and carry out a black political battle plan. It could, for example, identify vote-rich states and districts where liberal candidates are threatened and provide either support or opposition depending on the candidates' willingness to support black political objectives. A black political party could sort out the merits of black candidates and discourage them from competing with one another or from running as spoilers against white politicians who could be counted on to support the black legislative agenda. A black political party could organize target campaigns against those congressmen who still win elections on subtly disguised racist platforms. The game of politics is always a quasi-military operation; and the party supplies the necessary generals and troops.

Of great importance, too, is the fact that a black political party would enable blacks to keep political score. Political power has no presence until it is demonstrated. Right now, blacks have no way to show or prove their contribution to the defeat or election of a particular candidate. But if blacks were organized into a single political party, it would be relatively easy for them to prove their role in the outcome of any particular election. Once this kind of proof is on the table, elective power would be at hand and blacks could then set the date for political negotiations with the established powers who govern the country.

Finally, a black political party would provide a means—far superior to favorite son and other strategies—of developing and controlling black issues and black candidates. The presence of an established party, whose presence becomes an expected fixture in every election, legitimizes the always shaky but potentially powerful idea that it's proper to believe that one's political views should be influenced by one's race.

Even when there is no racist mayor to defeat, no Ku Klux Klan sympathizers to drive out of Congress, and no charismatic black candidate to support, a black political party would generate political energy and commitment. The party would perform the important functions of raising the political sights and morale of black people, educating them to realities of confrontation politics, exposing the racial hypocrisies of "friends in high places," promoting awareness of the current inability of the Democratic party to espouse black issues, and mobilizing the black vote. At the moment, blacks are politically divided, ideologically split, unsure of their moral position on such issues as school busing and affirmative action, unwilling to alienate powerful whites, and largely convinced that ethnic politics are not in their interests. A black political party could buffer many of these influences which cause blacks in the United States to be a textbook example of political apathy and division.

There are, of course, distinct disadvantages to the creation of an independent black party. The present system of funding political campaigns works against the third-party idea. By law, only the two major parties gain automatic access to television, a place on the ballot, and public funds. What is more, the two-party system is so deeply ingrained in the American political psyche that the two major parties are able to effectively block outside competition that might interfere with their alternating control of the machinery of government. Americans have, as it were, inner television sets capable of tuning to only two channels. Any extra broadcast sources tend to be received as static. This explains why most Americans saw John Anderson's independent candidacy in 1980 as little more than the efforts of a "spoiler" who was bent on rocking the boat and breaking the rules.

Aside from the practical problems of mounting a third-party effort, there are also distinct power disadvantages. A black party would deprive blacks of much of the legislative influence, however slight, that they have laboriously built since 1964. If blacks left the Democratic party to challenge the established lions in Congress, black congressmen would stand to lose most of the committee and subcommittee assignments they now hold.

THE POLITICS OF BLACK EMPOWERMENT

Undoubtedly, the most immediate harm to result from the formation of a black political party could be the election of a number of racial conservatives whom blacks would rather not have in public office. If a black political party nominated candidates for the House, the Senate, and the White House, and if black voters stuck by these candidates to the bitter end, the Democratic party would be deprived of an important part of its political base and would lose a number of elections it would otherwise have won. This being the case, a black political party that actually fielded candidates and expected blacks to vote for them would be electing few, if any, of their candidates. Blacks would take votes away from other candidates preferred by blacks and, in the process, would be helping candidates unsympathetic to black objectives to gain political office.

The principal argument against the creation of a black political party is its certainty to turn off liberal white voters whose ballots are currently helping elect black mayors and other public officials. Without the support of white voters, black Mayors Wilson Goode in Philadelphia, Thomas Bradley in Los Angeles, and Harold Washington in Chicago would not have been elected to office.

When the pros and cons of a black party are added up, the disadvantages, at least over the short term, seem far weightier than the advantages. Indeed, considerations such as the morale-boosting effect of an independent black party seem to vanish if one considers the severe decline in black political morale, which is bound to follow the realization that black strength in Congress, puny though it may be at present, has actually declined as a result of the creation of a black party. Few of the benefits of a black political party can be realized in the short run, which is precisely when most of the disadvantages will be felt. Whether any aggrieved group can, in all conscience, be asked to suffer such heavy short-run losses for the sake of hypothetical long-run gains is a difficult question. Despite all the problems posed by a third-party effort, many blacks appear to be discouraged by their traditional role of loyal appendages to the Democratic party. A 1980 poll showed that at least 31 percent of black voters would support a black political party and vote its ticket.[14] The theoretical black power advantages of the third-party thesis are huge; but for the moment, it appears that pie in the sky should be spurned in favor of smaller slices on the table.

The fact that, under present conditions, the idea of a permanent black political party is romantic and dysfunctional does not rule out partial use of the strategy. Blacks can employ the third-party tactic to make temporary forays into enemy territory, to spoil the electoral chances of conservatives and black political antagonists, and to run favorite sons in primaries as a means of gathering influence at national nominating conventions. Sooner or later, blacks must experiment with third-party initiatives. The most attractive feature of the idea is that it permits blacks to embrace the cardinal objective of all power users—to work oneself into a position where one can raise the stakes, and increase the opponent's risk while still retaining the ability to withdraw unharmed. The black prodigal's place of retreat is, of course, the Democratic party homeland, and always just in time to vote in national elections.

The 1978 senatorial election in Mississippi offers a pragmatic example of how an independent black candidate can be used tactically to develop black strength for future elections. Independent candidate Charles Evers, the black mayor of Fayette, pulled enough votes from conservative Democrat Maurice Dantin to enable the conservative Republican candidate Thad Cochran to become the first Mississippi Republican in history to be publicly elected to the United States Senate. Since blacks, who made up 37 percent of the state's population, had little to gain if either Dantin or Cochran were elected, Evers' candidacy offered a cost-free chance to demonstrate that the Democratic party of Mississippi could no longer dominate the state's politics without black support. Once this lesson was learned, Mississippi Democrats would have to choose between attending to the needs of black voters or watching more Republicans take the oath of office.

Divide and Conquer: Exploiting Ideological Differences Within the Major Political Parties

Both political parties have retained political power for themselves because, in the past, they have been able to prevent serious factionalism from developing within their ranks. Yet, obviously, if rifts in a major party were to occur, the bargaining power of special interests would then mount considerably. In this situation, the major parties would be struggling to build majority coalitions and would be aggressively bidding for the support of various constituent party factions, including blacks.

American voters have shown an increasing trend toward factionalism in recent years. Each day seems to bring fresh testimony to the increasing fragmentation of social groups within the United States. We see, particularly, large numbers of fringe and special-interest groups whose singular interests transcend membership in the traditional political parties. The modern pollster must take into account the votes of "hard hats," "white ethnics," "right-to-lifers," "Naderites," "environmentalists," "women's-libbers," and a host of other permanent or ad hoc groups. Independent from political parties, too, are the Israeli lobby, the automotive lobby, the oil lobby, the farm lobby, the civil service lobby, and the politically active religious fundamentalists. Irish Catholics, Italians, Czechs, Slovaks, Greeks, and Jews are more vocal today as individual ethnic units than as minority voices within an overriding political party. The Republican coalition of white-collar workers, midwestern farmers, and small businessmen is often as difficult to hold together as the Democratic coalition of the poor, blacks, blue-collar workers, Catholics, organized labor, and all-purpose liberals.

What this means to black political aspirations should be obvious. Power derives from unity; powerlessness from disunity. The political power of blacks mounts in direct proportion to the increasing fragmentation of other powers, including the major parties. As ideological polarization within parties proceeds, the time may be at hand when black voters, as one of the largest special-interest groups in the nation, can take advantage of a gradual breakdown of the two-party system. The bargaining power of blacks on legislative initiatives and political appointments would be considerable in a multiparty environment. This explains why, all other things being equal, blacks have a fundamental interest in encouraging the increasing fragmentation of the leading political parties.

Understandably, most politically sensitive blacks have ambivalent feelings about any development that weakens the Democratic party. After all, blacks have derived important benefits as wards of the Democratic party. Federal laws prohibiting discrimination in public facilities, housing, and credit have all resulted from Democratic initiatives. The Democrats fought for blacks in the great congressional debates over Title VII of the Civil Rights Act of 1964, the landmark legislation that opened up employment opportunities for blacks in occupations that had been wholly closed to them. The Voting Rights Act of 1965, the enabling legislation that now vests such a huge potential for political power in black voters, was pushed through Congress by Democrats. The great surge in black incomes during the 1960s can at least in part be explained by the black political awakening that took place at a time when minority pressures on the economic system were not only tolerated, but were nurtured by Democratic Presidents.

Yet in the early 1980s, the Democratic party was pressed by the increasing appeal of the New Right. In a panic over the loss of many of its constituents to appeals from the right, the Democratic party deserted many of its traditional liberal objectives. The subtle sabotage by the party leadership of the last remnants of the Humphrey-Hawkins full employment measure in 1978 highlighted the fact that traditional liberals had lost much of their influence within the party. Large numbers of liberal whites who had once joined blacks at the civil rights barricades came to regard the struggle for further progress as either boring, passé, or a threat to their own status and prerogatives. More than at any time in the preceding fifteen years, blacks faced the dilemma of choosing between two major political parties, both of which denied them a credible plan for racial progress.

Black voter ambivalence about the possibility of erosion of Democratic party unity is more than a matter of sentimentality about the days when Democratic strength produced legislation and executive orders working toward racial justice. Blacks in the 1980s correctly perceived the Democratic party as the only bulwark standing in the way of resegregation of public education and the dismantling or evasion of laws imposing affirmative employment duties on large corporations. Thus, the idea of fragmenting the Democratic coalition continues to pose serious dangers for blacks. The weakening of the Democratic party could win elections for many political conservatives and opponents of black rights. It follows, then, that blacks can achieve greater political power through increasing political party divisions *only if fragmentation occurs in both parties simultaneously or in the Republican party first*. This objective becomes then a major goal of black politics.

Black Power in Coalition Politics

Coalition building is a vital feature of almost any strategy of power augmentation. As black organizations look over the political landscape, they are faced with a wide assortment of possible groups with which alliances might be made. Many potential prospects are unsuitable or unsympathetic to black objectives. Among these are certain fundamentalist church groups, the farm lobby, gay activists, anti-abortion and anti-gun-control groups. Environmentalists also tend to make unreliable partners because their objectives often run counter to the black goals of full employment and rapid economic development.

On the other hand, blacks are in a position to make successful alliances with organized labor and with women's and senior citizens' groups. Both blacks and labor would benefit from fuller unionization in the South, where wages have been historically low. Both groups actively sought passage of the Humphrey-Hawkins full employment bill as well as other job development programs. Blacks and big labor tend to support similar initiatives in housing, health care, and public education; they tend to have similar interests in defeating the so-called right-to-work laws as well as legislative measures that would weaken collective bargaining rights. A very powerful alliance could be created by blacks and the women's movement, with both groups actively committed to the Equal Rights Amendment, the establishment of formal rules for minority seats at nominating conventions, reduced

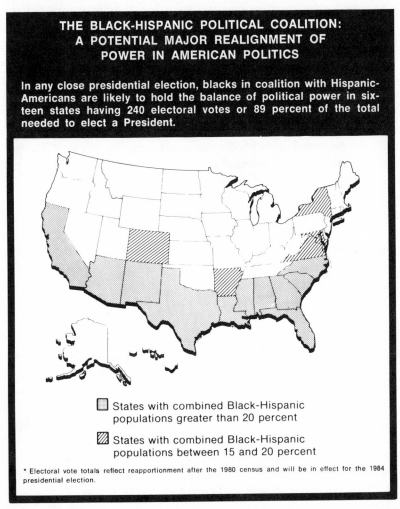

THE BLACK-HISPANIC POLITICAL COALITION: A POTENTIAL MAJOR REALIGNMENT OF POWER IN AMERICAN POLITICS

In any close presidential election, blacks in coalition with Hispanic-Americans are likely to hold the balance of political power in sixteen states having 240 electoral votes or 89 percent of the total needed to elect a President.

☐ States with combined Black-Hispanic populations greater than 20 percent

▨ States with combined Black-Hispanic populations between 15 and 20 percent

* Electoral vote totals reflect reapportionment after the 1980 census and will be in effect for the 1984 presidential election.

defense expenditures, and fuller minority participation in the work force and in corporate management. Only in rare circumstances do the political interests of tens of millions of elderly whites, with little means of support other than Social Security checks, have political interests that run contrary to the standard black agenda.

Unquestionably, the most effective political alliance blacks could possibly make would be one with Hispanic-Americans. Both groups have almost identical interests: full employment, breaking down racial isolation, welfare reform, restraints on racial bigotry, fuller minority participation in the political process, and quality schooling for the poor. Unfortunately, the issue that greatly divides these two natural allies is competition for jobs, which became tragically clear in the Miami riots of 1980. Moreover, no alliance could occur unless blacks overcame their opposition to the free immigration of competing Chicano labor into the United States. Massive gains would come into view if blacks and Hispanics were to bury the hatchet and collectively turn to the job of raising the economic status of both groups.

The potential force of a black-Hispanic political coalition is so impressive that it is tempting to explore the political implications of the combination despite the present unlikelihood of its realization. By 1985, it is expected that Hispanic voters will outnumber blacks. Hispanics are already a potent political force in California and Texas, states that together control 28 percent of the electoral votes required to elect a President. Blacks and Hispanics combined make up more than 30 percent of the population in five different states—Texas, Mississippi, South Carolina, New Mexico, and Louisiana. Assuming the continuation of two very strong major political parties, a minority coalition of blacks and Hispanics could dictate the outcomes of most elections in these states as well as in California, Florida, New York, and Illinois.

Since the Hispanic population, like its black counterpart, tends to be geographically concentrated, the coalition could decide the outcome of many congressional races. In the mid-1980s, perhaps five to ten congressional districts were ripe for the election of black congressmen. Add the Hispanic vote and a number of other minority congressmen might be sent to Washington. Looking into the late 1980s, a strong black-Hispanic alliance could produce upwards of thirty-five minority representatives in Congress.

In Congress, state legislatures, and city councils, local or nationwide black-Hispanic alliances would present formidable voting blocs. A group of minority legislators working in a tightly organized caucus, bound by agreement to vote as a bloc on issues of crucial importance to their constituents, would have irresistible bargaining power with other lawmakers. The feasibility of minority coalition politics is demonstrated by the performance of the Black and Puerto Rican Caucus in the New York State Assembly, which has already proven itself a powerful legislative force within the state.

In the late 1970s, when there were only fifteen full voting members of the Black Caucus and five in the Hispanic Caucus, Congressman Mickey

Leland of Texas was leading a fight to forge a coalition between the two groups in the House of Representatives. If formed, a coalition of blacks and Hispanics in the mid-1980s would produce a thirty-vote bloc of congressional votes.

If and when a coalition occurs, majority voters will face a political tidal wave. There are few strategies for minority political empowerment that offer greater promise than the creation of national alliances of black and Hispanic voters and of their publicly elected officials.

Blacks and the Republican Party

A traditional black aphorism describes the political dilemma of black voters under the American two-party system:

> "There are two things that will be the end to colored people—the boll weevil and the lesser of two evils."

The boll weevil refers, of course, to the destruction of the cotton economy of the South. The lesser of two evils refers to whichever political party, at any particular time in history, is able to convince black voters that while it may not be an advocate of black interests, it should be awarded the black vote as the party whose candidates will do blacks the least harm.

As shown earlier, blind acceptance of the lesser-of-two-evils thesis has consistently undermined the political influence of black voters. Since Franklin Roosevelt's presidency, blacks have consistently found the Democratic party to be the lesser of two evils, even in the early 1930s when the party refused to fight for strong antilynching measures in the South.

Disloyalty to the Democratic party continues to be unacceptable to most blacks, yet blacks and other racial minorities might, from time to time, cut through the no-place-else-to-go dilemma through a variety of temporary alliances with the GOP. In voter redistricting contests, particularly, blacks and Republicans often have the same political goal: the bunching of as many black voters as possible into a single congressional or state legislative voting district. For blacks, the reverse gerrymander strategy is to amass enough voting strength in the district to elect a black legislator. The Republican objective is to concentrate as many black (usually Democratic) voters as possible into a single district in order to make adjoining districts safe for GOP candidates. Of course, alliances between blacks and the GOP do not sit well with the Democratic party regulars. Yet, as long as blacks perceive that their political interests within legislative bodies are best represented by other blacks, and especially by black bloc-voting strategies, temporary alliances with Republican interests make good political sense. In most cases, black politics has the objective of establishing black political bases and electing black candidates from those bases. This being so, there are few circumstances where black political influence would be enhanced by supporting the Democratic position on the redistricting issue.

There are other circumstances where temporary alliances between blacks and Republicans may be desirable. For example, were Republicans to present blacks with the opportunity to defeat a politically racist or merely antiblack Democratic officeholder—examples in 1984 would be Democratic Congressmen Jamie Whitten of Mississippi, or Dan Daniel of Virginia—black voters would be foolish to decline proffered alliances, provided the Republican candidates' views were reasonably acceptable on racial and other issues that most concern blacks. Moreover, in cases where the Democratic party consistently nominates conservative candidates who are unacceptable to blacks, black voters may consider making a show of black political strength through a one-shot black voter shift to Republican ranks. When this happens, Democrats are likely to be more responsive to black interests in future elections. Finally, it is not uncommon that Republican political ideology expressly coincides with black economic interests. For example, the GOP may be supportive and willing to give political assistance to black efforts to establish inner-city "enterprise zones" or other minority self-help development efforts. Here, too, the short-term, black-GOP alliance is a useful and legitimate political expedient.

We may assume the truth of the proposition that one loses one's soul—and in the end one's power—by making alliances with the devil. But the Republican party must never be confused with Satan; at one point in American history the GOP was, in fact, a staunch friend of blacks. While always keeping a sharp eye out for the Trojan horses of adversary politics, blacks frequently stand to make important tactical gains when the GOP makes overtures of friendship.

When the Dinosaur Awakes: Empowerment Through Punitive Political Action

Even today, a large number of white supremacists walk the halls of Congress. In fact, some of the most powerful men in the country's legislative branch are outright racists. Headed by Senator Jesse Helms of North Carolina, there are several dozen individuals in Congress who hold poorly disguised beliefs that blacks are inferior to whites, who are opponents of the two races living together, and who are strong believers that politically active blacks are necessarily communist agitators. Many of the most stubborn opponents of racial equality are not vulnerable to efforts by blacks to unseat them because they come from states and districts with small black voting populations. Yet many of the most unyielding white supremacists represent congressional districts with black populations greater than 30 percent. It is in these districts that blacks must begin to use their dormant political muscle to defeat legislators who oppose the protection of black civil rights and the elevation of black people to equal power and status in our society.

In the past, black political strategy has aimed almost exclusively at electing blacks to Congress. This has met with some success in districts where blacks hold majority status or make up very large proportions of the population, but for a group far more often in the minority, the strategy has evident weaknesses. In 1984, only four black representatives, Ronald Dellums and Merv Dymally of California, Katie Hall of Indiana, and Alan Wheat of Missouri, held office in districts with a black electorate of less than 40 percent. Black strategy in congressional elections must therefore be expanded to include efforts to bench racial conservatives who hold public office and to block the election of others with similar ideologies. Indeed, given the demographics of ethnic voting power, blacks must recognize the fact that they will more often be in a position to say who will not go to Washington than to say who will. In terms of demonstrating the power of the black vote, defeating unfriendly legislators is just as important as getting one's brothers elected.

One of the most startling and inexcusable political failures of blacks has been their apathy in exposing and campaigning against overt racists running for public office. Even the most ugly haters often have dossiers that remain known only to a few voters. In 1980, Gerald Carlson, a white man, ran a successful Republican primary campaign for the Fifteenth Congressional District in Detroit, a city where 63 percent of the population is black. For nine months, he operated a "white-power hotline" featuring recorded telephone messages urging Dearborn whites to drive blacks from their neighborhoods. Here is Carlson's favorite example of his own rhetoric:

> "We had a case, here in Detroit, with a Negro whose eyes got bigger than his stomach. He was working for the government and he took off with more than a million dollars. Then he checked himself into a psychiatric clinic in Ferndale. I said the man was suffering from a disease called 'Negro-itis,' the inability of the Negro to function responsibly in positions in a white society. Then every time we had another incident, I'd say, 'Looks like we have another case of Negro-itis here.' " [15]

It was a foregone conclusion that Carlson would lose the election to the sixteen-year incumbent, Congressman William Ford, yet blacks never made Carlson an unacceptable embarrassment to the GOP. The failure of blacks to exploit, at a national level, the acceptance by the Republican party of a candidate running a campaign on the basis of throwing scraps of rhetorical red meat to white racists remains inexplicable. This was a superb opportunity for blacks to give a well-publicized thrashing to a confirmed racist.[16]

Very high political priority should be given to developing plans to defeat specifically targeted incumbent Democrats in primary elections and—particularly in general elections—the Republican officeholders who still remain staunch friends of Jim Crow. Concentrated efforts should be directed first at congressmen who, for one reason or another, are politically weak in their own districts. Rather than organize widely dispersed and probably unsuccessful efforts against a large number of political opponents, the preferred tactic should be to mount a few intense and widely publicized campaigns directed against one or two particularly inviting targets who are not only opposed to the progress of blacks but are politically vulnerable in their own right. In deposing segregationists who hold political office, as well as other opponents of an open society, there is no substitute for black power in support of the traditional equal-access virtues which for many white voters and major-party candidates have become largely poetry and rhetoric.

Blacks as Power Brokers in Third World Diplomacy

In a multiracial society such as exists in the United States, the economic and political power of ethnic groups at home are at times greatly influenced by circumstances abroad. Polish-, Irish-, German-, Jewish-, and Italian-Americans have all experienced this phenomenon. Recent changes in the balance of world power have conferred some domestic political power on American blacks. One of the fundamental facts of geopolitical life today is that the two great international superpowers, the Soviet Union and the United States, are locked in a struggle to win the friendship and support of the nonaligned nations of the world. A huge number of the uncommitted nations happen to be black and Moslem. Correctly or incorrectly, both superpowers perceive that the survival of their own political systems depends in large part on which way the nonaligned nations jump. In a nuclear age, the ideological struggle between democracy and communism seems less likely to be determined as a result of armed conflict than as a consequence of slow, diplomatic processes by which the great powers win or lose the friendship of the uncommitted nations. This courtship process clearly confers huge political power on the nonaligned nations which are the prizes in the contest. In theory, they are able to use their strategic position to extract foreign aid and trade concessions, and sometimes even to gain the occasional satisfaction of humiliating great powers.

THE POLITICS OF BLACK EMPOWERMENT

Where do American blacks stand with reference to the power that has fallen into the hands of Third World nations? Some American blacks have tried to set themselves up as power brokers between white America and the mostly black and Moslem Third World nations. The theory is that if, for example, blacks in the United States were in a position to win favors from Third World nations for the United States, it might be possible for U.S. blacks to win economic and political concessions for themselves in the United States as a bargained-for quid pro quo for their efforts abroad. Conversely, if the nonaligned nations saw American blacks as effective bargaining agents for their interests within the United States, these nations might be persuaded to cultivate black political support here by providing financial sustenance for the political and economic activities of American blacks.

Of course, there are no blacks in the Soviet Union whose presence in that country could retard or advance Russian interests in the Third World. But in the United States, there are over 27 million blacks who could potentially influence America's relations with the nonaligned nations. Some American blacks see here an opportunity to gain political leverage in the decision-making of the United States Government as well as in the governments of countries such as Nigeria, Libya, Algeria, Tanzania, Saudi Arabia, Iraq, and Iran. This potential influence tends to be confirmed by sporadic efforts of Arab nations to win American blacks to the Arab position on Israel. The general perception that some Third World nations look to American blacks as allies is reinforced by the fact that black Americans are usually exempted from standard Arab denunciations of American imperialism. Indeed, the United States Government itself has tended to encourage the use of American blacks as a bargaining wedge in advancing U.S. interest in Third World politics. The United States has consistently appointed blacks as ambassadors to Third World nations and has used blacks in high United Nations posts even though it has never placed them in posts of domestic power or authority in Washington.

The issue of foreign oil further enhances the potential for black political power in the United States. In 1979, 40 percent of all U.S. oil imports came from Nigeria, Algeria, and Libya. Through 1979, U.S. dependence on Nigerian oil had steadily increased to the point where Nigeria became the second largest foreign supplier of U.S. oil. In 1979, Nigeria made veiled threats to cut off the one million barrels of oil a day it then exported to the United States if the United States removed economic sanctions against the racist government of Zimbabwe-Rhodesia. In addition, Nigeria warmly welcomed UN Ambassador Andrew Young after three times refusing to receive Secretary of State Henry Kissinger. Despite lessening U.S. dependence on foreign oil, some blacks in the United States lick their chops at the prospect of oil-rich Moslem nations linking their oil exports with their international diplomatic objectives. If the most heady pan-African dreams came true, it is not beyond the realm of possibility that African and Moslem oil as well as African manganese, nickel, chrome, gold, and diamonds might be traded—with black leaders in America acting as brokers—for legislation or executive orders favorable to blacks in the United States. If blacks in the United States ultimately win greater influence in their own government, there is a possibility that African nations might make a direct alliance with American blacks, possibly even naming the Congressional Black Caucus as their bargaining representative. Pan-Africanism is a strong movement in the world, and there are a number of black leaders in the United States who would welcome an appointment by the Organization of African States as its official ambassador to Washington.

Blacks and whites who perceive such visions of grand power as subversive, impractical, and romantic must concede that strengthened ties between American blacks and Third World nations would provide American blacks with a greater voice in American government. Still, it is not yet clear what, if anything, blacks could gain from a greater involvement in foreign affairs. For the moment, most Nigerians and black Africans remain indifferent to the fate of American Negroes. A world oil glut has greatly reduced the political bargaining position of the petroleum-rich Moslem and African nations. In the foreseeable future, it is most unlikely that there will be any Arab funding of black political campaigns or of black inner-city community development in the United States. Blacks have almost no political influence over the policies of the U.S. Government, and African nations know this. American blacks in government who are sent as ambassadors to African nations tend to be perceived in Africa as messenger boys for the U.S. State Department and are treated as such by their host countries.

But the most serious impediment that blacks face in acting as foreign power brokers is not their powerlessness in the American political scene but the inherent conflict with their overriding allegiance to the United States. How far can blacks go in conducting de facto diplomatic relations while still remaining loyal to the country most of them love and defend? Blacks in the United States have a strong and legitimate interest in the well-being of their brothers in southern Africa. Also, as a disporportionate percentage of the poor in the United States, they have a manifest interest in the price of imported foreign oil. They have powerful motivation for making common cause with African and some Moslem nations. But what will happen when they discover that this common cause gives succor to nations in a position to blackmail the United States?

As blacks in the United States become increasingly frustrated with their inability to improve their lot through conventional means, it is likely that they will try to play their "African card." Already, the active involvement by blacks in foreign affairs seems to have breathed new strength into moribund black pressure groups such as the Southern Christian Leadership Conference. As blacks win greater political power in the United States, they may, in time, bootstrap this leverage to win greater influence in Africa and the Moslem world. But, for the moment, there is no black lobby with sufficient force to influence the United States Government or to win any African funding for black economic interests here. As far as African nations are concerned, blacks in the United States are ineffective, as well as illegitimate, bargaining agents for any nation or group. As long as this is the case, the Third World nations will remain essentially indifferent to the continuing second-class status of very large numbers of American blacks.

Black Power and the Curse of Separatism

The traditional debate over the kinds of strategies to be employed to improve the economic and social positions of blacks in America usually polarizes around two viewpoints. The *integrationist* position, which has the support of most American blacks, puts great emphasis on the "melting pot" theory of ethnic progress in the United States. Integrationists hold that blacks will get ahead by doing—and only by doing—those things that help them blend, in an economic, political, and social sense, with the greater society. The integrationist position therefore places great importance on enacting and enforcing laws to curb race discrimination in employment, housing, and education. Integrationists are considered political moderates in the sense that they usually oppose the use of public protest and other forms of direct action to accomplish their purposes. They lean, instead, on the established processes of courts, legislatures, and the executive branch, which they tend to view as the only legitimate forces available to help blacks progress and achieve equal status with whites.

Standing in sharp opposition to much of the integrationist position is a small—and in recent years increasingly less important—movement made up of the so-called *black separatists*. Separatists see race discrimination as an unavoidable and immutable fact of life throughout the world. Blacks, they feel, will remain economically and politically subordinate to whites as long as they live in the same nation and under laws that whites are able to make and interpret. Accordingly, in the separatist view, there is little prospect that whites will of their own accord adopt more than token measures to integrate society or to cause economic and educational institutions to accept blacks as fully participating members. The separatist position is that blacks will make their way most effectively by taking care of their own needs and rejecting help from generous-spirited whites who are really more interested in salving their consciences than in opening doors to equal power and participation.

The extreme separatist position (held by only a very few of those blacks who do favor separatist strategies) calls for black political self-determination, the deliberate creation of separate black communities, and, in some cases, even the physical withdrawal of blacks from the United States and the founding of an independent black nation or state. A far more important and moderate wing of the separatist position demands strategies favoring black solidarity, self-help, and self-reliance, but stops far short of advocating geographical isolation. The moderate separatists sometimes refer to their objectives as "black nation building," but this expression is largely metaphorical inasmuch as it does not imply either physical removal from the United States or black political self-determination. But the moderate separatist position does call on blacks to "go it alone" in the sense of developing and controlling their own schools, building up economic resources within their own neighborhoods, creating their own financial institutions, and in some cases taking political control of their communities. In either its radical or its moderate position, the black separatist movement views itself as profoundly pragmatic. It argues that for the time being there are, in fact, two societies in America, one black and one white, and it steers its course accordingly.

A striking irony in the black separatist movement is that many features of its ideology precisely mesh with the racial politics of traditional Jim Crow segregationists. Indeed, the fact that the arch segregationists of the South have always supported black separatist movements is a major reason most integrationists find the separatist movement so offensive and destructive to the aspirations of most blacks.

The separatist-integrationist conflict has divided black political theory for many generations. In many ways the ideological dispute is the force producing the enervating feuding within the ranks of the National Association for the Advancement of Colored People. Intense emotional feelings attach to these different ideologies and especially to the labels by which people have come to be known. Integrationists accuse separatists of polarizing the nation around the issue of race and of irresponsibly encouraging violence and racial backlash which can only harm black people. In recent years, both liberals and progressives have accused separatists of exploiting black anti-Semitism and isolating legitimate black civil rights organizations from traditional Jewish charitable and ideological support for liberal causes. On the other side, separatists denounce integrationists as "accommodationists," "Uncle Toms," and tools of the white power structure. Separatists insist that black progress over the past generation cannot be credited to the gentle pressures from the NAACP, but to the more intense forces mounted against white institutions by activist blacks. Undeniably, separatist strategies had a powerful impact during the black protest years of the 1960s, leading directly to federal support for black efforts to win entry into economic, educational, and political institutions. But in the past decade black separatism, in even its moderate forms, has found few advocates among either blacks or whites.

Although separatism may be a relatively unimportant ideology today, it still casts a giant and harmful shadow over the concept of black power. In the perception of the general public, the idea of black power has almost always been associated with the black separatist movement. For example, the Congress of Racial Equality (CORE), a black organization whose strategies in the 1960s emphasized black pressure and self-help tactics, was always viewed by the integrationist National Association for the Advancement of Colored People and by liberals generally as separatist, and to that extent a dangerous and seditious institution. Other black organizations that pressed the idea of black solidarity and self-help, such as the Southern Christian Leadership Conference and the Student Nonviolent Coordinating Committee, were also closely identified with black separatist policies. From the viewpoint of integrationists and traditional liberals, the Black Muslims stood as the most notorious examples of the dangers of black separatism and black power.

The important result is that in the public view, black separatism, black solidarity, black power, and black protest have become virtually synonymous labels, all carrying the pejorative implication of disloyalty to country and opposition to liberal integrationist orthodoxy. Unfortunately, this has meant that anyone opposing black separatism tended automatically to oppose all forms of black power, including even traditional nonviolent black political pressures with clearly integrationist aims. In any political debate, an advocate of nonviolent black power could be summarily disparaged and dismissed as a "separatist" and few people bothered to inquire beyond that label.

The invidious connection in the public mind between black separatism and black power has been nurtured further by real or apparent connections of both movements with Marxism. During the 1920s and 1930s, American communists called for black self-determination in the black belt of the southern states. In the 1960s, many black separatist organizations as well as traditional civil rights movements were disparaged as tools of the communist conspiracy. To this day, advocates of strong black political organizations functioning outside the two major political parties are viewed as profoundly subversive. To a considerable extent, the two major political parties in the United States have been able to garner black votes without having to compete for them by the simple expedient of labeling any independent black political movement as unpatriotic and disloyal. Although third parties generally are acceptable political tactics, *black* third parties conjure up memories of extremist pan-African movements as well as of black radical activists such as Bobby Seale, Eldridge Cleaver, and Angela Davis. A very large number of voters today see black candidates, black political organizations, and black voter unity as left-wing plots.

It is an unfortunate aspect of human psychology that the attitudes that shape the processes by which racial equality might be achieved are generally determined by the ghosts and legends of the past. The idea of black empowerment is constantly put on the defensive by pejorative labels having nothing to do with fact or good sense. When we carefully think through what is meant by black power, we arrive at a perfectly legitimate and moderate concept that advocates neither that blacks be separated from whites nor that blacks use violence or terror to achieve their aims. Black power, as properly conceived, is a nonviolent and evolutionary approach to black problems. Black power is in perfect harmony with American political theory, which encourages participatory democracy through the nonviolent competition among self-seeking pressure and special-interest groups. Moreover, properly conceived, black power makes no sense unless it has integrationist objectives that press for greater participation and influence in the affairs and activities of the nation as a whole. What is more, any sound and effective concept of black power can have no truck with violence simply because, as we saw in Chapter Three, black power always evaporates whenever it espouses or uses violence, terrorism, or other revolutionary tactics. As long as black power scrupulously rejects all violent tactics, its protest and direct-action strategies are perfectly compatible with the political freedoms guaranteed by the Constitution.

The true nature of legitimate black power emerges when we examine a number of strategies, tactics, and goals that most blacks would applaud. In the process, we shall see that the labels of "separatist" and "integrationist" have little if any meaning. Suppose blacks in a given community band together to take action against certain merchants who have displayed flagrantly racist employment practices. They decide to boycott the shops of the merchants in question as well as the business establishments of others who do business with them. While there may be differences of opinion as to the propriety of the secondary pressure on merchants who are not directly engaging in acts of racial discrimination, the direct boycott is a lawful and acceptable use of nonviolent black power. The collective protest strategy might have separatist overtones in the sense that it emphasizes black solidarity and collective action as a pressure mechanism, but its goal—fuller integration of blacks into the greater society—is clearly not in the least separatist.

Turning now to a more formal political context, suppose the Congressional Black Caucus uses its congressional power to vote as a bloc (or to trade its bloc of votes) in order to win firmer antidiscrimination legislation. Here again, black political solidarity, in a separatist sense, is being used to win integrationist objectives. It is difficult to see how this form of black power can be faulted as subversive of democratic principles when bloc-voting strategies lie at the very heart of traditional democratic processes. In precisely the same way, separatist tendencies may be at work whenever blacks organize political caucuses in order to press one of the major political parties to adopt a party platform acceptable to blacks. But the objectives of such separatist pressures are usually integrationist—enforcement of laws prohibiting racial segregation, protection of black voting rights, upgrading blacks in mainstream institutions. There is no denying that racial quotas for admission to institutions, affirmative-action employment programs, and targeted campaigns to elect blacks to public office have distinctly separatist aspects in their emphasis on ethnic identity and solidarity, but these tactics are improperly branded as separatist since their explicit purpose is fuller participation and integration.

In sum, all the examples I have given demonstrate that many, if not most, separatist and black power strategies have profoundly integrationist objectives. To be sure, blacks could use racial politics and black solidarity for segregationist or separatist purposes. This would be the case if, for example, black power and solidarity were employed to force whites out of their neighborhoods, to create all-black schools which exclude even those whites who are perfectly willing to integrate and pursue education together. It is safe to say, however, that except on the extreme fringe of the black movement, the separatist techniques of black power are rarely, if ever, employed to secure such separatist ends. The dreams and aspirations of most American blacks are decidedly integrationist. This is why so much harm is done to black objectives by the discrediting linkage that has been made between black power, black separatism, and black violence. It has become almost a holy writ among citizens and politicians that all three of these expressions refer to similar strategies and tactics.

As a result, the concepts of black separatism and its handmaiden "black power" (in the sense of black violence) have become rhetorical weapons that are used to trample and render illegitimate all the traditional and constitutionally protected nonviolent means by which minority groups have improved their lot in a democratic society. Since, in many ways, equal opportunities and equal rights are essentially a matter of equal power, this linkage has served as an effective way of dissuading blacks from using the one weapon that shows promise of helping them to become equal. In short, the concept of black power in all its permissible and nonviolent forms cannot do much for blacks until it first succeeds in disassociating itself in the public mind from the odious concepts of separatism as an objective, and violence as a means, of accomplishing full participation by blacks in all aspects of American society. Black solidarity and bloc voting must be seen not as racist or separatist, but as simply what they are—a means of acquiring power.

The Prospect for Solidarity

Plainly, blacks do not need theoretical politics. They do not need glowing but unrealistic tributes to black voter strength. They need practical politics. A person may be fully persuaded that pressure politics and other nonviolent coercive strategies offer a theoretical framework for producing greater racial equality in the United States. The person may further agree that dividing the opposition, experimenting with coalition politics, making third-party forays, and organizing drives to oust racial bigots from political office are, in theory, useful stratagems for making the economic and political system more accountable to the black race. But political power does not grow out of handbooks of strategy and tactics. It must be built by the hands of ordinary mortals working in the real world. Black power must be the end result of the actions of black people. And in the last analysis, that means black individuals, not some abstraction that one conveniently labels *the* black people. Where, we may well ask, in the cold and passionless world of individual self-interest, are consensus and solidarity to be found? How can blacks—historically, and for understandable reasons, a politically apathetic group—become vitally interested not only in politics, but specifically in black politics?

Let us consider in concrete terms some of the barriers to group solidarity. First, there are the unemployed black youths of the ghetto, whose sense of power may turn in the dysfunctional direction of violence. Are these young people, who often despise the free-enterprise system, expected to stand shoulder to shoulder with members of a frequently conservative black middle class that is often strongly opposed to any form of confrontation politics? Are the semiliterate and near-subsistence black agricultural workers of the South likely to stand together with the black welfare mothers, both of whom have good reason to fear that assertions of pressure will cause them to lose even their marginal economic positions or public assistance? Only a generation ago, most blacks were menials. Today, there are millions of blacks in blue collars, and more than ever before in button-down white-collar jobs. Are these upscale groups of employed blacks more likely to work in compliant obedience to current racial practices within the system or to stand together collectively to challenge some of its faults? There is now a small elite group of influential black businessmen who, as has been the case for many years, are staunch supporters of the status quo; they often vote the Republican ticket; often, too, they are persuaded that other blacks can make it on their own merits without bringing pressures to bear on the economic and educational systems. There are now a considerable number of up-and-coming young black lawyers and businessmen. Often their goals, like their white peers', are to earn an annual income of $100,000, own a Mercedes car, and send their children to private schools. Will they move to a comfortable suburb where their contribution to black political power is nil, or submit their children to the hazards of inner-city living where they can stand shoulder to shoulder with poor blacks and provide the votes necessary to take political control of a city? There are the black economic royalists who have made fortunes in basketball, football, baseball, and the entertainment and fashion industries. Are these successful groups likely to meet in common protest or convention with the lunch-counter agitators of the past? Within the black movement itself are profound disagreements regarding the proper route to equality. Where is there common ground among the black proponents of school busing to produce racially mixed schools and others who stand unalterably opposed and who argue instead for black control of inner-city education and increased funding of predominantly black schools?

Many other factors work to splinter blacks. How rapidly can a black consensus develop when black spokesmen are specifically rewarded and chosen to serve in government because of their express opposition to the politics of black solidarity? How likely is it that a black consensus will build in favor of sweeping welfare reform when there are thousands of black social workers who fear their jobs will vanish if blacks win for themselves and others a federally guaranteed minimum income? Is it likely that a black reunification movement will develop when, as today, millions of blacks have been persuaded by government and by other blacks that continued progress of blacks will be an automatic outcome of laissez-faire capitalism? Is a black consensus likely to develop when even civil rights activists fail to see the connection between Negro powerlessness and high rates of illegitimate births and broken families, low rates of educational achievement, and even lower rates of labor force participation?

How, in years to come, is nonviolent consensus force to be nurtured when the very concept of black power still conjures up images of the assassins in the United States who called themselves the Black Liberation Army? Huey Newton, Stokely Carmichael, David Hillard, and Bobby Hutton may go into exile or change their politics, but the destructive slogan of Eldridge Cleaver's 1968 Peace and Freedom Ticket—"If we don't get justice, we're going to tear this country apart"—is still deeply imprinted in the memory of both blacks and whites. How, indeed, is the idea of black solidarity to be sold to the tired old man sitting on the stoop of a tenement in Harlem?

For all these reasons, the forces running against the consensus that is necessary for a black political awakening are very great. But the pressures to band together are equally compelling. There are searing moral issues around which blacks can still be inspired to organize. Blacks in the United States have three times or more their share of hunger, drug addiction, and poverty. Infant mortalities, maternal deaths, and some infectious disease rates among blacks run two to seven times the rates of whites. The terrors and sinister activities of the white citizens' councils are still deeply embedded in black consciousness. Blacks have a common history of slavery, public lynchings, debt servitude, and unjust convictions of crimes committed by others. Greater black solidarity is being forged today by episodic reversions to the Jim Crow tradition of all-white juries acquitting whites in criminal trials when the evidence was overwhelming that serious crimes had been committed against blacks. Greater black unity is encouraged today by a growing Ku Klux Klan, the continuing presence of rearguard segregationist judges in the South, racially hostile police and military officers, and politicians running on avowedly states'-rights tickets. The small group of congressmen who have discovered a new license to make cloakroom jokes about what does "Fred" want instead of "what do the niggers want" are sowing the seeds of a new black solidarity. For scores of historic, as well as current, reasons the ties of brotherhood for blacks must always be stronger than labor and other special-interest groups that, despite comparable obstacles, have consistently maintained their solidarity.

Other forces, too, are likely to contribute a new black groundswell. Blacks of all economic classes are faced with the injustice of voting districts that are gerrymandered against them. They now observe that the federal government openly breaks its own laws against federal funding of segregated education when it seems expedient to do so. They see the government shutting down the machinery of racial integration and encouraging the re-segregation of public schools and state universities. No black person alive in the United States is exempt from the tens of thousands of white realtors who steer middle- and upper-class blacks away from the all-white suburbs with the superior schools and the many thousands of financial institutions that now deny credit by postal ZIP code rather than skin color.

History shows that conditions of injustice do not, by themselves, produce political consensus among the people who have been oppressed. More often, united protest action develops when people, black or white, discover, or have thrust upon them, a catalytic event that shapes the moral issue, takes possession of the mind, and consumes the attention of all. In the 1960s, electrifying acts of injustice—burnings of black churches, and murders of civil rights workers—galvanized otherwise passive spectators into freedom marchers. Dr. Martin Luther King had only a handful of supporters until the police in Birmingham used police dogs and fire hoses on defenseless children and nuns.

One cannot definitely foresee what event or issue will act as the catalyst for the next black consensus that will reignite a black awakening. However, the seeds of moral outrage—so often the driving force behind group protest—are visible. Persistent and indefensible conditions of malnutrition among blacks in many counties of the rural South may find their symbolic equivalent of the Pettus Bridge police assault on Negroes at Selma, Alabama in 1965. The flash point of black outrage may be a teenage unemployment rate reaching 60 percent or more. The social implications of the facts that blacks own not much more than one or 2 percent of the nation's wealth and control absolutely none of the instruments of corporate production may suddenly rise to the surface of black consciousness. Racial discrimination may some day be seen by black people in the United States for what it is, a brutal strike at the life chances of black children. The destabilizing misery of inner-city crime, drug addiction, burned-out housing, and intolerable infant mortality rates may one day mobilize millions of occupationally dispensable and now politically impotent black people. The grave danger is that this anger may once more take the form of rebellion and violence rather than concerted political action.

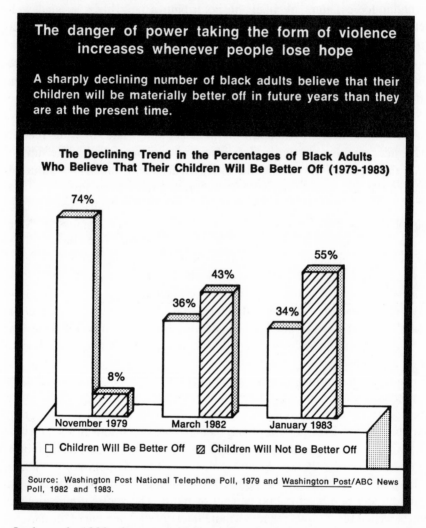

The danger of power taking the form of violence increases whenever people lose hope

A sharply declining number of black adults believe that their children will be materially better off in future years than they are at the present time.

The Declining Trend in the Percentages of Black Adults Who Believe That Their Children Will Be Better Off (1979-1983)

74%
55%
43%
36%
34%
8%

November 1979   March 1982   January 1983

☐ Children Will Be Better Off   ▨ Children Will Not Be Better Off

Source: Washington Post National Telephone Poll, 1979 and Washington Post/ABC News Poll, 1982 and 1983.

In the early 1980s there was no immediate issue in view that appeared to carry with it the immediate potential for producing a compelling stance of moral outrage. But then, only in hindsight does one ascertain that particular forces were bound to erupt. No person would have perceived twenty-five years ago that tens of thousands of blacks would risk life and limb over the right to use drinking fountains and restrooms in bus stations in the South. Almost no one would have predicted that thousands of other Negroes would submit themselves to physical beatings and police arrest over the unexciting issue of whether or not blacks should sit down with whites at privately owned lunch counters. Why did blacks in Selma, Alabama, in 1965, suddenly go to the ramparts over the drab, abstract, and traditionally worthless right to vote, an issue they had largely ignored for fifty years? Only a third of a human lifetime ago, the black population accepted with general equanimity state-enforced educational segregation as well as the private codes that wholly excluded them from admission to great universities and graduate schools.

In the slow march toward equality, blacks have always used the politics of pressure and self-help. Because these measures use nonviolent means to force whites to confront the perils of racial inequality, these tactics are the most noble and efficient hallmarks of the black political tradition. Often these corrective pressures have surfaced at the most unexpected times and for immediate reasons that in themselves appeared to be trivial. When they occur, they always swamp the conflicting political philosophies and clashing ambitions that keep blacks divided and weak. The question of whether these countervailing strategies will be employed again is not one of whether but of when.

Nonviolent Direct Action: The Backbone of the Black Bargaining Position

"Those who profess to favor freedom
And yet deprecate agitation
Are men who want crops
Without plowing the ground
They want rain without thunder and lightning
They want the ocean without the awful roar of its waters
Power concedes nothing without a demand
It never did, and it never will."

—Frederick Douglass
(August 4, 1857)

Introduction

PRIOR TO WORLD WAR II, the crushing forces of racial etiquette and obligation were sufficient to maintain the great majority of American Negroes as a controlled group of deferential and economically inferior menials. In fact, all four of the standard psychological characteristics of creature domestication were present in both the northern and southern states: constraint, segregation, protection, and taming. We have shown through a variety of proofs that the product of these political and psychological forces was the creation and perpetuation of a profoundly subordinate and economically backward racial caste. Except for the repressive codes of race, there was no adequate explanation for what had occurred. In fact, the economic consequences of racial caste were objectively measurable. By federal Census estimates in 1939, black incomes were approximately 37 percent of whites'. Yet, the group had enjoyed technical freedom for nearly three generations.

Suddenly and unpredictably, in the early 1940s, a number of black people in the United States began to break the psychological bonds of their place assignments; they questioned the etiquette of ethnic subordination; they stirred to their potential powers as a racial and political group. Beginning in

1941, with A. Philip Randolph's proposed march on Washington, Negro-Americans demonstrated for the first time that they could organize themselves for successful political confrontation. The pressure on the country mounted and became intense. So effective were black people in projecting the power of their collective will that in the early World War II years the nation had no choice but to rearrange its affairs to accommodate the demands of Negroes for wider admission into American institutions. Indeed, Negro skills and educational levels were essentially unchanged, but industrial employment suddenly opened up to them. Truly remarkable economic gains were then achieved. From 1939 to 1947, black incomes as a percentage of whites' rose from 37 to 51 percent. Beginning in the World War II years, important features of racial caste began to crumble as blacks moved into a whole range of occupations that had previously been closed to them. Yet, after the conclusion of the war, black political pressures and agitation abated. Whites successfully defended and often reestablished their traditional places of privilege and advantage in most areas of American society. Blacks, in turn, settled back once more into their traditional posture of collective obedience to the remaining, and still highly restrictive, codes of race.

A second black awakening in the nation occurred in 1955. Militant Negro groups in the South set out to extinguish the remaining rules of racial caste. Once more the chosen black political strategy was the application of shock to the American economic and social system. The events that followed are well known. Beginning with the Montgomery bus boycotts of the winter of 1955 and through the next decade, blacks pursued a host of direct-action strategies which contributed importantly to the huge economic, political, and social gains that carried on for the next decade and a half. The sit-in movement of 1957, the Freedom Rides of 1961, the Birmingham mass demonstrations, Bayard Rustin's march on Washington in 1963, and the Selma-Montgomery marches of 1965 led to legislated equal opportunity laws and government-assured voting rights. For the first time in American history, Negroes on the march captured public sentiment and briefly set the domestic agenda of the nation. In both northern and southern states, the gates were opened to restaurants, hotels, theaters and drinking fountains, and to many schools, business enterprises and neighborhoods that had been wholly closed to blacks. For black people the economic progress that followed was only short of spectacular. In merely four years, black incomes gained 13 percent on whites'. The number of black elected officials in the South increased nineteenfold in the ten years following the enactment of the Voting Rights Act of 1965. At last it appeared that Negro-Americans knew what they wanted to be and were taking powerful steps toward that end.

Voting, of course, had brought to blacks a brand-new form of power. Now that they had access to the ballot, many black people believed that traditional pressure and direct-action strategies were no longer useful or necessary. This was, indeed, a naive view of the forces of historical change. Blacks still did not have sufficient economic or political power in place. Only five years after the enactment of the Voting Rights Act, Negro economic fortunes began to decline. Select groups of blacks did well but, during the 1970s, blacks as a whole steadily lost ground to whites. Yet, confident of their influence as an important part of the progressive coalition of the Democratic party, most Negroes believed that economic equality for their race would be virtually an automatic outcome of the generosity of government liberalism and corporate philanthropy. In 1976, the short-term view of history would, indeed, have persuaded most progressives that blacks were at long last riding to equality on the policy coattails of President Carter, a head of state whom black voters had helped to elect.

But a new wave of voter conservatism severely curtailed President Carter's initial support of the black agenda. In early 1977, it became clear that blacks would have no influence in the Carter White House. As in the past, they were far removed from the levers of decisionmaking and would assume only the usual deputy posts that had traditionally been bestowed on Negro people. It became clear, too, that, while the rhetoric of racial justice was consistently broadcast from the White House, the President was not prepared to use the executive powers of his office to further open the economic or educational systems of the nation to entry by larger numbers of blacks. In fact, under President Carter, the influence of Negroes over government powers and policies, except in the federal judicial branch, would not greatly differ from what it had been under the Nixon and Ford administrations.

In the early 1980s, blacks found themselves even further removed from the centers of political power. A new, conservative government had come to office on a platform that was openly unsympathetic to the political objectives of the vast majority of black people. The Reagan Administration curtailed enforcement of laws against housing discrimination. It proposed to turn over the enforcement of civil rights laws to the states. It sought to reestablish a "right" of white children to the freedom to attend racially segregated schools. It undercut and threatened voting rights laws. It sought to reestablish tax exemption for racially discriminatory schools. It gave comfort to racial traditionalists who attacked the motives and achievements of Dr. Martin Luther King. At a time when most liberals and moderates hoped that racism was disappearing from American life, President Reagan played to the millions who continue to remain mean-spirited or racially prejudiced. Thus, in the early 1980s, black people stood by wholly power-less to prevent the implementation of government policies that made it considerably easier not to hire blacks, easier not to go to school with blacks, easier to fund institutions that denied admittance to blacks, easier to deny credit to blacks, and easier not to have to live next door to blacks.

Aside from obliterating much of the liberal agenda, the shift to the right in 1980 had one very important effect: a solid dose of racial conservatism in government concentrated the mind on fundamentals. For the vast major-ity of blacks, the election of an administration with no interest in their concerns was likely to act as a reminder to them that they have never been able to achieve major economic and social gains by depending exclusively on the sympathy and benevolence of liberal whites. From time to time, alliances with traditional progressives have produced important gains; but self-help is, and always has been, the best bet for blacks. It was likely then that the decline of the liberal wing of the Democratic party could, in the long run, turn out to be a useful political development for blacks. It forced them to rethink their position, to rely more on themselves, and to develop new means of bringing nonviolent pressure on American institutions—precisely the political strategy that in the past has always offered the best prospects for achieving permanent gains.

For our purposes here, we embrace the proposition that blacks will essen-tially win—and possibly only win—that which they seek out and claim for themselves. We accept, too, the view that the chances of black people being treated fairly and according to law will depend not only on the sense of fairness and integrity of those doing the judging, but also on the power of the people sitting in the dock. With these principles in mind, I have worked out in this chapter a number of direct-action strategies through which black people may come to share power in the United States. In later chapters we will turn to the other great powers at the disposal of black people: the judiciary, the executive, and the legislative forces. In recent years, these institutions, too, have turned their backs on the concerns of racial minor-ities. Yet, we shall see that there remain a number of important ways in which these branches of government may be moved to respond to, and in fact nurture, the powers and liberties of blacks.

Many of the proposals suggested in the following pages involve high risk; many are difficult to implement, and must not be tried without long deliber-ation and debate. Others will have easily predictable and useful con-sequences; they should be acceptable even to the most timid, and could be put in place right away. Against the background of conservative political attitudes of the early 1980s, some of my proposals may seem to border on fantasy. But shifts in power and attitudes occur very rapidly in this country. Moreover, group solidarity, wherever it occurs, has a way of happening suddenly and defying the prevailing conventional wisdom that holds that it can't happen.

Each of the measures I suggest is intended to empower blacks either individually or as a group and as a consequence to expand their economic and political choices. In all cases but one I have steered away from pressures for large money transfers and similar grants that so often create dependency, maintain client status, and diminish black strength. If our premise is correct that the possession of human power in all its complex and varied forms is the single most important dynamic that controls life opportunities and well-being, the measures suggested should be sound. The precedent of history strongly suggests that these strategies are almost certain to produce significant progress in the slow and painful struggle of blacks to break loose from the morbid state of apathy that currently afflicts them and to march gradually toward economic and political parity with whites.

Adopt a Standard Set of Indicators for Measuring Black Economic Progress

"A man with one watch knows what time it is;
a man with two watches is never quite sure."

—Lee Segall

IT IS VERY DIFFICULT, perhaps impossible, for people to be stirred to sympathy or indignation, much less provoked to action, by problems they cannot comprehend or with which they cannot find a personal identification. A whole nation can hang breathlessly upon the fate of a little boy buried alive in a cave or a little girl trapped in a well, but these same millions feel only a numbed indifference when thousands of faceless, unknown individuals die in a Turkish earthquake or starve to death in a famine in India.

Very large numbers of Americans feel a vague and unfocused sympathy for the struggle of blacks to achieve economic and social equality. But specific efforts to achieve economic parity often lack a sense of urgency because there is no single standard by which the public can measure either the progress blacks are making or the extent to which they are falling behind.

Some current statistics on the relative economic performance of blacks and whites show gains for blacks; more of them show losses. In this confusing welter of information and misinformation, one can hardly blame the average American for feeling that he is free to choose whatever version of these contradictory facts best suits his own preconceived notions and his private calculations of what is in his own best interest. The effect is, of course, profoundly political. Uncertainties about information tend to protect existing economic positions and arrangements. Confusing statistics and conflicting information disarm the efforts of blacks to organize around their grievances.

Much of this confusion could be eliminated if an index of black economic progress, modeled on such composite measures of the general economy as the consumer price index, were constructed and published on a regular basis. An index of black economic progress would serve a number of important purposes. It would regularly confront the American people with the disquieting fact of the persistent and huge disparity in the economic conditions of blacks and whites in the United States. Regular publication of the index would confront Presidents, legislators, and business leaders with harsh and stubborn facts that could neither be ignored nor swept under the rug. If the black condition as a whole were greatly deteriorating, politicians would no longer be able to hoodwink constituents by palming off a single statistic that indicates an improvement in the well-being of a limited demographic group as a fair picture of the overall situation. There would be strong reference points by which blacks could measure the kinds of government policies and economic activities that improved or worsened the economic gap between blacks and whites. For the first time, blacks would know where they stand, where they are going, and whether they are getting there at a satisfactory or an intolerably slow rate.

The question, next, is how one goes about developing a standard index of black economic trends. Which measures should be used and how should they be weighted and combined in order to give blacks the most accurate possible picture of their true economic standing?

In Chapters Eleven through Fourteen, we viewed the comparative economic strength of blacks and whites in the United States from four arbitrary, if conventional, perspectives. The measures we used were: the comparative incomes of blacks and whites; the relative percentage of blacks and whites living in poverty conditions; comparative black and white unemployment and employment participation; and finally, relative black-to-white holdings and control of wealth and capital goods. Until someone demonstrates otherwise, these economic measures are as good a starting point as any for constructing a suitable index of black economic progress. They might be augmented by other statistics such as:

- Comparative wealth of the races as measured by dividend and interest income.
- Comparative percentages by race of high school and college graduates.
- Comparative percentages by race of families receiving public assistance.
- The ratio of new business failures to new business start-ups, compared by race.
- The number of new loans to black businesses as a percentage of new loans to small businesses as a whole.
- The comparative percentages of people holding federal civil service positions with a GS ranking of 9 or higher.
- A measure of the extent to which the number of black corporate executives, with salaries large enough to be listed in Securities and Exchange Commission filings, falls short of the black percentage of the population as a whole.
- The ratio of black labor union membership to total population.
- The average workweek and wages of black production workers compared with white workers.
- Earnings by race of college graduates five years or less out of college.
- The comparative percentages by race of layoffs of industrial and construction workers.
- Gross receipts of black-controlled businesses compared with all business enterprises.
- Comparative poverty rates of female-headed black families and white families also headed by a woman.

Since the traditional pork-chop economic issues—comparative incomes, poverty and unemployment rates, and wealth statistics—are the most critical indicators of comparative economic well-being, these particular gauges would be heavily weighted—responsible, perhaps, for making up at least 50 percent of the index.

The index would not serve its purpose of synthesizing complex information unless it described reality in an accepted and meaningful way. Blacks would be obliged to identify and weigh those factors most important to their sense of economic, social, and political well-being. As long as blacks of all political persuasion still view themselves as a group with special economic, political, and social problems, a strong case can be made that they should be the judges of how they wish their progress to be measured.

The next question is who speaks for the black community in determining which economic indicators are important and which are less important or irrelevant. One might turn to the familiar black civil rights organizations, but many of them are not representative of blacks as a whole. For this reason, either a newly established caucus of black elected officials or the present Congressional Black Caucus would be a more logical starting point. The first step would be to choose a team of economists and statisticians and charge them with responsibility for constructing the index. While there will be profound differences between conservative and liberal blacks as to what, if anything, should be done about racial inequality, they should have much less difficulty agreeing on how to measure the inequality. Once the group had approved an economic barometer of the black economy, the readings would be published regularly by black elected officials and other private organizations interested in keeping the country's attention focused on the black economic condition. In time, it is likely that major newspapers would regularly publish the index, just as they now publish other economic information such as home-building trends and stock price averages.

To win greater legitimacy, authority, and public visibility, the index of black economic progress should ultimately be published by the federal government. Responsibility for securing this objective would naturally fall on the Congressional Black Caucus. The political task would be to persuade the government to require the U.S. Census Bureau to produce index figures on a regular basis.

To see how such a standardized measuring rod would work, let us propose a rudimentary index of black economic progress using only the three statistics presently collected and published on a regular basis by the Census Bureau or the Department of Labor. These are comparative income, unemployment, and poverty rates. For our first computation, these three factors would be weighted equally.

This approach to the composite index would show blacks, as compared with whites, doing about the same in 1979 (43.6 percent) as they were doing during the Eisenhower administration in 1959 (43.5 percent). If this result shocks the reader, it must be remembered that the situation of the black underclass has significantly worsened over the years. Although black family income as a percentage of white gained 5 percentage points during the period 1959-1979 and black unemployment remained fairly constant at 2.2 times the white rate, the other indicator, comparative poverty, lagged enough to offset the gain. In 1959, blacks were 2.9 times as likely as whites to be poor, but by 1979 blacks were 3.5 times more often in poverty.[1]

Already the proposed index changes perspectives. It limits and tends to put in proper place and proportion the highly trumpeted gains of a few

American blacks, and dredges up for view the increasingly large and invisible underclass of urban blacks.

Suppose we now conclude that greater weight should be given to family income trends because our subjective judgment tells us this is the most meaningful measure of black economic progress. We then weigh this factor twice as heavily as comparative poverty or unemployment rates. Using this computation, the long-term trend in the composite index comes out about the same, with blacks showing a totally unsatisfactory improvement of only 1.33 percentage points during the twenty-year period 1959-1979. A straight-line projection of this rate of improvement (.0665 percentage points a year) would not produce economic parity until the year 2629.[2]

This rather primitive composite index does not include a wealth factor. If this important gauge of a group's well-being were added to our mix, the overall level of the index would drop somewhat, since for many generations it appears that the wealth difference between the races has remained nearly constant at about three times the differences in comparative income, poverty, and employment.

Admittedly, the composite indicators I have used are very rudimentary. Yet they illustrate the function of any composite index in focusing the mind and permitting ordinary human intelligence to make some reasonable sense out of what otherwise appears to be statistical chaos. A single indicator—such as family income, in which blacks gained slightly on whites during our twenty-year period—can give a misleading picture, but such distortions disappear when multiple measures are combined, even as simply as we have just demonstrated.

A more sophisticated and probably more balanced index of comparative black-white economic performance indicator might allocate, in varying proportions, 50 percent to all the standard economic measures—comparative family incomes, unemployment, percent in poverty, and comparative wealth—with the other half of the index comprised of weighted subsidiary measures such as labor union membership, average weekly wages of production workers, or new small business start-ups, for example. Political factors such as percentages of blacks in legislative bodies, judgeships, and political offices could also be included in the index, as well as certain social indicators not usually associated with economic progress—comparative voter turnout by race, literacy rate, infant mortality, letter mail per capita, professional school enrollment ratios, or telephones per thousand people. Employing a great number of components would give the index greater stability and would reduce the effects of major fluctuations in particular components.

Designing a satisfactory composite black progress index is a challenging conceptual and statistical problem. Yet if an economic problem such as inflation in the United States economy as a whole is deemed to be measurable by a single leading index of seemingly unrelated components, the problem of comparing racial segments of the economy should yield to the same type of synthesis. In constructing an index of black economic progress, the problems of weighting various factors are no greater than those inherent in computing the Dow-Jones stock averages, where the heavy representation of certain highly valued securities and so-called blue-chip stocks frequently gives a distorted picture of what is happening to the "entire" market. Making the judgment, for example, that the same weight should be given to relative black and white family income and relative

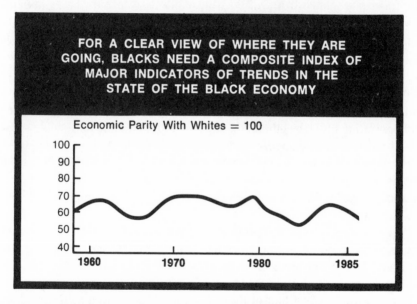

FOR A CLEAR VIEW OF WHERE THEY ARE GOING, BLACKS NEED A COMPOSITE INDEX OF MAJOR INDICATORS OF TRENDS IN THE STATE OF THE BLACK ECONOMY

Economic Parity With Whites = 100

numbers of blacks and whites in poverty is arbitrary, but no more arbitrary than stipulating that new manufacturers' orders be given a particular weight relative to layoffs when calculating the composite index of the twelve leading economic indicators.

It is clear that prevailing indifference to the problems of blacks—an apathy shared by many blacks as well as most whites—cannot be overcome simply by constructing an index of black economic progress. But the publication of information is necessary to set the stage for political action. Once a suitable index of the black condition has been designed and published, the press, public officials, and legislators would find the political message difficult to ignore. The political impact would be very great if the state of the index were reported regularly on national television and published regularly in influential journals such as *Business Week, The Wall Street Journal,* and *Time.*

Like all approximations of the truth, shorthand measures of complex differences must always be viewed with great caution. But so must one avoid being deceived by complicated sets of statistics that avoid distorting the truth at the cost of hiding it behind an impenetrable thicket of often contradictory numbers. Whenever there are people who have a continuing stake in confusion, it is essential that someone undertake the task of simplification and clarification. It goes without saying that there are many policymakers who benefit politically from selectively controlling the kind of information the world hears about racial differences in the United States. Predictably, they can be expected to raise a host of objections to the use of a standardized index of racial progress. But blacks as a group should not be deflected in this effort. They urgently need a cool, reliable, and dispassionate scorekeeper bound by a consistent, albeit somewhat arbitrary, set of rules. Posting the score on a monthly or even a semiannual basis denies racial extremists on the political right the power to overstate their case. Scorekeeping prevents irresponsible militants from concealing black progress. In particular, scorekeeping alerts educated and influential people in the United States to the undeniable truth of extreme and persisting black inequality.

Root Out and Ruthlessly Punish All Forms of Black Terrorism and Violence in the United States

"And Samson said 'Let me die with the Philistines.' Then he bowed with all his might; and the house fell upon the lords and upon all the people that were in it. So the dead he slew at his death were more than those whom he had slain during his life."

—*Judges* 16:30

TERRORISM HAS BECOME a worldwide epidemic. In the name of a "higher justice," innocent people are incinerated by partisans in a pub in Belfast. Afraid of having their kneecaps shot off by the Red Brigade, Italian businessmen travel in bulletproof cars. For a "higher good," school children are held hostage in Holland. For the noble goal of creating a Palestinian state, planeloads of passengers are brutally maimed or killed in the Tel Aviv airport. A whole nation turns itself into a pack of lawless kidnappers in order to make another nation pay for the sins of a deposed ruler. Hijacking, carnage, kidnapping, and murder have become standard—and often temporarily effective—weapons of minority groups. All over the world, despairing and often insane individuals glorify or condone murder because they see no prospect of victory for their causes through persuasion and legitimate political processes.

Many blacks in the United States see their own people herded into squalid ghettos, born into the world without a chance of finding decent employment, oppressed by the police, and increasingly ignored by their government. Finding no effective means of redress through traditional politics, they, too, are likely to turn again to violence, just as certain small but highly publicized segments of the black radical movement did during the politically tumultuous days of the Vietnam War. But this course of action would have chilling and tragic consequences. Widespread acts of violence committed by or on behalf of blacks would set back the black cause for generations to come.

If black people are to be successful in their endeavors to win political and economic influence in the United States, they must recognize three fundamental truths about violence as a form of power: violence in the form of political terrorism is morally wrong; it is not a necessary political strategy; nor is it effective when employed. In fact, the use of terrorism robs blacks of the ability to use all of the useful legitimate forms of political and economic power currently at their disposal.

Under all of the traditional concepts of justifiable civil disobedience, there is no case whatsoever for black terrorism in the United States. Terrorism conducted by underground partisans was justified in Nazi Germany, a society that had embarked on a policy of racial genocide. Nazi Germany, moreover, was a country from which all processes of law had disappeared. But neither of these conditions has ever been present in the United States. There are no preventive detentions of blacks in America, nor are blacks who speak out against racism either censored or imprisoned. There are no kangaroo courts which summarily order the jailing or execution of blacks accused of crime. On the contrary, blacks are guaranteed the right to march, to protest, to unionize, to vote, and, if they deem it necessary, to organize in protest a national strike of black workers in any or all private sectors of the economy. In the United States there are many other open avenues of political redress whose presence denies any conceivable moral claim to the right to use force or violence. Indeed, both federal and state governments have passed public laws punishing race discrimination and segregation. In many instances, the states have ordered favored treatment of blacks in employment, education, and commercial transactions. Congress, controlled by whites, has adopted voting rights measures that, in some instances, literally assure the election of blacks to public office. The most conservative Supreme Court in two generations has nevertheless upheld the constitutionality of most of these laws favoring blacks, including racially preferential government edicts. Finally, blacks have full access to the overriding powers of federal courts where, in only four years' time, the number of black judges has more than doubled. The United States offers none of the conditions where political philosophers have asserted a right of civil disobedience.

The use of nonviolent power has served blacks well in the past. The history of the black protest movement from 1955 to 1967 attests to this. Moreover, there are innumerable, and perfectly acceptable, economic and political strategies that blacks have never tried but which hold out great promise for helping them to reach equality in the United States. This is not to deny that social injustice still exists in the United States; but as long as established political processes offer means for redress, all acts of violence against the American brand of racism are fundamentally illegitimate and unjust.

What can be done to reduce the prospect of outbreaks of black political terrorism in the United States? Unfortunately, not much, except through education, propaganda, and indoctrination. The most impressive forces for instruction in nonviolence will always be provided by the spiritual leaders and heroes whom young blacks admire most.

Young blacks, particularly, must come to understand that terrorism is never justified in a nation that has not lost its sense of justice. They must be taught that acts of terrorism needlessly undermine the collective strength and sap the stamina of the group. They must be indoctrinated in the wisdom that violence invites retaliation and forfeits the moral prestige of black grievances, which otherwise would exert a powerful claim on the conscience of America. Because of the grave risk of political terrorism by militant black groups, parents, teachers, and community leaders must drill young blacks in the self-destructive ends of violence and in the spectacular power advantages of nonviolence. There should be intensive instruction in the alternative routes of political power. Blacks everywhere—church leaders, community leaders, teachers, entertainers, and police officers—should launch nationwide campaigns to expose, embarrass, and isolate those who advocate violence. Black athletes and celebrities must mount television campaigns showing why smart, "cool guys" organize strong political organizations rather than neighborhood gangs. Finally, of course, concerted political action must be taken to create economic and educational opportunities that turn the mind away from crime, violence, and terrorism.

Invoke Every Lawful Means to Integrate
Public Schools and Suburban Communities

"Three hounds sittin' by the front door starvin'
Lookin' thru the window at a roast beef carvin'
One started beggin'
One started bitchin'
One started makin'
Friends with the cook in the kitchen."

—"Skinnin' a Cat," lyrics by Peter Udell,
from the Broadway comedy *Purlie* (1970)

TO THE CASUAL MIND, the race-trait prejudgment and its driving engine, the psychological need for racial segregation and subordination, are simply unfortunate but forgivable human failings. Accordingly, government efforts to enforce a civic duty to integrate often appear to be an extreme but unwarranted restriction on human liberty. But this trivialization of the race prejudgment falls far from the mark. Racial discrimination must be understood as an ugly and repressive form of public power. This is the case not only because universally observed racial prejudice uses collective social codes and sanctions to assign inferior caste, but also because the sweep of the rules and conventions of the racial prejudgment corners people, boycotts them, and locks them out of all those places where important and necessary educational and economic and other human resources are found. To be specific, race discrimination says to black people: "You may not enter certain schools or colleges; you may enter only certain places of employment; you may borrow money or use capital but only in certain places and for certain purposes. And in extreme cases, the racial prejudgment says, "You may not enter a voting booth or put up your name for political office." It is, therefore, the *place restrictions*—the strict limits on human liberty and mobility—that are the most repressive aspect of the codes of racial control.

This is why the goal of formal mixing or integration is indispensable to black economic, political, and social progress. Lower caste status may not be cancelled without conferring on blacks wide-ranging and unrestricted powers *to enter places* —particularly those places where power is found.

In recent years, the value to black children of policies of racial integration of public schools has been seriously disputed. Many black people question whether integrated education improves the academic skills of their children.

There is increasing disillusionment also about the usefulness of active measures to integrate suburban and other predominantly white communities and institutions. Resigned to the determination of most whites to keep their communities white, an increasing number of blacks opt once more for separate but equal treatment: "Just give us equal expenditures for public (albeit segregated) education and we will be satisfied." Watching cities like Chicago delay integration until most whites have moved out, a few black scholars, including Derek Bell, Dean of the University of Oregon Law School, have suggested abandoning policies of racial integration in order to concentrate on the educational enrichment of black schools.

To yield on the issue of segregated schools and neighborhoods would be an error of catastrophic proportions, having profoundly harmful economic consequences for the future of the entire black population. The reason integrated education and living are indispensable to racial equality has more to do with economic opportunity and power than with traditional educational and social objectives. Without regard to family background and handicaps, the young person who grows up in a community of economically successful people will have greater economic power and success on that account alone. The distribution of economic power inherent in family connections, friendships, and luck, as well as superior information about economic opportunities, will always strongly favor those who are physically situated in the economic and social mainstream of our society. The right place to be is always in close proximity to the events and people who control employment opportunities, credit, admissions, and access to institutions of all kinds. The favorable place to be is at or near the place of residence or business of people who manage and call the shots in the political and economic systems. The preferred schools, colleges, or business schools to be in are the ones with strong links to the white-controlled business world. Because of prior segregation and racial subordination, these places of schooling and living are presently occupied almost exclusively by whites. Unless blacks have equal access, in space and time, to all of the physical playing fields of competition, equal opportunity rules will be of little avail, even to the most dedicated, hardworking, and gifted blacks.

The compelling reason for integrated living and education, therefore, is not the racially elitist notion that "white" is superior or the equally condescending idea that blacks learn more when they go to school with whites. Nor does school integration enrich the lives of black children today simply because black children in the past have, in the words of the Supreme Court, "been psychologically and emotionally harmed by white domination." The reason for affirmative racial integration is that physical presence in all of the places where important economic events take place is necessary to over-come the massive economic handicap of established racial isolation. Since whites, for the moment, control all economic, political, and professional power, the redistribution of that power along nonracial lines is not likely to occur other than in a racially integrated society. Only when full racial integration occurs—in the most literal, temporal, and spatial senses of the term—will success factors such as luck, connections, friendships, loyalties, nepotism, and access to information help blacks and whites on an equal basis.

Conservatives are fond of instructing blacks that they will get ahead by studying at night and taking two jobs. But the instructors fail to point out that blacks will also get ahead by living in integrated communities where business is conducted, where jobs are handed out, and where people use influence to help each other win admission to accrediting institutions. Observing all the established principles of human power and success in the economic struggle, blacks must insist on unrestricted human mobility for themselves. They must yield to nothing short of unqualified access to all of the places that are open to white people. They must use the courts, the legislatures, and all the available strategies of nonviolent direct action to close distance on and mix with whites wherever the latter have retreated or can be found. The albeit odious remedies of pupil busing and scrambling of school district boundaries must be pursued by all proper means. Anyone who carefully thinks through the close relationship of power to space and time must conclude that for blacks racial integration is *an indispensable requirement for achieving economic equality*.

From the standpoint of power and advantage, even self-chosen segregation within an integrated institution is almost invariably a distinctly inferior choice. Hence, the black student who rejects integration in favor of the feelings of solidarity and security he gets from joining an all-black fraternity sacrifices the economic, social, and political advantages available in an integrated or predominantly white fraternity. The same power disadvantage resides in all-black lodges, labor unions, neighborhoods, newspapers, cotillions, eating clubs, banks, and insurance companies. The clamor for all-black dormitories, sororities, and college eating tables isolates blacks from the power centers of this country in much the same way as would a successful back-to-Africa movement. Although separatist arrangements and institutions confer the useful benefits of self-sufficiency and group solidarity, they do so at the cost of the superior power and life opportunities that accrue to those who press on to integrate themselves and their friends into the powerful ways of the larger society. Measured in terms of access to power generally—and access to the power of information in particular—the price blacks pay for separatism and self-segregation far exceeds the benefits.

Fuller residential and school integration contributes to black empower-

---

THE INCREASING MIGRATION OF BLACKS TO THE SUBURBS: THE MOST IMPORTANT AND BENIGN OF ALL CURRENT DEMOGRAPHIC TRENDS

Urban political power may be blunted, but far more important economic and social gains should be created as increasing numbers of blacks leave the commercial backwaters of the inner cities and head for the economic and educational mainstream of the suburbs.

The Suburban Migration of Blacks
(1970-1980)

City	Black Suburban Population—1980	Increase in Black Suburban Population—1970 to 1980	Percent Black 1970	Percent Black 1980
New York	156,291	33,148	5.9%	7.6%
Los Angeles	398,069	158,048	6.2%	9.6%
Chicago	230,827	101,033	3.6%	5.6%
Philadelphia	245,527	54,216	6.7%	8.1%
Detroit	131,478	32,164	3.4%	4.2%
Dallas	65,955	24,923	3.6%	3.9%
Washington, D.C.	404,814	225,386	8.3%	16.7%
St. Louis	201,348	76,106	7.0%	10.6%
Pittsburgh	73,790	7,945	3.5%	4.0%
Baltimore	125,721	55,807	6.0%	9.1%
Atlanta	215,909	123,469	8.4%	13.5%
Cleveland	94,285	—49,648	3.4%	7.1%
San Diego	26,752	17,507	1.4%	2.7%
Newark	225,770	78,323	8.4%	13.8%

Source: U.S. Bureau of the Census, 1980 Census of the Population.

---

ment in another important respect. Integration is indispensable to shattering racial stereotypes. The black person who lives next door to whites and goes to school with their children is more likely to become known to whites and to be judged as an individual rather than as a lower-class person. He or she is less likely to be prejudged by the demeaning and inaccurate expectations many whites associate with people who have a black face. Only in day-to-day contact with blacks will whites learn that blacks are not less intelligent, less honest, or less human than whites. Through time, integrated living and integrated education are the most forceful weapons for breaking the stubborn and enduring mental habit of defining people's traits according to their race. These are weapons far more potent than the force of law.

Integrated education also contributes to the power of blacks in one other important respect. While it is a matter of dispute as to whether educational achievement scores of black children improve in a racially integrated school setting, it is certain that once white children are required to attend formerly black schools, the levels of educational resource allocation in these schools always rise. Nothing encourages white-controlled school boards and state assemblies to upgrade inner-city schools as effectively as putting a fair number of white children into these schools. Whites in power will always protect the opportunities of their own children, and integration thus forces them to attend to the needs of black youngsters at the same time.

Unfortunately, school busing remains the single most important means of creating a more fully integrated society. Pupil busing initiatives must be urged in the courts for all communities where school segregation is the result of official policy. Blacks must also press for much more drastic use of cutoffs of federal funding to racially segregated school districts, a strategy that depends, in the last analysis, on greater black and Hispanic political power on a national and local level.

Further, a serious legal attack must be launched against segregated higher education in state universities. More than a quarter of a century after the Supreme Court outlawed state-sponsored racial segregation in public education, the states of Texas, North Carolina, Alabama, South Carolina, Delaware, West Virginia, Ohio, Missouri, and Kentucky still maintain dual state university systems.[3] Finally, the tax-exemption privileges of the "seg" academies or private schools formed to avoid school integration laws should be challenged in the courts as well as by political means. The continuing grant of tax exemption to these schools is the unconscionable equivalent of a tax subsidy to them. Sooner or later, the simple and irrefutably fair principle of "Jim Crow on Your Own Dough" must become an enforced law in the United States.

In 1981, a civil rights counterrevolution was blunting government efforts to enforce the integration of neighborhoods and public schools. Soon after President Reagan took office, the U.S. Department of Justice settled the

Chicago School Board litigation, leaving the nation's second largest public school system with 250 schools that were all black or all Hispanic-American. Many other city schools in Chicago remained over 70 percent white. The Justice Department gave up its efforts to integrate Houston's inner-city black schools. Los Angeles abandoned its scheme for mandatory integration of its public schools and busing programs were cut back or stopped in Seattle and Dallas.[4] In the early 1980s, a battery of bills were introduced in Congress designed to end the power of government to require mandatory busing. Clearly, further efforts to achieve racial integration in education face formidable opposition.

In the 1960s, Malcolm X was fond of mocking integration as a word invented by a northern liberal. In 1981, the revival of his views was playing squarely into the hands of the large number of white Americans who have never lost their aversion to mixing white and black children in neighborhood schools. Fortunately, the National Association for the Advancement of Colored People had never retreated from its single-minded devotion to the racial integration of schools and neighborhoods.

Liberals who shaped the integrationist policies of so many school boards in the 1960s have now become a political minority. Many blacks, too, have come to accept a revisionist thesis that government efforts to end race discrimination cannot improve the lot of blacks. There is strong support among a number of black spokesmen for the position that civil rights groups should abandon further efforts toward affirmative integration and hand over white schools to whites. But this capitulation would betray an important constitutional principle: that the state may not, directly or indirectly, racially segregate children in public schools. The abdication of the right to an effective remedy for unlawful segregation would be pragmatically short-sighted and, in a most serious sense, economically destructive to future generations of black people.

Find a Leader Who Will Reunify Blacks and Set a National Black Agenda

"Before long there will be heard throughout the planet a formidable cry, rising like the howling of innumerable dogs to the stars, asking for someone or something to take command. . . ."

—Jose Ortega y Gasset (1930)

THE CONDITION OF BLACK POWERLESSNESS in the United States is due, in large part, to ideological and political disunity among Negro people. In recent years, particularly, there have been sharp and divisive disputes among blacks about objectives, policies, and strategies. The appropriate political tactics of black people are subject to fundamental internal differences. Should blacks take up political positions based on racial consciousness? Is the ballot to be used by black people merely as an effective means of self-defense, or should blacks turn minority voting power into an offensive weapon by which they evict race baiters from public office and take control of important centers of American political power? Disunifying differences have arisen among blacks over the legitimacy of government and private pressures to help Negroes catch up with whites. Equally enervating controversies rage over whether blacks benefit more from a laissez-faire economy or one where government intervenes on behalf of racial minorities. Even the basic causes of the black disadvantage have become the subject of bitter disputes among black people.

Ideological differences should not, nor can they, be repressed; yet the elimination of major differences and the attendant creation of a new black political consensus are indispensable to arriving at a state of political empowerment. But consensus, with the power that always attends it, rarely develops without the cohesive force of leadership. Like any other disorganized group, blacks need a moving spirit—a person who will bind them together, inform their efforts, articulate their moral position, organize them as a political force, write down an agenda, and set goals that will transcend their ideological differences.

Particularly, the leader must be adroit at blunting the sugar-coated ploys that political opponents use to pacify or disarm black people. The chief must be skilled at refuting exaggerated claims about the costs, or harms to Negroes, of preferential treatment, race-conscious quotas, and the use of government power to repress race discrimination and segregation. There must be either a chosen or a de facto political chief who is capable of acting decisively to undercut attempts to buy off blacks with token appointments and mere promises of good intentions and of better opportunities down the line. A leader must be discovered who will project the necessary moral force to persuade downtrodden and middle-class people alike to do what they don't want—or are afraid—to do, to convince them to declare and insist, "This is our program; this is the way we are going." The cause of black empowerment is no exception to the rule that political movements always require a binding force at the top in the form of a leader who keeps the ideology pure, plots the strategy, galvanizes the hesitant into action, and pushes the group ahead on a steady course.

Sporadic efforts to put pressure on institutions that have the ability to open opportunities and to make life better for blacks may, on occasion, sting an organization, shock the system, and produce some useful results. But political power is effective only when it is intelligently manipulated and controlled. For this reason, too, there must be a person or body that *commands* black power, someone who switches it off and on, who negotiates the terms under which others will feel, or be relieved of, its force.

While the chief function of the leader is spiritual—to inspire people to bleed and die in order to build and protect a black consensus—naming and celebrating a leader also produce the indispensable central black command post. In the black community there must be an overall political authority that establishes an official black position on issues such as voting rights, affirmative action, school busing, welfare reform, and minority economic development. To present an effective black political front there must be a single organ or committee with the standing and authority to negotiate with the Business Roundtable over the minority employment record of major corporations, to deal with the White House on executive orders of particular concern to black citizens, and to speak for a unified black vote in political bargaining with congressmen, state legislators, and government bureaucrats. All of this, of course, is a tall order; yet the ability of blacks to influence American institutions is likely to be modest until a leader of the highest order appears.

The importance of black political leadership—in the sense of the presence of a chosen or implicitly obeyed nation head who controls black votes—may be illustrated by the relationship of black voting power to the presidential power in early 1983. At that time, President Reagan's policy of soft-pedaling the enforcement of civil rights laws and his cutbacks in social programs, combined with the highest black unemployment rate in fifty years, had produced for him a calamitously low popularity rating among blacks. In the spring of 1983, only 9 percent of blacks approved of the President's performance in office. At the same time, a large so-called gender gap existed with regard to women voters. While 47 percent of Americans generally gave President Reagan a positive approval rating, only 36 percent of women expressed approval of the way the President was discharging his duties. While the gender gap that President Reagan faced was a serious threat to his political base, the approval rating of women was not so low that it was futile for President Reagan to try to repair it. Within a period of only a few weeks from the day the gender gap was widely publicized, two women were appointed to the Cabinet in quick succession. Elizabeth Dole was named Secretary of Transportation and Margaret Heckler was appointed Secretary of Health and Human Services. Since, for over two years, President Reagan had maintained a traditional all-male Cabinet, it was clear at the time that these sudden appointments were designed to placate women and bring them back into the GOP fold. But the sting of female voting power operated in this situation only because the President perceived that the female vote *might be recaptured*.

In the case of blacks, however, the voter approval rating was so low that the President—in common with most recent Republican Presidents—had altogether written off Negro ballots. To Republican political tacticians it appeared that the Negro vote was, in fact, structurally incapable of supporting the President, even on a temporary basis. This meant that blacks, unlike women voters, were objectively powerless because of general perceptions that they were totally defended against even the most persuasive efforts to swing their votes to the President or to his party. The result was that President Reagan made very few black appointments in government, often supported the political opponents of black people, and persisted in pursuing civil rights and economic policies inimical to most blacks. And he did this in considerable part because blacks—unlike women—never presented him with an opening where a Negro bargaining agent might, under special circumstances, shift masses of black votes to the President.

Therefore, an important function of a black leader would be to augment black political power by creating a credible prospect that black votes could, in fact, be swung to the GOP. It is possible then that a strong black political leader commanding a high degree of voter loyalty could confer significant political power on black people and make them count in the constant struggle to build coalitions and voting constituencies. If, for example, a designated black leader were perceived as having the power to control black votes and to bargain on their behalf, the White House would have a much greater interest in establishing policies and making appointments that take black objectives into account. Thus, in an exaggerated case, if a black leader with nationwide support were perceived as capable of shifting the black vote for the GOP from, say, 7 percent to 30 percent, black people would not only count in Republican party politics, but they would also begin to shed their orphan status in the Democratic party. The explanation for this, of course, is that political power grows not so much out of a large vote, but out of a *swing* vote. And it is the swing vote that cannot be produced without a political leader whom people trust and to whom they are willing to give their proxy, whether the balloting be in state, local, or national elections.

There are many black people today who contend that the question of who the black leader will be is the wrong question. The better questions, it is suggested, are: How can a multiplicity of black leaders cooperate to sustain the struggle? How can a collegial atmosphere be built among black organizations working together to create better life chances for Negro people? But these questions do not adequately address the proven preconditions of political empowerment. The indisputable fact is that, even in a participatory democracy, the generation of group power requires the presence of a central command that unites the members of the group. According to this rule there can be no effective black power in the United States unless most blacks in the country are prepared to point their fingers in one direction when whites ask of them, "Who here is in charge?"

Combine All Black Civil Rights Organizations Into a Unified and Independent Black Lobby

"One time over in Virginny dere was two ole niggers. Uncle Bob and Uncle Tom. Dey was mad at one 'nuther and one day dey decided to have a dinner and bury de hatchet. So dey sat down, and when Uncle Bob wasn't lookin' Uncle Tom put some poison in Uncle Bob's food, but he saw it and when Uncle Tom wasn't lookin', Uncle Bob he turned de tray roun' on Uncle Tom, and he gits the poison food."

—A Negro fable

FUNDED ON A SHOESTRING, riddled by infighting, and politically impotent, black self-help organizations today are pale leftovers of what was once a much stronger black political force. In better days, organizations such as the National Association for the Advancement of Colored People (NAACP) and the Southern Christian Leadership Conference (SCLC) led the struggle for voting rights, equal opportunity employment rules, and racial integration of schools and other public places. During the 1950s and 1960s, other black organizations, such as the Student Nonviolent Coordinating Committee (SNCC) and the Congress of Racial Equality (CORE), exerted considerable economic and political pressure on southern defenders of white supremacy and, in the process, made an important contribution to the improved economic and social status that blacks enjoy today. Currently, these once relatively powerful black organizations suffer from tired blood. Their political and economic policies are divided and often incoherent. Among black organizations, hidden agendas are as common as shared goals. Even when they share a single vision of the shape of their political strategies, black organizations are not strong enough to do what they believe is right and necessary. Professor Martin Kilson's remark in 1982—"The NAACP is in its twilight zone. The sun is setting on its head"—was equally applicable to most other black and so-called civil rights organizations.

The funding of most black organizations, as well as control of the organizations themselves, is often in the hands of well-meaning whites who advocate traditional liberal programs that succor blacks without empowering them. The agenda of most black organizations—often a mirror image of the benevolent progressivism of the editorial pages of the liberal press—is tired, paternalistic, and generally accommodating to the wishes of influential whites who shower blacks with degrees and awards but have no serious intention of sharing political, economic, or media power with them.

The impotence of black organizations is fiscal as well as spiritual and structural. One of the largest of these organizations, the National Urban League, had annual private funding in 1979 of about $12 million, a sum only slightly exceeding the annual receipts of the National Audubon Society. In that year, annual gifts to the NAACP were running at the rate of $5 million—less than the annual pledges made by alumni to many small private liberal arts colleges. The problems of black organizations may be summed up as follows: ideological divisions; inadequate funding shared by too many organizations; manipulation and control by large organizations essentially opposed to power-sharing; insufficient support by blacks; and the absence of a unified black political agenda.

The political empowerment of blacks begins by combining black pressure groups into a single action alliance. This develops the consensus power that appears only when a group speaks, negotiates, votes, and brings confrontation pressures through a single bargaining agency.

As unity is approached, black organizations must develop home-grown and black-nurtured status. Fiscal self-sufficiency must be achieved. Organizations such as the NAACP and the National Urban League must throw away their begging bowls and turn to political action. Even if withdrawal from fiscal dependency on large foundations sacrifices beloved assistance programs, the unified nationwide alliance of black organizations must free itself from the crippling effects of financial dependence on business and government charity. The importance of achieving self-funded status was highlighted in striking terms in 1981 when President Reagan's deep cuts in federal funding for social programs produced helpless dismay at the headquarters of black civil rights organizations, which faced massive layoffs of workers and operational cutbacks. This distress would not have occurred had the NAACP, and others, not been engaged, over the last ten years, in developing an unsustainable menu of band-aid and relief programs that depended on funding from others.

Attaining adequate political strength to influence legislation, as well as to affect the policies of administrative officials, ultimately depends on developing a system of tithing. In due course, blacks must begin to press other blacks to tithe a fixed percent of their incomes in favor of a single national black self-help organization. This objective is in the tradition of many other strong and successful pressure groups. At least 80 percent of all black organizational funding should come from blacks.[5] Despite severe economic problems, American blacks have sufficient financial strength to mount the most powerful lobbying organization the nation has ever seen. The personal income of blacks in the United States in 1981 was $138 billion. A mere one-half of one percent of this sum would produce $690 million a year, an amount more than 100 times the current annual budget of the NAACP.[6]

The mission of the national black lobbying organization would be standard: pressure, protest, and political action. The central organization must pose a constant political threat to elected officials who take unfavorable stands on black issues; it must launch new political initiatives and organize coalitions to support agreed-upon legislative objectives and seek to veto the objectives of opponents of wider liberties and opportunities for blacks. It must support congressmen, black or white, who are under attack by groups opposed to seeing blacks take up important positions in American society. In the style of other influential groups, the alliance must round up Negro votes, decide political tactics in elections, identify the candidates blacks should back, impose conditions for black political support, expose government efforts to co-opt black political power, and ensure that allies and supporters show up to vote in elections. The black organizational alliance must develop the black issues, build a consensus on them, and determine the broad agenda for the political empowerment of black America. Then, indeed, blacks would become a political *force* instead of a captive and uninfluential constituency within the liberal political establishment.

Adopt a Master Plan for Taking Up Positions in Strategic Sectors of the American Economy

. . . segregation is a complex of interlocking economic, political, legal, social, and ideological components maintained by the dominant group . . . [it is] a circular process by which custom becomes law and law creates custom. Between them they serve to keep the subjected groups in their place . . .

—C. Vann Woodward (1983)

WE SHOWED EARLIER how the possession of information plays an indispensable role in the exercise of human power. But the vast majority of people are unaware of the tremendous importance of information differences as they affect the economic life chances of particular groups or individuals. Black civil rights groups, particularly, are often so embroiled in efforts to maintain government aid or to defend or advance the minority legislative agenda that they neglect to notice the implications for public policy in the fact that even minor shifts in access to economic information may profoundly affect black incomes, employment, and wealth opportunities.

To illustrate, suppose hypothetically that in 1970 blacks in the United States had been able to see into the future. Suppose they had known that by the end of the decade, steel, tire, and other heavy industries would come on very hard times, with unemployment rates reaching 50 percent or more. Possessing this extraordinarily valuable information, black workers in large numbers could have systematically moved into jobs in other industries which in fact boomed during the decade of the 1970s.

If blacks had been blessed with information on the impending decline of heavy industry, the skill, education, and other front-runner advantages of whites as a group would have been almost completely blunted as skilled and semiskilled blacks claimed jobs as computer assembly-line workers, paralegals, and health care workers. Handicapped by inferior information, the traditional white advantages would have simply melted away; whites would have been left to their prized seniority privileges in the once large but now declining or dying "smokestack" industries. As a result, black incomes almost certainly would have made significant gains on white incomes during the decade. Even if blacks enjoyed only a 25 percent information advantage over whites, on this score alone relative economic differences between the two groups would have diminished significantly. It is difficult to imagine the prodigious gains blacks would have made if, in the decade of the 1970s, they had come to dominate the labor force in the health care and electronics industries instead of "hanging tough" in their precarious but hard-won positions in heavy manufacturing industries. Thus we see that educational advantages, job skills, and superior motivational attitudes among individuals or groups could, in theory, be almost nullified by a single countervailing advantage: the possession of superior information about economic events and trends.

The same information advantage could apply with equal force to capital formation and wealth acquisition. If, for some reason, blacks had had special knowledge of the extent to which OPEC would inflate domestic oil prices during the period 1973 to 1980, they might have invested their meager savings in the shares of domestic oil producers and, in the process, transferred many billions of dollars of wealth from whites to blacks.

Needless to say, these things do not happen in the real world. Nobody knows what is going to appear in tomorrow's or next year's *Wall Street Journal*. Yet from time to time, individuals and groups do acquire information advantages, and when they do they are almost certain to do much better than those with poor information or no information. The person who sees even dimly into the future will almost always come out on top even when other economic factors are working strongly against him. Because of our somewhat romantic beliefs in the ideology of equal opportunity, consensus opinion will always deny the existence of an information advantage, particularly if it is said to favor whites. But the fact remains that good information is often more important to economic success than traditional factors such as education, skill, hard work, self-discipline, and ambition.

Through the many generations when occupational restrictions prevented blacks from upgrading their employment opportunities, blacks had little need for serious economic information. Ideas, leads, or counsel about where and when there would be secure and profitable places to work made no difference to blacks. Because of occupational exclusions, they could do little to take advantage of good forecasts even when they had them. Today, a vast range of career opportunities is open to blacks. It has become critical for them to acquire and value good economic information. Whites, however, have always had superior access to economic information, and they have always prized this advantage. This explains in part why, for economic reasons alone, they value their often segregated clubs, school connections, business associations, and neighborhoods. Now that equal opportunity laws have created a new economic climate where information matters to blacks, they must find ways to neutralize the burden of their information handicap for the simple reason that achieving equal competence and skills will not produce racial equality unless blacks, pari passu with whites, are full participants in their access to the economic information network.

Looking at the matter in practical terms, it seems clear that whites are likely to maintain their superior access to economic information for many years to come. We have seen that it is very unlikely that equal opportunity laws, which simply require evenhanded treatment in judging qualifications, can overcome the huge advantage that whites have in being closer to the information grapevine that distributes job and career information as well as information about entrepreneurial and investment opportunities. Yet manifestly, the future of blacks will depend greatly on whether they find their way into, or avoid, certain declining or burgeoning industries and careers.

Any person who claims superior insights as to which industries will flourish or decline in the United States should be viewed with considerable suspicion. Yet, certain trends in the economic development of the United States have been repeatedly confirmed—and it is essential that blacks be aware of these developments and make plans to blunt the serious harms that technological change will almost surely impose on them.

For example, it is almost certain that over the next generation automation, robots, and microprocessor technology will greatly reduce the demand for unskilled and semiskilled labor. As machinery and robots are increasingly substituted for human labor, massive unemployment is likely to be a worldwide phenomenon. As in the past, the burden of this unemployment will fall first on blacks and other low-skilled groups whose jobs are easier to automate. The traditional 2-to-1 black-white unemployment ratio may well increase to 3 or 4 to 1. Black politicians in the early 1980s fretted publicly about the racial insensitivity of President Reagan and a veiled brand of neoracism that appeared in some debates in Congress, but few had identified the most formidable enemy of black people: *the imminent arrival of the steamroller of automated production*. The likelihood that a huge technologically illiterate black underclass was building in America was just as great a threat to the economic aspirations of Negro people as the catastrophic increase in the number of black female-headed families.

The danger signals of technological obsolescence are clear for everyone to see. Consider once again a few of the job categories in which blacks are heavily employed and which are likely to be whipsawed by the forces of automation. The coded stripes on packaged merchandise will almost certainly eliminate the jobs of 100,000 or more black checkout counter clerks in supermarkets and retail stores. New telecommunications equipment will end many tens of thousands of black jobs as telephone operators just as new word processor technology will greatly reduce demand for ordinary typists. Electronically controlled inventories will close down the jobs of tens of thousands of black stockroom workers while electronic mail and telecommunications should largely eliminate the need for messengers and reduce employment for huge numbers of black postal workers. The agricultural—and heavily black and Hispanic—labor force will drastically shrink as harvesting and planting technology become increasingly sophisticated. The expected reindustrialization of America may put some Americans back to work, but most of them will be in new technology-based industries requiring highly skilled workers rather than in heavy industry where black employment is relatively high and the threat of assembly-line robots most real. The most important point of all is that robots will have replaced huge numbers of black factory hands by 1990.

Over many years, blacks have tended to lose sight of economic trends and opportunities by listening to what whites have said, instead of watching what they were doing. In this tradition, blacks, today, who continue to prepare themselves for jobs in smokestack industries on assurances from the President that successful reindustrialization of the nation will provide plenty of work for all are likely to be greatly disappointed. As special, though not deliberate, targets of automated manufacturing, blacks will probably find themselves holding a large percentage of the most insecure jobs in the nation. Following historical precedent, whites, in turn, are more likely to use their front-runner advantages to move into more profitable and stable employment in new technology, leaving much of the unwanted and insecure work in post-industrial America to blacks and other less economically sophisticated groups.

The two-page chart lists the industries, job positions, and career activities where opportunities for blacks appear to be most promising. Also shown are a number of other industries and job positions where technology will almost certainly decimate the ranks of black workers.

Eighty years ago more than a third of all American workers were farmers. Today the figure is around 3 percent. After the turn of the century, America slowly became an industrial or manufacturing society. By 1950, half of the nation's work force were employed in industrial occupations. Thirty-four percent of all workers held manufacturing jobs alone. Thirty years later, jobs in the manufacturing industry accounted for only 22 percent of the country's total employment. In recent years, startling changes have occurred.[7] Half of all American workers are now involved in the *information industry*: the generation, processing, or distribution of information.[8] This means, almost certainly, that workers who are somehow involved with data processing, recordkeeping, market research, business and professional publishing, and communications should enjoy a continuing advantage in the future.

Predicting economic revolutions or change is a high-risk business. The importance of the printing press or the steam engine was not perceived until many generations after the invention. Yet it is almost certain that we are involved in a massive technological revolution today. Just as human labor was bypassed by tools and later by factory machines, it is likely now that

POINT ONE: BLACKS MUST GET OUT OF THE WAY OF ROBOTS

In the coming decade very large numbers of jobs now disproportionately held by blacks in these occupations will almost certainly disappear as a result of the substitution of machines for human labor.

Jobs Vulnerable to Robots

- Farm Laborers
- Mail Carriers
- Messengers
- Stock Clerks
- Food Counter Workers
- Steel Workers
- Dishwashers
- Key Punch Operators
- Bank Tellers
- Checkout Clerks
- Telephone Operators
- Assembly Line Workers
- Parking Lot Attendants
- Garbage Collectors
- Automobile Workers
- Welders
- Gardeners

- Meat Cutters
- Gas Station Attendants
- Railroad Workers
- Ticket Collectors
- Mass Transit Workers
- Utility Meter Readers
- Bottlers and Canners
- Fork Lift Operators
- Payroll Clerks
- File Clerks
- Textile Workers
- Shipping Clerks
- Elevator Operators
- Freight Handlers
- Clothing Ironers
- Stenographers

Source of projected employment growth: U.S. Bureau of Labor Statistics, Occupational Outlook Handbook, 1980.

POINT TWO: BLACKS MUST EQUIP THEMSELVES TO MOVE INTO THE JOBS THAT ROBOTS CREATE OR LEAVE UNMOLESTED

As professional jobs replace factory positions blacks will continue to drop behind whites unless they acquire the technical skills demanded by the automated society.

Employment Created by Robots

Occupation	Projected Employment Growth 1978-1990	Occupation	Projected Employment Growth 1978-1990
• Computer Programmers	73.6%	• Travel Agents	55.6%
• Systems Analysts	107.8%	• Paralegals	132.4%
• Electronic Technicians	45.4%	• Plumbers	20.0%
• Vocational Trainers	26.5%	• Nurses	50.3%
• Laboratory Technicians	43.9%	• Accountants	32.7%
• Crane Operators	40.4%	• Law Clerks	44.0%
• Appliance Repairers	24.1%	• Firemen	22.7%
• Health Care Technicians	45.0%	• Lithographers	45.8%
• Auto Body Repairers	27.0%	• Electricians	24.6%
• Physical Therapists	57.5%	• Tax Preparers	64.5%
• X-Ray Technicians	47.4%	• Mechanics	29.7%
• Bulldozer Operators	57.0%	• Policemen	23.2%

communications technology will bypass much of the human labor that is so important to economic well-being in traditional smokestack America. *This means that access to and control over knowledge and information may well replace ownership of industrial capital as the important source of economic power.* It is very difficult to overstate the importance of this trend to blacks. All of their political and economic strategies must take account of this remarkable development.

As economic power and wealth move away from traditional manufacturing activities, and as the value of traditional industrial capital shrinks in importance, vast stores of new wealth will be discovered in the information society of the future. Blacks must seize this opportunity to develop new entrepreneurial wealth by concentrating their training and entrepreneurial efforts in every aspect of data processing and telecommunications.

At the present time, the huge wealth advantage of whites is due, in large part, to their monopoly position in the ownership and control of traditional manufacturing capital. But, a striking opportunity may be presented where outside economic forces could largely neutralize the white wealth advantage. If, in fact, the capital of the future lies in the information society of computers and telecommunications, a truly fabulous opportunity window is presented to blacks to catch up with whites. If educational advantages can be held equal, the forces of deindustrialization—and the eventual end of the era of economic dominance by manufacturing capital—may deny whites their present almost insuperable advantage. The new technology emerging may permit each new generation of blacks to begin life much closer to the starting line that has always favored whites.

Organize Selective Boycotts Against Major Institutions That Persist in Employment and Credit Discrimination

"Through speech, assembly, and petition—rather than through riot or revolution, the protesters sought to change a social order that had consistently treated them as second-class citizens. Unless there is proof that they acted violently, the political boycott enjoys the full protections of the Constitution."

—Justice John Paul Stevens,
NAACP v. Claiborne Hardware Company,
458 U.S. 886 (1982)

THE POLITICALLY MOTIVATED BOYCOTT of goods and services is firmly embedded in the American tradition of political protest. Prior to the Civil War, abolitionists moved to end slavery by boycotting slave-made goods. During the Colonial period, boycotts were used to force repeal of the Stamp Act. The antisegregation movement of the 1960s was essentially launched through the Montgomery, Alabama bus boycotts organized by Dr. Martin Luther King, Jr. Credit is due to the economic pressure activities of the National Sharecroppers Fund rather than to the Mississippi state legislature for the fact that black women in Mississippi are currently earning the minimum wage for hoeing cotton instead of the $3 a day they were earning only a short time ago.

It has been many years since blacks in the United States have mounted a broad-based economic boycott in protest against whites-first hiring practices and other forms of economic injustice. Now euphemistically referred to as "selective purchasing campaigns," the boycott has fallen into disuse as a strategy for breaking down race discrimination and for increasing black participation in the American economy. Among possibly a majority of blacks, there exists a decided abhorrence of the boycott as a political strategy just as there is widespread opposition to nonviolent mass protest.

A decade or more ago, it was common to see placards reading, "Don't bank where you can't borrow," and "Don't purchase where you can't work." Not only have the signs and picket lines disappeared, but it is commonplace today for prominent blacks to lend their names and faces to support corporate tokenism used to delay the economic progress of black people. Large banks with truly miserable records of lending money to Negroes find no shortage of blacks willing to pose for advertisements touting paper commitments to equal opportunity.

Despite corporate publicity to the effect that "he hasn't laid a glove on us," Jesse Jackson's PUSH organization has used the boycott strategy with great success. In a little-publicized effort organized in 1981, Coca-Cola came off the shelves of 100 Chicago stores; the product was removed from vending machines in 194 city halls under black control. The result of the boycott was the signing of a landmark agreement by the Coca-Cola Company to advance blacks to holdings of 12.5 percent of management positions; to increase the number of black-owned Coke distributors from two to thirty-two; to deposit company funds in black banks; and to establish a venture capital fund for black entrepreneurs. PUSH has also signed similar agreements with Seven-Up, Kentucky Fried Chicken, Burger King, and Southland Corp.

Referring to the Coca-Cola agreement, Jesse Jackson stated, "We have concluded that we have become our own Equal Employment Opportunity

Commission," [9] a high-handed announcement, yet warranted to some extent by the Reagan Administration's efforts to wind down government enforcement of equal opportunity laws.

Daring, imaginative, highly targeted and well-planned boycotts have worked in the past. There is no reason to believe they will not work well in the future. There is no need to window dress these efforts with doubletalk about good-faith goals. The purpose of the boycott is explicit: to impose fixed ethnic employment, credit, contracting, and purchasing obligations on the remaining group of major corporations where opportunities for black employment or advancement have been limited or closed.

Standing behind the boycott strategy is black purchasing power of colossal proportions, which, in fact, currently ranks with that of whites living in most countries of the Western world. A nationwide mobilization of this $150 billion annual spending could usher in a new world of black opportunities for employment, entrepreneurship, and capital formation. In every major urban center, the economic power of blacks today far exceeds their strength of a quarter of a century ago when a small band of impoverished Negroes in Montgomery, Alabama organized a highly successful major boycott against a local bus company.

The major obstacle to successful application of boycott sanctions is quite simply the absence of a collective will among blacks to use those sanctions. The potential of the boycott strategy suffers from the fact that very large numbers of blacks and whites write it off as a deviant political effort conducted by an irresponsible minority fringe. Many black Americans today—particularly those who recently have moved into better jobs—are unwilling to risk tactics which they see as imperiling the individual gains already made. Understandably, too, the newly arrived middle-class black person, who at one time might have been counted upon for protest support, now has a much keener interest in moving up the economic ladder and in being "a go-along-no-troublemaking" member of the Rotary Club. Also, the black flirtation in the early 1980s with laissez-faire economic strategies has both obscured and denigrated the boycott as a valuable resource in the all-too-meager armory of black political weapons. Traditional economic interests have convinced large numbers of blacks that ethnic quotas—and protest activities used to win them—are harmful and subversive. Boycott proposals are more often crushed by clucks of disapproval in the black community than by opposition or retaliation by whites. The resulting neglect of the boycott strategy is particularly debilitating in conservative times, when the government's equal employment opportunity enforcement agencies are merely feigning opposition to the flagging minority employment and affirmative-action efforts of many large employers.

Should blacks decide to take a more active view of the potential of their economic power, the major boycott targets are both well-known and vulnerable. Most employers whom civil rights groups have challenged on grounds of lagging minority employment practices have a moss-backed management style that is ill-equipped to stave off a well-executed buyer's boycott. The most determined corporate defenders of jobs for whites first and of the traditional corporate right to choose when and where black people will be admitted to employment are usually counted among the ineptly navigated slow boats that have contributed to the recent decline in American capitalism. It would not be difficult to construct a successful boycott strategy against a number of these institutions which derive a very large percentage of their revenues from black consumers.

A few of the most notable and vulnerable offenders include Coors Breweries, Inc., Winn-Dixie Stores, American Home Products, Inc., Mobil Corp., Richardson-Vicks Inc., Nabisco Brands, Inc., Uniroyal, Inc., and Blue Bell, Inc. All sellers of branded consumer products, these corporations have been major race-relations laggards. Because of the consumer nature of their businesses, they are uniquely vulnerable to boycott sanctions. Banking and financial institutions that have displayed particularly objectionable practices and policies concerning blacks are led by Citicorp, Bank of America Corp., and a number of banks in southern cities. As retail institutions catering to individual customers, most banks are particularly exposed to depositor boycott strategies. In considering a renewed boycott strategy, blacks have a unique economic advantage. Black people as consumers tend to be far more loyal than whites to branded products. Products such as Listerine, Tide, Clorox, Minute Maid, Gold Medal, Campbell, and Maxwell House have huge black followings. Black purchases of these brands far exceed, on a relative basis, the economic loyalties of whites to these and other brands.[10]

One by one, the large corporations that are still reluctant to hire and promote blacks should be pressed, through nonviolent use of withheld economic purchase power, to meet reasonable standards for providing minority opportunities. The Supreme Court's 1982 opinion in *NAACP v. Claiborne Hardware*[11] publishes a clear rule that political protest taking the form of an economic boycott directed at racially motivated selection practices in American institutions will receive the full protection of the Constitution.

Use the Financial Power of Pension Funds to Blacklist Corporations That Persist in Denying Opportunities to Blacks

"Modern history will furnish innumerable examples of how the man succeeded best who knew best how to play the fox."

—Niccolo Machiavelli (1513)

A BURNING ECONOMIC ISSUE of the next decade will be the struggle for control of the huge fund of capital represented by the nation's pension fund investments. In the past, company management has enjoyed almost unilateral control over the investment of pension fund assets. But labor unions and other employees' associations have increasingly come to regard their pension funds as deferred wages; labor groups are demanding a voice in how these assets are to be invested.

The pension fund control issue is of major economic importance because of the magnitude of the sums involved. The nation's private employee benefit system, which in 1983 stood at about $1 trillion, is expected by the Department of Labor to reach $3 trillion by 1995. Obviously, whoever controls the deployment of these vast resources will also be a major influence on corporate employment, contracting, and investment practices.

Labor's challenge to management's right to control pension fund investments was triggered in part by the fact that in recent years a large part of institutional funds has been invested in nonunionized industry in the Sun Belt states. Insofar as those investments are viewed as undercutting the economies of the North (where union labor remains strong and where most pension money is generated), workers complain, with some justice, that they are, in effect, being forced to subsidize the loss of their own jobs. As a result, many labor officials are now bringing up the pension investment control question in collective bargaining negotiations. Lane Kirkland, president of the AFL-CIO, sounded the challenge in labor's fight for a role in pension investment planning when he declared in 1979, "We shall be pursuing every available means to ensure that pension money is invested creatively and constructively, to the benefit of workers and fair employers." [12]

In the struggle to win influence over pension fund investment decisions, blacks and Big Labor have similar objectives. Both have parallel interests in steering capital away from investment in the shares of corporations that violate federal health and safety rules. Both are keenly interested in withdrawing investment funds from nonunionized industry in the South, where underpaid and often predominantly black labor stands to gain most from greater unionization. But black labor has a special agenda that sometimes runs contrary to the policies of labor generally. For example, labor in gen-

BLACK PENSION POWER

Thirty large pension funds where blacks may be in a political position to withdraw investment capital from companies with consistently poor fair employment practices

Name of Pension Fund	Size of Fund—1980 (Assets in Millions)
California Public Employees	$17,958
Teachers Annuity and Insurance Association/ College Retirement Equities Fund	14,366
General Motors Corporation	12,973
New York State Employees	11,682
New York City Employees/Teachers	10,461
New York State Teachers	6,463
New Jersey Division of Investment	5,171
Ford Motor Company	4,900
United States Steel & Carnegie	4,700
Pennsylvania School Employees	4,393
Michigan State Employees	4,146
Los Angeles County Employees	2,539
Pennsylvania State Employees	2,340
Maryland Public Employees	2,100
New York City Teachers Annuity	1,438
Detroit Retirement System	1,336
Ohio School Employees	994
Los Angeles Fire & Police	705
Los Angeles City Employees	702
Chicago Teachers	600
Los Angeles Water & Power	557
Philadelphia Municipal Fund	550
Chicago Employees	521
Baltimore Employees	504
United Presbyterian Fund	472
Episcopal Church	400
Michigan Municipal Employees	312
United Church of Christ	263
Chicago Transit	250
Delaware Employees	207

Source of information on size of funds from: Pensions & Investments, January 21, 1980, pp. 1 & 13.

eral does not have a strong commitment to black objectives such as moving pension capital away from equal employment opportunity violators and denying capital to companies that ignore federal affirmative-action rules.

Big Labor has little interest in channeling pension money investments toward inner-city hospitals, black business, and job development in the cities; nor does American labor generally care much about withholding investment capital from U.S. companies that support South African apartheid.

At present, it appears that blacks in the United States are the beneficial owners of upwards of $60 billion of private pension assets. But blacks have no say whatsoever as to how these funds are invested. Blacks working in investment banking and securities investment counseling firms have almost no representation in high executive ranks, where most pension investment decisions are now made. Blacks lack a strong voice in any of the major labor unions that might influence the investment policies of pension funds. What can blacks do to change this?

Before they can slay pension fund dragons, blacks must exert much more influence in labor unions generally. Although blacks make up about 15 percent of all organized workers, they have very little representation in top labor union posts. Only if blacks successfully move into upper-rank labor union positions will they get the issues most vitally important to them placed on the bargaining table. Opportunities for winning greater bargaining leverage for blacks are particularly strong in the management ranks of large unions with major black membership, such as the United Auto Workers, the United Steelworkers, and the American Federation of State, County and Municipal Employees (AFSCME).

Where company, or bank-controlled, pension funds persist in investing pension monies in equal opportunity violators and in companies with strong links to South Africa, blacks should consider organizing work stoppages, consumer boycotts, and other standard direct-action techniques against the institutions that control the investment of these funds. There are strong equitable arguments in support of measures taken to prevent black-owned capital from being used to support institutions that block the economic or social advancement of blacks here or in other parts of the world. Nonviolent pressures to prevent black money from being used against blacks can scarcely be viewed as radical or excessive.

Unquestionably, the best opportunity for blacks to influence institutional investment power is through state retirement pension systems. It is here that one finds the largest concentrations of black workers. The forty largest state and local government pension plans in the United States had assets of about $130 billion in 1979. Blacks make up a significant percentage of the beneficiaries of many of these funds. For instance, the pension plan for New York State employees—16 percent of whom are black—had assets of about $17 billion in 1982 and ranked as the largest public fund in the country. In

California, where blacks make up approximately 9 percent of the state's payroll, blacks and Spanish-speaking Americans should be able to win considerable influence over the investment policies of the California Public Employees pension fund. The California fund is the third largest in the United States, with assets totaling nearly $14 billion in 1982. According to a 1979 Corporate Data Exchange study, these two funds (New York and California) alone had over $1 billion invested in companies that showed up as violators of EEO employment guidelines or provided economic comfort to South African apartheid.[13]

In 1983, two states—Massachusetts and Connecticut—had enacted laws calling for divestment of South African-related investments by public employee benefit funds. In addition, several cities had approved ordinances requiring divestment, including: Philadelphia, New York, Hartford, Grand Rapids, East Lansing, Berkeley, Gary, and Cambridge. Black political power is almost sovereign in many large cities. This gives black voters the almost certain ability to prevent public funds in these cities from being used to support enterprises that downgrade or exclude black people.

If blacks are successful in moving up to influential positions as directors and senior executives in large corporations and banks, then corporate pension funds are likely to begin to withdraw investments from corporations with backward racial policies. The giant private funds include General Motors, $16 billion; General Electric, $9 billion; IBM, $7 billion; Ford Motor Company, $6.6 billion; duPont, $6.1 billion; and U.S. Steel, $5.6 billion. A superficial glance at the stock portfolios of these pension funds shows major holdings in companies with employment policies and international activities repugnant to most blacks. Very large public pension fund investments in companies with poor ratings on minorities issues include familiar equal opportunity laggards: Mobil; Sears; Bank of America; Fluor; Phillips Petroleum; Texaco; Goodyear; and Standard Oil of California.

In the view of many people, and certainly in the perception of the banking community, the introduction of social criteria into pension fund investing is considered either outrageously irrelevant or wholly inimical to free-market principles. These views necessarily exclude racial justice as a proper investment consideration, just as they reject consideration of other public issues such as pollution and product safety. The free-enterprise system, it is said, recognizes no politics—only the bottom line of profit and loss. But this misstates the nature of our economy. The free-enterprise system in the United States has always responded to the collective power of race discrimination and, on this account, has excluded blacks from a wide range of economic, educational, and professional activities. American free enterprise has ignored open-market considerations in that—for a century or more and in many cases to this day—it has exhausted all white offerings of labor, goods, and entrepreneurship before it has turned to the offerings of blacks. Moreover, the marketplace—and investment decisions pursuant to its mandates—continues to recognize, and be influenced by, positions of unequal economic power that race discrimination has produced and kept in place. Moreover, the economic selection system continues to respond to the coercive power of other political and special-interest groups (farmers, environmentalists, and anti-nuclear power activists) whose objectives are political as well as economic. In investment decisions, as in other economic exchanges, the "bottom line" has always been defined not only by merit and profit, but also by political and kinship influence and other power arrangements in which black people never participated.

Uniquely, pension funds in the United States offer major economic and political leverage to blacks. And blacks, like other groups before them, must fight on grounds where they have strength. Pension monies that are beneficially owned by black people should not provide capital to organizations that either honor Jim Crow here or abroad or pay lip service only to the equal opportunity laws of the country.

Mount a National Campaign to Repudiate All Forms of Institutional Tokenism

"The rights and interest of the laboring man will be protected and cared for, not by the labor agitators, but by the Christian men to whom God in his infinite wisdom has given control of the property interests of the country."

—George F. Baer, spokesman for the mine owners during the 1902 Pennsylvania coal strike

TOKEN APPEARANCES, symbolic appointments, and nominal money allocations characterize the first stage of integrating any activity or society that has been closed to participation by an outcast or stigmatized group. Once the society has successfully passed through the stage of tokenism, it begins to assign roles, positions, and goods without regard to race or status. A society inclined toward change proceeds finally to a fully integrated state where there is full power-sharing with members of the formerly outcast group. The racial integration of the economy and of the political and education system may then be viewed as complete. In an event familiar to all,

Satchel Paige, a black man and possibly the greatest baseball pitcher of all time, made a token appearance in the 1948 World Series, pitching two-thirds of an inning. This appearance by Paige was a classic example of the role of tokenism in a society that was in the process of changing its rules of racial etiquette and its codes of ethnic participation in sports.

While tokenism is in itself a signal of racial progress, the practice also serves, ironically, as a serious form of racial constraint. When a society engages in tokenism, it is feeling its way toward change and is often pretending to be more integrated than it really is. At the same time, tokenism permits the society to delay integration and to bolster the status quo by assuring traditionalists that appearances by former outcasts in new positions should be treated as only "token" and that these appointments are being encouraged simply to appease various pressure groups. In applying superficial or band-aid solutions to fundamental racial problems, tokenism frustrates the grievance process and delays racial integration and participation. It co-opts the black agenda by appearing to endorse its goals. It provides effective cover for government programs aimed at making the corporate decision to employ minorities a voluntary matter. Successful integration does not occur until society's controlling groups no longer use token appearances by minorities, or other sops, either to delay racial integration or to pretend that society's institutions are fully integrated when this is not the case. Few people realize the extent to which tokenism is truly a powerful and ubiquitous opponent of the aspirations of black people.

Despite significant progress in recent years, institutions in the United States still observe many of the traditional ethnic codes of etiquette that assign Negroes to slots determined by race. While this is so, the practice of racial tokenism will continue to be a standard method of racial manipulation and control. Since the urban riots of the mid-to-late-1960s, many business and philanthropic bodies have become past masters at tossing odd scraps to black people—a job, a loan, a grant—and, in the process, whites (often in league with blacks) have successfully maintained public beliefs in the propriety of a social order, that, for the past decade, finds black incomes at a figure less than 60 percent of whites'. Despite these extreme and unwarranted economic differences, political pressures for a new deal for blacks are consistently defused by the iron law of power that you can't argue with Santa Claus.

At a time when the big stick of a strong central government has been rejected as a suitable policeman of equal opportunity laws, the co-opting power of tokenism has been discovered as a valuable instrument for protecting institutional liberty to pursue business as usual in race relations. Tokenism is particularly appealing to corporate managements because effectively publicized token appointments permit organizations to self-monitor their equal opportunity programs rather than submit their practices to outside judgments and oversight. In public affairs, tokenism is an effective means of avoiding power-sharing with black people because it permits governments and institutions to name token minority personnel to government posts and thereby convince the world that these institutions have a broad demographic base and represent the wishes and views of all groups within a particular society. Thus, often as a result of effective tokenism strategies, the great majority of blacks continue to entrust their economic and political destiny to the goodwill of people who, in fact, have little interest in racial progress. Blacks, in turn, fail to take useful measures to help themselves.

Looking over the corporate, foundation, educational, and political scene, we must conclude that racial tokenism is by no means a universal practice, but it is a common means of slowing up the entry of unwanted groups. Tokenism is universally harmful when it persists and prevents institutions from moving on to the final stage of full racial integration, which necessarily includes unrestricted participation by outcast groups in controlling the means of production and distribution.

The simple fact is that whites continue to practice tokenism for the reason that blacks continue to allow them to do so. Charles de Gaulle once said that in his relations with the United States, "saying no" was France's first step toward regaining respect. In the United States, blacks almost never say "no" to whites. They almost never say "no" when tokenism strategies invite them to join the black advisory councils of the many insurance companies that consistently refuse to write performance bonds for black contractors. Blacks rarely refuse invitations to become directors of the major metropolitan banks that consistently practice blatant credit redlining. Blacks all too readily accept the honor of acting as highly visible ballot counters at political conventions where Negroes as a whole are not effectively represented on the convention floor. There are no published reports of blacks refusing honorary degrees tendered by many of the state university systems in the South, where twenty-five years after the outlawing of segregated public education, separate campuses for the two races are still maintained. Even black advocates of strong enforcement measures in minority employment rarely decline awards of token and honorary status when large corporations identify them as "experts" and blunt pressures for racial reform by employing them as corporation consultants or advisers.

Empowerment and full participation require a widely adopted campaign to neutralize the economic and political force of tokenism. Black political and economic influence will not develop until blacks as a group decide to

BLACK POWER PREEMPTED: ENTICING BENEFITS ARE SOMETIMES OFFERED TO GIFTED PEOPLE WHO ARE PREPARED TO ACCEPT VISIBLE BUT LESS THAN INFLUENTIAL POSITIONS

Collective efforts to place more Negro people in important posts in government are frequently undercut by the ready willingness of many of the most accomplished black citizens to accept prestigious but powerless positions, where official authority is limited to acting as ambassadors to other black people.

Blacks Appointed as Ambassadors to Black Nations Abroad

AMBASSADOR	FOREIGN NATION	YEAR APPOINTED
Hon. Edward R. Dudley	Liberia	1949
Hon. Richard L. Jones	Liberia	1955
Hon. John H. Morrow	Guinea	1959
Hon. Mercer Cook	Niger	1961
Hon. Franklin Williams	Ghana	1965
Hon. Elliot Skinner	Upper Volta	1966
Hon. Samuel C. Adams	Niger	1968
Hon. Clinton E. Knox	Haiti	1969
Hon. Terrence A. Todman	Chad	1969
Hon. Clarence Ferguson	Uganda	1970
Hon. Charles J. Nelson	Botswana	1971
Hon. John E. Reinhardt	Nigeria	1971
Hon. O. Rudolph Aggrey	Senegal	1973
Hon. David B. Bolen	Botswana	1974
Hon. Theodore Britten	Barbados	1974
Hon. Ronald D. Palmer	Togo	1976
Hon. Charles A. Jones	Niger	1976
Hon. Wilbert LeMelle	Kenya	1977
Hon. Mabel M. Smythe	Cameroon	1977
Hon. Richard K. Fox	Trinidad and Tobago	1977
Hon. William B. Jones	Haiti	1977
Hon. Horace G. Dawson	Botswana	1979
Hon. Ann F. Holloway	Mali	1979
Hon. Walter C. Carrington	Senegal	1980
Hon. John A. Burroughs	Malawi	1981
Hon. Melvin Evans	Trinidad and Tobago	1981
Hon. Howard K. Walker	Togo	1982

treat the token gift as they would a case of the measles. Thus, when a metropolitan bank approaches black leaders in a particular community with a proposal to set up a small pool of funds to grant loans to minority businessmen, peer pressure should be brought to persuade all would-be takers in the black community to say, "Thank you very much, but we prefer instead that you publicize the names of your black loan officers with authority to lend over $100,000." Black leaders, whose sponsorship and praise are so eagerly sought by major corporations, may greatly benefit the vast majority of other blacks by refusing to act as industry's ambassadors to the ghetto, where their usual assignment is to convince other blacks that standard band-aid programs represent a serious commitment to economic change. A strong case can be made that blacks serve neither themselves nor other blacks by accepting decorative titles such as vice-chairman of national political committees of either the Democratic or Republican parties. In order to come to power, blacks as a group must decide to refuse all the token grants, prizes, and appointments that whites still use to regulate the progress of blacks and to maintain an economic order where Negro people hold an insignificant share of the power that goes with property, politics, and the control of capital.

Tokenism imperceptibly blends into the coercive process that we call "co-option." Here the power of another person is disarmed and turned against him. In the case of blacks in the United States and elsewhere, this happens when blacks are successfully convinced that they hold or share power when such is not the case. Charitable activities operating under such names as urban coalitions, national alliances of businessmen, associations to assist Negro dropouts, councils for business counseling, and institutes for intensive entrepreneurial training tend to have co-option effects and should be viewed with suspicion. These organizations are neither partially nor fully autonomous and, in many cases, tend to hold blacks back by demeaning the importance of black economic powers and by channeling black people into economic activities that experienced whites have long since abandoned. In contrast, there are genuinely black-controlled self-help organizations such as the Voter Education Project, the Southern Poverty Law Center, Opportunities Industrialization Centers, and the several dozen community development corporations in black communities. These latter projects are organized by blacks, controlled by blacks, and tend to help blacks gain economic and political strength rather than co-opt or repress blacks by rewarding those among them who discourage Negro efforts to become more influential in American society.

It is a sad fact that the fundamental decency of one man helping another without expecting a benefit in return has largely disappeared in the race relations industry of the modern liberal state. As a result, a very large number of acts of institutional charity, including "big-brother programs," inner-city pep rallies, Rosa Parks community service awards, black testimonials, and fund raisers, tend to be propaganda activities which, in one way or another, continue to appease blacks and to limit the use of political pressures by them. But this corruption of the milk of human kindness must not obscure for blacks the complex psychological processes by which strong people—often unwittingly—keep weak people at bay through gifts of food baskets, prizes, and offerings of nominal appointments.

In the course of the modern black freedom movement, Negroes have consistently defeated efforts to control them by collectively saying "no." During the heroic civil rights era of the late 1950s, they overcame the controls of racial separation by collectively defying mobs organized to keep them in segregated universities, restaurants, buses, and parks. They expunged the whites-only voting codes by collectively resisting the threats of southern sheriffs to punish them if they entered voting registrars' offices. At times, Negroes used collective acts of nonviolent civil disobedience as a potent means of subverting and repealing the strict economic rules by which whites kept certain types of industrial jobs to themselves. Today, whites no longer fear blacks who have liberty, but they do continue to fear blacks with power. And one of the most effective instruments that strong institutions have devised to regulate and repress black power is the stratagem of tokenism. If blacks decide to take up a much wider range of influential positions in the greater society, they must collectively refuse—and persuade their peers and associates to refuse—all the badges of tokenism that are proffered to them every day, and which none among them would truthfully mistake for genuine acts of power-sharing. By these means, they will begin to deal as negotiating equals with people in higher places who still are congenitally unable to share power but who are past masters at pretending to do so.

Create Disproportionate Gains for Black Labor by Unionizing the South

"The South is just waiting to be organized."

—Samuel Gompers (1898)

NEARLY 50 PERCENT OF ALL BLACKS and 47 percent of all black civilian laborers still live in the South. Blacks also represent a disproportionately large part of the southern labor force of major corporations. For example, at least 25 percent of the employees of the giant J.P. Stevens textile company are black. In fact, many other large plants in the South, particularly in the Carolinas, are manned predominantly by blacks. This means that as long

as job discrimination laws and affirmative-action requirements are enforced, the introduction of almost any new economic or political force that
has the effect of increasing southern wages generally will automatically
increase the wages of huge numbers of southern working blacks.[14]

The migration of jobs in recent years from the unionized North to the
nonunionized South makes it doubly important for blacks to get behind Big

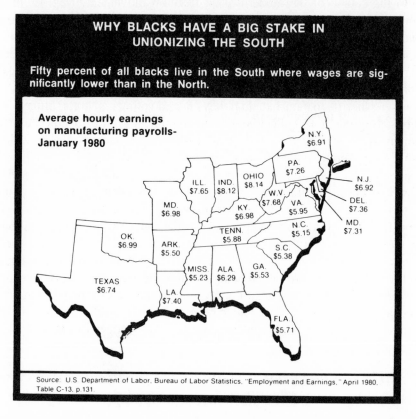

**WHY BLACKS HAVE A BIG STAKE IN
UNIONIZING THE SOUTH**

Fifty percent of all blacks live in the South where wages are significantly lower than in the North.

Average hourly earnings
on manufacturing payrolls-
January 1980

N.Y. $6.91
PA. $7.26
ILL. $7.65
IND. $8.12
OHIO $8.14
N.J. $6.92
MD. $6.98
W.V. $7.68
KY. $6.98
VA. $5.95
DEL. $7.36
MD. $7.31
OK. $6.99
ARK. $5.50
TENN. $5.88
N.C. $5.15
S.C. $5.38
TEXAS $6.74
MISS. $5.23
ALA. $6.29
GA. $5.53
LA. $7.40
FLA $5.71

Source: U.S. Department of Labor, Bureau of Labor Statistics, "Employment and Earnings," April 1980.
Table C-13, p.131.

Labor's efforts to organize the southern part of the country, where half of
all blacks live. Traditionally, wages in the South run $1 to $1.50 an hour
below the national average, in many cases as much as $2 to $3 an hour
below the well-paying, and often unionized, jobs in states north of the Ohio
River. It is the combination of circumstances, the very large regional difference in unionization, combined with the heavy concentration of blacks in
the South—the least organized and fastest-growing part of the nation's
economy—that yields the potential for large black gains if only wages in the
South generally can be improved.

For southern blacks, the potential income gains at stake in developing a southern strategy are huge. A major boost in the incomes of working blacks in the South would significantly reduce the *national* income gap between blacks and whites inasmuch as such a large percentage of the black population would be affected. If, as experienced elsewhere in the country, unionization of labor in the South added an annual increment of 20 percent to southern wages, the aggregate income of southern black workers would be increased by nearly $10 billion per year.[15] Black incomes nationwide would leap almost 7 percent.

It is clear, then, that blacks stand to make important gains by lending political and economic support to Big Labor's long-range target of organizing workers in the South. Blacks and Big Labor will not stand alone in this effort. It is likely that many midwestern and northern congressmen would support these efforts because it is the most heavily unionized states in the North that have lost the greatest numbers of jobs to the nonunionized South. The southern wage advantage continues to threaten the economies of the industrialized northern states; this gives most northern Democrats a vested interest in advancing organized labor's efforts to organize the South. In this way, the southern states would be forced to compete on an equal footing without the advantage of a cheap, nonunionized labor force.

Black support of organized labor's efforts to strengthen its position in the South may take any of the following forms:

- Black voter pressure to repeal the southern states' "right-to-work" laws that presently inhibit the organization of southern workers.

- Black lobbying and pressure for federal labor law reform, which would make it difficult for southern employers to unreasonably delay votes on union representation.

- Black consumer boycotts of companies that still hold to the traditional southern antiunion loyalty pledge.

- Black economic pressures on northern and southern banks, insurance companies, and pension funds that currently invest in and give financial support to southern manufacturing corporations that are staunch enemies of trade unions.

Many blacks have expressed skepticism as to whether unionization significantly raises black wages. Certainly, the unfavorable experience of blacks in some craft unions gives a measure of credibility to this argument. But indisputably, blacks still do much better when they are unionized than when they are not, both in absolute terms and relative to whites. In 1975, black hourly wages were 9 percent less than white wages within unions but 15 percent less than white wages outside unions. Also, while there are disputes about the effects of unionization on productivity and incentives, all economists agree that unionized workers have consistently kept pace with inflation more effectively than have nonunionized workers.[16]

An important side effect of the unionization of the South would be greater black influence within the AFL-CIO, in which blacks are still an uninfluential minority. The addition of large numbers of black voting members would tend to cause the AFL-CIO to take stronger political positions in support of black economic and political objectives.

As a strategy for increasing the economic bargaining power of black people in the country, the program to unionize the South has important psychological and political advantages. Unlike affirmative-action initiatives, special allocations to blacks of government-controlled resources, and other racially based pressures for improving the status of blacks, the strategy of unionizing the South will not be perceived by whites as an unfair handout to one ethnic group. Unionization of the South would, in fact, produce disproportionate gains for blacks, yet these advances would not be perceived nationwide as being a black program or as coming at the expense of whites.

Add Several Billion Dollars to Black Incomes by Unionizing Household Workers

"Among the people who have come forward to help the Vietnamese 'boat people' is Diane von Furstenberg. The designer has been making inquiries about how to go about hiring two refugees—preferably both of them women— for domestic work in her New York apartment. . . .'One can't help feeling for those people. If there's anything I possibly can do, and be helpful to me at the same time, I certainly will.' "

—*The New York Times* (1978)

AMERICANS CARE A GREAT DEAL about their homes and their children, but they pay very low wages to the people who look after them. In 1978, the median family income of domestic employees was $5,800, a figure well below the then established poverty level of $6,600.[17] Almost without exception, domestic employees work without benefit of sick pay, holidays, vacation, pension, or any form of job security.

Whatever one's views of the harms caused by strong unions, one cannot accuse them of neglecting to advance the wages of the unionized people in the United States who clean and scrub. Hotel maids in New York City, all unionized, earned $5.82 an hour plus liberal vacation and retirement allowances. In comparison, checking with agencies for domestic workers in New York City, one finds that the average hourly wage of nonunionized domestic workers in 1979 was around $3.75.

According to official government figures, in the early 1980s there were 345,000 black domestic workers in the United States, 33 percent of the total household domestic work force. Because so many domestic workers are paid cash in "off-the-record income," it is likely that government figures greatly underestimate the actual number of household workers. Probably, there are 50,000 or more black domestic workers in Chicago alone.[18]

Fear of government penalties for income tax evasion, suspicion about labor organizers, and frequent job changes have all combined to discourage grassroots organization of domestic workers. Yet, the potential gains to be made by unionization are staggering. If merely the black domestic workers who are known to the government were able to organize and secure the same pay scale as hotel maids, black income nationwide would be increased by $1.4 billion. If domestic wages were tripled, an additional $5 billion a year would be added to black incomes. Since blacks and Hispanics will be a disproportionate percentage of the household labor force for many decades to come, they can ill afford to pass up the possibility of such impressive gains while they continue to be so heavily represented in domestic work.[19]

According to the ethic of affluent America, the idea of a labor union for maids is shocking and subversive. But this opinion is difficult to defend in a country where collective bargaining is open to all workers except certain government employees. All that is necessary for the successful unionization of domestics is their awakening to the dependency of employees on their services, worker perception of the benefits to be obtained from collective organization, and the gathering of the necessary confidence and determination to sign up in the face of the wrath of employers.

Establish a Nationwide Black Litigation Agenda

"Justice is sovereign over both liberty and equality. You can have too much of either of the last two. But you can't have too much justice."

—Mortimer Adler (1983)

NO COUNTRY IN THE WESTERN WORLD confers so much power on its courts as does the United States. Federal courts are constitutionally empowered to

reverse the legislative commands of Congress. The courts have the constitutional authority to countermand many of the orders of a President. The
Supreme Court has power, and often uses it, to establish public policy on
critical racial issues such as school segregation, compensatory employment
of racial minorities, educational preferences, and voting rights.

Over the past twenty years, the judicial branch has contributed mightily
to the advancement of American blacks. On numerous occasions, the Supreme Court has stretched the Constitution to the limit—and sometimes
ignored its plain meaning—in order to remove racial barriers in public
education, political participation, and employment. In many instances,
these judicial decisions countermanded and ran contrary to the express
wishes of the President, the elected Congress, and large numbers—possibly
a majority—of white Americans.

This period of judicial activism ended abruptly during the presidency of
Richard Nixon. Supreme Court appointments made during the Nixon administration created the potential for a new conservative majority of judges.
In recent years the Court has not been disposed to employ judicial power to
redress the current harms of prior racial wrongs or to satisfy Negro grievances over current inequalities where there was no explicit proof of current
race discrimination. Nevertheless, many judicial remedies are still available
to blacks, particularly in certain instances that involve narrow issues of law.
These include such matters as white majority interference with, or dilution
of, black voting rights and explicit acts of race discrimination sponsored,
supported, or subsidized by the state. Unequal treatment in public education
and gross underrepresentation of blacks in public or government-assisted
employment are additional areas where blacks are likely to be successful in
litigation. Courts have only begun to probe the dimensions of public law
expressed in the Fifth, Thirteenth, and Fourteenth Amendments condemning racial discrimination, and prohibiting any government assistance
through tax exemptions, deductions, or direct support of a racially segregated activity. Even today, blacks still have considerable room to raise new
legal issues and to press old grievances that have not yet received judicial
probing or attention. Activating the power of the law continues to be an
important route to bringing greater equality of rights and opportunities to
black people.

Litigation strategy is profoundly pragmatic. It goes without saying that
blacks will increase their chances of winning favorable decisions if they
litigate in forums known to be positively disposed toward minority grievances. For example, the decisions of the Court of Appeals of the District

642

of Columbia Circuit, where much of the important litigation affecting federal civil rights occurs, continue to be heavily weighted in favor of racial minorities. In addition, there has been a nearly twofold increase over the past five years in the number of blacks and women serving on the federal bench. In the real politics of the judicial process, this means that minority rights issues are more likely than before to be decided in favor of blacks and other minorities at lower and intermediate judicial levels. Since the Supreme Court is burdened with an unprecedentedly heavy work load, the likelihood increases that the decisions of lower federal courts are also more likely than ever before to provide binding precedents.

Another aspect of the black litigation strategy is to frame legal issues under *state* constitutions and litigate them in those state courts known to be favorably disposed toward minorities. The current U.S. Supreme Court's dedication to states' rights should lead to less frequent review by the Supreme Court of decisions by state courts that expand the rights of blacks and other minorities, yet do so on the basis of interpretations of state constitutions. Important decisions expanding the economic rights of blacks have been handed down from the highest courts of New Jersey, California, Michigan, Illinois, and New York.

Ideally, most of the minority civil rights litigation agenda should be shouldered by the U.S. Department of Justice, which has the resources to support the very high cost of lawsuits. Unfortunately, blacks do not influence the Justice Department's discretion over which litigation it will pursue unless the President, at whose pleasure the Attorney General serves, is himself sympathetic to the black cause or politically concerned about the influence of black voters. At present, blacks simply don't have the political muscle to persuade a President to set an aggressive Justice Department litigation policy. Although this circumstance does not foreclose the possibility of successful privately initiated litigation, it does mean that under either a conservative or liberal President, the Department of Justice is a weak reed for blacks to lean on. For the immediate future, minority legal strategists must write off the possibility of much help from that quarter; they must press ahead with their own litigation agenda.

Whatever litigation strategy is adopted, it is important that it be centrally planned, coordinated, and executed. The Congressional Black Caucus could be an effective agent for setting strategy since it has some power to broker its legislative and electoral support of administration programs in exchange for favorable use of the executive branch's litigating discretion. On the other hand, the Legal Defense Fund, formerly affiliated with the NAACP, has been historically the most important and effective litigating agent for black people. In any case, the choice of which institution is to call the shots on black litigating strategy is much less important than that ultimate authority to shape and carry out a litigation plan be located in one place and that the designated litigating agent enjoy very wide financial and political support from black citizens.

The following list of proposed litigation tactics concentrates on areas where blacks appear to stand good chances of making some political and economic gains through the courts:

1. *Establish a nationwide plan to block continuing efforts on the part of whites to dilute black voting strength.* Southern resistance to voting rights reform has crystalized in the creation of so-called at-large voting districts which dissipate local minority electoral strength in thousands of southern town, city, and school board elections. Litigation aimed at forcing white-controlled state assemblies to convert at-large political units to single-member districts has had a good record of success. The same holds true of litigation attacking "dilutive annexations" in which centers of black political power are diffused by combining them with white majority voting districts. Litigation challenging these practices should be greatly expanded, especially in Texas, Georgia, North Carolina, and South Carolina.

2. *Press suits challenging the tax-exempt status of private clubs and trade associations.* As a general principle of law, federal or state subsidy or assistance may not support private institutions that engage in race discrimination. Statutes forbidding aid to segregation provide opportunities to challenge the tax-exempt status of many pension funds, charitable foundations, labor unions, private schools (particularly those formed to avoid public school desegregation orders), business trade associations, and clubs that discriminate against racial minorities. All of these organizations to some extent certify or qualify people and therefore confer power, and access to power. The integration of blacks into these institutions is critical to full access to the nation's economic opportunities, its information network, and to the overall goal of achieving black economic equality.

Challenges to the discriminatory practices of private organizations are likely to be most effective in cities where black political influence has produced the appointment of black judges as well as the enactment of local ordinances prohibiting race discrimination in private clubs, schools, trade unions, and other associations. Legal challenges should continue to be made, particularly against employers paying dues for white employees who gain an unfair business or employment advantage through membership in all-white clubs where business is transacted and names of members are referred to potential employers.

3. *Intensify efforts to challenge current standardized testing procedures in educational institutions.* Disproportionately large numbers of blacks continue to be assigned to low-track or slow learning groups in public schools, largely as a result of scores on so-called standardized tests of intelligence and learning ability. While there is no proof that these tests unfairly measure the educational attainments of blacks, it is clear that, because of prior employment and educational discrimination against blacks, these tests perpetuate the economic and educational advantages that are disproportionately held by whites. In predicting test results of various demographic groups, the income of the parent is the best indicator of how well children will do on tests. As long as white incomes run 40 percent or more higher than blacks', the black test disadvantage will be severe. In some cases, too, there is reason to believe that competence classifications based on test scores are used by some school administrators and employers as a means of excluding blacks from institutions or as a subterfuge for maintaining racially segregated classrooms in otherwise racially integrated public schools.

Blacks should continue to challenge standardized tests that favor upper-income students and, as a result, put stumbling blocks in the paths of blacks. The object of the litigation is not the mindless one of requiring test results to be ratably distributed among blacks and whites. The purpose, instead, is to block the use of the tests until their freedom from bias is proven and, in the meantime, to require institutions to evaluate candidates based on personal interviews and individual determinations of merit. The standardized test is a prime example of how apparently evenhanded selection policies prevailing in commercial and educational institutions provide each generation of young whites with a head start and slow down the efforts of blacks to catch up.

4. *Seek court-ordered cutoffs of federal contracting payments to employers who persist in race discrimination.* Under Title VI of the Civil Rights Act of 1964, more than twenty federal agencies that distribute funds to state, local, and private organizations are required to guarantee nondiscriminatory use of these funds. The agencies obliged to meet this standard include the Department of Agriculture, the Tennessee Valley Authority, the Department of Energy, and the General Services Administration. Not only do these agencies rarely live up to their Title VI responsibilities, but they are also almost never pressed by either the Justice Department, the Office of Federal Contract Compliance Programs, or private litigants to cut off funds to offending recipients of federal monies.

Although its enforcement efforts intensified somewhat under the Carter administration, the record of the Office of Federal Contract Compliance Programs, the government's chief enforcer of job discrimination and affirmative-action rules, has always been spotty. In the late 1970s, the General Accounting Office described the entire government enforcement effort as "so lax as to establish a policy of nonexistent enforcement." There continue to be many government contractors who persist in traditional discriminatory hiring practices and refuse to go beyond the merest tokenism in their efforts to comply with affirmative-action requirements. Judicial pressure may help stiffen some agency backbones; indeed, simply the threat of litigation is likely to cause some bureaucrats to sit up and take notice. The judicial remedy is the exclusive remedy at times when government is withdrawing from many of its traditional responsibilities for the oversight of fair employment practices.

It makes little sense for blacks to pour their hearts and souls into securing beneficial legislation if the laws, once passed, are neither enforced nor obeyed. The economic bargaining power of blacks increases if federal contractors learn that ignoring equal opportunity laws can be an expensive proposition.

5. *Challenge race discrimination in the legal and accounting professions.* The legal profession, particularly at the firm partnership level, continues to be one of the most formidable bastions of the American tradition of all-white professionalism. The accounting profession, with only a smattering of blacks, is only a few steps behind. To a large extent, both professions have been able to maintain their essentially all-white status. The reason seems to be that both groups are politically powerful and neither profession has ever been subjected to federal or state affirmative-action pressures. In fact, some very large law firms with annual revenues of tens of millions of dollars had the effrontery to publicly declare that federal race discrimination laws do not apply to their decisions to grant or deny partnership status to blacks and other minorities.

Because the courts have complete discretion over the qualifications of lawyers who wish to appear before them, an effort should be made, by application to the courts, to deny to any law firm practicing racial discrimination in the selection of associates or the admission of partners the right to represent a client before the Internal Revenue Service, in the United States Tax Court, or before any other government agency. The U.S. Tax Court and the Internal Revenue Service should use similar sanctions against the accounting profession. Even if unsuccessful, this test litigation would focus national attention on these important and influential professions where widespread discrimination against minorities still persists.

The importance to black people of winning proportionate representation in the 500,000-member legal profession cannot be overestimated. Lawyers traditionally become judges, legislators, governors, and Cabinet officers. In many respects, they control corporate America. The legal profession, more than any other, is the repository of both public and private power in the United States.

6. *Litigate the right of holders of public franchises to obtain utility rate increases as long as race discrimination persists and affirmative-action objectives are not met*. State and federal public service and regulatory agencies continue to renew operating franchises and to grant rate increases to utilities, without inquiring as to whether these quasi-public bodies comply with the fair employment laws of the nation. Yet the fact is that these industries have consistently been singled out as laggards in the employment and upgrading of minority workers. The threat of the loss of public broadcast franchises has been an effective enforcer of affirmative-action rules in the television industry, and the same enforcement lever should be used against public utilities and other employers holding public licenses.[20]

7. *Test the right of investment banking firms that have virtually all white executive personnel to profit from the sale of government securities*. The investment banking industry has lagged well behind other employers in bringing blacks into management and out of back-office positions. Despite the industry's increasing emphasis on merit appointments, traditional club attitudes are so pervasive that even today there are no blacks in senior line positions in any of the major investment banking firms. Successful litigation resulting in a court order denying the right to underwrite the sale of government-backed securities—or to use the facilities of the national securities exchanges—to firms failing to comply with established affirmative-action employment requirements would be a fast and effective way of breaking down the steep barriers of prejudice within the investment banking industry. The opportunities for blacks and public-interest groups to invoke state civil rights laws to curb underwriting privileges in state and local bond issues can be significant in some of the large states in the North where judicial friends of race discrimination are few: New York; Pennsylvania; Illinois; Michigan; Ohio; New Jersey; and Massachusetts.

8. *Press for the enforcement of federal statutes requiring affirmative federal contracting in favor of low-income communities*. Since its organization in 1964 as the Office of Economic Opportunity, the former

federal Community Services Administration has consistently ignored its mandate to assure that federal contract awards be made in such a manner as to favor community development corporations and other organizations in low-income communities. Similarly, the federal government's flagship program to foster minority business, the Small Business Administration's so-called 8A Plan, has, in many cases, been doing precisely the opposite of its intended purpose. The program has helped many wealthy and successful white contractors win contracts by using blacks as fronts for white-controlled firms. The legal obligations of both the Community Services Administration (now transferred to the Department of Commerce) and the Small Business Administration should be enforced through a skillfully framed legal action. Here again, the courts are the most effective agents to prevent hard-won minority legislative victories from being nullified by bureaucratic reluctance to enforce either the spirit or the letter of laws designed to strengthen black entrepreneurship and capital formation.

9. *Challenge bonding and "redlining" practices in the insurance industry.* A major handicap for black contractors has been the refusal of fidelity companies to bond minority contractors on the ground of unacceptable risk. This is only one aspect of the tendency of money institutions to starve efforts at capital formation in minority communities. Like most banks and other financial institutions, life insurance companies almost invariably cling to investment policies that generally discourage mortgage commitments to commercial and residential properties in minority communities. An effective challenge to these practices could be mounted in the form of litigation designed to deny these companies the right to write performance bonds covering government contracts, to insure military personnel or installations, or (in the case of life insurance companies) to administer Medicare/Medicaid contracts. The sanctions would be directed at the insurance carriers that (a) fail to adopt affirmative-action employment rules, (b) are not in compliance with federal anti-redlining mortgage investment rules, or (c) fail to show that they encourage minority contractor bonding applications.

10. *Challenge the right of the federal government to insure deposits of banks practicing employment discrimination.* Without federal deposit insurance, banks would be forced to close; without the benefit of highly profitable U.S. Treasury deposits, most large metropolitan banks would experience a serious financial squeeze. These federal benefits are the pressure points that can be used to change the racial practices of an industry that has consistently lagged behind other employers. Lawsuits aimed at stripping banks that are not in compliance with government minority employ-

ment and credit rules of their privileges to claim these government benefits would be a potent corrective measure. This is especially so if litigation is combined with political pressures on the bank regulatory agencies to secure federal and state administrative orders to the same effect. Financial institutions chartered in the public interest should not receive significant subsidies and benefits as long as they refuse to abide by the government's rules on fair employment and credit policies.

11. *Seek court orders blocking federal revenue-sharing payments to state and local units that practice race discrimination and maintain segregated facilities.* Under the banner of "states' rights," race discrimination and segregation persist in the administration of thousands of American cities, towns, and school districts. These violations of federal law exist despite the fact that the Federal Revenue Sharing Act authorizes the withholding of revenue-sharing funds from state and local governments that discriminate against or segregate minorities. At last count, 39,193 state and local units (many in the South where racial segregation policies are commonplace) were eligible to receive federal revenue-sharing funds totaling nearly $7 billion a year. Many local government units have become wholly dependent on these funds.[21]

Again, blacks should act on two fronts: put political pressure on the administrative branch to ensure that the Office of Federal Revenue Sharing withholds funds from offending state and local agencies; and challenge in the courts the right of the federal government to subsidize race discrimination or segregation in any form.

The litigation agenda I have suggested identifies only a few of the ways in which legal pressure may be applied to improve the economic and political opportunities of blacks. There are many other public and private activities that are ripe for challenge, including housing, land use, health care, law enforcement, and criminal justice.

A theme running through the overall black litigation strategy is the use of the judicial authority to reduce the instances where federal, state, or local governments reward segregation or race discrimination. The simple and self-evident proposition is that black taxpayers may not be constitutionally required to subsidize their own exclusion from the tax-exempt or tax-assisted institutions which, in many cases, are counted among the important power-conferring organizations in the nation.

In times when strong political forces are at work to remove the federal courts as the primary guardians of the rights of blacks, it is difficult to muster much enthusiasm for developing a national black litigation agenda. In coming years, black civil rights groups are likely to have their hands full simply resisting efforts on the part of racial conservatives to strip the courts of powers to reverse locally mandated separation of black and white children in public schools. Moreover, black public-interest advocates will be employing all their litigating resources in sustaining affirmative-action decrees and in sidetracking voluntary compliance programs and other initiatives that put the power to discriminate back in the hands of established institutions.

The unfavorable political climate for legislative change focuses attention on the urgent need for blacks to develop massive litigating skills and resources. Litigation reserves must be employed sparingly and only in those cases where important economic and political benefits are in the cards. Falling into the trap of embarking on indiscriminate or unsuccessful litigation would enable segregationists and even moderate backers of Jim Crow to win wider public support for curbing civil rights litigation and thereby limit blacks to the use of political and legislative strategies that require the persuasion of an overwhelmingly unsympathetic public of the merits of Negro grievances.

Organize a Black-Controlled Intelligence Agency and Strategy Center

"Give us a plan of action . . . a 10 Black Commandments, simple, strong, that we can carry in our memories no matter where we are and reach out and touch and feel the reassurance that there is behind everything we do a simple, moral, intelligent plan that must be fulfilled in the course of time. Even if all of our leaders, one by one, fall in battle, somebody will rise up and say, 'Brother, our leader died while we were on page three of the plan. Now that the funeral is over, let us proceed to page four.' "

—Ossie Davis, *Keynote Address,*
Congressional Black Caucus Dinner (1971)

THE COLLECTIVE OPINION of millions of blacks in America holds that it is the numerical minority position that keeps Negroes from claiming some power in this country. This conclusion wholly ignores the potential of minority power in a democracy. The fact is that black powerlessness is due in large measure to the inability of Negro people to develop a "win" scenario for taking up positions of power. This is not a failure of numbers; it is often a failure of *intelligence* operations. Blacks simply lack the information and plans necessary to set in place a strategy for becoming both strong and equal.

Intelligence power uniquely belongs to those who can read maps. In modern times, powerful people possess and read the mapped-out channels of the federal bureaucracy. They find, and skillfully interpret, the intricate charts of Wall Street finance, the complex folkways of large corporations, and the obscure roads of entry into credentializing institutions. They scout out the thickets of legislative and administrative bodies. Powerful people and groups tend to be the people who know the ropes because they have charted the maze of business, government, education, and banking.

Like other activities associated with power, expert training in map reading and other intelligence activities has been reserved for members of the white race. In recent years, many of the critical charts that describe the engines of power in the United States have been unlocked and made available for distant inspection by blacks. But few blacks have learned to use the charts and scrutinize the maps; few have discovered how to move comfortably through the maze of political and economic information that is indispensable to those who would locate, harness, or blunt institutional power.

In order to come to power and finally reach equality in the United States, blacks, too, must become expert map readers. To this end they must organize and *control* a competent and well-funded intelligence-gathering agency. Staffed by expert chart readers and intelligence operators, the intelligence unit is necessary to provide black leaders and strategists with all the charts and other strategic information that they need to "scope out" their problems, detect the presence of barriers, find ways of entering closed places, set agendas, plan political strategies, and act rationally to attain agreed-on objectives.

What kinds of information will this new black intelligence agency search out, analyze, and publish? Answers are needed to some very basic questions:

- What are the principal underlying causes of black inequality?

- What, in order of importance, are the current forces that pose the greatest obstacles to the progress of blacks?

- To what extent, if any, is racial inequality self-repairing if openly competitive and bias-free markets can be established?

- Are simple and well-enforced laws against racial bias in commercial and employment selections sufficient, in due course, to cause blacks to catch up to whites?

- What is the effect on blacks of minimum wage laws and similar protective legislation?

- How can standardized tests be prevented from perpetuating the economic and educational advantages of whites?

- To what extent do affirmative action and similar racially oriented policies reinforce race prejudice and otherwise hurt blacks?

- What states, cities, and congressional districts offer the best opportunities for building black political strength?

- What are the reasons for the disintegration of the black family?

- How is black progress to be measured?

A condition for making gains—or going somewhere other than where you are now—is necessarily knowing what is holding you back. Of particular importance to the empowerment and greater mobility of black America is the creation of carefully researched intelligence predictions of what kinds of political and economic strategies are likely to help black people. Do reforms such as family allowances, national health insurance, federal day-care assistance, and preferential employment rights—which on the surface appear so valuable to blacks—in fact undermine black motivation and thus help to perpetuate unequal poverty between the races? Are there circumstances where tax credits to industry and other "help the strong first" strategies produce worthwhile "trickle down" effects that create a greater demand for black labor? Are community development corporations an effective instrument for dealing with inner-city unemployment? How do the policies of major government agencies—the Federal Reserve Board and the Office of Management and Budget, for example—work for or against the economic goals of blacks? What, if anything, is to be done about the high rate of functional illiteracy among blacks? Would policies of controlled growth of the economy and severe environmental constraints have the effect of locking blacks into their present plight of grossly disproportionate poverty? Are strategies for the reindustrialization of the United States likely to open or close the overall black-white income gap? How are government policies subsidizing the manufacture of robots likely to affect the demand for black labor?

One of the most serious problems facing blacks is their chronic failure to deflect or escape enervating government and corporate policies that are readily imposed on them as a result of their inability to refute the seductive homilies and rhetoric of their opponents and professed friends. Slogans of the New Right such as "a rising tide raises all boats equally" have the ring of truth, but may or may not correctly describe what happens to the opportunities of unskilled blacks during a period of prosperity fueled by new technology and job automation. The black intelligence agency must be sufficiently sophisticated to detect and expose, where appropriate, tax policies and administrative rulings that do harm to the economic prospects of most blacks, but which are traditionally introduced and voted on with ringing preambles about racial justice and an abhorrence of policies that subsidize or encourage racial segregation.

The black intelligence agency must be staffed by expert economists, sociologists, political strategists and investigators who are sufficiently worldly and knowledgeable to challenge and, when needed, to refute the standard bromides and prescriptions issued by America's sociological "think tanks," which ponder the problems of minorities and repeatedly recommend public policies that perpetuate the power advantage of whites.

An important purpose of a black intelligence agency is to shape the black political agenda and plan its tactics. To this end, the black intelligence agency would lay out the possible scenarios for winning and losing in particular political campaigns and identify by polling the issues on which blacks can win and where they must inevitably lose. The agency must detect the "open windows" where black political power can move in and share control of institutions and cities, scout the political past of congressmen who are ardent opponents of black progress, and devise political strategies and rewards to convert opponents of black-backed legislation.

Another important role of the black intelligence agency would be to set straight the public record when black politicians act irresponsibly or dishonestly. For example, on numerous occasions the FBI and other government agencies have been falsely accused by publicity-seeking blacks of "genocidal" conspiracies against black people. The Atlanta murders of black children in 1981 were an example of this outrageous behavior. These excesses destroy the credibility of blacks as a race, reinforce white beliefs in the incompetence and unreliability of blacks, and do irreparable harm to the ability of black politicians to win elections. Blacks must have a reliable intelligence organization that will take public issue with irresponsible blacks and criticize their actions in ways that white organizations cannot undertake without being charged with racism.

The recommendation that blacks should organize a black-controlled intelligence agency is subject to misconceptions and misinterpretations. Although one function of the intelligence group would be to encourage the development of a black political consensus, the intelligence unit would not operate, in the totalitarian style, as a sort of ministry of information and thought. Information, as we all know, is subject to diverse interpretations and differing emphasis. This is why there can be, and are, liberal and conservative interpretations and analyses of each decade's Census report on racial statistics. But the fact remains that, so far, virtually all the political, sociological, and economic data in the United States have been collected by whites. Almost all extant racial information has been catalogued by whites and gathered and presented with a view to answering the questions that whites consider important and interesting about blacks.

The purpose of the black intelligence agency is, then, to permit blacks to assume control over the critical information that affects how they will shape their lives and policies, just as they must also assume greater control over employment, admissions, capital investments, and other forces that decide who gets what in the United States. The football coach does not rely on the coach of the opposing team for strategic information. The political candidate pays little heed to the published intentions of his opponent. So, too, once blacks intend to become politicized, they must free themselves from the important constraint that much of what they now know, or are likely to know, is controlled by government and private media power, which, at best, wants to help blacks but is endemically opposed to empowering them.

Since the dawn of history, power has been discovered by people who knew what they were doing. In the world today, the U.S.S.R. knows what it is doing. Despite some setbacks, OPEC knows what it is doing. Whites in America have built a position superior to blacks in part by knowing what they were doing and by using blacks to serve those goals whatever they might be. Blacks in America knew what they were doing at Selma in 1965; they knew what they were doing and what they wanted when they gathered at the steps of the Lincoln Memorial in 1963.

But blacks as a group no longer know what they are doing; black people in the early 1980s were uncertain, drifting and apathetic; they had very little understanding or interest in the mechanics of political and economic power; in many cases their inadequate knowledge of the forces holding them back has prevented them from developing useful and practical solutions to their problems. Too often they were squandering efforts on black studies programs instead of acquiring a clear-cut picture of the educational forces that were keeping them out of the mainstream; large numbers of blacks were glorifying "Black English" and the inferior syntax that so effectively separated them from communication with whites; they had failed to do their homework on their group strengths and weaknesses as well as on the similar traits and vulnerabilities of those who wished to hold them in place. In sum, large numbers of blacks in the early 1980s had retreated from the concrete purposes of the civil rights movement and in truth no longer knew where they were heading. At the same time, the American people as a whole didn't know what blacks wanted or what they were doing about what they wanted.

The strategic purpose of the black intelligence agency must be to define what blacks should do and how they might do it. With the aid of superb intelligence operations, they must develop a concrete and definite plan. And to this end, blacks, for the first time in American history, must—unfortunately perhaps—become first-class spies and sleuths.

Use Black Congressional Committee Positions to Publicly Expose the Practices of Corporations That Resist Equal Opportunity Goals

"We merely bring to the surface the hidden tension that is already alive. We bring it out into the open, where it can be seen and dealt with. Like a boil that can never be cured so long as it is covered up, but must be opened with all its ugliness to the natural medicines of air and light, injustice must be exposed, with all the tension its exposure creates, to the light of human conscience and the air of rationale opinion before it can be cured."

—Dr. Martin Luther King, in
A Letter From a Birmingham Jail (1963)

IN VIEW OF RECENT AND TRIUMPHANT SUCCESSES of the federal government in disarming legal and political pressures for racial integration and for the economic advancement of blacks, it is unlikely that bold new legislative measures to improve their status and bargaining power will be forthcoming in the immediate future. Moreover, on the issue of race discrimination, the American public has developed in recent years a very high threshold of disbelief. The public will suspend disbelief of charges of corporate racism, for example, only when the fictions and propaganda emanating from the

Chamber of Commerce and the White House are unmistakenly contradicted by hard proof. Despite this adverse political and psychological climate, highly publicized examples of racial discrimination in major institutions legitimize affirmative-action orders and lend support for continuing black pressures for stern enforcement measures that would otherwise antagonize a large number of Americans. Faced with overwhelming evidence of continuing unfair treatment of blacks, the general public may be persuaded that blacks are *currently* being treated unjustly. Once there is public recognition of unfair treatment, black power is ushered through the portals of acceptable authority. Court decisions, administrative measures, and legislative initiatives favorable to minority interests are more likely to follow.

The Congressional Black Caucus should become the focal point for a major effort to publicize the most flagrant examples of continuing race discrimination in business corporations and in other organizations whose activities critically affect the well-being of blacks. Liberated by government deregulation policies, many large corporations, in recent years, have completely ignored equal opportunity laws and their prior minority employment commitments. Traditional hiring practices that use the white-controlled grapevine and union halls have been reinstated. Yet, through public hearings, the Caucus could call these corporations to account, directing particular attention to companies with no black or minority employees. Even in years when public concerns for the advancement of minorities were strong, a study published in 1974 by former Federal Reserve Governor Andrew Brimmer showed that 27 percent of all corporations with 100 or more employees had no black workers whatsoever. In the early 1980s, a significant number of corporations continued to flagrantly ignore equal employment opportunity rules. Many did not even give lip service to affirmative-action requirements. The chief executives of a selected group of these business corporations should be subpoenaed, called to public account, and publicly examined at open congressional hearings.[22]

Highly placed Black Caucus members whose committee positions vest them with legislative subpoena powers should publicly examine the chief executives of all financial institutions with a record of no more than token commercial loans or mortgage credits to minority enterprises in inner-city communities. Widespread publicity should also be given to the large investment banking firms employing no minorities other than in menial or downscale positions. For many generations, films and other media have successfully misinstructed the public in a message that banks deny credit to widows and delight in foreclosing mortgages on orphans. But it is not generally realized that, for a century or more, banking institutions have, in fact, systematically excluded blacks from virtually all forms of banking credit

THE POWER TO PUBLICIZE
RACE DISCRIMINATION

In 1983, several black congressmen had the power to hold public hearings and to compel production of records and attendance of witnesses

Committee Chairman		1983
Ronald Dellums	District of Columbia Committee	
Louis Stokes	Standards of Official Conduct	
Parren Mitchell	Small Business	
Augustus Hawkins	House Administration	
Charles Rangel	Select Committee on Narcotics Abuse and Control	

Subcommittee Chairman		1983
Ronald Dellums	Armed Services Committee-Subcommittee on Military Installations and Facilities	
Walter Fauntroy	Banking Committee-Subcommittee on Domestic Monetary Policy	
Augustus Hawkins	Education and Labor Committee-Subcommittee on Employment Opportunities	
William Gray III	District of Columbia Committee-Subcommittee on Government Operations and Metropolitan Affairs	
Cardiss Collins	Government Operations Committee-Subcommittee on Government Activities and Transportation	
John Conyers	Judiciary Committee-Subcommittee on Criminal Justice	
Mickey Leland	Post Office and Civil Service Committee-Subcommittee on Postal Personnel and Modernization	
Charles Rangel	Ways and Means Committee-Subcommittee on Oversight	
William Clay	Post Office and Civil Service Committee-Subcommittee on Postal Operations and Services	
Julian Dixon	Appropriations Committee-Subcommittee on the District of Columbia	
Merv Dymally	District of Columbia Committee-Subcommittee on Judiciary and Education	
Harold Ford	Ways and Means Committee-Subcommitteee on Public Assistance and Unemployment Compensation	

and, in the process, have cut out the heart of virtually all black financial and entrepreneurial endeavors.

Individual committee chairmen and subcommittee chairmen, with the full committee's approval, have plenary powers to hold public hearings and to issue subpoenas to heads of corporations and financial institutions. These hearings would be far more useful to the minority cause if they were organized and called by white congressional leaders known for a generally moderate position on racial issues. In conservative times, the chance of this happening is unlikely. This means that the logical place to initiate public hearings on corporate resistance to racial integration is either in the House Education and Labor Subcommittee on Employment Opportunities or in the House Banking Subcommittee on Domestic Monetary Policy. In 1984, both of these committees of the House of Representatives were chaired by blacks.

Corporate executives appear to be less concerned about corporate fines for violations of equal opportunity laws than they are about public embarrassment when their high-minded public statements about racial fairness and open opportunity are exposed as false. For this reason, the public exposé is an effective means of routing out the commonplace but often covert practices that limit the opportunities of black people.

In the campaign to inform the public of persistent unequal treatment of blacks, the possibility of holding regional committee hearings should not be overlooked. Powerful political pressures would be directed against flagrant EEO offenders by holding regional hearings on corporate minority practices in cities with large black and Hispanic populations such as Chicago, Los Angeles, Houston, Philadelphia, and New York.

The carrot of reward power frequently works as effectively as the stick. Consequently, it is as important to publicize the good as it is to expose the bad. The laudable and aggressive affirmative-action policies of a number of corporations should be made known to the public and held up as a standard for the rest of the industry to emulate. Companies with a number of blacks in upscale and high-paying jobs include: Avon Products Inc.; Campbell Soup Co.; Chase Manhattan Bank; Connecticut Bank and Trust Co.; Eastern Airlines; Equitable Life Assurance Society, Inc.; Ford Motor Co.; Gannett, Inc.; General Electric Co.; General Mills, Inc.; General Motors Co. Other companies showing aggressive minority recruitment efforts are: International Business Machines, Inc.; Levi Strauss & Co.; Philadelphia National Bank; Philip Morris, Inc.; Pillsbury Inc.; Procter & Gamble Co.; Union Carbide Corp.; Weyerhaeuser Co.; and Xerox Corporation. Extensive publicity should also be given to the names of government contractors with strong and effective affirmative-action programs.

To organize successful hearings, committee staffs must obtain in advance from the Equal Employment Opportunity Commission and the Office of Federal Contract Compliance Programs—through subpoena if necessary—lists of chronic violators and their specific violations. Documented with the most critical and specific facts, hearings unambiguously exposing illegal corporate practices are likely to anger stockholders, put corporations in jeopardy of losing government and state contracts, lead to selective purchasing pressures on the part of blacks, and possibly stimulate class-action suits by employees. If public sentiment is sufficiently aroused, the hearings could, in time, persuade state legislatures, Congress, and the White House to tighten job discrimination laws and to grant broader enforcement powers to the Equal Employment Opportunity Commission.

A second, and far preferable, method of compelling disclosures of harmful institutional minority employment and other practices is through the use of the executive power of the President. Forcing public disclosure of corporate practices through executive order is not uncommon in other areas that affect the public interest. For example, in its campaign against contaminated food, the Department of Agriculture has regularly publicized the names of meat and poultry plants identified as "chronic problem plants." Similarly, prior to the freeze on government activism, serious violators of antipollution laws used to be publicly identified by the Environmental Protection Agency. As black political power mounts and as American Presidents become increasingly concerned with winning, or at least not alienating, minority voters, black elected officials will be in a better position to press for executive orders requiring, perhaps, the 500 largest corporations and the nation's major labor unions to publicly disclose the racial composition of their work forces and to publish progress reports on their compliance with affirmative-action initiatives.

Disclosure orders carry no deterrent effect unless new rules are adopted preventing the traditional corporate doublespeak that permits racial conservatives to create false appearances of minority employment. The present broad category descriptions of employees all too often encourage corporations to duck their obligation to integrate at all levels by the simple expedient of upgrading the job descriptions of minority employees. For example, when blacks are involved, laboratory messengers are often classified as "technicians," thus enabling the employer to lay claim to an impressively high percentage of blacks with impressive-sounding job titles. New position categories that are narrower in scope and that precisely describe the jobs covered would put an end to this sort of transparent cheating.

Among the nation's cynics it is believed that on emotional public issues such as school busing, affirmative action, and other policies designed to promote integration and fuller participation by blacks, people's minds already tend to be made up. Consequently, it is also believed that congressional hearings and other efforts to publicize acts of racial injustice do not change opinions or votes. But the conclusion that the prejudgment will carry the day is true only part of the time. In the 1981 House of Representatives hearings on the renewal of the Voting Rights Act, Illinois Congressman Henry J. Hyde, ranking Republican member of the House Judiciary Subcommittee on Civil and Constitutional Rights, opened the hearings with an admittedly strong personal hostility to the proposed extension of the Voting Rights Act. But civil rights groups produced a mass of impressive evidence showing continuing and flagrant violations of black voting rights in the South. This evidence included proof of forcing blacks to fill out ballots in view of white poll-watchers, police photographing persons who attempted to assist illiterate black voters, the harassment of black voters by "reidentification" legislation applied only to blacks, and concealed voting registrars' offices. Conservative Congressman Hyde's mind was changed by the undisputed evidence, and he ultimately wrote newspaper pieces advocating extension of the Voting Rights Act.[23]

Most measures to help blacks to better jobs—special educational programs and training of disadvantaged workers—do nothing to alter the persistent and apparently structural economic demand bias against blacks. But winning a comprehensive presidential minority employment *disclosure order* is a clear-cut measure that should reduce the bias in economic demand without tackling the formidable task of persuading Congress to enact tighter job discrimination laws. In many cases, antidiscrimination laws already on the books would go a long way to improve minority opportunities if only the laws were enforced. Public disclosure of how major institutions are advancing or ignoring blacks is an important step toward converting equal opportunity laws into potent instruments for better opportunities rather than into mere paper declarations.

Organize a Network of Nationwide Caucuses of Black Government and Corporate Employees

"Power tends to connect; absolute power tends to connect absolutely."

—Peter Newman (1979)

THE MERIT RULE underlying our competitive system—that individual skills and competence will determine how well a person will do in life—holds only partially true. As we have seen, even where race discrimination is not present the playing fields are not level; the unequal ability to use coercive power and other position advantages often produces overriding gains that improve incomes, create wealth, and supplement competency and diligence in the contest of pure competition. Whites have consistently constructed sloping playing fields for teams fielded by blacks. Hobbled by a long history of high illiteracy and low skills, blacks have suffered an extra handicap because their choices have been curbed by various forms of coercive power used by whites: state-sponsored race discrimination in employment; occupational codes and restrictions; exclusion from labor unions; unlawful evictions from political power; and enforced separation from the instruments of capital. For these reasons, a sensible strategy for improving the black economic position has two prongs. Blacks will make gains not only by improving their economic skills, but also by pursuing a host of non-violent coercive tactics that will strengthen them as a group, open doors for entry to institutions, and in the process gradually redress the balance of economic power.

One measure that would magnify black collective bargaining strength would be the organization of a nationwide system of black caucuses within all major corporations. A parallel system of black assemblies could be organized within federal and state government. Standing together as a group, black employees, in both public and private sectors, could press their employers to insist on strict enforcement of antidiscrimination laws. Organized black caucuses could lobby for stronger affirmative-action policies in recruiting, training, employing, and promoting blacks. These caucuses or assemblies would identify and publicize the names of banks and industrial corporations favorably disposed toward minorities as well as the identity of those holding blacks in traditional and downscale posts. Corporate decisions harmful to black interests—such as moving company offices from large cities to all-white suburban areas—could be effectively challenged by black caucuses and made subject to the bargaining process. Institutional violations of civil rights laws could be identified, publicized, and reported to the EEOC or to private civil rights litigation groups.

A black assembly within a particular corporation or organization would have access to parallel black assembly groups working in other corporate settings. This would enable the caucuses to monitor the minority practices of other organizations, thus making it more difficult for employers to raise fictitious obstacles to proposals for affirmative action and other minority advancement plans that had worked well elsewhere. If the black caucuses were all linked by a network of other black assemblies, then universities, hospitals, school boards, industrial firms, and financial organizations could be made more responsive to the goals of most black Americans.

There is a second virtue in the idea of black empowerment through caucusing within institutions. Local assemblies of black workers would significantly increase the general level of economic information within the black community and hence increase its collective power. Through the caucus network, more blacks would be informed of job openings. Through a nationwide assembly network, blacks could begin to build the kind of old-boy employment and referral network that, in the past, has so effectively served whites. A nationwide affiliation of black assemblies would offer blacks far superior information than they now receive on political opportunities, entrepreneurial openings, potential business partners, contracting opportunities, and sources of credit and investment funds.

At the moment, neither the Congressional Black Caucus, the NAACP, nor the National Urban League has adequate information, intelligence operations, or political contacts to effectively police the racial policies of government agencies. But black assemblies operating inside the federal and state governments could monitor civil rights enforcement policies in the many federal agencies and departments where blacks now work. If internal black assemblies were tracking their activities, government departments such as the Department of Labor and the Treasury Department would have difficulty in quietly cancelling equal opportunity compliance rules and soft-pedaling affirmative-action requirements. Organized collectively—and for that reason substantially protected from economic reprisals—assemblies of blacks in federal, state, and local government could publicize government minority practices, ventilate government connivances in violations of school integration orders, and provide a political counterbalance to unsympathetic government policies in health care, criminal justice, and housing.

In 1980, at least one prototype of a black assembly was functioning within the federal government. This was the Racial and Ethnic Minority Attorneys Caucus organized in the Justice Department. Representing approximately 150 minority group lawyers within the Justice Department, the Caucus charged the Department with discriminating against minority lawyers in hiring, training, and promotions. There is no report as to whether the charges had merit, and if they had, whether the grievances were satisfied. The Justice Department, which correctly called the action unprecedented, had agreed to discuss the complaint with the Caucus.

In the past, whites in positions of power and authority have often been able to limit the opportunities of blacks by keeping them removed from key places where major economic and political decisions were made. As literal outcasts, blacks simply did not know—or have the ability to find out—what was going on within the councils of political parties, executive suites of business enterprises, and ruling circles of educational institutions. Today, as a result of agitation and civil rights legislation, blacks have a considerable presence in these institutions. This new presence may be used as a stepping-stone to greater sharing of power, and to bring about wider participation by blacks in the affairs and decisions of the nation's institutions.

The arguments against the organization of black political units within large institutions fall into two categories: First, it may be said that the assembly strategy will hurt rather than help blacks, because caucus activity will be held against them when promotions within corporations are made. It is possible, too, that if blacks organize politically within large organizations, black people will be hurt because employers may respond by hiring only "tame" blacks so as to minimize "troublemaking" and "boat rocking" within the corporation. Black networking and caucusing may even produce a greater tendency on the part of corporations to "showcase" blacks in token appointments and intensify efforts to keep them from access to positions of authority. It is also likely that many talented blacks will perceive such assemblies as "fringe radical" groups with which they want no association. This, in turn, would deprive the assemblies of many gifted blacks who are accustomed to working their way up the ladder by testing their skills against whites. The position may be taken, finally, that black assemblies would be economically counterproductive from the point of view of the performance of institutions as a whole because the presence of collective bodies within hierarchical organizations tends to subvert the merit system, undermine the authority of the institution, impair its ability to get things done, and, in effect, confer a veto power on pressure groups.

All these positions have considerable merit, although the sincerity with which they are advanced is somewhat suspect as these contentions are precisely the same as those advanced against collective bargaining on the parts of workers generally, as well as against other self-help efforts on the parts of blacks.

No one knows for sure whether the assembly idea would work constructively for blacks and for the nation as a whole in the sense that reductions in racial inequalities are in the national interest. Certainly, there are many forces that tend to break up successful caucus solidarity—the tendency of blacks, like whites, to value individual advancement over group advancement; the fear of losing promotion opportunities as a result of bucking the system; the fear of inciting backlash sentiments among the white workers in the organization. On balance, experimentation with black assemblies seems warranted. If black assembly or caucus activities are limited to policing of institutional compliance with race discrimination and the use of a black information network to improve the quality of economic information available to blacks, the negative effects seem to be slight. To the extent that race discrimination and footdragging in the enforcement of antidiscrimination laws persist, a strong black assembly adversary posture might help blacks overcome these obstacles. As long as the nationwide black caucus strategy does not resort to sabotage or illegal pressures, standard collective techniques that enhance black power within institutions may not be summarily dismissed on the ground that tamer strategies would better suit whites. The network proposal should not be scrubbed simply because whites find it perverse of blacks to use collective pressures to try to lift themselves as a group, rather than simply to seek advancement as individual competitors. This is particularly true in settings where front-runner status and unequal power or advantage will almost certainly cause the vast majority of blacks to come in behind whites.

Reserve the Possibility of Mounting a National Strike of the Black Work Force in the Event of the Continuing Deterioration of the Black Economic Condition

"The right of men to leave their jobs is a test of freedom. . . . There are some things worse, much worse, than strikes—one of them is the loss of freedom."

—Dwight D. Eisenhower (1952)

THE HISTORY OF THE BLACK STRUGGLE for racial equality is instructive concerning the kinds of strategies useful today. The record of the past strongly suggests that blacks must always hold in reserve the possible political strategy of nonviolent mass confrontation conducted on a national scale. Over the years, the most significant examples of black progress—acceptance of Negroes in industrial employment, attainment of voting rights, integration of educational institutions, of retail stores and lunch counters, and of public facilities—have resulted from planned acts of nonviolent mass protest.

In the past, the essentially menial and agricultural nature of black employment—combined with a long-dormant black consciousness—limited the ability of blacks to use work stoppages and other collective economic measures to improve their status. But blacks today hold positions throughout the economic system. Removed from servant status, they are much closer, today, to the means of production. For that reason, black people have significant strength within the industrial system. This economic power includes necessarily the ability to mount a nationwide strike of black workers.

The high-risk strategy of a national strike would be warranted only under extreme conditions. One of these conditions might be serious government lawbreaking in the enforcement of employment discrimination laws. Grounds for a national strike by black workers might include the refusal of the government to protect Negro voting rights, the failure to punish Ku Klux Klan violence, or the unwillingness to prosecute lynchings and other criminal conspiracies against blacks. A united black leadership might set an outside limit to the present decline in the black-white income gap—a limit of, say, 50 percent or more—and agree to a one-week national labor stoppage in the event the limit was exceeded. A worsening of the black-white unemployment ratio to 3 or 4 to 1 or more might justify mass economic action. But government cutbacks in job training, subsidized housing, legal services for the poor, or mass transit would not provide acceptable ground for strong confrontation tactics. These would not be desperate circumstances warranting desperate action.

It is impossible to predict the political or economic impact of a national strike by 10 million or more black workers. The assembly lines of the automobile industry would be largely, if not completely, shut down, inasmuch as some of the United Automobile Workers locals in Detroit and other cities have minority memberships as high as 80 percent. There are very heavy concentrations of blacks working in steel mills, textile factories, banks, transportation, and service industries. The major impact of a national strike on the part of blacks would be felt in urban areas where in many cases it would not be feasible to use strikebreakers. Even if the economic effects were not great, a nationwide strike by black workers would focus national and international attention on black economic inequalities. A properly conducted strike would place significant political pressure on industry and the government to deal with black grievances. As was true of Gandhi's strategy of passive resistance against British authorities, black protest power would be protected—and for that reason stronger—because it, too, would be dealing with a decent and moral society.

There are unusually heavy concentrations of black workers in the civil service, the military, mass transit, hospitals, and the postal service. A black workers' strike affecting these government activities would seriously threaten the public interest. In most instances, the strike would also be illegal. By the majority view, the legitimacy of a properly elected government may not be challenged by civil disobedience. Thus, black workers would have little moral or legal standing to strike against the government. In fact, the ability of blacks to *limit* any strike to the private sector would be an effective demonstration of their collective will, discipline, and strength.

For most people, the prospect of a national strike mounted by any ethnic or political group has strong overtones of illegitimacy. But the American system protects the rights of aggrieved groups to band together for any lawful and nonviolent purpose. Beyond any question, the Constitution permits them to leave their jobs and withhold their work for economic or political gain. With the exception of no-strike covenants by public employees, there is no law, no moral injunction that prevents blacks from calling a general strike of the black work force. Concededly, the Teamsters' union may call or threaten a nationwide strike in order to raise truckers' wages above $25,000 a year. Where is the principle of justice or fairness that would deny blacks the right to call a strike to raise median incomes of black families above the current level of approximately $13,600 a year.

Indisputably, there are severe moral problems whenever one person suggests that another person engage in direct action. Even when protest is conducted through meticulously nonviolent means, these are dangerous and extreme measures whose consequences will fall most often not on the person who airs them, but on the direct actors who actually decide to provoke majority power. The only sure counsel that nonparticipants may offer to those who consider extreme measures to deal with desperate circumstances is that any collective act of protest be open and fully advertised in advance. Successful power's insistence on legitimacy demands this. In the words of the wily White House strategist for the New Deal, Thomas Corcoran: "It must be right down the main aisle . . . in broad daylight with a brass band behind me."

CHAPTER TWENTY-THREE

The Political Empowerment of Black America

"The way to play the game is to inch along, steal a base, bunt a man down, hit behind the runner, thread a needle . . . and don't look back."

—*Leroy Satchel Paige (1953)*

IN THE LAST CHAPTER, we explored a number of direct-action strategies that blacks could properly and lawfully use to acquire power *outside* of the formal framework of American politics. Because of the handicaps inherent in the minority political position, these direct pressures were often the powers that counted most. Public protest and nonviolent mass pressures not only produced greater Negro access to institutions and wider participation by blacks in the economic life of the nation, but also created important secondary political effects. Thus, confrontation strategies and mass demonstrations led to voting rights legislation; and voting rights, in turn, introduced blacks to the levers of formal politics. Here, in formal politics, constitutionally established powers of the sovereign could be activated so as to generate even greater political and economic gains. The coming to political power on the part of American blacks would be a classic example of the traditional sequence of group empowerment in a political democracy: protest; the grant of formal access to political institutions; and finally, the use of these political institutions to protect past gains and to create new ones.

Few events in recent times have arrived more unexpectedly and rapidly than the revolution in the political status and power of American blacks. In the decade of the 1970s, the number of black elected officials increased by nearly 300 percent. In the same period, the number of blacks holding judicial power almost doubled. In the ten years following the enactment of the Voting Rights Act of 1965, black representation in Congress increased threefold. In many cities and counties in the South, blacks hold some of the highest posts in local government; yet, in many of these places less than a generation earlier they had not even been permitted to enter voting booths.

In several northern state legislatures—New York State being the most important example—black caucuses of elected officials have assembled a large enough minority position to exact a worthwhile price for their votes. In the U.S. Congress, the Black Caucus is still growing and united. Getting by on family incomes less than 60 percent of whites', blacks are still profoundly underdeveloped in an economic sense, but in politics their force is considerable and mounting very rapidly.

There is a special reason that black interests are served through supplementing direct-action strategies with intensive manipulation of the political system. Protest activities are necessarily shrill and disruptive. Even peaceful and orderly demonstrations tend to be perceived by the general public as unacceptably rude and radical, a perception that robs direct action of much of its persuasive power. Since most political change in America comes from the middle, as well as from those power sources that are perceived as most legitimate, conventional politics should always be the preferred route. It is, then, the formal political process that not only confers formal or delegated power on blacks but also saves blacks from the awful dilemma of either acceptance of permanent inequality or the sure repression they face if they mount serious urban disturbances.

The strategic political moves I now suggest are some of the building blocks that are likely to establish the necessary black political base from which superior economic positions will also come into view. As we proceed, we shall see that for American blacks, Thomas Hobbes' vision of man's "restless desire of power" has economic and social virtues greatly transcending the mere craving to be strong. At a time when there is broad distrust of liberal values, the strategy of seeking power is clean and upfront. It refrains from tiresome criticisms of whites. It rejects the role of the pleading mendicant. It removes blacks from being put down as irresponsible spenders of public funds. The strategy simply embraces power as a critical determinant of well-being, and power acquisition as the single most effective means of achieving black progress.

Hold Annual Conventions of Black Leaders to Develop a United Black Political Front

"You make a winning plan and you make it happen."

—George Wiley (1977)

ACTION-SHY INTELLECTUALS with a common political axe to grind may be inclined to sit around, drink coffee or fruit juice, and talk politics; action-oriented people with the same political axe to grind sit instead in political conventions. The reason for this is that the convention is the essential political institution by which people who have been acting in a random, competitive, or powerless manner come together—often with great difficulty and after a period of feuding and schism—and finally achieve the blessed state of unity from which all group power flows.

Through the convention process, shared ideas become converted into shared and concerted action. Through the political convention, those people to whom low rank has been assigned build solidarity and power by achieving political consensus, shaping platform agenda, writing option papers, and choosing leaders. If black Americans finally decide to come to power in the United States, they, too, must periodically meet in convention. In order to unite under a single political banner, they must have leadership contests and resolve their differences before embarking on political bargaining transactions with their opponents. They must hammer out a common front on the issues that divide them, such as affirmative action, bloc voting, school busing, and inner-city community development. Reaching unity and speaking as a single voice on issues are the *strategic* purposes of the convention. From the dawn of history, people have come to power by suppressing competition, preventing polarization that works to the advantage of opponents, and seeking the power advantages of gathering in crowds. The political convention is simply democracy's expression of fundamental human power behavior.

If the broad black political goals and strategies can be settled, more specific tasks for the convention come to view. For *tactical* purposes, black political officials and community leaders must meet in full convention at least once a year, well in advance of the major political party primaries. The convention must identify congressional districts where blacks should run for office, where sympathetic white congressmen should be supported, and where black voting power should be organized to oust congressmen with voting records that consistently oppose black interests. On a regular basis, the tactical convention should name black favorite sons to run in the primaries so that they can attend the major-party nominating conventions with strings of delegates to be traded for important concessions from the candidates who need their votes. Further, the black political convention should develop and work out tactical alliances with Spanish-speaking Americans and other groups that have political objectives similar to their own.

Particularly, the black political convention must become an annual public demonstration of Negro capacity for strength and unity. After several hundred years of political apathy and submission, blacks continue to be thought of by most whites as ratifiers of policy rather than originators. The convention becomes then political theater for the skeptics who question whether blacks are capable of organizing on their own behalf. The convention demonstrates to the American public that black politics is serious business, not a fringe activity of black radicals.

The idea of a black convention is by no means new. The first convention of free blacks was organized by Richard Allen in the 1830s. Sixty-two delegates, representing Pennsylvania, New York, Connecticut, Massachusetts, Rhode Island, Delaware, Maryland, and New Jersey, met in Philadelphia in 1833 and adopted a platform advocating black emancipation in the United States and black colonizing in Canada. Over 100 years later, another major effort was mounted in the spring of 1972. Organized around a demand for a black reparations commission, a highly vocal but politically ineffectual black political convention met in Gary, Indiana. Two years later, in 1974, another national convention of blacks was called in Little Rock. The meeting was sparsely attended by black political leaders, who with good reason did not wish to be identified with the violent policies of the Black Panther party, the sponsor of the convention.

Traditionally, the black convention movement has foundered because of inadequate financing, poor attendance, and discord among the participants. Indeed, during times of particularly sharp divisions among black voters, black leaders have judiciously decided it would be better to hold no convention than to mount a session that would do little more than advertise black disunity. Thus, in early 1980, a presidential election year, *The New York Times* reported:

> "With many prominent blacks already committed to supporting one of the two leading contenders for the Democratic Presidential nomination, black political strategists have decided against a national political convention of their own and have instead settled on a meeting to determine 'agendas' for the next decade." [1]

The result of this decision to scrub the 1980 convention was the National Conference on a Black Agenda for the Eighties held in Richmond, Virginia in 1980. This mid-winter "nonconvention" was attended by over 1,000 black delegates representing approximately 300 organizations. Invitations to address the assembly were sent out to the major presidential candidates of both parties. Although the conference was held in the political primary season, ten or more viable presidential candidates still remained. None of them accepted the invitation to appear at the conference. Here was a significant statement of the political impotence of blacks in the United States in the early 1980s.

In the current climate where few blacks can agree on what's wrong or what to do next, the chances of bringing off a successful national black convention are poor. Yet the odds improve each time Census figures show black incomes falling further behind whites', and each time national and local elections show an increasing number of blacks going to the polls and balloting 90 percent or more for the same candidates. If blacks are to stand tall in American politics, the convention effort must be tried and retried until it succeeds. For this to happen, black people, in much greater numbers, will have to break the psychological hammerlock that ensures their loyalty to the Democratic party at all stages of the primary season. The great majority of blacks must decide to turn a deaf ear to the pleas of Democratic party regulars who see the black convention as a threat to the party's established coalition and who ask for black allegiance without offering a quid pro quo.

Encourage the Growth of Special-Interest and Splinter Groups Within the Two Main Political Parties

"Let the whites divide, what happens? Here is the dangerous and alien influence that holds the balance of power."

—Henry Grady (c. 1890)

AS SOCIETIES GROW OLDER, it seems that they often tend to lose their loyalty to many of the national symbols and beliefs that originally united their people. This phenomenon may now be occurring in the United States. Consider how, in recent years, Americans have been dividing into sharper ethnic, religious, geographic, and social factions. Political parties today are loose and fragile coalitions of groups such as farmers, unionized labor, urban blacks, blue-collar workers, southern conservatives, small-town whites, eastern liberals, and countless other permanent or ad hoc groups. This fragmentation produces a large number of unaffiliated voters loyal to neither party but often intensely interested in single issues such as abortion, capital punishment, handgun control, family values, nuclear power, and women's rights. Observing the divisive trends in his own party, House

Speaker "Tip" O'Neill remarked in 1978, "If this were France, the Democratic party would be five parties." [2]

In 1978, *Time* magazine pronounced somewhat prematurely, "Today the parties have virtually collapsed as a force in American politics." [3] The truth is that both political parties have survived and will continue to withstand all the supposed periods of "near extinction." Yet the forces of disaffiliation are very strong. Whatever the future of the two-party system in the United States, the continuation of divisive pressures within the two main parties will make it possible for blacks to achieve much greater political influence in future years. The increasing fragmentation of the two great power centers that govern the United States enables blacks for the first time to take advantage of the fundamental rule that minority power in a parliamentary democracy always increases whenever greater powers divide into competing political factions.

The effect of party fragmentation in enlarging the power of minority groups is best displayed in the continental system of multiparty politics. In Israel and Italy, where a free-for-all coalition system prevails, each special-interest group benefits from intraparty and interparty competition for its vote and, accordingly, finds itself enjoying considerable political influence. In Italy's parliament, party defections and alliances have been known to produce the election of a prime minister who was, in fact, the leader of a party claiming less than 10 percent of the popular vote.

Huge political leverage would accrue to American blacks under a European-type multiparty system. If, in the United States, there were four or five major parties instead of our present two, blacks as a unified voting body would be able to form their own political bloc without concerns about splitting the liberal vote and conferring election success on conservative candidates antagonistic or indifferent to black interests.

Consider some of the concrete gains that would flow from the fragmentation of the major parties. In the states, congressional districts, cities, and counties with large concentrations of minority voters, black party candidates would enjoy considerable success running in a field of three or more whites who might very well split the general vote, thus allowing the black party candidate to gain a plurality. In a presidential election contested by five or more major parties, a black entry could conceivably win the electoral votes of several states with large minority populations, possibly giving the black candidate the balance of power in a multiparty runoff in the Electoral College. Instead of retaining orphan status in the Democratic party, blacks would be aggressively courted by coalition builders seeking to assemble a majority. In the course of election campaigns, blacks could exchange their electoral strength for key political concessions from one or more of the other competing parties. Under a multiparty system, where the general electorate would be divided into many factions and parties, blacks, as a unified 11.5 percent of the population—concentrated in northern cities and in the South—could present established political interests with an extremely powerful and, in some cases, indigestible political force.

But blacks win strength only if *both* of the two main political parties divide. If the Republican party only were to split into conservative and moderate wings, the Democrats would be in such a commanding position that they would have even less reason than they do now to respond to black political and economic aspirations. And a split in the Democratic ranks without a similar split in the Republican party would simply confer elections on conservatives and deprive blacks of the even slight influence they currently have in the Democratic party. In other words, a black political bloc could play an influential role in American politics only if there were four or more parties or splinter groups present, all spinoffs from the original two-party system.

Whether a major structural change in American political parties is in the offing remains to be seen. Certainly, the low voter turnout registered in the 1980 presidential election showed that many millions of nonvoting American voters find no home in either of the two major parties. In this kind of political setting, the development of additional political parties and options would encourage greater political participation at the cost of little, if any, harm to American democratic traditions. It is commonplace but unproven wisdom to intone that the American political process functions best when the two major political parties hold a healthy duopoly of political power. Certainly, the system functions better for whites since they control both parties. But many blacks can be expected to look at the matter from a different perspective.

Divide and Conquer

The current political trend away from the unifying influence of the parties and toward single-issue politics seems to have an independent life, which neither blacks nor any other special-interest group can do very much to control. But black political strategists are in a position to encourage some of the splintering forces currently at work and, in the process, to come to hold power in their own right. Even if present trends toward the Balkanization of American political parties do not lead ultimately to the creation of a formal multiparty system, politicians seeking office would still be forced to put together a coalition of many one-issue groups in order to assemble a majority. In this political setting, blacks, as a very large unified voting bloc, would inevitably be in great political demand by other groups.

The divide-and-conquer strategy which southern whites have used so effectively against blacks is not a perfect fit on the other foot. As mentioned, a breakdown in the Democratic party coalition would only reinforce the power of conservatives to the detriment of the political objectives of the vast majority of blacks. Thus, the prime objective must be to encourage divisive tendencies inside the Republican party. Divisive forces are always present in the GOP. For many years, conservatives in the GOP have been balking at what they view as the leftward drift of the party. In 1983, for example, President Reagan was in danger of losing much of his conservative following as a result of raising taxes, increasing budget deficits, freezing military pay, failing to cut back the growth of government, abandoning Taiwan, and failing to stop busing or to restore prayer in schools. In every GOP administration, there is invariably a significant group of disaffected conservatives threatening to defect from Presidents whom they view as having betrayed campaign promises.

To encourage the process of party disaffiliation on the part of conservatives, blacks are most effective simply by pressing the standard black agenda. Unrelenting pressure for school busing, affirmative action, neighborhood racial integration, more black judges, and so forth, may, in combination with related initiatives that most conservatives abhor, succeed in separating from the GOP the large conservative wing which John Anderson called "the red necks of the Republican right." The populism, emotionalism, and religious fundamentalism of Republican loyalists such as Jesse Helms are increasingly jarring to the traditional corporate spirit of middle-of-the-road prudence embodied in the politics of George Bush or George Shultz. More than any other issue, continuing pressures for enforcement of antidiscrimination laws would be likely to exacerbate tensions between the moderate and conservative wings of the Republican party.

The withdrawal from the GOP in 1982 of some arch conservatives and the agitation of the Committee of Conservative Activists (COCA) for a brand-new party on the right hinted at the possibility of a division that could be highly favorable to black political interests. So, too, was the organization, in the early 1980s, of twenty moderate Republicans into the "gypsy moth" faction, which, in conjunction with the pressures from the New Right, was threatening to undermine a unified Republican front.

Ideological differences within the GOP may be expected to reemerge as they always have. Any efforts to revive the Rockefeller liberal wing of the Republican party should receive strong black support. The discontent of consumers and environmentalists within both parties should be exploited. Differences within the Democratic party among various urban, ethnic, and labor union groups also serve to strengthen black political influence and should not be discouraged. The more the women's movement, the gay rights movement, and the "right-to-life" movement—as well as the environmental and consumer movements—function outside the traditional political parties, the weaker the hold of the two-party system becomes. Blacks are strengthened in the process.

The objective of moving toward a multiparty political system must be viewed against the broader purpose of creating much more inter- and intra-party competition for the black vote. The proportionate representation of blacks in government is bound to increase significantly if they and other minorities successfully threaten majority coalitions and, particularly, if they erode or break down the present political duopoly of the Republican and Democratic parties under the two-party system. To be sure, efforts on the part of blacks to divide the major parties are likely to be attacked as a form of juvenile delinquency; yet, dividing one's opponents is a legitimate political tactic commonly used by patriotic pressure groups within any participatory democracy. But a rigid determination on the part of blacks to stay loyal to the Democratic party and tote its flag is simply a ticket to continuing political impotence.

Establish the Black Vote as an Independent Political Faction Within the Democratic Party

"What decides presidential elections is the 'swing' vote, not the 'base' vote of either party. . . . And blacks are decidely *not* part of the swing vote in the United States. In each of the last four elections they have voted roughly 9-1 Democratic."

—Patrick J. Buchanan,
The New York Post
(November 18, 1976)

DESPITE A GREAT DEAL OF HUFFING AND PUFFING about their new political clout, blacks, the nation's largest voting bloc, have very little political influence in the United States. We have seen that this impotence stems in large part from the limited choices presented by our two-party system. There is simply no place for blacks in a Republican party that opposes voting rights legislation, gun control, affirmative action, educational grants for the poor and minorities, and most of the other items at the head of the black agenda. As a result, the black vote "belongs" to the Democratic party. Because of its captive status, the black voter carries no weight within the party and is incapable of influencing the party's platform or political initiatives. Only the rhetoric of the Democratic party, today, supports the traditional black agenda.

Indeed, the strategy of publicly abhorring racial inequality while refraining from doing much about it makes good sense for the Democratic party. Democratic candidates can count on winning black votes without incurring the disadvantage of alienating other elements in the party that would develop if they seriously supported the black agenda. The Democratic party leadership is well aware that in the two-party system blacks have nowhere to go but home to the Democrats. Even when, as in recent years, the Democratic party condones racially restrictive voting rules in order to hold the allegiance of white voters in the South, blacks can do little more than resign themselves to accepting Democrats as the lesser of two evils. The black political dilemma was effectively described by political columnist Patrick J. Buchanan:

> "For almost any national Democrat, the black vote is a given. Even Daniel Patrick Moynihan, the Irishman from New York City's Hell's Kitchen, who used to punch third worlders in the United Nations, and who is the popularizer of benign neglect—a candidate purportedly the anathema of New York's black elite—concedes cheerfully in *Playboy*: 'I carried the black vote by a 5 to 1 margin.' "[4]

Blacks have often flirted with the idea of forming a separate political party. Political theory holds that if the nearly 18 million blacks old enough to vote were organized as a separate party, all other powerful interests in the United States would covet, and therefore bargain for, their vote. For political theoreticians, the third-party ideal has always offered the potential of a promised land of increased black voter turnout, widespread alliances with other special-interest groups, and black political independence.

But fond illusions must give way to harsh reality. Under present conditions, where political power is lodged in two parties, the idea of a permanent separate black political party is a blueprint for frustration. As we have already shown, in all close elections during the recent past, an independent black party would have served only to confer the presidency on the candidate least acceptable to blacks. A black third-party effort would almost certainly have produced a Ford victory over Carter in 1976 and a Nixon victory over Kennedy in 1960. In the past fifteen years, dozens of moderate and liberal Democratic congressmen would have lost to conservative Republicans had they not been able to hold the black votes that would have been lost if a strong black third party had been active in the elections. At the moment, the black third-party objective serves the same divisive and enervating political purpose as the efforts of Republican state legislators to dilute the influence of black votes for Democrats by gerrymandering black voters into voting districts that are still safe for Republicans.

For the moment, then, there are some positive benefits in remaining under the umbrella of the Democratic party. In election districts where black candidates have the potential to become winners, success is more likely if the candidate works within the framework of the party. Black Democrats, for instance, are able to secure financial assistance from the party's national campaign chest. A separate party effort would require separate fund-raising efforts—always a major obstacle for blacks—as well as difficult and costly efforts to secure a special place on ballots. In addition, the fact is that many white liberals will vote for a black candidate only if he or she is running as a traditional Democrat. There is the further disadvantage that, in the minds of many white voters, the very concept of a black political party triggers an instinctive backlash reaction because it is so easily confused with black racism, separatism, and the radical militancy of groups such as the Black Panther party.

In Congress, too, blacks who keep their Democratic affiliations stand a far better chance of winning political power derived from holding committee and subcommittee chairmanships. At the present time, black Democrats participate in electing the House Speaker, the members of the powerful Democratic Steering and Policy Committee, and holders of other key leadership posts. Functioning as regular party Democrats, blacks will have more influence over the policies of Democratic office seekers as well as over the initiatives of a sitting Democratic President than they could possibly have as members of an independent black political party.

What concrete measures might blacks take to have their cake and eat it, to stay in the Democratic party yet become a floating interest pressure group within the party? In forming the Congressional Black Caucus, blacks have already taken the first step toward greater political independence. The Caucus uses the Democratic party as its base, recognizes an essential loyalty to the party, yet reserves the right to vote against the party leadership on issues of particular concern to blacks.

To create a new political counterforce within the Democratic party, blacks might consider the following tactics:

• *Enforce a bloc voting strategy in the Congressional Black Caucus.* If all black representatives agreed to vote according to the wishes of the majority, the Caucus's votes would become a coveted political commodity capable of bringing a high price in the complex horse-trading of congressional give-and-take. Effective bloc voting by blacks in Congress and in the state legislatures would, in effect, establish a party within a party.

• *Present a unified black front in Democratic primaries.* Black political power is most effectively harvested during the primary season when the chances are greatest that a number of candidates will be competing for the black vote. If blacks run black favorite son candidates in primaries, press mainstream candidates in primary elections to commit to black issues, and if blacks are successful in forcing primary candidates who are white to seek out Black Caucus endorsements, black voters will automatically become a much more important force within the Democratic party.

• *Establish a network of black Democratic clubs to take control of party machinery in areas with large black populations.* If blacks are able to build strong local organizations capable of delivering black votes in large numbers to Democrats, black political negotiating strength will be greatly increased within the Democratic party.

• *Abstain, or even vote Republican, when black interests are ignored.* There are many election years when both political parties offer candidates wholly unacceptable to blacks. When this happens, blacks have little to lose in boycotting an election or even in temporarily switching their support to a select list of acceptable Republican candidates. Massive black abstentions from voting would also be a healthy form of political muscle-flexing. In 1972, organized labor, disenchanted with George McGovern, demonstrated the power of this tactic by sitting out the election and handing the Democrats one of the worst defeats in their history. Similarly, southern whites, a key faction in the Democratic party, switched their support to Nixon in 1972, then returned to the fold in 1976 when the party fielded a more acceptable candidate.

Since emancipation, blacks successively have been wards of the Republican and then of the Democratic party. Over this long period of more than 120 years, both parties have patted blacks on the head and told them to leave important political decisions to their elders. At no time have there been black defections from white-controlled political institutions. For blacks today, creative factionalism—the political technique of swinging in and out of a political party—offers a major opportunity for achieving major power status.

Forge a Nationwide Black-Hispanic Political Alliance as a Third Force in American Politics

"All government, indeed, every human benefit and enjoyment, every virtue and precedent act, is founded on compromise and barter."

—Edmund Burke,
Speech on Conciliation with America, 1775

SINCE THE BEGINNING OF TIME, oppressed or troubled people have turned to an ally for help. The political strategy of making an alliance with another group continues to be a standard means of winning rights and advantages that otherwise would be beyond reach. Power diplomacy's grand gesture of calling a press conference and announcing a treaty is one of the tough tactics of realpolitik that blacks have rarely employed or considered.

If it is agreed that blacks acting alone are unlikely to achieve more than part of their political objectives, where do they turn for support? Today, northern liberals—only a few decades ago the black person's most potent ally—are ideologically exhausted and show little interest in the plight of blacks. Blue-collar whites, corporate interests, farmers, merchants, small businessmen and "middle Americans" tend either to ignore black people or to be among the strong believers in their inadequacies. Environmentalists and consumerists often have somewhat elitist interests that run counter to the primary black objective of increasing their personal incomes. Formerly sympathetic Jewish interests have become profoundly resentful over black quotas and Negro support of Palestinians on Middle East issues.

Indisputably, the ideal alliance for blacks would be a political union with Hispanics. If significant minority power is to develop in the United States, it is very likely to take the shape of a black-Hispanic political coalition.

For blacks, the desirability of this alliance is shaped in large part by the huge number of voters that Hispanic-Americans bring to the bargaining table. Hispanic-Americans are by far the fastest-growing minority group in the United States. Official government statistics place the nation's Hispanic population at 14 million, roughly half that of blacks. But these figures fail to consider the huge number of undocumented Mexican immigrants who, in recent years, have entered the United States at the estimated rate of one million people per year. A more accurate tally of the Hispanic population would probably put the total closer to 20 million, or roughly 9 percent of the total American population. If present birth rates and immigration patterns continue, Hispanics will soon surpass blacks in numbers. In the next decade, Spanish-origin Americans, in all likelihood, will become the nation's largest minority.

Hispanic populations are concentrated in the Southwest, particularly in Texas, California, Arizona, and New Mexico. Over 40 percent of the population of New Mexico is Hispanic, while California, Texas, Arizona, and Colorado all have Spanish-origin populations of at least 13 percent. Over 1.5 million Mexican-Americans live in Los Angeles, home to more people of Mexican descent than any city in the world other than Mexico City. In both Texas (Hispanic population, 21 percent) and southern California, the *reconquista,* a Spanish political reconquest of the once Spanish Southwest, is a recurring political theme.

Large numbers of Hispanics live in other parts of the country as well, most notably in the New York City area, with a Puerto Rican community of about one million, and in south Florida where there is a very large Cuban-American population. Indeed, there are large Hispanic communities in almost every major American city. In Minneapolis-St. Paul, Mexican-Americans have already replaced blacks as the largest minority.

While the potential political power of Hispanics is vast, they, like blacks, hold few elective offices or other positions of influence. In 1984, only nine Hispanics served in Congress; none were in the Senate. The situation in California—a state with an Hispanic population exceeding 4 million—is typical of Hispanic underrepresentation in governing posts. While Hispanic-Americans make up almost 16 percent of California's population, they hold only 2 percent of the elected posts. In 1980, no Hispanic-American sat on the Los Angeles City Council. But Hispanic political power is growing. The mayors of Denver, San Antonio, and Miami are Hispanic, as are nine U.S. congressmen and New Mexico's governor.

The major obstacle to a black-Hispanic political alliance is quite simply the tensions of competition, which have markedly increased in recent years. The civil disturbances in Miami in 1980 point to increasing conflicts between blacks and Hispanics, focused on competition for starting-level jobs. While many undocumented Hispanic immigrants wash dishes, sweep floors, harvest crops, wash cars, bus tables, and do other menial work often

performed by blacks, the competition bites most painfully at higher economic levels. Flooding every major city in search of work, Hispanics are

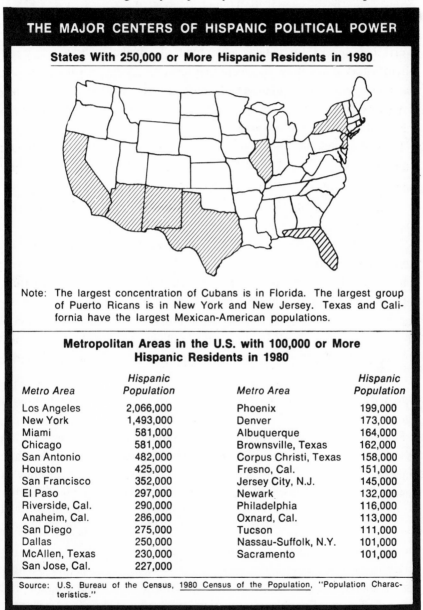

THE MAJOR CENTERS OF HISPANIC POLITICAL POWER

States With 250,000 or More Hispanic Residents in 1980

Note: The largest concentration of Cubans is in Florida. The largest group of Puerto Ricans is in New York and New Jersey. Texas and California have the largest Mexican-American populations.

Metropolitan Areas in the U.S. with 100,000 or More Hispanic Residents in 1980

Metro Area	Hispanic Population	Metro Area	Hispanic Population
Los Angeles	2,066,000	Phoenix	199,000
New York	1,493,000	Denver	173,000
Miami	581,000	Albuquerque	164,000
Chicago	581,000	Brownsville, Texas	162,000
San Antonio	482,000	Corpus Christi, Texas	158,000
Houston	425,000	Fresno, Cal.	151,000
San Francisco	352,000	Jersey City, N.J.	145,000
El Paso	297,000	Newark	132,000
Riverside, Cal.	290,000	Philadelphia	116,000
Anaheim, Cal.	286,000	Oxnard, Cal.	113,000
San Diego	275,000	Tucson	111,000
Dallas	250,000	Nassau-Suffolk, N.Y.	101,000
McAllen, Texas	230,000	Sacramento	101,000
San Jose, Cal.	227,000		

Source: U.S. Bureau of the Census, 1980 Census of the Population, "Population Characteristics."

pushing upward into construction, blue-collar, restaurant, and service
trades. In Miami, blacks—once a majority of the city's menial and service

workers—now hold only 2 percent of the jobs in hotels and restaurants. Understandably, blacks are angered when, as is often the case, they are refused jobs because they cannot speak Spanish. Cuban-Americans in particular have a strong entrepreneurial class that competes much more effectively than blacks for capital and credit. To make matters worse, an inflammatory black press has increased tensions. A 1979 article in *Ebony* magazine gave wide circulation to the questionable view that "the siphoning of jobs by [illegal aliens] is a major reason for the unemployment crisis among blacks, especially young black men."[5]

The state-provided menu of racial entitlements is also a source of intense interracial conflict. Blacks and Hispanics compete to fill quotas in government posts, foundations, corporations, school boards, and in educational institutions. Both groups compete for minority contract allotments, for low-cost housing, and, of course, for political office.

The competition between blacks and Hispanics not only inhibits the building of a political alliance, but also leads to divisive political initiatives that harm both groups. So intense, for example, is the job competition between blacks and Hispanics that a number of black leaders have announced support for legislative efforts to block the further immigration of Mexican aliens into the United States. For blacks this is a shortsighted and ultimately self-destructive policy. By supporting exclusionary immigration policies, blacks alienate a powerful political ally; they also adopt an ideological position that is fundamentally at war with black interests in creating a more open society.

Scarcity-dictated infighting provides the stage where whites, deliberately or unwittingly, fan the flames of conflict between Hispanics and blacks. A number of white politicians are adept at exacerbating racial tensions by raising the ogre of illegal Mexican immigration into the states. Since the spoils of the minority quota system are controlled entirely by whites, it is easy to pit the two major ethnic groups against one another as they reach for the same bone. Although the point is rarely publicized, established political interests have an important stake in encouraging competition between blacks and Hispanics—particularly in big cities and in the Southwest. In a number of melting-pot election districts, established Democrats survive in office only by spreading poison that keeps the two ethnic groups at each other's throats.

If either blacks or Hispanics are to address the issue of their power-lessness in America, they must end the competitive pressures now ener-vating both groups. A formal political alliance must be reached. They must collectively refuse further to strengthen the hands of political incum-bents by playing out the script that calls for blacks and Hispanics to compete for government handouts. There must be joint black-Hispanic political ef-forts to elect agreed-on minority political candidates; combined efforts must be launched to defeat majority candidates who attack the interests of either group; flying under a bipartisan banner blacks and Hispanics must press for greater employment opportunities for both groups, followed by joint control over how these advantages are shared. In every campus, factory, financial institution, city school board, and government contracting office, blacks and Hispanics will make the economic contest more equal by bargaining collectively for a greater collective share. Mutually assured impotence for both ethnic groups is the expectable outcome of current conflicts where whites in industry, education, and government negotiate separately with blacks and Hispanics over the minor spoils of ethnic allotments.

The Feasibility of Marriage

It is often said that the prospect of a black-Hispanic coalition ignores the realities of ethnic politics. But why should this be so? The forces driving blacks and Hispanics toward political union are much stronger than those keeping them apart. Both blacks and Hispanics endure very high rates of unemployment and poverty; both experience intense discrimination in the job, credit, and housing markets. Both groups tend to be disenfranchised by racially gerrymandered election districts, both are forced to put up with inferior public education, and both suffer from very high rates of disease, crime, drug addiction, and infant mortality. Blacks and Hispanics have a sturdy common interest in welfare reform, protected employment, main-taining a high level of public education, and in criminal justice reform. Neither group is in a position to accomplish its political objectives without the support and assistance of the other. Clearly, the pressures in favor of making a political alliance are much greater than those that keep blacks and Hispanics apart.

An impressive model for an effective black-Hispanic coalition already exists in the New York State Assembly. Here the Black-Puerto Rican Cau-cus has sixteen members out of a total of 150 state legislators, and thus controls almost one-fifth of the votes needed to pass bills. The Caucus wields considerable influence over any close assembly vote and has been able to use this influence to win concessions from the New York State Democratic leadership in return for Black-Puerto Rican Caucus support. Admittedly, black and Puerto Rican legislators in New York have an unusually high degree of common ground because, for the most part, they represent constituents who live in the same neighborhoods in New York City. Unquestionably, it will be considerably more difficult to weld a coalition between Mexican-Americans from rural Texas and blacks from the ghettos of northern cities. These groups tend to have sharply different life-styles, backgrounds, and opinions on such issues as immigration policy, abortion and bilingual education. Also, minority coalition-building in Florida will be a difficult task. Miami's Cuban population is already politically active and will not readily share power with blacks. Rural blacks in the counties near the Georgia and Alabama borders have little in common with the Cuban communities hundreds of miles to the south in Miami and Tampa. The likelihood of a political coalition between the nation's two largest minority groups is remote at present, but the political advantages that argue for a united Hispanic-black front are compelling.

The first step in forming a successful black-Hispanic coalition—whether at the state, local, or national level—is for the two groups to meet in a formal political convention. The convention should begin by developing the usual ingredients of unity: a commitment to work together, to iron out differences, to treat an attack on one group as an attack on the other; to develop tactics to prevent parties in power from creating divisions and competition between blacks and Hispanics. The convention would then proceed to work out a common political plan and a strategy to accomplish agreed-upon goals. The convention would address the difficult problems that cannot be resolved by the elementary rhetoric of cooperation. For example, convention leaders must agree on which political offices the minorities should seek and on who the candidates should be. Black candidates must be selected to run for some offices, Hispanics for others, each being firmly supported by the other. In any given city—such as New York City where blacks and Hispanics make up almost half the population—a black might be the sole minority candidate for mayor while an Hispanic candidate runs for city council president. The next year the roles would be reversed. Eschewing competition and, instead, taking turns at making political runs at the opposition should quite promptly lead both groups out of the political wilderness.

On the national level, a convention of blacks and Hispanics would formulate a joint strategy for building ethnic political power in presidential elections. The coalition would hear briefs in support of the presidential aspirants of the major parties; the joint alliance might very well decide to run favorite son candidates in various state primaries in an effort to win delegates to national party conventions. The nation's major parties would be confronted with a tightly knit Hispanic-black coalition, a political alliance potentially holding the balance of citizen voting power in Texas, California, New York, Florida, Arizona, and New Mexico, and thus controlling 145 electoral votes. In the face of an avalanche of united black and Hispanic voters, presidential candidates from both major parties—for the first time in history—would become politically accountable to the aims of the two largest and most disadvantaged groups in the United States.

An insight into the truly commanding force of a black-Hispanic political alliance may be had against the backdrop of any close presidential election. A united ethnic front, motivated to make a potent election statement against Republican policies toward minorities, could swing many elections to the Democratic candidate. For example, if both blacks and Hispanics were to cast 90 percent of their votes for the Democratic ticket (a percentage black voters have given the Democratic party in every election since 1964) and were to turn out to vote at rates similar to white voters, the Republican party would have to win a whopping 59 percent to 41 percent majority among white voters in order to achieve a majority of the popular vote. Even in the Roosevelt sweep in 1932 and Eisenhower's landslide reelection in 1956, the winner received only 57 percent of the popular vote.

The heavy concentration of Hispanics in the large electoral vote-rich states magnifies the political power of Spanish-origin Americans. Hispanic power, in fact, may be summed up in four words: California, Florida, New York and Texas—states with enough electoral votes to make or break any election. In California, a state with forty-seven electoral votes (more than 17 percent of the total required to win the presidency), Hispanics make up 16 percent of the electorate while blacks add another 7 percent of all voters. With a black-Hispanic coalition holding nearly a quarter of the possible vote, the Republicans would need a huge percentage of the white vote—upwards of 62 percent—in order to win the state if the black-Hispanic alliance produced voters in the same percentages as whites and cast 90 percent of its ballots for the Democrats.

In New York (36 electoral votes) and Florida (21 electoral votes) the black-Hispanic coalition could potentially cast a quarter of all votes, thus forcing the Republican candidate to win a 62-38 percent advantage among white voters in order to take these states. In Texas (29 electoral votes) black and Hispanic voters make up nearly one-third of the entire voting-age population. If these voters turned out at the same rate as white Texans and again cast 90 percent of their votes for the Democratic ticket, the Republican party would be hard-pressed to win the 70-30 percent majority it would need from white voters in order to carry Texas.

Four states—California, Florida, New York, and Texas—control 133 electoral votes or nearly half of the total required to win the presidency. Any

---

A UNITED BLACK-HISPANIC VOTING BLOC IN A PRESIDENTIAL ELECTION WOULD POSSESS FORMIDABLE IF NOT UNBEATABLE POLITICAL POWER

The conservative-libertarian alliance that stands opposed to most black political initiatives can win a presidential election without the black vote.

It can also win without the Hispanic vote.

But it will be extremely difficult for it to win the presidency without *both* votes.

Assumption: If blacks and Hispanics cast 90 percent of their votes for the Democratic ticket and:

Minority-to-White-Voter-Turnout Ratio Is:	White Vote Percentage the GOP Must Get to Win the Election Is:
1 to 1	59% to the GOP 41% to the Democrats
4 to 5	57% to the GOP 43% to the Democrats
3 to 5	55% to the GOP 45% to the Democrats

Note: In all six national elections that have taken place since 1964, over 87 percent of the black vote has been delivered to the Democratic nominee. In four of these elections (1964, 1976, 1980, and 1984) blacks gave over 90 percent of their votes to the Democratic candidate.

---

candidate carrying three of these four states would very likely be the winner of the presidential election. From time to time, blacks and Hispanics separately call for various economic and political reforms. Majority power invariably responds merely by deploring existing conditions and expressing grave concerns and sympathy. It is likely that rhetoric would be transformed into a dedicated majority commitment if blacks and Hispanics in these *four swing states* were to join forces and *jointly* call for the same reforms.

Mount a Massive Nationwide Campaign to Increase Black Registration and Voter Turnout

"It used to be southern politics was just 'nigger' politics, who could 'outnigger' the other—then you registered 10 to 15 percent in the community and folk would start saying 'Nigra,' and then you get 35 to 40 percent registered and it's amazing how quick they learned how to say 'Nee-grow,' and now that we've got 50, 60, 70 percent of the black votes registered in the South, everybody's proud to be associated with their black brothers and sisters."

—Andrew Young (1976)

ABSENT A MASSIVE DEFECTION by whites to the GOP, unregistered black voters have the potential power to take both the South and key northern industrial states away from the Republican ticket in any moderately close election. Yet, despite this capacity to control the outcomes of elections, it is almost impossible to win much enthusiasm among black people for the power of the ballot. In 1983, there were over 7 million voting-age blacks who remained unregistered to vote.

Despite all the complaints by blacks of voter harassment and election law discrimination, the main reason blacks do not vote is that *they choose not to do so*. In the 1978 midterm elections, the black turnout rate nationally was 37 percent; the white rate was 47 percent.[6] Even the striking statistical differences in black and white voting habits do not reveal the true depths of black voter apathy. In many parts of the country, black voter participation is almost nil. In New York City, for example, the vote in black precincts in the 1977 mayoralty race was one-quarter to one-half the vote in white precincts. In a largely black congressional district in Brooklyn, only 12 percent of the registered blacks voted in 1978. The story is much the same elsewhere. In Texas, only 27 percent of the eligible blacks voted in the 1976 presidential election; only 12 percent of the registered blacks went to the polls in Houston's Eighteenth Congressional District in 1978; in Mississippi's Fourth Congressional District, only 22,000 out of 104,000 eligible blacks voted in 1976, despite the fact that the incumbent was a strong opponent of black interests. Mayor Tom Bradley of Los Angeles could have been elected the first black state governor in 1982. He lost by less than 50,000 votes. Among the reasons, blacks did not turn out to vote in sufficient numbers. Repeatedly, voter apathy has been the essential cancer that has eaten away at black efforts to make important political gains.

As expected, voter apathy is most severe among young blacks. Only 27 percent of blacks ages 18 to 20 were registered in 1978 and only 15 percent actually voted. Although young whites also have poor voter participation rates, they register and vote in far greater percentages than do their black counterparts.[7]

The black voter apathy problem boils down to this. In common with other low-income groups, huge numbers of blacks are as ignorant of the power of voting as they would be about the workings of the committee system in

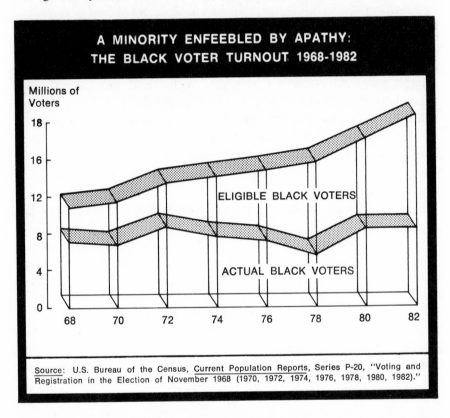

A MINORITY ENFEEBLED BY APATHY: THE BLACK VOTER TURNOUT 1968-1982

Millions of Voters

ELIGIBLE BLACK VOTERS

ACTUAL BLACK VOTERS

Source: U.S. Bureau of the Census, Current Population Reports, Series P-20, "Voting and Registration in the Election of November 1968 (1970, 1972, 1974, 1976, 1978, 1980, 1982)."

Congress. In most elections, the great mass of blacks—to a much greater degree than whites—look on political campaigns with total indifference. Perceiving major political parties as essentially similar, many highly educated blacks have adopted an attitude of total indifference to political campaigns. Among many blacks the view tends to be, "Why bother because whites will lead the country anyway." Perhaps because the repressive actions of whites are viewed as responsible for black inequality in the first place, there is a persisting tendency on the part of a great many blacks to believe that only whites have the power to redress the political balance.

As a result, politically inactive and nonvoting blacks become the single largest political party working against black interests.

In sharp contrast, other special-interest groups draw their political power not so much from their overall numbers but from their intense and often cunning political activity. The striking political power of the Jewish minority owes its force not only to Jewish money and political sophistication, but also to voter turnout rates that approach 75 percent. If blacks could organize themselves to turn out votes at anything like this rate, dozens of statewide and congressional elections would swing to the candidate preferred by blacks. For example, if 75 percent of the eligible black electorate had voted in 1976 and cast the same 90 percent of their votes for the Democratic ticket, seven additional states would have switched to the Carter column. The potential of the unregistered black vote is even more impressive in the Reagan-Carter contest in 1980. President Reagan's margins of victory in New York, Massachusetts, Alabama, Mississippi, Tennessee, Louisiana, North Carolina, South Carolina, Arkansas, Kentucky, and Virginia were *less in each state* than the number of unregistered blacks in the states.[8]

If black minority voter participation were increased by only 20 percent, blacks would immediately witness a significant increase in the number of legislators seeking their votes and a dramatic change in the voting habits of white legislators. State governors, elected judges, and public officials everywhere would toady to black people, not because Negro voters actually held the balance of power but because they *might* hold the balance. Even rock-ribbed racial conservatives would get a "touch of soul."

Easy Voter Registration

Voting rules in effect in most states discourage voting particularly by the poor and other groups lacking a political tradition and the motivation to vote. If these barriers were removed, the voting strength of blacks and other minority groups would mount considerably. A simple measure to increase black participation would cut registration red tape by the enactment of so-called easy voter-registration legislation. Minnesota and Wisconsin have already liberalized rules to require that prospective voters simply show up at the polls on election day holding only proof of age and residence. Laws permitting registration by mail would also be a boon to minorities, as would legislation authorizing deputized registrars to enter a community and sign up unregistered voters on the spot. A Michigan law enacted in 1979 permits the deputizing of high school principals to register seniors before they graduate. As governor of Georgia, Jimmy Carter signed a similar bill into law in 1971; in 1979, twenty other states were also considering similar easy voter-registration proposals.[9] Since blacks are registered to vote in much lower percentages than whites, blacks should unite behind all current efforts by civic groups to ease the voting process.

Most incumbent politicians appear to feel more comfortable with present election laws, which make voting difficult and tend to limit active voters to upper- and middle-class Americans who are well indoctrinated in the duty to vote. Because most incumbents believe that they have little to gain, and possibly a great deal to lose, if voting power increases among low-income groups, it is likely that burdensome voter-registration procedures will prevail for many years. If blacks are to strengthen their ranks at the polls, they will have to do so within a system that discourages voting by requiring certain archaic and potentially burdensome acts on the part of those who want to vote, such as presenting themselves in person at the voting registrar's office at some arbitrarily specified time before the election. In the absence of "easy" voting legislation, the most effective way to overcome these hurdles is by privately organized voter-registration drives staffed by a pool of volunteers who can provide transportation and other support.

A successful voter-registration drive usually makes use of intensive printed ads, radio spots, and neighborhood canvassing. The most effective drives generally target one specific area for a one-day intensive effort. Volunteers saturate a community by ringing door bells and telephones, handing out leaflets, and visiting popular gathering places and clubs. In the case of black voters, this task is somewhat simplified by the typical geographic concentrations of black people.

Voter-Registration Drives

In any political setting, black voter turnout is weak; yet the number of black voters who go to the polls will vary greatly with political circumstances—many of which can be controlled. In election after election, it has been demonstrated that the most effective method of getting out the black vote is to place a black candidate somewhere on the ballot. But voter apathy always reclaims the landscape whenever black voters are forced to choose between two or more garden-variety nonminority candidates. The point is illustrated by the 1981 New York City mayoralty primary. The black voter turnout in some Harlem districts was 25 percent higher than the citywide average due in part to black animosity toward the incumbent mayor, Edward Koch, but also because of the presence on the ballot of a respected black candidate, David Dinkins, who was running for Manhattan Borough President.

Even without a black candidate on the ballot, black voter turnout increases markedly whenever whites engage in old-fashioned racial politics. Efforts by state assemblies to water down the black vote inevitably increase it, just as a tough law-and-order platform, which blacks usually read as a covert form of racism, never fails to draw large numbers of blacks to the polls. For example, blacks effectively took advantage of a racially charged political atmosphere in Philadelphia in 1978. A charter referendum that would have allowed Mayor Frank Rizzo to run for a third term was voted down due to an extraordinarily large black voter turnout that resulted from the wide publicization given to the repressive policies of the Rizzo administration. To a great extent, therefore, effective black voter turnout drives must be opportunistic, exploiting throwbacks to Jim Crow, ill-conceived law-and-order rhetoric, and antiblack political blunders.

In theory, black newspapers and radio stations should play a role in improving black voter participation, but in fact the media force controlled by blacks is too insignificant to have much impact. The formation of strong neighborhood political organizations would contribute greater political force. In the same manner as other special-interest groups, black communities must organize effective block associations and political clubs to hold regular meetings to discuss local grievances, organize protests when needed, arrange for endorsements of candidates, and stage social events to encourage widespread community political participation. At election time, the clubs would mount registration drives, political rallies, and "get-out-the-vote" campaigns. Strong local clubs and associations also tend to produce voters through peer-group pressures. For the same reason, a revival of inner-city and rural community development corporations would also contribute to black neighborhood solidarity and voter participation. It is for this reason, perhaps, that community development self-help efforts on the part of the black poor have never been popular either with Republicans, who prefer to discourage strong voter turnouts among low-income people, or with Democrats, who have a strong preference for a tame, rather than active, black constituency within the liberal coalition.

There are few activities in life so arduous as the political organization of those whose lives have never been touched by or benefited from the political process. In voter-registration drives no short-term rewards are won, results are not easily perceived, and the work involved lacks the glamor associated with many other forms of political activity. Nevertheless, laborious voter-organization efforts are indispensable to the process of minority group empowerment. The successful history of the politicization of Irish-Americans provides an outstanding example of bootstrapping one's way to equality through political activity. Irish-Americans living in ethnic neighborhoods developed strong local political organizations, slowly won control of their neighborhoods, wards, and precincts, and eventually took control of the local city hall. Precisely the same course can and should be followed by blacks.

Computers, Walking Lists, and Loss Leaders

The traditional loss-leader approach to consumer marketing may be applied to the task of getting out the black vote. In this case, the loss leader is a political referendum or initiative taken directly to the people. "Hot" issues capable of pulling large numbers of blacks to the polls are proposals on open housing, gun control, discrimination in public health care, school segregation, and referendums that force citizens to face up to the many circumstances where the states and cities subsidize private organizations that exclude blacks. Requirements for submitting voter referendums on the ballot vary widely from state to state. In many areas, only the governing legislative body has the power to put a question on the ballot, but seventeen states and hundreds of counties and cities have provisions for publicly initiated referendums. Usually, the number of signatures required to place an initiative on the ballot corresponds with a stipulated percentage of the total vote cast in the last general election. In areas with large concentrations of eligible black voters, this minimum number of signatures is well within reach. Moreover, the campaign to collect signatures has independent political value and should help stimulate black interest in almost all elections.[10]

Other standard measures for getting out the minority vote include developing precinct walking lists that identify all the eligible black voters within each district, mailing of campaign literature to prospective voters during the week prior to the election, calling on potential voters at their homes or places of work, and providing transportation to the polls on election day. Transportation for black voters is important in rural areas of the Deep South, where polling places are typically—and sometimes deliberately—located many miles away from where black people live.

In politics as in economics, successful power seekers always insist upon greater access to modern technology and, particularly, electronic access to information. The voter data bank is the current political equivalent of the freedom riders of the 1950s. In cities and congressional districts where blacks have voting majorities or large pluralities, computer data banks should be installed. The data bank produces the names, addresses, and phone numbers of all blacks in any political subdivision. The data bank contains information on voting habits, party affiliations, financial contributions, and the names of potential voters requiring transportation. In countering the skillful use of computerized vote solicitation by conservatives and Jim Crow supporters, computerized voter information becomes a powerful resource for black political candidates. Instant access to the names of millions of black voters sharing a broad unity of political views provides liberal candidates generally, and particularly those who are trying to defeat or unseat politicians who have voting records unsympathetic to blacks, with an immensely potent political weapon. Moreover, for blacks, the data bank is an invaluable resource in mounting direct-action tactics such as protests, boycotts, and demonstrations. Today, blacks must link computers just as in 1964 they linked arms.

Concentrated voter education effort among black school children is a vital part of any successful long-term strategy for political empowerment of Negro voters. Here is another instance where racial segregation—this time in public education—tends to work to the political advantage of blacks. Every effort must be made to instill a sense of duty to vote among the millions of young black people currently attending essentially all-black schools. Modern political strategies and techniques must be taught. Students must be made aware of past black electoral successes and of the gains that have resulted when blacks have banded together and assumed political control of cities and public institutions. To counteract the messages of racial conservatives to the effect that blacks are never helped by political action or legislation, there must be instruction in the positive gains made by blacks as a result of voting rights legislation. Black elected officials must be encouraged to visit schools in their districts. Black teachers should make political issues a frequent topic of classroom discussions. Mock elections should be held during political campaign seasons. Children should be encouraged to press their parents to register and to vote and should report back to the class on the results of their efforts. School credit should be given to black teenagers who do volunteer work for a political campaign or civic organization. Just as one teaches the value of economic activity or of taking care of one's personal health, comprehensive instruction must be given in black schools on how and why the voting process is democracy's most powerful weapon for protecting rights and opportunities.

Black Media Leads the Charge

Despite the fact that Negro people have an almost insignificant presence in the world of media power, black press and broadcast media must assume prime responsibility for black voter education. The black media is the only communications force that is likely to expand political awareness by broadcasting editorial statements on the political records of officeholders who oppose black interests; the black press must provide the energy to activate the black vote by exposing public schemes to disenfranchise blacks, such as district gerrymandering and discriminatory election laws. The black media must issue report cards on the performance of elected officials in predominantly black districts. Few whites tune into the black media with the result that blacks can conduct political consciousness-raising campaigns with little risk of white backlash. Raising the political awareness of black voters is far more important to black empowerment and progress than current black media efforts to celebrate Negro culture and studies.

The dramatic 1983 upset victory achieved by Harold Washington in his campaign to become the first black mayor of Chicago demonstrated the payoff for blacks when they conduct successful voter-registration drives. The black voter-registration drive in Chicago conducted in the summer of 1982 increased black voter registration by 100,000 to about 600,000 voters. In the February Democratic mayoralty primary election, the black voter turnout surged to 80 percent of those registered. Aided by Chicago's unusually strong black media, the election was in Washington's hands despite the fact that he won only 6 percent of the white vote.

Enlarge the Black Legislative Bargaining Position by Doubling the Number of Congressional Seats Held by Blacks

" 'The [Black] Caucus has sixteen votes in the [New York State] Assembly,' one high-ranking Democrat said; 'How many bills do you think we would get passed if we didn't push for a welfare increase?' "

> —*The New York Times,* quoting a
> member of the New York State
> Assembly (January 21, 1979), p. 21

THROUGH THE SUCCESSFUL USE OF DIRECT ACTION and confrontation politics, blacks won the right to vote. The vote brought to blacks the ability to

694

influence the power of the state. But a share of that political power has never been realized in the place where it counts most: the United States Congress. Defeated in its efforts to win ratification of the Equal Rights Amendment, the women's movement realized finally that the problem was that there were not enough women in legislative positions. So, too, with blacks. One of the best ways to advance black legislative goals—and to protect blacks from the harm that state power can cause them—is to build a much larger and critical mass of black legislators in Congress. Possibly, in fact, the most straightforward way even to think about black political power is to ask simply, "How many blacks can we elect to Congress?"

Nine Congressional Districts Where Blacks Stand a Good Chance of Capturing Seats and Adding to Their Congressional Strength

1985

Current Representative and Party	State	District	Percent Black Voting-Age Population
Wyche Fowler (D)	Georgia	Fifth	60.5%
Peter Rodino (D)	New Jersey	Tenth	50.7%
Webb Franklin (R)	Mississippi	Second	48.0%
Corrine Boggs (D)	Louisiana	Second	58.0%
Wayne Dowdy (D)	Mississippi	Fourth	40.1%
Norman Sisisky (D)	Virginia	Fourth	37.3%
Robert Tallon (D)	South Carolina	Sixth	36.7%
Tim Valentine (D)	North Carolina	Second	36.5%
Gillis Long (D)	Louisiana	Eighth	35.7%

Black political representation in Congress continues to be in token proportions. In 1985, blacks held only nineteen voting seats in the House, thirty short of the number they would have held if they had racially proportionate representation. Blacks have no seats whatsoever in the Senate. A critical mass of at least thirty black congressmen, all united under the banner of the Congressional Black Caucus, would be required before blacks would have enough political strength to influence executive policy as well as to bargain for favorable legislation within Congress itself.

To field a strong political force of lawmakers in Washington, black elected officials and community leaders must organize a major effort in the key congressional districts to elect many more blacks to Congress. The Congressional Black Caucus should strive to elect at least eight new members within the next eight years. Campaigns should be targeted in congressional districts with very large black populations, especially districts where the current incumbent is politically vulnerable. In 1984, nine congressional districts with black voting-age populations greater than 35 percent were represented by whites. In some of these districts, to be sure, the incumbents who are white have favorable voting records on many issues of great concern to blacks. But support by liberal and concerned whites adds nothing as such to black legislative power. Congressmen sympathetic to black objectives do not vote as a bloc for the official Caucus position. When the congressional leadership looks for voting blocs to line up for or against any proposal, the liberal whites who usually vote on the side of blacks do not count in the Caucus bloc. The support of the non-Caucus members on any particular issue tends to be limited to that issue alone and for general negotiating purposes contributes very little to the collective political power of black people.

Georgia's Fifth Congressional District

Georgia's Fifth District, which encompasses much of Atlanta, presents the best opportunity to elect another black to the Congress. In 1972, Andrew Young was elected to the House from this district, but a special election was held to fill the vacancy when Young resigned his seat in 1977 to become Ambassador to the United Nations. Two prominent blacks, Ralph Abernathy of the Southern Christian Leadership Conference and John Lewis, the director of the Voter Education Project, were among eleven candidates seeking Young's seat. Because of a low turnout and divisions among black voters, the voters chose the then vice-mayor of Atlanta, Wyche Fowler. Fowler, who is white, has won reelection easily ever since. The Fifth District has nearly 230,000 eligible black voters, substantially more than the total vote Fowler received in 1982. Blacks now make up 60 percent of the district's population. Although Fowler has a favorable voting record on black concerns, blacks should go after this seat for the simple reason that they stand an excellent chance of winning it.

In 1982, it appeared that Julian Bond, the well-known Georgia state legislator, was set to challenge Fowler but unexpectedly bowed out of the race. Other black candidates, thinking Bond was a sure winner, declined to enter. When Bond suddenly dropped out, there was not enough time for blacks to organize another campaign and Fowler was able to win against only token opposition.

New Jersey's Tenth Congressional District

New Jersey's Tenth Congressional District in Newark and Georgia's Fifth are the only congressional districts in the United States with a majority black electorate that still send a white delegate to Congress. The Tenth District's Congressman, Peter Rodino, is extremely popular, not only with the white minority in the district but also with blacks. His voting record has almost invariably supported Black Caucus objectives. Undoubtedly, this explains why he has faced only one serious black challenge—in the 1972 primary, when two blacks split 42 percent of the vote. The district illustrates the perennial black dilemma: Whether to support a good friend of black people or to opt for greater black political power. Three blacks challenged Rodino in the 1980 primary, yet he received the support of the most prominent black leader in the district, Mayor Kenneth Gibson of Newark. A united effort by blacks behind a single black candidate will be needed to capture this seat. Rodino is now in his seventies and will in all likelihood retire soon. Blacks will almost certainly take control of this district on Rodino's retirement.

Mississippi's Second and Fourth Congressional Districts

Although Mississippi has a greater percentage of blacks than any other state, until 1984 artful gerrymandering by the Mississippi legislature insured that none of the state's five districts had a black voting majority. Since Mississippi requires a primary runoff contest when no candidate receives a majority of the primary vote, it was extremely difficult to nominate a black candidate in any Democratic primary—precisely the result most Mississippians intend.

Amazingly, blacks were able to secure the Democratic nomination in the Second District in 1982. The Mississippi legislature, under pressure from the courts and the Department of Justice, had to redraw congressional district lines following the 1980 Census. Previously, the state's black voters had been evenly distributed among four of the state's five districts, all approximately 35 to 40 percent black. Under the new redistricting plan, the Second District had a slim 53.7 black majority, but only a 48 percent black voting-age population. Under these circumstances, blacks made up a majority of the Democratic voters and were able to nominate a black candidate,

697

Robert Clark, a member of the Mississippi state legislature. But in the 1982 general election, Clark lost by a narrow 51-49 percent margin. In 1984, the Mississippi legislature redrew district lines once again and added thousands of additional black voters to the Second District. However, Clark was buried in the Reagan landslide. In 1986, he should win.

Facing the realities of a de facto all-white primary law, blacks in the Fourth District often run as independents in the general election. In 1978, Evan Doss, the black independent candidate, organized a strong campaign, and was expected to benefit from the well-publicized Senate campaign of Fayette Mayor Charles Evers. However, in a district with 104,000 eligible black voters comprising nearly 40 percent of the total electorate, Doss was able to muster only 25,000 votes and he finished a distant third.

In 1980, blacks in the Fourth District did much better. Leslie McLemore, the black independent running in the general election, actually ran ahead of the white Democratic candidate, polling 53,000 votes—30 percent of the total ballots cast. However, the Republican incumbent, Jon Hinson, who held one of the most virulent antiblack voting records in the Congress, was reelected by a margin of 16,000 votes. Hinson retired from the House in April 1981, after arrest on a sodomy charge. In the special election held to fill his seat, a large turnout by black voters was mainly responsible for the narrow upset victory by white Democrat Wayne Dowdy. While Dowdy, reelected twice, hasn't done much harm to blacks, blacks in Mississippi should concentrate on capturing the Fourth District. The growing strength of the black voters, generated by Jesse Jackson's candidacy in 1984, should encourage future efforts to win this seat in 1986.

Demographic changes have made a number of other congressional districts ripe for the election of blacks. For example, in December 1983, Louisiana, under federal court order, created a 58 percent black majority congressional district in New Orleans. Although the present incumbent, Congresswoman Lindy Boggs, is extremely popular with both white and black voters, this redistricting enables black voters in Louisiana to elect the first congressional representative in the state since Reconstruction and also to end the white monopoly in holdings of congressional seats in the states of the Deep South. Also, heavier concentrations of black voters in districts such as North Carolina's Second, South Carolina's Sixth and Virginia's Fourth should, in time, produce black congressmen. High black voter turnout rates have become common in these districts. Also, the 1982 election of black representatives to Congress from Gary, Indiana and Kansas City, Missouri from districts that were less than 25 percent black is encouraging.

The biracial political base of blacks elected from racially integrated districts frequently will raise delicate issues when these congressmen become loyal members of a Black Caucus voting bloc. But the appeal of black-elected officials to white constituents should mount as elected blacks gain the ability to use congressional power and patronage to confer benefits on all constituents within their districts.

It remains clear that a long-term strategy aimed at enlarging the size of the Congressional Black Caucus should rank near the head of the black political agenda. But a great deal of polling, campaign organization, and fundraising is required. Concrete plans should be mapped immediately to move in a firm and systematic way toward taking control of the districts where blacks already have the votes.

Mount Selective Campaigns to Unseat Congressmen Who Are Pandering to Segregationists or Voting Against Black Interests

"I float like a butterfly. . .
I sting like a bee."

—Muhammed Ali
(1970)

A DEMOCRACY KNOWS NO THREAT more effective in moderating the voting practices of an incumbent legislator than a serious challenge to his or her job. The direct challenge appeals to the primal human instinct of the politician: political survival.

Blacks have made many efforts to elect other blacks to office, but they have almost never mounted campaigns against elected officials who consistently foment hate and bigotry and use public office to delay the progress of black people. As a result, large numbers of congressmen—many of them from districts with very large concentrations of black voters—vote their racial bigotries with total elective impunity.

As a practical matter, black voter strength will never be respected until it demonstrates the ability to defeat its enemies as well as to defend its friends. For this reason, if for no other, blacks must establish a track record of successfully ending the political careers of lawmakers who continue to fight the rearguard action against racial integration as well as of those politicians who pander to racial bigotry under the guise of states' rights. Blacks must constantly remind elected officials that black voters are politically strong and that their goals and ambitions are not to be taken lightly.

Both conservative and liberal political action groups have successfully employed the tactic of moderating congressional voting behavior by threatening to turn opponents out of office. Perhaps the most successful of these

A core of strong legislative opponents of black advancement whom black voters might usefully remove from the United States Congress

United States Senators

Name and Party	State	Percent of Eligible Voters Who Are Black
Strom Thurmond (R)	South Carolina	27.3%
Thad Cochran (R)	Mississippi	31.0%
Jesse Helms (R)	North Carolina	20.3%
John Warner (R)	Virginia	17.5%

United States Representatives

Name and Party	State and District	Percent of Eligible Voters Who Are Black
Jamie Whitten (D)	Mississippi—1st	22.6%
Dan Daniel (D)	Virginia—5th	22.4%
William Dickinson (R)	Alabama—2nd	27.4%
Floyd Spence (R)	South Carolina—2nd	31.9%
G.V. Montgomery (D)	Mississippi—3rd	27.5%
William Nichols (D)	Alabama—3rd	25.2%

campaigns was the 1980 effort by the National Conservative Political Action Committee (NCPAC). In 1980, "Nick-pack," as the acronym is pronounced, defeated four of the six liberal incumbent United States senators whom it had targeted for defeat. NCPAC efforts flopped in the 1982 congressional elections, a consequence not of unsuitable strategy, but rather of mean, deceitful, and "hit-'em-anywhere-you-can" campaign tactics combined with extremist political goals much less appealing to the American political center than the struggle to eliminate racial bigotry in high places.

Black political influence would be markedly increased by the completion of a few successful campaigns to defeat congressional supporters of Jim

Crow. The logical targets are readily identifiable, and many are politically vulnerable. A number of senators and congressmen, predominantly from southern states, continue to oppose black interests in Congress despite the fact that they represent states and congressional districts with black populations as great as 35 percent. Secure in their beliefs that blacks will never organize successful campaigns to put them out of office, a few of these legislators have been explicitly racist in attitude and in public statements.

Do blacks have the power to remove some of these legislators from office? Emphatically, yes. As we saw in Chapter Twenty-one, there are at least eighty congressional districts in the country where black voters are a large enough percentage of the electorate to control most close elections. In scores of election contests in past years, black voters could easily have defeated incumbents who fed hate and bigotry to the American people; but blacks did not turn out at the polls to do so. To be sure, the powerful die-hard segregationists in Congress are not going to immediately sue for peace, or change their voting habits, simply because a group of impecunious black political organizers announce a plan to remove them from Congress. The obvious difficulty of the political task should not deter blacks from undertaking it. Win or lose, the effort builds black political strength.

"By God, he's as black as melted midnight. Get outta my way. This mongrel meeting ain't no place for a white man!"

— South Carolina Sen. Ellison Smith's exclamation as he walked out of 1936 Democratic National Convention in protest of invocation being offered by black Congressman Arthur Mitchell

---

The accompanying list identifies incumbent senators and representatives whose careers from the viewpoint of most blacks might be usefully ended. All of the federal legislators on the list have displayed insensitivity to black concerns; they have voting records almost consistently opposed to positions of the Congressional Black Caucus. Many are profoundly dedicated to perpetuating racial segregation; most consistently go out of their way to punish blacks and impugn their character; many of them are actively fighting rearguard action against racial equality. Some of them, in fact, believe that America would be better off if blacks were not in this country and are explicitly dedicated to reestablishing "a white Christian state" in the United States. These elected representatives have been selected not only because of their racially obnoxious voting records, but also because their constituencies contain significant numbers of black voters.

• *Sen. Strom Thurmond Republican South Carolina Term Expires: 1990*

Few politicians in the country have played the politics of race more skillfully than Republican Strom Thurmond of South Carolina. Before blacks became influential in southern politics, Thurmond openly appealed to the sentiments of white supremacists with angry rhetoric of racial hate. In 1948, Thurmond declared, "There are not enough troops in the Army to force southern people to admit Negroes into our theaters, swimming pools and homes." In opposition to the 1957 Civil Rights Act, he set a record for a one-man filibuster of twenty-four hours and eighteen minutes.[11] After the enactment of the Voting Rights Act of 1965 and the enfranchisement of black voters in South Carolina, Thurmond backed away from overt attacks on blacks. Like other former hard-line southern segregationists, his office makes sure that blacks get their Social Security checks on time. Because of this, many black voters from South Carolina don't seem to care if Thurmond actively plots to end voting rights protections and to cut welfare in one of the poorest states in the nation. Despite token gestures to the black community, Thurmond has adamantly opposed every major civil rights bill introduced in Congress.

"Wherever some people go the rat holes will follow. Wherever some people go, the slums will follow. We can take the people out of the slums, but we cannot take the slums out of the people."

—West Virginia Senator Robert L. Byrd (1964)

The GOP takeover of the Senate following the 1980 elections has greatly enhanced Thurmond's ability to do harm to blacks. As chairman of the Senate Judiciary Committee, Thurmond has a powerful post from which to lead efforts to stall voting rights protection, subvert enforcement of race discrimination laws, and curb the powers of the federal courts to break down dual school systems.

After announcing his intention to retire in 1984, Thurmond had second thoughts and won reelection easily. Thurmond is physically fit and may run again in 1990. To discourage six more years of racially reactionary representation, black voters in South Carolina might mount a "Dump Thurmond" campaign well in advance of the 1990 election. It will be recalled that in 1978 arch segregationist James Eastland of Mississippi withdrew his candidacy for the Senate when it became apparent that there would be an upswelling of black voter opposition. Like Eastland, Thurmond would have no choice but to take such a message to heart, for there are over 590,000 eligible black voters in South Carolina—more votes than the total Thurmond received in his 1978 reelection. Blacks make up over 27 percent of the South Carolina electorate and can obviously make the difference in a hotly contested statewide race. Jimmy Carter, for example, lost the white vote in South Carolina in 1976 but carried the state by over 100,000 votes on the strength of overwhelming support from the black community. South Carolina's other senator, moderate Democrat Ernest Hollings, has on occasion been saved from defeat by the loyal support of the black electorate.

The chances of unseating Thurmond appeared to improve in 1983, when Rev. I. DeQuincy Newman was elected (in a district two-thirds of whose voters were white) the first black state senator in South Carolina since 1888. In 1983, Thurmond, the Dixiecrat race-baiter of thirty-five years ago, voted in the U.S. Senate to create a national holiday honoring Martin Luther King, Jr. By Christmas of 1983, the senator, who had vilified blacks for his entire political life, had charmed thousands of black voters in South Carolina with new sewers in black communities, support for food stamps, and other scraps from the political pork barrel. Thurmond's efforts paid off as blacks failed to mount a challenge to his candidacy.

"These unconscionable maligners have tried to represent to the people that I favor the repeal of the poll tax making it possible for Negroes to participate in governmental affairs. This is the biggest lie that has been uttered against me in this campaign. I want to make it absolutely impossible for the Negro to vote . . . and thus guarantee white supremacy."

—Mississippi Senator Theodore Bilbo (1940)

• *Sen. Thad Cochran   Republican   Mississippi   Term Expires: 1990*

Thad Cochran represented Mississippi's Fourth Congressional District in the House for three terms before he was elected to the Senate in 1978. Adept at playing the politics of closet Jim Crow, Cochran has always treated black leaders with courtesy, has actively campaigned for black votes, has listened to the appeals of black constituents, and has even appointed blacks to his staff. In 1978, Cochran boasted that he had even learned the "soul handshake."[12] But his voting record is hard-core status quo for blacks. In 1973, Cochran opposed the position taken by the Congressional Black Caucus on all but one of forty-one roll call votes important to blacks. Despite the fact that he represented a congressional district with a black population greater than 40 percent, he opposed the Humphrey-Hawkins full employment bill, the Legal Services Corporation, public jobs programs, funds for education, public housing appropriations, and the District of Columbia voting representation amendment. Even prior to the Reagan presidency, Cochran, who represents the state with the highest poverty level in the country, was an ardent supporter of cutting budgets for food stamps, welfare, health care, and jobs programs.

Senator Cochran is an historical accident. Ironically, he owes his incumbency to the political efforts of Charles Evers, the black mayor of Fayette. In the 1978 election, Evers ran as an independent and pulled enough votes away from the Democratic nominee to allow Cochran to win with only 45 percent of the total vote. The racial polarity that has been the bane of the Democratic party in Mississippi was largely dissipated by Governor William F. Winter, who, in 1982, campaigned hard for black candidates throughout the state. However, Winter's campaign for the Senate never got off the ground and Cochran won handily.

"The Voting Rights Act allowed people with no more intelligence and not much more education than a six-year-old to vote."

—South Carolina Senator Strom Thurmond (1972)

• *Sen. Jesse Helms   Republican   North Carolina   Term Expires: 1990*

Once a solitary voice from the backwaters of the radical right, Republican Senator Jesse Helms of North Carolina, who Anthony Lewis has called the "meanest man in the United States Senate," has become an impressive force in government. Few senators on the Hill have shown greater contempt for the aspirations of black people. In the tradition of all die-hard segregationists, Helms has used states'-rights rhetoric to camouflage his stand against all initiatives aimed at improving the status and opportunities of Negro-Americans. In public statements, Helms still treats Negro voters as amusing but inconsequential pests.

His 1984 opponent, Democratic Governor James B. Hunt, was the strongest vote-getter in recent North Carolina history, a skilled politician, and controlled the strongest political machine in the South. Two-thirds of all voters in North Carolina are Democrats.

UNSEAT RACIAL CONSERVATIVES IN CONGRESS

"But you know and I know what's the best way to keep the nigger from voting. You do it the night before the election. I don't have to tell you any more than that. Redblooded men know what I mean."

—Senator Theodore Bilbo (1946)

The results of the 1978 election indicated that Helms was not popular with voters generally and should have been vulnerable in 1984. In 1978, Helms faced a weak Democratic opponent, outspent him 28 to 1, and was still able to muster only 54 percent of the total vote. It was thought that a well-financed Democratic campaign in 1984, by Hunt, would oust Helms from the Senate. However, Helms benefited from Reagan's huge win in North Carolina and held on to defeat Hunt by a narrow margin. In 1990, a nonpresidential election year, Helms could be in for a tough fight if the 850,000 eligible black voters can be mobilized into a unified voting bloc.

Alliances should be made with other interest groups that would also like to see Helms sent into retirement. Helms has consistently opposed measures favored by organized labor and environmental groups. As a staunch opponent of the ERA and abortion, Helms has angered women's groups. These special interests should be willing to support efforts to defeat Helms, but blacks, as 20 percent of the North Carolina electorate, must lead the fight.

Perhaps more than any other member of the Senate, Helms is the most highly visible and outspoken opponent of black interests. Unfortunately, some elements of the New Right movement in the United States have encouraged the belief among some younger politicians that political hay can be made by reviving old-fashioned "nigger politics." A successful campaign to defeat Helms would thoroughly scotch this political trend.

"Tell your brother that when I get Cox, he gets the nigger."

—Sen. James Eastland informing Robert F. Kennedy of his desire to have his former college roommate, Harold Cox, appointed to the federal bench in return for Eastland's approval of President Kennedy's nomination of Thurgood Marshall to the U.S. Circuit Court of Appeals (1961)

• *Sen. John Warner   Republican   Virginia   Term Expires: 1990*

Elected to the Senate in 1978, John Warner is an improvement over his predecessor, Senator William Scott, who once proclaimed that "the only reason we need ZIP codes is because niggers can't read." [13] In contrast, Warner makes a pointed effort to consult with black leaders, has blacks on his Senate staff, and provides generous constituent service to minorities in Virginia. But this should not mislead anyone as to his stand on black issues. Warner has been a consistent opponent of strong voting rights legislation. The Senator's position on racial progress is best illustrated by his performance as Secretary of the Navy in the Nixon administration when, by his own admission, he attempted to slow the integration of the Navy. During the summer of 1981, Warner recommended that the White House pick the next three Virginian federal judges from a list of thirteen white males, ending a three-month search that placed special emphasis on finding women and blacks.

Warner's election in 1978 was something of a fluke. After losing the GOP nomination, Warner was placed on the November ballot when the Republican candidate was killed in a plane crash. In the general election, the well-financed Warner was able to squeak through by less than 5,000 votes out of a total of 1.2 million cast. Black voters, who comprise over 17 percent of the electorate in Virginia, gave 91 percent of their votes to Warner's opponent, Andrew Miller. If blacks had been able to increase their turnout rate by only one percent, Warner would have been defeated.

Defeating Warner will be a difficult task for black voters, particularly since the Democratic party has not been able to find a strong nominee to run against him.

"The Ku Klux Klan is needed today as never before and I am anxious to see its rebirth in West Virginia. . . . It is necessary that the order be promoted immediately and in every state in the union."

—Letter written on April 8, 1946 by the current
Minority Leader of the U.S. Senate,
Robert C. Byrd of West Virginia

• *Rep. Jamie Whitten*   *Democrat*   *Mississippi*   *First District*

After forty years of service, Congressman Jamie Whitten is both a cagey politician and a seasoned segregationist. Whitten's social and racial views are illustrated by his 1972 statement that "all welfare families want is cola and candy." [14]

In 1978, Whitten was in line to assume the chairmanship of the powerful House Appropriations Committee, but there was much speculation that the liberal Democratic House leadership would attempt to deny him the post. As a result, Whitten's voting record moved dramatically toward the center, and he was able to assume the chairmanship without significant opposition. The next year, with his leadership position assured, Whitten ended his flirtation with soul, as well as his favors for the Black Caucus.

Whitten's long-standing opposition to black concerns includes voting against the Civil Rights Acts of 1957, 1960, and 1964, and the Voting Rights Act of 1965. In recent years, Whitten has supported efforts to prohibit school busing, to reduce appropriations for the U.S. Civil Rights Commission, and to prevent the Internal Revenue Service from investigating the tax-exempt status of southern private schools that exclude blacks.

Although they comprise 23 percent of the electorate, blacks in Whitten's district in northern Mississippi are not politically organized. Further complicating any effort to oust Whitten is the fact that as chairman of the House Appropriations Committee he will be able to manipulate black voters through his control of federal funds in his district.

"No more taxes. Limit spending. Put the niggers back to work."

—Connecticut State Representative Russell J. Reynolds, 1980, responding to a United Press International survey on state taxes

---

• *Rep. Dan Daniel* *Democrat* *Virginia* *Fifth District*

The last time Representative Dan Daniel of Virginia faced an opponent in either a primary or a general election was 1970. His ability to fend off any election challenge is remarkable in view of the facts that median family income in his district is about half the average in the suburban counties in the northern part of the state, that the average level of education is only nine years, and that he has compiled an extremely negative voting record on issues of importance to minorities and the poor. Daniel's attentiveness to constituent casework for blacks and whites appears to be his major preoccupation in Congress; he offered only one piece of legislation during the 1979 session.

It appears that Daniel's black constituents, who comprise close to 22 percent of the total electorate, may be largely unaware of his negative voting record and therefore judge his performance solely on the individual services his office provides. In fact, Daniel has opposed black interests to as great a degree as any Democrat with a comparably large black constituency. In one year, 1979, Daniel voted for a constitutional amendment to prohibit busing as well as for proposals to cut spending for food stamps, and against the African Development Fund and appropriations for the Departments of Labor and HEW. Daniel also voted to prevent the removal of tax-exempt status for segregated private schools, to limit affirmative action in education, to limit the civil rights responsibilities of health care facilities, against the creation of a national holiday to commemorate Martin Luther King, Jr., and against a fuel purchase assistance plan for the poor. In a 1979 survey of Congressional Black Caucus positions, Daniel supported the Caucus position on only one of eighteen votes.[15]

Organized labor may be an important ally of groups that would like to remove Daniel from Congress. Daniel's rural Virginia district is dominated by the largely nonunionized textile industry. Daniel has routinely scored very low on AFL-CIO surveys of congressional voting performance.

"All welfare families want is cola and candy."

—Mississippi Congressman Jamie Whitten
(1972)

• *Rep. William Dickinson Republican Alabama Second District*

The racial views of Congressman William Dickinson of Alabama are best illustrated by his charge on the floor of the House in 1965 that the Selma civil rights marchers were engaged in sexual orgies.[16] Attacks on blacks have been muted in recent years, but Dickinson continues to oppose the interests of his black constituents, who comprise about 27 percent of the eligible voters in his district.

Dickinson has been a passionate defender of racial segregation. In 1979 Dickinson introduced measures to prevent the IRS from withholding funds from private schools that discriminate on the basis of race, to prohibit school busing to achieve racial integration, and to curb the use of food stamps.

Dickinson has had some tough reelection battles in the past but has always managed to obtain a majority. In 1976, the number of eligible blacks who did not bother to vote was more than two and a half times Dickinson's margin of victory. In 1978, Dickinson won by an even smaller margin. But in 1980, just when it seemed that his popularity was on the decline, Dickinson benefited from the Reagan landslide and won 61 percent of the vote. In 1982, he barely survived a challenge in the general election. There are over 105,000 eligible black voters in the Second District, considerably more than Dickinson's total vote in 1982.

"The mental level of those people renders them incapable of suffrage."

—Senator James Eastland (1947)

• *Rep. Floyd Spence   Republican   South Carolina   Second District*

Floyd Spence of Lexington, South Carolina, a suburb of Columbia, the state capital, is a traditional "turn-back-the-clock" southern politician, elected from a district where over one-third of the eligible voters are black. Spence has opposed food stamps, community development grants, subsidized housing, increased revenue-sharing for poor rural areas, and various jobs programs. Moreover, Spence is a staunch opponent of easy voter registration and the District of Columbia voting representation amendment.

Due to overwhelming support from the predominantly white suburbs of Columbia, Spence has been able to survive a number of tough challenges over the years. But Spence can be beaten. In 1974, a black Democrat, Matthew Perry, now a federal judge, won 42 percent of the vote against Spence in the general election. In 1982, another black candidate attracted 41 percent of the vote. Slightly increased registration and turnout rates by black voters could elect a black congressman from South Carolina's Second District.

"In South Carolina, Negroes are voting in large numbers. Of course, they are not so well qualified as are the white people."

—Senator Strom Thurmond (1957)

• *Rep. G.V. Montgomery   Democrat   Mississippi   Third District*

Few representatives of the courtly southern tradition remain in Congress today. G.V. "Sonny" Montgomery, however, is a relic of the Old South with a voting record to match. Over 40 percent of Montgomery's constituents were black in 1980, many of them residing in some of the poorest rural counties of Mississippi. Yet Montgomery has steadfastly voted against nearly every measure of importance to minorities: welfare reform, food stamps, legal aid for the poor, busing, public jobs programs, attempts to limit mortgage redlining, housing and community development appropriations, and the District of Columbia voting representation amendment.

Many blacks were removed from his district during the 1980 reapportionment process. Yet, there are still nearly 100,000 eligible black voters in Congressman Montgomery's district. Montgomery frequently runs for election unopposed or with only token opposition. To defeat Montgomery, blacks will have to back the candidacy of a moderate white Democrat already popular in the district and must be prepared to deliver a massive bloc of black votes to the challenger.

"I am just as much opposed to Booker Washington as a voter, with all his Anglo-Saxon reenforcements, as I am to the coconut-headed, chocolate-covered, typical little coon, Andy Dotson, who blacks my shoes every morning. Neither is fit to perform the supreme function of citizenship."

—Mississippi Senator James K. Vardaman (1910)

• *Rep. Bill Nichols*　　　*Democrat*　　　*Alabama*　　　*Third District*

Congressman Bill Nichols has not faced a serious challenge at the polls since 1972. Although blacks make up more than a quarter of Nichols' constituents, they have made little or no attempt to remove him from office despite his opposition to black economic, social, and political interests on nearly every vote. Nichols has voted to end enforcement of minority hiring rules on federally financed construction projects and to cut the funding for the Office of Economic Opportunity, the Civil Rights Commission, and the food stamp program. He has voted to reduce the level of revenue-sharing funds targeted for poor rural areas, to drastically cut appropriations for HHS, to exempt health care facilities from civil rights responsibilities, and to prevent the Legal Services Corporation from participating in busing cases. Nichols rounds out a consistent antiblack voting record by opposition to federal jobs programs, the District of Columbia voting representation amendment and the Humphrey-Hawkins full employment initiative.

Nichols will be difficult to defeat because of great popularity in his district.

Conclusion

It must be conceded, as Senator John Danforth has observed, that the first priority of every politician is to get reelected, and the second priority is to let nothing get in the way of the first. But the fact that a shiver goes down the spine of most lawmakers when unexpected challengers appear should not lead to exaggerated notions of the potential of black voting power. Campaigns against bigots who hold public office are not likely to cause them to become overnight defenders of poor blacks. Nor are these campaigns likely to cause other dyed-in-the-wool segregationists to stop equivocating on civil rights or to mount strong commitments to racial integration. Yet, a series of well-planned and -publicized challenges is likely to erase or modify a number of the congressional votes that today are an important part of the political burden carried by the black race in the United States.

Here are some suggested guidelines for mounting campaigns to defeat racial hardliners and other politicians who exploit racial bigotry for political advantage:

- Concentrate campaign efforts in congressional districts where the black vote is a very large percentage of the electorate—more than 30 percent—e.g., Floyd Spence's district in South Carolina or Webb Franklin's in Mississippi.

- Mobilize the black vote by selecting politicians who have committed the political blunder of *publicly declared* racism. Make racial bigotry—not political conservatism—the critical campaign issue.

- Use modern media techniques of direct mail and newspaper, radio, and television advertising to show black and white voters why the congressman is a *public* embarrassment. Publicize the candidate's opposition to fundamental decency and fairness.

- In each political season, concentrate efforts and resources on a single candidate, one who is highly visible, politically vulnerable, and who symbolizes the rearguard defense of racial segregation.

- Choose a district or state where there are other powerful constituencies with reasons for getting rid of the congressman, and make the necessary political alliances to defeat the candidate.

- In most cases, the greatest enemy is not the congressman but *black voter apathy*. Combat this by mounting voter-registration drives, exploiting the candidate's racial attitudes, and by running black candidates for local offices.

- Occasionally campaign against a well-known symbol of racism whether or not there are large numbers of black voters in the incumbent's constituency. Enlist the support of liberals and other activists. Devote an entire year to exposing the racial attitudes and voting record of the prime opponent.
- Work heavily on the powerful theme that the candidate doesn't represent the people, but represents instead the forces of hate, bigotry, and violence.

Note: The quotes interspersed throughout this section have the following sources:

- Senator Ellison Smith's comments at the 1936 Democratic Convention were recorded in *The New York Times,* June 25, 1936, p. 1.
- Senator Byrd's pronouncement about the inability to take the slums out of the people is documented in *The New York Times Magazine,* Feb. 28, 1971, p. 9.
- Senator Theodore Bilbo's remarks during the 1940 election campaign appear in Steven F. Lawson, *Black Ballots* (New York: Columbia University Press, 1976), p. 99.
- Strom Thurmond's estimate of the effects of the Voting Rights Act was reported in *Ralph Nader's Congress Project-Citizens Look at Congress—Strom Thurmond* (Grossman Publishers, 1972), p. 9.
- Senator Theodore Bilbo's manly advice on how best to keep blacks from voting is reported in Steven F. Lawson, *Black Ballots,* p. 100.
- The statement of Senator Eastland regarding the appointment of Thurgood Marshall to the federal bench is reported in Jason Berry, *Amazing Grace* (New York: Saturday Review Press, 1973), p. 175.
- Senator Byrd's advocacy of the Ku Klux Klan is reported in Neal R. Pierce, *The Border South States* (New York: W.W. Norton Co., 1975).
- The comment by Connecticut State Representative Russell Reynolds was reported by *The New York Times,* Feb. 1, 1980, p. A1.
- Representative Jamie Whitten's statement regarding the buying habits of welfare families appeared in *Ralph Nader's Congress Project—Citizens Look at Congress—Jamie Whitten,* p. 8.
- Senator Eastland's views on black voting appear in Robert Sherill, *Gothic Politics of the Deep South* (New York: Grossman Publishers, 1968), p. 211.
- The opinion expressed by Senator Thurmond concerning the qualification of black voters was made on the floor of the Senate on August 28, 1957.
- Mississippi Senator James Vardaman's opposition to black voting rights in the early 1900s appeared in Paul Lewinson, *Race, Class and Party* (New York: Universal Library, 1965), pp. 84-85.

In Presidential Elections Concentrate Efforts to Increase Black Voter Activity and Political Strength in the Nine Major Swing States

"Nothing causes a prince to be so much esteemed as great enterprises and giving proof of prowess."

—Niccolo Machiavelli (1513)

IT IS A TRUISM THAT POWER DISSIPATES when it is dispersed over many fronts. Power builds, in turn, and is most effective, when it is concentrated at specific pressure points. The propositions hold true particularly when the pressure points are either inherently weak or defended by a *divided major-ity*. This rule about the workings of power exposes a number of political openings for blacks. In future elections, blacks will be in a position to build much greater overall strength simply by *concentrating efforts in selected states where the major parties have equal strength, and where because of the way votes are allocated by the Electoral College system, disproportionate black political leverage may be achieved.*

In each of five states—Alabama, Georgia, Louisiana, Mississippi, and South Carolina—blacks make up between 22 percent and 31 percent of the eligible voters. In another twelve—Arkansas, Delaware, Florida, Illinois, Maryland, Michigan, New Jersey, New York, North Carolina, Tennessee, Texas, and Virginia—the black electorate ranges from 10 to 19 percent of the total. The large and growing number of eligible black voters in these seventeen states makes them important playing grounds for black politics.

The political window is wide open in those states where GOP and Democratic voters are evenly split and, in consequence, where neither of the major parties is dominant. In Georgia, for example, 24 percent of the total electorate is black, but the Democratic party has been so strong that black voter influence has been negligible in general elections. Much the same has been true in Alabama, Arkansas, and the Carolinas. In Louisiana, black influence in general elections is sharply reduced by the state's unique open primary system. For minority voters to exert significant political influence in these states, they must unite prior to the primaries and be prepared to swing their votes to the Democratic primary candidate who shows the greatest promise of voting favorably on black concerns.

In several other southern states, however, black political power can effectively show its muscle in both the primaries and general elections. With the emergence of a stronger Republican party in many southern states, it has become more critical than in the past for southern Democrats to hold black voters. At the same time, southern Republicans have suddenly acquired an interest in the black vote, a vote they had written off in the days when they stood virtually no chance of winning elections in the South. Suddenly, both parties in the South are intensely courting blacks. In Mississippi, a state

Black political efforts should be concentrated in electoral vote-rich states where most presidential elections are won.

Large black voter populations may be a controlling force in nine states which have nearly 90 percent of the electoral votes needed to win the presidency.

Note: The swing states control 241 votes; 270 votes are needed for election. Electoral vote totals have been revised to reflect reapportionment after the 1980 census.

long dominated by the Democratic party, the GOP has made a remarkable comeback. Two of the state's five congressional districts are in Republican hands. Republican Gil Carmichael narrowly missed winning the 1975 gubernatorial election. In 1978, Thad Cochran, the first Mississippi Republican ever publicly elected to the United States Senate, was sworn into office, winning the seat because black independent Charles Evers pulled enough votes from the Democratic candidate to throw the election to Cochran. The important point is not that Evers lost the election but that his presence in the contest shifted the final outcome—a lesson that will undoubtedly not be lost on future Democratic hopefuls.

In Virginia, too, the resurgence of the Republican party has strengthened the position of blacks. After years of domination by Harry Byrd's Democratic machine, Virginia, the only state of the Old Confederacy to vote for Gerald Ford in 1976, has developed the strongest Republican party in the South. On the local level, Democrats continue to win a great majority of elected positions, but the GOP has come to dominate contests for congressional and state offices. Both U.S. senators and six of the state's ten congressmen were Republicans in 1985. In 1981, the son-in-law of former President Johnson, Charles Robb, was the first Democrat in Virginia to win the governor's chair in the past sixteen years. Due to the great strength of the GOP in Virginia, the power of the black electorate—about 16.5 percent of the voting population—has now become important to all the candidates. Many Republican candidates actively seek out black support because black voter turnout rates are very high in the state. In the 1976 presidential election, over 75 percent of the registered black voters participated—the highest turnout rate for blacks in the United States. Ninety percent of the registered blacks in Virginia's Fourth Congressional District went to the polls, a truly remarkable performance.

The Nine Swing States: Blacks Hold Power at the Margin

In presidential elections, blacks must concentrate their efforts in the big and heavily weighted electoral vote states with a significant minority population. Texas is the prime example. No Democratic candidate in this century has won the presidency without carrying Texas's electoral votes.

The potential political leverage of blacks is huge in three electoral vote-rich key states in the North whose electoral votes dominate any national election. These states are New York, Ohio, and Pennsylvania. If blacks were to do nothing nationwide but organize a large swing vote in these three states—which together provide nearly *one-third of the electoral votes necessary to win the presidency*—blacks would find themselves with immense negotiating influence over the presidential hopefuls in both major parties.

Expanding further the centers of potential black political power, the leverage of the "winner-take-all" effect of the Electoral College causes us to look to nine key states: California, Florida, Illinois, Michigan, New Jersey,

New York, Ohio, Pennsylvania, and Texas. Both major parties are strong in each of these states, which provides a good chance of success for black efforts to tip an election one way or the other. *These nine states alone control 241 of the 270 electoral votes needed to win the presidency.* Other than Richard Nixon in 1968, no President since Eisenhower has won an election without carrying half of the states in the industrial heartland: Illinois, Michigan, New York, New Jersey, Ohio, and Pennsylvania. If blacks can muster enough votes to swing half of these states to the black preferred candidate, they are likely to defeat any but the most extraordinarily popular presidential candidate.

The multiplier effect of concentrated political activity in the vote-rich states that control elections would increase manyfold if blacks were successful in the secondary strategy of forging a bloc-voting alliance with Hispanic-Americans. In fact, if the large concentrations of Hispanic voters in California, New York, and Texas were aligned with blacks in those states, the combination could virtually control the 112 electoral votes belonging to these states, or over *40 percent of the total needed for victory in a national election.*

It is interesting to contemplate the political consequences if blacks were to adopt a strategic policy of mass migrations to the key states. Black political power would increase in astronomical proportions if many black persons in the United States simply pulled up stakes and moved to one of the nine key states rich in electoral votes. The unlikelihood of this happening is exceeded only by the certainty that the Electoral College system would be changed if it did happen. But the image of a black mass migration to these states concentrates the mind on the important political leverage that minority groups possess as a result of the current Electoral College voting system. The idea gives sharp focus to our view of the vast unused strength blacks and Hispanics already hold in the major electoral vote-rich states.

Run Black Favorite Sons to Barter
at Nominating Conventions

"We must think and act anew. We must disenthrall ourselves."

—Abraham Lincoln

IN THE SPRING OF 1980, Mayor Coleman Young of Detroit shrewdly assessed the political dilemma facing most blacks: "After you get through booing [President Carter], who the hell are you going to vote for?" At election time, more often than other American citizens, blacks find themselves facing two unacceptable choices. One choice is the Republican candidate, backed by a political party fundamentally opposed to most of the political measures most blacks believe they need to improve their economic status. In most cases, the other choice will be a Democrat who is long on liberal rhetoric, and who professes a profound interest in advancing the black political agenda. But in all likelihood the Democratic candidate will, in practice, substantially ignore black political interests while attending to other more powerful and important constituencies within the Democratic party. In practical terms, the two-party system has evolved an effective and constitutional system for disenfranchising most blacks—almost as effective as the all-white primaries of a generation ago.

There is one means of at least partial escape from the orphan status conferred on blacks by the two-party system. Blacks can win greater influence within the Democratic party by running black favorite son candidates in state primaries and thereby confronting the Democratic leadership with a large bloc of black delegate strength. The black favorite son campaign strategy could deliver as many as 500 black delegates to almost any national Democratic convention; an alliance with Hispanic-Americans would add another 300 delegates or more. The aim, of course, is not to elect the black or the Hispanic candidate. The purpose is to exchange the favorite son candidate's votes for concessions from one of the mainstream candidates. This strategy would confer substantial bargaining power on blacks within the Democratic party and give minority groups a major source of political strength that they do not now have. The major candidates would come to terms with blacks in a manner never experienced before.

The current black strategy which weakly endeavors to bargain with either an already-nominated Democratic presidential candidate or a sitting Democratic President is futile. Once the primaries and conventions are over and the Democratic candidate has been selected, the ball game is also over for blacks. The Democratic party and its candidates will not respond to black interests unless and until blacks are organized to send off a few long shots across the bow before and during the national nominating convention. This means that blacks must make a total break with their traditional practice of taking a back seat during political primaries.

How much can be gained by controlling a sizable number of delegates is best exemplified by the political strategy of Mayor Richard Daley of Chicago. From 1956 to 1976, every Democrat knew that at each nominating convention Daley would control 100 or more delegates. All Democratic presidential aspirants took pains not to offend the powerful mayor because they knew he had the strength to make or break a candidacy. Even if the convention turned out to be so one-sided that Daley's 100 votes didn't mean

BLACK POLITICAL POWER COMES OF AGE: RUNNING TO BARTER INSTEAD OF TO WIN

While the black favorite son strategy may drain off some primary votes from liberal candidates, it provides overwhelming compensating advantages to black people in their efforts to build political strength and to influence the policies of the people who govern the United States.

- The favorite son strategy enables blacks to escape the "lesser-of-two-evils" dilemma of most general elections by forcing Democratic party regulars to negotiate with black interests during primary seasons and, in hotly contested primary contests, may even confer swing-vote power status on black voters.

- The nomination of black candidates generates massive increases in black voter registrations and political activity, leading in time to the election of many more black congressmen, mayors, and other black public officials.

- The "go-to-the-convention-and-negotiate" strategy creates black bargaining agents with the power to broker blacks voters' support for white political candidates who agree in turn to campaign for black candidates in congressional, mayoralty, and local elections.

- The favorite son strategy tends to produce indigestable blocs of black-controlled delegates at Democratic national nominating conventions, with the result that black people are more likely to have a major "say" on important votes over rules, credentials, and party platforms as well as on party nominations.

- Black favorite son candidates deflect media coverage away from the standard economic calamities of inflation, strikes, and unemployment and focus national attention instead on racial inequality, school segregation, ghetto poverty, and other black issues largely ignored by television, newspapers, and other media.

- The "running-to-barter" strategy provides black voters with a permanent political mechanism to punish white candidates who consistently win office with the help of black voters and later repudiate their prior commitments to black political goals.

- The appearance of strong black favorite sons breaks down racial stereotypes by displaying black candidates as serious political candidates for mainstream political posts rather than as second-class contenders for backwater positions as chiefs of poverty and ghetto communities.

- The black favorite son strategy represents an important structural advance in the evolution of black political power from the primitive stage of street protest to the more sophisticated world of elective politics.

anything, every Democrat interested in making a run for the presidency in the *next* election was obliged to court Daley. Politicians could never forget that in four years' time Daley might once again hold the balance of power through the 100 or more cards that he could always play.

Simple mathematics tells us that if Daley could derive so much strength from 100 delegates, the control of 400 or 500 delegates would give blacks truly important negotiating status. Facing the near certainty of a black favorite son effort, incumbent Presidents seeking a second term would have to think twice before deserting full employment, open housing, and school desegregation initiatives. Democratic presidential hopefuls would be far more inclined than they are at present to make commitments to the black agenda. Established power brokers would listen to blacks, and appoint them to chairs in campaign organizations, despite the fact that at that particular moment blacks were not delivering any political heat.

Even in uncontested primary campaigns, as in the case of a popular President assured of renomination, blacks must still run their favorite sons in Democratic primaries to show strength for the next election, when the black delegate voting bloc may count. Without regard to the question of influencing nomination choices, it is always important for blacks to maintain an effective convention voice in matters such as rules and procedures, credentials, platform, and, most important, the choice of the Vice-President.

Where the black favorite son candidate has a broad grassroots support among black voters (as was the case of Jesse Jackson's candidacy in the 1984 election), the power of the candidate to broker a convention becomes much stronger if he or she refuses to rule out the possibility of running as an independent candidate in the general election. This "win or ruin" posture or bluff is necessary to persuade Democratic party leaders to come to terms with the black vote. If, on the other hand, Democratic party regulars are convinced that the "scorched earth" tactic is mere posturing and that the black candidate will necessarily rejoin the Democratic ticket for the general election, the incentive to bargain with black interests is greatly reduced. In the early months of the 1984 presidential campaign, Jesse Jackson effectively confounded Democratic councils by nurturing his image as an egotistical and perhaps somewhat irrational mugwump. At the same time, Jackson's influence at the convention was undermined by a number of factors: his attack on Jewish interests, his criticism of the United States from abroad, Democratic concerns about defections of southern whites to the GOP, and the party's firm hold on the loyalty of Coretta King. Yet, the perception of Jackson as a possible spoiler was always a factor that tended to increase his bargaining position.

As in other instances where blacks leave the Democratic party fold and seek power in their own right, the favorite son tactic will be opposed on the ground that its delegate-gathering objectives will be overwhelmed by the countereffects of white voter or delegate backlash. This position, however, carries little weight. The favorite son strategy does not require black favorite sons to attract even one white vote. If blacks present a united front and vote for their favorite sons in the various state primaries and caucuses, they will win their share of delegates no matter what whites do. Moreover, any threat of white backlash will eventually ebb away as organized black political power—like labor voting power—becomes just another major special interest with which the Democratic party must come to terms in order to build the winning coalition it needs in order to win.

The favorite son strategy should not be confined to presidential elections. Black candidates may play influential roles as stalking horses in primary elections for senator, governor, and congressman, as well as in contests for other state and local offices. In voting districts where blacks are a majority, a black candidate enters the primary in order to win. The same is true also in many regions where blacks are a significant minority, perhaps 25 to 35 percent of the total population, particularly if there are several candidates who will split the white vote. In a great many more state assembly and congressional districts, however, blacks are too small a part of the population to elect black officeholders. Yet, in these districts blacks still comprise a large enough share of the electorate to swing many primary elections to the candidate of their choice. To be sure, in primaries where an incumbent is unopposed or faces only token opposition, there will be little blacks can do, because the favorite son strategy doesn't work without the presence of two or more viable white candidates competing for the black vote. If no candidate is willing to come to terms with black voters, the black favorite son may even remain in the race and act as a spoiler to ensure that in the next election the main candidates will actively bargain for black votes.

The realpolitik of the favorite son strategy may be looked at against the background of the 1980 presidential election. By running favorite sons, blacks could have seriously threatened Carter in the nominating contest where he was seriously challenged by Ted Kennedy. It is even possible that had blacks used the favorite son strategy they might have tipped the scale to Kennedy, in many ways a far superior candidate for blacks than Carter was. In a more sophisticated move, they might later have shifted their vote to independent John Anderson and intensified the pressure on President Carter, who was already losing liberal voters to Anderson.

A similar lapsed opportunity to force major candidates to come to terms with the black vote was presented in the 1984 presidential primaries when black political regulars undercut their then emerging political strength by an early repudiation of the candidacy of Jesse Jackson. The automatic black lineup behind Mondale bought nothing for black people. In the spring of the campaign year, neither Walter Mondale nor Gary Hart—always keeping an anxious eye on the conservative vote of boll weevil southern Democrats— had made favorable commitments to the black agenda. Yet, black mayors in the South and other black Democratic party loyalists rushed to endorse candidate Walter Mondale who had made political promises to virtually every special-interest group *except* black people. A few months later, orphan political status was solidly reestablished when blacks divided their votes in the Alabama and Georgia Democratic primaries. Mondale might indeed have been the superior candidate in a final convention selection, and blacks could have given him their support at that time, but no good purpose was served by the early rush by black voters to back Mondale and thereby harm their chances to establish black political power.

To achieve maximum convention bargaining power, black favorite sons must always aim for a brokered convention. To that end, black political solidarity must be maintained throughout the primary season. Defections from the consensus must be treated as serious breaches of loyalty to the cause of black progress. Successful delivery of a brokered convention demands that blacks *deny the mainstream candidates access to the black vote in all primaries preceding the convention.*

Black political power does not establish its credibility as a political force in current and future contests unless it displays delegate unity. This means that the vast majority of black delegates at the convention must at least temporarily stake out independence from the Democratic party leadership by conferring their first presidential nominating ballot vote on the black favorite son.

Use Black Political Strength to Bargain for Positions in the Inner Circles of the Executive Branch

"[N]o people can be free who themselves do not constitute an essential part of the ruling element of the country in which they live."

—Martin Delaney (1852)

THERE ARE PEOPLE in the United States who *decide* things. They decide, for example, whether it is time for the government to regulate or to deregulate.

They decide whether it is time for applications of supply-side economics or for the pursuit of more traditional Keynesian income policies. They decide whether to actively deal with problems of racial justice or to pursue policies of "business as usual" that ignore the economic problems of minority groups. They decide whether the country is to be put on a war footing or is to spend its resources on bread and butter. They decide whether the legal establishment of the country will oppose race-conscious remedies or get behind remedial measures to eliminate the damage of prior discrimination.

Traditionally, the people who decide things are members of a society's elite. They hold the highest posts in large corporations. They chair large foundations. They head the nation's prestigious educational institutions. They are the senior partners in influential law and investment banking firms. And, most particularly, they are the senior voices in government. As we have seen, blacks are almost never counted among the people who decide things in the United States.

By all the standard and accepted political means, blacks must prepare for, seek out, and win a critical mass of these high posts in government, industry, education, and the foundation world, where important decisions are made. When blacks achieve significant representation in the so-called establishment, it is very likely that then, too, economic differences between the races will diminish and blacks as a group will begin to approach economic equality with whites. When blacks do all the important things and make all the critical decisions that others in our society do, the *social* differences in the races, too, will almost certainly take care of themselves. It is possible that a very large black underclass will still persist, but the chances are much less likely once a powerful black elite has a strong and visible presence in every corner of American society.

Professor Michael de Haven Newsom of Howard University Law School has expressed the importance of this objective:

> "Only a strong, vibrant, confident, well-educated and self-assured black elite can guarantee that racial equality ever will be reached. . . . There must be a move to insinuate blacks in every aspect of American society. . . . There will be racial equality only when large numbers of black people can and do tell white people what to do." [17]

Obviously, there are many barriers that prevent blacks from moving into positions where things are decided—unequal education, the preference of whites to choose other whites for high positions, the discomfort that establishment whites feel in the presence of blacks. Other inhibiting forces include the loss of status whites feel when blacks are named to posts above or equal to them, and the absence of blacks from the old-boy selection network through which elites are traditionally selected. In recent years, moreover, whites have established further rules of racial etiquette—as such not considered racially discriminatory—which nevertheless regulate and retard the movement of black people into the higher reaches of government power.

As mentioned earlier, the practice of institutional tokenism is a formidable obstacle to the advancement of blacks. Since the late 1950s, when black people first began to appear in corporate and government boardrooms, tokenism has been the controlling rule in the making of black government appointments. The traditional candidate's promise to name more blacks to his administration commonly translates, after the election, into appointments of blacks to an array of unimportant protocol posts. Position opportunities abound for black ambassadors to African nations and/or black Cabinet or sub-Cabinet staffers who, in effect, act as ambassadors to domestic blacks. Agencies and departments such as HHS and HUD, where little policy is made and limited discretionary funds are available, usually find appointed blacks at the very top. The Minority Business Development Agency and the Equal Employment Opportunity Commission, neither of which has been vested by Congress with broad regulatory or adjudication powers, invariably are headed by blacks. But the inner circle of top White House advisers is and always has been completely white. Line authority in government, wherever found, is almost always reserved for white people.

The government practice of racial job stereotyping, and its companion policy, tokenism, has a profound and injurious effect on how whites perceive blacks and how blacks perceive themselves. For example, black government officials may make occasional appearances on influential television programs such as *Meet the Press* or *Issues and Answers,* but they never appear on these programs as experts on issues of monetary policy, defense, or energy regulation. The reason for this is not because there are no blacks who are expert on these issues, but rather because whites almost never consider appointing blacks to government posts requiring an expertise that is not related to being a black person. Hence, the racially stereotyped competence expectation, in which blacks are never consulted either in government or on television—except on issues of race, poverty, sports, and relations with Third World nations—defines and limits how blacks and whites think about each other's skills and places in the world.

In addition to using all available means to educate, sponsor, and finance black experts and elites, there are political steps that blacks can take to integrate the team at the top. First, the Congressional Black Caucus must work toward becoming a clearinghouse, or possibly the bargaining agent, for the appointment of blacks to high government positions. The intellectual position that a President should not be obliged to bargain with anyone over Cabinet and other appointments is a strong one. The difficulty with it is that the practice has always been otherwise. It is well known, for example, that in the first six months of the Reagan Administration, important presidential appointments were months behind schedule simply because of the inability of the White House to clear candidates with a then important conservative power, Senator Jesse Helms of North Carolina.

Black Caucus influence over presidential appointments would tend to undercut the presidential practice of co-opting blacks by appointing them to visible positions in the outer circle of government activity. To break the tokenists' lock on entry to government power, blacks could reach for appointments to more important government posts if they, in common with Senator Helms, became sympathetic to the value of employing a bargaining agent for government appointments. Particularly if the highly educated and influential black elite could be persuaded that collective bargaining on black appointments was desirable for raising the power and repute of blacks, the idea of political negotiation for government positions could win legitimacy for blacks just as has always been the case for whites.

Not only do blacks tend to get appointed to decorative posts, but they also tend to be offered positions where failure is likely because the position carries no powers to use sanctions necessary to produce results. Experienced politicians functioning in sophisticated groups such as the Black Caucus can spot these traps in advance and avoid them. For example, advancing the black bargaining position requires one to avoid appointments to the agencies and commissions that study and report but have no powers to take action. Blacks may take the position that if the government wishes to create an equal opportunity contracting commission and vest it with no regulatory authority, no binding rulemaking powers, no ability to punish lawbreakers—then let whites head it. And let whites accept the abuse and ridicule when its stated objectives fail—as they almost inevitably will. When government power is sincerely interested in intervening on the side of blacks, it will create agencies with the power to take effective action to expand the powers and choices of black people. Until then, it is proposed that blacks should refuse to take part in any charade designed to foster the illusions that blacks have governing authority and that they themselves are responsible for the failure of programs designed to help them.

An important reason for boycotting tokenism is successful resistance to the appointment of manifestly *unqualified* blacks to positions where blacks—because whites assign *collective* traits to the poor performance of *individual* blacks—bring disrepute to blacks generally. Until 1981, there was no record of black groups opposing the appointment of any unqualified black person to a federal government post of even secondary significance. A major break with tradition occurred when President Reagan, in June 1981, named William Bell, a black man, to be chairman of the Equal Employment Opportunity Commission. Bell, a man of little distinction, who had never held a responsible supervisory position, ran into a storm of opposition from black and Hispanic groups. The appointment of Bell failed to be confirmed, despite efforts by the Reagan Administration to divide blacks and Hispanics by passing the word that if Bell was confirmed an Hispanic would be named executive director of the EEOC.[18]

At first glance, it may seem perverse of blacks to refuse to accept ceremonial government appointments when only a few short decades ago the attainment by a black person of virtually any job in Washington that required wearing a suit to work would have been hailed as a significant victory. But the objective of full racial integration—and attendant power-sharing— requires full participation in government, and not simply the appearances of integration, which creates the illusion of full participation. By controlling the types of government positions black people are offered and accept, the force of tokenism as a delaying device may be overturned. Blacks gather strength by refusing to accept ambassadorships to black African nations and by refusing to accept the traditional black seats at HUD and HHS. By declining the proffer of virtually any job whose title includes the words "Human Development," "Welfare," "Community Relations," "Minority Affairs," or "Community Planning," blacks are in a position to make a powerful collective declaration that tokenism is an unacceptable instrument of racial control and place assignment. The refusal is sound political policy even when, as is often the case, it is proposed that the black appointment be made in a televised love fest staged in the White House Rose Garden.

In general, government posts may be placed in three categories of relative authority. At the very top are what we may call the "imperial posts," which carry some of the major powers usually associated with the sovereign. These include the President, the Secretaries of State and Defense, the Attorney General, the Chairman of the Joint Chiefs of Staff, the Directors of the FBI and the CIA, the Chief Justice, the Chairmen of the Federal Reserve Board and the Council of Economic Advisors, the Director of the Office of Management and Budget, the Assistants to the President for National Security Affairs, and the White House Chief of Staff. Below these positions there is a second layer of important posts that confer significant authority on those who hold them but lack the imperial authority that one finds at the very top. These are positions as Cabinet and sub-Cabinet officers and heads of administrative agencies, which in each case exercise some degree of regulatory, command, or adjudicating authority. Finally come the ceremonial posts, which usually offer their incumbents very little authority but often provide considerable glory, status, and public visibility. I have not classified the vice-presidency as one of the imperial posts, but it must be ranked very near, if not at, the top.

What then are the prospects for blacks attaining any of the highest posts in government?

The political expediencies resulting from rapidly mounting black political influence may cause a black person to be nominated to the vice-presidency in the near future. In retrospect, it appears probable that if a black person of national stature had been chosen instead of Senator Robert Dole as the Republican vice-presidential nominee in 1976, President Ford might have attracted enough black votes in states such as Ohio, Texas, Louisiana, and Mississippi to have won the election. Sophisticated voter polling and similar bottom-line calculations of alternative Electoral College outcomes may produce computerized tallies that point unmistakably to the political wisdom of a black vice-presidential candidate. But as long as a large body of white voters holds a low opinion of blacks as a group and fears them when they hold major powers, it appears that the selection of a black running mate would severely affect the electability of the person heading the ticket. The underground would constantly remind undecided voters that Vice-Presidents become *Presidents* when the latter die in office.

A high post that is unlikely to go to a black person for many years is the President's chief of staff. This conclusion is also true of other intimate White House advisers who make up the traditional White House breakfast gatherings. Well into the future, the President's chief of staff, his political point man, his congressional pulse takers, his claim brokers all will be white. Here, the President must have "his own man," a close and trusted friend. Only the passage of a full generation of a fully integrated society— where blacks and whites are brought up together as undifferentiated members of the same educational, neighborhood, and social networks—is likely to produce demographic conditions where there is any statistical probability that a black person will turn out to be a close and trusted associate of the President of the United States.

There are, however, two imperial posts that are not unreasonably beyond the reach of blacks. The first is the office of Attorney General, the chief legal officer of the United States. This post carries power of particular importance to blacks. The Attorney General sets the litigation agenda for the federal government. The Attorney General is highly influential in determining which cases will go to the Supreme Court as well as in selecting who will be appointed to the federal bench. The office of Attorney General has very broad discretionary judgment as to whether the weight of the federal government will be brought to bear on the enforcement of civil rights laws. In effect, the Attorney General's broad authority to delay bringing suits to compel integration, or to delay affirmative-action policies in the courts, gives him a unique degree of control over the nation's timetable for racial integration. Here, then, is a position of great weight and prestige for which hundreds of black judges and lawyers are highly qualified. Here, too, is a post where the nation appears to be psychologically prepared to accept the appointment of a black person. Rumors in early 1977 that Jimmy Carter might appoint a black Attorney General did not seem to ruffle many feathers in Congress.

The position of director of the Office of Management and Budget is another post at the top of government where a black incumbent would contribute in an important way to the powers and prestige of the black race. With approximately 700 employees, OMB is the largest unit in the Executive Office of the President. In many respects, the director of OMB—behind the President himself—holds the second most powerful position in Washington. Because the office possesses life-and-death budgetary power over other government agencies, OMB is in a unique position to press government officials to enforce antidiscrimination laws, to cut off federal subsidies of racially segregated public education, and to impose firm affirmative-action policies on federally regulated industries.

Despite setbacks resulting from the recent election of political conservatives, the long-term trend toward the fuller racial integration of government elites is a powerful one. In due course, the position of Attorney General or director of OMB will go to a black person. This is likely to happen for the same reason it was likely in 1981 that, at last, a woman would be appointed to the Supreme Court. For one overwhelming reason—the politician's desire to win black votes or to disarm their offensive use against one's candidacy—an aspiring presidential candidate will announce his intention, if elected, to appoint a black person to one of these high positions. And the likelihood of this happening is directly proportionate to the strength of the organization of black voters and its perceived ability to influence the outcome of presidential and other elections.

At the high but less than imperial levels of government, blacks have done only slightly better than they have at the highest levels. Throughout American history, only four blacks have served in any of these important posts: Thurgood Marshall as a Justice of the Supreme Court, William T. Coleman as Secretary of Transportation, and Emmett J. Rice and Andrew Brimmer, both of whom have served as Governors of the Federal Reserve Board. It is at this high—but not imperial—level of authority that blacks stand the best chance of making significant inroads in the future through concerted political action. To a large extent, the outcome will depend on the importance future Presidents attach to the issue of integration of government service and whether blacks continue to accept ceremonial appointments and, thereby, let high government off the hook. In this regard, the development by blacks of a vote-threatening political incentive to appoint blacks to high government positions will introduce blacks to new posts for which they have long been qualified and where, at long last, they will share some of the most important powers found in American society.

Reach for Numerical Parity in Holdings of Judicial and Law Enforcement Power

"Whoever has an absolute authority to interpret any law, it is he who is the lawgiver to all intents and purposes."

—Benjamin Hoadley

THE OVERWHELMINGLY WHITE COMPLEXION of the American law enforcement system has been one of the most visible public statements of the presence of racial caste in the United States. In both the North and South, white police officers, sheriffs, district attorneys, and judges were frequently the feared authority figures that enforced racial etiquette requiring blacks to yield access, opportunities, and positions to whites. For this reason, the explicit political goal of placing many more blacks in law enforcement posts has social and psychological implications that transcend the simple objective of equal black participation in jobs, professions, and in government positions. Every time a black person is appointed to the bench or an important law enforcement position, and performs with skill and self-assurance, one more nail is driven into the coffin of the negative race-trait expectation

In a nation whose Constitution grants judges next to imperial powers to make social policy, it is a matter of utmost importance to blacks who is entrusted with the judicial authority

One federal judge, Frank M. Johnson, Jr., acting alone in most cases, issued a stream of decisions that virtually turned the tide of southern resistance to the civil rights of blacks.

During the years 1956 to 1974, Judge Johnson:

- Ordered the racial integration of the public transportation system of the city of Montgomery. *Browder v. Gayle* (1956)
- Invalidated the city of Tuskegee's plan to dilute black voting strength by redrawing city boundaries so as to move concentrations of black voters out of the city limits. *Gomillion v. Lightfoot* (1961)
- Ordered that black persons be registered to vote if their application papers were equal to the performance of the least qualified white applicant accepted on the voting rolls. *United States v. Alabama* (1961)
- Required desegregation of the bus depots of the city of Montgomery. *Lewis v. Greyhound* (1961)
- Ordered the city of Montgomery to surrender its voting registration records to the United States Department of Justice. *United States v. City of Montgomery* (1961)
- Required the state of Alabama to reapportion state legislative districts to adhere to the "one man, one vote" principle. *Sims v. Frink* (1962)
- Mandated, in Alabama, the first statewide desegregation of public schools. *Lee v. Macon County Board of Education* (1963)
- Ordered Governor George Wallace to permit Dr. Martin Luther King's civil rights protest march from Selma to Montgomery. *Williams v. Wallace* (1965)
- Ruled that the state of Alabama must permit blacks to serve on juries. *White v. Crook* (1966)
- Declared the Alabama poll tax unconstitutional. *United States v. Alabama* (1966)
- Ordered the desegregation of the Montgomery chapter of the YMCA. *Smith v. YMCA of Montgomery* (1970)
- Required the state of Alabama to hire one black state trooper for every white state trooper until racial parity was achieved. *NAACP v. Dothard* (1974)

Note: Not one of these decisions by Judge Johnson was either reversed or significantly modified by the Fifth Circuit Court of Appeals or by the Supreme Court of the United States.

that still grips the minds of most whites and many black Americans. Black people serving as judges powerfully undermines the white sense of superiority; these holdings by blacks of judicial powers force upon people an often grudging concession that blacks have the stuff to do important work.

Today, the appearance of blacks in high positions in judicial and law enforcement bodies is commonplace. The appointment of thirty-eight black federal judges during the Carter presidency brought the percentage of blacks on the federal bench to a level comparable to their percentage of the nation's population. But nationwide, blacks fall far short of parity in the posts they hold in the law enforcement system. According to Labor Department statistics, blacks in 1979 held only 2.6 percent of the 21,000 judicial posts in the United States. While blacks comprise slightly less than 10 percent of the nation's police officers, they are probably less than one percent of the nation's police chiefs.[19]

There is nothing abstruse or difficult about the methods blacks should use to increase their representation in law enforcement bodies. Once again the logic is black politics. Black voting strength should be brought to bear to press the President, as well as state-elected officials, to appoint more blacks to the bench, particularly to positions on appellate courts. The black political power centers must be so strong that elected officials must be left with no political options but to nominate many more black lawyers as U.S. attorneys and state attorneys. Target campaigns should be launched to defeat elected officials in urban areas who do not vigorously support the goal of selecting many more blacks to serve as law enforcement officials. Finally, the election of more black mayors and other city officials should produce stricter affirmative-action rules governing the racial composition of police forces. Because the whites-first selection rule has been absolutely rigid in the past, the courts have shown a strong tendency to order compensatory hirings and training of blacks in law enforcement posts. Minority and civil rights groups have barely scratched the surface of the potential for securing strong affirmative-action policies in selecting law enforcement officers in communities with significant minority populations.

A major obstacle to the affirmative integration of law enforcement bodies exists in the southern states where powerful county sheriffs are in many respects the law. In 1979, only ten of the 1,145 sheriffs in the eleven states of the Old Confederacy were black. But this situation may readily be addressed. As long as voting rights are protected by the federal government, blacks have formidable political strength in the South. In scores of counties they have the clear voting power to elect black sheriffs.[20]

The drive for more black police officers and law enforcement officials may be greatly advanced by effective support propaganda. On the whole, most whites are not persuaded that affirmative-action policies in general employment are beneficial either to whites or to the greater productivity or well-being of the nation. In education, too, most whites believe that affirmative-action policies tend to be detrimental to educational standards. But police effectiveness is a different matter. Especially in cities where civil disturbances and crime tend to be identified with blacks, whites will readily assent to the proposition that fully integrated metropolitan police forces are likely to reduce the probability of urban disturbances. In this circumstance, black police will be viewed as more effective crime fighters than white law enforcement officers.

The goal of placing more blacks in law enforcement positions should be near the head of the black political agenda. This is not simply because courts and state attorneys' offices act as quasi-legislative bodies in the United States. It is because judges rank at the very pinnacle of prestige and honor in our society. It is, in fact, likely that race discrimination in the United States will be on its last legs not when a black person is appointed to head the Ford Foundation or when it is no longer necessary to extend the federal Voting Rights Act, but rather when whites everywhere barely notice whether the cop on the beat, or the judge sitting in juvenile court, is white or black.

Take Political Control of Ten or More Major Cities Where Blacks Are a Majority or Near Majority

"Blacks will do what whites do. Take a bunch of patronage jobs for themselves, the spoils of war. The City Hall budget will remain bloated with payments for 99-man sanitation trucks and firehouses full of checker players and the requisite 38 clerks needed to pass one building permit application. Nothing will change except the color of the faces of some of the loafers on the public payroll."

—Mayor Jane Byrne commenting in 1983 on the election of Harold Washington as mayor of Chicago

DISPOSABLE POWER—MILITARY, ECONOMIC, AND POLITICAL—involves the acquisition and control of bases. Black power is no exception. Large cities are clearly the most important potential power bases for American blacks. This is the ironic and bittersweet payoff for all the trauma and hardship that have resulted from the great black migration to the cities and the current abandonment of many cities by whites. The development of express strategies for taking political control of some of the nation's largest cities should now be one of the principal goals of black politics.

What is the nature of the power held by mayors? Territorial and political control of cities begin in city hall. Mayors control the allocation of city services such as fire and police protection and sanitation. City hall controls tax assessments, building and fire codes, health services, and consumer affairs. Mayors have a decisive say about which social programs to continue and which to cut, about how many policemen are going to patrol the streets and where. City halls and city councils control the distribution of large shares of federal revenue-sharing funds. Mayors hold considerable power to influence educational and school integration policies in public schools and other important services that affect the everyday lives of a city's residents. In many cities controlled by whites, blacks have to file lawsuits to force these cities to pave streets, unclog storm drains, and install streetlamps in black neighborhoods. When black mayors are in control, these services are far more likely to be supplied. To the extent that blacks govern large cities, racial discrimination against blacks in government policies and selections is blunted; to the extent city government is capable of affecting the quality of black life, blacks clearly have much better prospects under black administrations than under most white city governments.

The capture-the-cities strategy carries with it a broader political agenda. The circumstance of having a black mayor, or black-controlled city council, in charge of any major city almost always provides blacks an extended political power base at the federal and statewide level. Mayors often handpick the delegates to state conventions, who, in turn, nominate the candidates for statewide offices. To only a slightly lesser extent, mayors play an influential role in the selection of delegates to national nominating conventions. In addition, city hall controls many of the services in the election districts of both state legislators and U.S. congressmen. Through traditional back-room wheeling and dealing, city government is often in a good position to do some serious horse-trading with members of the legislative branches.

It is remarkable how often a lawmaker may be persuaded to rethink his opposition to a bill a mayor favors the moment the mayor threatens to close a public skating rink in the legislator's district. In the tradition of Mayor Richard Daley of Chicago, the power of city hall may be projected as a major force in national politics. In many cases, the handpicked choice of an incumbent black mayor is quite automatically nominated as the Democratic candidate from congressional districts in large cities. Watching Chicago

THIRTY MAJOR URBAN POWER BASES WHERE BLACKS MAY BE IN A POSITION TO ELECT HIGH OFFICIALS AND TO USE PARTY ORGANIZATION AND PATRONAGE TO PROJECT POLITICAL POWER INTO STATE AND NATIONAL POLITICS

City	Black Population—1980	Percent Black Population—1980
New York, New York	1,784,124	25.2%
*Chicago, Illinois	1,197,000	39.8%
*Detroit, Michigan	758,939	63.1%
*Philadelphia, Pennsylvania	638,878	37.8%
*Los Angeles, California	545,940	16.4%
*Washington, D.C.	448,229	70.2%
Houston, Texas	440,257	27.6%
Baltimore, Maryland	431,151	54.8%
*New Orleans, Louisiana	312,191	53.5%
Memphis, Tennessee	307,702	47.6%
*Atlanta, Georgia	282,912	66.6%
Cleveland, Ohio	251,347	43.8%
St. Louis, Missouri	206,386	45.6%
*Newark, New Jersey	191,743	58.2%
*Birmingham, Alabama	158,223	55.6%
Indianapolis, Indiana	152,647	21.8%
Milwaukee, Wisconsin	146,940	23.1%
Jacksonville, Florida	137,324	25.4%
Cincinnati, Ohio	130,467	33.8%
Boston, Massachusetts	126,229	22.4%
Columbus, Ohio	124,880	22.1%
Kansas City, Missouri	122,699	27.4%
*Richmond, Virginia	112,357	51.3%
*Charlotte, North Carolina	107,973	29.8%
Nashville, Tennessee	105,942	23.3%
Tampa, Florida	104,835	20.6%
Pittsburgh, Pennsylvania	101,813	20.3%
Jackson, Mississippi	95,357	47.0%
Buffalo, New York	85,116	26.6%
Shreveport, Louisiana	84,624	41.1%

* Indicates cities with an elected black mayor in 1984.

Mayor Harold Washington's easy nomination of Charles Hayes in the crowded 1983 First Congressional District Democratic primary, an opponent stated: "I stood in awe at the sound and crunch of the wheels of a new machine, and that machine rolled over us." [21] In view of Chicago's political power on the national political scene, it is likely that any Democrat who wants to be President of the United States will have to submit himself for clearance by Mayor Washington.

Black Mayors and Economic Gains

In a nation where the economic well-being of people is influenced to a great extent by who holds political power and the ability to manipulate patronage, the direct economic advantages to blacks in having a black mayor are huge. Despite high-minded rhetoric to the contrary, incumbent mayors and politicians control the spoils system of public employment; they always have issued, and always will deal out, the best jobs to their friends and supporters. In the American political-economic system of payoffs, kickbacks, patronage, and nepotism, blacks are free to play the game but only when they hold the political tickets.

Secondary economic gains also flow from black mayoralty power. On the whole, black mayors are more likely than their white counterparts to press affirmative-action programs in police departments, fire departments, and city government. In cities governed by black officials, the local banks, insurance companies, employment agencies, television stations, and other business enterprises are more likely to pay serious attention to compliance with rules and ordinances prohibiting employment and credit discrimination. As illustrated by most of the urban development contract awards made in recent years in the District of Columbia, black political control of cities produces important participation by black entrepreneurs in the exploitation of government franchises and redevelopment programs. A firm political hold on city hall, as well as on the contract awards controlled by city hall, may be the most effective route to prosperity and power for the black businessman—just as it was for the Irish, Polish, and Italian businessman before him.

The black community benefits not only when a black wins a mayoralty election, but even when a black runs for it unsuccessfully. Black voter participation automatically increases when a black is on the ballot and declines just as reflexively—both in numbers and cohesiveness—when there are no black candidates and no black-white issues. Thus, the mere presence of black mayoralty candidates tends to strengthen political black solidarity and increase the number of black votes in national and state elections.

Black mayors control city halls in Chicago, Los Angeles, Philadelphia, Birmingham, Charlotte, Detroit, Atlanta, Richmond, Newark, Oakland, New Orleans, Hartford, and Washington—thirteen cities with large minority populations. Other cities with very large numbers of eligible black voters—Memphis, Cleveland, Baltimore, and St. Louis—are likely to elect black mayors in the near future. If black populations in major urban centers were to form an effective political alliance with Hispanics, other large cities such as New York, Houston, and Dallas could easily elect minority mayors. In these cities, the black population percentage falls short of that of Baltimore or Memphis, but the total minority population in those cities is still 40 percent or more.

A large black population in a particular city is not necessarily the touchstone to the election of a black mayor. Even in these cities, cohesive black voting power will rarely produce a black mayor if whites unite behind a liberal, moderate or coalition candidate. In 1979, a black candidate, Charles Bowser, entered the Philadelphia mayoralty race against three whites. He appeared to be the likely winner until two of his opponents withdrew from the race just two weeks before the election, turning the contest into a one-on-one, black-against-white confrontation in which the white candidate, William Green, became a certain winner. The lesson is familiar: Do everything possible to divide the opposition. Blacks in large cities, as elsewhere, win elections when white candidates split the white vote.

Election laws present a serious obstacle to blacks winning control of many more cities. Established powers in Democratic politics have shrewdly protected themselves against insurgents. Most major cities in the North and the South require runoff elections if no candidate receives a majority vote in the original primary. In most instances, black candidates may expect to win no more than 15 percent of the white vote. This means that the runoff system makes it extremely difficult to elect black mayors in those cities with black populations of less than 40 percent.

Since blacks are a minority in most cities, a significant white crossover vote is usually needed to elect a black mayor. The chances of a crossover are greatly diminished when large or highly vocal white minority groups escalate racial sentiments. The anticipated backlash white vote of the magnitude that almost defeated Harold Washington in Chicago in 1983 tends to reduce the prospect of electing black mayors in heavily black populated and racially polarized cities such as Memphis, St. Louis, and Houston. Conversely, a significant white crossover is a realistic possibility in cities such as New Orleans and Los Angeles, communities with large numbers of white liberal voters.

White backlash voting was effectively squelched in the 1972 mayoralty campaign of A.J. Cooper in Pritchard, Alabama, and in the 1979 campaign that elected Richard Arrington mayor of Birmingham. In Cooper's campaign, posters and handbills distributed in the black community included a picture of the candidates, but no picture was used in white neighborhoods. John Dean, Cooper's campaign manager, explained the strategy for the white areas of Pritchard:

"[M]ake a deliberate effort not to become too black in orientation or message and efforts would be made to recruit local white volunteers to work in their community. The candidate would maintain a low profile in the white community to decrease any further public recognition of him and to reduce any perception on that community's part of the vigor of the campaign."[22]

In 1979, Richard Arrington, running for mayor in the much larger metropolitan area of Birmingham, used no television advertising because of concerns that the vision of a black candidate would draw to the polls white voters who normally would not have bothered to vote.[23] Recent voting behavior in Charlotte, Boston, and Philadelphia suggests that whites are now much less likely to be put off by a black face on the ballot.

Although defeated in the 1982 gubernatorial race in California, Thomas Bradley of Los Angeles has been the most impressive example of a black mayoralty candidate attracting large numbers of white votes. Running for mayor in a city with a black population of only 17 percent, Bradley's 1973 campaign pledge was "to serve all the people." He won 56 percent of the total vote. He was subsequently reelected in both 1977 and 1981 with 59 and 64 percent of the vote, respectively. The most dramatic example of a black mayoralty victory in the South was the 1977 triumph of Ernest N. Morial in New Orleans. Morial's campaign was so well run that the candidate not only made a clean sweep among the city's 42 percent black population, but also drew over one-fifth of the white vote.[24] White backlash voting—particularly when it is manipulated by racist political slogans—is usually exaggerated. Harold Washington in Chicago, Maynard Jackson in Atlanta, and Richard Arrington in Birmingham were all elected despite racist slogans playing on white fears of blacks in power.

Self-evidently, black politics must start somewhere. The cities are clearly places to begin. For whatever value precedent may be, Irish immigrants to the United States did not get their start in politics by electing a President of the United States. They first won control of their own neighborhoods, then districts, cities, party organizations, and some states. Eventually, an Irish-American captured the White House. Unquestionably, many years will pass before voters in the United States will be prepared to elect a black President. In the meantime, a few dozen black mayors—even when they operate from cash-poor cities of the underprivileged—would have very strong political claims on any Democrat who occupies the White House. This, in turn, should contribute to a host of favorable presidential executive orders, appointments, and general support of black economic and political objectives. Even Republican Presidents could not safely ignore the huge negative vote that could be produced by a large group of black mayors speaking for fifteen or more of the nation's largest cities. A sustained presidential attack on the rights and opportunities of minorities, such as occurred under President Reagan in the early 1980s, is not likely to recur if blacks show the political courage to reject the tempting perks and public glory of minor posts and make a major move, instead, to establish political beachheads as mayors of the major cities of the United States.

The immediate target cities for the election of black mayors are Cleveland, Baltimore, Memphis, and St. Louis.

Use Every Political Means to Outlaw "At-Large" Election Procedures

"As long as I count the votes, what are you going to do about it?"

—William March (Boss) Tweed (1871)

AT-LARGE ELECTION LAWS seriously undermine black voting strength. In an at-large voting system, members of the state legislature, county governing board, city council, school committee, and the like are not elected by individual districts or wards. Instead, officials are chosen by all voters in a large and often ethnically diverse political area. To win an election under an at-large system, a black candidate must appeal to the population at large instead of voters in the area where the candidate is running for office. The ability of minorities to vote as a bloc and carry their own neighborhoods is overwhelmed by the large vote totals amassed by white candidates in area-wide polling.

Mississippi provides a good example of how the at-large voting system erases black political power. For many years Mississippi held its elections for the state legislature on an at-large basis. Moreover, black areas of the state were gerrymandered to include large white populations. Under this system, as many as twelve legislators were elected from one district. In 1975, this system produced only one black in the 174-member legislature of the state. Yet, Mississippi's population was over 30 percent black. In 1979, after the state was forced to change its election laws to a system in which all legislators were elected from single-member districts, seventeen blacks were elected—a very dramatic increase, although still far below their percentage of the population.

The dilution of black voting strength through the use of at-large elections occurs at the municipal level as well. A 1979 study of cities with populations greater than 50,000 in which blacks made up at least 15 percent of the total showed that in those cities using an at-large system blacks won only 42 percent of the council seats their percentage of the population warranted.

THE SYSTEMATIC ELIMINATION OF AT-LARGE ELECTION PROCEDURES WOULD SIGNIFICANTLY BOOST BLACK VOTING STRENGTH

In 1979, elections for the Mississippi State Legislature were conducted under a single-member district system for the first time. The new system resulted in substantial increases in minority representation.

MISSISSIPPI HOUSE OF REPRESENTATIVES

	1975	1979
Number of Seats	122	122
Number of Districts	46	122
Number of Multi-Member Districts	34	0
Most Members from One District	12	1
Total Black Members	1	14

MISSISSIPPI SENATE

	1975	1979
Number of Seats	52	52
Number of Districts	33	52
Number of Multi-Member Districts	10	0
Most Members from One District	5	1
Total Black Members	0	3

Source: Joint Center for Political Studies, National Roster of Black Elected Officials, Washington, D.C., Vol.5, July, 1975, pp.125 & xiii and Vol.9, 1979, pp.128 & x-xi ; and Office of the Secretary of State, Jackson, Mississippi.

Conversely, blacks won 85 percent of their fair share of legislative seats in cities that elected their governing bodies by single-member districts or wards.[25]

In 1979, twenty-three states still used some form of at-large systems in elections for their state legislatures. Thirty-two states used at-large elections for county governing board contests. In 1976, 69 percent of all cities with over 5,000 people used at-large election systems.[26] The major states with handicapping at-large voting rules are South Carolina, Florida, and North Carolina. Cities that keep blacks at bay through at-large voting rules include Charlotte, Houston, Mobile, Dallas, and Indianapolis. South Carolina is the most flagrant example of the dilution of black voter strength through an at-large voting system. In 1980, South Carolina had forty-six counties and forty-six white state senators elected at-large, even though the statewide eligible black vote is 25 percent.

Decisions of the Supreme Court have not been favorable toward blacks' efforts to nullify at-large election rules. In 1971, the Court ruled that at-large systems may not be overturned as unconstitutional burdens of the right to vote unless there is an explicit showing that the at-large voting system was set up with discriminatory intent. In the case then before the Court, it was clear that blacks were grossly underrepresented in the Indiana state legislature because the entire city of Indianapolis elected its fifteen representatives and eight senators at-large. But the Court refused to strike down the election law because there was no documented proof that the system was conceived with the discriminatory purpose of diluting the black vote. In 1973, the Court clarified its ruling by declaring that discriminatory intent could be established by demonstrating a history of prior discrimination by the official governing body. This ruling seemingly gave blacks—especially in the South, where overt racism had been commonplace—a valuable precedent for further challenges to at-large election systems. But seven years later, the Court reversed its position, ruling once more that at-large systems are unconstitutional only if it is shown that the voting system was intentionally designed to discriminate against minorities. This ruling was a serious setback for black efforts to win proportionate political strength in the South. Until the Justices are persuaded to change their views or until the composition of the Court is favorably altered, blacks must explore other strategies for removing election laws that undercut their ability to vote as an ethnic bloc.[27]

If the most burdensome of the at-large election laws in the country were eliminated, past experience in particular states where reforms have taken place suggests that the total number of black elected officials in the country might be increased by 25 percent or more. Particularly, there would be massive increases of black political power in states such as South Carolina, Georgia, and Florida. But the at-large voting system will be extremely difficult to dismantle. The at-large election laws do not overtly disenfranchise blacks and therefore do not strike the ordinary citizen as blatantly unjust. Not only are the at-large election laws a cornerstone of white political dominance, but when a legislator votes to repeal such a law, his vote is frequently tantamount to voting himself out of office. In moving against at-large election laws, blacks necessarily will be playing a weak hand. The task is arduous but achievable: slowly building greater black representation and bargaining leverage in the state legislatures that maintain the at-large systems; careful research of the histories of the various at-large systems, and the preparation of sophisticated legal briefs showing discriminatory legislative intent; concentrated protest and public demonstrations in states where virtually all-white state legislatures maintain the most oppressive voting systems. As ever, the weak hand will be much stronger if blacks unite with other minorities and organize a formidable political bloc of ethnic groups that have a common interest in eliminating the debilitating effects of election laws whose covert racial purposes are well known to everyone.

The Legislation of
Black Power

"If you have the law, you don't need the crowd."
—Clarence Darrow (c. 1924)

IN RECENT YEARS, America's confidence in government process has steadily eroded. Remedial legislation—traditionally perceived as the most legitimate and effective use of state power—is widely held in disrepute. Critics of government point accusingly to a hobbling maze of employment, credit, safety, and environmental laws which they blame for low productivity, stagflation, persisting poverty, and economic decline. Yet, only a few years ago, we as a nation believed that we could reach for an approximation of social utopia if we could simply devise and enact an appropriate set of laws, rules, or regulations. We were confident, too, that problems of race and inequality were equally susceptible to legislative repair. Enact the right law and race discrimination and poverty would simply go away! Today, traditional liberalism, with its buoyant confidence in the wide-ranging benefits of corrective legislation, is everywhere on the defensive. Proposals for new laws to deal with social and economic problems are greeted with public derision. Suggestions for legislating wider opportunities or economic advantages for blacks and other minority groups are, in most cases, rejected out of hand.

Unquestionably, liberal excesses are partially to blame for much of this reactionary fervor. The 100,000 pages of new federal regulations published every year in the *Federal Register* are sufficient proof that government lawmaking has been running wild. There can be little question, too, that legislative aid packages which remove many of the market penalties for economic failure have hobbled the diligent, given comfort to the idle, and curbed our once proud entrepreneurial spirit. The dampening effects of government regulation persist whether the beneficiary of federal generosity is a failing industrial corporation or simply an individual who finds life more agreeable if he does not work. Nevertheless, the corrective legislative process continues to be indispensable to an orderly and just society. The recent revival of interest in the primacy of freedom over justice does not do away with the need for governments to take certain overriding steps to prevent people from harming one another, or to repair or redress harms already done. In particular, the use of state power, in the form of law and regulation, remains indispensable in settings where unfairly won positions of power or advantage do serious damage to the life chances of particular groups of people or where, as in the case of race discrimination and occupational restrictions, the self-regulating force of competition has been suspended and the precious right to compete has been repealed.

The intensity of the hostility toward government lawmaking runs especially strong when state power shows its face in the form of laws and regulations designed to benefit blacks. Job discrimination rules, equal pay provisions, and administrative orders requiring "black-first" hiring procedures—even when directed against organizations that for generations have always hired whites first—have come under bitter attack. In many cases, blacks themselves have joined the chorus condemning the social agenda that they, only a few years ago, held so dear. In the rush to expose the evils of a central government grown too strong, there is little room for making distinctions between good and bad government policy. Rarely are differentiations made between those laws that might, on the whole, be good for blacks and those laws that, on balance, appear to do blacks affirmative harm.

Legislation designed to benefit blacks and other minorities may be divided into two broad categories. There is, first, a set of laws aimed primarily at supporting and protecting people. It is true that many of these laws give rise to habits of dependency and a loss of personal strength and independence. In many respects, too, these laws are twentieth-century versions of the offensive racial codes and plantation practices that once purported to protect blacks by assigning them to menial, though secure, employment. But there is also a different category of laws whose principal effect is to empower blacks or to contribute to the expansion of their choices and self-sufficiency. In actual cases, the distinction between "protectionist" laws and "empowering" laws is sometimes blurred, but, as we shall see, the difference is nevertheless a valid and important one.

The difference is critical to all strategies for the empowerment and advancement of blacks.

Let us first identify some laws that appear to benefit blacks but on the whole do more harm than good because they create dependency and undermine initiative. In general, these laws are easy to spot because they deal with the *effects* of poverty or powerlessness rather than with their perceived

---

BE WARY OF PUBLISHED WISDOM THAT THERE ARE NO LEGISLATIVE SOLUTIONS TO BLACK PROBLEMS

Voting Rights Legislation: The Remarkable Results of the Most Effective Civil Rights Law Ever Enacted by Congress

- In the eight days immediately following the passage of the Voting Rights Act on August 6, 1965, more blacks were registered to vote in Selma, Alabama than had been registered in the previous sixty-five years of this century.

- In the four years following the enactment of the federal voting rights legislation, black voter registrations in the southern states increased by nearly 50 percent. By 1976, the number of registered black voters had nearly doubled.

- In 1965, there were less than 100 black elected officials in the seven southern states where the most flagrant voting abuses had occurred. By 1980, 1,813 blacks held elective office in these states.

- In 1965, only a handful of blacks sat in the state legislatures of the southern states. Within a decade after the enactment of federal voting rights legislation, 120 blacks held state legislative seats.

- Within a decade of the enactment of the Voting Rights Act, eighty-two black mayors had been elected in southern cities and towns, many of which had not seen a black elected official since Reconstruction.

Sources: Voter-registration figures in Selma, Alabama were reported in Steven Lawson, Black Ballots (New York: Columbia University Press, 1976). Voter-registration figures for the entire South were obtained from the Voter Education Project, Atlanta, Georgia. Data on the numbers of black elected officials are from The National Roster of Black Elected Officials (Washington, D.C.: Joint Center for Political Studies, 1981).

---

causes. More often than not, these laws provide security and protection at the expense of reducing choices or curbing assertions of human will or endeavor. Much welfare legislation, for example, oppresses and demeans its recipients, denying them economic choice and providing incentives that keep people on the dole. Many of our federal programs for public housing, urban renewal, food stamps, and welfare services fall into this category.

Under most of these legislative programs, people are awarded certain benefits provided they behave in certain debilitating ways, such as maintaining personal incomes or property holdings at or below the poverty level. Through these legislative manipulations, dependency is encouraged while self-help and self-advancement are discouraged. The case is strong that many of these laws should be repealed and rejected whenever proposed. Protectionist laws of this nature do much the same harm to assertions of will and self-help as do corporate welfare activities and food baskets for the poor.

Now let us look to some of the laws that greatly contribute to power, liberties, and self-sufficiency. Prominent among these are laws prohibiting discrimination against blacks in employment, credit, housing, or education. While admittedly restricting the freedoms of whites, these laws do so only by denying whites the liberty to judge the qualifications of people according to racial caste expectation rather than according to individual merit—a liberty whose pursuit, in most cases, carries no moral or ethical justification or commercial value to the nation. At the same time, these laws blocking race discrimination greatly expand the employment, educational, and other life choices of blacks. It is true that antidiscrimination laws do designate blacks and other minorities as a protected class, but the protection is only against the collective and oppressive economic power of others. Far from creating habits of dependency, affirmative-action rules, too, confer liberty and power on blacks by providing them with much wider economic choices than they would otherwise enjoy. This is true even when affirmative-action laws or policies take the form of explicit quotas that allocate preferential positions to blacks in employment, credit, or education.

Laws that compel whites to open their schools and neighborhoods to the admission of blacks are often cited as harmful to blacks. But this is not so. These laws introduce blacks to better education as well as to superior economic information and opportunities that exist only in the social and economic mainstream. These laws provide blacks with the chance to move in and within the same spaces as whites, a condition that we have shown is indispensable to placing blacks on an equal competitive footing with whites. Laws forcing the racial integration of schools and neighborhoods expand the potential of blacks by providing them with the opportunity to disprove the negative racial stereotypes held by whites and used by them to hold blacks back. Clearly, fair housing laws and other rules opening up schools, labor unions, trade associations and other institutions to blacks provide them with much greater mobility and wider choices in life. If blacks as a group have the power to move more of their members into integrated neighborhoods and schools where the main chances of life occur, then individual blacks will have a far better chance of winning more and better jobs and of being promoted or appointed more often to even better positions.

The range of public laws that indisputably expand the powers and choices of blacks is very broad. For example, a voting rights act confers the ability to use the sanction of the vote—and particularly the bloc vote—where no such power existed before. The proposal to confer full statehood rights on the District of Columbia would enable blacks to elect two black senators to a powerful political body, which at present has no black members. Outright federal grants to black-controlled community development corporations stand on the same footing inasmuch as they give poor blacks much wider economic choices and political powers. Laws breaking down racial restrictions in labor unions introduce blacks to the economic and political advantages of trade union power. A law that denies tax exemption to schools that discriminate against blacks raises the cost of race discrimination and, as a result, opens up educational resources and opportunities to blacks. Policies that expressly set aside government contracts for minority bidding provide blacks with much broader economic opportunities, including the chance, long denied them through law and custom, of significant capital formation. Mandatory allocations of radio and television broadcast licenses to blacks would confer access to society's powers of mass persuasion, an invaluable state-controlled power which blacks have never been permitted to hold in the past. In most cases the argument that these laws requiring preferential treatment hurt blacks is a smokescreen. Whatever racial stigma may attach to specially assigned privileges based on race is overcome manyfold by the huge expansion in black powers and opportunities which these laws deliver.

There are other legislative proposals where the expected results will be mixed. For example, a minimum wage law in and of itself could restrict the economic choices of young people, particularly blacks, but a minimum wage law *combined* with strong affirmative-action policies for hiring black teenagers would give many blacks far more economic freedoms and opportunities than they have ever enjoyed. One could go on and on, examining countless proposals to see which are patronizing and protectionist and which give rise to new freedoms and new powers. But it should already be abundantly clear that there are scores of ways in which the so-called allocative state is in a position to use public laws and regulations to expand the powers and choices of blacks and, particularly, to open doors to all those formerly closed spaces and playing fields that successful humans must have the ability to enter.

- Slavery formally abolished by resolution of Congress and ratified by the states.

—Thirteenth Amendment to the Constitution (1865)

- Negroes guaranteed equal citizenship rights including rights to enforce contracts, to own property, and to give testimony.

—The Civil Rights Act of 1866

- Federal fines or imprisonment imposed on law officials depriving former slaves of equal citizenship rights.

—The Civil Rights Act of 1866

- Southern states required to grant Negroes the right to vote as a condition to readmission into the Union.

—The Reconstruction Act of 1867

- No state may deny any citizen due process or equal protection of the laws.

—The Fourteenth Amendment to the Constitution (1868)

- States may not deny the right to vote because of race, color, or private servitude.

—The Fifteenth Amendment to the Constitution (1870)

- Private persons made subject to criminal punishments for harassing or intimidating citizens seeking to vote or to enjoy other constitutional rights.

—The Enforcement Act of 1870

- Federal examiners may be appointed by the federal courts to oversee elections in the South.

—Force Act of 1871 (repealed in large part by Congress in 1894)

- Private suits may be brought against state officials and police officers who deprive citizens of constitutional rights.

—Force Act of 1871

- The President authorized to use federal troops to prevent mob violence against Negroes and to protect their right to vote.

—Ku Klux Act (1871)

- Racial discrimination outlawed in public accommodations.

—Civil Rights Act of 1875 (ruled unconstitutional by the Supreme Court in 1883)

- United States Commission on Civil Rights established.

—Civil Rights Act of 1957

- Civil Rights Division of the Department of Justice established. Justice Department authorized to seek injunctions against civil rights violations.

—Civil Rights Act of 1957

- Federal courts may appoint examiners to help blacks register to vote. State election officials required to make voter-registration records available to the Department of Justice.

—Civil Rights Act of 1960

- Poll tax outlawed in all federal elections.

—Twenty-Fourth Amendment to the Constitution (1964)

- Race discrimination banned in public accommodations and in federally assisted programs.

—Civil Rights Act of 1964

- Congress creates the federal Equal Employment Opportunity Commission and bans race discrimination in private employment.

—Civil Rights Act of 1964

- Literacy tests for voter registration suspended in much of the South.

—Voting Rights Act of 1965

- The United States Attorney General empowered to send federal registrars and poll watchers into certain areas of the South with a history of voting rights abuses.

—Voting Rights Act of 1965

- Changes in election laws of six southern states and in certain counties in other states must be submitted to the U.S. Attorney General for advance approval.

—Voting Rights Act of 1965

- Race discrimination prohibited in the sale or rental of private housing.

—Civil Rights Act of 1968

- Equal Employment Opportunity Commission authorized to seek enforcement orders in federal courts.

—Equal Employment Opportunity Act of 1972

- Permanent ban on literacy tests in all elections.

—Voting Rights Act extension of 1975

- Tax-exempt status denied to social clubs and organizations whose membership requirements discriminate on the basis of race.

—Tax Amendments of 1976

Like the laws they make, institutions of government also tend to divide into those that empower and those that protect blacks. Generally speaking, the Department of Housing and Urban Development, the Department of Health and Human Services, and the Minority Business Development Agency tend to deal with the effects of disadvantage and repression and ultimately create more dependency than economic freedom. For this reason, blacks might be far better off if these institutions were abolished and the equivalent resources allocated to government strategies that do empower blacks. On the other hand, the Equal Employment Opportunity Commission and the Office of Federal Contract Compliance Programs are capable of major contributions to the economic and political bargaining strength of minorities, provided that the agencies have the necessary powers to command, adjudicate, and intervene in, or block, transactions that favor whites and in the process perpetuate inferior status for blacks.

We see then that nothing could be further from the truth than the notion, currently in vogue, that a strong central government tends to weaken the position of blacks. Quite the contrary, the clear need for expanded choices and powers in the black community may be addressed only by a strong central government aggressively legislating to remove the barriers of prior Jim Crow and to outlaw the many surrogate devices that the vast majority of whites continue to use to block Negroes from access to American institutions. For most blacks, then, it would be a serious political mistake to allow important parts of their agenda to be swept away by a conservative tide that indiscriminately attacks all interventions by the state on their behalf. The long history of benign results from congressional legislation on behalf of blacks—and the expanded political and economic opportunities it has delivered for more than a century—should be persuasive that further gains are highly dependent on corrective racial legislation. A successful move toward equality requires, further, the presence of a bipartisan congressional majority—of which blacks must form an essential element—strongly motivated to use legislative power to break resistance to racial integration and to block further efforts to restore a racially segregated way of life or to keep economic and political power away from blacks.

Doubters will suggest that a white-controlled Congress is not likely to enact new laws that increase the powers of blacks. But that opinion requires a very short view of American history. The chart highlights the scores of congressional enactments on the side of further powers and liberties for the American Negro. Not mentioned is the original liberating act of Congress of April 1862 in which 3,100 slaves in the District of Columbia were freed nearly nine months before Abraham Lincoln took executive action to emancipate blacks in the rest of the country.

The following proposals are offerred for consideration if and when blacks alone—or in alliance with Hispanics and others—are successful in gathering sufficient political strength to overcome resistance in both political parties to further legislation on behalf of groups whose unequal competitive positions may be traced to fundamental violations of the tenets of our political order. Each of these proposals, if enacted, would not only augment the political strength of blacks as a group but would also contribute in an important way to their economic power and advancement.

In developing these proposals, I have scrupulously avoided any legislative remedy that would provide blacks with permanent crutches, protect their dependent status, or grant them economic support while making them economically weak. For this reason, many of the standard items on the black legislative agenda will not appear here.

Magnify the Political Force of the Black Vote Through Universal Voter Registration

"America, be true to what you said on paper."
—Martin Luther King, Jr. (1968)

WHITES IN THE UNITED STATES outnumber blacks by a ratio of 8 to 1. Thus, it would at first appear that universal voter registration might dilute the little political influence blacks already have. In fact, the reverse is true. This is so because a far greater percentage of whites are currently registered than blacks. Universal registration would therefore add proportionately more blacks to the voting rolls. This, in turn, should result in much higher minority voter percentages. Major shifts in black voting power would occur particularly in a number of predominantly black southern congressional and state assembly districts where whites maintain political control only because very small percentages of blacks are registered or voting.[1]

A second and far more important reason why universal registration would enlarge black political power has to do with the *way* blacks vote. More than any other group in America, blacks vote as a bloc. In 1980, about 90 percent of all blacks voted for Jimmy Carter against the landslide winner Ronald Reagan. Four years earlier, 90 percent of all black voters also cast their ballots for Carter. In 1964, Lyndon Johnson received 97 percent of the black vote. No matter what the political affiliation of a candidate, blacks tend to *mass* their votes. In sixty-three of eighty-four elections for the House of Representatives monitored by the Joint Center for Political Studies in

1976, blacks supported either the Democrat or the Republican with at least 90 percent of their votes.[2] Since whites split their votes, any increase in black voting will have much more relative impact on election results than a corresponding increase in white registrations. The vaunted swing-vote potential of black people becomes a truly powerful weapon under a system where almost *everybody* votes.

Universal registration would further benefit the black voting bloc because easier access to voting would add very large numbers of young whites and poor whites to the voting rolls. All studies show that these two groups of whites, who currently vote in very low percentages, are much more likely than the white population generally to support the progressive candidates usually preferred by blacks. Stated another way, blacks would benefit because universal voter registration *tends to dilute the voting strength of the mostly conservative white middle class,* most of whom are already registered and can gain little from increases in registration.

Even more to the point, universal voter registration should strengthen the huge potential black vote in big cities. Fifty-six percent of the black population in the United States live in our central cities, compared with only 24 percent of the white population.[3] In urban areas, polling places are usually within easy walking distance; in most cases, potential voters do not face transportation problems. And because a campaign worker using a bullhorn atop an automobile may be heard by hundreds of people at one time in a city, massive get-out-the-vote techniques mobilize the urban and largely black vote much more efficiently than any comparable technique used in predominantly white suburbs and rural areas. Unleashing the presently untapped urban vote would add many millions of low-income and mostly black urban voters to the present black voting bloc.

A number of states have already enacted so-called easy voter-registration laws. In Wisconsin, anyone at the polls having a driver's license or other document proving age and residence may vote. Minnesota has put a similar law on the books, and in both states voter turnout has dramatically increased. In the 1976 presidential election, over 70 percent of the eligible voters in these two states went to the polls—the highest rates in the nation. In the 1978 midterm elections, Minnesota and Wisconsin again led the nation with turnout rates of 64 and 58 percent, respectively.[4]

Other states such as Maryland and Texas have simplified their registration systems to allow enrollment by mail. Another positive step is a drive being conducted by the NAACP and the Reverend Jesse Jackson to permit high school principals to register students before graduation. Michigan enacted such a law in August 1979, and many other states have similar bills pending in their legislatures. In New Jersey, county officials regularly visit public schools to register 18 year olds. Increased registration among high school seniors should have a dramatic effect on the low voter turnout rate in the heavily black 18-to-20 age group.

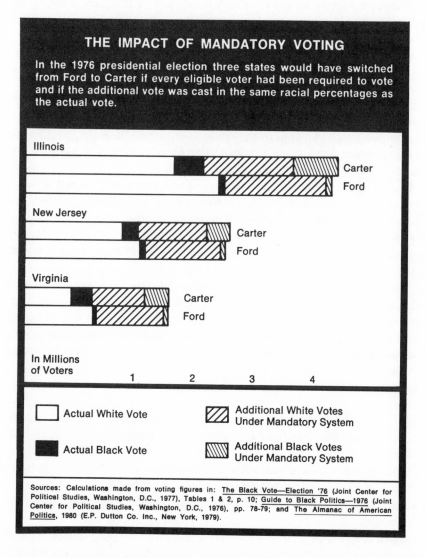

THE IMPACT OF MANDATORY VOTING

In the 1976 presidential election three states would have switched from Ford to Carter if every eligible voter had been required to vote and if the additional vote was cast in the same racial percentages as the actual vote.

Illinois

Carter

Ford

New Jersey

Carter

Ford

Virginia

Carter

Ford

In Millions of Voters   1   2   3   4

☐ Actual White Vote

■ Actual Black Vote

▨ Additional White Votes Under Mandatory System

▧ Additional Black Votes Under Mandatory System

Sources: Calculations made from voting figures in: The Black Vote—Election '76 (Joint Center for Political Studies, Washington, D.C., 1977), Tables 1 & 2, p. 10; Guide to Black Politics—1976 (Joint Center for Political Studies, Washington, D.C., 1976), pp. 78-79; and The Almanac of American Politics, 1980 (E.P. Dutton Co. Inc., New York, 1979).

Compulsory voting in federal elections would prove even more advantageous to blacks than universal registration. This is not an unusual procedure. Compulsory voting laws exist in Australia, Chile, and a number of African nations. The turnout in Italian elections is normally among the highest of the democratic countries. Failure to vote is registered in a citizen's file in city hall and may weigh against him if he seeks a government job.

Although Americans are not likely to abridge their freedom *not* to vote, it is interesting to superimpose the hypothesis of mandatory voting on recent elections and see how the outcomes might have been affected. The 1976 presidential election provides a telling illustration of the potential of universal registration and mandatory voting to affect election outcomes. If all Americans over 18 years of age had been required to vote in the 1976 presidential election and had cast their ballots in the same black-white proportion as actually occurred, the additional black vote for Carter, coupled with a near-even split of the white vote, would have shifted the states of Illinois, New Jersey, and Virginia to the Democratic ticket, giving Carter an easy 352-186 victory in the Electoral College.[5]

In a democracy, universal voter registration or voting is not a radical idea. Japanese voters do not even have to register to vote. Their names automatically go on electoral rolls when they become 20 years old, the legal voting age in Japan. Why should people object if the exercise of the most important right and responsibility offered by a democracy is made mandatory?

Wholly aside from racial considerations, there are very powerful reasons why, in the interests of international prestige and standing, the United States should press legislative initiatives to increase voter turnout. It is one of our great international embarrassments that the world's leading democracy has the lowest level of voter participation in the industrialized world, largely because no other country makes the voting process so difficult.[6]

Renew Political Pressures to Establish Federally Guaranteed Employment

"In the general course of human nature, a power over a man's subsistence amounts to a power over his will."

—Alexander Hamilton (1788)

A FEDERAL LAW GUARANTEEING EMPLOYMENT for everyone would, in a statistical sense, completely eliminate the huge unemployment gap between blacks and whites. With one stroke of the presidential pen, the economic factor, which is perhaps the single most important indicator of racial inequality, could be removed. Although full employment legislation would not affect the *quality* of black employment, the law would confer upon blacks a significant degree of economic power that they do not now possess. Millions of blacks would have the new freedom to choose work over idleness; and because of the very high rate of black unemployment, this new work option would be afforded to blacks in far greater percentages than it would be extended to whites. The creation of a genuine right-to-work law, which on its face would be racially neutral, would in fact greatly favor blacks.

In an economy where full employment became a first priority, America would reap both ideological and practical benefits. The society as a whole would gain if nearly half of all black teenagers were not unemployed and on the streets; everyone now loses as a result of higher crime rates and reduced educational incentives that the near-certain prospect of unemployment brings to teenagers in the cities. The argument is strong that the costs of crime and delinquency—and other social ills associated with unemployment—far exceed the costs to the government and to the economy as a whole of funding full employment legislation. Also, the nation's image abroad, which has reached a low point in recent years, is severely injured by the visible presence of a million or more unemployed blacks in the inner cities. In this light, the fact that the constitution of the Soviet Union guarantees the right to a job—a fact not neglected in Soviet propaganda directed to Third World nations—becomes a pervasive force in moving toward a right to assured employment in the United States. The successful economies of Japan and West Germany demonstrate that protected employment is not necessarily inconsistent with high productivity, an incentive to improve one's lot, and a sound currency.

Contrary to statements frequently made by the U.S. Chamber of Commerce and other advocates of unregulated free enterprise, the American people as a whole strongly support the proposition that the government should see that everybody who wants to work has a job. Except for the elderly, the ill, and single parents of young children whom American society is committed to support anyhow, the drive for guaranteed employment helps all citizens and should not be seen as a black or minority program.

Employment protection proposals are invariably loaded with traps for the unwary. It is important to analyze and project the likely effects of specific proposals for guaranteed employment. It is possible that a full employment plan might not work to equalize economic differences between the races at all, but might instead help the white unemployed more than the black unemployed. For example, government "job creation" tax subsidies to industry to encourage research and development expenditures tend to automate the country away from unskilled employment and toward skilled employment, with the probable result that black unemployment prospects would suffer compared with those of whites, who, by education and training, are much better equipped to deal with the pressures of technologically induced unemployment. In 1980, blacks were about 10 percent of the labor force but made up over 20 percent of the unemployed. Thus, a government employment strategy that had the effect of creating new jobs for blacks in proportion to their percentage of the population would not close the racial gap in the unemployment rates even though the program would bring down the

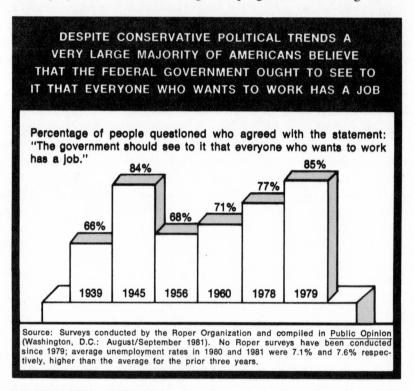

DESPITE CONSERVATIVE POLITICAL TRENDS A VERY LARGE MAJORITY OF AMERICANS BELIEVE THAT THE FEDERAL GOVERNMENT OUGHT TO SEE TO IT THAT EVERYONE WHO WANTS TO WORK HAS A JOB

Percentage of people questioned who agreed with the statement: "The government should see to it that everyone who wants to work has a job."

1939	1945	1956	1960	1978	1979
66%	84%	68%	71%	77%	85%

Source: Surveys conducted by the Roper Organization and compiled in Public Opinion (Washington, D.C.: August/September 1981). No Roper surveys have been conducted since 1979; average unemployment rates in 1980 and 1981 were 7.1% and 7.6% respectively, higher than the average for the prior three years.

unemployment rates for both groups. The gap between the black and white unemployment rates would close only if the jobs were somehow disproportionately allocated to blacks, or allocated to blacks in proportion to the percentage of blacks unemployed.

In practice, it is highly likely that a government job protection program would take the direct form of providing public-service jobs to the unemployed. In rural communities, many whites would claim these jobs rather than accept public assistance. But in urban areas, whites are much more likely than blacks to reject public-works jobs on the grounds that they are menial, demeaning, and "meant for blacks." It is to be expected, then, that a very large proportion of new government-created jobs would be created and accepted in heavily black-populated urban areas.

A reasonable assumption to make is that the proportion of black enrollment in public-service jobs would roughly equal blacks' participation in the Department of Labor's Job Corps training program for youths between the ages of 16 and 21. In 1967, approximately 70 percent of all Job Corps enrollees nationwide were minorities; 60 percent were black. If blacks claimed public-service jobs at the same rate that they enrolled in the Job Corps, they would obtain 600,000 out of, say, a million new jobs. This would have a huge positive impact on their unemployment rate. Although the long-term effect on the ability of blacks to make their way in the private economy is uncertain, a very large statistical reduction in the racial unemployment gap would necessarily result from the new legislation.[7]

In practice, then, it is impossible to predict with much certainty the racial composition of the new job holdings that would be created under public-service job legislation. Much depends on whether or not differing percentages of blacks and whites would prefer to stay on public-assistance programs of one sort or another rather than accept public-service employment. The conclusion is that strategists who engineer initiatives to help blacks catch up with whites would be ill-advised to embrace each and every guaranteed employment proposal on the assumption that all job-support legislation would alter the black-white unemployment ratio in favor of blacks.

If the government were to embark on a serious effort to provide employment security, practical politics would probably require it to manipulate the labor market by using tax incentives or monetary policies to reduce unemployment rather than to create jobs directly. Business generally prefers the indirect approach. But econometric studies made by the Federal Reserve Board show that direct government employment, dollar for dollar, is a far more efficient means of providing jobs than are government payments or tax credits to private enterprises.

Let us suppose that instead of adopting a direct public employment measure as a means of reducing unemployment, the government were to use Federal Reserve Board monetary policies to create a tight labor market. Since the present racial bias in the demand for labor could be expected to continue and relative black-white skill levels would remain unchanged, it is likely that blacks and whites would claim new jobs in the usual proportions. In this case, the standard 2-to-1 unemployment ratio would continue to prevail. Because of the government's action there would be far fewer blacks unemployed, but the black-white unemployment ratio would remain the same. Since whites have more education, greater access to coercive economic pressure such as trade unions power, and better referral connections with other whites who hold jobs, it is very likely that whites would disproportionately claim the jobs that an artificially heated-up economy would generate. In this event, the "fuller" employment legislation could actually cause the gap between black and white incomes to increase.

In short, blacks should not unqualifiedly support all government unemployment reduction proposals even though most of them have the merit of helping *some* blacks to become employed. Because blacks in very large numbers are poorly educated and handicapped by the stigma of race, they need a highly targeted full employment measure whose clear purpose and effect are to close the present racial unemployment gap. This legislative strategy which *disproportionately creates demand for black labor* should be of far greater benefit to black people than the current array of very costly training entitlements which do not significantly enlarge the economic power of blacks to claim work and have only marginal or symbolic value.

Launch a National Campaign to Eradicate Illiteracy

"You've got to be better, boy. You've got to move better."

—Justice Thurgood Marshall,
quoting Charles E. Houston,
former Dean of the Howard University Law School

IN THE PRE-CIVIL WAR SOUTH, slave owners advised other plantation owners not to bother to use fences or chains to prevent runaway slaves. "Keep them in captivity by ignorance" was the standard slaveowner's advice, as recounted by Frederick Law Olmstead. Accordingly, under the pragmatic rules of the antebellum South, it was always a crime to teach a slave to read. And, today, millions of blacks are tethered close to home and still remain in virtual bondage simply because of their illiteracy. Whites set blacks free, but a continuing legacy of human ignorance—exacerbated by a century of restricted economic opportunities, even for those who could read—still produces among millions of blacks the "habit of perfect dependency" which the plantation owner always sought to inculcate in his slaves.

A major Ford Foundation study issued in 1980 reported that 50 million American adults were either illiterate or near illiterate. Illiteracy affects blacks at least three times as often as whites. According to the National Assessment of Educational Progress, in 1975 *nearly 42 percent of 17-year-old* blacks were functionally illiterate, in the sense of lacking the reading skills necessary to get along in a society dominated by the printed word.[8]

Nothing but the most menial work is open to a person who cannot read. For an individual who cannot interpret a want ad or fill in a job application, all routes to employment are blocked. In this sense, the immediate barrier to black advancement is not racial discrimination but the simple inability to process information. Lacking the ability to change money, to read signs on buses and street corners, to read simple directions, and to fill out employment forms, millions of blacks—and whites, too, but in far lower proportions—live on the fringes of our economic system. Aside from its destructive effects on the human spirit generally, illiteracy plays a massive role in perpetuating inequality between whites and blacks.

What Jonathan Kozol calls "the pestilence of mass illiteracy" is not perceived as a racial issue. Thus, for blacks, Hispanics, and whites, the task of bringing pressure to bear on the government to take measures to eradicate illiteracy has the political advantage of serving all races. Some 50 million people in the United States would be profoundly helped if this critical national problem could be overcome. Yet, because the literacy gap between the races is huge, a strong and effective national campaign to eliminate illiteracy would disproportionately benefit blacks. Provided that economic and educational opportunities are held open by laws prohibiting race discrimination, success in establishing universal literacy is bound to help equalize the huge unemployment and poverty rate differences between whites and blacks, and at the same time greatly reduce the greater risk to blacks of hunger, disease, accident, and political and economic deception.

Most successful campaigns to abolish illiteracy have been mounted in totalitarian states such as Cuba and the People's Republic of China, nations where no value is placed on protecting the individual freedom *not* to learn to read. Even in the United States, where the government cannot constitutionally force people to become literate, there are many measures that can be taken to greatly reduce illiteracy. The plain fact is that even a government that can't mandate literacy *can* force schools to teach. The federal government has the power to spearhead a campaign against illiteracy by mandating much stricter academic standards that would effectively abolish automatic promotions at grade level. The government has the power to enforce school attendance laws, particularly in poor neighborhoods. It has the ability to provide massive public funding of remedial classes for slow readers, and particularly for schools in poor neighborhoods. There must be more intensive testing of youngsters to determine the presence of illiteracy at an early age when the problem is remediable. Parents, voters, and teachers must insist on basic standards of reading competence.

To make serious inroads into the problems of illiteracy, a massive campaign, spearheaded by blacks, should be mounted to stigmatize and erase the corruption of language that goes under the name of Black English. Particularly, academic credit should be denied for mock academic activities, which pollute the curriculums of many black schools. In these schools, intense reading courses should be substituted for the rote learning

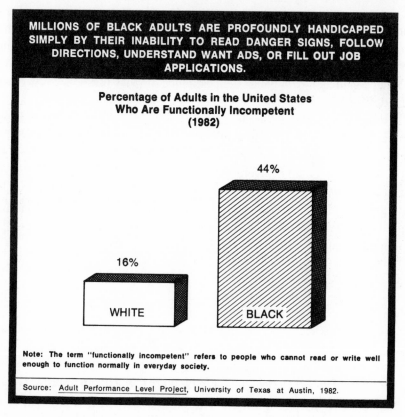

MILLIONS OF BLACK ADULTS ARE PROFOUNDLY HANDICAPPED SIMPLY BY THEIR INABILITY TO READ DANGER SIGNS, FOLLOW DIRECTIONS, UNDERSTAND WANT ADS, OR FILL OUT JOB APPLICATIONS.

Percentage of Adults in the United States Who Are Functionally Incompetent (1982)

44%

16%

WHITE

BLACK

Note: The term "functionally incompetent" refers to people who cannot read or write well enough to function normally in everyday society.

Source: Adult Performance Level Project, University of Texas at Austin, 1982.

of American civics and the many useless and self-pitying courses currently given under the rubric of the "black experience."

Under a national campaign to wipe out illiteracy, tens of thousands of young teachers could be trained and sent to work in poor communities, and scores of black folk heroes could be enlisted for a nationwide propaganda campaign to convince young people of the tragic consequences of remaining illiterate. Politically active community groups have the political power to fund reduced class sizes and employment of expanded numbers of qualified teachers in those critical early grades where literacy is achieved or allowed to slip away. Public pressure must be brought to bear on parents to take up the battle against illiteracy. Only parents can cut down the time children spend watching television and increase the time they spend doing homework. Higher standards, greater motivation to learn, and better attendance records are the products of involved and determined parents. Above all, a major commitment must be made to research and development aimed at creating a revolution in teaching methods and materials. Without this, a dramatic breakthrough in reducing illiteracy rates is unlikely. There is reason to be encouraged. In the mostly black District of Columbia public school system, where intensive new instruction programs have been introduced in recent years, there has been an almost uninterrupted upswing since 1977 in reading and math test scores.

Present rates of illiteracy among both blacks and whites are intolerable. The government must insist that every child and young adult who cannot read, write, or do simple arithmetic be provided effective training in these basic disciplines. The instruction may not be optional. Particularly, black parents cannot even begin to think seriously about reaching economic and social equality with whites until they decide at long last to deny their children the liberty not to learn to read.

It is one of the great ironies of the black condition that Negroes fought long and hard for the right to use two forms of human power: the power to vote and the power to protect and advance oneself through education. The tragic fact, however, is that millions of blacks, today, don't bother to exercise either of these important powers, which are so important to individual security, well-being, and advancement.

Assign the Highest Priority to the Enactment of a Nationwide Family Income Maintenance Plan

"Never insult an alligator until after you have crossed the river."
—Cordell Hull

COMPREHENSIVE WELFARE REFORM must always rank as a cornerstone of the black legislative agenda. It is true that improving the size and importance of the black middle class and strengthening black incomes generally are urgent objectives. Yet, closing the poverty gap between the races must be a central element in any black political strategy that aspires to achieve economic equality between blacks and whites.

A simple look at Census statistics leads us to the core of the problem. In 1979, 41 percent of all black children, ages 15 and under, were being raised in conditions of poverty. On a percentage basis, poor black households headed by a woman with at least one dependent child outnumbered similar white families nearly *nine to one*. What is more, poverty among the elderly is 2.7 times higher for blacks than for whites.[9] Clearly, political measures such as full employment legislation and affirmative-action employment initiatives do not, and cannot, help these groups of poor blacks because most of them could not work even if offered employment. For these people, the argument that the poor should buck up and earn their way like everybody else is simplistic and irrelevant. The only realistic means of dealing with the problems of these groups is through comprehensive welfare reform based on establishing a national income support plan that guarantees every American family an income at or above the poverty level.

Using Census Bureau figures that detail the extent of the income deficit of the nation's poor, we can estimate the annual cost to the taxpayer of a guaranteed income program. In 1979, an income maintenance program that brought the incomes of all the nation's poor up to the poverty threshold would have had an annual price tag of about $22 billion, assuming that current federal programs for the poor were maintained. Of this sum, it appears that about $6.6 billion, or 29 percent, would go to blacks.[10] As expected, then, blacks would claim a disproportionate share of the family income support appropriation.

Based on 1979 figures, an annual appropriation of $22 billion for income maintenance would represent about 4 percent of the national budget; it would increase present appropriations for the poor, including the accompanying administrative costs, by about 20 percent. Even adjusting for increased costs prevailing in the early 1980s, we are viewing important, but not massive, additions to the government budget. When the American people are prepared to readdress the issue of involuntary poverty—exacerbated as it will necessarily be by technologically induced unemployment of people with low or obsolete skills—blacks and other minorities must be politically strong and prepared to lead a legislative drive for income maintenance.

Howsoever great the blessings of government-protected income for the involuntary poor, one must keep in mind that the enactment of a comprehensive family income support plan would have very little effect on *overall* income inequality between the races. Even a $22 billion increase to the total national family income would amount to less than 2 percent of the more than $1.3 trillion of personal income earned each year in the United States. If, through government income maintenance, all incomes were brought up to the poverty level, the black share of the total family income would increase by only three-tenths of a percentage point, from about 6.7 percent to 7 percent.[11]

Although the federal income maintenance idea has the support of a number of conservative economists, including Nobel Laureate Professor Milton Friedman, the plan is unpopular in the country at large. Most Americans associate income maintenance with the despised and "outdated" Great Society programs that are believed to reward "welfare chiselers" and the so-called undeserving poor. Moreover—although the point is never publicly articulated—politicians are keenly aware of the extent to which income maintenance would strengthen the political hands of blacks and other minorities. Large numbers of political officeholders, particularly in southern states, will strongly oppose family income support measures since these reforms would deprive party leaders of their ability to influence black voters through control of jobs and the public dole, not to mention their ability to manipulate black politicians through the political leverage attached to discretionary disbursements of federal revenue-sharing funds. In addition, many employers, in both the North and the South, see income support as a marginally radical plot to deprive them of low-cost labor. Finally, even political liberals are reluctant to support major welfare reform in a period of decreasing government revenues and increasing public debt.

Even if inflation and other economic problems are brought under control—and all national defense priorities are met as well—there still remains a serious question of the effect of income support policies on incentives and productivity generally. Income maintenance studies conducted under federal auspices some years ago concluded that support payments did not appear to cause working people to work less. More recently, the so-called Seattle-Denver experiment suggested unfavorable effects. Conducted by the Stanford Research Institute, the study found that:

- A guaranteed income causes a modest reduction in work effort. Blacks and Hispanics who received a guaranteed income cut their work more than whites—double in some cases. The study could not explain why.
- Teenagers who were not heads of households worked less when offered guaranteed incomes. They did not use the extra time for schooling.
- Marriages broke up more often among families receiving income support payments. Depending on the support guarantee level, white families suffered breakups 18 to 63 percent more frequently; black families from 15 to 73 percent more frequently than those who were not receiving support.

The results of the Stanford study should give serious pause to anyone, black or white, advocating a guaranteed income program in this country. Also, the study reinforces the public's renewed interest in Darwinian economics and its skepticism about the efficacy of any federal interventions in the economy. The Stanford study, together with budgetary problems, will probably end—at least for the next several years—further consideration of fundamental welfare reform.

Despite the uncertainties that are still unresolved, the guaranteed minimum income issue should have priority over nearly all other social initiatives on the black agenda. If work incentive and marital breakup questions can be answered, there is no other pragmatically realizable legislation in view that could so strategically improve the economic position of the black race in the United States. In pressing the case for a guaranteed minimum income, blacks pursue not the narrow, partisan, and controversial goals of racial quotas or favoritism, but rather an almost universal and overriding principle of a just society: that every person should have a sufficient amount of money to pursue a decent human life.

Establish the Congressional Black Caucus as a Permanent Standing House Committee With Plenary Subpoena and Investigatory Powers

". . . every bondman in his own hand bears the power to cancel his captivity."

—William Shakespeare,
Julius Caesar (Act I, Sc. iii)

FEW PEOPLE ARE AWARE OF THE FACT that the Congressional Black Caucus, an unofficial association of twenty black congressmen, is currently the single most important black political force in the United States. Unlike most other black pressure groups, only the Caucus holds the highly legitimate power that derives from holdings of elective office. As an organized group of elected legislators, the Caucus symbolizes the social, political, and economic aspirations of a very large proportion of black Americans; it uniquely defines and legitimizes the issues and strategies that are important to the nation's largest minority group. As increasing numbers of blacks are elected to Congress, and as the Caucus becomes increasingly interested in brokering political power, it is likely to become the one black institution that is genuinely capable of moving the government to take measures that improve the life chances of blacks in the United States.

While the Caucus stands preeminent in the black power landscape, its influence is still not great. Yet, as the central focus point of black legislative force, the Caucus could take a number of steps to expand its authority and bargaining influence within the federal government.

First, the Caucus could seek *official* status within the legislative branch. To this end, the Caucus should mount a campaign in Congress to become a permanent standing committee of the House of Representatives. This goal is not merely symbolic. Creation of official status (which would require a vote of the majority of the House) would confer upon the Caucus many of the usual powers and sanctions of a legislative body. The most important of these are the powers to hold public hearings, to subpoena witnesses, to compel testimony, and to invoke the powers of the federal courts to punish witnesses who defy its processes.

If the Caucus held the traditional powers of a standing House committee, its investigatory processes could reach into the activities of all branches of government. The Caucus would have broad powers to examine Cabinet officers, agency heads, and other civil servants on how government policies affect issues critical to blacks and other minorities. The current flabby state of government enforcement of equal opportunity laws could be exposed to public view. No agency or department would be exempt from the Caucus's inquiries, including those that have usually succeeded in masking their racial policies from public scrutiny: the Department of Justice, the Federal Reserve Board, the Defense Department, the Office of Management and Budget, the Central Intelligence Agency, and the Federal Bureau of Investigation.

If the Caucus had subpoena powers, it could investigate, and open for public view, the activities of public institutions in the country whose rules, practices, and decisions profoundly affect the life chances of black people: school boards, police departments, zoning boards, and voting registrars. For the first time, too, a surveillance body acting for blacks and other minority groups would have direct access to information regarding the employment, contracting, and lending practices of large industrial corporations, pension funds, labor unions, life insurance companies, and banks. Placing the great power of state subpoena in black hands would be a landmark event. This first-time access to one of the great prerogatives of the sovereign would contribute immensely to the overall economic and political strength of black people.

In addition to lobbying for official legislative status, and the investigative powers that accompany it, the Caucus should also move to establish itself as the official spokesman for black civil rights groups in all dealings with the White House and other government agencies. At present, black political objectives are often put off or sidetracked by the Administration because black organizations compete with each other, and with the Caucus, as to who speaks for blacks. The axiom that empowerment requires unity also calls upon other black organizations to defer to the Caucus as the central clearinghouse and advisory board for evaluating presidential appointments and legislative proposals. The Caucus as a public body of *elected* black officials should become the single organization entrusted with the responsibility for formulating black political objectives and setting legislative, litigation, and voting strategies. In the primary season preceding the 1984 national elections, Jesse Jackson's campaign to register black voters—and, indeed, his chances of establishing blacks as a force in American politics—would have received a major boost if the Black Caucus had provided an early endorsement of his candidacy and maintained this support until the Democratic presidential nominating convention. It is difficult to overestimate the political bargaining leverage that would develop if the Caucus were to become the de jure or de facto spokesman for 27 million blacks.

To strengthen its hand within Congress, the Caucus should try to impose a mandatory bloc-voting strategy on its members. The Caucus would have much greater legislative influence in securing the enactment of its programs if other congressmen knew that a majority vote by Caucus members would determine how the entire bloc would vote on non-Caucus issues. Further, the Caucus could enlarge its bargaining powers in Congress as a whole through expanded use of the so-called Fauntroy strategy of lobbying congressmen elected from heavily black congressional districts to support Caucus positions and legislative objectives. In the past, blacks have rarely picked up political due bills from lawmakers who owed their jobs to the loyalty of black voters in their congressional districts. Finally, the Caucus might use its legislative position to secure the appointment of more blacks to influential positions on major congressional committees such as Ways and Means, Appropriations, and Rules. Bloc-voting by Caucus members provides the necessary power base. To reach maximum political strength, the Caucus must demand obedience to a strict party line. It must seek to become one to the best-organized special-interest groups within Congress.

Should the Caucus try to broaden its political base by seeking a permanent alliance with the Congressional Hispanic Caucus? Official committee status for minorities within Congress would stand a much better chance of acceptance in the House if a Committee for Minority Affairs were proposed instead of separate committees for blacks and Hispanics. Since there are at least thirty-two black, Oriental, and Spanish-origin congressional representatives in the House, a joint demand for official committee status would be politically difficult to ignore. The difficult question is whether the Black Caucus would have more to gain in a multi-ethnic alliance than in going it alone.

Opposition to converting the Black Caucus into a hard-bargaining and formally recognized unit in Congress is bound to be intense. Established political parties like to keep power to themselves and invariably oppose the proliferation of single-interest pressure groups and constituencies. In the House of Representatives in 1984 there was an Hispanic caucus, a steel caucus, a shipbuilding caucus, and a rural caucus, to name a few. Aside from the threat to established political interests, ethnic politics is frequently discredited as being racially divisive, harmful to liberal objectives and having no place in the American system. Whatever the merit of these criticisms, it is by no means clear that these considerations should require blacks to give up their political ambitions. If these ambitions include the acquisition of political power, it follows that blacks must strive for greater cohesion within the nation's lawmaking bodies just as they must work toward greater cohesion within the black body politic generally. Official status converts Black Caucus power into Black Caucus *authority*. Congressional recognition of the Caucus certifies and credentializes black political power. In the process, black bargaining strength would be greatly enhanced.

Punish Violations of Race Discrimination Laws With the Same Severe Penalties as Now Apply to Other Commercial Offenses

"Warrington Trently, this court has found you guilty of price-fixing, bribing a government official, and conspiring to act in restraint of trade. I sentence you to six months in jail, suspended. You will now step forward for the ceremonial tapping of the wrist."

—from a *New Yorker* cartoon (1978)

RACIAL DISCRIMINATION IS ESSENTIALLY A WRONG against capitalism. It suspends the free market and substitutes instead a cartel-type economic consensus that boycotts, downgrades, or excludes altogether black workers, borrowers, managers, and entrepreneurs. Race discrimination insists that the entire supply of white labor be consumed before any blacks are hired. Race discrimination maintains artificially low prices for black labor by herding blacks into menial tasks and forcing them to bid against each other for those jobs only. By limiting career opportunities, race discrimination inflicts low motivational aspirations on black people and stunts their economic and professional growth. Race discrimination in employment puts a freeze on black educational desires by telling young blacks to slow down or not to bother to prepare themselves for skilled employment where education and diligent preparation make a difference. As an arrogant form of monopoly power, codes of racial prejudgment enforce an economic caste system that contradicts the most fundamental ideals of the American system of open competition and unfettered opportunity. As a crime against free and open markets, race discrimination should be punished as a very severe infraction of our laws protecting the right to compete.

Wide publicity is usually given to back-pay settlements imposed on business institutions that have violated employment discrimination laws. To the layman, it appears that the deterrent effect of these judgments might be considerable since the payments often involve very large sums of money. But in the budgets of large corporations, the amounts paid are trivial—never more than a few pennies per share on the earnings of the corporation.

Even in cases involving the most willful and flagrant violations of anti-discrimination laws, the punitive damages and legal fees involved are usually treated by the company as simply another inevitable and acceptable cost of doing business. Of course, a certain amount of public embarrassment may result from an unfavorable court finding, but the corporate executives responsible for these violations of law are never denied promotions, nor do they lose positions or privileges, because of infractions of job bias rules. Ask a thousand business executives to solemnly swear that they will obey and enforce race discrimination laws and the vast majority will raise their hands and take the oath. But it is a rare corporation, indeed, where compliance with laws prohibiting race discrimination is considered by those executives with line operating authority a serious bottom-line matter.

Clearly, too, the penalties involved are not comparable to the penalties exacted for other commercial infractions of law where less than commensurate harm is done. In the case of many commercial offenses, fines and sometimes jail sentences are imposed directly on business executives. For example, under present federal law, corporate executives face the possibility of a $100,000 fine, three years in jail, or both for antitrust violations; $10,000 in fines, three years in jail, or both for infractions of food and drug laws; and $50,000 in fines, one year in jail, or both for infractions of consumer product safety laws. For violations of antidiscrimination laws, on the other hand, executives face no individual sanctions or penalties. Yet, race discrimination singles out certain groups of people, treats them as contaminated objects, restricts their life chances, and crushes their spirits in ways that infractions of antitrust laws can never do.

Despite the mountain of anti-job bias edicts that most traditional liberals support, race discrimination continues to be a cheap and effective screening device for selecting labor, setting promotions, and allocating credit and other benefits. Most whites would still prefer not to have blacks competing for their jobs or working in close proximity to them. A substantial minority of Americans continue to have an economic and psychological stake in protecting deeply entrenched beliefs that whites are inherently superior to blacks. If elected officials and voters were as serious about stamping out race discrimination as they are about punishing violators of antitrust laws, they would accord similar penalties for the two offenses. But they do not!

Every effort should be made by blacks, Hispanic-Americans, and women's groups to press for legislation that treats willful acts of racial discrimination as commercial crimes that are as serious as price fixing and securities violations—crimes for which personal fines and occasional jail sentences are now imposed on corporate executives.

If the government were to make race discrimination in employment sufficiently costly, employers and labor officials would quickly stop the practice. Unlike antitrust violations or other financial infractions—where there may be considerable profit to be made from successfully evading the law—the violation of antidiscrimination laws is something of a psychic luxury, offering very little in the way of financial payoffs to induce an executive to run the risk involved. It is difficult to imagine high-level corporate executives so committed to maintaining "white preferred" hiring policies that they would risk jail or personal fines on that account.

This is not to say that tough laws will immediately put an end to policies preferring whites, but the new legislation would mean that those engaging in willful acts of racial discrimination would be dealt with as social outlaws, since they would be obliged to bear the stigma of possible short jail sentences and large personal fines. As a result, American business and labor officials would at last be forced to view racial discrimination as an unacceptably costly enterprise as well as a public wrong of the gravest nature.

Provide the Equal Employment Opportunity Commission With Standard Regulatory and Enforcement Powers

> "First feed the people and then ask them to be virtuous."
> —Feodor Dostoyevsky (1880)

DESPITE VOLUBLE PROTESTS FROM BUSINESS EXECUTIVES over the tyrannical powers of the Equal Employment Opportunity Commission, the federal agency charged with enforcement of employment discrimination laws is not one of Washington's powerful agencies. Unlike many other government watchdog agencies, the EEOC does not hold administrative trials and determine fault or liability. None of its 3,200 lawyers and bureaucrats has the authority to issue a binding compliance order. EEOC has no power to compel any corporation—no matter how backward its racial hiring practices—to cease and desist or to undertake affirmative action in the employment of minorities. The Commission may not indict, punish, or impose penalties or sanctions for violations of the laws it supposedly administers.

The permitted functions of the EEOC are restricted to investigating complaints, conciliating disputes, and taking a party to court if it has cause to believe that race discrimination is taking place. Even before the onset of Reagan deregulation, the Commission was, in the words of Stephen Shulman, a former chairman of EEOC, "out to kill an elephant with a flygun." [12]

As we have shown earlier, blacks will win their place in the working world, not as a consequence of a nostalgic return to laissez-faire markets which have always kept them out, but through aggressive government police action directed against markets that are structurally geared to hiring whites first. Armed with the enforcement power granted to other government agencies, the Equal Employment Opportunity Commission could become an effective force for eliminating discrimination and pressing affirmative measures for advancing the economic status of minority groups. The powers the Commission needs are no broader than those of other government agencies such as the Federal Trade Commission and the National Labor Relations Board. The powers necessary include:

1. The power to hold hearings and to adjudicate cases involving charges of race discrimination.

2. The authority to issue cease and desist orders and to impose fines against employers and trade unions found guilty of discrimination.

3. The power to disclose publicly the minority employment statistics and affirmative-action practices of companies and unions within its jurisdiction.

4. The ability to originate proceedings before the National Labor Relations Board to suspend a labor union's collective bargaining privileges until discriminatory practices are removed.

5. The ability to develop and issue binding rules and regulations defining a "discriminatory practice" in much the same way that the NLRB is presently authorized to develop rules or laws as to the meaning of "unfair labor practices."

No watchdog agency is effective unless its sources of information on violations of law are assured. To protect company employees and executives who notify the EEOC of violations of job discrimination laws, the EEOC enabling law should be amended to include harsh punishment for retaliatory actions taken by employers who have been reported as EEO violators. The protection of informants is standard legislative practice in other matters of public concern such as federal safety and environmental protection laws. [13]

When the Reagan Administration came to power in 1981, it succeeded in convincing many Americans that the EEOC was an oppressive bureaucracy whose regulatory excesses had wickedly imposed low productivity on American industry by forcing it to hire incompetent and unqualified blacks. Casting about for a scapegoat on which to blame America's economic decline, very large numbers of Americans were prepared to embrace the thesis that liberal policies requiring favored treatment of ill-educated and unmotivated minorities had infected our economic system.

Without overtly espousing this somewhat racist view of economic decline, businessmen, particularly, were pleased to be relieved of many of the EEOC employment guidelines and were happy to return to their preferred packages of voluntary corporate aid programs to the racially underprivileged and charitable benefits for socially and economically disadvantaged people. Such was the magic of the new promise of "born again" free markets that large numbers of blacks, who were once intensely vocal about the importance of a strong EEOC, watched the deregulatory process with massive indifference as antidiscrimination rules were repealed or went unenforced. Remarkably, many blacks, too, succumbed to the allures of skillful government sloganeering to the effect that laws forbidding race discrimination interfered with the economic incentives of corporations to hire qualified blacks and therefore were the prime *cause* of black inequality.

For these reasons, it was clear, in the early 1980s, that no strengthening of the enforcement powers of the EEOC would take place without a major shift in national political attitudes about the destructive role that race discrimination plays in our society, accompanied by a strong assertion of coordinated political power by blacks, Hispanics, and women's groups. A vigorous EEOC, with broad powers to adjudicate complaints of racial discrimination in industry and to impose penalties for violations of the law, remains one of the most effective means of maximizing the price American business must pay either for excluding blacks or for putting them on a separate and inferior economic track.

Neutralize the White Wealth Advantage in Politics Through Public Financing of Election Campaigns

"A ruling group is a ruling group so long as it can nominate its successors."

—George Orwell (1945)

UNDER THE AMERICAN POLITICAL SYSTEM, access to wealth and private credit provides a huge advantage to any candidate for public office. The advantage arises not only from the constitutional interpretation that candidates are permitted to spend unlimited personal funds on their campaigns, but also from the circumstance that well-to-do candidates usually have an inside track in securing financial support from banks and well-funded political action groups that are skilled in finding ways to skirt federal and state restrictions on campaign contributions.

Since almost all wealth in this country is owned or controlled by whites, the wealth advantage in politics is necessarily a white advantage. Most blacks are obliged to run their political campaigns on a shoestring. Black candidates almost never have networks of wealthy friends and business associates. Blacks are almost never in position to call on major corporations to use their institutional muscle and influence to pressure executives and employees to pump money into political action fund-raising committees. Blacks individually, or organized as political action committees, are almost never in a position to borrow large sums of money to sustain or advance their political campaigns. Since blacks hold few elective posts, they almost never enjoy the superior fund-raising ability enjoyed by incumbents. Three-quarters of all the money contributed to congressional candidates in 1978 went to incumbents, 96 percent of whom were white. In 1978, not one of the fifty-one incumbent representatives in Congress who received over $70,000 from political action committees was a black person. In the few cases where blacks are already in office, they usually find their fund-raising constituency to be the poor, the unemployed, and even welfare recipients.[14]

The formidable fund-raising problems faced by almost all black politicians are illustrated by the 1978 senatorial campaign in Mississippi. Republican Thad Cochran and Democrat Maurice Dantin, both whites, each raised $500,000 for the contest while Charles Evers, a black independent, had great difficulty in reaching his meager campaign goal of $50,000. In 1978, Senator Jesse Helms of North Carolina raised over $7 million for his reelection bid—more than 140 times as much as Evers was able to collect.

BLACKS FACE POWERFUL HEADWINDS FROM WELL-FINANCED RIGHT-WING LOBBYING GROUPS

In 1982, six of the ten strongest political action committees in the United States spent over $25 million to advance conservative causes including dedicated opposition to equal opportunity laws, affirmative action, minority appointments, and elimination of racial segregation in education.

RANK	POLITICAL ACTION COMMITTEE	EXPENDITURES (1981-1982)
1	The Congressional Club	$9,627,600
2	National Conservative Political Action Committee	$9,003,800
3	Realtors Political Action Committee	$2,894,000
4	Fund for a Conservative Majority	$2,460,800
5	American Medical Political Action Committee	$2,374,700
6	National Committee for an Effective Congress	$2,261,900
7	Citizens for the Republic	$2,246,100
8	Committee for the Survival of a Free Congress	$2,197,900
9	Fund for a Democratic Majority	$1,803,300
10	Gun Owners of America Campaign Committee	$883,300

Source: The Federal Election Commission, Washington, D.C.

It is certain that Helms—a candidate strongly opposed to the political aspirations of most blacks—raised twice as much money in 1978 as all thirty-five black candidates for congressional offices combined. The black political candidates who have succeeded in raising substantial institutional funds are usually black mayoralty candidates in large cities where banks, insurance companies, and large corporations must concede the inevitability of the election of black mayors and, under the circumstances, have decided that it's best to be funding an almost sure winner.

The recent politicization of American corporations—together with the vast discretionary wealth at their disposal—has had a profoundly depressing effect on black political chances. The growth of corporate political action committees—$6.7 million raised in 1976 increasing to $67.7 million in 1980—benefits white candidates almost exclusively. Large corporations have discovered how to use their middle-management networks to raise

WHEN MONEY POWER LAUNCHES MEDIA BARRAGES AND PULLS THE LEVERS OF BALLOT BOXES BLACK CANDIDATES ARE LIKELY TO BE OUTFLANKED BY A 10-TO-1-OR-MORE DISADVANTAGE

A Representative Sampling of Recent Political Contests Involving Black Candidates

1983 Chicago Democratic Mayoralty Primary

Candidate	Campaign Receipts
Jane Byrne	$10,000,000
Richard Daley	2,000,000
Harold Washington	1,100,000

1978 Mississippi Senate Election

Thad Cochran	$ 1,100,000
Maurice Dantin	874,000
Charles Evers	135,000

1978 Congressional Election—Mississippi Fourth District

John Stennis	$ 311,000
Jon Hinson	249,000
Evan Doss	20,000

1978 Congressional Primary—Georgia Fifth District

Wyche Fowler	$ 142,000
Clint Deveaux	42,000

1980 Congressional Election—Mississippi Fourth District

Jon Hinson	$ 252,000
Britt Singletary	104,000
Lester McLemore	43,000

1980 Democratic Congressional Primary—New Jersey Tenth District

Peter Rodino	$ 213,000
Donald W. Payne	34,000
Golden E. Johnson	47,000

Note: Black candidates appear in boldface type.

Source: Campaign financial data obtained from the Federal Election Commission.

huge sums for mostly conservative candidates who are almost never black, or supported by most blacks. In short, blacks are greatly handicapped by the simple fact that most political money is in the hands of the GOP, a party that has not supported black political objectives for a century or more. In

1981, Republican committees raised about $73 million compared with only $9.9 million raised by Democrats.[15]

The wealth disadvantage of black candidates mounts each year as the result of massive increases in the costs of running for public office. In 1978, the average U.S. Senate candidate spent $920,000; the average House candidate, $104,000. Only a handful of blacks in the United States have access to resources of this magnitude. The extent to which the money problem hurts black electoral chances may be gauged from the fact that in 85 percent of the Senate races and 82 percent of the House races in 1978 the candidate who spent the most money during the general election campaign was the winner.[16]

It has been noted many times that well-entrenched members of Congress are unlikely to set up a political system in which anybody—black or white—can run against them at public expense. Yet, public financing of election campaigns should rank very high on the black legislative agenda. It is the single most effective way to eliminate the wealth disadvantage of the black candidate. Public financing of elections would negate the immense influence of well-heeled political action committees organized predominantly by corporate interests that are highly antagonistic to equal opportunity initiatives and to the other political and economic objectives of minority groups. Blacks are not likely to win many political offices unless this political disadvantage—whose origins are deep in the racial history of the United States—is curbed.

Despite the shift in political power toward blacks that would result under a system of public financing of political campaigns, the idea is not a black-white issue. Public financing of election contests is consistent with the most fundamental democratic principle—that public office should be awarded on the basis of merit rather than wealth; enactment of the measure would go a long way toward ridding our system of one of its most unpleasant and far-reaching biases, the intimate connection between money and political success.

Blacks, Hispanics, and other minority groups, whose political influence would mount if politics were divorced from wealth, should support bills such as the Obey-Railsback Amendment, which would limit the amount any political action committee could contribute to one candidate to $6,000 and the total amount any candidate could receive from all political action committees to $70,000. Passed by the House in October 1979, the amendment stalled in the Senate. It is highly unlikely that a conservative Senate will consider reviving the proposal. Many Senate incumbents owe their election to the financially potent political action committees of the New Right.

The national interest in campaign financing reforms spurred by the Watergate scandal has almost disappeared. With the nation now going through a period in which its leaders are determined to apply free-enterprise theory to almost every human endeavor, the interest in reducing the political advantages of the wealthy is not great. It appears that blacks and others who aspire to share political power must bide their time until once again the expectable national election scandal persuades the general electorate that the wealthy should no longer enjoy a favored opportunity to either write the laws or to buy the men and women who write them.

Abolish the Department of Housing and Urban Development and Transfer Its $30 Billion Annual Budget to Community Development and Other Self-Help Efforts in Poverty Communities

"You have sat here too long for any good you have been doing. Depart, I say, and let us have done with you. In the name of God, go."

—Oliver Cromwell (1658)

THE DEPARTMENT OF HOUSING and Urban Development is a classic example of a bankrupt social program of the Great Society. In terms of its 1983 budgetary authority of $30 billion, HUD ranks fourth among federal departments and agencies. Since its beginnings in 1966, the agency has become an increasingly bloated and ineffectual bureaucracy wholly oriented toward welfare, housing subsidies, and other oppressive palliatives for the poor. Like its sister agency, the Department of Health and Human Services, HUD concentrates on ministering to the needs of the poor rather than assisting them to gain the necessary powers to win a greater share of economic goods. HUD's housing programs represent traditional government accommodation to poverty rather than a stimulus to economic development and self-help efforts likely to put people in funds so they can then choose and buy their own housing. Despite eighteen years of inflated expectations and billions of dollars poured into model cities and other programs, the main beneficiaries of HUD programs have been the approximately 18,000 civil servants who work there, 23 percent of whom are black.

HUD is not simply an agency of awesome incompetence. It is also the embodiment of the demeaning government policy that so often places blacks in the backwaters of government power and then puts a black man or woman in charge of the ghetto. Over the years, three blacks have held the top position in HUD. In its HUD appointments the Reagan Administration has been true to tradition. Shortly after the presidential election, Samuel R. Pierce, Jr., a distinguished black lawyer from New York City, became Secretary of the Department of Housing and Urban Development. Six months later, Pierce's importance in the Cabinet became clear. President Reagan did not even recognize the face of his Cabinet Secretary at a White House conference of city officials.[17]

It would indeed be difficult to single out a government agency more worthy of extinction than HUD, an agency that has consistently pursued policies that perpetuate the dependency of large numbers of blacks and others. But money invested by government in the right places contributes to the liberties and powers of people, just as money spent in the wrong places weakens them and protects their dependent status. In this case the expenditure by HUD, over its eighteen-year life, has exceeded $300 billion. If HUD were scrapped, a large part of its huge budget could be shifted to community development corporations and other minority development efforts that have a demonstrated record of creating employment, fostering capital formation, and otherwise successfully dealing with the problems of poverty and low incomes.

Fund an Independent National Minority Development Corporation

"Give me a lever long enough
And a prop strong enough,
I can single handed move the world."

—Archimedes (c. 230 B.C.)

WE SAW IN CHAPTER TWO that power's essential trait is *risk reduction*. The commercial risks—either real or imagined—that presently act as major barriers to free commerce between whites and blacks could be overcome to a great degree if there were a major institution chartered and empowered to reduce or eliminate those risks. In a major step to remove those barriers, minority groups would make major employment and wealth gains if they were successful in pressing the President and Congress to fund a national minority development corporation (NMDC). The national minority development corporation would be capitalized by the U.S. Treasury with a minimum of $2.5 billion, an adequate but not large fund equal to approximately

$238 for every poor minority person in the nation.[18] The corporation would further be authorized to call upon the Treasury for additional capital funds up to $1.5 billion and would be granted U.S. agency-type public market borrowing powers of up to $20 billion.

The express purpose of the NMDC would be to ease and encourage economic transactions between the races in general, to strengthen the bargaining power of members of minority groups, and particularly to encourage wealth and capital formation in minority communities. The corporation would accomplish these goals by insuring risk in a wide variety of commercial transactions between whites and nonwhites. Like many other development bodies with a specific economic or political mission, the NMDC would need to have considerable independence from congressional and presidential oversight. It would be governed by appointed officials named possibly by United States congressmen representing congressional districts with minority populations of 20 percent or more. The national minority development corporation would be expressly chartered to act as a nationwide advocate of the economic rights and advancement of minority groups.

The Promissory Economy

The idea of a national minority development corporation may best be understood within the context of the vast economic distance between blacks and whites in this country. An advanced economy, which, for the most part, is driven by contractual relationships, actually contributes to this distance. In the United States, as in any free and well-developed economy, virtually all employment and commercial transactions occur under promissory relationships which look to the performance of a future act. People *promise* labor or managerial employment. People and institutions *agree* to borrow, lend, and repay money. People in commerce and institutions *contract* with others to supply goods and machinery. Investment capital is promised, and rewards are reciprocally promised or expected on the part of those who use or rent investment capital. Accordingly, *the instrument of the commercial promise is the principal mechanism for the distribution of income, goods, and capital.*

As a result, one's well-being within the society is highly dependent on whether or not one is, in fact, participating in the vast network of commercial and employment promises that are made every day.

In any given situation, the likelihood of a particular set of commercial promises being made and accepted is largely dependent on whether each party involved in the exchange of promises believes that the other party will perform his promise or keep his "part of the bargain." It follows that whenever significant fear, uncertainty, or ignorance arises about the possible completion of an offered promise, serious obstacles are presented to employment, investment, trade, and other exchanges.

Since the mercantile promise necessarily contemplates completion of a future act, the important question is always the *perceived expectation* about whether or not the promise will be fulfilled. This counts far more than the

---

THE RANGE OF RISK-REDUCTION ACTIVITIES OF A NATIONAL MINORITY DEVELOPMENT CORPORATION

Firming Up the Bargaining Power of Minority Groups to Enable Them to Negotiate Entry Into the Economic Mainstream

- Guarantee credits to assist minority groups to purchase large-scale business enterprises.
- Support minority job creation by providing broad credit guarantees and investment insurance to attract additional investment funds to inner-city and rural neighborhood development corporations.
- Indemnify established bonding companies against above-average losses on performance bonds of minority contractors.
- Underwrite credit risks on home mortgage loans developed by minority mortgage bankers for resale to large institutional investors.
- Guarantee inventory borrowings of minority retailers and wholesalers.
- Improve the ability of minority banks and savings institutions to attract deposits by providing a secondary market for their mortgages and other loans.

---

reality of the statistical probability that the promise will, in fact, be fulfilled. For instance, on Friday, June 20, 1969, the former Penn Central Company was insolvent. This meant that, objectively viewed, the company definitely could not and would not keep its promises to repay its debts. Nevertheless, on that same day the company borrowed tens of millions of dollars. This was possible because others still *believed* in the company's ability to keep its promises to repay its debts and to act responsibly in commercial transactions.

Just as a commercial promise may be incorrectly believed or credited, so may it be incorrectly disbelieved or discredited. For many generations, for example, it was widely believed in banking circles that a promise to repay a loan for the purchase of a non-income-producing chattel such as a piano, home appliance, or automobile was a promise not likely to be completed.

Accordingly, credit was not extended to finance the purchase of these particular goods. Time proved this banking policy to be mistaken, however, and today banks make handsome profits by financing pianos, automobiles, and appliances. The same principle applies to all other commercial transactions. I may or may not be awarded a job, be sold a machine, be offered an extension of credit, be entrusted with leased property, get my construction contract bonded, or receive a money deposit of funds depending on whether or not, at that particular point in time, my promise to perform work, pay for the machine, pay back the loan, pay rent, perform a contract, or return money *appears* to be credible in the eyes of the parties with whom I am dealing.

Since appearances and beliefs often count for more than reality in such transactions, a person or group that *appears* credible in fact possesses economic power and bargaining strength. Conversely, a person or group *perceived* as unreliable or incapable of keeping promises has no economic power. Obviously, any collective prejudgment holding that a certain group is a poor commercial risk will induce those subscribing to this prejudgment to refuse to make any economic transactions with the group thus stigmatized. Over a period of time, this perception has the capacity to reduce the group to the powerless and subservient economic status of an outcast class. In virtually all cases, the outcast group will function wholly outside the network of commercial promises that allocates goods and benefits within the economy.

Blacks Outside the Consensual Economic System

In the case of blacks in America, there was a long period of time, approximately 1619 to 1942, during which *they had no choice but to function almost entirely outside the normal consensual and other promissory commercial exchange relationships that drive the greater economy*. Because of the restrictive force of the race-trait prejudgment, even highly educated and skilled blacks were not entrusted with a great range of tasks and professional activities because their promise to perform a task was not viewed as credible. Thus, blacks operated almost entirely as low-skilled laborers, porters, janitors, and domestic servants, where they could readily be replaced if they failed to perform and where, because of the simplicity of the tasks assigned, long-term promises or assurances were not required.

During this long period when blacks functioned almost entirely outside the consensual system of exchanged promises that characterized the mainstream economy, credit was not extended to black people because of a collective belief on the part of lenders that black people were both unwilling and unable to repay debts. The commitment of a black person to perform a long-term lease or to carry out the terms of a manufacturing or construction contract was essentially a nonnegotiable promise. In this sense, nobody "bought" the promise because few people, including blacks themselves, believed that the promise would be fulfilled or honored. During this period, investment capital was not entrusted to black managers and entrepreneurs because no one believed the black man's commitment to make the capital grow and bear fruit. Deposits in black banks were not made by whites because of perceived risks about the possible incompletion of the black banker's promise to make a good return on the deposit. In many ways, the backward economy of the black American ghetto of today is an institutional statement of the long-standing lack of confidence on the part of whites in the ability of blacks to perform any important commercial or professional undertakings.

One way for blacks to overcome the immense handicap of having been labeled unfit for trust as employees, contractors, borrowers, or in any important promissory relationship would be for the state to simply *command* whites to accept blacks in undertakings where they have been habitually rejected. To a certain extent, this has occurred. In employment, credit extensions, and contracts, limited affirmative-action requirements have been imposed on commercial enterprises; but wide-ranging economic coercion is neither feasible nor constitutional.

A second and often more acceptable approach to the problem would be the creation of a large and financially credible organization to bridge the distance by standing behind and warranting the undertakings of blacks. This is the function of the national minority development corporation. The NMDC would be prepared to sponsor and guarantee a wide variety of undertakings by minority groups. For example, it would underwrite minority covenants to protect the value of capital, promises to repay loans, and undertakings to manufacture and deliver goods. It would certify and insure a contractor's pledge to construct a building, a merchant's promise to pay rent under a commercial lease, and a mortgage convenant secured by a minority-operated factory. The NMDC would be charged to identify a whole range of organizations in low-income and minority communities—community development corporations, minority banks, credit unions, retail and production cooperatives, contractors, entrepreneurs, and housing cooperatives—and where necessary, to underwrite their commercial undertakings as well as their capital and credit needs.

In view of the high-risk characteristics of its activities, the national minority development corporation would require sufficient capital and borrowing power to give it relatively permanent financial autonomy and strength. To advance its economic independence, the corporation would charge fees in order to strengthen its capital to support its various activities and services. In the same manner as a newly organized casualty or life insurance company, it would budget its undertakings so that its premium income would gradually build up a reserve against possible losses.

Since the national minority development corporation would be explicitly chartered to alter economic power relationships in favor of minority groups, the development corporation would necessarily undertake a number of politically unpopular actions. Its endeavors could cut deeply into white economic advantages and probably rouse opposition far more intense than garden-variety forms of affirmative action. To acquire the political independence needed to support controversial transactions, the NMDC would necessarily fail in its mission if it were regularly accountable to the electorate or to the changing moods of Congress. Of course, Congress could at any time take the drastic step of abolishing the NMDC, but short of that, the forces on Capitol Hill should not be in a position to modify the NMDC's strategies or its policies on an item-by-item basis any more than Congress sets the specific agenda of the Federal Reserve Board. Only by providing such a layer of insulation between the NMDC and its legislative creators could the corporation be guaranteed the political independence it would need to perform many of its politically unpopular chores.

The Opportunity Funding Corporation Experiment

A prototype of the NMDC began operations in 1970 as a private nonprofit corporation known as the Opportunity Funding Corporation. It was designed to develop, test, and demonstrate the feasibility of directing private investment into minority and capital-poor communities. As its central strategy, OFC employs a wide range of guarantee protection arrangements and risk-reduction devices to lower the level of loss assumed by private investors committing funds to low-income and minority communities.[19]

Initially capitalized at $7.4 million by the former Office of Economic Opportunity, OFC was able, in the course of a decade, to achieve considerable standing as a sound, effective, and cost-efficient development body without any significant expenditure of the taxpayers' money. By 1980, OFC had participated in risk-reduction financing of over 139 minority job-creation projects in thirty-two states.

The most important feature of the opportunity funding idea is the leverage effect by which it uses very limited federal funds to produce minority employment with a value many times greater than the government funds contributed. This leverage is illustrated by the record of OFC during the period 1970 to 1978. During these years, OFC received operating grants from the federal government totaling $2.2 million, in addition to the initial capitalization of $7.4 million, making a total of $9.6 million of funds received.

Compare these relatively minor costs with the huge benefits of the OFC program. OFC claims credit for having produced 3,600 new jobs during this period.[20] In view of the participation by others in this effort, OFC should possibly be credited with producing only one-third of that employment, or 1,200 jobs. Even at poverty-level wages of $6,000 a year, the income value of 1,200 jobs for one year is $7 million. If the jobs lasted three years, the value of the employment would be $21 million. Direct government public-service employment of the same 1,200 people over eight years, again at the poverty level of $6,000 a year, would cost the government upwards to $60 million—exactly six times what OFC spent to produce financially comparable results. Clearly, the leverage technique used by OFC is a highly efficient method of funding employment in low-income communities. Moreover, the minority employment that was created occurred entirely within the private sector and, for that reason, did not carry the stigmatizing effects of jobs directly created with federal money.

There are further secondary advantages to the OFC's lever-type approach to economic development. With capital of only $7.4 million, OFC produced in excess of $30 million of permanent private investment in low-income communities. In addition, OFC maintained over $5 million of its funds on deposit in some forty-five financial institutions, all situated in poverty communities. Through its emphasis on ventures with a developmental multiplier effect—that is to say, banks, new towns, and rural development projects—OFC's activities may safely be assumed to have resulted in a large number of additional derivative jobs. The accompanying chart shows the investment funds generated and matched against OFC's net losses—loss reserves less investment income—over the first ten years of operation.

Unfortunately, the potential benefits of a national minority development corporation to minority groups are far clearer than are the prospects of winning the legislation necessary to realize these benefits in the near future. In 1970, liberals held political power in Congress. At that time there was almost no cynicism about the ability of a wealthy nation to enact laws capable of eliminating racial inequality. In this climate the concept of a national minority development corporation might have moved swiftly through Congress. Today, however, an ever-worsening black economic condition coincides with a hardening of political attitudes against government measures to assist blacks to move into the economic mainstream.

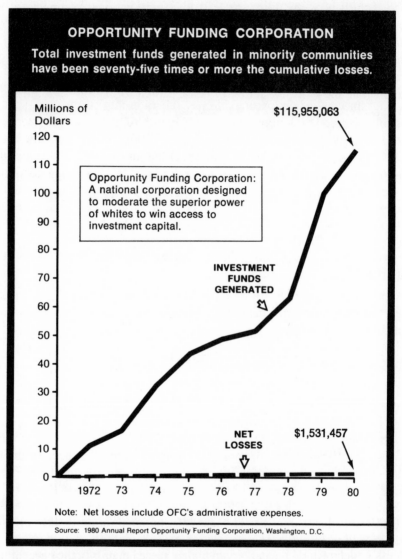

OPPORTUNITY FUNDING CORPORATION

Total investment funds generated in minority communities have been seventy-five times or more the cumulative losses.

Millions of Dollars

$115,955,063

Opportunity Funding Corporation: A national corporation designed to moderate the superior power of whites to win access to investment capital.

INVESTMENT FUNDS GENERATED

NET LOSSES

$1,531,457

1972 73 74 75 76 77 78 79 80

Note: Net losses include OFC's administrative expenses.

Source: 1980 Annual Report Opportunity Funding Corporation, Washington, D.C.

Given the current state of national apathy on issues of racial inequality, no President is likely to press Congress to establish a national minority development corporation, nor would Congress enact such legislation if it were proposed.

In time, the public mood is certain to shift. Forces such as the burgeoning political influence of blacks, the continuing deterioration of the black economic position, and mounting public concerns about the resumption of urban disturbances are likely to lead to a new national commitment to strengthen the minority economic position. Even if the nation as a whole decides to renew its commitment to improving the economic status of racial minorities, it is still unlikely that the national minority development corporation idea will be pursued unless blacks and other minority groups come to appreciate the indispensability of black capital formation—and the economic power it generates—to the realization of overall racial equality.

Moderate Wealth Differences Between Blacks and Whites Through Comprehensive Estate Tax Reform

"The meek shall inherit the earth, but not its mineral rights."
—John Paul Getty (1892-1976)

DESPITE THE PRESENCE ON THE STATUTE BOOKS of supposedly punitive estate taxes, wealthy Americans have never allowed these taxes to interfere with their ability to transmit large sums of wealth to succeeding generations. Clearly, this capacity to pass on wealth to heirs often conflicts with the Jeffersonian ideals on which the Republic was founded. In theory, natural ability and hard work should be the principal determinants of economic success, but in practice wealth transferred to children and grandchildren confers unearned political, economic, and educational advantages, and to a great extent assures them the ability to claim superior positions and opportunities for which others with lesser inheritances may be better qualified.

The idea of placing a lid on the ability of very wealthy families to transmit large amounts of wealth to their children is profoundly opposed by rich and poor alike. Yet, by restricting somewhat the amount of wealth that could be transferred from one generation to another, we would tend to prevent the development of privileged classes and protect the American ideal whereby success is determined by individual ability rather than inherited wealth or position. Instead of liberalizing estate duties—as has been the trend in recent years—these laws should be tightened. This could be done without eroding the incentives of the person who makes the money. Present wealth inequalities in America are so extreme as to be indefensible, and they appear to be increasing. A 1969 study by the Internal Revenue Service reported that people with wealth of more than $5 million—the top .008 percent of the population—own as much combined property as the bottom half of all families.

For these reasons the issue of estate tax reform transcends racial considerations and would be socially desirable in any society that seriously aspires to be a genuine meritocracy. And this would be true even if blacks had already achieved economic parity with whites. But blacks have a special interest in pressing for heavier and more tightly enforced inheritance levies. In the United States, upwards of 98 percent of all real estate, business assets, stocks, and bonds are in white hands. Virtually all of the means of production are controlled by whites. Long-term trends show no perceptible closing of the immense wealth gap between blacks and whites.[21] Heavier estate duties would level some of these extreme economic differences between the races, negate somewhat the white wealth advantage, and make it possible for young blacks to compete on a more equal footing with young whites.

From the black viewpoint, the most important reform in the estate tax laws would be simply to close some of the major loopholes so that inherited wealth is really taxed at the rates which the public is led to believe already prevail. One could well start by eliminating the so-called stepped-up basis estate tax rule which allows heirs (including widows who now receive property without limit as to amounts wholly free of estate taxes in their husbands' estates) to sell appreciated wealth without paying any capital gains taxes whatsoever. The size of this loophole may be gauged from the fact that more money may be lost to the government by this means than is collected from all capital gains taxes—about $20 billion a year. The closing of this glaring loophole in the federal estate tax laws would be a first small step in moving toward the ideal of giving each generation a fresh start in life.

Ultimately, major estate tax reforms should be contemplated to bring America closer to Jefferson's ideal of an aristocracy of merit. Some dollar limit—say $5 million per child—would be imposed on the ability of the wealthy to pass their wealth on to future generations. Parents have a legitimate interest in providing for the security of their children, but there is no compelling reason why any child needs to start off life with more than a $5 million nest egg.

The standard argument against a ceiling on inheritable wealth is its possible harmful effects on work incentives, innovation, and new capital formation. There is no denying that people work hard to buy their children a superior education, to set them up in business, or simply to make them rich. These are rights and benefits that the nation should protect. But there is no evidence whatsoever that the privilege of passing on unlimited wealth to offspring is essential to maintaining the economic incentives that produce innovation, efficiency, and new wealth. The need to endow one's children with sums above $5 million each is not an incentive but a symptom of pure addiction to wealth. In a society that values open opportunity for all—and is further dedicated to the proposition that no person's vote should be more valuable than another's—there is no rational justification for not taxing away inheritances above these truly immense sums.

Fundamental estate tax reform is not likely to occur in the foreseeable future. Still, it deserves an important place on the black agenda, along with other goals that may have to wait a long time before they are realized. Blacks, in particular, have an interest in promoting any inheritance tax reform that will cut back the massive inherited wealth disadvantage resulting from the historical circumstances that, at a critical stage in the development of American capitalism, only whites were permitted to compete for the accumulation of industrial, mineral, communications and banking wealth.

Revive the Community Development Corporation as an Instrument for Building Economic and Political Power in Minority Communities

"Historically no poor migrant groups in any country, at any time, have climbed out of poverty on therapeutic ladders proffered by an elite."

—Charles Hampden-Turner (1974)

DESPITE A BRIEF FLIRTATION in the mid-1960s with the idea of empowerment of the poor, most government programs for low-income people—including programs for job training, housing assistance, and welfare support—appear to have weakened the economic position of the intended beneficiaries. As government has taken increasingly greater responsibility for the problems of the poor and of minority groups, the people who were supposed to be helped have become increasingly dependent on the crutches of social services and assistance and probably less able than before to deal with their problems. To this extent, the conservative thesis that exposes and abhors the enervating effects of the federal dole is undoubtedly correct.

Standing in sharp contrast to the consistent failures of governments, corporations, and private charities to improve the position of so-called disadvantaged people are the striking successes of programs based on the principle of local initiative and self-help. In general, the most effective self-help programs for the poor have been those carried out through the mechanism of the community development corporation (CDC). As a community-based organization cooperatively owned and controlled by community residents, the CDC concentrates its efforts on capital formation, job creation, and building economic and political bargaining power, particularly in the inner cities and in rural poverty areas.

Originally conceived by the Congress of Racial Equality (CORE) in conjunction with a number of Republican legislative planners, the CDC idea was first articulated in the Community Self-Determination Bill, which excited a great deal of liberal interest in the mid-1960s. Although the bill was never enacted by Congress, the CDC idea was put into effect on an experimental basis through the former federal Office of Economic Opportunity.

The CDC: Consensus Power Institutionalized

In essence, the CDC gathers political and economic power by operating as a consensus builder. It is an economic and political organization around which poor, dependent, and discouraged people may gather, affiliate, and act collectively to use collective power to achieve common goals. As a body, the CDC deals with social and economic problems through concerted but nonviolent action. It uses group pressure in much the same way that a labor union, a political party, a consumer cooperative, or a lobbying organization does.

Federal funding acts as the catalyst, making it possible for the CDC to employ organizers, to fund self-help efforts, to acquire business enterprises, and to use communications media to mobilize collective action and to motivate members of the group. The power of the community development corporation—and, in most cases, its success in its self-help programs—is a direct function of the extent to which the federal funding is provided on a certain and unconditional basis. Reliable, no-strings-attached funding allows the CDC to operate without fear of manipulation by the central funding organization. On the other hand, funding that is either uncertain or conditional upon state and federal program approvals tends to draw power away from the CDC to the distant bureaucracies that control the purse strings. A mature CDC, like any other strong business or political organization, ultimately seeks to become self-funded through the payment of dues by its members. This autonomous fiscal position is a necessary condition for the development by the CDC of the collective bargaining tactics that characterize economic and political power generally.

It may be useful to think of the CDC as essentially a labor union for low-income and minority groups. A properly functioning CDC generates economic power because it creates economic demand for the work, services, and products of its members. Relying upon federal funding and possibly upon its own secondary borrowing ability, the CDC is able to establish labor-intensive enterprises that employ local people. If, for example, a large metropolitan bank wishes to "do good works" in the ghetto, the CDC acts as the bargaining agent for determining the conditions under which these works will be done. If, for political or eleemosynary reasons, a large federal contractor wishes to establish a manufacturing plant in a low-income community, the local CDC may negotiate the terms of entry and may act as a bargaining agent for local employees. The CDC may organize product boycotts against corporations with poor minority employment records. It may use peer pressure, and play upon feelings of community loyalty, to persuade local residents to patronize CDC-operated banks, markets, and automobile dealerships. The CDC may organize community-based labor unions to bargain in the larger economy for jobs for its members.

In the eyes of charitable organizations and of coalitions of businessmen bound on good-works missions for the poor, the confrontational attitude of the CDC appears to be both ungrateful and counterproductive. But the posture of independence and confrontation is simply a natural outcome of the rules of empowerment that insist that affluent people—or for that matter rather distant and unresponsive government and private agencies—can or will do very little to reduce racial inequality unless they are responding to pressure, sanctions, or economic need.

The CDC Controls Territory

A successful CDC develops the power that usually accompanies the control of territory. Although the CDC is not a political unit, it tends to acquire some elements of economic and political sovereignty. For example, by virtue of a CDC's territorial influence, the contractors working on a government-subsidized office building constructed in a low-income community may have to come to terms with the governing CDC as to numbers of minority workers to be employed on the construction site. Private developers who wish to take advantage of various government incentives in poverty areas may be obliged to negòtiate with a local CDC as to the number of store locations in a project that will be operated by local entrepreneurs rather than by absentee merchants. The CDC may require that building maintenance and insurance contracts in its territory be placed through CDC-controlled enterprises. The CDC's power in the community sometimes means that schools and social services may come under CDC influence and thus become more accountable to its members. To the extent the CDC actually owns retail stores, lending institutions, day-care centers, nursing homes, food markets, and liquor stores, it becomes accountable to its community members as to how those institutions operate and affect the lives of members.

The CDC as a Nursery for Black Capital Formation

The CDC strives to become a center for capital formation, which in turn produces greater economic self-sufficiency and independence in a community. By establishing locally controlled banking and savings units, the CDC reverses the "export effect" of branches of large metropolitan banks and loan companies that remit to the outside economy funds derived from deposits and profits earned within the community. In many cases, the CDC acquires ownership or control of some local housing. To this extent, rental income is held for internal property improvement and reinvestment, instead of being remitted to absentee landlords. The CDC also serves as a permanent coalition for pressing large financial institutions to comply with the federal Community Reinvestment Act requiring private financial institutions to reinvest certain funds in low-income communities. By providing a new capital base within the community, the CDC can help to establish new organizations such as cable television units, community-controlled construction companies, transportation facilities, office buildings, venture capital organizations, shopping centers, industrial plants, theaters, and restaurants.

The CDC as a Broker of Political Power

While its stated objectives are social and economic change, the CDC necessarily becomes a center for the organization of community political power. Like the federally funded community action agencies before them, CDCs organize political consensus. In black communities, CDCs work to create a unified local black electorate. A successful CDC identifies candidates who will best serve blacks, raises money for them, and gets out the community vote in primaries and general elections. A well-oiled CDC lobbies for better police and municipal services and mounts campaigns to retire mayors who have neglected municipal services in minority communities.

As the organization responsible for spearheading bloc-voting strategies, the CDC has considerable leverage in influencing the governing bodies that control public schools, fire departments, ambulance services, and hospitals. The CDC may mediate between police headquarters and the community when civil disturbances and other problems arise in a low-income community. Even the merchant usurer or loan shark unlawfully exploiting unsophisticated consumers may be obliged to deal with the community development corporation, which has ready access to the courts and law enforcement authorities if its complaints are not promptly and effectively acted upon.

The community development corporation often becomes the focal point for the organization of a strong community commitment to the prevention of crime. Obviously, individual residents of low-income neighborhoods have no power to jail the narcotics dealers who prey on the young members of their community; acting alone, they have no way to punish marauding juveniles who terrorize senior citizens. Of course, neither CDCs nor their members have official power to discipline the cop "on the take," to curb vandalism, merchant exploitation, or loan-sharking. But the CDC may organize "block watchers" to police neighborhoods, it may pressure city hall to curb crime and to enforce criminal laws. The CDC may use its political influence to make city government respond to the needs of the low-income community.

CDCs in Operation

The community development corporation concept of group self-help through the use of leveraged federal economic development grants is a far more cost-effective means of dealing with chronic unemployment than are present welfare and job training efforts. Moreover, the CDC, which in practice employs people who have never held jobs before, may in time succeed in removing many workers from an otherwise dependent condition. Knowledgeable congressmen, the General Accounting Office, and private evaluators generally agree that a well-managed and adequately funded CDC can produce impressive economic gains in a poverty community. Approximately thirty-six urban community development corporations operated during the decade 1968 to 1978. All were organized with federal funding under the so-called special impact provisions of the original 1964 federal law that established the federal Office of Economic Opportunity. Most neighborhood development corporations have operated in urban settings such as the black ghetto and the Mexican-American barrio, but CDCs have also

GOVERNMENT-ENGINEERED ETHNIC POWER

Urban community development corporations funded from 1968 to 1978

Urban Community Development Corporation	Total Government Funding 1968-1978
Hough, Cleveland, Ohio	$11,422,000
Bedford Stuyvesant, Brooklyn, New York	53,879,000
United, Durham, North Carolina	3,477,000
Harlem Commonwealth, New York, New York	28,132,000
Union Sarah EDC, St. Louis, Missouri	5,548,000
ICBIF, Detroit, Michigan	1,800,000
Pyramidwest, Chicago, Illinois	18,953,000
PIC/PDC, Washington, D.C.	1,525,000
Denver CDC, Denver, Colorado	6,253,000
East Boston CDC, East Boston, Mass.	6,100,000
UIC, Seattle, Washington	152,000
ECCO, Columbus, Ohio	900,000
Greater Roxbury Development Corp., Mass.	4,574,000
N.J. Dept. of Community Affairs	2,140,000
Bergen-Greenville Development Corp., N.J.	1,360,000
N.Y. Office of Community Development	825,000
Memphis Area Chamber of Commerce, Tenn.	5,520,000
CDC of Kansas City, Missouri	1,060,000
CAO, Buffalo, New York	4,255,000
Hunts Point CLDC, Bronx, New York	4,030,000
CEDC of Nassau County, New York	6,920,000
MAUC, San Antonio, Texas	13,192,000
TELACU, East Los Angeles, California	3,350,000
SRC, Racine, Wisconsin	2,050,000
San Juan CDC, San Juan, Puerto Rico	1,650,000
Anacostia EDC, Washington, D.C.	3,923,000
Chicanos Por La Causa, Phoenix, Arizona	1,323,000
Black People's Unity EDC, Camden, N.J.	774,000
Chinese EDC, Boston, Massachusetts	213,000
Eastside Community Inv., Indianapolis, Ind.	198,000
Operation Life CDC, Las Vegas, Nevada	231,000
POCD, Pensacola, Florida	228,000
Southside Community Inv., Minneapolis, Minn.	208,000
SSUC, Oakland, California	552,000
UMCC, Omaha, Nebraska	150,000
Milwaukee CDC, Milwaukee, Wisconsin	—
TOTAL	**$196,870,000**

Source: Center for Community Economic Development Review, Cambridge, Massachusetts, Summer 1979.

been established by poor whites in Appalachia and by black farmers in rural areas of the South. Like most new business enterprises, their record of success is mixed. By the late 1970s, eight of the original thirty-six CDCs had ceased operations, but the other twenty-eight were still in existence— some of them relatively healthy, others barely holding their own.

The community development corporation strategy has special political and economic advantages for blacks. Since the CDC effort is designed to help all those who are poor, it is a racially neutral program and therefore does not present the constitutional problems posed by preferential government allocations to blacks. Yet the impact of CDC programs benefits blacks disproportionately since blacks are in poverty three or more times as often as whites, black youths are unemployed three times as often as white youths, and blacks are heavily concentrated in urban areas where community development programs tend to be concentrated. Because intensive CDC funding helps blacks disproportionately, the strategy, when successful, tends to close the black-white poverty gap.

From the point of view of poor blacks, a strong case can be made that the community development corporation remains the single most promising and cost-efficient plan for creating jobs and reducing chronic unemployment in the inner cities and rural poverty areas. For this reason, a black political agenda should call for the reinstatement of federal funding of community development corporations in rural and urban low-income neighborhoods. New federal appropriations for self-help neighborhood economic development units should be raised from the 1979 level of $35 million to at least $1 billion a year.

Enterprise Zones

Traditional alternatives to community development corporations propose business aid from the outside rather than self-help efforts originating from within poverty neighborhoods. Under most alternative plans, large corporations would be persuaded to locate their own job-producing factories in distressed urban areas rather than to finance efforts by blacks to form locally owned and controlled enterprises. In lieu of encouraging black-owned banks and other capital-formation activities by minority groups, the standard alternative to the CDC calls for incentives to large metropolitan banks that encourage them to extend credit to inner-city blacks.

The most recent of the business-oriented alternatives to community development corporations is the proposed creation of federally designated "enterprise zones." In enterprise zone areas, federal tax incentives that provide jobs and credit in these communities would be offered to business.

Firms operating in the enterprise zones would receive generous benefits such as the elimination of capital gains taxes on investments, partial tax exemption on income, and tax credits for the employment of workers formerly on welfare rolls.

While there is reason to doubt that tax incentives will be enough to overcome the costs and risks of doing business in distressed urban areas, enterprise zone tax incentives might cause some large corporations to set up plants in inner-city areas. It is possible, too, that some firms participating in the program might even find the effort financially profitable. But these programs would add nothing to black economic independence or strength and, for this reason, are unlikely to assist blacks in closing the economic gap. Paying the rich to come to the aid of the poor may relieve the poor of some economic distress, but it does not appear to be a useful formula for helping poor blacks gather the economic strength to catch up with whites.

The CDC and Access to Playing Fields of Competition

The confrontational aspects of community development tactics are profoundly disturbing to most people who have a misty and romantic vision of capitalism's abhorrence of coercive power. But, the soundness of the CDC concept rests in the dual nature of the rules of power governing American capitalism. The first rule is that people who have economic bargaining power in the sense of being skilled and highly motivated workers tend to earn more than those who have less market influence because they are unskilled and unmotivated. A second and equally important rule—one not intended by laissez-faire economists—is that access to coercive power also dictates who will do well. People who command tend to do better, in an economic sense, than those who obey. And this is true even when those who command are not particularly well endowed with traditional economic skills. As long as both forms of economic power govern material well-being, blacks must concentrate on gathering both forms of economic strength. Of all the ideas so far advanced for black empowerment in the second sense, the CDC appears to be most valuable for low-income black people. The CDC provides the necessary economic base for mounting the political and economic power blacks need to enter an economy that still obeys many of the exclusionary rules of race. It provides them with some of the wherewithal to deal with well-defended economic and educational advantages heretofore won by whites under a 100-year-old system where public law and private codes demanded and ensured the subordination of black people. Once unrestricted entry onto the playing fields of competition is won, the more traditional powers deriving from skill and competence may operate to ensure that Negro people may compete more effectively and on fairer terms with the seasoned power holders who have staked out and hold virtually all of the positions of economic and political advantage.

Use Every Constitutional Means to Outlaw Runoff Primaries and Gerrymandered Voting Districts

"The requirement of an absolute majority made it almost impossible for a black candidate to win in the Democratic party primaries."

—Clifton McCleskey,
The Government and Politics of Texas
(Boston: Little, Brown & Co., 1972), p. 49

SINCE THE RECONSTRUCTION PERIOD, whites have used a variety of legislative tricks and extralegal procedural devices to block the election of blacks to Congress and to state and local office. As a result of Supreme Court rulings banning these practices and congressional enactment of the Voting Rights Act of 1965, many of the roadblocks that impeded the development of black political power have been eliminated. But the heavy hand of the past continues to control the present. Voting rules and structures set up generations ago for the purpose of ensuring the election of whites still remain on the statute books. Although couched in nonracial terms, these rules continue to restrict or dilute the black voting franchise.

The geographic distribution of black voters highlights the importance of these voting restrictions. Fifty percent of the black population of the United States still live in the South. Yet, there are only two black U.S. congressmen from the eleven states of the Old Confederacy; there is no black congressman from the five heavily black populated states of the Deep South. No black holds any major state office in the South despite the presence of 13 million black citizens in the region. Yet, because blacks are so highly concentrated geographically in the South, as many as twenty additional black United States congressmen could be elected from the southern states if there were an unfettered electoral system. How might this come about?

The drawing and redrawing of racially gerrymandered congressional voting districts have been the slickest and most successful of the tricks used by southern state legislatures to disarm black voters. Although blacks in the South are clearly the majority in many regions, district lines have been drawn by white-controlled state assemblies in such ways as to create a political map in which nearly all congressional districts in the South have a white majority.

The racial gerrymander has been under steady constitutional attack in the courts. Because of flagrantly racist intent, it is probable that whites who control the southern state legislatures will eventually be forced by the courts to redraw their districts to increase the percentage of black voters. As a result of court-ordered voting reforms, additional blacks are likely to be elected to Congress.

Still, even if racial gerrymandering were eliminated, conservatives in the South have a bag full of other tricks for keeping blacks out of public office, particularly congressional office. The key element in this second line of defense is the runoff primary system which prevails in most southern states. Despite the reemergence of the Republican party in recent elections, much of the South remains a Democratic stronghold, especially on the local level. In a great many instances, victory in the Democratic primary is tantamount to election. So much is this the case that even in the 1980 Republican sweep, eighteen incumbent Democratic congressmen in the South faced no GOP opponent in the general election and twenty-five other Democratic con- gressional candidates won landslide victories against only token Republican opposition.

Unlike general elections where the presence of two major parties usually limits the contest to two serious contenders, a primary often presents a crowded field of candidates vying for the same office. In any given primary, it is often possible to win the party nomination with a small percentage, say 25 to 30 percent of the primary vote. As a result, it follows that even in a gerrymandered congressional district that includes a significant black mi- nority, a black candidate could win the Democratic nomination—and in all likelihood the subsequent general election—if whites split their votes among many candidates.

After World War II, it became clear to segregationists in the South that blacks would eventually win the vote and thereby pose a considerable threat to Jim Crow. To ensure that this would not occur, the runoff primary system was instituted. In this system, if no candidate receives a majority of the total vote cast in the first primary, the top two finishers must square off in a second contest. A classic example of how the runoff primary defeats black candidates occurred in the 1982 congressional election in North Carolina. In the Second District, where blacks make up about 36 percent of the regis- tered Democrats, H.M. Michaux, a black candidate, led the field in the first primary but was unable to obtain a majority of the total vote cast. In the runoff election, Michaux was beaten by the white candidate, Tim Valentine, who had finished second in the original primary contest. Valentine went on to win a landslide victory in the general election. Black voter apathy was not the problem since blacks in the district are well organized and achieve among the highest voter turnout rates in the country. Plainly and simply, Michaux was defeated by the runoff primary law which gives whites a second chance to defeat a successful black candidate.

In 1984, the runoff primary system was in effect in only nine mostly southern states: Alabama, Arkansas, Florida, Georgia, Mississippi, North Carolina, Oklahoma, South Carolina, and Texas. The fact that in the states of the North and West, without exception, a simple plurality is required to win primaries for state and congressional elections is strong evidence that the runoff system was designed to give political protection to the racial biases of southern voters rather than to institute a representative form of elective government.

For these reasons, the runoff primary system is constitutionally vulnerable and its elimination is one of the most important steps to win greater black representation in Congress and in other elective offices. Although the United States Constitution delegates the power to establish election procedures to the state legislatures, it also allows Congress to alter the voting procedures by which its members are elected. Thus, Congress could enter the picture—as it did in 1965 when it enacted the Voting Rights Act—and nullify the runoff primary systems for congressional races in the southern states.[22]

A major effort of blacks and Hispanics should be organized to press for legislation or litigation curtailing the runoff election system. In this campaign, blacks should enlist the support of other groups adversely affected by the runoff rules. In Texas, for example, there are three congressional districts with significant Hispanic minorities that could conceivably nominate a Spanish-American candidate for Congress if the white vote were split between two or more candidates. Similarly, the Cuban-American population in Miami might also be interested in the effort because Florida's runoff system effectively blocks the nomination of a Cuban-American in that state. In addition, women's groups should also be enlisted to support the elimination of the runoff system. In 1980 only two women were elected to Congress from any state that held a runoff primary. A clear example of the harm done by the runoff primary to women candidates was the 1979 gubernatorial contest in Mississippi. But for the runoff system, Evelyn Gandy would have won the Democratic nomination for governor of Mississippi in 1979, as she led the six-candidate field in the preliminary election.

However, in the runoff, former Lieutenant Governor William Winter defeated Gandy in a one-on-one, man-against-woman contest and went on to win the general election.

In enacting the Voting Rights Act in 1965 and in extending it three times, in 1970, 1975, and 1982, Congress has shown its capacity to legislate on voting rights over powerful conservative objections. If minority groups succeed in gaining greater influence on Capitol Hill, they might succeed in pressing Congress to once again take upon itself the task of reversing discriminatory election rules. Despite setbacks in many elections, beleaguered Democrats will show the usual resilience and once again become formidable contenders for power. When this happens, blacks and other minorities must play coalition politics within the Democratic party to accomplish a pivotal political objective.

Black Power Engineered by the Chief of State

"One man with courage makes a majority."
—Andrew Jackson (b. 1767)

FROM THE MOMENT high school students enter their first civics class they are solemnly taught that under the American system, Congress makes the laws and then the President carries them out. But that's not an accurate description of how our government works. Unlike most Western democracies, the American constitutional system confers broad legislative powers on its chief of state. In fact, since the presidency of Franklin Roosevelt, it has been customary for American Presidents to personally legislate many of the economic and social policies that they think are good for us. And they do this through the process of White House executive order rather than by seeking formal legislation through Congress.

These unique legislative powers of American Presidents are of profound importance to black people. Under the President's constitutional powers, there is hardly a school board, police station, voting registrar's office, hospital, or university whose policies toward racial minorities may not be controlled by the discretionary lawmaking authority of the White House. On a routine basis, the minority employment practices of the nation's labor unions, utilities, banks, and manufacturing plants are regulated by sweeping and penetrating edicts issued by the President. In fact, the centralized power of the President over the economy is so comprehensive that virtually any institution that does business with the federal government, holds a license from it, receives federal tax exemption, or accepts any form of federal aid must comply with policies established by executive directives from the White House.

In practice, of course, there are limits on the powers of what has come to be known as the imperial presidency. Strong, charismatic leaders may press the presidential authority quite far. Weaker leaders are seldom successful in probing the bounds of their constitutional powers. Wholly aside from legal or constitutional considerations, pragmatic limits are established by that which the people, on a case-by-case basis, feel to be fair, just, or necessary. Nonetheless, the executive power in the United States is indeed a commanding force, unparalleled in its reach except in totalitarian states.

In addition to the general powers that go with the office of President, the Constitution expressly confers on the President almost exclusive powers over government purchasing and contracting. This very broad discretionary authority permits the President, if he so chooses, to interrupt and redirect the normal flow of employment, credit, investment, and commerce. Under the procurement power, the President may impose broad affirmative-action requirements on most of the nation's large industrial and financial corporations that do business with the government. In fact, since the presidency of Franklin Roosevelt, the executive power over government procurement has traditionally provided the essential constitutional footing for many of the most important and far-reaching presidential lawmaking edicts. And, historically, the lever of the government procurement authority has been the most effective presidential force for opening new doors to minorities and providing them with much wider participation in the economic and educational lives of the nation.

There is still more to the constitutional powers of the President. Broad legislative authority flows from the President's powers to set budgets, to administer law enforcement, and to appoint high officials. These executive powers are consistently used to control the content as well as the administration of the law. For example, the President's constitutional responsibility to enforce civil rights statutes gives him comprehensive, though merely implied, powers to require disclosure of the minority employment and credit practices of public and private organizations. His power to appoint or dismiss high government officials confers on the President the additional power to control the policies, interpretations, and rulings of these officials. The President's ability to use the prestige of his office to influence voting by citizens and legislators permits him to protect his executive orders from legislative opposition or reversal. His ability to endorse candidates for state or local offices is both a tempting carrot and a powerful stick in recruiting support for White House policies and edicts.

One aspect of the executive power is particularly important to black people. The nonexecutive branches of government usually require action by a number of officials before any law may be enacted or definitively interpreted. In Congress, for example, a majority decision is necessary, and the majority is always composed of whites. In the courts, too, definitive decisions in appellate cases are invariably made by a white majority. No matter how effectively minority groups maneuver in order to cast the deciding vote in a contest among greater powers, the minority position is necessarily subordinate to the will of others. But the presidential power is different. If, on any particular issue, blacks are able to win the support of the President, a broad range of new freedoms and powers might be conferred on black people. For the President sits on the throne. He acts unilaterally. Before issuing his all-potent executive orders, he need consult only himself.

Blacks, in common with most citizens, more often have read the Constitution literally. They have looked to the courts and Congress as the exclusive places where they might repeal the private codes of race and repair the unhealed wounds of centuries of racial subordination. But in many ways, the powers of the executive branch—and the sensibilities and policies of the person who is in the White House—are forces that are more important to the goal of racial progress. American history is teeming with examples. For black Americans, the most significant law ever published in the United States was neither an act of Congress nor a decree of the Supreme Court. The Emancipation Proclamation was a unilateral executive order issued by President Lincoln. This great Proclamation has been followed by a host of other presidential orders and decrees dealing with racial segregation and subordination. In most cases, the purposes of these orders were either to move toward more equal treatment of blacks in private transactions or, in even more cases, affirmatively to open America's public institutions more fully to entry by blacks.

The idea that the presidential power should be used to improve the fortunes of the masses dates to the presidency of Franklin Roosevelt. But, as the chart on the next page shows, the idea that the same power should be used to elevate the status of black people is of much earlier origin. The long history of presidential executive orders issued on behalf of the Negro stands as powerful evidence of the value to blacks of an enduring constitutional tradition under which American Presidents, inspired by a strong sense of mission to establish racial justice—as well, perhaps, as by personal ambitions to win for themselves a revered place in history—have taken unilateral measures to curb the racial prejudices of the American people.

In the early 1980s—for the first time since the Hoover presidency—the powers of the executive branch were being used to undercut and slow the progress of blacks into the economic, residential, and educational life of the nation. But the inexorable drive toward racial equality—a trend whose dimensions are worldwide—is not likely to be interrupted for long in the

NEVER UNDERESTIMATE THE POWER OF THE CHIEF

The Historical Use of De Facto Legislation by the President to Advance the Status and Powers of Blacks

- All slaves set free by presidential order.
  —Emancipation Proclamation—President Lincoln (1863)
- Employment discrimination in defense industries banned.
  —Executive Order 8802—President Roosevelt (1941)
- Fair Employment Practices Commission established.
  —Executive Order 9346—President Roosevelt (1943)
- Armed Forces desegregated.
  —Executive Order 9981—President Truman (1948)
- Departments of Defense and Commerce may not discriminate by race in awarding government contracts.
  —Executive Order 10210—President Truman (1951)
- Tennessee Valley Authority ordered to pursue racially neutral policies in awarding federal contracts.
  —Executive Order 10231—President Truman (1951)
- Civil Defense Administration must award contracts without discriminating by race.
  —Executive Order 10243—President Truman (1951)
- Interior Department ordered to end all race discrimination in licensing and contracting.
  —Executive Order 10298—President Truman (1951)
- Government Contracting Commission established to monitor racial practices in contracting orders.
  —Executive Order 10479—President Eisenhower (1953)
- Employment discrimination by the United States government prohibited.
  —Executive Order 10925—President Kennedy (1961)
- Government mortgage insurance may not be issued to home builders who practice race discrimination.
  —Executive Order 11063—President Kennedy (1962)
- Employment discrimination by all federal contractors prohibited.
  —Executive Order 11114—President Kennedy (1963)
- Any federal contractor awarded government business of $500,000 or more may be required to institute an affirmative employment action plan.
  —Executive Order 11246—President Johnson (1965)
- Employers have affirmative obligations to employ minorities on construction projects where any federal assistance is provided.
  —Executive Order 11375—President Johnson (1967)
- Federal departments and agencies must set plans for equal employment opportunity.
  —Executive Order 11478—President Nixon (1969)
- The absence of local discriminatory housing practices should be considered as a criteria in selecting sites of federal facilities.
  —Executive Order 11512—President Nixon (1970)
- Federal agencies are required to use all formal and informal means to remedy violations of the Fair Housing Act.
  —Executive Order 12259—President Carter (1980)

United States. Looking to a day when Presidents may once again be disposed to employ public power to confer more positions of value, power, and prestige on blacks in the United States, we now ask, what kinds of executive orders might blacks want to urge upon future Presidents? Once blacks acquire significant political bargaining strength in the United States, what is the shape of an executive agenda that they might press upon future elected chiefs? What, particularly, are the potential landmark initiatives that Presidents might use, not simply to open up many more economic opportunities to blacks but, more important, to draw them closer to sharing control with whites over the basic forces that drive American capitalism.

Stimulate a Massive Upsurge in Black Capital Formation Through a Sweeping Presidential Order Setting Preferential Rights to Government Awards

"Behold, I have set before thee an open door. . . ."

—Revelations 3:8

BECAUSE OF CIRCUMSTANCES unique to their past, blacks still overwhelmingly see themselves as working for others. As formerly protected and dependent people, Negroes, much more often than whites, perceive themselves as hired hands who should seek safe employment in large corporations in preference to taking the risks of independent entrepreneurship. Indeed, disproportionately large numbers of black parents appear to have an undue reverence for the status of employment in established business enterprises and look suspiciously on their children marrying young men or women who aspire to become business proprietors rather than workers or administrators. Often, according to my experience, many well-educated blacks (in common perhaps with white women) suffer near-morbid feelings of fear when confronted with the need to cope with the standard commercial documents of American capitalism. These crippling attitudes are, in large measure, one of the enduring harms of long-standing racial customs and commercial practices which, in effect, protected blacks from entrepreneurial careers, as well as from other vicissitudes and benefits of economic liberty.

It is self-evident that no subordinate group may be viewed as equal unless its members hold a significant number of positions in every important part of the economy. Accordingly, blacks must become entrepreneurs just as they must become managers and administrators. They must own and manage capital just as they must also work for the capital controlled or owned by others. Not only is the formation of new wealth in Negro hands objectively necessary for overall racial equality, but it is also indispensable to changing all the negative perceptions that stand in the way of the willingness of whites to permit black people to enter all of the economic and political playing fields of our competitive society.

In a precedent-setting, albeit tentative, congressional effort to draw blacks and other racial minorities into the mainstream of American capitalism, Congress enacted the Public Works Employment Act of 1977. This law—probably the most striking legislative achievement of the Congressional Black Caucus—conferred undisguised preferential ethnic bidding advantages as to a specific set of federal contract appropriations. This legislation, whose explicit racial requirement for contract awards has been upheld by the Supreme Court, required that 10 percent of a $4 billion federal works appropriation be set aside for exclusive bidding by minority contractors.[1] The 1977 Act covered only a very small part of the overall federal procurement authority, about one-half of one percent. Nevertheless, the law was a giant step forward in establishing the legislative legitimacy, as well as the formal constitutionality, of express actions by the government to reserve special places and bidding advantages to blacks and other minorities.

On many occasions in the past the Supreme Court has ruled that the President, too, has broad constitutional powers to use his authority over government purchasing to advance social goals unrelated to the national procurement effort. Since the purchasing authority of the executive branch is constitutionally created, the President's use of his contracting powers does not depend on congressional authorization. Particularly as long as Congress has not explicitly legislated *against* affirmative procurement privileges, it appears that any President, acting through the usual executive order, could set aside large-scale awards and bidding rights for minority groups.

It is well known that over the past 100 years the federal procurement policy openly excluded qualified black people from government contract bidding privileges. The government broke its own laws by denying a class of its citizens the rights and privileges of competing for government contracts. In view of these past policies of the executive branch—whose actions are deeply implicated in the capital-bereft position of black people today—the Supreme Court is likely to decide that the President would be acting well within the scope of his constitutional authority if he were to adopt aggressive executive efforts to redress the effects of past discrimination.

Because of the importance of wealth parity to the goal of overall economic equality, blacks, at the earliest date, should lobby for a comprehensive and truly landmark presidential procurement order. The order should require all corporations holding federal contracts with a value of $50 million or more to make firm commitments to subcontract fixed percentages of all prime contract awards for (1) community economic development corporations serving government-designated low-income areas, (2) minority business enterprises, and (3) any enterprise designated by the Department of Labor as drawing the majority of its labor force from government-certified areas of poverty and high unemployment.

To cushion shock to the federal procurement system, and to neutralize opposition from current government contractors, the fixed percentage of subcontracting appropriations set aside for minorities might start at one percent during the first year and rise to the maximum of 5 percent after five years. Black wealth is currently a small fraction of the national mean. The minority order would remain in effect until Census statistics showed black holdings of capital assets, securities, and other financial assets had reached at least 50 percent of the national norm. Strong medicine, indeed! But necessary and appropriate in a circumstance where, as we have shown, there are no satisfactory explanations for the massive black-white wealth gap other than a century of rigid racial rules—both public and private—as to who was permitted to seek, use, and exploit capital.

Abundant administrative precedents exist for using government purchasing power to strengthen special segments of society. Examples of similar unilateral presidential orders are: Executive Order No. 8802, President Roosevelt's 1941 order establishing a policy of nondiscrimination in defense industries; Executive Orders 11246, 11378, and 11141, requiring government contractors to refrain from discrimination in hiring; Executive Order 11598, requiring contractors to report job openings to agencies helping job-hunting veterans; Defense Manpower Power Policy No. 4, issued by the Office of Defense Mobilization in 1952, requiring prime government contractors to set up formal programs to attract subcontractors from low-employment areas.

The so-called Philadelphia Plan, designed to increase minority employment in the construction industry, is another strong precedent for a far-reaching minority contracting executive order. The Philadelphia Plan was implemented in 1969 by executive order of President Nixon. It required government contractors to set affirmative-action plans for employment of minority workers in the construction trades. In the early 1970s, Congress explicitly refused to rescind the Philadelphia Plan, and the executive order establishing the plan was later upheld by a federal court of appeals.[2]

To avoid constitutional questions that still complicate minority contracting orders, the first expression of the presidential contracting authority need not explicitly specify blacks or other racial minorities as its target groups. Instead, the order might require simply that the stipulated percentage of contracts be awarded to community development corporations funded by the federal government under the authority of the Economic Opportunity Act of 1964. Since the vast majority of government-assisted community development corporations have been organized by blacks and other minorities in inner-city and rural poverty areas, the presidential contracting order would disproportionately benefit blacks and other minorities without making them explicit, and possibly unconstitutional, beneficiaries of the order.

No matter what one's view of the propriety of using government power to force-feed black capital formation, the allocation to minorities of such small percentages of the federal contracting budget may appear, on its face, to be fiscally inconsequential. In fact, very large sums of money would be involved. In 1980, federal government procurement alone was $100 billion. If merely one-half of one percent of all government procurement expenditures were allocated to inner-city and rural community development corporations, their development and job-creating revenues would increase from the present figure of a few million to more than half a billion dollars a year.

In winning, finally, the enactment of the Public Works Employment Act of 1977, the Congressional Black Caucus first broke with the traditional "band-aid" agendas, whose purposes were often to render social services and give comfort and relief to poor blacks. It was the first break, too, with the government's superficial minority capitalism efforts that assisted black people to function as petty entrepreneurs—as gas station proprietors and soul food operatives on the fringes of the American economy. As an economic empowerment strategy—and a first step, also, to introduce blacks to big-league capitalism—the 1977 congressional contracting initiative was sound and should be pressed further. Mandatory minority contracting awards offer huge potential for generating new capital formation, employment, and entrepreneurship in low-income communities. As the new minority contracting rule takes hold, and government-created demand opportunity increases, new minority enterprises will form, and the quality of managerial experience in the black community will multiply greatly.

While many blacks have made significant gains in recent decades, unequal economic power relationships remain untouched. There are no indications whatsoever that the huge differences between blacks and whites in access to capital and control of wealth and economic power will be equalized through income strategies or normal competitive forces. These massive differences—established in part through constitutionally improper processes by which the federal government expressly excluded blacks from competing for government land grants and franchise awards—are likely to remain in place and hold back income gains as well as capital formation. Indefinite black inequality is already in the pipeline unless, through the force of a reverse reallocation process, the federal fiscal powers are used, in expressly targeted ways, to allot business revenues, capital, and credit for the use of blacks and other minorities. As a strategy for securing a place for blacks in the world of capital ownership and management, the mandatory procurement edict would be far more effective than special training programs for minority entrepreneurs who, as things stand now, will almost certainly lose out in virtually every open competition for credit, capital, and market share.

Require All Major Corporations to Adopt Firm Fifteen-Year Minority Employment Plans

"Government enjoys the unrestricted power to produce its own supplies, to determine those with whom it will deal, and to fix the terms and conditions upon which it will make needed purchases."

—Justice Hugo Black in
Perkins v. Lukens Steel Co.,
310 U.S. 113, 127 (1940)

A MAJOR ECONOMIC HANDICAP facing blacks continues to be the dual quality of the American labor market. Labor demand continues to issue from two compartments: black and white. Blacks have unequal power to sell their labor in the marketplace because, among other reasons, major employers continue to prefer white workers to black workers. Even when blacks have diligently pursued high school educations, their incomes and employment participation rates fall far short of whites of similar or lower educational backgrounds. Blacks with some college education are still barely doing as well as whites with high school educations. In the case of teenagers, the statistical evidence is very strong that, even in times of healthy economic demand, employers will hire almost all available white youngsters before turning to young blacks. Under established and increasingly unregulated markets, there are almost no built-in incentives to persuade American industry to seek out, train, employ, and promote black Americans. For these reasons it appears that, except for the highly educated black elites who continue to do well, a reversal in the catastrophic ten-year drop in black employment participation rates is not likely to occur unless government power intervenes and forces a major demand shift toward all categories of black labor.

In the early 1980s, a major campaign was launched to discredit affirmative action. A new national administration ideologically committed to voluntary approaches to racial problems was soft-pedaling enforcement of laws against race discrimination. It had also withdrawn from all efforts to expand or upgrade black employment through quotas, preferences, or timetables. Despite the suspension of government efforts to help people at the bottom, it would be a serious mistake for blacks to write off any prospect for using their political power to bring about a major new presidential initiative to improve both the rate and the quality of black employment.

Here, the successful precedent of history is very strong. Four decades ago, President Roosevelt, acting in response to the intense pressures of a threatened protest march on Washington, issued a sweeping executive order requiring defense contractors to open employment to blacks. Unprecedented and politically unpopular, this extraordinary executive order, for the first time, opened up industrial employment to blacks in America. This presidential order was followed by dozens of other White House proclamations, each securing for Negroes new points of entry into the economic system. Admittedly, this series of presidential edicts significantly restricted the liberties of white employers and, in a great many cases, provided favored economic treatment for blacks. Yet, most people identified these presidential orders with the American sense of fair play, and came to accept them as permanent fixtures of the country's social and political consensus.

It is likely that future political pressures—stemming perhaps from renewed protest and political activities on the part of blacks—will produce further presidential orders in the field of minority employment. The continuing decline in black incomes relative to whites' and the persistent deterioration of the black-white unemployment ratio are likely to be additional catalysts that would persuade a future President to require American industry to bid much more aggressively for minority employees. But past history shows that government compulsion, rather than voluntary corporate job pledges, will be necessary to achieve significant results. To be sure, there will be the usual pro forma hiring efforts, flag-waving, and good citizenship awards even if the government takes no action. But only a very naive person, or one wholly unacquainted with American economic history, would expect that a new spirit of altruism will persuade the heads of large corporations to adopt new racial priorities that still run against the wishes of the vast majority of their executives and employees.

Set a Fifteen-Year Timetable for Major Corporations

If the White House were to decisively move to use the executive powers to improve the ability of blacks to bargain for employment, what kind of presidential order might be devised? The main thrust should be strict affirmative-action rules imposed on all large corporations with sales of over $1 billion. These corporations would be required to submit and observe firm commitments for bringing minority employment in all job categories up to parity with minority population percentages *within fifteen years*. Unlike all prior affirmative-action plans, this order would require specified action in accordance with a rigid timetable. Almost all of the large corporations affected by the order would either be government contractors or otherwise be receiving sufficient government benefits and assistance to come within the scope of the presidential authority. Despite major economic problems in the large smokestack industries, these large, and typically multinational, corporations are generally in a much better position than are smaller enterprises to bear the economic burdens of stringent affirmative-action rules. Moreover, presidential orders targeted at large enterprises only would still affect a very large proportion of the American labor force. Taken together, companies with $1 billion or more in sales embrace, perhaps, 60 percent or more of the nation's work force. As shown in Chapter Nineteen, all previous experience with race-conscious affirmative-action programs and preferences in minority employment shows that these measures produce demonstrable and far-reaching gains for blacks.

To assist public and private monitoring of compliance with the presidential order, each corporation would be required to make an annual public report showing the racial composition of all levels of its work force. Corporations affected by the order would be obliged to obtain periodic certification from the Department of Labor's Office of Federal Contract Compliance Programs that the company had complied with its own affirmative-action plan. Intolerable bureaucracy and red tape? Yes! Costly for some industries breathing heavily because of shortsighted business policies in the past? Yes! But these detriments are a superior choice to a deteriorating black economic condition, reinforcement of the black underclass, and a dangerous buildup of rage in the black community. Since people rarely do what they find costly or unpleasant, good-faith efforts and volunteerism are mere slogans to justify inaction. Without government certification of compliance with the executive order, no corporation should be eligible to bid on any federal contract.

A strictly enforced fifteen-year affirmative-action order applied to major corporations avoids most of the constitutional problems raised in recent Supreme Court decisions invalidating government-ordered reverse discrimination. First, the order imposes a firm fifteen-year timetable but sets no annual quotas. Second, the order is directed at government contracting, an activity that has historically been marked by a discrete and provable history of race discrimination. Finally, the fifteen years allotted for compliance would provide sufficient room for protecting the seniority rights of white employees. As long as fixed quotas are avoided, rulings of the Supreme Court permit considerable latitude in shaping affirmative-action measures.

The likely effects of a comprehensive government affirmative-action order applied to all stages of the private employment ladder must be distinguished from those to be expected of traditional full employment bills. Full employment legislative initiatives usually contemplate the creation of low-level public-service jobs and other downscale employment to soak up the excess and unwanted labor for which the free-market economy provides little demand. Accordingly, full employment edicts would reduce the *unemployment* gap between blacks and whites but would do little to close the black-white income gap. In contrast, a comprehensive minority employment order, which imposes strict affirmative-action requirements at all levels of employment, grapples with the entire hierarchy of black economic activity. It opens the middle and upper levels of private employment to blacks and should have the effect of gradually pulling black incomes closer to income and employment parity with whites.

Integrating the Executive Suite

What is the justification for applying government-ordered affirmative action to minority employment in higher management positions? It is commonly believed that blacks are already making good progress into senior management roles. But this progress is greatly overstated in corporate advertising and public relations campaigns. Nationwide, blacks are grossly underrepresented in executive positions. "Manager" is the title of the highest-ranking black in most corporations, with black managers traditionally appointed to paper-shuffling and auxiliary positions such as urban affairs and equal employment opportunity responsibility. In the early 1980s, one could identify only a handful of blacks in senior management of major corporations, with none whatsoever in the top executive ranks. It is true that as a result of intense affirmative-action pressure blacks, over the past twenty years, have moved from entry-level jobs into some middle-management roles. But there is no indication in any but a handful of large corporations that top management will voluntarily open its executive suites to black executives exercising line authority at the highest levels. As was the case in the initial entry by black managers, it is likely that strict affirmative action will be necessary before blacks move into the very high posts where white prerogatives have been so well guarded by tradition and etiquette. The abysmally slow progress into top corporate ranks on the part of black executives—many of them now twenty years or more out of business or law school—confirms that conclusion.

Opponents of affirmative action sometimes concede that strict minority employment rules may provide job opportunities for blacks with some skills and work experience, but the position is taken that these policies don't help the great mass of urban or rural blacks with no training or employment experience. This conclusion is merely assumed; it has never been proven or tested. Moreover, the conclusion that affirmative action won't help unskilled blacks defies the expectable effects of the laws of labor supply and demand. If, as a result of intensive affirmative-action policies established by large corporations, heavy labor demand is targeted for blacks in positions requiring minimal or moderate skills, it is reasonable to conclude that unskilled blacks will gradually be motivated to seek the education and training necessary to move into these positions. Low-skill positions in construction trades, in warehouses, and in factories would gradually be claimed by young blacks who were given a prior claim on this work. People are not likely to continue to choose disadvantage if economic demand patterns are rearranged in such a way as to pay them to rise from disadvantage. If the problems of lower-class urban blacks—low aspirations, poor work habits, and high levels of functional illiteracy—are rooted in past practices of race discrimination whose effects have been to blunt or nullify the desire on the part of so many blacks to seek and prepare themselves for nonmenial work, there seems to be no reason, reciprocally, why affirmative employment demands targeted specifically toward this group won't ultimately persuade them that it is advantageous to change their habits. To say that affirmative action won't help the great masses of untrained young blacks is to assume the conclusion. One cannot prejudge the economic behavior of the group until the work opportunity is created and in sight.

By 1980 most large corporations had accepted the overall concept of affirmative action. But the prospect of extending or tightening the rules faced the stone wall of newly appointed government officials fundamentally hostile to equal opportunity laws. Minorities had their hands full simply defending attacks on existing job-bias and affirmative-action rules. The superior strategy for blacks in the early 1980s was to look in another direction, that of building black and Hispanic political strength in preparation for a day when economic and political circumstances would be more favorable toward pressing forward with a major new government assault or the racial bias in the labor market.

Liberals and conservatives, alike, incorrectly identify affirmative action and other forms of government compulsion with the failed social programs of the past. As shown in Chapter Nineteen, large and measurable economic and educational gains by blacks are the direct consequence of affirmative intervention in traditional selection processes. Reasonable racial quotas are good policy, they achieve what they seek to accomplish, they don't violate civil rights statutes, they serve the ends of economic justice, and they are *fair* according to the basic tenets of our political order. For many years to come, the use of government power to establish affirmative-action employment policies will remain a key link in the process of chipping away at the enduring and unwarranted advantage of being born in the United States with a white skin.

Charter Fifty New Minority-Owned Broadcast Television Stations in Leading Viewing Areas

"The only people who can truly enjoy freedom of the press are those who own one."

—A.J. Liebling (1947)

MODERN TELEVISION is the single most important instrument of mass persuasion ever developed by man. The average American adult watches television three hours a day, the average child four or more. The opinions of hundreds of millions of people are controlled, in very large part, by what they hear and see on television. More than any other public medium, television shapes the opinions that whites have about blacks and that blacks have about themselves. Yet, at present, black participation in the power of this crucial opinion-molding process is minuscule. Blacks have no control or influence whatsoever over the racial images that go out over the screen. If, as I contend here, the three great powers in the nation are political, economic, and media, it is difficult to conceive of blacks reaching parity with whites in terms of political and economic power without their having, also, a firm hold on media power.

In 1980 there were only three black-controlled VHF (channels 2 to 13) television stations in the United States—WLBT-TV, an NBC affiliate in Jackson, Mississippi; WNEC-TV in Rochester, New York; and WAEO-TV in the small city of Rhinelander, Wisconsin. There was no black-controlled television outlet in any of the major cities with large black populations. Under FCC pressure, blacks have been brought into the usual token and low-level positions of employment at the major television and radio stations, but at both the local and network levels, management and programming policy remain entirely in the hands of whites. Of the 500 or so vice-presidents at the three major networks, only six were members of a minority group. Not one was in the news division. Of the country's 800 commercial TV stations, only two had black general managers, four have black station managers, and three had black news directors.[3]

It is difficult to overestimate the importance of the media to black political power. Black radio and newspapers have always been active in get-out-the-vote campaigns. They are the essential means by which black people with political inclinations find out what is going on. The black media provide accounts of political developments and perspectives overlooked by the major broadcasters. Black radio in Chicago was viewed as indispensable to the election of Harold Washington as mayor of Chicago in 1983.

Bootstrapping Media Power
Through Administrative Order

Despite unfavorable political conditions prevailing in the early 1980s, the best prospect for blacks to acquire a share of the power of mass communication is still through federal administrative order. Since 1975, the Federal Communications Commission has been studying the possibility of issuing new VHF channel licenses in ninety-six major television markets. White House pressure on the FCC, combined with the appointment of more FCC commissioners favoring expanding media opportunities for minorities, could produce a large number of new VHF license allocations to blacks and Hispanics. But the prospect for new government orders addressing the issue of minority participation in broadcasting media will remain dim unless blacks and Hispanics win sufficient political power to persuade the political party in power to press for the necessary television station franchise awards. It is frequently asked what black presidential candidates gain by running to barter in primary campaigns that they can't win. Collapsing a strong minority candidacy in favor of a mainstream candidate who commits, upon election to the presidency, to award even a handful of VHF television licenses to minority ownership would introduce blacks to major media power and be well worth the effort and expense of the minority candidacy campaign.

There are few areas of the economy where there is greater justification for government action to redress the effects of past discrimination. Since the very beginning of the broadcasting industry, the hugely valuable and powerful monopoly privileges of federal license grants have been issued without charge—and under federal policies where white skin color was an implicit requirement of qualification for a license. Unlike white media owners, the scores of successful and affluent black newspaper proprietors of past decades were never considered eligible to receive the federal grant of an urban television or radio broadcast license. The current objection to compensatory minority allocation quotas of airwave privileges is not persuasive in an industry where government allocation quotas—100 percent in favor of whites—have always prevailed.

Broadcast License Challenges: Picking Up Small Change

A second although less satisfactory route to greater communications power is available to blacks. The Federal Communications Act provides the machinery for legal challenges to the renewal of existing broadcast licenses. The traditional ground for challenges has been that station owners were not adequately serving the needs of the population in their viewing areas. One successful challenge of this nature resulted in a black takeover of station WLBT-TV in Jackson, Mississippi, where blacks make up more than 40 percent of the population in the viewing area. In 1964, the Communications Office of the United Church of Christ filed a petition with the Federal Communications Commission charging white owners of WLBT with race discrimination. The petition stated that the station did not allow blacks to appear on local programs, did not announce black community events, and presented a biased view on race-related issues. The station's license was vacated by the United States District Court of the District of Columbia in 1969. After ten years of legal maneuvering, the FCC, in 1979, finally awarded the license to a majority black group headed by Aaron Henry, head of the Mississippi chapter of the National Association for the Advancement of Colored People.[4]

BROADCAST COMMUNICATIONS POWER IN ALL MAJOR CITIES IS CONTROLLED BY WHITES

In 1980, there were no black-owned VHF television stations in any of these cities with large black populations.

CITY	Percent Black—1980	CITY	Percent Black—1980
Gary, IN	70.8%	Wilmington, DE	51.1%
Washington, DC	70.3%	Savannah, GA	49.0%
Atlanta, GA	66.6%	Memphis, TN	47.6%
Detroit, MI	63.1%	Oakland, CA	46.9%
Newark, NJ	58.2%	Charleston, SC	46.5%
Birmingham, AL	55.6%	St. Louis, MO	45.6%
New Orleans, LA	55.3%	Chicago, IL	39.8%
Baltimore, MD	54.8%	Philadelphia, PA	37.8%
Camden, NJ	53.0%	Houston, TX	27.6%
Richmond, VA	51.3%	New York, NY	25.2%

In the early 1980s, it appeared that cumbersome remedies against race discrimination in the broadcast industry were to be replaced by no remedies at all. Free-market zealotism prevailing at the FCC produced new rules that would relieve holders of TV broadcast licenses of their obligations to serve community needs. The FCC moved to permit station owners to renew their broadcast licensing by postcard. Until the political pendulum swings back, blacks and other minorities will be severely limited in their ability to use existing law as a means of establishing beachheads in broadcasting media.

One may ask how black media power is enhanced by challenges to television station franchises. The answer is that even unsuccessful legal challenges to existing station licenses are likely to have a salutary effect on the policies of station owners. Stations in serious danger of losing their licenses are more likely to increase their news coverage of black political activities;

racial slurs on the airwaves are likely to be curtailed and stations subject to civil rights pressures are likely to moderate some of the standard "Sambo" stereotypes which most blacks feel have a harmful effect on their children. But the strategy of influencing station broadcasting policies by challenging station licenses will, at best, have marginal effects. In redressing the immense imbalance of communications power in the United States, there is no effective substitute for the creation of several dozen black-owned television stations in the major urban markets.

Capital No Obstacle

If, in the next few years, a half dozen new VHF licenses were allocated by the federal government to black groups, it is clear that the initial capital needs of the licensees could be met. This is so largely because the license itself is a capital asset of very great value, sufficient to support large-scale funding for capital equipment and other purposes. Several nonprofit organizations already exist whose purpose is to assist minorities in meeting the capital requirements for entering the broadcasting industry. Indeed, one of the important objectives of the national minority development corporation proposed in Chapter Twenty-four would be to assist major transfers of broadcasting licenses to minority ownership.

Broadcast television not only represents power to shape public opinion, it is also very big business in the United States. Established television interests look benignly upon the awarding of orphan stations located in minority viewing areas to minority ownership, but intense resistance on the ground of qualifications is encountered when minority licenses are sought in large cities where any license is worth $100 million or more. As black political power mounts, it is likely that the federal government will make every effort to satisfy minority pressures to win a foothold in television broadcasting by offering cosmetic reforms. It is almost certain, too, that minorities will be offered allocations of "soul" radio stations as well as the widely available ultra-high-frequency television outlets, channels 14 to 83, where reception is weak and audiences relatively small. But the minority political opportunity must not be squandered by settling for token broadcasting awards. Instead, blacks and Hispanics must amass sufficient political strength so that they are in a position to claim, in due time, a significant share of the nation's government-awarded media power.

For reasons that are well known, cable television now poses a serious competitive threat to conventional broadcast television. As in over-the-air broadcast television, the major companies with strong cable positions are large, well capitalized, and controlled exclusively by whites. In many large cities, cable franchises have been awarded on explicitly political grounds. If viable cable television had appeared on the scene ten years later than it did, urban blacks would undoubtedly have had sufficient political strength to have claimed major cable franchises in many large metropolitan areas. But once again—as in the case of other business opportunities opened up by technological change—blacks were ill-equipped to compete with big powers. Once more they have been left at the starting gate. Most desirable major metropolitan areas already have cable or are in the process of being wired. Well-chronicled fiscal problems and high unemployment rates have chased off the giant cable operators as bidders in Detroit, St. Louis, and Cleveland. Once more, black operators will be left holding the inner cities and the economic backwaters. Short of major reallocations of franchises already held, it is probably too late for blacks to acquire a significant position in the upscale cable television industry.[5]

Media Power Under Free Markets

The recent history of allocations of cable television franchise monopolies teaches two important lessons about the flow of power. First, cable television allotments show why political power is indispensable, if not a precondition, to economic power. Whether the next important government award be satellite communications rights or, merely, permission to drill for oil in the Grand Canyon, black political power must be strong enough to bargain for its share when the next round of public allocations of franchises takes place. Second, the history of cable television awards shows irrefutably that even when race discrimination is no longer practiced, the groups that already hold economic and political power are invariably in a superior position to claim the next round of economic advantages. Not only are established groups in a superior position to use political power to pick off the economic plums, but they and their associates will also leverage off prior advantage to assure them forward access to prime financing, technological support, and customer bases necessary to exploit the newest publicly granted monopoly. Except in the case of entry into activities where capital costs are low, competition as an ultimate equalizer of the positions of groups with unequal power holdings is pure myth. In the cold light of economic reality, power and advantage almost always beget additional power and advantage. And this is a prime reason why blacks will be committing a monumental political blunder if, as most industrialists and government leaders urge, they reject government backing and media allotments and, instead, wistfully hitch their wagons to the promised advantages of freely competitive markets.

Abolish the Federal Minority Business Development Agency and Substitute a Presidential Order Using All the Federal Fiscal Powers to Stimulate Large-Scale Minority Capital Formation

"Look, under the Constitution I have the right to earn as much money as I am capable of. Let's be realistic. One, I've only two years of college education. Two, I'm black. And, three, I'm not very smart, although I have a lot of common sense. My time is now. I sign a six-year contract and then, maybe, just maybe, I might have two or three more years. What happens to George McGinnis then? I don't want to be a stockbroker. I don't want to wear a suit and tie and work 8 to 5. I don't see why it's so complicated. Here's one pile of money and there's another. One pile is larger."

—George McGinnis,
professional basketball player (1977)

A CENTRAL FEATURE of the American private free-enterprise system is that it is only partially private. Large-scale public-sector grants, gifts, awards— and frequently outright raids on the public treasury—have been an integral part of the creation of much of the private wealth in this country. Curiously, many of the champions of unregulated markets—often the people who object most vehemently to the use of the government's fiscal powers to encourage wealth formation by blacks—hardly notice that many of the "free enterprises" that they cherish so dearly have their origins in outright federal grants of public franchises, licensed business monopolies, and privileges to exploit public resources. In view of America's conspicuous history of open-handed government subsidy and support of wealth accumulation efforts limited to whites only, there is considerable moral force on the side of the position that calls upon the government to take modest steps to even things up by using its huge fiscal powers in large-scale efforts to assist blacks in acquiring capital.

Because of consistent government practices in past years of granting its fiscal favors to whites only, there should be considerable latitude, under recent Supreme Court decisions, for upholding preferential government support of wealth accumulation efforts on the part of blacks. In adopting policies that would provide special drawing rights for blacks, there would be no break with any free-enterprise precedent; for no such precedent exists except in the minds of ideologues who choose to ignore the consistently symbiotic relationship between government and private wealth in the history of capital formation in the United States.

For most Americans the idea of large-scale wealth in the hands of blacks—major banks, industrial firms, and utilities—is almost beyond imagination. Yet, due to the needs of conscience, as well as of practical politics, whites, in recent years, have found it necessary to *appear* to be doing something about encouraging black business ownership and entrepreneurship. For the past fifteen years, the federal government has more or less successfully created the appearance of being active in accelerating black capital formation without actually incurring the detriments of doing anything sufficiently costly or decisive enough to produce significant results. The Commerce Department's Minority Business Development Agency, formerly the Office of Minority Business Enterprise (OMBE), has been the essential player in this charade. MBDA has no budgetary authority to offer incentives for minority entrepreneurship. Its powers are limited to exhorting whites to help blacks, and to issuing press releases—many of them false or misleading—about the extent of government aid to minority business.

MBDA, a misbegotten and egregiously incompetent agency, with its armies of employees and consultants, should be disbanded. From the minority viewpoint, it is distinctly preferable to have no government agency chartered to assist minorities than to have a sham institution that causes blacks and others to believe that government power is working on behalf of black capital acquisition when, in fact, it is not.

As a first step, then, the Minority Business Development Agency should be eliminated by White House executive order. Once blacks and Hispanics have sufficient political strength to have White House power working in their interests, a second step is taken to win a comprehensive executive order fostering large-scale wealth and capital formation in minority and low-income communities. Under this plan, the entire fiscal force of the executive branch would be deployed to initiate large-scale government loan guarantees and credits to enable blacks to develop wide-ranging business, financial, and banking activities.

Mandate Black Capital Formation

An explicit goal of an effective minority wealth development plan—an objective that, admittedly, is not politically feasible in the foreseeable future—should be fundamental realignments of economic power among blacks and whites. To this end, government financial assistance and guarantees would ensure that blacks and other minorities would be in a position, from time to time, to acquire *major instruments of capital*. This would include partial or complete control of some strong industrial corporations, including banks, mortgage companies, utilities, and insurance companies, as well as significant petroleum, agricultural, and mining interests. To be sure, major wealth transfers are usually reserved for revolutions. Yet, this need not be the case. The recent congressional enactment of major government tax subsidies for so-called employee stock ownership plans (ESOPs) shows that a democratic government subject to political pressures from populists, and "have-nots" is capable of using its legislative powers to stimulate wealth transfers to groups that are capital-poor.

A successful minority wealth development plan must make an end run around tokenism's customary efforts to make blacks settle for ragtag enterprises that whites don't want. Sufficient political power must be mounted to suspend all further support for the inner-city rib shops that currently pass as "black capitalism." Industry and government officials must be blocked from making points with minority voters by using government-backed loans to a minority purchaser as a bailout device for transferring failing or near-bankrupt divisions of major corporations to black ownership. Government policy must be directed toward capital formation rather than toward the rhetoric of capital formation.

The minority wealth development plan should also include government backing of blacks in acquiring media power in the field of mass communications. Here, as already mentioned, the regulatory agencies should be called upon to redress past racial discrimination in government franchise awards by allocating one-half or more of all *new* federally granted business monopolies such as television, radio, microwave, and satellite communications facilities to minority entrepreneurs. Similarly, one-tenth or more of all new contracts for the exploitation of federal timberlands, coal, uranium, and oil deposits should be set aside for exclusive bidding by minorities. Preferential rights should be awarded to exploit and develop frontier territories such as the 5 million acres of federally owned property in Alaska currently classified as commercial land, as well as the 45 million acres of existing commercially classified timberlands in Colorado, Oregon, Idaho, and Montana. There are 700 million acres of public lands—more than a third of all land west of the Mississippi River—owned by the American people as a whole. This land is rich in oil, gas, coal, and precious mineral deposits. If these treasures are to be exploited, a modest proportion should be set aside for blacks who, for a century or more, were openly excluded by the federal government from staking out any claim to government properties in the past.

Timber, oil, and other interests, which have benefited mightily from public grants and franchises, often take the position that government allocations to minority businesses make the beneficiary dependent on the government. But the thesis that special set-asides of government contracts hurt blacks is plainly untrue. Moreover, whites have always aggrandized their wealth holdings—and surely done themselves no harm—by using political power to win franchises, contracts, and other allotments from the public treasury. So, too, should blacks. A contemporary case in point may be made in the District of Columbia. Here blacks have successfully mixed politics and economics to build their own old-boy network. To the distress of established white real estate developers, as well as of a liberal press opposed to the appearance of a minor-league black spoils system, black lawyers and politicians have acquired ownership of government-assisted commercial real estate developments without putting up any money. A strong, propertied black middle class is being developed in the District because blacks are now manipulating the political economy in the same manner as have whites for the past century or more. Here is a textbook case where a racial group has acquired access to government-created wealth and is doing much better because of it.

Any high school student is able to appreciate the fact that the principal economic problems of blacks have been low incomes and under-employment. Approximately 30 percent of all black families are living below the poverty level. Under these circumstances, government efforts to aggrandize black wealth may appear irrelevant. But, as shown earlier, greater personal wealth and greater control of corporate wealth are critical to the overall goal of racial economic quality. If the basic premise is accepted that income differences between the races should be gradually reduced, measures designed simply to raise black incomes will not be enough because these measures rarely deal with interracial power relationships. Steps will have to be taken to influence large-scale allocations of capital which, in turn, will have important side effects on who gets what and how much. Like others in our society, blacks must have the ability to influence capital to their advantage and, in the same manner as other groups, to prevent capital from being used by others to their disadvantage. Even if blacks were to achieve equal stations in the business and professional life of the nation and thus reach earned-income parity with whites, caste status is likely to persist as long as wealth positions remain grossly unequal.

Attacks on affirmative action and similar strategies that impose hardships on whites summarily label these policies "egalitarian" or "Marxist." People with bona fide claims for redress are silenced by charges that the corrective policies they advocate are designed to make everybody equal. But this charge misstates the objectives of affirmative action. In the American economic scheme, individual inequalities in wealth are both intended and desirable. A strong case can be made for the conclusion that everybody is better off when successful people are allowed to keep the benefits of their industry, skill, and imagination. Accordingly, a government assault on unequal wealth as such is not permissible. Even after several centuries of government policies that allocated all public wealth to whites, blacks are not thereby entitled to a redistribution of this wealth. But when the state chooses *in the future* to use its manifest powers to create more wealth through the award of public franchise or subsidies, the position is very strong that blacks should have a first claim on these new allotments.

Blacklist for Federal Funding Any Public or Private Activity Where Racial Segregation Is Practiced

"No money shall be drawn from the treasury, but in consequence of appropriations made by law. . . ."

—The United States Constitution
Article 1, Section 9, Paragraph 6

AN ACT OF CONGRESS expressly bars federal financial aid or government subsidy to any activity where racial discrimination is practiced. Yet no federal agency has expressly been assigned responsibility for enforcing this law, and the mandate of the statute has been largely ignored. Nevertheless, the law stands as potentially the single most powerful weapon for undercutting many of the ways that whites—both unintentionally and by design—use the power and wealth of the state to assist and subsidize other whites and to keep blacks off protected turfs and territories.[6]

On a nationwide basis, federal tax dollars subsidize racial discrimination. Federal education grants go to racially segregated public schools; government funding is received by many private hospitals that do not admit blacks; federally subsidized highways are built by contractors who routinely exclude blacks from work crews. Each year, many billions of dollars are channeled to police departments, fire departments, school boards, court systems, and voter-registration offices that have never employed, or even considered employing, a black official. Suburban communities that adopt housing rules and zoning measures with the express purpose of keeping blacks out of their neighborhoods are recipients each year of hundreds of millions of dollars of federal community development grants.

Enforcing federal laws prohibiting government support of race discrimination would require no complicated new enforcement machinery or new layers of federal bureaucracy. The President controls the disbursement of federal revenues; he is charged, also, under the Constitution with the enforcement of all the laws of the United States. By simple executive directive the President has the power to direct the Office of Management and Budget to block disbursements of government money to activities where administrative hearings have found proof of race discrimination.

Instead of placing the burden of proving explicit race discrimination on the Office of Management and Budget, the presidential order could require advance compliance prior to government funding. All federal or state agencies—and, for that matter, all states, cities, towns, hospitals, school boards, and other grantees—would be obliged to file documentary proof of compliance with laws against racial discrimination as well as with applicable affirmative-action rules. This is precisely the principle that the federal government already applies to environmental matters, where the burden of proof falls upon developers who must show, in environmental impact statements, that the projects they are proposing will not harm the public. There seems to be no reason why this enforcement approach, which has worked so well to protect trees and water fowl, shouldn't be used to protect the opportunities of blacks and other minority Americans. As long as the determination not to subsidize race discrimination is firm, the budgetary discretion that rewards compliance with antidiscrimination laws by granting funds—and punishes noncompliance by withholding money—can be a potent weapon for recruiting wider participation by blacks in the American economy.

During the Carter administration, a tentative step was taken toward the use of budgetary powers for civil rights objectives. In the fall of 1979, the Office of Management and Budget set up a civil rights office "to ensure a consistency in agency enforcement of civil rights issues." However, OMB's civil rights office has done little but occupy office space.

In the early 1980s, policies of the federal government strongly defended established territorial and power relationships between blacks and whites. Neither the Office of Management and Budget nor any other department of the executive branch was likely to interfere with the liberty of whites to attend segregated schools, to enter racially restricted hospitals, or to use local rules to keep blacks out of their neighborhoods. In fact, until blocked by the courts, the inclinations of the Reagan Administration were to affirmatively fund private colleges whose rules denied admission to Negro people. But for future Presidents, for whom racial inequalities may be a more pressing issue, the critical pressure point has been identified. Any administration seriously interested in stopping the flow of federal money to state, local, and private business activities that engage in race discrimination should turn to OMB as the all-powerful place in government where the money spigot is turned on and off. Minority groups may in fact gain far more by directing their attention to OMB than to the courts or the legislatures. OMB is inherently a superb, but long-neglected, lever for enforcing race discrimination laws.

Require Publication of a Minority Impact Statement Prior to the Adoption of Any Law or Regulation That Might Have a Disproportionate Effect on Minority Groups

"One Law for the Lion and the Ox is Oppression."

—William Blake (c. 1800)

FOR A CENTURY OR MORE, the federal government was a direct and active agent of racial discrimination in the United States. Race was an explicit criterion for the award of wide-ranging benefits including contracts, education, employment, mortgage insurance, and government franchises. State-ordered racial discrimination which constrains or limits the freedoms of minority groups is now fully acknowledged as unconstitutional behavior. Nevertheless, many public laws are passed that on the surface are racially neutral yet, for one reason or another, have a disproportionately harmful impact on blacks and other racial groups. In many cases, these apparently evenhanded laws open up the economic or educational gap between blacks and whites. The damage to minorities usually occurs when goods or benefits are allocated by government rules or criteria technically free of racial bias, yet where the categories used to assign benefits or penalties reinforce unequal racial positions for the reason that blacks are already underrepresented or overrespresented in particular categories or positions. Most civil rights litigants, as well as other government watchdog groups, generally scrutinize proposed rules or legislation only for explicit racial discrimination. Hence, the secondary form of discriminatory impact effect is commonly overlooked.

A few examples will clarify the process by which a rule free of explicit racial bias nevertheless has a punitive impact on blacks. A racially neutral law protecting, say, on-site picketing in the construction industry will probably help more whites than blacks to bargain for greater wages for the reason that, historically, the construction industry and its unions have been all-white working preserves. So, too, a routine increase in Social Security taxes, or similar federal tax burdens on employment, may hurt black workers much more than whites because increased wage costs may persuade employers to automate more jobs, thereby eliminating more of the low-skill jobs disproportionately held by blacks. Similarly, increases in federal minimum wage requirements, long thought to be a boon for the struggling low-paid worker, more often benefit white unionized workers with protected jobs, while displacing low-skilled black teenagers with no seniority and unprotected jobs.

The ordinance of a municipality or of a state university may exclude blacks from opportunities without many people knowing it. Thus, a fiercely defended all-white suburb, such as Cicero, Illinois, that adopts a rule requiring residence as a condition for obtaining municipal jobs is, in practice, making race a requirement for public employment. The consequences of a new rule may not be clear until all circumstances are exposed and examined. For instance, an institution that adopts a new rule requiring its applicants to have Scholastic Aptitude Test scores of no less than 650, as is the case in the University of Maryland, is in effect—though not without valid educational purpose—restricting admission of blacks nationwide. But we don't know this unless we also know that blacks score 100 points or more lower than whites on standardized tests. We see then that equal treatment may really be unequal whenever blacks are disproportionately members of any class that is the object of legislation or administrative rule.

Tax policy is an important area of government subsidy where ostensibly racially neutral legislation reinforces and probably opens up the economic gap between blacks and whites. For example, every time Congress liberalizes the tax deduction for interest paid on home mortgages and other loans, it is making legislation carrying a massive racial bias. This tax subsidy—enjoyed almost entirely by whites—is in the magnitude of $19 billion a year. The reason for the bias is that employment and credit discrimination against blacks in the past leave blacks owning only a tiny fraction of American real estate and, as a group, relatively unable to take advantage of the interest deduction subsidy disproportionately claimed by white homeowners. For the same reason, the residential property tax deduction—a federal subsidy of over $8 billion a year to homeowners—goes almost entirely into the pockets of whites. The same racially skewed tax benefits go to parents who put money aside in tax-exempt accounts to finance their children's college educations. Only a tiny percentage of black families have incomes large enough to claim the economic subsidy stipulated by the requirement of high family income. Similarly, the federal tax credit support for manufacturers who automate—and thereby eliminate jobs requiring only limited skills—may be an important factor in keeping black unemployment at twice the white rate. Yet, on its face the law carries no racial bias.

Note finally the steep federal tax cut of 1981, which provided a textbook example of a law that was racially neutral on its face while in fact granting virtually all of its benefits to whites. When the maximum tax rate on unearned income of wealthy individuals was cut from 70 percent to 50 percent, the action was virtually the equivalent of *cutting taxes of whites only*. The number of blacks with sufficient dividend income to qualify for the 70 percent tax was insignificant. Thus, by a stroke of the legislative pen, the white wealth advantage was reinforced by many billions of dollars without any public awareness of what had occurred.

Generally speaking, courts strike down on constitutional grounds only explicit or documentable acts of race discrimination by the state. Nobody pays much attention to laws or regulations that disproportionately hurt blacks provided overt bias is not present. Blacks are essentially powerless to block, or even know about, a great deal of legislation that potentially is extremely harmful to them. Nor, in fact, can they or anyone else determine in advance the likely consequences for minorities of many proposed new policies and laws.

Of course, the waiting list for litigants challenging racial bias in government would be quadrupled if every law having a negative impact on black people could be subject to constitutional attack. Yet, at the very minimum, government procedures should be established that would oblige federal officials and lawmakers to consider before acting the possible racial consequences of what they are doing. Officials should be required to project as best they can, and to publicize, the likely impact on racial minorities of proposed new government regulations or legislative initiatives. This policy should also apply to the repeal of any law or regulation that could have a disproportionately negative impact on minority groups.

A first step in effectively tracking and publicizing the racial impact of new laws and rules would be the adoption of a congressional resolution requiring the General Accounting Office to file and publish a minority impact statement before a congressional committee reports out any new bill that might disproportionately affect the economic status of minorities. Moreover, independent administrative agencies such as the Federal Reserve Board, the Interstate Commerce Commission, the Federal Trade Commission, and particularly the Internal Revenue Service and the Department of

Energy should be required to publish minority impact statements in advance of issuing new rules and regulations. Advance minority impact statements should be required particularly for all proposed legislation that would affect taxation, manpower, education, health, housing, energy, commerce, and monetary policy.

The filing of minority impact statements would not block legislation unfavorable to blacks but it would at least give minorities advance notice of whatever the government knows or doesn't know on the subject, and would alert minority groups to the possible need to lobby against trends in government policy that are unfavorable to minority interests. The requirement would even up somewhat the huge information disadvantage which, as we have seen, is one of the most serious aspects of the handicaps of race.

There seems to be a phenomenon of political behavior that when powerful people set about to help others they usually end up helping themselves. Particularly, when well-intentioned whites try to help blacks with minimum wage laws, low-cost housing programs, or tax incentives for hiring the so-called hard-core unemployed, the economics of the transaction may reinforce racial inequalities just as much as do unfettered market transactions. Forced disclosure of the effects of government kindness gives minorities an opportunity to protect themselves from their benefactors. Clearly, then, proposed legislation which is explicitly earmarked to *help* minority groups should not be excepted from the impact statement requirement.

Strip Labor Unions That Discriminate Against Blacks of Collective Bargaining Privileges

"[Inequalities in advantages and disadvantages are created] . . . in the three following ways. First, by restraining the competition in some employments to a smaller number than would otherwise be disposed to enter into them; secondly, by increasing it in others beyond what it naturally would be; and, thirdly, by obstructing the free circulation of labor and stock, both from employment to employment and from place to place."

—Adam Smith,
The Wealth of Nations (1776)

DESPITE THE DEPLETED RANKS and diminished clout of organized labor, workers represented by labor organizations earn significantly more than those who are not. Also, unionized employees are more effective in keeping up with inflation, or even in making wage gains in excess of inflation, than are nonunionized workers. Currently, nearly three-fifths of new union contracts include built-in cost-of-living adjustments that give unionized workers a much better chance to keep pace with price increases. Recent declines in union power should not obscure the massive economic force that trade unions exercise over who gets what in the American economy.

Surprisingly, 35 percent of all black male workers belong to labor unions, while only 29 percent of all white male workers are unionized. Black women are also more likely to be unionized than are white women, with 23 percent of black female workers represented by labor organizations, compared with only 15 percent of white female workers.[7] Despite the larger percentages of blacks in unionized jobs, whites have a much firmer grip on higher-paying unionized positions controlled by the great labor powerhouses such as the Teamsters Union and the various unions controlling the skilled commercial building trades. It is likely that black earnings gains relative to white are held back in considerable part because the stronger collective bargaining units—as well as those units bargaining for high wage earners—are disproportionately bargaining on behalf of whites.

Unions often support liberal political initiatives similar to those urged by blacks. This creates the inaccurate public impression that unions always welcome blacks to their membership. But the fact is that a fundamental goal of any labor monopoly is to ration membership, and the rationing or screening device that is used is often skin color. Organized labor has a long history of discrimination against blacks. It still enjoys considerable freedom to discriminate because it is a powerful voting constituency that elected public officials are reluctant to challenge. Some labor organizations such as the automobile and packing house workers have very large black memberships. But many large unions—particularly among the AFL craft unions—have few minority members. The most flagrant violators of equal opportunity laws have generally been the trade organizations of plumbers, carpenters, sheetmetal workers, electrical workers, ironworkers, pipefitters, utility workers, lathers, rubber workers, and teamsters. Also, labor unions have been far more skillful than employers generally in so-called motorcycle compliance with antidiscrimination laws where one black worker is put on a motorcycle and, for the benefit of the federal EEO inspector, is shuttled from one job to another all day long. To date, the National Labor Relations Board has never used its powers to revoke the certification of a union found to have discriminated on the basis of race.[8] And the complex love-hate relationship that exists between blacks and organized labor appears to have prevented black civil rights groups from effectively challenging union employment practices.

The underrepresentation of blacks in many unions may be redressed in a number of ways. The prestige of the office of the President, as well as his power to appoint National Labor Relations Board members, should be used to press the Board to adopt a policy of suspending or rescinding union certification and collective bargaining privileges of unions denying equal representation and membership to minority workers. At the same time, civil rights groups should seek cease-and-desist court orders against the major unions that habitually discriminate against blacks. Minority groups should also lobby for much greater public disclosure of minority membership in major unions. Labor unions should be pressed to publicize and submit for outside audit the impact on black workers of seniority rules, apprenticeship training programs, and other arrangements for hiring, firing, and laying off employees. In most cases, full disclosure of the racial composition of labor union membership could be accomplished by a White House executive order requiring unions participating in government contract work to make the necessary disclosures.

If the NLRB fails to take firm action against union discrimination, as is likely to be the case, the Congressional Black Caucus should lobby the White House to invoke law enforcement powers of the Department of Justice and of the Department of Labor to block further race discrimination in the major craft unions. To this end, the Caucus and other black civil rights organizations should carefully scrutinize the racial views of presidential nominees to the all-powerful post of General Counsel of the National Labor Relations Board. In the new political environment in which blacks and Hispanics may account for 20 percent of the votes nationwide, a Republican in doubt of reelection, or troubled about the reelection prospects of GOP candidates at the state and local level, might be tempted to adopt a firm antidiscriminatory labor union admissions policy, and possibly capture enough minority votes to swing an election—or thwart a defeat.

As a legalized workers' monopoly protected by the Wagner Act, organized labor is one of the great economic, industrial, and political powers in the nation. Full political and economic equality for blacks is inconceivable without full participation by them in the immense economic and political power held by organized labor. The very heart of union power is its legally protected right to bargain collectively on behalf of its members. Challenging this right would threaten a union's very reason for being. Hence, the strategy of depriving recognition and legal bargaining status to those unions still inclined toward Jim Crow is the most effective method of enabling racial minorities to win much greater access to the political and economic benefits of trade union power.

Adopt Strict Affirmative-Action Rules Affecting the 75 Million Jobs in Government-Regulated Industries

"Mr. President, time is running out. You are busy. We want specifically to talk to you about the problem of jobs for Negroes in defense industries. Our people are being turned away at factory gates because they are colored. They can't live with this thing. What are you going to do about it?"

"Well, Phil," the President said, "what do you want me to do?"

"Mr. President, we want you to do something that will enable Negro workers to get work in these plants."

The President said he would do something. "I'll call up the heads of the various defense plants and have them see to it that Negroes are given the same opportunity to work in defense plants as any other citizen in the country."

"We want you to do more than that," Randolph said.

"We want something concrete, something tangible, definite, positive, affirmative."

"What do you mean?"

"Mr. President, we want you to issue an executive order making it mandatory that Negroes be permitted to work in these plants."

> —From Lerone Bennett's *Great Moments in Black History: The Day They Didn't March,* describing a 1940 meeting between President Roosevelt and A. Philip Randolph, *Ebony,* Feb. 1977, p. 128

THE POWER OF THE President to open up black employment opportunities in federally regulated industries far exceeds his executive authority over private enterprise generally. While past Presidents have consistently chipped away at the white economic advantage through a series of results-oriented affirmative-action orders affecting employment of government contractors, none has significantly used either his executive or his appointive powers to harness the powers of government over regulated industries so as to expand the participation of minorities in American economic life.

The potential impact of the executive power in this very large part of the labor marketplace may be gauged from the fact that somewhere between two-thirds and three-quarters of the economy of the United States is controlled by the 1,000 or so largest industrial corporations, banks, utilities, and financial organizations. Virtually all of these institutions are in some way either beneficiaries of federal aid or regulated by an agency or department of the federal government. This means that 75 percent or more of the entire United States work force, representing close to 75 million jobs, is employed in industries subject to some form of direct government regulation. Were the government to commit itself simply to imposing affirmative-action obligations in those areas of the economy where it already enjoys comprehensive regulatory authority, its action could produce a strikingly new economic climate where many more of the best paid and most secure jobs in the nation are held by blacks.

Public utilities and a number of other regulated industries are permitted by law to pass on their extra labor and training costs to customers. Accordingly, one might expect that these industries would be effective warriors in the effort to find more jobs for blacks. But this is not the case. Instead of being paragons of nondiscrimination, the regulated industries continue to be among the poorest performers in employing and upgrading blacks.[9] Thus we have the anomalous situation where those government agencies that have the most comprehensive and clear-cut powers to advance blacks are, in fact, the agencies that have made the least effort. The determination of many large utilities to pursue minority hiring and upgrading on their own terms and pace could be reversed if blacks were to apply voter pressure on Presidents and presidential candidates, demanding tighter affirmative-action rules in these industries where old-fashioned government regulatory authority is present.

Using the Federal Agencies to Suppress Race Discrimination

There are a number of federal agencies or departments with significant power to expand minority opportunities in regulated industries. For example, the President has virtually total control over policies of the Department of Labor because its head is a Cabinet officer who serves at the pleasure of the President. As a result, the President could readily require the Department of Labor to withdraw federal funds from state employment offices that screen out minorities. State employment agencies that are largely supported by the federal government, as well as private employment agencies usually regulated by the states, are responsible for job placements of a very high percentage of the civilian work force. Both public and private agencies have a long history of racial discrimination, often serving as unlawful racial screening devices for corporations, banks, law firms, and others unwilling to risk the legal action that could result from direct interviews and rejections of minority job applicants. Title VI of the Civil Rights Act of 1964 explicitly authorizes the Department of Labor to withdraw funds from state employment offices known to violate equal opportunity laws.[10] If blacks had the power of the White House working on their behalf, the Department of Labor could become a positive force for the advancement of blacks.

Like the Department of Labor, the Securities and Exchange Commission has ample authority to enact rules suppressing race discrimination in the securities industry. The problem facing civil rights groups has been the SEC's unwillingness to require minority employment commitments from stock exchanges and securities brokers, dealers, and underwriters. The Commission has never taken any steps to curb racial bias in the securities industry, despite the fact that the industry has been identified by the Equal Employment Opportunity Commission as a major laggard in providing greater opportunities for blacks and other minorities.[11]

Counting as they do for almost nothing in the money industry, blacks also find their interests at the Treasury Department totally ignored. The U.S. Treasury is a department of the federal government that could make important commitments to blacks if the President were on their side. The influence of the White House over Treasury policies is nearly absolute since the Secretary of the Treasury serves at the pleasure of the President. Traditionally, Treasury Department heads have been former bankers inclined primarily to serve the interests of the banking industry. Even during periods when heavy government regulation was in vogue, there has been no record of any Secretary of the Treasury showing serious interest in using the fiscal powers of his office to redress racial inequities in the economy. In 1965, the White House issued Executive Order 11246 requiring banks, as federal contractors, to take affirmative action to remedy job discrimination in the banking industry. In theory, this order permits the Treasury to terminate the federal contractor status of any bank that fails to comply with affirmative-action rules. However, like many similar orders, this rule has served less as an enforcement measure than as a means of persuading minorities that the government has a commitment to them. Like other federal agencies, the Treasury is well-decorated with in-house civil rights officials; neither they nor higher Treasury officials have ever seriously used their powers to increase the cost to banks of credit discrimination against black people or to purge banking institutions of their persisting habits of dealing only with their own kind.

A President seriously committed to using the authority of the Treasury to help remove blacks from the catfish economy in which they now function and introduce them into the mainstream of the world of banking and finance could require a number of measures. Where flagrant job and credit discrimination are evident, the President could require the Secretary of the Treasury to revoke a bank's authorization to serve as a depository for federal funds. In addition, the White House could make public—or seek the legal authority to make public—the minority employment reports that banks file yearly with the Treasury Department. The White House could also require the

Treasury to test its legal authority to adopt rules that would withhold revenue-sharing and other federal funds from any institutions that persist in overt race discrimination in education, housing, and health care.

Other departments and agencies whose activities have a serious impact on blacks include the Interstate Commerce Commission, the Department of Energy, the Federal Communications Commission, and the Department of Transportation. These government units have direct regulatory jurisdiction over a private work force of 20 million or more. Good jobs are available for racial minorities in constructing highways, building mass transit, operating trucks, buses, and railroads, generating electrical power, and operating telephone and television communications systems. Looking into the late 1980s, America will be spending trillions of dollars in rebuilding its roads and bridges. Unless black political power mounts very fast, black workers and construction firms are not likely to claim an important slice of the redevelopment pie. A White House executive order could blunt or reverse the political forces that inexorably confer these benefits on whites.

Few organizations are so minimally involved in federal aid as to be immune to equal opportunity oversight. For example, large supermarket chains are virtually federal contractors subject to the jurisdiction of the Department of Agriculture, a department that has shown a marked lack of enthusiasm for guarding interests other than those of the food and farming industry. It appears that the judges of the federal courts, the tax courts, the Court of Claims, and patent courts have not been asked to determine whether the privilege of representing clients may be denied to law firms that continue to practice race discrimination in the selection of partners or associates. Nor has the distinct preference of the large architectural and engineering firms for employing whites ever been raised as an issue in awarding federal contracting for new government buildings.

We have shown earlier in this book how, in a wide range of settings and circumstances, the economic, social, and political status of blacks improved *because* of strong remedial action by the federal government. Free enterprise has *never* shown itself as a powerful champion of fair employment, minority access to credit or investment capital, or Negro entry into trade unions. While the federal government has a proven record as a powerful workhorse on behalf of black economic progress, the capacity of the state to influence the regulated sector of the economy has been largely untapped. Here in the domain of regulated industry is a major presidential opportunity to take overriding measures to draw many more black people out of the backwaters of the American economy.

Require the Nation's Largest Banks to Earmark
Funds for Disadvantaged Sectors of the Economy

"Institutions tend to reproduce themselves unless something interferes with the process. Build an institution white for racist reasons and it will tend to continue white even when the racism that founded it abates—unless, again, something interferes with that process. That outside interference is what I think of as affirmative action and I'm prepared to defend it."

—William Raspberry (1981)

A CENTRAL DEFECT OF THE ECONOMY OF THE URBAN GHETTO is the fact there is no capital base. There is no wealth to start with, and people and institutions in these areas lack the economic power to bid for outside capital or to secure business or real estate credit through established private money markets. Since racial inequality is most often thought of in terms of jobs and employment, few people have an adequate appreciation of how much the huge deficiency in holdings of wealth and capital contributes to the weakness of black incomes and undermines black economic and political bargaining strength.

To attack this problem directly, a modest national affirmative-action plan should be established for banking credit. Preferential fund allocations should be made in poor and minority communities. The requirement would apply only to large banking institutions with $1 billion or more in assets—banks that avail themselves of the standard benefits of government assistance and subsidies. In 1979, approximately 200 banks in the United States had resources in excess of $1 billion. The total assets of these institutions were nearly $1 trillion. This comprised about 60 percent of all banking assets in the country. The federal assistance and subsidies invariably drawn on by these large banking institutions usually consist of federal deposit insurance, federal loan and mortgage insurance, federal reserve window or rediscount borrowing privileges, as well as direct federal deposits from the U.S. Treasury.[12]

A punchlist of eligible enterprises would be designated that would qualify for purposes of meeting the affirmative-action lending requirements. These would include federally funded community development corporations serving low-income communities, housing units, hospitals, day-care units, and shopping centers serving communities designated as low income by the Census Bureau, and, of course, minority business enterprises.

Under prevailing credit markets, the preferred borrower is the large corporate business. Even in periods of tight credit, these institutions usually borrow easily and frequently, while the small occasional borrower is last in the credit line and experiences difficulty in finding funds. This particular bias in credit markets is not necessarily a matter of racial discrimination. The bias arises from differences in credit risk as well as from the established lending practices of large financial institutions that typically prefer to deal with and seek out regular and established borrowers.[13]

There is, however, a different type of credit bias that operates against borrowers according to their social or ethnic class. The excluded groups tend to be blacks, women, and racial minorities. Thus, while most small institutions have difficulty in borrowing, blacks and other minorities have found access to credit doubly or triply difficult because they have skin color, smaller size, and higher risk all working against them. Even in an economy where there is no racial bias in credit allocations, blacks and other minorities do not bid successfully for funds.

To overcome the effects of general credit bias—although not the effects of the preference for white borrowers—many industrialized countries have designated preferred economic sectors where specific privileges are granted to borrowers who are ordinarily far down the line for loanable funds. In the United States, too, the government has provided special borrowing privileges for certain sectors of the economy that are normally credit-starved. These arrangements have included government lending programs, government credit guarantees, favorable bank reserve requirements, and credit subsidies for "preferred" loans. In most instances, the beneficiaries have been farmers, contractors in the housing and defense fields, the shipping industry, and failing institutions with large numbers of jobs at stake. There have also been some special credits earmarked for blacks and minorities— programs marked more by flag-waving than by major appropriations.

In the United States, there has been some experimentation too with the use of state-owned banks to help underdeveloped sectors of the economy. One bank of this nature still exists in North Dakota. Also, many states deposit public monies in commercial banks on the condition that the banks make "socially desirable" loans. Laws have been passed in some states, too, curbing so-called redlining practices that limit credit in the inner city. And extensive laws have been enacted that require financial institutions to make loan disclosures according to ZIP codes and geographical regions. As a step toward restoring credit to areas unable to compete for funds, the federal Community Reinvestment Act conditions certain banking privileges on findings that banks have satisfactorily served the communities in which they do business.

The most direct approach, and probably the most effective from the standpoint of racial minorities, would be a strong government program of affirmative action in the lending practices of major banks. Acting in concert, the various federal banking regulatory agencies could require regulated financial institutions—limited perhaps to those with resources over $1 billion—to establish firm annual lending commitments to sectors of the economy that have traditionally been outside the credit mainstream.

The justification for affirmative action in lending practices, targeted mainly at minority groups, is found in the long history of the "whites only" lending rule in the banking industry. Credit discrimination has been to commercial banks what job discrimination has been to employers. If one had records going back many years, few banks could show other than token lending to minority enterprises; until recently, banks have made almost no mortgage loans on properties in black communities. Indeed, the banking industry has been repeatedly cited by government agencies for its regressive racial practices.[14]

Unless outside White House or congressional pressures are brought to bear, there is little likelihood of government administrative action to advance minority borrowing opportunities. The Senate Banking Committee has studied the antidiscrimination activities of the four principal bank regulatory bodies—the Federal Reserve Board, the Federal Deposit Insurance Corporation, the Federal Home Loan Bank Board, and the Comptroller of the Currency. A Senate study, issued in 1976, showed that none of the four agencies had issued a cease-and-desist order against any bank, none had required a lender to adopt an affirmative-action program to redress a past pattern of discrimination, none had referred any credit discrimination case to the Department of Justice, and the three principal bank agencies had ignored Justice Department and HUD efforts to persuade them to initiate compliance programs in the institutions they regulated.[15]

It is common in the United States for regulatory agencies to come under control of the industries they regulate. And the banking regulatory agencies have always been in the pocket of the banks. It is clear that affirmative lending requirements—or for that matter strictly enforced rules against credit bias—will not be imposed by the banking regulatory agencies unless overriding pressure is brought to bear by higher authority. For this reason, a strong White House commitment is required if there is to be a significant reversal of policies that sequester virtually all commercial and mortgage credit to whites. The authority of the President, as well as his control over banking agency budgets and appointments, gives him sufficient political leverage to make new banking policy.

The Federal Deposit Insurance Corporation, the agency with jurisdiction over the federal deposit insurance benefits that almost all banks require in order to do business, appears to be the place where the concept of affirmative lending orders should be initiated. In view of the generous benefits that the public grants to large financial institutions—interest-free deposits, government deposit insurance, federally insured mortgages, and Federal Reserve borrowing privileges—it would not be unreasonable to require these large institutions to earmark a modest one percent of their deposits to the preferred sectors of the economy. A mere one percent of the deposits of the commercial banks with assets over $1 billion would produce a considerable fund for minority development, about $10 billion a year. For each individual bank, however, the sums involved would be so small as to have little, if any, adverse effect on either their strength or their profitability.

Understandably, banks and financial institutions find enforced credit allocations to be singularly offensive. They often contend, in fact, that the allocations interfere with free markets to the detriment of the minority groups that are supposed to benefit by the rules. There is no evidence to support this claim. Throughout the entire history of the nation, prior to the enactment of laws prohibiting credit discrimination, our system of supposedly free and open markets consistently denied credit to even highly qualified blacks. And even when racial bias is not present, unequal bargaining power distinctly works against smaller and particularly minority borrowers.

Currently, blacks face strong pressures from the political right for repeal of many of the legislative and administrative rules that have created some special openings and places for black people. Affirmative action, already under intense attack, is not likely to be extended to banking credit in the foreseeable future. But the idea should nevertheless rank high on the black agenda. The passion of liberals for delivering self-satisfying aid and social programs to black people, and the tendency of racial conservatives to use the rule that the state must remain neutral as a rubric for maintaining the subordinate status of blacks, must not be permitted to obscure the clear need for black people to use the power of the state to help them establish economic power and position in all the important centers of American capitalism.

Conclusion

IT IS COMMONLY BELIEVED that the American people are unalterably opposed to strong presidential efforts on behalf of blacks. In fact, however, the idea of giving blacks a special break does not seem to violate any deeply held principles of most Americans. To be sure, the person who pays heavy taxes and works hard for a living often resents having the government use his tax money "to support drones who are unwilling to work." But just as often, the taxpayer assents to the inherent fairness of giving a temporary head start to those who have had a singularly raw deal in the past. No matter how vehemently a conservative government proclaims the inevitable success of the proud individualist who is hardworking and ambitious, most people have the pragmatic good sense to know that the determinants of success are more complex. They know too that a group whose initiative and independence have been crushed for two centuries by lynching parties, mob justice, abominable public education, and rigid rules of economic caste is not likely to recover through a simple strategy of grit, pluck and trying harder.

This conclusion that whites tend to be sympathetic to efforts to help blacks overcome the negative tilt to our economy is confirmed by most polls of public attitudes of conservative voters. For example, the CBS News-*New York Times* poll made prior to the 1980 presidential election showed that nearly 60 percent of those who voted for President Reagan thought that the Carter government was paying either the right amount or not enough attention to the needs of blacks and other minorities.[16] A President with the will, energy, and determination to press for gradual redress of the social balance on behalf of blacks would not run into much opposition from the American people.

Conclusion

The Black Power Imperative

"Free men set themselves free."

—*James Oppenheim*
The Slave *(1915)*

VIEWING THE WORLD as it is rather than as we might like it to be, we reaffirm our original proposition. Economic success tends to be a story about power. From the beginning of recorded history—down through the Middle Ages, into the period of modern capitalism, as well as under contemporary Marxist regimes—life chances have always been better for the powerful. In most societies there is a tendency to deny this conclusion. Great powers customarily pledge allegiance to more estimable values such as the pursuit of equality, efficiency, merit, altruism, or social justice. These values do indeed have an important influence on who gets what. In free-market economies, particularly, the powers of individual merit and competence are the major determinants of economic well-being. Yet the fact remains that in most places in the world, including the United States, coercive power is a mighty economic force. There appear to be few records in history of any tribe or nation where the largest share of economic goods and valued positions has not been claimed by those individuals and groups that were economically and politically strong and that had the most secure hold on society's instruments of coercion.

I have never thought it was right that this should be so. And the fact that this is so does not make it right. But if those groups in American society that persistently lag behind the majority—particularly those whose competitive powers have been repressed by the coercive forces of racial subordination and disrepute—are to devise useful strategies to catch up, they must shape their policies and build their lives not on myths and slogans published by the powerful, but on truth and experience about themselves and about how the world around them actually distributes its economic rewards and penalties.

In this light, very high rates of black unemployment, grossly unequal incomes, grotesquely disparate shares of education, and massive black underrepresentation in political institutions may be understood not simply as a reflection of unequal skills, industry, motivation, or training but as symptoms of an awesome deficiency in the overall capacity of black people to influence the economic and political decisions of others. We conclude, then, that blacks in America are unlikely to overcome the afflictions of racial contempt and caste simply by adopting the traditional American virtues of diligence, entrepreneurship, and the pursuit of greater skills. In the tradition of many other ethnic outsiders who have achieved rank equal to the majority, blacks must also become competent in all of the accepted forms of economic and political power that a democracy holds open to its citizens and protects for their benefit and advancement.

This conclusion suggests, too, that, from the vantage point of blacks, it would be a seriously inhibiting mistake for them to treat America simply as an ideologically flawed society that somehow needs a new set of human values and incentives. Rather, the United States should be seen by them for what it is, a liberal but traditional society which, like almost all societies before it, is responsive to the self-seeking needs and wishes of those groups and individuals who, through competence or position, have the ability to persuade others to share, or part with, valued positions and resources. The struggle by blacks to take an equal place in the economy must not be seen as an effort to overturn or humanize capitalism but rather as an effort to move onto its playing fields, become part of its powerful institutions, and to share all the perquisites and prerogatives of those who run and regulate it. Under these circumstances, blacks move toward equal wealth and station not simply because it is right and just that they do so but because their struggle for economic justice is well armed with all the human powers, both collective and individual, that others use to enlarge their opportunities and strengthen their competitive positions.

Over a long span of history, two distinct forms of power, operating simultaneously or sequentially, have shaped efforts in the United States to provide blacks with an equal economic and social position: power employed by blacks and power brought to bear by whites on behalf of blacks. We may identify these forces as the politics of white compassion and the politics of black self-help. Moved as it is by changing levels of guilt, the politics of compassion has been a fitful and unreliable force for the advancement of

American blacks. Only by a whisker did plantation Negroes in the last century escape the plans of northern abolitionists to trade their guilt for an independent South where slavery would continue without threatening northern consciences.

The politics of black self-help has been an irregular process too. But it has operated as a more reliable agent of racial progress. Good things have always happened to black people when they have acted powerfully and in their own interests. In recent history, the self-help strategy first emerged in the civil rights protest movement pioneered by A. Philip Randolph in 1941. This movement advanced further in the Freedom Rides of the late 1950s, and the Greensboro, North Carolina sit-ins of the early 1960s; it culminated in the voting rights marches of the 1960s led by Dr. Martin Luther King. These pressures and demonstrations of black solidarity engaged the support of influential whites, unlocked a closed society, and propelled many blacks out of their semifeudal economic state into the industrial economy of twentieth-century America. Yet, without benefit of organized pressure and agitation, it is almost inconceivable that the single-minded dedication of blacks to education, making themselves competent, and other forms of individual self-improvement would have produced the great strides that blacks have made over the past forty years.

The most recent surge of black power declined and died not as a result of King's assassination in 1968, but at the hands of the Black Panthers and other insurgents. Their apocalyptic rhetoric and sinister tactics discredited black power, aborted a strong and courageous movement, and handed responsibility for black progress back to orthodox liberalism. As blacks increasingly became regarded as objects of concern and compassion, rather than as powerful persons with whom society had to come to terms, the once vigorous black power movement in the nonviolent tradition of Randolph and King became moribund, decadent, and sometimes corrupt. In its place was a liberal agenda that was set largely by whites. The nation's commitment to improve the status of black people came to take the form of massive government aid and services. Going into the 1980s, tens of billions of dollars a year were being spent on federal succor and support programs whose main effect was to protect black economic weakness and to preserve a developing culture of dependency. The once powerful black civil rights groups which, a decade earlier, had led blacks forward were effectively placed on the dole of government aid and corporate largesse. Such was the enfeebled and dependent state of black America that a full thirty years after Rosa Parks had refused to give up her seat on a racially segregated

Birmingham bus, blacks in the mid-1980s were still waiting for their former oppressors to complete the rescue operation. Embroiled in debilitating conflict and competition over alms and old overcoats donated by the powerful, blacks had collapsed politically. With no unified lobbying force in place, they took their assigned places at political nominating conventions and voted loyally for an enfeebling agenda set by their protectors in the Democratic party. Afraid of retribution and backlash, black people showed little capacity to act powerfully for any economic or political purpose. The idea that once more they might chart their course, and raise the collective level of all their people, through unity, collective determination, and self-help had been virtually scrubbed off the political map of black America.

The decline in black pressures was reflected in economic status. During the decade of the 1970s, black economic winnings of the 1960s were curtailed and in many cases liquidated. Selected individual blacks were inducted into middle-management positions, but the forces of automation and technology had now overtaken millions of black people and left them unpropertied and unwanted in the backwaters of the post-industrial society. In the mid-1980s, blacks by virtually every standard economic measure were losing ground to whites. As the nation's political center shifted to the right, the politics of compassion was also spent and ineffective. Fifteen years ago, the American conscience had been profoundly moved by racial inequality. Two decades later, the American people took little note of the wretched life prospects of most black children. It was clear that the nation would discuss and deal with black problems only if she were obliged to do so.

Today, the simple truth is that blacks have no sturdy ally in government or in either political party. They derive little comfort from the standard competitive drives of the American marketplace for labor or capital which continues, as always, to be a risk-averse system that, in the absence of compulsion, takes few chances on the talents of black people. Liberal whites who once joined black activists on the barricades of the civil rights movement show no capacity or inclination to provide blacks with the powers and backing they need to move forward in their struggle for equality.

Once more, blacks in America must turn to the politics of ethnic solidarity and self-help. As a group, black people must determine in caucus or convention what goals and tactics are going to serve their interests for the balance of the century. They must find and certify a trailblazing leader who will lay down a proper set of marching orders and make the black agenda effective by connecting it with the public interest and the American sense of fair play. Awakening to the pleasures of elective politics, blacks must multiply their political and economic strength by making political and economic alliances with other groups that share common burdens and aspirations.

The new voting power of upwards to 17 million adult black people must be used to bench racial conservatives who take economic power away from blacks by protecting organizations that persist in using skin color as a qualification for employment, credit, or admission to bodies that issue passports to wealth, connections, and power. When, as they must, blacks decide to cast their votes as a bloc, the ballots must go not to office-seekers who will provide the best safety nets but rather to the candidates who will use the powers of government to lead black children into all-white classrooms, take federal money away from racially segregated institutions, and back black entrepreneurs in their efforts to rise out of the bush leagues of American capitalism. For blacks, the progressive ideas of the past have been the palliatives of food stamps, rent subsidies, training grants and corporate philanthropy. The ideas of the future must be political and economic empowerment through capital formation, enforced affirmative action, and shared control of the political and fiscal mechanisms of the state.

The importance of political power to the economic progress of black people must never obscure the rule that market capitalism honors the industrious ways of the beaver just as faithfully as it defers to the potent habits of the lion. Operating in a society where liberalism's protection and prejudice's power have insidiously combined to stifle the ambitions of young people, blacks must inspire their children to cultivate power's traits of hard work, competence, self-reliance, and innovation. To support a new drive among young blacks for greater achievements in education and employment, black voting strength must be used to repeal and redirect the federal incentives that discourage labor, pay bonuses to men who leave their families, and undermine incentives for work, training, and preparation. At the same time, blacks must demonstrate how restrictive forces of job reservation, embargoes on credit and investment capital, boycotts mounted against the black entrepreneur, state-supported controls of black academic aspirations, and the eviction of blacks from political power have combined to gather all economic and political power into the hands of white people. Only by redefining the moral vulnerability of the white majority will blacks in the United States establish their right to use the countervailing strength they need to break the lock that whites continue to hold over the power to decide who gets what.

Mindful always that they live, and must compete, in a world of great powers, blacks will cease to entreat the lion to restrain his greed or share his meals. Instead, they will organize a nationwide network of political power centers, lobbying units, and self-help organizations. They will use technology and planning to build a national political organization superior to anything previously known in American politics. They will seek and win all of the far-reaching powers and advantages that go with proficiency in politics, competence in technology, and the control of property and capital. In tactically favorable circumstances, they will take control of the black vote, deny it to whites, and use this power to bargain for policy concessions that advance the political and economic status of black people. Needing no reminders of the marginal gains made during periods in American history when pressures abated, blacks will decisively repudiate the nostrums of free-market zealots whose seductive homilies undermine the quest for position and power by entrusting the life prospects of black children to volunteers, philanthropists, and markets unguarded against race discrimination.

A new political weapon of stunning potential has revealed itself to black and white America. Its origins date probably to the presidential contest of 1948 when Harry Truman, a good friend to black people, won his election through voting margins provided by blacks in three pivotal states. This power is not a mere token of the lust of black people to be strong. Nor is it a cynical effort to use political force to revive the spoils system or to redistribute wealth. Black power is, instead, a legitimate and principled power. In seeking to reapportion opportunity, it bargains on behalf of grievances deeply rooted in nearly four centuries of ugly racial codes. It strives to repair the harms of vigilante prohibitions that have stripped millions of black people of much of their economic potential and left them trading with unequal currency and competing from profoundly unequal bargaining positions. Unlike the majority powers that made it necessary, black power is scrupulously dedicated to nonviolence and the rule of law.

Driven by ambitions to overcome the overwhelming economic advantages that go with being a white person in the United States, black power agitates and it prods. It does political combat with its opponents and maneuvers to turn them out of office. It marches, it boycotts, and it frequently makes a nuisance of itself. Keeping its eye always on the unpleasant world where coercive power is an important arbiter of economic success, it measures the life chances of black people not simply in terms of equal freedoms or opportunities, but in terms of equal powers. To this end it reaches for, and finally achieves, equal standing and respect for the black race by using every nonviolent means at its disposal to see that the positive racial attitudes we now begin to observe around us are everywhere and equally reflected in the distribution of society's power.

Source Notes

Part One

Chapter Two. The Dynamics of Contemporary Power

1. The "black dot" system of racial coding used by the Detroit Edison Company is part of the court record in Stamps v. Detroit Edison Co., 365 F. Supp. 87 (E.D. Mich. 1973).

2. The failure of the Office of Federal Contract Compliance Programs to enforce its rules is described in the Report of the United States Commission on Civil Rights, *The Federal Civil Rights Enforcement Effort—1974* (Washington, D.C.: U.S. Government Printing Office, 1975), pp. 298-299.

Part Two

Chapter Six. Power in Classifying People: To Each According to His Group

1. The statement of the natural inferiority of the Negro was made by Supreme Court Chief Justice Roger B. Taney in Scott v. Sanford, 60 U.S. (19 Howard) 393 (1857).

Chapter Seven. The Ethnic Prejudgment as Power: To Each According to His Race

1. Gordon Allport's classic work on race discrimination develops a similar sequence of evasive tactics by which individuals tend to defend race prejudgments. See Gordon W. Allport, *The Nature of Prejudice* (Cambridge: Addison-Wesley, 1954).

Chapter Eight. Mob Justice: Majority Power Codifies the Race-Trait Belief System

1. An account of the race riots in East St. Louis, Illinois may be found in Richard Kluger, *Simple Justice* (New York: Vintage Books, 1975), p. 111.

2. Racial epithets threatening blacks in the North have been reported frequently. For a collection of the most offensive examples, see *Washington Post*, Sept. 29, 1973, p. A3 ; *New York Times*, April 23, 1972, p. 57; *Newsweek*, Sept. 22, 1975, p. 25.

3. The news quotation referring to the IBM executive's family is from *New York Times*, Aug. 9, 1979, p. 1.

4. The racial configuration of Detroit's public schools is part of the U.S. Supreme Court opinion in Bradley v. Milliken, 418 U.S. 717 (1974).

5. The Levittown sales agreement was discussed in *Newsweek*, Oct. 11, 1976, p. 86.

6. For a discussion of racial discrimination within desegregated school systems, see David L. Kirp, "Schools as Sorters: The Constitutional and Policy Implications of Student Classification," *Pennsylvania Law Review*, Vol. 121 (1973), pp. 705, 760, 766.

7. Discriminatory lending policies by financial institutions in Boston and New York City are reported in *Boston Globe,* Sept. 14, 1971, p. 3, and *New York Times,* May 2, 1972, p. 46.

8. The statistics concerning the building trades are drawn from *Black Enterprise,* July 1972, p. 19.

9. The quotation specifying North American Aviation's hiring policy on the eve of World War II is from *The Pittsburgh Courier,* June 28, 1941, p. 6.

10. Racial discrimination in employment practices within the Supreme Court is described in Nina Tottenberg, "The Supreme Court: The Last Plantation," *New York Times,* July 24, 1974, p. 26.

11. The racial hiring codes of congressmen were publicized by the *Fort Worth Star Telegram,* Aug. 18, 1974, p. 1. For a follow-up article, see *Washington Post,* Aug. 24, 1974, p. A18.

Chapter Nine. The State as an Outlaw: The Eviction of Blacks From Political Power

1. The provisions of state constitutions in the South prior to 1865 are discussed in G. James Fleming, "The Negro in American Politics," in *The American Negro Reference Book,* John P. Davis, ed. (Englewood Cliffs: Prentice-Hall, Inc., 1966), pp. 414-418.

Denial of the voting franchise to blacks in the northeastern states is described in Leon F. Litwack, *North of Slavery* (Chicago: University of Chicago Press, 1961), p. 91.

2. Repressive actions taken against blacks in the former Confederate states are described in "A Brief History of the Negro in the United States," in *The American Negro Reference Book,* p. 41.

3. Registration figures for blacks in the South are reviewed in Roger Butterfield, *The American Past* (New York: Simon and Schuster, 1976), p. 187.

4. The opinion that blacks held the balance of power in the South was expressed in Butterfield, *The American Past,* p. 188; the contrary view is found in John Hope Franklin, *Reconstruction: After the Civil War* (Chicago: University of Chicago Press, 1961), p. 133.

5. Information on state legislatures during the Reconstruction period is found in Fleming, "The Negro in American Politics," in *The American Negro Reference Book,* p. 421.

The Joint Center for Political Studies, a black political research organization, compiled the data for the 1868 to 1890 period in *National Roster of Black Elected Officials: 1976* (Washington, D.C.: Joint Center, 1976).

6. In The Slaughterhouse Cases, 16 Wall, 36 (1876), the Supreme Court distinguished between national and state citizenship rulings that the Fourteenth Amendment did not incorporate all civil rights and liberties of the federal Bill of Rights into state citizenship rights.

7. The story of how Florida rigged elections against blacks after instituting the poll tax and the multiple-ballot box system is told in Hugh D. Price, *The Negro and Southern Politics* (New York: New York University Press, 1957), p. 16.

8. The quotation from Senator Bilbo's letter to election officials is from Hodding Carter, "The Man from Mississippi—Bilbo," *New York Times Magazine,* June 30, 1946, p. 12.

9. The definition of habeas corpus appears in Steven F. Lawson, *Black Ballots: Voting Rights in the South, 1944-1969* (New York: Columbia University Press, 1976), p. 86.

The recollection of Andrew Young is told in Jack Bass and Walter DeVries, *The Transformation of Southern Politics* (New York: Basic Books, 1976), p. 42.

10. The quotation from Carter Glass appears in Paul Lewinson, *Race, Class and Party* (New York: Grosset and Dunlap, 1965), p. 86.

11. Data on the effects of new laws dealing with black voter registration in Louisiana and Virginia are found in C. Vann Woodward, *Origins of the New South, 1877-1913* (Baton Rouge: Lousiana State University Press, 1951), pp. 14-15.

12. The story of how the white citizens' councils in southern communities intimidated black registrants is told in *Hearings on Civil Rights,* February 13, 1957, p. 1026, held by the House Committee on the Judiciary, 85th Cong., 1st Sess. (Feb. 13, 1957).

13. A brilliant account of the politics of purchased accommodation is William H. Chafe, *Civilities and Civil Rights: Greensboro, North Carolina, and the Black Struggle for Freedom* (New York: Oxford University Press, 1980). See particularly Chapter 1, in which the author shows how Burlington Industries, Cone Mills, Carolina Steel and Iron Company, and Jefferson Standard Life Insurance Company spearheaded an economic campaign in the 1950s to reward black leaders in North Carolina who advocated compliance with traditional codes of racial subordination.

14. In Grovey v. Townsend, 225 U.S. 45 (1935), the Supreme Court ruled that denial of a ballot to a Negro in a primary election, pursuant to a resolution adopted by the Texas Democratic State Party Convention restricting party membership to whites, was not state action under the provisions of the Fourteenth Amendment.

15. The Supreme Court declared the all-white primary unconstitutional in Smith v. Allwright, 321 U.S. 649 (1944). The Court decided that the right of a citizen of the United States to vote in a primary for the nomination of candidates for the U.S. Senate and House is an integral part of the elective process, a right secured by the federal Constitution, and may not be abridged on account of race or color.

The quotation from Herman Talmadge is taken from *The Atlanta Constitution,* Aug. 19, 1948, p. 5.

16. The data on the black population in congressional districts were found in U.S. Bureau of the Census, *1980 Census of the Population.*

17. The racial motivation for the redistricting of Mississippi is described in *Washington Post,* June 1, 1982, p. A6.

18. The Supreme Court upheld the at-large election system in Mobile v. Bolden, 446 U.S. 55 (1980). The Supreme Court relied on a rule developed in the 1970s, stating that it was not enough to demonstrate a racially discriminatory effect; it was necessary to show that the racial discrimination was the intention of those who passed the law.

19. President Grant's warning to Congress about the tactics of violence and intimidation practiced by southern states against black voters was delivered in his Message to Congress, Dec. 5, 1870. It is quoted in Franklin, *Reconstruction: After the Civil War,* p. 166.

The account of events in Crittenden County, Arkansas appears in Lawson, *Black Ballots: Voting Rights in the South, 1944-1969*, p. 7.

20. Accounts of violence directed against blacks are found in Lawson, *Black Ballots: Voting Rights in the South, 1944-1969*, pp. 7, 100.

21. The murder of Isaac Nixon by two Klansmen and their subsequent acquittal are also recounted in Lawson, *Black Ballots: Voting Rights in the South, 1944-1969*, p. 132.

22. The cross-burning in Liberty County, Florida, is described in Price, *The Negro and Southern Politics*, p. 43. Price, at pp. 33-58, discusses black registration in Florida in the 1940s and 1950s and correlates the racial composition of counties with levels of black voter registration. The author also documents the sharp decline in the 1940s and 1950s of black registration in the Republican party.

23. The comment of the southern senator on Massachusetts voters is from Litwack, *North of Slavery*, p. 84.

24. The buying of black votes in Springfield is described in Ray S. Baker, "What Is a Lynching?" in *Racism at the Turn of the Century*, Donald P. Denevi and Doris A. Holmes, eds. (San Rafael: Leswing Press, 1973).

DuBois' statement about the Philadelphia clubs comes from W.E.B. DuBois, *The Philadelphia Negro* (originally published in 1899) (New York: Schocken Books, 1967), p. 378.

Machine politics in Philadelphia in 1940 are described in Ralph J. Bunche, *The Political Status of the Negro in the Age of FDR* (Chicago: University of Chicago Press, 1973), p. 594.

25. The story of how Kennedy dealt with Dawson without damaging his support among black voters is told in Arthur M. Schlesinger, Jr., *A Thousand Days* (Boston: Houghton Mifflin Co., 1965), p. 144.

26. Black representation at Republican national conventions is discussed in Jackson R. Champion, *Blacks in the Republican Party?* (Washington, D.C.: Les Champs Publishers, 1976), p. 25.

27. The selection in 1924 of the first black delegate and, in 1936, of the first black to second a nomination is discussed in Milton Morris, *The Politics of Black America* (New York: Harper & Row, 1975), pp. 193-194.

The recent percentages of black delegates are taken from *Guide to Black Politics, 1976* (Washington, D.C.: Joint Center for Political Studies, 1976), pp. 28, 34.

Chapter Ten. Control Through Racial Defamation, Tokenism, and Discrediting Black Power

1. Jefferson's opinion that blacks were inferior to whites is from Dan Lacy, *The White Use of Blacks in America* (New York: Atheneum, 1972), p. 46.

Jefferson's attitude toward the accomplishments of Benjamin Banneker is found in *The Works of Thomas Jefferson*, Vol. 5, Paul Leiscester Ford, ed. (New York: G.P. Putnam's Sons, 1892-1899), pp. 261, 377-378.

2. The excerpt from Lincoln's debate in 1858 with Douglas at Quincy, Illinois is from *Lincoln: Complete Works*, John Hay and John G. Nicolay, eds. (Charleston: The Century Co., 1894), pp. 369, 370, 457-478.

The excerpt from Lincoln's address to Negro leaders at the White House is contained in "Address on Colonization to a Deputation of Negroes," in *The Collected Works of Abraham Lincoln*, Vol. 5, Roy P. Basler, ed. (New Brunswick: Rutgers University Press, 1953), pp. 371-372.

3. The quotations from Roosevelt and Taft are contained in Melvin Steinfeld, *Our Racist Presidents* (San Ramon, Cal.: Consensus Publications, 1972), pp. 201-212.

4. The quote from Woodrow Wilson is in Eli Ginzberg and Alfred S. Eichner, *The Troublesome Presence* (London: The Free Press, 1964), p. 275.

5. The presidential attacks on immigrants are described in Seymour Martin Lipset and Earl Rabb, "An Appointment with Watergate," *Commentary*, Sept. 1973; the conversation between Earl Warren and President Eisenhower is recounted by the Chief Justice in *The Memoirs of Earl Warren* (Garden City: Doubleday and Co., Inc., 1977), p. 291.

6. The quotation from Senator William Scott appears in Neal R. Pierce, *The Border South States* (New York: W.W. Norton Co., 1975), p. 82.

7. Taney's statement of caste is found in Scott v. Sandford, 60 U.S. (19 Howard) 393 (1857).

8. Judge Cox's comments about the intelligence level of blacks are reported in *The American Lawyer*, July 1979, p. 29.

9. The standard thesis of white racial superiority appears in *Encyclopedia Britannica*, Vol. 19 (11th ed., 1910), p. 344.

10. The story of how Flossie separated Jujube from the white dolls is recounted in Laura Lee Hope, *The Bobbsey Twins* (New York: Grosset & Dunlap, 1904), pp. 56-57.

11. The portrayal of blacks on television programs is described in *Window Dressing on the Set: Women and Minorities in Television,* Report of the United States Commission on Civil Rights (Washington, D.C., 1979); the data on comedy roles are from that study and are found in Table 2.5 of the study, entitled "Proportion of Major Characters in Serious vs. Comic Roles by Race and Sex."

12. For an excellent analysis of *Roots* as an example of how mass racial mythology may be swiftly defined and shaped, see William Grieder, "Shared Legacy: Why Whites Watched 'Roots,'" *Washington Post*, Feb. 3, 1977, p. B1.

13. The activities of the New York Coalition of Businessmen on behalf of Harlem youth are described in *New York Times*, July 19, 1969, p. 60.

14. Corporate good citizenship activities on behalf of blacks are described in *Response, the Newsletter of Corporate Responsibility*, March 1980, p. 7.

15. Booker T. Washington's famous Atlanta Compromise speech is contained in "Atlanta Compromise Address," in *The Booker T. Washington Papers*, Louis R. Harlan, ed. (Urbana: University of Illinois Press, 1972), pp. 72-75.

16. The quotation from William Lloyd Garrison is from Robert Cruden, *The Negro in Reconstruction* (Englewood Cliffs: Prentice-Hall, 1969), p. 36.

Part Three

Chapter Eleven. Black and White Incomes: 350 Years to Equality

1. The median may be understood as follows: in a list of numbers, for instance, 2, 3, 4, 7, 8, in ascending order, the median for that list is the number that divides the list into two equal-sized groups (in this case, two numbers each). In this example the median is 4. The two groups are 2 and 3 and 7 and 8. However, in the same list the average is 4.8, which is the sum of the five numbers divided by the number of numbers in the list—in this case, 5:

$$\frac{2+3+4+7+8}{5} = 4.8$$

2. We must omit nonmoney income in our comparisons because we have no means to measure it. The Census Bureau, for methodology and practical reasons, does not collect this information in its income surveys. As the bulk of available income data comes from the Census Bureau, we must exclude noncash forms of income. It is unlikely that this omission produces an overstatement of income differences.

3. Differences between white and black families' median income is found in U.S. Department of Commerce, Bureau of the Census, *Current Population Reports*, Series P-60, No. 134, "Money Income and Poverty Status of Families and Persons in the United States: 1981" (Advance Report), Table 1, p. 7.

Although of little use to social and economic analysts, mean (average) figures are available from the Census Bureau. In 1981 the black mean family income was $16,696 or

$10,238 below the white mean of $26,934. The mean figures for blacks and whites are both significantly higher than the median figures. This is so because in most population groups, the few families at the top with truly enormous incomes (say, in excess of $1 million) always pull up the average, or mean, income figure enough to make it significantly higher than the median.

4. Figures from the 1940 census are contained in *Current Population Reports,* Series P-60, No. 5, "Income of Families and Persons in the United States: 1947," Table 13.

5. The comparisons between white and nonwhite family incomes during the Truman, Eisenhower, and Kennedy administrations come from data contained in *Current Population Reports,* Series P-60, No. 101, "Money Income in 1974 of Families and Persons in the United States," Table 13, p. 24.

The term "nonwhite" includes Orientals and some Hispanics in addition to blacks. Orientals as a group have the highest median income of any group in the country, so that their inclusion in the nonwhite group somewhat biases the figure.

"White" includes a large number of Chicanos and Hispanics, so that the figures for this group are somewhat biased downward by recent Spanish-speaking immigrants. The term "Anglo-white" is generally taken to mean persons of Northwest European descent and, of course, derives from the fact that the first sizable group of immigrants to this country were British of Anglo-Saxon descent. In distinguishing persons of Spanish origin from these so-called Anglo-whites, it is important to keep in mind the times at which their respective immigrations occurred. The last major Anglo-white immigration was over sixty years ago, whereas there are still sizable numbers of immigrants today from countries where the native language is Spanish.

6. The improvement of black economic conditions during the presidency of Lyndon Johnson is indicated by data in *Current Population Reports,* Series P-23, No. 54, "The Social and Economic Status of the Black Population in the United States: 1974," Table 9, p. 25.

7. Changes in black economic conditions between 1966 and 1981 are contained in *Current Population Reports,* Series P-60, No. 134, Table 1, p. 6; and Series P-23, No. 54, Table 9, p. 25.

Observe that a straight-line projection of the trend over the seventeen-year period, 1964-1981, shows blacks gaining 0.1235 percent per year relative to whites. Since blacks must gain 43.6 percentage points in order to close the income gap, the projected year when blacks will reach equality is 2334.

8. The dollar gap between total black and total white income in the United States can be calculated from *Current Population Reports,* Series P-60, No. 125, "Money Income and Poverty Status of Families and Persons in the United States: 1979" (Advance Report), Table 10, p. 21.

9. Median income figures for black and white families in 1964 and 1979 are documented in *Current Population Reports,* Series P-23, No. 54, Table 9, p. 25; and Series P-60, No. 125, Table 1, p. 7.

10. A good example of the absurdities involved in using percentage increases when gains are made from a low starting point is illustrated in the following conversation at a meeting of the Massachusetts State Advisory Committee to the United States Commission on Civil Rights in Boston, June 1969:

"Mr. Tobin: Total membership in the Union (Plumbers' Union No. 12, in Boston) . . . is approximately 1,200 working on building construction.
Rev. Drinan: And the minority membership is what?

Mr. Tobin: Eleven apprentices and two journeymen.
Rev. Drinan: How does that compare with ten or fifteen years ago?
Mr. Tobin: Excellent. In other words, it is a hundred percent improvement."

U.S. Commission on Civil Rights, *Contract Compliance and Equal Employment Opportunity in the Construction Industry, 1969*, pp. 266-267.

11. Over the fifteen-year period 1964 to 1979, the dollar gap between black and white families grew by $5,742, from $3,134 to $8,876. Thus, the gap has increased annually by approximately $383. The dollar gap is calculated from statistics contained in *Current Population Reports*, Series P-23, No. 54, Table 9, p. 25; Series P-60, No. 125, Table 1, p. 7.

12. The female-head-of-household statistic and its correlation with family income is found in *Current Population Reports*, Series P-23, No. 54, Table 15, p. 32; and Series P-60, No. 125, Tables 1, 12, pp. 7, 22.

13. In 1979, the Census Bureau listed three classifications of family type: husband-wife families, male single-parent families, and female single-parent families. Black husband-wife families had incomes that were 77 percent of similar white families. For male single-parent families (4 percent of all black families and 3 percent of all white families), blacks had median incomes that were 70 percent of whites'. Thus, eliminating all female-headed families would at best reduce the income shortfall from 43 percent to 23 percent.

The Census classifications are contained in *Current Population Reports*, Series P-60, No. 125, Table 1, p. 7.

14. Data on the median incomes of black and white families by marital status are from *Current Population Reports*, Series P-60, No. 125, Table 1, p. 7.

15. Two factors largely explain the difference in median age between whites and blacks: (1) a much higher birth rate for blacks, far exceeding the excessive infant mortality rate among them; (2) a significantly higher mortality rate among older blacks. In 1979, 27.3 percent of all blacks were under the age of 14, compared with only 20.1 percent of whites. In the same year, 11.4 percent of whites were over the age of 65, compared with only 7.9 percent of blacks. (The nonwhite life expectancy at birth in 1974 was 5.7 years less than that for whites.) Offsetting the overall lower age of blacks is the fact that in 1978, 66.2 percent of all black families were headed by a person in their prime earning years of 25-54, compared with 61.8 percent of all white families.

The calculation that demonstrates that the black-white family income would decrease by only 3.3 percentage points if black family heads had the same age distribution as white family heads was made as follows:

Age	White Age Distribution	×	Median Black Family Income of Age Group	=	Age Differential
14-24	.064		$ 5,646		$ 361.34
25-34	.228		10,738		2,448.26
35-44	.201		13,476		2,708.68
45-54	.190		15,124		2,873.56
55-64	.166		12,401		2,058.57
65+	.151		6,877		1,038.43
					$11,488.84

In 1978, black median family income of $10,879 was 59.2 percent of the white median of $18,368. If black family heads had the ·same age distribution as whites and earned the median income of the blacks in each age group, black median family income would rise $610 to $11,489. This would be 62.5 percent of the white median. Thus the black-white income ratio would improve 3.3 percentage points from 59.2 percent to 62.5 percent.

The figures showing that for every different age group blacks earn less than whites are as follows:

Median Family Income by Age

Age	Black	White	Black Income as a Percentage of White Income
14-24	$ 5,646	$12,741	44.3
25-34	10,738	18,151	59.2
35-44	13,476	21,089	63.9
45-54	15,124	23,480	64.4
55-64	12,401	20,002	62.0
65+	6,877	10,433	65.9

SOURCE: *Current Population Reports,* Series P-60, No. 123, "Money Income in 1978 of Families and Persons in the United States," Table 2, p. 32, Table 20, p. 89.

16. The calculation of the income gap, assuming blacks were dispersed throughout the country in the same proportion as whites, was made as follows:

Region	White Population Distribution		Median Black Family Income for Region		Regional Differential
Northeast	.225	×	$12,079	=	$ 2,717.78
North Central	.276		13,128		3,623.33
South	.314		10,795		3,389.63
West	.185		13,179		2,438.12
					$12,168.86

In 1979, black median family income of $11,648 was 56.8 percent of the white median of $20,524. If black families had the same regional distribution as white families and earned the median black income of each region, black median family income would rise $521 to $12,169. This would be 59.3 percent of the white median of $20,524. Thus the black-white income gap would improve by 2.5 percentage points from 56.8 percent to 59.3 percent.

Data on geographical differentials between blacks and whites are found in *Current Population Reports,* Series P-60, No. 125, Table 1, p. 7.

17. Figures demonstrating that the black-white income gap would not change drastically if all blacks earned what southern blacks earned or what blacks in the North Central region earned in 1979 are as follows:

Black median family income	= $11,648
White median family income	= $20,524

If all blacks earned what southern blacks earned:

Black median family income	= $10,795
White median family income	= $20,524
Black income as a percentage of white	= 52.6%

If all blacks earned what blacks in the North Central region earned:

Black median family income	= $13,128
White median family income	= $20,524
Black income as a percentage of white	= 64.0%

SOURCE: *Current Population Reports,* Series P-60, No. 125, Table 1, p. 7.

18. In 1979, 10.3 percent of all families were black, yet they earned only 6.7 percent of all family income. If estimated figures for in-kind benefits are added ($4.5 billion for blacks and $11.5 billion for whites), black families would still earn only 7 percent of all family income.

Statistics on the amount of family income earned by blacks, and whites nationally were computed from data in *Current Population Reports,* Series P-60, No. 125, Table 6, p. 15.

19. The estimates on unreported income compiled by the Census Bureau are contained in *Current Population Reports,* Series P-60, No. 123, Table A-4, p. 297.

20. The fact that black earnings from wages and salaries are a higher percentage of their total income than white earnings from wages and salaries is found in *Current Population Reports,* Series P-60, No. 129, Table 34, p. 138.

21. The types of income received by blacks and whites are found in *Current Population Reports,* Series P-60, No. 129, Table 34, p. 138.

22. The middle-class status of blacks and whites using incomes of $20,000 or more as the threshold is found in *Current Population Reports,* Series P-60, No. 125, Table 4, p. 7.

23. The trend involving black movement into the middle class is calculated using data from *Current Population Reports,* Series P-60, No. 125, Table 4, p. 14.

24. The quotation stating that a majority of black Americans are now in the middle class is from Ben J. Wattenberg and Richard Scammon, "Black Progress and Liberal Rhetoric," *Commentary*, April 1973, p. 35.

25. The definition by the Bureau of Labor Statistics that $7,214 represented the lower standard budget for a family of four is found in Bureau of Labor Statistics, Bulletin 1570, p. vii.

26. The 1970 Census Bureau conclusions that for young black and white families outside the South incomes for blacks and whites were "more or less equal" are contained in Series P-23, No. 39, "Differences Between Incomes of White and Negro Families by Work Experience of Wife and Region: 1970, 1969, and 1959," p. 1: "There was no apparent difference in 1970 between the incomes of white and Negro husband and wife families outside the South where the head was under 35 years old."

27. The statement by Daniel P. Moynihan that outside the South, in young families with both husband and wife working, black incomes were higher than white, is from Daniel P. Moynihan, "The Schism in Black America," *The Public Interest* (Spring 1972), p. 10.

28. The very small percentage of the black population involved in Moynihan's analysis can be calculated using data from *Current Population Reports,* Series P-23, No. 39, Table 1, p. 6.

29. The differences between working time and mean earnings of black and white women in the Moynihan group are contained in *Current Population Reports,* Series P-23, No. 39, Table 4, p. 13. Median income figures are not available for this group. However, in general, the relationship between black and white mean figures is close enough to that between the median figures to enable us to use the means as proxies. *Current Population Reports,* Series P-23, No. 54, Table 21, p. 39.

30. The increase in family income provided by working wives for black and white families can be calculated from data in *Current Population Reports,* Series P-23, No. 39, Table 20, p. 38.

· 31. Mean figures are used here because medians are not available. Means are sufficiently comparable to be acceptable for rough comparisons, since the general relationship of means to medians is well known. When the incomes of a broad group of people are being assessed, the mean is inflated by the very few large incomes at the extreme. For such large groups, the mean will *always* exceed the median. Were medians available for husbands with working wives, they would be even lower than the means cited here.

Technically, the black and white incomes compared here are for total family income. But since the husband is the sole earner in this case, it is a good approximation of his earning ability.

The income data comparing white and black men with working wives and the performance of men whose wives worked with those whose wives did not are contained in *Current Population Reports,* Series P-23, No. 39, Tables 1, 5, pp. 8, 14.

32. The skewing of Moynihan's population sample in terms of an urban bias favoring blacks can be determined by examining the tables in *Current Population Reports,* Series P-60, No. 101, Table 16, p. 27. In 1970, the figures were: metropolitan areas—white median, $11,203, black median, $7,140; nonmetropolitan (rural)—white median, $8,661, black median, $4,397; for these data, see Series P-23, No. 75, "Social and Economic Characteristics of the Metropolitan and Nonmetropolitan Population: 1977 and 1970," Table 3, p. 30.

33. Data for black and white families with incomes of over $50,000 are contained in *Current Population Reports,* Series P-60, No. 75, "Money Income in 1969 of Families and Persons in the United States"; Series P-60, No. 125, Table 6, p. 15.

34. Data for black and white families with incomes over $75,000 are contained in Series P-60, No. 125, Table 6, p. 15.

35. The compensation of the highest-paid chief executives in 1978 is contained in *Forbes,* June 11, 1979, p. 117.

Chapter Twelve. People in Poverty: The Expanding Black Underclass

1. The source on poverty thresholds for nonfarm families in 1979 is U.S. Department of Commerce, Bureau of the Census, *Current Population Reports,* Series P-60, No. 125, "Money Income and Poverty Status of Families and Persons in the United States: 1979" (Advance Report), Table 17, p. 28.

The original definition of poverty was developed by the Social Security Administration in 1964 and was later revised by a federal interagency committee in 1969. The poverty concept is based primarily on the observation that the average poor family spends about one-third of its income on food. The cost of feeding a family of a certain size and type for one year is the cornerstone of the poverty threshold computation. The Department of Agriculture devised a nutritionally adequate food plan. Its cost for a family of a certain size and type was computed, and then the threshold was set at three times the cost. Farm families were originally thought to spend 70 percent of what nonfarm families spent on food; this was later changed to 85 percent. The threshold figures are revised annually, based on the Consumer Price Index.

For a discussion of the poverty threshold concept and its relationship to other economic indicators, see *Current Population Reports,* Series P-60, No. 102, "Characteristics of the Population Below the Poverty Level: 1974," pp. 1-11, 143-144.

2. In 1979, government data indicated that there were 58,385,000 families in the United States. Of these, 6,041,000 were black, or 10.3 percent. The total number of families below the poverty level was 5,292,000, and of these, 1,666,000 were black; 31.5 percent of all families below the poverty level were black.

3. In 1979, the Census Bureau estimated there were 6,041,000 black families. Of these, 2,430,000 were female-headed, or 40.2 percent. Of the 51,350,000 white families, only

5,952,000, or 11.6 percent, were female-headed. There were 1,666,000 black families in poverty, of which 1,195,000 were female-headed, or 71.7 percent. Of the total number of female-headed families in poverty, 2,568,000, or 46.5 percent, were black. It is not clear the extent to which males who are actually present conceal themselves from the Census out of fear that Census accounting would diminish the amount of benefits available to the family under public assistance, particularly if the male is employed.

4. Statistics on the poverty rates of black and white male- and female-headed families are found in *Current Population Reports,* Series P-60, No. 124, "Characteristics of the Population Below the Poverty Level: 1978"; Series P-60, No. 125.

Here is the calculation of the comparative black-white poverty rate if blacks had the same percentage of female-headed families as whites.

Family Type	Distribution of White Families	×	Black Poverty Rates	=	Family Type Differential
Male head	88.4%		13.0%		11.492%
Female head	11.6%		49.2%		5.707%
					17.199%

The black family poverty rate would drop from 27.6 percent to 17.2 percent, which is still 2.5 times the white poverty rate of 6.8 percent.

5. Statistics on the number of children in black and white families are found in *Current Population Reports,* Series P-60, No. 123, "Money Income in 1978 of Families and Persons in the United States," Table 2, p. 32.

This large number of children accounts for much of the "age gap" between blacks and whites. If the population over 16 only is considered, the age gap between the two races shrinks to three years.

6. Poverty rates for black and white families and individuals according to age can be calculated from *Current Population Reports,* Series P-60, No. 125, Tables 20, 21, pp. 33, 34.

7. Black and white poverty rates by age group are found in *Current Population Reports,* Series P-60, No. 125, Tables 20, 21, pp. 33, 34. The actual black family poverty rate in 1979 was 27.6 percent. One may calculate what the rate would be without the age disparity in the following manner:

Age of Head	Distribution of White Ages	×	Black Poverty Rate	=	Age Differential
15-24	.061%		50.1%		3.06%
25-34	.230		29.8		6.85
35-44	.207		25.0		5.18
45-54	.184		22.8		4.20
55-59	.091		17.6		1.60
60-64	.074		23.8		1.76
65 +	.154		26.0		4.00
					26.65

Adjusted black poverty rate: 26.65

26.65 divided by the white rate of 6.8 percent shows a gap of 3.9 to 1. Calculations for individuals were made in the same manner as for families.

8. Any size black family is more likely to live in poverty than a similar white family, according to *Current Population Reports,* Series P-60, No. 125, Table 21, p. 34.

9. The rates of poverty for black and white families with similar levels of education are found in *Current Population Reports*, Series P-60, No. 125, Table 21, p. 34.

10. The rates of poverty among young blacks and whites ages 22 to 34 are found in *Current Population Reports*, Series P-60, No. 124, Table 13, p. 55.

11. The data on poor blacks and whites in metropolitan areas come from *Current Population Reports*, Series P-60, No. 125, Table 22, p. 36; No. 102, Table 3; No. 115, Table 41, p. 172.

12. Research demonstrating that the cost of comparable goods and services is greater in black inner-city areas is contained in David Caplovitz, *The Poor Pay More* (Glencoe: The Free Press, 1963); also see John Kain and John Quigley, "Housing Market Discrimination, Home Ownership and Saving Behavior," paper presented at the American Economic Association Annual Meeting, Dec. 29, 1969.

The data on poor black families in New York City were provided by the Bureau of the Census, Dec. 1978.

13. Herbert Stein's statement that "there is very little poverty in the United States" is taken from *Wall Street Journal*, Oct. 28, 1976.

14. The figure for the mean income deficit of poor families in 1979 is taken from *Current Population Reports*, Series P-60, No. 125, Table 23, p. 37.

15. Calculations of the estimated black poverty rate when in-kind benefits are included are made from information in *Current Population Reports*, Series P-60, No. 125, Table 23, p. 37.

The assumption is that blacks and whites each receive $5 billion of in-kind benefits, although if blacks received the same proportion as their percentage of poor families they would receive only $3 billion.

If the $5 billion were evenly distributed among poor black families, it would equal about $3,000 per family. This added income would pull 60 percent of poor blacks out of poverty, making an adjusted black poverty rate of 11 percent.

For whites, the additional $5 billion would amount to about $1,500 per poor family and would pull 45 percent of the poor white families out of poverty, making the adjusted white poverty rate 4.1 percent. Black families would still be in poverty 2.7 times as often as white families.

16. The Bureau of the Census calculations that excluded transfer payments from income statistics are contained in U.S. Department of Commerce, Bureau of the Census, *Current Population Survey*, unpublished data from March 1975 and March 1976.

17. For the percentage of black and white families below the poverty line receiving money assistance from the government, see *Current Population Reports*, Series P-60, No. 124, Table 38, p. 150.

18. The sources of income received by blacks and whites above and below the poverty line are described in *Current Population Reports*, Series P-60, No. 124, Table 38, p. 162. The data can be summarized in the following manner:

PERCENTAGE OF FAMILIES BY RACE AND POVERTY STATUS
RECEIVING SOME INCOME FROM VARIOUS SOURCES

	Whites		Blacks	
		Below Poverty		Below Poverty
Type of Income	*Total*	*Level*	*Total*	*Level*
Wages and salaries	83.89	52.2	82.1	53.9
Nonfarm self-employment	13.6	12.2	3.9	1.4
Farm self-employment	4.25	6.2	0.8	1.0

PERCENTAGE OF FAMILIES BY RACE AND POVERTY STATUS
RECEIVING SOME INCOME FROM VARIOUS SOURCES
(Continued)

| | Whites | | Blacks | |
| | | Below Poverty | | Below Poverty |
Type of Income	Total	Level	Total	Level
Social Security	23.2	24.0	22.3	21.2
Public assistance	3.9	30.6	23.5	58.2
Supplemental security income	2.1	8.2	8.3	12.1
Other transfers	14.2	9.4	13.0	6.3
Dividends, interest, and rent	64.3	22.7	24.6	4.4
Private pensions, government pensions, alimony, annuities, etc.	19.5	12.4	14.5	10.0

MEAN FAMILY INCOME BY RACE AND POVERTY STATUS
FROM VARIOUS SOURCES

| | Whites | | Blacks | |
| | | Below Poverty | | Below Poverty |
Type of Income	Total	Level	Total	Level
Wages and salaries	$19,053	$2,908	$13,327	$2,835
Nonfarm self-employment	10,845	− 270	5,747	NA
Farm self-employment	5,874	−1,266	NA	NA
Social Security	4,389	2,736	3,369	2,388
Public assistance	2,362	2,642	2,481	2,512
Supplemental security income	1,629	1,519	1,674	1,622
Other transfers	1,696	1,495	1,584	1,208
Dividends, interest, and rent	1,518	292	546	NA
Private pensions, government pensions, alimony, annuities, etc.	3,967	1,452	2,692	1,364

19. The percentage of black and white families below the poverty line depending entirely on earnings is given in *Current Population Reports,* Series P-60, No. 124, Table 37, p. 154.

20. Data on people living on income less than 125 percent of the official poverty level are contained in *Current Population Reports,* Series P-60, No. 125, Table 19, p. 32.

21. Calculations based on $10,000 as the poverty threshold were made using data from *Current Population Reports,* Series P-60, No. 125, Table 3, p. 13.

22. Data on poverty status by race were not regularly collected until 1966. However, in 1959 the Census Bureau conducted a 1-in-1,000 sample of the 1960 Census to determine the poverty status of blacks. For consistency, figures for white poverty in 1959 are taken from the same sample. The findings appeared in *Current Population Reports,* Series P-60, No. 119, Table 4, p. 21, Table A-1, p. 204.

23. Data on the increase in black families below the poverty line in the 1969 to 1979 period can be computed from *Current Population Reports,* Series P-60, No. 124, Table 4, p. 24.

24. The percentage of black children under 18 being reared in families with income below the poverty line is found in *Current Population Reports,* Series P-60, No. 125, Table 20, p. 33.

Chapter Thirteen. Black Unemployment:
More Than Twice as Often and Still Losing Ground

1. According to the Bureau of Labor Statistics, the unemployment rate "measures those presently seeking full- or part-time work as a percentage of the total civilian labor force." The "civilian labor force" consists of all presently employed or seeking work.

2. Comparisons between white and nonwhite unemployment rates are presented in U.S. Department of Labor, *Employment and Training Report of the President—1978,* Table A-5, p. 190; U.S. Bureau of Labor Statistics, *Employment and Earnings,* Vol. 27, No. 1, Jan. 1980, Table 6, p. 163. Prior to 1972, figures for blacks are not available, so data for nonwhites are used.

Although blacks constitute over 90 percent of nonwhites, the economic resilience of other nonwhites such as the Chinese and Japanese gives an unemployment rate for nonwhites lower than for blacks alone. In 1979, for example, the unemployment rate for nonwhites was 11.3 percent, for blacks only the rate was 12.2 percent.

The inclusion of the recently arrived Spanish-speaking in the *white* groups gives an unemployment rate for whites that is higher than for Anglo-whites taken alone. In official figures, these factors understate the unemployment gap between blacks and whites.

The 1982 data are from the U.S. Bureau of Labor Statistics, *The Employment Situation: August 1982,* USDL-82-310, Table A-2.

3. For nonwhite unemployment rates during the Depression, see U.S. Department of Commerce, Bureau of the Census, *Fifteenth Census of the United States, 1930: Unemployment,* Vol. 2, Table 6, p. 232; *Sixteenth Census of the United States, 1940,* "Labor Force, Employment and Personal Characteristics," Table 1, p. 17. In 1940, the nonwhite unemployment rate was 17.9 percent versus 14.3 percent for whites.

4. The data on the 2-to-1 ratio between unemployed blacks and whites, which have prevailed for thirty years, are found in *Employment and Training Report of the President—1978,* Table A-18, p. 210; and *Employment and Earnings,* Vol. 27, No. 1, Jan. 1980, Table 6, p. 163.

5. Unemployment rates by sex as well as by race are contained in U.S. Bureau of Labor Statistics, *Handbook of Labor Statistics, 1974,* Bulletin No. 1825, Table 63, p. 151; *Employment and Earnings,* Vol. 27, No. 1, Tables 5-6, pp. 162-163.

6. Information on teenage unemployment is found in *Employment and Training Report of the President—1978,* Table A-5, p. 190; *Employment and Earnings,* Vol. 27, No. 1, Tables 5-6, and Vol. 28, No. 1, Table 5.

7. The statistics on the percentages of white and nonwhite teenagers who held jobs in 1954 and 1980 are documented in *Employment and Training Report of the President—1979,* Table A-5; *Employment and Earnings,* Vol. 28, No. 1, Jan. 1981, Table 3, p. 164.

8. For criticism of Labor Department calculations, see Ben J. Wattenberg, *The Real America: A Surprising Examination of the Union* (New York: G.P. Putnam's Sons, 1976), p. 129.

9. The data on white and nonwhite married men are found in *Employment and Earnings,* Vol. 27, No. 1, Table 10, p. 165.

10. The argument that the difference in median age between whites and blacks accounts for much of the higher unemployment rate of blacks is contained in Thomas Sowell, *Race and Economics* (New York: David McKay Co., Inc., 1975), p. 151.

11. Data showing that at every age level black men are twice as likely to be unemployed as white men appear in *Employment and Earnings,* Vol. 27, No. 1, Tables 3-5, pp. 158-162.

For all males in the labor force over the age of 16, the median age for blacks in 1979 was 34.4 years; for whites 35.3 years. For black women it was 33.2 years; for white women 34.2 years.

12. Data showing that blacks between the ages of 20 and 29 have completed about the same number of years of school as whites are found in U.S. Department of Commerce, Bureau of the Census, *Current Population Reports,* Series P-20, No. 314, "Educational Attainment in the United States: March 1976 and 1977," Table 2, pp. 24-25.

The fact that there have been no corresponding gains in employment is documented in *Employment and Earnings,* Vol. 27, No. 1, Tables 3, 5, pp. 158-162. Within the 20-29 age group the black-white difference in median years of school completed is 0.2 to 0.5 years.

13. Data showing that black college graduates are twice as likely to be unemployed as their white counterparts appear in U.S. Bureau of Labor Statistics, *Special Labor Force Report,* No. 225, "Educational Attainment of Workers: Some Trends from 1973 to 1978," Table 1, p. 55.

In 1978, blacks with one to three years of college were unemployed at the rate of 10.4 percent, or 2.5 times the rate of similar whites (4.1 percent). For college graduates, black unemployment was 4.6 percent, and white unemployment was 2.3 percent.

14. Unemployment rates for various groups such as Hispanics and Asians can be found in *Current Population Reports,* Series P-20, No. 249, "Characteristics of the Population by Ethnic Origin: March 1972 and 1971," Table 7, p. 24; *1970 Census of the Population,* PC(2)-1G, "Japanese, Chinese and Filipinos in the United States," Tables 4, 19, pp. 13, 72; *Employment and Training Report of the President—1978,* Table A-18, p. 210; *Special Labor Force Report,* No. 225, Tables 1, 3, pp. 55, 57.

15. Information about labor force participation since 1948 is found in *Employment and Training Report of the President—1977,* Table A-4, p. 142; *Employment and Earnings,* Vol. 27, No. 1, Table 4, p. 160.

16. Labor participation rates for men between the ages of 35 and 44 are presented in *Employment and Training Report of the President—1978,* Table A-4, p. 186; *Employment and Earnings,* Vol. 27, No. 1, Table 4, p. 160.

In 1948, 89.5 percent of men aged 55 to 64 and 46.8 percent of men over 65 were in the labor force. By 1979, these figures were down to 73 percent and 20 percent, respectively.

17. The decline of the participation rate for young black males is documented in *Employment and Training Report of the President—1978,* Table A-4, pp. 187-188; *Employment and Earnings,* Vol. 27, No. 1, Table 4, p. 160.

18. The rise in black unemployment rates during recessionary periods is documented in *Employment and Training Report of the President—1978,* Table A-18, p. 210.

19. The high unemployment rates found in metropolitan poverty areas are documented in *Employment and Earnings,* Vol. 27, No. 1, Tables 1, 58, p. 201.

20. For an analysis of the lengthy recovery period blacks face after a recession, see Andrew Brimmer, "Economic Developments in the Black Community," *The Public Interest* (Winter 1974), p. 148.

21. The conditions of poverty in which over 40 percent of black children are being raised are described in Charles Hamden-Turner, *From Poverty to Dignity: A Strategy for Poor Americans* (Garden City: Doubleday, 1974).

22. On the importance of role models in the development of entrepreneurial skills, see Edward Roberts, "Entrepreneurship and Technology," in *Factors in the Transfer of Technology,* W.H. Gruber and Donald G. Marquis, eds. (Cambridge, Mass.: M.I.T. Press, 1969), pp. 219-237.

23. The occupational structure of the black community is outlined in *The Statistical History of the United States,* Series D705-714 (New York: Basic Books, Inc., 1976), p. 163.

24. The information on black occupational progress in the 1960 to 1979 period is documented by the U.S. Bureau of the Census, *1960 Census of the Population, Special Studies,* PC(2)-7A, "Occupational Characteristics," Table 3, p. 21; and *Employment and Earnings,* Vol. 27, No. 1, Jan. 1980, Table 22, p. 180.

25. The quotation on the occupational progress of blacks since World War II is from Richard B. Freeman, *Black Elite: The New Market for Highly Educated Black Americans* (New York: McGraw-Hill, 1976), pp. 1, 34.

26. The small percentage of blacks who have completed college is found in *Current Population Reports,* Series P-20, No. 314, "Educational Attainment in the United States: March 1977 and 1976," Table 1, p. 7.

27. The concentration of black workers in menial positions is shown in *Employment and Earnings,* Vol. 27, No. 1, Table 23, p. 174.

28. The difference between black and white occupational structures is contained in *Employment and Earnings,* Vol. 27, No. 1, Table 22, p. 173.

29. On the Census data recounting the change in percentage of black technical and professional workers, see *1960 Census of the Population, Special Studies,* Table 3, p. 21; *1970 Census of the Population, Special Studies,* PC(2)-7A, "Occupational Characteristics," Table 2, p. 12.

30. The data on the percentages of blacks employed in various professional and technical occupations in 1970 are contained in *1970 Census of the Population, Special Studies,* PC(2)-7A, Table 2, p. 12.

31. Data on nonwhite "white-collar workers" in both 1960 and 1979 are from *Employment and Earnings,* Vol. 27, No. 1, Table 22, p. 173; *1960 Census of the Population, Special Studies,* Table 3, p. 21.

32. The survey of 1,000 corporations, banks, utilities, and insurance companies that did not find a single black among the top executives or board members is discussed in Theodore Cross, "A Firm Negative on Affirmative Action," *Business and Society Review* (Spring 1977), p. 82.

Ebony magazine's annual survey of the "100 Most Influential Black Americans," which did not list any blacks who served as an officer in a major corporation, appeared in the May 1978 issue on p. 64.

33. On the black supervisor of Ford Motor Company's Chicago plant, see "Big Man at Ford," *Ebony,* March 1977, p. 62.

The low percentage of black lawyers is documented in *National Law Journal,* July 2, 1979, p. 1.

34. The statistics used to calculate the shortfall in black earnings are contained in *Employment and Earnings,* Vol. 27, No. 1, Table 44, p. 191; and *Current Population Reports,* Series P-60, No. 123, "Money Income in 1978 of Families and Persons in the United States," Table 62, p. 269.

Chapter Fourteen. Latecomers to the Feast: The Black-White Wealth Gap

1. The statement by Dr. James Freeman Clarke on the importance of having "colored people rich as Croesus" is from Martin R. Delang, *Condition, Elevation, Emigration, and*

Destiny of the Colored People of the United States Politically Considered (Boston, 1859), pp. 42-45.

2. The economic success of blacks in fields such as catering, life insurance, tailoring, sailmaking, and provisioning is described in Abram L. Harris, *The Negro as Capitalist: A Study of Banking and Business Among American Negroes* (Philadelphia: The American Academy of Political and Social Science, 1936); see also Pat Patterson, "Two Hundred Years of Economic Development," *Black Enterprise,* June 1976, p. 99.

The analysis of the 1870 Census appears in Lee Soltow, *Men and Wealth in the United States, 1850-1870* (New Haven: Yale University Press, 1975).

3. Comparisons of wealth of blacks and whites indicating that in 1870 white males had thirty-six times the wealth of black males are contained in Soltow, *Men and Wealth in the United States, 1850-1870,* p. 144.

For the population figures necessary to compute per capita wealth, see U.S. Bureau of the Census, *Negro Population in the United States: 1790-1915* (New York: Arno Press, 1968), p. 53.

The wealth gap between the races in 1870 may be understated due to the exclusion of women. There were wealthy white women in 1870, but almost no black women had accumulated significant assets.

4. The federal Office of Economic Opportunity surveys of American households that found blacks owned about 2 percent of all assets are presented and evaluated in Henry S. Terrell, "Wealth Accumulation of Black and White Families: The Empirical Evidence," *Journal of Finance* (May 1971).

See also the review of the survey estimates in Andrew F. Brimmer, "Economic Integration and the Progress of the Negro Community," *Ebony,* Aug. 1970, p. 119.

5. The fact that the average wealth for nonwhites in 1962 was less than for whites in 1870 is found in Soltow, *Men and Wealth in the United States, 1850-1870,* p. 145.

6. Census Bureau figures for income from dividends, interest, and rent are contained in U.S. Department of Commerce, Bureau of the Census, *Current Population Reports,* Series P-60, No. 124, "Characteristics of the Population Below the Poverty Level: 1978," Table 38, p. 162.

7. The Brimmer study on black wealth is discussed in *Black Enterprise*, Oct. 1983, p. 41.

The estimates of average black and white wealth in 1979 were contained in William P. O'Hare, "Wealth and Economic Status," *FOCUS* (Washington, D.C.: Joint Center for Political Studies, June 1983).

See also *Wall Street Journal,* June 20, 1983, p. 3.

8. The surprising fact that at every income level a greater percentage of black families than white families owns life insurance is found in Survey Research Center, *Survey of Consumer Finances* (Ann Arbor: University of Michigan, 1966). Of course, the total per capita value of the policies held by blacks is minuscule compared with the value of policies held by whites. Also, compared with whites, a larger percentage of the black population *as a whole* is uninsured.

9. The data on black spending habits are from Marcus Alexis, George Haines, and Leonard Simon, *Survey of Consumer Finances* (Ann Arbor: University of Michigan Press, 1981).

10. On the greater tendency of blacks to think of savings in terms of "rainy days," see Milton Friedman, *A Theory of the Consumption Function* (Princeton: Princeton University Press, 1957), pp. 79-85.

11. Figures on the receipts of black firms are from *U.S. Bureau of the Census, 1977 Survey of Minority Owned Business Enterprises, MB77-1*, "Minority Owned Businesses— Black," Table 1A, p. 10.

The information on gross receipts of all firms in the United States was obtained from Internal Revenue Service, *Statistics of Income, 1977: Business Income Tax Returns*, Washington, D.C.

12. Data on the combined annual sales of the twenty-five largest black businesses are from *Black Enterprise*, June 1983, p. 68. Information on the sales of the 500 largest industrial corporations in the United States is from *Fortune*, May 2, 1983, p. 226.

In 1982, Exxon had sales of $97,172,523,000.

13. The large number of service enterprises and automobile dealerships is shown in the annual survey of black businesses appearing in *Black Enterprise*, June 1983, p. 68.

The high number of barber shops and beauty shops is documented in *1977 Survey of Minority Owned Business Enterprises, MB77-1*, Table 1A, p. 10.

The poor growth prospects for minority-owned businesses are examined in Andrew F. Brimmer, "The Road Ahead: Outlook for Blacks in Business," paper read before the Annual Meeting of the Association for the Study of Negro Life and History, Cincinnati, Ohio, Oct. 19, 1972.

14. The conclusion that black businesses cannot employ large numbers of blacks is reached in Andrew F. Brimmer and Henry S. Terrell, paper read before the Meeting of the American Economic Association, New Orleans, Louisiana, Dec. 29, 1969.

Data on the 100 largest black businesses are from *Black Enterprise*, June 1983, p. 68, and data on employment in all black-owned enterprises are from *1977 Survey of Minority Owned Business Enterprises, MB77-1*, Table 1A, p. 10.

Statistics on black employment in general are from *Employment and Earnings*, Vol. 29, No. 1.

Information on employment by American Telephone and Telegraph, Inc., comes from its Press Relations Department.

15. Information about the thirty-eight black-owned life insurance companies and forty-four banks is found in *Black Enterprise*, June 1983, pp. 103, 145.

Data on the assets of the largest banks in the country are from *Polk's World Bank Directory* (Fall 1982), pp. vii-viii.

Statistics on white-owned insurance companies and their assets are found in *Fortune*, June 13, 1983.

16. For a study of black banks that demonstrates their insignificant impact on the black community, see Samuel I. Doctors, "The Impact of Minority Banks on Communities," *The Bankers Magazine* (Spring 1975), pp. 84-91.

17. The fact that not one of the top 500 corporations had a black serving in one of its highest posts is documented in "A Firm Negative on Affirmative Action," *Business and Society Review* (Spring 1977), p. 82.

The results of the survey conducted by the Race Relations Information Center were reported in *New York Times*, Oct. 1, 1970, p. 61.

In 1977, a black executive vice-president was employed at the Girard Bank and Trust Company in Philadelphia and a black senior vice-president was employed at the Connecticut Bank and Trust Company in Hartford and at the First Pennsylvania Bank in Philadelphia. A considerable number of additional black vice-presidents of banks have been appointed since 1977.

18. The $4.0 trillion figure on institutional wealth can be broken down as follows: $1.87 trillion in commercial banks and mutual savings banks; $1 trillion in pension funds; $459 billion in savings and loan associations; $600 billion in life insurance companies. Figures are from *Polk's World Bank Directory* (Spring 1980), p. vii; *Pensions and Investments*, Jan. 21, 1980, p. 1; and *Moody's Bank and Finance Manual* (1979).

Black-owned and -operated banks, savings and loans, and life insurance companies are, of course, an exception to the general rule that blacks do not control black assets. But the total wealth in these institutions is only $2.7 billion, or about one percent of the total of attributed black wealth I have estimated to be in the hands of life insurance companies, banks, savings and loans, and pension funds generally.

19. The loan policies of the Interstate Building Association are described in *Washington Post*, May 9, 1975, p. A28.

20. The tiny percentage of black security salespersons in the investment banking and brokerage industries shows in data from the U.S. Equal Employment Opportunity Commission, *Equal Employment Opportunity Report—1973*, Vol. 1, "Job Patterns for Minorities and Women in Private Industry," Table 2, p. 138.

On the subject of blacks in investment banking, see also Ron Howell, "Who Are the Blacks at the Top of the Money Business?" *Ebony*, Nov. 1979, p. 158.

21. The figures for government contracts to the private sector were obtained from the U.S. Office of Management and Budget.

22. On the 1.9 percent of the District of Columbia construction money awarded to minority firms, see *Washington Post*, Oct. 24, 1974, p. A1.

Contrary to popular belief, new companies do not necessarily become large by "pulling themselves up by their bootstraps." Enterprises such as the Rand Corporation, Reynolds Aluminum, and the aircraft industries were virtually created by government grants. See J. Stefan Dupree and A. Sanford Lakoff, *Science and the Nation* (Englewood Cliffs: Prentice-Hall, 1962).

23. The decline in land ownership by blacks from 15 million acres in 1915 to less than 5 million acres today is discussed in William E. Nelson, Jr., "Black Political Power and the Decline of Black Land Ownership," *The Review of Black Political Economy* (Spring 1978), p. 253.

This decline was documented on "Going Going Gone" *CBS Reports*, produced by Philip Burton, broadcast originally on July 5, 1978 (transcript available from CBS News, New York City).

24. On the substantial real estate holdings by blacks prior to the great northward migration, see Earl Caldwell, "Gaining Ground on Black Property," *Black Enterprise*, May 1978, p. 22.

25. The appreciation of home values is contained in the *Real Estate Status Report* (National Association of Realtors, Sept. 19, 1979), p. 1.

26. The 1967 federal Office of Economic Opportunity study discussed earlier in this chapter identified blacks as owning 2 percent of all assets. Using this figure for wealth appreciation in farmland and home ownership during the 1970s is justified for the following reasons. First, blacks own about one-half of one percent of all farmland. Second, since blacks are nearly twice as often renters, a reliable estimate would be that blacks own perhaps 5 percent of the total single-family homes. Finally, the value of these black-owned homes is probably less than 5 percent of the total because black single-family homes are more apt to be located in the rural South and in depressed urban areas where property values are generally lower.

The calculation of per capita wealth accumulation in real estate was made as follows: in 1970, the average price per acre was $193 and there were approximately one billion acres of farmland for a total of $193 billion; in 1979, for the same number of acres the average price per acre was $559 for a total value of $559 billion.

In 1970, the value of all single-family homes was $890 billion, while in 1979, the value was $2,300 billion.

The total value of farms and single-family homes thus increased during the decade from $1,083 billion to $2,859 billion. If 98 percent of this wealth belonged to whites, their share in the decade increased from $1,061,340,000,000 to $2,801,820,000,000, while the 2 percent share of blacks meant an increase from $21,660,000,000 to $57,180,000,000. Among the 177,700,000 whites in the United States in 1970, the per capita wealth in farms and single-family homes was $5,973, but by 1979, whites (187,000,000 in number) had increased such per capita wealth to $14,983.

27. The $581 billion increase in the value of U.S. oil reserves was calculated using data obtained from the Independent Petroleum Association of America in Washington, D.C. The figures on white wealth generally are from the 1967 federal Office of Economic Opportunity study as reported by Terrell, "Wealth Accumulation of Black and White Families: The Empirical Evidence," p. 367. This study showed the total family wealth in the United States to be approximately $1.1 trillion and black wealth to be $22.7 billion.

28. The report of black farmers in Louisiana finding oil on their land is reported in *Washington Post*, Oct. 11, 1981, p. A1.

29. The Forbes 400 Wealthiest Families are listed in *Forbes,* Sept. 27, 1982, p. 48.

30. For a detailed account of the mineral deposits on Indian lands, see James Cook, "New Hope on the Reservations," *Forbes,* Nov. 9, 1981, p. 108. The vast coal resources in the United States (one-third of which may be on Indian-owned land) are discussed in *U.S. News and World Report,* Aug. 13, 1979.

31. The Brimmer study on black and white wealth in 1982 is referred to in *Black Enterprise*, Oct. 1983, p. 41. The study of aggregate black wealth in 1979 appears in O'Hare, "Wealth and Economic Status," *FOCUS.*

32. On the gains blacks have made in the American economy between 1964 and 1973, see Edward D. Irons, "Is it Now?" paper read before a meeting of the Financial Management Association, Oct. 25, 1974; *Black Enterprise,* June 1976, p. 35; *1977 Survey of Minority Owned Businesses,* MB72-1, "Minority Owned Businesses—Black," Table 1, pp. 14-15, 18-19.

Chapter Fifteen. The United States Congress: The Backwaters of Black Politics

1. Adam Clayton Powell's career as a member of Congress is discussed in Mark J. Green, *Who Runs Congress?* (New York: Grossman Publishers, 1972), pp. 178-180.

2. A good account of Jim Crow practices involving congressional facilities appears in William "Fishbait" Miller, *Fishbait: Memoirs of a Congressional Doorkeeper* (Englewood Cliffs: Prentice-Hall, 1977), p. 188.

3. In 1977, 1978, and 1979, Thurmond voted to curtail the authority of the courts to order busing to accomplish school integration, to prohibit legal services attorneys from working on school desegregation cases, to cut funds for public housing, to remove $2 billion from food stamp appropriations, and to cut nearly $4 billion from public jobs programs.

Data on Thurmond's share of the black vote in 1978 are documented in *Election '78—Implications for Black America* (Washington, D.C.: Joint Center for Political Studies, 1979), Table 14, p. 23.

4. For information on the voting records of members of Congress in dealing with race-related issues, see Theodore Cross and Robert Bruce Slater, *A Black Voter's Guide to the 1978 Election* (New York: Business and Society Review, 1978).

Information on the share of black votes received by Senator Levin is contained in *Election '78—Implications for Black America*, Table 14, p. 23.

5. On the role of congressional staff members as a kind of "invisible government" within the legislature, see Harrison Fox and Susan Hammond, *Congressional Staffs: The Invisible Force in American Lawmaking* (New York: The Free Press, 1977); also Michael Malbin, *Unelected Representatives* (New York: Basic Books, 1980).

6. The survey of blacks in professional positions on Senate staffs is based on interviews with leadership aides in both parties and on material provided by the Ad Hoc Committee of Black Senate Legislative Staff.

7. Information about the racial composition of the staff employees serving Ohio's representatives is from *The Journal Herald* (Dayton, Ohio), Feb. 14, 1977, and conversation with the author of the article, Andrew Alexander.

8. On Congress' exemption of itself from equal opportunity laws, see Title VII of the Civil Rights Act, which forbids job discrimination on the basis of race, color, sex, or national origin; the Equal Pay Act, which forbids paying men more than women for equal work; and the Fair Labor Standards Act, which sets minimum wages and overtime requirements. These laws do not apply to offices of United States Senators or Representatives.

9. Information on blacks at the state political level is based on data in *National Roster of Black Elected Officials*, Vol. 10 (Washington, D.C.: Joint Center for Political Studies, 1979), pp. x, xi, xii, xvi.

Data on black candidates in the 1978 election are from *Election '78—Implications for Black America*, Table 2, p. 6.

10. Information about seats held by blacks in state legislatures is from *National Roster of Black Elected Officials*, pp. 1-2.

11. Information about black officials in state legislatures or county governing boards is found in *National Roster of Black Elected Officials*, pp. 1-238.

12. The 1975 study of county governing boards in black majority counties appears in *Black Political Participation: A Look at the Numbers* (Washington, D.C.: Joint Center for Political Studies, 1975), Table II.

13. Information about black mayors is from *National Roster of Black Elected Officials*, pp. xv, 1-238.

Political conditions existing in these small southern towns are discussed in Kenneth S. Colburn, *Southern Black Mayors: Local Problems and Federal Response* (Washington, D.C.: Joint Center for Political Studies, 1975).

14. Information about black officials on school boards is found in *National Roster of Black Elected Officials*, p. xi.

The percentages and the consequences of blacks holding school board seats is discussed in *The Fifty State School Board Association*, 1979, p. 3.

As of October 1978, according to figures from the Boston School Committee, there were 37,738 blacks in the Boston schools, 28,716 whites, and 8,709 Hispanics.

Chapter Sixteen. Blacks in the Executive Branch: Walter Mittys and Lord High Nobodies

1. A description of the ceremonial duties assigned to Morrow and the quotation from him appear in Everett Frederick Morrow, *Black Man in the White House: A Diary of the White House Years by the Administrative Officer for Special Projects, The White House, 1955-1961* (New York: Coward-McCann, 1963), pp. 21, 55, 88.

2. Attorney General Robert Kennedy's evaluation of Taylor is recorded in Arthur M. Schlesinger, Jr., *Robert Kennedy and His Times* (Boston: Houghton Mifflin Co., 1978), p. 313.

3. Harry S. Dent, *The Prodigal South Returns to Power* (New York: John Wiley and Sons, 1978), pp. 15, 134, 181.

4. Carter's promise to cut the White House staff and its increase by 30 percent are noted in *Time,* April 25, 1977, p. 21.

5. Mitchell's comments are reported in *New York Times,* May 14, 1978.

6. On Louis Martin's appointment and duties in the Carter administration as White House Special Assistant for Minority Affairs, see *Washington Post,* Oct. 18, 1978, p. B3.

7. The racial composition of the Office of Management and Budget during the Carter administration is contained in U.S. Civil Service Commission, *Equal Employment Opportunity Statistics* (Nov. 1977), No. SM70-77B, pp. 42-43.

8. The racial composition of the National Security Council Staff during the Carter administration is found in *Equal Employment Opportunity Statistics,* pp. 38-39.

9. No black has ever held a high position in the FBI, and until 1978, no black had ever been in charge of any of the Bureau's many field offices. Less than 3 percent of all FBI agents were black as of February 1979. SOURCE: FBI Office of Public Affairs.

Eight percent of the total CIA work force was black in November 1978—about only 3.4 percent of the professional staff compared with 17.6 percent of the clerical staff. SOURCE: CIA Office of Public Information.

Of the military services, the Army has always had the highest proportion of blacks in its officer corps, yet they were only 2.8 percent of all Army officers in 1957 and 3.8 percent in 1972, during the Vietnam War. Even in September 1978, when the enlisted ranks were 29.2 percent black, blacks comprised only 6.4 percent of all officers. SOURCE: Department of the Army.

10. The fact that Arthur A. Fletcher was the seventh black to be offered the position of Assistant Secretary of Labor by Nixon is recounted in Arthur A. Fletcher, "The Black Dilemma if Nixon Wins," *Wall Street Journal,* Sept. 25, 1972.

11. For a lively account of black expectations of appointments in the Carter administration, see Robert Shrum, "Carter and the Blacks," *New Times,* Jan. 21, 1977, pp. 22-25.

12. An assessment of Young's appointment is made in Robert Shrum, "Carter and the Blacks," pp. 22-25; Young's career until that point is highlighted in *Current Biography,* June 1977, pp. 7-9.

13. The quotation about Young not being an administration spokesman on Africa is from *The Economist,* April 23, 1977.

14. The quotation by Kissinger about Andrew Young is from the *Atlanta Journal,* July 14, 1978.

15. The thirteen independent agencies classified as the major "command" or "regulatory" bodies are: the Civil Aeronautics Board (to be abolished in 1985); the Commodity Futures Trading Commission; the Environmental Protection Agency; the Federal Communications

Commission; the Federal Home Loan Bank Board; the Federal Maritime Commission; the Federal Mine Safety and Health Review Commission; the Federal Trade Commission; the Interstate Commerce Commission; the National Labor Relations Board; the Nuclear Regulatory Commission; the Occupational Safety and Health Review Commission; and the Securities and Exchange Commission.

16. The findings of the House of Representatives study on the Federal Reserve Board underrepresentation of blacks at the regional banks are found in *Washington Post*, April 10, 1976, p. F1.

17. Statistics on the very high rate of employment of blacks in government in 1977 compared with their proportion in the general population come from *Equal Employment Opportunity Statistics*, p. 2; *Civil Service News*, Aug. 13, 1976, Table 8. In November 1975, 63,401 of the 180,766 government employees in the nation's capital were black. Figures for the military are as of September 30, 1978, and were supplied by the Department of Defense.

18. On black employment in the national government in 1912, see John P. Davis, ed., *The American Negro Reference Book* (Englewood Cliffs: Prentice-Hall, Inc. 1966), pp. 426-427. The salary figures for 1977 are from *Equal Employment Opportunity Statistics*, p. 2.

19. The heavy concentration of blacks at the lower end of the General Services pay scale is documented in *Equal Employment Opportunity Statistics*.

20. The pledge made by Meese that Reagan would put black appointees in nontraditional roles is reported in *Washington Post*, Dec. 15, 1980, p. A-6.

21. Mr. Garrett's comment about "It's a fireman-type job . . ." can be found in *Wall Street Journal*, June 13, 1983, pp. 1, 17.

22. For a discussion of the black appointments made by the Reagan Administration, see *Black Enterprise*, July 1981, pp. 21-22.

23. A description of the March 24, 1970 meeting on desegregation is contained in "Nixon Delivers on Desegregation," in Dent, *The Prodigal South Returns to Power*, Ch. 6.

Chapter Seventeen. The Power to Decide: Black Robes and White Judges

1. Chief Justice Mansfield's opinion outlawing slavery in England is Somerset v. Steward, Lofft 1, 19, 98 Eng. Rep. 499 (K.B. 1772).

The Supreme Court opinion holding that blacks had "no rights which the white man was bound to respect" was Scott v. Sandford, 19 Howard 393 (1857).

2. The quotation about federal judges being formed in a society that segregated everything from maternity wards to cemeteries is from Donald S. Strong, *Negroes, Ballots and Judges* (University of Alabama Press, 1968), p. 68.

3. The record of appointments to the federal judiciary by Presidents Carter and Reagan may be found in U.S. Civil Rights Commission, "Equal Opportunity in Presidential Appointments," June 1983.

4. Senator Eastland's offer to Kennedy on the subject of "getting the nigger" is from Jason Berry, *Amazing Grace* (New York: Saturday Review Press, 1973), p. 175.

5. Information about the number of black judges serving in the states is from *National Roster of Black Elected Officials*, Vol. 9 (Washington, D.C.: Joint Center for Political Studies, 1979), pp. 1-239.

6. Racial bias in the exercise of police discretion is reviewed in Thomas M. Uhlman, *Racial Justice* (Lexington: D.C. Heath and Co., 1979), pp. 3-4.

The quotation from the Amnesty International report on police brutality appeared in *New York Times,* Dec. 10, 1980, p. A7.

7. Information on the number of minority police officers is found in John Egerton, "Minority Policemen—How Many Are There?" *Race Relations Reporter* (Nov. 1974).

For statistics on the number of minority police in the New York Police Department and their rank in the force, as well as the impact on minorities of retirements at the highest ranks, see James I. Alexander, *Blue Coats Black Skin—The Black Experience in the New York City Police Department Since 1891* (Hicksville: Exposition Press, 1978), pp. 113-114.

8. Statistics on the number of sheriffs in the United States and the percentage of those who are black may be found in *National Roster of Black Elected Officials.*

9. Documentation of U.S. attorney appointments by Presidents Carter and Reagan is in "Equal Opportunity in Presidential Appointments."

10. On overt racism within the FBI under Hoover, see Sandford J. Ungar, *FBI: An Uncensored Look Behind the Walls* (Boston: Little, Brown and Co. 1975), pp. 406-411; also Arthur M. Schlesinger, Jr., *Robert Kennedy and His Times* (Boston: Houghton Mifflin Co., 1978), pp. 291-292.

11. Information on the number of blacks who are special agents or agents-in-charge of field offices of the FBI was obtained from the Office of Public Affairs, Federal Bureau of Investigation, Washington, D.C.

12. Statistics on the number of black attorneys and law school students in the United States are from the Public Affairs Office, American Bar Association; see also Walter J. Leonard, *Black Lawyers* (Boston: Senna and Shih, 1977), and U.S. Bureau of Labor Statistics, *Employment and Earnings,* Vol. 27, No. 1, Jan. 1980, Table 23, p. 174.

13. Data on black partners in the nation's fifty largest firms are from *National Law Journal,* July 1, 1979, p. 1.

14. The survey of the sixty-eight leading law firms in New York, Washington and Los Angeles is in *Legal Times,* Aug. 8, 1983, p. 37.

15. For details of the lawsuit against the Cravath firm, see Lucido v. Cravath, Swaine and Moore, N.Y. Dkt. No. 75-6341 (S.D.N.Y. 1975).

16. For information on the racial composition of federal prisoners, see C. Schweber-Koren, "Prison Education," and Richard W. Velde, "Blacks and Criminal Justice Today," in *Blacks and Criminal Justice,* Charles E. Owens and Jimmy Bell, eds. (Lexington: Lexington Books, 1977); see also *New York Times,* Nov. 9, 1980, p. 1.

17. Statistics on executions and occupants of death row were obtained from *Criminology and the Criminal Justice System: Old and New*, appearing in transcript of Workshop of the Afro-American Studies Program (Boston University, 1976); also the Law Enforcement Assistance Administration, *Sourcebook of Criminal Justice Statistics—1978* (June 1979).

18. The Southern Poverty Law Center study demonstrating that the race of the victim played a role in the severity of the sentence was reported in *New York Times,* Nov. 14, 1978.

19. Information on disparities in sentencing for income tax evasion based on race of the offender appears in Basil Patterson, "Blacks and the Judicial System," *From the Black Bar: Voices for Equal Justice,* Gilbert Ware, ed. (New York: Capricorn Books, 1976), p. 185.

Part Four

Chapter Eighteen. Majority Power as the Cause of Black Inequality

1. The insignificant representation of blacks in high management positions is discussed in Chapter Thirteen.

2. The token representation of blacks in construction trades is reported in William B. Gould, *Black Workers in White Unions* (Ithaca: Cornell University Press, 1977), p. 281.

3. The reasons for the successes of West Indian blacks in the United States are analyzed in three works by Thomas Sowell: *Race and Economics* (New York: David McKay Co., 1975), pp. 96-97, 132-133; "Myths About Minorities," *Commentary*, Aug. 1979, pp. 33-34; and "The Other Blacks: Leaders or 'Leaders'?" *New York Times*, April 12, 1979, p. A21.

4. For a revealing account of blacks as scholars, scientists, and kingdom builders both before and after the period of Rome, see John Henrik Clarke, "Africa in Early World History," *Ebony*, Aug. 1976, p. 125.

5. The quotation about the commercial achievements of early Africans is found in John Hope Franklin, *From Slavery to Freedom*, 6th ed. (New York: Alfred A. Knopf, 1947), p. 18.

6. The passage about the skills of West Africans brought to America in slave ships is found in Eugene D. Genovese, *Roll, Jordan Roll: The World* (New York: Pantheon Books, 1974), pp. 389, 404-405.

7. Information on occupational positions of blacks prior to the Civil War appears in Charles H. Wesley, *Compendium of the Census of 1850, Negro Labor in the United States, 1850-1925* (New York: Russell and Russell, 1967), p. 142.

A comprehensive account of the activities of blacks in the economy prior to the Civil War may be found in Herbert Hill, *Black Labor and the American Legal System* (Washington: Bureau of National Affairs, 1967), pp. 1-34; see also Franklin, *From Slavery to Freedom*.

On Irish-American and Italian-American incomes, see U.S. Department of Commerce, Bureau of the Census, *Current Population Reports*, Series P-20, No. 249, "Characteristics of the Population by Ethnic Origin: March 1972 and 1971," Table 9, p. 26; Series P-60, No. 85, "Money Income in 1971 of Families and Persons in the United States," Table 3, p. 24.

8. The percentage of blacks in the construction trades is taken from Gould, *Black Workers in White Unions*, p. 282.

9. The quotation dealing with the Negro family is from Daniel P. Moynihan, *The Negro Family: The Case for National Action* (Washington, D.C.: Office of Policy Planning and Research, U.S. Department of Labor, March 1965).

10. The evidence that nuclear families and stable marriages typified black families under slavery was first advanced in Herbert G. Gutman, *The Black Family in Slavery and Freedom, 1750-1925* (New York: Pantheon, 1976). The quotation is from H. Gutman, "The Black Family Reconsidered," *New York Times*, Pts. I and II, Sept. 22, 23, 1976, p. 41, each edition.

11. Data on black and white family income, poverty, and unemployment are found in *Current Population Reports*, Series P-60, No. 125, "Money Income and Poverty Status of Families and Persons in the United States: 1979" (Advance Report), Tables 1 and 16, pp. 7, 27; Series P-23, No. 80, "The Social and Economic Status of the Black Population in the United States: An Historical View, 1790-1978," Tables 143-144, pp. 198-99; *Employment and Earnings*, Vol. 27, No. 1, Jan. 1980, Table 10, p. 166.

12. The data on black and white husband-wife families may be found in *Current Population Reports*, Series P-60, No. 125, Table 1, p. 7.

13. The quotation regarding blacks, Puerto Ricans, and Mexicans is from Edward C. Banfield, *The Unheavenly City Revisited* (Boston: Little Brown and Co., 1974), p. 68.

14. A useful review of Professor Sowell's arguments appeared in William Raspberry's column in *Washington Post*, May 24, 1976; see also Stanley H. Masters, *Black-White*

Income Differentials: Empirical Studies and Policy Implications (Institute for Research on Poverty Monograph Series, New York: Academic Press, 1975), p. 50.

15. The incomes and the poverty status of the black population in the South are documented in *Current Population Reports*, Series P-60, No. 125, Tables 1, 20, pp. 7, 32.

16. The size of the black population in various large northern cities in 1930 is found in U.S. Bureau of the Census, *Negro Population in 1930: A Listing of the 695 Cities and Urban Places Having 1,000 or More Negro Inhabitants*, p. 2.

The menial occupational characteristics of blacks are found in U.S. Bureau of the Census, *Statistical Abstract of the United States—1978*, Table 680, p. 419.

17. For a discussion of the "recent immigrant" theory of black inequality, see Thomas Sowell, *Race and Economics* (New York: David McKay Co., 1975), p. 84.

The data on various ethnic groups are from *Current Population Reports*, Series P-20, No. 249, Table 9, p. 26; also Series P-60, No. 85, Table A, p. 1.

18. The regional comparisons of black income as a percentage of white income are from *Current Population Reports*, Series P-23, No. 38, "The Social and Economic Status of Negroes in the United States: 1970," Table 18, p. 27; Series P-60, No. 125, Table 1, p. 7.

19. The impact of northern migration on southern black men is explored in Masters, *Black-White Income Differentials*, p. 51; also Larry H. Long and Lynne R. Heltman, "Migration and Income Differences Between Black and White Men in the North," *American Journal of Sociology*, Vol. 80 (1975), p. 1391.

20. The fact that in 1977 black college graduates were earning less than white high school graduates is documented in *Current Population Reports*, Series P-60, No. 118, Table 47, p. 188; No. 123, "Money Income in 1978 of Families and Persons in the United States," Table 50, p. 216.

21. The disparity in poverty rates between highly educated blacks and whites is found in *Current Population Reports*, Series P-60, No. 124, "Characteristics of the Population Below the Poverty Level: 1978," Table 33, p. 145.

22. The fact that young blacks made no progress in closing the income gap on young whites in the 1970-1977 period is found in *Current Population Reports*, Series P-60, No. 80; Series P-60, No. 118.

23. Data indicating that blacks now stay in school and complete the same number of years as whites do are contained in *Current Population Reports*, Series P-20, No. 314, "Educational Attainment in the United States: March 1977 and 1976," Table 1, p. 7; and Series P-23, No. 38, Tables 20, 65, pp. 29, 79; and Series P-60, No. 118, Table 20, p. 71. Income data are from *Current Population Reports*, Series P-60, No. 118, Table 2, p. 14.

24. In 1978, the overall nonwhite unemployment rate was 11.9 percent. In 1948, 5.9 percent of the nonwhite labor force was unemployed. See U.S. Department of Labor, *Employment and Training Report of the President—1977*, Table A-18, p. 166; and U.S. Bureau of Labor Statistics, *Employment and Earnings*, Table 6, p. 163.

25. The quotation about Negroes turning into whites is from Edward Banfield, *The Unheavenly City* (Boston: Little Brown and Co., 1968), p. 73. The modified version appeared in Banfield, *The Unheavenly City Revisited*.

26. On the closings of racially integrated schools, see *Washington Post*, Dec. 30, 1981, p. C1.

27. The results of studies of lending discrimination by the Federal Home Loan Bank Board, the Federal Reserve Board, and the Controller of the Currency were reported in *New York Times*, Aug. 19, 1975.

The practice of racially segregating classes within desegregated schools is described in David L. Kirp, "Schools as Sorters: The Constitutional and Policy Implications of Student Classifications," *University of Pennsylvania Law Review,* Vol. 121 (1973), pp. 705-760.

28. The large percentage of blacks in various menial occupations is documented in U.S. Bureau of the Census, *1970 Census of Population, Special Studies,* PC(2)-7A, "Occupational Characteristics," Table 2, pp. 12-19.

29. Census figures show that blacks continued to be excluded from professional and managerial positions and remained employed in largely menial work. See U.S. Bureau of the Census, *A Social-Economic Grouping of the Gainful Workers in the United States,* 1938. For a detailed analysis of these data, see Masters, *Black-White Income Differentials.*

30. Data showing that black college graduates earned less than white high school graduates until 1978 are found in *Current Population Reports,* Series P-60, No. 118, Table 47, p. 184; No. 123, Table 50, p. 212.

31. Information on the experience of ethnic groups is found in *Current Population Reports,* Series P-60, No. 118, Table 10, p. 32; *1970 Census of the Population, Special Studies,* PC(2)-1G, "Japanese, Chinese and Filipinos in the United States," Table 9, p. 42; and Andrew Greeley, *The American Catholic* (New York: Basic Books, 1977), Tables 3, 3A, p. 57.

32. The conversation between the Howard and Radcliffe students is recounted in Susan Jacoby, "Blacks and Jews: End of the Affair," *The Nation,* Dec. 1, 1979, p. 553.

33. Data on the income of whites, blacks, Chinese-Americans, and Japanese-Americans are found in *Current Population Reports,* Series P-60, No. 118, Table 10, p. 32; and *1970 Census,* PC(2)-1G, Table 9, p. 42.

34. Milton Friedman's statement is from a Public Television Broadcast entitled *Free to Choose,* Jan. 1980.

35. In 1969, blacks who graduated from college had mean incomes that were 16 percent higher than those who had only one to three years of college. White college graduates had incomes 26 percent over whites who had only some college. By 1977, whites who finished college had incomes 40 percent higher than those who had one to three years, while black college graduates improved their incomes by only 25 percent over those students that had not graduated.

The statistics are found in *Current Population Reports,* Series P-23, No. 38, Table 25, p. 34; and Series P-60, No. 118, Table 47, p. 184.

Chapter Nineteen. The Scars of Memory: Racial Inequality in a Discrimination-Free Society

1. Information on the effect of black population concentrations in large cities on white high school enrollments between 1967 and 1977 is found in *New York Times,* Nov. 21, 1977; for a discussion, see Diane Ravitch, "Wasted Decade," *New Republic,* Nov. 5, 1977, p. 13.

2. Information on white control of 99 percent of all elected offices is contained in *National Roster of Black Elected Officials* (Washington, D.C.: Joint Center for Political Studies, 1979).

3. A description of the layoffs in the New York City government that decimated the black work force is found in *New York Times,* Jan. 29, 1975, p. 17.

On the possible elimination of all black pilots, co-pilots, or flight engineers by Trans World Airlines, see *New York Times,* Feb. 20, 1976, p. 1.

An account of how seniority rules are capable of undoing years of job equality gains in state employment appears in *Washington Post,* March 9, 1982, p. A7.

4. The development of the mechanical tobacco defoliator is described in *New York Times,* Oct. 4, 1971, p. 46; on the mechanical tomato harvester, see *Business Week,* Jan. 30, 1978, p. 69.

5. Government grants to universities for agricultural development aimed at the replacement of farm labor are described in *New York Times,* Feb. 11, 1980, p. A14; on the development of harvesting machines by the state university of California, see *The Nation,* Feb. 16, 1980, p. 170.

6. The position that advancing technology may be beneficial to black unskilled workers is developed in Edward C. Banfield, *The Unheavenly City Revisited* (Boston: Little Brown and Co., 1974), p. 103.

7. The quotation beginning "the balance of power . . ." is from a letter written by John Adams to James Sullivan, May 26, 1776.

The Homestead Act was in force until 1974. Although no reliable statistics are available, it is unlikely that many blacks took part in the program.

8. The position that discrimination against blacks would be greater if blacks were better educated is made in Gary S. Becker, *The Economics of Discrimination,* 1st ed. (Chicago: The University of Chicago Press, 1971). Becker states: "[E]vidence clearly shows that discrimination is greater against older and better-educated nonwhites. (This does not imply that older and better-educated whites discriminate more than those who are younger and less educated. . . .)" *Ibid.,* p. 124.

9. The information about black schooling and the failure of educational gains to produce monetary rewards is found in U.S. Department of Commerce, Bureau of the Census, *Current Population Reports,* Series P-23, No. 38, "The Social and Economic Status of Negroes in the United States, 1970," Tables 20 and 65, pp. 29, 79; Series P-20, No. 314, "Educational Attainment in the United States: March 1977 and 1976," Table 1, p. 7; and Series P-60, No. 123, "Money Income in 1978 of Families and Persons in the United States," Table 20, p. 89.

10. Data that confirm the failure of improved education among young blacks to reduce relative unemployment rates are contained in U.S. Bureau of the Census, *United States Census of the Population, 1950,* Vol. 4, Special Reports, Part 5, Chapter B, "Education," Table 5, p. 42; and *Current Population Reports,* Series P-20, No. 314, Table 1, p. 7; and U.S. Department of Labor, *Employment and Training Report of the President—1978,* Table A-20.

The poverty statistics cited in connection with the effects of education are documented in *Current Population Reports,* Series P-60, No. 125, "Money Income and Poverty Status of Families and Persons in the United States: 1979" (Advance Report), Table 21, p. 34.

11. Data on unemployment rates of black and white high school graduates are from U.S. Bureau of Labor Statistics, *Special Labor Force Reports,* No. 240, "Educational Attainment of Workers, 1979," Table M, p. A-23.

12. Data on the employment performance by college-educated black men are from *Special Labor Force Reports,* No. 225, "Educational Attainment of Workers—Some Trends From 1973 to 1978," Table M, p. A-19.

13. In 1979, 56 percent of all blacks lived inside central cities, nearly half in high poverty areas, according to *Current Population Reports,* Series P-60, No. 125, Table 20, p. 33.

14. Data on the number of Supreme Court Justices who attended Princeton, Harvard, or Yale were obtained from the Clerk of the Supreme Court. See also "The Supreme Court's Princeton Seat," *Princeton Alumni Weekly,* Sept. 26, 1977.

15. Documentation of the fact that children from poor families score significantly lower on standardized tests than do children from middle- and upper-income households is reported in *College Bound Census, 1973-1974,* College Entrance Examination Board, Princeton, N.J., 1974.

16. The results of the Pentagon competency test are described in Office of the Assistant Secretary of Defense for Manpower, Reserve Affairs and Logistics, *Profile of American Youth: 1980 Nationwide Administration of the Armed Services Vocational Aptitude Battery* (Washington, D.C., 1982), Table C-1, page 77.

The number of black students scoring 700 or higher on the SAT in 1983 was reported in *New York Times,* June 10, 1984.

17. The use of examinations by nineteen states in 1979 for high school graduation, and test results in Tampa, Florida, are discussed in *Newsweek,* May 28, 1979, pp. 97-98.

18. The effects of competency tests on prospective black teachers are described in *Washington Post,* April 26, 1983, p. A2.

19. The quotation from the study on freshmen entering college in 1975 is reported in Robert L. Jacobson, "Standardized Testing and Cultural Bias," *The Chronicle of Higher Education,* July 25, 1977, pp. 3-4.

20. The lower scores of blacks on the Scholastic Aptitude Test are reported by the College Entrance Examination Board in *Report of the Advisory Panel on Scholastic Aptitude Test Decline* (New York, 1977), p. 15. The statement on black scores made by the president of the University of North Carolina is reported in *New York Times,* Dec. 13, 1977, p. 15.

In 1977, the Educational Testing Service in Princeton, New Jersey, made an analysis of minority enrollment in law schools and found that minority admissions would drop 60 to 80 percent if race or ethnic identity were ignored in admissions policy. See Robert Shrum, "Racist Tests: The Hidden Issue of Bakke," *New Times,* Feb. 6, 1978, p. 9.

21. The results of IQ tests in five southeastern states are reported in Arthur Jensen, *Bias in Mental Testing* (New York: The Free Press, 1980), pp. 98-100.

22. The National Science Foundation study on how blacks are being left behind in access to computers is described in *Washington Post,* Sept. 12, 1983, p. A1.

23. The fact that black male college graduates under 35 make up less than one percent of the black population is from *Current Population Reports,* Series P-20, No. 314, Table 1, p. 7; and Series P-60, No. 116, Table 19, p. 25.

24. The results of studies on the occupational progress of blacks relative to whites are reported in Becker, *The Economics of Discrimination,* Ch. 9; and in Dale L. Heistand, *Economic Growth and Employment Opportunities for Minorities* (New York: Columbia University Press, 1964), pp. 51 et seq.

25. The quotation of Walter Williams is from *Time,* Jan. 21, 1980, p. 66.

26. Unemployment figures for teenage workers in 1954 and 1980 were obtained from *Employment and Training Report of the President—1977,* Table A-5, p. 146, and the U.S. Bureau of Labor Statistics, *Employment and Earnings,* Jan. 1981, Tables 5 and 6, pp. 168-169.

27. On the dramatic increase in the 1970s of black men in managerial positions, see U.S. Bureau of the Census, *1960 and 1970 Census of the Population, Special Studies,* PC(2)-7A, "Occupational Characteristics," and U.S. Bureau of Labor Statistics, *Employment and Earnings,* Jan. 1980.

28. The Labor Department study on affirmative action is summarized in *Washington Post,* June 20, 1983, p. A3.

Chapter Twenty. Reverse Discrimination: The Case for Countervailing Power

1. The statement urging protection of the liberty to be racially prejudiced is from Milton Friedman, *Capitalism and Freedom* (Chicago: University of Chicago Press, 1962), p. 111 (emphasis added).

2. The information about blacks working in the mining, manufacturing, and transportation industries in the nineteenth century and as craftsmen is from Herbert Hill, *Black Labor and the American Legal System, Vol. I—Race, Work, and the Law* (Washington, D.C.: The Bureau of National Affairs, Inc., 1977), pp. 6ff.

3. The dollar gap of $67 billion may be computed as follows: In 1979, blacks had money income of $113.9 billion; whites had $1,459.3 billion. Blacks, making up approximately 11.5 percent of the population, had only 7.2 percent of the total national money income of $1,573.2 billion. Had blacks earned a percentage of the national income equal to their percentage of the population, they would have had money income of $180.9 billion instead of the $113.9 billion they actually had.

Thus, the total dollar gap in 1979 is the difference between what they would have had, $180.9 billion, and what they actually had, $113.9 billion, or $67 billion. The source of figures for this computation is U.S. Bureau of the Census, *Current Population Reports,* Series P-60, No. 125, "Money Income and Poverty Status of Families and Persons in the United States: 1979" (Advance Report), Table 10, p. 21.

4. The quotation about "Mozart murdered" is from Antoine de Saint-Exupery, *Wind, Sand and Stars,* trans. Lewis Galantiere, in *Airman's Odyssey* (New York: Reynal and Hitchcock, 1942), pp. 204-206.

5. The language excluding the black race from "civilized government and the family of nations" appeared in the opinion of Supreme Court Chief Justice Taney in the case of Scott v. Sanford, 19 Howard 393 (1857).

Part Five

Chapter Twenty-One. The Politics of Empowerment and the Bases of Black Strength

1. The five black members of Congress who have been elected in four of the forty-two southern districts in which blacks made up 20 percent or more of the eligible voters are Andrew Young from Georgia's Fifth Congressional District (C.D.), 1972 to 1976; Barbara Jordan, Texas's Eighteenth C.D., 1972 to 1978; Parren Mitchell, Maryland's Seventh C.D., 1970- ; Harold Ford, Tennessee's Eighth C.D., 1974- ; and Mickey Leland, Texas's Eighteenth C.D., 1978—.

2. The following table, prepared from data furnished by the Joint Center for Political Studies, illustrates the effect of the black vote on Carter's 1976 presidential campaign in the South.

1976 Election Results in Selected Southern States

State	Carter Victory Margin	Estimated Black Vote for Carter	Percent Black Vote for Carter
Florida	186,087	261,797	94.9
Louisiana	77,308	264,615	93.6
Maryland	86,638	149,794	91.5

1976 Election Results in Selected Southern States
(Continued)

State	Carter Victory Margin	Estimated Black Vote for Carter	Percent Black Vote for Carter
Mississippi	11,537	122,819	87.4
South Carolina	101,492	166,907	90.4
Texas	155,246	259,202	96.8

SOURCE: *The Black Vote—Election 1976* (Washington, D.C.: Joint Center for Political Studies, 1977), Table II, p. 10.

3. The information on the 1966 and 1968 elections is from Mark R. Levy and Michael S. Kramer, *The Ethnic Factor* (New York: Simon and Schuster, 1972), pp. 53-56; for the 1976 figures on black voters influencing the 1976 elections see *The Black Vote—Election 1976* (Washington, D.C.: Joint Center for Political Studies, 1977).

4. Taking the black vote for Carter and comparing it with his margin of victory in each state, we may compute that in thirteen states Carter lost the white vote but, nevertheless, carried the state. In Florida, Carter won 94.9 percent of 261,797 black votes. He won the state by only 186,087 votes; clearly, the black vote put Carter over the top in Florida. The source for these data is *The Black Vote—Election 1976,* Table II, p. 10.

5. The support Truman received in 1948 from black voters, which enabled him to defeat Dewey, is discussed in Levy and Kramer, *The Ethnic Factor,* pp. 41-42.

6. Black support for John F. Kennedy in 1960 in Illinois, Texas, Michigan, New Jersey, Missouri, and North Carolina is discussed in Levy and Kramer, *The Ethnic Factor,* pp. 44-45. In fact, Kennedy won the electoral vote 303 to 219 with fifteen southern electors bolting the Democratic party and casting their ballots for Harry Byrd of Virginia. Had the twenty-seven electoral votes of Illinois and the thirteen electoral votes of Missouri switched to Nixon, the final Electoral College tally would have read: Kennedy—263, Nixon—259, Byrd—15.

No candidate would have amassed the 269 electoral votes required to win in 1960, and the Constitution mandates that the choice would have been made in the House of Representatives.

7. Data on the percentages of eligible whites and blacks casting votes in the 1976 election are from U.S. Department of Commerce, Bureau of the Census, *Current Population Reports,* Series P-20, No. 322, "Voting and Registration in the Election of November 1976," Table 2, p. 14; the estimates of black turnouts in primaries are from *Guide to Black Politics—1976* (Washington, D.C.: Joint Center for Political Studies, 1976), p. 79.

8. Data on black and Jewish turnouts in the 1976 senatorial primary in New York State are from *New York Times,* Sept. 14, 1976. There were 1,622,000 eligible black voters in the state, and approximately 100,000 voted, for a participation rate of 6.2 percent.

9. The 1976 campaign memorandum to Morris Udall on the influence of Jewish voters was reported in *Washington Post,* March 13, 1976, p. 19.

10. The low rates of voting by blacks are contained in *Current Population Reports,* Series P-20, No. 332, "Voting and Registration in the Election of November 1978" (Advance Report), Table 1, p. 5.

11. The fact that the black voting rate, had it approximated the rates of other groups, could have given Carter a landslide victory in the Electoral College is found in data from *The Black Vote—Election 1976,* Table II, p. 10. For example, in California, Ford received 3,882,244 votes to Carter's 3,742,284 votes. Blacks cast 441,579 votes in California, 92.2

percent for Carter, 5.8 percent for Ford, and 2 percent for other candidates. Only 41 percent of the eligible blacks went to the polls. If 75 percent of the eligible blacks had voted, the black vote would have increased by 367,671. If these additional blacks had voted in the same percentage as those who did cast ballots, it would have added 338,993 votes to Carter's column and 21,325 votes to Ford's. The revised result for the state of California would then be 4,081,277 or 50.1 percent for Carter to Ford's 3,903,569, or 47.9 percent, with 2 percent of the vote going to other candidates. Thus, the forty-five electoral votes of the state of California would have gone to Carter.

Similar calculations producing the same results can be made for the other states mentioned.

12. Information on the number of Jews in the House and Senate comes from *Congressional Quarterly Weekly Reports*, Jan. 13, 1979, pp. 43-52.

13. The calculation that the number of eligible blacks who did not vote in 1976 was greater than the winning margin achieved by either candidate in twenty-five states is made by taking the total black voting age population of a state and subtracting the estimated turnout of black voters. The remainder is the number of eligible blacks not voting. One can then compare this figure with the victory margin of the candidate who carried the state. See figures from *Guide to Black Politics—1976*, p. 78.

14. The 1980 poll results showing that at least 31 percent of the black voters would support a black political party and vote its ticket are found in *Black Enterprise*, Aug. 1980, p. 53.

15. The excerpt from Gerald Carlson's "White-Power Hotline" was reported in *Washington Post*, Aug. 18, 1980, p. 1.

16. Remarkably, Carlson received more than 50,000 votes, or 32 percent of the total vote cast. In California's Forty-third C.D., another racist, Thomas Metzger, a Ku Klux Klan sympathizer, received over 45,000 votes as the Democratic party candidate in 1980.

Chapter Twenty-Two. Nonviolent Direct Action: The Backbone of the Black Bargaining Position

1. The figures on black income, poverty, and unemployment in 1959 and 1979 are from U.S. Department of Commerce, Bureau of the Census, *Current Population Reports*, Series P-60, No. 123, "Money Income in 1978 of Families and Persons in the United States," No. 124, "Characteristics of the Population Below the Poverty Level: 1978," No. 125, "Money Income and Poverty Status of Families and Persons in the United States: 1979" (Advance Report); Series P-23, No. 54, "The Social and Economic Status of the Black Population in the United States: 1974"; *Employment and Training Report of the President—1978;* and U.S. Bureau of Labor Statistics, *Employment and Earnings*, Vol. 27, No. 1, Jan. 1980.

2. The following tabulations show comparative rankings of blacks and whites according to three yardsticks: family incomes; unemployment rates of the civilian labor force; and percentage of the population in poverty. The income ratio is devised by comparing black family income as a percentage of white. The ratios for unemployment and poverty, being negative factors, are compared by taking the white rates as a percentage of the black rates. The mean of these three factors becomes the composite equality ratio. Income figures are for blacks only from 1964 to 1979. Poverty figures are for blacks only from 1966 to 1979. All other figures are for "blacks and other races," of which blacks make up about 90 percent of the total.

Year	Family Income	Unemployment	Poverty	Composite Equality Ratios Weighted Equally	Income 2x
1979	56.75	45.13	28.80	43.56	46.86
1978	59.23	43.70	28.43	43.79	47.65
1977	57.13	47.32	28.43	44.29	47.50
1976	59.58	53.43	29.26	47.39	50.41
1975	61.53	56.11	30.99	49.54	52.54
1974	58.46	50.50	28.34	45.77	48.94
1973	57.71	48.31	26.75	44.26	47.62
1972	59.43	50.00	27.02	45.48	48.97
1971	60.34	54.54	30.46	48.44	51.42
1970	61.34	54.87	29.55	48.59	51.78

3. State university systems that still maintain separate campuses based on race include, most notably, the Universities of North Carolina, Texas, Alabama, South Carolina, Delaware, West Virginia, Ohio, Missouri, and Kentucky. See *Washington Post,* Aug. 10, 1979, p. A6.

4. Descriptions of the Reagan counterrevolution in the policies of government toward the integration of public schools appear in *The Economist,* Sept. 5, 1981, p. 21, and *New York Times,* Aug. 29, 1981, p. 1.

5. Robert S. Browne, a leading black economist, appears to be the first advocate of black tithing in favor of black self-help organizations. Address, April 5, 1975, The Seventh Annual Conference in African Heritage Studies.

6. Statistics on the total money income earned by blacks are from *Current Population Reports,* Series P-60, No. 125, Table 10, p. 21.

The operating budget of the NAACP was obtained through the Public Information Department, National Association for the Advancement of Colored People, New York, N.Y.

7. The percentage of the work force employed in the manufacturing industry during the twentieth century is documented in *The Statistical History of the United States* (New York: Basic Books, 1976), p. 137.

8. An excellent account of the growth of the information industry may be found in *The Economist,* Dec. 27, 1980, p. 20.

9. The Coca-Cola boycott story appears in William Raspberry, *Washington Post,* Aug. 31, 1981, p. A15.

10. A study of black consumer brand preferences was conducted in 1980 by the Wellington Group of Haddon Heights, New Jersey. The results were reported in *Advertising Age,* May 18, 1981.

11. The historic boycott decision decided by the Supreme Court was NAACP v. Claiborne Hardware, 458 U.S. 886 (1982).

12. Lane Kirkland's statement that pension fund investments would become an issue in collective bargaining negotiations appeared in *Fortune,* Dec. 31, 1979, p. 64.

13. The assets of the forty largest state and local government pension plans are reported in *Pensions and Investments Age,* Jan. 24, 1983, p. 1. The statistics on the black percentage of the state work force in New York and California were obtained from the New York State Civil Service Commission, Career Opportunities Department, Albany, N.Y., and the State of California, Department of Personnel, Management Information, Sacramento, California.

The policies of pension funds holding shares in companies violating EEO guidelines or doing business with South Africa are discussed in *Pension Investments: A Social Audit* (New York: Corporate Data Exchange, 1979).

According to the CDE study, equal employment opportunity violators included Bank of America, Blue Bell, Coor's, Merrill Lynch, Safeway, and Uniroyal.

14. In 1978, of all the 11,963,000 nonwhites in the civilian labor force, 5,614,000 or 47 percent, lived in the states which the Census Bureau includes in its definition of the South. SOURCE: U.S. Bureau of Labor Statistics, *Employment and Earnings,* Vol. 26, No. 1, Table 4; and *Geographic Profile of Employment and Unemployment: States, 1978—Metropolitan Areas, 1977-1978,* Table 1.

15. In 1978, the mean income of the 7,818,000 southern blacks over 14 years of age who had some income was $5,811. Thus, the total money income of southern blacks was $45.5 billion. If black incomes increased 20 percent as a result of unionization, total black income would rise to $55.5 billion.

This calculation was made from figures documented in *Current Population Reports,* Series P-60, No. 123, Table 45, p. 189.

16. For an account of how unionized workers are better equipped to keep pace with inflation, see Richard B. Freeman and James L. Medoff, "The Two Faces of Unionism," *The Public Interest* (Fall 1979).

17. The median family income of domestics and the poverty level figures are for heads of households. See *Current Population Reports,* Series P-60, No. 123, Table 39, p. 160.

18. The official government figures on the number of black domestic workers in the United States are from *Employment and Earnings,* Vol. 28, No. 1, Jan. 1981, Table 23, p. 180.

19. The computations on the increase in overall black income in the United States resulting from increased pay for domestic work were calculated as follows: at a wage of $5.82 an hour (the rate earned by hotel maids) and $11.25 an hour (triple the present rate of $3.75 an hour). At $11.25 an hour, increased wages would add an additional $5 billion of income for blacks annually.

20. In 1970, the utilities industry had the lowest percentage of black employees of any industry with over 500,000 employees. Remarkably, a third of all utility companies that filed reports with the EEOC in 1970 had no black employees at all. See William B. Gould, *Black Workers in White Unions* (Ithaca: Cornell University Press, 1977), p. 410.

21. Federal revenue-sharing statistics are from the public affairs department of the U.S. Department of the Treasury, Office of Revenue Sharing.

22. The data showing that more than one-quarter of all corporations with 100 or more employees had no black workers on their payrolls are from Andrew F. Brimmer, "Prospects for Black Employment," United States Federal Reserve Board (May 5, 1974).

The racial practices of major corporations are not easily rated on a scale of backwardness. Much of this confusion is due to the inability to obtain reliable information and deceptive public relations. Based on personal research, EEOC complaints, and general reputation, my own list of corporations with insensitive racial policies or poor records in minority participation include: American Brands Inc.; American Home Products Inc.; Blue Bell Inc.; Coor's Breweries Inc.; Dart and Kraft Inc.; Dresser Industries Inc.; Fluor Inc.; Great Atlantic and Pacific Tea Co.; K-mart Inc.; Kimberly-Clark Corp; Mars Inc.; Merrill Lynch, Pierce, Fenner & Smith, Inc.; Mobil Oil Corp.; Nabisco Brands Inc.; Richardson-Vicks, Inc.; Standard Oil of California Inc.; Texaco Inc.; Uniroyal Inc.; and Winn-Dixie Stores Inc.

23. The story of Congressman Hyde's conversion on minority voting rights is told in Henry J. Hyde, "Why I Changed My Mind on the Voting Rights Act," *Washington Post,* July 26, 1981, p. D7.

Chapter Twenty-Three.
The Political Empowerment of Black America

1. The article reporting the decision by black leaders not to hold a national political convention in 1980 appeared in *New York Times,* Jan. 26, 1980, p. 38.

2. House Speaker O'Neill's quotation about Democrats consisting of five parties appeared in *Time,* Nov. 20, 1978, p. 42.

3. The article on the collapse of political parties as a force in American politics appeared in *Time,* Nov. 20, 1978, p. 42.

4. On the black vote as a "given" for Democratic candidates, see Patrick J. Buchanan, *New York Times,* April 5, 1977, p. 33.

5. An assertion that illegal aliens were responsible for the unemployment crisis among young blacks appeared in Jacquelyne J. Jackson, "Illegal Aliens: Big Threat to Black Workers," *Ebony,* April 1979.

For information on friction between blacks and Hispanics in Miami, see *Time,* Oct. 16, 1978, p. 52.

6. On black voter turnout rates in the 1978 midterm elections, see U.S. Department of Commerce, Bureau of the Census, *Current Population Reports,* Series P-20, No. 332, "Voting and Registration in the Election of November 1978" (Advance Report), Table 1, p. 4.

7. On selected black voter turnouts in New York, Houston, and Mississippi, see *Election '78: Implications for Black America* (Washington, D.C.: Joint Center for Political Studies, 1979), Table 3, p. 7; *The Black Vote—Election '76* (Washington: D.C.: Joint Center for Political Studies, 1977), Tables 2 and IV, pp. 10, 12.

The low voter turnout of blacks, ages 18 to 20, is documented in *Current Population Reports,* Series P-20, No. 332, Table 1, p. 4.

8. The seven states that would have switched from Ford to Carter in the 1976 presidential election had blacks raised their turnout rate to 75 percent of the eligible electorate were: California, Illinois, Michigan, New Jersey, Oklahoma, Oregon, and Virginia. For information on how the revised vote was calculated, see Chapter Twenty-one, note 11.

On the relationship of unregistered black voters to President Reagan's 1980 victory margin, see Paul Delaney, "Voting: The New Black Power," *New York Times Magazine,* Nov. 27, 1983, pp. 34, 38.

9. The twenty states considering bills to deputize school officials as voting registrars were: Arkansas, California, Connecticut, Delaware, Illinois, Indiana, Kansas, Kentucky, Louisiana, New Jersey, New Mexico, New York, North Carolina, Ohio, Pennsylvania, South Carolina, Tennessee, Texas, Virginia, and Wisconsin.

10. The seventeen states permitting public referendums were: Arkansas, Arizona, California, Colorado, Florida, Illinois, Massachusetts, Michigan, Missouri, Montana, Nebraska, Nevada, North Dakota, Ohio, Oklahoma, Oregon, and South Dakota.

11. Strom Thurmond's threat that the South would not capitulate to the integration demands of the federal government appeared in the March 17, 1978, syndicated column of Rowland Evans and Robert Novak entitled, "South Carolina's New Strom Thurmond."

12. An account of Thad Cochran's effort to woo black voters during the 1978 senatorial campaign in Mississippi appeared in *New York Times,* Nov. 13, 1978.

13. Former Senator William Scott's insulting remark about blacks who work for the postal service appears in Neal R. Pierce, *The Border South States* (New York: W.W. Norton Co., 1975), p. 82.

14. Whitten's analysis of the needs of welfare families is documented by Anne Millet in *Ralph Nader's Congress Project: A Citizen's Look at Congress—Jamie L. Whitten* (Washington, D.C.: Grossman Publishers, 1972).

15. Copies of the 1979 and the 1978 surveys of key votes mentioned throughout this section may be obtained from The National Newspaper Publishers Association, 770 National Press Building, Washington, D.C. 20045. The 1973 survey, also mentioned frequently throughout the text, appeared in *FOCUS* (Washington, D.C.: Joint Center for Political Studies, April 1973).

16. Representative Dickinson's charge of sex orgies on the part of civil rights marchers in Selma, Alabama, appears in the *Congressional Record*, 89th Cong., Vol. 3, Pt. 5, pp. 633f, and Pt. 6, pp. 8592-8600.

17. The Newsome quote is from a talk at the Charles H. Houston Forum, Amherst College, Amherst, Massachusetts, Spring 1981.

18. For an account of the furor over Bell's nomination to be chairman of the EEOC, see *Washington Post*, Nov. 13, 1981.

19. Statistics on the percentage of black judges and police officers in 1979 in the United States are from U.S. Bureau of Labor Statistics, *Employment and Earnings*, Vol. 27, No. 1, Jan. 1980, Table 23, p. 174.

20. Information on the ten black sheriffs in the South is from *National Roster of Black Elected Officials*, Vol. 9 (Washington, D.C.: Joint Center for Political Studies, 1979).

21. The comment of the power of Chicago Mayor Harold Washington's political machine appears in *Washington Post*, July 28, 1983, p. A8.

22. The statement by John Dean, campaign manager for Mayor Cooper of Pritchard, Alabama, about maintaining a low profile in the white community is from John Dean, *The Making of a Black Mayor* (Washington, D.C.: Joint Center for Political Studies, 1973), p. 10.

23. Richard Arrington's campaign strategies in the Birmingham, Alabama mayoralty campaign are described in *New York Times*, Oct. 31, 1979, p. A16.

24. The story of Ernest Morial's campaign victory in New Orleans is told in *New York Times*, Nov. 14, 1977, p. 40.

25. The effects of at-large elections in cities with populations greater than 50,000 are documented in Barbara L. Berry and Thomas R. Dye, "The Discriminatory Effects of At-Large Elections," *Florida State University Law Review* (Winter 1979), pp. 85-122.

26. The statistic that 69 percent of all cities with populations greater than 5,000 used at-large systems is from Berry and Dye, "The Discriminatory Effects of At-Large Elections," p. 87.

27. The test of discriminatory intent by the state legislature in drawing district lines was announced by the Supreme Court in Whitcomb v. Chavis, 403 U.S. 124 (1971).

Evidence of prior state discrimination supporting the finding of intent to discriminate in drawing district lines was permitted as evidence in White v. Regester, 412 U.S. 755 (1973).

The U.S. Supreme Court returned to the strict evidentiary standard of racial intent in Mobile v. Bolden, 446 U.S. 55 (1980).

Chapter Twenty-Four. The Legislation of Black Power

1. Information on percentages of whites and blacks registered to vote in 1978 is found in U.S. Department of Commerce, Bureau of Census, *Current Population Reports*, Series

P-20, No. 332, "Voting and Registration in the Election of November 1978" (Advance Report), Table B, p. 3.

2. Details on the tendency of blacks to vote as a bloc for a single candidate in congressional and other elections appears in *The Black Vote—Election '76* (Washington, D.C.: Joint Center for Political Studies, 1977), Table IV, p. 12.

3. Population data on the concentration of the black population in large central cities appear in *Current Population Reports*, Series P-60, No. 125, "Money Income and Poverty Status of Families and Persons in the United States: 1979" (Advance Report), Table 20, p. 33.

4. On statewide voter turnout rates, see *Current Population Reports*, Series P-20, No. 332, Table 2, p. 6.

5. The calculations on how mandatory 18-year-old voting would have shifted three states to Carter in 1976 are based on voting figures appearing in *The Black Vote—Election '76*, Tables 1 & 2, p. 10; *Guide to Black Politics—1976* (Washington, D.C.: Joint Center for Political Studies, 1976), pp. 78-79; and *The Almanac of American Politics: 1980* (New York: E.P. Dutton Co., Inc.), 1979.

6. Voter turnouts in general elections held in foreign countries through 1978 were as follows:

	Percent of Eligible Voters Who Voted
Malta	94.4
Australia	92.6
Austria	91.9
Sweden	91.4
Italy	90.8
Iceland	90.3
West Germany	89.9
Belgium	88.3
Denmark	88.2
Holland	87.5
France	83.5
Norway	83.8
New Zealand	82.7
Israel	78.2
Ireland	75.7
Canada	74.9
Britain	72.8
Japan	72.6
India	60.5
United States (1976)	54.4
Switzerland	51.7
United States (1978)	37.0

SOURCE: *The Economist*, Nov. 11, 1978.

7. The racial composition of Job Corps enrollees in 1967 is from U.S. Department of Labor, Employment and Training Administration, Job Corps National Office, *Job Corps in Brief*, 1967.

8. The fact that 42 percent of 17-year-old blacks were functionally illiterate was reported in *The National Assessment of Educational Progress, 1974-1975* (Denver, Colorado: Education Commission of the States, 1976).

9. In 1979, poor black families headed by a woman with at least one child constituted 18.1 percent of all black families in the United States. Poor white families headed by a woman with at least one child made up only 2.0 percent of all white families. For people 65 years and over, 35.5 percent of blacks were poor compared to 13.2 percent of similar whites. *Current Population Reports,* Series P-60, No. 125, Tables 20 & 21, pp. 33-35.

10. The calculation of the annual cost to the taxpayers of an income tax maintenance program that brought those in poverty up to the poverty threshold is made as follows:

Number of poor families	5,292,000
Mean income deficit	× $2,697
Total deficit	$14,272,524,000
Number of poor black families	1,666,000
Mean income deficit	× $2,854
Total black deficit	$ 4,754,764,000

In addition to families, there were 5.6 million poor people not living with any relative. To bring these people up to the poverty threshold would cost another $8.3 billion.

Number of poor unrelated individuals	5,575,000
Mean income deficit	× $1,488
Total deficit	$ 8,295,600,000
Number of poor black unrelated individuals	1,155,000
Mean income deficit	× $1,617
Total black deficit	$ 1,849,848,000

Adding together the figures for families and unrelated individuals, it would cost approximately $22.6 billion for an income plan that would pull everyone up to the poverty threshold. Of this, $6.6 billion would go to blacks. *Current Population Reports,* Series P-60, No. 125, Table 23, p. 37.

11. In 1979, black families had total money income of $88.2 billion, or 6.7 percent of the national total of $1.307 trillion. As shown in the previous calculation, bringing all poor black families up to the poverty threshold would add $4.8 billion to the total black income figure. Under such a plan, which would add $14.3 billion to the total national family income, total black income would be $93 billion, or 7 percent of the national total of $1.321 trillion. *Current Population Reports,* Series P-60, No. 125, Tables 6 & 23, pp. 15, 37.

12. The assessment of the enforcement abilities of the EEOC by its former chairman Stephen Shulman appears in "Official Bias: A Note on the Equal Employment Opportunity Commission," *Barron's,* July 17, 1967, p. 1.

13. Employee protection sections in laws passed by Congress include the following: Occupational Safety and Health Act of 1979 (Pub. L. No. 91-596, § 11c), the Federal Water Pollution Control Act Amendments of 1972 (Pub. L. No. 92-500, § 507), the Safe Drinking Water Act of 1974 (Pub. L. No. 93-523, § 1450), the Toxic Substances Control Act of 1976 (Pub. L. No. 94-469), § 23), the Resource Conservation and Recovery Act of 1976 (Pub. L. No. 94-580, § 7001), the Clean Air Act Amendments of 1977 (Pub. L. No. 95-99, § 312), the Federal Mine Safety and Health Act of 1977 (Pub. L. No. 95-164, § 105(c)), and the Nuclear Regulatory Commission Authorization Act of 1978 (Pub. L. No. 95-601, § 10).

14. Information on political contributions to congressional candidates in 1978 is found in *Congressional Quarterly Weekly Report,* Oct. 20, 1979, p. 2338.

15. For a good discussion of the scope and influence of corporate fund-raising, see Thomas B. Edsall, "Why the Republicans Can't Lose," *Washington Post,* Jan. 17, 1982, p. D1.

16. Information on the election success of candidates spending the most money appears in *New York Times,* Jan. 18, 1979, p. A19.

17. An account of Secretary Pierce's first six months in office, including the fact that the President did not recognize the Secretary at a White House reception, appeared in *New York Times,* July 16, 1981, p. A20.

18. In 1979, according to the Census Bureau there were 10.5 million minority persons in poverty. Dividing this figure by $2.5 billion yields $238 for every poor minority person in the nation. The poverty statistics appear in *Current Population Reports,* Series P-60, No. 125, Table 20, p. 33.

19. Examples of some of the activities the Opportunity Funding Corporation has assisted are:

- Providing $500,000 in venture capital support to the Southern Agricultural Corporation. This project was initiated by a consortium of southern economic development groups, the Rockefeller Brothers Fund, and OFC to finance the acquisition and operation of substantial commercial farming ventures by minorities in the Southeast.
- Offering of $500,000 in loan guarantees to provide long-term financing of an investment company to assist in financing the acquisition and expansion of a broadcast foundation (SYNCOM), as well as industry sources (CBS and Capital Cities Communications).
- Partial guaranty of a loan by the Bank of America which enabled some seventy Mexican-American migrant families to acquire a large strawberry farming operation near Salinas, California.
- Eighty percent guaranty of $500,000 in capital notes provides by Boston's major banks to inject capital into New England's only black bank when it was threatened with failure.
- Partial guaranty of a bank line of credit to support an intertribal fish marketing operation developed by the Lummi Indian tribe in Marietta, Washington.
- A $100,000 guaranty, enabling a vitally needed nursing home in the black community of Denver to obtain a long-term real estate equipment loan of $600,000 from a private lender, thus rescuing the nursing home from bankruptcy and preserving its $250,000 annual payroll.
- Providing $500,000 of equity and loan capital to facilitate the participation of Washington, D.C.'s minority community as owners of 70 percent of the company which will develop Fort Lincoln, Washington's $250 million new-town-in-town.

20. OFC's assertion that it produced 3,600 new jobs between 1970 to 1978 appears in Opportunity Funding Corporation, *Annual Report,* 1978, p.2.

21. For a detailed discussion of trends in the black-white wealth gap, see Chapter Fourteen.

22. Article 1, Section 4 of the United States Constitution provides:

"The times, places and manner of holding elections for senators and representatives shall be prescribed in each state by the legislature thereof; *but the Congress may at any time by law make or alter such regulations. . . ."* [Emphasis added.]

Thus, an act of Congress abolishing the runoff primary would appear to be constitutional.

Chapter Twenty-Five. Black Power Engineered by the Chief of State

1. The Supreme Court case upholding racial criteria in awarding government contracts in Fullilove v. Klutznick, 448 U.S. 448 (1980).

2. The administrative regulations issued by the Department of Labor creating the Philadelphia Plan were upheld by the Supreme Court as a valid exercise of the executive authority under the Civil Rights Act of 1964. See Contractors Ass'n of Eastern Pennsylvania v. Schultz, 442 F.2d 159 (3d Cir.), *cert. denied,* 404 U.S. 854 (1971).

3. For a summary of the penetration of blacks into the television industry, see United States Conference on Civil Rights, "Window Dressing on the Set: An Update" (Washington, D.C., Jan. 1979).

The statistics on black representation in the television industry are from "Blackout in Television," *Columbia Journalism Review* (Nov./Dec. 1982), pp. 38-44.

4. The unfair treatment of blacks on Mississippi television is documented in the United Church of Christ petition filed with the FCC (April 15, 1964).

5. The extent of black penetration into the cable television market is documented in *Panorama,* Jan. 1981, p. 95. In 1980, the only black-owned cable television system operated in a section of Columbus, Ohio, and served only 12,000 subscribers.

6. Title VI of the Civil Rights Act of 1964 (Pub. L. No. 88-352), Section 601, provides: "No person in the United States shall, on the ground of race, color or national origin, be excluded from participation in, be denied the benefits of, or be subjected to discrimination under any program or activity receiving Federal financial assistance."

7. Information on the percentages of workers belonging to unions, broken down by race and sex, appears in U.S. Department of Labor, Bureau of Labor Statistics, Report No. 556, "Earnings and Other Characteristics of Organized Workers" (May 1977), p. 1.

8. National Labor Relations Board decisions in which unions have been found to have discriminated on the basis of race include Hughes Tool Co., 147 N.L.R.B. 1573 (1964), and Bell & Howell Co., 213 N.L.R.B. 79 (1974). For other cases and an analysis of how the NLRB handles them, see William B. Gould, "Framework of Employment Discrimination Law: An Introduction," in *Black Workers in White Unions,* Ch. 2 (Ithaca, N.Y.: Cornell University Press, 1977).

9. The tendency of regulated industries to have unfavorable minority employment records is discussed in Thomas Sowell, *Race and Economics* (New York: David McKay, Inc. 1975), pp. 166-167.

10. On employment office discrimination, see the studies cited in Robert H. Olson, Jr., "Employment Discrimination Litigation: New Priorities in the Struggle for Black Equality," *Harvard Civil Rights Law Review* (Dec. 1970), pp. 46-47. This article details the ways in which public and private agencies have used racially discriminatory patterns of interviewing and placing for the benefit of private employers.

11. The U.S. Equal Employment Opportunity Commission identified the securities industry as lagging in efforts to provide equal employment opportunity to minorities in "Job Patterns for Minorities and Women in Private Industry," in *Equal Employment Opportunity Report—1973,* Vol. 1.

12. The total assets of the 200 largest banking institutions are shown in *Rand McNally International Bankers Directory* (1979 ed.).

13. For an excellent analysis of why money markets prefer the larger borrower and tend to exclude the smaller one, see Staff of the Committee on Banking and Currency, House of Representatives, *Foreign Experience With Monetary Policies to Promote Economic and Social Priority Programs,* 92d Cong., 2d Sess.

14. The citations of widespread and intense racial discrimination in the banking industry appear in annual editions of *Equal Employment Opportunity Reports* (Washington, D.C.: U.S. Equal Employment Opportunity Commission).

15. On the absence of effective antidiscrimination enforcement activities in the four principal bank regulatory agencies, see *Report on Fair Lending Enforcement by the Four Federal Financial Regulatory Agencies From the Senate Committee on Banking, Housing and Urban Affairs,* 94th Cong., 2d Sess. (Washington, D.C.: Government Printing Office, 1976).

16. The CBS News-*New York Times* poll of American attitudes toward the federal government's attention to minority concerns was conducted on October 16-20, 1980. The results were analyzed in *Public Opinion,* Dec.-Jan. 1981.

Selected Reading

Allport, Gordon W. *The Nature of Prejudice*. Cambridge, Mass.: Addison-Wesley, 1954.

Arendt, Hannah. *Eichmann in Jerusalem*. New York: Viking, 1963.

Arrow, Kenneth J. "Models of Discrimination." In *Racial Discrimination in Economic Life*. Edited by Anthony H. Pascal. Lexington, Mass.: Lexington Books, 1972.

Baldwin, James. *The Fire Next Time*. New York: The Dial Press, 1963.

Banfield, Edward C. *The Unheavenly City*. Boston: Little Brown, 1970.

Becker, Gary S. *The Economics of Discrimination*. Chicago: University of Chicago Press, 1957.

Bell, Daniel. *The Coming of Post-Industrial Society*. New York: Basic Books, 1973.

Bennett, Lerone, Jr. *Black Power U.S.A.* Chicago: Johnson Publishing Co., 1967.

Bentham, Jeremy. *An Introduction to the Principles of Morals and Legislation*. New York: Hafner, 1948.

Berle, Adolph A., and Means, Gardiner C. *The Modern Corporation and Private Property*. New York: Macmillan, 1932.

Bettelheim, Bruno, and Janowitz, Morris. *Dynamics of Prejudice*. New York: Harper, 1950.

Bittker, Boris I. *The Case for Black Reparations*. New York: Random House, 1973.

Browne, Robert. "The Economic Basis for Reparations to Black America." In *The Review of Black Political Economy*. Vol. 2. 1972.

Chafe, William H. *Civilities and Civil Rights: Greensboro, North Carolina, and the Black Struggle for Freedom*. New York: Oxford University Press, 1980.

Clark, Kenneth B. *Dark Ghetto: Dilemmas of Social Power*. New York: Harper & Row, 1965.

Cleage, Albert B., Jr. *The Black Messiah*. New York: Sheed and Ward, 1968.

Cleaver, Eldridge. *Soul on Ice*. New York: McGraw-Hill, 1968.

Commons, John R. *The Economics of Collective Action.* Madison, Wis.: The University of Wisconsin Press, 1950.

Cruse, Harold. *The Crisis of the Negro Intellectual.* New York: William Morrow & Co., 1967.

Dahl, Robert. *Who Governs? Democracy and Power in an American City.* New Haven, Conn.: Yale University Press, 1961.

Delany, Martin R. "The Condition, Elevation, Emigration, and Destiny of the Colored People of the United States, Politically Considered." In *American Negro: His History and Literature Series.* New York: Arno Press, 1968.

DuBois, W.E.B. *Selected Writings.* Edited by Walter Wilson. New York: New American Library, 1970.

Eastland, Terry, and Bennett, William J. *Counting by Race.* New York: Basic Books, 1979.

Erikson, Erik. *Gandhi's Truth: On the Origins of Militant Nonviolence.* New York: W.W. Norton & Co., 1969.

Fanon, Frantz. *Black Skin, White Masks.* Translated by Charles Lam Markmann. New York: Grove Press, 1967.

Fogel, Robert William, and Engerman, Stanley L. *Time on the Cross.* Boston: Little, Brown, 1974.

Franklin, John Hope. *From Slavery to Freedom.* New York: Alfred A. Knopf, 1941.

Frazier, E. Franklin. *Black Bourgeoisie.* New York: Free Press, 1957.

Frederickson, George M. *White Supremacy: A Comparative Study in American and South African History.* New York: Oxford University Press, 1981.

Freeman, Richard B. *Black Elite.* New York: McGraw-Hill, 1976.

Friedman, Milton. *Capitalism and Freedom.* Chicago: University of Chicago Press, 1962.

Fromm, Erich. *Escape From Freedom.* New York: Rinehart, 1941.

Galbraith, John Kenneth. *The Affluent Society.* Boston: Houghton Mifflin, 1971.

Galbraith, John Kenneth. *The New Industrial State.* New York: Signet, 1967.

Genovese, Eugene D. *In Red and Black.* New York: Vintage Books, 1968.

Gibbon, Edward. *The Decline and Fall of the Roman Empire.* Edited by Dero A. Saunders. New York: Viking Press, 1952.

Gilder, George. *Wealth and Poverty.* New York: Basic Books, 1981.

Glazer, Nathan. *Affirmative Discrimination.* New York: Basic Books, 1975.

Glazer, Nathan, and Moynihan, Daniel P. *Beyond the Melting Pot*. Cambridge: M.I.T. and Harvard University Press, 1963.

Goodman, Paul. *Growing Up Absurd; Problems of Youth in the Organized System*. New York: Random House, 1960.

Gould, William B. *Black Workers in White Unions: Job Discrimination in the United States*. Ithaca, N.Y.: Cornell University Press, 1977.

Gutman, Herbert C. *The Black Family in Slavery and Freedom, 1750-1925*. New York: Pantheon Books, 1976.

Hampden-Turner, Charles. *Radical Man: The Process of Psycho-Social Development*. New York: Doubleday-Anchor, 1971.

Harris, Abram L. *The Negro as Capitalist*. Gloucester, Mass.: Peter Smith, 1968.

Hayek, Friedrich A. *The Road to Serfdom*. Chicago: University of Chicago, 1944.

Heilbroner, Robert L. *The Worldly Philosophers*. New York: Simon & Schuster, 1953.

Hiestand, Dale L. *Discrimination in Employment: An Appraisal of the Research*. Ann Arbor, Mich.: Institute of Labor and Industrial Relations, University of Michigan-Wayne State University, 1970.

Hill, Herbert. *Black Labor and the American Legal System*. Washington: The Bureau of National Affairs, 1977.

Hobbes, Thomas. *Leviathan*. New York: E.P. Dutton, 1950.

Horney, Karen. *The Neurotic Personality of Our Time*. New York: W.W. Norton, 1937.

Jaynes, Julian. *The Origin of Consciousness in the Breakdown of the Bicameral Mind*. Boston: Houghton Mifflin, 1976.

Jencks, Christopher. *Who Gets Ahead?* New York: Basic Books, 1979.

Jencks, Christopher, et al. *Inequality: A Reassessment of the Effect of Family and Schooling in America*. New York: Basic Books, 1972.

Jordan, Winthrop D. *White Over Black*. Baltimore: Penguin Books, 1969.

de Jouvenal, Bertrand. *The Ethics of Redistribution*. New York: Harper & Row, 1973.

de Jouvenal, Bertrand. *On Power: Its Nature and the History of Its Growth*. Translated by J.F. Huntington. New York: Viking, 1949.

Kelso, Louis, and Hetter, Patricia. *Two-Factor Theory: The Economics of Reality*. New York: Vintage Books, 1967.

Kluger, Richard. *Simple Justice: The History of Brown v. Board of Education: Black America's Struggle for Equality*. New York: Alfred A. Knopf, 1976.

Kohlberg, Lawrence. *Moral Development: Stages in the Development of Moral Thought and Action*. New York: Holt, Rinehart & Winston, 1984.

Lacy, Dan. *The White Use of Blacks in America*. New York: McGraw-Hill, 1972.

Laski, Harold. *The State in Theory and Practice*. New York: Viking, 1935.

Lasswell, Harold D. *Politics: Who Gets What, When, How*. New York: Meridian Books 1958.

Lekachman, Robert. *Greed Is Not Enough*. New York: Pantheon Books, 1982.

Lester, Julius. *Look Out Whitey! Black Power's Gon' Get Your Mama*. New York: Dial Press, 1968.

Levitan, Sar A.; Johnston, William B.; and Taggart, Robert. *Still a Dream*. Cambridge: Harvard University Press, 1974.

Lewis, Anthony, *Gideon's Trumpet*. New York: Random House, 1964.

Liebow, Elliot. *Tally's Corner: A Study of Negro Streetcorner Men*. Boston: Little, Brown, 1967.

Lindblom, Charles E. *Politics and Markets*. New York: Basic Books, 1977.

Litwack, Leon F. *North of Slavery, The Negro in the Free States, 1790-1860*. Chicago: University of Chicago Press, 1961.

Locke, John. *Two Treatises of Government*. Edited by Peter Laslett. 2d ed. Cambridge: Cambridge University Press, 1967.

Lomax, Louis E. *The Negro Revolt*. New York: Harper & Row, 1962.

Machiavelli, *The Prince*. Translated and edited by Mark Musa. New York: St. Martin's Press, 1964.

Malcolm X with the assistance of Alex Haley. *The Autobiography of Malcolm X*. New York: Grove Press, 1966.

May, Rollo. *Power and Innocence*. New York: W.W. Norton & Co., 1972.

McClelland, David C. *The Achieving Society*. Princeton, N.J.: Van Nostrand, 1961.

Milgram, Stanley. *Obedience to Authority*. New York: Harper & Row, 1974.

Mills, C. Wright. *Power, Politics and People*. New York: Ballantine Books, 1963.

Mosca, Gaetano. *The Ruling Class*. New York and London: McGraw-Hill, 1939.

Moynihan, Daniel P. *Maximum Feasible Misunderstanding*. New York: Free Press, 1969.

Moynihan, Daniel P., ed. *On Understanding Poverty*. New York: Basic Books, 1969.

Moynihan, Daniel P. *The Politics of a Guaranteed Income: The Nixon Administration and the Family Assistance Plan.* New York: Random House, 1973.

Myrdal, Gunnar. *An American Dilemma.* New York: Harper, 1944.

Nozick, Robert. *Anarchy, State, and Utopia.* New York: Basic Books, 1974.

Parsons, Talcott, "The Distribution of Power in American Society," *World Politics* (Oct. 1957), p. 10.

Patterson, H. Orlando. *Ethnic Chauvinism: The Reactionary Impulse.* New York: Stein & Day, 1977.

Phillips, Ulrich B. *The Slave Economy of the Old South.* Baton Rouge: Louisiana State University Press, 1968.

Piven, Frances Fox, and Cloward, Richard A. *Regulating the Poor.* New York: Pantheon, 1971.

Rawls, John. *A Theory of Justice.* Cambridge: Belknap Press of Harvard University Press, 1971.

Riesman, David, et al. *The Lonely Crowd.* New Haven, Conn.: Yale University Press, 1950.

Rosengarten, Theodore. *All God's Dangers: The Life of Nate Shaw.* New York: Alfred A. Knopf, 1974.

Russell, Bertrand. *Power: A New Social Analysis.* New York: W.W. Norton & Co., 1938.

Ryan, William. *Blaming the Victim.* New York: Pantheon Books, 1971.

Sanders, Marion K. *The Professional Radical: Conversations With Saul Alinsky.* New York: Harper & Row, 1965.

Schuchter, Arnold. *White Power, Black Freedom.* Boston: Beacon Press, 1968.

Schumpeter, Joseph A. *Capitalism, Socialism and Democracy.* New York: Harper & Row, Torchbooks, 1950.

Sennett, Richard, and Cobb, Jonathan. *The Hidden Injuries of Class.* New York: Alfred A. Knopf, 1972.

Silberman, Charles E. *Crisis in Black and White.* New York: Random House, 1964.

Skinner, B.F. *Beyond Freedom and Dignity.* New York: Random House, 1964.

Smith, Adam. *The Wealth of Nations.* Baltimore: Penguin Books, 1970.

Sowell, Thomas. *Ethnic America.* New York: Basic Books, 1981.

Sowell, Thomas. *Markets and Minorities.* New York: Basic Books, 1981.

Thurow, Lester. *Poverty and Discrimination.* The Brookings Institution, 1969.

Tillich, Paul. *Love, Power and Justice*. New York: Oxford University Press, 1954.

Turnbull, Collin. *The Forest People*. New York: Simon & Schuster, 1961.

Veblen, Thorstein. *The Theory of the Leisure Class*. New York: Modern Library, 1934 (first published 1899).

Washington, Booker T. *Up From Slavery*. Garden City, N.Y.: Doubleday, 1963.

Weber, Max. *From Max Weber: Essays in Sociology*. Translated by H.H. Gerth and C. Wright Mills. Fairlawn, N.J.: Oxford University Press, 1946.

Weber, Max. *The Theory of Social and Economic Organization*. Translated by A.M. Henderson and Talcott Parsons. New York: Free Press, 1947.

Wilson, James Q. *Negro Politics: The Search for Leadership*. New York: Free Press, 1960.

Wilson, William Julius. *The Declining Significance of Race*. Chicago: The University of Chicago Press, 1978.

Woodson, Carter G. *The Education of the Negro Prior to 1861*. New York: Arno Press, 1968.

Woodward, C. Vann. *The Strange Career of Jim Crow*. New York: Oxford University Press, 1955.

Wright, Richard. *Native Son*. New York: Harper, 1940.

Wrong, Dennis H. *Power*. New York: Harper & Row, 1979.

Index

INDEX

Bush, George, 354, 674
Business Roundtable, 615
Busing, for school desegregation, 309, 433, 608; *see also* Segregation
Byrd, Harry F., 714

C

Cabinet; *see* Executive branch
Calhoun, John, 334-5
Callaway, Louis M., 255
Campbell Soup Co., 626, 658
Capitalism, 39; and black business, 268-76, 284; and class, 91-3; and community development corporations, 788, 792-3; and Jews, 418; and self-interest, 39-41; and struggle for power, 41-4; theory of, 71-8, 126, 189, 285, 421-2
Cardozo, Benjamin, 416
Carlson, Gerald, 577
Carmichael, Gil, 714
Carmichael, Stokely, 536, 588
Carnegie, Andrew, 393, 454
Carswell, G. Harrold, 310, 347
Carter, Jimmy, 153, 302, 448, 460, 690, 821; and black vote, 542-3, 550, 555-7, 559, 563, 565, 689, 703, 716, 720, 749, 752; Cabinet appointments, 347-9, 727; and campaign promises, 347, 595; judicial appointments, 365-6, 371, 730; and White House staff, 335-9
Caste, 93, 356-8
Census Bureau, 143, 531, 600, 654, 671, 832; and employment, 237-8, 249, 252-4, 256; and income, 191, 193, 204, 207, 218; and poverty, 218, 222-3, 225, 227, 760; and wealth, 261-3, 265-6, 268, 270
Central Intelligence Agency, 763
Chase Manhattan Bank, 92, 167, 170, 658
Chiles, Lawton, 312
Chinese-Americans, 420-1
Chisholm, Shirley, 153, 293, 295, 561
Chrysler Corporation, 167
Citicorp, 171, 273, 627
Citronelle Oil Field, 278
Civil Rights Act of 1957, 702, 707
Civil Rights Act of 1964, 123, 563, 571, 645, 707, 829

Civil rights organizations, 419, 615; funding of, 616-7; ineffectiveness of, 615-7
Clark, Jim, 531
Clark, Ramsey, 331
Clark, Robert, 618, 698
Clarke, James Freeman, 260
Clarke, John Henrik, 385
Class, 83-93; and coercion, 84-7; and free markets, 91-3; and prejudice, 88-93; race controversy, vs., 398-401; and racism, 84-93
Classifications, as a form of power, 81-93, 96-7
Clay, Cassius, 157
Clay, William, 151, 294, 553
Cleaver, Eldridge, 302, 584, 588
Clement, William, 563
Clorox Co., 626
Coalition politics, 572-5, 679-86, 711; *see also* Black-Hispanic alliance
Coca-Cola Co., 625, 627
Cochran, Thad, 312, 570, 703-4, 714-5, 771
Coercion, and class traits, 84-7; and competition, 65-70; and consensus, 73; as economic power, 72-8; and freedom, 6-7; and groups, 17-8; as influence or "pull," 441-3; and labor unions, 73-4; and legitimacy, 47; and pension funds, 632; and political power, 71-78; and power generally, 17-8, 63-5, 429; and prejudice, 100-2; and threats, 26-9
Coleman, William T., 177, 344, 346, 728
Collective action, 22-4, 536-40, 596-660
Collective agreements, 109-10
College Entrance Examination Board, 472-3
Collins, Cardiss, 294, 552
Collins, George W., 294
Collins, Marva, 353
Collins, Robert F., 367
Commerce, Department of, 648
Committee of Conservative Activists, 674
Committee on Equal Employment Opportunity, 351
Community development corporations, 785-93
Community Reinvestment Act, 833
Community Services Administration, 351, 648

893

INDEX

Democratic party, black influence on, 566-70, 595, 675-9, 717-21; black loyalty to, 671; conventions, 152-3, 551-3, 555; diversity of, 671-5; and labor, 566, 639-40; and the New Right, 571-2; and Populists, 136-7; promoting disunity within, 570-2; and southern politics, 140, 142, 713; and tokenism, 636

Democratic Steering and Policy Committee, 677

Dent, Harry S., 333

Denton, Jeremiah, 312

Dependency, and black organizations, 615-7; and black powerlessness, 41-2, 531-5; and legislation, 744; and power, 6-7

DePriest, Oscar, 288

Desegregation; see Segregation

Detroit Edison Company, 19

Devine, Samuel, 563

Dewey, Thomas, 557

Dickinson, William, 307, 563

Diggs, Charles, 294, 298

Dinkins, David, 691

Direct action; see Collective action

Discrimination, and the armed forces, 123; as behavior, 497-503; as blacklisting offenders, 820-2; as cause of black inequality, 379-428; and children, 590-9; as coercive power, 106; and competition, 68-70; in Congress, 123-4; and corporations, 165, 658-60, 765-7; as a criminal offense, 765-7; in education, 398; in the executive branch, 327-58; as government policy, 123-4; in housing, 116-7, 119; illegitimacy of, 53-7; in labor unions, 121-3; in the legal profession, 646-7; and seniority, 438-41; and tokenism, 165-9

Disenfranchisement of black voters, 134-6, 138-47

Dixon, Julian, 294-5, 552

Doar, John, 347

Dole, Elizabeth, 613

Dole, Robert, 726

Domestic employees, unionization of blacks, 640-1

Doss, Evan, 698

Double primaries; see Runoff primaries

Douglas, Stephen A., 156

Douglass, Frederick, 179, 416, 533

Dowdy, Wayne, 698

Dredd Scott, *Scott v. Sanford* (60 U.S. 393), 90, 158, 359

Drew, Dr. Charles Richard, 162

DuBois, W.E.B., 150, 162, 173, 277, 385, 416

du Pont de Nemours, E.I. Inc., 453, 631

Dymally, Mervyn, 295, 552, 577

E

East, John, 312

Eastern Airlines, 658

Eastland, James, 353-4, 702

Ebony, 254, 281, 682

Economic growth, 476-82

Economic indicators, black, 597-603

Economic Opportunity Act, 804

Economist, The, 349, 473

Education, and affirmative action, 441, 488, 518; black-white differences, 396-7; as cause of black inequality; 395-8; and computers, 474-5; and discrimination, 398; and employment, 240-1, 396-7, 466; as force for equality, 463-8; and income, 396-8, 413, 464-5; and poverty, 222-3, 396-7, 468; and standardized tests, 117, 382-4, 407, 468-73, 645, 823; and teachers, 407, 441; and voting, 693; and wealth, 467

Educational Testing Service, 468

Einstein, Albert, 105

Eisenhower, Dwight D., 157, 193, 290, 326, 329, 716

Eizenstat, Stuart, 336

Elections, at-large, 145, 644, 737-40; congressional, 134-5, 287-96, 540-4, 560-3, 576-8, 675-8, 687-8, 694-711; financing of, 553, 677, 770-4; presidential, 542-60, 563, 565, 713-6, 749, 752; primaries (*see* Primary elections); runoffs, 145-6, 697, 794-6; senatorial, 308; and wealth, 460-2

Electoral College, 444-9, 544-9, 563, 672, 715-6, 726

Emancipation Proclamation, 114, 800

Emergency Land Fund, 456

Emerson, Ralph Waldo, 96

INDEX

Fowler, Wyche, 307, 696-7
Fraunces, Samuel, 261
Frankfurter, Felix, 346
Franklin, John Hope, 386
Franklin, Webb, 711
Freedom, 497-503; and economic power, 64-5; and power, 5-14
Freedom Rides, 538
Freeman, Richard B., 250
Freud, Sigmund, 162
Friedman, Milton, 267, 421, 497-8, 500, 761

G

Gandy, Evelyn, 795
Gannett Inc., 658
Gardner, James, 543
Garrett, Thaddeus, 354
Garrison, William Lloyd, 184
de Gaulle, Charles, 634
General Accounting Office, 646, 789, 824
General Electric Inc., 631, 658
General Mills Inc., 658
General Motors Inc., 91, 204, 631
General Services Administration, 350, 645
Genetic inferiority, and scientific racism, 380-5
Genovese, Eugene, 386
Gerrymandering, 117, 136, 142-4, 151-2, 308, 361, 520, 677, 697, 737, 793-4
Giannini, A.P., 393, 454
Gibbon, Edward, 34
Gibson, Kenneth, 553, 697
Glass, Carter, 139
Goode, William, 323, 569
Goodyear Tire & Rubber Co., 631
Government contracts, 492, 658, 801-5, 828-31
Grady, Henry, 133, 284
Grant, Ulysses S., 147
Gray, William, 294-5, 552
"Great Society," 292-3, 423
Green, Dennis, 337, 341
Green, William, 735
Greyhound Corp., 167
Griffin, Robert, 309, 314
Gutman, Herbert G., 389
Guyer, Tennyson, 124

H

Haldeman, H.R., 328
Hall, Katie, 295, 577
Harding, Warren G., 157
Harriman, Averell, 343
Harris, Patricia R., 344, 348
Hart, Gary, 721
Hart, Sam, 355
Harvard Business School, 168
Hastie, William H., 365, 416
Hatcher, Andrew, 330
Hatcher, Richard, 337, 553
Hawkins, Augustus, 294, 298, 300, 552
Hayes, Charles, 295, 553, 733
Hayes-Tilden Compromise, 134-5
Haynesworth, Clement F., 309-10
Health and Human Services, Department of, 343, 351, 708, 723, 725, 748, 774
Hearst Corporation, 453
Hebert, F. Edward, 302
Heckler, Margaret, 613
Heflin, Howard, 312
Helms, Jesse, 312, 576, 674, 704-5, 724, 771
Henry, Aaron, 813
Hill, John, 563
Hillard, David, 588
Hinson, Jon, 698
Hispanic-Americans, and alliance with blacks, 574-5, 670-86, 716; elected officials, 680; as recent immigrants, 393; voting power of, 554-5
Hitler, Adolph, 105
Hobbes, Thomas, 3, 668
Hollings, Ernest, 312, 543, 703
Homestead Act, 76, 456
Hooks, Benjamin, 346, 356
Hoover, Herbert, 157, 327, 566
Hoover, J. Edgar, 371
Hopkins, Harry, 328
House Administration Committee, 294, 298
House Appropriations Committee, 294, 300, 301, 307, 706
House Armed Services Committee, 293, 302
House Assassinations Committee, 303
House Banking Subcommittee on Domestic Monetary Policy, 294, 300, 658
House District of Columbia Committee, 290, 292-4, 298

INDEX

O

P

About the Author

Theodore Cross, lawyer and editor of *Business and Society Review*, has been a foremost spokesman for black economic development. In 1969, the publication of his book *Black Capitalism* (McKinsey Foundation Book Award, 1969), which *Black Enterprise* magazine called "the catalytic work on minority capitalism," shaped a number of new federal programs, including the Washington-based Opportunity Funding Corporation, which the author designed in 1970 at the request of the White House.

The author has been a consultant to the Department of Health and Human Services, the former Office of Economic Opportunity, and the White House. He has lectured on minority economics and law at Harvard, Cornell, and the University of Virginia. He is a trustee of Amherst College, Chairman of the Investment Committee of its Board of Trustees, and a past Public Governor of the American Stock Exchange. He is a graduate of Harvard Law School, where he was an editor of *The Harvard Law Review*.

He is married to Mary Cross, a photographer and free-lance journalist. They live in Princeton, New Jersey.